T0189193

Foreword

Hosting the European Conference on Computer Vision (ECCV 2020) was certainly an exciting journey. From the 2016 plan to hold it at the Edinburgh International Conference Centre (hosting 1,800 delegates) to the 2018 plan to hold it at Glasgow's Scottish Exhibition Centre (up to 6,000 delegates), we finally ended with moving online because of the COVID-19 outbreak. While possibly having fewer delegates than expected because of the online format, ECCV 2020 still had over 3,100 registered participants.

Although online, the conference delivered most of the activities expected at a face-to-face conference: peer-reviewed papers, industrial exhibitors, demonstrations, and messaging between delegates. In addition to the main technical sessions, the conference included a strong program of satellite events with 16 tutorials and 44 workshops.

Furthermore, the online conference format enabled new conference features. Every paper had an associated teaser video and a longer full presentation video. Along with the papers and slides from the videos, all these materials were available the week before the conference. This allowed delegates to become familiar with the paper content and be ready for the live interaction with the authors during the conference week. The live event consisted of brief presentations by the oral and spotlight authors and industrial sponsors. Question and answer sessions for all papers were timed to occur twice so delegates from around the world had convenient access to the authors.

As with ECCV 2018, authors' draft versions of the papers appeared online with open access, now on both the Computer Vision Foundation (CVF) and the European Computer Vision Association (ECVA) websites. An archival publication arrangement was put in place with the cooperation of Springer. SpringerLink hosts the final version of the papers with further improvements, such as activating reference links and supplementary materials. These two approaches benefit all potential readers: a version available freely for all researchers, and an authoritative and citable version with additional benefits for SpringerLink subscribers. We thank Alfred Hofmann and Aliaksandr Birukou from Springer for helping to negotiate this agreement, which we expect will continue for future versions of ECCV.

August 2020

Vittorio Ferrari
Bob Fisher
Cordelia Schmid
Emanuele Trucco

Preface

Welcome to the proceedings of the European Conference on Computer Vision (ECCV 2020). This is a unique edition of ECCV in many ways. Due to the COVID-19 pandemic, this is the first time the conference was held online, in a virtual format. This was also the first time the conference relied exclusively on the Open Review platform to manage the review process. Despite these challenges ECCV is thriving. The conference received 5,150 valid paper submissions, of which 1,360 were accepted for publication (27%) and, of those, 160 were presented as spotlights (3%) and 104 as orals (2%). This amounts to more than twice the number of submissions to ECCV 2018 (2,439). Furthermore, CVPR, the largest conference on computer vision, received 5,850 submissions this year, meaning that ECCV is now 87% the size of CVPR in terms of submissions. By comparison, in 2018 the size of ECCV was only 73% of CVPR.

The review model was similar to previous editions of ECCV; in particular, it was double blind in the sense that the authors did not know the name of the reviewers and vice versa. Furthermore, each conference submission was held confidentially, and was only publicly revealed if and once accepted for publication. Each paper received at least three reviews, totalling more than 15,000 reviews. Handling the review process at this scale was a significant challenge. In order to ensure that each submission received as fair and high-quality reviews as possible, we recruited 2,830 reviewers (a 130% increase with reference to 2018) and 207 area chairs (a 60% increase). The area chairs were selected based on their technical expertise and reputation, largely among people that served as area chair in previous top computer vision and machine learning conferences (ECCV, ICCV, CVPR, NeurIPS, etc.). Reviewers were similarly invited from previous conferences. We also encouraged experienced area chairs to suggest additional chairs and reviewers in the initial phase of recruiting.

Despite doubling the number of submissions, the reviewer load was slightly reduced from 2018, from a maximum of 8 papers down to 7 (with some reviewers offering to handle 6 papers plus an emergency review). The area chair load increased slightly, from 18 papers on average to 22 papers on average.

Conflicts of interest between authors, area chairs, and reviewers were handled largely automatically by the Open Review platform via their curated list of user profiles. Many authors submitting to ECCV already had a profile in Open Review. We set a paper registration deadline one week before the paper submission deadline in order to encourage all missing authors to register and create their Open Review profiles well on time (in practice, we allowed authors to create/change papers arbitrarily until the submission deadline). Except for minor issues with users creating duplicate profiles, this allowed us to easily and quickly identify institutional conflicts, and avoid them, while matching papers to area chairs and reviewers.

Papers were matched to area chairs based on: an affinity score computed by the Open Review platform, which is based on paper titles and abstracts, and an affinity score computed by the Toronto Paper Matching System (TPMS), which is based on the paper's full text, the area chair bids for individual papers, load balancing, and conflict avoidance. Open Review provides the program chairs a convenient web interface to experiment with different configurations of the matching algorithm. The chosen configuration resulted in about 50% of the assigned papers to be highly ranked by the area chair bids, and 50% to be ranked in the middle, with very few low bids assigned.

Assignments to reviewers were similar, with two differences. First, there was a maximum of 7 papers assigned to each reviewer. Second, area chairs recommended up to seven reviewers per paper, providing another highly-weighed term to the affinity scores used for matching.

The assignment of papers to area chairs was smooth. However, it was more difficult to find suitable reviewers for all papers. Having a ratio of 5.6 papers per reviewer with a maximum load of 7 (due to emergency reviewer commitment), which did not allow for much wiggle room in order to also satisfy conflict and expertise constraints. We received some complaints from reviewers who did not feel qualified to review specific papers and we reassigned them wherever possible. However, the large scale of the conference, the many constraints, and the fact that a large fraction of such complaints arrived very late in the review process made this process very difficult and not all complaints could be addressed.

Reviewers had six weeks to complete their assignments. Possibly due to COVID-19 or the fact that the NeurIPS deadline was moved closer to the review deadline, a record 30% of the reviews were still missing after the deadline. By comparison, ECCV 2018 experienced only 10% missing reviews at this stage of the process. In the subsequent week, area chairs chased the missing reviews intensely, found replacement reviewers in their own team, and managed to reach 10% missing reviews. Eventually, we could provide almost all reviews (more than 99.9%) with a delay of only a couple of days on the initial schedule by a significant use of emergency reviews. If this trend is confirmed, it might be a major challenge to run a smooth review process in future editions of ECCV. The community must reconsider prioritization of the time spent on paper writing (the number of submissions increased a lot despite COVID-19) and time spent on paper reviewing (the number of reviews delivered in time decreased a lot presumably due to COVID-19 or NeurIPS deadline). With this imbalance the peer-review system that ensures the quality of our top conferences may break soon.

Reviewers submitted their reviews independently. In the reviews, they had the opportunity to ask questions to the authors to be addressed in the rebuttal. However, reviewers were told not to request any significant new experiment. Using the Open Review interface, authors could provide an answer to each individual review, but were also allowed to cross-reference reviews and responses in their answers. Rather than PDF files, we allowed the use of formatted text for the rebuttal. The rebuttal and initial reviews were then made visible to all reviewers and the primary area chair for a given paper. The area chair encouraged and moderated the reviewer discussion. During the discussions, reviewers were invited to reach a consensus and possibly adjust their ratings as a result of the discussion and of the evidence in the rebuttal.

After the discussion period ended, most reviewers entered a final rating and recommendation, although in many cases this did not differ from their initial recommendation. Based on the updated reviews and discussion, the primary area chair then made a preliminary decision to accept or reject the paper and wrote a justification for it (meta-review). Except for cases where the outcome of this process was absolutely clear (as indicated by the three reviewers and primary area chairs all recommending clear rejection), the decision was then examined and potentially challenged by a secondary area chair. This led to further discussion and overturning a small number of preliminary decisions. Needless to say, there was no in-person area chair meeting, which would have been impossible due to COVID-19.

Area chairs were invited to observe the consensus of the reviewers whenever possible and use extreme caution in overturning a clear consensus to accept or reject a paper. If an area chair still decided to do so, she/he was asked to clearly justify it in the meta-review and to explicitly obtain the agreement of the secondary area chair. In practice, very few papers were rejected after being confidently accepted by the reviewers.

This was the first time Open Review was used as the main platform to run ECCV. In 2018, the program chairs used CMT3 for the user-facing interface and Open Review internally, for matching and conflict resolution. Since it is clearly preferable to only use a single platform, this year we switched to using Open Review in full. The experience was largely positive. The platform is highly-configurable, scalable, and open source. Being written in Python, it is easy to write scripts to extract data programmatically. The paper matching and conflict resolution algorithms and interfaces are top-notch, also due to the excellent author profiles in the platform. Naturally, there were a few kinks along the way due to the fact that the ECCV Open Review configuration was created from scratch for this event and it differs in substantial ways from many other Open Review conferences. However, the Open Review development and support team did a fantastic job in helping us to get the configuration right and to address issues in a timely manner as they unavoidably occurred. We cannot thank them enough for the tremendous effort they put into this project.

Finally, we would like to thank everyone involved in making ECCV 2020 possible in these very strange and difficult times. This starts with our authors, followed by the area chairs and reviewers, who ran the review process at an unprecedented scale. The whole Open Review team (and in particular Melisa Bok, Mohit Unyal, Carlos Mondragon Chapa, and Celeste Martinez Gomez) worked incredibly hard for the entire duration of the process. We would also like to thank René Vidal for contributing to the adoption of Open Review. Our thanks also go to Laurent Charling for TPMS and to the program chairs of ICML, ICLR, and NeurIPS for cross checking double submissions. We thank the website chair, Giovanni Farinella, and the CPI team (in particular Ashley Cook, Miriam Verdon, Nicola McGrane, and Sharon Kerr) for promptly adding material to the website as needed in the various phases of the process. Finally, we thank the publication chairs, Albert Ali Salah, Hamdi Dibeklioglu, Metehan Doyran, Henry Howard-Jenkins, Victor Prisacariu, Siyu Tang, and Gul Varol, who managed to compile these substantial proceedings in an exceedingly compressed schedule. We express our thanks to the ECVA team, in particular Kristina Scherbaum for allowing open access of the proceedings. We thank Alfred Hofmann from Springer who again serve as the publisher. Finally, we thank the other chairs of ECCV 2020, including in particular the general chairs for very useful feedback with the handling of the program.

August 2020

Andrea Vedaldi
Horst Bischof
Thomas Brox
Jan-Michael Frahm

Organization

General Chairs

Vittorio Ferrari   Google Research, Switzerland
Bob Fisher   University of Edinburgh, UK
Cordelia Schmid   Google and Inria, France
Emanuele Trucco   University of Dundee, UK

Program Chairs

Andrea Vedaldi   University of Oxford, UK
Horst Bischof   Graz University of Technology, Austria
Thomas Brox   University of Freiburg, Germany
Jan-Michael Frahm   University of North Carolina, USA

Industrial Liaison Chairs

Jim Ashe   University of Edinburgh, UK
Helmut Grabner   Zurich University of Applied Sciences, Switzerland
Diane Larlus   NAVER LABS Europe, France
Cristian Novotny   University of Edinburgh, UK

Local Arrangement Chairs

Yvan Petillot   Heriot-Watt University, UK
Paul Siebert   University of Glasgow, UK

Academic Demonstration Chair

Thomas Mensink   Google Research and University of Amsterdam, The Netherlands

Poster Chair

Stephen Mckenna   University of Dundee, UK

Technology Chair

Gerardo Aragon Camarasa   University of Glasgow, UK

Tutorial Chairs

Carlo Colombo   University of Florence, Italy
Sotirios Tsaftaris   University of Edinburgh, UK

Publication Chairs

Albert Ali Salah   Utrecht University, The Netherlands
Hamdi Dibeklioglu   Bilkent University, Turkey
Metehan Doyran   Utrecht University, The Netherlands
Henry Howard-Jenkins   University of Oxford, UK
Victor Adrian Prisacariu   University of Oxford, UK
Siyu Tang   ETH Zurich, Switzerland
Gul Varol   University of Oxford, UK

Website Chair

Giovanni Maria Farinella   University of Catania, Italy

Workshops Chairs

Adrien Bartoli   University of Clermont Auvergne, France
Andrea Fusiello   University of Udine, Italy

Area Chairs

Lourdes Agapito   University College London, UK
Zeynep Akata   University of Tübingen, Germany
Karteek Alahari   Inria, France
Antonis Argyros   University of Crete, Greece
Hossein Azizpour   KTH Royal Institute of Technology, Sweden
Joao P. Barreto   Universidade de Coimbra, Portugal
Alexander C. Berg   University of North Carolina at Chapel Hill, USA
Matthew B. Blaschko   KU Leuven, Belgium
Lubomir D. Bourdev   WaveOne, Inc., USA
Edmond Boyer   Inria, France
Yuri Boykov   University of Waterloo, Canada
Gabriel Brostow   University College London, UK
Michael S. Brown   National University of Singapore, Singapore
Jianfei Cai   Monash University, Australia
Barbara Caputo   Politecnico di Torino, Italy
Ayan Chakrabarti   Washington University, St. Louis, USA
Tat-Jen Cham   Nanyang Technological University, Singapore
Manmohan Chandraker   University of California, San Diego, USA
Rama Chellappa   Johns Hopkins University, USA
Liang-Chieh Chen   Google, USA

Yung-Yu Chuang	National Taiwan University, Taiwan
Ondrej Chum	Czech Technical University in Prague, Czech Republic
Brian Clipp	Kitware, USA
John Collomosse	University of Surrey and Adobe Research, UK
Jason J. Corso	University of Michigan, USA
David J. Crandall	Indiana University, USA
Daniel Cremers	University of California, Los Angeles, USA
Fabio Cuzzolin	Oxford Brookes University, UK
Jifeng Dai	SenseTime, SAR China
Kostas Daniilidis	University of Pennsylvania, USA
Andrew Davison	Imperial College London, UK
Alessio Del Bue	Fondazione Istituto Italiano di Tecnologia, Italy
Jia Deng	Princeton University, USA
Alexey Dosovitskiy	Google, Germany
Matthijs Douze	Facebook, France
Enrique Dunn	Stevens Institute of Technology, USA
Irfan Essa	Georgia Institute of Technology and Google, USA
Giovanni Maria Farinella	University of Catania, Italy
Ryan Farrell	Brigham Young University, USA
Paolo Favaro	University of Bern, Switzerland
Rogerio Feris	International Business Machines, USA
Cornelia Fermuller	University of Maryland, College Park, USA
David J. Fleet	Vector Institute, Canada
Friedrich Fraundorfer	DLR, Austria
Mario Fritz	CISPA Helmholtz Center for Information Security, Germany
Pascal Fua	EPFL (Swiss Federal Institute of Technology Lausanne), Switzerland
Yasutaka Furukawa	Simon Fraser University, Canada
Li Fuxin	Oregon State University, USA
Efstratios Gavves	University of Amsterdam, The Netherlands
Peter Vincent Gehler	Amazon, USA
Theo Gevers	University of Amsterdam, The Netherlands
Ross Girshick	Facebook AI Research, USA
Boqing Gong	Google, USA
Stephen Gould	Australian National University, Australia
Jinwei Gu	SenseTime Research, USA
Abhinav Gupta	Facebook, USA
Bohyung Han	Seoul National University, South Korea
Bharath Hariharan	Cornell University, USA
Tal Hassner	Facebook AI Research, USA
Xuming He	Australian National University, Australia
Joao F. Henriques	University of Oxford, UK
Adrian Hilton	University of Surrey, UK
Minh Hoai	Stony Brooks, State University of New York, USA
Derek Hoiem	University of Illinois Urbana-Champaign, USA

Timothy Hospedales	University of Edinburgh and Samsung, UK
Gang Hua	Wormpex AI Research, USA
Slobodan Ilic	Siemens AG, Germany
Hiroshi Ishikawa	Waseda University, Japan
Jiaya Jia	The Chinese University of Hong Kong, SAR China
Hailin Jin	Adobe Research, USA
Justin Johnson	University of Michigan, USA
Frederic Jurie	University of Caen Normandie, France
Fredrik Kahl	Chalmers University, Sweden
Sing Bing Kang	Zillow, USA
Gunhee Kim	Seoul National University, South Korea
Junmo Kim	Korea Advanced Institute of Science and Technology, South Korea
Tae-Kyun Kim	Imperial College London, UK
Ron Kimmel	Technion-Israel Institute of Technology, Israel
Alexander Kirillov	Facebook AI Research, USA
Kris Kitani	Carnegie Mellon University, USA
Iasonas Kokkinos	Ariel AI, UK
Vladlen Koltun	Intel Labs, USA
Nikos Komodakis	Ecole des Ponts ParisTech, France
Piotr Koniusz	Australian National University, Australia
M. Pawan Kumar	University of Oxford, UK
Kyros Kutulakos	University of Toronto, Canada
Christoph Lampert	IST Austria, Austria
Ivan Laptev	Inria, France
Diane Larlus	NAVER LABS Europe, France
Laura Leal-Taixe	Technical University Munich, Germany
Honglak Lee	Google and University of Michigan, USA
Joon-Young Lee	Adobe Research, USA
Kyoung Mu Lee	Seoul National University, South Korea
Seungyong Lee	POSTECH, South Korea
Yong Jae Lee	University of California, Davis, USA
Bastian Leibe	RWTH Aachen University, Germany
Victor Lempitsky	Samsung, Russia
Ales Leonardis	University of Birmingham, UK
Marius Leordeanu	Institute of Mathematics of the Romanian Academy, Romania
Vincent Lepetit	ENPC ParisTech, France
Hongdong Li	The Australian National University, Australia
Xi Li	Zhejiang University, China
Yin Li	University of Wisconsin-Madison, USA
Zicheng Liao	Zhejiang University, China
Jongwoo Lim	Hanyang University, South Korea
Stephen Lin	Microsoft Research Asia, China
Yen-Yu Lin	National Chiao Tung University, Taiwan, China
Zhe Lin	Adobe Research, USA

Haibin Ling	Stony Brooks, State University of New York, USA
Jiaying Liu	Peking University, China
Ming-Yu Liu	NVIDIA, USA
Si Liu	Beihang University, China
Xiaoming Liu	Michigan State University, USA
Huchuan Lu	Dalian University of Technology, China
Simon Lucey	Carnegie Mellon University, USA
Jiebo Luo	University of Rochester, USA
Julien Mairal	Inria, France
Michael Maire	University of Chicago, USA
Subhransu Maji	University of Massachusetts, Amherst, USA
Yasushi Makihara	Osaka University, Japan
Jiri Matas	Czech Technical University in Prague, Czech Republic
Yasuyuki Matsushita	Osaka University, Japan
Philippos Mordohai	Stevens Institute of Technology, USA
Vittorio Murino	University of Verona, Italy
Naila Murray	NAVER LABS Europe, France
Hajime Nagahara	Osaka University, Japan
P. J. Narayanan	International Institute of Information Technology (IIIT), Hyderabad, India
Nassir Navab	Technical University of Munich, Germany
Natalia Neverova	Facebook AI Research, France
Matthias Niessner	Technical University of Munich, Germany
Jean-Marc Odobez	Idiap Research Institute and Swiss Federal Institute of Technology Lausanne, Switzerland
Francesca Odone	Università di Genova, Italy
Takeshi Oishi	The University of Tokyo, Tokyo Institute of Technology, Japan
Vicente Ordonez	University of Virginia, USA
Manohar Paluri	Facebook AI Research, USA
Maja Pantic	Imperial College London, UK
In Kyu Park	Inha University, South Korea
Ioannis Patras	Queen Mary University of London, UK
Patrick Perez	Valeo, France
Bryan A. Plummer	Boston University, USA
Thomas Pock	Graz University of Technology, Austria
Marc Pollefeys	ETH Zurich and Microsoft MR & AI Zurich Lab, Switzerland
Jean Ponce	Inria, France
Gerard Pons-Moll	MPII, Saarland Informatics Campus, Germany
Jordi Pont-Tuset	Google, Switzerland
James Matthew Rehg	Georgia Institute of Technology, USA
Ian Reid	University of Adelaide, Australia
Olaf Ronneberger	DeepMind London, UK
Stefan Roth	TU Darmstadt, Germany
Bryan Russell	Adobe Research, USA

Kwang Moo Yi	University of Victoria, Canada
Zhaozheng Yin	Stony Brook, State University of New York, USA
Chang D. Yoo	Korea Advanced Institute of Science and Technology, South Korea
Shaodi You	University of Amsterdam, The Netherlands
Jingyi Yu	ShanghaiTech University, China
Stella Yu	University of California, Berkeley, and ICSI, USA
Stefanos Zafeiriou	Imperial College London, UK
Hongbin Zha	Peking University, China
Tianzhu Zhang	University of Science and Technology of China, China
Liang Zheng	Australian National University, Australia
Todd E. Zickler	Harvard University, USA
Andrew Zisserman	University of Oxford, UK

Technical Program Committee

Sathyanarayanan
  N. Aakur
Wael Abd Almgaeed
Abdelrahman
  Abdelhamed
Abdullah Abuolaim
Supreeth Achar
Hanno Ackermann
Ehsan Adeli
Triantafyllos Afouras
Sameer Agarwal
Aishwarya Agrawal
Harsh Agrawal
Pulkit Agrawal
Antonio Agudo
Eirikur Agustsson
Karim Ahmed
Byeongjoo Ahn
Unaiza Ahsan
Thalaiyasingam Ajanthan
Kenan E. Ak
Emre Akbas
Naveed Akhtar
Derya Akkaynak
Yagiz Aksoy
Ziad Al-Halah
Xavier Alameda-Pineda
Jean-Baptiste Alayrac

Samuel Albanie
Shadi Albarqouni
Cenek Albl
Hassan Abu Alhaija
Daniel Aliaga
Mohammad
  S. Aliakbarian
Rahaf Aljundi
Thiemo Alldieck
Jon Almazan
Jose M. Alvarez
Senjian An
Saket Anand
Codruta Ancuti
Cosmin Ancuti
Peter Anderson
Juan Andrade-Cetto
Alexander Andreopoulos
Misha Andriluka
Dragomir Anguelov
Rushil Anirudh
Michel Antunes
Oisin Mac Aodha
Srikar Appalaraju
Relja Arandjelovic
Nikita Araslanov
Andre Araujo
Helder Araujo

Pablo Arbelaez
Shervin Ardeshir
Sercan O. Arik
Anil Armagan
Anurag Arnab
Chetan Arora
Federica Arrigoni
Mathieu Aubry
Shai Avidan
Angelica I. Aviles-Rivero
Yannis Avrithis
Ismail Ben Ayed
Shekoofeh Azizi
Ioan Andrei Bârsan
Artem Babenko
Deepak Babu Sam
Seung-Hwan Baek
Seungryul Baek
Andrew D. Bagdanov
Shai Bagon
Yuval Bahat
Junjie Bai
Song Bai
Xiang Bai
Yalong Bai
Yancheng Bai
Peter Bajcsy
Slawomir Bak

Mahsa Baktashmotlagh
Kavita Bala
Yogesh Balaji
Guha Balakrishnan
V. N. Balasubramanian
Federico Baldassarre
Vassileios Balntas
Shurjo Banerjee
Aayush Bansal
Ankan Bansal
Jianmin Bao
Linchao Bao
Wenbo Bao
Yingze Bao
Akash Bapat
Md Jawadul Hasan Bappy
Fabien Baradel
Lorenzo Baraldi
Daniel Barath
Adrian Barbu
Kobus Barnard
Nick Barnes
Francisco Barranco
Jonathan T. Barron
Arslan Basharat
Chaim Baskin
Anil S. Baslamisli
Jorge Batista
Kayhan Batmanghelich
Konstantinos Batsos
David Bau
Luis Baumela
Christoph Baur
Eduardo
  Bayro-Corrochano
Paul Beardsley
Jan Bednavr'ik
Oscar Beijbom
Philippe Bekaert
Esube Bekele
Vasileios Belagiannis
Ohad Ben-Shahar
Abhijit Bendale
Róger Bermúdez-Chacón
Maxim Berman
Jesus Bermudez-cameo

Florian Bernard
Stefano Berretti
Marcelo Bertalmio
Gedas Bertasius
Cigdem Beyan
Lucas Beyer
Vijayakumar Bhagavatula
Arjun Nitin Bhagoji
Apratim Bhattacharyya
Binod Bhattarai
Sai Bi
Jia-Wang Bian
Simone Bianco
Adel Bibi
Tolga Birdal
Tom Bishop
Soma Biswas
Mårten Björkman
Volker Blanz
Vishnu Boddeti
Navaneeth Bodla
Simion-Vlad Bogolin
Xavier Boix
Piotr Bojanowski
Timo Bolkart
Guido Borghi
Larbi Boubchir
Guillaume Bourmaud
Adrien Bousseau
Thierry Bouwmans
Richard Bowden
Hakan Boyraz
Mathieu Brédif
Samarth Brahmbhatt
Steve Branson
Nikolas Brasch
Biagio Brattoli
Ernesto Brau
Toby P. Breckon
Francois Bremond
Jesus Briales
Sofia Broomé
Marcus A. Brubaker
Luc Brun
Silvia Bucci
Shyamal Buch

Pradeep Buddharaju
Uta Buechler
Mai Bui
Tu Bui
Adrian Bulat
Giedrius T. Burachas
Elena Burceanu
Xavier P. Burgos-Artizzu
Kaylee Burns
Andrei Bursuc
Benjamin Busam
Wonmin Byeon
Zoya Bylinskii
Sergi Caelles
Jianrui Cai
Minjie Cai
Yujun Cai
Zhaowei Cai
Zhipeng Cai
Juan C. Caicedo
Simone Calderara
Necati Cihan Camgoz
Dylan Campbell
Octavia Camps
Jiale Cao
Kaidi Cao
Liangliang Cao
Xiangyong Cao
Xiaochun Cao
Yang Cao
Yu Cao
Yue Cao
Zhangjie Cao
Luca Carlone
Mathilde Caron
Dan Casas
Thomas J. Cashman
Umberto Castellani
Lluis Castrejon
Jacopo Cavazza
Fabio Cermelli
Hakan Cevikalp
Menglei Chai
Ishani Chakraborty
Rudrasis Chakraborty
Antoni B. Chan

Kwok-Ping Chan
Siddhartha Chandra
Sharat Chandran
Arjun Chandrasekaran
Angel X. Chang
Che-Han Chang
Hong Chang
Hyun Sung Chang
Hyung Jin Chang
Jianlong Chang
Ju Yong Chang
Ming-Ching Chang
Simyung Chang
Xiaojun Chang
Yu-Wei Chao
Devendra S. Chaplot
Arslan Chaudhry
Rizwan A. Chaudhry
Can Chen
Chang Chen
Chao Chen
Chen Chen
Chu-Song Chen
Dapeng Chen
Dong Chen
Dongdong Chen
Guanying Chen
Hongge Chen
Hsin-yi Chen
Huaijin Chen
Hwann-Tzong Chen
Jianbo Chen
Jianhui Chen
Jiansheng Chen
Jiaxin Chen
Jie Chen
Jun-Cheng Chen
Kan Chen
Kevin Chen
Lin Chen
Long Chen
Min-Hung Chen
Qifeng Chen
Shi Chen
Shixing Chen
Tianshui Chen

Weifeng Chen
Weikai Chen
Xi Chen
Xiaohan Chen
Xiaozhi Chen
Xilin Chen
Xingyu Chen
Xinlei Chen
Xinyun Chen
Yi-Ting Chen
Yilun Chen
Ying-Cong Chen
Yinpeng Chen
Yiran Chen
Yu Chen
Yu-Sheng Chen
Yuhua Chen
Yun-Chun Chen
Yunpeng Chen
Yuntao Chen
Zhuoyuan Chen
Zitian Chen
Anchieh Cheng
Bowen Cheng
Erkang Cheng
Gong Cheng
Guangliang Cheng
Jingchun Cheng
Jun Cheng
Li Cheng
Ming-Ming Cheng
Yu Cheng
Ziang Cheng
Anoop Cherian
Dmitry Chetverikov
Ngai-man Cheung
William Cheung
Ajad Chhatkuli
Naoki Chiba
Benjamin Chidester
Han-pang Chiu
Mang Tik Chiu
Wei-Chen Chiu
Donghyeon Cho
Hojin Cho
Minsu Cho

Nam Ik Cho
Tim Cho
Tae Eun Choe
Chiho Choi
Edward Choi
Inchang Choi
Jinsoo Choi
Jonghyun Choi
Jongwon Choi
Yukyung Choi
Hisham Cholakkal
Eunji Chong
Jaegul Choo
Christopher Choy
Hang Chu
Peng Chu
Wen-Sheng Chu
Albert Chung
Joon Son Chung
Hai Ci
Safa Cicek
Ramazan G. Cinbis
Arridhana Ciptadi
Javier Civera
James J. Clark
Ronald Clark
Felipe Codevilla
Michael Cogswell
Andrea Cohen
Maxwell D. Collins
Carlo Colombo
Yang Cong
Adria R. Continente
Marcella Cornia
John Richard Corring
Darren Cosker
Dragos Costea
Garrison W. Cottrell
Florent Couzinie-Devy
Marco Cristani
Ioana Croitoru
James L. Crowley
Jiequan Cui
Zhaopeng Cui
Ross Cutler
Antonio D'Innocente

Rozenn Dahyot
Bo Dai
Dengxin Dai
Hang Dai
Longquan Dai
Shuyang Dai
Xiyang Dai
Yuchao Dai
Adrian V. Dalca
Dima Damen
Bharath B. Damodaran
Kristin Dana
Martin Danelljan
Zheng Dang
Zachary Alan Daniels
Donald G. Dansereau
Abhishek Das
Samyak Datta
Achal Dave
Titas De
Rodrigo de Bem
Teo de Campos
Raoul de Charette
Shalini De Mello
Joseph DeGol
Herve Delingette
Haowen Deng
Jiankang Deng
Weijian Deng
Zhiwei Deng
Joachim Denzler
Konstantinos G. Derpanis
Aditya Deshpande
Frederic Devernay
Somdip Dey
Arturo Deza
Abhinav Dhall
Helisa Dhamo
Vikas Dhiman
Fillipe Dias Moreira
  de Souza
Ali Diba
Ferran Diego
Guiguang Ding
Henghui Ding
Jian Ding

Mingyu Ding
Xinghao Ding
Zhengming Ding
Robert DiPietro
Cosimo Distante
Ajay Divakaran
Mandar Dixit
Abdelaziz Djelouah
Thanh-Toan Do
Jose Dolz
Bo Dong
Chao Dong
Jiangxin Dong
Weiming Dong
Weisheng Dong
Xingping Dong
Xuanyi Dong
Yinpeng Dong
Gianfranco Doretto
Hazel Doughty
Hassen Drira
Bertram Drost
Dawei Du
Ye Duan
Yueqi Duan
Abhimanyu Dubey
Anastasia Dubrovina
Stefan Duffner
Chi Nhan Duong
Thibaut Durand
Zoran Duric
Iulia Duta
Debidatta Dwibedi
Benjamin Eckart
Marc Eder
Marzieh Edraki
Alexei A. Efros
Kiana Ehsani
Hazm Kemal Ekenel
James H. Elder
Mohamed Elgharib
Shireen Elhabian
Ehsan Elhamifar
Mohamed Elhoseiny
Ian Endres
N. Benjamin Erichson

Jan Ernst
Sergio Escalera
Francisco Escolano
Victor Escorcia
Carlos Esteves
Francisco J. Estrada
Bin Fan
Chenyou Fan
Deng-Ping Fan
Haoqi Fan
Hehe Fan
Heng Fan
Kai Fan
Lijie Fan
Linxi Fan
Quanfu Fan
Shaojing Fan
Xiaochuan Fan
Xin Fan
Yuchen Fan
Sean Fanello
Hao-Shu Fang
Haoyang Fang
Kuan Fang
Yi Fang
Yuming Fang
Azade Farshad
Alireza Fathi
Raanan Fattal
Joao Fayad
Xiaohan Fei
Christoph Feichtenhofer
Michael Felsberg
Chen Feng
Jiashi Feng
Junyi Feng
Mengyang Feng
Qianli Feng
Zhenhua Feng
Michele Fenzi
Andras Ferencz
Martin Fergie
Basura Fernando
Ethan Fetaya
Michael Firman
John W. Fisher

Matthew Fisher
Boris Flach
Corneliu Florea
Wolfgang Foerstner
David Fofi
Gian Luca Foresti
Per-Erik Forssen
David Fouhey
Katerina Fragkiadaki
Victor Fragoso
Jean-Sébastien Franco
Ohad Fried
Iuri Frosio
Cheng-Yang Fu
Huazhu Fu
Jianlong Fu
Jingjing Fu
Xueyang Fu
Yanwei Fu
Ying Fu
Yun Fu
Olac Fuentes
Kent Fujiwara
Takuya Funatomi
Christopher Funk
Thomas Funkhouser
Antonino Furnari
Ryo Furukawa
Erik Gärtner
Raghudeep Gadde
Matheus Gadelha
Vandit Gajjar
Trevor Gale
Juergen Gall
Mathias Gallardo
Guillermo Gallego
Orazio Gallo
Chuang Gan
Zhe Gan
Madan Ravi Ganesh
Aditya Ganeshan
Siddha Ganju
Bin-Bin Gao
Changxin Gao
Feng Gao
Hongchang Gao

Jin Gao
Jiyang Gao
Junbin Gao
Katelyn Gao
Lin Gao
Mingfei Gao
Ruiqi Gao
Ruohan Gao
Shenghua Gao
Yuan Gao
Yue Gao
Noa Garcia
Alberto Garcia-Garcia
Guillermo
    Garcia-Hernando
Jacob R. Gardner
Animesh Garg
Kshitiz Garg
Rahul Garg
Ravi Garg
Philip N. Garner
Kirill Gavrilyuk
Paul Gay
Shiming Ge
Weifeng Ge
Baris Gecer
Xin Geng
Kyle Genova
Stamatios Georgoulis
Bernard Ghanem
Michael Gharbi
Kamran Ghasedi
Golnaz Ghiasi
Arnab Ghosh
Partha Ghosh
Silvio Giancola
Andrew Gilbert
Rohit Girdhar
Xavier Giro-i-Nieto
Thomas Gittings
Ioannis Gkioulekas
Clement Godard
Vaibhava Goel
Bastian Goldluecke
Lluis Gomez
Nuno Gonçalves

Dong Gong
Ke Gong
Mingming Gong
Abel Gonzalez-Garcia
Ariel Gordon
Daniel Gordon
Paulo Gotardo
Venu Madhav Govindu
Ankit Goyal
Priya Goyal
Raghav Goyal
Benjamin Graham
Douglas Gray
Brent A. Griffin
Etienne Grossmann
David Gu
Jiayuan Gu
Jiuxiang Gu
Lin Gu
Qiao Gu
Shuhang Gu
Jose J. Guerrero
Paul Guerrero
Jie Gui
Jean-Yves Guillemaut
Riza Alp Guler
Erhan Gundogdu
Fatma Guney
Guodong Guo
Kaiwen Guo
Qi Guo
Sheng Guo
Shi Guo
Tiantong Guo
Xiaojie Guo
Yijie Guo
Yiluan Guo
Yuanfang Guo
Yulan Guo
Agrim Gupta
Ankush Gupta
Mohit Gupta
Saurabh Gupta
Tanmay Gupta
Danna Gurari
Abner Guzman-Rivera

JunYoung Gwak
Michael Gygli
Jung-Woo Ha
Simon Hadfield
Isma Hadji
Bjoern Haefner
Taeyoung Hahn
Levente Hajder
Peter Hall
Emanuela Haller
Stefan Haller
Bumsub Ham
Abdullah Hamdi
Dongyoon Han
Hu Han
Jungong Han
Junwei Han
Kai Han
Tian Han
Xiaoguang Han
Xintong Han
Yahong Han
Ankur Handa
Zekun Hao
Albert Haque
Tatsuya Harada
Mehrtash Harandi
Adam W. Harley
Mahmudul Hasan
Atsushi Hashimoto
Ali Hatamizadeh
Munawar Hayat
Dongliang He
Jingrui He
Junfeng He
Kaiming He
Kun He
Lei He
Pan He
Ran He
Shengfeng He
Tong He
Weipeng He
Xuming He
Yang He
Yihui He

Zhihai He
Chinmay Hegde
Janne Heikkila
Mattias P. Heinrich
Stéphane Herbin
Alexander Hermans
Luis Herranz
John R. Hershey
Aaron Hertzmann
Roei Herzig
Anders Heyden
Steven Hickson
Otmar Hilliges
Tomas Hodan
Judy Hoffman
Michael Hofmann
Yannick Hold-Geoffroy
Namdar Homayounfar
Sina Honari
Richang Hong
Seunghoon Hong
Xiaopeng Hong
Yi Hong
Hidekata Hontani
Anthony Hoogs
Yedid Hoshen
Mir Rayat Imtiaz Hossain
Junhui Hou
Le Hou
Lu Hou
Tingbo Hou
Wei-Lin Hsiao
Cheng-Chun Hsu
Gee-Sern Jison Hsu
Kuang-jui Hsu
Changbo Hu
Di Hu
Guosheng Hu
Han Hu
Hao Hu
Hexiang Hu
Hou-Ning Hu
Jie Hu
Junlin Hu
Nan Hu
Ping Hu

Ronghang Hu
Xiaowei Hu
Yinlin Hu
Yuan-Ting Hu
Zhe Hu
Binh-Son Hua
Yang Hua
Bingyao Huang
Di Huang
Dong Huang
Fay Huang
Haibin Huang
Haozhi Huang
Heng Huang
Huaibo Huang
Jia-Bin Huang
Jing Huang
Jingwei Huang
Kaizhu Huang
Lei Huang
Qiangui Huang
Qiaoying Huang
Qingqiu Huang
Qixing Huang
Shaoli Huang
Sheng Huang
Siyuan Huang
Weilin Huang
Wenbing Huang
Xiangru Huang
Xun Huang
Yan Huang
Yifei Huang
Yue Huang
Zhiwu Huang
Zilong Huang
Minyoung Huh
Zhuo Hui
Matthias B. Hullin
Martin Humenberger
Wei-Chih Hung
Zhouyuan Huo
Junhwa Hur
Noureldien Hussein
Jyh-Jing Hwang
Seong Jae Hwang

Sung Ju Hwang
Ichiro Ide
Ivo Ihrke
Daiki Ikami
Satoshi Ikehata
Nazli Ikizler-Cinbis
Sunghoon Im
Yani Ioannou
Radu Tudor Ionescu
Umar Iqbal
Go Irie
Ahmet Iscen
Md Amirul Islam
Vamsi Ithapu
Nathan Jacobs
Arpit Jain
Himalaya Jain
Suyog Jain
Stuart James
Won-Dong Jang
Yunseok Jang
Ronnachai Jaroensri
Dinesh Jayaraman
Sadeep Jayasumana
Suren Jayasuriya
Herve Jegou
Simon Jenni
Hae-Gon Jeon
Yunho Jeon
Koteswar R. Jerripothula
Hueihan Jhuang
I-hong Jhuo
Dinghuang Ji
Hui Ji
Jingwei Ji
Pan Ji
Yanli Ji
Baoxiong Jia
Kui Jia
Xu Jia
Chiyu Max Jiang
Haiyong Jiang
Hao Jiang
Huaizu Jiang
Huajie Jiang
Ke Jiang

Lai Jiang
Li Jiang
Lu Jiang
Ming Jiang
Peng Jiang
Shuqiang Jiang
Wei Jiang
Xudong Jiang
Zhuolin Jiang
Jianbo Jiao
Zequn Jie
Dakai Jin
Kyong Hwan Jin
Lianwen Jin
SouYoung Jin
Xiaojie Jin
Xin Jin
Nebojsa Jojic
Alexis Joly
Michael Jeffrey Jones
Hanbyul Joo
Jungseock Joo
Kyungdon Joo
Ajjen Joshi
Shantanu H. Joshi
Da-Cheng Juan
Marco Körner
Kevin Köser
Asim Kadav
Christine Kaeser-Chen
Kushal Kafle
Dagmar Kainmueller
Ioannis A. Kakadiaris
Zdenek Kalal
Nima Kalantari
Yannis Kalantidis
Mahdi M. Kalayeh
Anmol Kalia
Sinan Kalkan
Vicky Kalogeiton
Ashwin Kalyan
Joni-kristian Kamarainen
Gerda Kamberova
Chandra Kambhamettu
Martin Kampel
Meina Kan

Christopher Kanan
Kenichi Kanatani
Angjoo Kanazawa
Atsushi Kanehira
Takuhiro Kaneko
Asako Kanezaki
Bingyi Kang
Di Kang
Sunghun Kang
Zhao Kang
Vadim Kantorov
Abhishek Kar
Amlan Kar
Theofanis Karaletsos
Leonid Karlinsky
Kevin Karsch
Angelos Katharopoulos
Isinsu Katircioglu
Hiroharu Kato
Zoltan Kato
Dotan Kaufman
Jan Kautz
Rei Kawakami
Qiuhong Ke
Wadim Kehl
Petr Kellnhofer
Aniruddha Kembhavi
Cem Keskin
Margret Keuper
Daniel Keysers
Ashkan Khakzar
Fahad Khan
Naeemullah Khan
Salman Khan
Siddhesh Khandelwal
Rawal Khirodkar
Anna Khoreva
Tejas Khot
Parmeshwar Khurd
Hadi Kiapour
Joe Kileel
Chanho Kim
Dahun Kim
Edward Kim
Eunwoo Kim
Han-ul Kim

Hansung Kim
Heewon Kim
Hyo Jin Kim
Hyunwoo J. Kim
Jinkyu Kim
Jiwon Kim
Jongmin Kim
Junsik Kim
Junyeong Kim
Min H. Kim
Namil Kim
Pyojin Kim
Seon Joo Kim
Seong Tae Kim
Seungryong Kim
Sungwoong Kim
Tae Hyun Kim
Vladimir Kim
Won Hwa Kim
Yonghyun Kim
Benjamin Kimia
Akisato Kimura
Pieter-Jan Kindermans
Zsolt Kira
Itaru Kitahara
Hedvig Kjellstrom
Jan Knopp
Takumi Kobayashi
Erich Kobler
Parker Koch
Reinhard Koch
Elyor Kodirov
Amir Kolaman
Nicholas Kolkin
Dimitrios Kollias
Stefanos Kollias
Soheil Kolouri
Adams Wai-Kin Kong
Naejin Kong
Shu Kong
Tao Kong
Yu Kong
Yoshinori Konishi
Daniil Kononenko
Theodora Kontogianni
Simon Korman

Adam Kortylewski
Jana Kosecka
Jean Kossaifi
Satwik Kottur
Rigas Kouskouridas
Adriana Kovashka
Rama Kovvuri
Adarsh Kowdle
Jedrzej Kozerawski
Mateusz Kozinski
Philipp Kraehenbuehl
Gregory Kramida
Josip Krapac
Dmitry Kravchenko
Ranjay Krishna
Pavel Krsek
Alexander Krull
Jakob Kruse
Hiroyuki Kubo
Hilde Kuehne
Jason Kuen
Andreas Kuhn
Arjan Kuijper
Zuzana Kukelova
Ajay Kumar
Amit Kumar
Avinash Kumar
Suryansh Kumar
Vijay Kumar
Kaustav Kundu
Weicheng Kuo
Nojun Kwak
Suha Kwak
Junseok Kwon
Nikolaos Kyriazis
Zorah Lähner
Ankit Laddha
Florent Lafarge
Jean Lahoud
Kevin Lai
Shang-Hong Lai
Wei-Sheng Lai
Yu-Kun Lai
Iro Laina
Antony Lam
John Wheatley Lambert

Xiangyuan lan
Xu Lan
Charis Lanaras
Georg Langs
Oswald Lanz
Dong Lao
Yizhen Lao
Agata Lapedriza
Gustav Larsson
Viktor Larsson
Katrin Lasinger
Christoph Lassner
Longin Jan Latecki
Stéphane Lathuilière
Rynson Lau
Hei Law
Justin Lazarow
Svetlana Lazebnik
Hieu Le
Huu Le
Ngan Hoang Le
Trung-Nghia Le
Vuong Le
Colin Lea
Erik Learned-Miller
Chen-Yu Lee
Gim Hee Lee
Hsin-Ying Lee
Hyungtae Lee
Jae-Han Lee
Jimmy Addison Lee
Joonseok Lee
Kibok Lee
Kuang-Huei Lee
Kwonjoon Lee
Minsik Lee
Sang-chul Lee
Seungkyu Lee
Soochan Lee
Stefan Lee
Taehee Lee
Andreas Lehrmann
Jie Lei
Peng Lei
Matthew Joseph Leotta
Wee Kheng Leow

Gil Levi
Evgeny Levinkov
Aviad Levis
Jose Lezama
Ang Li
Bin Li
Bing Li
Boyi Li
Changsheng Li
Chao Li
Chen Li
Cheng Li
Chenglong Li
Chi Li
Chun-Guang Li
Chun-Liang Li
Chunyuan Li
Dong Li
Guanbin Li
Hao Li
Haoxiang Li
Hongsheng Li
Hongyang Li
Houqiang Li
Huibin Li
Jia Li
Jianan Li
Jianguo Li
Junnan Li
Junxuan Li
Kai Li
Ke Li
Kejie Li
Kunpeng Li
Lerenhan Li
Li Erran Li
Mengtian Li
Mu Li
Peihua Li
Peiyi Li
Ping Li
Qi Li
Qing Li
Ruiyu Li
Ruoteng Li
Shaozi Li

Sheng Li
Shiwei Li
Shuang Li
Siyang Li
Stan Z. Li
Tianye Li
Wei Li
Weixin Li
Wen Li
Wenbo Li
Xiaomeng Li
Xin Li
Xiu Li
Xuelong Li
Xueting Li
Yan Li
Yandong Li
Yanghao Li
Yehao Li
Yi Li
Yijun Li
Yikang LI
Yining Li
Yongjie Li
Yu Li
Yu-Jhe Li
Yunpeng Li
Yunsheng Li
Yunzhu Li
Zhe Li
Zhen Li
Zhengqi Li
Zhenyang Li
Zhuwen Li
Dongze Lian
Xiaochen Lian
Zhouhui Lian
Chen Liang
Jie Liang
Ming Liang
Paul Pu Liang
Pengpeng Liang
Shu Liang
Wei Liang
Jing Liao
Minghui Liao

Renjie Liao
Shengcai Liao
Shuai Liao
Yiyi Liao
Ser-Nam Lim
Chen-Hsuan Lin
Chung-Ching Lin
Dahua Lin
Ji Lin
Kevin Lin
Tianwei Lin
Tsung-Yi Lin
Tsung-Yu Lin
Wei-An Lin
Weiyao Lin
Yen-Chen Lin
Yuewei Lin
David B. Lindell
Drew Linsley
Krzysztof Lis
Roee Litman
Jim Little
An-An Liu
Bo Liu
Buyu Liu
Chao Liu
Chen Liu
Cheng-lin Liu
Chenxi Liu
Dong Liu
Feng Liu
Guilin Liu
Haomiao Liu
Heshan Liu
Hong Liu
Ji Liu
Jingen Liu
Jun Liu
Lanlan Liu
Li Liu
Liu Liu
Mengyuan Liu
Miaomiao Liu
Nian Liu
Ping Liu
Risheng Liu

Sheng Liu
Shu Liu
Shuaicheng Liu
Sifei Liu
Siqi Liu
Siying Liu
Songtao Liu
Ting Liu
Tongliang Liu
Tyng-Luh Liu
Wanquan Liu
Wei Liu
Weiyang Liu
Weizhe Liu
Wenyu Liu
Wu Liu
Xialei Liu
Xianglong Liu
Xiaodong Liu
Xiaofeng Liu
Xihui Liu
Xingyu Liu
Xinwang Liu
Xuanqing Liu
Xuebo Liu
Yang Liu
Yaojie Liu
Yebin Liu
Yen-Cheng Liu
Yiming Liu
Yu Liu
Yu-Shen Liu
Yufan Liu
Yun Liu
Zheng Liu
Zhijian Liu
Zhuang Liu
Zichuan Liu
Ziwei Liu
Zongyi Liu
Stephan Liwicki
Liliana Lo Presti
Chengjiang Long
Fuchen Long
Mingsheng Long
Xiang Long

Yang Long
Charles T. Loop
Antonio Lopez
Roberto J. Lopez-Sastre
Javier Lorenzo-Navarro
Manolis Lourakis
Boyu Lu
Canyi Lu
Feng Lu
Guoyu Lu
Hongtao Lu
Jiajun Lu
Jiasen Lu
Jiwen Lu
Kaiyue Lu
Le Lu
Shao-Ping Lu
Shijian Lu
Xiankai Lu
Xin Lu
Yao Lu
Yiping Lu
Yongxi Lu
Yongyi Lu
Zhiwu Lu
Fujun Luan
Benjamin E. Lundell
Hao Luo
Jian-Hao Luo
Ruotian Luo
Weixin Luo
Wenhan Luo
Wenjie Luo
Yan Luo
Zelun Luo
Zixin Luo
Khoa Luu
Zhaoyang Lv
Pengyuan Lyu
Thomas Möllenhoff
Matthias Müller
Bingpeng Ma
Chih-Yao Ma
Chongyang Ma
Huimin Ma
Jiayi Ma

K. T. Ma
Ke Ma
Lin Ma
Liqian Ma
Shugao Ma
Wei-Chiu Ma
Xiaojian Ma
Xingjun Ma
Zhanyu Ma
Zheng Ma
Radek Jakob Mackowiak
Ludovic Magerand
Shweta Mahajan
Siddharth Mahendran
Long Mai
Ameesh Makadia
Oscar Mendez Maldonado
Mateusz Malinowski
Yury Malkov
Arun Mallya
Dipu Manandhar
Massimiliano Mancini
Fabian Manhardt
Kevis-kokitsi Maninis
Varun Manjunatha
Junhua Mao
Xudong Mao
Alina Marcu
Edgar Margffoy-Tuay
Dmitrii Marin
Manuel J. Marin-Jimenez
Kenneth Marino
Niki Martinel
Julieta Martinez
Jonathan Masci
Tomohiro Mashita
Iacopo Masi
David Masip
Daniela Massiceti
Stefan Mathe
Yusuke Matsui
Tetsu Matsukawa
Iain A. Matthews
Kevin James Matzen
Bruce Allen Maxwell
Stephen Maybank

Filip Radenovic
Petia Radeva
Venkatesh
  B. Radhakrishnan
Ilija Radosavovic
Noha Radwan
Rahul Raguram
Tanzila Rahman
Amit Raj
Ajit Rajwade
Kandan Ramakrishnan
Santhosh
  K. Ramakrishnan
Srikumar Ramalingam
Ravi Ramamoorthi
Vasili Ramanishka
Ramprasaath R. Selvaraju
Francois Rameau
Visvanathan Ramesh
Santu Rana
Rene Ranftl
Anand Rangarajan
Anurag Ranjan
Viresh Ranjan
Yongming Rao
Carolina Raposo
Vivek Rathod
Sathya N. Ravi
Avinash Ravichandran
Tammy Riklin Raviv
Daniel Rebain
Sylvestre-Alvise Rebuffi
N. Dinesh Reddy
Timo Rehfeld
Paolo Remagnino
Konstantinos Rematas
Edoardo Remelli
Dongwei Ren
Haibing Ren
Jian Ren
Jimmy Ren
Mengye Ren
Weihong Ren
Wenqi Ren
Zhile Ren
Zhongzheng Ren

Zhou Ren
Vijay Rengarajan
Md A. Reza
Farzaneh Rezaeianaran
Hamed R. Tavakoli
Nicholas Rhinehart
Helge Rhodin
Elisa Ricci
Alexander Richard
Eitan Richardson
Elad Richardson
Christian Richardt
Stephan Richter
Gernot Riegler
Daniel Ritchie
Tobias Ritschel
Samuel Rivera
Yong Man Ro
Richard Roberts
Joseph Robinson
Ignacio Rocco
Mrigank Rochan
Emanuele Rodolà
Mikel D. Rodriguez
Giorgio Roffo
Grégory Rogez
Gemma Roig
Javier Romero
Xuejian Rong
Yu Rong
Amir Rosenfeld
Bodo Rosenhahn
Guy Rosman
Arun Ross
Paolo Rota
Peter M. Roth
Anastasios Roussos
Anirban Roy
Sebastien Roy
Aruni RoyChowdhury
Artem Rozantsev
Ognjen Rudovic
Daniel Rueckert
Adria Ruiz
Javier Ruiz-del-solar
Christian Rupprecht

Chris Russell
Dan Ruta
Jongbin Ryu
Ömer Sümer
Alexandre Sablayrolles
Faraz Saeedan
Ryusuke Sagawa
Christos Sagonas
Tonmoy Saikia
Hideo Saito
Kuniaki Saito
Shunsuke Saito
Shunta Saito
Ken Sakurada
Joaquin Salas
Fatemeh Sadat Saleh
Mahdi Saleh
Pouya Samangouei
Leo Sampaio
  Ferraz Ribeiro
Artsiom Olegovich
  Sanakoyeu
Enrique Sanchez
Patsorn Sangkloy
Anush Sankaran
Aswin Sankaranarayanan
Swami Sankaranarayanan
Rodrigo Santa Cruz
Amartya Sanyal
Archana Sapkota
Nikolaos Sarafianos
Jun Sato
Shin'ichi Satoh
Hosnieh Sattar
Arman Savran
Manolis Savva
Alexander Sax
Hanno Scharr
Simone Schaub-Meyer
Konrad Schindler
Dmitrij Schlesinger
Uwe Schmidt
Dirk Schnieders
Björn Schuller
Samuel Schulter
Idan Schwartz

William Robson Schwartz
Alex Schwing
Sinisa Segvic
Lorenzo Seidenari
Pradeep Sen
Ozan Sener
Soumyadip Sengupta
Arda Senocak
Mojtaba Seyedhosseini
Shishir Shah
Shital Shah
Sohil Atul Shah
Tamar Rott Shaham
Huasong Shan
Qi Shan
Shiguang Shan
Jing Shao
Roman Shapovalov
Gaurav Sharma
Vivek Sharma
Viktoriia Sharmanska
Dongyu She
Sumit Shekhar
Evan Shelhamer
Chengyao Shen
Chunhua Shen
Falong Shen
Jie Shen
Li Shen
Liyue Shen
Shuhan Shen
Tianwei Shen
Wei Shen
William B. Shen
Yantao Shen
Ying Shen
Yiru Shen
Yujun Shen
Yuming Shen
Zhiqiang Shen
Ziyi Shen
Lu Sheng
Yu Sheng
Rakshith Shetty
Baoguang Shi
Guangming Shi

Hailin Shi
Miaojing Shi
Yemin Shi
Zhenmei Shi
Zhiyuan Shi
Kevin Jonathan Shih
Shiliang Shiliang
Hyunjung Shim
Atsushi Shimada
Nobutaka Shimada
Daeyun Shin
Young Min Shin
Koichi Shinoda
Konstantin Shmelkov
Michael Zheng Shou
Abhinav Shrivastava
Tianmin Shu
Zhixin Shu
Hong-Han Shuai
Pushkar Shukla
Christian Siagian
Mennatullah M. Siam
Kaleem Siddiqi
Karan Sikka
Jae-Young Sim
Christian Simon
Martin Simonovsky
Dheeraj Singaraju
Bharat Singh
Gurkirt Singh
Krishna Kumar Singh
Maneesh Kumar Singh
Richa Singh
Saurabh Singh
Suriya Singh
Vikas Singh
Sudipta N. Sinha
Vincent Sitzmann
Josef Sivic
Gregory Slabaugh
Miroslava Slavcheva
Ron Slossberg
Brandon Smith
Kevin Smith
Vladimir Smutny
Noah Snavely

Roger
D. Soberanis-Mukul
Kihyuk Sohn
Francesco Solera
Eric Sommerlade
Sanghyun Son
Byung Cheol Song
Chunfeng Song
Dongjin Song
Jiaming Song
Jie Song
Jifei Song
Jingkuan Song
Mingli Song
Shiyu Song
Shuran Song
Xiao Song
Yafei Song
Yale Song
Yang Song
Yi-Zhe Song
Yibing Song
Humberto Sossa
Cesar de Souza
Adrian Spurr
Srinath Sridhar
Suraj Srinivas
Pratul P. Srinivasan
Anuj Srivastava
Tania Stathaki
Christopher Stauffer
Simon Stent
Rainer Stiefelhagen
Pierre Stock
Julian Straub
Jonathan C. Stroud
Joerg Stueckler
Jan Stuehmer
David Stutz
Chi Su
Hang Su
Jong-Chyi Su
Shuochen Su
Yu-Chuan Su
Ramanathan Subramanian
Yusuke Sugano

Masanori Suganuma
Yumin Suh
Mohammed Suhail
Yao Sui
Heung-Il Suk
Josephine Sullivan
Baochen Sun
Chen Sun
Chong Sun
Deqing Sun
Jin Sun
Liang Sun
Lin Sun
Qianru Sun
Shao-Hua Sun
Shuyang Sun
Weiwei Sun
Wenxiu Sun
Xiaoshuai Sun
Xiaoxiao Sun
Xingyuan Sun
Yifan Sun
Zhun Sun
Sabine Susstrunk
David Suter
Supasorn Suwajanakorn
Tomas Svoboda
Eran Swears
Paul Swoboda
Attila Szabo
Richard Szeliski
Duy-Nguyen Ta
Andrea Tagliasacchi
Yuichi Taguchi
Ying Tai
Keita Takahashi
Kouske Takahashi
Jun Takamatsu
Hugues Talbot
Toru Tamaki
Chaowei Tan
Fuwen Tan
Mingkui Tan
Mingxing Tan
Qingyang Tan
Robby T. Tan

Xiaoyang Tan
Kenichiro Tanaka
Masayuki Tanaka
Chang Tang
Chengzhou Tang
Danhang Tang
Ming Tang
Peng Tang
Qingming Tang
Wei Tang
Xu Tang
Yansong Tang
Youbao Tang
Yuxing Tang
Zhiqiang Tang
Tatsunori Taniai
Junli Tao
Xin Tao
Makarand Tapaswi
Jean-Philippe Tarel
Lyne Tchapmi
Zachary Teed
Bugra Tekin
Damien Teney
Ayush Tewari
Christian Theobalt
Christopher Thomas
Diego Thomas
Jim Thomas
Rajat Mani Thomas
Xinmei Tian
Yapeng Tian
Yingli Tian
Yonglong Tian
Zhi Tian
Zhuotao Tian
Kinh Tieu
Joseph Tighe
Massimo Tistarelli
Matthew Toews
Carl Toft
Pavel Tokmakov
Federico Tombari
Chetan Tonde
Yan Tong
Alessio Tonioni

Andrea Torsello
Fabio Tosi
Du Tran
Luan Tran
Ngoc-Trung Tran
Quan Hung Tran
Truyen Tran
Rudolph Triebel
Martin Trimmel
Shashank Tripathi
Subarna Tripathi
Leonardo Trujillo
Eduard Trulls
Tomasz Trzcinski
Sam Tsai
Yi-Hsuan Tsai
Hung-Yu Tseng
Stavros Tsogkas
Aggeliki Tsoli
Devis Tuia
Shubham Tulsiani
Sergey Tulyakov
Frederick Tung
Tony Tung
Daniyar Turmukhambetov
Ambrish Tyagi
Radim Tylecek
Christos Tzelepis
Georgios Tzimiropoulos
Dimitrios Tzionas
Seiichi Uchida
Norimichi Ukita
Dmitry Ulyanov
Martin Urschler
Yoshitaka Ushiku
Ben Usman
Alexander Vakhitov
Julien P. C. Valentin
Jack Valmadre
Ernest Valveny
Joost van de Weijer
Jan van Gemert
Koen Van Leemput
Gul Varol
Sebastiano Vascon
M. Alex O. Vasilescu

Subeesh Vasu
Mayank Vatsa
David Vazquez
Javier Vazquez-Corral
Ashok Veeraraghavan
Erik Velasco-Salido
Raviteja Vemulapalli
Jonathan Ventura
Manisha Verma
Roberto Vezzani
Ruben Villegas
Minh Vo
MinhDuc Vo
Nam Vo
Michele Volpi
Riccardo Volpi
Carl Vondrick
Konstantinos Vougioukas
Tuan-Hung Vu
Sven Wachsmuth
Neal Wadhwa
Catherine Wah
Jacob C. Walker
Thomas S. A. Wallis
Chengde Wan
Jun Wan
Liang Wan
Renjie Wan
Baoyuan Wang
Boyu Wang
Cheng Wang
Chu Wang
Chuan Wang
Chunyu Wang
Dequan Wang
Di Wang
Dilin Wang
Dong Wang
Fang Wang
Guanzhi Wang
Guoyin Wang
Hanzi Wang
Hao Wang
He Wang
Heng Wang
Hongcheng Wang

Hongxing Wang
Hua Wang
Jian Wang
Jingbo Wang
Jinglu Wang
Jingya Wang
Jinjun Wang
Jinqiao Wang
Jue Wang
Ke Wang
Keze Wang
Le Wang
Lei Wang
Lezi Wang
Li Wang
Liang Wang
Lijun Wang
Limin Wang
Linwei Wang
Lizhi Wang
Mengjiao Wang
Mingzhe Wang
Minsi Wang
Naiyan Wang
Nannan Wang
Ning Wang
Oliver Wang
Pei Wang
Peng Wang
Pichao Wang
Qi Wang
Qian Wang
Qiaosong Wang
Qifei Wang
Qilong Wang
Qing Wang
Qingzhong Wang
Quan Wang
Rui Wang
Ruiping Wang
Ruixing Wang
Shangfei Wang
Shenlong Wang
Shiyao Wang
Shuhui Wang
Song Wang

Tao Wang
Tianlu Wang
Tiantian Wang
Ting-chun Wang
Tingwu Wang
Wei Wang
Weiyue Wang
Wenguan Wang
Wenlin Wang
Wenqi Wang
Xiang Wang
Xiaobo Wang
Xiaofang Wang
Xiaoling Wang
Xiaolong Wang
Xiaosong Wang
Xiaoyu Wang
Xin Eric Wang
Xinchao Wang
Xinggang Wang
Xintao Wang
Yali Wang
Yan Wang
Yang Wang
Yangang Wang
Yaxing Wang
Yi Wang
Yida Wang
Yilin Wang
Yiming Wang
Yisen Wang
Yongtao Wang
Yu-Xiong Wang
Yue Wang
Yujiang Wang
Yunbo Wang
Yunhe Wang
Zengmao Wang
Zhangyang Wang
Zhaowen Wang
Zhe Wang
Zhecan Wang
Zheng Wang
Zhixiang Wang
Zilei Wang
Jianqiao Wangni

Anne S. Wannenwetsch
Jan Dirk Wegner
Scott Wehrwein
Donglai Wei
Kaixuan Wei
Longhui Wei
Pengxu Wei
Ping Wei
Qi Wei
Shih-En Wei
Xing Wei
Yunchao Wei
Zijun Wei
Jerod Weinman
Michael Weinmann
Philippe Weinzaepfel
Yair Weiss
Bihan Wen
Longyin Wen
Wei Wen
Junwu Weng
Tsui-Wei Weng
Xinshuo Weng
Eric Wengrowski
Tomas Werner
Gordon Wetzstein
Tobias Weyand
Patrick Wieschollek
Maggie Wigness
Erik Wijmans
Richard Wildes
Olivia Wiles
Chris Williams
Williem Williem
Kyle Wilson
Calden Wloka
Nicolai Wojke
Christian Wolf
Yongkang Wong
Sanghyun Woo
Scott Workman
Baoyuan Wu
Bichen Wu
Chao-Yuan Wu
Huikai Wu
Jiajun Wu

Jialin Wu
Jiaxiang Wu
Jiqing Wu
Jonathan Wu
Lifang Wu
Qi Wu
Qiang Wu
Ruizheng Wu
Shangzhe Wu
Shun-Cheng Wu
Tianfu Wu
Wayne Wu
Wenxuan Wu
Xiao Wu
Xiaohe Wu
Xinxiao Wu
Yang Wu
Yi Wu
Yiming Wu
Ying Nian Wu
Yue Wu
Zheng Wu
Zhenyu Wu
Zhirong Wu
Zuxuan Wu
Stefanie Wuhrer
Jonas Wulff
Changqun Xia
Fangting Xia
Fei Xia
Gui-Song Xia
Lu Xia
Xide Xia
Yin Xia
Yingce Xia
Yongqin Xian
Lei Xiang
Shiming Xiang
Bin Xiao
Fanyi Xiao
Guobao Xiao
Huaxin Xiao
Taihong Xiao
Tete Xiao
Tong Xiao
Wang Xiao

Yang Xiao
Cihang Xie
Guosen Xie
Jianwen Xie
Lingxi Xie
Sirui Xie
Weidi Xie
Wenxuan Xie
Xiaohua Xie
Fuyong Xing
Jun Xing
Junliang Xing
Bo Xiong
Peixi Xiong
Yu Xiong
Yuanjun Xiong
Zhiwei Xiong
Chang Xu
Chenliang Xu
Dan Xu
Danfei Xu
Hang Xu
Hongteng Xu
Huijuan Xu
Jingwei Xu
Jun Xu
Kai Xu
Mengmeng Xu
Mingze Xu
Qianqian Xu
Ran Xu
Weijian Xu
Xiangyu Xu
Xiaogang Xu
Xing Xu
Xun Xu
Yanyu Xu
Yichao Xu
Yong Xu
Yongchao Xu
Yuanlu Xu
Zenglin Xu
Zheng Xu
Chuhui Xue
Jia Xue
Nan Xue

Tianfan Xue
Xiangyang Xue
Abhay Yadav
Yasushi Yagi
I. Zeki Yalniz
Kota Yamaguchi
Toshihiko Yamasaki
Takayoshi Yamashita
Junchi Yan
Ke Yan
Qingan Yan
Sijie Yan
Xinchen Yan
Yan Yan
Yichao Yan
Zhicheng Yan
Keiji Yanai
Bin Yang
Ceyuan Yang
Dawei Yang
Dong Yang
Fan Yang
Guandao Yang
Guorun Yang
Haichuan Yang
Hao Yang
Jianwei Yang
Jiaolong Yang
Jie Yang
Jing Yang
Kaiyu Yang
Linjie Yang
Meng Yang
Michael Ying Yang
Nan Yang
Shuai Yang
Shuo Yang
Tianyu Yang
Tien-Ju Yang
Tsun-Yi Yang
Wei Yang
Wenhan Yang
Xiao Yang
Xiaodong Yang
Xin Yang
Yan Yang

Yanchao Yang
Yee Hong Yang
Yezhou Yang
Zhenheng Yang
Anbang Yao
Angela Yao
Cong Yao
Jian Yao
Li Yao
Ting Yao
Yao Yao
Zhewei Yao
Chengxi Ye
Jianbo Ye
Keren Ye
Linwei Ye
Mang Ye
Mao Ye
Qi Ye
Qixiang Ye
Mei-Chen Yeh
Raymond Yeh
Yu-Ying Yeh
Sai-Kit Yeung
Serena Yeung
Kwang Moo Yi
Li Yi
Renjiao Yi
Alper Yilmaz
Junho Yim
Lijun Yin
Weidong Yin
Xi Yin
Zhichao Yin
Tatsuya Yokota
Ryo Yonetani
Donggeun Yoo
Jae Shin Yoon
Ju Hong Yoon
Sung-eui Yoon
Laurent Younes
Changqian Yu
Fisher Yu
Gang Yu
Jiahui Yu
Kaicheng Yu

Ke Yu
Lequan Yu
Ning Yu
Qian Yu
Ronald Yu
Ruichi Yu
Shoou-I Yu
Tao Yu
Tianshu Yu
Xiang Yu
Xin Yu
Xiyu Yu
Youngjae Yu
Yu Yu
Zhiding Yu
Chunfeng Yuan
Ganzhao Yuan
Jinwei Yuan
Lu Yuan
Quan Yuan
Shanxin Yuan
Tongtong Yuan
Wenjia Yuan
Ye Yuan
Yuan Yuan
Yuhui Yuan
Huanjing Yue
Xiangyu Yue
Ersin Yumer
Sergey Zagoruyko
Egor Zakharov
Amir Zamir
Andrei Zanfir
Mihai Zanfir
Pablo Zegers
Bernhard Zeisl
John S. Zelek
Niclas Zeller
Huayi Zeng
Jiabei Zeng
Wenjun Zeng
Yu Zeng
Xiaohua Zhai
Fangneng Zhan
Huangying Zhan
Kun Zhan

Xiaohang Zhan
Baochang Zhang
Bowen Zhang
Cecilia Zhang
Changqing Zhang
Chao Zhang
Chengquan Zhang
Chi Zhang
Chongyang Zhang
Dingwen Zhang
Dong Zhang
Feihu Zhang
Hang Zhang
Hanwang Zhang
Hao Zhang
He Zhang
Hongguang Zhang
Hua Zhang
Ji Zhang
Jianguo Zhang
Jianming Zhang
Jiawei Zhang
Jie Zhang
Jing Zhang
Juyong Zhang
Kai Zhang
Kaipeng Zhang
Ke Zhang
Le Zhang
Lei Zhang
Li Zhang
Lihe Zhang
Linguang Zhang
Lu Zhang
Mi Zhang
Mingda Zhang
Peng Zhang
Pingping Zhang
Qian Zhang
Qilin Zhang
Quanshi Zhang
Richard Zhang
Rui Zhang
Runze Zhang
Shengping Zhang
Shifeng Zhang

Shuai Zhang
Songyang Zhang
Tao Zhang
Ting Zhang
Tong Zhang
Wayne Zhang
Wei Zhang
Weizhong Zhang
Wenwei Zhang
Xiangyu Zhang
Xiaolin Zhang
Xiaopeng Zhang
Xiaoqin Zhang
Xiuming Zhang
Ya Zhang
Yang Zhang
Yimin Zhang
Yinda Zhang
Ying Zhang
Yongfei Zhang
Yu Zhang
Yulun Zhang
Yunhua Zhang
Yuting Zhang
Zhanpeng Zhang
Zhao Zhang
Zhaoxiang Zhang
Zhen Zhang
Zheng Zhang
Zhifei Zhang
Zhijin Zhang
Zhishuai Zhang
Ziming Zhang
Bo Zhao
Chen Zhao
Fang Zhao
Haiyu Zhao
Han Zhao
Hang Zhao
Hengshuang Zhao
Jian Zhao
Kai Zhao
Liang Zhao
Long Zhao
Qian Zhao
Qibin Zhao

Qijun Zhao
Rui Zhao
Shenglin Zhao
Sicheng Zhao
Tianyi Zhao
Wenda Zhao
Xiangyun Zhao
Xin Zhao
Yang Zhao
Yue Zhao
Zhichen Zhao
Zijing Zhao
Xiantong Zhen
Chuanxia Zheng
Feng Zheng
Haiyong Zheng
Jia Zheng
Kang Zheng
Shuai Kyle Zheng
Wei-Shi Zheng
Yinqiang Zheng
Zerong Zheng
Zhedong Zheng
Zilong Zheng
Bineng Zhong
Fangwei Zhong
Guangyu Zhong
Yiran Zhong
Yujie Zhong
Zhun Zhong
Chunluan Zhou
Huiyu Zhou
Jiahuan Zhou
Jun Zhou
Lei Zhou
Luowei Zhou
Luping Zhou
Mo Zhou
Ning Zhou
Pan Zhou
Peng Zhou
Qianyi Zhou
S. Kevin Zhou
Sanping Zhou
Wengang Zhou
Xingyi Zhou

Yanzhao Zhou
Yi Zhou
Yin Zhou
Yipin Zhou
Yuyin Zhou
Zihan Zhou
Alex Zihao Zhu
Chenchen Zhu
Feng Zhu
Guangming Zhu
Ji Zhu
Jun-Yan Zhu
Lei Zhu
Linchao Zhu
Rui Zhu
Shizhan Zhu
Tyler Lixuan Zhu

Wei Zhu
Xiangyu Zhu
Xinge Zhu
Xizhou Zhu
Yanjun Zhu
Yi Zhu
Yixin Zhu
Yizhe Zhu
Yousong Zhu
Zhe Zhu
Zhen Zhu
Zheng Zhu
Zhenyao Zhu
Zhihui Zhu
Zhuotun Zhu
Bingbing Zhuang
Wei Zhuo

Christian Zimmermann
Karel Zimmermann
Larry Zitnick
Mohammadreza
  Zolfaghari
Maria Zontak
Daniel Zoran
Changqing Zou
Chuhang Zou
Danping Zou
Qi Zou
Yang Zou
Yuliang Zou
Georgios Zoumpourlis
Wangmeng Zuo
Xinxin Zuo

Additional Reviewers

Victoria Fernandez
  Abrevaya
Maya Aghaei
Allam Allam
Christine
  Allen-Blanchette
Nicolas Aziere
Assia Benbihi
Neha Bhargava
Bharat Lal Bhatnagar
Joanna Bitton
Judy Borowski
Amine Bourki
Romain Brégier
Tali Brayer
Sebastian Bujwid
Andrea Burns
Yun-Hao Cao
Yuning Chai
Xiaojun Chang
Bo Chen
Shuo Chen
Zhixiang Chen
Junsuk Choe
Hung-Kuo Chu

Jonathan P. Crall
Kenan Dai
Lucas Deecke
Karan Desai
Prithviraj Dhar
Jing Dong
Wei Dong
Turan Kaan Elgin
Francis Engelmann
Erik Englesson
Fartash Faghri
Zicong Fan
Yang Fu
Risheek Garrepalli
Yifan Ge
Marco Godi
Helmut Grabner
Shuxuan Guo
Jianfeng He
Zhezhi He
Samitha Herath
Chih-Hui Ho
Yicong Hong
Vincent Tao Hu
Julio Hurtado

Jaedong Hwang
Andrey Ignatov
Muhammad
  Abdullah Jamal
Saumya Jetley
Meiguang Jin
Jeff Johnson
Minsoo Kang
Saeed Khorram
Mohammad Rami Koujan
Nilesh Kulkarni
Sudhakar Kumawat
Abdelhak Lemkhenter
Alexander Levine
Jiachen Li
Jing Li
Jun Li
Yi Li
Liang Liao
Ruochen Liao
Tzu-Heng Lin
Phillip Lippe
Bao-di Liu
Bo Liu
Fangchen Liu

Hanxiao Liu
Hongyu Liu
Huidong Liu
Miao Liu
Xinxin Liu
Yongfei Liu
Yu-Lun Liu
Amir Livne
Tiange Luo
Wei Ma
Xiaoxuan Ma
Ioannis Marras
Georg Martius
Effrosyni Mavroudi
Tim Meinhardt
Givi Meishvili
Meng Meng
Zihang Meng
Zhongqi Miao
Gyeongsik Moon
Khoi Nguyen
Yung-Kyun Noh
Antonio Norelli
Jaeyoo Park
Alexander Pashevich
Mandela Patrick
Mary Phuong
Bingqiao Qian
Yu Qiao
Zhen Qiao
Sai Saketh Rambhatla
Aniket Roy
Amelie Royer
Parikshit Vishwas
    Sakurikar
Mark Sandler
Mert Bülent Sarıyıldız
Tanner Schmidt
Anshul B. Shah

Ketul Shah
Rajvi Shah
Hengcan Shi
Xiangxi Shi
Yujiao Shi
William A. P. Smith
Guoxian Song
Robin Strudel
Abby Stylianou
Xinwei Sun
Reuben Tan
Qingyi Tao
Kedar S. Tatwawadi
Anh Tuan Tran
Son Dinh Tran
Eleni Triantafillou
Aristeidis Tsitiridis
Md Zasim Uddin
Andrea Vedaldi
Evangelos Ververas
Vidit Vidit
Paul Voigtlaender
Bo Wan
Huanyu Wang
Huiyu Wang
Junqiu Wang
Pengxiao Wang
Tai Wang
Xinyao Wang
Tomoki Watanabe
Mark Weber
Xi Wei
Botong Wu
James Wu
Jiamin Wu
Rujie Wu
Yu Wu
Rongchang Xie
Wei Xiong

Yunyang Xiong
An Xu
Chi Xu
Yinghao Xu
Fei Xue
Tingyun Yan
Zike Yan
Chao Yang
Heran Yang
Ren Yang
Wenfei Yang
Xu Yang
Rajeev Yasarla
Shaokai Ye
Yufei Ye
Kun Yi
Haichao Yu
Hanchao Yu
Ruixuan Yu
Liangzhe Yuan
Chen-Lin Zhang
Fandong Zhang
Tianyi Zhang
Yang Zhang
Yiyi Zhang
Yongshun Zhang
Yu Zhang
Zhiwei Zhang
Jiaojiao Zhao
Yipu Zhao
Xingjian Zhen
Haizhong Zheng
Tiancheng Zhi
Chengju Zhou
Hao Zhou
Hao Zhu
Alexander Zimin

Contents – Part XIII

Fashion Captioning: Towards Generating Accurate Descriptions with Semantic Rewards

XuewenYang[1]([✉]), Heming Zhang[2], Di Jin[3], Yingru Liu[1], Chi-Hao Wu[2], Jianchao Tan[4], Dongliang Xie[5], Jue Wang[6], and Xin Wang[1]

[1] Stony Brook University, Stony Brook, USA
xuewen.yang@stonybrook.edu
[2] USC,Los Angeles, USA
[3] MIT, Cambridge, USA
[4] Kwai Inc., Washington, USA
[5] BUPT, Beijing, China
[6] Megvii, Beijing, China

Abstract. Generating accurate descriptions for online fashion items is important not only for enhancing customers' shopping experiences, but also for the increase of online sales. Besides the need of correctly presenting the attributes of items, the expressions in an enchanting style could better attract customer interests. The goal of this work is to develop a novel learning framework for accurate and expressive fashion captioning. Different from popular work on image captioning, it is hard to identify and describe the rich attributes of fashion items. We seed the description of an item by first identifying its attributes, and introduce *attribute-level semantic* (ALS) reward and *sentence-level semantic* (SLS) reward as metrics to improve the quality of text descriptions. We further integrate the training of our model with maximum likelihood estimation (MLE), attribute embedding, and Reinforcement Learning (RL). To facilitate the learning, we build a new FAshion CAptioning Dataset (FACAD), which contains 993K images and 130K corresponding enchanting and diverse descriptions. Experiments on FACAD demonstrate the effectiveness of our model (Code and data: https://github.com/xuewyang/Fashion_Captioning).

Keywords: Fashion · Captioning · Reinforcement Learning · Semantics

1 Introduction

Motivated by the quick global growth of the fashion industry, which is worth trillions of dollars, extensive efforts have been devoted to fashion related research over the last few years. Those research directions include clothing attribute

Electronic supplementary material The online version of this chapter (https://doi.org/10.1007/978-3-030-58601-0_1) contains supplementary material, which is available to authorized users.

© Springer Nature Switzerland AG 2020
A. Vedaldi et al. (Eds.): ECCV 2020, LNCS 12358, pp. 1–17, 2020.
https://doi.org/10.1007/978-3-030-58601-0_1

prediction and landmark detection [24,36], fashion recommendation [40], item retrieval [23,37], clothing parsing [7,14], and outfit recommendation [5,11,25].

Accurate and enchanting descriptions of clothes on shopping websites can help customers without fashion knowledge to better understand the features (attributes, style, functionality, benefits to buy, etc.) of the items and increase online sales by enticing more customers. However, manually writing the descriptions is a non-trivial and highly expensive task. Thus, the automatic generation of descriptions is in urgent need. Since there exist no studies on generating fashion related descriptions, in this paper, we propose specific schemes on *Fashion Captioning*. Our design is built upon our newly created *FAshion CAptioning Dataset* (FACAD), the first fashion captioning dataset consisting of over 993K images and 130K descriptions with massive attributes and categories. Compared with general image captioning datasets (e.g. MS COCO [4]), the descriptions of fashion items have three unique features (as can be seen from Fig. 1), which makes the automatic generation of captions a challenging task. First, fashion captioning needs to describe the fine-grained attributes of a single item, while image captioning generally narrates the objects and their relations in the image (e.g., a person in a dress). Second, the expressions to describe the clothes tend to be long so as to present the rich attributes of fashion items. The average length of captions in FACAD is 21 words while a sentence in the MS COCO caption dataset contains 10.4 words in average. Third, FACAD has a more enchanting expression style than MS COCO to arouse greater customer interests. Sentences like "pearly", "so-simple yet so-chic", "retro flair" are more attractive than the plain or "undecorated" MS COCO descriptions.

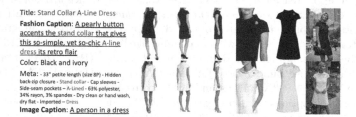

Fig. 1. An example for Fashion Captioning. The images are of different perspectives, colors and scenarios (shop-street). Other information contained include a title, a description (caption) from a fashion expert, the color info and the meta info. Words in color denotes the attributes used in sentence.

The image captioning problem has been widely studied and achieved great progress in recent years. An encoder-decoder paradigm is generally followed with a deep convolutional neural network (CNN) to encode the input images and a Long Short Term Memory (LSTM) decoder to generate the descriptions [2,15,17,18,39]. The encoder-decoder model is trained via maximum likelihood estimation (MLE), which aims to maximize the likelihood of the next word given the previous words. However, MLE-based methods will cause the model to generate "unmatched" descriptions for the fashion items, where sentences cannot precisely describe the attributes of items. This is due to two reasons.

First, MLE treats the attribute and non-attribute words equally. Attribute words are not emphasized and directly optimized in the training process, however, they are more important and should be considered as the key parts in the evaluation. Second, MLE maximizes its objective word-by-word without considering the global semantic meaning of the sentence. This shortcoming may lead to generating a caption that wrongly describes the category of the item.

To generate better descriptions for fashion items, we propose two semantic rewards as the objective to optimize and train our model using Reinforcement Learning (RL). Specifically, we propose an *attribute-level semantic* (ALS) reward with an attribute-matching algorithm to measure the consistency level of attributes between the generated sentences and ground-truth. By incorporating the semantic metric of attributes into our objective, we increase the quality of sentence generation from the semantic perspective. As a second procedure, we propose a *sentence-level semantic* (SLS) reward to capture the semantic meaning of the whole sentence. Given a text classifier pretrained on the sentence category classification task, the high level features of the generated description, i.e., the category feature, should stay the same as the ground-truth sentence. In this paper, we use the output probability of the generated sentence as the groundtruth category as the SLS reward. Since both ALS reward and SLS reward are non-differentiable, we seek RL to optimize them.

In addition, to guarantee that the image features extracted from the CNN encoder are meaningful and correct, we design a visual attribute predictor to make sure that the predicted attributes match the ground-truth ones. Then attributes extracted are used as the condition in the LSTM decoder to produce the words of description. This work has three main contributions.

1. We build a large-scale fashion captioning dataset FACAD of over 993K images which are comprehensively annotated with categories, attributes and descriptions. To the best of our knowledge, it is the first fashion captioning dataset available. We expect that this dataset will greatly benefit the research community, in not only developing various fashion related algorithms and applications, but also helping visual language related studies.
2. We introduce two novel rewards (ALS and SLS) into the Reinforcement Learning framework to capture the semantics at both the attribute level and the sentence level to largely increase the accuracy of fashion captioning.
3. We introduce a visual attribute predictor to better capture the attributes of the image. The generated description seeded on the attribute information can more accurately describe the item.

2   Related Work

Fashion Studies. Most of the fashion related studies [5,7,23,24,33,36,40] involve images. For outfit recommendation, Cucurull *et al.* [5] used a graph convolutional neural network to model the relations between items in a outfit set, while Vasileva *et al.* [33] used a triplet-net to integrate the type information into the recommendation. Wang *et al.* [36] used an attentive fashion grammar network for landmark detection and clothing category classification. Yu *et al.* [40]

introduced the aesthetic information, which is highly relevant with user preference, into clothing recommending systems. Text information has also been exploited. Han *et al.* [11] used title features to regularize the image features learned. Similar techniques were used in [33]. But no previous studies focus on fashion captioning.

Image Captioning. Image captioning helps machine understand visual information and express it in natural language, and has attracted increasingly interests in computer vision. State-of-the-art approaches [2,15,17,39] mainly use encoder-decoder frameworks with attention to generate captions for images. Xu *et al.* [39] developed soft and hard attention mechanisms to focus on different regions in the image when generating different words. Johnson *et al.* [17] proposed a fully convolutional localization network to generate dense regions of interest and use the generated regions to generate captions. Similarly, Anderson *et al.* [2] and Ma *et al.* [26] used an object detector like Faster R-CNN [29] or Mask R-CNN [12] to extract regions of interests over which an attention mechanism is defined. Regardless of the methods used, image captioning generally describes the contents based on the relative positions and relations of objects in an image. Fashion Captioning, however, needs to describe the implicit attributes of the item which cannot be easily localized by object detectors.

Recently, policy-gradient methods for Reinforcement Learning (RL) have been utilized to train deep end-to-end systems directly on non-differentiable metrics [38]. Commonly the output of the inference is applied to normalize the rewards of RL. Ren *et al.* [30] introduced a decision-making framework utilizing a *policy network* and a *value network* to collaboratively generate captions with reward driven by visual-semantic embedding. Rennie *et al.* [31] used self-critical sequence training for image captioning. The reward is provided using CIDEr [35] metric. Gao *et al.* [8] extended [31] by running a n-step self-critical training. The specific metrics used in RL approach are hard to generalize to other applications, and optimizing specific metrics often impact other metrics severely. However, the semantic rewards we introduce are general and effective in improving the quality of caption generation.

3   The FAshion CAptioning Dataset

We introduce a new dataset - FAshion CAptioning Dataset (FACAD) - to study captioning for fashion items. In this section, we will describe how FACAD is built and what are its special properties.

3.1   Data Collection, Labeling and Pre-Processing

We mainly crawl fashion images with detailed information using Google Chrome, which can be exploited for the fashion captioning task. Each clothing item has on average 6–7 images of various colors and poses. The resolution of the images is 1560×2392, much higher than other fashion datasets.

In order to better understand fashion items, we label them with rich categories and attributes. An example category of clothes can be "dress" or "T-shirt", while an attribute such as "pink" or "lace" provides some detailed information about a specific item. The list of the categories is generated by picking the last word of the item titles. After manual selection and filtering, there are 472 total valuable categories left. We then merge similar categories and only keep ones that contain over 200 items, resulting in 78 unique categories. Each item belongs to only one category. The number of items contained by the top-20 categories are shown in Fig. 2a.

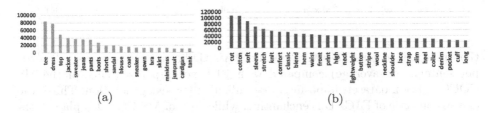

(a)   (b)

Fig. 2. (a) Number of items in the top-20 categories. (b) Number of items in the top-30 attributes.

Since there are a large number of attributes and each image can have several attributes, manual labeling is non-trivial. We utilize the title, description and meta data to help label attributes for the items. Specifically, we first extract the nouns and adjectives in the title using Stanford Parser [32], and then select a noun or adjective as the attribute word if it also appears in the caption and meta data. The total number of attributes we extracted is over 3000 and we only keep those that appear in more than 10 items, resulting in a list of 990 attributes. Each item owns approximately 7.3 attributes. We show the number of items that are associated with the top-30 attributes in Fig. 2b.

To have clean captions, we tokenize the descriptions using NLTK tokenizer[1] and remove the non-alphanumeric words. We lowercase all caption words.

3.2 Comparison with Other Datasets

The statistics of our FACAD is shown in Table 1. Compared with other fashion datasets such as [9,10,24,42,43], FACAD has two outstanding properties. First, it is the biggest fashion datasets, with over 993K diverse fashion images of all four seasons, ages (kids and adults), categories (clothing, shoes, bag, accessories, etc.), angles of human body (front, back, side, etc.). Second, it is the first dataset to tackle captioning problem for fashion items. 130K descriptions with average length of 21 words was pre-processed for future researches.

Compared with MS COCO [4] image captioning dataset, FACAD is different in three aspects. First, FACAD contains the fine-grained descriptions of attributes of fashion-related items, while MS COCO narrates the objects and

---

[1] https://www.nltk.org/api/nltk.tokenize.html.

Table 1. Comparison of different datasets. ∗ Image sizes are approximate values. CAT: category, AT: attribute, CAP: caption, FC: fashion captioning, IC: image captioning, CLS: fashion classification, SEG: segmentation, RET: retrieval.

Datasets	# img	Img size∗	# CAT	# AT	# CAP	Avg len	Style	Task
FACAD	993K	1560 × 2392	78	990	130K	21	enchanting	FC
MS COCO [4]	123K	640 × 480	–	–	616K	10.4	Plain	IC
VG [21]	108K	500 × 500	-	-	5040K	5.7	Plain	IC
DFashion [9,24]	800K	700 × 1000	50	1000	-	-	-	CLS
Moda [42]	55K	-	13	-	-	-	-	SEG
Fashion AI [43]	357K	512 × 512	6	41	-	-	-	CLS
Fashion IQ [10]	77K	300 × 400	3	1000	-	-	-	RET

their relations in general images. Second, FACAD has longer captions (21 words per sentence on average) compared with 10.4 words per sentence of the MS COCO caption dataset, imposing more difficulty for text generation. Third, the expression style of FACAD is enchanting, while that of MS COCO is plain without rich expressions. As illustrated in Fig. 1, words like "pearly", "so-simple yet so-chic", "retro flair" are more attractive than the plain MS COCO descriptions, like "a person in a dress". This special enchanting style is important in better describing an item and attracting more customers, but also imposes another challenge for building the caption models.

4 Respecting Semantics for Fashion Captioning

In this section, we first formulate the basic fashion captioning problem and its general solution using Maximum Likelihood Estimation (MLE). We then propose a set of strategies to increase the performance of fashion captions: 1) learning specific fashion attributes from the image; 2) establishing attribute-level and sentence-level semantic rewards so that the caption can be generated to be more similar to the ground truth through Reinforcement Learning (RL); 3) alternative training with MLE and RL to optimize the model.

4.1 Basic Problem Formulation

We define a dataset of image-sentence pairs as $\mathcal{D} = \{(X, Y)\}$. Given an item image X, the objective of Fashion Captioning is to generate a description $Y = \{y_1, \ldots, y_T\}$ with a sequence of T words, $y_i \in V^K$ being the i-th word, V^K being the vocabulary of K words. The beginning of each sentence is marked with a special <BOS> token, and the end with an <EOS> token. We denote $\mathbf{y}_i$ as the embedding for word y_i. To generate a caption, the objective of our model is to minimize the negative log-likelihood of the correct caption using maximum likelihood estimation (MLE):

$$\mathcal{L}_{MLE} = -\sum_{t=1}^{T} \log p(y_t | y_{1:t-1}, X). \tag{1}$$

As shown in Fig. 3, we use an encoder-decoder architecture to achieve this objective. The encoder is a pre-trained CNN, which takes an image as the input and extracts B image features, $\mathbf{X} = \{\mathbf{x}_1, \ldots, \mathbf{x}_B\}$. We dynamically re-weight the input image features $\mathbf{X}$ with an attention matrix γ to focus on specific regions of the image at each time step t [39], which results in a weighted image feature $\mathbf{x}_t = \sum_{i=1}^{B} \gamma_t^i \mathbf{x}_i$. The weighted image feature is then fed into a decoder which is a Long Short-Term Memory (LSTM) network for sentence generation. The decoder predicts one word at a time and controls the fluency of the generated sentence. More specifically, when predicting the word at the t-th step, the decoder takes as input the embedding of the generated word y_{t-1}, the weighted image feature $\mathbf{x}_t$ and the previous hidden state $\mathbf{h}_{t-1}$. The initial memory state and hidden state of the LSTM are initialized by an average of the image features fed through two feed-forward networks f_c and f_h which are trained together with the whole model: $\mathbf{c}_0 = f_c(\frac{1}{B} \sum_{i=1}^{B} \mathbf{x}_i)$, $\mathbf{h}_0 = f_h(\frac{1}{B} \sum_{i=1}^{B} \mathbf{x}_i)$. The decoder then outputs a hidden state $\mathbf{h}_t$ (Eq. 2) and applies a linear layer f and a *softmax* layer to get the probability of the next word (Eq. 3):

$$\mathbf{h}_t = LSTM([\mathbf{y}_{t-1}; \mathbf{x}_t], \mathbf{h}_{t-1}) \qquad (2)$$

$$p_\theta(y_t | y_{1:t-1}, \mathbf{x}_t) = softmax(f(\mathbf{h}_t)) \qquad (3)$$

where [;] denotes vector concatenation.

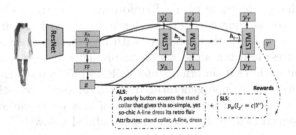

Fig. 3. The proposed model architecture and rewards.

4.2 Attribute Embedding

To make sure that the caption correctly describes the item attributes, we introduce an attribute feature $\mathbf{z}$ into the model, which modifies Eq. 1 into:

$$\mathcal{L}_{MLE} = -\sum_{t=1}^{T} \log p(y_t | y_{1:t-1}, \mathbf{z}, X). \qquad (4)$$

This objective aims at seeding sentence generation with the attribute feature of the image. To regularize the encoder to output attribute-correct features, we add a visual attribute predictor to the encoder-decoder model. As each item in the FACAD has its attributes shown in the captions, the predictor can be trained by solving the problem of multi-label classification. The trained model can be applied to extract the attributes of an image to produce the caption.

Figure 3 illustrates the attribute prediction network. We attach a feed-forward (FF) network to the CNN feature extractor, and its output is fed into a sigmoid layer to produce a probability vector and calculate multi-class multi-label loss. We can then modify Eq. 2 and Eq. 3 to include the attribute embedding as:

$$\mathbf{h}_t = LSTM([\mathbf{y}_{t-1}; \mathbf{x}_t; \mathbf{z}], \mathbf{h}_{t-1}) \tag{5}$$

$$p_\theta(y_t|y_{1:t-1}, \mathbf{x}_t, \mathbf{z}) = softmax(f_h(\mathbf{h}_t)) \tag{6}$$

where $\mathbf{z}$ is the attribute features before the output layer, $[;]$ denotes vector concatenation.

4.3 Increasing the Accuracy of Captioning with Semantic Rewards

Simply training with MLE can force the model to generate most likely words in the vocabulary, but not help decode the attributes that are crucial to the fashion captioning. To solve this issue, we propose to exploit two semantic metrics to increase the accuracy of fashion captioning: an attribute-level semantic reward to encourage our model to generate a sentence with more attributes in the image, and a sentence-level semantic reward to encourage the generated sentence to more accurately describe the category of a fashion item. Because optimizing the two rewards is a non-differentiable process, during the MLE training, we supplement fashion captioning with a Reinforcement Learning (RL) process.

In the RL process, our encoder-decoder network with attribute predictor can be viewed as an *agent* that interacts with an external *environment* (words and image features) and takes the *action* to predict the next word. After each action, the agent updates its internal *state* (cells and hidden states of the LSTM, attention weights, etc.). Upon generating the *end-of-sequence* (<EOS>) token, the agent observes a *reward* r as a judgement of how good the overall decision is. We have designed two levels of rewards, as defined below:

Attribute-Level Semantic (ALS) Reward. We propose the use of *attribute-level semantic* (ALS) reward to encourage our model to locally generate as many correct attributes as possible in a caption. First, we need to represent an attribute with a phrase. We denote a contiguous sequence of n words as an n-gram, and we only consider $n = 1, 2$ since nearly all the attributes contain 1 or 2 words. We call an n-gram that contains a correct attribute a tuple t_n. That is, a tuple t_n in the generated sentence contains the attribute in the groundtruth sentence and results in an attribute "Match". We define the proportion of "Matching" for attributes of n words in a generated sentence as: $P(n) = \frac{Match(n)}{H(n)}$, where $H(n)$ is the total number of n-grams contained by a sentence generated. An n-gram may or may not contain an attribute. For a generated sentence with M words, $H(n) = M + 1 - n$. The total number of "Matches" is defined as:

$$Match(n) = \sum_{t_n} \min(C_g(t_n), C_r(t_n)) \tag{7}$$

where $C_g(t_n)$ is the number of times a tuple t_n occurs in the generated sentence, and $C_r(t_n)$ is the number of times the same tuple t_n occurs in the groundtruth caption. We use min() to make sure that the generated sentence does not contain more repeated attributes than the groundtruth. We then define the ALS reward as:

$$r_{ALS} = \beta\{\prod_{n=1}^{2} P(n)\}^{\frac{1}{n}} \tag{8}$$

where β is used to penalize short sentences which is defined as:

$$\beta = \exp\{\min(0, \frac{l-L}{l})\} \tag{9}$$

where L is the length of the groundtruth and l is the length of the generated sentence. When the generated sentence is much shorter than the groundtruth, although the model can decode the correct attributes with a high reward, the sentence may not be expressive with an enchanting style. We thus leverage a penalization factor to discourage this.

Sentence-Level Semantic (SLS) Reward. The use of attribute-level semantic score can help generate a sentence with more correct attributes, which thus increases the similarity of the generated sentence with the groundtruth one at the local level. To further increase the similarity between the generated sentence and groundtruth caption at the global level, we consider enforcing a generated sentence to describe an item with the correct category. This design principle is derived based on our observation that items of the same category share many attributes, while those of different categories often have totally different sets of attributes. Thus, a sentence generally contains more correct attributes if it can describe an item with a correct category.

To achieve the goal, we pretrain a text category classifier p_ϕ, which is a 3-layer text CNN, using captions as data and their categories as labels (ϕ denotes the parameters of the classifier). Taking the generated sentence $Y' = \{y'_1, \ldots, y'_T\}$ as inputs, the text category classifier will output a probability distribution $p_\phi(l_{Y'}|Y')$, where $l_{Y'}$ is the category label for Y'. The sentence-level semantic reward is defined as:

$$r_{SLS} = p_\phi(l_{Y'} = c|Y') \tag{10}$$

where c is the target category of the sentence.

Overall Semantic Rewards. To encourage our model to improve both the ALS reward and the SLS reward, we use an overall semantic reward which is a weighted sum of the two:

$$r = \alpha_1 r_{ALS} + \alpha_2 r_{SLS} \tag{11}$$

where α_1 and α_1 are two hyper-parameters.

Computing Gradient with REINFORCE. The goal of RL training is to minimize the negative expected reward:

$$\mathcal{L}_r = -\mathbb{E}_{Y' \sim p_\theta}[r(Y')] \tag{12}$$

To compute the gradient $\nabla_\theta \mathcal{L}_r(\theta)$, we use the REINFORCE algorithm [38] to calculate the expected gradient of a non-differentiable reward function. To reduce the variance of the expected rewards, the gradient can be generalized by incorporating a *baseline b*:

$$\nabla_\theta \mathcal{L}_r(\theta) = -\mathbb{E}_{Y' \sim p_\theta}[(r(Y') - b)\nabla_\theta \log p_\theta(Y')] \tag{13}$$

In our experiments, the expected gradient is approximated using H samples from p_θ and the baseline is the average reward of all the H sampled sentences:

$$\nabla_\theta \mathcal{L}_r(\theta) \simeq -\frac{1}{H}\sum_{j=1}^{H}[(r_j(Y'_j) - b)\nabla_\theta \log p_\theta(Y'_j)] \tag{14}$$

where $b = \frac{1}{H}\sum_{j=1}^{H} r(Y'_j)$, $Y'_j \sim p_\theta$ is the j-th sampled sentence from model p_θ and $r_j(Y'_j)$ is its corresponding reward.

4.4 Joint Training of MLE and RL.

In practice, rather than starting RL training from a random policy model, we warm-up our model using MLE and attribute embedding objective till converge. We then integrate the pre-trained MLE, attribute embedding, and RL into one model to retrain until it converges again, following the overall loss function:

$$\mathcal{L} = \mathcal{L}_{MLE} + \lambda_1 \mathcal{L}_r + \lambda_2 \mathcal{L}_a \tag{15}$$

with λ_1 and λ_2 being two hyper-parameters.

5   Experiments

5.1   Basic Setting

Dataset and Metrics. We run all methods over FACAD. It contains 993K images and 130K descriptions, and we split the whole dataset, with approximately 794K image-description pairs for training, 99K for validation, and the remaining 100K for test. Images for the same item share the same description. The number of images associated with one item varies, ranging from 2 to 12. As several images in FACAD (e.g., clothes shown in different angles) share the same description, instead of randomly splitting the dataset, we ensure that the images with the same caption are contained in the same data split. We lowercase all sentences and discard non-alphanumeric characters. For words in the training set, we keep the ones that appear at least 5 times, making a vocabulary of 15807 words.

For fair and thorough performance measure, we report results under the commonly used metrics for image captioning, including BLEU [27], METEOR [6], ROUGEL [22], CIDEr [35], SPICE [1]. In addition, we compare the attributes in the generated captions with those in the test set as ground truth to find the average precision rate for each attribute using mean average precision (mAP). To evaluate whether the generated captions belong to the correct category, we report the category prediction accuracy (ACC). We pre-train a 3-layer text CNN [19] as the category classifier p_ϕ, achieving a classification accuracy of 90% on testset.

Network Architecture. As shown in Fig. 3, we use a ResNet-101 [13], pre-trained on ImageNet to encode each image feature. Since there is a large domain shift from ImageNet to FACAD, we fine tune the conv4_x and the conv5_x layers to get better image features. The features output from the final convolutional layer are used to further train over FACAD. We use LSTM [16] as our decoder. The input node dimension and the hidden state dimension of LSTM are both set to 512. The word embeddings of size 512 are uniformly initialized within $[-0.1, 0.1]$. After testing with several combinations of the hyper-parameters, we set the $\alpha_1 = \alpha_2 = 1$ to assign equal weights to both rewards, and $\lambda_1 = \lambda_2 = 1$ to balance MLE, attribute prediction and RL objectives during training. The number of samplings in RL training is $H = 5$.

Training Details. All the models are trained according to the following procedure, unless otherwise specified. We initialize all models by training using MLE objective with cross entropy loss with ADAM [20] optimizer at an initial learning rate of 1×10^{-4}. We anneal the learning rate by a factor of 0.9 every two epochs. After the model training converges on the MLE objective, if RL training is further needed in a method, we switch to MLE + RL training till another converge. The overall process takes about 4 days on two NVIDIA 1080 Ti GPUs.

Baseline Methods. To make fair comparisons, we take image captioning models based both on MLE training and training with MLE+RL. For all the baselines, we use their published codes to run the model, performing a hyperparameter search based on the original author's guidelines. We follow their own training schemes to train the models.

MLE-Based Methods. **CNN-C**[3] is a CNN-based image captioning model which uses a masked convolutional decoder for sentence generation. **SAT** [39] applies CNN-LSTM with attention, and we use its hard attention method. **BUTD** [2] combines the bottom-up and the top-down attention, with the bottom-up part containing a set of salient image regions, each is represented by a pooled convolutional feature vector. **LBPF** [28] uses a look back (LB) approach to introduce attention value from the previous time step into the current attention generation and a predict forward (PF) approach to predict the next two words in one time step. **TRANS** [15] proposes the use of geometric attention for image objects based on Transformer [34].

MLE + RL Based Methods. **AC** [41] uses actor-critic Reinforcement Learning algorithm to directly optimize on CIDEr metric. **Embed-RL** [30] utilizes a "policy" and a "value" network to jointly determine the next best word. **SCST** [31] is a self-critical sequence training algorithm. **SCNST** [8] is a n-step self-critical training algorithm extended from [31]. We use 1-2-2-step-maxpro variant which achieved best performance in the paper.

5.2   Performance Evaluations

Results on Fashion Captioning. Our Semantic Rewards guided Fashion Captioning (SRFC) model achieves the highest scores on all seven metrics. Specifically, it provides 1.7, 1.4, 3.5, 7.4, 1.2, 0.054 and 0.042 points of improvement over the best baseline SCNST on BLEU4, METEOR, ROUGEL, CIDEr, SPICE, mAP and ACC respectively, demonstrating the effectiveness of our proposed model in providing fashion captions. The improvement mainly comes from 3 parts, attribute embedding training, ALS reward and SLS reward. To evaluate how much contribution each part provides to the final results, we remove different components from SRFC and see how the performance degrades. For SRFC without attribute embedding, our model experiences the performance drops of 0.8, 0.6, 1.0, 3.0, 0.3, 0.011 and 0.021 points. After removing ALS, the performance of SRFC drops 1.3, 0.8, 1.5, 4.6 and 0.6 points on the first five metrics. For the same five metrics, the removing of SLS results in higher performance degradation, which indicates that the global semantic reward plays a more important role in ensuring accurate description generation. More interestingly, removing ALS produces a larger drop in mAP, while removing SLS impacts more on ACC. This means that ALS focuses more on producing correct attributes locally, while SLS helps ensure the global semantic accuracy of the generated sentence. Removing both ALS and SLS leads to a large decrease of the performance on all metrics, which suggests that most of the improvement is gained by the proposed two semantic rewards. Finally, with the removal of all three components, the performance of our model is similar to that of the baselines without using any proposed techniques. This demonstrates that all three components are necessary to have a good performance on fashion captioning.

Results with Subjective Evaluation As fashion captioning is used for online shopping systems, attracting customers is a very important goal. Automatically evaluating the ability to attract customers is infeasible. Thus, we perform human evaluation on the attraction of generated captions from different models. 5 human judges of different genders and age groups are presented with 200 samples each. Among five participants, two are below 30, two are from 40 to 50 years old, one is over 60. They all have online shopping experiences. Each sample contains an image, 10 generated captions from all 10 models, with the sequence randomly shuffled. Then they are asked to choose the most attractive caption for each sample. To show the agreement rate, we calculate Fleiss' kappa based on our existing experimental results, with the rate is in the range of [0.6,0.8] indicating consistent agreement, while the range [0.4, 0.6] showing moderate agreement. The agreement rates for different models are SRFC (ours) (0.63), SCNST (0.61), SCST (0.62), Embed-RL (0.54), AC (0.56), TRANS (0.52), LBPF (0.55), BUTD (0.53), SAT (0.55), CNN-C (0.54). The results in Table 3 show that our model produces the most attractive captioning (Table 2).

Table 2. Fashion captioning results - scores of different baseline models as well as different variants of our proposed method. **A:** attribute embedding learning. We highlight the **best** model in bold.

Model	BLEU4	METEOR	ROUGEL	CIDEr	SPICE	mAP	ACC
CNN-C [3]	18.7	18.3	37.8	97.5	16.9	0.133	0.430
SAT [39]	19.1	18.5	38.6	98.4	17.0	0.144	0.433
BUTD [2]	19.9	19.7	39.7	100.1	17.7	0.162	0.439
LBPF [28]	22.2	21.3	43.2	105.3	20.6	0.173	0.471
TRANS [15]	21.2	20.8	42.3	104.5	19.8	0.167	0.455
AC [41]	21.5	20.1	42.8	106.1	19.9	0.166	0.443
Embed-RL [30]	20.9	20.4	42.1	104.7	19.0	0.170	0.459
SCST [31]	22.0	21.2	42.9	106.2	20.5	0.184	0.467
SCNST [8]	22.5	21.8	43.7	107.4	20.7	0.186	0.470
SRFC	**24.2**	**23.2**	**47.2**	**114.8**	**21.9**	**0.240**	**0.512**
SRFC−A	23.4	22.6	46.2	111.8	21.6	0.239	0.491
SRFC−ALS	22.9	22.4	45.7	110.2	21.3	0.233	0.487
SRFC−SLS	22.6	22.2	45.3	109.7	21.1	0.234	0.463
SRFC−ALS−SLS	20.2	19.9	41.5	102.1	18.1	0.178	0.448
SRFC−A−ALS−SLS	19.9	18.7	38.2	98.5	17.1	0.146	0.434

Table 3. Human evaluation on captioning attraction. We highlight the **best** model in bold.

Model	CNN-C	SAT	BUTD	LBPF	TRANS	AC	Embed-RL	SCST	SCNST	SRFC
% best	7.7	7.9	8.1	10.0	8.8	8.4	8.5	10.2	10.7	**19.7**

Qualitative Results and Analysis. Figure 4 shows two qualitative results of our model against SCNST and ground truth. In general, our model can generate more reasonable descriptions compared with SCNST for the target image in the middle column. In the first example, we can see that our model generates a description with more details than SCNST, which only correctly predicted the category and some attributes of the target item.

By providing two other items of the same category and their corresponding captions, we have two interesting observations. First, our model generates descriptions in two steps, it starts learning valuable expressions from similar items (in the same category) based on attributes extracted, and then applies these expressions to describe the target one. Taking the first item (top row of Fig. 4) as an example, our model first gets the correct attributes of the image, i.e., *italian sport coat, wool, silk*. Then it tries to complete a diverse description by learning from the captions of those items with similar attributes. Specifically, it uses *a richly textured blend* and *handsome* from the first item (left column) and *framed with smart notched lapel* (right column) from the second item to make a new description for the target image. The second observation is that our model can enrich description generation by focusing on the attributes identified even if they are not presented in the groundtrue caption. Even though the *notched lapel* is not described by the ground-truth caption, our model correctly discovers this attribute and generates *framed with smart notched lapel* for it. This is because that *notched lapel* is a frequently referred attribute for items of the category *coat*, and this attribute appears in 11.4% descriptions. Similar phenomena can be found for the second result. The capability of extracting the correct attributes owes to the *Attribute Embedding Learning* and *ALS* modules. The *SLS* can help our model generate diverse captions by referring to those from other items with the same category and similar attributes.

Fig. 4. Two qualitative results of SRFC compared with the groundtruth and SCNST. Two target items and their corresponding groundtruth are shown in the red dash-dotted boxes in the middle column. The black dash-dotted boxes contain the captions generated by our model and SCNST. Our model diversely learns different expressions from the other items (on the first and third columns) to describe the target item.

6   Conclusion

In this work, we propose a novel learning framework for *fashion captioning* and create the first fashion captioning dataset FACAD. In light of describing fashion items in a correct and expressive manner, we define two novel metrics ALS and SLS, based on which we concurrently train our model with MLE, attribute embedding and RL training. Since this is the first work on fashion captioning, we apply the evaluation metrics commonly used in the general image captioning. Further research is needed to develop better evaluation metrics.

Acknowledgements. This work is supported in part by the National Science Foundation under Grants NSF ECCS 1731238 and NSF CCF 2007313.

References

1. Anderson, P., Fernando, B., Johnson, M., Gould, S.: SPICE: semantic propositional image caption evaluation. In: Leibe, B., Matas, J., Sebe, N., Welling, M. (eds.) ECCV 2016. LNCS, vol. 9909, pp. 382–398. Springer, Cham (2016). https://doi.org/10.1007/978-3-319-46454-1_24

2. Anderson, P., et al.: Bottom-up and top-down attention for image captioning and visual question answering. In: The IEEE Conference on Computer Vision and Pattern Recognition (CVPR) (2018)
3. Aneja, J., Deshpande, A., Schwing, A.G.: Convolutional image captioning. In: 2018 IEEE/CVF Conference on Computer Vision and Pattern Recognition (2018)
4. Chen, X., et al.: Microsoft COCO captions: Data collection and evaluation server (2015)
5. Cucurull, G., Taslakian, P., Vazquez, D.: Context-aware visual compatibility prediction. In: The IEEE Conference on Computer Vision and Pattern Recognition (CVPR) (June 2019)
6. Denkowski, M., Lavie, A.: Meteor universal: Language specific translation evaluation for any target language. In: Proceedings of the 9th Workshop on Statistical Machine Translation (2014)
7. Gabale, V., Prabhu Subramanian, A.: How to Extract Fashion Trends from Social Media? A Robust Object Detector With Support For Unsupervised Learning. arXiv e-prints (2018)
8. Gao, J., Wang, S., Wang, S., Ma, S., Gao, W.: Self-critical n-step training for image captioning. In: The IEEE Conference on Computer Vision and Pattern Recognition (CVPR) (2019)
9. Ge, Y., Zhang, R., Wu, L., Wang, X., Tang, X., Luo, P.: A versatile benchmark for detection, pose estimation, segmentation and re-identification of clothing images. In: CVPR (2019)
10. Guo, X., Wu, H., Gao, Y., Rennie, S., Feris, R.: The fashion IQ dataset: Retrieving images by combining side information and relative natural language feedback. arXiv preprint arXiv:1905.12794 (2019)
11. Han, X., Wu, Z., Jiang, Y.G., Davis, L.S.: Learning fashion compatibility with bidirectional LSTMs. In: ACM Multimedia (2017)
12. He, K., Gkioxari, G., Dollár, P., Girshick, R.B.: Mask R-CNN. 2017 IEEE International Conference on Computer Vision (ICCV) (2017)
13. He, K., Zhang, X., Ren, S., Sun, J.: Deep residual learning for image recognition. In: 2016 IEEE Conference on Computer Vision and Pattern Recognition (CVPR) (2016)
14. He, Y., Yang, L., Chen, L.: Real-time fashion-guided clothing semantic parsing: a lightweight multi-scale inception neural network and benchmark. In: AAAI Workshops (2017)
15. Herdade, S., Kappeler, A., Boakye, K., Soares, J.: Image captioning: transforming objects into words. In: Advances in Neural Information Processing Systems, vol. 32 (2019)
16. Hochreiter, S., Schmidhuber, J.: Long short-term memory. Neural Comput. **9**(8), 1735–1780 (1997)
17. Johnson, J., Karpathy, A., Fei-Fei, L.: DenseCap: fully convolutional localization networks for dense captioning. In: Proceedings of the IEEE Conference on Computer Vision and Pattern Recognition (2016)
18. Karpathy, A., Fei-Fei, L.: Deep visual-semantic alignments for generating image descriptions. IEEE Trans. Pattern Anal. Mach. Intell. **39**, 664–676 (2017)
19. Kim, Y.: Convolutional neural networks for sentence classification. In: Proceedings of the 2014 Conference on Empirical Methods in Natural Language Processing (EMNLP) (2014)
20. Kingma, D.P., Ba, J.: Adam: A method for stochastic optimization (2015)

21. Krishna, R., et al.: Visual genome: connecting language and vision using crowd-sourced dense image annotations. Int. J. Comput. Vis. **123**, 32–73 (2017). https://doi.org/10.1007/s11263-016-0981-7
22. Lin, C.Y.: ROUGE: A package for automatic evaluation of summaries. In: Text Summarization Branches Out (2004)
23. Liu, S., et al.: Hi, magic closet, tell me what to wear! In: Proceedings of the 20th ACM International Conference on Multimedia (2012)
24. Liu, Z., Luo, P., Qiu, S., Wang, X., Tang, X.: DeepFashion: powering robust clothes recognition and retrieval with rich annotations. In: Proceedings of IEEE Conference on Computer Vision and Pattern Recognition (CVPR) (2016)
25. Lu, Z., Hu, Y., Jiang, Y., Chen, Y., Zeng, B.: Learning binary code for personalized fashion recommendation. In: The IEEE Conference on Computer Vision and Pattern Recognition (CVPR) (June 2019)
26. Ma, C.Y., Kadav, A., Melvin, I., Kira, Z., Alregib, G., Graf, H.: Attend and interact: Higher-order object interactions for video understanding (2017)
27. Papineni, K., Roukos, S., Ward, T., Zhu, W.J.: BLEU: a method for automatic evaluation of machine translation. In: Proceedings of the 40th Annual Meeting of the Association for Computational Linguistics (2002)
28. Qin, Y., Du, J., Zhang, Y., Lu, H.: Look back and predict forward in image captioning. In: The IEEE Conference on Computer Vision and Pattern Recognition (CVPR) (2019)
29. Ren, S., He, K., Girshick, R., Sun, J.: Faster R-CNN: towards real-time object detection with region proposal networks. In: Advances in Neural Information Processing Systems, vol. 28 (2015)
30. Ren, Z., Wang, X., Zhang, N., Lv, X., Li, L.J.: Deep reinforcement learning-based image captioning with embedding reward (2017)
31. Rennie, S.J., Marcheret, E., Mroueh, Y., Ross, J., Goel, V.: Self-critical sequence training for image captioning. In: IEEE Conference on Computer Vision and Pattern Recognition (CVPR) (2017)
32. Socher, R., Bauer, J., Manning, C.D., Ng, A.Y.: Parsing with compositional vector grammars. In: Proceedings of the 51st Annual Meeting of the Association for Computational Linguistics (Volume 1: Long Papers) (2013)
33. Vasileva, M.I., Plummer, B.A., Dusad, K., Rajpal, S., Kumar, R., Forsyth, D.: Learning type-aware embeddings for fashion compatibility. In: Ferrari, V., Hebert, M., Sminchisescu, C., Weiss, Y. (eds.) ECCV 2018. LNCS, vol. 11220, pp. 405–421. Springer, Cham (2018). https://doi.org/10.1007/978-3-030-01270-0_24
34. Vaswani, A., et al.: Attention is all you need. In: Advances in Neural Information Processing Systems, vol. 30 (2017)
35. Vedantam, R., Zitnick, C.L., Parikh, D.: CIDEr: consensus-based image description evaluation. In: CVPR (2015)
36. Wang, W., Xu, Y., Shen, J., Zhu, S.C.: Attentive fashion grammar network for fashion landmark detection and clothing category classification. In: 2018 IEEE/CVF Conference on Computer Vision and Pattern Recognition (2018)
37. Wang, Z., Gu, Y., Zhang, Y., Zhou, J., Gu, X.: Clothing retrieval with visual attention model. In: 2017 IEEE Visual Communications and Image Processing (VCIP), pp. 1–4 (2017)
38. Williams, R.J.: Simple statistical gradient-following algorithms for connectionist reinforcement learning. Mach. Learn. **8**, 229–256 (1992). https://doi.org/10.1007/BF00992696

39. Xu, K., et al.: Show, attend and tell: Neural image caption generation with visual attention. In: Proceedings of the 32nd International Conference on Machine Learning (2015)
40. Yu, W., Zhang, H., He, X., Chen, X., Xiong, L., Qin, Z.: Aesthetic-based clothing recommendation. In: Proceedings of the 2018 World Wide Web Conference (2018)
41. Zhang, L., et al.: Actor-critic sequence training for image captioning. In: NIPS workshop (2017)
42. Zheng, S., Yang, F., Kiapour, M.H., Piramuthu., R.: ModaNet: a large-scale street fashion dataset with polygon annotations. In: ACM Multimedia (2018)
43. Zou, X., Kong, X., Wong, W., Wang, C., Liu, Y., Cao, Y.: FashionAI: a hierarchical dataset for fashion understanding. In: CVPRW (2019)

Reducing Language Biases in Visual Question Answering with Visually-Grounded Question Encoder

Gouthaman KV(✉) and Anurag Mittal

Indian Institute of Technology Madras, Chennai, India
{gkv,amittal}@cse.iitm.ac.in

Abstract. Recent studies have shown that current VQA models are heavily biased on the language priors in the train set to answer the question, irrespective of the image. E.g., overwhelmingly answer "what sport is" as "tennis" or "what color banana" as "yellow." This behavior restricts them from real-world application scenarios. In this work, we propose a novel model-agnostic question encoder, Visually-Grounded Question Encoder (VGQE), for VQA that reduces this effect. VGQE utilizes both visual and language modalities equally while encoding the question. Hence the question representation itself gets sufficient visual-grounding, and thus reduces the dependency of the model on the language priors. We demonstrate the effect of VGQE on three recent VQA models and achieve state-of-the-art results on the bias-sensitive split of the VQAv2 dataset; VQA-CPv2. Further, unlike the existing bias-reduction techniques, on the standard VQAv2 benchmark, our approach does not drop the accuracy; instead, it improves the performance.

Keywords: Deep-learning · Visual Question Answering · Language bias

1 Introduction

Visual Question Answering (VQA) is a good benchmark for context-specific reasoning and scene understanding that requires the combined skill of Computer Vision (CV) and Natural Language Processing (NLP). Given an image and a question in natural language, the task is to answer the question by understanding cues from both the question and the image. Tackling the VQA problem requires a variety of scene understanding capabilities such as object and activity recognition, enumerating objects, knowledge-based reasoning, fine-grained recognition, and common sense reasoning, etc. Thus, such a multi-domain problem yields a good measure of whether computers are reaching capabilities similar to humans.

With the success of deep-learning in CV and NLP, several datasets [3,14,15, 19,21,42], and models [2,4–6,22] have been proposed to solve VQA. Most of these

Electronic supplementary material The online version of this chapter (https://doi.org/10.1007/978-3-030-58601-0_2) contains supplementary material, which is available to authorized users.

models perform well in the existing benchmark datasets where the train and test sets have similar answer distribution. However, recent studies show that these models often rely on the statistical correlations between the question patterns & the most frequent answer in the train set, and shows poor generalized performance (i.e., poor performance on a test set with different answer distributions than the train set [1]). In other words, they are heavily biased on the language modality. E.g., most of the existing models overwhelmingly answer "tennis" by seeing the question pattern "what sport is..." or answer the question "what color of the banana?" as "yellow" even though it is a "green banana," By definition and design, the VQA models need to merge the visual and textual modalities to answer the question. However, in practice, they often answer the question without considering the image modality, i.e., they tend to have less image grounding and rely more on the question. This undesirable behavior restricts the existing VQA models being applicable in practical scenarios.

One reason for this behavior is the strong language biases that exist in the available VQA datasets [3,14]. Hence, the models trained on these datasets will often rely on such biases [1,7,9,32,33,39]. E.g., in the most popular and large VQAv2 dataset [14], a majority of the "what sport is" question is linked to "tennis." Hence, upon training, the model will blindly learn the superficial correlations between the "what sport is" language pattern from the question, and the most frequent answer "tennis." Unfortunately, it is hard to avoid these biases from the train set when collecting real-world samples due to the annotation cost. Instead, we require methods that force the model to look at the image and question equally to predict the answer. Since the main source of bias is the over-dependency of the models on the language side, some approaches such as [7,9,32], tried to overcome this by reducing the contribution from the language side. On the other hand, some approaches [1,33,39] tried to improve the visual-grounding of the model in order to reduce the language-bias. All of these existing bias reduction methods cause a performance reduction in the standard benchmark VQA datasets.

A common pipeline in existing VQA models is to encode the image and question separately and then fuse them to predict the answer. Typically the image is encoded using a pre-trained CNN (e.g., ResNet [16], VGGNet [35], etc.), and the question is encoded by sending the word-level features to an RNN (GRU [10] or LSTM [18]). In this approach, while encoding the question, it only considers the language modality, and such a question representation has not contained any distinguishable power based on the content in the image. In other words, the question representation is not grounded in the image. E.g., with this scheme, the question "what sport is this?" has the same encoded representation irrespective of whether the image contains "tennis," "baseball," or "skateboarding," etc. Since the majority of such questions are linked to the answer "tennis" in the train set, the model will learn a strong correlation between the question pattern "what sport is" to the answer "tennis," irrespective of the image. This leads to overfitting the question representation to the most frequent answer, and the model will ignore the image altogether.

In this paper, we propose a generic question encoder for VQA, the Visually-Grounded Question Encoder (VGQE), that reduces this problem. VGQE encodes

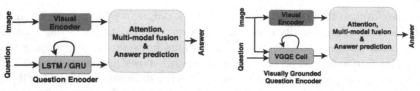

(a) A generic VQA model with a traditional question encoder.

(b) A generic VQA model with VGQE.

Fig. 1. A VQA model with a traditional question encoder vs. with VGQE: A traditional question encoder uses only the language modality while encoding the question, whereas VGQE uses both language and visual modalities to encode the question.

the question by considering not only the linguistic information from the question but also the visual information from the image. A visual comparison of a generic VQA model with a traditional question encoder and with VGQE is shown in Fig. 1. The VGQE explicitly forces the model to look at the image while encoding the question. For each question word, VGQE finds the important visual feature from the image and generates a visually-grounded word-embedding vector. This word embedding vector contains the language information from the question word and the corresponding visual information from the image. These visually-grounded word-embedding vectors are then passed to a sequence of RNN cells (inside VGQE) to encode the question. Since VGQE considers both the modalities equally, the encoded question representation will get sufficient distinguishing power based on the visual counterpart. For e.g., with VGQE, in the case of the "what sport is this" question, the model can easily distinguish the question for "baseball," "tennis," or "skateboarding," etc. As a result, the question representation itself is heavily influenced by the image, and the learning of the correlation between specific language patterns and the most frequent answers in the train set can be reduced.

The VGQE is generic and easily adaptable to any existing VQA models, i.e., replace the existing traditional language-based question encoder in the model with VGQE. In this paper, we demonstrate the ability of VGQE to reduce the language bias on three recent best performing baseline VQA models, i.e., MUREL [6], UpDn [2] and BAN [22]. We did extensive experiments on the VQA-CPv2 dataset [1] and demonstrate the ability of VGQE to push the baseline models to achieve state-of-the-art results. The VQA-CPv2 dataset is specifically designed to test the VQA model's capacity to overcome the language biases from the train set. Further, we show the effect of VGQE in the standard VQAv2 benchmark as well. Unlike existing bias reduction techniques [1,7,9,32,39], VGQE does not show any drop in the accuracy on the standard VQAv2 dataset; instead, it improves the performance.

2   Related Works

A major role in the success of deep-learning models lies in the availability of large datasets. Most of the existing real-world datasets for various problems will have some form of biases, and it is hard to avoid this at the time of dataset collection, due to the annotation cost. Consequently, the models trained on these datasets often over-fit to the biases between the inputs and ground truth annotations from the train set. Researchers tried different procedures to mitigate this problem in various domains. For instance, some methods focused on the biases in captioning models [17], gender biases in multi-label object classification [43], biases in ConvNets and ImageNet [36], etc. Since our work focuses on reducing the language biases in VQA models, in the following, we discuss the related works lying on the same line.

Approaches in the Dataset Side: In VQA, various datasets have been proposed so far such as [3,14,21,24]. The main source of bias in these datasets are from the language side, i.e., the question. There exist strong correlations between some of the word patterns in the question and the frequent answer words in the dataset. For e.g., in the large and popular VQAv1 dataset [3], there exist strong language priors such as "what color..." to "white," "is there..." to "yes," "how many..." to "2", etc. To reduce the language biases in VQAv1, in [14], the authors introduced a more balanced VQAv2 dataset, by adding at least two similar images with different answers for each question. However, with this additional refinement also, there still exists a considerable amount of language biases that can be leveraged by the model during training. In [1,8,27], the authors empirically show that a question-only model (without using the image) trained on VQAv2 shows reasonable performance, indicating the strong language priors in the dataset. In [1], the authors show that since the train and test answer distributions of VQAv2 are still similar, and the models that solely memorize language biases in the train set show acceptable performance while testing. In this regard, they introduced a diagnostic dataset, the VQA-CP (VQA under Changing Priors), to measure the language bias learned by the VQA models. This dataset is constructed with vastly different answer distributions between the train and test splits. Hence the models that rely heavily on the language priors in the train set will show poor performance while testing. [1] empirically shows that most of the existing best performing VQA models on the VQAv2 dataset show a significant drop in the accuracy when tested on the new test split from VQA-CPv2. E.g., a model with ≈66% accuracy in the standard VQAv2 shows only ≈40% accuracy in the bias sensitive VQA-CPv2.

Approaches in the Architecture Side: Several approaches have been considered in the literature to remove such biases. In [1], the authors propose a specific VQA model built upon [40], the GVQA model, consists of specially designed architectural restrictions to prevent the model from relying on the question-answer correlations. This model is complicated in design and requires multi-stage training, which makes it challenging to adapt to existing VQA models. In [7,32], the authors propose different regularization techniques that can be applied via the question encoder to reduce the bias. In [32], the authors added an adversary question-only branch to the model, and it is supposed to find the amount of bias that exists in the question. Then, a gradient negation of the question-only branch loss is applied to remove answer discriminative features from the question representation of the original model. They also propose a difference of entropy (DoE) loss captured between the output distributions of the VQA model and the additional question-only branch. In [7], the authors propose a similar approach as in [32], named RUBi, where instead of using the DoE and question-only loss, they mask (using the *sigmoid* operation) the output from the question-only branch and element-wise multiplying it with the output of the original model, to dynamically adapt the value of the classification loss to reduce the bias. However, both of these regularization approaches show a decrease in the performance on the standard VQAv2 benchmark, while reducing the bias. In [33], the authors propose a tuning method, called HINT, that is used to improve the visual-grounding of the existing model. Specifically, they tuned the model with manually annotated attention maps from the VQA-HAT dataset [11]. Similar to this, in [39], the authors propose a tuning approach called SCR, which uses additional manually annotated attention maps (from the VQA-HAT [11]) or textual explanations (from the VQA-X dataset [20]) to improve the visual-grounding of the model. However, both of these approaches [33,39] require additional manually annotated data, and collecting the same is expensive. Also, these approaches reduce the performance on the standard VQAv2. Recently, in [9], the authors proposed an approach based on language-attention and is built upon the GVQA model [1]. The language attention module splits the question into three language phrases: question type, referring objects, and specific features of the referring object. These phrases further utilized to infer the answers from the image. They claim that splitting the question into different language phrases reduces the learning of the bias. However, this approach also shows a reduction in the performance on VQAv2.

The prior works are trying to overcome the bias either by reducing the contribution from the language side as in [7,9,32], or by improving the visual-grounding by tuning with additional manually annotated data as in [33,39]. One common drawback of all of these methods is that they show a significant drop in the performance on the standard VQAv2 benchmark while reducing the bias. On the contrary, our approach improves the representation power of the question encoder to make visually-grounded question encodings to reduce the bias. The advantage of such an approach is that it is not only model-agnostic but also does not sacrifice the performance on the standard VQAv2 benchmark. Also, it does not require any additional manually annotated data or tuning.

Traditional Question Encoders and Pitfall: The widely adopted question encoding scheme in VQA is passing the word-level features to a recurrent sequence model (LSTM [18] or GRU [10]) and taking the final state vector as the encoded question. Some early works use one-hot representations of question words and pass through an LSTM such as in [3,13,41], or GRU as in [4]. The drawback of using the one-hot vector representations of question words is the manual creation of the word vocabulary. Later, the usage of pre-trained word embedding vectors such as GloVe [30], BERT [12], etc., becomes popular, since they do not require any word vocabulary and also rich in linguistic understanding. This question encoding scheme, i.e., pass the pre-trained word

embeddings of the question words to some RNNs, is the currently popular approach in VQA [2,5,6,22,28,29]. However, recently, with the success of Transformer based models in various NLP tasks [12], usage of Multi-modal Transformers (MMT) are becoming popular, such as ViLBERT [26], LXMERT [37],
etc. These are co-attention models working on top of the Transformers [38],
where while encoding the question, the words are prioritized with the guidance
of the visual information.

The above-mentioned question-encoding schemes only use the language
modality, i.e., the word-embeddings of the question words. As a result, the
encoded question contains only the linguistic information from the question, and
it cannot distinguish the questions based on their visual counterpart. This situation forces the model to learn the unwanted correlations between the language
patterns in the questions, and the most frequent answers in the train set without considering the image which leads to a language side biased model. On the
contrary, our question encoder, the VGQE, considers both visual and language
modalities equally and generate visually-grounded question representations. A
VQA model with such a question representation can reduce the over-dependency
on the language priors in the train set.

The VGQE is also related to approaches such as FiLM [31], in terms of the
early usage of the complementary information. The FiLM uses the question context to influence the image encoder, whereas VGQE uses the visual information
inside the question encoder.

3   Visually-Grounded Question Encoder (VGQE)

We follow the widely-adopted RNN based question encoding scheme in VQA as
the base. In VGQE, instead of the traditional RNN cell, a specially designed
cell called the VGQE cell is used. A VGQE cell takes the word embedding of
the current question word and finds its relevant visual counterpart feature from
the image, then creates a visually-grounded question word embedding. This new
word embedding is passed to an RNN cell to encode the sequence information.

Before going into the VGQE cell details, we explain the image and question
feature representations used by the model. The image is represented by two sets
of features $V = \{v_i \in \mathbb{R}^{d_v}\}_{i \in [1,k]}$ and $L = \{l_i \in \mathbb{R}^{d_w}\}_{i \in [1,k]}$ corresponding to the
CNN features of objects and embeddings of the class labels respectively, where
k is the total number of objects. The question is represented as a sequence of
words with corresponding word embedding vectors, the word embedding of the
t^{th} question word is being denoted by $q_t \in \mathbb{R}^{d_w}$.

3.1   VGQE Cell

The basic building block of the proposed question encoder is the VGQE cell. This
is analogous to the RNN cell (LSTM [18] or GRU [10]) in the traditional approach. An illustration of the VGQE cell at time t is shown in Fig. 2. Each VGQE
cell takes the object-level features V, L, the current question word embedding q_t

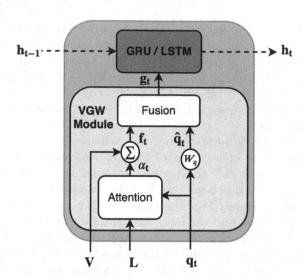

Fig. 2. VGQE cell at time t: VGW module finds the visually-grounded word embedding g_t for the current question word q_t and the RNN cell (GRU or LSTM) encodes the sequential information in the question. V and L are the sets of object-level features.

and the previous state context vector h_{t-1}, and then outputs the current state context vector h_t. The context vector h_t is then pass to the next VGQE cell in sequence. Mathematically we represent a VGQE cell as follows:

$$h_t = \text{VGQE}(V, L, q_t, h_{t-1}) \tag{1}$$

A VGQE cell consists of two modules: the Visually-Grounded Word embedding (VGW) module and a traditional RNN cell (GRU [10] or LSTM [18]). The VGW module is responsible for finding the visually-grounded word embedding vector g_t for the current question word embedding q_t. Then, g_t is passed to the RNN cell to encode the question sequence information.

VGW Module: This module is the crux of the VGQE cell, where the visually-grounded word embedding g_t for the current question word q_t is extracted. It works in two stages: 1) *Attention* and 2) *Fusion*. The first stage calculates the visual counterpart feature f_t of the question word embedding q_t, while in the fusion stage, f_t and q_t are fused to generate the visually-grounded word embedding vector g_t.

Attention: This module takes the set of object-label features L and the current question word q_t as inputs and outputs a relevance score vector $\alpha_t \in \mathbb{R}^k$. Each of the k values in α_t tells the relevance of the corresponding object from the image in the context of the current question word q_t. Then, one single visual feature vector f_t is extracted by taking the weighted sum over the set of object CNN features V, where the weights are defined by α_t. Mathematically, the above steps are formulated as follows:

$$f_t = \sum_{i=1}^{k} \alpha_t[i] * v_i \tag{2}$$

$$\alpha_t = softmax(w_a^T(W(\mathbf{L} * (\mathbb{1}q_t))^T))$$

where $*$ is element-wise multiplication, $v_i \in V$ is the ith object CNN feature vector, $\alpha_t \in \mathbb{R}^k$ and $f_t \in \mathbb{R}^{d_v}$ are the object-relevance score vector and the visual counter part feature for the current question word q_t respectively, $\alpha_t[i]$ is the relevance of the ith object at time t, $\mathbf{L} \in \mathbb{R}^{k \times d_w}$ is the matrix representation of the set of object-label features, $w_a \in \mathbb{R}^{d_w}$ and $W \in \mathbb{R}^{d_w \times d_w}$ are learnable parameters and $\mathbb{1}$ is a column vector of length k consists all ones.

Fusion: In this stage, the word-level visual feature f_t is grounded to the word-level language feature q_t. This results in the visually-grounded word embedding vector g_t. For fusion, any multi-modal fusion function F_m such as element-wise multiplication, bi-linear fusion [4,5,13,23,41] etc. can be used. In this paper, we use the BLOCK fusion as F_m, which is a recently proposed best performing bi-linear multi-modal fusion method [5]. The formal representation of the visually-grounded word embedding vector g_t is as follows:

$$g_t = F_m(f_t, \hat{q}_t; \Theta) \tag{3}$$

where F_m is the multi-modal fusion function (in our case BLOCK) with Θ as the learnable parameters, the vector $\hat{q}_t = W_q(q_t)$ is the fine-tuned word embedding vector with W_q as the learnable parameters of a two-layer network that projects from d_w-space to d-space, and f_t is the visual feature as defined in Eq. (2). The fused vector g_t contains relevant language information from the word embedding q_t and visual information from f_t; in other words, g_t is a visually-grounded word embedding vector. For the same question word (e.g., banana), the g_t vector will vary according to their visual counterpart (as a result, the "green banana" and "yellow banana" will get distinguishable representations in the question.).

The output from the VGW module, the visually-grounded word embedding vector g_t along with the previous state context vector h_{t-1}, is then passed to a traditional RNN cell to generate the current state question context vector h_t.

3.2   Using VGQE Cell to Encode the Question

In the proposed question encoder, we use the VGQE cell instead of the traditional RNN cell. An illustration of a generic VQA model with VGQE is shown in Fig. 3. The visual encoder encodes the image as in the original model. The question is encoded using VGQE instead of the existing question encoder. The question word embeddings are passed through a sequence of VGQE cells along with the object-level features (V and L) and take the final state representation as the encoded question. In this paper, we use GRU as the RNN cell inside the VGQE cell. Other question-encoder adaptations using variants of RNN, such as LSTM, are also possible, with appropriate changes in the RNN cell of VGQE. Since, in VGQE, the question words are grounded on its visual counterpart, the encoded

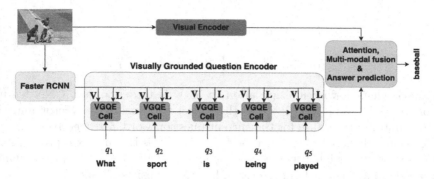

Fig. 3. An illustration of a generic VQA model with VGQE

questions itself contain sufficient visual-grounding. Hence, they become robust enough to reduce the correlation between specific language patterns and the most frequent answers in the train set.

3.3   Baseline VQA Architecture

In this paper, we adopt the same baseline as used in prior work [7], to perform various experiments, also to make a fair comparison. This baseline is a simplified version of the MUREL VQA model [6]. The word embeddings are passed to a GRU [10] to encode the question. Then, each of the object CNN features $v_i \in V$ are bi-linearly fused (using BLOCK fusion [5]) with the encoded question to get the question-aware object features. A max-pool operation over these features gives a single vector that later used by the answer prediction network.

4   Experiments and Results

4.1   Experimental Setup

We train and evaluate the models on the VQA-CPv2 dataset [1]. This dataset is designed to test the robustness of VQA models in dealing with language biases. The train and test sets of VQA-CPv2 have totally different answer distributions; hence a model that strongly depends on the language priors in the train set will perform poorly on the test set. We also use the VQAv2 dataset to train and evaluate the models on the standard VQA benchmark. We use the VQA accuracy [3] as the evaluation metric.

We use the object-level CNN features provided in [2] as V ($d_v = 2048$). We use the pre-trained Glove [30] for the object-label features L and question word embeddings q_t ($d_w = 300$). We train the model using Adamw [25] with $weightdecay = 2 * 10^{-5}$ and cross-entropy loss. Further implementation details are provided in the supplementary material.

Table 1. Comparison with existing models on VQA-CPv2.

Model	Overall	Yes/no	Number	Other
GVQA [1]	31.30	57.99	13.68	22.14
RAMEN [34]	39.21	-	-	-
BAN [22]	39.31	-	-	-
MUREL [6]	39.54	42.85	13.17	45.04
UpDn [2]	39.74	42.27	11.93	46.05
UpDn+Q-Adv+DoE [32]	41.17	65.49	15.48	35.48
UpDn+HINT [33]	46.73	67.27	10.61	45.88
UpDn+LangAtt [9]	48.87	70.99	18.72	45.57
UpDn+SCR (VQA-X) [39]	49.45	**72.36**	10.93	**48.02**
Baseline [7]	38.46	42.85	12.81	43.20
Baseline+RUBi [7]	47.11	68.65	20.28	43.18
Baseline+VGQE	**50.11**	66.35	**27.08**	46.77

4.2   Results

Comparison with State-of-the-Art Models: In Table 1, we compare VGQE against existing state-of-the-art bias reduction techniques in VQA-CPv2. We can see that our approach achieves a new state-of-the-art. With VGQE, we improved the baseline model (that uses the traditional GRU based question encoder) accuracy from 38.46 to 50.11. This performance also corresponds to a notable improvement from the RUBi approach [7], where they also use the same baseline. Our approach outperforms the UpDn based approaches [9,32,33,39] as well. Comparing with GVQA, a specific model designed for VQA-CP, our generic approach outperforms with a +18.81 gain in the accuracy.

Question-Type-Wise Results: In Table 2, we show the comparison of some of the question-type-wise results of the baseline and with VGQE (+VGQE) models. The baseline model shows comparatively poor performance than the model with VGQE. Since most of the time, the baseline model with a traditional question encoder tries to memorize the language biases in the train set. We can see that, in all the question-types, the incorporation of VGQE reduces such biases and improves performance. To further clarify this, in Fig. 4, we visualize the answer distributions of some of the question-types in the VQA-CPv2 train & test sets and outputs of the baseline & baseline+VGQE models (less frequent answers are ignored for better visualization). It is clear from the visualizations that the baseline model learns the language biases in the train set and predicts the answer without considering the image. The incorporation of VGQE helps to reduce such biases and to answer by grounding the question onto the image. E.g., from Fig. 4, consider the case of the "Do you" type questions. Most of such questions are linked to the answer "no" in the train set; in other words, there is a strong correlation between the "Do you" language pattern and the answer "no." We can see that most of the time, the baseline model predicts the answer "no" upon

Table 2. Performance comparison between the baseline and VGQE corresponding to some of the question-types in the VQA-CPv2 test set. VGQE reduces the learning of unwanted question pattern-answer correlations and improves the performance. All numbers are VQA accuracy values.

Question type	Baseline	+VGQE
Do you	30.7	93.19
Can you	29.04	52.54
What are the	39.8	48.52
What color are the	28.32	64.42
What sport is	88.39	93.19
What is the person	57.40	63.65
What time	39.28	57.88
What room is	80.34	92.87
What is in the	29.34	35.84
Where are the	19.87	31.88
What brand	28.54	47.19
How many	12.91	19.65
How many people	36.62	50.03
Does the	31.91	77.39
Which	26.73	39.0
Why	12.28	14.76

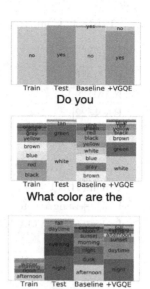

Fig. 4. Answer distributions from train & test sets of VQA-CPv2, and outputs of baseline & baseline+VGQE models, for some question types from Table 2. We can see that VGQE helps the model to reduce the learning of bias from the train set. (Color figure online)

seeing the pattern "Do you," without considering the image. This indicates that the baseline model relies on the strong correlation between the language pattern "Do you" and the answer "no," rather than looking at the image. In contrast, the incorporation of VGQE helps to reduce such learning of biases and to predict the answer by considering the image as well.

On comparing the performance gain among the question types, we can see that the questions that start with "why" show relatively less improvement. Since these questions usually require common sense reasoning (e.g., Why people wear the hat?), and in such cases, the VGQE cannot improve much from the baseline. **Qualitative Results:** In Fig. 5, we show some qualitative comparisons between the baseline (Base) and baseline+VGQE (Ours) models. Figure 5(a), shows the case of the "What color are the" question pattern, where the train set has heavy biases towards the colors "black", "red", "blue","brown", and "yellow" (see Fig. 4). In Fig. 5(b) and (c), we show the cases of the same question asked for different images. The question "What sport is being played?" has a bias on "tennis" ($\approx$63.2%) and "soccer" ($\approx$17.5%) whereas "What color is the fire hydrant?" is biased towards the colors "yellow" ($\approx$46%), "white" ($\approx$12%) and

Q: What color are the   Q: What color are the   Q: What color are the
bananas. **GT**: green,   umbrellas. **GT**: white,   cabinets. **GT**: white,
Ours:green,**Base**: yellow. **Ours**:white,**Base**: blue. **Ours**:white, **Base**: brown.

(a) **Question Pattern:** What color are the

GT: frisbee,   **GT**: baseball,   **GT**: baseball,
Ours: frisbee,   **Ours**: baseball,   **Ours**: baseball,
Base: soccer   **Base**: tennis   **Base**: tennis

(b) **Common Question:** What sport is being played?

GT: red,   **GT**: red,   **GT**: red,
Ours: red, **Base**: yellow **Ours**: red, **Base**: white.   **Ours**: red, **Base**: black

(c) **Common Question:** What color is the fire hydrant?

Fig. 5. Some qualitative comparisons of our model (Baseline+VGQE) with Baseline. **Ours**, **Base** and **GT** represents the baseline+VGQE, baseline and the ground truth, respectively. Best viewed in color. (Color figure online)

"black" ($\approx$10%) in the train set [1]. These visualizations further show that incorporating VGQE helps the baseline model to reduce the learning of biases.

In Fig. 6, we show a visualization of the grounded image regions at each time step of VGQE with the same question ("What sport is being played?") but different images. We can see that the question words are grounded onto the relevant visual counterparts. Hence, the same words will get different representations based on the image. For e.g., the word "sport" is grounded on the "baseball" player in the first case, whereas it is grounded on the "frisbee" player in the second case. Hence, even though the question is the same, the VGQE generates different visually-grounded question representations.

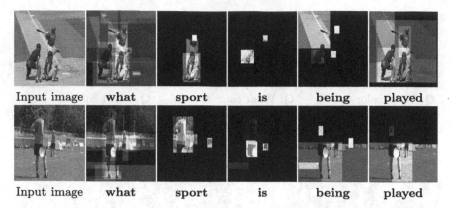

Fig. 6. A visualization of the grounded visual regions at each time step of VGQE with the same question ("What sport is being played?") but different images. The same words will get different visually-grounded embeddings based on the visual counterpart.

4.3   Performance of VGQE on Other Baselines

The proposed question encoder, the VGQE, can be easily incorporated into any existing VQA model, i.e., replace the existing question encoder with VGQE (See Fig. 3 for an illustration). We have already shown the effectiveness of VGQE on the MUREL baseline (see Table 1). In this section, we show (see Table 3) the impact of VGQE on two more recent best performing models as well:

– **UpDn** [2]: This VQA model is based on question guided visual attention. The word embeddings are pass to a GRU to encode the question. The image is encoded using visual attention guided by the question representation, over the set of object CNN features V. Then, both encoded image and question are combined using element-wise multiplication and pass to the answer predictor.
– **BAN** [22]: This model is based on bi-linear co-attention maps between the objects and question words. The question word embeddings are passed through a GRU. Then all the GRU cell outputs and the object-level CNN features are given to a co-attention module, the BAN. This module will give a combined vector which later used by the answer predictor.

In both models, we replaced the traditional GRU-based question encoder with VGQE. Note that, unlike other model-agnostic bias reduction methods, VGQE does not require a new question-only branch as in [7,32] or tuning with additional annotated data as in [33,39], while training. The results are shown in Table 3. We can see that, in both models, VGQE consistently improves the performance (39.74 to 48.75 in UpDn [2] and 39.31 to 50.0 in BAN [22]) on VQA-CPv2, showing that here also VGQE reduces the language-bias.

Table 3. Effect of VGQE on UpDn [2] and BAN [22] models, on VQA-CPv2 and VQAv2 val.

Model	VQA-CPv2	VQAv2 val
UpDn [2]	39.74	63.48
UpDn+Q-Adv [32]	40.08	60.53
UpDn+DoE [32]	40.43	63.43
UpDn+Q-Adv+DoE [32]	41.17	62.75
UpDn+RUBi [7]	44.23	-
UpDn+HINT [33]	46.73	63.38
UpDn+LangAtt [9]	48.87	57.96
UpDn+SCR [39]	48.47	62.3
UpDn+SCR (HAT) [39]	49.17	62.2
UpDn+SCR (VQA-X) [39]	**49.45**	62.2
UpDn+VGQE	48.75	**64.04**
BAN [7,22]	39.31	65.36
BAN+VGQE	**50.00**	**65.73**

Table 4. Comparison of performance of the baseline model with RUBi and VGQE on VQAv2 val set. RUBi shows a drop in the accuracy whereas VGQE does not show any drop.

Model	VQAv2 val
Baseline [7]	63.10
+RUBi [7]	61.16
+VGQE	**63.18**

4.4 Performance of VGQE on the Standard VQAv2 Benchmark

Existing bias reduction techniques such as [7, 9, 32, 33, 39] show a reduction in the performance on the standard VQAv2 benchmark. For instance, in Table 3, the best performing UpDn based models on VQA-CPv2, such as UpDn+LangAtt [9] reduce the accuracy in the VQAv2 val set from 63.48 to 57.96 & UpDn+SCR [39] reduces it from 63.48 to 62.2. Note that, UpDn+SCR reduces the performance even though it uses additional manually annotated data (HAT or VQA-X). Also, in Table 4, adding RUBi to the baseline model decreases the accuracy from 63.10 to 61.16. On the contrary, VGQE does not sacrifice the performance on the standard VQAv2 benchmark. Interestingly, VGQE slightly improves the performance of the respective models; from 63.48 to 64.04, 63.10 to 63.18 and 65.36 to 65.73 in UpDn [2], baseline [7] and BAN [22] respectively. We ascribe this to the following; VGQE adds a robust and visually-grounded question representation to the model without damaging its existing reasoning power.

5 Conclusion

Current VQA models rely heavily on the language priors that exists in the train set, without considering the image. Such models that fail to utilize both modalities equally would likely perform poorly in real-world scenarios. We propose VGQE, a novel question-encoder that utilizes both the modalities equally and generates visually-grounded question representations. Such question representations have sufficient distinguishing power based on the visual counterpart and help the models to reduce the learning of language biases from the train set. We did extensive experiments on the bias sensitive VQA-CPv2 dataset and achieved a new state-of-the-art. The VGQE is model agnostic and can easily incorporate into existing VQA models without the need for additional manually annotated data and training. We experimented with three best performing VQA models, and deliver consistent performance improvement in all of them. Further, unlike existing bias reduction techniques, VGQE does not sacrifice the original model's performance on the standard VQAv2 benchmark.

References

1. Agrawal, A., Batra, D., Parikh, D., Kembhavi, A.: Don't just assume; look and answer: overcoming priors for visual question answering. In: Proceedings of the IEEE Conference on Computer Vision and Pattern Recognition, pp. 4971–4980 (2018)
2. Anderson, P., et al.: Bottom-up and top-down attention for image captioning and visual question answering. In: IEEE conference on Computer Vision and Pattern Recognition, pp. 6077–6086 (2018)
3. Antol, S., et al.: VQA: visual question answering. In: Proceedings of the IEEE International Conference on Computer Vision, pp. 2425–2433 (2015)
4. Ben-Younes, H., Cadene, R., Cord, M., Thome, N.: MUTAN: multimodal tucker fusion for visual question answering. In: Proceedings of the IEEE International Conference on Computer Vision, vol. 3 (2017)
5. Ben-Younes, H., Cadene, R., Thome, N., Cord, M.: BLOCK: bilinear superdiagonal fusion for visual question answering and visual relationship detection. Proc. AAAI Conf. Artif. Intell. **33**, 8102–8109 (2019)
6. Cadene, R., Ben-Younes, H., Cord, M., Thome, N.: MUREL: multimodal relational reasoning for visual question answering. In: IEEE Conference on Computer Vision and Pattern Recognition, pp. 1989–1998 (2019)
7. Cadene, R., Dancette, C., Cord, M., Parikh, D., et al.: RUBi: reducing unimodal biases for visual question answering. In: Advances in Neural Information Processing Systems, pp. 839–850 (2019)
8. Chao, W.L., Hu, H., Sha, F.: Being negative but constructively: Lessons learnt from creating better visual question answering datasets. arXiv preprint arXiv:1704.07121 (2017)
9. Jing, C., Wu, Y., Zhang, X., Jia, Y., Wu, Q.: Overcoming language priors in VQA via decomposed linguistic representations. In: 2020 34th AAAI Conference on Artificial Intelligence (2020)
10. Cho, K., Van Merriënboer, B., Bahdanau, D., Bengio, Y.: On the properties of neural machine translation: Encoder-decoder approaches. arXiv preprint arXiv:1409.1259 (2014)
11. Das, A., Agrawal, H., Zitnick, L., Parikh, D., Batra, D.: Human attention in visual question answering: do humans and deep networks look at the same regions? Comput. Vis. Image Underst. **163**, 90–100 (2017)
12. Devlin, J., Chang, M.W., Lee, K., Toutanova, K.: BERT: pre-training of deep bidirectional transformers for language understanding. In: Conference of the North American Chapter of the Association for Computational Linguistics: Human Language Technologies (2019)
13. Fukui, A., Park, D.H., Yang, D., Rohrbach, A., Darrell, T., Rohrbach, M.: Multimodal compact bilinear pooling for visual question answering and visual grounding. In: Conference on Empirical Methods in Natural Language Processing, pp. 457–468 (2016)

14. Goyal, Y., Khot, T., Summers-Stay, D., Batra, D., Parikh, D.: Making the V in VQA matter: elevating the role of image understanding in visual question answering. In: IEEE Conference on Computer Vision and Pattern Recognition, pp. 6904–6913 (2017)
15. Gurari, D., et al..: VizWiz grand challenge: answering visual questions from blind people. In: Proceedings of the IEEE Conference on Computer Vision and Pattern Recognition, pp. 3608–3617 (2018)
16. He, K., Zhang, X., Ren, S., Sun, J.: Deep residual learning for image recognition. In: Proceedings of the IEEE Conference on Computer Vision and Pattern Recognition, pp. 770–778 (2016)
17. Hendricks, L.A., Burns, K., Saenko, K., Darrell, T., Rohrbach, A.: Women also snowboard: overcoming bias in captioning models. In: Ferrari, V., Hebert, M., Sminchisescu, C., Weiss, Y. (eds.) ECCV 2018. LNCS, vol. 11207. Springer, Cham (2018). https://doi.org/10.1007/978-3-030-01219-9_47
18. Hochreiter, S., Schmidhuber, J.: Long short-term memory. Neural Comput. 9(8), 1735–1780 (1997)
19. Hudson, D.A., Manning, C.D.: GQA: a new dataset for real-world visual reasoning and compositional question answering. In: Conference on Computer Vision and Pattern Recognition (CVPR) (2019)
20. Huk Park, D., et al.: Multimodal explanations: justifying decisions and pointing to the evidence. In: Proceedings of the IEEE Conference on Computer Vision and Pattern Recognition, pp. 8779–8788 (2018)
21. Kafle, K., Kanan, C.: An analysis of visual question answering algorithms. In: ICCV (2017)
22. Kim, J.H., Jun, J., Zhang, B.T.: Bilinear attention networks. In: Advances in Neural Information Processing Systems, pp. 1564–1574 (2018)
23. Kim, J.H., On, K.W., Lim, W., Kim, J., Ha, J.W., Zhang, B.T.: Hadamard product for low-rank bilinear pooling. In: ICLR (2017)
24. Krishna, R., et al.: Visual genome: connecting language and vision using crowd-sourced dense image annotations. Int. J. Comput. Vis. 123(1), 32–73 (2017)
25. Loshchilov, I., Hutter, F.: Decoupled weight decay regularization. In: International Conference on Learning Representations (2019). https://openreview.net/forum?id=Bkg6RiCqY7
26. Lu, J., Batra, D., Parikh, D., Lee, S.: ViLBERT: pretraining task-agnostic visiolinguistic representations for vision-and-language tasks. In: Advances in Neural Information Processing Systems, pp. 13–23 (2019)
27. Manjunatha, V., Saini, N., Davis, L.S.: Explicit bias discovery in visual question answering models. In: Proceedings of the IEEE Conference on Computer Vision and Pattern Recognition, pp. 9562–9571 (2019)
28. Nguyen, D.K., Okatani, T.: Improved fusion of visual and language representations by dense symmetric co-attention for visual question answering. In: IEEE Conference on Computer Vision and Pattern Recognition, pp. 6087–6096 (2018)
29. Gao, P., You, H., Zhang, Z., Wang, X., Li, H.: Multi-modality latent interaction network for visual question answering. In: Proceedings of the IEEE International Conference on Computer Vision (2019)
30. Pennington, J., Socher, R., Manning, C.: GloVe: global vectors for word representation. In: Conference on Empirical Methods in Natural Language Processing, pp. 1532–1543 (2014)
31. Perez, E., Strub, F., De Vries, H., Dumoulin, V., Courville, A.: FiLM: visual reasoning with a general conditioning layer. In: 32nd AAAI Conference on Artificial Intelligence (2018)

32. Ramakrishnan, S., Agrawal, A., Lee, S.: Overcoming language priors in visual question answering with adversarial regularization. In: Advances in Neural Information Processing Systems, pp. 1541–1551 (2018)
33. Selvaraju, R.R., et al.: Taking a hint: leveraging explanations to make vision and language models more grounded. In: Proceedings of the IEEE International Conference on Computer Vision, pp. 2591–2600 (2019)
34. Shrestha, R., Kafle, K., Kanan, C.: Answer them all! Toward universal visual question answering models. In: Proceedings of the IEEE Conference on Computer Vision and Pattern Recognition, pp. 10472–10481 (2019)
35. Simonyan, K., Zisserman, A.: Very deep convolutional networks for large-scale image recognition. arXiv preprint arXiv:1409.1556 (2014)
36. Stock, P., Cisse, M.: ConvNets and ImageNet beyond accuracy: understanding mistakes and uncovering biases. In: Ferrari, V., Hebert, M., Sminchisescu, C., Weiss, Y. (eds.) ECCV 2018. LNCS, vol. 11210, pp. 504–519. Springer, Cham (2018). https://doi.org/10.1007/978-3-030-01231-1_31
37. Tan, H., Bansal, M.: LXMERT: learning cross-modality encoder representations from transformers. In: Proceedings of the 2019 Conference on Empirical Methods in Natural Language Processing and the 9th International Joint Conference on Natural Language Processing (EMNLP-IJCNLP), pp. 5103–5114 (2019)
38. Vaswani, A., et al.: Attention is all you need. In: Advances in neural information processing systems, pp. 5998–6008 (2017)
39. Wu, J., Mooney, R.: Self-critical reasoning for robust visual question answering. In: Advances in Neural Information Processing Systems, pp. 8601–8611 (2019)
40. Yang, Z., He, X., Gao, J., Deng, L., Smola, A.: Stacked attention networks for image question answering. In: Proceedings of the IEEE Conference on Computer Vision and Pattern Recognition, pp. 21–29 (2016)
41. Yu, Z., Yu, J., Fan, J., Tao, D.: Multi-modal factorized bilinear pooling with co-attention learning for visual question answering. In: Proceedings of the IEEE International Conference on Computer Vision, vol. 3 (2017)
42. Zellers, R., Bisk, Y., Farhadi, A., Choi, Y.: From recognition to cognition: visual commonsense reasoning. In: Proceedings of the IEEE Conference on Computer Vision and Pattern Recognition, pp. 6720–6731 (2019)
43. Zhao, J., Wang, T., Yatskar, M., Ordonez, V., Chang, K.W.: Men also like shopping: Reducing gender bias amplification using corpus-level constraints. arXiv preprint arXiv:1707.09457 (2017)

Unsupervised Cross-Modal Alignment for Multi-person 3D Pose Estimation

Jogendra Nath Kundu$^{(\boxtimes)}$, Ambareesh Revanur, Govind Vitthal Waghmare, Rahul Mysore Venkatesh, and R. Venkatesh Babu

Video Analytics Lab, Indian Institute of Science, Bangalore, India
jogendrak@iisc.ac.in

Abstract. We present a deployment friendly, fast bottom-up framework for multi-person 3D human pose estimation. We adopt a novel neural representation of multi-person 3D pose which unifies the position of person instances with their corresponding 3D pose representation. This is realized by learning a generative pose embedding which not only ensures plausible 3D pose predictions, but also eliminates the usual keypoint grouping operation as employed in prior bottom-up approaches. Further, we propose a practical deployment paradigm where paired 2D or 3D pose annotations are unavailable. In the absence of any paired supervision, we leverage a frozen network, as a teacher model, which is trained on an auxiliary task of multi-person 2D pose estimation. We cast the learning as a cross-modal alignment problem and propose training objectives to realize a shared latent space between two diverse modalities. We aim to enhance the model's ability to perform beyond the limiting teacher network by enriching the latent-to-3D pose mapping using artificially synthesized multi-person 3D scene samples. Our approach not only generalizes to in-the-wild images, but also yields a superior trade-off between speed and performance, compared to prior top-down approaches. Our approach also yields state-of-the-art multi-person 3D pose estimation performance among the bottom-up approaches under consistent supervision levels.

1 Introduction

Multi-person 3D human pose estimation aims to simultaneously isolate individual persons and estimate the location of their semantic body joints in a 3D space. This challenging task can aid a wide range of applications related to human behavior understanding such as surveillance [56], group activity recognition [30], sports analytics [12], etc. Existing multi-person pose estimation approaches can be broadly classified into two categories namely, top-down and bottom-up. In top-down approaches [7, 36, 47, 48], the first step is to detect persons using an off-the-shelf detector which is followed by predicting a 3D pose for each person using a

---

J.N. Kundu and A. Revanur—equal contribution. | *Webpage*: https://sites.google.com/view/multiperson3D.

Electronic supplementary material The online version of this chapter (https://doi.org/10.1007/978-3-030-58601-0_3) contains supplementary material, which is available to authorized users.

© Springer Nature Switzerland AG 2020
A. Vedaldi et al. (Eds.): ECCV 2020, LNCS 12358, pp. 35–52, 2020.
https://doi.org/10.1007/978-3-030-58601-0_3

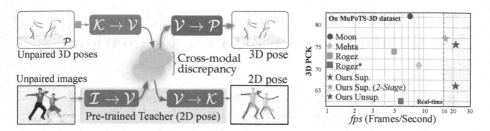

Fig. 1. We aim to realize a shared latent space $\mathcal{V}$ which embeds samples from varied input modalities *i.e.* the unpaired images and unpaired 3D poses. Auto-encoding pathway: $\mathcal{K} \rightarrow \mathcal{V} \rightarrow \mathcal{P}$. Distillation pathway: from $\mathcal{I} \rightarrow \mathcal{V} \rightarrow \mathcal{K}$ to camera projection of $\mathcal{I} \rightarrow \mathcal{V} \rightarrow \mathcal{P}$. Inference: $\mathcal{I} \rightarrow \mathcal{V} \rightarrow \mathcal{P}$ (red shadow). (Color figure online)

Fig. 2. We achieve a superior trade-off between speed and performance against the prior arts (Rogez [48], Rogez* [47], Mehta [34], Moon [36]). See Sect. 5

single-person 3D pose estimator. Such approaches [47,48] are usually incapable of inferring absolute camera-centered distance of each human as they miss the global context. In contrast, the bottom-up approaches [34] first locate the body joints, and then assign them to each individual person via a keypoint grouping operation. The bottom-up approaches yield suboptimal results as compared to top-down approaches, but have a superior run-time advantage against top-down methods [18,46]. In this paper, we aim to leverage the computational advantage of bottom-up approaches while effectively eliminating the keypoint grouping operation via an efficient 3D pose representation. This results in a substantial gain in performance while maintaining an optimal computational overhead.

Almost all multi-person 3D pose estimation approaches access large-scale datasets with 3D pose annotations. However, owing to the difficulties involved in capturing 3D pose in wild outdoor environments, many of the 3D pose datasets are captured in indoor settings. This restricts diversity in the corresponding images (*i.e.* limited variations in background, attires and pose performed by actors) [14,15]. However, 2D keypoint annotations [19,20] are available even for in-the-wild multi-person outdoor images. Hence, several approaches aim to design 2D-to-3D pose lifters [4,32] by relying on an off-the-shelf, Image-to-2D pose estimator. Such approaches usually rely on geometric self-consistency of the projected 2D pose obtained from the lifter output, while imposing adversarial prior to assure plausible 3D pose predictions [4,16]. However, the generalizability of such approaches is limited owing to the dataset bias exhibited by the primary Image-to-2D pose estimator which is trained in a fully-supervised fashion.

Our Problem Setting. Consider a scenario where a pretrained Image-to-2D pose estimator is used for the goal task of 3D pose estimation. There are two challenges that must be tackled. First, a pretrained Image-to-2D estimator would exhibit a dataset bias towards the training data. Thus, the deployment of such a model in an unseen environment (*e.g.* dancers in unusual costumes) is not guaranteed to result in an optimal performance. This curtails the learning of the 2D-to-3D pose lifter, especially in the absence of paired images from the unseen environment. Second, along with the Image-to-2D model, one can not expect to be provided with its labeled training dataset owing to proprietary [29,37] or even memory [9,26] constraints. Considering these two challenges, the problem boils down to performing domain adaptation by leveraging the pretrained Image-to-2D network (*a.k.a* the teacher network) in an unsupervised fashion, *i.e. in the absence of any paired 2D or 3D pose annotations*. Further, acknowledging the limitations of existing 2D-to-3D pose lifters, we argue that the 3D pose lifter should access the latent convolutional features instead of the final 2D pose output; owing to its greater task transferability [28].

Though it is easy to obtain unpaired multi-person images, acquiring a dataset of unpaired multi-person 3D pose is inconvenient. To this end, we synthesize multi-person 3D scenes by randomly placing the single-person 3D skeletons in a 3D grid as shown in Fig. 3B. We also formalize a systematic way to synthesize single-person 3D pose by accessing plausible ranges of parent-relative joint angle limits provided by biomechanic experts. This eradicates our dependency even on an unpaired 3D skeleton dataset. Our idea of creating artificial samples stems from the concept of domain randomization [42,53] which is shown to be effective for generalizing deep models to unseen target environments. The core hypothesis is that the multi-person 3D pose distribution characterized by the artificially synthesized 3D pose scenes would subsume the unknown target distribution. Note that the proposed joint angle sampling would allow sampling of minimal implausible single-person poses as it does not adhere to the strong pose-conditioned joint angle priors formalized by Akhter *et al.* [2].

We posit the learning framework as a cross-modal alignment problem (see Fig. 1). To this end, we aim to realize a shared latent space $\mathcal{V}$, which embeds samples from varied input modalities [6], such as unpaired multi-person image $\mathcal{I}$ and unpaired multi-person 2D pose $\mathcal{K}$ (*i.e.* camera projection on multi-person 3D pose $\mathcal{P}$). Our training paradigm employs an auto-encoding loss on $\mathcal{P}$ (via $\mathcal{K} \to \mathcal{V} \to \mathcal{P}$ pathway), a distillation loss on $\mathcal{K}$ (via $\mathcal{I} \to \mathcal{V} \to \mathcal{P} \to \mathcal{K}$ pathway) and an additional adaptation loss (non-adversarial) to minimize the cross-modal discrepancy at the latent space $\mathcal{V}$. In further training iterations, we stop the limiting distillation loss and fine-tune the model on a self-supervised criteria based on the equivariance property [49] of spatial-transformations on the image and its corresponding 2D pose representation. Extensive experiments of our ablations and comparisons against prior arts establish the superiority of this approach. In summary, our contributions are as follows:

- We propose an efficient bottom-up architecture that yields fast and accurate single-shot multi-person 3D pose estimation performance with structurally infused articulation constraints to assure valid 3D pose output. In absence of paired supervision we cast the learning as a cross-modal alignment problem and propose training objectives to realize a shared latent space between two diverse data-flow pathways.
- We enhance the model's ability to perform even beyond the limiting teacher network as a result of the enriched latent-to-3D-pose mapping using artificially synthesized multi-person 3D scene samples.

– Our approach not only yields *state-of-the-art* multi-person 3D pose estimation performance among the prior bottom-up approaches but also demonstrates a superior trade-off between speed and performance.

2   Related Work

Multi-person 2D pose estimation works can be broadly classified into top-down and bottom-up methods. Top-down methods such as [5,11,39,54] first detect the persons in the image and then estimate their poses. On the other hand, bottom-up methods [3,13,38,40,44] predict the pose of all persons in a single-shot. Cao *et al.* [3] use a non-parametric representation Part Affinity Field (PAF) and Part Confidence Map (PCM) to learn association between 2D keypoints and persons in the image. Similarly, Kocabas *et al.* [18] proposed a bottom-up approach using pose residual network for estimating both keypoints and human detections simultaneously.

Many approaches have been proposed for solving the problem of single-person 3D human pose estimation [23–25,41,51,55]. Vnect [35] is the first realtime 3D human pose estimation work that infers the pose by parsing location-maps and joint-wise heatmaps. Martinez *et al.* [32] proposed an effective approach to directly lift the ground-truth 2D poses to 3D poses. Few methods have been proposed so far for Multi-person 3D pose estimation. In [47,48], Rogez *et al.* proposed a top-down approach based on localization, classification and regression of 3D joints. These modules are pipelined to predict the final pose of all persons in the image. Mehta *et al.* [34] proposed a single-shot approach to infer 3D poses of all people in the image using PAF-PCM representation. To handle occlusions, they introduced Occlusion Robust Pose Maps (ORPM) which allows full body pose inference under occlusions. Moon *et al.* [36] proposed the first top-down camera-centered 3D pose estimation. Their framework contains three modules: DetectNet localizes multiple persons in the image, RootNet estimates camera-centered depth of root joint and PoseNet estimates root relative 3D pose of the cropped person. In RootNet, they use pinhole camera projection model to estimate absolute camera-centered depth. Dabral *et al.* [7] proposed a 2D to 3D lifting based approach for camera-centric predictions. Rogez *et al.* [47,48] and Moon *et al.* [36] crop the detected person instances from the image and they do not leverage the global context information. All prior state-of-the-art works [7,34,36,47,48] require paired supervision. See Table 1 for a characteristic comparison against prior works.

Table 1. Characteristic comparison against prior works. **without paired supervision** implies the method does not need access to annotations.

Methods	Single shot	w/o paired supervision	Camera centric
Rogez [47]	✗	✗	✗
Mehta [34]	✓	✗	✗
Rogez [48]	✗	✗	✗
Dabral [7]	✗	✗	✓
Moon [36]	✗	✗	✓
Ours	✓	✓	✓

Cross-Modal Distillation. Gupta *et al.* [10] proposed a novel method for enabling cross-modal transfer of supervision for tasks such as depth estimation. They propose alignment of representations from a large labeled modality to a sparsely labeled modality. In [50], Spurr *et al.* demonstrated the effectiveness of cross-modal alignment of latent space for the task of hand pose estimation. In a related work [43], Pilzer *et al.* proposed an unsupervised distillation based depth estimation approach via refinement of cycle-inconsistency.

3   Approaches

Our prime objective is to realize a learning framework for the task of multi-person 3D pose estimation without accessing any paired data (*i.e.* images with the corresponding 2D or 3D pose annotations). To achieve this, we plan to distill the knowledge from a frozen teacher network which is trained for an auxiliary task of multi-person 2D landmark estimation. Furthermore, in contrast to the general top-down approaches in fully-supervised scenarios, we propose an effective single-shot, bottom-up approach for multi-person 3D pose estimation. Such an architecture not only helps us maintain an optimal computational overhead but also lays a suitable ground for cross-modal distillation.

3.1   Architecture

Aiming to design a single-shot end-to-end trainable architecture, we draw motivation from the real-time object detectors such as YOLO [46]. The output layer in YOLO divides the output spatial map into a regular grid of cells. The multi-dimensional vector at each grid location broadly represents two important attributes. Firstly, a confidence value indicating the existence of an object centroid in the corresponding input image patch upon registering the grid onto the spatial image plane. Secondly, a parameterization of the object properties, such as class probabilities and attributes related to the corresponding bounding box. In similar lines, for multi-person 3D pose estimation, each grid location of the output layer represents a heatmap indicating existence of a human pelvis location (or root) followed by a *parameterization* of the corresponding root-relative 3D pose. Here, the major challenge is how to parameterize root-relative human 3D pose in the efficient manner. We explicitly address it in the following subsection.

3.1.1   Parameterizing 3D Pose via Pose Embedding.

Root relative human 3D pose follows a complex structured articulation. Moreover, defining a parameterization procedure without accounting for the structural plausibility of the 3D pose would further add up to the inherent 2D to 3D ambiguity. Acknowledging this, we aim to devise a parameterization which selectively decodes anthropomorphically plausible human poses spanning a continuous latent manifold (see Fig. 3A). One of the effective ways to realize the above objective is to train a generative network which models the most fundamental form of human pose variations. Thus, we disentangle the root-relative

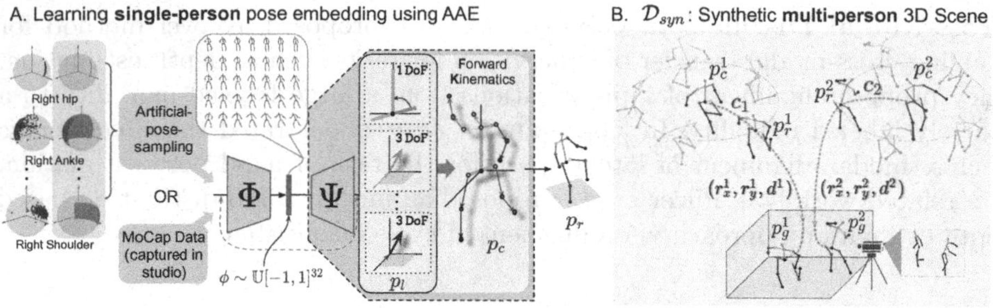

A. Learning **single-person** pose embedding using AAE   **B.** $\mathcal{D}_{syn}$: Synthetic **multi-person** 3D Scene

Fig. 3. A. Learning continuous pose-embedding on MoCap or Artificially sampled pose dataset. **B.** Creating $\mathcal{D}_{syn}$: Each canonical pose p_c is rigidly transformed through rotation and translation operation to form random 3D scenes.

pose p_r into its rigid and non-rigid factors. The non-rigid factor, also known as the canonical pose p_c is designed to be view-invariant. The rigid transformation is defined by the parameters c as required for the corresponding rotation matrix. In further granularity, according to the concept of forward kinematics [58], movement of each limb is constrained by the parent-relative joint-angle limits and the scale invariant fixed relative bone lengths. Thus, the unit vectors corresponding to each joint defined at their respective parent-relative local coordinate system [2] is regarded as the most fundamental form of 3D human pose which is denoted by p_l. Note that, the transformation $p_l \rightarrow p_c$ is a fully-differentiable series of forward kinematic operations. We train a generative network [21,22] following the learning procedure of adversarial auto-encoder $\{\Phi, \Psi\}$ (AAE [31]) on samples of p_l acquired from either a MoCap [1] dataset or via a proposed *Artificial-pose-sampling* procedure (see Fig. 3A). It is important to note that we consider a uniform prior distribution *i.e.* $\mathbb{U}[-1, 1]^{32}$. This ensures that any random vector $\phi \in [-1, 1]^{32}$ decodes (via Ψ) an anthropomorphically plausible human pose. (See Suppl)

In the proposed *Artificial-pose-sampling* procedure, we use a set of joint angle limits (4 angles *i.e.* the allowed range of polar and azimuthal angles in the parent relative local pose representation) provided by the biomechanic experts. The angle for each limb is independently sampled from a uniform distribution defined by the above range values (see the highlighted regions on the sphere for each body joint in Fig. 3A). Note that, the proposed joint angle sampling would allow sampling of minimal implausible single-person poses as it does not adhere to the pose-conditioned joint angle limits formalized by Akther *et al.* [2]. (See Suppl)

3.1.2   Neural Representation of Multi-person 3D Pose.

The last layer output of the single-shot latent to multi-person 3D pose mapper $\mathcal{H}$, denoted as s, is a 3D tensor of size $H \times W \times M$ (see block $\mathcal{M}$ Fig. 4B). The number of channels constitutes of 4 distinct components. The M dimensional vector for each grid location r^i constitutes of 4 distinct components viz,

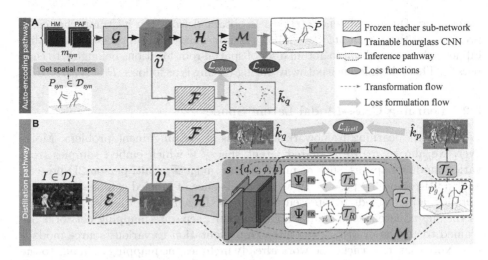

Fig. 4. Proposed data-flow pathways. Distillation is performed from the teacher, $\{\mathcal{E}, \mathcal{F}\}$ to the student $\{\mathcal{H}\}$. Weights of $\mathcal{H}$ and $\mathcal{F}$ are shared across both the pathways.

a) a scalar heatmap intensity indicating existence of a skeleton pelvis denoted as h^i, **b)** a 32 dimensional 3D pose embedding ϕ^i, **c)** 6 dimensional rigid transformation parameters c^i (sin and cos component of 3 rotation angles), and **d)** a scalar absolute depth d^i associated with the skeleton pelvis. Note that, the last 3 components are interpretable only in presence of a pelvis at the corresponding grid location as denoted by the first component. Here, ϕ^i is obtained through a *tanh* nonlinearity thus constraining it to decode (via frozen Ψ AAE from Subsect. 3.1.1) only plausible 3D human poses.

The model accesses a set of 2D pelvis key-point locations belonging to each person in the corresponding input image, denoted as $\{r^i\}_{i=1}^N$. Here, N denotes the total number of persons. These spatial locations are obtained either as estimated by the teacher network or from the ground-truth depending on its availability. For each selected location r^i, the corresponding ϕ^i and c^i are pooled from the relevant grid location to decode (via Ψ) the corresponding root-relative 3D pose, p_r^i. First, the canonical pose, p_c^i is obtained by applying forward kinematics (denoted as FK in Fig. 4B in module $\mathcal{M}$) on the decoded local vectors obtained from the pose embedding ϕ^i. Following this, p_r^i is obtained after performing rigid transformation using c^i, *i.e.* $\mathcal{T}_R$ in Fig. 4B. Finally, the global 3D pose scene, $\hat{P} = \{p_g^i\}_{i=1}^N$, is constructed by translating the root-relative 3D poses to their respective root locations in the camera centered global coordinate system, *i.e.* $\mathcal{T}_G$ in Fig. 4B. The 3D translation for each person i is obtained using (r_x^i, r_y^i, d^i), where r_x^i and r_y^i are the X and Y component obtained as a transformation of the spatial root location r^i. In Fig. 4B, the series of fixed (non-trainable) differentiable operations to obtain $\hat{P}$ from the CNN output s is denoted as $\mathcal{M}$. A weak perspective camera transformation, $\mathcal{T}_K$, of P provides us the corresponding multi-person 2D key-points denoted by $\hat{k}_p$.

Inference. During inference, (r_x^i, r_y^i) is obtained from the heatmap channel h predicted at the output of $\mathcal{F}$. We follow the non-maximum suppression algorithm inline with Cao et al. [3] to obtain a set of spatial root locations belonging to each person. Thus, the inference pathway during testing is as follows, $\hat{P} = \mathcal{M} \circ \mathcal{H} \circ \mathcal{E}(I)$.

3.2   Learning Cross-Modal Latent Space

We posit the learning framework as a cross-modal alignment problem. Moreover, we aim to realize a shared latent space, $\mathcal{V}$ which embed samples from varied modality spaces, such as multi-person image $\mathcal{I}$, multi-person 2D pose $\mathcal{K}$, and multi-person 3D pose $\mathcal{P}$. However, in absence of labeled samples (or paired samples) an intermediate representation of the frozen teacher network is treated as the shared latent embedding. Following this, separate mapping networks are trained to encode or decode the latent representation to various source modalities. Note that, the teacher network already includes the mapping of image to the latent space, $\mathcal{E} : \mathcal{I} \rightarrow \mathcal{V}$ and latent space to multi-person 2D pose, $\mathcal{F} : \mathcal{V} \rightarrow \mathcal{K}$. We train two additional mapping networks, viz. a) multi-person 2D pose to latent space, $\mathcal{G} : \mathcal{K} \rightarrow \mathcal{V}$ and b) latent space to multi-person 3D pose, $(\mathcal{M} \circ \mathcal{H}) : \mathcal{V} \rightarrow \mathcal{P}$. Also note that, $(\mathcal{T}_K \circ \mathcal{M} \circ \mathcal{H}) : \mathcal{V} \rightarrow \mathcal{K}$.

Available Datasets. We have access to two unpaired datasets viz. a) unpaired multi-person images $I \sim \mathcal{D}_I$ and b) unpaired multi-person 3D pose samples $P_{syn} \sim \mathcal{D}_{syn}$. Though it is easy to get hold of unpaired multi-person images, acquiring a dataset of unpaired multi-person 3D pose is inconvenient. Acknowledging this, we propose a systematic procedure to synthesize a large-scale multi-person 3D pose dataset from a set of plausible single-person 3D poses. A multi-person 3D pose sample constitute of a certain number of persons (samples of p_l^i) with random rigid transformations (c^i) placed at different locations (i.e. r_x^i, r_y^i, d^i) in a 3D room. This is illustrated in Fig. 3B. Here, samples of p_l can be obtained either from a MoCap dataset or by following *Artificial-pose-sampling*.

Broadly, we use two different data-flow pathways as shown in Fig. 4. Here, we discuss how these pathways support an effective cross-modal alignment.

a) Cross-Modal Distillation Pathway for $I \sim \mathcal{D}_I$. The objective of distillation pathway is to instill the knowledge of mapping an input RGB image to the corresponding multi-person 2D pose (i.e. from the teacher network $\hat{k}_q = \mathcal{F}(v)$ where $v = \mathcal{E}(I)$) into the newly introduced 3D pose estimation pipeline. Here, $\hat{k}_q$ is obtained after performing bipartite matching inline with Cao et al. [3]. We update the parameters of $\mathcal{H}$ by imposing a distillation loss between $\hat{k}_q$ and the perceptively projected 2D pose $\hat{k}_p = \mathcal{T}_K \circ \mathcal{M} \circ \mathcal{H}(v)$, i.e. $\mathcal{L}_{distl} = |\hat{k}_p - \hat{k}_q|$.

b) Auto-encoding Pathway for $P_{syn} \sim \mathcal{D}_{syn}$. In the auto-encoding pathway, the objective is to reconstruct back the synthesized samples of multi-person 3D poses via the shared latent space. Owing to the spatially structured latent representation, for each non-spatial P_{syn} we first generate the corresponding multi-person spatial heatmap (HM) and Part Affinity Map (PAF) inline with Cao et al. [3], denoted by m_{syn} in Fig. 4A. Note that m_{syn} represents the 2D keypoint locations of k_{syn} which is the obtained as the camera projection of the P_{syn}. Following this, we obtain $\tilde{P} = \mathcal{M} \circ \mathcal{H}(\tilde{v})$ where $\tilde{v} = \mathcal{G}(m_{syn})$. Parameters of both $\mathcal{G}$ and $\mathcal{H}$ are updated to minimize $\mathcal{L}_{recon} = |P_{syn} - \tilde{P}|$.

c) **Cross-Modal Adaptation.** Notice that, $\mathcal{H}$ is the only common model updated in both pathways. Here, $\mathcal{L}_{distl}$ is computed against the noisy teacher prediction that too in the 2D pose space. In contrast, $\mathcal{L}_{recon}$ is computed against the true ground-truth 3D pose thus devoid of the inherent 2D to 3D ambiguity. As a result of this disparity, the model $\mathcal{H}$ differentiates between the corresponding input distributions, *i.e.* between $\mathbb{P}(v)$ and $\mathbb{P}(\tilde{v})$, thereby learning separate strategies favouring the corresponding learning objectives. To minimize this discrepancy, we rely on the frozen teacher sub-network $\mathcal{F}$. We hypothesize that, the energy computed via $\mathcal{F}$, *i.e.* $|\mathcal{F}(\tilde{v}) - m_{syn}|$ would be low if the associated input distribution of $\mathcal{F}$, *i.e.* $\mathbb{P}(v = \mathcal{E}(I))$ aligns with the output distribution of $\mathcal{G}$, *i.e.* $\mathbb{P}(\tilde{v} = \mathcal{G}(m_{syn}))$. Accordingly, we propose to minimize $\mathcal{L}_{adapt} = |\mathcal{F} \circ \mathcal{G}(m_{syn}) - m_{syn}|$ to realize an effective cross-modal alignment.

Training Phase-1. We update $\mathcal{G}$ and $\mathcal{H}$ to minimize all the three losses discussed above, *i.e.* $\mathcal{L}_{recon}$, $\mathcal{L}_{distl}$ and $\mathcal{L}_{adapt}$ each with different Adam [17] optimizers.

3.3   Learning Beyond the Teacher Network

We see a clear limitation in the learning paradigm discussed above. The inference performance of the final model is limited by the dataset bias infused in the teacher network. We recognize $\mathcal{L}_{distl}$ as the prime culprit which limits the ability of $\mathcal{H}$ by not allowing it to surpass the teacher's performance. Though one can rely on $\mathcal{L}_{recon}$ to further improve $\mathcal{H}$, this would degrade performance in the inference pathway as a result of increase in discrepancy between v and $\tilde{v}$. Considering this, we propose to freeze $\mathcal{G}$ thereby freezing its output distribution $\mathbb{P}(\tilde{v} = \mathcal{G}(m_{syn}))$ in the second training phase.

Furthermore, in absence of the regularizing $\mathcal{L}_{distl}$ we use a self-supervised consistency loss to regularize $\mathcal{H}$ for the unpaired image samples. For each image I we form a pair (I, I') where $I' = T_s(I)$ is the spatially transformed version (*i.e.* image-flip, random-crop, or in-place rotation) of I. Here, T_s represents the differentiable spatial transformation. Next, we propose a consistency loss based on the equivariance property [49] of the corresponding multi-person 2D pose, *i.e.*

$$\mathcal{L}_{ss} = |T_s \circ T_K \circ \mathcal{M} \circ \mathcal{H} \circ \mathcal{E}(I) - T_K \circ \mathcal{M} \circ \mathcal{H} \circ \mathcal{E} \circ T_s(I)|$$

The above loss is computed at the root-locations extracted using the teacher network for the original image I. Whereas, for I' we use the spatial transformation T_s on the extracted root locations of the original image.

Training Phase-2. We update the parameters of $\mathcal{H}$ ($\mathcal{G}$ is kept frozen from the previous training phase) to minimize two loss terms *i.e.* $\mathcal{L}_{recon}$ and $\mathcal{L}_{ss}$.

Table 2. Quantitative analysis of different ablations of our approach on MuPoTS-3D. *Unpaired* means that there is no ground truth annotation available for an image. *Paired* means that there is a corresponding annotation available for an image. 3DPCK is Percentage of Correct 3D Keypoints predicted within 15 cm. (higher 3DPCK is better). "sup." stands for supervision. MuCo-3DHP [34] is used in fifth column. Red color indicates that configuration is less preferable for low data regime. (*Best viewed in color*).

Methods	Artificial poses (Ψ_{arti})	MoCap poses (Ψ_{mocap})	Paired **multi person** 2D sup.	Composed **multi person** 3D sup.	3DPCK
Ours: learning without any paired supervision. Using 2D predictions from teacher					
$\mathcal{L}_{distl}$ (no $\mathcal{D}_{syn}$)	✔	✗	✗	✗	53.3
$+\mathcal{L}_{recon}$	✔	✗	✗	✗	57.6
$+\mathcal{L}_{adapt}$	✔	✗	✗	✗	61.9
$+\mathcal{L}_{ss}$	✔	✗	✗	✗	64.2
Ours-Us	✗	✔	✗	✗	66.1
Ours: weakly supervised learning methods. Using paired 2D supervision only					
with Ψ_{arti}	✔	✗	✔	✗	66.4
Ours-Ws	✗	✔	✔	✗	67.9
Ours: supervised learning methods. Using both paired 2D and 3D supervision					
No $\mathcal{D}_{syn}$	✗	✔	✔	✔	71.1
Ours-Fs	✗	✔	✔	✔	75.8

4   Experiments

In this section, we describe the experiments and results of the proposed approach on several benchmark datasets. Through quantitative and qualitative analysis, we demonstrate the practicality and performance of our method.

4.1   Implementation Details

First, we explain the implementation details of synthetic dataset creation. Next, we provide the training details for learning the neural representation.

3D Skeleton Dataset. *Artificial-pose-sampling* is performed by sampling uniformly from joint wise angle limits defined at local parent relative [2] spherical coordinate system (see Fig. 3A) *i.e.* $[\theta_1, \theta_2]$, and $[\gamma_1, \gamma_2]$. For example, right-hip joint $\theta_1 = \theta_2 = \pi$ (*i.e.* 1-DoF) and $\gamma_1 = \pi/3$, $\gamma_2 = 2\pi/3$ (See Suppl). Using these predefined limits, we construct a full 3D pose (via FK). A total of 1M poses are sampled for training Ψ_{arti}. Further, 100k synthetic multi-person pose scenes are created by sampling upto 4 single-person 3D poses per scene. Note that, the $\mathcal{D}_{syn}$ dataset can also utilize 3D poses from single-person 3D dataset such as Human 3.6M [14] and MPI-INF-3DHP [33], when accessible.

Training. First, we train a pose decoder (see Sect. 3.1.1) either on artificial pose dataset (Ψ_{arti}) or MoCap 3D dataset (Ψ_{mocap}). The AAE modules are trained

Table 3. Comparison of 3DPCK$_{rel}$ on MuPoTS-3D sequences. Our methods are highlighted in gray background color. Underlined values indicate that our unpaired learning (*Ours-Us*) approach performs better on that sequence. *Ours-Fs* (fully-supervised) achieves state-of-the-art in bottom up methods. *Ours-Us* approach performs competitively even when compared with prior fully supervised approaches.

Methods	S1	S2	S3	S4	S5	S6	S7	S8	S9	S10	S11	S12	S13	S14	S15	S16	S17	S18	S19	S20	Avg
Accuracy for all groundtruths																					
Rogez[47]	67.7	49.8	53.4	59.1	67.5	22.8	43.7	49.9	31.1	78.1	50.2	51.0	51.6	49.3	56.2	66.5	65.2	62.9	66.1	59.1	53.8
Rogez[48]	87.3	61.9	67.9	74.6	78.8	48.9	58.3	59.7	78.1	89.5	69.2	73.8	66.2	56.0	74.1	82.1	78.1	72.6	73.1	61.0	70.6
Dabral[7]	85.1	67.9	73.5	76.2	74.9	52.5	65.7	63.6	56.3	77.8	76.4	70.1	65.3	51.7	69.5	87.0	82.1	80.3	78.5	70.7	71.3
Mehta[34]	81.0	60.9	64.4	63.0	69.1	30.3	65.0	59.6	64.1	83.9	68.0	68.6	62.3	59.2	70.1	80.0	79.6	67.3	66.6	67.2	66.0
Ours-Us	76.8	61.8	61.2	63.0	68.7	20.3	67.3	65.2	59.5	83.6	62.4	66.0	52.7	54.9	57.5	73.6	70.9	70.1	70.4	60.8	63.3
Ours-Ws	79.6	62.3	54.2	55.9	69.3	36.1	69.1	67.7	58.4	80.2	75.3	68.7	53.6	56.5	59.6	77.4	76.7	69.6	69.2	64.1	65.2
Ours-Fs	85.5	84.1	66.7	70.5	77.4	68.6	74.8	77.9	69.1	80.0	78.4	75.4	61.1	60.9	71.3	81.4	85.1	73.4	74.9	63.5	74.0
Accuracy only for matched groundtruths																					
Rogez[47]	69.1	67.3	54.6	61.7	74.5	25.2	48.4	63.3	69.0	78.1	53.8	52.2	60.5	60.9	59.1	70.5	76.0	70.0	77.1	81.4	62.4
Rogez[48]	88.0	73.3	67.9	74.6	81.8	50.1	60.6	60.8	78.2	89.5	70.8	74.4	72.8	64.5	74.2	84.9	85.2	78.4	75.8	74.4	74.0
Dabral[7]	85.8	73.6	61.1	55.7	77.9	53.3	75.1	65.5	54.2	81.3	82.2	71.0	70.1	67.7	69.9	90.5	85.7	86.3	85.0	91.4	74.2
Mehta[34]	81.0	65.3	64.6	63.9	75.0	30.3	65.1	61.1	64.1	83.9	72.4	69.9	71.0	72.9	71.3	83.6	79.6	73.5	78.9	90.9	70.8
Ours-Us	76.8	66.6	62.1	63.9	73.5	20.3	67.3	67.8	59.5	83.6	62.4	66.0	56.0	63.5	59.5	75.2	70.9	73.0	73.1	80.8	66.1
Ours-Ws	79.6	66.0	55.5	56.4	74.8	36.1	69.1	69.6	58.4	80.2	75.3	68.7	56.7	66.4	61.6	78.9	76.7	72.8	71.7	83.0	67.9
Ours-Fs	85.5	86.5	66.7	70.5	81.2	68.6	74.8	79.5	69.1	80.0	78.4	75.4	64.0	68.6	73.7	82.9	85.1	76.4	77.4	72.8	75.8

using a batch size of 32, with a learning rate of 1e−4 using Adam optimizers till convergence (See Suppl). The decoder Ψ is frozen for rest of the training. For training the neural representation, we choose the pretrained network of Cao *et al.* [3] as the teacher network. We consider upto stage-1 "conv5-4-CPM" layer of [3] as $\mathcal{E}$. We concatenate the predictions of both heatmap and Part Affinity Field branches to obtain an embedding space of size $28 \times 28 \times 1024$. We consider module $\mathcal{F}$ as from stage-1 "conv5-5-CPM" layer upto stage-2 "Mconv7-stage2" layer of [3]. Using this teacher model, we train the modules $\{\mathcal{H}, \mathcal{G}\}$ by minimizing the losses $\mathcal{L}_{distl}$, $\mathcal{L}_{recon}$, $\mathcal{L}_{adapt}$, $\mathcal{L}_{ss}$ using separate Adam optimizers for each of the losses. We use a learning rate of 1e−4 upto 100k iterations and 1e−5 for the following 500k iterations while using a fixed batch size of 8 throughout the training. Further, we use batches of images from $\mathcal{D}_{syn}$ and $\mathcal{D}_I$ in alternate iterations while training the network. The input image size for $\mathcal{D}_I$ is $224 \times 224 \times 3$ and input PAF representation [3] is of shape $28 \times 28 \times 43$ for $\mathcal{D}_{syn}$. All transformations $\mathcal{T}_K$, $\mathcal{T}_R$, $\mathcal{T}_G$ have been implemented using TensorFlow and are designed to be completely differentiable end-to-end. We have trained the entire pipeline on a Tesla-V100 GPU card in Nvidia-DGX station (See Suppl).

4.2 Ablation Studies

In order to study the effectiveness of our method, we perform extensive ablation study by varying levels of supervision, as shown in Table 2. For all the ablations, we have used MuCo-3DHP images [34] as $\mathcal{I}$. Depending on the supervision setting, we either access none (for unsup. setting), a small fraction (semi sup. setting) or a complete set (full sup. setting) of 3D annotations in MuCo-3DHP dataset.

Ours-Us (Using *Unpaired* images only): Our baseline model (see Table 2) trained without accessing any annotated labels gives an overall 3DPCK of 53.3.

Table 4. Joint wise analysis of $3DPCK_{rel}$ on MuPoTS-3D (higher is better). Underlined values indicate that our unpaired learning (*Ours-Us*) performs better on that joint

Methods	Hd.	Nck.	Sho.	Elb.	Wri.	Hip	Kn.	Ank.	Avg
Rogez[47]	<u>49.4</u>	<u>67.4</u>	<u>57.1</u>	<u>51.4</u>	41.3	<u>84.6</u>	<u>56.3</u>	<u>36.3</u>	<u>53.8</u>
Mehta[34]	62.1	81.2	77.9	<u>57.7</u>	47.2	**97.3**	<u>66.3</u>	47.6	66.0
Ours-Us	52.9	79.0	72.2	57.9	45.3	89.9	66.9	45.1	63.3
Ours-Ws	59.9	84.2	78.0	60.6	42.3	91.5	67.2	45.5	65.2
Ours-Fs	**63.4**	**85.5**	**84.2**	**70.4**	**56.8**	95.0	**78.2**	**59.0**	**74.0**

Table 5. We report Camera Centric absolute $3DPCK_{abs}$ metric on MuPoTS-3D. B/U means Bottom-up. *fps* is runtime frames/second.

Methods	B/U	$3DPCK_{abs}$ (↑)	*fps* (↑)
Moon* [36]	✗	9.6	7.3
Moon [36]	✗	**31.5**	7.3
Ours-Us	✔	23.6	**21.2**
Ours-Ws	✔	24.3	**21.2**
Ours-Fs	✔	28.1	**21.2**

Table 6. Comparison of Absolute MPJPE (lower is better) on Human 3.6M evaluated on S9 and S11. The table is split into three parts: single-person 3D pose estimation approaches (No. 1 to 6), multi-person 3D pose estimation *top-down* approaches (No. 7 to 10), multi-person 3D pose estimation *bottom-up* approaches (No. 11 and 12). Our approach performs better than previous bottom-up multi-person pose estimation methods.

No.	Methods	Dir.	Dis.	Eat	Gre.	Phon.	Pose	Pur.	Sit	SitD.	Smo.	Phot.	Wait	Walk	WaD.	WaP.	Avg
	Single-person approaches																
1.	Martinez [32]	51.8	56.2	58.1	59.0	69.5	55.2	58.1	74.0	94.6	62.3	78.4	59.1	65.1	49.5	52.4	62.9
2.	Zhou [57]	54.8	60.7	58.2	71.4	62.0	53.8	55.6	75.2	111.6	64.1	65.5	66.0	51.4	63.2	55.3	64.9
3.	Sun [51]	52.8	54.8	54.2	54.3	61.8	53.1	53.6	71.7	86.7	61.5	67.2	53.4	47.1	61.6	53.4	59.1
4.	Dabral [8]	44.8	50.4	44.7	49.0	52.9	43.5	45.5	63.1	87.3	51.7	61.4	48.5	37.6	52.2	41.9	52.1
5.	Hossain [45]	44.2	46.7	52.3	49.3	59.9	47.5	46.2	59.9	65.6	55.8	59.4	50.4	52.3	43.5	45.1	51.9
6.	Sun [52]	47.5	47.7	49.5	50.2	51.4	43.8	46.4	58.9	65.7	49.4	55.8	47.8	38.9	49.0	43.8	49.6
	Multi-person approaches																
7.	Rogez [47]	76.2	80.2	75.8	83.3	92.2	79.0	71.7	105.9	127.1	88.0	105.7	83.7	64.9	86.6	84.0	87.7
8.	Rogez [48]	55.9	60.0	64.5	56.3	67.4	71.8	55.1	55.3	84.8	90.7	67.9	57.5	47.8	63.3	54.6	63.5
9.	Dabral [7]	52.6	61.0	58.8	61.0	69.5	58.8	57.2	76.0	93.6	63.1	79.3	63.9	51.5	71.4	53.5	65.2
10.	Moon[36]	51.5	56.8	51.2	52.2	55.2	47.7	50.9	63.3	69.9	54.2	57.4	50.4	42.5	57.5	47.7	54.4
11.	Mehta[34]	58.2	67.3	61.2	65.7	75.8	62.2	64.6	82.0	93.0	68.8	84.5	65.1	57.6	72.0	63.6	69.9
12.	*Ours-Fs*	55.8	61.4	58.4	71.9	67.6	65.2	67.7	86.7	84.3	68.3	78.9	67.9	51.8	77.9	55.2	67.9

We observe that $\mathcal{L}_{adapt} + \mathcal{L}_{ss}$ gives a non-trivial boost of 4–6%. This demonstrates the importance of cross-modal alignment and self-supervised consistency.

Ours-Ws (*Weakly supervised*): When supervised weakly by 2D ground truth ($\mathcal{L}_{2D} = |k_p - \hat{k}_p|$), our approach obtains a 3DPCK of 67.9. Further, the performance of our approach that uses Ψ_{arti} is on par with our performance with Ψ_{mocap} indicating that ϕ_{arti} has rich representation space, equivalent to ϕ_{mocap}.

Ours-Fs (*Fully supervised*): When we access the full training dataset of MuCo-3DHP and impose a 3D reconstruction loss by using $\mathcal{L}_{3D} = |P - \hat{P}|$, we obtain a 3DPCK of 75.8, which is significantly better than the prior arts.

Table 7. 2D keypoint result comparison of our student model with teacher network on MuPoTS-3D. ↑ indicates that higher is better and ↓ indicates that lower is better.

Methods	IoU (↑)	2D-MPJPE (↓)	2D-PCK (↑)
Teacher (Cao [3])	60.1	38.0	66.6
$\mathcal{L}_{distl}$ (no $\mathcal{D}_{syn}$)	51.9	49.6	60.3
Ours-Fs	81.6	19.5	74.7

Table 8. Complexity analysis on MuPoTS-3D. B/U stands for bottom-up approach. ↑ indicates that higher is better and ↓ indicates that lower is better.

Methods	B/U	3DPCK (↑)	fps (↑)	Model size (↓)
Mehta [34]	✔	70.8	8.8	> 25.7M
Moon [36]	✗	82.5	7.3	34.3M
Ours-Fs	✔	75.8	21.2	17.1M

4.3   Datasets and Quantitative Evaluation

MuCo-3DHP Training Set and MuPoTS-3D Test Set. Mehta et.al [34] proposed creation of training dataset by compositing images from 3D single-person dataset MPI-INF-3DHP [33]. MPI-INF-3DHP is created by marker-less motion capture for 8 subjects using 14 cameras. MuPoTS-3D [34] is a multi-person 3D pose test dataset that contains 20 sequences capturing upto 3 persons per frame. Each of these sequences include challenging human poses and also capture real world interactions of persons. For evaluating multi-person 3D person pose, $3DPCK_{rel}$ (Percentage of Correct Keypoints) is widely employed [34,36,47]. In the root-relative system, a joint keypoint prediction is considered as a correct prediction if the joint is present within the range of 15cm. For evaluating absolute location of human joints in camera coordinates, [36] proposed $3DPCK_{abs}$ in which a prediction is considered correct when the joint is within the range of 25cm. In Table 3 we have compared the results of our method against the state-of-the-art methods. Our fully supervised approach yields state-of-the-art bottom-up performance (75.8 v/s Mehta [34] 70.8) while being faster than the top-down approaches. In Table 4 we present joint-wise 3DPCK on MuPoTS-3D dataset. We compare against [36] on $3DPCK_{abs}$ metric in Table 5 as it is the only work that reported on $3DPCK_{abs}$.

Human 3.6M [14]. This dataset consists of 3.6 million video frames of single person 3D poses that have been collected in laboratory setting. In Table 6, we show results on Protocol 2: MPJPE calculation on after alignment of root. As shown in Table 6, our approach outperforms bottom-up multi-person works (Mehta [34] 69.9 v/s Ours 67.9) and performs on par with top-down approaches (Rogez [48] 63.5 and Dabral [7] 65.2).

5   Discussion

Fast and Accurate Inference. In Table 8, we provide runtime complexity analysis of our model in comparison to prior works. All top-down approaches [36,47,48] depend on a person detector model. Hence these methods have low *fps* in comparison to bottom-up approaches (See Fig. 2). We outperform the previous bottom-up approach by a large margin in terms of 3DPCK, *fps* and model

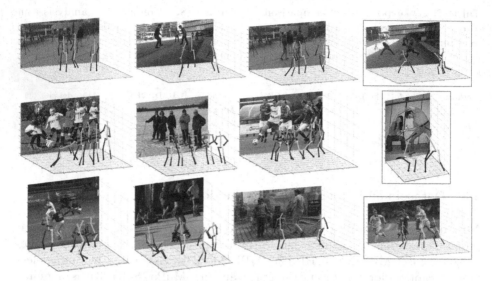

Fig. 5. Qualitative results on MuPoTS-3D (1st row), MS-COCO (2nd row), and "in-the-wild" images (3rd row) of our approach. Our approach is able to effectively handle inter-person occlusion and make reliable predictions for crowded images. Pink box highlights some failure cases. 1st row: presence of self-occlusion, 2nd row: rare multi-person interaction and 3rd row: joint location ambiguity.

size. We achieve a superior real-time computation capability because our approach effectively eliminates the keypoint grouping operation usually performed in bottom-up approaches [3,34]. All *fps* numbers reported in Table 8 were obtained on a Nvidia RTX 2080 GPU. In Table 8, we also show the total number of parameters of the model used during inference time.

Is Student Network Limited by Teacher Network? In Table 7 we report results of 2D pose estimation on both teacher model ($\hat{k}_q$) and student model ($\hat{k}_p$) by evaluating IoU, 2D-MPJPE and 2D-PCK on MuPoTS-3D dataset. We observe that a student model trained by minimizing $\mathcal{L}_{distl}$ alone performs sub-optimally in comparison to the teacher. This result is not surprising as the student model is restricted by knowledge of the teacher model. However, in our complete loss formulation (*Ours-Fs*) our approach outperforms the teacher on the 2D task, validating the hypothesis that our approach can learn beyond the teacher network.

Qualitative Results. We show qualitative results on the MS-COCO [27], MuPoTS-3D and frames taken from YouTube videos and other "in-the-wild" sources in Fig. 5. As seen in the Fig. 5, our model produces correct predictions on images with different camera viewpoints and on those images containing challenging elements such as inter-person occlusion. These qualitative results show that our model has generalized well on unseen images.

Two-Stage Refinement for Performance-Speed Tradeoff. Top-down frameworks yield better performance as compared to the bottom-up approach while having substantial computational overhead [18]. To this end we realize a hybrid framework which would provide flexibility based on the requirement. For example, the current single-shot (or single-stage) operates in a substantial computational superiority. To further improve its performance, we propose an additional pass of each detected persons through the full pipeline (Fig. 6). Here, we train a separate $\mathcal{H}'$ for the single-person pose estimation task which is operated on the cropped image patches of single human instances obtained from the *Stage-1* predictions. By training the $\mathcal{H}'$ network we obtain a 3DPCK of 76.9 (v/s *Ours-Fs* 75.8) with a runtime *fps* of 16.6 (v/s *Ours-Fs* 21.2 *fps*). (See Table 3 and Fig. 2)

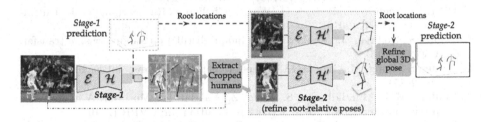

Fig. 6. A hybrid framework for two-stage refinement which treats *Stage-1* output as a person detector while *Stage-2* performs single-person 3D pose estimation.

6 Conclusion

In this paper we have introduced an unsupervised approach for multi-person 3D pose estimation by infusing structural constraints of human pose. Our bottom-up approach has real-time computational benefits and can estimate the pose of persons in camera-centric coordinates. Our method can benefit from future improvements on 2D pose estimation works in a plug-and-play fashion. Extending such a framework for multi-person human mesh recovery and extraction of appearance related mesh texture remains to be explored in future.

Acknowledgement. This project is supported by a Indo-UK Joint Project (DST/INT/UK/P-179/2017), DST, Govt. of India and a WIRIN project.

References

1. CMU graphics lab motion capture database. http://mocap.cs.cmu.edu/
2. Akhter, I., Black, M.J.: Pose-conditioned joint angle limits for 3D human pose reconstruction. In: CVPR (2015)

3. Cao, Z., Simon, T., Wei, S.E., Sheikh, Y.: Realtime multi-person 2D pose estimation using part affinity fields. In: CVPR (2017)
4. Chen, C.H., Tyagi, A., Agrawal, A., Drover, D., Stojanov, S., Rehg, J.M.: Unsupervised 3D pose estimation with geometric self-supervision. In: CVPR (2019)
5. Chen, Y., Wang, Z., Peng, Y., Zhang, Z., Yu, G., Sun, J.: Cascaded pyramid network for multi-person pose estimation. In: CVPR (2018)
6. Chung, Y.A., Weng, W.H., Tong, S., Glass, J.: Unsupervised cross-modal alignment of speech and text embedding spaces. In: NeurIPS (2018)
7. Dabral, R., Gundavarapu, N.B., Mitra, R., Sharma, A., Ramakrishnan, G., Jain, A.: Multi-person 3D human pose estimation from monocular images. In: 3DV (2019)
8. Dabral, R., Mundhada, A., Kusupati, U., Afaque, S., Sharma, A., Jain, A.: Learning 3D human pose from structure and motion. In: Ferrari, V., Hebert, M., Sminchisescu, C., Weiss, Y. (eds.) ECCV 2018. LNCS, vol. 11213, pp. 679–696. Springer, Cham (2018). https://doi.org/10.1007/978-3-030-01240-3_41
9. Dhar, P., Singh, R.V., Peng, K.C., Wu, Z., Chellappa, R.: Learning without memorizing. In: CVPR (2019)
10. Gupta, S., Hoffman, J., Malik, J.: Cross modal distillation for supervision transfer. In: CVPR (2016)
11. Huang, S., Gong, M., Tao, D.: A coarse-fine network for keypoint localization. In: ICCV (2017)
12. Ibrahim, M.S., Muralidharan, S., Deng, Z., Vahdat, A., Mori, G.: A hierarchical deep temporal model for group activity recognition. In: CVPR (2016)
13. Insafutdinov, E., Pishchulin, L., Andres, B., Andriluka, M., Schiele, B.: DeeperCut: a deeper, stronger, and faster multi-person pose estimation Model. In: Leibe, B., Matas, J., Sebe, N., Welling, M. (eds.) ECCV 2016. LNCS, vol. 9910, pp. 34–50. Springer, Cham (2016). https://doi.org/10.1007/978-3-319-46466-4_3
14. Ionescu, C., Papava, D., Olaru, V., Sminchisescu, C.: Human3.6M: large scale datasets and predictive methods for 3D human sensing in natural environments. TPAMI **36**(7), 1325–1339 (2013)
15. Joo, H., et al.: Panoptic studio: a massively multiview system for social motion capture. In: ICCV (2015)
16. Kanazawa, A., Black, M.J., Jacobs, D.W., Malik, J.: End-to-end recovery of human shape and pose. In: CVPR (2018)
17. Kingma, D.P., Ba, J.: Adam: a method for stochastic optimization. In: ICLR (2014)
18. Kocabas, M., Karagoz, S., Akbas, E.: MultiPoseNet: fast multi-person pose estimation using pose residual network. In: Ferrari, V., Hebert, M., Sminchisescu, C., Weiss, Y. (eds.) ECCV 2018. LNCS, vol. 11215, pp. 437–453. Springer, Cham (2018). https://doi.org/10.1007/978-3-030-01252-6_26
19. Kundu, J.N., Rahul, M.V., Ganeshan, A., Babu, R.V.: Object Pose estimation from monocular image using multi-view keypoint correspondence. In: Leal-Taixé, L., Roth, S. (eds.) ECCV 2018. LNCS, vol. 11131, pp. 298–313. Springer, Cham (2019). https://doi.org/10.1007/978-3-030-11015-4_23
20. Kundu, J.N., Ganeshan, A., MV, R., Prakash, A., Babu, R.V.: iSPA-Net: iterative semantic pose alignment network. In: ACM Multimedia (2018)
21. Kundu, J.N., Gor, M., Babu, R.V.: BiHMP-GAN: bidirectional 3D human motion prediction GAN. In: AAAI (2019)
22. Kundu, J.N., Gor, M., Uppala, P.K., Babu, R.V.: Unsupervised feature learning of human actions as trajectories in pose embedding manifold. In: WACV (2019)
23. Kundu, J.N., Patravali, J., Babu, R.V.: Unsupervised cross-dataset adaptation via probabilistic amodal 3D human pose completion. In: WACV (2020)

24. Kundu, J.N., Seth, S., Jampani, V., Rakesh, M., Babu, R.V., Chakraborty, A.: Self-supervised 3D human pose estimation via part guided novel image synthesis. In: CVPR (2020)
25. Kundu, J.N., Seth, S., Rahul, M., Rakesh, M., Babu, R.V., Chakraborty, A.: Kinematic-structure-preserved representation for unsupervised 3D human pose estimation. In: AAAI (2020)
26. Li, Z., Hoiem, D.: Learning without forgetting. TPAMI **40**(12), 2935–2947 (2017)
27. Lin, T.-Y., et al.: Microsoft COCO: common objects in context. In: Fleet, D., Pajdla, T., Schiele, B., Tuytelaars, T. (eds.) ECCV 2014. LNCS, vol. 8693, pp. 740–755. Springer, Cham (2014). https://doi.org/10.1007/978-3-319-10602-1_48
28. Long, M., Cao, Y., Wang, J., Jordan, M.: Learning transferable features with deep adaptation networks. In: ICML (2015)
29. Lopes, R.G., Fenu, S., Starner, T.: Data-free knowledge distillation for deep neural networks (2017)
30. Luvizon, D.C., Picard, D., Tabia, H.: 2D/3D pose estimation and action recognition using multitask deep learning. In: CVPR (2018)
31. Makhzani, A., Shlens, J., Jaitly, N., Goodfellow, I., Frey, B.: Adversarial autoencoders. arXiv preprint arXiv:1511.05644 (2015)
32. Martinez, J., Hossain, R., Romero, J., Little, J.J.: A simple yet effective baseline for 3D human pose estimation. In: ICCV (2017)
33. Mehta, D., et al.: Monocular 3D human pose estimation in the wild using improved CNN supervision. In: 3DV (2017)
34. Mehta, D., et al.: Single-shot multi-person 3D pose estimation from monocular RGB. In: 3DV (2018)
35. Mehta, D., et al.: VNect: real-time 3D human pose estimation with a single RGB camera. ACM TOG **36**(4), 1–14 (2017)
36. Moon, G., Chang, J.Y., Lee, K.M.: Camera distance-aware top-down approach for 3D multi-person pose estimation from a single RGB image. In: ICCV (2019)
37. Nayak, G.K., Mopuri, K.R., Shaj, V., Radhakrishnan, V.B., Chakraborty, A.: Zero-shot knowledge distillation in deep networks. In: ICML (2019)
38. Newell, A., Huang, Z., Deng, J.: Associative embedding: end-to-end learning for joint detection and grouping. In: NIPS (2017)
39. Newell, A., Yang, K., Deng, J.: Stacked hourglass networks for human pose estimation. In: Leibe, B., Matas, J., Sebe, N., Welling, M. (eds.) ECCV 2016. LNCS, vol. 9912, pp. 483–499. Springer, Cham (2016). https://doi.org/10.1007/978-3-319-46484-8_29
40. Nie, X., Feng, J., Zhang, J., Yan, S.: Single-stage multi-person pose machines. In: ICCV (2019)
41. Pavlakos, G., Zhou, X., Derpanis, K.G., Daniilidis, K.: Coarse-to-fine volumetric prediction for single-image 3D human pose. In: CVPR (2017)
42. Peng, X.B., Andrychowicz, M., Zaremba, W., Abbeel, P.: Sim-to-real transfer of robotic control with dynamics randomization. In: ICRA (2018)
43. Pilzer, A., Lathuiliere, S., Sebe, N., Ricci, E.: Refine and distill: exploiting cycle-inconsistency and knowledge distillation for unsupervised monocular depth estimation. In: CVPR (2019)
44. Pishchulin, L., et al.: DeepCut: joint subset partition and labeling for multi person pose estimation. In: CVPR (2016)
45. Hossain, M.R.I., Little, J.J.: Exploiting temporal information for 3D human pose estimation. In: Ferrari, V., Hebert, M., Sminchisescu, C., Weiss, Y. (eds.) ECCV 2018. LNCS, vol. 11214, pp. 69–86. Springer, Cham (2018). https://doi.org/10.1007/978-3-030-01249-6_5

46. Redmon, J., Divvala, S., Girshick, R., Farhadi, A.: You only look once: unified, real-time object detection. In: CVPR (2016)
47. Rogez, G., Weinzaepfel, P., Schmid, C.: LCR-Net: localization-classification-regression for human pose. In: CVPR (2017)
48. Rogez, G., Weinzaepfel, P., Schmid, C.: LCR-Net++: multi-person 2D and 3D pose detection in natural images. TPAMI **42**, 1146–1161 (2019)
49. Schmidt, U., Roth, S.: Learning rotation-aware features: from invariant priors to equivariant descriptors. In: CVPR (2012)
50. Spurr, A., Song, J., Park, S., Hilliges, O.: Cross-modal deep variational hand pose estimation. In: CVPR (2018)
51. Sun, X., Shang, J., Liang, S., Wei, Y.: Compositional human pose regression. In: ICCV (2017)
52. Sun, X., Xiao, B., Wei, F., Liang, S., Wei, Y.: Integral human pose regression. In: Ferrari, V., Hebert, M., Sminchisescu, C., Weiss, Y. (eds.) ECCV 2018. LNCS, vol. 11210, pp. 536–553. Springer, Cham (2018). https://doi.org/10.1007/978-3-030-01231-1_33
53. Tobin, J., Fong, R., Ray, A., Schneider, J., Zaremba, W., Abbeel, P.: Domain randomization for transferring deep neural networks from simulation to the real world. In: IROS (2017)
54. Xiao, B., Wu, H., Wei, Y.: Simple baselines for human pose estimation and tracking. In: Ferrari, V., Hebert, M., Sminchisescu, C., Weiss, Y. (eds.) ECCV 2018. LNCS, vol. 11210, pp. 472–487. Springer, Cham (2018). https://doi.org/10.1007/978-3-030-01231-1_29
55. Yasin, H., Iqbal, U., Kruger, B., Weber, A., Gall, J.: A dual-source approach for 3D pose estimation from a single image. In: CVPR (2016)
56. Zheng, L., Zhang, H., Sun, S., Chandraker, M., Yang, Y., Tian, Q.: Person re-identification in the wild. In: CVPR (2017)
57. Zhou, X., Huang, Q., Sun, X., Xue, X., Wei, Y.: Towards 3D human pose estimation in the wild: a weakly-supervised approach. In: ICCV (2017)
58. Zhou, X., Sun, X., Zhang, W., Liang, S., Wei, Y.: Deep kinematic pose regression. In: Hua, G., Jégou, H. (eds.) ECCV 2016. LNCS, vol. 9915, pp. 186–201. Springer, Cham (2016). https://doi.org/10.1007/978-3-319-49409-8_17

Class-Incremental Domain Adaptation

Jogendra Nath Kundu$^{(\boxtimes)}$, Rahul Mysore Venkatesh, Naveen Venkat,
Ambareesh Revanur, and R. Venkatesh Babu

Video Analytics Lab, Indian Institute of Science, Bangalore, India
jogendrak@iisc.ac.in

Abstract. We introduce a practical Domain Adaptation (DA)
paradigm called Class-Incremental Domain Adaptation (CIDA). Existing DA methods tackle domain-shift but are unsuitable for learning novel
target-domain classes. Meanwhile, class-incremental (CI) methods enable
learning of new classes in absence of source training data, but fail under
a domain-shift without labeled supervision. In this work, we effectively
identify the limitations of these approaches in the CIDA paradigm. Motivated by theoretical and empirical observations, we propose an effective
method, inspired by prototypical networks, that enables classification
of target samples into both shared and novel (one-shot) target classes,
even under a domain-shift. Our approach yields superior performance as
compared to both DA and CI methods in the CIDA paradigm.

1 Introduction

Deep models have been shown to outperform human evaluators on image recognition tasks [15]. However, a common assumption in such evaluations is that
the training and the test data distributions are alike. In the presence of a larger
domain-shift [43] between the training and the test domains, the performance of
deep models degrades drastically resulting from the domain-bias [18,50]. Moreover, the recognition capabilities of such models is limited to the set of learned
categories, which further limits their generalizability. Thus, once a model is
trained on a source training dataset (the *source* domain), it is essential to further
upgrade the model to perform well in the test environment (the *target* domain).

For example, consider a *self-driving car* installed with an *object recognition
model* trained on urban scenes. Such a model will underperform in rural landscapes (test environment) where objects differ in their visual appearance and
the surrounding context. Moreover, the model will also misclassify objects from
unseen categories (*a.k.a* target-private categories) into one of the learned classes.
This is a direct result of the domain-shift between urban and rural environments.

J. N. Kundu and R. M. Venkatesh are Equal contribution.

Electronic supplementary material The online version of this chapter (https://
doi.org/10.1007/978-3-030-58601-0_4) contains supplementary material, which is available to authorized users.

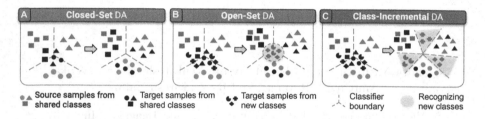

Fig. 1. Problem Setting. A) Closed-set DA assumes a shared label-set between the source and the target domains. **B)** Open-set DA rejects target samples from unseen categories into a single *unknown* class. **C)** In Class-Incremental DA, we aim to recognize both shared and new target classes by assigning a unique semantic label to each class.

A naive approach to address this problem would be to fine-tune [28] the model on an annotated dataset drawn from the target environment. However, this is often not a practical solution as acquiring label-rich data is an expensive process. Moreover, for an efficient model upgrade, it is also imperative that the model supports adaptation to new domains and tasks, without re-training on the source training data [7,28] from scratch. Motivated by these challenges, in this paper we ask "how to effectively upgrade a trained model to the target domain?".

In the literature, this question has been long-standing. A line of work called Unsupervised Domain Adaptation (UDA) [2,3,5,21,22,25,31,51] has emerged that offers an elegant solution to the domain-shift problem. In UDA, the usual practice [10,37] is to obtain a labeled source dataset and unlabeled targets samples, to perform adaptation under the co-existence of samples from both the domains. However, most UDA methods [10,12,44,52] assume that the two domains share the same label space (as shown in Fig. 1A), making them impractical in real-world where a target domain potentially contains unseen categories (*in the self-driving car example, novel objects occur in the deployed environment*). To this end, open-set DA [1,24,36,45] and universal DA [23,54] have gained attention, where the target domain is allowed to have novel (target-private) classes not present in the source domain. These target-private samples are assigned an "*unknown*" label (see Fig. 1B). As a result, target-private samples with diverse semantic content get clustered together in a single "*unknown*" class in the latent space.

While UDA methods tackle the domain-shift problem, these require simultaneous access to both source and target domain samples, which makes them unsuitable in cases where the source training data is proprietary [24,32,34] (*e.g. in a self-driving car*), or simply unavailable during model upgrade [7,23,28]. Moreover, these methods can only detect new target categories as a single *unknown* class [36], and cannot assign individual semantic labels to such categories (Fig. 1C). Thus, these methods do not truly facilitate model upgrade (*e.g. adding new classes to the recognition model*) thereby having a limited practical use-case.

Another line of work consists of Class-Incremental (CI) learning methods [4,28,38,42,53] which aim at adding new classes to a trained model while preserving the performance on the previously learned classes. Certain methods [7] achieve this even without accessing the source training data (hereon, we call such methods as *source-free*). However, these methods are not tailored to address domain-shift (*thus, in our example, the object recognition model would still underperform in rural scenarios*). Moreover, many of these methods [4,7,41] require the target data to be labeled, which is impractical for real world applications.

To summarize, UDA and CI methods address different challenges under separate contexts and neither of them alone suffices practical scenarios. A characteristic comparison against prior arts is given in Table 1. Acknowledging this gap between the available solutions and their practical usability, in this work we introduce a new paradigm called Class-Incremental Domain Adaptation (CIDA) with the best of both worlds. While formalizing the paradigm, we draw motivation from both UDA and CI and address their limitations in CIDA.

In CIDA, we aim to adapt a source-trained model to the desired target domain in the presence of domain-shift as well as unseen classes using a minimal amount of

Table 1. Characteristic comparison based on the support for *source-free* (**SF**), class-incremental (**CI**) model upgrade under domain-shift (**DA**).

Method	SF	CI	DA
DANN [11]	✗	✗	✓
OSBP [45]	✗	✗	✓
UAN [54]	✗	✗	✓
STA [29]	✗	✗	✓
LETR [33]	✗	✓	✓
E2E [4]	✗	✓	✗
iCaRL [41]	✗	✓	✗
LwF-MC [7]	✓	✓	✗
LwM [7]	✓	✓	✗
Ours	✓	✓	✓

labeled data. To this end, we propose a novel training strategy which enables a *source-free* upgrade to an unlabeled target domain by utilizing one-shot target-private samples. Our approach is motivated by prototypical networks [48] which exhibit a simpler inductive bias in the limited data regime. We now review the prior arts and identify their limitations to design a suitable approach for CIDA. Our contributions are as follows:

- We formalize a novel Domain Adaptation paradigm, Class-Incremental Domain Adaptation (CIDA), which enables the recognition of both shared and novel target categories under a domain-shift.
- We discuss the limitations of existing approaches and identify the challenges involved in CIDA to propose an effective training strategy for CIDA.
- The proposed solution is motivated by theoretical and empirical observations and outperforms both UDA and CI approaches in CIDA.

2   Background

Before formalizing the CIDA paradigm, we review the prior methods and study their limitations. In the UDA problem, we consider a labeled source domain with the label-set $\mathcal{C}_s$ and an unlabeled target domain with the label-set $\mathcal{C}_t$. The goal is to improve the task-performance on the target domain by transferring the task-relevant knowledge from the source to the target domain.

The most popular UDA approach [11,25,30,46,49,52] is to learn a predictor $h(x) = g \circ f(x)$ having a domain-agnostic feature extractor f that is common to both the domains, and a classifier g which can be learned using source supervision. These methods align the latent features $f(\cdot)$ of the two domains and use the classifier g to predict labels for the target samples. A theoretical upper bound [2] for the target-domain risk of such predictors is as follows,

$$\epsilon_t(g) \leq \epsilon_s(g) + \frac{1}{2}d_{\mathcal{H}\Delta\mathcal{H}}(s,t) + \lambda \tag{1}$$

where, given a hypothesis space $\mathcal{H}$, ϵ_s and ϵ_t denote the expected risk of the classifier $g \in \mathcal{H}$ in the source and the target domains respectively, and $d_{\mathcal{H}\Delta\mathcal{H}} = 2\sup_{g,g'\in\mathcal{H}}|\epsilon_s(g,g') - \epsilon_t(g,g')|$ measures the distribution shift (or the domain discrepancy) between the two domains and $\lambda = \min_{g\in\mathcal{H}} \epsilon_s(g)+\epsilon_t(g)$ is a constant that measures the risk of the optimal joint classifier.

Notably, UDA methods aim to minimize the upper bound of the target risk (Eq. 1) by minimizing the distribution shift $d_{\mathcal{H}\Delta\mathcal{H}}$ in the latent space $f(\cdot)$, while preserving a low source risk ϵ_s. This works well under the closed-set assumption (*i.e.* $\mathcal{C}_s = \mathcal{C}_t$). However, in the presence of target-private samples (*i.e.* samples from $\mathcal{C}'_t = \mathcal{C}_t \setminus \mathcal{C}_s$), a direct enforcement of such constraints often degrades the performance of the model, even on the shared categories - a phenomenon known as negative transfer [35]. This is due to two factors. Firstly, a shared feature extractor (f), which is expected to generalize across two domains, acts as a bottleneck to the performance on the target domain. Secondly, a shared feature extractor enforces a common semantic granularity in the latent space ($f(\cdot)$) across both the domains. This is especially unfavorable in CIDA, where the semantic space must be modified to accommodate target-private categories (see Fig. 3).

Why are UDA methods insufficient? Certain UDA methods [29,54] tackle negative transfer by detecting the presence of target-private samples and discarding them during domain alignment. As a result, these samples (with diverse semantic content) get clustered into a single *unknown* category. While this improves the performance on the shared classes, it disturbs the semantic granularity of the latent space (*i.e.* $f(\cdot)$), making the model unsuitable for a class-incremental upgrade. This additional issue must be tackled in CIDA.

To demonstrate this effect, we employ the state-of-the-art open-set DA method STA [29] for image recognition on the Amazon $\rightarrow$ DSLR task of Office [43] dataset. A possible way to extend STA for CIDA would be to collect the target samples that are predicted as *unknown* (after adaptation) and obtain few-shot labeled samples from this set (by randomly labeling, say, 5% of the samples). One could then train a classifier using these labeled samples. We follow this approach and over 5 separate runs, we calculate the class-averaged accuracy. The model achieves an accuracy of $95.9 \pm 0.3\%$ on the shared classes, while only $17.7 \pm 3.5\%$ on the target-private classes. See Suppl. for experimental details. This clearly indicates that the adaptation disturbs the granularity of the semantic space [20], which is no more useful for discriminating among novel target categories.

Why are CI methods insufficient? Works such as [4,33,41] use an exemplary set to receive supervision for the source classes C_s along with labeled samples from target-private classes. [33] aims to address domain-shift using labeled samples. However, the requirement of the source data during model upgrade is a severe drawback for practical applications [28]. While [7] is *source-free*, it still assumes access to labeled target samples, which may not be viable in practical deployment scenarios. As we show in Sect. 4, these methods yield suboptimal results in the presence of limited labeled data. Nevertheless, most CI methods are not geared to tackle domain-shift. Thus, the assumption that the source-model is proficient in classifying samples in C_s [7], will not hold good for the target domain. To the best of our knowledge, the most closely related CI work is [8] that uses a reinforcement-learning based framework to select source samples during one-shot learning. However, [8] assumes non-overlapping label sets $(C_s \cap C_t = \phi)$, and does not consider the effect of negative transfer during model upgrade.

Why do we need CIDA? Prior arts independently address the problem of class-incremental learning and unsupervised adaptation in seperate contexts, by employing learning procedures specific to the problem at hand. As a result of this specificity, they are not equipped to address practical scenarios (*such as the self-driving car example* in Sect. 1). Acknowledging their limitations, we propose CIDA where the focus is to improve the performance on the target domain to achieve class-incremental recognition in the presence of domain-shift. This makes CIDA more practical and more challenging than the available DA paradigms.

What do we assume in CIDA? To realize a concrete solution, we make the following assumptions that are within the bounds of a practical DA setup. Firstly, considering that the labeled source dataset may not be readily available to perform a model upgrade, we consider the *adaptation step to be source-free*. Accordingly, we propose an effective source-model training strategy which allows *source-free* adaptation to be implemented in practice. Secondly, as the target domain may be label-deficient, we pose CIDA as an Unsupervised DA problem wherein the *target samples are unlabeled*. However, conceding that it may be impractical to discover semantics for unseen target classes in a completely unsupervised fashion, we assume that we can obtain a single labeled target sample for each target-private class C_t' (*one-shot target-private* samples). This can be perceived as the knowledge of new target classes that must be added during the model upgrade. Finally, the overarching objective in CIDA is to *improve the performance in the target domain* while the performance on the source domain remains secondary.

The assumptions stated above can be interpreted as follows. In CIDA, we first quantify the upgrade that is to be performed. We identify "what domain-shift is to be tackled?" by collecting unlabeled target domain samples, and determine "what new classes are to be added?" by obtaining one-shot target-private samples. This deterministic quantification makes CIDA different from UDA and CI methods, and enhances the reliability of a *source-free* adaptation algorithm. In the next section, we formalize CIDA and describe our approach to solve the problem.

3   Class-Incremental Domain Adaptation

Let $\mathcal{X}$ and $\mathcal{Y}$ be the input and the label spaces. The source and the target domains are characterized by the distributions p and q on $\mathcal{X} \times \mathcal{Y}$. We denote the set of labeled source samples as $\mathcal{D}_s = \{(\mathbf{x}_s, y_s) : (\mathbf{x}_s, y_s) \sim p\}$ with label set $\mathcal{C}_s$ and the set of unlabeled target samples as $\mathcal{D}_t = \{\mathbf{x}_t : \mathbf{x}_t \sim q_{\mathcal{X}}\}$ with label-set $\mathcal{C}_t$, where $q_{\mathcal{X}}$ denotes the marginal input distribution and $\mathcal{C}_s \subset \mathcal{C}_t$. The set of target-private classes is denoted as $\mathcal{C}_t' = \mathcal{C}_t \setminus \mathcal{C}_s$. See Suppl. for a notation table. To perform class-incremental upgrade, we are given one target sample from each target-private category $\{(\tilde{\mathbf{x}}_t^c, \tilde{y}_t^c)\}_{c \in \mathcal{C}_t'}$ (one-shot target-private samples). Further, we assume that source samples are unavailable during model upgrade [23,24,28]. Thus, the goal is to train a model on the source domain, and later, upgrade the model (address domain-shift and learn new classes) for the target domain. Accordingly, we formalize a two-stage approach as follows,

1. **Foresighted source-model training.** It is imperative that a source-trained model supports *source-free* adaptation. Thus, during source training, we aim to suppress the domain and category bias [18] that culminates from overconfident class-predictions. Specifically, we augment the model with the capability of out-of-distribution [27] detection. This step is inspired by prototypical networks that have a simpler inductive bias in the limited data regime [48]. Finally, the source-model is shipped along with prototypes as meta-data, for performing a future *source-free* upgrade.
2. **Class-Incremental DA.** During CIDA, we aim to align the target samples from shared classes with the high-source-density regions in the latent space, allowing the reuse of the source classifier. Further, we must accommodate new target classes in the latent space while preserving the semantic granularity. We achieve both these objectives by learning a target-specific latent space in which we obtain learnable centroids called *guides* that are used to gradually steer the target features into separate clusters. We theoretically argue and empirically verify that this enables a suitable ground for CIDA.

3.1   Foresighted Source-Model Training

The architecture for the source model contains a feature extractor f_s and a $(|\mathcal{C}_s| + 1)$-class classifier g_s (see Fig. 2A). We denote the latent-space by $\mathcal{U}$. A naive approach to train the source-model would be using the cross-entropy loss,

$$\mathcal{L}_{vanilla} : \underset{(\mathbf{x}_s, y_s) \sim p}{\mathbb{E}} l_{ce}\left(g_s \circ f_s(\mathbf{x}_s), y_s\right) \tag{2}$$

where, ∘ denotes composition. However, enforcing $\mathcal{L}_{vanilla}$ alone biases the model towards source domain characteristics. As a result, the model learns highly discriminative features and mis-classifies out-of-distribution samples into one of the learned categories $(\mathcal{C}_s)$ with high confidence [24]. For e.g., an MNIST image classifier is shown to yield a predicted class-probability of 91% on random input [16]. We argue that such effects are due to the domain and category bias culminating from the overconfident predictions. Thus, we aim to suppress this bias in the presence of the source samples for a reliable *source-free* upgrade.

We note two requirements for a source-trained model suitable for CIDA. First, we must penalize overconfident predictions [40] which is a crucial step to enable generalization over unseen target categories. This will aid in mitigating the effect of negative-transfer (discussed in Sect. 2). Second, we aim for *source-free* adaptation in CIDA, which calls for an alternative to source samples. We satisfy both these requirements using class-specific gaussian prototypes [9,48] as follows.

a) Gaussian Prototypes. We define a Gaussian Prototype for a class c as $\mathcal{P}_s^c = \mathcal{N}(\boldsymbol{\mu}_s^c, \boldsymbol{\Sigma}_s^c)$ where $\boldsymbol{\mu}_s^c$ and $\boldsymbol{\Sigma}_s^c$ are the mean and the covariance obtained over the features $f(\mathbf{x}_s)$ for samples $\mathbf{x}_s$ in class c. In other words, a Gaussian Prototype is a multivariate Gaussian prior defined for each class in the latent space $\mathcal{U}$. Similarly, a global Gaussian Prototype is defined as $\mathcal{P}_s = \mathcal{N}(\boldsymbol{\mu}_s, \boldsymbol{\Sigma}_s)$, where $\boldsymbol{\mu}_s$ and $\boldsymbol{\Sigma}_s$ are calculated over the features $f_s(\mathbf{x}_s)$ for all source samples $\mathcal{D}_s$. We hypothesize that at the $\mathcal{U}$-space, we can approximate the class semantics using these Gaussian priors which can be leveraged for *source-free* adaptation.

To ensure that this Gaussian approximation is accurate, we explicitly enforce the source features to attain a higher affinity towards these class-specific Gaussian priors. We refer to this as the *class separability* objective defined as,

$$\mathcal{L}_{s1}: \mathop{\mathbb{E}}_{(\mathbf{x}_s, y_s) \sim p} -\log \left(\exp\left(\mathcal{P}_s^{y_s}(\mathbf{u}_s)\right) / \sum_{c \in \mathcal{C}_s} \exp\left(\mathcal{P}_s^c(\mathbf{u}_s)\right) \right) \tag{3}$$

where $\mathbf{u}_s = f(\mathbf{x}_s)$, and the term inside the logarithm is the posterior probability of a feature $\mathbf{u}_s$ corresponding to its class y_s (obtained as the softmax over likelihoods $\mathcal{P}_s^c(\mathbf{u}_s)$). In effect, $\mathcal{L}_{s1}$ drives the latent space to form well-separated, compact clusters for each class $c \in \mathcal{C}_s$. We verify in Sect. 4 that compact clusters enhance the reliability of a *source-free* model upgrade, where the clusters must rearrange to attain a semantic granularity suitable for the target domain.

b) Negative Training. While $\mathcal{L}_{s1}$ enforces well-separated feature clusters, it does not ensure tight decision boundaries, without which the classifier misclassifies out-of-distribution (OOD) samples [27] with high confidence. This overconfidence issue must be resolved to effectively learn new target categories. Certain prior works [55] suggest that a Gaussian Mixture Model based likelihood threshold could effectively detect OOD samples. We argue that additionally, the classifier g_s should also be capable of assigning a low confidence to OOD samples [27], forming tight decision boundaries around the source clusters (as in Fig. 2A).

We leverage the Gaussian Prototypes to generate *negative* feature samples to model the low-source-density (OOD) region. The *negative* samples are denoted as

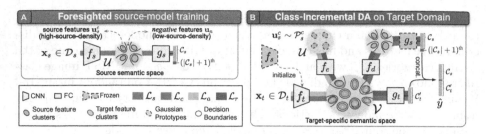

Fig. 2. Our Approach. A) The source-model is trained with an additional $(|\mathcal{C}_s| + 1)^{\text{th}}$ class representing out-of-distribution (OOD) region. **B)** During CIDA, we learn a target-specific feature extractor f_t (to minimize domain-shift) and classifier g_t (to learn $\mathcal{C}'_t$). The adaptation process aligns the shared classes, and separates the target-private classes. Colored lines represent the gradient pathway for each loss.

$\mathcal{D}_n = \{(\mathbf{u}_n, y_n) : (\mathbf{u}_n, y_n) \sim r\}$ where r is the distribution of the OOD regime. More specifically, we obtain the samples $\mathbf{u}_n$ from the global Gaussian Prototype $\mathcal{P}_s$ which are beyond 3-σ confidence interval of all class-specific Gaussian Prototypes $\mathcal{P}_s^c$ (see Suppl. for an algorithm). These *negative* samples correspond to the $(|\mathcal{C}_s| + 1)^{\text{th}}$ category and the classifier g_s is trained to assign a low confidence to such samples (see Fig. 2A). Thus, the cross-entropy loss in Eq. 2 is modified as:

$$\mathcal{L}_{s2} : \underset{(\mathbf{x}_s, y_s) \sim p}{\mathbb{E}} l_{ce}(g_s \circ f_s(\mathbf{x}_s), y_s) \quad + \underset{(\mathbf{u}_n, y_n) \sim r}{\mathbb{E}} l_{ce}(g_s(\mathbf{u}_n), y_n) \qquad (4)$$

By virtue of $\mathcal{L}_{s2}$, the classifier g_s assigns a high source-class confidence to samples in $\mathcal{D}_s$, and a low source-class confidence to samples in $\mathcal{D}_n$. Thus, g_s learns compact decision boundaries (as shown in Fig. 2A).

c) Optimization. We train $\{f_s, g_s\}$ via alternate minimization of $\mathcal{L}_{s1}$ and $\mathcal{L}_{s2}$ using Adam [19] optimizers (see Suppl.). Effectively, the total loss $\mathcal{L}_s = \mathcal{L}_{s1} + \mathcal{L}_{s2}$ enforces the Cluster Assumption at the $\mathcal{U}$-space (via $\mathcal{L}_{s1}$) that enhances the model's generalizability [6,14], and, mitigates the overconfidence issue (via $\mathcal{L}_{s2}$) thereby reducing the discriminative bias towards the source domain. We update the Gaussian Prototypes and the *negative* samples at the end of each epoch. Once trained, the source-model is ready to be shipped along with the Gaussian Prototypes as meta-data. Note, in contrast to source data, Gaussian Prototypes are cheap and can be readily shared (similar to BatchNorm [17] statistics).

3.2 Class-Incremental DA on the Target Domain

Following the CIDA paradigm during the model upgrade, we have access to a source model $\{f_s, g_s\}$ and its meta-data (Gaussian Prototypes $\mathcal{P}_s^c$), unlabeled target samples $\mathcal{D}_t$, and one-shot target-private samples $\{(\tilde{\mathbf{x}}_t^c, \tilde{y}_t^c)\}_{c \in \mathcal{C}'_t}$. We now formalize an approach that tightens the target risk bound (Eq. 1) exploiting a foresighted source-model trained using $\mathcal{D}_s \cup \mathcal{D}_n$. Recall that the bound comprises of three terms - source risk (ϵ_s), distribution shift ($d_{\mathcal{H}\Delta\mathcal{H}}$) and the constant λ.

a) **Learning target features.** A popular strategy for UDA is to learn domain-agnostic features [29,45,47]. However, as argued in Sect. 2, in CIDA we must learn a target-specific latent space (annotated as $\mathcal{V}$ in Fig. 2B) which attains a semantic granularity suitable for the target domain. To this end, we introduce a target-specific feature extractor f_t that is initialized from f_s. Informally, this process "initializes the $\mathcal{V}$-space from the $\mathcal{U}$-space". Thereafter, we gradually rearrange the feature clusters in the $\mathcal{V}$-space to learn suitable target semantics. To receive stable gradients, g_s is kept frozen throughout adaptation. Further, we introduce a classifier g_t to learn the target-private categories $\mathcal{C}'_t$ (see Fig. 2B).

b) **Domain projection.** The key to effectively learn target-specific semantics is to establish a transit mechanism between the $\mathcal{U}$-space (capturing the semantics of the learned classes $\mathcal{C}_s$) and the $\mathcal{V}$-space (where $\mathcal{C}_t$ must be learned). We address this using the domain projection networks $f_e : \mathcal{U} \rightarrow \mathcal{V}$ and $f_d : \mathcal{V} \rightarrow \mathcal{U}$. Specifically, we obtain feature samples from the Gaussian Prototypes $\mathbf{u}_s^c \sim \mathcal{P}_s^c$ for each class $c \in \mathcal{C}_s$ (called as proxy-source samples). Thereafter, we formalize the following losses to minimize the source risk (ϵ_s in Eq. 1) during adaptation,

$$\mathcal{L}_{r1} : \mathop{\mathbb{E}}_{\mathbf{u}_s^c \sim \mathcal{P}_s^c} l_{ce}(\hat{y}(\mathbf{u}_s^c), c) \quad ; \quad \mathcal{L}_{r2} : \mathop{\mathbb{E}}_{\mathbf{u}_s^c \sim \mathcal{P}_s^c} l_2(f_d \circ f_e(\mathbf{u}_s^c), \mathbf{u}_s^c)^2 \tag{5}$$

where l_2 is the euclidean distance and the output $\hat{y}(\cdot)$ is the concatenation (Fig. 2B) of logits pertaining to $\mathcal{C}_s$ ($g_s \circ f_d \circ f_e(\mathbf{u}_s^c)|_{c \in \mathcal{C}_s}$) and those of $\mathcal{C}_t$ ($g_t \circ f_e(\mathbf{u}_s^c)$). The total loss $\mathcal{L}_r = \mathcal{L}_{r1} + \mathcal{L}_{r2}$ acts as a regularizer, where $\mathcal{L}_{r1}$ preserves the semantics of the learned classes in the $\mathcal{V}$-space, while $\mathcal{L}_{r2}$ prevents degenerate solutions. In Sect. 4, we show that $\mathcal{L}_r$ mitigates catastrophic forgetting [13] (by minimizing ϵ_s in Eq. 1) that would otherwise occur in a *source-free* scenario.

c) **Semantic alignment using guides.** We aim to align target samples from shared classes $\mathcal{C}_s$ with the high source-density region (proxy-source samples) and disperse the target-private samples away into the low source-density region (*i.e.* the *negative* regime). Note, as the source model was trained on $\mathcal{D}_s$ augmented with $\mathcal{D}_n$, this process would entail the minimization of $d_{\mathcal{H}\Delta\mathcal{H}}$ (Eq. 1) measured between the target and the augmented source distributions in the $\mathcal{V}$-space.

To achieve this, we obtain a set of $|\mathcal{C}_t|$ *guides* ($\mathbf{v}_g^c$) that act as representative centers for each class $c \in \mathcal{C}_t$ in the $\mathcal{V}$-space. We model the euclidean distance to a *guide* as a measure of class confidence, using which we can assign a pseudo class-label [26] to the target samples. These pseudo-labels can be leveraged to rearrange the target features into separate compact clusters (Fig. 3B-F). Note that $\mathcal{L}_{s1}$ (*class separability* objective) enforced during the source training is crucial to improve the reliability of the *guides* during adaptation.

We consider the features of the one-shot target-private samples $f_t(\tilde{\mathbf{x}}_s^c)$ as the *guides* for the target-private classes. Further, since $\mathcal{V}$ is initialized from $\mathcal{U}$, one might consider the source class-means $\boldsymbol{\mu}_s^c$ as the *guides* for the shared classes. However, we found that a fixed *guide* representation (*e.g.* $\boldsymbol{\mu}_s^c$) hinders the placement of target-private classes. Thus, we obtain trainable *guides* for the shared classes as $f_e(\boldsymbol{\mu}_s^c)$, by allowing f_e to modify the placement of the *guides* in

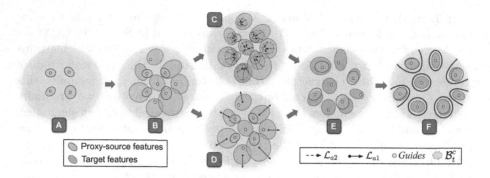

Fig. 3. Semantic Alignment using *guides* **in** $\mathcal{V}$**-space. A)** $\mathcal{V}$ is initialized from $\mathcal{U}$. **B)** Domain-shift between target and proxy-source features. **C)** $\mathcal{L}_{a2}$ steers the confident target samples ($\mathcal{B}_t^c$) towards the corresponding *guides* ($\mathbf{v}_g^c$). **D)** $\mathcal{L}_{a1}$ separates the clusters, making space for target-private classes. **E)** This rearrangement aligns the shared classes while separating the target-private classes. **F)** The classifiers $\{g_s, g_t\}$ recognize all target classes by assigning an individual semantic label to each class.

the $\mathcal{V}$-space (Fig. 3). This allows all the *guides* to rearrange and steer the target clusters in the $\mathcal{V}$-space as the training proceeds. To summarize, the *guides* are computed as $\mathbf{v}_g^c = f_e(\boldsymbol{\mu}_s^c) \ \forall c \in \mathcal{C}_s$, and, $\mathbf{v}_g^c = f_t(\tilde{\mathbf{x}}_t^c) \ \forall c \in \mathcal{C}_t'$.

To minimize $d_{\mathcal{H}\Delta\mathcal{H}}$ (Eq. 1), we must first detect the target-shared and target-private samples and then perform feature alignment. To this end, for a target feature $\mathbf{v}_t = f_t(\mathbf{x}_t)$, we obtain the euclidean distance d to its nearest *guide*, and assign a pseudo-label k corresponding to the class represented by the *guide* as, $d = \min_{c \in \mathcal{C}_t} \ l_2(\mathbf{v}_t, \mathbf{v}_g^c)$, and, $k = \arg \min_{c \in \mathcal{C}_t} l_2(\mathbf{v}_t, \mathbf{v}_g^c)$.

Using pseudo-labeled samples we obtain Gaussian Prototypes $\mathcal{P}_t^c = \mathcal{N}(\boldsymbol{\mu}_t^c, \boldsymbol{\Sigma}_t^c) \ \forall c \in \mathcal{C}_t$ in the $\mathcal{V}$-space (as done in Sect. 3.1a), and enforce the *class separability* objective. Further, for each *guide* $\mathbf{v}_g^c$ ($c \in \mathcal{C}_t$), we define a set $\mathcal{B}_t^c$ of the closest n-percent target samples based on the distance d (see Suppl. for the algorithm). Notionally, $\mathcal{B}_t^c$ represents the confident target samples which are then pulled closer to $\mathbf{v}_g^c$. These two losses are defined as,

$$\mathcal{L}_{a1} : \underset{\mathbf{x}_t \sim q_\mathcal{X}}{\mathbb{E}} - \log \left(\exp\left(\mathcal{P}_t^k(\mathbf{v}_t)\right) / \sum_{c \in \mathcal{C}_t} \exp\left(\mathcal{P}_t^c(\mathbf{v}_t)\right) \right) ; \ \mathcal{L}_{a2} : \underset{\mathbf{x}_t \sim \mathcal{B}_t^c}{\mathbb{E}} l_2(\mathbf{v}_t, \mathbf{v}_g^c)^2 \quad (6)$$

The total adaptation loss is $\mathcal{L}_a = \mathcal{L}_{a1} + \mathcal{L}_{a2}$. Overall, $\mathcal{L}_a$ pulls the target-shared samples towards the high source-density region and separates the target-private clusters away from the high source-density regions (Fig. 3B-E). This results in a superior alignment thereby minimizing $d_{\mathcal{H}\Delta\mathcal{H}}$. Particularly, the separation caused by $\mathcal{L}_{a1}$ minimizes the negative influence of target-private samples during adaptation, thereby preventing negative transfer [29]. $\mathcal{L}_{a2}$ ensures compact feature clusters which aids in preserving the semantic granularity across the target classes.

d) Learning target-private classes. Finally, to learn new target classes, we apply cross-entropy loss on the confident target samples $\mathcal{B}_t^c$ ($c \in \mathcal{C}_t$) as,

$$\mathcal{L}_c : \mathop{\mathbb{E}}_{\mathbf{x}_t \sim \mathcal{B}_t^c} l_{ce}(\hat{y}(\mathbf{v}_t), c) \tag{7}$$

where the output $\hat{y}(\cdot)$ is obtained similar to that in Eq. 5, by concatenating the logits $g_s \circ f_d(\mathbf{v}_t)|_{c \in \mathcal{C}_s}$ and $g_t(\mathbf{v}_t)$. We verify in Suppl. that the precision of pseudo-labels for target samples in $\mathcal{B}_t^c$ is high. Thus, the loss $\mathcal{L}_c$ along with $\mathcal{L}_{r1}$ can be viewed as conditioning the classifier $\{g_s, g_t\}$ to deliver a performance close to that of the optimal joint classifier (with the minimal risk λ).

e) Optimization. We pre-train $\{f_e, f_d\}$ to a near-identity function with the losses $l_2(\mathbf{u}_s^c, f_e(\mathbf{u}_s^c))^2$ and $l_2(\mathbf{u}_s^c, f_d(\mathbf{u}_s^c))^2$, where $\mathbf{u}_s \sim \mathcal{P}_s^c \; \forall c \in \mathcal{C}_s$ and l_2 is the euclidean distance (similar to an auto-encoder). The total loss employed is $\mathcal{L}_t = \mathcal{L}_a + \mathcal{L}_c + \mathcal{L}_r$, which tightens the bound in Eq. 1 as argued above, yielding a superior adaptation guarantee. Instead of directly enforcing $\mathcal{L}_t$ at each iteration, we alternatively optimize each loss using separate Adam [19] optimizers in a round robin fashion (*i.e.* we cycle through the losses $\{\mathcal{L}_{a1}, \mathcal{L}_{a2}, \mathcal{L}_c, \mathcal{L}_{r1}, \mathcal{L}_{r2}\}$ and minimize a single loss at each iteration). Since each optimizer minimizes its corresponding loss function independently, the gradients pertaining to each loss are adaptively scaled via the higher order moments [19]. This allows us to avoid hyperparameter search for loss scaling. See Suppl. for the training algorithm.

4 Experiments

We conduct experiments on three datasets. **Office** [43] is the most popular benchmark containing 31 classes across 3 domains - Amazon (**A**), DSLR (**D**) and Webcam (**W**). **VisDA** [39] contains 12 classes with 2 domains - Synthetic (**Sy**) and Real (**Re**) with a large domain-shift. **Digits** dataset is composed of MNIST (**M**), SVHN (**S**) and USPS (**U**) domains. See Suppl. for label-set details.

a) Evaluation. We consider two setups for target-private samples - i) one-shot, and, ii) few-shot (5% labeled). In both cases, we report the mean target accuracy over $\mathcal{C}_t$ (ALL) and $\mathcal{C}_t'$ (PRIV), over 5 separate runs (with randomly chosen one-shot and few-shot samples). We compare against prior UDA methods DANN [11], OSBP [45], UAN [54], STA [29], and CI methods E2E [4], LETR [33], iCaRL [41], LwF-MC [7], LwM [7]. To evaluate UDA methods in CIDA, we collect the target samples predicted as *unknown* after adaptation. We annotate a few of these samples following the few-shot setting, and train a separate target-private classifier (TPC) similar in architecture to g_t. At test time, a target sample is first classified into $\mathcal{C}_s \cup \{unknown\}$, and if predicted as *unknown*, it is further classified by the target-private classifier. We evaluate the prior arts only in the few-shot setting since they require labeled samples for reliable model upgrade.

b) Implementation. See Suppl. for the architectural details and an overview of the training algorithms for each stage. A learning rate of 0.0001 is used for the Adam [19] optimizers. For the source-model training, we use equal number of source and *negative* samples per batch. For adaptation, we set

Table 2. Baseline Comparisons. Results on **Office**, **Digits** and **VisDA** for CIDA using **one-shot** target-private samples.

Method	Office $|\mathcal{C}_s| = 20, |\mathcal{C}_t| = 31$													
	A→D		A→W		D→A		D→W		W→A		W→D		Avg	
	ALL	PRIV	ALL	PRIV	ALL	PRIV	ALL	PRIV	ALL	PRIV	ALL	PRIV	ALL	PRIV
Ours-a	69.1	66.7	58.2	55.9	60.6	58.1	70.2	68.9	59.4	57.6	80.4	80.0	66.4	64.5
Ours-b	69.5	71.9	58.2	60.4	60.9	61.1	73.3	75.6	61.1	62.3	81.7	82.8	67.5	69.0
Ours-c	70.4	70.1	60.4	58.7	61.7	60.4	75.4	73.8	61.7	61.2	85.9	84.8	69.3	68.1
Ours-d	73.7	73.6	64.8	64.6	64.4	63.9	80.9	80.7	63.6	61.8	90.1	89.6	72.9	72.4
Ours	73.3	73.1	63.6	62.6	64.1	64.3	80.3	79.4	63.7	62.8	89.5	88.4	72.4	71.8
Method	Digits ($|\mathcal{C}_s| = 5, |\mathcal{C}_t| = 10$)								VisDA ($|\mathcal{C}_s| = 6, |\mathcal{C}_t| = 12$)					
	S→M		M→U		U→M		Avg		Sy→Re		Re→Sy		Avg	
	ALL	PRIV	ALL	PRIV	ALL	PRIV	ALL	PRIV	ALL	PRIV	ALL	PRIV	ALL	PRIV
Ours-a	41.2	38.7	64.9	63.5	63.1	62.6	56.4	54.9	52.3	51.4	50.9	49.6	51.6	50.5
Ours-b	42.4	42.9	66.1	67.2	63.9	64.7	57.5	58.3	53.1	53.6	51.1	51.4	52.1	52.5
Ours-c	44.5	43.8	69.4	69.3	65.3	64.5	59.7	59.2	54.3	54.0	52.3	51.9	53.3	52.9
Ours-d	46.5	45.3	72.7	72.2	69.4	68.8	62.9	62.1	56.6	56.3	55.8	55.4	56.2	55.8
Ours	46.4	45.7	72.5	71.6	69.4	68.6	62.8	61.9	56.4	56.3	55.8	55.7	56.1	56.0

$n = 20\%$ for confident samples. At test time, the prediction for a target sample $\mathbf{x}_t$ is obtained as arg max over the logits pertaining to $\mathcal{C}_s$ ($g_s \circ f_d \circ f_t(\mathbf{x}_t)|_{c \in \mathcal{C}_s}$) and $\mathcal{C}_t$ ($g_t \circ f_t(\mathbf{x}_t)$).

4.1 Discussion

a) Baseline Comparisons. To empirically verify the effectiveness of our approach, we implement the following baselines. See Suppl. for illustrations of the architectures. The results are summarized in Table 2.

i) *Ours-a*: To corroborate the need for a target-specific feature space, we remove $\{f_e, f_d\}$, and discard the loss $\mathcal{L}_{r2}$. Here, the $\mathcal{V}$-space is common to both the target and the proxy-source samples. Thus, the *guides* for the shared classes are the fixed class-means ($\boldsymbol{\mu}_s^c$), and the only trainable components are f_t and g_t. In doing so, we force the target classes to acquire the semantics of the source domain which hinders the placement of target-private classes and degrades the target-private accuracy. However, in our approach (*Ours*), trainable *guides* allow the rearrangement of features which effectively minimizes the $d_{\mathcal{H}\Delta\mathcal{H}}$ (in Eq. 1).

ii) *Ours-b*: To study the regularization of the sampled proxy-source features, we modify our approach by removing $\mathcal{L}_r$. We observe a consistent degradation in performance resulting from a lower target-shared accuracy. This verifies the role of $\mathcal{L}_r$ in mitigating catastrophic forgetting (*i.e.* by minimizing ϵ_s in Eq. 1).

iii) *Ours-c*: We modify our approach by removing $\mathcal{L}_{a2}$ that produces compact target clusters. We find that the target-private accuracy decreases, verifying the need for compact clusters to preserve the semantic granularity across the target classes. Note, *Ours-c* (having trainable *guides* for $\mathcal{C}_s$) outperforms *Ours-a* (having frozen *guides* for $\mathcal{C}_s$), even in the absence of $\mathcal{L}_{a2}$.

Table 3. Comparison against prior arts. Results on **Office** ($|\mathcal{C}_s| = 10, |\mathcal{C}_t| = 20$) for CIDA. Unsup. denotes the method is unsupervised (on target). SF denotes model upgrade is *source-free*. Note, non-*source-free* methods access labeled source data. Results are grouped based on access to i) few-shot and ii) one-shot target-private samples.

Method	SF	Unsup.	A→D		A→W		D→A		D→W		W→A		W→D		Avg	
			ALL	PRIV	ALL	PRIV	ALL	PRIV	ALL	PRIV	ALL	PRIV	ALL	PRIV	ALL	PRIV
Using few-shot target-private samples (5% labeled)																
DANN+TPC	✗	✔	54.3	21.4	52.4	16.7	48.2	19.8	61.4	24.3	57.9	21.1	56.5	38.0	55.1	23.6
OSBP+TPC	✗	✔	51.6	13.9	49.2	9.5	58.8	14.3	55.5	18.4	49.1	13.6	64.0	29.1	54.7	14.5
STA+TPC	✗	✔	56.6	17.7	51.2	10.2	54.8	16.5	59.6	21.8	54.7	15.9	67.4	35.4	57.4	19.6
UAN+TPC	✗	✔	56.2	24.4	54.8	21.2	57.3	24.7	62.6	29.5	59.2	28.9	68.4	42.8	59.8	28.6
iCaRL	✗	✗	63.6	63.2	54.3	53.8	56.9	56.1	65.4	65.2	57.5	56.8	76.8	77.5	62.4	62.1
E2E	✗	✗	64.2	61.9	55.6	53.2	58.8	58.4	66.3	66.5	57.9	56.6	76.5	73.2	63.2	60.8
LETR	✗	✔	71.3	68.5	58.4	57.6	58.2	58.4	70.3	69.8	62.0	60.7	84.2	82.9	67.4	66.3
LwM	✔	✗	66.5	66.2	56.3	55.9	57.6	56.8	68.4	68.3	59.8	59.4	78.4	78.1	64.5	61.9
LwF-MC	✔	✗	64.3	63.8	55.6	55.1	55.5	55.7	67.6	67.7	59.4	59.0	77.3	76.9	63.3	63.0
*Ours**	✔	✔	**78.8**	**74.3**	**70.1**	**69.8**	**66.9**	**67.1**	**85.0**	**84.6**	**67.2**	**65.3**	**90.4**	**90.8**	**76.4**	**75.3**
Using one-shot target-private samples																
Ours-a	✔	✔	67.4	64.1	56.2	53.4	60.1	57.8	69.2	68.3	57.1	55.6	77.9	76.5	65.0	62.3
Ours-b	✔	✔	68.4	70.2	57.5	59.6	60.6	60.8	70.9	72.4	58.4	58.7	79.8	80.2	65.9	67.0
Ours-c	✔	✔	70.0	69.3	59.5	57.4	61.5	60.2	73.1	71.4	61.8	60.1	82.3	81.1	68.0	66.6
Ours	✔	✔	**72.2**	**72.6**	**62.1**	**62.0**	**62.6**	**61.8**	**78.5**	**78.7**	**62.1**	**62.4**	**87.8**	**87.6**	**70.7**	**70.8**

iv) *Ours-d:* To establish the reliability of the Gaussian Prototypes, we perform CIDA using the source dataset, *i.e.* using the features $f_s(\mathbf{x}_s)$ instead of the sampled proxy-source features. The performance is similar to *Ours*, confirming the efficacy of the Gaussian Prototypes in modelling the source distribution. This is owed to $\mathcal{L}_{s1}$ that enhances the reliability of the Gaussian approximation.

b) Comparison against prior arts. We compare against prior UDA and CI approaches in Table 3. Further, we run a variation of our approach with few-shot (5% labeled) target-private samples (*Ours**), where the *guides* for $\mathcal{C}_t'$ are obtained as the class-wise mean features of the few-shot samples.

UDA methods exploit unlabeled target samples but require access to labeled source samples during adaptation. They achieve a low target-private (PRIV) accuracy owing to the loss of semantic granularity. This effect is evident in open-set methods, where target-private samples are forced to be clustered into a single *unknown* class. However in DANN and UAN, such a criterion is not enforced, instead a target sample is detected as *unknown* using confidence thresholding. Thus, DANN and UAN achieve a higher PRIV accuracy than STA and OSBP.

The performance of most CI methods in CIDA is limited due to the inability to address domain-shift. LETR, E2E and iCaRL require labeled samples from both the domains during the model upgrade. E2E exploits these labeled samples to re-train the source-trained model with all classes ($\mathcal{C}_t$). However, the need to generalize across two domains degrades the performance on the target domain where target-shared samples are unlabeled. In contrast, LwM and LwF-MC learn a separate target model, by employing a distillation loss using the target samples.

However, distillation is not suitable under a domain-shift since the source model is biased towards the source domain characteristics that cannot be generalized for the target domain. In LETR, the global domain statistics across the two domains are aligned. However, such a global alignment is prone to the negative influence of target-private samples which limits its performance.

Our method addresses these limitations and outperforms both UDA and CI methods. The foresighted source-model training suppresses domain and category bias by addressing the overconfidence issue. Then, a gradual rearrangement of features in a target-specific semantic space allows the learning of target-private classes while preserving the semantic granularity. Furthermore, the regularization from the proxy-source samples mitigates catastrophic forgetting. Thus our approach achieves a more stable performance in CIDA, even in the challenging *source-free* scenario. See Suppl. for a discussion from the theoretical perspective.

c) Effect of class separability objective. We run an ablation on the **A→D** task (Table 3) without enforcing $\mathcal{L}_{s1}$ during the source-model training. The accuracy post adaptation is 68.6% (PRIV = 70.4%) as compared to 72.2% (PRIV = 72.6%) in *Ours*. This suggests that the *class separability* objective (enforcing the Cluster Assumption) helps in generalization to the target domain.

d) Effect of negative training. On the **A→D** task (Table 3), a source-model trained with *negative* samples $(\mathcal{D}_s \cup \mathcal{D}_n)$ achieves a source accuracy of 96.7%, while that trained without *negative* samples yields 96.9%. Thus, there is no significant drop on the source performance due to negative training. However, this aids in generalizing the model to novel target classes. Specifically, a source-model trained with *negative* samples (*Ours*) yields 72.2% (PRIV = 72.6%) after adaptation, while that without *negative* training achieves 67.4% (PRIV = 62.3%) after adaptation. The performance gain in *Ours* is attributed to the mitigation of the overconfidence issue thereby reliably classifying target-private samples.

e) Sensitivity to hyperparameters. In Fig. 4, we plot the target accuracy post adaptation for various hyperparameter values for the task **A→D**. Empirically, we found that a 3-σ confidence interval for *negative* sampling was most effective in capturing the source distribution (Fig. 4A). We choose an equal number of source (N_{src}) and *negative* (N_{neg}) samples in a batch during source training to avoid the bias caused by imbalanced data. Figure 4C shows the sensitivity to the batch size ratio N_{src}/N_{neg}. Further, the hyperparameter n is marginally stable around $n = 20\%$ (Fig. 4D) which was used across all experiments. Finally, the trend in Fig. 4B is a result of the challenging one-shot setting.

f) Two-step model upgrade. We extend our approach to perform two-step model upgrade under CIDA on **Office** (See Suppl. for details). First a source model ($\{f_s, g_s\}$) is trained on the 10 classes of Amazon (**A**) which is upgraded to the 20 classes of DSLR (**D**) thereby learning $\{f_t, g_t, f_e, f_d\}$. We upgrade this DSLR-specific model to the Webcam (**W**) domain, having 20 classes shared with (**A+D**), and 11 new classes. This is done by learning feature extractor f_{t_2}, classifier g_{t_2}, and domain projection networks $\{f_{e_2}, f_{d_2}\}$ learned between the latent spaces of f_t and f_{t_2}. We observe an accuracy of 79.9% on **W**, which is

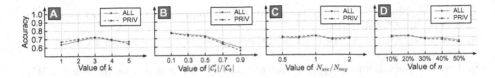

Fig. 4. Sensitivity for A → D task (Office). **A)** Confidence interval $k\text{-}\sigma$ for *negative* sampling. **B)** Fraction of target-private classes $|\mathcal{C}'_t|/|\mathcal{C}_t|$ during CIDA. **C)** Batch size ratio of source (N_{src}) and *negative* (N_{neg}) samples during source-training. **D)** Percentage of confident target samples for $\mathcal{B}^c_t$ during CIDA. Note the scale of the axes.

close to that obtained by directly adapting from 20 classes of DSLR to 31 classes in Webcam (80.3%, Table 2). This corroborates the practical applicability of our approach to multi-step model upgrades. See Suppl. for a detailed discussion.

5   Conclusion

We proposed a novel Domain Adaptation paradigm (CIDA) addressing class-incremental learning in the presence of domain-shift. We studied the limitations of prior approaches in the CIDA paradigm and proposed a two-stage approach to address CIDA. We presented a foresighted source-model training that facilitates a *source-free* model upgrade. Further, we demonstrated the efficacy of a target-specific semantic space, learned using trainable *guides*, that preserves the semantic granularity across the target classes. Finally, our approach shows promising results on multi-step model upgrades. As a future work, the framework can be extended to a scenario where a series of domain-shifts and task-shifts are observed.

Acknowledgement. This work is supported by a Wipro PhD Fellowship and a grant from Uchhatar Avishkar Yojana (UAY, IISC_010), MHRD, Govt. of India.

References

1. Baktashmotlagh, M., Faraki, M., Drummond, T., Salzmann, M.: Learning factorized representations for open-set domain adaptation. In: ICLR (2019)
2. Ben-David, S., Blitzer, J., Crammer, K., Kulesza, A., Pereira, F., Vaughan, J.W.: A theory of learning from different domains. Mach. Learn. **79**(1–2), 151–175 (2010)
3. Ben-David, S., Blitzer, J., Crammer, K., Pereira, F.: Analysis of representations for domain adaptation. In: NeurIPS (2007)
4. Castro, F.M., Marin-Jimenez, M.J., Guil, N., Schmid, C., Alahari, K.: End-to-end incremental learning. In: ECCV (2018)
5. Chang, W.G., You, T., Seo, S., Kwak, S., Han, B.: Domain-specific batch normalization for unsupervised domain adaptation. In: CVPR (2019)
6. Chapelle, O., Zien, A.: Semi-supervised classification by low density separation. In: AISTATS (2005)

7. Dhar, P., Singh, R.V., Peng, K.C., Wu, Z., Chellappa, R.: Learning without memorizing. In: CVPR (2019)
8. Dong, N., Xing, E.P.: Domain adaption in one-shot learning. In: ECML-PKDD (2018)
9. Fort, S.: Gaussian prototypical networks for few-shot learning on omniglot (2017). arXiv preprint arXiv:1708.02735
10. Ganin, Y., Lempitsky, V.: Unsupervised domain adaptation by backpropagation. In: ICML (2015)
11. Ganin, Y., Ustinova, E., Ajakan, H., Germain, P., Larochelle, H., Laviolette, F., Marchand, M., Lempitsky, V.: Domain-adversarial training of neural networks. JMLR **17**(1), 2030–2096 (2016)
12. Gong, B., Shi, Y., Sha, F., Grauman, K.: Geodesic flow kernel for unsupervised domain adaptation. In: CVPR (2012)
13. Goodfellow, I.J., Mirza, M., Xiao, D., Courville, A., Bengio, Y.: An empirical investigation of catastrophic forgetting in gradient-based neural networks (2013). arXiv preprint arXiv:1312.6211
14. Grandvalet, Y., Bengio, Y.: Semi-supervised learning by entropy minimization. In: NeurIPS (2005)
15. He, K., Zhang, X., Ren, S., Sun, J.: Delving deep into rectifiers: Surpassing human-level performance on imagenet classification. In: ICCV (2015)
16. Hendrycks, D., Gimpel, K.: A baseline for detecting misclassified and out-of-distribution examples in neural networks. In: ICLR (2017)
17. Ioffe, S., Szegedy, C.: Batch normalization: Accelerating deep network training by reducing internal covariate shift. In: ICML (2015)
18. Khosla, A., Zhou, T., Malisiewicz, T., Efros, A.A., Torralba, A.: Undoing the damage of dataset bias. In: ECCV (2012)
19. Kingma, D.P., Ba, J.L.: Adam: A method for stochastic optimization. In: ICLR (2014)
20. Kundu, J.N., Gor, M., Agrawal, D., Babu, R.V.: GAN-Tree: An incrementally learned hierarchical generative framework for multi-modal data distributions. In: ICCV (2019)
21. Kundu, J.N., Lakkakula, N., Babu, R.V.: UM-Adapt: Unsupervised multi-task adaptation using adversarial cross-task distillation. In: ICCV (2019)
22. Kundu, J.N., Uppala, P.K., Pahuja, A., Babu, R.V.: Adadepth: Unsupervised content congruent adaptation for depth estimation. In: CVPR (2018)
23. Kundu, J.N., Venkat, N., Rahul, M.V., Venkatesh Babu, R.: Universal source-free domain adaptation. In: CVPR (2020)
24. Kundu, J.N., Venkat, N., Revanur, A., Rahul, M.V., Venkatesh Babu, R.: Towards inheritable models for open-set domain adaptation. In: CVPR (2020)
25. Kuroki, S., Charoenphakdee, N., Bao, H., Honda, J., Sato, I., Sugiyama, M.: Unsupervised domain adaptation based on source-guided discrepancy. In: AAAI (2019)
26. Lee, D.H.: Pseudo-label: The simple and efficient semi-supervised learning method for deep neural networks. In: Workshop on Challenges in Representation Learning at ICML (2013)
27. Lee, K., Lee, H., Lee, K., Shin, J.: Training confidence-calibrated classifiers for detecting out-of-distribution samples. In: ICLR (2018)
28. Li, Z., Hoiem, D.: Learning without forgetting. TPAMI **40**(12), 2935–2947 (2017)
29. Liu, H., Cao, Z., Long, M., Wang, J., Yang, Q.: Separate to adapt: Open set domain adaptation via progressive separation. In: CVPR (2019)
30. Long, M., Cao, Y., Wang, J., Jordan, M.I.: Learning transferable features with deep adaptation networks. In: ICML (2015)

31. Long, M., Zhu, H., Wang, J., Jordan, M.I.: Unsupervised domain adaptation with residual transfer networks. In: NeurIPS (2016)
32. Lopes, R.G., Fenu, S., Starner, T.: Data-free knowledge distillation for deep neural networks. In: LLD Workshop at NeurIPS (2017)
33. Luo, Z., Zou, Y., Hoffman, J., Fei-Fei, L.F.: Label efficient learning of transferable representations across domains and tasks. In: NeurIPS (2017)
34. Nayak, G.K., Mopuri, K.R., Shaj, V., Radhakrishnan, V.B., Chakraborty, A.: Zero-shot knowledge distillation in deep networks. In: ICML (2019)
35. Pan, S.J., Yang, Q.: A survey on transfer learning. IEEE Trans. Knowl. Data Eng. **22**, 1345–1359 (2009)
36. Panareda Busto, P., Gall, J.: Open set domain adaptation. In: ICCV (2017)
37. Pei, Z., Cao, Z., Long, M., Wang, J.: Multi-adversarial domain adaptation. In: AAAI (2018)
38. Peng, H., Li, J., Song, Y., Liu, Y.: Incrementally learning the hierarchical softmax function for neural language models. In: AAAI (2017)
39. Peng, X., Usman, B., Kaushik, N., Hoffman, J., Wang, D., Saenko, K.: Visda: The visual domain adaptation challenge (2017). arXiv preprint arXiv:1710.06924
40. Pereyra, G., Tucker, G., Chorowski, J., Kaiser, Ł., Hinton, G.: Regularizing neural networks by penalizing confident output distributions. In: ICLR (2017)
41. Rebuffi, S.A., Kolesnikov, A., Sperl, G., Lampert, C.H.: iCaRL: Incremental classifier and representation learning. In: CVPR (2017)
42. Ruping, S.: Incremental learning with support vector machines. In: ICDM (2001)
43. Saenko, K., Kulis, B., Fritz, M., Darrell, T.: Adapting visual category models to new domains. In: ECCV (2010)
44. Saito, K., Watanabe, K., Ushiku, Y., Harada, T.: Maximum classifier discrepancy for unsupervised domain adaptation. In: CVPR (2018)
45. Saito, K., Yamamoto, S., Ushiku, Y., Harada, T.: Open set domain adaptation by backpropagation. In: ECCV (2018)
46. Sankaranarayanan, S., Balaji, Y., Castillo, C.D., Chellappa, R.: Generate to adapt: Aligning domains using generative adversarial networks. In: CVPR (2018)
47. Shu, Y., Cao, Z., Long, M., Wang, J.: Transferable curriculum for weakly-supervised domain adaptation. In: AAAI (2019)
48. Snell, J., Swersky, K., Zemel, R.: Prototypical networks for few-shot learning. In: NeurIPS (2017)
49. Sun, B., Saenko, K.: Deep coral: Correlation alignment for deep domain adaptation. In: ECCV Workshops (2016)
50. Torralba, A., Efros, A.A.: Unbiased look at dataset bias. In: CVPR (2011)
51. Tzeng, E., Hoffman, J., Saenko, K., Darrell, T.: Adversarial discriminative domain adaptation. In: CVPR (2017)
52. Tzeng, E., Hoffman, J., Zhang, N., Saenko, K., Darrell, T.: Deep domain confusion: Maximizing for domain invariance (2014). arXiv preprint arXiv:1412.3474
53. Wu, Y., Chen, Y., Wang, L., Ye, Y., Liu, Z., Guo, Y., Fu, Y.: Large scale incremental learning. In: CVPR (2019)
54. You, K., Long, M., Cao, Z., Wang, J., Jordan, M.I.: Universal domain adaptation. In: CVPR (2019)
55. Zheng, Z., Hong, P.: Robust detection of adversarial attacks by modeling the intrinsic properties of deep neural networks. In: NeurIPS (2018)

Anti-bandit Neural Architecture Search for Model Defense

Hanlin Chen[1], Baochang Zhang[1(✉)], Song Xue[1], Xuan Gong[2], Hong Liu[3],
Rongrong Ji[3], and David Doermann[2]

[1] Beihang University, Beijing, China
{hlchen,bczhang}@buaa.edu.cn
[2] University at Buffalo, Buffalo, USA
[3] Xiamen University, Fujian, China

Abstract. Deep convolutional neural networks (DCNNs) have dominated as the best performers in machine learning, but can be challenged by adversarial attacks. In this paper, we defend against adversarial attacks using neural architecture search (NAS) which is based on a comprehensive search of denoising blocks, weight-free operations, Gabor filters and convolutions. The resulting anti-bandit NAS (ABanditNAS) incorporates a new operation evaluation measure and search process based on the lower and upper confidence bounds (LCB and UCB). Unlike the conventional bandit algorithm using UCB for evaluation only, we use UCB to abandon arms for search efficiency and LCB for a fair competition between arms. Extensive experiments demonstrate that ABandit-NAS is about twice as fast as the state-of-the-art NAS method, while achieving an 8.73% improvement over prior arts on CIFAR-10 under PGD-7.

Keywords: Neural architecture search (NAS) · Bandit · Adversarial defense

1 Introduction

The success of deep learning models [4] have been demonstrated on various computer vision tasks such as image classification [18], instance segmentation [25] and object detection [36]. However, existing deep models are sensitive to adversarial attacks [6,16,37], where adding an imperceptible perturbation to input images can cause the models to perform incorrectly. Szegedy et al. [37] also observe that these adversarial examples are transferable across multiple models such that adversarial examples generated for one model might mislead other models as well. Therefore, models deployed in the real world scenarios are susceptible to adversarial attacks [24]. While many methods have been proposed to defend against these attacks [7,37], improving the network training process proves to be one of the most popular. These methods inject adversarial examples into the training data to retrain the network [1,16,21]. Similarly, pre-processing

© Springer Nature Switzerland AG 2020
A. Vedaldi et al. (Eds.): ECCV 2020, LNCS 12358, pp. 70–85, 2020.
https://doi.org/10.1007/978-3-030-58601-0_5

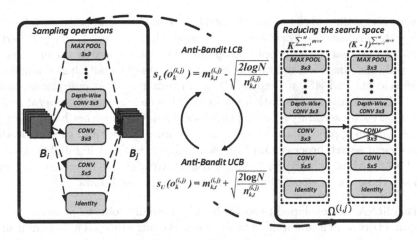

Fig. 1. ABanditNAS is mainly divided into two steps: sampling using LCB and abandoning based on UCB.

defense methods modify adversarial inputs to resemble clean inputs [22,35] by transforming the adversarial images into clean images before they are fed into the classifier.

Overall, however, finding adversarially robust architectures using neural architecture search (NAS) shows even more promising results [7,11,27,29]. NAS has attracted a great attention with remarkable performance in various deep learning tasks. In [7] the researchers investigate the dependence of adversarial robustness on the network architecture via NAS. A neural architecture search framework for adversarial medical image segmentation is proposed by [29]. [27] leverages one-shot NAS [3] to understand the influence of network architectures against adversarial attacks. Although promising performance is achieved in existing NAS based methods, this direction still remains largely unexplored.

In this paper, we consider NAS for model defense by treating it as a multi-armed bandit problem and introduce a new anti-bandit algorithm into adversarially robust network architecture search. To improve the robustness to adversarial attacks, a comprehensive search space is designed by including diverse operations, such as denoising blocks, weight-free operations, Gabor filters and convolutions. However, searching a robust network architecture is more challenging than traditional NAS, due to the complicated search space, and learning inefficiency caused by adversarial training. We develop an anti-bandit algorithm based on both the upper confidence bound (UCB) and the lower confidence bound (LCB) to handle the huge and complicated search space, where the number of operations that define the space can be 9^{60}! Our anti-bandit algorithm uses UCB to reduce the search space, and LCB to guarantee that every arm is fairly tested before being abandoned.

Making use of the LCB, operations which have poor performance early, such as parameterized operations, will be given more chances but they are thrown away once they are confirmed to be bad. Meanwhile, weight-free operations will be compared with parameterized operations only when they are well trained. Based on the observation that the early optimal operation is not necessarily the optimal one in the end, and the worst operations in the early stage usually has a worse performance at the end [45], we exploit UCB to prune the worst operations earlier, after a fair performance evaluation via LCB. This means that the operations we finally reserve are certainly a near optimal solution. On the other hand, with the operation pruning process, the search space becomes smaller and smaller, leading to an efficient search process. Our framework shown in Fig. 1 highlights the anti-bandit NAS (ABanditNAS) for finding a robust architecture from a very complicated search space. The contributions of our paper are as follows:

- ABanditNAS is developed to solve the adversarially robust optimization and architecture search in a unified framework. We introduce an anti-bandit algorithm based on a specific operation search strategy with a lower and an upper bound, which can learn a robust architecture based on a comprehensive operation space.
- The search space is greatly reduced by our anti-bandit pruning method which abandons operations with less potential, and significantly reduces the search complexity from exponential to polynomial, i.e., $\mathcal{O}(K^{|\mathcal{E}_\mathcal{M}| \times v})$ to $\mathcal{O}(K^2 \times T)$ (see Sect. 3.4 for details).
- Extensive experiments demonstrate that the proposed algorithm achieves better performance than other adversarially robust models on commonly used MNIST and CIFAR-10.

2   Related Work

Neural Architecture Search (NAS). NAS becomes one of the most promising technologies in the deep learning paradigm. Reinforcement learning (RL) based methods [46,47] train and evaluate more than $20,000$ neural networks across 500 GPUs over 4 days. The recent differentiable architecture search (DARTS) reduces the search time by formulating the task in a differentiable manner [23]. However, DARTS and its variants [23,41] might be less efficient for a complicated search space. To speed up the search process, a *one-shot* strategy is introduced to do NAS within a few GPU days [23,31]. In this one-shot architecture search, each architecture in the search space is considered as a sub-graph sampled from a super-graph, and the search process can be accelerated by parameter sharing [31]. Though [7] uses NAS with reinforcement learning to find adversarially robust architectures that achieve good results, it is insignificant compared to the search time. Those methods also seldom consider high diversity in operations closely related to model defense in the search strategy.

Adversarial Attacks. Recent research has shown that neural networks exhibit significant vulnerability to adversarial examples. After the discovery of adversarial examples by [16,37] proposes the Fast Gradient Sign Method (FGSM) to generate adversarial examples with a single gradient step. Later, in [21], the researchers propose the Basic Iterative Method (BIM), which takes multiple and smaller FGSM steps to improve FGSM, but renders the adversarial training very slow. This iterative adversarial attack is further strengthened by adding multiple random restarts, and is also incorporated into the adversarial training procedure. In addition, projected gradient descent (PGD) [26] adversary attack, a variant of BIM with a uniform random noise as initialization, is recognized to be one of the most powerful first-order attacks [1]. Other popular attacks include the Carlini and Wagner Attack [6] and Momentum Iterative Attack [10]. Among them, [6] devises state-of-the-art attacks under various pixel-space l_p norm-ball constraints by proposing multiple adversarial loss functions.

Model Defense. In order to resist attacks, various methods have been proposed. A category of defense methods improve network's training regime to counter adversarial attacks. The most common method is adversarial training [21,28] with adversarial examples added to the training data. In [26], a defense method called Min-Max optimization is introduced to augment the training data with first-order attack samples. [38] investigates fast training of adversarially robust models to perturb both the images and the labels during training. There are also some model defense methods that target at removing adversarial perturbation by transforming the input images before feeding them to the network [1,17,22]. In [8,12], the effect of JPEG compression is investigated for removing adversarial noise. In [30], the authors apply a set of filters such as median filters and averaging filters to remove perturbation. In [42], a ME-Net method is introduced to destroy the adversarial noise and re-enforce the global structure of the original images. With the development of NAS, finding adversarially robust architectures using NAS is another promising direction [7], which is worth in-depth exploration. Recently, [29] designs three types of primitive operation set in the search space to automatically find two-cell architectures for semantic image segmentation, especially medical image segmentation, leading to a NAS-Unet backbone network.

In this paper, an anti-bandit algorithm is introduced into NAS, and we develop a new optimization framework to generate adversarially robust networks. Unlike [19] using bandits to produce black-box adversarial samples, we propose an anti-bandit algorithm to obtain a robust network architecture. In addition, existing NAS-based model defense methods either target at different applications from ours or are less efficient for object classification [7,11,27,29].

3   Anti-bandit Neural Architecture Search

3.1   Search Space

Following [23,45,47], we search for computation cells as the building blocks of the final architecture. Different from these approaches, we search for v ($v > 2$) kinds of cells instead of only normal and reduction cells. Although it increases the search space, our search space reduction in ABanditNAS can make the search efficient enough. A cell is a fully-connected directed acyclic graph (DAG) of M

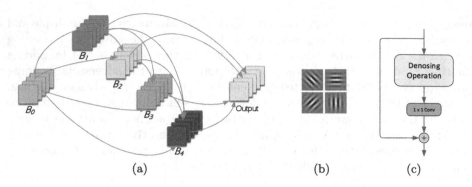

(a)   (b)   (c)

Fig. 2. (a) A cell containing four intermediate nodes B_1, B_2, B_3, B_4 that apply sampled operations on the input node B_0. B_0 is from the output of the previous cell. The output node concatenates the outputs of the four intermediate nodes. (b) Gabor Filter. (c) A generic denoising block. Following [40], it wraps the denoising operation with a 1×1 convolution and an identity skip connection [18].

nodes, $i.e.$, $\{B_1, B_2, ..., B_M\}$ as shown in Fig. 2a. Each node B_i takes its dependent nodes as input, and generates an output through the selected operation $B_j = o^{(i,j)}(B_i)$. Here each node is a specific tensor ($e.g.$, a feature map in convolutional neural networks) and each directed edge (i, j) between B_i and B_j denotes an operation $o^{(i,j)}(.)$, which is sampled from $\Omega^{(i,j)} = \{o_1^{(i,j)}, ..., o_K^{(i,j)}\}$. Note that the constraint $i < j$ ensures that there are no cycles in a cell.. Each cell takes the output of the previous cell as input, and we define this node belonging to the previous cell as the input node B_0 of the current cell for easy description. The set of the operations Ω consists of $K = 9$ operations. Following [23], there are seven normal operations that are the 3×3 max pooling, 3×3 average pooling, skip connection (identity), 3×3 convolution with rate 2, 5×5 convolution with rate 2, 3×3 depth-wise separable convolution, and 5×5 depth-wise separable convolution. The other two are 3×3 Gabor filter and denoising block. Therefore, the size of the whole search space is $K^{|\mathcal{E}_\mathcal{M}| \times v}$, where $\mathcal{E}_\mathcal{M}$ is the set of possible edges with M intermediate nodes in the fully-connected DAG. The search space of a cell is constructed by the operations of all the edges, denoted as $\{\Omega^{(i,j)}\}$. In our case with $M = 4$ and $v = 6$, together with the input node, the total number of cell structures in the search space is $9^{(1+2+3+4) \times 6} = 9^{10 \times 6}$.

Gabor Filter. Gabor wavelets [14,15] were invented by Dennis Gabor using complex functions to serve as a basis for Fourier transform in information theory applications. The Gabor wavelets (kernels or filters) in Fig. 2b are defined as: $\exp(-\frac{x'^2 + \gamma^2 y'^2}{2\sigma^2}) \cos(2\pi \frac{x'}{\lambda} + \psi)$, where $x' = x \cos\theta + y \sin\theta$ and $y' = -x \sin\theta + y \cos\theta$. We set σ, γ, λ, ψ and θ to be learnable parameters. Note that the symbols used here apply only to the Gabor filter and are different from the symbols used in the rest of this paper. An important property of the wavelets is that the product of its standard deviations is minimized in both time and frequency domains. Also, robustness is another important property which we use here [32].

Denoising Block. In [40], the researchers suggest that adversarial perturbations on images can result in noise in the features. Thus, a denoising block Fig. 2c is used to improve adversarial robustness via feature denoising. Similarly, we add the non-local mean denoising block [5] to the search space to denoise the features. It computes a denoised feature map z of an input feature map x by taking a weighted mean of the features over all spatial locations $\mathcal{L}$ as $z_p = \frac{1}{C(x)} \sum_{\forall q \in \mathcal{L}} f(x_p, x_q) \cdot x_q$, where $f(x_p, x_q)$ is a feature-dependent weighting function and $C(x)$ is a normalization function. Also, the denosing block needs huge computations because of the matrix multiplication between features.

It is known that adversarial training is more challenging than that of natural training [33], which adds an additional burden to NAS. For example, adversarial training using the F-step PGD attack needs roughly $F + 1$ times more computation. Also, more operations added to the search space are another burden. To solve these problems, we introduce operation space reduction based on the UCB bandit algorithm into NAS, to significantly reduce the cost of GPU hours, leading to our efficient ABanditNAS.

3.2 Adversarial Optimization for ABanditNAS

Adversarial training [26] is a method for learning networks so that they are robust to adversarial attacks. Given a network f_θ parameterized by θ, a dataset (x_e, y_e), a loss function l and a threat model Δ, the learning problem is typically cast as the following optimization problem: $\min_\theta \sum_e \max_{\delta \in \Delta} l(f_\theta(x_e + \delta), y_e)$, where δ is the adversarial perturbation. A typical choice for a threat model is to take $\Delta = \{\delta : \|\delta\|_\infty \leq \epsilon\}$ for some $\epsilon > 0$, where $\|\cdot\|_\infty$ is some l_∞-norm distance metric and ϵ is the adversarial manipulation budget. This is the l_∞ threat model used by [26] and what we consider in this paper. The procedure for adversarial training is to use attacks to approximate the inner maximization over Δ, followed by some variation of gradient descent on the model parameters θ. For example, one of the earliest versions of adversarial training uses the Fast Gradient Sign Method (FGSM) [16] to approximate the inner maximization. This could be seen as a relatively inaccurate approximation of the inner maximization for l_∞ perturbations, and has the closed form solution: $\theta = \epsilon \cdot \text{sign}\left(\nabla_x l(f(x), y)\right)$.

A better approximation of the inner maximization is to take multiple, smaller FGSM steps of size α instead. However, the number of gradient computations caused by the multiple steps is proportional to $\mathcal{O}(EF)$ in a single epoch, where E is the size of the dataset and F is the number of steps taken by the PGD adversary. This is F times greater than the standard training which has $\mathcal{O}(E)$ gradient computations per epoch, and so the adversarial training is typically F times slower. To speed up the adversarial training, we combine the FGSM with random initialization [39].

3.3 Anti-bandit

In machine learning, the multi-armed bandit problem [2,34] is a classic reinforcement learning (RL) problem that exemplifies the exploration-exploitation trade-off dilemma: shall we stick to an arm that gave high reward so far (exploitation) or rather probe other arms further (exploration)? The Upper Confidence Bound (UCB) is widely used for dealing with the exploration-exploitation dilemma in the multi-armed bandit problem. For example, the idea of bandit is exploited to improve many classical RL methods such as Monte Carlo [20] and Q-learning [13]. The most famous one is AlphaGo [34], which uses the Monte Carlo Tree Search (MCTS) algorithm to play the board game Go but based on a very powerful computing platform unavailable to common researchers. Briefly, the UCB algorithm chooses at trial the arm k that maximizes

$$\hat{r}_k + \sqrt{\frac{2 \log N}{n_k}}, \tag{1}$$

where $\hat{r}_k$ is the average reward obtained from arm k, and n_k is the number of times arm k has been played up to trial N. The first term in Eq. 1 is the value term which favors actions that look good historically, and the second is the exploration term which makes actions get an exploration bonus that grows with $\log N$. The total value can be interpreted as the upper bound of a confidence interval, so that the true mean reward of each arm k with a high probability is below this UCB.

The UCB in bandit is not applicable in NAS, because it is too time-consuming to choose an arm from a huge search space (a huge number of arms, e.g., 9^{60}), particularly when limited computational resources are available. To solve the problem, we introduce an anti-bandit algorithm to reduce the arms for the huge-armed problem by incorporating both the upper confidence bound (UCB) and the lower confidence bound (LCB) into the conventional bandit algorithm. We first define LCB as

$$\hat{r}_k - \sqrt{\frac{2 \log N}{n_k}}. \tag{2}$$

LCB is designed to sample an arm from a huge number of arms for one more trial (later in Eq. 3). A smaller LCB means that the less played arm (a smaller n_k) is given a bigger chance to be sampled for a trial. Unlike the conventional bandit based on the maximum UCB (Eq. 1) to choose an arm, our UCB (Eq. 6) is used to abandon the arm operation with the minimum value, which is why we call our algorithm anti-bandit.

Our anti-bandit algorithm is specifically designed for the huge-armed bandit problem by reducing the number of arms based on the UCB. Together with the LCB, it can guarantee every arm is fairly tested before being abandoned.

3.4   Anti-bandit Strategy for ABanditNAS

As described in [43,45], the validation accuracy ranking of different network architectures is not a reliable indicator of the final architecture quality. However, the experimental results actually suggest a nice property that if an architecture performs poorly in the beginning of training, there is little hope that it can be part of the final optimal model [45]. As the training progresses, this observation

---

Algorithm 1: ABanditNAS

Input: Training data, validation data, searching hyper-graph, adversarial
perturbation δ, adversarial manipulation budget ϵ, $K = 9$,
hyper-parameters α, $\lambda = 0.7$, $T = 3$.

Output: The remaining optimal structure;

1   $t = 0$; $c = 0$;

2   Get initial performance $m_{k,0}^{(i,j)}$;

3   **while** $(K > 1)$ **do**

4      $c \leftarrow c + 1$;

5      $t \leftarrow t + 1$;

6   Calculate $s_L(o_k^{(i,j)})$ using Eq. 3;

7   Calculate $p(o_k^{(i,j)})$ using Eq. 4;

8   Select an architecture by sampling one operation based on $p(o_k^{(i,j)})$ from $\Omega^{(i,j)}$ for every edge;

9   // Train adversarially the selected architecture

10   **for** $e = 1, ..., E$ **do**

11         $\delta = \text{Uniform}(-\epsilon, \epsilon)$;

12         $\delta \leftarrow \delta + \alpha \cdot \text{sign}\left(\nabla_x l(f(x_e + \delta), y_e)\right)$;

13         $\delta = \max\left(\min(\delta, \epsilon), -\epsilon\right)$;

14         $\theta \leftarrow \theta - \nabla_\theta l(f_\theta(x_e + \delta), y_e)$;

15   **end**

16   Get the accuracy a on the validation data;

17   Update the performance $m_{k,t}^{(i,j)}$ using Eq. 5;

18   **if** $c = K * T$ **then**

19   Calculate $s_U(o_k^{(i,j)})$ using Eq. 6;

20   Update the search space $\{\Omega^{(i,j)}\}$ using Eq. 7;

21         $c = 0$;

22         $K \leftarrow K - 1$;

23   **end**

24 **end**

---

is more and more certain. Based on this observation, we derive a simple yet effective operation abandoning method. During training, along with the increasing epochs, we progressively abandon the worst performing operation for each edge. Unlike [45] which just uses the performance as the evaluation metric to decide which operation should be pruned, we use the anti-bandit algorithm described next to make a decision about which one should be pruned.

Following UCB in the bandit algorithm, we obtain the initial performance for each operation in every edge. Specifically, we sample one from the K operations in $\Omega^{(i,j)}$ for every edge, then obtain the validation accuracy a which is the initial performance $m_{k,0}^{(i,j)}$ by training adversarially the sampled network for one epoch, and finally assigning this accuracy to all the sampled operations.

By considering the confidence of the kth operation with the UCB for every edge, the LCB is calculated by

$$s_L(o_k^{(i,j)}) = m_{k,t}^{(i,j)} - \sqrt{\frac{2\log N}{n_{k,t}^{(i,j)}}}, \tag{3}$$

where N is to the total number of samples, $n_{k,t}^{(i,j)}$ refers to the number of times the kth operation of edge (i,j) has been selected, and t is the index of the epoch. The first item in Eq. 3 is the value term which favors the operations that look good historically and the second is the exploration term which allows operations to get an exploration bonus that grows with $\log N$. The selection probability for each operation is defined as

$$p(o_k^{(i,j)}) = \frac{\exp\{-s_L(o_k^{(i,j)})\}}{\sum_m \exp\{-s_L(o_m^{(i,j)})\}}. \tag{4}$$

The minus sign in Eq. 4 means that we prefer to sample operations with a smaller confidence. After sampling one operation for every edge based on $p(o_k^{(i,j)})$, we obtain the validation accuracy a by training adversarially the sampled network for one epoch, and then update the performance $m_{k,t}^{(i,j)}$ which historically indicates the validation accuracy of all the sampled operations $o_k^{(i,j)}$ as

$$m_{k,t}^{(i,j)} = (1-\lambda)m_{k,t-1}^{(i,j)} + \lambda * a, \tag{5}$$

where λ is a hyper-parameter.

Finally, after $K * T$ samples where T is a hyper-parameter, we calculate the confidence with the UCB according to Eq. 1 as

$$s_U(o_k^{(i,j)}) = m_{k,t}^{(i,j)} + \sqrt{\frac{2\log N}{n_{k,t}^{(i,j)}}}. \tag{6}$$

The operation with the minimal UCB for every edge is abandoned. This means that the operations that are given more opportunities, but result in poor performance, are removed. With this pruning strategy, the search space is significantly reduced from $|\Omega^{(i,j)}|^{10\times 6}$ to $(|\Omega^{(i,j)}|-1)^{10\times 6}$, and the reduced space becomes

$$\Omega^{(i,j)} \leftarrow \Omega^{(i,j)} - \{\arg\min_{o_k^{(i,j)}} s_U(o_k^{(i,j)})\}, \forall(i,j). \tag{7}$$

The reduction procedure is carried out repeatedly until the optimal structure is obtained where there is only one operation left in each edge. Our anti-bandit search algorithm is summarized in Algorithm 1.

Complexity Analysis. There are $\mathcal{O}(K^{|\mathcal{E}_M|\times v})$ combinations in the process of finding the optimal architecture in the search space with v kinds of different cells. In contrast, ABanditNAS reduces the search space for every $K * T$ epochs. Therefore, the complexity of the proposed method is

$$\mathcal{O}(T \times \sum_{k=2}^{K} k) = \mathcal{O}(TK^2). \tag{8}$$

4   Experiments

We demonstrate the robustness of our ABanditNAS on two benchmark datasets (MNIST and CIFAR-10) for the image classification task, and compare ABanditNAS with state-of-the-art robust models.

4.1   Experiment Protocol

In our experiments, we search architectures on an over-parameterized network on MNIST and CIFAR-10, and then evaluate the best architecture on corresponding datasets. Unlike previous NAS works [23,31,41], we learn six kinds of cells, instead of two, to increase the diversity of the network.

Search and Training Settings. In the search process, the over-parameterized network is constructed with six cells, where the 2nd and 4th cells are used to double the channels of the feature maps and halve the height and width of the feature maps, respectively. There are $M = 4$ intermediate nodes in each cell. The hyperparameter T which denotes the sampling times is set to 3, so the total number of epochs is $\sum_{k=2}^{K} k*T$. The hyperparameter λ is set to 0.7. A large batch size of 512 is used. And we use an additional regularization cutout [9] for CIFAR-10. The initial number of channels is 16. We employ FGSM adversarial training combined with random initialization and $\epsilon = 0.3$ for MNIST, and $\epsilon = 0.031$ for CIFAR-10. We use SGD with momentum to optimize the network weights, with an initial learning rate of 0.025 for MNIST and 0.1 for CIFAR-10 (annealed down to zero following a cosine schedule), a momentum of 0.9 and a weight decay of 3×10^{-4} for MNIST/CIFAR-10.

After search, the six cells are stacked to get the final networks. To adversarially train them, we employ FGSM combined with random initialization and $\epsilon = 0.3$ on MNIST, and use PGD-7 with $\epsilon = 0.031$ and step size of 0.0078 on CIFAR-10. Next, we use ABanditNAS-V to represent ABanditNAS with V cells in the training process. The number V can be different from the number v. The initial number of channels is 16 for MNIST, and 48 for CIFAR-10. We use a batch size of 96 and an additional regularization cutout [9] for CIFAR-10. We employ the SGD optimizer with an initial learning rate of 0.025 for MNIST and 0.1 for CIFAR-10 (annealed down to zero following a cosine schedule without restart), a momentum of 0.9, a weight decay of 3×10^{-4}, and a gradient clipping at 5. We train 150 epochs for MNIST and CIAFR-10.

White-Box vs. Black-Box Attack Settings. In an adversarial setting, there are two main threat models: white-box attacks where the adversary possesses complete knowledge of the target model, including its parameters, architecture and the training method, and black-box attacks where the adversary feeds perturbed images at test time, which are generated without any knowledge of the target model, and observes the output. We evaluate the robustness of our proposed defense against both settings. The perturbation size ϵ and step size are the same as those in the adversarial training for both the white-box and black-box attacks. The numbers of iterations for MI-FGSM and BIM are both set

Table 1. Robustness of ABanditNAS under FGSM and PGD attacks on MNIST.

Architecture	Clean (%)	FGSM (%)	PGD-40 (%)	PGD-100 (%)	# Params (M)	Search Cost (GPU days)	Search Method
LeNet [26]	98.8	95.6	93.2	91.8	3.27	-	Manual
LeNet (Prep. + Adv. train [42])	97.4	-	94.0	91.8	0.06147	-	Manual
UCBNAS	99.5	98.67	96.94	95.4	0.082	0.13	Bandit
UCBNAS (pruning)	99.52	98.56	96.62	94.96	0.066	0.08	Bandit
ABanditNAS-6	**99.52**	**98.94**	**97.01**	**95.7**	**0.089**	**0.08**	Anti-Bandit

Table 2. Robustness of our model in the white-box and black-box settings on MNIST and CIFAR-10. Here ϵ is the perturbation size. PGD means PGD-40 for MNIST and PGD-7 for CIFAR-10. 'copy' means we use a copied network to generate black-box adversarial examples, and 'ResNet-18' means using ResNet-18 to generate black-box adversarial examples.

Structure	Clean	White-Box			Black-Box		
		MI-FGSM	BIM	PGD	MI-FGSM	BIM	PGD
MNIST ($\epsilon = 0.3$)							
LeNet [26] (copy)	98.8	–	–	93.2	–	–	96.0
ABanditNAS-6 (copy)	**99.52**	97.41		97.63	**97.58**	99.09		99.12	**99.02**
CIFAR-10 ($\epsilon = 0.031$)							
Wide-ResNet [26] (copy)	87.3	–		–	50.0	–		–	64.2
NASNet [7] (copy)	**93.2**	–		–	50.1	–		–	75.0
ABanditNAS-6 (copy)	87.16	48.77	47.59	50.0	74.94	75.78	76.13
ABanditNAS-6 (ResNet-18)	87.16	48.77	47.59	50.0	77.06	77.63	78.0
ABanditNAS-10 (ResNet-18)	90.64	**54.19**	**55.31**	**58.74**	**80.25**	**80.8**	**81.26**

to 10 with a step size and a standard perturbation size the same as those in the white-box attacks. We evaluate ABanditNAS against transfer-based attack where a copy of the victim network is trained with the same training setting. We apply attacks similar to the white-box attacks on the copied network to generate black-box adversarial examples. We also generate adversarial samples using a ResNet-18 model, and feed them to the model obtainedly ABanditNAS.

4.2 Results on Different Datasets

MNIST. Owing to the search space reduction by anti-bandit, the entire search process only requires 1.93 h on a single NVIDIA Titan V GPU. For MNIST, the structure searched by ABanditNAS is directly used for training. We evaluate the trained network by 40 and 100 attack steps, and compare our method with LeNet [26] and MeNet [42] in Table 1. From these results, we can see that ABandit-NAS using FGSM adversarial training with random initialization is more robust than LeNet with PGD-40 adversarial training, no matter which attack is used. Although MeNet uses matrix estimation (ME) as preprocessing to destroy the adversarial structure of the noise, our method still performs better. In addition,

Table 3. Validation accuracy and robustness of various models trained on CIFAR-10. Note that the search cost of NASNet which is unknown is estimated based on [7]. 'PGD-10' means the result of VGG-16 is under PGD-10 attack which comes from [44].

Architecture	Clean (%)	MI-FGSM (%)	PGD-7 (%)	PGD-20 (%)	# Params (M)	Search Cost (GPU days)	Search Method
VGG-16 [44]	85.16	–	46.04 (PGD-10)	–	–	–	Manual
ResNet [26]	79.4	–	47.1	43.7	0.46	–	Manual
Wide-ResNet [26]	87.3	-	50.0	45.8	45.9	–	Manual
NASNet [7]	93.2	–	50.1	–	–	~7 × 2000	RL
UCBNAS (pruning)	89.54	53.12	54.55	45.33	8.514	0.08	Bandit
ABanditNAS-6	87.16	48.77	50.0	45.9	**2.892**	0.08	Anti-Bandit
ABanditNAS-6 (larger)	87.31	52.01	51.24	45.79	12.467	0.08	Anti-Bandit
ABanditNAS-10	90.64	**54.19**	**58.74**	**50.51**	5.188	0.08	Anti-Bandit

our method has the best performance (99.52%) on the clean images with a strong robustness. For the black-box attacks, Table 2 shows that they barely affect the structures searched by ABanditNAS compared with other models, either manually designed or searched by NAS. As illustrated in Fig. 3a, with the increase of the perturbation size, our network's performance does not drop significantly, showing the robustness of our method.

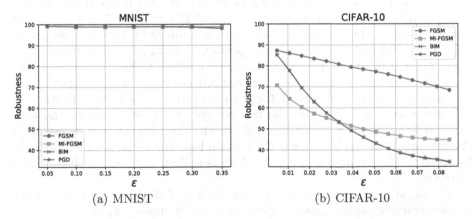

(a) MNIST   (b) CIFAR-10

Fig. 3. Robustness of ABanditNAS against different white-box attacks for various perturbation budgets.

We also apply the conventional bandit which samples operations based on UCB to search the network, leading to UCBNAS. The main differences between UCBNAS and ABanditNAS lie in that UCBNAS only uses UCB as an evaluation measure to select an operation, and there is no operation pruning involved. Compared with UCBNAS, ABanditNAS can get better performance and use less search time under adversarial attacks as shown in Table 1. Also, to further

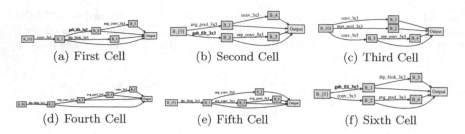

(a) First Cell   (b) Second Cell   (c) Third Cell

(d) Fourth Cell   (e) Fifth Cell   (f) Sixth Cell

Fig. 4. Detailed structures of the best cells discovered on CIFAR-10 using FGSM with random initialization.

demonstrate the effectiveness of our ABanditNAS, we use UCBNAS with pruning to search for a robust model, which not only uses UCB to select an operation, but also prune operation of less potential. Although UCBNAS (pruning) is as fast as ABanditNAS, it has worse performance than ABanditNAS because of unfair competitions between operations before pruning.

CIFAR-10. The results for different architectures on CIFAR-10 are summarized in Table 3. We use one Titan V GPU to search, and the batch size is 512. The entire search process takes about 1.94 h. We consider $V = 6$ and $V = 10$ cells for training. In addition, we also train a larger network variant with 100 initial channels for $V = 6$. Compared with Wide-ResNet, ABanditNAS-10 achieves not only a better performance (50.0% vs. 58.74%) in PGD-7, but also fewer parameters (45.9 M vs. 5.188 M). Although the result of VGG-16 is under PGD-10, ABanditNAS-10 achieves a better performance under more serious attack PGD-20 (46.04% vs. 50.51%). When compared with NASNet[1] which has a better performance on clean images, our method obtains better performance on adversarial examples with a much faster search speed ($\sim$7 $\times$ 2000 vs. 0.08). Note that the results in Table 3 are the best we got, which are unstable and need more trials to get the results. Table 2 shows the black-box attacks barely affect the networks obtained by ABanditNAS, much less than those by other methods. In addition, Fig. 3b illustrates ABanditNAS is still robust when the disturbance increases.

For the structure searched by ABanditNAS on CIFAR-10, we find that the robust structure prefers pooling operations, Gabor filters and denosing blocks (Fig. 4). The reasons lie in that the pooling can enhance the nonlinear modeling capacity, Gabor filters can extract robust features, and the denosing block and mean pooling act as smoothing filters for denosing. Gabor filters and denosing blocks are usually set in the front of cell by ABanditNAS to denoise feature encoded by the previous cell. The setting is consistent with [40], which demonstrates the rationality of ABanditNAS.

---

[1] Results are from [7].

4.3 Ablation Study

The performances of the structures searched by ABanditNAS with different values of the λ are used to find the best λ. We train the structures under the same setting.

Effect on the Hyperparameter λ: The hyperparameter λ is used to balance the performance between the past and the current. Different values of λ result in similar search costs. From Fig. 5, we can see that when $\lambda = 0.7$, ABanditNAS is most robust.

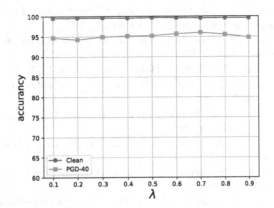

Fig. 5. The performances of the structures searched by ABanditNAS with different values of the hyperparameters T and λ.

5 Conclusion

We have proposed an ABanditNAS approach to design robust structures to defend adversarial attacks. To solve the challenging search problem caused by the complicated huge search space and the adversarial training process, we have introduced an anti-bandit algorithm to improve the search efficiency. We have investigated the relationship between our strategy and potential operations based on both lower and upper bounds. Extensive experiments have demonstrated that the proposed ABanditNAS is much faster than other state-of-the-art NAS methods with a better performance in accuracy. Under adversarial attacks, ABanditNAS achieves much better performance than other methods.

Acknowledgments. Baochang Zhang is also with Shenzhen Academy of Aerospace Technology, Shenzhen, China, and he is the corresponding author. He is in part Supported by National Natural Science Foundation of China under Grant 61672079, Shenzhen Science and Technology Program (No.KQTD2016112515134654).

References

1. Athalye, A., Carlini, N., Wagner, D.: Obfuscated gradients give a false sense of security: Circumventing defenses to adversarial examples. In: ICML (2018)
2. Auer, P., Cesa-Bianchi, N., Fischer, P.: Finite-time analysis of the multiarmed bandit problem. Mach. Learn. 47, 235–256 (2002)
3. Bender, G., Kindermans, P.J., Zoph, B., Vasudevan, V., Le, Q.V.: Understanding and simplifying one-shot architecture search. In: ICML (2018)
4. Bengio, Y., Goodfellow, I., Courville, A.: Deep learning. Citeseer (2017)
5. Buades, A., Coll, B., Morel, J.: A non-local algorithm for image denoising. In: CVPR (2005)
6. Carlini, N., Wagner, D.: Towards evaluating the robustness of neural networks. In: 2017 IEEE Symposium on Security and Privacy (2017)
7. Cubuk, E.D., Zoph, B., Schoenholz, S.S., Le, Q.V.: Intriguing properties of adversarial examples. In: ICLR (2017)
8. Das, N., Shanbhogue, M., Chen, S., Hohman, F., Chen, L., Kounavis, M.E., Chau, D.H.: Keeping the bad guys out: Protecting and vaccinating deep learning with jpeg compression (2017). arXiv
9. DeVries, T., Taylor, G.W.: Improved regularization of convolutional neural networks with cutout (2017). arXiv
10. Dong, Y., Liao, F., Pang, T., Su, H., Zhu, J., Hu, X., Li, J.: Boosting adversarial attacks with momentum. In: CVPR (2018)
11. D.V. Vargas, S.Kotyan: Evolving robust neural architectures to defend from adversarial attacks (2019). arXiv
12. Dziugaite, G.K., Ghahramani, Z., Roy, D.M.: A study of the effect of jpg compression on adversarial images (2016). arXiv
13. Even-Dar, E., Mannor, S., Mansour, Y.: Action elimination and stopping conditions for the multi-armed bandit and reinforcement learning problems. J. Mach. Learn. Res. 7, 1079–1105 (2006)
14. Gabor, D.: Electrical engineers part iii: Radio and communication engineering. J. Inst. Electr. Eng. - Part III: Radio Commun. Eng. 1945–1948 93, 1 (1946)
15. Gabor, D.: Theory of communication. part 1: The analysis of information. J. Inst. Electr. Eng. Part III: Radio Commun. Eng. 93, 429–441 (1946)
16. Goodfellow, I.J., Shlens, J., Szegedy, C.: Explaining and harnessing adversarial examples (2014). arXiv
17. Gupta, P., Rahtu, E.: Ciidefence: Defeating adversarial attacks by fusing class-specific image inpainting and image denoising. In: ICCV (2019)
18. He, K., Zhang, X., Ren, S., Sun, J.: Deep residual learning for image recognition. In: CVPR (2016)
19. Ilyas, A., Engstrom, L., Madry, A.: Prior convictions: Black-box adversarial attacks with bandits and priors. In: ICLR (2018)
20. Kocsis, L., Szepesvari, C.: Bandit based monte-carlo planning. In: Proceedings of the 17th European Conference on Machine Learning (2006)
21. Kurakin, A., Goodfellow, I., Bengio, S.: Adversarial examples in the physical world. In: ICLR (2016)
22. Liao, F., Liang, M., Dong, Y., Pang, T., Hu, X., Zhu, J.: Defense against adversarial attacks using high-level representation guided denoiser. In: CVPR (2018)
23. Liu, H., Simonyan, K., Yang, Y.: Darts: Differentiable architecture search. In: ICLR (2018)

24. Liu, Y., Chen, X., Liu, C., Song, D.: Delving into transferable adversarial examples and black-box attacks. In: ICLR (2016)
25. Long, J., Shelhamer, E., Darrell, T.: Fully convolutional networks for semantic segmentation. In: CVPR (2015)
26. Madry, A., Makelov, A., Schmidt, L., Tsipras, D., Vladu, A.: Towards deep learning models resistant to adversarial attacks. In: ICLR (2017)
27. Guo, M., Yang, Y., Xu, R., Liu, Z.: When NAS meets robustness: In search of robust architectures against adversarial attacks. In: CVPR (2020)
28. Na, T., Ko, J.H., Mukhopadhyay, S.: Cascade adversarial machine learning regularized with a unified embedding. In: ICLR (2017)
29. Dong, N., Xu, M., Liang, X., Jiang, Y., Dai, W., Xing, E.: Neural architecture search for adversarial medical image segmentation. In: MICCAI (2019)
30. Osadchy, M., Hernandez-Castro, J., Gibson, S., Dunkelman, O., Pérez-Cabo, D.: No bot expects the deepcaptcha! introducing immutable adversarial examples, with applications to captcha generation. IEEE Trans. Inf. Forensics Secur. **12**, 2640–2653 (2017)
31. Pham, H., Guan, M.Y., Zoph, B., Le, Q.V., Dean, J.: Efficient neural architecture search via parameter sharing. In: ICML (2018)
32. Pérez, J.C., Alfarra, M., Jeanneret, G., Bibi, A., Thabet, A.K., Ghanem, B., Arbeláez, P.: Robust gabor networks (2019). arXiv
33. Shafahi, A., Najib, M., Ghiasi, M.A., Xu, Z., Dickerson, J., Studer, C., Davis, L.S., Taylor, G., Goldstein, T.: Adversarial training for free! In: NIPS (2019)
34. Silver, D., et al.: Mastering the game of go without human knowledge. In: Nature (2017)
35. Pouya, S., Maya, K., Rama, C.: Defense-GAN: Protecting classifiers against adversarial attacks using generative models. In: ICLR (2018)
36. Szegedy, C., Liu, W., Jia, Y., Sermanet, P., Reed, S., Anguelov, D., Erhan, D., Vanhoucke, V., Rabinovich, A.: Going deeper with convolutions. In: CVPR (2015)
37. Szegedy, C., Zaremba, W., Sutskever, I., Bruna, J., Erhan, D., Goodfellow, I., Fergus, R.: Intriguing properties of neural networks. In: ICLR (2013)
38. Wang, J., Zhang, H.: Bilateral adversarial training: Towards fast training of more robust models against adversarial attacks. In: ICCV (2019)
39. Wong, E., Rice, L., Kolter, J.Z.: Fast is better than free: Revisiting adversarial training. In: ICLR (2020)
40. Xie, C., Wu, Y., Maaten, L.V.D., Yuille, A.L., He, K.: Feature denoising for improving adversarial robustness. In: CVPR (2019)
41. Xu, Y., Xie, L., Zhang, X., Chen, X., Qi, G., Tian, Q., Xiong, H.: PC-DARTS: Partial channel connections for memory-efficient differentiable architecture search. In: ICLR (2019)
42. Yang, Y., Zhang, G., Katabi, D., Xu, Z.: ME-Net: Towards effective adversarial robustness with matrix estimation. In: ICML (2019)
43. Ying, C., Klein, A., Real, E., Christiansen, E., Murphy, K., Hutter, F.: Nas-bench-101: Towards reproducible neural architecture search. In: ICML (2019)
44. Zhang, C., Liu, A., Liu, X., Xu, Y., Yu, H., Ma, Y., Li, T.: Interpreting and improving adversarial robustness with neuron sensitivity (2019). arXiv
45. Zheng, X., Ji, R., Tang, L., Wan, Y., Zhang, B., Wu, Y., Wu, Y., Shao, L.: Dynamic distribution pruning for efficient network architecture search (2019). arXiv
46. Zoph, B., Le, Q.V.: Neural architecture search with reinforcement learning. In: ICLR (2016)
47. Zoph, B., Vasudevan, V., Shlens, J., Le, Q.V.: Learning transferable architectures for scalable image recognition. In: CVPR (2018)

Wavelet-Based Dual-Branch Network for Image Demoiréing

Lin Liu[1,2], Jianzhuang Liu[2], Shanxin Yuan[2(✉)], Gregory Slabaugh[2], Aleš Leonardis[2], Wengang Zhou[1], and Qi Tian[3]

[1] University of Science and Technology of China, Hefei, China
[2] Noah's Ark Lab, Huawei Technologies, Shenzhen, China
shanxin.yuan@huawei.com
[3] Huawei Cloud BU, Beijing, China

Abstract. When smartphone cameras are used to take photos of digital screens, usually moiré patterns result, severely degrading photo quality. In this paper, we design a wavelet-based dual-branch network (WDNet) with a spatial attention mechanism for image demoiréing. Existing image restoration methods working in the RGB domain have difficulty in distinguishing moiré patterns from true scene texture. Unlike these methods, our network removes moiré patterns in the wavelet domain to separate the frequencies of moiré patterns from the image content. The network combines dense convolution modules and dilated convolution modules supporting large receptive fields. Extensive experiments demonstrate the effectiveness of our method, and we further show that WDNet generalizes to removing moiré artifacts on non-screen images. Although designed for image demoiréing, WDNet has been applied to two other low-level vision tasks, outperforming state-of-the-art image deraining and deraindrop methods on the Rain100h and Raindrop800 data sets, respectively.

Keywords: Deep learning · Image demoiréing · Wavelet

1 Introduction

A smartphone has become an indispensable tool in daily life, and the popularity of mobile photography has grown supported by advancements in photo quality. It has become increasingly common to take photos of digital screens in order to quickly save information. However, when a photo is taken of a digital screen, moiré patterns often appear and contaminate the underlying clean image. These moiré patterns are caused by the interference between the camera's color filter array (CFA) and the screen's subpixel layout. In general, moiré patterns are likely to appear when two repetitive patterns interfere with each other. For example, moiré artifacts can appear when the repetitive patterns in textiles and building's bricks interfere with camera's CFA. Removing moiré patterns is challenging, as moiré patterns are irregular in shape and color, and can span a large range

Electronic supplementary material The online version of this chapter (https://doi.org/10.1007/978-3-030-58601-0_6) contains supplementary material, which is available to authorized users.

© Springer Nature Switzerland AG 2020
A. Vedaldi et al. (Eds.): ECCV 2020, LNCS 12358, pp. 86–102, 2020.
https://doi.org/10.1007/978-3-030-58601-0_6

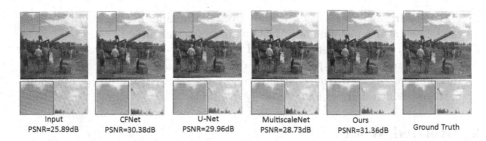

| Input | CFNet | U-Net | MultiscaleNet | Ours | |
| PSNR=25.89dB | PSNR=30.38dB | PSNR=29.96dB | PSNR=28.73dB | PSNR=31.36dB | Ground Truth |

Fig. 1. Qualitative comparison among CFNet [32], U-Net [42], MultiscaleNet [53] and our network on the TIP2018 data set [53]. Ours is trained in the wavelet domain and removes the moiré patterns significantly better.

of frequencies. Unlike other image restoration tasks, such as image denoising [27,54,67], image demosaicing [9,34] and super resolution [19,20,22,69], where the challenge is mainly in removing high-frequency noise and recovering details, image demoiréing requires not only recovering high frequency image details, but also removing moiré patterns with frequencies spanning a large range.

Most existing image restoration methods [21,42,69] working in the RGB domain are not tailored to image demoiréing, though a few attempts [14,32,53] have been made to tackle it recently. Sun *et al.* [53] proposed a multi-resolution network to remove moiré patterns of different frequencies/scales. Liu *et al.* [32] developed a coarse-to-fine network and trained it on a synthetic dataset and refined real images with GAN. He *et al.* [14] utilized the edge information and appearance attributes of moiré patterns to demoiré. However, all the existing methods (working in the RGB domain) have difficulty in distinguishing moiré patterns from the real image content, and in dealing with low-frequency moiré patterns [53]. Figure 1 shows some qualitative comparisons among four methods (including ours). We argue that image demoiréing can be more easily handled in the frequency domain. Wavelet-based methods have been explored in computer vision and shown good performance, e.g., in classification [7,38], network compression [11,28], and face super-resolution [19]. However, due to their task-specific design, these methods cannot be directly used for image demoiréing.

In this paper, we propose to remove moiré patterns in the frequency domain, where the input image with moiré patterns is first decomposed into different frequency bands using a wavelet transform. After the wavelet transform, moiré patterns are more apparent in certain wavelet subbands, where they can be more easily removed (see Fig. 3 for example). Our model, working in the frequency domain, is a dual-branch network with dense branches and dilated branches, which are responsible for restoring the close-range and far-range information, respectively. We also design a spatial attention mechanism called a *direction perception module* in the dense branches to highlight the areas with moiré patterns.

In this paper, we make following contributions:

1. We propose a novel wavelet-based and dual-branch neural network for image demoiréing. We also propose a spatial attention mechanism called direction perception module (DPM) to highlight the areas with moiré patterns.

2. Our network achieves the best results on the demoiréing task. Our trained model can also remove moiré artifacts on non-screen images.
3. Our new architecture generalises well to other low-level vision tasks, such as deraining and deraindrop, where we also obtain state-of the-art results.
4. In addition, we built a new urban-scene data set with more types of moiré patterns, which will be made publicly available.

2   Related Work

In this section, we give a brief review of the most relevant work for image demoiréing.

Moiré Pattern Removal. Early image demoiréing work [33,43,46,48,61] focused on certain specific moiré patterns. Sidorov et al. [48] presented a spectral model to address monotonous and monochrome moiré patterns. Other work tried to remove striped moiré artifacts [43,47,56] or dotted artifacts [25,46,51] in scanned or X-ray images. Yang et al. [61] and Liu et al. [33] removed moiré artifacts using low-rank and sparse matrix decomposition. But their methods focus on textile moiré patterns and cannot handle low-frequency moiré patterns. Compared to these methods, our approach can deal with a much larger range of moiré patterns as we do not make presumptions about the moiré patterns. Contemporary models [14,32,53,70] and recent challenges [64–66] cast image demoiréing as an image restoration problem addressed using deep learning. Recently Liu et al. [32] built a coarse-to-fine convolutional neural network to remove moiré patterns from photos taken of screens. But the method mainly used synthetic data for network training and focuses on removing moiré patterns in text scenes. Sun et al. [53] proposed a multi-resolution convolutional neural network for demoiréing and released an associated dataset. He et al. [14] labeled the data set in [53] with three attribute labels of moiré patterns, which is beneficial to learn diverse patterns. This method, along with [32,53], works in the RGB domain and in a multi-scale manner. Such a strategy has limited capacity to correctly distinguish moiré patterns from true image content. In contrast, our method works in the wavelet domain, and we introduce a novel network design, resulting in stronger moiré pattern removal while restoring image details.

Wavelet-Based Methods. Wavelet-based methods have been explored in some computer vision tasks, including classification [7,29,38,57], network compression [11,28], face aging [36], super-resolution [19,35], style transfer [63], etc. Fujieda et al. [7] proposed wavelet CNNs that utilize spectral information to classify the textures. Liu et al. [36] used a wavelet-based method to capture age-related texture details at multiple scales in the frequency domain. Our work is the first to use a wavelet transform to remove moiré patterns in the frequency domain. Compared with Fourier transform and discrete cosine transform, wavelet transform considers both spatial domain information and frequency domain information. With the wavelet composition, different wavelet bands represent such a broad range of frequencies, which can not be achieved by a few convolutional layers even with large kernels.

The most relevant in the above studies is [19] for using wavelets for face super-resolution, where a neural network is deployed to predict the wavelet coefficients. But predicting the wavelet coefficients of a moiré-free image from its moiré image in the RGB domain is difficult. Moiré patterns cover a wide range in both space and frequency domains, making it hard to distinguish moiré patterns from true scene textures. For photo-realistic style transfer, Yoo *et al.* [63] regarded the wavelet transform and wavelet inverse transform as a pooling layer and an unpooling layer respectively , with the aim of preserving their structural information. However, this technique [63] may not be suitable for image demoiréing, where moiré patterns can have strong structural information overlaid with true image contents. Our work runs directly in the wavelet domain. Wavelet transform and inverse wavelet transform are used outside of the network.

Dual-Branch Design. Dual-branch network structure design makes use of two branches, complementing each other [6,8,40,45]. It has been used in image super-resolution [40], classification [8], segmentation [6] and person-re-ID [45]. Gao *et al.* [8] proposed a dual-branch network for polarimetric synthetic aperture radar image classification. One branch is used to extract the polarization features and the other to extract the spatial features. Fu *et al.* [6] proposed a dual attention network with a position attention module and a channel attention module for scene segmentation. For image super-resolution, the dual branch in [40] can give consideration to easy image regions and hard image regions at the same time. All existing dual-branch networks have different branches, each focusing on certain image features, which only merge at the end of the network. In our design, the two branches iteratively communicate with each other to achieve a better representation.

Texture Removal. Texture removal [13,50,68] is related to demoiréing, as moiré patterns can be viewed as a special type of texture. Methods using local filters attempted to remove certain textures while maintaining other high-frequency structures [13,50,68]. Subr *et al.* [50] smoothed texture by averaging two manifolds from local minima and maxima. Both Ham *et al.* [13] and Zhang *et al.* [68] used dynamic guidance and a fidelity term for image filtering. Multiple strategies to smooth texture were used in [1,24,49]. Optimization-based methods were also exploited [52,58,59]. Sun *et al.* [52] and Xu *et al.* [58] used l_0 minimization to retrieve structures from images. Xu *et al.* [59] optimized a global function with relative total variation regularization. However, these texture removal methods focus on the structure of the image and remove some repeated and identical or similar patterns. They do not address moiré patterns that span a much wider range of frequencies and appear in varied shapes and directions.

3   Our Method

The architecture of **WDNet** is shown in Fig. 2. The original RGB image input is first transformed into the **W**avelet domain, where a **D**ual-branch **Net**work is used to remove the moiré patterns. The final RGB image output is obtained by applying the inverse wavelet transform to the network's output. The dual-branch network has seven dual-branch modules, each including a dense branch

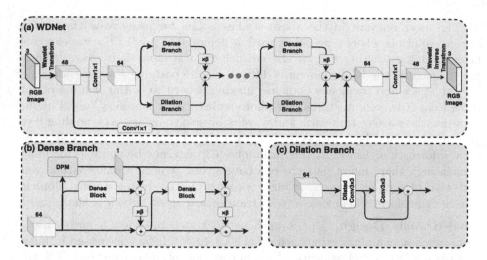

Fig. 2. The architecture of the proposed WDNet (a) consisting of two kinds of branches, the dense branch (b) for restoring the close-range information and the dilation branch (c) for restoring the far-range information. Working in the wavelet domain can better remove the moiré patterns and retain the details. The numbers of channels are given in the figure.

and a dilation branch. A ResNet [15] style skip connection is made. The dense and dilation branches are responsible for acquiring moiré information in different frequency ranges; the former detects close-range patterns and the latter detects far-range patterns.

3.1   Working in the Wavelet Domain

Our network operates in the wavelet domain to remove moiré patterns. We employ 2D fast wavelet transform (FWT) to decompose the input RGB image into a sequence of wavelet subbands (coefficients) of a common smaller size, but with different frequency content. We choose the simplest Haar wavelet as the basis for the wavelet transform. A Haar wavelet transform can be efficiently computed and suitable for our task. The FWT iteratively applies low-pass and high-pass decomposition filters along with downsampling to compute the wavelet coefficients where the low-pass filter $= \left(1/\sqrt{2}, 1/\sqrt{2}\right)$ and the high-pass filter $= \left(1/\sqrt{2}, -1/\sqrt{2}\right)$. In each level of the transform, we use the high-pass filter and the low-pass filter along the rows to transform an image to two images, and then we apply the same filters along the columns of these two images, obtaining four images in total. The equations to derive the subbands can be found in [10].

As shown in Figs. 3(c) and (d), the wavelet subbands at different levels correspond to different frequencies. Moiré patterns are conspicuous only in certain wavelet subbands. For example, in Fig. 3(e), the difference between (c) and (d) shows that the first three wavelet subbands of the first column in Fig. 3(c) contain obvious and different moiré patterns. From our experiments, we find that

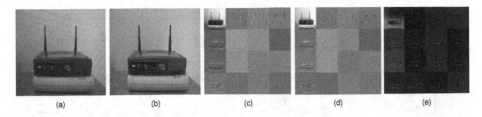

Fig. 3. (a) An image with moiré patterns. (b) The ground truth of (a). (c) Wavelet subbands transformed from the gray-level image of (a). (d) Wavelet subbands transformed from the gray-level image of (b). (e) Difference between (c) and (d).

wavelet subbands with higher frequencies usually contain fewer moiré patterns. These wavelet subbands provide important information to recover the details for moiré pattern-free images.

In our method, the wavelet transform level is set to 2. The original RGB input is transformed into 48 subbands, with 16 subbands for each color channel. As such, another benefit of working in the wavelet domain is that the spatial size of the original image ($H \times W \times 3$) is reduced by a quarter in both the width and height ($(H/4) \times (W/4) \times 48$). The reduced spatial size consequently reduces the computation in the deep network. Besides, we concatenate all the 48 channels instead of processing the high and low frequency bands individually, because moire patterns for each image vary a lot, it is difficult to find a threshold to manually separate them.

3.2 Dense Branch

DenseNet [18] can alleviate the problem of vanishing gradient and reduce the number of network parameters through the design of bypass connections and feature reuse. In low-level vision, dense blocks have been used in deraining and dehazing [12,44], and image super-resolution with the Residual Dense Network (RDN) [69] or other networks [22].

As shown in Fig. 2(b), we design each dense branch by adding a new Direction Perception Module (DPM) to the residual dense module borrowed from RDN [69]. The residual dense module has two small dense blocks each with 5 convolutional layers. In the same dense block, the input of each layer contains the output of all previous layers. DPM is used to find the directions of moiré patterns and will be explained in Sect. 3.4 in detail. The output of DPM and each dense block are multiplied, weighted by a factor β, and then the result is added to the input. This design can effectively find the locations of close-range moiré patterns.

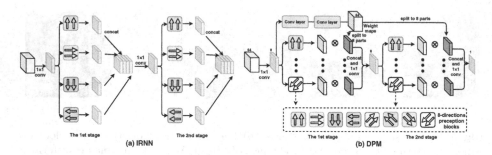

Fig. 4. (a) Image recurrent neural network (IRNN). (b) Our direction perception module (DPM) with two stages, each with 8 directions.

3.3 Dilation Branch

Subsampling or pooling feature maps can enlarge receptive fields, but loses some details. Dilated convolution is used to overcome this problem. In each of our dilation branches (Fig. 2(c)), there are two layers: a 3×3 dilated convolution layer with a dilation rate $d_{k+2} = d_k + d_{k+1}$, followed by a traditional 3×3 convolution, where k is the index of a dilation branch with $d_1 = 1$ and $d_2 = 2$. The rationale for this design is explained below.

When multiple dilated convolutions with a fixed dilation rate (say, 2) are applied successively, many pixels are not involved in the convolutions and a special kind of artifact called *gridding* appears [55]. Alternatively, a hybrid design using dilation rates (1,2,3,1,2,3,...) [55] is not suitable for our task because these dilations are not large enough to cover general moiré patterns. Therefore, we design our dilation rates according to the Fibonacci series (e.g., (1,2,3,5,8,13,21) when there are 7 dilation branches). Additionally, we apply a traditional 3×3 convolution on the output of the dilated convolution to further reduce any gridding artifact (Fig. 2(c)).

3.4 Direction Perception Module

We propose a Direction Perception Module (DPM) by improving the Image Recurrent Neural Network (IRNN) [2,17,60], as shown in Fig. 4. The two-stage four-directional IRNN (Fig. 4(a)) architecture enhances the use of contextual information, where the first stage in IRNN aims to produce feature maps that acquire neighboring contextual information and the second stage in IRNN further gathers the global information. However, in IRNN, in the feature maps at the end of the first stage, a pixel can only obtain information in the vertical and horizontal directions, but not in other directions.

As shown in Fig. 4(b), we improve IRNN in two aspects. First, we extend the 4-direction perception to 8-direction perception by including 4 more diagonal directions to enhance the detection ability of slanting moiré patterns. The moiré patterns in other directions are detected in the second stage. Second, the weight maps are used to distinguish the importance of information in different directions. Unlike IRNN which learns direction-aware features in the embedded space, we use DPM to generate the attention map which highlights moiré pattern spatial distributions and is supervised by L_a discussed in Sect. 3.6. The combination of the two convolution layers and the eight-direction perception blocks is equivalent to an attention operation.

Loss Function. The loss function of the whole network is defined as follows:

$$L = \lambda_1 L_a + \lambda_2 L_{l_1} + \lambda_3 L_p + \lambda_4 L_w, \tag{1}$$

where L_{l_1} is the l_1 loss between the image and its ground-truth in the RGB domain, L_p is the perceptual loss [23], and the other parts are described below.

Wavelet Loss. Let $C = (c_1, c_2, ..., c_N)$ and $\hat{C} = (\hat{c}_1, \hat{c}_2, ..., \hat{c}_N)$ be the ground-truth and the estimated wavelet subbands, respectively. Two wavelet-based losses, MSE loss l_{MSE} and detail loss l_{detail}, are defined as follows:

$$l_{\text{MSE}} = \gamma_1 \sum_{i=1}^{3} \|\hat{c}_i - c_i\|^2 + \gamma_2 \sum_{i=4}^{N} \|\hat{c}_i - c_i\|^2, \tag{2}$$

where the first term is for the low-frequency components, and the second for the high-frequency ones, and γ_1 and γ_2 are two weighting factors.

$$l_{detail} = \sum_{i=4}^{N} \max\left(\alpha |c_i|^2 - |\hat{c}_i|^2, 0\right), \tag{3}$$

which is inspired by the work in super-resolution [19] to prevent the wavelet coefficients from converging to 0 and therefore retaining the high-frequency details of the image. α is a positive number and set to 1.2 in this work. Setting α to a value greater than 1 can effectively prevent $\hat{c}_i$ from converging to 0. Different from the loss function in [19], ours does not have a bias value ϵ, because we found that ϵ has little effect on the final results. Besides, the value of ϵ in [19] was set to 0 in their source code. The network's wavelet loss L_w is then:

$$L_w = l_{\text{MSE}} + l_{detail}. \tag{4}$$

Attention Loss. We further apply the attention loss L_a as:

$$L_a = \|A - d(M)\|_2^2, \tag{5}$$

where A is the output of the DPM in the network and M is the mask of the moiré patterns, which is computed by thresholding the difference between the moiré-contaminated image and the ground-truth. $d(\cdot)$ is a downsampling operation to ensure that the mask and A have the same size. The threshold is set to 15 in this work.

4   Experiments

We compare WDNet with state-of-the-art methods, and conduct user studies for image demoiréing. We also demonstrate that WDNet when trained only for screen image demoiréing can also remove moiré artifacts on non-screen images. Finally, we apply WDNet to two other tasks, deraining and de-raindrop, to show that our method generalizes well to other frequency-based low-level vision tasks.

4.1   Implementation Details

Throughout our experiments, the input is a $256 \times 256 \times 3$ RGB image, which is then transformed into 48 different-level wavelet subbands with the size of 64×64 by a Haar wavelet transform. We use seven dual-branch modules and add DPM into the 4th dense branch to perceive moiré patterns. Our model is implemented in PyTorch and runs on a NVIDIA Tesla V100 GPU. The batch size is set to 16 during training. Adam [26] is used to search the minimum of the loss function. The learning rate of the generator is 0.0002 and reduced by one-tenth for every 20 epochs. In Eqs. (1) and (2), the parameters λ_1, λ_2, λ_3, λ_4, γ_1 and γ_2 are empirically set to 1, 5, 10, 200, 0.01 and 1.1 respectively. The method of *eye* initialization in [69] is used to initialize the weights of WDNet. The value of β throughout the paper is set to 0.2. The dense branch has more parameters than the dilation branch. Setting β to 0.2 makes the weights of the dilation branch's parameters larger, which can maintain the details of the original image.

4.2   Datasets and State-of-the-Art Methods

We perform experiments on two datasets, TIP2018 [53] and a new London's Buildings. The TIP2018 dataset contains 100,000+ image pairs with about 800×800 resolution and the moiré-free images come from the ImageNet ISVRC 2012 dataset. The new dataset London's Buildings was built by us recently and will be publicly released. It is an urban-scene data set and its images contain bricks, windows and other regular patterns which are prone to generate moiré patterns. We use mobile phones and screens different from those used in the TIP2018 data set and thus provide additional diversity of moiré patterns. London's Buildings includes 400 training pairs and 60 testing pairs with about 2300×1700 resolution. The 256×256 images used in training are resized (in TIP2018) or cropped (in London's buildings) from the original higher-resolution images. We conduct two experiments on the TIP2018 data set, TestA and TestB. TestB follows the same setting as in [53]. TestA is a subset of TestB and this subset contains 130 hard samples from the same camera.

We compare our model with MuiltiscaleNet [53], CFNet [32], Pix2pix [21], U-Net [42], MopNet [14], and ResNet-34 [15]. For fair comparison, when a network is trained on the TIP2018 data set, we use the same setting as in [53]. We faithfully reimplement MuiltiscaleNet [53] and CFNet [32] based on their papers. Note that since MopNet is very recent work without its code released, we can only compare with it in one experiment where [14] gives its result on TIP2018.

Table 1. Quantitative comparison on TIP2018. The best results are in **bold**.

Test set		Pix2pix	U-Net	CFNet	MultiscaleNet	MopNet	WDNet
TestA	PSNR/SSIM	25.32/0.756	25.80/0.803	25.52/0.810	26.11/0.801	−/−	**27.88/0.863**
TestB	PSNR/SSIM	25.74/0.825	26.49/0.864	26.09/0.863	26.99/0.871	27.75/0.895	**28.08/0.904**

Table 2. Quantitative comparison on London's Building.

	U-Net	MultiscaleNet	ResNet	CFNet	WDNet
PSNR/SSIM	23.48/0.790	23.64/0.791	23.87/0.780	23.22/0.764	**25.41/0.839**

Table 3. User study. The preference rate shows the percentage of comparisons in which the users prefer our results.

	WDNet>CFNet	WDNet>U-Net	WDNet>MultiscaleNet
Preference rate	83.7%	82.1%	80.5%

4.3 Comparison with the State-of-the-Art

For quantitative comparison, we choose the PSNR and SSIM. As shown in Tables 1 and 2, our method outperforms the state-of-the-art on both datasets. Note that our model outperforms the most recent MopNet [14] by 0.33 dB, even though MopNet uses additional annotation (labelling TIP2018 with three attribute labels of moiré patterns) for training. We show some qualitative results in Figs. 5 and 6, where there are different kinds of moiré patterns appearing in the input images. Our WDNet most effectively removes the moiré patterns. For the computation consumption, CFNet, MultiscaleNet, U-Net, MopNet and WDNet take 58.2 ms, 5.7 ms, 3.8 ms, 71.8 ms and 14.6 ms, respectively, to restore a 256 × 256 image on one NVIDIA Tesla P100 GPU.

User Studies. We also conduct a user study with 10 users to compare the visual quality of the results generated by the models. During the study, two images I_1 and I_2, respectively obtained by our model and another model, and the corresponding moiré-free image (ground truth) I, are shown to a user who is asked to choose one from I_1 and I_2 which is closer to I. There are 100 triplets of these images randomly selected from TIP2018 to compare two models and the results are reported in Table 3.

Removal of Moiré Artifacts on Non-screen Images. Moiré artifacts may also appear on objects with dense repetitive textures, such as buildings and clothes. This kind of moiré artifacts usually does not always appear on the whole image. In Fig. 7, we show some results of directly applying our WDNet model trained on TIP2018 without fine-tuning on non-screen images. It shows that our method is effective in removing this kind of moiré patterns as well.

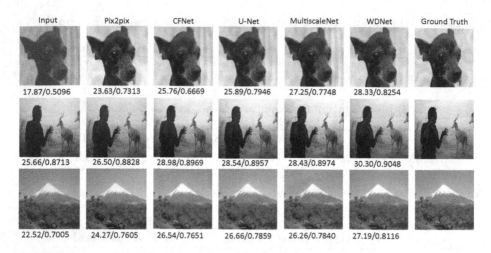

Fig. 5. Visual comparison among Pix2pix [21], CFNet [32], U-Net [42], MuiltiscaleNet [53] and our model WDNet, evaluated on images from the TIP2018 data set. The numbers under the images are PSNR/SSIM.

Fig. 6. Visual comparison on an image from the London's Building data set.

Fig. 7. Some results on non-screen images.

4.4   Ablation Studies

To conduct ablation studies to quantify the contributions of the components of WDNet, the TestA dataset is used in the experiments. To understand the restoration strategy between the two branches in the dual-branch architecture, we examine the feature maps of WDNet. At layer six, we normalize each channel of the feature map, and then sum up the values channel-wise to obtain a heat map. As shown in Fig. 8, the dense branch focuses on the local moiré patterns (interlaced bright and dark areas), while the dilation branch focuses on the

Fig. 8. The heat maps of the feature maps outputted from the two branches of the 6th layer.

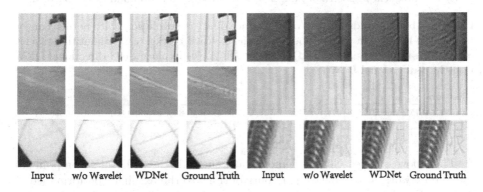

Fig. 9. Visual comparison between WDNet and WDNet without wavelet transform. These patches show that the former restores the details better and removes more moiré patterns.

whole areas contaminated by the moiré patterns due to its larger receptive field. It demonstrates that the two types of branches are responsible for the acquisition of the close-range and far-range information and jointly restore the image.

To test the effectiveness of the dense branches, we replace the dense blocks of them with ResNet blocks. To test the dilation branches, we replace the dilated convolutions with normal convolutions. As shown in Table 4, both the dense and dilation branches play an important role in WDNet. When the dense branches or the dilation branches are replaced, the PSNR decreases by 0.52 dB or 1.05 dB, respectively. The PSNR decreases by 0.41 dB when we remove the DPM module and the attention loss, and by 0.27 dB when we remove the weight maps in DPM. In addition, to compare the 8-directional DPM with the 4-directional IRNN, using the latter makes the PSNR decrease by 0.19 dB.

In order to verify whether working in the wavelet domain is better than in the RGB domain, we design a network by removing the wavelet transform and wavelet inverse transform from WDNet, without the wavelet loss during training. These two networks are compared at the same computation amount and the results are shown in Table 4. A visual comparison is shown in Fig. 9. From Table 4 and Fig. 9, we can see that the complete model best achieves moiré pattern removal. The wavelet transform can help to keep the edges and prevent the details from blurring.

(a) Rain Streak   (b)   (c) Rain Drop   (d)   (e) Moire Pattern   (f)

Fig. 10. Frequency spectra of images of rain streak, rain drop and moiré pattern.

Table 4. Ablation study on TestA. (a) Replace dilated convolutions with normal convolutions. (b) Replace the dense blocks with the residual blocks. (c) Without the wavelet and inverse wavelet transform. (d) Without DPM. (e) Replace the 8-directional DPM with the 4-directional IRNN.

Network	a	b	c	d	e	Complete model
PSNR/SSIM	26.83/0.858	27.36/0.856	27.03/0.859	27.47/0.853	27.69/0.857	27.88/0.863

The above studies clearly demonstrate that all the WDNet's components and the network design have their contributions to the excellent performance of WDNet. We also perform an experiment to explore the effect of different wavelet transform levels on the network's performance with the same network parameters. For levels 1, 2 and 3, the PSNR/SSIM are 27.24/0.866, 27.88/0.863, and 27.94/0.843, respectively. As the number of levels increases, the PSNR increases, but the SSIM decreases. The reason for such an interesting phenomenon will be left as the future work. Some recent related work such as [3] shows that perceptual quality and distortion (PSNR) may conflict with each other, particularly for image restoration tasks.

4.5   Extension to Deraining and Deraindrop

We show that our network also has advantages over the state-of-the-art methods in some other low-level vision tasks, such as deraining and deraindrop. Deraining methods can be divided into traditional methods and deep-learning methods. Traditional methods [4,37] remove rain streaks in images by designing some hand-crafted priors. Deep-learning methods [16,30,62] use convolutional neural networks to learn the rain streak features automatically. Yang *et al.* [62] created a multi-task network to jointly detect and remove rain. And Li *et al.* [30] proposed a recurrent neural network, where useful information in previous stages is beneficial to the rain removal in later stages. However, few deep-learning methods study how to use the feature of the rain streaks in the frequency domain to derain. In Fig. 10, similar to moiré patterns, rain streaks include high-frequency and low-frequency patterns, depending on the severity of the rain and distance to the camera. However, unlike moiré patterns, which can have different orientations in the same image, the directions of rain streaks are more consistent, resulting in an easier image restoration task. Like demoiréing, after the wavelet

Table 5. Quantitative comparison on Rain100h.

Method	DSC [37]	JORDER_R [62]	DID_MDN [69]	RESCAN [30]	DAFNet [16]	WDNet(Ours)
PSNR/SSIM	15.6/0.5446	23.45/0.749	24.53/0.799	26.45/0.845	28.44/0.874	**28.60/0.878**

Table 6. Quantitative comparison on Raindrop800.

Method	Eigen [5]	Pix2pix [21]	A^2Net [31]	AttentiveGAN [39]	Quan's [41]	WDNet (Ours)
PSNR/SSIM	23.90/0.80	28.85/0.84	30.79/0.93	31.52/0.92	31.44/**0.93**	**31.75/0.93**

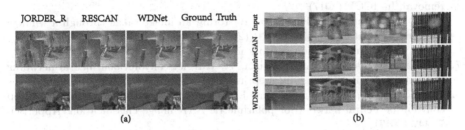

Fig. 11. (a) Visual deraining comparison among JORDER_R, RESCAN and WDNet. (b) Visual deraindrop comparison between AttentiveGAN and WDNet.

transform, different types of rain steaks in the RGB domain are easier to distinguish in the wavelet domain.

We train WDNet on the Rain100h data set [62] for deraining and on the Raindrop800 data set [39] for deraindrop, and test it on the corresponding test sets. Though the textures of the rain/raindrop and moiré patterns are very different in color and structure, our WDNet method can also remove them well. The results are given in Table 5, Table 6 and Fig. 11, which show that our WDNet performs better than the state-of-the-art. More visual results are given in the material.

5   Conclusion

We have proposed a novel wavelet-based dual-branch network (WDNet) to remove moiré patterns. Working in the wavelet domain can restore more details and is more effective at moiré pattern removal than in the RGB domain. WDNet's dense branches and dilation branches are responsible for the acquisition of close-range and far range information, respectively. The new DPM module inside some dense branches can better perceive slanting moiré patterns. WDNet substantially outperforms other state-of-the-art models. Moreover, it obtains the best results in two other low-level vision tasks, deraining and deraindrop. In addition, we built a new urban-scene data set with challenging types of moiré patterns, which will be made publicly available. Our future work includes applications of WDNet on other vision tasks such as denoising and demosaicing.

References

1. Bao, L., Song, Y., Yang, Q., Yuan, H., Wang, G.: Tree filtering: efficient structure-preserving smoothing with a minimum spanning tree. TIP **23**, 555–569 (2013)
2. Bell, S., Lawrence Zitnick, C., Bala, K., Girshick, R.: Inside-outside net: detecting objects in context with skip pooling and recurrent neural networks. In: CVPR (2016)
3. Blau, Y., Michaeli, T.: The perception-distortion tradeoff. In: CVPR (2018)
4. Chang, Y., Yan, L., Zhong, S.: Transformed low-rank model for line pattern noise removal. In: ICCV (2017)
5. Eigen, D., Krishnan, D., Fergus, R.: Restoring an image taken through a window covered with dirt or rain. In: CVPR (2013)
6. Fu, J., et al.: Dual attention network for scene segmentation. In: CVPR (2019)
7. Fujieda, S., Takayama, K., Hachisuka, T.: Wavelet convolutional neural networks for texture classification. arXiv preprint arXiv:1707.07394 (2017)
8. Gao, F., Huang, T., Wang, J., Sun, J., Hussain, A., Yang, E.: Dual-branch deep convolution neural network for polarimetric SAR image classification. Appl. Sci. **7**, 447 (2017)
9. Gharbi, M., Chaurasia, G., Paris, S., Durand, F.: Deep joint demosaicking and denoising. TOG **35**, 1–12 (2016)
10. Gonzalez, R.C., Woods, R.E.: Digital Image Processing, 3rd edn. Prentice-Hall, Upper Saddle River (2007)
11. Gueguen, L., Sergeev, A., Kadlec, B., Liu, R., Yosinski, J.: Faster neural networks straight from JPEG. In: NeurIPS (2018)
12. Guo, T., Cherukuri, V., Monga, V.: Dense123'color enhancement dehazing network. In: CVPRW (2019)
13. Ham, B., Cho, M., Ponce, J.: Robust image filtering using joint static and dynamic guidance. In: CVPR (2015)
14. He, B., Wang, C., Shi, B., Duan, L.Y.: Mop moire patterns using MopNet. In: ICCV (2019)
15. He, K., Zhang, X., Ren, S., Sun, J.: Deep residual learning for image recognition. In: CVPR (2016)
16. Hu, X., Fu, C.W., Zhu, L., Heng, P.A.: Depth-attentional features for single-image rain removal. In: CVPR (2019)
17. Hu, X., Fu, C.W., Zhu, L., Qin, J., Heng, P.A.: Direction-aware spatial context features for shadow detection and removal. TPAMI (2019)
18. Huang, G., Liu, Z., Van Der Maaten, L., Weinberger, K.Q.: Densely connected convolutional networks. In: CVPR (2017)
19. Huang, H., He, R., Sun, Z., Tan, T.: Wavelet-SRNet: a wavelet-based CNN for multi-scale face super resolution. In: ICCV (2017)
20. Isobe, T., et al.: Video super-resolution with temporal group attention. In: CVPR (2020)
21. Isola, P., Zhu, J.Y., Zhou, T., Efros, A.A.: Image-to-image translation with conditional adversarial networks. In: CVPR (2017)
22. Jang, D.W., Park, R.H.: DenseNet with deep residual channel-attention blocks for single image super resolution. In: CVPRW (2019)
23. Johnson, J., Alahi, A., Fei-Fei, L.: Perceptual losses for real-time style transfer and super-resolution. In: Leibe, B., Matas, J., Sebe, N., Welling, M. (eds.) ECCV 2016. LNCS, vol. 9906, pp. 694–711. Springer, Cham (2016). https://doi.org/10.1007/978-3-319-46475-6_43

24. Karacan, L., Erdem, E., Erdem, A.: Structure-preserving image smoothing via region covariances. TOG **32**, 1–11 (2013)
25. Kim, T.H., Park, S.I.: Deep context-aware descreening and rescreening of halftone images. TOG **37**, 1–12 (2018)
26. Kingma, D.P., Ba, J.: Adam: a method for stochastic optimization. arXiv preprint arXiv:1412.6980 (2014)
27. Lefkimmiatis, S.: Universal denoising networks: a novel CNN architecture for image denoising. In: CVPR (2018)
28. Levinskis, A.: Convolutional neural network feature reduction using wavelet transform. Elektronika ir Elektrotechnika **19**, 61–64 (2013)
29. Li, Q., Shen, L., Guo, S., Lai, Z.: Wavelet integrated CNNs for noise-robust image classification. In: CVPR (2020)
30. Li, X., Wu, J., Lin, Z., Liu, H., Zha, H.: Recurrent squeeze-and-excitation context aggregation net for single image deraining. In: ECCV (2018)
31. Lin, H., Fu, X., Jing, C., Ding, X., Huang, Y.: A^2Net: Adjacent aggregation networks for image raindrop removal. arXiv preprint arXiv:1811.09780 (2018)
32. Liu, B., Shu, X., Wu, X.: Demoiréing of camera-captured screen images using deep convolutional neural network. arXiv preprint arXiv:1804.03809 (2018)
33. Liu, F., Yang, J., Yue, H.: Moiré pattern removal from texture images via low-rank and sparse matrix decomposition. In: VCIP (2015)
34. Liu, L., Jia, X., Liu, J., Tian, Q.: Joint demosaicing and denoising with self guidance. In: CVPR (2020)
35. Liu, P., Zhang, H., Zhang, K., Lin, L., Zuo, W.: Multi-level wavelet-CNN for image restoration. In: CVPRW (2018)
36. Liu, Y., Li, Q., Sun, Z.: Attribute-aware face aging with wavelet-based generative adversarial networks. In: CVPR (2019)
37. Luo, Y., Xu, Y., Ji, H.: Removing rain from a single image via discriminative sparse coding. In: ICCV (2015)
38. Oyallon, E., Belilovsky, E., Zagoruyko, S.: Scaling the scattering transform: deep hybrid networks. In: ICCV (2017)
39. Qian, R., Tan, R.T., Yang, W., Su, J., Liu, J.: Attentive generative adversarial network for raindrop removal from a single image. In: CVPR (2018)
40. Qin, J., Xie, Z., Shi, Y., Wen, W.: Difficulty-aware image super resolution via deep adaptive dual-network. In: ICME (2019)
41. Quan, Y., Deng, S., Chen, Y., Ji, H.: Deep learning for seeing through window with raindrops. In: ICCV (2019)
42. Ronneberger, O., Fischer, P., Brox, T.: U-Net: Convolutional networks for biomedical image segmentation. In: Navab, N., Hornegger, J., Wells, W.M., Frangi, A.F. (eds.) MICCAI 2015. LNCS, vol. 9351, pp. 234–241. Springer, Cham (2015). https://doi.org/10.1007/978-3-319-24574-4_28
43. Sasada, R., Yamada, M., Hara, S., Takeo, H., Shimura, K.: Stationary grid pattern removal using 2D technique for moiré-free radiographic image display. In: Medical Imaging (2003)
44. Shen, L., Yue, Z., Chen, Q., Feng, F., Ma, J.: Deep joint rain and haze removal from a single image. In: ICPR (2018)
45. Si, J., et al.: Dual attention matching network for context-aware feature sequence based person re-identification. In: CVPR (2018)
46. Siddiqui, H., Boutin, M., Bouman, C.A.: Hardware-friendly descreening. TIP **19**, 746–757 (2009)
47. Sidorov, D.N., Kokaram, A.C.: Removing moire from degraded video archives. In: ESPC (2002)

48. Sidorov, D.N., Kokaram, A.C.: Suppression of moiré patterns via spectral analysis. In: VCIP (2002)
49. Su, Z., Luo, X., Deng, Z., Liang, Y., Ji, Z.: Edge-preserving texture suppression filter based on joint filtering schemes. TMM **15**, 535–548 (2012)
50. Subr, K., Soler, C., Durand, F.: Edge-preserving multiscale image decomposition based on local extrema. TOG **28**, 1–9 (2009)
51. Sun, B., Li, S., Sun, J.: Scanned image descreening with image redundancy and adaptive filtering. TIP **23**, 3698–3710 (2014)
52. Sun, Y., Schaefer, S., Wang, W.: Image structure retrieval via l_0 minimization. TVCG **24**, 2129–2139 (2017)
53. Sun, Y., Yu, Y., Wang, W.: Moiré photo restoration using multiresolution convolutional neural networks. TIP **27**, 4160–4172 (2018)
54. Tai, Y., Yang, J., Liu, X., Xu, C.: MemNet: a persistent memory network for image restoration. In: ICCV (2017)
55. Wang, P., et al.: Understanding convolution for semantic segmentation. In: WACV (2018)
56. Wei, Z., Wang, J., Nichol, H., Wiebe, S., Chapman, D.: A median-Gaussian filtering framework for Moiré pattern noise removal from X-ray microscopy image. Micron **43**, 170–176 (2012)
57. Williams, T., Li, R.: Wavelet pooling for convolutional neural networks. In: ICLR (2018)
58. Xu, L., Lu, C., Xu, Y., Jia, J.: Image smoothing via L0 gradient minimization. TOG **30**, 11 (2011)
59. Xu, L., Yan, Q., Xia, Y., Jia, J.: Structure extraction from texture via relative total variation. TOG **31**, 1–10 (2012)
60. Xu, X., et al.: Rendering portraitures from monocular camera and beyond. In: ECCV (2018)
61. Yang, J., Liu, F., Yue, H., Fu, X., Hou, C., Wu, F.: Textured image demoiréing via signal decomposition and guided filtering. TIP **26**, 3528–3541 (2017)
62. Yang, W., Tan, R.T., Feng, J., Liu, J., Guo, Z., Yan, S.: Deep joint rain detection and removal from a single image. In: CVPR (2017)
63. Yoo, J., Uh, Y., Chun, S., Kang, B., Ha, J.W.: Photorealistic style transfer via wavelet transforms. In: CVPR (2019)
64. Yuan, S., Timofte, R., Leonardis, A., Slabaugh, G.: NTIRE 2020 challenge on image demoireing: methods and results. In: CVPRW (2020)
65. Yuan, S., Timofte, R., Slabaugh, G., Leonardis, A.: AIM 2019 challenge on image demoireing: dataset and study. In: ICCVW (2019)
66. Yuan, S., et al.: AIM 2019 challenge on image demoireing: methods and results. In: ICCVW (2019)
67. Zhang, K., Zuo, W., Chen, Y., Meng, D., Zhang, L.: Beyond a Gaussian denoiser: residual learning of deep CNN for image denoising. TIP **26**, 3142–3155 (2017)
68. Zhang, Q., Shen, X., Xu, L., Jia, J.: Rolling guidance filter. In: Fleet, D., Pajdla, T., Schiele, B., Tuytelaars, T. (eds.) ECCV 2014. LNCS, vol. 8691, pp. 815–830. Springer, Cham (2014). https://doi.org/10.1007/978-3-319-10578-9_53
69. Zhang, Y., Tian, Y., Kong, Y., Zhong, B., Fu, Y.: Residual dense network for image super-resolution. In: CVPR (2018)
70. Zheng, B., Yuan, S., Slabaugh, G., Leonardis, A.: Image demoireing with learnable bandpass filters. In: CVPR (2020)

Low Light Video Enhancement Using Synthetic Data Produced with an Intermediate Domain Mapping

Danai Triantafyllidou$^{(\boxtimes)}$, Sean Moran, Steven McDonagh, Sarah Parisot, and Gregory Slabaugh

Huawei Noah's Ark Lab, London, UK
danaitri22@gmail.com, sean.j.moran@gmail.com,
{steven.mcdonagh,sarah.parisot,gregory.slabaugh}@huawei.com

Abstract. Advances in low-light video RAW-to-RGB translation are opening up the possibility of fast low-light imaging on commodity devices (*e.g.* smartphone cameras) without the need for a tripod. However, it is challenging to collect the required paired short-long exposure frames to learn a supervised mapping. Current approaches require a specialised rig or the use of *static* videos with no subject or object motion, resulting in datasets that are limited in size, diversity, and motion. We address the data collection bottleneck for low-light video RAW-to-RGB by proposing a data synthesis mechanism, dubbed *SIDGAN*, that can generate abundant dynamic video training pairs. SIDGAN maps videos found 'in the wild' (*e.g.* internet videos) into a low-light (short, long exposure) domain. By generating dynamic video data synthetically, we enable a recently proposed state-of-the-art RAW-to-RGB model to attain higher image quality (improved colour, reduced artifacts) and improved temporal consistency, compared to the same model trained with only static real video data.

1 Introduction

Low-light imaging (less than 5 lux) is a challenging scenario for camera image signal processor (ISP) pipelines due to the low photon count, low signal-to-noise ratio (SNR) and profound colour distortion [6]. The ISP is responsible for forming a high-quality RGB image with minimal noise, pleasing colors, sharp detail, and good contrast from the originally captured RAW data. Recently there has been growing research interest in end-to-end deep neural network architectures for modelling the entire ISP pipeline, both in well-lit [40] and low-light scenarios [6].

A major bottleneck in the learning of deep models for end-to-end RAW-to-RGB mapping is the availability of data. Existing models require a large amount of manually collected paired data (RAW sensor data and its corresponding RGB image) for training. However, collecting suitable amounts of paired data is often time consuming, error prone (*e.g.* misaligned pairs), and expensive. Chen *et al.* [5]

Electronic supplementary material The online version of this chapter (https://doi.org/10.1007/978-3-030-58601-0_7) contains supplementary material, which is available to authorized users.

A. Vedaldi et al. (Eds.): ECCV 2020, LNCS 12358, pp. 103–119, 2020.
https://doi.org/10.1007/978-3-030-58601-0_7

Ground Truth   SID motion   Ours (SIDGAN)

Fig. 1. Comparing the image quality with SID motion [20]. Training with synthetic data provides a more capable colour reproduction

resort to using a tripod to collect static videos for training. In [20] a novel optical system is designed to obtain dark and bright paired frames of the same scene simultaneously, but this rig is not publicly available, requires expertise to operate and only works if the scene is adequately illuminated. These challenges result in datasets that are limited in size, diversity in scene type, content and motion. This in turn typically produces models offering only limited colour reproduction and temporal consistency on real dynamic video (Fig. 1 and Sect. 4). In this paper, we address the training data bottleneck for learning the RAW-to-RGB mapping, with a specific focus on low-light dynamic synthetic video data generation. Low-light video enhancement provides an ideal testbed for studying the potential of synthetic data as it is highly challenging to manually collect such data. In contrast to pre-existing work, we propose **S**eeing **I**n the **D**ark **GAN** (SIDGAN), a synthetic low-light video data generation pipeline leveraging Generative Adversarial Networks (GANs) [14].

GANs have proved to be a powerful modelling paradigm for learning complex high dimensional data manifolds for many types of real-world data such as natural images. The data distribution is modelled by framing learning as a competition between a generator network and a discriminator network. The generator attempts to produce samples from the desired data distribution that are as realistic as possible such that the discriminator network is fooled into classifying the synthetic samples as being real. The ensuing minimax game between the two networks can lead to a generator network that produces realistic samples from the data manifold. SIDGAN builds on the CycleGAN work of Zhu *et al.* [50] who demonstrate how to learn an unpaired mapping between two disparate domains (*e.g.* two sets of images with different styles). However, different to their work, we extend the mapping to three domains using a pair of CycleGANs while leveraging a weak supervisory signal in the form of an *intermediate* domain that has a paired data relationship with one of the remaining two domains. We argue that for an effective mapping between two domains that are very distant (*e.g.* internet videos and short exposure frames from a completely different sensor), that it is best to leverage an intermediate domain. Our approach is illustrated in Fig. 2.

Our main contributions are three-fold:

- **Semi-supervised dual CycleGAN with intermediate domain mapping**: Mapping directly from internet videos (Fig. 2, domain A) to short exposure (domain C) is difficult due to the large domain gap and lack of paired training examples. Instead, we bridge the gap using an intermediate long exposure domain (domain B) for which we have paired data (between domains B and C). This decomposes a difficult problem into two simpler problems, the latter with supervision.
- **Data abundance for RAW-to-RGB video**: The Dual CycleGAN allows synthesis of abundant video data in order to train high capacity models with, typically unavailable, dynamic and domain specific paired training data.
- **A practical strategy to combine synthetic and real data**: We propose an effective three-step training and fine-tuning scheme to address the remaining domain gap between synthetically generated and real video data. Combining our dynamic synthetic data with static real data yields a forward RAW-to-RGB video model with superior temporal consistency and colour reproduction compared to the same model trained with only real data.

2   Related Work

Low-light image and video quality enhancement topics are closely related to our contributions. In addition to these areas, we briefly review intermediate domain mappings, synthetic image generation and learning with unpaired data.

Low-Light Image Enhancement. A large body of work exists on low-light image enhancement, spanning histogram equalization (HE) techniques [3,17,34] and approaches grounded in Retinex theory [21,22,25,49]. Classical enhancement methods often make use of statistical techniques that typically rely on strong modeling assumptions, which may not hold true in real world scenes or scenarios. Deep learning techniques have also been readily applied to low-light image enhancement in recent years. The work of LLNet [28] employed an autoencoder towards low-light image denoising. Further convolutional works have used multiscale feature maps [45] and brightness transmission image priors [44] to enhance image contrast with strong qualitative results *c.f.* classical approaches.

Low-Light Video Enhancement. The video enhancement problem is more recent and has received comparatively less attention. Analogous to static images, statistical Retinex theory has also been applied to video [27,47]. Framing the problem in a joint-task setting was investigated by [23]; coupling low-light enhancement with denoising. Network based learning is also considered for video; Lv *et al.* [30] propose a multi-branch low-light enhancement network, applicable to both image and video domains. As earlier highlighted, learning-based mapping of (low-light) RAW-to-RGB work is highly relevant for our direction; Chen *et al.* [5,6] learn this transformation considering both images and, latterly, video.

Capture of real video data in this problem setting is prohibitively expensive. However, as noted, systems have been proposed that can capture both bright and dark videos of identical scene content, providing training pairs for low-light video models. Jiang *et al.* [20] collected data and employed a standard CNN to learn enhancement mappings for the transformation from low-light raw camera sensor data to bright RGB videos. Collected data was relatively small by deep learning standards (179 video pairs), illustrating the arduous burden of real-world video collection in scenarios that involve complex capture setups and custom hardware (here beam splitters and relay lenses). Uncommon specialist hardware, operator expertise requirements and support for (only) adequately illuminated scenes can be considered the main disadvantages of video enhancement work that depends exclusively on real-world data.

Intermediate Domain Mappings. The concept of harnessing intermediate domain bridges can be considered powerful and related strategies have been employed in a number of scenarios [8,13,15,26,43]. In addition to visual domains, evidence in support of the broader applicability of this family of strategies is also found in machine translation tasks [10], where intermediate domains enabled extension of bilingual systems to become multilingual. Relevant synthetic data work [7], that we draw from, leverages chains of image mappings ("indirect-paths") to gain a supervisory signal towards improving super-resolution. Combining intermediate domain mappings with synthetic data offers a promising direction for problem domains where acquisition of paired imagery, and therefore direct supervisory signal, is challenging.

Synthetic Data Augmentation. The use of synthetic data for model training and testing can be considered popular and datasets have been created for a multitude of image processing and computer vision problems [9,11,32,37]. Early work performed successful scene text recognition with simplistic data generation [19] and, more recently, the benefits of combining synthetic data with Generative Adversarial Networks (GANs) [14] have been actively explored.

The work of [51] explores GAN data augmentation, generating artificial images using conditional Generative Adversarial Networks (cGANs). By conditioning on segmentation masks, realistic images were generated for their task (leaf segmentation), and related performance improved by $\sim$16% *c.f.* without synthetic augmentation. In [12] a semi-supervised adversarial framework is used to generate photorealistic facial images. By introducing pairwise adversarial supervision, two-way domain adaptation is constrained using only small paired real (and synthetic) images along with a large volume of unpaired data. Performance improves, due to the synthetic imagery, and consistently betters that of a face recognition network trained with Oxford VGG Face data. In [46] both paired and unpaired training data is utilised simultaneously in conjunction with generative models. Two generators and four discriminators are employed in a hybrid setting and qualitatively strong results, on multiple image-to-image translation tasks, are reported. Mixed and fully unsupervised approaches [29] begin to show great promise in faithfully generalising to real-world image distributions that are naturally sample-scarce or where data is otherwise hard to collect. These results motivate the use of inexpensive synthetic data for training GAN based tools. The need to collect large amounts of hand-annotated real-world data is avoided yet performance can surpass that of training with real-data exclusively.

In contrast to these successes, recent work [36] reports interesting findings when employing generative models (*e.g.* BigGAN), for data augmentation. Image classification error performance (Top-1 and Top-5) improves only marginally when additional synthetic data is added to an ImageNet training set. As GAN tools begin to be employed to aid downstream tasks, metrics that appropriately measure *downstream task performance* must be utilised *c.f.* solely evaluating synthetic sample image quality. Towards this our current work considers quantitative downstream performance evaluation, providing evidence towards the efficacy of our proposed data generation strategy (Sect. 4).

3   Learning the Low-Light Video RAW-to-RGB Mapping

Our objective is to learn short-to-long exposure mappings that provide accurate colour reproduction and temporal consistency. Given the lack of available real short, long exposure video pairs we propose a two-step approach that leverages *data synthesis*. The first step (Sect. 3.1), involves training a dual CycleGAN model for the purposes of data synthesis. The dual CycleGAN maps video frames to a domain characterised by short exposure images. A domain bridge (*e.g.* long exposure images) is used to regularise the mapping with available paired supervision. The trained CycleGAN permits videos 'from the wild' to be projected into the long and then short exposure domains, thereby generating the necessary paired supervision. Our second step, detailed in Sect. 3.2, utilises this synthetic data to train a forward model capable of mapping low-light video RAW to long exposure RGB. Finally, Sect. 3.3 provides details on synthetic data generation network architectures.

3.1   Synthetic Data Generation Using an Intermediate Domain

SIDGAN is modelled as a set of two CycleGANs in a dual configuration that learns the domain distributions for three domains; A, B and C. The model architecture is shown in Fig. 2 and our domain B-C CycleGAN is shown in more detail in Fig. 4. Domain A is characterised by a set of video frames defined by probability distribution p_A. The set of N videos from this domain $\{V_i\}_{i=1}^{N} \sim p_A$ are available for training. Similarly, we also consider M long exposure still images $\{L_i\}_{i=1}^{M} \sim p_B$ (domain B) and T short exposure still images $\{S_i\}_{i=1}^{T} \sim p_C$ (domain C). The remainder of this section details how the sample sets are leveraged in order to learn a mapping from domain A to domain C via bridge domain B.

The A-B CycleGAN learns, in a conditional GAN fashion, an *unpaired* mapping between domains A and B, transforming a set of RGB videos to a domain characterised by a set of RGB images (*i.e.* long exposure images) using generators G_{AB} and G_{BA}. This unsupervised CycleGAN does not require explicit sample pairings. Discriminator D_A attempts to distinguish generated video frames $\hat{V}=G_{BA}(L)$, $L \sim p_B$ from real video frames drawn from the input distribution $V \sim p_A$ in Domain A (Eq. 1). Discriminator D_B tries to differentiate synthetic

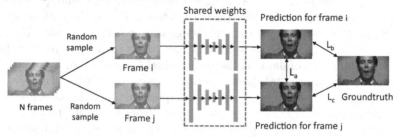

Fig. 2. Step 1: We use SIDGAN generators (G_{AB}, G_{BC}) to map Vimeo videos (domain A) into the long (domain B), then short (domain C) exposure domains, giving our synthetic training dataset. **Step 2:** The forward model can be very different from the generators of SIDGAN *e.g.* leveraging a mechanism for exploiting the temporal domain in the synthetic video data

long exposure still images $\hat{L} = G_{AB}(V)$, $V \sim p_A$ from real long exposure images $L \sim p_B$, drawn from Domain B (Eq. 2).

$$\mathcal{L}_{GAN}(G_{BA}, D_A) = \mathbb{E}_{L \sim p_B}[\log(1 - \log(D_A(G_{BA}(L))))] + \mathbb{E}_{V \sim p_A}[\log(D_A(V))] \tag{1}$$

$$\mathcal{L}_{GAN}(G_{AB}, D_B) = \mathbb{E}_{V \sim p_A}[\log(1 - \log(D_B(G_{AB}(V))))] + \mathbb{E}_{L \sim p_B}[\log(D_B(L))] \tag{2}$$

We regularise the mappings between domains such that G_{AB}, G_{BA} are approximate inverses of one another by employing a cycle consistency loss [50] (Eq. 3) (Fig. 3):

$$\mathcal{L}_{cyc}(G_{AB}, G_{BA}) = \mathbb{E}_{L \sim p_B}\|[G_{AB}(G_{BA}(L)) - L]\|_1 \tag{3}$$
$$+ \mathbb{E}_{V \sim p_A}\|[G_{BA}(G_{AB}(V)) - V]\|_1.$$

Domain A   Domain B   Domain C

Fig. 3. Generating synthetic long and short exposure frame pairs in two steps: **Step 1:** Project videos from domain A to our sensor-specific long exposure domain B using generator G_{AB}. **Step 2:** Project the translated image from step 1 to the sensor-specific short exposure domain C using generator G_{BC}

Following [42,50], we find it also important to add an identity loss $\mathcal{L}_{identity}$ in order to prevent colour inversion:

$$\mathcal{L}_{identity}(G_{AB}, G_{BA}) = \mathbb{E}_{V \sim p_A} \|[G_{BA}(V) - V]\|_1 + \mathbb{E}_{L \sim p_B} \|[G_{AB}(L) - L]\|_1. \quad (4)$$

Our final loss combines the introduced individual loss terms as a weighted combination, with individual components weighted by hyperparameters λ_1, λ_2 (Eq. 5):

$$\mathcal{L}(G_{AB}, G_{BA}, D_A, D_B) = \mathcal{L}_{GAN}(G_{BA}, D_A) + \mathcal{L}_{GAN}(G_{AB}, D_B) \quad (5)$$
$$+ \lambda_1 \mathcal{L}_{cyc}(G_{AB}, G_{BA}) + \lambda_2 \mathcal{L}_{identity}(G_{AB}, G_{BA}).$$

In contrast to the domain A-B mapping, the B-C CycleGAN is *paired* (supervised) and employs generators G_{BC} and G_{CB}. This component of our dual CycleGAN model is responsible for mapping long exposure RGB images to short exposure counterparts. This domain mapping is paired as, in contrast to dynamic video, it is easier to collect short-long exposure pairs for still images by using a tripod and varying camera exposure time. SIDGAN leverages this supervision, using intermediate domain B, with the aim of enhancing the quality of the target task; mapping dynamic videos (domain A) to short exposure (domain C). The B-C CycleGAN component employs a loss (Eq. 6), analogous to that of the domain A-B mapping, and additionally incorporates a $\mathcal{L}_{sup}$ term (Eq. 7), harnessing the supervisory signal that is available.

$$\mathcal{L}(G_{BC}, G_{CB}, D_B, D_C) = \mathcal{L}_{GAN}(G_{CB}, D_B) + \mathcal{L}_{GAN}(G_{BC}, D_C) \quad (6)$$
$$+ \lambda_1 \mathcal{L}_{cyc}(G_{BC}, G_{CB}) + \lambda_2 \mathcal{L}_{sup}(G_{BC}, G_{CB})$$

Given a set of M short-long exposure pairs $\{(S_i, L_i)\}_{i=1}^M$, the supervised term $\mathcal{L}_{sup}(G_{BC}, G_{CB})$ is defined as:

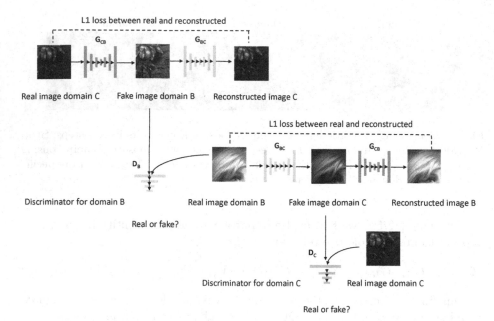

Fig. 4. Visualisation of our Domain B-C CycleGAN, a sub-component of the complete dual CycleGAN architecture found in Fig. 2

$$\mathcal{L}_{sup}(G_{BC}, G_{CB}) = \mathbb{E}_{L \sim p_B} \|[G_{BC}(L) - S]\|_1 + \mathbb{E}_{S \sim p_C} \|[G_{CB}(S) - L]\|_1. \quad (7)$$

Our experimental evaluation (Sect. 4), demonstrates that a significant boost in translation quality is achieved when leveraging intermediate domain B to aid the weakly supervised CycleGAN mapping.

3.2   Training Low-Light RAW-to-RGB Forward Models

Our forward model training, fine-tuning schemes leverage a mixture of real and synthetic video data to learn a short-to-long exposure video mapping. We aim to extract an understanding of the correct colour and luminance distribution from real data (static video) while learning temporal consistency from the synthetic data (dynamic video). Our approach is shown in Fig. 2. In the first step, synthetic data is generated by taking internet videos and passing them through generators G_{AB} and G_{BC}; using the process described previously (Sect. 3.1). In the second, step this synthetic video data is mixed with real data to train the forward model, adhering to the following three training and fine tuning steps:

1. **Training**: Train a forward model solely on real static video data
2. **Fine Tuning a**: Fine tune solely on synthetic dynamic video data
3. **Fine Tuning b**: Fine tune on real static video data

Our following experimental work (Sect. 4), employs a RAW-to-RGB forward model that follows the architecture of the SID motion model [5], reproduced in Fig. 2. However, we note that our previously introduced synthetic data generation process is agnostic to specific model architectures. The model samples two frames from a static video and has three L_1 loss terms acting on the VGG features [41] of the two predicted frames ($\mathcal{L}_a$) and the two predicted frames and the groundtruth long exposure frame ($\mathcal{L}_b$, $\mathcal{L}_c$). As the training data is a static video there is no object and subject motion between frames, with noise being the only differentiator. We comment that while using our generator G_{CB} to model the short-to-long exposure mapping would also be possible, we instead leverage a temporal consistency term in the forward model to exploit the temporal dimension of the synthetic video generated using the dual CycleGAN (Sect. 3.1).

3.3 GAN Architectures for Data Generation

Generators G_{AB}, G_{BA}, G_{BC}, G_{CB} are modelled on the popular U-Net architecture [38]. In comparison to alternatives *e.g.* ResNet, we corroborate previous work [6] and find that the encoder-decoder architecture of the U-Net to be amenable to high-quality image translation. Nevertheless, we modify the components of the U-Net to further increase the quality of the produced images. Our final generators are comprised of 5 convolutional blocks with a stride of 1 followed by 2×2 max pooling layers. Upsampling is performed using a nearest neighbour bilinear interpolation followed by a 1×1 convolution, which we found important to reduce the prevalence of checkerboard (upsampling) artifacts.

The discriminators D_A, D_B, D_C are all PatchGAN discriminators [18] which attempt to penalize structure at the scale of patches by classifying them as real or fake. The discriminators ingest 192×192 patches which correspond to a receptive field that covers 75% of the input image. Finally, we note that CycleGANs in our dual CycleGAN setup are optimised independently. Joint training is theoretically possible but poses a more difficult optimisation problem and exhausted our available GPU memory in practice.

4   Experimental Results

4.1   Datasets and Implementation Details

We employed the Vimeo-90K dataset [48] to translate real-world videos into our low-light sensor specific domain. The dataset has $91,701$ septuplet samples, each containing 7 video frames of resolution 448×255. For the sensor-specific long and short exposure domains (*i.e.* domains B and C), we use the Dark Raw Video (DRV) dataset [5], which contains 224 low-light raw video data and corresponding long-exposure images. Our intermediate domain B is represented by the long exposure DRV RGB images while for domain C we use the provided preprocessed DRV short exposure RAW video frames.

(KID 5.06)   (KID 4.78)   (KID 4.68)   (KID 3.99)

Fig. 5. Evolution of the KID distance during the unpaired training of CycleGAN$_{AB}$. The KID distance correlates well with visual quality and is used for model selection

Data is pre-processed using the pipeline of Chen *et al.* [5] which involves RAW-to-RGB conversion by averaging green pixels in each two-by-two block, black level subtraction, 2×2 binning, and global digital gain. Furthermore, noise is reduced using VBM4D [31] and pixel values are linearly scaled using exposure value (EV) difference. We resize the DRV long and short exposure RGB images such that resolution matches that of Vimeo-90K and normalize images in $[-1, 1]$. Experimentally we find that training on large patches is crucial in order to capture the global statistics and learn the correct white balance. For this reason, both CycleGAN$_{AB}$ and CycleGAN$_{BC}$ are trained using 256×256 crops corresponding to 50% of the resized DRV frames. We randomly select 400 Vimeo-90K videos and train our Dual CycleGAN, retaining the original train/val/test partitions of the DRV dataset. Finally, our forward RAW-to-RGB model is trained using the train partition of the DRV dataset and 9, 366 synthetic videos.

Models are implemented using Tensorflow and Keras [1, 2] and trained using an NVidia Tesla V100 GPU with 32 GB memory. Our CycleGAN models are trained initially for 50 epochs with a learning rate 10^{-4} which then linearly decays for a further 20 epochs. Hyperparameters λ_1, λ_2 are found by empirical search and set to values 6.0, 6.0 in Eq. 5, and values 10.0, 10.0 in Eq. 6, respectively. The batch size is set to 1 and our forward model is trained using the training scheme described in Sect. 3.2 for a total of 1000 epochs. We employ a learning rate of 10^{-4} for the initial 500 epochs and reduce this to 10^{-5} for the latter half of training.

4.2   Synthetic Data Quality Evaluation

We distinguish between the unpaired task that pertains to CycleGAN$_{AB}$ and the paired RGB-to-RAW mapping of CycleGAN$_{BC}$. Since CycleGAN$_{AB}$ is responsible for mapping videos from any source to our sensor-specific domain, no ground truth information is available for this task. In order to numerically evaluate generators G_{AB} and G_{BA} we adopt the following metrics: Fréchet Inception Distance (FID) [16] and Kernel Inception distance (KID) [4]. For CycleGAN$_{BC}$, we use the available ground truth; long and short exposure pairs of the test partition (DRV dataset) and evaluate performance using standard metrics; Peak Signal-to-Noise Ratio (PSNR), Structural Similarity (SSIM) (Fig. 6).

Ground Truth   Unsup. (PSNR 24.0)   Semi-sup. (PSNR 27.2)

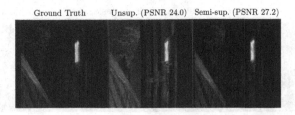

Fig. 6. Comparing CycleGAN with the proposed semi-supervised CycleGAN. Our semi-supervised variant shows better translation performance by exploiting the ground truth information in the optimization objective

We observe experimentally that the KID correlates better than FID with the visual quality of the generated samples (see Fig. 5) and we base final selection of models G_{BA} and G_{AB} solely on KID score. Our generator G_{BC}, responsible for mapping long exposure (domain B) to short exposure (domain C), achieves 27.28 dB PSNR and 0.88 SSIM and G_{CB} performance is 25.28 dB and 0.74, respectively. Quantitative results allude to the fact that long exposure captures more photons and images better represent scene colors and contrast. Intuitively the problem can be regarded as more ill-posed when mapping in the short to long direction. We also observe by ablation that training without the supervised term (Eq. 7) resulted in significantly lower performance ($\sim$4 dB less), providing evidence in support of our choice to decompose the data synthesis task into two separate learning problems and exploit the available paired data via the intermediate domain mapping. Figure 7 provides example predictions for generators G_{CB} and G_{BC}. We compare our trained RAW-to-RGB forward model against state-of-the-art approaches for low-light image and video processing. Following [20], we evaluate the performance on the static videos of the DRV dataset and examine both the image quality and the temporal stability of our method.

4.3   Output Image and Video Quality Evaluation

Image Quality: For consistent comparison with previous work [5], we compare the fifth frame of our output video with the respective long exposure ground truth image and evaluate the performance in terms of average PSNR and SSIM over the 49 DRV test videos. We compare performance with recent methods SID [6] and SID motion [5] as well as common baselines that combine performant denoising algorithms (VBM4D [31], KPN [33]) with traditional non-learning based enhancement tools (here using Rawpy[1]). Results are summarised in Table 1. Baselines are observed to perform poorly for this challenging task. Our forward model, trained purely on synthetic data, achieves a PSNR of 21.53 dB and SSIM of 0.70. We attribute this fairly weak performance to a well understood domain shift between synthetic and real data [35,39]. However, we observe

---

[1] https://pypi.org/project/rawpy/.

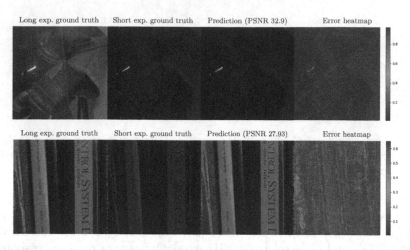

Fig. 7. First row: Mapping from domain B (long exposure) to domain C (short exposure) using generator G_{BC}. Second row: Mapping from domain C (short exposure) to domain B (long exposure) using generator G_{CB}

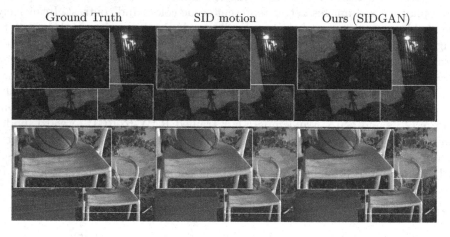

Fig. 8. Comparing the image quality with SID motion [5]. Note the improved colours in the marked regions (Color figure online)

that training the model by adding a small fraction of real data (with a real : synthetic data ratio of 1 : 45) successfully diminishes this domain gap yielding 28.94 dB PSNR and 0.83 SSIM, constituting state-of-the-art performance on the DRV dataset (Fig. 8).

Temporal Consistency: The DRV dataset contains static raw videos, thus temporal stability can be measured by computing temporal PSNR (TPSNR) and temporal SSIM (TSSIM) between pairs of consecutive frames, in similar fashion to [6]. Results are presented in Table 2. Our model offers competitive results when evaluated under these temporal metrics and we attribute strong performance to the extra information provided by our dynamic video synthetic

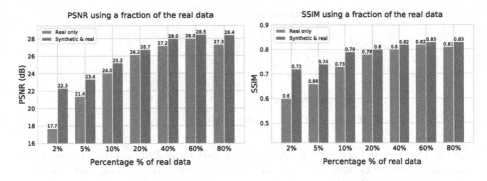

Fig. 9. The effect of real : synthetic training data ratios using portions of the DRV dataset. Left: PSNR, right: SSIM

Table 1. Output image quality on the DRV static dataset

Model	PSNR↑	SSIM↑
Input+Rawpy	12.94	0.165
VBM4D+Rawpy	14.77	0.315
KPN+Rawpy	18.81	0.540
SID w/o VBM4D	27.32	0.799
SID	27.69	0.803
SID Motion (real only)	28.26	0.815
SIDGAN (synthetic only)	21.53	0.704
SIDGAN (synthetic + real)	**28.94**	**0.830**

data. We further evaluate dynamic video temporal stability by introducing synthetic training data, in a varying ratio with (scarce) real data. Average temporal warping error [24] is reported in Table 3. Largest improvements are observed when available real data is scarcest.

4.4 Real Training Data Quantity and Ratios

The addition of real image data was shown to help close synthetic training distribution domain gaps, resulting in quantitative improvements (Sect. 4.3). We further investigate the effect of adding real image data quantities in relation to synthetic data. Subsets of the DRV real dataset comprising 2%, 5%, 10%, 20% 40%, 60% and 80% are randomly sampled and model performance is evaluated when training solely on these real data subsets. We additionally train models on a set of 9, 366 synthetic videos, generated by SIDGAN, and then fine-tune with the aforementioned real data subsets accordingly. All models are trained for 1000 epochs using identical hyperparameters. PSNR and SSIM performance is reported in Fig. 9. We observe that the addition of our synthetic data significantly boosts performance; increasing PSNR from 17.70 to 22.32, from 21.35 to 23.35

Table 2. Output video quality on the DRV static dataset

Model	TPSNR↑	TSSIM↑
SID [9] w/o VBM4D	33.72	0.939
SID	37.05	0.961
SID Motion (real only)	38.31	**0.974**
SIDGAN (synthetic + real)	**39.34**	0.966

Table 3. Dynamic video quality evaluation with varying real data ratios. Training the same model using increasing fractions of real data only (SID motion) and real data and synthetic data (SIDGAN).

Model	$E_{warp} \times 10^{-5}$ ↓
SID Motion (2% real DRV data)	55.9
SID Motion (5% real DRV data)	54.3
SID Motion (20% real DRV data)	35.6
SID Motion (100% real DRV data)	29.3
SIDGAN (2% real DRV data + synthetic)	31.2
SIDGAN (5% real DRV data + synthetic)	32.7
SIDGAN (20% real DRV data + synthetic)	32.2
SIDGAN (100% real DRV data + synthetic)	**28.2**

and from 24.04 to 25.19 for the cases of 2%, 5% and 10%, respectively. As the fraction of real data is increased, the gap in performance reduces indicating that the addition of our synthetic data again offers largest benefit in scenarios where real data is scarce.

5   Conclusions

We introduce **S**eeing **I**n the **D**ark **GAN** (SIDGAN), a data synthesis method addressing the training data bottleneck encountered when learning models for RAW-to-RGB problems. SIDGAN comprises two CycleGANs in order to leverage an intermediate domain mapping. Tasks that involve mapping between domains containing disparate appearance yet also lacking paired samples, can benefit from *intermediate domain* mappings that possess a paired data relationship with one of the original domains. We show that this strategy is capable of increasing the strength of the training signal and results in significant improvements for the investigated low-light RAW-to-RGB problem. Such tools may be widely applicable for domain mapping instances where data collection of directly paired samples between the domains of interest proves difficult or impossible.

References

1. Keras: deep learning for humans. https://github.com/keras-team/keras
2. Abadi, M., et al.: TensorFlow: large-scale machine learning on heterogeneous distributed systems. CoRR abs/1603.04467 arXiv:1603.04467 (2016)
3. Arici, T., Dikbas, S., Altunbasak, Y.: A histogram modification framework and its application for image contrast enhancement. IEEE Trans. Image Process. **18**(9), 1921–1935 (2009)
4. Borji, A.: Pros and cons of GAN evaluation measures. CoRR abs/1802.03446 arXiv:1802.03446 (2018)
5. Chen, C., Chen, Q., Do, M.N., Koltun, V.: Seeing motion in the dark. In: The IEEE International Conference on Computer Vision (ICCV), October 2019
6. Chen, C., Chen, Q., Xu, J., Koltun, V.: Learning to see in the dark. In: Proceedings of the IEEE Conference on Computer Vision and Pattern Recognition, pp. 3291–3300 (2018)
7. Chen, S., et al.: Unsupervised image super-resolution with an indirect supervised path. In: Proceedings of the IEEE/CVF Conference on Computer Vision and Pattern Recognition (CVPR) Workshops, June 2020
8. Cui, Z., Li, W., Xu, D., Shan, S., Chen, X., Li, X.: Flowing on Riemannian manifold: domain adaptation by shifting covariance. IEEE Trans. Cybern. **44**(12), 2264–2273 (2014)
9. Dosovitskiy, A., et al.: FlowNet: learning optical flow with convolutional networks. In: Proceedings of the IEEE International Conference on Computer Vision, pp. 2758–2766 (2015)
10. Escolano, C., Costa-jussà, M.R., Fonollosa, J.A.R.: Towards interlingua neural machine translation. CoRR abs/1905.06831 arXiv:1905.06831 (2019)
11. Gaidon, A., Wang, Q., Cabon, Y., Vig, E.: Virtual worlds as proxy for multi-object tracking analysis. In: Proceedings of the IEEE Conference on Computer Vision and Pattern Recognition, pp. 4340–4349 (2016)
12. Gecer, B., Bhattarai, B., Kittler, J., Kim, T.K.: Semi-supervised adversarial learning to generate photorealistic face images of new identities from 3D morphable model. In: Proceedings of the European Conference on Computer Vision (ECCV), pp. 217–234 (2018)
13. Gong, R., Li, W., Chen, Y., Gool, L.V.: DLOW: Domain flow for adaptation and generalization. In: Proceedings of the IEEE/CVF Conference on Computer Vision and Pattern Recognition (CVPR), June 2019
14. Goodfellow, I., et al.: Generative adversarial nets. In: Ghahramani, Z., Welling, M., Cortes, C., Lawrence, N.D., Weinberger, K.Q. (eds.) Advances in Neural Information Processing Systems 27, pp. 2672–2680. Curran Associates, Inc. (2014). http://papers.nips.cc/paper/5423-generative-adversarial-nets.pdf
15. Gopalan, R., Li, R., Chellappa, R.: Domain adaptation for object recognition: an unsupervised approach. In: 2011 International Conference on Computer Vision, pp. 999–1006. IEEE (2011)
16. Heusel, M., Ramsauer, H., Unterthiner, T., Nessler, B., Klambauer, G., Hochreiter, S.: GANs trained by a two time-scale update rule converge to a Nash equilibrium. CoRR abs/1706.08500 arXiv:1706.08500 (2017)
17. Ibrahim, H., Kong, N.S.P.: Brightness preserving dynamic histogram equalization for image contrast enhancement. IEEE Trans. Consum. Electron. **53**(4), 1752–1758 (2007)

18. Isola, P., Zhu, J.Y., Zhou, T., Efros, A.A.: Image-to-image translation with conditional adversarial networks. arxiv (2016)
19. Jaderberg, M., Simonyan, K., Vedaldi, A., Zisserman, A.: Synthetic data and artificial neural networks for natural scene text recognition. In: Workshop on Deep Learning, NIPS (2014)
20. Jiang, H., Zheng, Y.: Learning to see moving objects in the dark. In: The IEEE International Conference on Computer Vision (ICCV), October 2019
21. Jobson, D.J., Rahman, Z.U., Woodell, G.A.: A multiscale retinex for bridging the gap between color images and the human observation of scenes. IEEE Trans. Image Process. **6**(7), 965–976 (1997)
22. Jobson, D.J., Rahman, Z.U., Woodell, G.A.: Properties and performance of a center/surround retinex. IEEE Trans. Image Process. **6**(3), 451–462 (1997)
23. Kim, M., Park, D., Han, D.K., Ko, H.: A novel approach for denoising and enhancement of extremely low-light video. IEEE Trans. Consum. Electron. **61**(1), 72–80 (2015)
24. Lai, W.S., Huang, J.B., Wang, O., Shechtman, E., Yumer, E., Yang, M.H.: Learning blind video temporal consistency. In: European Conference on Computer Vision (2018)
25. Land, E.H.: The retinex theory of color vision. Sci. Am. **237**(6), 108–129 (1977)
26. Li, Y., Peng, X.: Learning domain adaptive features with unlabeled domain bridges. arXiv preprint arXiv:1912.05004 (2019)
27. Liu, H., Sun, X., Han, H., Cao, W.: Low-light video image enhancement based on multiscale retinex-like algorithm. In: 2016 Chinese Control and Decision Conference (CCDC), pp. 3712–3715. IEEE (2016)
28. Lore, K.G., Akintayo, A., Sarkar, S.: LLNet: a deep autoencoder approach to natural low-light image enhancement. Pattern Recogn. **61**, 650–662 (2017)
29. Lugmayr, A., Danelljan, M., Timofte, R.: Unsupervised learning for real-world super-resolution. arXiv preprint arXiv:1909.09629 (2019)
30. Lv, F., Lu, F., Wu, J., Lim, C.: MBLLEN: Low-light image/video enhancement using CNNs. In: British Machine Vision Conference (BMVC) (2018)
31. Maggioni, M., Boracchi, G., Foi, A., Egiazarian, K.O.: Video denoising, deblocking, and enhancement through separable 4-D nonlocal spatiotemporal transforms. IEEE Trans. Image Process. **21**, 3952–3966 (2012)
32. McDonagh, S., Klaudiny, M., Bradley, D., Beeler, T., Matthews, I., Mitchell, K.: Synthetic prior design for real-time face tracking. In: 2016 Fourth International Conference on 3D Vision (3DV), pp. 639–648. IEEE (2016)
33. Mildenhall, B., Barron, J.T., Chen, J., Sharlet, D., Ng, R., Carroll, R.: Burst denoising with kernel prediction networks. CoRR abs/1712.02327 arXiv:1712.02327 (2017)
34. Nakai, K., Hoshi, Y., Taguchi, A.: Color image contrast enhancement method based on differential intensity/saturation gray-levels histograms. In: 2013 International Symposium on Intelligent Signal Processing and Communication Systems, pp. 445–449. IEEE (2013)
35. Nowruzi, F.E., Kapoor, P., Kolhatkar, D., Hassanat, F.A., Laganiere, R., Rebut, J.: How much real data do we actually need: analyzing object detection performance using synthetic and real data. arXiv preprint arXiv:1907.07061 (2019)
36. Ravuri, S., Vinyals, O.: Seeing is not necessarily believing: limitations of BigGANs for data augmentation (2019)

37. Richter, S.R., Vineet, V., Roth, S., Koltun, V.: Playing for data: ground truth from computer games. In: Leibe, B., Matas, J., Sebe, N., Welling, M. (eds.) ECCV 2016. LNCS, vol. 9906, pp. 102–118. Springer, Cham (2016). https://doi.org/10.1007/978-3-319-46475-6_7

38. Ronneberger, O., Fischer, P., Brox, T.: U-Net: Convolutional networks for biomedical image segmentation. In: Medical Image Computing and Computer-Assisted Intervention (MICCAI), LNCS, vol. 9351, pp. 234–241. Springer, Heidelberg (2015). https://doi.org/10.1007/978-3-319-24574-4_28, http://lmb.informatik.uni-freiburg.de/Publications/2015/RFB15a, arXiv:1505.04597 [cs.CV]

39. Sankaranarayanan, S., Balaji, Y., Jain, A., Nam Lim, S., Chellappa, R.: Learning from synthetic data: addressing domain shift for semantic segmentation. In: Proceedings of the IEEE Conference on Computer Vision and Pattern Recognition, pp. 3752–3761 (2018)

40. Schwartz, E., Giryes, R., Bronstein, A.M.: DeepISP: towards learning an end-to-end image processing pipeline. IEEE Trans. Image Process. **28**(2), 912–923 (2019)

41. Simonyan, K., Zisserman, A.: Very deep convolutional networks for large-scale image recognition. In: Bengio, Y., LeCun, Y. (eds.) 3rd International Conference on Learning Representations, ICLR 2015, San Diego, CA, USA, May 7–9, 2015, Conference Track Proceedings (2015). arXiv:1409.1556

42. Taigman, Y., Polyak, A., Wolf, L.: Unsupervised cross-domain image generation. In: 5th International Conference on Learning Representations, ICLR 2017, Toulon, France, April 24–26, 2017, Conference Track Proceedings. OpenReview.net (2017). https://openreview.net/forum?id=Sk2Im59ex

43. Tan, B., Zhang, Y., Pan, S.J., Yang, Q.: Distant domain transfer learning. In: Thirty-first AAAI Conference on Artificial Intelligence (2017)

44. Tao, L., Zhu, C., Song, J., Lu, T., Jia, H., Xie, X.: Low-light image enhancement using CNN and bright channel prior. In: 2017 IEEE International Conference on Image Processing (ICIP), pp. 3215–3219. IEEE (2017)

45. Tao, L., Zhu, C., Xiang, G., Li, Y., Jia, H., Xie, X.: LLCNN: a convolutional neural network for low-light image enhancement. In: 2017 IEEE Visual Communications and Image Processing (VCIP), pp. 1–4. IEEE (2017)

46. Tripathy, S., Kannala, J., Rahtu, E.: Learning image-to-image translation using paired and unpaired training samples. In: Jawahar, C.V., Li, H., Mori, G., Schindler, K. (eds.) ACCV 2018. LNCS, vol. 11362, pp. 51–66. Springer, Cham (2019). https://doi.org/10.1007/978-3-030-20890-5_4

47. Wang, D., Niu, X., Dou, Y.: A piecewise-based contrast enhancement framework for low lighting video. In: Proceedings 2014 IEEE International Conference on Security, Pattern Analysis, and Cybernetics (SPAC), pp. 235–240. IEEE (2014)

48. Xue, T., Chen, B., Wu, J., Wei, D., Freeman, W.T.: Video enhancement with task-oriented flow. CoRR abs/1711.09078 arXiv:1711.09078 (2017)

49. Ying, Z., Li, G., Ren, Y., Wang, R., Wang, W.: A new low-light image enhancement algorithm using camera response model. In: Proceedings of the IEEE International Conference on Computer Vision Workshops, pp. 3015–3022 (2017)

50. Zhu, J.Y., Park, T., Isola, P., Efros, A.A.: Unpaired image-to-image translation using cycle-consistent adversarial networks. In: Proceedings of the IEEE International Conference on Computer Vision, pp. 2223–2232 (2017)

51. Zhu, Y., Aoun, M., Krijn, M., Vanschoren, J., Campus, H.T.: Data augmentation using conditional generative adversarial networks for leaf counting in Arabidopsis plants. In: BMVC, p. 324 (2018)

Non-local Spatial Propagation Network for Depth Completion

Jinsun Park[1], Kyungdon Joo[2], Zhe Hu[3], Chi-Kuei Liu[3], and In So Kweon[1(✉)]

[1] Korea Advanced Institute of Science and Technology, Daejeon, Republic of Korea
{zzangjinsun,iskweon77}@kaist.ac.kr
[2] Robotics Institute, Carnegie Mellon University, Pittsburgh, USA
kjoo@andrew.cmu.edu
[3] Hikvision Research America, Santa Clara, USA
zhu@ucmerced.edu

Abstract. In this paper, we propose a robust and efficient end-to-end non-local spatial propagation network for depth completion. The proposed network takes RGB and sparse depth images as inputs and estimates non-local neighbors and their affinities of each pixel, as well as an initial depth map with pixel-wise confidences. The initial depth prediction is then iteratively refined by its confidence and non-local spatial propagation procedure based on the predicted non-local neighbors and corresponding affinities. Unlike previous algorithms that utilize fixed-local neighbors, the proposed algorithm effectively avoids irrelevant local neighbors and concentrates on relevant non-local neighbors during propagation. In addition, we introduce a learnable affinity normalization to better learn the affinity combinations compared to conventional methods. The proposed algorithm is inherently robust to the mixed-depth problem on depth boundaries, which is one of the major issues for existing depth estimation/completion algorithms. Experimental results on indoor and outdoor datasets demonstrate that the proposed algorithm is superior to conventional algorithms in terms of depth completion accuracy and robustness to the mixed-depth problem. Our implementation is publicly available on the project page (https://github.com/zzangjinsun/NLSPN_ECCV20).

Keywords: Depth completion · Non-local · Spatial propagation network

1 Introduction

Depth estimation has become an important problem in recent years with the rapid growth of computer vision applications, such as augmented reality, unmanned aerial vehicle control, autonomous driving, and motion planning. To obtain a reliable depth prediction, information from various sensors is utilized,

Electronic supplementary material The online version of this chapter (https://doi.org/10.1007/978-3-030-58601-0_8) contains supplementary material, which is available to authorized users.

© Springer Nature Switzerland AG 2020
A. Vedaldi et al. (Eds.): ECCV 2020, LNCS 12358, pp. 120–136, 2020.
https://doi.org/10.1007/978-3-030-58601-0_8

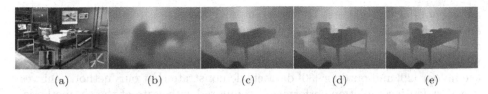

(a)   (b)   (c)   (d)   (e)

Fig. 1. Example of the depth completion on the NYU Depth V2 dataset [29]. (a) RGB image and a few samples of the estimated non-local neighbors. Depth completion results by (b) direct regression [21], (c) local propagation [9], and (d) non-local propagation (ours), respectively, and (e) the ground truth.

e.g., RGB cameras, radar, LiDAR, and ultrasonic sensors [2,3]. Depth sensors, such as LiDAR sensors, produce accurate depth measurements with high frequency. However, the density of the acquired depth is often sparse due to hardware limitations, such as the number of scanning channels. To overcome such limitations, there have been a lot of works to estimate dense depth information based on the given sparse depth values, called *depth completion.*

Early methods for depth completion [10,30] rely only on sparse measurement. Therefore, their predictions suffer from unwanted artifacts, such as blurry and mixed-depth values (*i.e.*, mixed-depth problem). Because RGB images show subtle changes of color and texture, recent methods use RGB images as the guidance to predict accurate dense depth maps.

Direct depth completion algorithms [21,30] take RGB or RGB-D images and directly infer a dense depth using a deep convolutional neural network (CNN). These direct algorithms have shown superior performance compared to conventional ones; however, they still generate blurry depth maps near depth boundaries. Soon after, this phenomenon is alleviated by recent affinity-based spatial propagation methods [9,32]. By learning affinities for local neighbors and iteratively refining depth predictions, the final dense depth becomes more accurate. Nonetheless, previous propagation networks [9,19] have an explicit limitation that they have a fixed-local neighborhood configuration for propagation. Fixed-local neighbors often have irrelevant information that should not be mixed with reference information, especially on depth boundaries. Hence, they still suffer from the mixed-depth problem in the depth completion task (see Fig. 1(c)).

To tackle the problem, we propose a Non-Local Spatial Propagation Network (NLSPN) that predicts non-local neighbors for each pixel (*i.e.*, where the information should come from) and then aggregates relevant information using the spatially-varying affinities (*i.e.*, how much information should be propagated), which are also predicted from the network. By relaxing the fixed-local neighborhood configuration, the proposed network can avoid irrelevant local neighbors affiliated with other adjacent objects. Therefore, our method is inherently robust to the mixed-depth problem. In addition, based on our analysis of conventional affinity normalization schemes, we propose a learnable affinity normalization method that has a larger representation capability of affinity combinations. It enables more accurate affinity estimation and thus improves the propagation among non-local neighbors. To further improve robustness to outliers from input and inaccurate initial prediction, we predict the confidence of the initial dense depth simultaneously, and it is incorporated into the affinity normalization to minimize the propagation of unreliable depth values. Experimental results on the indoor [29] and outdoor [30] datasets demonstrate that our method achieves superior depth completion performance compared with state-of-the-art methods.

2   Related Work

Depth Estimation and Completion. The objective of depth estimation is to generate dense depth predictions based on various input information, such as a single RGB image, multi-view images, sparse LiDAR measurements, and so on. Conventional depth estimation algorithms often utilize information from a single modality. Eigen *et al.* [11] used a multi-scale neural network to predict depth from a single image. In the method introduced by Zbontar and LeCun [35], the deep features of image patches are extracted from stereo rectified images, and then the disparity is determined by searching for the most similar patch along the epipolar line. Depth estimation with accurate but sparse depth information (*i.e.*, depth completion) has been intensively explored as well. Uhrig *et al.* [30] proposed sparsity invariant CNNs to predict a dense depth map given a sparse depth image from a LiDAR sensor. Ma and Sertac [21] introduced a method to construct a 4D volume by concatenating RGB and sparse depth images and then feed it into an encoder-decoder CNN for the final prediction. Chen *et al.* [7] adopted a fusion of 2D convolution and 3D continuous convolution to effectively consider the geometric configuration of 3D points.

Spatial Propagation Network. Although direct depth completion algorithms have demonstrated decent performance, sparse-to-dense propagation with accurate guidance from different modalities (*e.g.*, an RGB image) is a more effective way to obtain dense prediction from sparse inputs [9,17,22,32]. Liu *et al.* [19] proposed a spatial propagation network (SPN) to learn local affinities. The SPN learns task-specific affinity values from large-scale data, and it can be applied to a variety of high-level vision tasks, including depth completion and semantic segmentation. However, the individual three-way connection in four-direction is adopted for spatial propagation, which is not suitable for considering all local neighbors simultaneously. This limitation was overcome by Cheng *et al.* [9], who proposed a convolutional spatial propagation network (CSPN) to predict affinity values for local neighbors and update all the pixels simultaneously with their local context for efficiency. However, both the SPN and the CSPN rely on fixed-local neighbors, which could be from irrelevant objects. Therefore, the propagation based on those neighbors would result in mixed-depth values, and the iterative propagation procedure used in their architectures would increase the impact. Moreover, the fixed neighborhood patterns restrict the usage of relevant but wide-range (*i.e.*, non-local) context within the image.

Non-local Network. The importance of non-local information has been widely explored in various vision tasks [5,28,31,34]. Recently, a non-local block in deep

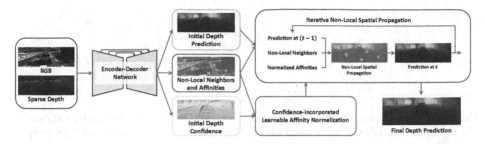

Fig. 2. Overview of the proposed algorithm. The encoder-decoder network is built upon the residual network [13]. Given RGB and sparse depth images, an initial dense depth and its confidence, non-local neighbors, and corresponding affinities are predicted from the network. Then non-local spatial propagation is conducted iteratively with the confidence-incorporated learnable affinity normalization.

neural networks was proposed by Wang *et al.* [31]. It consists of pairwise affinity calculation and feature-processing modules. The authors demonstrated the effectiveness of non-local blocks by embedding them into existing deep networks for video classification and image recognition. These methods showed significant improvement over local methods.

Our Work. Unlike previous algorithms [9,19,32], our network is trained to predict non-local neighbors with corresponding affinities. In addition, our learnable affinity normalization algorithm searches for the optimal affinity space, which has not been explored in conventional algorithms [6,9,19]. Furthermore, we incorporate the confidence of the initial dense depth prediction (which will be refined by propagation procedure) into affinity normalization to minimize the propagation of unconfident depth values. Fig. 2 shows an overview of our algorithm. Each component will be described in subsequent sections in detail.

3 Non-local Spatial Propagation

The goal of spatial propagation is to estimate missing values and refine less confident values by propagating neighbor observations with corresponding affinities (*i.e.*, similarities). Spatial propagation has been utilized as one of the key modules in various computer vision applications [16,17,24]. In particular, spatial propagation is suitable for the depth completion task [9,19,32], and its superior performance compared to direct regression algorithms has been demonstrated [21,30]. In this section, we first briefly review the local SPNs and their limitations, and then describe the proposed non-local SPN.

3.1 Local Spatial Propagation Network

Let $\mathbf{X} = (x_{m,n}) \in \mathbb{R}^{M \times N}$ denote a 2D map to be updated by spatial propagation, where $x_{m,n}$ denotes the pixel value at (m, n). The propagation of $x_{m,n}$ at the

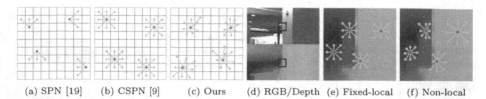

(a) SPN [19]   (b) CSPN [9]   (c) Ours   (d) RGB/Depth (e) Fixed-local (f) Non-local

Fig. 3. Visual comparison of SPNs. (a)-(c) Examples of neighbor configurations of the (a) SPN [19], (b) CSPN [9], and (c) NLSPN (ours), where purple and light purple pixels denote reference and neighboring pixels, respectively. Compared to the others, our neighbor configuration is highly flexible, and can be fractional. (d)-(f) Comparison of fixed-local and non-local configurations for various situations. The fixed-local configuration (e) cannot utilize relevant information beyond the fixed-local region. In contrast, the non-local configuration (f) avoids this problem effectively by predicting and utilizing relevant neighbors at various distances without limitation.

step t with its local neighbors, denoted by $\mathcal{N}_{m,n}$, is defined as follows:

$$x_{m,n}^t = w_{m,n}^c x_{m,n}^{t-1} + \sum_{(i,j)\in\mathcal{N}_{m,n}} w_{m,n}^{i,j} x_{i,j}^{t-1}, \tag{1}$$

where (m,n) and (i,j) are the coordinates of reference and neighbor pixels, respectively; $w_{m,n}^c$ represents the affinity of the reference pixel; and $w_{m,n}^{i,j}$ indicates the affinity between the pixels at (m,n) and (i,j). The first term in the right-hand side represents the propagation of the reference pixel, while the second term stands for the propagation of its neighbors weighted by the corresponding affinities. The affinity of the reference pixel $w_{m,n}^c$ (*i.e.*, how much the original value will be preserved) is obtained as

$$w_{m,n}^c = 1 - \sum_{(i,j)\in\mathcal{N}_{m,n}} w_{m,n}^{i,j}. \tag{2}$$

Spatial Propagation Network. The original SPN [19] is formulated on the configuration of three-way local connections, where each pixel is linked to three adjacent pixels from the previous row or column (see Fig. 3(a)). For instance, the local neighbors of the pixel at (m,n) for top-to-bottom propagation (*i.e.*, vertical) in the SPN, denoted by $\mathcal{N}_{m,n}^S$, are defined as follows:

$$\mathcal{N}_{m,n}^S = \{x_{m+p,n+q} \mid p = -1, q \in \{-1,0,1\}\}. \tag{3}$$

The local neighbors for other directions (*i.e.*, bottom-to-top, left-to-right and right-to-left) can be defined in similar ways. Figure 3(a) shows several examples of $\mathcal{N}^S$ for other directions. Note that the SPN updates rows or columns in $\mathbf{X}$ sequentially. Thus, a natural limitation of the three-way connection is that it does not explore information from all the directions simultaneously.

Convolutional Spatial Propagation Network. To consider all the possible propagation directions together, the original SPN propagates in four directions individually. Then it utilizes max-pooling to integrate those predictions [19]. The CSPN [9] addresses the inefficiency issue by simplifying separate propagations via convolution operation at each propagation step. For the CSPN with a 3×3 local window size, the local neighbors $\mathcal{N}_{m,n}^{\mathrm{CS}}$ are defined as follows:

$$\mathcal{N}_{m,n}^{\mathrm{CS}} = \{x_{m+p,n+q} \mid p \in \{-1,0,1\}, q \in \{-1,0,1\}, (p,q) \neq (0,0)\}. \tag{4}$$

Figure 3(b) shows some examples of $\mathcal{N}^{\mathrm{CS}}$. For more details of each network (the SPN and the CSPN), please refer to earlier works [9,19].

3.2 Non-local Spatial Propagation Network.

The SPN and the CSPN are effective in propagating information from more confident areas into less confident ones with data-dependent affinities. However, their potential improvement is inherently limited by the fixed-local neighborhood configuration (Fig. 3(e)). The fixed-local neighborhood configuration ignores object/depth distribution within the local area; thus, it often results in mixed-depth values of foreground and background objects after propagation. Although affinities predicted from the network can alleviate the depth mixing between irrelevant pixels to a certain degree, they can hardly avoid incorrect predictions and hold up the use of appropriate neighbors beyond the local area.

To resolve the above issues, we introduce a deep neural network that estimates the neighbors of each pixel beyond the local region (*i.e.*, non-local) based on color and depth information within a wide area. The non-local neighbors $\mathcal{N}_{m,n}^{\mathrm{NL}}$ are defined as follows:

$$\mathcal{N}_{m,n}^{\mathrm{NL}} = \{x_{m+p,n+q} \mid (p,q) \in f_\phi(\mathbf{I}, \mathbf{D}, m, n), \ p, q \in \mathbb{R}\}, \tag{5}$$

where $\mathbf{I}$ and $\mathbf{D}$ are the RGB and sparse depth images, respectively, and $f_\phi(\cdot)$ is the non-local neighbor prediction network that estimates K neighbors for each pixel, under the learnable parameters ϕ. We adopt an encoder-decoder CNN architecture for $f_\phi(\cdot)$, which will be described in Sect. 5.1. It should be noted that p and q are real numbers in Eq. 5; thus, the non-local neighbors can be defined to sub-pixel accuracy, as illustrated in Fig. 3(c).

Figure 3(f) shows some examples of appropriate and desired non-local neighbors near depth boundaries. In the fixed-local setup, affinity learning learns how to encourage the influence of the related pixels and suppress that of unrelated ones simultaneously. On the contrary, affinity learning with the non-local setup concentrates on relevant neighbors, and this facilitates the learning process.

4   Confidence-Incorporated Affinity Learning

Affinity learning is one of the key components in SPNs, which enables accurate and stable propagation. Conventional affinity-based algorithms utilize color

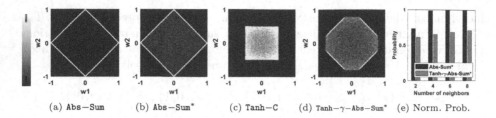

(a) Abs−Sum   (b) Abs−Sum*   (c) Tanh−C   (d) Tanh−γ−Abs−Sum*   (e) Norm. Prob.

Fig. 4. Illustration of affinity normalization schemes. (a)-(d) Affinity distribution after various normalization schemes for the 2-neighbor case. Color bar is shown on the left. (e) Probabilities of normalization with different strategies for each number of neighbors. Please refer to the text for details.

statistics or hand-crafted features [16,17,27]. Recent affinity learning methods [9,18,19] adopt deep neural networks to predict affinities and show substantial performance improvement. In these methods, affinity normalization plays an important role to stabilize the propagation process.

In this section, we analyze the conventional normalization approach and its limitation, and then propose a normalization approach in a learnable way. Moreover, we incorporate the confidence of the initial prediction during normalization to suppress negative effects from unreliable depth values during propagation.

4.1   Affinity Normalization

The purpose of affinity normalization is to ensure stability during propagation. For stability, the norm of the temporal Jacobian of x, $\partial x^t / \partial x^{t-1}$ should be equal to or less than one [19]. Under the spatial propagation formulation in Eq. 1, this condition would be satisfied if $\sum_{(i,j)\in\mathcal{N}_{m,n}} |w_{m,n}^{i,j}| \leq 1$, $\forall m, n$. To enforce the condition, previous works [9,19] normalize affinities by the absolute-sum (dubbed Abs−Sum) as follows:

$$w_{m,n}^{i,j} = \hat{w}_{m,n}^{i,j} / \sum_{(i,j)\in\mathcal{N}_{m,n}} |\hat{w}_{m,n}^{i,j}|, \tag{6}$$

where $\hat{w}$ denotes the raw affinity before normalization. Although the stability condition is satisfied by Abs−Sum, it has a problem in that the viable combinations of normalized affinities are biased to a narrow high-dimensional space.

Without loss of generality, we first analyze the biased affinity problem using a toy example of the 2-neighbor case and then present solutions to the issue. In the 2-neighbor case, we denote affinities of the two neighbors as w_1 and w_2 with a slight abuse of notation. We assume that the unnormalized affinities are sampled from the standard normal distribution, $N(0, 1)$ for simplicity.

For the Abs−Sum, the normalized affinities lie on the lines satisfying $|w_1| + |w_2| = 1$ (referred to as A_1), as shown in Fig. 4(a). This limits the usage of potentially advantageous affinity configuration within the area $|w_1| + |w_2| < 1$ (referred to as A_2). To fully explore the affinity configuration $|w_1| + |w_2| \leq 1$,

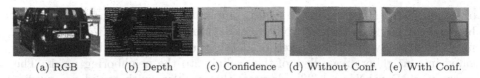

(a) RGB   (b) Depth   (c) Confidence   (d) Without Conf.   (e) With Conf.

Fig. 5. Example of propagation with and without confidence incorporation.

a simple remedy is to apply Eq. 6 only when $\sum_i |w_i| > 1$ (noted as Abs−Sum*). Figure 4(b) shows the affinity distribution of our simple remedy. However, the affinities normalized by Abs−Sum* still have a high chance to fall on A_1. Indeed, with the increasing number of neighbors K, the affinities are more likely to lie on A_1. (*e.g.*, the normalization probability is 0.985 when $K = 4$). Figure 4(e) (blue bars) shows the probability of affinities falling on A_1 with various K values.

One way to reduce the bias is to limit the range of raw affinities [20], for example, to $[-1/C, 1/C]$ using the hyperbolic tangent function ($\tanh(\cdot)$) with a normalization factor C. We refer to this normalization procedure as Tanh−C, which is defined as follows:

$$w_{m,n}^{i,j} = \tanh(\hat{w}_{m,n}^{i,j})/C, \qquad C \geq K, \tag{7}$$

where the condition $C \geq K$ enforces the normalized affinities to guarantee $\sum_{(i,j)\in\mathcal{N}_{m,n}} |w_{m,n}^{i,j}| \leq 1$; therefore, this condition ensures stability. Figure 4(c) shows the affinity distribution of Tanh−C when $C = 2$. With a sacrifice of boundary values, Tanh−C enables a more balanced affinity distribution. Moreover, the optimal value of C in Tanh−C may vary depending on the training task, *e.g.*, the number of neighbors, the activation functions, and the dataset.

To determine the optimal value for the task, we propose to learn the normalization factor together with non-local affinities, and apply the normalization only when $\sum_{(i,j)\in\mathcal{N}_{m,n}} |w_{m,n}^{i,j}| > 1$. The affinity of the proposed normalization, referred to as Tanh−γ−Abs−Sum*, is defined as follows:

$$w_{m,n}^{i,j} = \tanh(\hat{w}_{m,n}^{i,j})/\gamma, \quad \gamma_{min} \leq \gamma \leq \gamma_{max}, \tag{8}$$

where γ denotes the learnable normalization parameter, and γ_{min} and γ_{max} are the minimum and maximum values that can be empirically set. Figure 4(d) shows an example of Tanh−γ−Abs−Sum* when $\gamma = 1.25$. Here, Tanh−γ−Abs−Sum* can be viewed as a mixture of Abs−Sum* and Tanh−C (see Figs. 4(b) and (c)). The probability of affinities falling on the boundary with respect to the number of neighbors with $\gamma = K/2$ is shown in Fig. 4(e) (yellow bars). Compared to Abs−Sum*, Tanh−γ−Abs−Sum* still has a chance to avoid normalization, and it allows us to explore more diverse affinities with a larger number of neighbors.

4.2   Confidence-Incorporated Affinity Normalization

In the existing propagation frameworks [9, 16–19, 27], the affinity depicts the correlation between pixels and provides guidance for propagation based on similarity. In this case, each pixel in the map is treated equally without consideration of its reliability. However, in the depth completion task, different pixels should be weighted based on their reliability. For example, information from unreliable pixels (*e.g.*, noisy pixels and pixels on depth boundaries) should not be propagated into neighbors regardless of their affinity to the neighboring pixels. The recent work DepthNormal [32] addresses this problem with confidence prediction. It utilizes confidence as a mask for the weighted summation of input and prediction for seed point preservation. However, it does not fully prevent the propagation of incorrect depth values because weighted summation is conducted before each propagation separately.

In this work, we consider the confidence map of pixels and combine it with affinity normalization. That is, we predict not only the initial dense depth but also its confidence, and then the confidence is incorporated into affinity normalization to reduce disturbances from unreliable depths during propagation. The affinity of the confidence-incorporated Tanh$-\gamma-$Abs$-$Sum* is defined as follows:

$$w_{m,n}^{i,j} = c^{i,j} \cdot \text{tanh}(\hat{w}_{m,n}^{i,j})/\gamma, \tag{9}$$

where $c^{i,j} \in [0,1]$ denotes the confidence of the pixel at (i,j).

Figure 5(d) shows an example of a confidence-agnostic depth estimation result. Some noisy input depth points generate unreliable depth values with low confidences (see Fig. 5(c)). Without using confidence, the noisy and less confident pixels would harm their neighbor pixels during propagation and lead to unpleasing artifacts (see Fig. 5(d)). After the incorporation of confidence into normalization, our algorithm can successfully eliminate the impact of unconfident pixels and generate more accurate depth estimation, as shown in Fig. 5(e).

5   Depth Completion Network

In this section, we describe network architecture and loss functions for network training. The proposed NLSPN mainly consists of two parts: (1) an encoder-decoder architecture for the initial depth map, a confidence map and non-local neighbors prediction with their raw affinities, and (2) a non-local spatial propagation layer with a learnable affinity normalization.

5.1   Network Architecture

The encoder-decoder part of the proposed network is built upon residual networks [13], and it extracts high-level features from RGB and sparse depth images. Additionally, we adopt the encoder-decoder feature connection strategy [9,26] to simultaneously utilize low-level and high-level features.

In Fig. 2, we provide an overview of our algorithm. Features from the encoder-decoder network are shared for the initial dense depth, confidence, non-local neighbor, and raw affinity estimation. Then non-local spatial propagation is conducted in an iterative manner. As described in Sect. 3.2, non-local neighbors can have fractional coordinates. To better incorporate fractional coordinates into

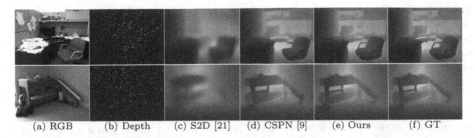

| (a) RGB | (b) Depth | (c) S2D [21] | (d) CSPN [9] | (e) Ours | (f) GT |

Fig. 6. Depth completion results on the NYUv2 dataset [29]. Note that sparse depth images are dilated for visualization.

training, differentiable sampling [15,36] is adopted during propagation. We note that our non-local propagation can be efficiently calculated by deformable convolutions [36]. Therefore, each propagation requires a simple forward step of deformable convolution with our affinity normalization. Please refer to the supplementary material for the detailed network configuration.

5.2   Loss Function

For accurate prediction of the dense depth map, we train our network with ℓ_1 or ℓ_2 loss as a reconstruction loss with the ground truth depth as follows:

$$L_{recon}(\mathbf{D}^{gt}, \mathbf{D}^{pred}) = \frac{1}{|\mathcal{V}|} \sum_{v \in \mathcal{V}} | \ d_v^{gt} - d_v^{pred} \ |^{\rho}, \tag{10}$$

where $\mathbf{D}^{gt}$ is the ground truth depth; $\mathbf{D}^{pred}$ is the prediction from our algorithm; and d_v, $\mathcal{V}$, and $|\mathcal{V}|$ denote the depth values at pixel index v, valid pixels of $\mathbf{D}^{gt}$, and the number of valid pixels, respectively. Here, ρ is set to 1 for ℓ_1 loss and 2 for ℓ_2 loss. Note that we do not have any supervision on the confidence because there is no ground truth; therefore, it is indirectly trained based on L_{recon}.

6   Experimental Results

In this section, we first describe implementation details and the training environment. After that, quantitative and qualitative comparisons to previous algorithms on indoor and outdoor datasets are presented. We also present ablation studies to verify the effectiveness of each component of the proposed algorithm.

The proposed method was implemented using PyTorch [23] with NVIDIA Apex [1] and trained with a machine equipped with Intel Xeon E5-2620 and 4 NVIDIA GTX 1080 Ti GPUs. For all our experiments, we adopted an ADAM optimizer with $\beta_1 = 0.9$, $\beta_2 = 0.999$, and the initial learning rate of 0.001. The network training took about 1 and 3 d on the NYU Depth V2 [29] and KITTI Depth Completion [30] datasets, respectively. We adopted the ResNet34 [13] as our encoder-decoder baseline network. The number of non-local neighbors was

Table 1. Quantitative evaluation on the NYUv2 [29] dataset. Results are borrowed from each paper. Note that S2D [21] uses 200 sampled depth points per image as the input, while the others use 500.

Method	RMSE (m)	REL	$\delta_{1.25}$	$\delta_{1.25^2}$	$\delta_{1.25^3}$
S2D [21]	0.230	0.044	97.1	99.4	99.8
[21]+Bilateral [4]	0.479	0.084	92.4	97.6	98.9
[21]+SPN [19]	0.172	0.031	98.3	99.7	99.9
DepthCoeff [14]	0.118	0.013	99.4	**99.9**	-
CSPN [9]	0.117	0.016	99.2	**99.9**	100.0
CSPN++ [8]	0.116	-	-	-	-
DeepLiDAR [25]	0.115	0.022	99.3	**99.9**	100.0
DepthNormal [32]	0.112	0.018	99.5	**99.9**	100.0
Ours	**0.092**	**0.012**	**99.6**	**99.9**	**100.0**

Table 2. Quantitative evaluation on the KITTI DC test dataset [30]. The results from other methods are obtained from the KITTI online evaluation site.

Method	RMSE (mm)	MAE	iRMSE	iMAE
CSPN [9]	1019.64	279.46	2.93	1.15
DDP [33]	832.94	203.96	2.10	0.85
NConv [12]	829.98	233.26	2.60	1.03
S2D [21]	814.73	249.95	2.80	1.21
DepthNormal [32]	777.05	235.17	2.42	1.13
DeepLiDAR [25]	758.38	226.50	2.56	1.15
FuseNet [7]	752.88	221.19	2.34	1.14
CSPN++ [8]	743.69	209.28	2.07	0.90
Ours	**741.68**	**199.59**	**1.99**	**0.84**

set to 8 for a fair comparison to other algorithms using 3×3 local neighbors. The number of propagation steps was set to 18 empirically. Other training details will be described for each dataset individually. For the quantitative evaluation, we utilized the following commonly used metrics [9,21,29]:

- RMSE (mm) : $\sqrt{\frac{1}{|\mathcal{V}|} \Sigma_{v \in \mathcal{V}} \left| d_v^{gt} - d_v^{pred} \right|^2}$
- MAE (mm) : $\frac{1}{|\mathcal{V}|} \Sigma_{v \in \mathcal{V}} \left| d_v^{gt} - d_v^{pred} \right|$
- iRMSE (1/km) : $\sqrt{\frac{1}{|\mathcal{V}|} \Sigma_{v \in \mathcal{V}} \left| 1/d_v^{gt} - 1/d_v^{pred} \right|^2}$
- iMAE (1/km) : $\frac{1}{|\mathcal{V}|} \Sigma_{v \in \mathcal{V}} \left| 1/d_v^{gt} - 1/d_v^{pred} \right|$

- REL : $\frac{1}{|\mathcal{V}|} \Sigma_{v \in \mathcal{V}} \left| (d_v^{gt} - d_v^{pred})/d_v^{gt} \right|$
- δ_τ : Percentage of pixels satisfying
$\max \left(\frac{d_v^{gt}}{d_v^{pred}}, \frac{d_v^{pred}}{d_v^{gt}} \right) < \tau$

6.1   NYU Depth V2

The NYU Depth V2 dataset [29] (NYUv2) consists of RGB and depth images of 464 indoor scenes captured by a Kinect sensor. For the training data, we utilized a subset of $\sim$50K images from the official training split. Each image was downsized to 320×240, and then 304×228 center-cropping was applied. We trained the model for 25 epochs with ℓ_1 loss, and the learning rate decayed by 0.2 every 5 epochs after the first 10 epochs. We set the batch size to 24. The official test split of 654 images was used for evaluation and comparisons.

In Fig. 6, we present some depth completion results obtained for the NYUv2 dataset. As in previous works [9,21], 500 depth pixels were randomly sampled from a dense depth image and used as the input along with the corresponding RGB image. For comparison, we provide results from the Sparse-to-Dense (S2D) [21] and the CSPN [9]. The S2D (Fig. 6(c)) generates blurry depth images, as it is a direct regression algorithm. Compared to the S2D, the CSPN and our method generate depth maps with substantially improved accuracy thanks to the

Fig. 7. Depth completion results on the KITTI DC dataset [30]. (a) RGB, (b) Sparse depth, (c) CSPN [9], (d) DepthNormal [32], (e) DeepLiDAR [25], (f) FuseNet [7], (g) CSPN++ [8], (h) Ours. Note that sparse depth images are dilated for visualization.

iterative spatial propagation procedure. However, the CSPN suffers from mixed-depth problems, especially on tiny or thin structures. In contrast, our method well preserves tiny structures and depth boundaries using non-local propagation.

Table 1 shows the quantitative evaluation of the NYUv2 dataset. The proposed algorithm achieves the best result and outperforms other methods by a large margin (RMSE 0.020m). Compared to geometry-agnostic methods [9,19,21], geometry-aware ones [8,14,25,32] show better performance in general. The proposed algorithm can be also viewed as a geometry-aware algorithm because it implicitly explores geometrically relevant neighbors for propagation.

6.2 KITTI Depth Completion

The KITTI Depth Completion (KITTI DC) dataset [30] consists of over 90K RGB and LiDAR pairs. We ignored regions without LiDAR projection (*i.e.*, top 100 pixels) and center-cropped 1216 × 240 patches for training. The proposed network was trained for 25 epochs with both ℓ_1 and ℓ_2 losses to balance RMSE and MAE, and the initial learning rate decayed by 0.4 every 5 epochs after the first 10 epochs. We used a batch size of 25 for the training.

Table 2 shows the quantitative evaluation of the KITTI DC dataset. Similar to the results obtained for the NYUv2, geometry-aware algorithms [7,8,25,32] perform better in general compared to geometry-agnostic methods [9,21]. Since

Fig. 8. Examples of non-local neighbors predicted by our network.

Table 3. Quantitative evaluation on the KITTI DC validation set [30] with various configurations. Please refer to the text for details.

	Neighbors	Affinity	Norm	Conf	RMSE (mm)
(a)	$\mathcal{N}^{CS}$	Learned	Abs−Sum	No	908.4
(b)				Yes	891.6
(c)			Tanh−γ−Abs−Sum*	No	896.4
(d)				Yes	890.4
(e)	$\mathcal{N}^{NL}$	Color			930.3
(f)		Learned	Abs−Sum	No	903.1
(g)				Yes	889.5
(h)			Abs−Sum*		886.0
(i)			Tanh−C		886.4
(j)			Tanh−γ−Abs−Sum*	No	891.3
(k)				Binary	892.9
(l)				Weighted	884.8
(m)				Yes	884.1

LiDAR sensor noise (*i.e.*, mixed foreground and background points as shown in Fig. 5) is inevitable, the predicted confidence is highly beneficial to eliminate the impact of the noise. DepthNormal [32] utilizes confidence values as a mask for weighted summation during refinement. However, its confidence mask does not totally prevent incorrect values from propagating into neighboring pixels. On the contrary, the proposed confidence-incorporated affinity normalization effectively restricts the propagation of erroneous values during propagation. We note that the proposed method outperformed all the peer-reviewed methods in the KITTI online leaderboard when we submitted the paper.

Figure 7 shows some examples of predicted dense depth with highlighted challenging areas. Those areas usually contain small structures near depth boundaries, which can be easily affected by the mixed-depth problem. Compared to the other methods (Figs. 7(c)-(g)), our algorithm (Fig. 7(h)) handles those challenging areas better with the help of non-local neighbors.

6.3   Ablation Studies

We conducted ablation studies to verify the role of each component of our network, including non-local propagation, affinity normalization, and the confidence-incorporated propagation. For all the experiments, we used a set of 10K images sampled from the KITTI DC training dataset for training and evaluated the performance on the full validation dataset. The network was trained for 20 epochs with center-cropped patches of 912×228 for fast training, and the batch size was set to 12. Other settings were set the same as those mentioned in Sect. 6.2.

Non-local Neighbors. Figure 8 visualizes some examples of non-local neighbors predicted by our algorithm. Compared to fixed-local neighbors, our predicted non-local neighbors have higher flexibility in the selection of neighbor pixels. In particular, non-local neighbors are selected from chromatically and geometrically relevant locations near the depth boundaries (*e.g.*, same objects or planes). Moreover, we collected the statistics of the depth variance of neighboring pixels to show the relevance of the selected neighbors. On the KITTI DC validation set, the average depth variances for fixed-local and non-local neighbor configurations were 22.7 mm and 11.6 mm, respectively. The small variance of the non-local neighbor configuration demonstrates that the proposed method is able to select more relevant neighbors for propagation.

The quantitative results obtained for the network with fixed-local $\mathcal{N}^{CS}$ and that with non-local neighbors $\mathcal{N}^{NL}$ are shown in Table 3. These networks were also tested with two normalization techniques: (1) with Abs−Sum (Table 3(b) and (g)), and (2) with Tanh−γ−Abs−Sum* (Table 3(d) and (m)). The proposed method with non-local neighbors consistently outperformed that with fixed-local neighbors, demonstrating the superiority of the non-local framework.

Affinity Normalization and Confidence Incorporation. To validate the proposed affinity normalization algorithm, we compare it with three different affinity normalization methods (*cf.*, Sect. 4). Table 3(g)-(i), and (m) assessed the performance using the same network but different affinity normalization methods. The model with Abs−Sum does not perform well due to the limited range of affinity combinations, as shown in Fig. 4(a). When relaxing the normalization condition while maintaining the stability condition (Abs−Sum*), the performance was improved thanks to the wider area of feasible affinity space and better affinity distribution (Fig. 4(b)). Tanh−C strengthens the stability condition without explicit normalization. However, as shown in Fig. 4(c), the resulting affinity values reside in a smaller affinity space (*i.e.*, in a K-dimensional hypercube with edge size $2/K$); therefore, it achieved a slightly worse performance compared to Abs−Sum*. The proposed Tanh−γ−Abs−Sum* was able to alleviate this limitation with a learnable normalization parameter γ. The learned γ compromises between Abs−Sum* and Tanh−C, and can boost the performance. Note that the final γ values (initialized with $\gamma = K = 8$) trained on the NYUv2 (Sect. 6.1) and the KITTI DC (Sect. 6.2) datasets were 5.2 and 6.3, respectively. This observation indicates that the optimal γ varies based on the training environment.

We also compared the performance of the network with and without confidence, to verify the importance of confidence incorporation. In addition, we tested two alternative confidence-aware networks (1) by generating a binary mask from confidence with a threshold of 0.5 and (2) with the weighted summation approach of DepthNormal [32], and applying each method during the propagation to eliminate the effect of outliers. The comparison results are shown in Table 3(j)-(m). The proposed confidence-incorporated affinity normalization (Table 3(m)) outperforms the others due to its capability of suppressing propagation from unreliable pixels. The mask-based (Table 3(k)) and weighted summation (Table 3(l)) approaches show worse performance compared to that of ours, indicating that the hard-thresholding and weighted summation approaches are not optimal for encouraging propagation from relevant pixels but suppressing that from irrelevant pixels. Note that the proposed confidence-incorporated

Table 4. Comparison of the number of network parameters. Note that only methods with publicly available implementations [9, 12, 21, 25, 32, 33] are included.

Method	CSPN [9]	DDP [33]	NConv [12]	S2D [21]	DepthNormal [32]	DeepLiDAR [25]	Ours
# Params. (M)	17.41	28.99	0.36	42.82	28.99	53.44	25.84

approach is effective for both the network with $\mathcal{N}^{NL}$ and that with $\mathcal{N}^{CS}$ (Table 3(a)-(d)). These results demonstrate the effectiveness of our confidence incorporation.

Further Analysis. To verify the importance of learned affinities, we further evaluated the proposed method with conventional affinities calculated based on the Euclidean distance between color intensities. As shown in Table 3(e) and (m), the network using learned affinities performed much better than the network using the hand-crafted one. In addition, we provide the number of network parameters of the compared methods in Table 4. The proposed method achieved superior performance with a relatively small number of network parameters. Please refer to the supplementary material for additional experimental results, visualizations, and ablation studies.

7   Conclusion

We have proposed an end-to-end trainable non-local spatial propagation network for depth completion. The proposed method gives high flexibility in selecting neighbors for propagation, which is beneficial for accurate propagation, and it eases the affinity learning problem. Unlike previous algorithms (*i.e.*, fixed-local propagation), the proposed non-local spatial propagation efficiently excludes irrelevant neighbors and enforces the propagation to focus on a synergy between relevant ones. In addition, the proposed confidence-incorporated learnable affinity normalization encourages more affinity combinations and minimizes harmful effects from incorrect depth values during propagation. Our experimental results demonstrated the superiority of the proposed method.

Acknowledgement. This work was partially supported by the National Information Society Agency for construction of training data for artificial intelligence (2100-2131-305-107-19).

References

1. NVIDIA Apex. www.github.com/nvidia/apex
2. TESLA Autopilot. www.tesla.com/autopilot
3. UBER ATG. www.uber.com/us/en/atg
4. Barron, J.T., Poole, B.: The fast bilateral solver. In: Leibe, B., Matas, J., Sebe, N., Welling, M. (eds.) ECCV 2016. LNCS, vol. 9907, pp. 617–632. Springer, Cham (2016). https://doi.org/10.1007/978-3-319-46487-9_38

5. Buades, A., Coll, B., Morel, J.M.: A non-local algorithm for image denoising. In: Proceedings of IEEE Conference on Computer Vision and Pattern Recognition (CVPR) (2005)
6. Chen, L.C., Barron, J.T., Papandreou, G., Murphy, K., Yuille, A.L.: Semantic image segmentation with task-specific edge detection using CNNs and a discriminatively trained domain transform. In: Proceedings of IEEE Conference on Computer Vision and Pattern Recognition (CVPR) (2016)
7. Chen, Y., Yang, B., Liang, M., Urtasun, R.: Learning joint 2D–3D representations for depth completion. In: Proceedings of IEEE International Conference on Computer Vision (ICCV) (2019)
8. Cheng, X., Wang, P., Guan, C., Yang, R.: CSPP++: learning context and resource aware convolutional spatial propagation networks for depth completion. In: Proceedings of AAAI Conference on Artificial Intelligence (AAAI) (2020)
9. Cheng, X., Wang, P., Yang, R.: Depth estimation via affinity learned with convolutional spatial propagation network. In: Ferrari, V., Hebert, M., Sminchisescu, C., Weiss, Y. (eds.) ECCV 2018. LNCS, vol. 11220, pp. 108–125. Springer, Cham (2018). https://doi.org/10.1007/978-3-030-01270-0_7
10. Chodosh, N., Wang, C., Lucey, S.: Deep convolutional compressed sensing for Lidar depth completion. In: Proceedings of Asian Conference on Computer Vision (ACCV) (2018)
11. Eigen, D., Puhrsch, C., Fergus, R.: Depth map prediction from a single image using a multi-scale deep network. In: Proceedings of Advances in Neural Information Processing Systems (2014)
12. Eldesokey, A., Felsberg, M., Khan, F.S.: Confidence propagation through CNNs for guided sparse depth regression. IEEE Trans. Pattern Anal. Mach. Intell. (TPAMI) (2019)
13. He, K., Zhang, X., Ren, S., Sun, J.: Deep residual learning for image recognition. In: Proceedings of IEEE Conference on Computer Vision and Pattern Recognition (CVPR) (2016)
14. Imran, S., Long, Y., Liu, X., Morris, D.: Depth coefficients for depth completion. In: Proceedings of IEEE Conference on Computer Vision and Pattern Recognition (CVPR) (2019)
15. Jaderberg, M., Simonyan, K., Zisserman, A., et al.: Spatial transformer networks. In: Proceedings of Advances in Neural Information Processing Systems (2015)
16. Krähenbühl, P., Koltun, V.: Efficient inference in fully connected CRFs with Gaussian edge potentials. In: Proceedings of Advances in Neural Information Processing Systems (2011)
17. Levin, A., Lischinski, D., Weiss, Y.: A closed form solution to natural image matting. In: Proceedings of IEEE Conference on Computer Vision and Pattern Recognition (CVPR) (2006)
18. Liu, F., Shen, C., Lin, G.: Deep convolutional neural fields for depth estimation from a single image. In: Proceedings of IEEE Conference on Computer Vision and Pattern Recognition (CVPR) (2015)
19. Liu, S., De Mello, S., Gu, J., Zhong, G., Yang, M.H., Kautz, J.: Learning affinity via spatial propagation networks. In: Proceedings of Advances in Neural Information Processing Systems (2017)
20. Liu, S., Pan, J., Yang, M.-H.: Learning recursive filters for low-level vision via a hybrid neural network. In: Leibe, B., Matas, J., Sebe, N., Welling, M. (eds.) ECCV 2016. LNCS, vol. 9908, pp. 560–576. Springer, Cham (2016). https://doi.org/10.1007/978-3-319-46493-0_34

21. Ma, F., Karaman, S.: Sparse-to-dense: depth prediction from sparse depth samples and a single image. In: Proceedings of IEEE International Conference on Robotics and Automation (ICRA) (2018)
22. Park, J., Tai, Y.W., Cho, D., Kweon, I.S.: A unified approach of multi-scale deep and hand-crafted features for defocus estimation. In: Proceedings of IEEE Conference on Computer Vision and Pattern Recognition (CVPR) (2017)
23. Paszke, A., et al.: Automatic differentiation in PyTorch. In: NIPS Autodiff Workshop (2017)
24. Perona, P., Malik, J.: Scale-space and edge detection using anisotropic diffusion. IEEE Trans. Pattern Anal. Mach. Intell. (TPAMI) (1990)
25. Qiu, J., et al.: Deeplidar: deep surface normal guided depth prediction for outdoor scene from sparse Lidar data and single color image. In: Proceedings of IEEE Conference on Computer Vision and Pattern Recognition (CVPR) (2019)
26. Ronneberger, O., Fischer, P., Brox, T.: U-net: convolutional networks for biomedical image segmentation. In: Proceedings of International Conference on Medical Image Computing and Computer Assisted Intervention (MICCAI) (2015)
27. Saxena, A., Chung, S.H., Ng, A.Y.: Learning depth from single monocular images. In: Proceedings of Advances in Neural Information Processing Systems (2006)
28. Shim, G., Park, J., Kweon, I.S.: Robust reference-based super-resolution with similarity-aware deformable convolution. In: Proceedings of IEEE Conference on Computer Vision and Pattern Recognition (CVPR) (2020)
29. Silberman, N., Hoiem, D., Kohli, P., Fergus, R.: Indoor segmentation and support inference from RGBD images. In: Fitzgibbon, A., Lazebnik, S., Perona, P., Sato, Y., Schmid, C. (eds.) ECCV 2012. LNCS, vol. 7576, pp. 746–760. Springer, Heidelberg (2012). https://doi.org/10.1007/978-3-642-33715-4_54
30. Uhrig, J., et al.: Sparsity invariant CNNs. In: International Conference on 3D Vision (3DV) (2017)
31. Wang, X., Girshick, R., Gupta, A., He, K.: Non-local neural networks. In: Proceedings of IEEE Conference on Computer Vision and Pattern Recognition (CVPR) (2018)
32. Xu, Y., Zhu, X., Shi, J., Zhang, G., Bao, H., Li, H.: Depth completion from sparse Lidar data with depth-normal constraints. In: Proceedings of IEEE International Conference on Computer Vision (ICCV) (2019)
33. Yang, Y., Wong, A., Soatto, S.: Dense depth posterior (DDP) from single image and sparse range. In: Proceedings of IEEE Conference on Computer Vision and Pattern Recognition (CVPR) (2019)
34. Yoon, K.J., Kweon, I.S.: Adaptive support-weight approach for correspondence search. IEEE Trans. Pattern Anal. Mach. Intell. (TPAMI) (2006)
35. Zbontar, J., LeCun, Y., et al.: Stereo matching by training a convolutional neural network to compare image patches. J. Mach. Learn. Res. 17, 1–32 (2016)
36. Zhu, X., Hu, H., Lin, S., Dai, J.: Deformable ConvNets v2: more deformable, better results. In: Proceedings of IEEE Conference on Computer Vision and Pattern Recognition (CVPR) (2019)

DanbooRegion: An Illustration Region Dataset

Lvmin Zhang[1,2], Yi Ji[2(✉)], and Chunping Liu[2(✉)]

[1] Style2Paints Research, Suzhou, China
lvminzhang@acm.org, lvminzhang@siggraph.org
[2] Soochow University, Suzhou, China
{jiyi,cpliu}@suda.edu.cn

Abstract. Region is a fundamental element of various cartoon animation techniques and artistic painting applications. Achieving satisfactory region is essential to the success of these techniques. Motivated to assist diversiform region-based cartoon applications, we invite artists to annotate regions for in-the-wild cartoon images with several application-oriented goals: (1) To assist image-based cartoon rendering, relighting, and cartoon intrinsic decomposition literature, artists identify object outlines and eliminate lighting-and-shadow boundaries. (2) To assist cartoon inking tools, cartoon structure extraction applications, and cartoon texture processing techniques, artists clean-up texture or deformation patterns and emphasize cartoon structural boundary lines. (3) To assist region-based cartoon digitalization, clip-art vectorization, and animation tracking applications, artists inpaint and reconstruct broken or blurred regions in cartoon images. Given the typicality of these involved applications, this dataset is also likely to be used in other cartoon techniques. We detail the challenges in achieving this dataset and present a human-in-the-loop workflow namely Feasibility-based Assignment Recommendation (FAR) to enable large-scale annotating. The FAR tends to reduce artist trails-and-errors and encourage their enthusiasm during annotating. Finally, we present a dataset that contains a large number of artistic region compositions paired with corresponding cartoon illustrations. We also invite multiple professional artists to assure the quality of each annotation.

Keywords: Artistic creation · Fine art · Cartoon · Region processing

1 Introduction

Starting from the composition impression within traditional on-paper drawing crafts, and popularized in fashion strategies beyond modern digital creation workflows, the fundamental art element "region" continuously contributes to the distinctive feeling and unique style beyond multifarious artworks. Nowadays, diversified cartoon processing techniques and commercial cartoon animation workflow facilitate the usage of such important regions.

Electronic supplementary material The online version of this chapter (https://doi.org/10.1007/978-3-030-58601-0_9) contains supplementary material, which is available to authorized users.

Fig. 1. Example of our region annotating principles created manually by artists.

Aimed at assisting various cartoon image processing techniques, we invite artists to manually annotate regions in cartoon illustrations and digital arts. We observe the demands of real-world cartoon creation workflows and diversiform professional cartoon editing software, and our motivation is based on the demands of related applications. To be specific, we encourage artists to achieve the following application-oriented goals.

Firstly, artists are encouraged[1] to produce object outlines and objects' surface regions by distinguishing and eliminating lighting-and-shadow boundaries. The motivation is to aid in a variety of cartoon rendering/relighting [16,47] and illumination decomposition [2,5] applications that require the painted object surfaces to be segmented into independent regions, whereas the edges of light and shadow should not interfere the segmentation. Artists can identify these patterns manually, *e.g.*, in Fig. 1-(a), artists outline the boy face and erase the shadow edge, and these manual data are helpful for algorithms to identify object edges and shadow edges.

Secondly, artists are encouraged to clean up texture or deformation patterns and emphasize cartoon structural lines. The motivation is to help an increasing number of line inking [41–43] and sketch-based editing [38,48,56] tools that are dedicated to achieving cartoon lines faithful to artist perception, plus texture removal [11,54] and structure extraction [28] scenarios that are aimed at eliminating texture patterns and tones. Artists can determine salient structures and texture patterns in illustrations, *e.g.*, in Fig. 1-(b), artists trace the cloth structure and erase the folding texture, and these data created by artists manually are technically useful.

Thirdly, artists are encouraged to reconstruct, reorganize, and inpaint vague, broken, or missing regions in illustrations. The motivation is to assist a majority of cartoon digitization [27], cartoon topology construction [14,35], and cartoon or clip-art vectorization [57] workflows, where the cartoon regions are required to

---

[1] Although we *encourage* artists to follow these suggestions, they are not absolutely constrained to do so, in order to capture a realistic distribution of artistic region compositions.

be separated as completely as possible, and simultaneously, the closure of these regions has to be ensured. Many in-the-wild illustrations have missing, broken, or blurred regions, *e.g.*, in Fig. 1-(c), the ambiguous hair structure is troublesome for vision techniques to interpret, whereas artists can distinguish and manage these regions from human perception.

More importantly, we would like to point out that, given the typicality of the mentioned applications, our dataset is also likely to be used in many other cartoon processing techniques. This is not only because that region is an ubiquitous element in cartoon image processing and this dataset enables many problems to be studied in a data-driven manner, but also because that the availability of the manual data created by real artists is likely to facilitate researches to study the artist perceptual vision in various scenarios, *e.g.*, to study how artists compose the regions when creating their artworks.

To this end, we elaborate the challenges in achieving this dataset, and propose the Feasibility-based Assignment Recommendation (FAR) workflow to enable large-scale annotating. We also present a brief examination where we study the performance of applications using this dataset in many tasks including animation tracking, cartoon intrinsic decomposition, and sketch colorization.

2   Background

Related Datasets. Many computer vision or graphics datasets exist in the field of cartoon and creative arts. For example, [61] is a dataset with sketches of semantic segmentations, [21] is a clip-art dataset with class labels, [52] provides artistic images with attributes, [40] is for artistic renderings of 3D models with computer-generated annotations. [3, 36] are existing tools and strategies to collect large datasets of segmented images. [6] discusses how to combine crowd-sourcing and computer vision to reduce the amount of manual annotations. [19,34,60] are proposed as applications for these datasets.

Cartoon Image Segmentation. Previous cartoon image segmentation problems are routinely solved within two paradigms. The first paradigm [12,17,57] is to handcraft region priors and solve the regions using traditional algorithms. The second paradigm [20,28,55] is to synthesize task-specific datasets and train neural networks with the synthesized data. Our dataset enables the third paradigm: addressing the cartoon image segmentation problem with full access to real data from professional artists in a data-driven manner.

Region-Based Cartoon Application. Various cartoon applications can benefit from our artist annotated regions. Firstly, cartoon image segmentation methods [57] and clip-art vectorizing applications [27] can use a learning-based backend trained on our dataset. Then, manga structure extraction [28], cartoon inking [41–43], and line closure [29,30] literatures can also benefit from our region boundaries. Besides, a data-driven region extraction model can be used in cartoon image editing and animating [45]. Moreover, our regions can be used in

Fig. 2. Selected annotations from professional artists and the corresponding annotating time. We show perceptually satisfying results that are carefully selected from the dataset.

proxy construction [16,47] to achieve nonphotorealistic rendering. When applied to animations, our region data can benefit cartoon tracking problems like [59]. Our object boundary annotations can assist cartoon intrinsic decomposition [2,5]. Finally, artistic region compositions can be applied to line drawing color filling applications [46,48,56], or cleaning up the color composition in existing illustrations [18].

Photography Segmentation and Region Evaluation Metrics. Although the other "photography" segmentation problems are also extensively studied in non-cartoon image processing works [1,12,13,17,32,39,53], a dominant majority of cartoon processing literatures [28–30,41–43] have reached the consensus that those photography segmentation methods are far from satisfactory when handling cartoons. Nevertheless, the photography region evaluation metrics are still technically rooted and effective when applied to cartoon region datasets. We build our benchmark upon those standard region evaluation metrics and make it consistent to previous region processing literatures.

3   The DanbooRegion Dataset

We introduce a dataset of illustration and region annotation pairs. Specifically, each pair consists of an in-the-wild illustration downloaded from the Danbooru-2018 [15], accompanied by a region map of all pixels marked with a limited number of mutually exclusive indices indicating the structural regions in the original illustration. All samples are provided as RGB images at 1024-px resolution and 8-bit depth, and the region maps are provided as int-32 index images.

The major uniqueness of the presented dataset is that our annotations are carefully created by 12 professional artists. We show several cherry-picked examples in Fig. 2. Our annotations have achieved several results. Firstly, artists produce object outlines and objects' surface regions free from shadow or highlight interference, as shown in Fig. 2-(a, f). Secondly, artists clean up the texture or deformation patterns to obtain structural boundary lines, as shown in Fig. 2-(b, c). Thirdly, artists reconstruct, reorganize, and inpaint the broken or vague regions in illustrations, as shown in Fig. 2-(d, e). As we have mentioned before, these results can benefit various cartoon applications like cartoon intrinsic image, relighting, coloring, inking, shading, vectorizing, tracking, and so on.

We take special care of the annotation quality. Our dataset consists of 5377 region annotation pairs, and the quality of each sample is assured by at least 3 professional artists. In general, 2577 annotations are acknowledged by 5 artists as usable, 1145 annotations are assured by 4 artists, and the remaining 1655 annotations are assured by 3 artists. Furthermore, from the perspective of annotation approach, 154 annotations are painted by artists manually, 146 annotations are collected by aligning and refining publicly available online illustration and line drawing pairs, and the remaining 5077 annotations are achieved using a human-in-the-loop annotation approach. The high-quality region annotations are perceptually satisfying and practically applicable to diversiform downstream tasks related to illustration, cartoon, manga, and painting.

4   Feasibility-Based Assignment Recommendation

The objective of our data collection is to gather a large number of illustrations with paired region annotations. Those regions should be either created by artists manually, or coarsely generated by algorithms and then carefully refined by artists. All region annotations must be acknowledged by multiple professional artists as practically usable. Our source illustrations are downloaded from Danbooru-2018 [15] and 12 artists are invited as our annotators. To reduce artist labor, we use a human-in-the-loop workflow: artists create annotations for neural networks to learn, and neural networks estimate coarse annotations for artists to refine.

In order to benefit related applications by achieving our aforementioned goals, we have to face several problems. Firstly, when annotating cartoon object outlines and objects' surface regions, we find many downloaded illustrations are of low quality, and do not have decent and worthwhile object outlines for artists to annotate. Secondly, when cleaning up the texture or deformation patterns and emphasizing cartoon structural lines, we find many sampled images are not related to cartoon, and their texture patterns or structure lines are not suitable for the dataset. Thirdly, when reconstructing, reorganizing, and inpainting the broken or vague regions, we find many illustrations have too many regions, which are impractical and cannot be annotated within an acceptable amount of time. We provide examples in later experiments, where we also show that these problems can disable large-scale annotating because manually solving these problems can significantly waste artists' labor and discourage their enthusiasm.

These problems are non-trivial because of the following reasons. (1) These problems are caused by a large number of intertwined factors, which require huge efforts if engineered one-by-one independently. For example, to identify low-quality or non-cartoon images, the intertwined factors may include color distribution, shape geometry, texture style, semantic feature, and much more. (2) It depends on human perception to determinate whether an illustration can be annotated. For example, there is no fixed threshold to determine how many regions should be considered as impractical to annotate. (3) The involved problem modeling requires assumptions or prior knowledge, making it foreseeably challenging for feature engineering approaches to discriminate illustrations that are not suitable for our dataset.

We present an interactive solution: neural networks learning artist behaviors. Corresponding to the above reasons, our solution has several advantages: (1) It is a joint solution that does not model the intertwined factors independently. (2) It involves human perception. (3) It learns the dataset priors in a data-driven manner. To be specific, we allow artists to give up several types of illustrations during the annotating workflow, and train neural networks to learn artists' giving-up behavior. Firstly, we allow artists to give up low-quality illustrations with no worthwhile object outlines and objects' surface regions. Secondly, we allow artists to give up non-cartoon images without cartoon texture and cartoon inking lines. Thirdly, we allow artists to give up illustrations with too many regions that are impractical to reconstruct, reorganize, or inpaint. Simultaneously, we label these given-up illustrations as "infeasible" and the remaining illustrations as "feasible". We train neural networks with these "feasibility" labels to characterize future illustrations. We name this workflow after Feasibility-based Assignment Recommendation (FAR).

As shown in Fig. 3, the FAR architecture has unique purposes. Firstly, to improve object outline and surface region annotation quality, we need to discard low-quality illustrations as adequately as possible. Therefore, instead of applying a fixed threshold to the CNN output, we rank a batch of illustrations and only view the best one as feasible. Secondly, to aid in cartoon structural region annotating and cartoon texture eliminating, the non-cartoon images should be recognized accurately. Thus, we use the features from different convolutional layers to achieve a reliable multiple-scale estimation. Thirdly, to assist artists to reconstruct broken or vague regions, we need to avoid impractical images with too many regions to annotate. Accordingly, we use the global average pooling to approximate global counting operations in deep convolutional features.

Overview. As shown in Fig. 3, we use a CNN to rank the illustration feasibility and give artists the best one. Then, we record whether that assignment is finished (then labeled as positive) or given up (then labeled as negative), and train the CNN with the recorded labels. In this way, the FAR model is optimized progressively to recommend artists with feasible illustration assignments.

Generating Assignment. Each time when an artist queries a new assignment, we randomly sample 100 illustrations in Danbooru and rank their feasibility. Then, we feed the best illustration to the Coarse CNN (Fig. 3) to get a coarse annotation. After that, the illustration and coarse annotation are packaged into an assignment for the awaiting artist. Herein, the Coarse CNN is a U-net [37] trained with the *region-from-normal* approach.

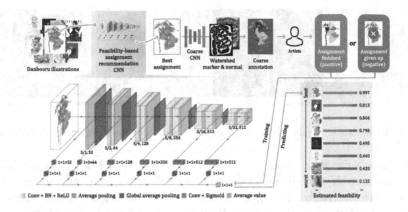

Fig. 3. Feasibility-based Assignment Recommendation (FAR) workflow. We show the neural network architectures and the visualized components within the FAR workflow.

Normal-from-Region Transform. As shown in Fig. 4, given an input region annotation X, the *normal-from-region* transform is aimed at produce a transformed map Y, which is a concatenation of a normal map N and a watershed marker W. The transform includes the following steps: *Step 1:* Compute the boundary of the region annotation X to get the boundary map B. *Step 2:* Compute the Zhang-Sun-Skeleton [58] of the region annotation X to get the skeleton map S. *Step 3:* Initialize a random field D_{rand}. If one pixel belongs to boundary in B, that pixel will be marked as zero. If one pixel belongs to skeleton in S, that pixel will be marked as one. The remaining pixels are be marked with random value sampled from random uniform distribution between zero and one. *Step 4:* Optimize the random field D_{rand} to get the displacement map D. We uses a routine Gaussian energy

$$E_{\text{displacement}} = \sum_p ||(D_{rand})_p - (g(D_{rand}))_p||_1$$

$$+ \sum_{i \in \{i | B_i = 1\}} ||(D_{rand})_i - 0||_1$$

$$+ \sum_{j \in \{j | S_j = 1\}} ||(D_{rand})_j - 1||_1 \qquad (1)$$

where p, i, and j are possible pixel positions, $g(\cdot)$ is a Gaussian (sigma is 1.0) filter, and $|| \cdot ||_1$ is the L1 Euclidean distance. This energy can be flexibly solved by gradient descent. *Step 5:* Compute the normal map N using the displacement map D. We use a standard *normal-from-height* [25] algorithm to achieve the normal. *Step 6:* Compute the watershed marker W by binarizing the displacement map D. We use the threshold 0.618. *Step 7:* Concatenate the normal map N and the watershed marker W into the final output Y.

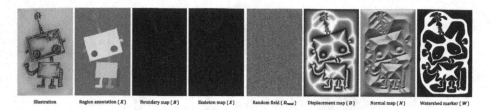

Illustration   Region annotation (X)   Boundary map (B)   Skeleton map (S)   Random field (D_{rand})   Displacement map (D)   Normal map (N)   Watershed marker (W)

Fig. 4. Visualization of involved maps in the region-normal transform algorithms.

Region-from-Normal Transform. Given the concatenated Y, we split it into the normal map N and the watershed marker W. After that, we run the watershed [33] with the marker W filling the map N. The results are the reconstructed regions. Note that when the marker W is predicted from neural networks, *e.g.*, the Coarse CNN, we may use morphology methods to remove some possible noise. In particular, we enforce all white regions in W to be bigger than 64 connected pixels.

Handling Assignment. Artists are allowed to give up any assignment, and in this case, the assignment feasibility is labeled as "0". Otherwise, the feasibility is labeled as "1", and artists refine the coarse annotations. Firstly, artists refine the region estimation to outline object surface regions free from lighting-and-shadow boundaries. Secondly, artists eliminate texture and emphasize cartoon structural lines in the estimated coarse regions. Thirdly, artists retouch the region estimation to reconstruct, reorganize, and inpaint broken or vague regions in the original illustration.

Instructions Given to the Artists. We present an artist guidelines in the supplementary material. The artists draw regions following their daily digital painting region composition workflow and the principles in §1. Herein, the digital painting region composition workflow refers to the workflow where artists compose there regions before drawing an illustration or filling colors in an artwork. We provide several on line resources of such workflow in the reference [7,31].

Initialization. We manually collect 300 low-quality or non-cartoon images as infeasible labels, and then collect another 300 feasible illustrations. In the feasible illustrations, 154 are high-ranking artworks in Danbooru, and 12 artists annotate them manually. The remaining 146 are cartoon images paired with line drawings searched with Google Images, enabling artists to directly align and refine the boundary lines into usable regions.

Detailed Workflow. At the beginning, we use the initial 300 feasible labels and 300 infeasible labels to train the FAR ranking network for 25 epochs, and use the 300 initial annotations to train the Coarse CNN for 20 epochs. After that, we view 100 annotations as one loop. When each loop is finished, we train FAR ranking network and Coarse CNN on the new data for 50 epochs, and train them on all old-and-new data for 20 epochs. We use Adam [26] ($l_r = 5e - 4$) for

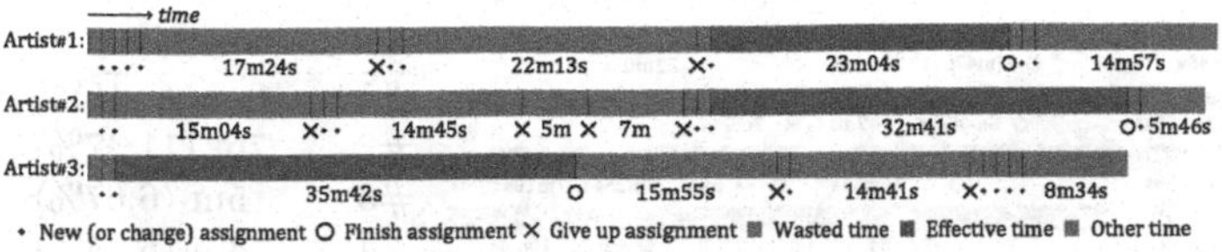

Fig. 5. Visualization of a naive annotation workflow by simply asking artists to handle all assignments one-by-one. Each time an artist finish or give up an assignment, a new assignment is then automatically assigned to that artist.

optimization, with each batch containing 8 randomly cropped 256×256 samples. Artists refine regions by drawing or erasing region boundaries, and merging or spiting region blocks. These editing strategy can be achieved using the software including PhotoShop, ClipStudio, *etc.*

Quality Assurance. After each loop, all 12 artists are invited to check the annotation quality in that loop. Artists are allowed to remove any annotations when they find low-quality ones. This quality assurance stage finishes when each annotation is assured by at least 3 artists as practically usable.

Significance of FAR. As shown in Fig. 5, we compare FAR to a naive workflow without the assignment recommendation but directly asking artists to annotate illustrations one-by-one. Artists are also allowed to give up infeasible assignments, and the configuration of the Coarse CNN remains unchanged. Our observation is that the decision of whether to give up is much more difficult than it seems to be, and even professional artists are likely to waste a significant amount of time in trials-and-errors, supported by two evidences: (1) Artists need a period of time to check each illustration assignment before they can judge whether to give up. This checking time causes a huge waste within a large number of assignments, *e.g.*, the artist #1 (Fig. 5) has given up (or change) more than 10 illustrations in the visualized workflow. (2) Even if the artist has decided to cope with one assignment, it is still possible that the assignment will be given up finally. In many cases, only after trying can an artist determine whether the annotating is feasible, *e.g.*, the artist #1 (Fig. 5) have wasted about 70% time (53 min) in the workflow. This can cause even worse wastes, discourages artist enthusiasm, and disable large-scale annotating.

On the contrary, by using FAR to recommend artists with feasible assignments, the amount of wasted time can be significantly reduced. We present a recorded workflow as shown in Fig. 6, and we focus on the behaviors of the artist #1. We can see that only 10 min are wasted in the beginning 79 min. The success of such effective workflow comes from the fact that many infeasible assignments are discriminated by FAR, and the consecutive success also protect artist enthusiasm and keep them encouraged.

Furthermore, we provide examples of infeasible illustrations discriminated by FAR in Fig. 7, where we also visualize the heat-map computed with Grad-Cam++ [8]. For example, as shown in Fig. 7-(b), several illustrations have too

→ time

Artist 1:
· 10m21s ○   28m48s   ○· 7m47s ○ 10m05s ✕·· 21m03s
Artist 2:
· 14m35s ○   25m59s   ○ 8m08s ○··· 7m14s ✕· 7m54s
Artist 3:
··· 7m51s ○   35m26s   ○   14m34s   ○··· 5m ✕ 7m25s ○ 7m10s
Artist 4:
·· 7m18s ○ 10m45s ○ 7m02s ○···   40m55s   ○ 4m ✕ 10m41s
Artist 5:
15m01s ○   25m56s   ○ 8m16s ○·· 5m ✕· 6m ✕·   23m22s

· New (or change) assignment ○ Finish assignment ✕ Give up assignment ■ Wasted time ■ Effective time ■ Other time

Artist	Wasted time
#1	10m (13.15%)
#2	7m (11.47%)
#3	5m (6.67%)
#4	4m (5.13%)
#5	11m (13.41%)

Fig. 6. Visualization of the annotation workflow using the FAR technique. The statistics are collected at the beginning of each artist's workflow.

(a) Non-cartoon images   (b) Illustrations with too many dense regions   (c) Low-quality Illustrations

Infeasible ——   —— Feasible

Fig. 7. Examples of the infeasible illustrations discriminated by FAR and the Grad-Cam++ heat-map visualization.

many regions that are impractical to annotate, and the FAR model successfully identifies those dense regions (marked with red in the heat-maps in Fig. 7-(b)). These evidences show that the FAR model has learned functional features to discriminate infeasible assignments.

Analysis of Dataset Quality. We perform an user study to analyze the final quality of the presented dataset. We invite the involved 12 artists to score 600 random region maps using the standards in Fig. 8. Each artist score 50 region maps. We also visualize the region quantity in each region map. A vast majority (80%) of the annotations in our dataset is usable or only need minor corrections, and about 20% annotations are aesthetically pleasing and can be used in professional artwork production workflows. We also note that the elimination of bad samples is still an unsolved open problem and this dataset still includes many "unfinished" or even "bad" annotations. Besides, results show that most region maps have more than 25 but less than 175 regions.

5 Benchmark

In this section, we first discuss the evaluation metrics for the presented dataset, and then test the performance of several possible candidates. The benchmark is presented in Table 1.

Metric. The metrics Average Precision (AP), Optimal Image Scale (OIS), and Optimal Dataset Scale (ODS) are widely considered as the standard metrics

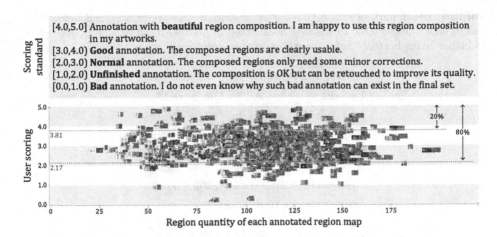

Fig. 8. User study result on annotation quality. The x-axis is the quantity of regions in each region map, while the y-axis is the user scoring with the above scoring standard.

in a dominant majority of region processing literature [1,12,13,17,32,39,53]. AP/OIS/ODS are mathematically rooted and particularly effective when evaluating region maps. It is notable that our problem is different from semantic segmentation tasks, *i.e.*, because the region classification labels are not available, so that many well-known metrics (*e.g.*, IoU) are not applicable. The effectiveness of AP/OIS/ODS has been proved by solid foundations including Holistically-nested Edge Detection [53] (HED), NYU-ObjectRegion [32], Berkeley-BSDS500 [1], and so on.

We include a brief review on AP/OIS/ODS to aid in reproducibility. Given a ground truth region map and an estimated one, AP is the average proportion of the true-positive pixels (correct region boundary pixels) in all positive pixels (all estimated region boundary pixels). We resize region maps to 256px when computing AP. It is obvious that AP is sensitive to image scale. Even computed on same region maps, different resizing scale causes remarkable indeterminacy. To address this problem, OIS searches all possible scales for each independent sample and report the optimal precision, whereas ODS searches all possible scales for the entire test set and report the optimal precision. Moreover, ODS is routinely considered as the best metric by many typical region processing works including HED [53], BSDS500 [1], and so on.

Experimental Setting. In the 5377 annotations, the quality of 2577 annotations are assured by 5 professional artists. In order to capture an accurate distribution of artist perception beyond artwork regions, we use the first 1000 in those 2577 annotations as our test set, with the remaining 4377 annotations being the training set. As to data augmentation, we use random left-and-right flipping and random rotation. We then randomly crop image data into 256×256 samples during the online training. It is notable that all non-deep-learning methods are directly tested on our test set.

Table 1. Benchmark of region boundary precision. Scores are in orange if below 0.65 and in blue if above 0.65. Best scores are marked in bold with red background. ↑ refers to higher being better. * refers to *region-from-normal* approaches.

CNN + Unet-decoder[37] + L2 loss		
Encoder	AP ↑	OIS ↑	ODS ↑
VGG16*[44]	0.710	**0.744**	0.731
VGG19*[44]	0.642	0.716	0.647
Resnet56*[22]	**0.722**	0.737	**0.732**
Resnet110*[22]	0.641	0.725	0.692
Densenet121*[23]	0.645	0.663	0.648
Image-to-image translation		
Model	AP ↑	OIS ↑	ODS ↑
Pix2Pix*[24]	0.562	0.663	0.642
CRN*[9]	0.546	0.606	0.548
Pix2PixHD*[51]	0.568	0.667	0.57
Traditional algorithm		
Algorithm	AP ↑	OIS ↑	ODS ↑
Mean Shift [12]	0.518	0.592	0.524
NCuts [13]	0.428	0.547	0.515
Felz-Hutt [17]	0.404	0.517	0.466
SWA [39]	0.377	0.568	0.538
Quad-Tree [1]	0.17	0.247	0.219
gPb-owt-ucm [1]	0.633	0.651	0.640
CartoonVec [57]	0.536	0.614	0.614
Dense instance segmentation		
Method	AP ↑	OIS ↑	ODS ↑
TensorMask [10]	0.454	0.519	0.495

Algorithm Candidate. We test the performance of traditional segmentation algorithms [1,12,13,17,39], including Vectorizing Cartoon Animations (CartoonVec) [57], by directly applying them to the test set. Then, using the aforementioned *region-from-normal* approach, we test the performance of image-to-image translation methods [9,24,51] by training them to predict region normals and markers. In the same way, we also include the baseline performance of VGG [44], Resnet [22], and Densenet [23], by using them as the encoder of U-net [37], and we train them with a standard L2 loss on region normals and markers. Instance segmentation methods can also be applied to our problem. To the best of our knowledge, TensorMask [10] is the only instance segmentation method that does not require region classification labels and can be trained on arbitrary number of regions. Therefore, we also train TensorMask on our dataset and report its performance.

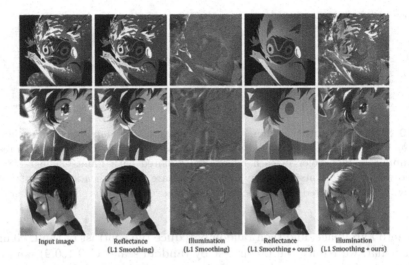

| Input image | Reflectance (L1 Smoothing) | Illumination (L1 Smoothing) | Reflectance (L1 Smoothing + ours) | Illumination (L1 Smoothing + ours) |

Fig. 9. Intrinsic cartoon images. We show the reflectance maps and the illumination maps decomposed using L1 smoothing with naive regions in [5] and our regions.

Human Performance. Different artists may produce slightly different region annotations even for one same illustration. Therefore, we also invite the 12 involved artists to annotate 36 random test illustrations again (each artist with 3 illustrations), and report the human performance: 0.785(OIS), 0.782(ODS).

Result. We have several interesting discoveries in this benchmark: (1) Learning-based models generally report higher scores than traditional algorithms. This indicates that data-driven approaches seem to be more faithful to artist perception when generating the regions. (2) Shallow models like VGG16 and Resnet56 outperform deep models like VGG19 and Resnet110. This may because deep models tend to over-fit the dataset, and stronger data augmentation might be necessary. (3) The instance segmentation method, TensorMask, does not report impressive performances. This may because the regions in our dataset is denser than most instance segmentation datasets, and instance segmentation methods like TensorMask are not well-suited for our problem.

6   Application

Cartoon Intrinsic Images. We present a region-based L1 intrinsic decomposition [5] as in Fig. 9. We can see that our data-driven region segmentation enables L1 smoothing to achieve more adequate decomposition when compared to the naive L1 smoothing. In particular, we directly train a Pix2PixHD [51] for this application. After the training, the estimated normal maps and watershed marker maps can be translated to regions using the *normal-from-region* approach. One notice is that we use a special data augmentation method to augment the luminance domain of the images to avoid luminance over-fitting, by converting the RGB

Fig. 10. Sketch colorization cleaning-up. *The regions in this figure are achieved interactively by user.* We use the estimated regions to clean up the sketch colorization results by sampling median color in each region. (a) Colored with PaintsChainer [48]. (b) Colored with Style2Paints [56]. The pointed hints are color indications for interactive coloring, while the dotted hints indicates that its covered regions should be merged.

image into Lab image, and then randomly reduce the contrast of the L channel. In particular, we reduce the L contrast by random scalar $U(0.1, 0.9)$, and then translate the Lab image back to RGB image. In order to make the estimated region boundary a bit more smoother (regions produced by watershed is not very smooth in most cases), we use the method [4] to simplify the topology of our region boundary. This is achieved by translating the region map into a vectorized map and then rasterize it back. We carefully tune the parameters of [4] and the smoothing weights to achieve our results in Fig. 9.

Flat Sketch Colorization and Color Cleaning-Up. Our dataset enables learning-based sketch colorization solutions [48,56] to be "cleaned-up" so as to adapt to the flat "cel-colorization" workflows like LazyBrush [46], by enabling neural networks to learn to reconstruct broken or vague regions. We present flat colorization and cleaning-up examples as shown in Fig. 10. We train a Pix2PixHD [51] for the application, and the estimation can be translated to regions using the *normal-from-region* approach. For data augmentation, we use the high-frequency augmentation. This is to encourage the neural networks to learn to reconstruct broken or ambiguous regions, and avoid the neural networks to over-fit the high-frequency edges in the input image. We apply a Bilateral Filter [49] to the training input image with a random number in $U(20, 1000)$ for the Bilateral spacial sigma, and $U(20, 1000)$ for the Bilateral color sigma. We also allow users to merge some regions in the region map by drawing some "dotted" lines. We use a fine-tuned selected search [50] to merge some small regions. The regions are also processed with [4] to simplify the topology of region boundary and make the resulting region looks smooth, by translating the region map into a vectorized map and rasterize it back. The smoothing parameters are tuned for Fig. 10.

7 Conclusion

We presented a dataset of illustration and region composition pairs annotated by real-life artists. Our dataset is unique in that it is faithful to artist perception, and is costumed to benefit diversiform cartoon processing applications.

All annotations are created from in-the-wild cartoon illustrations, and the quality of each annotation is assured by multiple artists. We provide the details of our data collection pipeline, which leverages a novel human-in-the-loop annotation workflow, namely Feasibility-based Assignment Recommendation (FAR), that is designed to improve the feasibility of involved assignments and enable the large-scale annotating. We demonstrate the usage of our dataset in a variety of applications like cartoon tracking, cartoon intrinsic images, and sketch colorization. Finally, we provide considerations for further researches in related avenue.

References

1. Arbeláez, P., Maire, M., Fowlkes, C., Malik, J.: Contour detection and hierarchical image segmentation. IEEE Trans. Pattern Anal. Mach. Intell. **33**(5), 898–916 (2011)
2. Bell, S., Bala, K., Snavely, N.: Intrinsic images in the wild. ACM Trans. Graph. (SIGGRAPH) **33**(4), 1–12 (2014)
3. Bell, S., Upchurch, P., Snavely, N., Bala, K.: OpenSurfaces: a richly annotated catalog of surface appearance. ACM Trans. Graph. (SIGGRAPH) **32**(4), 1–17 (2013)
4. Bessmeltsev, M., Solomon, J.: Vectorization of line drawings via polyvector fields. ACM Trans. Graph. **38**(1), 1–12 (2019). https://doi.org/10.1145/3202661
5. Bi, S., Han, X., Yu, Y.: An L1 image transform for edge-preserving smoothing and scene-level intrinsic decomposition. ACM Trans. Graph. **34**(4) (2015). https://doi.org/10.1145/2766946. https://doi.org/10.1145/2766946
6. Branson, S., Van Horn, G., Perona, P.: Lean crowdsourcing: combining humans and machines in an online system. In: The IEEE Conference on Computer Vision and Pattern Recognition (CVPR), July 2017
7. caydett: Cel shading tutorial by caydett (2018). https://www.deviantart.com/caydett/art/Cel-Shading-Tutorial-270935090
8. Chattopadhay, A., Sarkar, A., Howlader, P., Balasubramanian, V.N.: GradCAM: generalized gradient-based visual explanations for deep convolutional networks. In: WACV. IEEE, March 2018. https://doi.org/10.1109/wacv.2018.00097
9. Chen, Q., Koltun, V.: Photographic image synthesis with cascaded refinement networks. In: ICCV (2017)
10. Chen, X., Girshick, R., He, K., Dollar, P.: TensorMask: a foundation for dense object segmentation. In Arxiv (2019)
11. Cho, H., Lee, H., Kang, H., Lee, S.: Bilateral texture filtering. ACM Trans. Graph. **33**(4), 1–8 (2014). https://doi.org/10.1145/2601097.2601188
12. Comaniciu, D., Meer, P.: Mean shift: a robust approach toward feature space analysis. IEEE Trans. Pattern Anal. Mach. Intell. **24**(5), 603–619 (2002). https://doi.org/10.1109/34.1000236
13. Cour, T., Benezit, F., Shi, J.: Spectral segmentation with multiscale graph decomposition. In: CVPR. IEEE (2005). https://doi.org/10.1109/cvpr.2005.332
14. Dalstein, B., Ronfard, R., van de Panne, M.: Vector graphics animation with time-varying topology. ACM Trans. Graph. **34**(4) (2015). https://doi.org/10.1145/2766913
15. DanbooruCommunity: Danbooru 2017: a large-scale crowdsourced and tagged anime illustration dataset (2018)

16. Dvorožňák, M., Nejad, S.S., Jamriška, O., Jacobson, A., Kavan, L., Sýkora, D.: Seamless reconstruction of part-based high-relief models from hand-drawn images. In: Proceedings of International Symposium on Sketch-Based Interfaces and Modeling (2018)

17. Felzenszwalb, P.F., Huttenlocher, D.P.: Efficient graph-based image segmentation. IJCV **59**, 167–181 (2004)

18. Fourey, S., Tschumperle, D., Revoy, D.: A fast and efficient semi-guided algorithm for flat coloring line-arts. In: EUROGRAPHICS (2018)

19. Gao, C., Liu, Q., Xu, Q., Wang, L., Liu, J., Zou, C.: SketchyCOCO: image generation from freehand scene sketches. In: The IEEE/CVF Conference on Computer Vision and Pattern Recognition (CVPR), June 2020

20. Gao, S., et al.: A data-synthesis-driven method for detecting and extracting vague cognitive regions. Int. J. Geograph. Inf. Sci., 1–27 (2017). https://doi.org/10.1080/13658816.2016.1273357

21. Garces, E., Agarwala, A., Gutierrez, D., Hertzmann, A.: A similarity measure for illustration style. ACM Trans. Graph. (SIGGRAPH 2014) **33**(4), 1–9 (2014)

22. He, K., Zhang, X., Ren, S., Sun, J.: Deep residual learning for image recognition. In: 2016 IEEE Conference on Computer Vision and Pattern Recognition (CVPR). IEEE, June 2016. https://doi.org/10.1109/cvpr.2016.90

23. Huang, G., Liu, Z., van der Maaten, L., Weinberger, K.Q.: Densely connected convolutional networks. In: 2017 IEEE Conference on Computer Vision and Pattern Recognition (CVPR). IEEE, July 2017. https://doi.org/10.1109/cvpr.2017.243

24. Isola, P., Zhu, J.Y., Zhou, T., Efros, A.A.: Image-to-image translation with conditional adversarial networks. In: CVPR (2017)

25. Kender, J.R., Smith, E.M.: Shape from Darkness: Deriving Surface Information from Dynamic Shadows, chap. 3, pp. 378–385. Jones and Bartlett Publishers Inc, USA (1992)

26. Kingma, D.P., Ba, J.: Adam: a method for stochastic optimization. Computer Science (2014)

27. Lalonde, J.F., Hoiem, D., Efros, A.A., Rother, C., Winn, J., Criminisi, A.: Photo clip art. ACM Trans. Graph. (TOG) **26**(3), 3 (2007). https://doi.org/10.1145/1276377.1276381

28. Li, C., Liu, X., Wong, T.T.: Deep extraction of manga structural lines. ACM Trans. Graph. **36**(4), 1–12 (2017)

29. Liu, C., Rosales, E., Sheffer, A.: Strokeaggregator: consolidating raw sketches into artist-intended curve drawings. ACM Trans. Graph. **37**, 1–15 (2018)

30. Liu, X., Wong, T.T., Heng, P.A.: Closure-aware sketch simplification. ACM Trans. Graph. **34**(6), 168:1–168:10 (2015)

31. MicahBuzan: Cel shading tutorial (2020). https://www.micahbuzan.com/cel-shading-tutorial/

32. Silberman, N., Hoiem, D., Kohli, P., Fergus, R.: Indoor segmentation and support inference from RGBD images. In: Fitzgibbon, A., Lazebnik, S., Perona, P., Sato, Y., Schmid, C. (eds.) ECCV 2012. LNCS, vol. 7576, pp. 746–760. Springer, Heidelberg (2012). https://doi.org/10.1007/978-3-642-33715-4_54

33. Neubert, P., Protzel, P.: Compact watershed and preemptive SLIC: on improving trade-offs of superpixel segmentation algorithms. In: ICPR (2014)

34. Ren, H., Li, J., Gao, N.: Two-stage sketch colorization with color parsing. IEEE Access **8**, 44599–44610 (2020)

35. Rivière, M., Okabe, M.: Extraction of a cartoon topology. In: ACM SIGGRAPH 2014 Posters on - SIGGRAPH 2014. ACM Press (2014). https://doi.org/10.1145/2614217.2614260

36. Ronchi, M.R., Perona, P.: Describing common human visual actions in images. In: Proceedings of the British Machine Vision Conference (BMVC), pp. 52.1–52.12. BMVA Press, September 2015. https://doi.org/10.5244/C.29.52. https://dx.doi.org/10.5244/C.29.52

37. Ronneberger, O., Fischer, P., Brox, T.: U-Net: convolutional networks for biomedical image segmentation. In: Navab, N., Hornegger, J., Wells, W.M., Frangi, A.F. (eds.) MICCAI 2015. LNCS, vol. 9351, pp. 234–241. Springer, Cham (2015). https://doi.org/10.1007/978-3-319-24574-4_28

38. Sangkloy, P., Lu, J., Fang, C., Yu, F., Hays, J.: Scribbler: controlling deep image synthesis with sketch and color. In: CVPR (2017)

39. Sharon, E., Galun, M., Sharon, D., Basri, R., Brandt, A.: Hierarchy and adaptivity in segmenting visual scenes. Nature **442**(7104), 810–813 (2006). https://doi.org/10.1038/nature04977

40. Shugrina, M., et al.: Creative flow+ dataset. In: The IEEE Conference on Computer Vision and Pattern Recognition (CVPR), June 2019

41. Simo-Serra, E., Iizuka, S., Ishikawa, H.: Mastering sketching: adversarial augmentation for structured prediction. ACM Trans. Graph. **37**(1), 1–13 (2018)

42. Simo-Serra, E., Iizuka, S., Ishikawa, H.: Real-time data-driven interactive rough sketch inking. ACM Trans. Graph. **37**, 1–14 (2018)

43. Simo-Serra, E., Iizuka, S., Sasaki, K., Ishikawa, H.: Learning to simplify: fully convolutional networks for rough sketch cleanup. ACM Trans. Graph. **35**(4), 1–11 (2016)

44. Simonyan, K., Zisserman, A.: Very deep convolutional networks for large-scale image recognition. In: TPAMI (2014)

45. Sýkora, D., Buriánek, J., Žára, J.: Sketching cartoons by example. In: Proceedings of Eurographics Workshop on Sketch-Based Interfaces and Modeling, pp. 27–34 (2005)

46. Sykora, D., Dingliana, J., Collins, S.: LazyBrush: flexible painting tool for hand-drawn cartoons. Comput. Graph. Forum **28**(2), 599–608 (2009)

47. Sýkora, D., et al.: Ink-and-ray: bas-relief meshes for adding global illumination effects to hand-drawn characters. ACM Trans. Graph. **33**(2), 16 (2014)

48. TaiZan: Paintschainer tanpopo. PreferredNetwork (2016)

49. Tomasi, C., Manduchi, R.: Bilateral filtering for gray and color images. In: Sixth International Conference on Computer Vision (IEEE Cat. No.98CH36271). Narosa Publishing House (1998). https://doi.org/10.1109/iccv.1998.710815

50. Uijlings, J.R.R., van de Sande, K.E.A., Gevers, T., Smeulders, A.W.M.: Selective search for object recognition. IJCV **104**, 154–171 (2013)

51. Wang, T.C., Liu, M.Y., Zhu, J.Y., Tao, A., Kautz, J., Catanzaro, B.: High-resolution image synthesis and semantic manipulation with conditional GANs. In: CVPR (2018)

52. Wilber, M.J., Fang, C., Jin, H., Hertzmann, A., Collomosse, J., Belongie, S.: Bam! the behance artistic media dataset for recognition beyond photography. In: The IEEE International Conference on Computer Vision (ICCV), October 2017

53. Xie, S., Tu, Z.: Holistically-nested edge detection. In: CVPR (2015)

54. Xu, L., Yan, Q., Xia, Y., Jia, J.: Structure extraction from texture via relative total variation. ACM Trans. Graph. **31**(6), 1 (2012). https://doi.org/10.1145/2366145.2366158

55. Xu, N., Price, B., Cohen, S., Huang, T.: Deep image matting. In: CVPR. IEEE, July 2017. https://doi.org/10.1109/cvpr.2017.41

56. Zhang, L., Li, C., Wong, T.T., Ji, Y., Liu, C.: Two-stage sketch colorization. ACM Trans. Graph. **37**, 1–14 (2018)

57. Zhang, S.H., Chen, T., Zhang, Y.F., Hu, S.M., Martin, R.R.: Vectorizing cartoon animations. TVCG **15**, 618–629 (2009)
58. Zhang, T.Y., Suen, C.Y.: A fast parallel algorithm for thinning digital patterns. Commun. ACM **27**, 236–239 (1984)
59. Zhu, H., Liu, X., Wong, T.T., Heng, P.A.: Globally optimal toon tracking. ACM Trans. Graph. **35**(4), 75:1–75:10 (2016)
60. Zou, C., Mo, H., Gao, C., Du, R., Fu, H.: Language-based colorization of scene sketches. ACM Trans. Graph. (Proceedings of ACM SIGGRAPH Asia 2019) **38**(6), 233:1–233:16 (2019)
61. Zou, C., et al.: SketchyScene: richly-annotated scene sketches. In: Ferrari, V., Hebert, M., Sminchisescu, C., Weiss, Y. (eds.) ECCV 2018. LNCS, vol. 11219, pp. 438–454. Springer, Cham (2018). https://doi.org/10.1007/978-3-030-01267-0_26

Event Enhanced High-Quality Image Recovery

Bishan Wang, Jingwei He, Lei Yu$^{(\boxtimes)}$, Gui-Song Xia, and Wen Yang

Wuhan University, Wuhan, China
{wangbs,jingwei_he,ly.wd,guisong.xia,yangwen}@whu.edu.cn

Abstract. With extremely high temporal resolution, event cameras have a large potential for robotics and computer vision. However, their asynchronous imaging mechanism often aggravates the measurement sensitivity to noises and brings a physical burden to increase the image spatial resolution. To recover high-quality intensity images, one should address both denoising and super-resolution problems for event cameras. Since events depict brightness changes, with the enhanced degeneration model by the events, the clear and sharp high-resolution latent images can be recovered from the noisy, blurry and low-resolution intensity observations. Exploiting the framework of sparse learning, the events and the low-resolution intensity observations can be jointly considered. Based on this, we propose an explainable network, an event-enhanced sparse learning network (**eSL-Net**), to recover the high-quality images from event cameras. After training with a synthetic dataset, the proposed eSL-Net can largely improve the performance of the state-of-the-art by **7–12 dB**. Furthermore, without additional training process, the proposed eSL-Net can be easily extended to generate continuous frames with frame-rate as high as the events.

Keywords: Event camera · Intensity reconstruction · Denoising · Deblurring · Super resolution · Sparse learning

1 Introduction

Unlike the standard frame-based cameras, the event camera is a bio-inspired sensor that produce asynchronous "events" with very low latency (1 μs), leading to extremely high temporal resolution [4,17,18,27,31]. Naturally, it is immune to motion blurs and has highly appealing promise for low/high-level vision tasks [1,25,33]. However, the generated event streams can only depict the scene changes instead of the absolute intensity measurements. Meanwhile, the asynchronous data-driven mechanism also prohibits directly applying existing algorithms designed for standard cameras to event cameras. Thus the high-quality

---

B. Wang and J. He—Equal contribution.

Electronic supplementary material The online version of this chapter (https://doi.org/10.1007/978-3-030-58601-0_10) contains supplementary material, which is available to authorized users.

A. Vedaldi et al. (Eds.): ECCV 2020, LNCS 12358, pp. 155–171, 2020.
https://doi.org/10.1007/978-3-030-58601-0_10

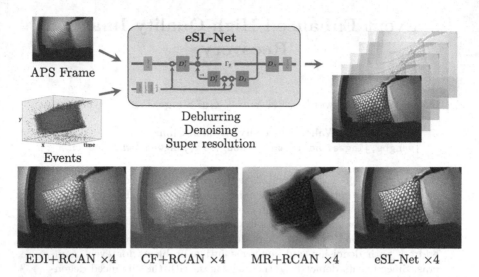

Fig. 1. Our eSL-Net reconstructs high-resolution, sharp and clear intensity images for event cameras by APS frames and the corresponding event sequences. The eSL-Net performs much better than EDI [25], CF [30] and MR [19] superimposing a SR network RCAN [38].

intensity image reconstruction from event streams is essentially required for visualization and provides great potentials to bridge the event camera to many high-level vision tasks that have been solved with standard cameras [13,15,16,19,29].

In order to achieve the low latency property, event cameras capture brightness changes of each pixels independently [4,12]. This mechanism aggravates the measurement sensitivity to noises and brings a physical burden to increase the image spatial resolution. Thus, the recovering of high-quality images from event cameras is a very challenge problem, where the following issues should be addressed simultaneously.

- **Low frame-rate and blurry intensity images:** The APS (Active Pixel Sensor) frames are with relatively low frame-rate ($\geq$5 ms latency). And the motion blur is inevitable when recording highly dynamic scenes.
- **High level and mixed noises:** The thermal effects or unstable light environment can produce a huge amount of noisy events. Together with the noises from APS frames, the reconstruction of intensity image would fall into a mixed noises problem.
- **Low spatial-resolution:** The leading commercial event cameras are typically with very low spatial-resolution. And there is a balance between the spatial-resolution and the latency.

To address the problem of noises for recovering images from event cameras, various methods have been proposed. Barua et al. [3] firstly proposed a learning-based approach to smooth the image gradient by imposing sparsity regularization, then exploited Poisson integration to recover the intensity image from denoised image gradient. Instead of sparsity, Munda et al. [19] introduced the manifold regularization imposed on the event time surface and proposed a real-time intensity reconstruction algorithm. With these hand-crafted regularizations, the noises can be largely alleviated, however, some artifacts (e.g. blurry edges) are meanwhile produced. Recent works turn to convolutional neural network (CNN) for event-based intensity reconstruction, where the network is trained end-to-end with paired events and intensity images [5,13,29,35]. Implicitly, the convolutional kernels with trained parameters are commonly able to reduce the noises. However, the man-made networks are often lack of physical mean and thus difficult to deal with both events and APS frames [5].

Besides the noise issue, a super-resolution algorithm is also urgent at present phase to further improve intensity reconstructions for high-level vision tasks, e.g. face recognition, but few of progress has been made in this line yet. Even though one can apply existing super-resolution algorithms to the low-resolution intensity frames (reconstructed), a comprehensive approach will be more desirable.

To the best of our knowledge, few study is able to simultaneously resolve all above three tasks, leaving an open problem: *Is it possible to find a unified framework to consider denoising, debluring and super-resolution simultaneously?* To answer this question, we propose to employ a powerful tool *sparse learning* to address the three tasks. General degeneration model for blurry images with noises and low-resolution, often assumes the whole image shares the same blurring kernel. However, events record intensity changes at a very high temporal resolution, which can enhance the degeneration model effectively to represent motion blur effect. The enhanced degeneration model provides a road to recover HR sharp and clear latent images from APS frames and their event sequences. We can solve the model by casting it to the framework of sparse learning, which also leads to its natural ability to resist noise. In this paper, we propose the **eSL-Net** to recover high-quality images for event cameras (Fig. 1). Specially, the eSL-Net trained by our synthetic dataset can be generalized to real scenes and without additional training process the eSL-Net can be easily extended to generate high frame-rate videos by transforming the event sequence. Experimental results show the proposed eSL-Net can improve high-quality intensity reconstruction.

Overall, our contributions are summarized as below:

- We propose an event enhanced degeneration model for the high-quality image recovery based on event cameras. Based on this, exploiting the framework of sparse learning, we propose an explainable network, an event-enhanced sparse learning network (eSL-Net), to recover the high-quality images from event cameras.
- Without retraining process, we propose an easy method to extend the eSL-Net for high frame-rate and high-quality video recovery.
- We build a synthetic dataset for event camera to connect events, LR blurry images and the HR sharp clear images.

Dataset, code, and more results are available at: https://github.com/ShinyWang33/eSL-Net.

2   Related Works

Event-Based Intensity Reconstruction: Early attempts of reconstructing intensity from pure events are commonly based on the assumption of brightness constancy, i.e. static scenes [15]. The intensity reconstruction is then addressed by simultaneously estimating the camera movement, optical flow and intensity gradient [16]. In [6], Cook et al. propose a bio-inspired and interconnected network to simultaneously reconstruct intensity frames, optical flow and angular velocity for small rotation movements. Later on, Bardow et al. [2] formulate the intensity change and optical flow in a unified variational energy minimization framework. By optimization, one can simultaneously reconstruct the video frames together with the optical flow. On the other hand, another research line on intensity reconstruction is the direct event integration method [19,25,30], which does not rely on any assumption about the scene structure or motion dynamics.

While the APS frames contain relatively abundant textures, events and APS frames can be used as complementary sources for event-based intensity reconstruction. In [30], events are approximated as the time differential of intensity frames. Based on this, a complementary filter is proposed as a fusion engine and nearly continuous-time intensity frames can be generated. Pan et al. [25] have proposed an event-based deblurring approach by relating blurry APS frames and events with an event-based double integration (EDI) model. Afterwards, a multiple-frame EDI model is proposed for high-rate video reconstruction by further considering frame-to-frame relations [24].

Event-Based Super-Resolution: Even though event cameras have extremely high temporal frequency, the spatial (pixel) resolution is relative low and yet not easy to be resolved physically [12]. Few of progress has been made to event-based super-resolution. To the best of our knowledge, only one very recent work [5], called SRNet, has been released when we are preparing this manuscript. Comparing to SRNet, our proposed approach differs in the following aspects: (1) we proposed a unified framework to simultaneously resolve the tasks including denoising, deblurring and superresolution, while SRNet [5] cannot directly deal with blurring or noisy inputs; (2) the proposed network is completely interpretable with meaningful intermediate processes; (3) our framework reconstructs the intensity frame by fusing events and APS frames, while SRNet is proposed for reconstruction from pure events.

3   Problem Statement

3.1   Events and Intensity Images

Event camera triggers events whenever the logarithm of the intensity changes over a pre-setting threshold c,

$$\log(\boldsymbol{I}_{xy}(t)) - \log(\boldsymbol{I}_{xy}(t - \Delta t)) = p \cdot c \tag{1}$$

where $\boldsymbol{I}_{xy}(t)$ and $\boldsymbol{I}_{xy}(t - \Delta t)$ denote the instantaneous intensities at time t and $t - \Delta t$ for a specific pixel location (x, y), Δt is the time since the last event at this pixel location, $p \in \{+1, -1\}$ is the polarity representing the direction (increase or decrease) of the intensity change. Consequently, an event is made up of (x, y, t, p).

In order to facilitate expression of events, for every location (x, y) in the image, we define $e_{xy}(t)$ as a function of continuous time t such that:

$$e_{xy}(t) \triangleq p\delta(t - t_0) \tag{2}$$

whenever there is an event (x, y, t_0, p). Here, $\delta(\cdot)$ is the Dirac function [8]. As a result, a sequence of discrete events is turned into a continuous time signal.

In addition to event sequence, many event cameras e.g., DAVIS [4], can provide grey-scale intensity images simultaneously with slower frame-rate. And mathematically, the f-th frame of the observed intensity image $\boldsymbol{Y}[f]$ during the exposure interval $[t_f, t_f + T]$ could be modeled as an average of sharp clear latent intensity images $\boldsymbol{I}(t)$ [25]:

$$\boldsymbol{Y}[f] = \frac{1}{T} \int_{t_f}^{t_f + T} \boldsymbol{I}(t) dt \tag{3}$$

Suppose that $\boldsymbol{I}_{xy}(t_r)$ is the sharp clear latent intensity image at any time $t_r \in [t_f, t_f + T]$, we have the following relationship according to (1) and (2), $\log(\boldsymbol{I}_{xy}(t)) = \log(\boldsymbol{I}_{xy}(t_r)) + c \int_{t_r}^{t} e_{xy}(s) ds$, then

$$\boldsymbol{Y}_{xy}[f] = \frac{\boldsymbol{I}_{xy}(t_r)}{T} \int_{t_f}^{t_f + T} \exp\left(c \int_{t_r}^{t} e_{xy}(s) ds\right) dt \tag{4}$$

Since each pixel can be treated separately, subscripts x, y are often omitted henceforth. Finally, considering the whole pixels, we can get a simple model connecting events, the observed intensity image and the latent intensity image:

$$\boldsymbol{Y}[f] = \boldsymbol{E}(t_r) \odot \boldsymbol{I}(t_r) \tag{5}$$

with $\boldsymbol{E}(t_r) = \frac{1}{T} \int_{t_f}^{t_f + T} \exp(c \int_{t_r}^{t} e(s) ds) dt$ being double integral of events at time t_r [25] and $\odot$ denoting the Hadamard product.

3.2   Event Enhanced Degeneration Model

Practically, the non-ideality of sensors and the relative motion between cameras and target scenes may largely degrade the quality of the observed intensity image $\boldsymbol{Y}[f]$ and make it noisy and blurry. Moreover, even though event cameras have extremely high temporal resolution, the spatial pixel resolution is relatively low due to the physical limitations. With these considerations, (5) becomes:

$$\begin{aligned} \boldsymbol{Y}[f] &= \boldsymbol{E}(t_r) \odot \boldsymbol{I}(t_r) + \varepsilon \\ \boldsymbol{I}(t_r) &= \boldsymbol{P}\boldsymbol{X}(t_r) \end{aligned} \tag{6}$$

with ε the measuring noise which can be assumed to be white Gaussian, $\boldsymbol{P}$ the downsampling operator and $\boldsymbol{X}(t_r)$ the latent clear image with high-resolution (HR) at time t_r. Consequently, (6) is the degeneration model where events are exploited to introduce the motion information.

Given the observed image $\boldsymbol{Y}[f]$, the corresponding triggered events and the specified time $t_r \in [t_f, t_f + T]$, our goal is to reconstruct a high quality intensity image $\boldsymbol{X}$ at time t_r. Obviously, it is a multi-task and ill-posed problem where denoising, deblurring and super-resolution should be addressed simultaneously.

In the following, we will first address the problem of reconstructing single high quality intensity image from events and a degraded LR blurry image. Then, the method to extend to generate high frame-rate video is addressed in Sect. 5.

4   Event Enhanced High-Quality Image Recovery

4.1   Event-Enhanced Sparse Learning

Many methods were proposed for image denoising, deblurring and SR [9,11,23,37]. However, most of them can not be applied for event cameras directly due to the asynchronous data-driven mechanism. Thanks to the sparse learning, we could integrate the events into sparsity framework and reconstruct satisfactory images to solve the aforementioned problems.

In this section, the expression of the time t_r and frame index f is temporally removed for simplicity. Then we arrange the image matrices as column vectors, i.e., $\boldsymbol{Y} \in \mathbb{R}^{N \times 1}$, $\boldsymbol{I} \in \mathbb{R}^{N \times 1}$, $\varepsilon \in \mathbb{R}^{N \times 1}$ and $\boldsymbol{X} \in \mathbb{R}^{sN \times 1}$, thus the blurring operator can be represented as $\boldsymbol{E} = \mathrm{diag}(e_1, e_2, \ldots, e_N) \in \mathbb{R}^{N \times N}$, where $e_1, e_2, \ldots, e_N$ are the elements of original blurring operator, so does $\boldsymbol{P} \in \mathbb{R}^{N \times sN}$, where s denotes the downsampling scale factor and N denotes the product of height H and width W of the observed image $\boldsymbol{Y}$. Then, according to (6), we have:

$$\begin{aligned} \boldsymbol{Y} &= \boldsymbol{E}\boldsymbol{I} + \varepsilon \\ \boldsymbol{I} &= \boldsymbol{P}\boldsymbol{X} \end{aligned} \tag{7}$$

The reconstruction from the observed image $\boldsymbol{Y}$ to HR sharp clear image $\boldsymbol{X}$ is highly ill-posed since the inevitable loss of information in the image degeneration process. Inspired by the success of Compressed Sensing [10], we assume that LR sharp clear image $\boldsymbol{I}$ and HR sharp clear image $\boldsymbol{X}$ can be sparsely represented on LR dictionary $\boldsymbol{D}_I$ and HR dictionary $\boldsymbol{D}_X$, i.e., $\boldsymbol{I} = \boldsymbol{D}_I \boldsymbol{\alpha}_I$ and $\boldsymbol{X} = \boldsymbol{D}_X \boldsymbol{\alpha}_X$ where $\boldsymbol{\alpha}_I$ and $\boldsymbol{\alpha}_X$ are known as sparse codes. Since the downsampling operator $\boldsymbol{P}$ is linear, LR sharp clear image $\boldsymbol{I}$ and HR sharp clear image $\boldsymbol{X}$ can share the same sparse code, i.e. $\boldsymbol{\alpha} = \boldsymbol{\alpha}_I = \boldsymbol{\alpha}_X$ if the dictionaries $\boldsymbol{D}_I$ and $\boldsymbol{D}_X$ are defined properly. Therefore, given an observed image $\boldsymbol{Y}$, we first need to find its sparse code on $\boldsymbol{D}_I$ by solving the LASSO [32] problem below:

$$\arg\min_{\alpha} \frac{1}{2} \|\boldsymbol{Y} - \boldsymbol{E}\boldsymbol{D}_I \boldsymbol{\alpha}\|_2^2 + \lambda \|\boldsymbol{\alpha}\|_1 \tag{8}$$

where $\| \cdot \|_p$ denotes the ℓ_p-norm, and λ is a regularization coefficient.

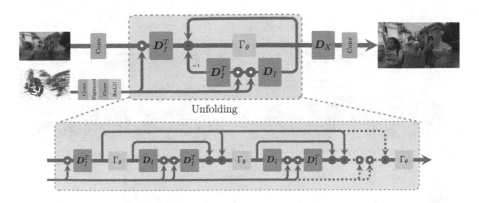

Fig. 2. eSL-Net framework

To solve (8), a common approach is to use iterative shrinkage thresholding algorithm (ISTA) [7]. At the n-th iteration, the sparse code is updated as:

$$
\begin{aligned}
\boldsymbol{\alpha}_{n+1} &= \Gamma_{\frac{\lambda}{L}}(\boldsymbol{\alpha}_n + \frac{1}{L}(\boldsymbol{ED_I})^T(\boldsymbol{Y} - \boldsymbol{ED_I}\boldsymbol{\alpha}_n)) \\
&= \Gamma_{\frac{\lambda}{L}}(\boldsymbol{\alpha}_n - \frac{1}{L}\boldsymbol{D_I^T}\boldsymbol{E}^T\boldsymbol{ED_I}\boldsymbol{\alpha}_n + \frac{1}{L}\boldsymbol{D_I^T}\boldsymbol{E}^T\boldsymbol{Y})
\end{aligned}
\tag{9}
$$

where L is the Lipschitz constant, $\Gamma_\theta(\beta) = \text{sign}(\beta)\max(|\beta| - \theta, 0)$ denotes the element-wise soft thresholding function. After obtaining the optimum solution of sparse code $\boldsymbol{\alpha}^*$, we could finally recover HR sharp clear image $\boldsymbol{X}$ by:

$$
\boldsymbol{X} = \boldsymbol{D_X}\boldsymbol{\alpha}^*
\tag{10}
$$

where $\boldsymbol{D_X}$ is the HR dictionary.

4.2 Network

Inspired by [14], we can solve the sparse coding problem efficiently by integrating it into the CNN architecture. Therefore we propose an Event-enhanced Sparse Learning Net (**eSL-Net**) to solve problems of noise, motion blur and low spatial resolution in a unified framework.

The basic idea of eSL-Net is to map the update steps of event-based intensity reconstruction method to a deep network architecture that consists of a fixed number of phases, each of which corresponds to one iteration of (9). Therefore eSL-Net is an interpretable deep network.

The whole eSL-Net architecture is shown as Fig. 2. Obviously the most attractive part in the network is iteration module corresponding to (9) in the green box. According to [26], when the coefficient in (9) is limited to nonnegative, ISTA is not affected. It is easy to find the equality of the soft nonnegative thresholding operator Γ_θ and the ReLU activation function. We use ReLU layer to implement Γ_θ.

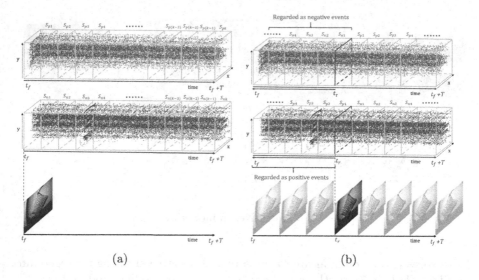

Fig. 3. (a) The method of transforming the event sequence to input event frames when eSL-Net is trained. The upper part is positive event sequence and the lower part is negative event sequence. (b) The method of transforming the event sequence to input event frames when eSL-Net outputs the latent frame at time t_r.

Convolution is a special kind of matrix multiplication, therefore we use convolution layers to implement matrix multiplication. Then the plus node in the green box with three inputs represents $\alpha_n - \frac{1}{L}D_I^T E^T E D_I \alpha_n + \frac{1}{L}D_I^T E^T Y$ in (9).

According to (5), E is double integral of events. In discrete case, the continuous integral turns into discrete summation. More generally, we use the weighted summation, convolution, to replace integral. As a result, through two convolution layers with suitable parameters, the event sequence input can be transformed to approximative E. What's more, convolution has some de-noise effect on event sequences.

Finally, the output of the iterative module, optimum sparse encoding α^*, is passed through a HR dictionary according to (10). In eSL-Net, we use convolution layers followed by shuffle layer to implement HR dictionary D_X, due to the fact that the shuffle operator, arranging the pixels of different channels, can be regarded as a linear operator.

4.3   Network Training

Because the network expects image-like inputs, we divide the time duration of the event sequence into k equal-scale portions, and then $2k$ grayscale frames, $S_{pi}(x,y)$, $S_{ni}(x,y)$, $i = 1, 2, .., k$ are formed respectively by merging the positive and negative events in each time interval, which is shown in Fig. 3(a). $S_{pi}(x,y)$ is the amount of positive events at (x,y) and $S_{ni}(x,y)$ is the amount of negative events at (x,y). The input tensor (obtained by concatenating $Y, S_{p1}, S_{n1}, S_{p2}$,

S_{n2}, ..., S_{pk}, S_{nk}), of size $(1 + 2 \times k) \times H \times W$ is passed through eSL-Net and size of output is $1 \times sH \times sW$ (s is upscale factor of the image).

As shown in Fig. 2, the eSL-Net is then fed with a pair of inputs including the f-th frame of the observed LR blurry and noisy intensity image $Y[f]$ and its corresponding event sequence triggered between the time interval $[t_f, t_f + T]$. With such inputs, the output is the HR sharp and clear intensity image X at time t_f, as shown in Fig. 3(a).

Loss: we use ℓ_1 loss which is a common loss in many image reconstruction methods. By minimizing ℓ_1 loss, our network effectively learns to make the output closer to the desired image. And ℓ_1 loss makes training process more stable.

5   High Frame-Rate Video Generation

With the f-th observed LR image frame $Y[f]$ and the corresponding event sequence triggered during $[t_f, t_f + T]$, it is possible to reconstruct the latent intensity image $X(t_f)$ by the trained eSL-Net, as shown in Fig. 3(a). Thus, the eSL-Net is trained for reconstructing the latent image at t_f.

$$X(t_f) = \text{eSL-Net}\,(Y[f], E(t_f))$$

In order to reconstruct the latent intensity image $X(t_r)$ of $t_r \neq t_f$, one should get the learned double integral of events $E(t_r)$ at time t_r. Let us consider the (4), the definition of the double integral implies that all events $e_{xy}(s)$ are fed into the network keeping the polarity and the order unchanged when $t_r = t_f$, but when $t_r \neq t_f$ the polarity and the order of the input events with timestamp less than t_r should be reversed. It is worth noting that this reversion has special physical mean for event cameras where the polarity and order of the produced events respectively represent the direction and the relative time of the brightness change. So when reconstructing the latent intensity image $X(t_r)$ with the trained network for $X(t_f)$, we need to re-organize the input event sequence to match the pattern of the polarity and the order as in the training phase.

Consequently, instead of retraining the network, we propose a very simple preprocessing step for the input event sequence to reconstruct the latent intensity image $X(t_r)$ for any $t_r \in [t_f, t_f + T]$. As shown in Fig. 3(b), the preprocessing step is only reversing the polarities and the orders of events with timestamp less than t_r. After that, the resulted new event sequence is then merged into frames as the inputs of eSL-Net. Theoretically, we can generate a video with frame-rate as high as the DVS's (Dynamic Vision Sensor) eps (events per second).

6   Dataset Preparation

In order to train the proposed eSL-Net, a mass of LR blurry noisy images with corresponding HR ground-truth images and event sequences are required. However, there exists no such large-scale dataset. This encourages us to synthesize a new dataset with LR blurry noisy images and the corresponding HR sharp clear images and events. And Sect. 7 shows that, although trained on synthetic data, the eSL-Net is able to be generalized to real-world scenes [25].

HR Clear Images: We choose the continuous sharp clear images with resolution of 1280 × 720 from GoPro dataset [20] as our ground truth.

LR Clear Images: LR sharp clear images with resolution of 320 × 180 are obtained by sampling HR clear images with bicubic interpolation, that are used as ground truth for the eSL-Net without SR.

LR Blurry Images: The GoPro dataset [20] also provides LR blurry images, but we have to regenerate them due to the ignorance of exposure time. Mathematically, during the exposure, a motion blurry image can be simulated by averaging a series of sharp images at a high frame rate [21]. However, when the frame rate is insufficient, e.g. 120 fps in GoPro [20], simple time averaging would lead to unnatural spikes or steps in the blur trajectory [36]. To avoid this issue, we first increase the frame-rate of LR sharp clear images to 960 fps by the method in [22], and then generate LR blurry images by averaging 17 continuous LR sharp clear images. Besides, to better simulate the real situation, we add additional white Gaussian noise with standard deviation $\sigma = 4$ ($\sigma = 4$ is the approximate mean of the standard deviations of many smooth patches in APS frames in the real dataset) to the LR blurry images.

Event Sequence: To simulate events, we resort to the open ESIM [28] which can generate events from a sequence of input images. For a given LR blurry image, we input the corresponding LR sharp clear images (960 fps) and obtain the corresponding event sequence. We add 30% (30% is artificially calculated approximate ratio of noise events to effective events in simple real scenes) noisy events with uniform random distribution to the sequence.

The entire synthetic dataset contains four parts:

- **HR clear images dataset** consists of 25650 HR sharp clear frames with various contents, locations, natural and handmade objects, from 270 video, each of which contains 95 images. It is used as ground truth in training and testing of network.
- **LR clear images dataset** consists of 25650 LR sharp clear frames from 270 video. It is used as ground truth in training and testing of network without SR.
- **LR blurry images dataset** consists of 25650 LR blurry noisy frames from 270 video correspondingly, which simulates the APS frames of the event camera with motion blur and noises.
- **Event sequences dataset** consists of event sequences corresponding to LR blurry frames. LR blurry images dataset and event sequences dataset are used as inputs of the eSL-Net.

According to partitions of GoPro dataset [20], images and event sequences in the synthetic dataset from 240 videos are used for training and the rest from 30 videos for testing.

Table 1. Quantitative comparison of our outputs without SR to EDI, CF and MR on the synthetic testing dataset.

Methods	EDI	CF	MR	eSL-Net
PSNR(dB)	22.42	19.75	13.76	**30.23**
SSIM	0.6228	0.4131	0.4960	**0.8703**

Table 2. Quantitative comparison of our outputs to EDI, CF and MR with SR method on the synthetic testing dataset.

Methods	EDI+RCAN 4×	CF+RCAN 4×	MR+RCAN 4×	eSL-Net 4×
PSNR(dB)	12.88	12.89	12.89	**25.41**
SSIM	0.4647	0.4638	0.4643	**0.6727**

7 Experiments

We train our proposed eSL-Net on the synthetic training dataset for 50 epoches using NVIDIA Titan-RTX GPUs, and compare it with state-of-the-art event-based intensity reconstruction methods, including EDI [25], complementary filter method (CF) [30] and manifold regularization method (MR) [19]. All methods are evaluated on the synthetic testing dataset and some real scenes [25] to verify intensity reconstruction capability. For the metrics, we use PSNR and SSIM [34] for quantitative comparison while the visual effect of the reconstructed images for qualitative comparison. In the end, we will test the ability of our method to reconstruct high frame-rate video frames in Sect. 5.

7.1 Intensity Reconstruction Experiments

Note that EDI, CF and MR can not super resolve the intensity images. Thus for fair comparison, we first replace the HR dictionary D_X with a LR dictionary (delete shuffle layers) in eSL-Net to demonstrate the basic ability of intensity reconstruction. Besides, to demonstrate the ability to solve three problems of denoising, deblurring and super resolution simultaneously, the eSL-Net is compared with EDI, CF and MR armed with an excellent SR network RCAN [38].

For the results without SR, the quantitative comparison is tabulated in Table 1. One can see that our method outperforms others by a large margin, especially for CF and MR. Note that since results of CF and MR are terrible in the beginning frames of videos, we only choose the middle reconstruction results (16–90 frames) of each video when calculating PSNR and SSIM. The qualitative results are shown in Fig. 4 and Fig. 5. Our method consistently achieves the best visual performance in terms of effectively denoising and deblurring.

For the results with SR, we show the quantitative results in Table 2. Compared with Table 1, all methods become worse when solving the three problems simultaneously. The reason why is that increased resolution aggravates the

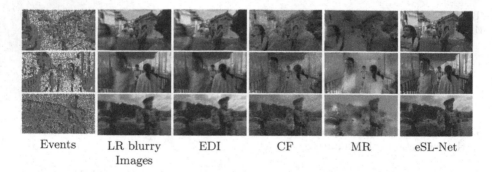

| Events | LR blurry Images | EDI | CF | MR | eSL-Net |

Fig. 4. Qualitative comparison of our outputs without SR to EDI, CF and MR on the synthetic testing dataset.

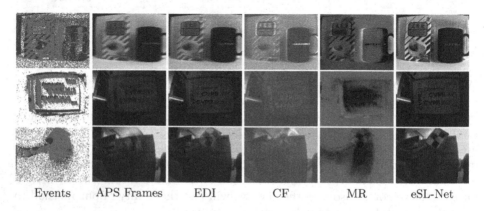

| Events | APS Frames | EDI | CF | MR | eSL-Net |

Fig. 5. Qualitative comparison of our outputs without SR to EDI, CF and MR on the real dataset [25].

adverse effects of noise and blur. Even though, our method is still able to maintain a good performance, which means noise, motion blur, low-resolution are well solved simultaneously in our eSL-Net. And the visual comparisons on synthetic and real datasets verifies this inference, as shown in Fig. 6 and Fig. 7. Compared to other methods superimposing a complex SR network, our method performs much better on edge recovery and noise removal after super resolution, which proves the superiority of our method.

7.2 High Frame-Rate Video Experiments

Theoretically, we can generate a video with frame-rate as high as the DVS's eps. However, when the frame-rate is too high, there are only a few events in the interval of two continuous frames, which results in a subtle difference between the reconstructed two frames, and even difficulty to distinguish them. Therefore, in order to balance the frame-rate and the visual effect, in our experiments, our

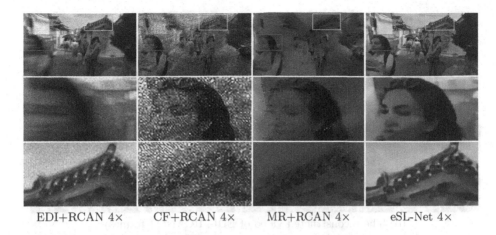

EDI+RCAN 4×   CF+RCAN 4×   MR+RCAN 4×   eSL-Net 4×

Fig. 6. Qualitative comparison of our outputs to EDI, CF and MR with SR method on the synthetic testing dataset.

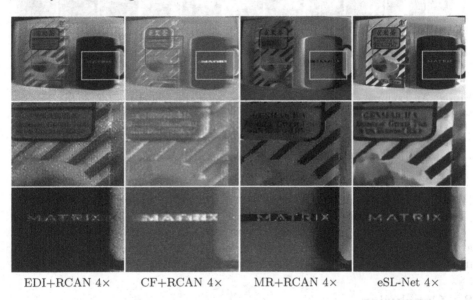

EDI+RCAN 4×   CF+RCAN 4×   MR+RCAN 4×   eSL-Net 4×

Fig. 7. Qualitative comparison of our outputs to EDI, CF and MR with SR method on the real dataset [25].

method generates continuous frames with frame-rate 21 times higher than the original APS frames. To show the changes among frames more clearly, 11 frames are taken at equal intervals from continuous frames recovered from an image and an event sequence by eSL-Net, as shown in Fig. 8(e), which demonstrates the effectiveness of our method on HR and high-frame-rate video reconstruction.

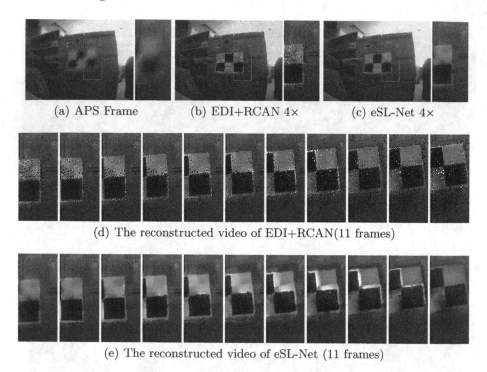

(a) APS Frame   (b) EDI+RCAN 4×   (c) eSL-Net 4×

(d) The reconstructed video of EDI+RCAN(11 frames)

(e) The reconstructed video of eSL-Net (11 frames)

Fig. 8. An example of the reconstructed result on the real dataset [25]. (a) The LR blurry and noisy input image. On the right is the zoom in of the marked rectangular. (b) The reconstructed frame by EDI with SR of scale 4. (c) The reconstructed frame by eSL-Net with SR of scale 4. (d)–(e) show selected 11 frames of the reconstructed video through EDI+RCAN and eSL-Net from (a) and an event sequence respectively.

Without retraining, our method is able to generate continuous frames while preserving more realistic and richer details.

Figure 8 shows qualitative comparisons between our method and EDI+RCAN about high frame-rate video reconstruction on real dataset. Obviously, our method is superior in edge recovery and noise removal.

8   Conclusion

In this paper, we proposed a novel network named **eSL-Net** for high-quality image reconstruction from event cameras. Enhanced by events, the degeneration model of event cameras can easily cope with the motion blur, noises and low spatial resolution problems. Particularly, exploiting sparse learning framework, we proposed an explainable network, i.e. eSL-Net, which is obtained by unfolding the iterative soft thresholding algorithm. Besides, the eSL-Net can be easily extended to generate high frame-rate videos only by a simple transform of the event steam. Experiments on synthetic and real-world data demonstrate the effectiveness and superiority of our eSL-Net.

Acknowledgement. The research was partially supported by the National Natural Science Foundation of China under Grants 61871297, and the Fundamental Research Funds for the Central Universities under Grants 2042020kf0019.

References

1. Almatrafi, M.M., Hirakawa, K.: DAViS camera optical flow. IEEE Trans. Comput. Imag. **6**, 396–407 (2020)
2. Bardow, P., Davison, A.J., Leutenegger, S.: Simultaneous optical flow and intensity estimation from an event camera. In: Proceedings of the IEEE Conference on Computer Vision and Pattern Recognition, pp. 884–892 (2016)
3. Barua, S., Miyatani, Y., Veeraraghavan, A.: Direct face detection and video reconstruction from event cameras. In: 2016 IEEE Winter Conference on Applications of Computer Vision (WACV), pp. 1–9. IEEE (2016)
4. Brandli, C., Berner, R., Yang, M., Liu, S.C., Delbruck, T.: A 240×180 130 db 3 μs latency global shutter spatiotemporal vision sensor. IEEE J. Solid State Circ. **49**(10), 2333–2341 (2014)
5. Choi, J., Yoon, K.J., et al.: Learning to super resolve intensity images from events. In: CVPR 2020. arXiv preprint arXiv:1912.01196 (2019)
6. Cook, M., Gugelmann, L., Jug, F., Krautz, C., Steger, A.: Interacting maps for fast visual interpretation. In: The 2011 International Joint Conference on Neural Networks, pp. 770–776. IEEE (2011)
7. Daubechies, I., Defrise, M., De Mol, C.: An iterative thresholding algorithm for linear inverse problems with a sparsity constraint. Commun. Pure Appl. Math. **57**(11), 1413–1457 (2004)
8. Dirac, P.A.M.: The Principles of Quantum Mechanics. No. 27. Oxford University Press, London (1981)
9. Dong, C., Loy, C.C., He, K., Tang, X.: Image super-resolution using deep convolutional networks. IEEE Trans. Pattern Anal. Mach. Intell. **38**(2), 295–307 (2015)
10. Donoho, D.L., et al.: Compressed sensing. IEEE Trans. Inf. Theory **52**(4), 1289–1306 (2006)
11. Elad, M., Aharon, M.: Image denoising via sparse and redundant representations over learned dictionaries. IEEE Trans. Image Process. **15**(12), 3736–3745 (2006)
12. Gallego, G., et al.: Event-based vision: a survey. arXiv preprint arXiv:1904.08405 (2019)
13. Gehrig, D., Loquercio, A., Derpanis, K.G., Scaramuzza, D.: End-to-end learning of representations for asynchronous event-based data. In: Proceedings of the IEEE International Conference on Computer Vision, pp. 5633–5643 (2019)
14. Gregor, K., LeCun, Y.: Learning fast approximations of sparse coding. In: Proceedings of the 27th International Conference on International Conference on Machine Learning, pp. 399–406 (2010)
15. Kim, H., Handa, A., Benosman, R., Ieng, S., Davison, A.: Simultaneous mosaicing and tracking with an event camera. In: BMVC 2014-Proceedings of the British Machine Vision Conference (2014)
16. Kim, H., Leutenegger, S., Davison, A.J.: Real-time 3D reconstruction and 6-DoF tracking with an event camera. In: Leibe, B., Matas, J., Sebe, N., Welling, M. (eds.) ECCV 2016. LNCS, vol. 9910, pp. 349–364. Springer, Cham (2016). https://doi.org/10.1007/978-3-319-46466-4_21

17. Lichtsteiner, P., Posch, C., Delbruck, T.: A 128 × 128 120 db 15 μs latency asynchronous temporal contrast vision sensor. IEEE J. Solid State Circ. **43**(2), 566–576 (2008)
18. Liu, S.C., Delbruck, T.: Neuromorphic sensory systems. Curr. Opin. Neurol. **20**(3), 288–295 (2010)
19. Munda, G., Reinbacher, C., Pock, T.: Real-time intensity-image reconstruction for event cameras using manifold regularisation. Int. J. Comput. Vis. **126**(12), 1381–1393 (2018)
20. Nah, S., et al.: NTIRE 2019 challenge on video deblurring and super-resolution: dataset and study. In: Proceedings of the IEEE Conference on Computer Vision and Pattern Recognition Workshops (2019)
21. Nah, S., Hyun Kim, T., Mu Lee, K.: Deep multi-scale convolutional neural network for dynamic scene deblurring. In: Proceedings of the IEEE Conference on Computer Vision and Pattern Recognition, pp. 3883–3891 (2017)
22. Niklaus, S., Mai, L., Liu, F.: Video frame interpolation via adaptive separable convolution. In: Proceedings of the IEEE International Conference on Computer Vision, pp. 261–270 (2017)
23. Pan, J., Sun, D., Pfister, H., Yang, M.H.: Blind image deblurring using dark channel prior. In: Proceedings of the IEEE Conference on Computer Vision and Pattern Recognition, pp. 1628–1636 (2016)
24. Pan, L., Hartley, R., Scheerlinck, C., Liu, M., Yu, X., Dai, Y.: High frame rate video reconstruction based on an event camera. arXiv preprint arXiv:1903.06531 (2019)
25. Pan, L., Scheerlinck, C., Yu, X., Hartley, R., Liu, M., Dai, Y.: Bringing a blurry frame alive at high frame-rate with an event camera. In: Proceedings of the IEEE Conference on Computer Vision and Pattern Recognition, pp. 6820–6829 (2019)
26. Papyan, V., Romano, Y., Elad, M.: Convolutional neural networks analyzed via convolutional sparse coding. J. Mach. Learn. Res. **18**(1), 2887–2938 (2017)
27. Posch, C., Matolin, D., Wohlgenannt, R.: A QVGA 143 dB dynamic range frame-free PWM image sensor with lossless pixel-level video compression and time-domain CDS. IEEE J. Solid State Circ. **46**(1), 259–275 (2010)
28. Rebecq, H., Gehrig, D., Scaramuzza, D.: ESIM: an open event camera simulator. In: Conference on Robot Learning, pp. 969–982 (2018)
29. Rebecq, H., Ranftl, R., Koltun, V., Scaramuzza, D.: Events-to-video: Bringing modern computer vision to event cameras. In: Proceedings of the IEEE Conference on Computer Vision and Pattern Recognition, pp. 3857–3866 (2019)
30. Scheerlinck, C., Barnes, N., Mahony, R.: Continuous-time intensity estimation using event cameras. In: Jawahar, C.V., Li, H., Mori, G., Schindler, K. (eds.) ACCV 2018. LNCS, vol. 11365, pp. 308–324. Springer, Cham (2019). https://doi.org/10.1007/978-3-030-20873-8_20
31. Son, B., et al.: A 640× 480 dynamic vision sensor with a 9μm pixel and 300meps address-event representation. In: 2017 IEEE International Solid-State Circuits Conference (ISSCC), pp. 66–67. IEEE (2017)
32. Tibshirani, R.: Regression shrinkage and selection via the lasso. J. Royal Stat. Soc. Ser. B Method. **58**(1), 267–288 (1996)
33. Vidal, A.R., Rebecq, H., Horstschaefer, T., Scaramuzza, D.: Ultimate SLAM? Combining events, images, and IMU for robust visual SLAM in HDR and high-speed scenarios. IEEE Robot. Autom. Lett. **3**(2), 994–1001 (2018)
34. Wang, Z., Simoncelli, E.P., Bovik, A.C.: Multiscale structural similarity for image quality assessment. In: The Thrity-Seventh Asilomar Conference on Signals, Systems & Computers, 2003, vol. 2, pp. 1398–1402. IEEE (2003)

35. Wang, Z.W., Jiang, W., He, K., Shi, B., Katsaggelos, A., Cossairt, O.: Event-driven video frame synthesis. In: Proceedings of the IEEE International Conference on Computer Vision Workshops (2019)
36. Wieschollek, P., Hirsch, M., Scholkopf, B., Lensch, H.: Learning blind motion deblurring. In: Proceedings of the IEEE International Conference on Computer Vision, pp. 231–240 (2017)
37. Zhang, K., Zuo, W., Chen, Y., Meng, D., Zhang, L.: Beyond a gaussian denoiser: residual learning of deep CNN for image denoising. IEEE Trans. Image Process. **26**(7), 3142–3155 (2017)
38. Zhang, Y., Li, K., Li, K., Wang, L., Zhong, B., Fu, Y.: Image super-resolution using very deep residual channel attention networks. In: Ferrari, V., Hebert, M., Sminchisescu, C., Weiss, Y. (eds.) ECCV 2018. LNCS, vol. 11211, pp. 294–310. Springer, Cham (2018). https://doi.org/10.1007/978-3-030-01234-2_18

PackDet: Packed Long-Head Object Detector

Kun Ding[1(✉)], Guojin He[1], Huxiang Gu[2,3], Zisha Zhong[2], Shiming Xiang[2], and Chunhong Pan[2]

[1] Aerospace Information Research Institute, Chinese Academy of Sciences, Beijing, China
kding1225@gmail.com, hegj@radi.ac.cn
[2] National Laboratory of Pattern Recognition, Institute of Automation, Chinese Academy of Sciences, Beijing, China
zisha.zhong@ia.ac.cn, {smxiang,chpan}@nlpr.ia.ac.cn
[3] Beijing EvaVisdom Tech, Beijing, China
guhuxiang@evavisdom.com

Abstract. State-of-the-art object detectors exploit multi-branch structure and predict objects at several different scales, although substantially boosted accuracy is acquired, low efficiency is inevitable as fragmented structure is hardware unfriendly. To solve this issue, we propose a packing operator (PackOp) to combine all head branches together at spatial. Packed features are computationally more efficient and allow to use cross-head group normalization (GN) at handy, leading to notable accuracy improvement against the common head-separate GN. All of these are only at the cost of less than 5.7% relative increase on runtime memory and introduction of a few noisy training samples, however, whose side-effects could be diminished by good packing patterns design. With PackOp, we propose a new anchor-free one-stage detector, PackDet, which features a single deeper/longer but narrower head compared to the existing methods: multiple shallow but wide heads. Our best models on COCO `test-dev` achieve better speed-accuracy balance: 35.1%, 42.3%, 44.0%, 47.4% AP with 22.6, 16.9, 12.4, 4.7 FPS using MobileNet-v2, ResNet-50, ResNet-101, and ResNeXt-101-DCN backbone, respectively. Codes will be released.(https://github.com/kding1225/PackDet)

Keywords: Object detection · Anchor-free · Packing features · Long head

1 Introduction

Object detection is a task of simultaneously locating and recognizing objects given an image, which serves as a very fundamental task in computer vision and is a building block of many other tasks, *e.g.*, instance segmentation [7]. Due to the

Electronic supplementary material The online version of this chapter (https://doi.org/10.1007/978-3-030-58601-0_11) contains supplementary material, which is available to authorized users.

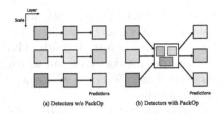

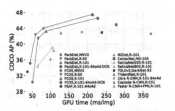

Fig. 1. A concept figure shows how to use PackOp to existing object detectors. PackOp stitches multi-scale features at spatial and performs forwarding all at once, which is faster. However, PackOp blends features at boundary, which will generate noisy data.

Fig. 2. *Single-model* and *single-scale* performance of different detectors on COCO **test-dev** set. Compared to the state-of-the-art method FCOS, PackDet that integrates PackOp in head can not only improve accuracy, but also decrease inference latency.

advance of deep learning techniques, more finely-annotated data and stronger computational power, object detection has achieved dramatic improvements, both on accuracy [13,29,30] and speed [29].

Prevailing detection pipelines use one or more stages of localization and classification, termed one-stage [18,30] and multi-stage [2,26] detectors. More stages generally lead to better localization and recognition accuracy at the cost of slower speed [2]. At different stages, currently two opposite techniques are developed: anchor-based [26,38] and anchor-free detectors [30,43]. The former pre-defines a large number of prior boxes with various sizes to cover the true scale space of objects, while the latter does not use any prior boxes. Enumerating all combinations results in one-stage anchor-based [16], one-stage anchor-free [30], multi-stage anchor-based [26], and multi-stage anchor-free [37,43] approaches. Considering the superiority of better computational efficiency and generalization ability, one-stage anchor-free detectors have drawn increasing attention [31,42].

Due to large scale-variation of objects, feature pyramid networks (FPN) and multi-branch structure have become the workhorses of state-of-the-art detectors [15,16,30,37]. FPN fuses and produces a series of feature maps with different scales, whereon objects of a certain range of size are predicted. However, the fragmented multi-branch structure is not hardware friendly and leads to suboptimal computation efficiency on mainstream deep learning frameworks, *e.g.*, PyTorch, despite of their intensive optimization of asynchronous computation.

To reduce the structure fragments and speed up computation, we develop a packing operator (termed PackOp, ref. Fig. 4 for the implementation) that combines all branches and the associated computations together, avoiding costly for-loops over all heads one by one. A concept figure of utilizing PackOp is shown in Fig. 1, obviously, PackOp can be easily integrated into existing FPN-based detectors. Though PackOp is simple, it could further squeezes the power of modern deep learning frameworks, especially for the cases of using more branches, deeper heads, thinner feature maps and smaller input images (ref. Fig. 8). Surprisingly, it is observed that detecting objects on packed features leads to improved accuracy.

We attribute this to the usage of cross-head GN (CH-GN) that is previously ignored and only head-separate GN (HS-GN) is explored. CH-GN works better than HS-GN because of more accurate mean and variance computed across all heads. The side effects incurred by PackOp include increased runtime memory cost, but which is tiny and could be acceptable, and the incorporation of noisy features, whose negative effect could be mitigated with good packing patterns.

Accordingly, we propose a new anchor-free one-stage detector, called Pack-Det. Owing to PackOp, the network structure of PackDet is much simpler, as shown in Fig. 3. PackDet first combines multi-scale feature maps into a packed feature map by PackOp, and then feeds the packed features to a shared head, two separate heads (localization and classification head) and the prediction layers, sequentially. A deep but narrow structure of shared head is explored, which consists of many times of repetition of a basic convolution block that contains one convolution, one CH-GN and one activation.

Extensive experiments are conducted on COCO detection dataset to demonstrate the effectiveness of PackDet. Our best models on COCO `test-dev` achieve 35.1%, 42.3%, 44.0%, 47.4% AP with 22.6, 16.9, 12.4, 4.7 FPS on GTX 1080Ti GPU using MobileNet-v2, ResNet-50, ResNet-101, and ResNeXt-101-DCN backbone, respectively, which are better speed-accuracy balance points (ref. Fig. 2) compared to state-of-the-art anchor-free one-stage approaches, *e.g.*, FCOS [30].

2   Related Work

One-stage and Multi-stage Object Detectors. Single-stage detectors use both bounding box regression and multi-class classification once, respectively, without further refinements in modeling. They are usually quite fast in inference and more favorable for mobile applications. Early one-stage detectors are less satisfactory in accuracy despite of striking FPS (frames per second) numbers, such as YOLO [23,24], SSD [18], DSSD [5]. Subsequent researches of one-stage detectors focus on improving accuracy, while trying to keep the advantage of high efficiency. Related techniques include designing better loss function to solve class-imbalance problem (*e.g.*, RetinaNet [16]), enhancing the multi-scale features (*e.g.*, M2Det [40]), searching network architectures (*e.g.*, NAS-FCOS [31] and EfficientDet [29]). The most common multi-stage detectors use two stages, one is region proposal network and the other is region-wise refinement network. Faster-RCNN [26] is among the earliest methods of this category, and many successors, *e.g.*, R-FCN [3], FPN [15] and TridentNet [13], further strengthen and enrich the two-stage framework. More stages are studied in Cascade R-CNN [2], and significantly improved accuracy is observed, but suffering from longer latency.

Anchor-based and Anchor-free Object Detectors. Anchor boxes serve as scale prior of object distribution and are extensively adopted in both one-stage and multi-stage detectors, such as Fast-RCNN [6], Faster-RCNN [26], YOLO [24], SSD [18]. Anchor boxes can also be learned from data, *e.g.*, MetaAnchor [36], OptAnchor [41]. Pre-defined prior boxes are suspected to have generalization problem and are less computational efficient, thus anchor-free methods begin to resuscitate. Based on feature pyramid networks and other novel ideas, recent work such as FCOS [30], FSAF [43], CenterNet [4], consistently demonstrate that it is possible to drop prior boxes while maintaining a promising result.

Multi-head Object Detectors. To tackle the large scale-variation, state-of-the-art detectors adopt feature pyramid structure (termed *neck*) and detect objects of different scales at the most suitable feature map, unanimously, such as FPN [15], TridentNet [13], SSD [18]. For each feature map, a multi-layer sub-network (termed *head*) is commonly applied to extract task-oriented object-level features. For sake of higher FPS, heads are often limited to a shallow and wide structure, *e.g.*, Faster-RCNN [26], light-head RCNN [14], RetinaNet [16]. By contrast, this work explores deeper and narrower head structure.

Normalization Techniques in Object Detection. Normalization can ease the deep neural networks training and has become a foundation of many algorithms, including object detection. The most commonly-used method is batch normalization (BN) [11], and its variants, freezing BN and synchronized BN [22]. Group norm (GN) [34] is recently proposed as an alternative for BN when batch size is relatively small, which is very appropriate for the tasks like object detection where only small batch is affordable subjected to high image resolution and limited GPU memory. GN is widely adopted in newest detectors [30,31,37] to normalize the layers in heads, which are newly-added and untransferable from a pre-trained classification model. However, in these methods, mean and variance are separately computed for different heads.

3   PackDet: Packed Long-Head Object Detector

This section elaborates the proposed packed long-head detector. We first summarize the overall network architecture (Sect. 3.1), and then detail all parts of PackDet, including packing operator (Sect. 3.2), head structure (Sect. 3.3), learning targets (Sect. 3.4) and loss functions (Sect. 3.5).

3.1   Network Architecture

As shown in Fig. 3, PackDet has a concise fully convolutional structure, consisting of a backbone, an FPN neck, a packing operator (PackOp), a shared head, a classification head and a localization head. An input image $I \in \mathbb{R}^{3 \times H \times W}$ is first fed to the backbone to extract visual features. After that, similar to existing multi-scale detectors [16,30], three feature maps $C_{l+3}, l \in [0,3)$ of strides $8, 16, 32$ are combined to generate five features $P_{l+3} \in \mathbb{R}^{C \times h_l \times w_l}, l \in [0,5)$ of stride $8, 16, 32, 64, 128$, respectively, with h_l the height and w_l the width of P_{l+3}. Here, we denote $[a, b)$ as the set containing all integers no less than a and smaller than b. P_6 and P_7 are obtained by consecutively applying convolution operations on P_5, and P_3–P_5 are generated in a top-down manner [16].

Unlike existing methods that construct a branch for per feature map, we first stitch all features together at spatial and obtain a big feature map, denoted

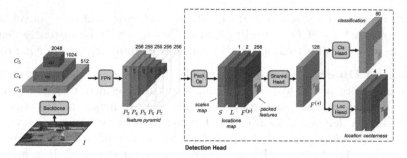

Fig. 3. Overview of PackDet with ResNet-50 as the backbone. PackOp stitches multiple feature maps (P_3–P_7) into a patchwork ($F^{(p)}$), see Fig. 4 for more details; shared head and separate heads: Figure 6; loss computation: Section 3.5.

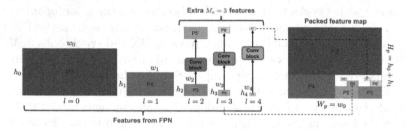

Fig. 4. The procedure of PackOp. Some lines are not drawn in case of cluttering.

as $F^{(p)}$, and only use one main branch subsequently. The packed feature $F^{(p)}$ is passed to a shared head to generate a new feature map $F^{(s)}$. We explore a deep and narrow structure for this shared head, while keeping the spatial size unchanged. $F^{(s)}$ is further fed to two separate heads to generate the classification and localization prediction, respectively.

3.2 Packing Operator

To reduce the structure fragments in FPN-like head, a packing operator (PackOp) is proposed, which places multi-scale feature maps into a cubic container, *i.e.*, packed feature map, while avoiding overlaps between any two feature maps. This problem is similar to the rectangle packing problem [9] that seeks an enclosing rectangle of minimal area to contain a given set of rectangles without overlap. Rectangle packing is proved to be a NP-completeness problem [12]. Considering the hardness of optimization and the searched solutions may not result in high detection accuracy, we find feasible solutions manually by exploiting the rules found by experiments.

The general case of PackOp with extra M_e (especially, $M_e = 3$) features is explained in Fig. 4. The new features P'_5, P'_6, P'_7 are generated by applying three convolution blocks (*i.e.*, conv-gn-relu) with different initial values to P_5, P_6, P_7, respectively. After that, all the $M_e + 5$ feature maps $F_l, l \in [0, M_e + 5)$ are placed

Table 1. Coordinates of F_l in $F^{(p)}$. $x_l^0, y_l^0, x_l^1, y_l^1$ are top-left horizontal, top-left vertical, bottom-right horizontal, bottom-right vertical coordinate, respectively.

l	F_l	Source	W_l	H_l	x_l^0	y_l^0	x_l^1	y_l^1
0	F_0	P_3	w_0	h_0	0	0	w_0	h_0
1	F_1	P_4	w_1	h_1	0	h_0	w_1	h_0+h_1
2	F_2	P_5	w_2	h_2	w_0-w_2	$h_0+h_1-h_2$	w_0	h_0+h_1
3	F_3	P_6	w_3	h_3	$w_0-w_2-w_3$	$h_0+h_1-h_2-h_3$	w_0-w_2	$h_0+h_1-h_2$
4	F_4	P_7	w_4	h_4	$w_0-w_2-w_3-w_4$	$h_0+h_1-h_2-h_3-h_4$	$w_0-w_2-w_3$	$h_0+h_1-h_2-h_3$
5	F_5	P_5'	w_2	h_2	w_1	$h_0+h_1-h_2$	w_1+w_2	h_0+h_1
6	F_6	P_6'	w_3	h_3	w_0-w_3	$h_0+h_1-h_2-h_3$	w_0	$h_0+h_1-h_2$
7	F_7	P_7'	w_4	h_4	$w_0-w_3-w_4$	$h_0+h_1-h_2-h_3-h_4$	w_0-w_3	$h_0+h_1-h_2-h_3$

```python
def PackOp(xs, boxes, levels, locations, Hp, Wp):
    # xs: feature map F_l, l=0,1,...,M-1, F_l: (N, C, H_l, W_l)
    # boxes: positions in packed feature map, (M, 4)
    # levels: level l for each feature map F_l, (M,)
    # locations: grid points per feature map, (N, 2, H_l, W_l)
    # Hp,Wp: height and width of packed feature map
    N, C = xs[0].shape[:2]
    pack_map = xs[0].new_zeros(N, C, Hp, Wp)
    scales_map = xs[0].new_zeros(N, 1, Hp, Wp)
    locations_map = -xs[0].new_ones(N, 2, Hp, Wp)
    for x, box, l, loc in zip(xs, boxes, levels, locations):
        x0, y0, x1, y1 = box
        pack_map[..., y0:y1, x0:x1] = x
        scales_map[..., y0:y1, x0:x1] = l
        locations_map[..., y0:y1, x0:x1] = loc
    return pack_map, scales_map, locations_map
```

Fig. 5. PyTorch code of PackOp.

into a big tensor $F^{(p)} \in \mathbb{R}^{C \times H_p \times W_p}$ according to pre-defined placing coordinates, as listed in Table 1. Accordingly, we obtain $H_p = H_0 + H_1$ and $W_p = W_0$. Apart from $F^{(p)}$, PackOp also computes two extra tensors, a scales map $S \in \mathbb{R}^{H_p \times W_p}$ recording the associated scale information of all pixels in $F^{(p)}$, and a locations map $L \in \mathbb{R}^{2 \times H_p \times W_p}$ recording the position of $F^{(p)}$'s pixels mapped back to the original image. S and L are necessary for computing supervision targets and decoding predictions. PackOp can be easily implemented with a few lines of PyTorch code, as is shown in Fig. 5.

As will be shown in our experiments (ref. Fig. 8), the proposed approach has universality in speeding up FPN-like head structure. Although this work explores the efficiency in object detection task, the underlying idea could also be applied to other tasks/methods as long as FPN-like multi-branch structure is adopted. It is worth noting that our work is quite different from architecture search [31,33], though which could also reduce network latency, as it generally focuses on discovering network structure automatically by optimizing accuracy-speed trade-off. More similar work include jigsaw based unsupervised learning [32] and

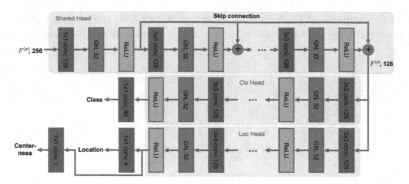

Fig. 6. The head architecture of PackDet (PackOp is not shown).

mixup-based data augmentation [39], but they have distinct differences to our method and are proposed in different contexts and for different applications. The idea of packing has already appeared in earlier work, such as [10,21]. However, the packing operations therein are performed in image space to make convnet feature pyramids faster to compute. Most recently, mosaic data augmentation is proposed in YOLOv4 [1], which combines 4 training images into one in certain ratios. The underlying idea also shares some similarities to ours, but also being performed in image space.

3.3   Packed Long Head

The overall head structure excluding PackOp is shown in Fig. 6. It contains three parts: shared head, classification head and localization head.

The shared head takes as an input $F^{(p)} \in \mathbb{R}^{C \times H_p \times W_p}$ and outputs $F^{(s)} \in \mathbb{R}^{C_s \times H_p \times W_p}$ with C_s the channel number of the output feature map. A dimension reduction block $R(\cdot)$ (1x1conv-gn-relu) is first applied to reduce the dimension, and then T_1 convolution blocks with 3×3 convolution $CB_i^1(\cdot), i \in [0, T_1)$ are performed sequentially, *i.e.* $F^{(s)} = CB_{T_1-1}^1(\cdots(CB_0^1(F^{(d)}), F^{(d)}), F^{(d)})$, where $F^{(d)} \triangleq R(F^{(p)})$ is the dimension reduced feature map. Therein, a skip connection from $F^{(d)}$ at each block is adopted. In all blocks, the spatial dimension is kept fixed, as objects should be detected at every positions determined by the locations map L that is intuitively unsuitable for interpolation.

Generally speaking, detection and classification are two quite different tasks and need task-specific features. To this end, two separate heads are stacked on top of the shared head: classification head and localization head. The structure of these two heads are identical to that of the shared head besides removed skip connections and fewer convolution blocks. We perform classification on the output of classification head and regression+centerness prediction on localization head (ref. Sect. 3.4). For convenience, let T_2 denote the number of convolution blocks used in classification/localization head.

PackDet uses deeper while narrower head structure, that is to say, $T_1 + T_2$ is relatively large, *e.g.*, 14, and C_s is relatively small, *e.g.*, 128. By contrast, exist-

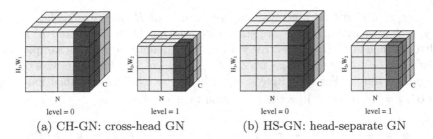

Fig. 7. Comparison between cross-head and head-separate normalization methods with group normalization (GN) taken as an example. Pixels with same color are normalized by the same statistics computed on the values of these pixels.

ing methods like FCOS [30] and RetinaNet [16] use shallow and wide heads. For instance, FCOS uses 4 convolution blocks (denoted as T) for both classification and localization head, the channel size (denoted as C) is set to be 256. The number of convolution parameters (excluding the last prediction layers) in PackDet's heads is $CC_s + (9T_1 + 18T_2)C_s^2$, and $18TC^2$ in FCOS's heads. The convolution FLOP count of PackDet's and FCOS's heads are proportional to $[CC_s + (9T_1 + 18T_2)C_s^2]H_pW_p$ and $18TC^2\sum_{l=0}^{4}H_lW_l$, respectively. Considering $\sum_{l=0}^{4}H_lW_l/H_pW_p \approx 0.89$, under the settings $T = 4, T_1 = 12, T_2 = 2, C = 256, C_s = 128$, PackDet's heads should have fewer parameters and FLOPs

Compared to processing all heads separately, PackOp slightly increases runtime memory cost by $\beta = 1 - \sum_{l=0}^{M-1}H_lW_l/H_pW_p$, relatively. For the case $M_e = 0$, β is about 11.2%; for the case $M_e = 3$, it is about 5.7%. While considering backbone, neck and head as a whole, the relative increment might be smaller. For example, when ResNet-50 serves as the backbone and M_e is 3, the GPU memory cost is only increased by 5.5%, relatively.

PackDet's heads perform convolution operations on packed feature maps, which inevitably incorporates some noisy features by mixing up spatially close features. The noisy data may mess the training procedure, and finally lead to worse performance. However, as will be demonstrated in the experiments, by carefully designing the packing pattern, this side-effect can be largely mitigated.

Due to the usage of packed features, feature normalization at each convolution block is performed across different heads. Figure 7 compares the differences between cross-head GN (CH-GN) and the common head-separate GN (HS-GN). In CH-GN, the statistics are computed based on values from all scales, which are more accurate and facilitate to get better accuracy (ref. Fig. 9).

3.4 Learning Targets

Considering the ij-th element of L, the associated feature stride is $2^{S_{i,j}+3}$ and the corresponding space location mapped back to the original image is $(L_{0,i,j}, L_{1,i,j}) = (2^{S_{i,j}+3}(j + 0.5), 2^{S_{i,j}+3}(i + 0.5))$. Following the improved version of FCOS [30], box shrinking strategy is adopted to reduce noisy positive samples. For this end, let $B = (c, x, y, w, h)$ be a ground-truth box, and

$B_s = (c, x, y, w', h')$ be a central shrunk version of B, where c is the class id, (x, y) is box center, w and h are the width and height of B, w' and h' are the width and height of B_s, respectively. Pixel (i, j) denotes a positive sample when $x - w'/2 \leq L_{0,i,j} \leq x + w'/2, y - h'/2 \leq L_{1,i,j} \leq y + h'/2$ holds, otherwise denotes a negative sample. For a positive sample, let $c_{i,j}^* = c$ be the classification target and $\mathbf{o}^*_{i,j} = (o^l, o^t, o^r, o^b)$ be the regression target, where

$$o^l = \frac{1}{2^{S_{i,j}+3}}[L_{0,i,j} - (x - w/2)], \quad o^t = \frac{1}{2^{S_{i,j}+3}}[L_{1,i,j} - (y - h/2)],$$

$$o^r = \frac{1}{2^{S_{i,j}+3}}[(x + w/2) - L_{0,i,j}], \quad o^b = \frac{1}{2^{S_{i,j}+3}}[(y + h/2) - L_{1,i,j}]. \quad (1)$$

o^l, o^t, o^r, o^b are the stride-normalized distances between $(L_{0,i,j}, L_{1,i,j})$ and the left, top, right, bottom boundaries of B, respectively. Like [30], centerness is also predicted to filter out low-quality boxes. For a position (i, j) that associates to a positive sample, the ground-truth centerness target is defined as $t_{ij}^* = \sqrt{\min(o^l, o^r)/\max(o^l, o^r) \cdot \min(o^t, o^b)/\max(o^t, o^b)}$. At test stage, centerness is used for down-weighting the scores of boxes that are far away from center.

3.5 Loss Functions

Assume that at location (i, j) the predicted class distribution vector is $\mathbf{p}_{i,j}$, the predicted class-agnostic bounding box offset vector is $\mathbf{o}_{i,j}$ and the predicted centerness is $t_{i,j}$, the following multi-task loss is adopted:

$$L(\{\mathbf{p}_{i,j}\}, \{\mathbf{o}_{i,j}\}, \{t_{i,j}\}) = \frac{1}{N_{\text{pos}}} \sum_{ij} L_{\text{cls}}(\mathbf{p}_{i,j}, c_{i,j}^*)$$

$$+ \frac{1}{N_{\text{pos}}} \sum_{ij} I_{c_{i,j}^* > 0} L_{\text{reg}}(\mathbf{o}_{i,j}, \mathbf{o}_{i,j}^*) + \frac{1}{N_{\text{pos}}} \sum_{ij} I_{c_{i,j}^* > 0} L_{\text{cen}}(t_{i,j}, t_{i,j}^*), \quad (2)$$

where $L_{\text{cls}}, L_{\text{reg}}, L_{\text{cen}}, N_{\text{pos}}$ denote classification loss, regression loss, centerness loss and the number of positive samples, respectively. Focal loss [16], GIoU loss [27], and binary cross entropy loss are used for $L_{\text{cls}}, L_{\text{reg}}, L_{\text{cen}}$, respectively.

3.6 Implementation Details

Training Details. The network initialization follows the tradition in [16,30]. Please refer to these work for more details. PackDet is trained with stochastic gradient descent (SGD) algorithm. Unless specified, all models are trained use a batch size of 16 and the 1x training strategy:[1] 1) use 90K iterations and initial learning rate of 0.01; 2) reduce learning rate by a factor 10 at iterations 60K and 80K, respectively. Unless otherwise specified, images are resized to have shorter side being 800 and longer size no more than 1333, meanwhile, only horizontal image flipping is applied. By default, we use $T_1 = 12$, $T_2 = 2$ and $C_s = 128$, which results in a long head with narrow feature maps.

---

[1] https://github.com/facebookresearch/maskrcnn-benchmark.

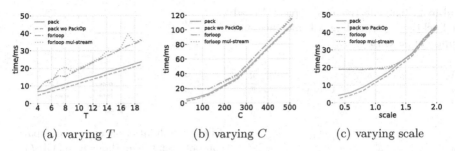

(a) varying T (b) varying C (c) varying scale

Fig. 8. GPU time comparison with varying T, C and scale s. The scales $\{2.0, 1.8, 1.6, 1.4, 1.2, 1.0, 0.8, 0.6, 0.4\}$ are used to resize input tensors. The default value of T, C, s are $10, 128, 1.0$, respectively.

Inference Details. At testing time, an image is fed to the network to get three tensors: a class score map ($K \times H_p \times W_p$, $K = 80$ for COCO), a box offset map ($4 \times H_p \times W_p$) and a centerness map ($H_p \times W_p$). We first threshold the element-wise product of class score map and centerness map by 0.05 to obtain some candidate objects. After that, predictions of the same scale are filtered to keep only top-1000 most confidential results. Finally, the predictions from all scales are merged followed by non-maximum suppression (NMS) with a threshold of 0.5 to generate the final results.

4   Experiments

We conduct experiments on COCO detection benchmark [17]. The `trainval35k` set is used for training, and the `minival` set is used for ablation study. For state-of-the-art comparison, we report COCO AP on the `test-dev` split.

4.1   Ablation Study

Benchmark PackOp's Speed. To validate the effectiveness of PackOp as a universal speeder for multi-branch structure, we benchmark the latency of forwarding on a multi-branch network. The network consists of 8 branches and each is a sequence of T convolution blocks (conv-gn-relu). The input tensors for all branches have the same batch size of 2 and channel number C. Their spatial dimensions are $(100, 100)$, $(50, 50)$, $(25, 25)$, $(13, 13)$, $(7, 7)$, $(25, 25)$, $(13, 13)$, and $(7, 7)$, respectively. All convolutions have the same kernel size of $3 \times 3 \times C$, padding of 1, and stride of 1. We consider two methods for forwarding: 1) loop over the branches one by one; 2) pack all branches and run forwarding only once.

We use PyTorch-1.1.0, CUDA-9.0, cuDNN-7.3.0, and perform forwarding on a single GTX 1080Ti GPU. Elapsed time is recorded by `torch.cuda.Event()` and the average time over 30 trials is reported. The results are shown in Fig. 8, where `pack wo PackOp` denotes the packing method excluding the PackOp time, `pack` is the same method counts this time, and `forloop` denotes the branch-by-branch method. Multiple CUDA streams are also tried for `forloop` and the

Table 2. The effectiveness of packed head in PackDet for speeding up inference and improving accuracy.

M_e	tr-pack	ts-pack	ch-gn	Time	AP	AP_{50}	AP_{75}	No.
0				67.4	38.9	56.7	42.2	①
0		✓		63.1	22.9	35.9	24.5	②
0			✓	68.9	39.5	57.2	42.7	③
0	✓	✓	✓	64.4	39.7	57.5	43.1	④
3				75.0	39.4	56.8	42.9	⑤
3		✓		65.2	25.9	39.7	28.1	⑥
3			✓	74.0	39.7	57.4	43.0	⑦
3	✓	✓	✓	65.3	40.1	57.5	43.3	⑧

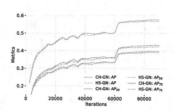

Fig. 9. Validation accuracy comparison between the methods using CH-GN and HS-GN. M_e is set to be 0.

corresponding method is called `forloop mul-stream`. Specifically, two CUDA streams are used as more streams do not make distinct difference. From Fig. 8, the following conclusions can be drawn: 1) PackOp is quite efficient to execute; 2) using multiple CUDA streams takes no effect on speed; 3) the speedup effect is more considerable for deeper but narrower network and smaller spatial size. We have also tried two other deep learning frameworks, TensorFlow and MXNet, and similar results are obtained. Please refer to supplementary for more details.

Speeding up PackDet by PackOp. To validate the effect of PackOp in speeding up forward computation, we slightly modify the packed head structure as shown in Fig. 6: PackOp is dropped and all the convolution blocks are computed using nested two-level for-loops over layers and branches. The results are listed in Table 2, where `tr-pack` and `ts-pack` denote whether PackOp is used in train and test stage, respectively. When `ch-gn` is checked, it means CH-GN is used, otherwise HS-GN is used. M_e means how many extra feature maps are added, it should be 0 or 3 (ref. Fig. 4). The listed times denote the inference time (in ms). By comparing line 1 to line 4, the relative reduction of inference time is 4.5%. With more branches, this number is larger, *i.e.*, 12.9% for $M_e = 3$ (ref. line 5 and 8 in Table 2). More results with varying input and channel size are given in the supplementary material. As a result, PackOp is indeed capable to speed up the network inference, and the more branches used the larger gain obtained.

The Usefulness of Test Time Packing. It is possible to train a multi-branch detector in a traditional manner without using PackOp but use it in test stage. Nevertheless, our experimental results demonstrate that this strategy is suboptimal. By comparing the results of line 1 and 2 (or line 5 and 6) in Table 2, we see that AP degrades significantly even though testing time also has a large drop, which could be attributed to the bias between training and testing.

Effect of Packed Convolution and Normalization. In Table 2, line 3 and 7 correspond to the method without using PackOp, while CH-GN is adopted. This is implemented by first concatenating the spatially flattened feature maps

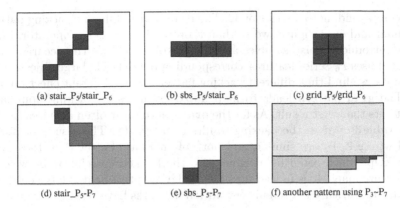

(a) stair_P_5/stair_P_6 (b) sbs_P_5/stair_P_6 (c) grid_P_5/grid_P_6

(d) stair_P_5-P_7 (e) sbs_P_5-P_7 (f) another pattern using P_3~P_7

Fig. 10. Different packing patterns being compared. (f) uses P_3–P_7 for packing. Different colors denote feature map of different scales. **sbs**: side-by-side.

from all scales of the same layer and then applying the naive GN, followed by a split operation. By comparing line 1 to line 3 (or line 5 to line 7), we find that CH-GN improves AP visibly. As the main difference between PackDet and the detectors using multi-branch structure lies in whether packed convolution and normalization are utilized or not, we believe that CH-GN does contribute to the accuracy improvement. However, there is still a small AP margin between the results of line 3 and line 4 (or line 7 and line 8). We conjecture that the correlation between the highest three scales are captured, at least in some degree, which are helpful for detecting large objects.

Packing Extra Features. In Table 2, by comparing the results in line 4 and 8, using extra three features increases 0.4% absolute AP. Thus, we conclude that the prediction results from different feature maps of the same scale should have some complementarity. How to use more feature maps and if extra improvements can be obtained are two open questions, we leave these for future work.

Packing Patterns Comparison. Different packing patterns may lead to different results. For example, to pack feature maps P_3–P_7, the pattern shown in Fig. 10(f) is also valid. However, when it is used in PackDet's head, the resultant AP is 39.3%, which is lower than the number 39.7% given in Table 2 (line 4). Thus, it is necessary to study what kind of rules should be followed to design good packing patterns. For this aim, we manually design five patterns for the following experiments, as shown in Fig. 10(a)–(e). (a)–(c) use features of same scale for packing. Feature map P_5 (or P_6) and its processed versions by different convolution blocks are used. (d) and (e) use P_5, P_6, P_7 for packing.

The results of same scale packing are shown in Table 3(a) and Table 3(b), where **pack** means if all branches are merged for forwarding in both train and test stage, and **ch-gn** denotes if CH-GN is adopted. For separate branches, CH-GN is performed as the manner mentioned before. Table 3(a) uses P_5-series features, corresponding to a stride of 32. The results with different packing patterns are similar and only slightly worse than those without packing operator, implying the introduced noisy samples are unable to degenerate the accuracy a lot. Table 3(b) uses P_6-series features, corresponding to relatively large objects. From the results, we find that different packing patterns have different effect on accuracy. The grid pattern leads to more mixed samples at packing boundaries, thus, it gets the worst result. As for the stair pattern, it often acquires the best result. Table 3(c) gives the packing results using P_3–P_7. The results of sbs_P_5-P_7 and stair_P_5-P_7 are similar, and both of them are better than those without PackOp, which could be attributed to the learned correlation between the three feature maps. It is indeed possible as the receptive field is large enough to cover all these feature maps and convolution networks have strong representative ability.

Table 3. Results of different packing patterns using (a) P_5 and its variants, (b) P_6 and its variants, and (c) P_5–P_7. sbs: side-by-side.

(a)

Pattern	Pack	ch-gn	AP	AP_{50}	AP_{75}
stair_P_5	✓	✓	14.6	22.3	15.5
sbs_P_5	✓	✓	14.2	22.0	15.0
grid_P_5	✓	✓	14.1	21.8	14.8
grid_P_5			14.7	22.5	15.6
grid_P_5		✓	14.8	22.9	15.6

(b)

Pattern	Pack	ch-gn	AP	AP_{50}	AP_{75}
stair_P_6	✓	✓	12.6	17.9	13.2
sbs_P_6	✓	✓	9.3	13.3	10.0
grid_P_6	✓	✓	4.1	6.6	4.2
grid_P_6			12.7	18.2	13.4
grid_P_6		✓	12.8	18.4	13.5

(c)

Pattern	Pack	ch-gn	AP	AP_{50}	AP_{75}
sbs_P_5-P_7	✓	✓	24.7	34.4	26.6
stair_P_5-P_7			24.4	34.2	26.3
stair_P_5-P_7		✓	24.4	34.3	26.4
stair_P_5-P_7	✓	✓	24.6	34.5	26.4

We summarize the rules of thumb for designing good packing patterns as follows: 1) It is not a good idea to put feature maps with the same high scale together; 2) Putting feature maps with the same low scale is feasible; 3) Putting several large-stride feature maps of different scales is helpful for improving accuracy. Reviewing Fig. 4 again, the designed packing pattern uses stair-like structure as much as possible and no feature maps of the same high scale are put near each other. As a result, PackDet could not only enjoy the speedup brought from PackOp, but also minimize its side effects.

Table 4. *Single-model and single-scale* results *vs.* state of the arts on COCO `test-dev` set. FPS is measured on a single GTX 1080Ti GPU card with a batch size of 1.

Method	Input size	Backbone	Anchor free	MS train	FPS	AP	AP$_{50}$	AP$_{75}$	AP$_S$	AP$_M$	AP$_L$
Multi-Stage:											
Faster R-CNN+FPN [15]	~1000×600	R-101			10.0	36.2	59.1	39.0	18.2	39.0	48.2
Cascade R-CNN [2]	~1300×800	R-101			7.8	42.8	62.1	46.3	23.7	45.5	55.2
TridentNet [13]	~1200×800	R-101	✓		2.7	42.7	63.6	46.5	23.9	46.6	56.6
TridentNet [13]	~1200×800	R-101-DCN	✓		1.3	46.8	67.6	51.5	28.0	51.2	60.5
Libra R-CNN [20]	~1300×800	X-101-64x4d			5.4	43.0	64.0	47.0	25.3	45.6	54.6
One-Stage:											
YOLOv3 [25]	608×608	DarkNet-53		✓	27.3	33.0	57.9	34.4	18.3	35.4	41.9
RetinaNet500 [16]	~832×500	R-101		✓	15.4	34.4	53.1	36.8	14.7	38.5	49.1
RetinaNet800 [16]	~1300×800	R-101		✓	9.5	39.1	59.1	42.3	21.8	42.7	50.2
CenterNet [4]	511×511	HG-104	✓	✓	3.6	44.9	62.4	48.1	25.6	47.4	57.4
M2Det [40]	512×512	R-101		✓	9.2	38.8	59.4	41.7	20.5	43.9	53.4
FSAF [43]	~1300×800	X-101-64x4d	✓	✓	4.2	42.9	63.8	46.3	26.6	46.2	52.7
FCOS [30]	~1300×800	MNV2	✓	✓	19.8	30.4	47.5	32.2	19.1	34.3	33.7
FCOS [30]	~1300×800	R-50	✓	✓	15.0	41.4	60.2	44.7	24.8	44.2	50.6
FCOS [30]	~1300×800	R-101	✓	✓	11.3	43.2	62.2	46.9	26.1	46.2	53.6
FCOS [30]	~1300×800	X-101-64x4d-DCN	✓	✓	4.4	46.5	65.7	50.5	28.9	49.2	58.1
PackDet	~1300×800	MNV2	✓	✓	22.6	35.1	51.6	38.1	19.1	37.0	44.0
PackDet	~1300×800	R-50	✓	✓	16.9	42.3	60.3	45.9	24.7	45.0	53.7
PackDet◇□	~1300×800	R-101	✓	✓	12.0	43.5	61.9	47.3	26.4	46.4	53.7
PackDet□	~1300×800	R-101	✓	✓	11.2	43.7	61.9	47.6	25.8	46.9	55.3
PackDet	~1300×800	R-101	✓	✓	12.4	44.0	62.3	47.8	25.6	47.3	55.7
PackDet	~1300×800	X-101-64x4d-DCN	✓	✓	4.7	47.4	66.3	51.5	28.9	50.5	60.1

◇: $M_e = 0$; □: without train/test packing or CH-GN; R: ResNet [8]; X: ResNeXt [8]; MNV2: MobileNet-v2 [28]; HG: Hourglass [19]; DCN: Deformable Convolutional Network [44]; **Input Size**: input image size; **Anchor Free**: whether no anchors are used; **MS Train**: whether multi-scale training is used.

4.2 Comparison to State of the Art

We further compare PackDet to state-of-the-art multi-stage and single-stage methods on COCO `test-dev` set. Following previous work, PackDet uses the 2x learning schedule, which runs 180K iterations with the learning rate change points tuned proportionally w.r.t. the 1x schedule. In addition, the shorter side of input images are randomly re-scaled to the range [640, 800]. Note that, when MobileNet-v2 [28] is used as the backbone, synchronous BN will be adopted as it boosts accuracy remarkably. Unless otherwise specified, M_e is set to be 3, train packing, test packing and CH-GN are all adopted.

The numerical results of different methods are shown in Table 4 and the speed-accuracy curves are plotted in Fig. 2. We can see that PackDet achieves better speed-accuracy trade-offs compared to the state-of-the-art anchor-free one-stage method FCOS. For example, when X-101-64x4d-DCN backbone is adopted, PackDet acquires 47.4% AP with 4.7 FPS, which outperforms FCOS notably, *i.e.*, 46.5% AP with 4.4 FPS. The speed and accuracy superiority of PackDet is more considerable for small backbones. For example, with MobileNet-v2 as the backbone, PackDet improves the baseline FCOS by a large margin, *i.e.*, 4.7% absolute AP and 2.8 FPS increase. These results imply that a single packed deep and narrow head is competitive to multiple shallow and wide heads in terms of both accuracy and speed. Finally, we will argue the accuracy improvements of PackDet are not caused by more model parameters as PackDet has fewer parameters than FCOS. Actually, PackDet could reduce about 0.7M parameters with the same backbone.

5   Conclusions

In this paper, we presented a packing operator called PackOp that puts a group of feature maps into a cubic container. With PackOp, a new detector PackDet was proposed, which packs all branches together for fast forwarding. Beside the speed advantage, the parallelized structure is also favorable for handy cross-head normalization that facilitates to get better accuracy. Extensive experiments demonstrated PackOp is effective in speedup and PackDet could get better accuracy-speed trade-off against state of the arts. Future work include searching the packing pattern and applying PackOp to other tasks, such as instance segmentation and keypoints detection.

Acknowledgement. This research was financially supported by National Natural Science Foundation of China (61731022, 91646207) and the Strategic Priority Research Program of the Chinese Academy of Sciences (XDA19090300). We would like to thank Rui Yang and Chaoyi Liu from EvaVisdom Tech for the inspiring discussions. We also thank the anonymous reviewers for their valuable suggestions.

References

1. Bochkovskiy, A., Wang, C.Y., Liao, H.Y.: YOLOv4: Optimal speed and accuracy of object detection. arXiv:2004.10934 (2020)
2. Cai, Z., Vasconcelos, N.: Cascade R-CNN: delving into high quality object detection. In: CVPR (2018)
3. Dai, J., Li, Y., He, K., et al.: R-FCN: object detection via region-based fully convolutional networks. In: NeurIPS (2016)
4. Duan, K., Bai, S., Xie, L., et al.: CenterNet: Keypoint triplets for object detection. arXiv:1904.08189 (2019)
5. Fu, C., Liu, W., Ranga, A., et al.: DSSD: Deconvolutional single shot detector. arXiv:1701.06659 (2017)
6. Girshick, R.B.: Fast R-CNN. In: ICCV (2015)
7. He, K., Gkioxari, G., Dollár, P., et al.: Mask R-CNN. In: ICCV (2017)
8. He, K., Zhang, X., Ren, S., et al.: Deep residual learning for image recognition. In: CVPR (2016)
9. Huang, E., Korf, R.E.: New improvements in optimal rectangle packing. In: IJCAI (2009)
10. Iandola, F., Moskewicz, M., Karayev, S., et al.: DenseNet: Implementing efficient convnet descriptor pyramids. arXiv:1404.1869 (2014)
11. Ioffe, S., Szegedy, C.: Batch normalization: accelerating deep network training by reducing internal covariate shift. In: ICML (2015)
12. Korf, R.E.: Optimal rectangle packing: initial results. In: ICAPS (2003)
13. Li, Y., Chen, Y., Wang, N., et al.: Scale-aware trident networks for object detection. In: ICCV (2019)
14. Li, Z., Peng, C., Yu, G., et al.: Light-head R-CNN: In defense of two-stage object detector. arXiv:1711.07264 (2017)
15. Lin, T., Dollár, P., Girshick, R.B., et al.: Feature pyramid networks for object detection. In: CVPR (2017)

16. Lin, T., Goyal, P., Girshick, R.B., et al.: Focal loss for dense object detection. In: ICCV (2017)
17. Liu, T.-Y., et al.: Microsoft COCO: common objects in context. In: Fleet, D., Pajdla, T., Schiele, B., Tuytelaars, T. (eds.) ECCV 2014. LNCS, vol. 8693, pp. 740–755. Springer, Cham (2014). https://doi.org/10.1007/978-3-319-10602-1_48
18. Liu, W., et al.: SSD: single shot multibox detector. In: Leibe, B., Matas, J., Sebe, N., Welling, M. (eds.) ECCV 2016. LNCS, vol. 9905, pp. 21–37. Springer, Cham (2016). https://doi.org/10.1007/978-3-319-46448-0_2
19. Newell, A., Yang, K., Deng, J.: Stacked hourglass networks for human pose estimation. In: Leibe, B., Matas, J., Sebe, N., Welling, M. (eds.) ECCV 2016. LNCS, vol. 9912, pp. 483–499. Springer, Cham (2016). https://doi.org/10.1007/978-3-319-46484-8_29
20. Pang, J., Chen, K., Shi, J., et al.: Libra R-CNN: towards balanced learning for object detection. In: CVPR (2019)
21. Papandreou, G., Kokkinos, I., Savalle, P.A.: Untangling local and global deformations in deep convolutional networks for image classification and sliding window detection. arXiv:1412.0296 (2014)
22. Peng, C., Xiao, T., Li, Z., et al.: MegDet: a large mini-batch object detector. In: CVPR (2018)
23. Redmon, J., Divvala, S.K., Girshick, R.B., et al.: You only look once: unified, real-time object detection. In: CVPR (2016)
24. Redmon, J., Farhadi, A.: YOLO9000: better, faster, stronger. In: CVPR (2017)
25. Redmon, J., Farhadi, A.: YOLOv3: An incremental improvement. arXiv:1804.02767 (2018)
26. Ren, S., He, K., Girshick, R.B., et al.: Faster R-CNN: towards real-time object detection with region proposal networks. In: NeurIPS (2015)
27. Rezatofighi, H., Tsoi, N., Gwak, J., et al.: Generalized intersection over union: a metric and a loss for bounding box regression. In: CVPR (2019)
28. Sandler, M., Howard, A.G., Zhu, M., et al.: MobileNetV2: inverted residuals and linear bottlenecks. In: CVPR (2018)
29. Tan, M., Pang, R., Le, Q.V.: EfficientDet: scalable and efficient object detection. arXiv:1911.09070 (2019)
30. Tian, Z., Shen, C., Chen, H., et al.: FCOS: Fully convolutional one-stage object detection. arXiv:1904.01355 (2019)
31. Wang, N., Gao, Y., Chen, H., et al.: NAS-FCOS: Fast neural architecture search for object detection. arXiv:1906.04423 (2019)
32. Wei, C., Xie, L., Ren, X., et al.: Iterative reorganization with weak spatial constraints: solving arbitrary Jigsaw puzzles for unsupervised representation learning. In: CVPR (2019)
33. Wu, B., Dai, X., Zhang, P., et al.: FBNet: hardware-aware efficient ConvNet design via differentiable neural architecture search. In: CVPR (2019)
34. Wu, Y., He, K.: Group normalization. In: Ferrari, V., Hebert, M., Sminchisescu, C., Weiss, Y. (eds.) ECCV 2018. LNCS, vol. 11217, pp. 3–19. Springer, Cham (2018). https://doi.org/10.1007/978-3-030-01261-8_1
35. Xie, S., Girshick, R.B., Dollár, P., et al.: Aggregated residual transformations for deep neural networks. In: CVPR (2017)
36. Yang, T., Zhang, X., Li, Z., et al.: MetaAnchor: learning to detect objects with customized anchors. In: NeurIPS (2018)
37. Yang, Z., Liu, S., Hu, H., et al.: RepPoints: Point set representation for object detection. arXiv:1904.11490 (2019)

38. Zhang, S., Wen, L., Bian, X., et al.: Single-shot refinement neural network for object detection. In: CVPR (2018)
39. Zhang, Z., He, T., Zhang, H., et al.: Bag of freebies for training object detection neural networks. arXiv:1902.04103 (2019)
40. Zhao, Q., Sheng, T., Wang, Y., et al.: M2Det: a single-shot object detector based on multi-level feature pyramid network. In: AAAI (2019)
41. Zhong, Y., Wang, J., Peng, J., et al.: Anchor box optimization for object detection. arXiv:1812.00469 (2018)
42. Zhu, C., Chen, F., Shen, Z., et al.: Soft anchor-point object detection. arXiv, arXiv:1911.12448 (2019)
43. Zhu, C., He, Y., Savvides, M.: Feature selective anchor-free module for single-shot object detection. In: CVPR (2019)
44. Zhu, X., Hu, H., Lin, S., et al.: Deformable ConvNets v2: more deformable, better results. In: CVPR (2019)

A Generic Graph-Based Neural Architecture Encoding Scheme for Predictor-Based NAS

Xuefei Ning[1], Yin Zheng[2], Tianchen Zhao[3], Yu Wang[1]($\boxtimes$), and Huazhong Yang[1]

[1] Department of Electronic Engineering, Tsinghua University, Beijing, China
yu-wang@tsinghua.edu.cn
[2] Weixin Group, Tencent, Shenzhen, China
foxdoraame@gmail.com
[3] Department of Electronic Engineering, Beihang University, Beijing, China

Abstract. This work proposes a novel Graph-based neural ArchiTecture Encoding Scheme, a.k.a. GATES, to improve the predictor-based neural architecture search. Specifically, different from existing graph-based schemes, GATES models the operations as the transformation of the propagating information, which mimics the actual data processing of neural architecture. GATES is a more reasonable modeling of the neural architectures, and can encode architectures from both the "operation on node" and "operation on edge" cell search spaces consistently. Experimental results on various search spaces confirm GATES's effectiveness in improving the performance predictor. Furthermore, equipped with the improved performance predictor, the sample efficiency of the predictor-based neural architecture search (NAS) flow is boosted.

Keywords: Neural architecture search (NAS) · Predictor-based NAS

1 Introduction

Recently, Neural Architecture Search (NAS) has received extensive attention due to its capability to discover neural network architectures in an automated manner. Substantial studies have shown that the automatically discovered architectures by NAS are able to achieve highly competitive performance.

Generally speaking, there are two key components in a NAS framework, the *architecture searching module* and the *architecture evaluation module*. Specifically, the architecture evaluation module provides the signals of the architecture performance, e.g., accuracy, latency, etc., which are then used by the architecture searching module to explore architectures in the search space. In the seminal work of [25], the architecture evaluation is conducted by training every candidate architecture

Electronic supplementary material The online version of this chapter (https://doi.org/10.1007/978-3-030-58601-0_12) contains supplementary material, which is available to authorized users.

© Springer Nature Switzerland AG 2020
A. Vedaldi et al. (Eds.): ECCV 2020, LNCS 12358, pp. 189–204, 2020.
https://doi.org/10.1007/978-3-030-58601-0_12

until convergence, and thousands of architectures need to be evaluated during the architecture search process. As a result, the computational burden of the whole NAS process is extremely large. There are two directions to address this issue, which focus on improving the searching and evaluation module, respectively. 1) Evaluation: accelerating the evaluation of each individual architecture, and in the meanwhile, keep the evaluation meaningful in the sense of ranking correlation; 2) Searching: increasing the sample efficiency so that fewer architectures are needed to be evaluated for discovering a good architecture.

To improve the sample efficiency of the architecture searching module, a promising idea is to learn an approximated performance predictor, and then utilize the predictor to sample architectures that are more worth evaluating. We refer to these NAS methods [8,13,21] as the predictor-based NAS methods, and their general flow will be introduced in Sect. 3.1. The generalization ability of the predictor is crucial to the sample efficiency of predictor-based NAS flows. Our work follows the line of research of predictor-based NAS, and focus on improving the performance predictor of neural architectures.

A performance predictor predicts the performance of architectures based on the encoding of them. Existing neural architecture encoding schemes include the sequence-based scheme and the graph-based scheme. The sequence-based schemes [8,13,21] rely on specific serialization of the architecture. They model the topological information only implicitly, which deteriorates the representational power and interpretability of the predictor. Existing graph-based schemes [4,19] usually apply graph convolutional networks (GCN) [6] to encode the neural architectures. For the "operation on node" (OON) search spaces, in which the operations (e.g., Conv3x3) are on the nodes of the directed acyclic graph (DAG), GCN can be directly applied to encode architectures. Nevertheless, since a neural architecture is a "data processing" graph, where the operations behave as the data processing functions (e.g., Conv3x3, MaxPool), existing methods' modeling of operations as the node attributes in OON search spaces is not suitable. Instead of modeling the operations as node attributes, a more natural solution is to treat them as the transforms of the node attributes (i.e., mimic the processing of the information). On the other hand, for the "operation on edge" (OOE) search spaces,[1] the handling of edge information in the existing graph-based scheme [4] is even more unsatisfying regarding its poor generalizability and flawed handling of architecture isomorphism.

In this work, we propose a general encoding scheme: *Graph-based neural ArchiTecture Encoding Scheme (GATES)*, which is suitable for the representation learning of data processing graphs such as neural architectures. Specifically, to encode a neural architecture, GATES models the information flow of the actual data processing of the architecture. First, GATES models the input information as the attributes of the input nodes. And the input information will be propagated along the architecture DAG. The data processing of the operations (e.g., Conv3x3, MaxPool) are modeled by GATES as different transforms of the information. Finally, the output information is used as the embedding of

---

[1] Figure 2 illustrates the OON and OOE search spaces.

the cell architecture. Since the encoding process of GATES mimics the actual computation flow of the architectures, GATES intrinsically maps isomorphic architectures to the same representation. Moreover, GATES can encode architectures from both the OON and OOE cell search spaces in a consistent way. Due to the superior representational ability of GATES, the generalization ability of the architecture performance predictor using GATES is significantly better than other encoders. Experimental results confirm that GATES is effective in improving the architecture performance predictors. Furthermore, by utilizing the improved performance predictor, the sample efficiency of the NAS process is improved.

2   Related Work

2.1   Architecture Evaluation Module

One commonly used technique to accelerate architecture evaluation is parameter sharing [15], where a super-net is constructed such that all architectures in the search space share a superset of weights and the training costs of architectures are amortized to an "one-shot" super-net training. Parameter sharing dramatically reduces the computational burden and is widely used by recent methods. However, recent studies [12,17] find that the ranking of architecture candidates with parameter sharing does not reflect their true rankings well, which dramatically affects the effectiveness of the NAS algorithm. Moreover, the parameter sharing technique is not generally applicable, since it is difficult to construct the super-net for some search spaces, for example, in NAS-Bench-101 [24], one operation can have different output dimensions in different candidate architectures. Due to these limitations, this work does not use the parameter sharing technique, and focus on improving the sample efficiency of the architecture searching module.

2.2   Architecture Searching Module

To improve the sample efficiency of the architecture search module, a variety of search strategies have been used, e.g., RL-based methods [3,15,25], Evolutionary methods [9,16], gradient-based method [7,10], Monte Carlo Tree Search (MCTS) method [14], etc.

A promising direction to improve the sample efficiency of NAS is to utilize a performance predictor to sample new architectures, a.k.a. *predictor-based NAS*. An early study [8] trains a surrogate model (predictor) to identify promising architectures with increasing complexity. NASBot [5] design a distance metric in the architecture space and exploits gaussian process to get the posterior of the architecture performances. Then, it samples new architectures based on the acquisition function calculated using the posterior. NAO [13] trains an LSTM-based autoencoder together with a performance predictor based on the latent representation. After updating the latent representation following the predictor's gradients, NAO decodes the latent representation to sample new architectures.

2.3 Neural Architecture Encoders

Existing neural architecture encoding schemes include the sequence-based and the graph-based schemes. In the sequence based scheme, the neural architecture is *flattened* into a string encoding the architecture decisions, then encoded using either an LSTM [8,13,21] or a Multi-Layer Perceptron (MLP) [8,21]. In these methods, the topological information could only be modeled implicitly, which deteriorates the encoder's representational ability. Also, the search efficiency would deteriorate since these encoders could not guarantee to map isomorphic architectures [20,24] to the same representation, and data augmentation and regularization tricks are utilized to alleviate this issue [13].

Recently, the graph-based encoding scheme that utilizes the topological information explicitly has been used to get better performance. In these graph-based schemes, graph convolutional networks (GCN) [6] are usually used to embed the graphs to fixed-length vector representations. For the "operation on node" search spaces, in which the operations (e.g., Conv3x3) are on the nodes of the DAG, GCN can be directly applied [19] to encode architectures, i.e., using adjacency matrix and operation embedding of each node as the input. However, for the "operation on edge" search spaces, in which the operations are on the edges, GCN cannot be applied directly. A recent study [4] proposes an ad-hoc solution for the ENAS search space. They represent each node by the concatenation of the operation embeddings on the input edges. This solution is contrived and cannot be generalized to search spaces where nodes could have different input degrees. Moreover, since the concatenation is not commutative, this encoding scheme could not handle isomorphic architectures correctly. In brief, existing graph-based encoding schemes are specific to different search spaces, and a generic approach for encoding the neural architectures is desirable in the literature.

3 Method

3.1 Predictor-Based Neural Architecture Search

The principle of predictor-based NAS is to increase the sample efficiency of the NAS process, by utilizing an approximated performance predictor to sample architectures that are more worth evaluating. Generally speaking, the flow of predictor-based NAS could be summarized as in Algorithm 1 and Fig. 1.

In line 6 of Alg. 1, the architecture candidates are sampled based on the approximated evaluation of the predictor. Utilizing a more accurate predictor, we could choose better architectures for further evaluation. The better the generalization ability of the predictor is, the fewer architectures are needed to be exactly evaluated to get a highly accurate predictor. Therefore, the generalization ability of the predictor is crucial for the efficiency and effectiveness of the NAS method.

The model design (i.e., how to encode the neural architectures) of the predictor is crucial to its generalization ability. We'll introduce our main effort to improve the predictor from the "model design" aspect in the following section.

Algorithm 1. The flow of predictor-based neural architecture search

---

1: $\mathcal{A}$: Architecture search space
2: P : $\mathcal{A} \to \mathbb{R}$: Performance predictor that outputs the predicted performance given the architecture
3: $N^{(k)}$: Number of architectures to sample in the k-th iteration

4: k = 1
5: **while** $k \leq$ MAX_ITER **do**
6:     Sample a subset of architectures $S^{(k)} = \{a_j^{(k)}\}_{j=1,\cdots,N^{(k)}}$ from $\mathcal{A}$, utilizing P
7:     Evaluate architectures in $S^{(k)}$, get $\tilde{S}^{(k)} = \{(a_j^{(k)}, y_j^{(k)})\}_{j=1,\cdots,N^{(k)}}$ (y is the performance)
8:     Optimizing P using the ground-truth architecture evaluation data $\tilde{S} = \cup_{i=1}^k \tilde{S}^{(i)}$
9: **end while**
10: Output $a_{j*} \in \cup_{i=1}^k S^{(i)}$ with best corresponding y_{j*}; Or, $a^* = \text{argmax}_{a \in \mathcal{A}} P(a)$

3.2   GATES: A Generic Neural Architecture Encoder

A performance predictor P is a model that takes a neural architecture a as input, and outputs a predicted score $\hat{s}$. Usually, the performance predictor is constructed by an encoder followed by an MLP, as shown in Eq. 1. The encoder Enc maps a neural architecture into a continuous embedding space, and its design is vital to the generalization ability of the performance predictor. Existing encoders include the sequence-based ones (e.g., MLP, LSTM) and the graph-based ones (e.g., GCN). We design a new graph-based neural architecture encoder GATES that is more suitable for modeling neural architectures.

$$\hat{s} = P(a) = \text{MLP}(\text{Enc}(a)) \tag{1}$$

To encode a cell architecture into an embedding vector, GATES follows the ideology of modeling the information flow in the architecture, and uses the output information as the embedding of the architecture. The notations are summarized in Table 1.

Specifically, we models the input information as the embedding of the input nodes $E \in \mathbb{R}^{n_i \times h_i}$, where n_i is the number of input nodes, and h_i is the embed-

Table 1. Notations of GATES. E, EMB, W_o and W_x are all trainable parameters

n_i	Number of input nodes: 1, 1, 2 for NAS-Bench-101, NAS-Bench-201 and ENAS, respectively
N_o	Number of operation primitives
h_o	Embedding size of operation
h_i	Embedding size of information
$E \in \mathbb{R}^{n_i \times h_i}$	The embedding of the information at the input nodes
EMB $\in \mathbb{R}^{N_o \times h_o}$	The operation embeddings
$W_o \in \mathbb{R}^{h_o \times h_i}$	The transformation matrix on the operation embedding
$W_x \in \mathbb{R}^{h_i \times h_i}$	The transformation matrix on the information

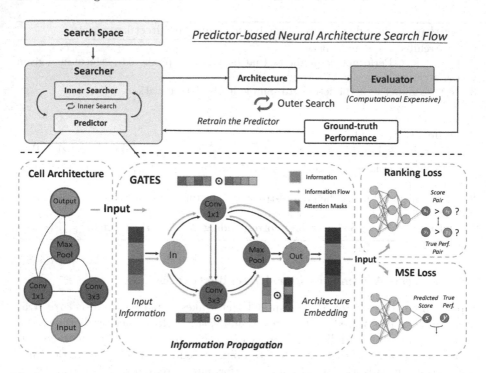

Fig. 1. The overview of the proposed algorithm. Upper: The general flow of the predictor-based NAS. Lower: Illustration of the encoding processes of GATES of an OON cell architecture

ding size of the information. The information (embedding of the input nodes) is then "processed" by the operations and "propagates" along the DAG.

The encoding process of GATES goes as follows: Upon each unary operation o (e.g., `Conv3x3`, `MaxPool`, etc.), the input information x_{in} of this operation is processed by a linear transform W_x and then elementwise multiplied with a soft attention mask $m = \sigma(\text{EMB}(o)W_o) \in \mathbb{R}^{1 \times h_i}$.

$$x_{\text{out}} = m \odot x_{\text{in}}W_x \tag{2}$$

where $\odot$ denotes the elementwise multiplication. And the mask m is calculated from the operation embedding $\text{EMB}(o) = \text{onehot}(o)^T \text{EMB} \in \mathbb{R}^{1 \times h_o}$.

Multiple pieces of information are aggregated at each node using summation. Finally, after obtaining the virtual information at all the nodes, the information at the output node is used as the embedding of the entire cell architecture. For search spaces with multiple cells (e.g., normal and reduce cells in ENAS), GATES encodes each cell independently, and concatenate the embeddings of cells as the embedding of the architecture.

Figure 2 illustrates two examples of the encoding process in the OON and OOE search spaces. As can be seen, the encoding process of GATES mimics the actual feature map computation. For example, in the example of the OON search

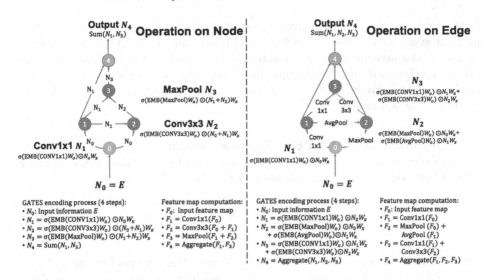

Fig. 2. Feature map (F_i) computation and GATES encoding process (N_i). Left: The "operation on node" cell search space, where operations (e.g., Conv3x3) are on the nodes of the DAG (e.g., NAS-Bench-101 [24], randomly wired search space [22]). Right: The "operation on edge" cell search space, where operations are on the edges of the DAG. (e.g., NAS-Bench-201 [2], ENAS [15])

space, the actual feature map computation at node 2 is $F_2 = \text{Conv3x3}(F_0 + F_1)$, where F_i is the feature map at node i. To model the information processing of this feature map computation, GATES calculates the information (node embedding) at node 2 by $N_2 = \sigma(\text{EMB}(\text{Conv3x3})W_o) \odot (N_0 + N_1)W_x$, where $\sigma(\cdot)$ is the sigmoid function, and $W_o \in \mathbb{R}^{h_o \times h_i}$ is a transformation matrix that transforms the h_o-dim operation embedding into a h_i-dim feature. That is to say, the summation of feature maps $F_0 + F_1$ corresponds to the summation of the virtual information $N_0 + N_1$, and the data processing function $o(\cdot)$ (Conv3x3) corresponds to a transform $f(\cdot)$ that processes the information $x = N_0 + N_1$ by $f_o(x) = \sigma(\text{EMB}(o)W_o) \odot xW_x$.

Intuitively, to model a cell architecture, GATES models the operations in the architecture as the "soft gates" that control the flow of the virtual information, and the output information is used as the embedding of the cell architecture. The key difference between GATES and GCN is: In GATES, the operations (e.g., Conv3x3) are modeled as the processing of the node attributes (i.e., virtual information), whereas GCN models them as the node attributes themselves.

The representational power of GATES for neural architectures comes from two aspects: 1) The more reasonable modeling of the operations in data-processing DAGs. 2) The intrinsic proper handling of DAG isomorphism. The discussion and experiments on how GATES handles the isomorphism are in the "Discussion on Isomorphism" section in the appendix.

In practice, to calculate the information propagation following the topological order of different graphs in a batched manner, we use a stack of GATES layers.

In the forward process of each layer, one step of information propagation is taken place at every node. That is to say, if a graph is input to a GATES encoder with N layers, the information is propagated and aggregated for N steps along the graph. The batched formulas and specific implementations of a GATES layer for OON and OOE search spaces are elaborated in the "Implementation of GATES" section in the appendix.

The Optimization of GATES. The most common practice [8,13] to train the architecture performance predictors is to minimize the Mean Squared Error (MSE) between the predictor outputs and the true performances.

$$L(\{a_j, y_j\}_{j=1,\cdots,N}) = \sum_{j=1}^{N}(P(a_j) - y_j)^2 \qquad (3)$$

where a_j denotes one architecture, and y_j denotes the true performance of a_j.

In NAS applications, what is really required to guide the search of architectures is the relative ranking order of architectures rather than the absolute performance values. In this paper, we adopt Kendall's Tau ranking correlation [18] as the measure as the direct criterion for evaluating architecture predictors. And since ranking losses are better surrogate losses [1,11,23] for the ranking correlation than the regression loss, in addition to the MSE loss, we use a hinge pair-wise ranking loss with margin $m = 0.1$ to train the predictors.[2]

$$L(\{a_j, y_j\}_{j=1,\cdots,N}) = \sum_{j=1}^{N} \sum_{i,y_i > y_j} \max[0, m - (P(a_i) - P(a_j))] \qquad (4)$$

3.3   Neural Architecture Search Utilizing the Predictor

We follow the flow in Algorithm 1 to conduct the architecture search. There are multiple ways of utilizing the predictor P to sample architectures (line 6 in Alg. 1), i.e., the choice of the inner search method. In this work, we use two inner search methods for sampling architecture for further evaluation:[3]

- Random sample n architectures from the search space, then choose the best k among them according to the evaluation of the predictor.
- Search with Evolutionary Algorithm (EA) for n steps, and then choose the best k with the highest predicted scores among the seen architectures.

Compared with the evaluation (line 7 in Alg. 1) in the outer search process, the evaluation of each architecture in the inner search process is very efficient with only a forward pass of the predictor. The sample ratio $r = \frac{n}{k}$ indicates the

---

[2] A more comprehensive comparison of the MSE regression loss and multiple ranking losses is shown in the appendix.

[3] Note that this inner search component could be easily substituted with other search strategies.

equivalent number of the architectures need to be evaluated by the predictor to make one sample decision. And it is not the case that bigger r leads to better sample efficiency of the overall NAS process. If n is too large (the limiting case is to exhaustive test the whole search space with $n = |\mathcal{A}|$), the sampling process would overfit onto exploiting the current performance predictor and fails to explore. Therefore, there is a trade-off between exploration and exploitation controlled by n, which we verify in Sect. 4.3.

4   Experiments

The experiments in Sect. 4.1 and Sect. 4.2 verify the effectiveness of the GATES encoder on both the OON and OOE search spaces. Then, in Sect. 4.3, we demonstrate that by utilizing GATES, the sample efficiency of the NAS process surpasses other searching strategies, including the predictor-based methods with other baseline encoders. Finally, in Sect. 4.4, we apply the proposed algorithm to the ENAS search space.

4.1   Predictor Evaluation on NAS-Bench-101

Setup. NAS-Bench-101 [24] provides the performances of the 423k unique architectures in a search space. The NAS-Bench-101 search space is an OON search space, in which sequence based encoding schemes [21], and graph based encoding schemes [19] are proposed for encoding architectures. We use the Kendall's Tau ranking correlation [18] as the measure for evaluating the architecture performance predictors. The first 90% (381262) architectures are used as the training data, and the other 42362 architectures are used for testing.[4]

We conduct a more comprehensive comparison of the MSE loss and multiple ranking losses on NAS-Bench-101, and the results are shown in the appendix. We find that compared to the MSE loss, ranking losses bring consistent improvements, and hinge pair wise loss is a good choice. Therefore, in our experiments, unless otherwise stated, the hinge pairwise loss with margin 0.1 is used to train all the predictors.

Results. Table 2 shows the comparison of the GATES encoder and various baseline encoders trained using different proportions of the training data. As can be seen, GATES could achieve higher Kendall's Taus on the testing architectures than the baseline encoders consistently with different training proportions. The advantages are especially significant when there are few training architectures. For example, when only 190 (0.05%) architectures are seen by the performance predictor, utilizing the same training settings, GATES achieves a test Kendall's Tau of *0.7634*, whereas the Kendall's Tau results achieved by MLP, LSTM, and the best GCN variant are 0.3971, 0.5509 and 0.5343, respectively. This demonstrates the surpassing generalization ability of the GATES encoder, which

---

[4] See "Setup and Additional Results" section in the appendix for more details.

Table 2. The Kendall's Tau of using different encoders on the NAS-Bench-101 dataset. The first 90% (381262) architectures in the dataset are used as the training data, and the other 42362 architectures are used as the testing data

Encoder	Proportions of 381262 training samples							
	0.05%	0.1%	0.5%	1%	5%	10%	50%	100%
MLP [21]	0.3971	0.5272	0.6463	0.7312	0.8592	0.8718	0.8893	0.8955
LSTM [21]	0.5509	0.5993	0.7112	0.7747	0.8440	0.8576	0.8859	0.8931
GCN (w.o. global node)	0.3992	0.4628	0.6963	0.8243	0.8626	0.8721	0.8910	0.8952
GCN (global node) [19]	0.5343	0.5790	0.7915	0.8277	0.8641	0.8747	0.8918	0.8950
GATES	**0.7634**	**0.7789**	**0.8434**	**0.8594**	**0.8841**	**0.8922**	**0.9001**	**0.9030**

Table 3. N@K on NAS-Bench-101. All predictors are trained with 0.1% of the training data (i.e., 381 architectures)

Encoder	Ranking loss		Regression loss	
	N@5	N@10	N@5	N@10
MLP [21]	57 (0.13%)	58 (0.13%)	1397 (3.30%)	552 (1.30%)
LSTM [21]	1715 (4.05%)	1715 (4.05%)	1080 (2.54%)	312 (0.73%)
GCN [19]	2025 (4.77%)	1362 (3.21%)	405 (0.95%)	405 (0.95%)
GATES	**22 (0.05%)**	**22 (0.05%)**	**27 (0.05%)**	**27 (0.05%)**

enables one to learn a good performance predictor for unseen architectures after evaluating only a small set of architectures.

In the Kendall's Tau measure, all discordant pairs are treated equally. However, in NAS applications, the relative rankings among the poorly performing architectures are not of concern. Therefore, we compare different predictors in the form of other measures that have a more direct correspondence with the NAS flow: 1) N@K: The best true ranking among the top-K architectures selected according to the predicted scores. 2) Precision@K: The proportion of true top-K architectures among the top-K predicted architectures. Table 3 and Fig. 3(a) show these two measures of the predictors with different encoders on the testing set of NAS-Bench-101. As can be seen, GATES achieves consistently better performances than other encoders across different Ks.

4.2   Predictor Evaluation on NAS-Bench-201

Setup. NAS-Bench-201 [2] is another NAS benchmark that provides the performances of 15625 architectures in an OOE search space. In our experiments, we use the first 50% (7813) as the training data, and the remaining 7812

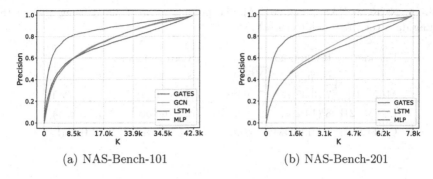

(a) NAS-Bench-101   (b) NAS-Bench-201

Fig. 3. Precision@K

Table 4. The Kendall's Tau of using different encoders on the NAS-Bench-201 dataset. The first 50% (7813) architectures in the dataset are used as the training data, and the other 7812 architectures are used as the testing data

Encoder	Proportions of 7813 training samples				
	1%	5%	10%	50%	100%
MLP [21]	0.0974	0.3959	0.5388	0.8229	0.8703
LSTM [21]	0.5550	0.6407	0.7268	0.8791	0.9002
GATES	**0.7401**	**0.8628**	**0.8802**	**0.9192**	**0.9259**

architectures as the testing data. Since GCN encoders could not be directly applied to the OOE search spaces, we compare GATES with the sequence-based encoders: MLP and LSTM (Table 4).[5]

Results. Table 2 shows the evaluation results of GATES. GATES could achieve significantly higher ranking correlations than the baseline encoders, especially when there are only a few training samples. For example, with 78 training samples, "GATES + Pairwise loss" could achieve a Kendall's Tau of 0.7401, while the best baseline result is 0.5550 ("LSTM + Pairwise loss").

The N@K and Precision@K measures on NAS-Bench-201 are shown in Table 5 and Fig. 3(b), respectively. We can see that GATES can achieve an N@5 of 1 on the 7812 testing architectures, with either ranking loss or regression loss. And, not surprisingly, GATES outperforms the baselines consistently on the Precision@K measure too.

---

[5] We also implement an ad-hoc solution of applying GCN on OOE architectures referred to as the Line Graph GCN solution, in which the graph is first converted to a line graph. See "Setup and Additional Results" section in the appendix for more details.

Table 5. N@K on NAS-Bench-201. All the predictors are trained using 10% of the training data (i.e., 781 architectures)

Encoder	Ranking loss		Regression loss	
	N@5	N@10	N@5	N@10
MLP [21]	7 (0.09%)	7 (0.09%)	1538 (19.7%)	224 (3.87%)
LSTM [21]	8 (1.02%)	2 (0.01%)	250 (6.65%)	234 (2.99%)
GATES	**1 (0.00%)**	**1 (0.00%)**	**1 (0.00%)**	**1 (0.00%)**

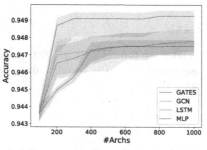 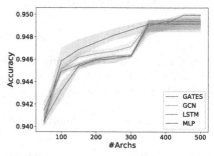

a) RS inner search method ($r = 500$)   (b) EA inner search method ($r = 100$)

Fig. 4. Comparison of predictor-based NAS with different encoders: The best validation accuracy during the search process over 10/15 runs for the RS and EA inner serach method, respectively. r is the sample ratio (see Sect. 3.3)

4.3   Neural Architecture Search on NAS-Bench-101

Equipped with a better performance predictor, the sample efficiency of the predictor-based NAS process can be significantly improved. To verify that, we conduct the architecture search on NAS-Bench-101 using various searching strategies. As the baseline of our method, we run a random search, regularized evolution [16], and predictor-based NAS methods equipped with the baseline encoders (i.e., LSTM, MLP, GCN).

Comparison of Sample Efficiency. The results of running predictor-based NAS methods with different encoders are shown in Fig. 4. We conduct experiments with two inner search methods: random search, and evolutionary algorithm. In each stage, 100 random samples are used to train the predictor (50 for evolutionary algorithm), and the predictor is trained for 50 epochs with hinge ranking loss. When using random search, $n = 2500$ architectures are randomly sampled, and the top $k = 5$ architectures with high predicted scores are chosen to be further evaluated by the ground truth evaluator. When using the evolutionary algorithm for the inner search, n is set to 100, and k is set to 1. And the population and tournament size is 20 and 5, respectively. We can see that the sample efficiency using GATES surpasses the baselines with different inner

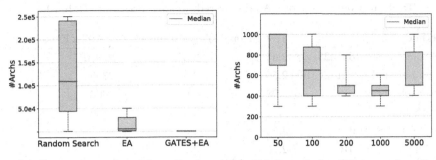

(a) Comparison of search methods   (b) Ablation study of the sample ratio r

Fig. 5. Left: Number of architectures evaluated to acquire the best validation accuracy on NAS-Bench-101 over 100 runs. We use the mean validation accuracy as the search reward. GATES-powered predictor-based NAS is 511.0× and 59.25× more sample efficient than random search and regularized evolution. Right: Number of architectures evaluated to acquire the best validation accuracy over 10 runs with different r

search methods. This verifies the analysis that utilizing a better neural architecture encoder in the predictor-based NAS flow leads to better sample efficiency.

The comparison of the sample efficiency of two baseline searching strategies and the predictor-based method with GATES is shown in Fig. 5(a). The median counts of evaluated architectures of RS, Regularized EA and GATES-powered NAS over 100 runs are 220400, 23700 and 400 (50 as the granularity), respectively. GATES-powered NAS is 551.0× and 59.25× more sample efficient than the random search and evolution algorithm.

Ablation Study of the Sample Ratio r. The ablation study of the sample ratio r (Sect. 3.3) is shown in Fig. 5(b). We run GATES-powered predictor-based search with evolutionary algorithm, and shows the architectures needed to evaluate before finding the architecture with the best validation accuracy. We can see that the sample ratio r should be neither too big nor too small, since a too small n leads to bad exploitation and a too large n leads to bad exploration.

4.4   Neural Architecture Search in the ENAS Search Space

In this section, we apply our method on the ENAS search space. This search space is an OOE search space that is much larger than the benchmark search spaces. We first randomly sample 600 architectures and train them for 80 epochs. Then we train a GATES predictor using the performance of the 600 architectures and use it to sample 200 architectures, by randomly sampling 10k architectures and taking the top 200 with the highest predicted scores (sample ratio $r = 50$). After training these 200 architectures for 80 epochs, we pick the architecture with the best validation accuracy. Finally, after the channel and layer augmentation, the architecture is trained from scratch for 600 epochs.

Table 6. Comparison of NAS-discovered architectures on CIFAR-10

Method	Test Error (%)	#Params (M)	#Archs Evaluated
NASNet-A + cutout [25]	2.65	3.3	20000
AmoebaNet-B + cutout [16]	2.55	2.8	27000
NAONet [13]	2.98	28.6	1000
PNAS [8]	3.41	3.2	1160
NAONet-WS† [13]	3.53	2.5	–
DARTS+cutout† [10]	2.76	3.3	–
ENAS + cutout† [15]	2.89	4.6	–
Ours + cutout	2.58	4.1	800

The comparison of the test errors of different architectures is shown in Table 6, and the discovered architecture is shown in the appendix. As can be seen, our discovered architecture can achieve a test error rate of 2.58%, which is better than those architectures discovered with parameter sharing evaluation. Compared to the other methods, much fewer samples are truly evaluated to discover an architecture with better or comparable performance. When transferred to ImageNet, the discovered architecture achieves a competitive top-1 error of 24.1% with 5.6M parameters.

5   Conclusion

In this paper, we propose GATES, a graph-based neural architecture encoder with better representation ability for neural architectures. Due to its reasonable modeling of the neural architectures and intrinsic ability to handle DAG isomorphism, GATES significantly improves the architecture performance predictor for different cell-based search spaces. Utilizing GATES in the predictor-based NAS flow leads to consistent improvements in sample efficiency. Extensive experiments demonstrate the effectiveness and rationality of GATES. Employing GATES to encode architectures in larger or hierarchical topological search spaces is an interesting future direction.

Acknowledgments. This work was supported by National Natural Science Foundation of China (No. 61832007, 61622403, 61621091, U19B2019), Beijing National Research Center for Information Science and Technology (BNRist). The authors thank Novauto for the support.

References

1. Chen, W., Liu, T.-Y., Lan, Y., Ma, Z., Li, H.: Ranking measures and loss functions in learning to rank. In: Bengio, Y., Schuurmans, D., Lafferty, J.D., Williams, C.K.I., Culotta, A. (eds.) Advances in Neural Information Processing Systems 22, pp. 315–323. Curran Associates, Inc., New York (2009)

2. Dong, X., Yang, Y.: Nas-bench-201: extending the scope of reproducible neural architecture search. In: International Conference on Learning Representations (2020). https://openreview.net/forum?id=HJxyZkBKDr

3. Guo, Y., et al.: Breaking the curse of space explosion: towards effcient nas with curriculum search. In: International Conference on Machine Learning (2010)

4. Guo, Y., et al.: Nat: neural architecture transformer for accurate and compact architectures. In: Advances in Neural Information Processing Systems, pp. 735–747 (2019)

5. Kandasamy, K., Neiswanger, W., Schneider, J., Poczos, B., Xing, E.P.: Neural architecture search with Bayesian optimisation and optimal transport. In: Advances in Neural Information Processing Systems, pp. 2016–2025 (2018)

6. Kipf, T.N., Welling, M.: Semi-supervised classification with graph convolutional networks. arXiv preprint arXiv:1609.02907 (2016)

7. Lian, D., et al.: Towards fast adaptation of neural architectures with meta learning. In: International Conference on Learning Representations (2020)

8. Liu, C., et al.: Progressive neural architecture search. In: Ferrari, V., Hebert, M., Sminchisescu, C., Weiss, Y. (eds.) ECCV 2018. LNCS, vol. 11205, pp. 19–35. Springer, Cham (2018). https://doi.org/10.1007/978-3-030-01246-5_2

9. Liu, H., Simonyan, K., Vinyals, O., Fernando, C., Kavukcuoglu, K.: Hierarchical representations for efficient architecture search. arXiv preprint arXiv:1711.00436 (2017)

10. Liu, H., Simonyan, K., Yang, Y.: Darts: Differentiable architecture search. arXiv preprint arXiv:1806.09055 (2018)

11. Liu, T.Y., et al.: Learning to rank for information retrieval. Found. Trends® Inf. Retrieval 3(3), 225–331 (2009)

12. Luo, R., Qin, T., Chen, E.: Understanding and improving one-shot neural architecture optimization. arXiv preprint arXiv:1909.10815 (2019)

13. Luo, R., Tian, F., Qin, T., Chen, E., Liu, T.Y.: Neural architecture optimization. In: Bengio, S., Wallach, H., Larochelle, H., Grauman, K., Cesa-Bianchi, N., Garnett, R. (eds.) Advances in Neural Information Processing Systems 31, pp. 7816–7827. Curran Associates, Inc. (2018). http://papers.nips.cc/paper/8007-neural-architecture-optimization.pdf

14. Negrinho, R., Gordon, G.: Deeparchitect: automatically designing and training deep architectures. arXiv preprint arXiv:1704.08792 (2017)

15. Pham, H., Guan, M.Y., Zoph, B., Le, Q.V., Dean, J.: Efficient neural architecture search via parameter sharing. arXiv preprint arXiv:1802.03268 (2018)

16. Real, E., Aggarwal, A., Huang, Y., Le, Q.V.: Regularized evolution for image classifier architecture search. Proc. AAAI Conf. Artificial Intell. 33, 4780–4789 (2019)

17. Sciuto, C., Yu, K., Jaggi, M., Musat, C., Salzmann, M.: Evaluating the search phase of neural architecture search. arXiv preprint arXiv:1902.08142 (2019)

18. Sen, P.K.: Estimates of the regression coefficient based on Kendall's tau. J. Am. Stat. Assoc. 63(324), 1379–1389 (1968)

19. Shi, H., Pi, R., Xu, H., Li, Z., Kwok, J.T., Zhang, T.: Multi-objective neural architecture search via predictive network performance optimization. arXiv preprint arXiv:1911.09336 (2019)

20. Stagge, P., Igel, C.: Neural network structures and isomorphisms: random walk characteristics of the search space. In: 2000 IEEE Symposium on Combinations of Evolutionary Computation and Neural Networks. Proceedings of the First IEEE Symposium on Combinations of Evolutionary Computation and Neural Networks (Cat. No. 00), pp. 82–90. IEEE (2000)

21. Wang, L., Zhao, Y., Jinnai, Y., Fonseca, R.: Alphax: exploring neural architectures with deep neural networks and monte carlo tree search. arXiv preprint arXiv:1805.07440 (2018)
22. Xie, S., Kirillov, A., Girshick, R., He, K.: Exploring randomly wired neural networks for image recognition. In: Proceedings of the IEEE International Conference on Computer Vision, pp. 1284–1293 (2019)
23. Xu, Y., et al.: Renas:relativistic evaluation of neural architecture search (2019)
24. Ying, C., Klein, A., Real, E., Christiansen, E., Murphy, K., Hutter, F.: Nas-bench-101: towards reproducible neural architecture search. arXiv preprint arXiv:1902.09635 (2019)
25. Zoph, B., Le, Q.V.: Neural architecture search with reinforcement learning. In: ICLR (2017). https://arxiv.org/abs/1611.01578

Learning Semantic Neural Tree
for Human Parsing

Ruyi Ji[1,2], Dawei Du[3], Libo Zhang[1(✉)], Longyin Wen[4], Yanjun Wu[1], Chen Zhao[1], Feiyue Huang[5], and Siwei Lyu[3]

[1] Institute of Software Chinese Academy of Sciences, Beijing, China
libo@iscas.ac.cn
[2] University of Chinese Academy of Sciences, Beijing, China
[3] University at Albany, State University of New York, Albany, NY, USA
[4] JD Finance America Corporation, Mountain View, CA, USA
[5] Tencent Youtu Lab, Shanghai, China

Abstract. In this paper, we design a novel semantic neural tree for human parsing, which uses a tree architecture to encode physiological structure of human body, and design a coarse to fine process in a cascade manner to generate accurate results. Specifically, the semantic neural tree is designed to segment human regions into multiple semantic sub-regions (*e.g.*, face, arms, and legs) in a hierarchical way using a new designed attention routing module. Meanwhile, we introduce the semantic aggregation module to combine multiple hierarchical features to exploit more context information for better performance. Our semantic neural tree can be trained in an end-to-end fashion by standard stochastic gradient descent (SGD) with back-propagation. Several experiments conducted on four challenging datasets for both single and multiple human parsing, *i.e.*, LIP, PASCAL-Person-Part, CIHP and MHP-v2, demonstrate the effectiveness of the proposed method. Code can be found at https://isrc.iscas.ac.cn/gitlab/research/sematree.

Keywords: Human parsing · Semantic neural tree · Semantic segmentation

1 Introduction

Human parsing aims to recognize each semantic part, *e.g.*, arms, legs and clothes, which is one of the most fundamental and critical problems in analyzing human with various applications, such as video surveillance, human-computer interaction, and person re-identification. With the development of convolutional neural networks (CNN) on semantic segmentation task, human parsing has obtained significant accuracy improvement recently. Most of previous algorithms [3,9,28,40]

R. Ji and D. Du—denotes equal contribution.

Electronic supplementary material The online version of this chapter (https://doi.org/10.1007/978-3-030-58601-0_13) contains supplementary material, which is available to authorized users.

© Springer Nature Switzerland AG 2020
A. Vedaldi et al. (Eds.): ECCV 2020, LNCS 12358, pp. 205–221, 2020.
https://doi.org/10.1007/978-3-030-58601-0_13

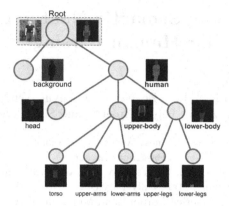

Fig. 1. Category hierarchy used in the PASCAL-Person-Part dataset [4].

attempt to assign each pixel with the predefined semantic labels, such as *arm* and *leg*. However, each semantic label is considered independently, which fails to consider context relations among different semantic labels, *e.g.*, the *upper-body* region is formed by the *torso*, *upper-arms* and *lower-arms* regions, see Fig. 1. Thus, exploiting the intrinsic physical structure of human body is an effective way to improve the segmentation accuracy.

Inspired from human perception [17], we argue that it is reasonable to use the hierarchical structure network to exploit discriminative features of human body to solve the human parsing task. Thus, we design a semantic neural tree network to encode the physical structure of human body, and design a coarse to fine process in a cascade manner. The coarse to fine process in a hierarchical design is helpful to improve the performance of human parsing. As an example in Fig. 1, we introduce a virtual category *upper-body*, and first distinguish the *upper-body* from the *head* and *lower-body* pixels. After that, we segment the *torso*, *upper-arms*, and *lower-arms* regions from the segmented *upper-body* region. Thus the hierarchical design in the cascade manner can generate more accurate results.

In this paper, we design a novel semantic neural tree (SNT) for human parsing, which uses a tree architecture to encode physiological structure of human body and design a coarse to fine process in a cascade manner. According to the topology structure of annotations in different datasets, we can design different tree architecture in a similar spirit. For the leaf node of each path in the tree, our goal is to distinguish just a few categories. In general, the proposed semantic neural tree consists of four components, *i.e.*, the backbone network for feature extraction, attention routing modules for sub-category partition, semantic aggregation modules for discriminative feature representation and prediction modules for generating parsing results, laid in several levels. That is, we segment human regions into multiple semantic sub-regions in a hierarchical way using the attention routing module. After that, we introduce the semantic aggregation module to combine multiple hierarchical features to exploit more context information. We generate the parsing result by aggregating the discriminative feature maps from each leaf node. Our SNT is trained in an end-to-end fashion using the standard stochastic gradient descent (SGD) with back-propagation [19].

Several experiments are conducted on four challenging datasets, *i.e.*, LIP [22], Pascal-Person-Part [4], CIHP [9] and MHP-v2 [41], demonstrating that our SNT method achieves favorable performance against the state-of-the-art methods for both single and multiple human parsing. Meanwhile, we also carry out ablation experiments to validate the effectiveness of the components in our SNT. The main contributions are summarized as follows, (1) We propose a semantic neural tree for human parsing, which integrates the physiological structure of human body into a tree architecture, and design a coarse to fine process in a cascade manner; (2) We introduce the semantic aggregation module to combine multiple hierarchical features to exploit more context information; (3) The experimental results on several challenging single and multiple human parsing datasets demonstrate that the proposed method achieves favorable performance against the state-of-the-art methods.

2 Related Work

Semantic Segmentation. Towards accurate scene understanding, many researchers [1–3,26,40] propose semantic segmentation methods based on the fully convolutional network (FCN) [29]. Zhao *et al.* [40] propose the pyramid scene parsing network (PSPNet) to capture the capability of global context information by different-region based context aggregation. In [26], the multi-path refinement network is developed to extract all the information available along the down-sampling process to enable high-resolution prediction using long-range residual connections. Besides, Chen *et al.* [2] introduce atrous spatial pyramid pooling (ASPP) to segment objects at multiple scales accurately. Improved from [2], they apply the depth-wise separable convolution to both ASPP and decoder modules to refine the segmentation results especially along object boundaries [3]. Recently, the meta-learning technique is applied in image prediction focused on the tasks of scene parsing, person-part segmentation, and semantic image segmentation, resulting in better performance [1]. However, these semantic segmentation methods are constructed without considering the relations among semantic sub-categories, leading to limited performance for human parsing with fine-grained sub-categories.

Human Parsing. Furthermore, human parsing can be regarded as a fine-grained semantic segmentation task. To adapt to the human parsing task, more useful modules are proposed and combined in the semantic segmentation methods. Ruan *et al.* [28] improve the PSPNet [40] by using the global context embedding module for multi-scale context information. Zhao *et al.* [41] employ three Generative Adversarial Network-like networks to perform semantic saliency prediction, instance-agnostic parsing and instance-aware clustering respectively. However, the aforementioned methods prefer to construct complex network for more discriminative representation, but consider little about semantic structure of human body when designing the network.

The semantic structure information is essential in human parsing. Gong *et al.* [9] consider instance-aware edge detection to group semantic parts into distinct person instances. Liang *et al.* [22] propose a novel joint human parsing and pose estimation network, which imposes human pose structures into the parsing results without resorting to extra supervision. In [8], the hierarchical graph transfer learning is incorporated upon the parsing network to encode the underlying label semantic structures and propagate relevant semantic information. Different from them without exploring human hierarchy, we take full use of the category label hierarchy and propose a new tree architecture to learn semantic regions in a coarse to fine process.

It is worth mentioning that some previous methods [24,33–35] use body physical structure information to improve the human parsing accuracy. Wang *et al.* [35] introduce hierarchical poselets to represent the rigid parts, covering large portions of the human body. Liang *et al.* [24] formulate the human parsing task as the active template regression problem, which uses the linear combination of the learned mask templates to represent each body item. The aforementioned two methods rely on keypoints detection to exploit the intrinsic structure information of human body, which brings extra computational overhead and relies on additional keypoints annotations in the training phase. The method [33] uses tree-like topology in network structure to fuse the information from three levels, *i.e.*, down-top, top-down, which assembles information from three inference processes over the hierarchy. Wang *et al.* [34] explore three categories of part relations, *i.e.*, decomposition, composition, and dependency, to simultaneously exploit the representation learning capacity of deep graph networks and the hierarchical human structures. In contrast to the method [34] focusing on the particular relations between nodes, our method designs the neural tree to encode the physical structure of human body in a coarse-to-fine manner. Meanwhile, different branches in the same hierarchy focus on different subregions of human body, and different hierarchies focus on human body with different receptive fields.

Neural Tree. The decision tree (DT) is an effective model and widely applied in machine learning tasks. As the inherent of the interpretability, it is usually regarded as an auxiliary tool to insight into the mechanism of neural network. However, the simplicity of identity function used in these methods means that input data is never transformed and thus each path from root to leaf node on the tree does not perform representation learning, limiting their performance. To integrate non-linear transformations into DTs, Kontschieder *et al.* [18] propose the stochastic and differentiable decision tree model based neural decision forest. Similarly, Xiao *et al.* [38] develop a neural decision tree with a multi-layer perceptron network at the root transformer. In contrast, our model focuses on the "topology structure" of annotations (see Fig. 1). That is, the proposed model have a flexible semantic topology depending on certain dataset.

3   Methodology

The goal of the proposed Semantic Neural Tree (SNT) method is to classify local parts of human along the path from root to leaf, and then fuse the feature maps before each leaf node to form the global representation for parsing prediction. We depart each sample $x \in X$ with the parsing label $y \in Y$. Notably, our

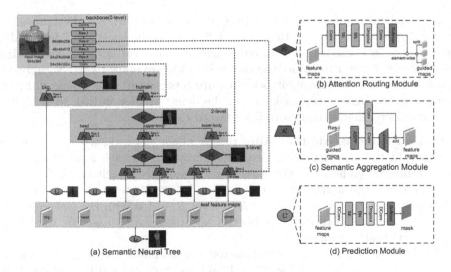

Fig. 2. The tree architecture of our SNT model used on the LIP dataset [22]. The blue dashed lines indicate that the semantic aggregation module in each level merges the features from different layers in the backbone. The purple double arrows denote the supervision for the attention routing and prediction modules. Best view in color.

model is not a full binary tree, because the topology of model is determined by the semantics of dataset. Based on our tree architecture, we group the parsing labels into category label hierarchy. For example, as shown in Fig. 2(a), the virtual category label *head* consists of several child category labels *face*, *hair* and *hat* in the LIP dataset [22].

Our model consists of four modules, the backbone network, the attention routing module, the semantic aggregation module, and the prediction module. Specifically, the backbone network is used to extract features in the proposed method. The attention routing module is designed to generate masks to determine the root-to-leaf computation paths. In this way, different branches in the same hierarchy of the tree focus on different subregions of human body, and different hierarchies in the tree network focus on human body with different receptive fields. Meanwhile, the semantic aggregation module integrates ASPP and SE modules to enforce the network to exploit discriminative features. After that, the prediction module is used to generate the parsing results for each category. We organize these four modules in a tree architecture and solve the parsing task in a coarse-to-fine process for accurate results.

3.1 Architecture

Backbone Network. Similar to the previous works, we rely on residual blocks of ResNet-101 network [13] to extract discriminative features of human in each sub-category. Our SNT can also work on other pre-trained networks, such as DenseNet [15] and Inception [32]. Specifically, we remove the global average pooling and fully connected layers from the network and use the truncated ResNet-101 network [13], *i.e.*, Res-j, ($j = 1, 2, 3, 4$), as the backbone. Meanwhile, followed by the backbone, we add one convolutional layer with the kernel size 1×1 and stride size 1 to reduce the channels of feature maps Res-4. Notably, as shown in Fig. 2, we employ multi-scale feature representation as a powerful tool to improve the ResNet-101 backbone in the dense prediction task with highly localized discriminative regions in fine-grained categories.

Attention Routing Module. After the backbone network, we need to solve how to split the tree structure. Given the sample x, in each level of the tree architecture, we employ the attention routing module to split the higher-level category labels and output the corresponding intermediate masks. That is, the i-th attention routing module at the k-th level R_i^k is fed with the feature maps $\phi_i^{k-1}(x)$ at the $(k-1)$-th level. To this end, we supervise R_i^k based on the labels of pre-set virtual categories.

As shown in Fig. 2(b), the attention routing module starts from one convolutional layer with the kernel size 1×1 and one Squeeze-and-Excitation (SE) layer [14]. Thus we can reduce the computational complexity and enforce the model to pay more attention to discriminative regions. After that, we use one dropout layer with the drop rate 0.5, one convolutional layer with the kernel size 1×1 and one softmax layer to output the mask of the pixel-level human parts $\Psi_i^k(x) = \{\psi_1^k(x), \cdots, \psi_I^k(x)\}$ such that $\psi_i^k(x) \in [0, 1]$. Notably, the channels of the mask consists of foreground channels and background channel, where I denotes the channel number of $\Psi_i^k(x)$. The foreground channels denote the sub-category labels at node i while background channel is defined as the other labels excluded from the sub-category labels at node i. With supervision on the masks, we can guide and split the feature maps at the k-th level into several semantic sub-categories, *i.e.*, $\Phi_i^k(x) = \{\phi_1^k(x), \cdots, \phi_I^k(x)\}$.

Semantic Aggregation Module. Followed by the attention routing module R_i^k, our goal is to extract discriminative feature representation for sub-categories. To this end, multi-scale feature representation is an important and effective strategy, *e.g.*, skip-connections in the U-Net architecture [3]. Besides, the convolution with stride larger than one and the pooling operations will shrink feature maps, resulting in information loss in details such as the edge or small parts.

To alleviate these issues, we introduce the semantic aggregation module A_i^k to deal with the feature maps $\phi_i^k(x)$. Specifically, we first adapt atrous spatial pyramid pooling (ASPP) [2] to concatenate the features from multiple atrous convolutional layers with different dilation rates arranged in parallel. Specifically, the ASPP module is built to deal with the guided feature maps after the semantic router with dilation rates $[1, 6, 12, 18]$ to form multi-scale features. To aggregate multi-scale feature, we also use the upsampling layer to increase the spatial size of feature while halve the number of channels. After that, we use the addition operation to fuse the multi-scale features from the ASPP module and the residual features of the backbone Res-j at the j-th stage (see Fig. 2(c)). Thus we can learn more discriminative feature maps $\hat{\phi}_i^k(x)$ for prediction.

Prediction Module. Based on the feature maps after semantic aggregation $\hat{\phi}_i^k(x)$, we use the prediction modules L_i^k in different levels to generate the parsing result for each sub-category. As shown in Fig. 2(d), the prediction module includes one deformable convolutional layer [43] with the kernel size 3×3, one SE layer [14], one batch normalization layer, one dropout layer with drop rate 0.5 and another deformable convolutional layer [43] with the kernel size 3×3. Finally, the softmax layer is used to output an estimate for conditional distribution for each pixel. For each leaf node at the k-th level, we can predict the local part parsing result $\varphi_i^k(x)$.

Moreover, we combine all the feature maps of each leaf node $\hat{\phi}_i^k(x)$. Specifically, we remove the background channel in every leaf feature map and then concatenate the rest foreground channels, $i.e.$, background, head, torso, arms, legs and shoes in Fig. 2(a), such that the overall number of channels is equal to the number of categories. Thus we can predict the final parsing result $\mathcal{P}(x)$ by using the prediction module L_0.

3.2 Loss Function

Class imbalance is an important issue that results in reduced performance easily. A common solution is to perform the hard negative mining strategy that samples hard examples or more other sampling/reweighing schemes during training phase. Since we aggregate several sub-categories into one virtual category in coarse levels, more severe class imbalance may exist in our hierarchical tree model. To deal with this issue, we adopt a simple category re-weighting strategy. Specifically, based on the ground-truth mask, we calculate percentage of pixels belonging to each category in every batch. Without doubt, the background is overwhelming compared with other categories. Therefore we consider the loss of pixels belonging to each category using the corresponding weight as $\mathcal{W}_{\mathcal{X}^j} = 1 - \sum_i \mathcal{C}_{\mathcal{X}_i^j} / \sum_j \sum_i \mathcal{C}_{\mathcal{X}_i^j}$, where $\mathcal{C}_{\mathcal{X}_i^j}$ indicates the i-th pixel belongs to the j-th category in $\mathcal{X}$ module in the current batch. $\mathcal{X}$ modules consist of the attention routing module (R), leaf node parsing (L) and final parsing (L_0). Based on the weights, we use three loss terms on the attention routing module, each leaf node, and the final output after prediction modules to train the whole network in an end-to-end manner, which is computed as

$$\mathcal{L} = \sum_i \sum_k \mathcal{L}_{R_i^k}(\Psi_i^k(x), \bar{y}_i^k, \mathcal{W}_R) + \omega_1 \cdot \sum_i \sum_k \mathcal{L}_{L_i^k}(\varphi_i^k(x), \dot{y}_i^k, \mathcal{W}_L)$$
$$+ \omega_2 \cdot \mathcal{L}_{L_0}(\mathcal{P}(x), y^*, \mathcal{W}_{L_0}), \tag{1}$$

where $\mathcal{L}_{R_i^k}(\cdot, \cdot, \cdot)$ denotes the re-weighted cross-entropy loss between the masks $\Psi_i^k(x)$ generated by the attention routing module R_i^k and the corresponding ground-truth $\bar{y}_i^k$ at the k-th level. $\mathcal{L}_{L_i^k}(\cdot, \cdot, \cdot)$ denotes the re-weighted cross-entropy loss between the output map $\varphi_i^k(x)$ by the leaf node and the corresponding ground-truth map $\dot{y}_i^k$ at the k-th level. $\mathcal{L}_{L_0}(\cdot, \cdot, \cdot)$ denotes the re-weighted cross-entropy loss between the final parsing result $\mathcal{P}(x)$ and the global parsing label y^*. The factors ω_1 and ω_2 are used to balance the attention routing module, leaf node parsing and final parsing. $\mathcal{W}_R$, $\mathcal{W}_L$ and $\mathcal{W}_P$ are category weights on router module, leaf node and global parsing, respectively. It is worth mentioning that the channel number of $\bar{y}_i^k$ is equal to the number of sub-category labels of node i at the k-th level, and the channel number of y^* is equal to the total number of labels.

3.3   Handling Multiple Human Parsing

To handle multiple human parsing, we integrate our method with the off-the-shelf instance segmentation framework, as similar as that in [28]. Specifically, we first employ the Mask R-CNN [12] pre-trained on MS-COCO dataset [27] to segment human instances from images. Then, we train three SNT sub-models to obtain global and local human parsing results with different size of input images, *i.e.*, one global sub-model and two local sub-models. The global sub-model is trained on the whole images without distinguishing each instance; while the other two local sub-models are input by segmented instance patches from Mask R-CNN [12] and ground-truth respectively. Notably, we use the same architecture for the three sub-models. Finally, both the global and local results from these sub-models are combined to output multiple human parsing results by late fusion. That is, we concatenate the feature maps before leaf node on each sub-branches in our network. Followed by the prediction module, we can estimate the category for each pixel under the supervision of cross-entropy loss function.

4   Experiment

Following the previous works [8,9,28,42], we compare our method with other state-of-the-art methods on the validation set of two single human parsing datasets (*i.e.*, LIP [22] and Pascal-Person-Part [4]) and two multiple human parsing datasets (*i.e.*, CIHP [9] and MHP-v2 [41]). Different evaluation datasets have different definitions of the topology of human body. Note that the physical structure of human body is intrinsic, such as head, arms, and legs. Thus, the annotations of human body can be easily obtained based on the uniform definition of the tree topology of human body.

Implementation Details. We implement the proposed framework in PyTorch. All models are trained on a workstation with a 3.26 GHz Intel processor, 32 GB memory, and one Nvidia V100 GPU. Following the previous works, we adopt the ResNet-101 [13] that is pre-trained on the ImageNet dataset [5] as the backbone network. For a fair comparison, we set input size of images 384×384 for single person parsing while 473×473 for multiple person parsing. For data argumentation, we adopt the strategy of random scaling (from 0.5 to 1.5), random rotation, random cropping and left-right flipping the training data. We use the SGD algorithm to train the network with 0.9 momentum, and 0.0005 weight

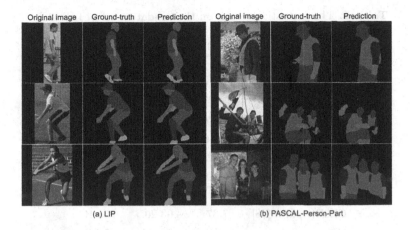

Fig. 3. Some visualized examples of single human parsing.

decay. The learning rate is initialized to 0.001 and adjusted by exponential learning rate decay policy (gamma is 0.9). Notably, the warming up policy is applied for training. That is, we use the learning rate of 0.0001 to warm up the model in the first 10 epochs, and then increase learning rate up to 0.001 linearly. The model is optimized in 200 epochs. In the loss function (1), the weights ω_1 and ω_2 are set as 1.5 and 2.0 empirically.

Metrics. First, we employ the mean IoU metric (mIOU) to evaluate the global-level predictions in single human parsing datasets (*i.e.*, LIP [22] and Pascal-Person Part [4]). Then, we use three metrics (*i.e.*, AP^r, AP^p and PCP) to evaluate the instance-level predictions in multiple human parsing. The AP^r score denotes the area under the precision-recall curve based on the limitation of different IoU thresholds (*e.g.*, 0.5, 0.6, 0.7) [11]. PCP elaborates how many body parts are correctly predicted of a certain person [20]. AP^p computes the pixel-level IoU of semantic part categories within a person. Similar to the previous works, we use the metrics of mIoU and AP^r to evaluate the performance on the CIHP dataset [9] while PCP and AP^p to evaluate the performance on the MHP-v2 dataset [41]. AP^r_m denotes the mean value.

4.1   Single Human Parsing

We compare the performance of single human parsing of our proposed method with other state-of-the-arts on the LIP [22] and Pascal-Person-Part [4] datasets. The qualitative human parsing results are visualized in Fig. 3.

Evaluation on LIP Dataset. The LIP dataset defines 6 body parts and 13 clothes categories, including 50, 462 images with pixel-level annotations. 30, 462 training and 10, 000 validation images are provided with publicly available annotations. As shown in Fig. 2, we construct the tree architecture in 3-level. As

Table 1. The evaluation results on the validation set of LIP [22].

Method	Pixel acc.	Mean acc.	mIoU
Attention+SSL [10]	–	–	44.73
DeepLab [2]	84.09	55.62	44.80
MMAN [30]	–	–	46.81
SS-NAN [39]	87.60	56.00	47.92
MuLA [31]	**88.50**	60.50	49.30
PSPNet [40]	86.23	61.33	50.56
JPPNet [21]	86.39	62.32	51.37
CE2P [28]	–	–	52.56
CE2P(w/flip) [28]	87.37	63.20	53.10
Ours	88.10	**70.41**	**54.86**

Table 2. The evaluation results on the validation set of LIP [22] in each category.

Method	bkg	hat	hair	glove	glasses	u-clothes	dress	coat	socks	pants	
Attention+SSL [10]	84.6	59.8	67.3	29.0	21.6	65.3	29.5	51.9	38.5	68.0	
DeepLab [2]	84.1	59.8	66.2	28.8	23.9	65.0	33.7	52.9	37.7	68.0	
PSPNet [40]	86.1	63.5	68.0	39.1	23.8	68.1	31.7	56.2	44.5	72.7	
MMAN [30]	84.8	57.7	65.6	30.1	20.0	64.2	28.4	52.0	41.5	71.0	
JPPNet [21]	86.3	63.6	70.2	36.2	23.5	68.2	31.4	55.7	44.6	72.2	
CE2P [28]	87.4	64.6	72.1	38.4	32.2	68.9	32.2	55.6	48.8	73.5	
Ours	**88.2**	**66.9**	**72.2**	**42.7**	**32.3**	**70.1**	**35.6**	**57.5**	**48.9**	**75.2**	
Method	j-suit	scarf	skirt	face	l-arm	r-arm	l-leg	r-leg	l-shoe	r-shoe	mIoU
Attention+SSL [10]	24.5	14.9	24.3	71.0	52.6	55.8	40.2	38.8	28.1	29.0	44.7
DeepLab [2]	26.1	17.4	25.2	70.0	50.4	53.9	39.4	38.3	27.0	28.4	44.8
PSPNet [40]	28.7	15.7	25.7	70.8	59.7	62.3	54.9	54.5	42.3	42.9	50.6
MMAN [30]	23.6	9.7	23.2	69.5	55.3	58.1	51.9	52.2	38.6	39.0	46.8
JPPNet [21]	28.4	18.8	25.1	73.4	62.0	63.9	58.2	58.0	44.0	44.1	51.4
CE2P [28]	27.2	13.8	22.7	74.9	64.0	65.9	59.7	58.0	45.7	45.6	52.6
Ours	**33.4**	**21.4**	**27.4**	**74.9**	**66.8**	**68.1**	**60.3**	**59.8**	**47.6**	**48.1**	**54.8**

presented in Table 1, we can conclude that our method achieves the best performance in terms of all the three metrics. Since semantic segmentation methods (e.g., DeepLab [2] and PSPNet [40]) consider little about fine-grained classification in the human parsing task, they perform not well. Moreover, the CE2P method [28] improves PSPNet [40] by adding the context embedding branch, achieving 53.10 mIOU score. Our method exceeds CE2P by 1.76% in terms of mIOU score. It indicates that our method can learn discriminative representation of each sub-category for human parsing. Moreover, as shown in Table 2, our method obtain the best mIOU score in each sub-category. Notably, our method achieves considerable accuracy improvement compared with the other methods in some ambiguous sub-categories, e.g., glove, j-suit, and shoe.

Table 3. The evaluation results on the validation set of Pascal-Person-Part [4].

Method	head	torso	u-arms	l-arms	u-legs	l-legs	bkg	mIoU
HAZN [36]	80.79	**80.76**	45.65	43.11	41.21	37.74	93.78	57.54
Attention+SSL [10]	83.26	62.40	47.80	45.58	42.32	39.48	94.68	59.36
Graph LSTM [25]	82.69	62.68	46.88	47.71	45.66	40.93	94.59	60.16
SE LSTM [23]	82.89	67.15	51.42	48.72	51.72	45.91	97.18	63.57
Part FCN [37]	85.50	67.87	54.72	54.30	48.25	44.76	95.32	64.39
DeepLab [2]	-	-	-	-	-	-	-	64.94
MuLA [31]	-	-	-	-	-	-	-	65.10
SAN [16]	86.12	73.49	59.20	56.20	51.39	49.58	96.01	64.72
WSHP [7]	87.15	72.28	57.07	56.21	52.43	50.36	97.72	67.60
DeepLab v3+ [3]	-	-	-	-	-	-	-	67.84
PGN [9]	**90.89**	75.12	55.83	64.61	55.42	41.57	95.33	68.40
Graphonomy [8]	-	-	-	-	-	-	-	69.12
Compositional Fusion [33]	88.02	72.01	**64.31**	63.52	55.61	**54.96**	96.02	70.76
DPC [1]	88.81	74.54	63.85	63.73	57.24	54.55	96.66	71.34
Ours	89.01	74.63	62.90	**64.70**	**57.53**	54.62	**97.74**	**71.59**

Evaluation on Pascal-Person-Part Dataset. The PASCAL-Person-Part
dataset [4] is originally from the PASCAL VOC-2010 dataset [6], and then
extended for human parsing with 6 coarse body part labels. It consists of $1,716$
training images and $1,817$ testing images ($3,533$ images in total). As shown
in Fig. 1, we construct the tree architecture in 3-level. Specifically, the virtual
category *human* consists of three sub-categories, *i.e.*, *head*, *upper-body* including torso, upper-arms and lower-arms and *lower-body* including upper-legs and
lower-legs. We report the performance on the Pascal-Person-Part dataset in
Table 3. Similar to the trend in the LIP dataset [22], the semantic segmentation methods, *e.g.*, DeepLab [2] and DeepLab v3+ [3], perform inferior mIoU
score, *i.e.*, less than 68.00. Moreover, the Graphonomy method [8] learns and
propagates compact high-level graph representation among the labels within
one dataset, resulting in better 69.12 mIoU score. Besides, DPC [1] achieves
better performance with 71.34 mIoU score. This is because it employs meta-
learning to search optimal efficient multi-scale network for human parsing. Our
SNT method obtains the best overall mIoU score of 71.59 and best mIoU scores
in terms of *l-arms* and *u-legs* among all the compared methods, which indicates
the effectiveness of our proposed tree network.

4.2   Multiple Human Parsing

Furthermore, we evaluate the proposed method on two large-scale multiple
human parsing datasets, *i.e.*, CIHP [9] and MHP-v2 [41]. For a fair comparison,
we apply same Mask R-CNN model to output instance segmentation masks.
Then, we use the global parsing and two local parsing models for human parsing as in [28]. Following the [28], final results are obtained by fusing the results
from three branch models with a refinement process. Some visual results are

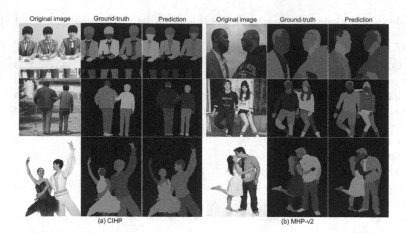

Fig. 4. Some visualized examples of multiple human parsing.

Table 4. The evaluation results on the validation set of CIHP [9].

Method	mIoU	$AP_{0.5}^r$	$AP_{0.6}^r$	$AP_{0.7}^r$	AP_m^r
PGN [9]	55.89	35.80	28.60	20.50	33.60
M-CE2P [28]	59.50	48.69	40.13	29.74	42.83
Ours	**60.87**	**49.27**	**41.98**	**33.00**	**43.96**

shown in Fig. 4, which indicates that our method can also generate precise and fine-grained results in multiple human parsing scenes.

Evaluation on CIHP Dataset. The CIHP dataset [9] is the largest multi-person human parsing dataset with $38,280$ diverse human images, *i.e.*, $28,280$ training, $5,000$ validation and $5,000$ test images. We use the same topology (*i.e.*, 3-level tree structure as shown in Fig. 2) in the LIP dataset [22] to perform human parsing because the two datasets share the same sub-category semantic annotations. As shown in Table 4, our method outperforms other compared methods (*i.e.*, PGN [9] and M-CE2P [28]), achieving AP_m^r score of 43.96. It is worth mentioning that SNT outperforms M-CE2P [28] in terms of $AP_{0.7}^r$ score by considerable improvement, *i.e.*, 29.74 vs. 33.00. It indicates that our method facilitates improving the segmentation accuracy of human instances.

Evaluation on MHP-v2 Dataset. The MHP-v2 dataset [41] includes $25,403$ annotated images with 58 fine-grained semantic category labels. Since this dataset has more labels than the LIP dataset [22], we construct the tree architecture in 5-level. As shown in Table 5, the semantic segmentation method Mask R-CNN [12] has the worst performance compared to other methods. NAN [42] achieves the AP_m^p score of 42.77, but much inferior performance in both $PCP_{0.5}$ and $AP_{0.5}^p$ scores. Our method achieves comparable state-of-the-art performance

Table 5. The performance on the validation set of MHP-v2 [41].

Method	$PCP_{0.5}$	$AP^p_{0.5}$	AP^p_m
Mask R-CNN [12]	25.12	14.50	-
MH-Parser [23]	26.91	18.05	-
NAN [42]	34.37	24.87	42.77
M-CE2P [28]	**43.77**	34.47	42.70
Ours	43.50	**34.76**	**43.03**

Table 6. Effect of the height of the tree on the LIP dataset [22].

height of the tree	pixel acc. (%)	mean acc. (%)	mIoU (%)
0	84.81	57.12	46.34
1	86.84	64.03	52.15
2	87.42	65.58	53.32
3	**88.10**	**70.41**	**54.86**
4	86.92	64.34	51.42

with M-CE2P [28] in terms of three metrics. It indicates that the coarse to fine process in a hierarchical design can facilitate improving the accuracy.

4.3 Ablation Study

We study the influence of some important parameters and components of our SNT method as follows. The experiment is conducted on the LIP dataset [22].

Height of the Tree. The height of the tree k indicates the complexity of the network. To explore the optimal height, we design five variants with different heights of the tree, see Fig. 2(a). If the height is equal to 0, only the ResNet-101 backbone is used for human parsing. As presented in Table 6, we can observe there is a sharp decline in mean accuracy and mIoU score. We find that our method with 3-level achieves the best performance, i.e., 54.86% mIoU score. The performance of our method sharply drops, using deeper or shallower tree architectures. If we set the tree height $k \leq 2$, there are limited number of parameters in our model, not enough to represent the significant variations of human body. Meanwhile, if we set $k = 4$, too many parameters with limited number of training data cause overfitting.

Effectiveness of Prediction Module. To analyze prediction module in the proposed network, we construct a variant of our method, i.e., "ours w/o pred". As shown in Fig. 2(d), the "ours w/o pred" method indicates that we combine the prediction results of each leaf node for final parsing result without the prediction module. If we do not use the prediction module to generate the final parsing result, we can observe a sharp decrease in mIoU score, i.e., 50.02 vs. 54.86. It

Table 7. Variants of the SNT method on the LIP dataset [22].

variant	pixel acc. (%)	mean acc. (%)	mIoU (%)
Ours w/o mask	86.84	64.03	52.15
Ours w/o skip	87.42	65.58	53.32
Ours w/o pred	85.34	63.22	50.02
Ours w/o reweight	87.92	66.42	54.73
Ours w/o warming up	87.95	70.21	54.75
Ours	**88.10**	**70.41**	**54.86**

is essential to achieve accurate parsing result based on the context information among every sub-categories.

Effectiveness of Semantic Aggregation Module. To verify the effectiveness of the semantic aggregation module, we construct the "ours w/o skip" method, which indicates that we do not combine the residual blocks from the backbone in semantic aggregation (see Fig. 2(c)). According to Table 7, we can conclude that the skip-connection from the backbone (see the dashed blue lines in Fig. 2(a)) can bring 1.54% mIoU improvement. This is because the skip-connection in our network can exploit multi-scale representation for sub-categories.

Effectiveness of Attention Routing Module. To study the effect of the attention routing module, the "ours w/o mask" indicates that we further remove the attention mask in the attention routing module from the "ours w/o skip" method (see Fig. 2(b)). That is, we directly split the feature maps into several semantic maps for the next level. As presented in Table 7, the "ours w/o skip" method achieves 1.17% improvement in mIoU score compared with the "ours w/o mask" method. It demonstrates the attention mask can enforce the tree network focus on discriminative representation for specific sub-category semantic information.

Effectiveness of Reweighting Strategy. To verify the effect of the reweighting strategy, we construct a variant by removing the reweighting strategy. That is, we train the network with equal weights of different categories. As presented in Table 7, the "ours w/o reweight" method drops 3.99% mean acc. score compared with our method, which demonstrates the effectiveness of the reweighting strategy.

Effectiveness of Warming up Strategy. To demonstrate the influence of the warming up policy, we construct a variant of the proposed method by removing the warming up policy, denoted as "ours w/o warming up". Specifically, the average accuracy of the "ours w/o warming up" method on the LIP dataset drops 0.2% compared to the proposed method, which demonstrates the effectiveness of the warming up policy.

5   Conclusion

In this paper, we propose a novel semantic tree network for human parsing. Our method can encode physiological structure of human body and segment multiple semantic sub-regions in a hierarchical way. Extensive experiments on four challenging single and multiple human parsing datasets indicate the effectiveness of the proposed semantic tree structure. Our method can learn discriminative feature representation and exploit more context information for sub-categories effectively. For future work, we plan to optimize the tree architecture for better performance by neural architecture search techniques.

Acknowledgements. This work was supported by the Key Research Program of Frontier Sciences, CAS, Grant No. ZDBS-LY-JSC038, the National Natural Science Foundation of China, Grant No. 61807033. Libo Zhang was supported by Youth Innovation Promotion Association, CAS (2020111), and Outstanding Youth Scientist Project of ISCAS.

References

1. Chen, L., et al.: Searching for efficient multi-scale architectures for dense image prediction. In: NeurIPS, vol, abs/1809.04184 (2018)
2. Chen, L., Papandreou, G., Kokkinos, I., Murphy, K., Yuille, A.L.: Deeplab: semantic image segmentation with deep convolutional nets, atrous convolution, and fully connected CRFs. TPAMI **40**(4), 834–848 (2018)
3. Chen, L.-C., Zhu, Y., Papandreou, G., Schroff, F., Adam, H.: Encoder-decoder with atrous separable convolution for semantic image segmentation. In: Ferrari, V., Hebert, M., Sminchisescu, C., Weiss, Y. (eds.) ECCV 2018. LNCS, vol. 11211, pp. 833–851. Springer, Cham (2018). https://doi.org/10.1007/978-3-030-01234-2_49
4. Chen, X., Mottaghi, R., Liu, X., Fidler, S., Urtasun, R., Yuille, A.L.: Detect what you can: detecting and representing objects using holistic models and body parts. In: CVPR, pp. 1979–1986 (2014)
5. Deng, J., Dong, W., Socher, R., Li, L., Li, K., Li, F.: ImageNet: a large-scale hierarchical image database. In: CVPR, pp. 248–255 (2009)
6. Everingham, M., Gool, L.V., Williams, C.K.I., Winn, J.M., Zisserman, A.: The pascal visual object classes (VOC) challenge. IJCV **88**(2), 303–338 (2010)
7. Fang, H., Lu, G., Fang, X., Xie, J., Tai, Y., Lu, C.: Weakly and semi supervised human body part parsing via pose-guided knowledge transfer. CoRR abs/1805.04310 (2018)
8. Gong, K., Gao, Y., Liang, X., Shen, X., Wang, M., Lin, L.: Graphonomy: universal human parsing via graph transfer learning. In: CVPR, pp. 7450–7459 (2019)
9. Gong, K., Liang, X., Li, Y., Chen, Y., Yang, M., Lin, L.: Instance-level human parsing via part grouping network. In: Ferrari, V., Hebert, M., Sminchisescu, C., Weiss, Y. (eds.) ECCV 2018. LNCS, vol. 11208, pp. 805–822. Springer, Cham (2018). https://doi.org/10.1007/978-3-030-01225-0_47
10. Gong, K., Liang, X., Zhang, D., Shen, X., Lin, L.: Look into person: self-supervised structure-sensitive learning and a new benchmark for human parsing. In: CVPR, pp. 6757–6765 (2017)

11. Hariharan, B., Arbeláez, P., Girshick, R., Malik, J.: Simultaneous detection and segmentation. In: Fleet, D., Pajdla, T., Schiele, B., Tuytelaars, T. (eds.) ECCV 2014. LNCS, vol. 8695, pp. 297–312. Springer, Cham (2014). https://doi.org/10.1007/978-3-319-10584-0_20

12. He, K., Gkioxari, G., Dollár, P., Girshick, R.B.: Mask R-CNN. In: ICCV, pp. 2980–2988 (2017)

13. He, K., Zhang, X., Ren, S., Sun, J.: Deep residual learning for image recognition. In: CVPR, pp. 770–778 (2016)

14. Hu, J., Shen, L., Sun, G.: Squeeze-and-excitation networks. In: CVPR, pp. 7132–7141 (2018)

15. Huang, G., Liu, Z., Weinberger, K.Q.: Densely connected convolutional networks. CoRR abs/1608.06993 (2016)

16. Huang, Z., Wang, C., Wang, X., Liu, W., Wang, J.: Semantic image segmentation by scale-adaptive networks. IEEE Trans. Image Process. **29**, 2066–2077 (2019). https://doi.org/10.1109/TIP.2019.2941644

17. Kimchi, R.: Primacy of wholistic processing and global/local paradigm: a critical review. Psychol. Bull. **112**(1), 24 (1992)

18. Kontschieder, P., Fiterau, M., Criminisi, A., Bulò, S.R.: Deep neural decision forests. In: ICCV, pp. 1467–1475 (2015)

19. LeCun, Y., et al.: Backpropagation applied to handwritten zip code recognition. Neural Comput. **1**(4), 541–551 (1989)

20. Li, J., Zhao, J., Wei, Y., Lang, C., Li, Y., Feng, J.: Towards real world human parsing: multiple-human parsing in the wild. CoRR abs/1705.07206 (2017)

21. Liang, X., Gong, K., Shen, X., Lin, L.: Look into person: joint body parsing & pose estimation network and a new benchmark. CoRR abs/1804.01984 (2018)

22. Liang, X., Gong, K., Shen, X., Lin, L.: Look into person: Joint body parsing & pose estimation network and a new benchmark. TPAMI **41**(4), 871–885 (2019)

23. Liang, X., Lin, L., Shen, X., Feng, J., Yan, S., Xing, E.P.: Interpretable structure-evolving LSTM. CoRR abs/1703.03055 (2017)

24. Liang, X., et al.: Deep human parsing with active template regression. CoRR abs/1503.02391 (2015)

25. Liang, X., Shen, X., Feng, J., Lin, L., Yan, S.: Semantic object parsing with graph LSTM. In: Leibe, B., Matas, J., Sebe, N., Welling, M. (eds.) ECCV 2016. LNCS, vol. 9905, pp. 125–143. Springer, Cham (2016). https://doi.org/10.1007/978-3-319-46448-0_8

26. Lin, G., Milan, A., Shen, C., Reid, I.D.: Refinenet: multi-path refinement networks for high-resolution semantic segmentation. In: CVPR, pp. 5168–5177 (2017)

27. Lin, T.-Y., et al.: Microsoft COCO: common objects in context. In: Fleet, D., Pajdla, T., Schiele, B., Tuytelaars, T. (eds.) ECCV 2014. LNCS, vol. 8693, pp. 740–755. Springer, Cham (2014). https://doi.org/10.1007/978-3-319-10602-1_48

28. Liu, T., et al.: Devil in the details: towards accurate single and multiple human parsing. CoRR abs/1809.05996 (2018)

29. Long, J., Shelhamer, E., Darrell, T.: Fully convolutional networks for semantic segmentation. In: CVPR, pp. 3431–3440 (2015)

30. Luo, Y., et al.: Macro-micro adversarial network for human parsing. In: Ferrari, V., Hebert, M., Sminchisescu, C., Weiss, Y. (eds.) ECCV 2018. LNCS, vol. 11213, pp. 424–440. Springer, Cham (2018). https://doi.org/10.1007/978-3-030-01240-3_26

31. Nie, X., Feng, J., Yan, S.: Mutual learning to adapt for joint human parsing and pose estimation. In: Ferrari, V., Hebert, M., Sminchisescu, C., Weiss, Y. (eds.) ECCV 2018. LNCS, vol. 11209, pp. 519–534. Springer, Cham (2018). https://doi.org/10.1007/978-3-030-01228-1_31

32. Szegedy, C., Vanhoucke, V., Ioffe, S., Shlens, J., Wojna, Z.: Rethinking the inception architecture for computer vision. CoRR abs/1512.00567 (2015)
33. Wang, W., Zhang, Z., Qi, S., Shen, J., Pang, Y., Shao, L.: Learning compositional neural information fusion for human parsing. In: ICCV (2019)
34. Wang, W., Zhu, H., Dai, J., Pang, Y., Shen, J., Shao, L.: Hierarchical human parsing with typed part-relation reasoning. In: CVPR (2020)
35. Wang, Y., Tran, D., Liao, Z.: Learning hierarchical poselets for human parsing. In: CVPR, pp. 1705–1712 (2011)
36. Xia, F., Wang, P., Chen, L.-C., Yuille, A.L.: Zoom better to see clearer: human and object parsing with hierarchical auto-zoom net. In: Leibe, B., Matas, J., Sebe, N., Welling, M. (eds.) ECCV 2016. LNCS, vol. 9909, pp. 648–663. Springer, Cham (2016). https://doi.org/10.1007/978-3-319-46454-1_39
37. Xia, F., Wang, P., Chen, X., Yuille, A.L.: Joint multi-person pose estimation and semantic part segmentation. In: CVPR, pp. 6080–6089 (2017)
38. Xiao, H.: NDT: neual decision tree towards fully functioned neural graph. CoRR abs/1712.05934 (2017)
39. Zhang, R., Tang, S., Zhang, Y., Li, J., Yan, S.: Scale-adaptive convolutions for scene parsing. In: ICCV, pp. 2050–2058 (2017)
40. Zhao, H., Shi, J., Qi, X., Wang, X., Jia, J.: Pyramid scene parsing network. In: CVPR, pp. 6230–6239 (2017)
41. Zhao, J., Li, J., Cheng, Y., Sim, T., Yan, S., Feng, J.: Understanding humans in crowded scenes: deep nested adversarial learning and a new benchmark for multi-human parsing. In: ACM MM, pp. 792–800 (2018)
42. Zhao, J., et al.: Understanding humans in crowded scenes: deep nested adversarial learning and a new benchmark for multi-human parsing. CoRR abs/1804.03287 (2018)
43. Zhu, X., Hu, H., Lin, S., Dai, J.: Deformable convnets V2: more deformable, better results. In: CVPR, pp. 9308–9316 (2019)

Sketching Image Gist: Human-Mimetic Hierarchical Scene Graph Generation

Wenbin Wang[1,2], Ruiping Wang[1,2(✉)], Shiguang Shan[1,2],
and Xilin Chen[1,2]

[1] Key Laboratory of Intelligent Information Processing of Chinese Academy
of Sciences (CAS), Institute of Computing Technology, CAS, Beijing 100190, China
wenbin.wang@vipl.ict.ac.cn, {wangruiping,sgshan,xlchen}@ict.ac.cn
[2] University of Chinese Academy of Sciences, Beijing 100049, China

Abstract. Scene graph aims to faithfully reveal humans' perception of
image content. When humans analyze a scene, they usually prefer to
describe image gist first, namely major objects and key relations in a
scene graph. This humans' inherent perceptive habit implies that there
exists a hierarchical structure about humans' preference during the scene
parsing procedure. Therefore, we argue that a desirable scene graph
should be also hierarchically constructed, and introduce a new scheme
for modeling scene graph. Concretely, a scene is represented by a human-
mimetic **H**ierarchical **E**ntity **T**ree (HET) consisting of a series of image
regions. To generate a scene graph based on HET, we parse HET with
a Hybrid Long Short-Term Memory (Hybrid-LSTM) which specifically
encodes hierarchy and siblings context to capture the structured information embedded in HET. To further prioritize key relations in the scene
graph, we devise a Relation Ranking Module (RRM) to dynamically
adjust their rankings by learning to capture humans' subjective perceptive habits from objective entity saliency and size. Experiments indicate
that our method not only achieves state-of-the-art performances for scene
graph generation, but also is expert in mining image-specific relations
which play a great role in serving downstream tasks.

Keywords: Image gist · Key relation · Hierarchical Entity Tree ·
Hybrid-LSTM · Relation Ranking Module

1 Introduction

In an effort to thoroughly understand a scene, scene graph generation (SGG)
[10,42] in which objects and pairwise relations should be detected, has been on
the way to bridge the gap between low-level recognition and high-level cognition, and contributes to tasks like image captioning [25,40,44], VQA [1,36], and
visual reasoning [31]. While previous works [16,17,28,36,39,42,43,49,50,53] have

Electronic supplementary material The online version of this chapter (https://
doi.org/10.1007/978-3-030-58601-0_14) contains supplementary material, which is
available to authorized users.

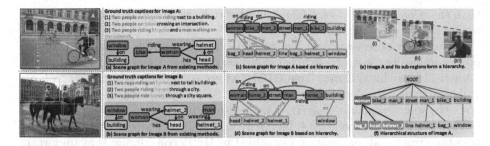

Fig. 1. Scene graphs from existing methods shown in (a) and (b) fail in sketc.hing the image gist. The hierarchical structure about humans' perception preference is shown in (f), where the bottom left highlighted branch stands for the hierarchy in (e). The scene graphs in (c) and (d) based on hierarchical structure better capture the gist. Relations in (a) and (b), and purple arrows in (c) and (d), are top-5 relations, while gray ones in (c) and (d) are secondary. (Color figure online)

pushed this area forward, the generated scene graph may be still far from perfect, e.g., they seldom consider whether the detected relations are what humans want to convey from the image or not. As a symbolic representation of an image, the scene graph is expected to record the image content as complete as possible. More importantly, a scene graph is not just for being admired, but for supporting downstream tasks, such as image captioning, where a description is supposed to depict the major event in the image, or the namely **image gist**. This characteristic is also one of the humans' inherent habits when they parse a scene. Therefore, an urgently needed feature of SGG is to assess the relation importance and prioritize the relations which form the major events that humans intend to preferentially convey, i.e., **key relations**. This is seldom considered by existing methods. What's worse, the universal phenomenon of unbalanced distribution of relationship triplets in mainstream datasets exacerbates the problem that the major event cannot be found out. Let's study the quality of top relations predicted by existing state-of-the-art methods (e.g., [49]) and check whether they are "key" or not. In Fig. 1(a)(b), two scene graphs shown with top-5 relations for image A and B are mostly the same although major events in A and B are quite different. In other words, existing methods are deficient in mining image-specific relations, but biased towards trivial or self-evident ones (e.g., ⟨woman, has, head⟩ can be obtained from commonsense without observing the image), which fail in conveying image gist (colored parts in ground truth captions in Fig. 1), and barely contribute to downstream tasks.

Any pair of objects in a scene can be considered relevant, at least in terms of their spatial configurations. Faced with such a massive amount of relations, how do humans choose relations to describe the images? Given picture (ii) in Fig. 1(e), a zoom-in sub-region of picture (i), humans will describe it with ⟨woman, riding, bike⟩, since woman and bike belong to the same perceptive level and their interaction forms the major event in (ii). When it comes to picture (iii), the answers would be ⟨woman, wearing, helmet⟩ and ⟨bag, on, woman⟩, where helmet and bag are finer details of woman and belong to an inferior perceptive level. It suggests that there naturally exists a hierarchical structure about humans' perception preference, as shown in Fig. 1(f).

Inspired by observations above, we argue that a desirable scene graph should be hierarchically constructed. Specifically, we represent the image with a human-mimetic Hierarchical Entity Tree (HET) where each node is a detected object and each one can be decomposed into a set of finer objects attached to it. To generate the scene graph based on HET, we devise Hybrid Long Short-Term Memory (Hybrid-LSTM) to encode both hierarchy and siblings context [36,49] and capture the structured information embedded in HET, considering that important related pairs are more likely to be seen either inside a certain perceptive level or between two adjacent perceptive levels. We further intend to evaluate the performances of different models on key relation prediction but the annotations of key relations are not directly available from existing datasets. Therefore, we extend Visual Genome (VG) [13] to VG-KR dataset which contains indicative annotations of key relations by drawing support from caption annotations in MSCOCO [21]. We devise a Relation Ranking Module to adjust the rankings of relations. It captures humans' subjective perceptive habits from objective entity saliency and size, and achieves ultimate performances on mining key relations.[1]

2   Related Works

Scene Graph Generation (SGG) and Visual Relationship Detection (VRD), are the two most common tasks aiming at extracting interaction between two objects. In the field of VRD, various studies [3,15,24,27,46,47,50–52] mainly focus on detecting each relation triplet independently rather than describe the structure of the scene. The concept of scene graph is firstly proposed in [10] for image retrieval. Xu et al. [42] define SGG task and creatively devise message passing mechanism for scene graph inference. A series of succeeding works struggle to design various approaches to improve the graph representation. Li et al. [17] induce image captions and object information to jointly address multitasks. [22,36,39,49] draw support from useful context construction. Yang et al. [43] propose Graph-RCNN to embed the structured information. Qi et al. [28] employ a self-attention module to embed a weighted graph representation. Zhang et al. [53] propose contrastive losses to resolve the related pair configuration ambiguity. Zareian et al. [48] creatvely treat the SGG as an edge role assignment problem. Recently, some methods try to borrow advantages from using knowledge [2,5] or causal effect [35] to diversify the predicted relations. Liang et al. [19] prune the dominant and easy-to-predict relations in VG to alleviate the annihilation problem of rare but meaningful relations.

Structured Scene Parsing, has been paid much attention in pursuit of higher-level scene understanding. [6,20,30,33,45,55] construct various hierarchical structures for their specific tasks. Unlike existing SGG studies that indiscriminately detect relations no matter whether they are concerned by humans or not,

---

[1] Source code and dataset are available at http://vipl.ict.ac.cn/resources/codesor https://github.com/Kenneth-Wong/het-eccv20.git.

our work introduces the idea of hierarchical structure into SGG task, and try to give priority to detect key relations, then the trivial ones for completeness.

Saliency vs. Image Gist. An extremely rich set of studies [8,14,23,37,38,54] focus on analyzing where humans gaze and find visually salient objects (high contrast of luminance, hue, and saturation, center position [9,12,41], etc..). It's notable that the visually salient objects are related but not equal to objects involved in image gist. He et al. [7] explore gaze data and find that only 48% of fixated objects are referred in humans' descriptions about the image, while 95% of objects referred in descriptions are fixated. It suggests that objects referred in a description (i.e., objects that humans think important and should form the major events/image gist) are almost visually salient and reveal where humans gaze, but what humans fixate (i.e., visually salient objects) are not always what they want to convey. We provide some examples in supplementary materials to help to understand this finding. Naturally, we need to emphasize that the levels in our HET reflect the perception priority level rather than the object saliency. Besides, this finding supports us to obtain the indicative annotations of key relations with the help of image caption annotations.

3   Proposed Approach

3.1   Overview

The scene graph $\mathcal{G} = \{\mathcal{O}, \mathcal{R}\}$ of an image $\mathcal{I}$ contains a set of entities $\mathcal{O} = \{o_i\}_{i=1}^N$ and their pairwise relations $\mathcal{R} = \{r_k\}_{k=1}^M$. Each r_k is a triplet $\langle o_i, p_{ij}, o_j \rangle$ where $p_{ij} \in \mathcal{P}$ and $\mathcal{P}$ is the set of all predicates. As illustrated in Fig. 2, our approach can be summarized into four steps. (i) We apply Faster R-CNN [29] with VGG16 [32] backbone to detect all the entity proposals and each of them possesses its bounding box $b_i \in \mathbb{R}^4$, 4,096-dimensional visual feature v_i, and the class probability vector q_i from the softmax output. (ii) In Sect. 3.2, HET is constructed by organizing the detected entities according to their perceptive levels. (iii) In Sect. 3.3, we design the Hybrid-LSTM network to parse HET, which firstly encodes the structured context then decodes it for graph inference. (iv) In Sect. 3.4, we improve the scene graph generated in (iii) with our devised RRM which further adjusts the rankings of relations and shifts the graph focus to the relations between entities that are close to top perceptive levels of HET.

3.2   Het Construction

We aim to construct a hierarchical structure whose top-down levels are accord with the perceptive levels of humans' inherent scene parsing hierarchy. From a massive number of observations, it can be found that entities with larger sizes are relatively more likely to form the major events in a scene (this will be proved effective through experiments). Therefore, we arrange larger entities as close to the root of HET as possible. Each entity can be decomposed into finer entities that make up the inferior level.

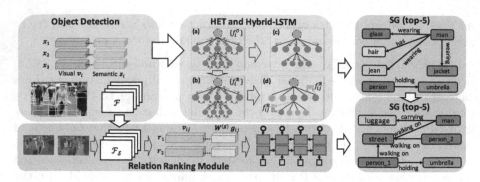

Fig. 2. An overview of our method. An object detector is firstly applied to give support to HET construction. Then Hybrid-LSTM is leveraged to parse HET, and specifically contains 4 processes, (a) entity context encoding, (b) relation context encoding, (c) entity context decoding, and (d) relation context decoding. Finally, RRM predicts a ranking score for each triplet which further prioritizes the key relations in the scene graph. (Color figure online)

Concretely, HET is a multi-branch tree $\mathcal{T}$ with a virtual root o_0 standing for the whole image. All the entities are sorted in descending order according to their sizes and we get an orderly sequence $\{o_{i_1}, o_{i_2}, \ldots, o_{i_N}\}$. For each entity o_{i_n}, we consider entities with larger size, $\{o_{i_m}\}, 1 \leq m < n$, and calculate the ratio

$$P_{nm} = \frac{I\left(o_{i_n}, o_{i_m}\right)}{A(o_{i_n})}, \tag{1}$$

where $A(\cdot)$ denotes the size of the entity and $I(\cdot, \cdot)$ is the intersection area of two entities. If P_{nm} is larger than threshold T, o_{i_m} will be a candidate parent node of o_{i_n} since o_{i_m} contains most part of o_{i_n}. If there is no candidate, the parent node of o_{i_n} is set as o_0. If there are more than one, we further determine the parent with two alternative strategies:

Area-first Strategy (AFS). Considering that entity with a larger size has a higher probability to contain more details or components, the candidate with the largest size is selected to be a parent node.

Intersection-first Strategy (IFS). We compute ratio

$$Q_{nm} = \frac{I\left(o_{i_n}, o_{i_m}\right)}{A(o_{i_m})}. \tag{2}$$

A larger Q_{nm} means that o_{i_n} is relatively more important to o_{i_m} than to other candidates. Therefore, o_{i_m} where $m = \arg\max_k Q_{nk}$ is chosen as parent of o_{i_n}.

3.3 Structured Context Encoding and Scene Graph Generation

The interpretability of HET implies that important relations are more likely to be seen between entities either inside a certain level or from two adjacent levels.

Therefore, both hierarchical connection [36] and sibling association [49] are useful for context modeling. Our Hybrid-LSTM encoder is proposed, which consists of a bidirectional multi-branch TreeLSTM [34] (Bi-TreeLSTM) for encoding the hierarchy context, and a bidirectional chain LSTM [4] (Bi-LSTM) for encoding the siblings context. We use two identical Hybrid-LSTM encoders to encode two types of context for each entity, one is **entity context** which helps predict the information of entity itself, and the other is **relation context** which plays a role in inferring the relation when interacting with other potential relevant entities. For brevity we only provide a detailed introduction of entity context encoding (Fig. 2(a)). Specifically, the input feature x_i of each node o_i is concatenation of visual feature v_i and weighted sum of semantic embedding vectors, $z_i = W_e^{(1)} q_i$, where $W_e^{(1)}$ is word embedding matrix initialized from GloVe [26]. For the root node o_0, v_0 is obtained with the whole-image bounding box, while z_0 is initialized randomly.

The hierarchy context (blue arrows in Fig. 2(a)) is encoded as:

$$C = \text{BiTreeLSTM}(\{x_i\}_{i=0}^{N}), \tag{3}$$

where $C = \{c_i\}_{i=0}^{N}$ and each $c_i = \left[\overrightarrow{h_i^{\mathcal{T}}}; \overleftarrow{h_i^{\mathcal{T}}}\right]$ is the concatenation of the top-down and bottom-up hidden states of Bi-TreeLSTM:

$$\overrightarrow{h_i^{\mathcal{T}}} = \text{TreeLSTM}\left(x_i, \overrightarrow{h_p^{\mathcal{T}}}\right), \tag{4a}$$

$$\overleftarrow{h_i^{\mathcal{T}}} = \text{TreeLSTM}\left(x_i, \left\{\overleftarrow{h_j^{\mathcal{T}}}\big| j \in C(i)\right\}\right), \tag{4b}$$

where $C(\cdot)$ denotes the set of children nodes while subscript p denotes the parent of node i.

The siblings context (red arrows in Fig. 2(a)) is encoded within each set of children nodes which share the same parent:

$$S = \text{BiLSTM}(\{x_i\}_{i=0}^{N}), \tag{5}$$

where $S = \{s_i\}_{i=0}^{N}$ and each $s_i = \left[\overrightarrow{h_i^{\mathcal{L}}}; \overleftarrow{h_i^{\mathcal{L}}}\right]$ is concatenation of forward and backward hidden states of Bi-LSTM:

$$\overrightarrow{h_i^{\mathcal{L}}} = \text{LSTM}\left(x_i, \overrightarrow{h_l^{\mathcal{L}}}\right), \quad \overleftarrow{h_i^{\mathcal{L}}} = \text{LSTM}\left(x_i, \overleftarrow{h_r^{\mathcal{L}}}\right), \tag{6}$$

where l and r stand for left and right sibling which share the same parent with i. We further concatenate hierarchy and siblings context to obtain the entity context, $f_i^{\mathcal{O}} = [c_i; s_i]$. Missing branches or siblings are padded with zero vectors.

The relation context is encoded (Fig. 2(b)) in the same way as entity context except that the input of each node is replaced by $\{f_i^{\mathcal{O}}\}_{i=0}^{N}$. Another Hybrid-LSTM encoder is applied to get the relation context $\{f_i^{\mathcal{R}}\}_{i=0}^{N}$.

To generate a scene graph, we should decode the context to obtain entity and relation information. In HET, a child node strongly depends on its parent, i.e., information of parent node is helpful for prediction of child node. Therefore, to predict entity information, we decode entity context in a top-down manner following Eq. (4a) as shown in Fig. 2(c). For node o_i, the input $\boldsymbol{x}_i$ in Eq. (4a) is replaced with $[\boldsymbol{f}_i^O; \boldsymbol{W}_e^{(2)} \boldsymbol{q}_p]$, where $\boldsymbol{W}_e^{(2)}$ is word embedding matrix and $\boldsymbol{q}_p$ is the predicted class probability vector of the parent of o_i. The output hidden state is fed into a softmax classifier and bounding box regressor to predict entity information of o_i. To predict the predicate p_{ij} between o_i and o_j, we feed $\boldsymbol{f}_{ij}^{\mathcal{R}} = [\boldsymbol{f}_i^{\mathcal{R}}; \boldsymbol{f}_j^{\mathcal{R}}]$ to an MLP classifier (Fig. 2(d)). As a result, a scene graph is generated, and for each triplet containing subject o_i, object o_j and predicate p_{ij}, we obtain their scalar scores s_i, s_j, and s_{ij}.

3.4   Relation Ranking Module

So far, we obtain the hierarchical scene graph based on HET. As we collect the key relation annotations (Sect. 4.1), we intend to further maximize the performance on mining key relations with supervised information, and explore the advantages brought by HET. Consequently, we design a Relation Ranking Module (RRM) to prioritize key relations. As analyzed in **Related Works**, regions of humans' interest can be tracked under the guidance of *visual saliency* although they do not always form the major events that humans want to convey. Besides, the *size*, which guides HET construction, not only is an important reference for estimating the perceptive level of entities, but also is found helpful to rectify some misleadings in humans' subjective assessment on the importance of relations (see supplementary materials). Therefore, we propose to learn to capture humans' subjective assessment on the importance of relations under the guidance of visual saliency and entity size information.

We firstly employ DSS [8] to predict the pixel-wise saliency map (**SM**) $\mathcal{S}$ for each image. To effectively collect entity size information, we propose a pixel-wise area map (**AM**) $\mathcal{A}$. Given the image $\mathcal{I}$ and its detected N entities $\{o_i\}_{i=1}^N$ with bounding boxes $\{\boldsymbol{b}_i\}_{i=1}^N$ (specially o_0 and $\boldsymbol{b}_0$ for the whole image), the value a_{xy} of each position (x, y) on $\mathcal{A}$ is defined as the minimum normalized size of entities which cover (x, y):

$$a_{xy} = \begin{cases} \min\left\{ \left. \dfrac{A(o_i)}{A(o_0)} \right| i \in \mathcal{X} \right\}, \text{if } \mathcal{X} \neq \emptyset \\ 0, \text{otherwise}, \end{cases} \tag{7}$$

where $\mathcal{X} = \{i | (x, y) \in \boldsymbol{b}_i, 0 < i \leq N\}$. The sizes of both $\mathcal{S}$ and $\mathcal{A}$ are the same as that of input image $\mathcal{I}$. We apply adaptive average pooling (AAP($\cdot$)) to smooth and down-sample these two maps to align with the shape of conv5 feature map $\mathcal{F}$ from Faster-RCNN, and obtain the attention embedded feature map $\mathcal{F}_S$:

$$\mathcal{F}_S = \mathcal{F} \odot (\text{AAP}(\mathcal{S}) + \text{AAP}(\mathcal{A})), \tag{8}$$

where $\odot$ is the Hadamard product.

We predict a score for each triplet to adjust their rankings. The input contains visual representation for a triplet, $v_{ij} \in \mathbb{R}^{4096}$, which is obtained by RoI Pooling on $\mathcal{F}_S$. Besides, the geometric information is also an auxiliary cue for estimating the importance. For a triplet containing subject box b_i and object box b_j, the geometric feature g_{ij} is defined as a 6-dimensional vector following [11]:

$$g_{ij} = \left[\frac{x_j - x_i}{\sqrt{w_i h_i}}, \frac{y_j - y_i}{\sqrt{w_i h_i}}, \sqrt{\frac{w_j h_j}{w_i h_i}}, \frac{w_i}{h_i}, \frac{w_j}{h_j}, \frac{b_i \cap b_j}{b_i \cup b_j} \right], \tag{9}$$

which is projected to a 256-dimensional vector and concatenated with v_{ij}, resulting in the final representation for a relation $r_{ij} = [v_{ij}; W^{(g)} g_{ij}]$ where $W^{(g)} \in \mathbb{R}^{256 \times 6}$ is projection matrix. Then we use a bi-directional LSTM to encode global context among all the triplets so that ranking score of each triplet can be reasonably adjusted considering scores of other triplets. Concretely, the ranking score t_{ij} for a pair (o_i, o_j) is achieved as:

$$\{h_{ij}^{\mathcal{R}}\} = \text{BiLSTM}\left(\{r_{ij}\}\right), \tag{10}$$

$$t_{ij} = W_2^{(r)} \text{ReLU}(W_1^{(r)} h_{ij}^{\mathcal{R}}). \tag{11}$$

$W_1^{(r)}$ and $W_2^{(r)}$ are weights of two fully connected layers. The ranking score is fused with classification scores so that both the confidences of three components of a triplet and ranking priority are considered, resulting in the final ranking confidence $\phi_{ij} = s_i \cdot s_j \cdot s_{ij} \cdot t_{ij}$, which is used for re-ranking the relations.

3.5 Loss Function

We adopt the cross-entropy loss for optimizing Hybrid-LSTM networks. Let e' and l' denote the predicted label of entity and predicate respectively, e and l denote the ground truth labels. The loss is defined as:

$$\mathcal{L}_{CE} = \mathcal{L}_{entity} + \mathcal{L}_{relation} = -\frac{1}{Z_1} \sum_i e_i' \log(e_i) - \frac{1}{Z_2} \sum_i \sum_{j \neq i} l_{ij}' \log(l_{ij}). \tag{12}$$

When the RRM is applied, the final loss function is the sum of $\mathcal{L}_{CE}$ and ranking loss $\mathcal{L}(\mathcal{K}, \mathcal{N})$, which is used to maximize the margin between the ranking confidences of key relations and those of secondary ones:

$$\mathcal{L}_{Final} = \mathcal{L}_{CE} + \mathcal{L}(\mathcal{K}, \mathcal{N}) = \mathcal{L}_{CE} + \frac{1}{Z_3} \sum_{r \in \mathcal{K}, r' \in \mathcal{N}} \max(0, \gamma - \phi_r + \phi_{r'}), \tag{13}$$

where γ denotes margin parameter, $\mathcal{K}$ and $\mathcal{N}$ stand for the set of key and secondary relations, r and r' are relations sampled from $\mathcal{K}$ and $\mathcal{N}$ with ranking confidences ϕ_r and $\phi_{r'}$. Z_1, Z_2, and Z_3 are normalization factors.

4 Experimental Evaluation

4.1 Dataset, Evaluation and Settings

VRD [24], is the benchmarking dataset for visual relationship detection task, which contains 4,000/1,000 training/test images and covers 100 object categories and 70 predicate categories.

Visual Genome (VG), is a large-scale dataset with rich annotations of objects, attributes, dense captions and pairwise relationships, containing 75,651/32,422 training/test images. We adopt the most widely used version of VG, namely VG150 [42], which covers 150 object categories and 50 predicate categories.

VG200 and VG-KR. We intend to collect the indicative annotations of key relations based on VG. Inspired by the finding illustrated in **Related Works**, we associate the relation triplets referred in caption annotations in MSCOCO [21] with those from VG. The details of our processing and more statistics are provided in supplementary materials.

Evaluation, Settings, and Implementation Details. For conventional SGG following triplet-match rule (only if three components of a triplet match the ground truth will it be a correct one), we adopt three universal protocols [42]: PREDCLS, SGCLS, and SGGEN. All protocols use Recall@K (R@K = 20, 50, 100) as a metric. When evaluating key relation prediction, there are some variations. First, we only evaluate with PREDCLS and SGCLS protocols to eliminate the interference of errors from object detector, and add a tuple-match rule (only the subject and object are required to match the ground truth) to investigate the ability to find proper pairs. Second, we introduce a new metric, **Key Relation Recall (kR@K)**, which computes recall rate on key relations. As the number of key relations is usually less than 5 (see supplementary materials), the K in kR@K is set to 1 and 5. When evaluating on VRD, we use RELDET and PHRDET [47], and report R@50 and R@100 at 1, 10, and 70 predicates per related pair. The details about the hyperparameters settings and implementation are provided in supplementary materials.

4.2 Ablation Studies

Ablation studies are separated into two sections. The first part is to explore some variants of HET construction. We conduct these experiments on VG150. The complete version of our model is **HetH**, which is configured with IFS and Hybrid-LSTM. The second part is an investigation into the usage of SM and AM in RRM. Experiments are carried out on VG-KR. The complete version is **HetH-RRM**, whose implementation follows Eq. (8).

Ablation study on HET construction. We firstly compare **AFS** and **IFS** for determining the parent node. Then we investigate the effectiveness of the chain LSTM encoder in Hybrid-LSTM. The ablative models mentioned above are shown in Table 1 as **HetH-AFS** (i.e. replace IFS by AFS), and **HetH**

Table 1. Results table (%) on VG150 and VG200. The results of the full version of our method are highlighted.

	R@	SGGEN			SGCLS			PREDCLS		
		20	50	100	20	50	100	20	50	100
VG150	VRD [24]	–	0.3	0.5	–	11.8	14.1	–	27.9	35.0
	IMP [42]	-	3.4	4.2	–	21.7	24.4	–	44.8	53.0
	IMP† [42,49]	14.6	20.7	24.5	31.7	34.6	35.4	52.7	59.3	61.3
	Graph-RCNN [43]	–	11.4	13.7	–	29.6	31.6	–	54.2	59.1
	MemNet [39]	7.7	11.4	13.9	23.3	27.8	29.5	42.1	53.2	57.9
	MOTIFS [49]	21.4	27.2	30.3	32.9	35.8	36.5	58.5	65.2	67.1
	KERN [2]	–	27.1	29.8	–	36.7	37.4	–	65.8	67.6
	VCTree-SL [36]	21.7	27.7	31.1	35.0	37.9	38.6	59.8	66.2	67.9
	HetH-AFS	21.2	27.1	30.5	33.7	36.6	37.3	58.1	64.7	66.6
	HetH w/o chain	21.5	27.4	30.7	32.9	35.9	36.7	57.5	64.5	66.5
	HetH	**21.6**	**27.5**	**30.9**	**33.8**	**36.6**	**37.3**	**59.8**	**66.3**	**68.1**
VG200	MOTIFS [49]	15.2	19.9	22.8	24.5	26.7	27.4	52.5	59.0	61.0
	VCTree-SL [36]	14.7	19.5	22.5	24.2	26.5	27.1	51.9	58.4	60.3
	HetH	**15.7**	**20.4**	**23.4**	**25.0**	**27.2**	**27.8**	**53.6**	**60.1**	**61.8**

Table 2. Results table (%) of key relation prediction on VG-KR.

kR@	Triplet match				Tuple match			
	SGCLS		PREDCLS		SGCLS		PREDCLS	
	1	5	1	5	1	5	1	5
VCTree-SL	5.7	14.2	11.4	30.2	8.4	22.2	16.1	46.4
MOTIFS	5.9	14.5	11.3	30.0	8.5	21.8	16.0	46.2
HetH	**6.1**	**15.1**	**11.6**	**30.4**	**8.6**	**22.7**	**16.4**	**47.1**
MOTIFS-RRM	8.6	16.4	16.7	33.8	13.8	26.3	27.9	57.1
HetH-RRM	**9.2**	**17.1**	**17.5**	**35.0**	**14.6**	**27.3**	**28.9**	**59.1**
RRM-Base	8.4	16.8	16.2	33.7	13.4	26.8	26.6	57.2
RRM-SM	9.0	16.9	17.2	34.5	14.3	27.1	28.6	58.7
RRM-AM	8.9	16.9	16.9	34.4	14.1	27.0	28.1	58.2

w/o chain. We observe that using IFS together with Hybrid-LSTM encoder has the best performances, which indicates that HET would be more reasonable using IFS. It's noteworthy that if the Bi-TreeLSTM encoder is abandoned, the Hybrid-LSTM encoder would almost degenerate to MOTIFS. Therefore, through comparisons between HetH and MOTIFS, HetH and HetH w/o chain, it implies that both hierarchy and siblings context should be encoded in HET.

Table 3. Results table (%) on VRD.

R@	RELDET						PHRDET					
	k = 1		k = 10		k=70		k = 1		k = 10		k = 70	
	50	100	50	100	50	100	50	100	50	100	50	100
ViP [15]	17.32	20.01	—	–	–	–	22.78	27.91	–	–	–	–
VRL [18]	18.19	20.79	–	–	–	–	21.37	22.60	–	–	–	–
KL-Dist [47]	19.17	21.34	22.56	29.89	22.68	31.89	23.14	24.03	26.47	29.76	26.32	29.43
Zoom-Net [46]	18.92	21.41	–	–	21.37	27.30	24.82	28.09	–	–	29.05	37.34
RelDN-L_0 [53]	24.30	27.91	26.67	32.55	26.67	32.55	31.09	36.42	33.29	41.25	33.29	41.25
RelDN [53]	25.29	28.62	28.15	33.91	28.15	33.91	31.34	36.42	34.45	42.12	34.45	42.12
HetH	22.42	24.88	26.88	31.69	26.88	31.81	30.69	35.59	**35.47**	**42.94**	**35.47**	**43.05**

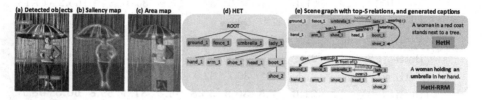

Fig. 3. Qualitative Results of HetH and HetH-RRM. In (e), the pink entities are involved in top-5 relations, and the purple arrows are key relations matched with ground truth. The purple numeric tags next to the relations are the rankings, and "1" means that the relation gets the highest score. (Color figure online)

Ablation study on RRM. In order to explore the effectiveness of saliency and size, we ablate HetH-RRM with the following baselines: (1) **RRM-Base:** v_{ij} is extracted from $\mathcal{F}$ rather than $\mathcal{F}_S$, (2) **RRM-SM:** only $\mathcal{S}$ is used, and (3) **RRM-AM:** only $\mathcal{A}$ is used. Results in Table 2 suggest that both saliency and size information indeed contributes to discovering key relations, and the effect of saliency is slightly better than that of the size. The hybrid version achieves the highest performances. From the following qualitative analysis, we can see that with the guidance of saliency and rectification effect of size, RRM further shifts the model's attention to key relations significantly.

4.3   Comparisons with State-of-the-Arts

For scene graph generation, we compare our **HetH** with the following state-of-the-art methods: **VRD** [24] and **KERN** [2] use knowledge from language or statistical correlations. **IMP** [42], **Graph-RCNN** [43], **MemNet** [39], **MOTIFS** [49] and **VCTree-SL** [36] mainly devise various message passing methods for improving graph representations. For key relation prediction, we mainly evaluate two latest works, MOTIFS and VCTree-SL on VG-KR. Besides, we further incorporate RRM to MOTIFS, namely **MOTIFS-RRM**, to explore the transferability of RRM. Results are shown in Table 1 and 2. We give statistical significance of the results in the supplementary materials.

Quantitative Analysis. In Table 1, when evaluated on **VG150**, HetH dominantly surpasses most methods. Compared to MOTIFS and VCTree-SL, HetH using multi-branch tree structure outperforms MOTIFS and yields comparable recall rate with VCTree-SL which uses a binary tree structure. It indicates that hierarchical structure is superior to plain one in terms of modeling context. We observe that HetH achieves better performances compared to VCTree-SL under PREDCLS protocol, while there exists a slight gap under SGCLS and SGGEN protocols. This is mainly because our tree structure is generated with artificial rules and some incorrect subtrees inevitably emerge due to occlusion in 2D images, while VCTree-SL dynamically adjusts its structure in pursuit of higher performances. Under SGCLS and SGGEN protocols in which object information is fragmentary, it is difficult for HetH to rectify the context encoded from wrong structures. However, we argue that our interpretable and natural multi-branch tree structure is also adaptive to the situation when there is an increment of object and relation categories but fewer data. It can be seen from evaluation results on **VG200** that the HetH outperforms MOTIFS by 0.67 mean points and VCTree-SL by 1.1 mean points. On the contrary, in this case, the data are insufficient for dynamic structure optimization.

As SGG task is highly related to VRD task, we apply HetH on **VRD** and the comparison results are shown in Table 3. Both the HetH and RelDN [53] use pretrained weights on MSCOCO, while only [46] states that they use ImageNet pretrained weights and others remain unknown. It's shown that our method yields competitive results and even surpasses state-of-the-arts under some metrics.

When it comes to key relation prediction, we directly evaluate HetH, MOTIFS, and VCTree-SL on **VG-KR**. As shown in Table 2, HetH substantially performs better than other two competitors, suggesting that the structure of HET provides hints for judging the importance of relations, and parsing the structured information in HET indeed capture humans' perceptive habits.

In pursuit of ultimate performances on mining key relations, we jointly optimize the HetH with RRM under the supervision of key relation annotations in VG-KR. From Table 2, both HetH-RRM and MOTIFS-RRM achieve significant gains, and HetH-RRM is better than MOTIFS-RRM, which proves the superiority of HetH again, and shows excellent transferability of RRM.

Qualitative Analysis. We visualize intermediate results in Fig. 3(a-d). HET is well constructed and close to human's analyzing process. In the area map, regions of *arm*, *hand*, and *foot* get small weights because of their small sizes. Actually, relations like ⟨*lady, has, arm*⟩ are indeed trivial. As a result, RRM suppresses these relations. More cases are provided in supplementary materials.

4.4   Analyses About het

We conduct additional experiments to validate whether HET has a potential to reveal humans' perceptive habits. As shown in Fig. 4(a), we compare the **depth distribution** of top-5 predicted relations (represented by tuple (d_{o_i}, d_{o_j}) consisting of the depths of two entities, and the depth of root is defined as 1.)

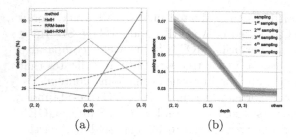

Strtg.	Metric	HetH-RRM
EP	kR@1	**17.5**
	kR@5	**35.0**
	speed	0.22
SP	kR@1	15.8
	kR@5	31.2
	speed	**0.18**

(a)   (b)

Fig. 4. (a) Depth distribution of top-5 predicted relations. (b) The ranking confidence of relations from different depths obtained from RRM-base. Sampling is repeated five times.

Fig. 5. Comparison between EP and SP. The inference speed (seconds/image) is evaluated with a single TITAN Xp GPU).

of HetH, RRM-base and HetH-RRM. After applying RRM, there is a significant increment on the ratio of depth tuples $(2, 2)$ and $(2, 3)$, and a drop on $(3, 3)$. This phenomenon is also observed in Fig. 3(e). Previous experiments have proved that RRM obviously upgrades the rankings of key relations. In other words, relations which are closer to the root of HET are regarded as key ones by RRM. We also analyze the ranking confidence (ϕ) of relations from different depths with the RRM-base model (to eliminate the confounding effect caused by AAP information). We sample 10,000 predicted relation triplets from each depth five times. In Fig. 4(b), the ranking confidence decreases as the depth increases. Therefore, different levels of HET indeed indicate different perceptive importance of relations. This characteristic makes it possible to reasonably adjust the scale of a scene graph. If we want to limit the scale of a scene graph but keep its ability to sketc.h image gist as far as possible, it is feasible for our hierarchical scene graph since we just need to cut off some secondary branches of HET, but is difficult to realize in an ordinary scene graph. We give an example in the supplementary materials.

Besides, different from traditional **Exhausted Prediction (EP,** predict relation for every pair of entities) during inference stage, we adopt a novel **Structured Prediction (SP)** strategy, in which we only predict relations between parent and children nodes, and any two sibling nodes that share the same parent. In Fig. 5, we compare the performances and inference speed between EP and SP for HetH-RRM. Despite the slight gap in terms of performances, the interpretability of connections in HET makes SP feasible to take a further step towards efficient inference, getting rid of the $O(N^2)$ complexity [16] of EP. Further researches need to be conducted to balance performance and efficiency.

Table 4. Results of image captioning on VG-KR.

Num.	Model	B@1	B@2	B@3	B@4	ROUGE-L	CIDEr	SPICE	Avg. Growth
all	GCN-LSTM	72.0	54.7	40.5	30.0	52.9	91.1	18.1	
20	HetH-Freq	73.1	55.7	41.0	30.1	53.5	94.0	18.8	0.06
	HetH	74.9	**58.4**	**43.9**	**32.8**	54.9	101.7	19.8	
	HetH-RRM	**75.0**	58.2	43.7	32.7	**55.1**	**102.2**	**19.9**	
5	HetH-Freq	70.7	53.2	38.6	28.0	51.7	84.4	17.2	1.57
	HetH	72.5	55.4	41.2	30.5	53.1	92.6	18.5	
	HetH-RRM	**73.7**	**56.7**	**42.3**	**31.5**	**54.0**	**97.5**	**19.1**	
2	HetH-Freq	68.1	50.8	36.8	26.5	50.2	76.5	15.5	2.10
	HetH	70.8	53.4	39.2	28.7	51.8	86.4	17.6	
	HetH-RRM	**72.3**	**55.2**	**41.0**	**30.4**	**53.1**	**92.2**	**18.4**	

5   Experiments on Image Captioning

Do key relations really make sense? We conduct experiments on one of the downstream tasks of SGG, i.e., image captioning, to verify it.[2]

Experiments are conducted on VG-KR since it has caption annotations from MSCOCO. To generate captions, we select different numbers of predicted top relations and feed them into the LSTM backend following [44]. We reimplement the complete **GCN-LSTM** [44] model and evaluate it on VG-KR since it's one of the state-of-the-art methods and is most related to us. As shown in Table 4, our simple frequency baseline, **HetH-Freq** (the rankings of relations are accord with their frequency in training data), with 20 top relations input, outperforms GCN-LSTM because GCN-LSTM conducts graph convolution using relations as edges, which is not as effective as our method in terms of making full use of relation information. After applying RRM, there is consistent performance improvement on overall metrics. This improvement is more and more significant as the number of input top relations reduces. It's reasonable since the impact of RRM centers at top relations. It suggests that our model provides more essential content with as few relations as possible, which contributes to efficiency improvement. The captions presented in Fig. 3(e) shows that key relations are more helpful for generating a description that highly fits the major events in an image.

6   Conclusion

We propose a new scene graph modeling formulation and make an attempt to push the study of SGG towards the target of practicability and rationalization. We generate a human-mimetic hierarchical scene graph inspired by humans' scene parsing procedure, and further prioritize the key relations as far as possible.

---

[2] We briefly introduce here and details are provided in supplementary materials.

Based on HET, a hierarchcal scene graph is generated with the assistance of our Hybrid-LSTM. Moreover, RRM is devised to recall more key relations. Experiments show outstanding performances of our method on traditional scene graph generation and key relation prediction tasks. Besides, experiments on image captioning prove that key relations are not just for appreciating, but indeed play a crucial role in higher-level downstream tasks.

Acknowledgements. This work is partially supported by Natural Science Foundation of China under contracts Nos. 61922080, U19B2036, 61772500, CAS Frontier Science Key Research Project No. QYZDJ-SSWJSC009, and Beijing Academy of Artificial Intelligence No. BAAI2020ZJ0201.

References

1. Antol, S., et al.: VQA: Visual question answering. In: Proceedings of the IEEE International Conference on Computer Vision (ICCV), pp. 2425–2433 (2015)
2. Chen, T., Yu, W., Chen, R., Lin, L.: Knowledge-embedded routing network for scene graph generation. In: Proceedings of the IEEE Conference on Computer Vision and Pattern Recognition (CVPR), pp. 6163–6171 (2019)
3. Dai, B., Zhang, Y., Lin, D.: Detecting visual relationships with deep relational networks. In: Proceedings of the IEEE Conference on Computer Vision and Pattern Recognition (CVPR), pp. 3298–3308 (2017)
4. Graves, A., Schmidhuber, J.: Framewise phoneme classification with bidirectional LSTM and other neural network architectures. Neural Networks **18**(5–6), 602–610 (2005)
5. Gu, J., Zhao, H., Lin, Z., Li, S., Cai, J., Ling, M.: Scene graph generation with external knowledge and image reconstruction. In: Proceedings of the IEEE Conference on Computer Vision and Pattern Recognition (CVPR), pp. 1969–1978 (2019)
6. Han, F., Zhu, S.C.: Bottom-up/top-down image parsing with attribute grammar. IEEE Trans. Pattern Anal. Mach. Intell. (TPAMI) **31**(1), 59–73 (2008)
7. He, S., Tavakoli, H.R., Borji, A., Pugeault, N.: Human attention in image captioning: dataset and analysis. In: Proceedings of the IEEE International Conference on Computer Vision (ICCV), pp. 8529–8538 (2019)
8. Hou, Q., Cheng, M.M., Hu, X., Borji, A., Tu, Z., Torr, P.: Deeply supervised salient object detection with short connections. In: Proceedings of the IEEE Conference on Computer Vision and Pattern Recognition (CVPR), pp. 3203–3212 (2017)
9. Itti, L., Koch, C., Niebur, E.: A model of saliency-based visual attention for rapid scene analysis. IEEE Trans. Pattern Anal. Mach. Intell. (TPAMI) **11**, 1254–1259 (1998)
10. Johnson, J., et al.: Image retrieval using scene graphs. In: Proceedings of the IEEE Conference on Computer Vision and Pattern Recognition (CVPR), pp. 3668–3678 (2015)
11. Kim, D.J., Choi, J., Oh, T.H., Kweon, I.S.: Dense relational captioning: triple-stream networks for relationship-based captioning. In: Proceedings of the IEEE Conference on Computer Vision and Pattern Recognition (CVPR), pp. 6271–6280 (2019)
12. Klein, D.A., Frintrop, S.: Center-surround divergence of feature statistics for salient object detection. In: Proceedings of the IEEE International Conference on Computer Vision (ICCV), pp. 2214–2219 (2011)

13. Krishna, R., et al.: Visual genome: connecting language and vision using Crowdsourced dense image annotations. Int. J. Comput. Vision (IJCV) **123**(1), 32–73 (2017). https://doi.org/10.1007/s11263-016-0981-7

14. Li, G., Yu, Y.: Visual saliency based on multiscale deep features. In: Proceedings of the IEEE Conference on Computer Vision and Pattern Recognition (CVPR), pp. 5455–5463 (2015)

15. Li, Y., Ouyang, W., Wang, X., Tang, X.: Vip-cnn: visual phrase guided convolutional neural network. In: Proceedings of the IEEE Conference on Computer Vision and Pattern Recognition (CVPR), pp. 7244–7253 (2017)

16. Li, Y., Ouyang, W., Zhou, B., Shi, J., Zhang, C., Wang, X.: Factorizable net: an efficient subgraph-based framework for scene graph generation. In: Ferrari, V., Hebert, M., Sminchisescu, C., Weiss, Y. (eds.) ECCV 2018. LNCS, vol. 11205, pp. 346–363. Springer, Cham (2018). https://doi.org/10.1007/978-3-030-01246-5_21

17. Li, Y., Ouyang, W., Zhou, B., Wang, K., Wang, X.: Scene graph generation from objects, phrases and region captions. In: Proceedings of the IEEE International Conference on Computer Vision (ICCV), pp. 1261–1270 (2017)

18. Liang, X., Lee, L., Xing, E.P.: Deep variation-structured reinforcement learning for visual relationship and attribute detection. In: Proceedings of the IEEE Conference on Computer Vision and Pattern Recognition (CVPR), pp. 4408–4417 (2017)

19. Liang, Y., Bai, Y., Zhang, W., Qian, X., Zhu, L., Mei, T.: VrR-VG: refocusing visually-relevant relationships. In: Proceedings of the IEEE International Conference on Computer Vision (ICCV), pp. 10403–10412 (2019)

20. Lin, L., Wang, G., Zhang, R., Zhang, R., Liang, X., Zuo, W.: Deep structured scene parsing by learning with image descriptions. In: Proceedings of the IEEE Conference on Computer Vision and Pattern Recognition (CVPR), pp. 2276–2284 (2016)

21. Lin, T.-Y., et al.: Microsoft COCO: common objects in context. In: Fleet, D., Pajdla, T., Schiele, B., Tuytelaars, T. (eds.) ECCV 2014. LNCS, vol. 8693, pp. 740–755. Springer, Cham (2014). https://doi.org/10.1007/978-3-319-10602-1_48

22. Lin, X., Ding, C., Zeng, J., Tao, D.: GPS-net: graph property sensing network for scene graph generation. In: Proceedings of the IEEE Conference on Computer Vision and Pattern Recognition (CVPR), pp. 3746–3755 (2020)

23. Liu, N., Han, J., Yang, M.H.: PiCANet: learning pixel-wise contextual attention for saliency detection. In: Proceedings of the IEEE Conference on Computer Vision and Pattern Recognition (CVPR), pp. 3089–3098 (2018)

24. Lu, C., Krishna, R., Bernstein, M., Fei-Fei, L.: Visual relationship detection with language priors. In: Leibe, B., Matas, J., Sebe, N., Welling, M. (eds.) ECCV 2016. LNCS, vol. 9905, pp. 852–869. Springer, Cham (2016). https://doi.org/10.1007/978-3-319-46448-0_51

25. Lu, J., Yang, J., Batra, D., Parikh, D.: Neural baby talk. In: Proceedings of the IEEE Conference on Computer Vision and Pattern Recognition (CVPR), pp. 7219–7228 (2018)

26. Pennington, J., Socher, R., Manning, C.: Glove: global vectors for word representation. In: Proceedings of the 2014 Conference on Empirical Methods in Natural Language Processing (EMNLP), pp. 1532–1543 (2014)

27. Peyre, J., Laptev, I., Schmid, C., Sivic, J.: Weakly-supervised learning of visual relations. In: Proceedings of the IEEE International Conference on Computer Vision (ICCV), pp. 5179–5188 (2017)

28. Qi, M., Li, W., Yang, Z., Wang, Y., Luo, J.: Attentive relational networks for mapping images to scene graphs. In: Proceedings of the IEEE Conference on Computer Vision and Pattern Recognition (CVPR), pp. 3957–3966 (2019)

29. Ren, S., He, K., Girshick, R., Sun, J.: Faster R-CNN: Towards real-time object detection with region proposal networks. In: Advances in Neural Information Processing Systems (NIPS), pp. 91–99 (2015)
30. Sharma, A., Tuzel, O., Jacobs, D.W.: Deep hierarchical parsing for semantic segmentation. In: Proceedings of the IEEE Conference on Computer Vision and Pattern Recognition (CVPR), pp. 530–538 (2015)
31. Shi, J., Zhang, H., Li, J.: Explainable and explicit visual reasoning over scene graphs. In: Proceedings of the IEEE Conference on Computer Vision and Pattern Recognition (CVPR), pp. 8376–8384 (2019)
32. Simonyan, K., Zisserman, A.: Very deep convolutional networks for large-scale image recognition. arXiv preprint arXiv:1409.1556 (2014)
33. Socher, R., Lin, C.C., Manning, C., Ng, A.Y.: Parsing natural scenes and natural language with recursive neural networks. In: Proceedings of the 28th International Conference on Machine Learning (ICML 2011), pp. 129–136 (2011)
34. Tai, K.S., Socher, R., Manning, C.D.: Improved semantic representations from tree-structured long short-term memory networks. In: Proceedings of the 53rd Annual Meeting of the Association for Computational Linguistics and the 7th International Joint Conference on Natural Language Processing (Vol. 1: Long Papers), pp. 1556–1566 (2015)
35. Tang, K., Niu, Y., Huang, J., Shi, J., Zhang, H.: Unbiased scene graph generation from biased training. In: Proceedings of the IEEE Conference on Computer Vision and Pattern Recognition (CVPR), pp. 3716–3725 (2020)
36. Tang, K., Zhang, H., Wu, B., Luo, W., Liu, W.: Learning to compose dynamic tree structures for visual contexts. In: Proceedings of the IEEE Conference on Computer Vision and Pattern Recognition (CVPR), pp. 6619–6628 (2019)
37. Wang, L., Lu, H., Ruan, X., Yang, M.H.: Deep networks for saliency detection via local estimation and global search. In: Proceedings of the IEEE Conference on Computer Vision and Pattern Recognition (CVPR), pp. 3183–3192 (2015)
38. Wang, T., Borji, A., Zhang, L., Zhang, P., Lu, H.: A stagewise refinement model for detecting salient objects in images. In: Proceedings of the IEEE International Conference on Computer Vision (ICCV), pp. 4019–4028 (2017)
39. Wang, W., Wang, R., Shan, S., Chen, X.: Exploring context and visual pattern of relationship for scene graph generation. In: Proceedings of the IEEE Conference on Computer Vision and Pattern Recognition (CVPR), pp. 8188–8197 (2019)
40. Wu, Q., Shen, C., Wang, P., Dick, A., van den Hengel, A.: Image captioning and visual question answering based on attributes and external knowledge. IEEE Trans. Pattern Anal. Mach. Intell. (TPAMI) 40(6), 1367–1381 (2018)
41. Xie, Y., Lu, H., Yang, M.H.: Bayesian saliency via low and mid level cues. IEEE Trans. Image Proc. (TIP) 22(5), 1689–1698 (2012)
42. Xu, D., Zhu, Y., Choy, C.B., Fei-Fei, L.: Scene graph generation by iterative message passing. In: Proceedings of the IEEE Conference on Computer Vision and Pattern Recognition (CVPR), pp. 5410–5419 (2017)
43. Yang, J., Lu, J., Lee, S., Batra, D., Parikh, D.: Graph R-CNN for scene graph generation. In: Ferrari, V., Hebert, M., Sminchisescu, C., Weiss, Y. (eds.) ECCV 2018. LNCS, vol. 11205, pp. 690–706. Springer, Cham (2018). https://doi.org/10.1007/978-3-030-01246-5_41
44. Yao, T., Pan, Y., Li, Y., Mei, T.: Exploring visual relationship for image captioning. In: Ferrari, V., Hebert, M., Sminchisescu, C., Weiss, Y. (eds.) Computer Vision – ECCV 2018. LNCS, vol. 11218, pp. 711–727. Springer, Cham (2018). https://doi.org/10.1007/978-3-030-01264-9_42

45. Yao, T., Pan, Y., Li, Y., Mei, T.: Hierarchy parsing for image captioning. In: Proceedings of the IEEE International Conference on Computer Vision (ICCV), pp. 2621–2629 (2019)
46. Yin, G., et al.: Zoom-net: mining deep feature interactions for visual relationship recognition. In: Ferrari, V., Hebert, M., Sminchisescu, C., Weiss, Y. (eds.) ECCV 2018. LNCS, vol. 11207, pp. 330–347. Springer, Cham (2018). https://doi.org/10.1007/978-3-030-01219-9_20
47. Yu, R., Li, A., Morariu, V.I., Davis, L.S.: Visual relationship detection with internal and external linguistic knowledge distillation. In: Proceedings of the IEEE International Conference on Computer Vision (ICCV), pp. 1974–1982 (2017)
48. Zareian, A., Karaman, S., Chang, S.F.: Weakly supervised visual semantic parsing. In: Proceedings of the IEEE Conference on Computer Vision and Pattern Recognition (CVPR), pp. 3736–3745 (2020)
49. Zellers, R., Yatskar, M., Thomson, S., Choi, Y.: Neural motifs: scene graph parsing with global context. In: Proceedings of the IEEE Conference on Computer Vision and Pattern Recognition (CVPR), pp. 5831–5840 (2018)
50. Zhang, H., Kyaw, Z., Chang, S.F., Chua, T.S.: Visual translation embedding network for visual relation detection. In: Proceedings of the IEEE Conference on Computer Vision and Pattern Recognition (CVPR), pp. 5532–5540 (2017)
51. Zhang, H., Kyaw, Z., Yu, J., Chang, S.F.: PPR-FCN: weakly supervised visual relation detection via parallel pairwise R-FCN. In: Proceedings of the IEEE International Conference on Computer Vision (ICCV), pp. 4233–4241 (2017)
52. Zhang, J., Kalantidis, Y., Rohrbach, M., Paluri, M., Elgammal, A., Elhoseiny, M.: Large-scale visual relationship understanding. Proc. AAAI Conf. Artif. Intell. (AAAI) **33**, 9185–9194 (2019)
53. Zhang, J., Shih, K.J., Elgammal, A., Tao, A., Catanzaro, B.: Graphical contrastive losses for scene graph parsing. In: Proceedings of the IEEE Conference on Computer Vision and Pattern Recognition (CVPR), pp. 11535–11543 (2019)
54. Zhang, L., Zhang, J., Lin, Z., Lu, H., He, Y.: CapSal: leveraging captioning to boost semantics for salient object detection. In: Proceedings of the IEEE Conference on Computer Vision and Pattern Recognition (CVPR), pp. 6024–6033 (2019)
55. Zhu, L., Chen, Y., Lin, Y., Lin, C., Yuille, A.: Recursive segmentation and recognition templates for image parsing. IEEE Trans. Pattern Anal. Mach. Intell. (TPAMI) **34**(2), 359–371 (2011)

Burst Denoising via Temporally Shifted Wavelet Transforms

Xuejian Rong[1,2]([✉]), Denis Demandolx[1], Kevin Matzen[1], Priyam Chatterjee[1],
and Yingli Tian[2]

[1] Facebook, Seattle, USA
{xrong,denisd,matzen,priyamc}@fb.com
[2] CUNY, New York, USA
ytian@ccny.cuny.edu

Abstract. Mobile photography has made great strides in recent years. However, low light imaging remains a challenge. Long exposures can improve signal-to-noise ratio (SNR) but undesirable motion blur can occur when capturing dynamic scenes. Consequently, imaging pipelines often rely on computational photography to improve SNR by fusing multiple short exposures. Recent deep network-based methods have been shown to generate visually pleasing results by fusing these exposures in a sophisticated manner, but often at a higher computational cost.

We propose an end-to-end trainable burst denoising pipeline which jointly captures high-resolution and high-frequency deep features derived from wavelet transforms. In our model, precious local details are preserved in high-frequency sub-band features to enhance the final perceptual quality, while the low-frequency sub-band features carry structural information for faithful reconstruction and final objective quality. The model is designed to accommodate variable-length burst captures via temporal feature shifting while incurring only marginal computational overhead, and further trained with a realistic noise model for the generalization to real environments. Using these techniques, our method attains state-of-the-art performance on perceptual quality, while being an order of magnitude faster.

Keywords: Burst denoising · Wavelet transform · Deep learning

1 Introduction

Image and video denoising are fundamental low-level vision tasks that have been studied for decades. Noise reduction is even more critical with the explosive growth of mobile cameras with small apertures and sensors that have limited light capture capabilities, making it difficult to acquire images in low light conditions. An effective denoising model could improve the visual quality of captures under such constraints, and immediately underpins many downstream computer vision and image processing applications.

Electronic supplementary material The online version of this chapter (https://doi.org/10.1007/978-3-030-58601-0_15) contains supplementary material, which is available to authorized users.

© Springer Nature Switzerland AG 2020
A. Vedaldi et al. (Eds.): ECCV 2020, LNCS 12358, pp. 240–256, 2020.
https://doi.org/10.1007/978-3-030-58601-0_15

The traditional approach to dealing with noise under low light situations is to increase the shutter time, allowing the sensor to collect more light to reduce the dominant photon noise. However, this approach requires that the camera be stable during the exposure and cannot handle object motion and corresponding motion blur well. An alternate approach is to capture multiple short-exposure frames (or bursts) to approximately capture an equivalent number of photons as long exposure, while also avoiding motion blur. Although producing a final high SNR image requires image registration which adds computational overhead, with advances in camera technology and dedicated compute units, burst capturing mode is now quite popular (e.g. Deep Fusion [1] and Night Sight [2].)

In the last decade, researchers have proposed various multi-frame noise reduction techniques for burst captures or videos [3–6]. Many recently proposed burst denoising techniques employ deep learning to improve the state-of-the-art [7–12]. However, they are typically not efficient enough for potential deployment (especially on edge devices). Subsequently, they are often trained and evaluated on unrealistic noise models which do not generally account for the signal-dependent and spatially correlated nature of actual noise [13].

In this paper, we propose a more practical end-to-end trainable burst denoising pipeline, which produces visually pleasing results while being significantly faster than the state-of-the-art. Specifically, we start from a 2D model which is capable of encoding high-frequency and high-resolution features from each burst frame, and then extend it to a pseudo-3D model to handle an arbitrary length of burst frame sequence, as presented in Sect. 3 in detail. Our proposed 2D model utilizes both high-resolution and high-frequency deep features, and is trained with realistic noise modeling. The motivation is that the high-resolution features have been validated in recent literature [14–16] to be drastically beneficial for preserving fine and detailed information during representation encoding, which is critical for image restoration tasks, especially for denoising. Moreover, an explicit feature decomposition is expected to guarantee the preserving of local details since the implicit decomposition of multi-scale high-resolution architectures might not be enough. After constructing the 2D model, it is further extended to handle burst frames of varying lengths using channel-wise temporal feature shifts, which utilizes temporal cues through all burst frames with limited overhead.

For any burst denoising solution to be practical, it needs to address a few major challenges. Firstly, it needs to be efficient, especially when considering resource constrained devices. Second, it needs to be flexible and scalable, being able to handle an arbitrary length of burst frames. Third, it needs to not only pursue objective quality, but also enhance perceptual quality and balance the trade-off between them as indicated in [17]. Our proposed approach is designed under the guideline to address all these challenges.

Our main contributions are summarized as follows:

Performance: Multi-frame denoising tasks are notably efficiency-demanding, and usually require real-time efficiency on terminals and edge devices. We present a novel, end-to-end trainable, deep convolutional burst denoising framework capable of achieving state-of-the-art performance both qualitatively and quantitatively. Additionally, reduced computational requirements demonstrate the efficiency of our model.

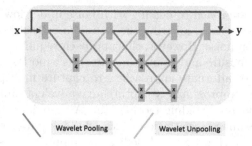

Fig. 1. Our proposed architecture for processing one corrupted frame, x, to recover one reconstructed frame, y. Inter-frame communication is facilitated through mechanisms illustrated in Fig. 2.

Features: To our knowledge, this is the first work that brings up the joint high-resolution and high-frequency feature extraction and fusion in denoising tasks. Systematic ablation studies and experiments are conducted to validate the efficacy of extracted features on burst denoising.

Flexibility: Our model can be used in both single-image (photo) and multi-image input (burst captures or videos) scenarios. For the multi-image input scenario, it could work in either a bidirectional offline manner (burst captures) or a unidirectional online manner (real-time video streams).

2   Background and Related Work

Single-Image Denoising. Image denoising has been extensively studied, with many traditional methods being proposed to take advantage of the specific statistics of natural images for reducing noise, including anisotropic diffusion [18], bilateral filters [19], total variation methods [20], domain transform methods such as wavelet transform [21,22], non-local patch-based methods [23], sparsity-based methods [24], and notably, the BM3D method [25]. Due to the popularity of deep neural networks, image denoising algorithms [26–33] have achieved a significant boost in performance. Notable denoising neural networks, DnCNN [26], and IrCNN [28] predict the residual noise present in the image instead of the denoised image, and recently, CBDNet [13] was proposed as a blind denoising model for real photographs. However, it is typically not satisfyingly effective and efficient to apply single-image denoising methods on multi-image data to generate consistent non-flickering results, without utilizing temporal cues.

Multi-image Denoising. Beyond the longstanding single-image denoising problem, many algorithms have also been proposed for multi-image (burst or video) denoising. Many ideas are shared between the two tasks, though burst denoising methods usually tend to generate or select one denoised frame as output, while video denoising methods aim to generate frame-by-frame output. When burst images or videos are available, noise can be reduced using spatial and temporal correlations. For example, BM3D has been extended to videos by filtering 3D blocks formed by grouping similar 2D patches (VBM3D) [4] or 4D blocks formed by grouping similar spatio-temporal volumes (VBM4D) [5]. [34] proposed a video denoising approach via the empirical Bayesian estimation of space-time patches. Liu et al. [6] in the case of processed images and Hasinoff et al. [10] in the case of raw images showed how to achieve good denoising performance in terms of PSNR and much higher speeds by exploiting temporal redundancy and averaging time-consistent pixels. Godard et al. [7] proposed a recurrent network for multi-frame denoising, where the burst sequence needs to be pre-warped to the reference frame. Mildenhall et al. [8] designed a convolutional network architecture that predicts spatially varying kernels for each of the input frames. These adaptive kernels can be applied to the input burst to correct for small misalignment and generate a clean output. Kokkinos et al. [11] proposed an iterative approach for both burst denoising and demosaicking tasks. Xu et al. [35] extended this approach to 3D deformable kernels for video denoising to sample pixels across the spatial-temporal space. We focus on the burst denoising task in this paper.

Wavelets in Convolutional Networks. Wavelets were originally proposed to separate data into different space-frequency components for component-wise analysis at multiple scales, and has been widely used in various image processing tasks [36]. Recently, different works have been proposed to incorporate wavelets with CNNs on various tasks, including deep feature dimension reduction [37], style transfer [38], super-resolution [39], and image denoising [27]. Different with most previous wavelet-based denoising networks which interleave wavelet transform with convolutional layers, we focus on utilizing wavelet transforms only by replacing the feature rescaling step similar to [37] and [38] to explicitly decompose the convolutional features to high-frequency and low-frequency sub-band features, and incorporate with the multi-scale network design.

The rest of this paper is organized as follows: Sect. 3 presents our proposed model for burst denoising, including the 2D model for feature extraction, and extended pseudo-3D model for temporal feature fusion. The data preparation and noise modeling are described in detail in Sect. 4. Section 5 demonstrates and analyzes the experimental results. Limitations and failure cases are presented in Sect. 5.6. We conclude this paper in Sect. 6.

3 Methodology

3.1 Overview

Our focus in this work is to generate a single high-quality clean image from a burst of $2N$ noisy frames ($\{X_0, ..., X_{2N-1}\}$) captured by a handheld camera. We consider X_N or X_{N+1}, namely the center frame, as the reference frame. We focus on the 8-bit sRGB camera output images as input instead of RAW images since most phones do not retain raw photos (even when supported). To be more practical, we developed our model to process images that are pre-processed by

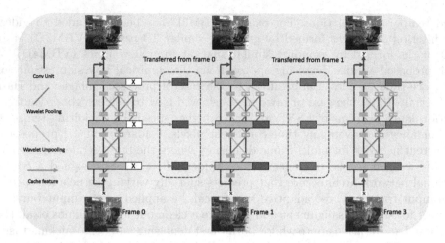

Fig. 2. The main schematic of our proposed model in unidirectional process-ing mode. For each burst frame, the 2D model will individually extract high-resolution and high-frequency features for later fusion. Then interleaved Temporal Shift Modules facilitate inter-frame communication and extend the 2D model to a full pseudo-3D model. As the forward pass of each per-frame branch is executed, a subset of activa-tions are stored in a separate buffer and the corresponding activations from the previous frame are copied to take their place.

an imaging pipeline. This is more challenging since the noise model is often considerably altered by different operations such as demosaicking, tone-mapping, and denoising.

In accordance with the goals for our burst denoising task, we designed a new deep learning-based pipeline to process noisy bursts. In the following subsections, we introduce our network architecture, high-resolution and high-frequency fea-ture extraction, temporal feature fusion mechanism, adaptive and conditional versions of the model, and training objective. The architecture of our proposed model is demonstrated in Fig. 2 using the unidirectional frame-by-frame pro-cessing manner as an example. The whole pipeline starts from the 2D model to extract high-frequency and high-resolution features from each burst frame, and is extended to the pseudo-3D version through temporal feature shifting. We explored different options for the 2D feature extraction and 3D feature aggrega-tion, and will present in detail in the following subsections. Specifically, Sect. 3.2 demonstrates the design for maintaining high-resolution features and explicitly separating high-frequency features, and Sect. 3.3 further demonstrate the differ-ent feature fusion regimes along the temporal dimension.

3.2 Features Matter in Burst Denoising

We first introduce how we built the 2D model for extracting the high-resolution and high-frequency features from each frame. This proposed 2D model can be directly used for the single image denoising task if needed.

High-Resolution Features. Recently high-to-low convolution and on-the-fly fusion techniques have been proposed for various computer vision tasks [14–16]. This helps maintain high-resolution representations through the whole convolutional feature extraction process. Our 2D model builds upon HRNet [15], one of the recently proposed multi-resolution convolution and fusion architectures, for high-resolution feature encoding. Our motivation is that the high-resolution features are expected to enhance the objective quality of the generated best denoised frame, while maintaining local detail. Our 2D network structure is illustrated below containing 3 parallel streams.

$$
\begin{aligned}
\mathcal{N}_{11} &\rightarrow \mathcal{N}_{21} \rightarrow \mathcal{N}_{31} \\
&\searrow \mathcal{N}_{22} \rightarrow \mathcal{N}_{32} \\
&\qquad\quad \searrow \mathcal{N}_{33}
\end{aligned}
\tag{1}
$$

where $\mathcal{N}_{s,r}$ is a sub-stream in the sth stage and r is the resolution index. The resolution index of the first stream is $r = 1$. The resolution of index r is $\frac{1}{2^{r-1}}$ of the resolution of the first stream. The highest resolution features are preserved along the top stream $\mathcal{N}_{s,1}$, and fused along with other streams at last.

High-Frequency Features. Besides maintaining high-resolution features, to achieve high visual quality, a denoising model should faithfully recover the structural information of a given noisy frame while removing noise. Though the aforementioned multi-scale architectures [14–16] are usually designed to implicitly decompose features into different frequencies, we find that an explicit decomposition is also beneficial to the multi-frame denoising task. (see Sect. 5).

Inspired by recent work on wavelet pooling and unpooling for convolutional networks [37,38], we propose to integrate wavelet decomposition along with the branch of high-resolution features in the multi-scale learning. That being that, the maintained high-resolution features are explicitly decomposed to different frequency bands, and processed on-the-fly before fused by wavelet unpooling. With several popular wavelets designs being proposed before, we finally choose Haar wavelet to efficiently split the original features into channels that capture different frequency bands. It results in better denoising and corresponding signal reconstruction. Specifically in our model, Haar wavelet pooling has four kernels, $\{LL^{\top}\ LH^{\top}\ HL^{\top}\ HH^{\top}\}$, where the low and high pass filters are

$$
L^{\top} = \frac{1}{\sqrt{2}}\begin{bmatrix} 1\ 1 \end{bmatrix}, \quad H^{\top} = \frac{1}{\sqrt{2}}\begin{bmatrix} -1\ 1 \end{bmatrix}.
\tag{2}
$$

Thus, unlike common pooling operations, the output of the Haar wavelet pooling has four channels. Here, the low-pass filter captures smooth surface and texture while the high-pass filters extract vertical, horizontal, and diagonal edge-like information. For simplicity, we denote the output of each kernel as LL, LH, HL, and HH, respectively.

One favorable property of wavelet pooling is that the original signal can be reconstructed by mirroring its operation; i.e., wavelet unpooling, as illustrated in detail in the supplementary doc. More precisely, wavelet unpooling can fully recover the original signal by performing a component-wise transposed-convolution. With this property, our proposed model can reconstruct an image with minimal information loss and noise amplification. In contrast, there is no exact inverse for max-pooling so that it is difficult for the encoder-decoder alike networks in previous work to fully recover the signal. To sum, both the high-resolution and high-frequency design are utilized in our final 2D model capable of frame-by-frame denoising, which will be further extended to a (pseudo-) 3D model for multi-frame burst denoising as instructed in Sect. 3.3.

3.3   Temporal Fusion of Deep Features

In this subsection, we introduce the different temporal feature fusion mechanisms we utilized for aggregating the information from all burst frames, including the conventional 3D convolution, and two pseudo-3D regimes, temporal max-pooling and temporal feature shifting. The final model adopts the temporal feature shifting as the feature fusion mechanism.

3D Convolution. For multi-frame feature extraction, there usually exist two flavors of 3D convolution methods, i.e. either feeding all frames into the network at once (offline mode), or feeding a certain number of frames (e.g. 3 or 5) in a unidirectional sliding window manner (online mode). For burst denoising, the 3D network aggregates all frames and jointly learn spatio-temporal features. However, 3D CNNs are computationally expensive [40] and more prone to over-fitting. As a result, we use 3D convolution as one version of our feature fusion regime, and further investigate 2 pseudo-3D learning mechanisms for the ablation study.

Temporal Max-Pooling. Compared to relatively computationally intensive real 3D convolutions, pseudo-3D convolution strategies such as temporal max-pooling have been recently proposed as an alternative for handling feature fusion. Zaheer et al. [41] and Qi et al. [42] show that any function that maps an unordered set into a regular vector (or an image) can be approximated by a neural network. Aittala et al. [9] successfully applied this idea to the burst deblurring task. In this version of our model, the individual input frame of the set are first processed separately by identical neural networks with tied weights, yielding a vector (or an image) of features for each. The features are then pooled by a symmetric operation, by evaluating either the mean or maximum value of each feature across the members. This scheme gives the individual frames in the burst a principled mechanism to contribute their local feature capturing the likely content of the sharp image.

Temporal Feature Shifting. Another alternative to 3D convolution method, the Temporal Shift Module (TSM) [43] has been successfully used for video understanding, and is ported as a feature fusion mechanism for our burst denoising model. Specifically, given a burst image sequence B, we take all $2N$ frames $\{X_0, ..., X_{2N-1}\}$ in the sequence. The aforementioned 2D CNN baseline model would process each of the frames individually with no temporal modeling, and the output results are averaged to give the final burst denoising prediction. In contrast, the TSM module has the same parameters and time cost of computation as 2D model. During inference, the frames are processed independently similar to 2D CNNs. The TSM is then inserted in each residual block (similar to temporal max-pooling) which enables temporal information fusion at no computational overhead. In our final model, TSM shifts a small proportion (typically 1/8) of channels along the temporal dimension, enabling the temporal multiply-accumulate to be computed inside the 2D convolution of channels instead of using an explicit time dimension. The temporal shift can be either uni- or bi-directional. In contrast to temporal max-pooling, TSM's can preserve information ordering. This allows the model to handle scene motion and object motion appearing in consecutive burst frames. For each inserted temporal shift module, the temporal receptive field will be enlarged by 2, as if running a convolution with the kernel size of 3 along the temporal dimension. Hence, the final integrated model has a very large temporal receptive field to conduct highly complicated temporal modeling.

Using the unidirectional temporal feature shifting for burst image denoising has some unique advantages. First, for each frame, we only need to replace and cache 1/8 of the features, without any extra computations. Hence, the latency of per-frame prediction is almost the same as the 2D CNN baseline. Both 3D Convolution and Temporal max-pooling methods need all the frames to be fed in the network at once for the inference, which leads to increased latency. Additionally, the temporal feature shifting enables temporal fusion on the fly at all levels, improving the model's robustness to scene motions. In contrast, most online methods only allow late temporal fusion after feature extraction.

3.4   Loss Function

With ground truth reference image Y and the denoised frame $\hat{Y}$ in linear space, we directly use a L_1 loss on both the pixel intensities and gradient intensities to train the proposed denoising network:

$$\ell(\hat{Y}, Y) = \lambda_1 \left\| \hat{Y} - Y \right\|_1 + \lambda_2 \left\| \nabla \hat{Y} - \nabla Y \right\|_1. \tag{3}$$

which tries to make the average of all denoising estimations close to the ground truth Y, with $\lambda_1 + \lambda_2 = 1$ (both set to a constant of 0.5 in our experiments). For fair comparisons with previous approaches, we do not utilize any adversarial training mechanism or perceptual loss in the proposed model to favor the perceptual metric. [8] proposed to add annealing loss for multi-frame training to avoid the convergence at an undesirable local minima in training, which we finally did not use as we have not noticed significant differences in our experiments.

4   Data Preparation

4.1   Camera Pipeline

In this work, we follow the camera simulation pipeline in [44] to model realistic noise, and generate noisy burst sequences for all the synthetic training samples.

Gaussian noise modeling   Realistic noise modeling

Fig. 3. Noisy image comparison between Gaussian noise modeling and our realistic noise modeling with inverse ISP.

We encourage readers to check our brief review in the *supplementary document* for more details of the camera pipeline we choose and corresponding comparisons. Specifically for the noise modeling, following [44], the noise parameters and factors (Gaussian and Poisson noise as additive and multiplicative operations) are randomly determined for all training samples, as 0–0.1 for Gaussian standard deviation, 0–0.02 for Poisson multiplication factor, with post-processing. For static burst synthesis, slight camera motion is simulated with random cropping and jittering (2–8 pixels) of a single image from the DIV2K dataset. Unfortunately, scene/object motion cannot be easily added without extra processing such as inpainting and depth/boundary prediction. For dynamic burst synthesis, we only add noises since camera and object motion already exist in the original data of the Vimeo90K dataset.

4.2 Datasets and Synthetic Burst Generation

DIV2K Dataset. DIV2K (DIVerse 2K resolution high-quality images) [45] is a dataset composed of 800 high (2K) resolution images for training with 100 images each for validation and testing respectively (the testing set is not publicly available). We used the available high-resolution images with the *static* noisy bursts synthesis for training and testing respectively.

Vimeo90K Dataset. Vimeo90K [46] is built upon 5, 846 selected videos from *vimeo.com*, which covers large variety of scenes and actions. The subset we used for training contains 91, 701 7-frame sequences, extracted from 39K selected video clips. We used all available 91, 701 7-frame sequences (original clean images) with our realistic noise modeling for the *dynamic* noisy bursts synthesis and training (original data containing various camera and scene/object motion as demonstrated on the dataset page). Note that though our proposed model supports by design bursts of arbitrary size, this is not the case for the network proposed in [8]. For a fair comparison, we duplicate the last frame in each 7-frame sequence to generate a 8-frame burst for training.

Real Noisy Burst Captures. We also captured a collection of realistic burst sequences with a handheld device. Most of the bursts are captured under low-light conditions where burst denoising is typically most useful. There are no ground-truth clean frames available for this set. We used these real noisy data to qualitatively evaluate the generalization capability of our model trained on synthetic bursts with realistic noise modeling.

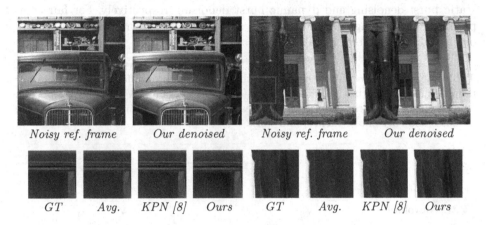

Noisy ref. frame   *Our denoised*   *Noisy ref. frame*   *Our denoised*

GT   Avg.   KPN [8]   Ours   GT   Avg.   KPN [8]   Ours

Fig. 4. The qualitative comparison of our burst denoising model with state-of-the-arts on synthetic burst captures. Our method well preserves the local details while avoiding the over-smooth issue. It also introduces less distortion than KPN in terms of the perceptual quality.

5 Experimental Results

5.1 Overview

After setting up the burst denoising benchmarks, we conducted various experiments for the ablation study on different modules of our model, burst image denoising, and efficiency analysis. We would like to compare our method to two most recent deep learning based approaches [11,47]. However, there is no model or testing data released from [47] as a preprint work. The proposed method in [11] strictly depends on the Enhanced Correlation Coefficient (ECC) estimation of the warping matrix that aligns every observation to the reference frame while all the other methods, including our proposed model, do not have this requirement. While there is no easy way to conduct a fair comparison with similar training regimes, we qualitatively evaluate our method on the public released testing set from [11] (see supplementary), and also tested its computational efficiency in Table 3 for a better experimental completeness.

Implementation and Training Details. We implement our method using PyTorch [48]. The full proposed model is trained on two NVIDIA GeForce RTX 2080 Ti GPU with 11 GB of memory each. We use the Adam optimizer [49] and the batch size is 16. The initial learning rate is 10^{-3} and is reduced to 3×10^{-5} after 80 epochs, which takes around 26 h in total. For the burst image denoising experiments, most DIV2K and Vimeo90K data are utilized for training, and the remaining DIV2K and Vimeo90K data are used for testing on static burst denoising and dynamic burst denoising respectively. For fair comparisons, all learning-based approaches such as KPN are trained from scratch on the DIV2K/Vimeo90K based data,

Table 1. *Ablation study.* Investigation of the contribution of different modules in our proposed model. The best results in PSNR (dB) on values on DIV2K [45] are reported. The + symbol indicates the optional modules, and the × symbols indicates the exclusive modules and only one of them would work.

Model								
+ high-res feature				✓		✓	✓	✓
+ high-freq feature					✓	✓	✓	✓
× 3D convolution	✓					✓		
× Temporal max-pooling		✓					✓	
× Temporal feature shifting			✓	✓	✓			✓
PSNR (in dB)	32.35	32.18	32.34	32.79	32.75	32.82	32.73	**32.88**

Evaluation Metrics. We evaluate our proposed model and state-of-the-art methods based on the standard Peak Signal-to-Noise Ratio (PSNR) and Structural Similarity (SSIM) image quality metrics. Furthermore, there usually exists a trade-off between objective quality and perceptual quality in image restoration tasks, as indicated in [17] and [39]. Compared with other burst denoising approaches, our model better preserves the local details in reconstruction due to utilizing the high-resolution and high-frequency features, thus is prone to better perceptual quality and alleviates the commonly occurred over-smoothing issues such as in VBM4D [5]. Therefore, besides the two objective metrics, we also introduce one recently popular deep learning-based perceptual metric, namely Learned Perceptual Image Patch Similarity (LPIPS) [50], for a more comprehensive comparison and analysis. LPIPS is more sensitive to the distortions from deep learning-based representations, and prone to the human perceptual judgments. For fair comparisons, we do not utilize any adversarial training mechanism or perceptual loss in the proposed model to favor this metric.

5.2   Ablation Study

To comprehensively analyze the contributions and significance of different modules in our proposed method, we first quantitatively assess our full model with a

Table 2. *The mean PSNR, SSIM, and LPIPS burst denoising results of our proposed model compared with state-of-the-art algorithms evaluated on the synthetic static burst denoising data generated from DIV2K (left) anddynamic data generated from Vimeo90K (right).*

Method	PSNR↑	SSIM↑	LPIPS↓	PSNR↑	SSIM↑	LPIPS↓
Noisy reference frame	23.38	0.6841	0.3361	23.33	0.5337	0.4255
Burst average	24.73	0.6923	0.3159	21.39	0.5164	0.4513
VBM4D [5]	30.81	0.8637	0.2166	27.05	0.6922	0.2869
VNLB [34]	31.52	0.8841	0.1824	27.44	0.7043	0.2720
KPN [8]	32.64	**0.8920**	0.1772	**28.67**	**0.7319**	**0.2357**
Our proposed	**32.88**	0.8855	**0.1742**	28.61	0.7246	0.2366

set of ablations on a synthetic test set, followed by an analysis of its interpretability. We choose the basic U-Net like residual denoising model as the baseline backbone 2D model for ablation study in feature encoding. The main designs we aim to analyze in our model include: 1) High-resolution feature encoding: w/ or w/o the three-stage multi-scale high-resolution convolutional network; 2) High-frequency feature encoding: w/ or w/o the interleaved wavelet pooling and unpooling operations to explicitly decompose the feature maps. For temporal feature fusion, only one mechanism will be integrated with 2D backbones to produce the final denoised output.

As illustrated in Table 1, when we directly utilize the baseline backbone model without preserving high-resolution and decomposing high-frequency features, the denoising network performs fairly well on the testing data. Both the high-resolution and high-frequency features would consistently boost the denoising performance, though the high-resolution features tend to make slightly more contributions.

As to the temporal feature fusion mechanisms, temporal feature shifting performs comparably well as the 3D convolution with the baseline model, and both outperforms the temporal max-pooling mechanism. However, temporal feature shifting demonstrates the capability to be better integrated with high-resolution and high-frequency features, most possibly due to the ability to learn shifting the most salient features temporally, and better aggregate cues from all available burst frames. Combining all the best practices, our full model achieves the top performance on the testing benchmark.

5.3   Burst Denoising Qualitative Evaluation

We evaluate different methods first on *static* noisy bursts derived from DIV2k, and then on *dynamic* noisy bursts derived from Vimeo90K. Here, *static* means the noisy bursts are generated by altering a single image with random jitter, disturbance, and shifts, then, finally, realistic noise is added. Therefore, these bursts contain no scene motion, only camera motion. In contrast, the *dynamic* noisy bursts contain scene motion that cannot be fully modeled by camera stabilization alone.

Figure 4 shows examples of the denoising results from the proposed model and state-of-the-arts. As claimed in recent kernel sampling based methods such as [8] and [47], the patch-based methods such as VBM4D, and direct prediction based deep learning methods which directly synthesize the denoising results (either producing the clean or residual image) is prone to generate over-smoothed results, and lose the local detail. However, the qualitative results validate the efficacy of our method, which effectively adopts the high-quality features, and faithfully synthesizes and reconstructs the details.

Also, the slight simulated camera motion are equally well tackled by our proposed model, though the kernel-sampling based methods such as KPN are naturally more robust to slight disturbances, and still outperforms the proposed method by a little margin on Vimeo90K dataset.

Table 3. *Comparison of inference latency (running time per frame) during testing.* We report the time of each method to denoise one color frame of resolution 720×720. For burst denoising, the overall latency can be computed by multiplying the per-frame latency with the total number of burst frames (e.g., 8 in our experiments). All deep learning based methods are evaluated on one single NVIDIA GeForce RTX 2080 Ti GPU. *Note: Values displayed for [34] and [11] do not include the time required for pre-processing (e.g., motion or warping matrix estimation), which can be time costing.

Method	Latency (s) ↓	Megapixels/s ↑
VNLB* [34]	387.24	0.0052
VBM4D [5]	131.49	0.0153
KPN (GPU) [8]	0.597	0.8685
Iterative (GPU)* [11]	0.140	3.7029
Our Proposed (GPU)	**0.064**	**8.1403**

5.4   Burst Denoising Quantitative Evaluation

Furthermore, we quantitatively evaluate our model along with state-of-the-arts on both the *static* and *dynamic* testing set, and the results are demonstrated in Table 2. Generally, our proposed model performs comparably decently with KPN on different evaluation metrics. In terms of the objective quality (PSNR and SSIM), KPN leads a slight margin, especially on the *dynamic* data which contain scene and object motion. However, our proposed model consistently outperforms all state-of-the-arts in terms of perceptual quality, evaluated by the deep learning based metric *LPIPS*.

5.5 Algorithm Efficiency

While achieving comparable performances on burst denoising, we further evaluate all models on efficiency. As illustrated in Table 3, benefiting from the efficient pseudo-3D feature fusion design, our model is significantly faster than state-of-the-arts. Empirically, the speed-up is mainly due to the concise network design and the way temporality is handled. The Haar wavelet transform is efficient, though bringing an increase of space complexity (more intermediate feature maps to store) of the model.

5.6 Limitations

The main limitation of our proposed model is that it is still trained in a non-blind denoising fashion without taking a noise estimation map as input from an individual noise estimator such as the ones proposed in [13,51], thus lacking the capability of adaptive noise-aware burst denoising which is recently popular in single-image denoising methods. Figure 2 in the *supplementary document* demonstrates a failure of our model on a severely corrupted burst, which is considerably noisier than examples seen during training. The model struggles to recover the corrupted detail, but instead produces unsatisfactory artifacts. Integrating the proposed model with a noise level estimation mechanism is a promising future research direction to mitigate this problem.

5.7 Generalization to Real Burst Captures

Finally, we evaluate the generalization capability of our model on real burst noisy frames. The results qualitatively validates that our proposed model performs reasonably well on real noisy burst captures, while only being trained on synthetic data with realistic noise modeling. We aim to collect more real noisy bursts along with corresponding long-exposure shots as the ground truth, though the problem is that this regime only works for static scenes.

6   Conclusion and Future Work

We propose the first unified end-to-end trainable deep burst denoising framework which effectively utilizes high-resolution and high-frequency features. The proposed model excels both quantitatively and qualitatively, while facilitating joint spatial-temporal modeling through burst frames at no extra cost. Compared to the prior state-of-the-art, our the proposed framework is more scalable, lighter, and faster, thus enabling low-latency burst denoising on edge devices.

Inspired by recent work on extreme low-light image [52] and video [53] enhancement, our future work is to support burst shots captured in the extreme dark environments where noise is significantly amplified. Also, we aim to incorporate a noise estimator for burst captures to support blind (noise-aware) denoising.

References

1. A Deep Look into the iPhone's new Deep Fusion Feature. https://tinyurl.com/deepfusion. Accessed 04 Nov 2019
2. Night Sight: Seeing in the Dark on Pixel Phones. https://tinyurl.com/googlenightsight. Accessed 04 Nov 2019
3. Buades, T., Lou, Y., Morel, J.M., Tang, Z.: A note on multi-image denoising. In 2009 International Workshop on Local and Non-Local Approximation in Image Processing, pp. 1–15. IEEE (2009)
4. Liu, C., Freeman, W.T.: A high-quality video denoising algorithm based on reliable motion estimation. In: Daniilidis, K., Maragos, P., Paragios, N. (eds.) ECCV 2010. LNCS, vol. 6313, pp. 706–719. Springer, Heidelberg (2010). https://doi.org/10.1007/978-3-642-15558-1_51
5. Maggioni, M., Boracchi, G., Foi, A., Egiazarian, K.: Video denoising, deblocking, and enhancement through separable 4-d nonlocal spatiotemporal transforms. IEEE Trans. Image Process. (TIP) **21**(9), 3952–3966 (2012)
6. Liu, Z., Yuan, L., Tang, X., Uyttendaele, M., Sun, J.: Fast burst images denoising. ACM Trans. Graphics (TOG) **33**(6), 232 (2014)
7. Godard, C., Matzen, K., Uyttendaele, M.: Deep burst denoising. In: Ferrari, V., Hebert, M., Sminchisescu, C., Weiss, Y. (eds.) ECCV 2018. LNCS, vol. 11219, pp. 560–577. Springer, Cham (2018). https://doi.org/10.1007/978-3-030-01267-0_33
8. Mildenhall, B., Barron, J.T., Chen, J., Sharlet, D., Ng, R., Carroll, R.: Burst denoising with kernel prediction networks. In: CVPR, pp. 2502–2510 (2018)
9. Aittala, M., Durand, F.: Burst image deblurring using permutation invariant convolutional neural networks. In: Ferrari, V., Hebert, M., Sminchisescu, C., Weiss, Y. (eds.) ECCV 2018. LNCS, vol. 11212, pp. 748–764. Springer, Cham (2018). https://doi.org/10.1007/978-3-030-01237-3_45
10. Hasinoff, S.W., et al.: Burst photography for high dynamic range and low-light imaging on mobile cameras. ACM Trans. Graphics (TOG) **35**(6), 192 (2016)
11. Kokkinos, F., Lefkimmiatis, S.: Iterative residual CNNS for burst photography applications. In: CVPR, pp. 5929–5938 (2019)
12. Dai, J., et al.: Deformable convolutional networks. In: ICCV, pp. 764–773 (2017)
13. Guo, S., Yan, Z., Zhang, K., Zuo, W., Zhang, L.: Toward convolutional blind denoising of real photographs. In: CVPR, pp. 1712–1722 (2019)
14. Ke, T.W., Maire, M., Yu, S.X.: Multigrid neural architectures. In: CVPR, pp. 6665–6673 (2017)
15. Wang, J., et al.: Deep High-resolution Representation Learning for Visual Recognition. arXiv preprint arXiv:1908.07919 (2019)
16. Chen, Y., et al.: Drop an octave: reducing spatial redundancy in convolutional neural networks with octave convolution. arXiv preprint arXiv:1904.05049 (2019)
17. Blau, Y., Michaeli, T.: The perception-distortion tradeoff. In: Proceedings of the IEEE Conference on Computer Vision and Pattern Recognition, pp. 6228–6237 (2018)
18. Weickert, J.: Anisotropic diffusion in image processing. Teubner, Stuttgart (1998)
19. Tomasi, C., Manduchi, R.: Bilateral filtering for gray and color images. In: ICCV, pp. 839–846 (1998)
20. Rudin, L.I., Osher, S., Fatemi, E.: Nonlinear total variation based noise removal algorithms. Physica D **60**(1–4), 259–268 (1992)
21. Antonini, M., Barlaud, M., Mathieu, P., Daubechies, I.: Image coding using wavelet transform. IEEE Trans. Image Process. (TIP) **1**(2), 205–220 (1992)

22. Portilla, J., Strela, V., Wainwright, M.J., Simoncelli, E.P.: Image denoising using scale mixtures of Gaussians in the wavelet domain. Trans. Img. Proc. **12**(11), 1338–1351 (2003)
23. Buades, A., Coll, B., Morel, J.M.: A non-local algorithm for image denoising. In: CVPR, vol. 2, pp. 60–65. IEEE (2005)
24. Elad, M., Aharon, M.: Image denoising via learned dictionaries and sparse representation. In: CVPR, vol. 1, pp. 895–900. IEEE (2006)
25. Dabov, K., Foi, A., Katkovnik, V., Egiazarian, K.: Image denoising by sparse 3-D transform-domain collaborative filtering. IEEE Trans. Image Process. (TIP) **16**, 2080–2095 (2007)
26. Zhang, K., Zuo, W., Chen, Y., Meng, D., Zhang, L.: Beyond a Gaussian denoiser: residual learning of deep CNN for image denoising. IEEE Trans. Image Process. (TIP) **26**(7), 3142–3155 (2017)
27. Liu, P., Zhang, H., Zhang, K., Lin, L., Zuo, W.: Multi-level wavelet-CNN for image restoration. In: CVPR Workshop, pp. 773–782 (2018)
28. Zhang, K., Zuo, W., Gu, S., Zhang, L.: Learning deep CNN denoiser prior for image restoration. In: CVPR, pp. 3929–3938 (2017)
29. Laine, S., Lehtinen, J., Aila, T.: High-quality self-supervised deep image denoising. arXiv preprint arXiv:1901.10277 (2019)
30. Batson, J., Royer, L.: Noise2Self: blind denoising by self-supervision. In: ICML, pp. 524–533 (2019)
31. Anwar, S., Barnes, N.: Real image denoising with feature attention. In: ICCV (2019)
32. Cha, S., Moon, T.: Fully convolutional pixel adaptive image denoiser. In: Proceedings of the IEEE International Conference on Computer Vision, pp. 4160–4169 (2019)
33. Gu, S., et al.: Self-guided network for fast image denoising. In: ICCV (2019)
34. Arias, P., Morel, J.M.: Video denoising via empirical Bayesian estimation of space-time patches. J. Math. Imaging Vis. **60**(1), 70–93 (2018)
35. Xu, J., Huang, Y., Liu, L., Zhu, F., Hou, X., Shao, L.: Noisy-as-clean: learning unsupervised denoising from the corrupted image. arXiv preprint arXiv:1906.06878 (2019)
36. Wang, J.Z.: Wavelets and imaging informatics: a review of the literature. J. Biomed. Inform. **34**(2), 129–141 (2001)
37. Williams, T., Li, R.: Wavelet pooling for convolutional neural networks. In: ICLR (2018)
38. Yoo, J., Uh, Y., Chun, S., Kang, B., Ha, J.W.: Photorealistic style transfer via wavelet transforms. In: ICCV (2019)
39. Deng, X., Yang, R., Xu, M., Dragotti, P.L.: Wavelet domain style transfer for an effective perception-distortion tradeoff in single image super-resolution (2019)
40. Kendall, A., Martirosyan, H., Dasgupta, S., Henry, P.: End-to-end learning of geometry and context for deep stereo regression. In: ICCV (2017)
41. Zaheer, M., Kottur, S., Ravanbakhsh, S., Poczos, B., Salakhutdinov, R.R., Smola, A.J.: Deep sets. In: NeurIPS, pp. 3391–3401 (2017)
42. Qi, C.R., Yi, L., Su, H., Guibas, L.J.: Pointnet++: deep hierarchical feature learning on point sets in a metric space. In: NeurIPS, pp. 5099–5108 (2017)
43. Lin, J., Gan, C., Han, S.: TSM: temporal shift module for efficient video understanding. In: ICCV (2019)
44. Jaroensri, R., Biscarrat, C., Aittala, M., Durand, F.: Generating training data for denoising real RGB images via camera pipeline simulation. arXiv preprint arXiv:1904.08825 (2019)

45. Agustsson, E., Timofte, R.: Ntire 2017 challenge on single image super-resolution: dataset and study. In: CVPR Workshop (2017)
46. Xue, T., Chen, B., Wu, J., Wei, D., Freeman, W.T.: Video enhancement with task-oriented flow. Int. J. Comput. Vis. (IJCV) **127**(8), 1106–1125 (2019)
47. Xu, X., Li, M., Sun, W.: Learning deformable kernels for image and video denoising. arXiv preprint arXiv:1904.06903 (2019)
48. Steiner, B., et al.: PyTorch: An imperative style, high-performance deep learning library. NeurIPS **32** (2019)
49. Kingma, D.P., Ba, J.: Adam: a method for stochastic optimization. arXiv preprint arXiv:1412.6980 (2014)
50. Zhang, R., Isola, P., Efros, A.A., Shechtman, E., Wang, O.: The unreasonable effectiveness of deep features as a perceptual metric. In: CVPR (2018)
51. Zhou, Y., et al.: When AWGN-based denoiser meets real noises. arXiv preprint arXiv:1904.03485 (2019)
52. Chen, C., Chen, Q., Xu, J., Koltun, V.: Learning to see in the dark. In: CVPR, pp. 3291–3300 (2018)
53. Chen, C., Chen, Q., Do, M., Koltun, V.: Seeing motion in the dark. In: ICCV (2019)

JSSR: A Joint Synthesis, Segmentation, and Registration System for 3D Multi-modal Image Alignment of Large-Scale Pathological CT Scans

Fengze Liu[1,2], Jinzheng Cai[1], Yuankai Huo[1,3], Chi-Tung Cheng[4],
Ashwin Raju[1], Dakai Jin[1], Jing Xiao[5], Alan Yuille[2], Le Lu[1], ChienHung Liao[4],
and Adam P. Harrison[1(✉)]

[1] PAII Inc., Bethesda, MD 20817, USA
tiger.lelu@gmail.com, adampharrison070@paii-labs.com
[2] Johns Hopkins University, Baltimore, MD 21218, USA
[3] Vanderbilt University, Nashville, TN 37235, USA
[4] Chang Gung Memorial Hospital, Linkou, Taoyuan City, Taiwan, ROC
[5] Ping An Technology, Shenzhen, China

Abstract. Multi-modal image registration is a challenging problem that is also an important clinical task for many real applications and scenarios. As a first step in analysis, deformable registration among different image modalities is often required in order to provide complementary visual information. During registration, semantic information is key to match homologous points and pixels. Nevertheless, many conventional registration methods are incapable in capturing high-level semantic anatomical dense correspondences. In this work, we propose a novel multi-task learning system, JSSR, based on an end-to-end 3D convolutional neural network that is composed of a generator, a registration and a segmentation component. The system is optimized to satisfy the implicit constraints between different tasks in an unsupervised manner. It first synthesizes the source domain images into the target domain, then an intra-modal registration is applied on the synthesized images and target images. The segmentation module are then applied on the synthesized and target images, providing additional cues based on semantic correspondences. The supervision from another fully-annotated dataset is used to regularize the segmentation. We extensively evaluate JSSR on a large-scale medical image dataset containing 1,485 patient CT imaging studies of four different contrast phases (i.e., 5,940 3D CT scans with pathological livers) on the registration, segmentation and synthesis tasks. The performance is improved after joint training on the registration and segmentation tasks by 0.9% and 1.9% respectively compared to a highly competitive and accurate deep learning baseline. The registration also consistently outperforms conventional state-of-the-art multi-modal registration methods.

© Springer Nature Switzerland AG 2020
A. Vedaldi et al. (Eds.): ECCV 2020, LNCS 12358, pp. 257–274, 2020.
https://doi.org/10.1007/978-3-030-58601-0_16

1   Introduction

Image registration attempts to discover a spatial transformation between a pair of images that registers the points in one of the images to the homologous points in the other image [37]. Within medical imaging, registration often focuses on inter-patient/inter-study mono-modal alignment. Another important and (if not more) frequent focal point is multi-channel imaging, *e.g.*, dynamic-contrast computed tomography (CT), multi-parametric magnetic resonance imaging (MRI), or positron emission tomography (PET) combined with CT/MRI. In this setting, the needs of intra-patient multi-modal registration are paramount, given the unavoidable patient movements or displacements between subsequent imaging scans. For scenarios where deformable misalignments are present, *e.g.*, the abdomen, correspondences can be highly complex. Because different modalities provide complementary visual/diagnosis information, proper and precise anatomical alignment benefits human reader's radiological observation and is crucial for any downstream computerized analyses. However, finding correspondences between homologous points is usually not trivial because of the complex appearance changes across modalities, which may be conditioned on anatomy, pathology, or other complicated interactions.

Unfortunately, multi-modal registration remains a challenging task, particularly since ground-truth deformations are hard or impossible to obtain. Methods must instead learn transformations or losses that allow for easier correspondences between images. Unsupervised registration methods, like [3,9], often use a local modality invariant feature to measure similarity. However these low-level features may not be universally applicable and cannot always capture high level semantic information. Other approaches use generative models to reduce the domain shift between modalities, and then apply registration based on direct intensity similarity [33]. A different strategy learns registrations that maximize the overlap in segmentation labels [3,12]. This latter approach is promising, as it treats the registration process similarly to a segmentation task, aligning images based on their semantic category. Yet, these approaches rely on having supervised segmentation labels in the first place for every deployment scenario.

Both the synthesis and segmentation approaches are promising, but they are each limited when used alone, especially when fully-supervised training data is not available, *i.e.*, no paired multi-modal images and segmentation labels, respectively. As Fig. 1 elaborates, the synthesis, segmentation, and registration tasks are linked together and define implicit constraints between each other. That motivates us to develop a joint synthesis, segmentation, and registration (JSSR) system which satisfies these implicit constraints. JSSR is composed of a generator, a segmentation, and a registration component that performs all three tasks simultaneously. Given a fixed image and moving image from different modalities for registration, the generator can synthesize the moving image to the same modality of the fixed image, conditioned on the fixed image to better reduce the domain gap. Then the registration component accepts the synthesized image from the generator and the fixed image to estimate a deformation field. Lastly, the segmentation module estimates the segmentation map for the moving image, fixed image and synthesized image. During the training procedure, we optimize several consistency losses including (1) the similarity between the fixed image and the warped synthesized image; (2) the similarity between the segmentation maps of the warped moving image and the fixed image; (3) an adversarial loss for generating high fidelity images; and (4) a smoothness loss to regularize the deformation field. To stop the segmentation module from providing meaningless segmentation maps, we regularize the segmentation by training it on fully supervised data obtained from a different source than the target data, e.g., public data. We evaluate our system on a large-scale clinical liver CT image dataset containing four phases per patient, for unpaired image synthesis, multi-modal image registration, and multi-modal image segmentation tasks. Our system outperforms the state-of-the-art conventional multi-modal registration methods and significantly improves the baseline model we used for the fother two tasks, validating the effectiveness of joint learning.

We summarize our main contributions as follows:

- We propose a novel joint learning approach for multi-modal image registration that incorporates the tasks of synthesis, registration and segmentation. Each task connects to the other two tasks during training, providing mutually reinforcing supervisory signals.
- We evaluate and validate the performance improvement of baseline methods for synthesis and segmentation after joint training by our system, demonstrating the effectiveness of our joint training setup and revealing the possibility of obtaining a better overall system by building upon and enhancing the baseline models.
- Our system consistently and significantly outperforms state-of-the-art conventional multi-modal registration approaches based on a large-scale multi-phase CT imaging dataset of 1,485 patients (each patient under four different intravenous contrast phases, i.e., 5,940 3D CT scans with various liver tumors).
- While we use supervised data from *single-phase* public data to regularize our segmentation, our method does not use or rely upon any manual segmentation labels from the target *multi-phase* target CT imaging dataset. Compared to approaches expecting target segmentation labels, JSSR enjoys better scalability and generalizability for varied clinical applications.

2   Related Work

Multi-modal Image Registration. Multi-modal image registration has been widely studied and applied in medical imaging. Existing registration methods can be based on additional information, e.g., landmarks [28,32] or a surface [40], or they can operate directly on voxel intensity values without any additional constraints introduced by the user or segmentation [23]. For voxel-based methods, there are two typical strategies. One is to transform each image using self-similarity measurements that are invariant across modalities. These include local

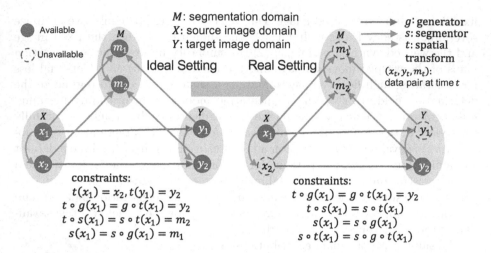

Fig. 1. The relationship between the synthesis, segmentation and registration tasks. In the ideal setting, spatially transformed examples from each domain, and their segmentation labels, are fully available. In more realistic settings, only one example is available from each domain, each under a different spatial transform. Moreover, segmentation labels are not available. Should segmentation, synthesis, and spatial transform *mappings* be available, the constraints in the ideal case can be mapped to analogous constraints in the real case.

self-similarities [29] or the modality independent neighbourhood descriptor [8]. Notably the DEEDS algorithm [7,9,10] employed a discrete dense displacement sampling for deformable registration using self-similarity context (SSC) [11]. The other common strategy is to map both modalities into a shared space and measure the mono-modal difference. Prominent examples include mutual information [21] and normalized mutual information [31] similarity measures that can be applied directly on cross-modal images. However, such methods can suffer from low convergence rates and loss of spatial information. [4] employed a convolutional neural network (CNN) to learn modality invariant features using a small amount of supervision data. [5] used Haar-like features from paired multimodality images to fit a random forest regression model for bi-directional image synthesis, and [22,33] applied CycleGANs to reduce the gap between modalities for better alignment. Recently [1] developed a joint synthesis and registration framework on natural 2D images.

Recently a variety of deep learning-based registration methods have been proposed. Because ground truth deformation fields are hard to obtain, unsupervised methods, like [3,20,34,35], are popular. These all rely on a CNN with a spatial transformation function [16]. These unsupervised methods mainly focus on mono-modal image registration. Some methods make use of correspondences between labelled anatomical structures to help the registration process [12]. [3] also showed how the segmentation map can help registration. However, in many cases the segmentation map is not available, which motivates us to combine the registration and segmentation components together.

Multi-task Learning Methods. As the registration, synthesis, segmentation tasks are all related with each other, there are already several works that explore combining them together. [22,33,36] used CycleGANs to synthesize multi-modal images into one modality, allowing the application of mono-modal registration methods. [17] projected multi-modal images into a shared feature space and registered based on the features. [27] made use of a generative model to disentangle the appearance space from the shape space. [19,26,39] combined a segmentation model with a registration model to let them benefit each other, but the focus was on mono-modal registration. [43] performed supervised multi-phase segmentation based on paired multi-phase images but did not jointly train the registration and segmentation. [14,41,42] used a generative model to help guide the segmentation model. In contrast, our work combines *all three* of the tasks together to tackle multi-modal registration problem in the most general setting where the deformation ground truth, paired multi-modal images and segmentation maps are *all unavailable*.

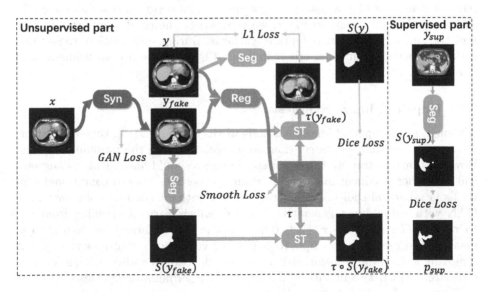

Fig. 2. The JSSR system. We denote the generator, segmentation, registration module and spatial transform as Syn, Seg, Reg and ST respectively.

3   Methodology

Given a moving image $x \in \mathcal{X}$ and fixed image $y \in \mathcal{Y}$ from different modalities, *but from the same patient*, we aim to find a spatial transformation function

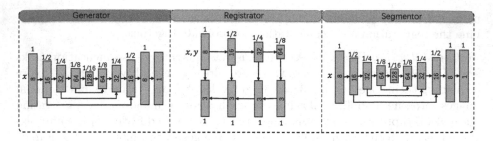

Fig. 3. The model structure for each component. We use a 3D PHNN [6] for registration and 3D VNet [25] for segmentation and the generator.

τ that corrects for any misalignments between the two. We tackle this multi-modal image registration problem in a fully unsupervised way to meet common applications settings, where none of the ground truth deformation fields, segmentation maps, or paired multi-modal images are available. As Fig. 1 depicts, image synthesis, segmentation and registration can be related together via a set of constraints. Motivated by this, we develop a system consisting of three parts: a generator G, a registration module Φ and a segmentation module S. By satisfying the constraints in Fig. 1, we can satisfy the conditions for a correct registration, segmentation and image synthesis. During optimization, these three tasks will benefit from each other. Refer to Fig. 2 for the overall framework of our system.

3.1   Unpaired Image Synthesis

Although good unpaired image synthesis works exist, e.g., [13], they may generate a variety of different target domain images based on the random sampling. However, for registration, the synthesized images should have identical anatomical and other pertinent modality-invariant properties. Thus, a conditional synthesis is a natural choice. Similar to [15], but without random noise, we use a GAN with a dual-input generative model G which learns a mapping from x, y to $\tau^{-1}(y)$, $G : \{x, y\} \rightarrow \tau^{-1}(y)$. Here τ is the true deformation from x to y, meaning the generator attempts to generate a version of x that looks like y, but removing any spatial transformation between the two. In reality, τ itself must be estimated, which we will outline in Sect. 3.2. A discriminator D is also equipped to detect the fake images from the generator.

The objective of the conditional GAN is

$$\mathcal{L}_{GAN}(G, D) = E_y \log D(y) - E_{x,y} \log D(G(x, y)). \tag{1}$$

In a classical paired GAN setup, we would use $E_y \log D(\tau^{-1}(y))$, but this is not available, so use unpaired synthesis, based on the assumption that spatial transform τ does not alter the likelihood of any one sample. We also add another appearance-based loss to benefit the GAN objective:

$$\mathcal{L}_{L1}^{syn}(G) = E_{x,y} ||\tau^{-1}(y) - G(x, y)||_1. \tag{2}$$

The final objective for the synthesis part is

$$G^* = \arg\min_G \max_D \mathcal{L}_{L1}^{syn}(G) + \lambda_{syn}\mathcal{L}_{GAN}(G, D). \tag{3}$$

3.2 Multi-modal Image Registration

For two images x and y, the registration module learns a function $\Phi : x, y \to \tau$ where τ is a spatial transformation function [16], also called the deformation field. For mono-modal registration, the L_1 loss can be used to estimate a deformation field that directly matches the intensities between the fixed image and warped image. Here we are registering two images from different modalities. [3] proposed to use a cross-modal similarity measure like cross-correlation [2]. Instead, if we assume a generative model is available to transform x into the $\mathcal{Y}$ domain, then we can use a simple mono-modal similarity measure:

$$\mathcal{L}_{L1}^{reg}(\Phi) = E_{x,y}||\tau(G(x, y)) - y||_1, \tag{4}$$

where $\tau = \Phi(G(x, y), y)$, and G is the generator that synthesizes images from $\mathcal{X}$ to $\mathcal{Y}$. Another smoothness term is added to prevent non-realistic deformation:

$$\mathcal{L}_{smooth}(\Phi) = E_{x,y} \sum_{v \in \Omega} ||\nabla\tau_v||^2, \tag{5}$$

where v represents the voxel location and $\nabla\tau_v$ calculates the differences between neighboring voxels of v. We use the same implementation for the smoothness term as in [3]. The final objective is:

$$\Phi^* = \arg\min_\Phi \mathcal{L}_{L1}^{reg}(\Phi) + \lambda_{reg}\mathcal{L}_{smooth}(\Phi). \tag{6}$$

Of course, we cannot optimize this objective without a G. However, to get a good G, we need a good Φ as discussed in Sect. 3.1, which makes this problem a chicken-and-egg conundrum. One way is to optimize the two objectives from the synthesis and registration modules together, which leads to

$$\begin{aligned}
\Phi^*, G^* &= \arg\min_{\Phi, G} \mathbb{F}(\Phi, G) \\
&= \arg\min_{\Phi, G} \max_D \mathcal{L}_{L1}^{reg}(\Phi, G) + \mathcal{L}_{L1}^{syn}(\Phi, G) \\
&\quad + \lambda_{reg}\mathcal{L}_{smooth}(\Phi, G) + \lambda_{syn}\mathcal{L}_{GAN}(G, D) \\
&\approx \arg\min_{\Phi, G} \max_D 2\mathcal{L}_{L1}^{reg}(\Phi, G) \\
&\quad + \lambda_{reg}\mathcal{L}_{smooth}(\Phi, G) + \lambda_{syn}\mathcal{L}_{GAN}(G, D).
\end{aligned} \tag{7}$$

However, there is no guarantee that we can get the optimal solution by minimizing $\mathbb{F}(\Phi, G)$. Actually there is a trivial solution that minimizes $\mathbb{F}(\Phi, G)$, which is when $G(x, y) = y$ and $\Phi(G(x, y), y) = \Phi(y, y) = I$, i.e., the identity transform. To mitigate this, we add skip connections from the source domain to keep the spatial information in the structure of generator, as shown in Fig. 3.

3.3 Multi-modal Image Segmentation

We enforce segmentation-based constraints for two reasons. Firstly, as noted in [3], the additional information of segmentation maps can help guide the registration process. However, [3] assumes the segmentation maps are available for the target dataset, which we do not assume. Secondly, as noted by others [19,26,39,41,42], synthesis and registration can benefit segmentation, which can help develop better segmentation models on datasets without annotation.

We denote the segmentation model as a function $S : x \to p$, where $p \in \mathcal{P}$ represents the segmentation map domain. Based on the constraint between synthesis, registration and segmentation tasks, we define the objective as:

$$\mathcal{L}_{dice}^{reg}(S, \Phi, G) = E_{x,y} 1 - Dice[\tau(S(G(x,y))), S(y)], \tag{8}$$

where $\tau = \Phi(G(x,y), y)$ and $Dice(x,y) = \frac{2x^T y}{x^T x + y^T y}$ is the widely used measurement for the similarity between two binary volumes. This loss term connects three components together and in the experiments afterwards we show this crucial toward the whole system's performance.

To make (8) work properly, we need the segmentation to be as accurate as possible. However only with the consistency loss, the segmentation module is not able to learn meaningful semantic information. For instance, a segmentation module that predicts all background can trivially minimize (8). To avoid this, we use fully supervised data, e.g., from public sources, to regularize the segmentation. Importantly, because (8) is only applied on the $\mathcal{Y}$ domain, we need only use supervised data from one modality, e.g., if we are registering dynamic contrast CT data, we need only fully-supervised segmentation maps from the more ubiquitous venous-phase CTs found in public data. Thus, the supervision loss is defined as

$$\mathcal{L}_{dice}^{sup}(S) = E_{y_{sup}} 1 - Dice[S(y_{sup}), p_{sup})], \tag{9}$$

where $y_{sup} \in \mathcal{Y}$ is in the same modality with $y \in \mathcal{Y}$, but the two datasets do not overlap. $p_{sup} \in \mathcal{P}_{sup}$ is the corresponding annotation. The total loss provided by the segmentation module is

$$\mathbb{H}(S, \Phi, G) = \mathcal{L}_{dice}^{reg}(S, \Phi, G) + \mathcal{L}_{dice}^{sup}(S). \tag{10}$$

3.4 Joint Optimization Strategy

Based on previous sections, the final objective for our whole system is

$$\Phi^*, G^*, S^* = \arg \min_{\Phi, G, S} \mathbb{F}(\Phi, G) + \lambda_{seg} \mathbb{H}(S, \Phi, G). \tag{11}$$

In order to provide all the components with a good initial point, we first train S on the fully-supervised data, $\{y_{sup}, p_{sup}\}$ and also train Φ and G using (7) on the unsupervised data. Finally, we jointly optimize all modules by (11). When optimizing (7) and (11), we use the classic alternating strategy for training GAN models, which alternately fixes Φ, G, S and optimizes for D and then fixes D and optimizes for the others.

4 Experiments

Datasets. We conduct our main experiments on a large-scale dataset of 3D dynamic contrast multi-phase liver CT scans, extracted from the archives of the Chang Gung Memorial Hospital (CGMH) in Taiwan. The dataset is composed of 1485 patient studies and each studies consists of CT volumes of four different intravenous contrast phases: venous, arterial, delay, and non-contrast. The studied population is composed of patients with liver tumors who underwent CT imaging examinations prior to an interventional biopsy, liver resection, or liver transplant. Our end goal is to develop a computer-aided diagnosis system to identify the pathological subtype of any given liver tumor. Whether the analysis is conducted by human readers or computers, all phases need to be precisely pre-registered to facilitate downstream analysis, which will observe the dynamic contrast changes within liver tumor tissues across the sequential order of non-contrast, arterial, venous and delay CTs.

The different phases are obtained from the CT scanner at different time points after the contrast media injection and will display different information according to the distribution of contrast media in the human body. The intensity value of each voxel in the CT image, measured by the Hounsfield Unit (HU), is an integer ranging from $-1000HU$ to $1000HU$, which will also be affected by the density of contrast media. The volume size of the CT image is $512 \times 512 \times L$, where L can vary based on how the image was acquired. The z-resolution is 5 mm in our dataset. Since the venous phase is one of the most informative for diagnosis, and is also ubiquitous in public data, we choose it as the anchor phase and register images from other three phases to it. Consequently, we also synthesize the other three phases images to the venous phase. We divide the dataset into 1350/45/90 patients for training, validation and testing, respectively, and we manually annotate the liver masks on the validation and testing sets for evaluation. *Note that there are in total* $1485 \times 4 = 5940$ *3D CT scans (all containing pathological livers) used in our work. To the best of our knowledge, this is the largest clinically realistic study of this kind to-date.* For the supervised part, we choose a public dataset, i.e., **MSD** [30], that contains 131 CT images of venous phase with voxel-wise annotations of the liver and divide it into 100/31 for training and validation. We evaluate the performance of all three registration, synthesis and segmentation tasks to measure the impact of joint training.

4.1 Baseline

We compare with several strong baselines for all three tasks:

- For image synthesis, we choose **Pix2Pix** [15]. We approximately treat the multi-phase CT scans from the same patient as paired data, so that we can better compare to see how incorporating registration can benefit the synthesis module when there is no paired data.

- For image registration, we first compare with **Deeds** [9], one of the best registration methods to date for abdominal CT [38]. The advantage of learning-based methods compared with conventional ones is often on the speed of inference, but we can also show performance improvement. We also compare with the learning-based **VoxelMorph** [3] with local cross-correlation to handle multi-modal image registration.
- For the segmentation task, we compare with **VNet** [25], which is a popular framework in medical image segmentation.

Table 1. Evaluation for the registration task on the CGMH liver dataset in terms of Dice score, HD (mm), ASD (mm), and GPU/CPU running time (s). Standard deviations are in parentheses.

	Dice ↑			HD95 ↓		
	Arterial	Delay	Non-contrast	Arterial	Delay	Non-contrast
Initial state	90.94 (7.52)	90.52 (8.08)	90.08 (6.74)	7.54 (4.89)	7.86 (5.83)	7.87 (4.37)
Affine [24]	92.01 (6.57)	91.69 (6.80)	91.52 (5.48)	6.81 (4.83)	6.95 (5.32)	6.73 (3.63)
Deeds [9]	94.73 (2.10)	94.70 (1.91)	94.73 (1.90)	4.74 (1.96)	4.76 (1.69)	4.62 (1.05)
VoxelMorph [3]	94.28 (2.53)	94.23 (3.15)	93.93 (2.58)	5.29 (2.33)	5.42 (3.25)	5.40 (2.48)
JSynR-Reg	94.81 (2.35)	94.71 (2.62)	94.57 (2.52)	4.93 (2.14)	5.07 (3.06)	4.87 (2.30)
JSegR-Reg	95.52 (1.76)	95.39 (2.14)	95.37 (1.80)	4.47 (2.21)	4.70 (3.24)	4.45 (1.85)
JSSR-Reg	**95.56**(1.70)	**95.42**(2.00)	**95.41**(1.72)	**4.44** (2.19)	**4.65** (3.14)	**4.35** (1.60)
	ASD ↓			Time ↓		
	Arterial	Delay	Non-contrast	Arterial	Delay	Non-contrast
Initial state	2.12 (1.86)	2.27 (2.19)	2.37 (1.77)	–/–	–/–	–/–
Affine [24]	1.74 (1.58)	1.86 (1.89)	1.87 (1.41)	–/7.77	–/7.77	–/7.77
Deeds [9]	1.01 (0.44)	1.01 (0.39)	0.99 (0.36)	–/41.51	–/41.51	–/41.51
VoxelMorph [3]	1.10 (0.53)	1.12 (0.87)	1.20 (0.67)	1.71/1.76	1.71/1.76	1.71/1.76
JSynR-Reg	0.95 (0.45)	0.98 (0.72)	0.98 (0.56)	3.14/1.76	3.14/1.76	3.14/1.76
JSegR-Reg	0.80 (0.37)	0.83 (0.59)	0.83 (0.40)	3.14/1.76	3.14/1.76	3.14/1.76
JSSR-Reg	**0.79** (0.36)	**0.83** (0.56)	**0.82** (0.37)	1.71/1.76	1.71/1.76	1.71/1.76

4.2 Implementation Details

We conduct several preprocessing procedures. First, since the CT images from different phases, even for the same patient, have different volume sizes, we crop the maximum intersection of all four phases based on the physical coordinates to make their size the same. Second, we apply rigid registration using [24] between the four phases, using the venous phase as the anchor. Third, we window the intensity values to $-200HU$ to $200HU$ and normalize to -1 to 1, and then we resize the CT volume to $256 \times 256 \times L$ to fit into GPU memory. For the public dataset, we sample along the axial axis to make the resolution also $5\,mm$, and then apply the same intensity preprocessing.

The structure of each component is shown in Fig. 3. We choose 3D V-Net [25] for the generator and segmentation module and 3D PHNN [6] for the registration. To optimize the objectives, we use the Adam solver [18] for all the modules, setting the hyper parameters to $\lambda_{seg} = \lambda_{reg} = 1$, $\lambda_{syn} = 0.02$. We choose different learning rates for different modules in order to better balance the training:. 0.0001, 0.001, 0.1, and 0.1 for the generator, registration module, segmentation module, and discriminator, respectively. Another way to balance the training is to adjust the loss term weights. However, there are loss terms that relate with multiple modules, which makes it more complex to control each component separately. We train on the Nvidia Quadro RTX 6000 GPU with 24 GB memory, with instance normalization and batch size 1. The training process takes about 1.4 GPU days.

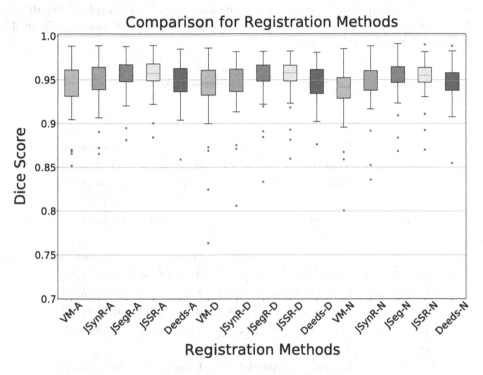

Fig. 4. Box-plots for the registration results (DSC). Suffixes indicate the moving phases (A, D, N for arterial, delay, non-contrast). VM stands for VoxelMorph.

4.3   Main Results

Multi-modal Image Registration. We summarize the results of registration task in Table 1. We use the manual annotations of the test set and evaluate the similarity between those of fixed image, which is always in the venous phase here, and the warped labels of the moving images chosen from arterial, delay and non-contrast. The similarity is measured using the Dice score, 95% hausdorff distance (HD), and the average surface distance (ASD). We also report the consumed time on GPU/CPU in sec for each method. We use the term "Initial State" to refer to the result before applying any registration and "Affine" to the result after rigid registration. We denote our joint system as JSSR and JSSR-Reg is only the registration part of JSSR. We also compare two ablations of JSSR. JSynR, which only contains the generator and registration module, is optimized using (7). JSegR has the segmentation and registration module instead. More details will be discussed in Sect. 5. As can be seen, our JSSR method outperforms Deeds by 0.83% by average Dice, while executing much faster in terms of inference. Also by taking advantage of the joint training, JSSR achieves significantly higher results than VoxelMorph (exceeded by 1.28%) with comparable inference time. We can observe gradual improvements from VoxelMorph to JSynR to JSSR, which demonstrates the successive contributions of joint training. Figure 4 depicts a box plot of these results.

Table 2. Evaluation for the synthesis and segmentation tasks on the CGMH liver dataset in terms of average Dice score

Dice ↑	VNet [25]			
	Venous	Arterial	Delay	Non-contrast
No-synthesis	90.47 (6.23)	89.47 (7.05)	89.88 (6.38)	89.38 (6.38)
Pix2Pix [15]	90.47 (6.23)	76.50 (17.77)	79.60 (13.13)	67.48 (15.97)
JSynR-Syn	90.47 (6.23)	89.69 (7.09)	90.01 (6.27)	90.15 (6.21)
JSSR-Syn	90.47 (6.23)	89.44 (7.15)	89.76 (6.34)	89.31 (7.57)
Dice ↑	JSegR-Seg			
	Venous	Arterial	Delay	Non-contrast
No-synthesis	91.88 (4.84)	90.91 (5.06)	91.18 (4.68)	91.12 (4.72)
Pix2Pix [15]	91.88 (4.84)	89.59 (5.51)	87.78 (5.78)	89.59 (5.51)
JSynR-Syn	91.88 (4.84)	91.15 (4.93)	91.37 (4.56)	91.36 (4.54)
JSSR-Syn	91.88 (4.84)	91.12 (4.99)	91.30 (4.63)	91.39 (4.53)
Dice ↑	JSSR-Seg			
	Venous	Arterial	Delay	Non-contrast
No-synthesis	92.24 (3.88)	91.25 (4.10)	91.34 (3.76)	91.37 (3.81)
Pix2Pix [15]	92.24 (3.88)	85.30 (7.11)	84.68 (9.29)	79.89 (8.49)
JSynR-Syn	92.24 (3.88)	91.42 (4.06)	91.58 (3.64)	91.67 (3.67)
JSSR-Syn	92.24 (3.88)	91.39 (4.10)	91.51 (3.72)	91.60 (3.69)

Multi-modal Image Segmentation and Synthesis. Table 2 presents the synthesis and segmentation evaluations. Following the practice of [15], we evaluate the synthesis model by applying the segmentation model on the synthesized image. The intuition is that the better the synthesized image is, the better the segmentation map can be estimated. We evaluate with three segmentation models. The VNet baseline is trained on the MSD dataset with full supervision. JSegR-Seg is the segmentation part of JSegR as described in Sect. 5. JSSR-Seg is the segmentation module of our JSSR system. For each segmentation model, we test it on different synthesis model, thus comparing all possible synthesis/segmentation combinations. For "No-Synthesis", we directly apply the segmentation model on original images. For the three synthesis models, we test the segmentation model on the original venous image and also on the "fake" venous images synthesized from arterial, delay, non-contrast phases. From the No-Synthesis lines we can observe a clear performance drop when directly applying the segmentation model to arterial, delay and non-contrast phases, since the supervised data is all from the venous phase. For Pix2Pix, the performance goes through different levels of reduction among different segmentation algorithms and is not as high as the Non-Synthesis. That may be caused by artifacts introduced by the GAN model and the L1 term is providing less constraint since there is no paired data. Comparing the JSynR-Syn and JSSR-Syn generators, the performance is improved by creating true paired data via the registration process, but even so, it is just comparable to No-Synthesis. For JSynR-Syn, the JSynR is not jointly learned with a segmentation process, so the performance for synthesized images does not necessarily go up. For JSSR-Syn, however, it means the constraints we are using for optimizing the system does not bring enough communication between the generator and segmentor to improve the former. Even so, we can improvements from VNet to JSegR-Seg to JSSR-Seg on both the No-Synthesis and various synthesis options, indicating that the segmentation process can still benefit from a joint system, which includes the synthesis module. Please refer to Fig. 5 for qualitative examples of JSSR registration, synthesis and segmentation results.

5   Ablation and Discussion

JSegR Vs JSSR. We implement JSegR as another ablation. The purpose is to explore the importance of the synthesis module for the JSSR system. Since JSegR does not have a generator, the registration module takes images from different phases directly as input. The segmentation consistency term in (8) is then replaced with

$$\mathcal{L}_{dice}^{reg}(S, \Phi) = E_{x,y} 1 - Dice[\tau(S(x)), S(y)], \qquad (12)$$

where $\tau = \Phi(x, y)$. This framework is similar to [39], which jointly learned the registration and the segmentation module. In our case, though, x, y are in a different domain and the annotations are unavailable. This method is expected to struggle, since x, y are in different phases. However, as shown in Table 2, the

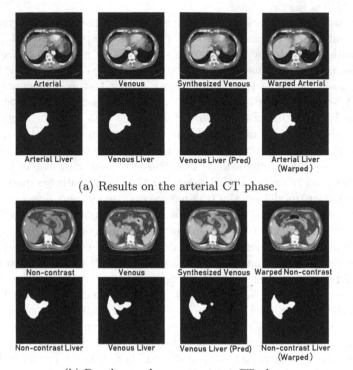

(a) Results on the arterial CT phase.

(b) Results on the non-contrast CT phase.

Fig. 5. Qualitative examples of JSSR synthesis, segmentation and registration.

performance drop across phases is not too severe even for the baseline VNet. Correspondingly, JSegR can achieve a higher result on registration than JSynR and performs close to JSSR, which demonstrates the great importance of incorporating semantic information into the registration.

Extra Constraints. The constraints detailed in Fig. 1 are not the only possible constraints. For instance, constraints can be added to ensure consistency between "register first" vs "register last" pipelines:

$$\mathcal{L}_{L1}^{reg}(\Phi, G) = E_{x,y}||G(\tau(x), y) - \tau(G(x, y))||_1. \tag{13}$$

However, each constraint introduces additional complexity. Future work should explore whether (13), or other constraints, can boost performance further.

6   Conclusion

In this paper, we propose a novel JSSR system for multi-modal image registration. Our system takes advantages of joint learning based on the intrinsic connections between the synthesis, segmentation and registration tasks. The optimization can be conducted end-to-end with several unsupervised consistency loss and each component benefits from the joint training process. We evaluate the JSSR system on a large-scale multi-phase clinically realistic CT image dataset without any segmentation annotations. After joint training, the performance of registration and segmentation increases by 0.91% and 1.86% respectively on the average Dice score for all the phases. Our system outperforms the recent Voxel-Morph algorithm [3] by 1.28%, and the state-of-the-art conventional multi-modal registration method [9] by 0.83%, but has considerably faster inference time.

Acknowledgements. This work was partially supported by the Lustgarten Foundation for Pancreatic Cancer Research. The main work was done when F. Liu was a research Intern at PAII Inc. We thank Zhuotun Zhu and Yingda Xia for instructive discussions.

References

1. Arar, M., Ginger, Y., Danon, D., Bermano, A.H., Cohen-Or, D.: Unsupervised multi-modal image registration via geometry preserving image-to-image translation. In: Proceedings of the IEEE/CVF Conference on Computer Vision and Pattern Recognition, pp. 13410–13419 (2020)
2. Avants, B.B., Epstein, C.L., Grossman, M., Gee, J.C.: Symmetric diffeomorphic image registration with cross-correlation: evaluating automated labeling of elderly and neurodegenerative brain. Med. Image Anal. **12**(1), 26–41 (2008)
3. Balakrishnan, G., Zhao, A., Sabuncu, M.R., Guttag, J., Dalca, A.V.: VoxelMorph: a learning framework for deformable medical image registration. IEEE Trans. Med. Imaging **38**(8), 1788–1800 (2019)
4. Blendowski, M., Heinrich, M.P.: Learning interpretable multi-modal features for alignment with supervised iterative descent. In: International Conference on Medical Imaging with Deep Learning, pp. 73–83 (2019)
5. Cao, X., Yang, J., Gao, Y., Guo, Y., Wu, G., Shen, D.: Dual-core steered non-rigid registration for multi-modal images via bi-directional image synthesis. Med. Image Anal. **41**, 18–31 (2017)
6. Harrison, A.P., Xu, Z., George, K., Lu, L., Summers, R.M., Mollura, D.J.: Progressive and multi-path holistically nested neural networks for pathological lung segmentation from CT images. In: Descoteaux, M., Maier-Hein, L., Franz, A., Jannin, P., Collins, D.L., Duchesne, S. (eds.) MICCAI 2017. LNCS, vol. 10435, pp. 621–629. Springer, Cham (2017). https://doi.org/10.1007/978-3-319-66179-7_71
7. Heinrich, M., Maier, O., Handels, H.: Multi-modal multi-atlas segmentation using discrete optimisation and self-similarities. CEUR Workshop Proceedings (2015)

8. Heinrich, M.P., et al.: MIND: modality independent neighbourhood descriptor for multi-modal deformable registration. Med. Image Anal. **16**(7), 1423–1435 (2012)
9. Heinrich, M.P., Jenkinson, M., Brady, S.M., Schnabel, J.A.: Globally optimal deformable registration on a minimum spanning tree using dense displacement sampling. In: Ayache, N., Delingette, H., Golland, P., Mori, K. (eds.) MICCAI 2012. LNCS, vol. 7512, pp. 115–122. Springer, Heidelberg (2012). https://doi.org/10.1007/978-3-642-33454-2_15
10. Heinrich, M.P., Jenkinson, M., Brady, M., Schnabel, J.A.: MRF-based deformable registration and ventilation estimation of lung CT. IEEE Trans. Med. Imaging **32**(7), 1239–1248 (2013)
11. Heinrich, M.P., Jenkinson, M., Papież, B.W., Brady, S.M., Schnabel, J.A.: Towards realtime multimodal fusion for image-guided interventions using self-similarities. In: Mori, K., Sakuma, I., Sato, Y., Barillot, C., Navab, N. (eds.) MICCAI 2013. LNCS, vol. 8149, pp. 187–194. Springer, Heidelberg (2013). https://doi.org/10.1007/978-3-642-40811-3_24
12. Hu, Y., et al.: Weakly-supervised convolutional neural networks for multimodal image registration. Med. Image Anal. **49**, 1–13 (2018)
13. Huang, X., Liu, M.Y., Belongie, S., Kautz, J.: Multimodal unsupervised image-to-image translation. In: Proceedings of the European Conference on Computer Vision (ECCV), pp. 172–189 (2018)
14. Huo, Y., et al.: SynSeg-Net: synthetic segmentation without target modality ground truth. IEEE Trans. Med. Imaging **38**(4), 1016–1025 (2018)
15. Isola, P., Zhu, J.Y., Zhou, T., Efros, A.A.: Image-to-image translation with conditional adversarial networks. In: Proceedings of the IEEE Conference on Computer Vision and Pattern Recognition, pp. 1125–1134 (2017)
16. Jaderberg, M., Simonyan, K., Zisserman, A., et al.: Spatial transformer networks. In: Advances in Neural Information Processing Systems, pp. 2017–2025 (2015)
17. Ketcha, M.D., et al.: Learning-based deformable image registration: effect of statistical mismatch between train and test images. J. Med. Imaging **6**(4), 044008 (2019)
18. Kingma, D.P., Ba, J.: Adam: a method for stochastic optimization. In: 3rd International Conference on Learning Representations, ICLR 2015, San Diego, CA, USA, 7–9 May 2015, Conference Track Proceedings (2015)
19. Li, B., et al.: A hybrid deep learning framework for integrated segmentation and registration: evaluation on longitudinal white matter tract changes. In: Shen, D., et al. (eds.) MICCAI 2019. LNCS, vol. 11766, pp. 645–653. Springer, Cham (2019). https://doi.org/10.1007/978-3-030-32248-9_72
20. Li, H., Fan, Y.: Non-rigid image registration using fully convolutional networks with deep self-supervision. arXiv preprint arXiv:1709.00799 (2017)
21. Maes, F., Collignon, A., Vandermeulen, D., Marchal, G., Suetens, P.: Multimodality image registration by maximization of mutual information. IEEE Trans. Med. Imaging **16**(2), 187–198 (1997)
22. Mahapatra, D., Antony, B., Sedai, S., Garnavi, R.: Deformable medical image registration using generative adversarial networks. In: 2018 IEEE 15th International Symposium on Biomedical Imaging (ISBI 2018), pp. 1449–1453. IEEE (2018)
23. Maintz, J.A., Viergever, M.A.: An overview of medical image registration methods. In: Symposium of the Belgian Hospital Physicists Association (SBPH/BVZF), vol. 12, pp. 1–22. Citeseer (1996)
24. Marstal, K., Berendsen, F., Staring, M., Klein, S.: SimpleElastix: a user-friendly, multi-lingual library for medical image registration. In: Proceedings of the IEEE Conference on Computer Vision and Pattern Recognition Workshops (2016)

25. Milletari, F., Navab, N., Ahmadi, S.A.: V-Net: fully convolutional neural networks for volumetric medical image segmentation. In: 2016 Fourth International Conference on 3D Vision (3DV), pp. 565–571. IEEE (2016)
26. Qin, C., et al.: Joint learning of motion estimation and segmentation for cardiac MR image sequences. In: Frangi, A.F., Schnabel, J.A., Davatzikos, C., Alberola-López, C., Fichtinger, G. (eds.) MICCAI 2018. LNCS, vol. 11071, pp. 472–480. Springer, Cham (2018). https://doi.org/10.1007/978-3-030-00934-2_53
27. Qin, C., Shi, B., Liao, R., Mansi, T., Rueckert, D., Kamen, A.: Unsupervised deformable registration for multi-modal images via disentangled representations. In: Chung, A.C.S., Gee, J.C., Yushkevich, P.A., Bao, S. (eds.) IPMI 2019. LNCS, vol. 11492, pp. 249–261. Springer, Cham (2019). https://doi.org/10.1007/978-3-030-20351-1_19
28. Rohr, K., Stiehl, H.S., Sprengel, R., Buzug, T.M., Weese, J., Kuhn, M.H.: Landmark-based elastic registration using approximating thin-plate splines. IEEE Trans. Med. Imaging 20(6), 526–534 (2001)
29. Shechtman, E., Irani, M.: Matching local self-similarities across images and videos. In: 2007 IEEE Conference on Computer Vision and Pattern Recognition (2007)
30. Simpson, A.L., et al.: A large annotated medical image dataset for the development and evaluation of segmentation algorithms. arXiv preprint arXiv:1902.09063 (2019)
31. Studholme, C., Hill, D.L., Hawkes, D.J.: An overlap invariant entropy measure of 3D medical image alignment. Pattern Recogn. 32(1), 71–86 (1999)
32. Sultana, S., Song, D.Y., Lee, J.: A deformable multimodal image registration using PET/CT and TRUS for intraoperative focal prostate brachytherapy. In: Fei, B., Linte, C.A. (eds.) Medical Imaging 2019: Image-Guided Procedures, Robotic Interventions, and Modeling, vol. 10951, pp. 383–388. International Society for Optics and Photonics, SPIE (2019). https://doi.org/10.1117/12.2512996
33. Tanner, C., Ozdemir, F., Profanter, R., Vishnevsky, V., Konukoglu, E., Goksel, O.: Generative adversarial networks for MR-CT deformable image registration. arXiv preprint arXiv:1807.07349 (2018)
34. de Vos, B.D., Berendsen, F.F., Viergever, M.A., Sokooti, H., Staring, M., Išgum, I.: A deep learning framework for unsupervised affine and deformable image registration. Med. Image Anal. 52, 128–143 (2019)
35. de Vos, B.D., Berendsen, F.F., Viergever, M.A., Staring, M., Išgum, I.: End-to-end unsupervised deformable image registration with a convolutional neural network. In: Cardoso, M.J., et al. (eds.) DLMIA/ML-CDS -2017. LNCS, vol. 10553, pp. 204–212. Springer, Cham (2017). https://doi.org/10.1007/978-3-319-67558-9_24
36. Wei, D., et al.: Synthesis and inpainting-based MR-CT registration for image-guided thermal ablation of liver tumors. In: Shen, D., et al. (eds.) MICCAI 2019. LNCS, vol. 11768, pp. 512–520. Springer, Cham (2019). https://doi.org/10.1007/978-3-030-32254-0_57
37. Woods, R.P.: Handbook of Medical Image Processing and Analysis (2009)
38. Xu, Z., et al.: Evaluation of six registration methods for the human abdomen on clinically acquired CT. IEEE Trans. Biomed. Eng. 63(8), 1563–1572 (2016)
39. Xu, Z., Niethammer, M.: DeepAtlas: joint semi-supervised learning of image registration and segmentation. In: Shen, D., et al. (eds.) MICCAI 2019. LNCS, vol. 11765, pp. 420–429. Springer, Cham (2019). https://doi.org/10.1007/978-3-030-32245-8_47
40. Yang, X., Akbari, H., Halig, L., Fei, B.: 3D non-rigid registration using surface and local salient features for transrectal ultrasound image-guided prostate biopsy. Proc. SPIE Int. Soc. Opt. Eng. 7964, 79642V–79642V (2011). https://doi.org/10.1117/12.878153

41. Zhang, Z., Yang, L., Zheng, Y.: Translating and segmenting multimodal medical volumes with cycle-and shape-consistency generative adversarial network. In: Proceedings of the IEEE Conference on Computer Vision and Pattern Recognition (2018)
42. Zheng, H., et al.: Phase collaborative network for multi-phase medical imaging segmentation. ArXiv abs/1811.11814 (2018)
43. Zhou, Y., et al.: Hyper-pairing network for multi-phase pancreatic ductal adenocarcinoma segmentation. In: Shen, D., et al. (eds.) MICCAI 2019. LNCS, vol. 11765, pp. 155–163. Springer, Cham (2019). https://doi.org/10.1007/978-3-030-32245-8_18

SimAug: Learning Robust Representations from Simulation for Trajectory Prediction

Junwei Liang[1]([⊠])(iD), Lu Jiang[2], and Alexander Hauptmann[1]

[1] Carnegie Mellon University, Pittsburgh, USA
{junweil,alex}@cs.cmu.edu
[2] Google Research, Mountain View, USA
lujiang@google.com

Abstract. This paper studies the problem of predicting future trajectories of people in unseen cameras of novel scenarios and views. We approach this problem through the real-data-free setting in which the model is trained only on 3D simulation data and applied out-of-the-box to a wide variety of real cameras. We propose a novel approach to learn robust representation through augmenting the simulation training data such that the representation can better generalize to unseen real-world test data. The key idea is to mix the feature of the hardest camera view with the adversarial feature of the original view. We refer to our method as *SimAug*. We show that *SimAug* achieves promising results on three real-world benchmarks using zero real training data, and state-of-the-art performance in the Stanford Drone and the VIRAT/ActEV dataset when using in-domain training data. Code and models are released at https://next.cs.cmu.edu/simaug.

Keywords: Trajectory prediction · 3D simulation · Robust learning · Data augmentation · Representation learning · Adversarial learning

1 Introduction

Future trajectory prediction [1,19,27,31,37,38,56] is a fundamental problem in video analytics, which aims at forecasting a pedestrian's future path in the video in the next few seconds. Recent advancements in future trajectory prediction have been successful in a variety of vision applications such as self-driving vehicles [4,7,8], safety monitoring [38], robotic planning [50,51], among others.

A notable bottleneck for existing works is that the current model is closely coupled with the video cameras on which it is trained, and generalizes poorly on new cameras with novel views or scenes. For example, prior works have proposed various models to forecast a pedestrian's trajectories in video cameras of different types such as stationary outdoor cameras [1,19,32,35,40,47], drone cameras [13,33,56], ground-level egocentric cameras [50,61,73], or dash cameras [8,45,60]. However, existing models are all separately trained and tested within one or two

© Springer Nature Switzerland AG 2020
A. Vedaldi et al. (Eds.): ECCV 2020, LNCS 12358, pp. 275–292, 2020.
https://doi.org/10.1007/978-3-030-58601-0_17

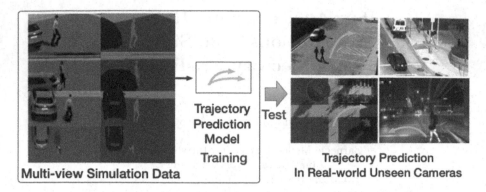

Fig. 1. Illustration of pedestrian trajectory prediction in unseen cameras. We propose to learn robust representations only from 3D simulation data that could generalize to real-world videos captured by unseen cameras.

datasets, and there have been no attempts at successfully generalizing the model across datasets of novel camera views. This bottleneck significantly hinders the application whenever there is a new camera because it requires annotating new data to fine-tune the model, resulting in a procedure that is not only expensive but also tardy in deploying the model.

An ideal model should be able to disentangle human behavioral dynamics from specific camera views, positions, and scenes. It should produce robust trajectory prediction despite the variances in these camera settings. Motivated by this idea, in this work, we learn a robust representation for future trajectory prediction that can generalize to unseen video cameras. Different from existing works, we study a *real-data-free* setting where a model is trained only on synthetic data but tested, out of the box, on unseen real-world videos, without further re-training or fine-tuning the model. Following the success of learning from simulation [15,52,55,59,67,79], our synthetic data is generalized from a 3D simulator, called CARLA [14], which anchors to the static scene and dynamic elements in the VIRAT/ActEV videos [47]. By virtue of the 3D simulator, we can generate multiple views and pixel-precise semantic segmentation labels for each training trajectory, as illustrated in Fig. 1. Meanwhile, following the previous works [37,56], scene semantic segmentation is used instead of RGB pixels to alleviate the influence of different lighting conditions, scene textures, subtle noises produced by camera sensors, etc. At test time, we extract scene features from real videos using pretrained segmentation models. The use of segmentation features is helpful but is insufficient for learning robust representation for future trajectory prediction.

To tackle this issue, we propose a novel data augmentation method called *SimAug* to augment the features of the simulation data with the goal of learning robust representation to various semantic scenes and camera views in real videos. To be specific, first, after representing each training trajectory by high-level scene semantic segmentation features, we defend our model from adversarial examples generated by white-box attack methods [18]. Second, to overcome the changes in camera views, we generate multiple views for the same trajectory, and encourage the model to focus on overcoming the "hardest" view to which the model has learned. Following [22,24], the classification loss is adopted and the view with the highest loss is favored during training. Finally, the augmented trajectory is computed as a convex combination of the trajectories generated in previous steps. Our trajectory prediction backbone model is built on a recent work called Multiverse [37]. The final model is trained to minimize the empirical vicinal risk over the distribution of augmented trajectories. Our method is partially inspired by recent robust deep learning methods using adversarial training [12,29], Mixup [77], and MentorMix [22].

We empirically validate our model, which is trained only on simulation data, on three real-world benchmarks for future trajectory prediction: VIRAT/ActEV [2,47], Stanford Drone [53], and Argoverse [8]. These benchmarks represent three distinct camera views: 45-degree view, top-down view and dashboard camera view with ego-motions. The results show our method performs favorably against baseline methods including standard data augmentation, adversarial learning, and imitation learning. Notably, our method achieves better results compared to the state-of-the-art on the VIRAT/ActEV and Stanford Drone benchmark. Our code and models are released at https://next.cs.cmu.edu/simaug. To summarize, our contribution is threefold:

- We study a new setting of future trajectory prediction in which the model is trained only on synthetic data and tested, out of the box, on any unseen real video with novel views or scenes.
- We propose a novel and effective approach to augment the representation of trajectory prediction models using multi-view simulation data.
- Ours is the first work on future trajectory prediction to demonstrate the efficacy of training on 3D simulation data, and establishes new state-of-the-art results on three public benchmarks.

2 Related Work

Trajectory Prediction. Recently there is a large body of work on predicting person future trajectories in a variety of scenarios. Many works [1,37,38, 56,72,78] focused on modeling person motions in videos recorded with stationary cameras. Datasets like VIRAT/ActEV [47], ETH/UCY [32,40] and Stanford Drone [53] have been used for evaluating pedestrian trajectory prediction. For example, Social-LSTM [1] added social pooling to model nearby pedestrian trajectory patterns. Social-GAN [19] added an adversarial network [17] on Social-LSTM to generate diverse future trajectories. Several works focused on learning the effects of the physical scene, e.g., people tend to walk on the sidewalk instead of grass. Kitani et al. [27] used Inverse Reinforcement Learning to forecast human trajectory. SoPhie [56] combined deep neural network features from scene semantic segmentation model and generative adversarial network (GAN) using attention to model person trajectory. More recent works [28,38,42,73] have attempted to predict person paths by utilizing individuals' visual features instead of considering them as points in the scene. For example, Liang et al. [37] proposed to use abstract scene semantic segmentation features for better generalization. Meanwhile, many works [4,21,31,33,44,51,57,81] have been proposed for top-down view videos for trajectory prediction. Notably, the Stanford Drone Dataset (SDD) [53] is used in many works [13,33,56] for trajectory prediction with drone videos. Other works have also looked into pedestrian prediction in dashcam videos [28,31,45,60] and first-person videos [61,73]. Many vehicle trajectory datasets [6,8,74] have been proposed as a result of self-driving's surging popularity.

Learning from 3D Simulation Data. As the increasing research focus in 3D computer vision [14,20,34,52,54,58,80], many research works have used 3D simulation for training and evaluating real-world tasks [3,9,15,26,37,59,62,63, 69,83]. Many works [15,48,59] were proposed to use data generated from 3D simulation for video object detection, tracking, and action recognition analysis. For example, Sun et al. [62] proposed a forecasting model by using a gaming simulator. AirSim [58] and CARLA [14] were proposed for robotic autonomous controls for drones and vehicles. Zeng et al. [76] proposed to use 3D simulation for adversarial attacks. RSA [79] used randomized simulation data for human action recognition. The ForkingPaths dataset [37] was proposed for evaluating multi-future trajectory prediction. Human annotators were asked to control agents in a 3D simulator to create a multi-future trajectory dataset.

Robust Deep Learning. Traditional domain adaptation approaches [5,16,25,65] may not be applicable as our target domain is considered "unseen" during training. Methods for learning using privileged information [30,39,41,66] is not applicable for a similar reason. Closest to ours is robust deep learning methods. In particular, our approach is inspired by the following methods: (i) *adversarial training* [18,43,70,76] to defend the adversarial attacks generated on-the-fly during training using gradient-based methods [11,18,43,64]; (ii) data augmentation methods to overcome unknown variances between training and test examples such as Mixup [77], MentorMix [22], AugMix [12], etc.; (iii) example re-weighting or selection [23,24,36,46,49] to mitigate network memorization. Different from prior work, ours uses 3D simulation data as a new perspective for data augmentation and is carefully designed for future trajectory prediction.

3   Approach

In this section, we describe our approach to learn robust representation for future trajectory prediction, which we call *SimAug*. Our goal is to train a model only on simulation training data that can effectively predict the future trajectory in the real-world test videos that are unseen during training.

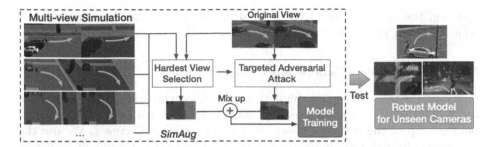

Fig. 2. Overview of our method *SimAug* that is trained on simulation and tested on real unseen videos. Each training trajectory is represented by multi-view segmentation features extracted from the simulator. *SimAug* mixes the feature of the hardest camera view with the adversarial feature of the original view.

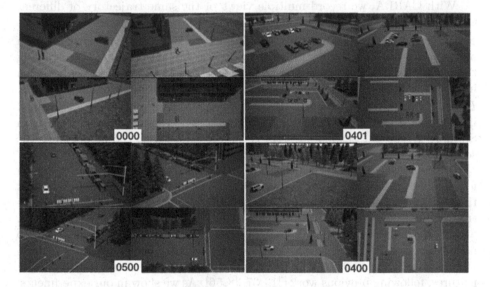

Fig. 3. Visualization of the multi-view 3D simulation data used in *SimAug* training. Data generation process is described in Sect. 3.2. We use 4 camera views from 4 scenes defined in [37]. "0400" and "0401" scene have overlapping views. The top-left views are the original views from VIRAT/ActEV dataset.

3.1   Problem Formulation

We focus on predicting the locations of a single agent for multiple steps into the future. Given a sequence of historical video frames $V_{1:h}$ of the past h steps and the past agent locations $L_{1:h}$ in training, we learn a probabilistic model on simulation data to estimate $P(L_{h+1:T}|L_{1:h}, V_{1:h})$ for $T - h$ steps into the future. At test time, our model takes as input an agent's observable past $(V_{1:h}, L_{1:h})$ in real videos to predict the agent's future locations $L_{h+1:T} = \{y_{h+1}, \ldots, y_T\}$, where y_t is the location coordinates. As the test real videos are unseen during training, the model is supposed to be invariant to the variances in semantic scenes, camera views, and camera motions (Fig. 2).

3.2 Training Data Generation from Simulation

Our model is trained only on simulation data. To ensure high-level realism, the training trajectories are generated by CARLA [14], an open-source 3D simulator built on top of the state-of-the-art game engine *Unreal Engine 4*. We use the trajectories from the Forking Paths dataset [37] that are semi-manually recreated from the VIRAT/ActEV benchmark that projects real-world annotations to the 3D simulation world. Note that it is not our intention to build an exact replica of the real-world scene, nor it is necessary to help train a model for real-world tasks as suggested in previous works [15,37,54,79].

With CARLA, we record multiple views of the same trajectory of different camera angles and positions. For a trajectory $(V_{1:T}, L_{1:T})$ in original view, let $S = \{(V_{1:T}^{(i)}, L_{1:T}^{(i)})\}_{i=1}^{|S|}$ denote a set of additional views for the same trajectory. In our experiments, we use four camera parameters pre-specified in [37], including three 45-degree views and one top-down view. We use a total of 4 scenes shown in Fig. 3. The ground-truth location varies under different camera views i.e. $L_{1:T}^{(i)} \neq L_{1:T}^{(j)}$ for $i \neq j$. Note that these camera positions and angles are defined in [37] specifically for VIRAT/ActEV dataset. The top-down view cameras in Stanford Drone dataset [53] are still considered unseen to the model since the scenes and camera positions are quite different.

In simulation, we also collect the ground-truth scene semantic segmentation for $K = 13$ classes including sidewalk, road, vehicle, pedestrian, etc. At test time, we extract the semantic segmentation feature from real videos using a pre-trained model with the same number of class labels per pixel. To be specific, we use the Deeplab model [10] trained on the ADE20k [82] dataset and keep its weights frozen. To bridge the gap between real and simulated video frames, we represent all trajectory $V_{1:T}$ as a sequence of scene semantic segmentation features, following previous works [13,37,38,56]. As we show in our experiments, the use of segmentation features is helpful but is still insufficient for learning the robust representation.

3.3 Multi-view Simulation Augmentation (*SimAug*)

In this subsection, we first describe *SimAug* for learning robust representations. Our trajectory prediction backbone model is built on the Multiverse model [37] and will be discussed in Sect. 3.4.

Given a trajectory in its original view $(V_{1:T}, L_{1:T})$, we generate a set of additional views in $S = \{(V_{1:T}^{(i)}, L_{1:T}^{(i)})\}_{i=1}^{|S|}$ as described in the previous section, where $V_t^{(i)}$ represents the scene semantic feature of view i at time t. $L_{1:T}^{(i)}$ is a sequence of ground-truth locations for the i-th view.

Each time given a camera view, we use it as an anchor to search for the "hardest" view that is most inconsistent with what the model has learned.

Inspired by [24], we use the classification loss as the criteria and compute:

$$j^* = \operatorname*{argmax}_{j \in [1, |\mathcal{S}|]} \{\mathcal{L}_{cls}(V_{1:h} + \delta, L_{h+1:T}^{(j)})\}, \tag{1}$$

where δ is the ℓ_∞-bounded random perturbation applied to the input features. $\mathcal{L}_{cls}$ is the location classification loss used in our backbone Multiverse model and will be discussed in the next subsection.

Then for the original view, we generate an adversarial trajectory by the targeted-FGSM attack [29]:

$$V_{1:h}^{adv} = V_{1:h} - \epsilon \cdot \mathrm{sign}(\nabla_{V_{1:h}} \mathcal{L}_{cls}(V_{1:h} + \delta, L_{h+1:T}^{(j^*)})), \tag{2}$$

where ϵ is the hyper-parameter. The attack tries to make the model predict the future locations in the selected "hardest" camera view rather than the original view. In essence, the resulting adversarial feature is "warped" to the "hardest" camera view by a small perturbation. By defending against such adversarial trajectory, our model learns representations that are robust against variances in camera views.

Finally, we mix up the trajectory locations of the selected view and the adversarial trajectory locations by a convex combination function [77] over their features and one-hot location labels.

$$V_{1:h}^{aug} = \lambda \cdot V_{1:h}^{adv} + (1 - \lambda) \cdot V_{1:h}^{(j^*)}$$
$$y_t^{aug} = \lambda \cdot \text{one-hot}(y_t) + (1 - \lambda) \cdot \text{one-hot}(y_t^{(j^*)}) \quad \forall t \in [h+1, T] \tag{3}$$
$$L_{h+1:T}^{aug} = [y_{h+1}^{aug}, \dots, y_T^{aug}]$$

where $[y_{h+1}, \cdots, y_T] = L_{h+1:T}$ are the ground-truth locations of the original view. The one-hot$(\cdot)$ function projects the location in xy coordinates into an one-hot embedding over the predefined grid used in our backbone trajectory prediction model. Please find the details in [37]. Following [77], λ is drawn from a Beta distribution Beta(α, α) controlled by the hyper-parameter α.

The algorithm for training with one training step is listed in Algorithm 1. To train robust models to various camera views and semantic scenes, we learn representations over augmented training trajectories to overcome (i) feature perturbations (Step 3 and 5) (ii) targeted adversarial attack (Step 5), and (iii) the "hardest" feature from other views (Step 4). By the mix-up operation in Eq. (3), our model is trained to minimize the empirical vicinal risk over a new distribution constituted by the generated augmented trajectories, which is proved to be useful in improving model robustness to real-world distributions under various settings [22].

3.4 Backbone Model for Trajectory Prediction

We employ Multiverse [37] as our backbone network, a state-of-the-art multi-future trajectory prediction model. Although we showcase the use of *SimAug* to

---

Algorithm 1: Multi-view Simulation Adversarial Augmentation (*SimAug*)

Input   : Mini-batch of trajectories; hyper-parameters α and ϵ
Output: Classification loss $\mathcal{L}_{\text{cls}}$ computed over augmented trajectories

---

1 **for** *each trajectory* $(V_{1:T}, L_{1:T})$ *in the mini-batch* **do**
2 | Generate trajectories from additional views $\mathcal{S} = \{(V_{1:T}^{(i)}, L_{1:T}^{(i)})\}$;
3 | Compute the loss for each camera view $\mathcal{L}_{\text{cls}}(V_{1:h} + \delta, L_{h+1:T}^{(j)})$;
4 | Select the view with the largest loss j^* by Eq. (1) ;
5 | Generate an adversarial trajectory $V_{1:h}^{adv}$ by Eq. (2);
6 | Mix up $(V_{1:h}^{adv}, L_{h+1:T})$ and $(V_{1:h}^{(j^*)}, L_{h+1:T}^{(j^*)})$ by Eq. (3);
7 | Compute $\mathcal{L}_{\text{cls}}$ over the augmented trajectory $(V_{1:h}^{aug}, L_{h+1:T}^{aug})$ from Step 6;
8 **end**
9 **return** averaged $\mathcal{L}_{\text{cls}}$ over the augmented trajectories

---

improve the robustness of Multiverse, *SimAug* is a general approach that can be applied to other trajectory prediction models.

Input Features. The model is given the past locations, $L_{1:h}$, and the scene, $V_{1:h}$. Each ground-truth location L_t is encoded by an one-hot vector $y_t \in \mathbb{R}^{HW}$ representing the nearest cell in a 2D grid of size $H \times W$. In our experiment, we use a grid scale of 36×18. Each video frame V_t is encoded as semantic segmentation feature of size $H \times W \times K$ where $K = 13$ is the total number of class labels as in [37,38]. As discussed in the previous section, we use *SimAug* to generate augmented trajectories $(V_{1:h}^{aug}, L_{1:h}^{aug})$ as our training features.

History Encoder. A convolutional RNN [68,71] is used to get the final spatial-temporal feature state $H_t \in \mathbb{R}^{H \times W \times d_{enc}}$, where d_{enc} is the hidden size. The context is a concatenation of the last hidden state and the historical video frames, $\mathcal{H} = [H_h, V_{1:h}]$.

Location Decoder. After getting the context $\mathcal{H}$, a coarse location decoder is used to predict locations at the level of grid cells at each time-instant by:

$$\hat{y}_t = \text{softmax}(f_c(\mathcal{H}, H_{t-1}^c)) \in \mathbb{R}^{HW} \tag{4}$$

where f_c is the convolutional recurrent neural network (ConvRNN) with graph attention proposed in [37] and H_t^c is the hidden state of the ConvRNN. Then a fine location decoder is used to predict a continuous offset in $\mathbb{R}^2$, which specifies a "delta" from the center of each grid cell, to get a fine-grained location prediction:

$$\hat{O}_t = \text{MLP}(f_o(\mathcal{H}, H_{t-1}^o)) \in \mathbb{R}^{HW \times 2}, \tag{5}$$

where f_o is a separate ConvRNN and H_t^o is its hidden state. To compute the final prediction location, we use

$$\hat{L}_t = Q_g + \hat{O}_{tg} \tag{6}$$

where $g = \operatorname{argmax} \hat{y}_t$ is the index of the selected grid cell, $Q_g \in \mathbb{R}^2$ is the center of that cell, and $\hat{O}_{tg} \in \mathbb{R}^2$ is the predicted offset for that cell at time t.

Training. We use *SimAug* (see Sect. 3.3) to generate $L_{h+1:T}^{aug} = \{y_{h+1}^{aug}, \ldots, y_T^{aug}\}$ as labels for training. For the coarse decoder, the cross-entropy loss is used:

$$\mathcal{L}_{\text{cls}} = -\frac{1}{T} \sum_{t=h+1}^{T} \sum_{c=1}^{HW} y_{tc}^{aug} \log(\hat{y}_{tc}) \tag{7}$$

For the fine decoder, we use the original ground-truth location label $L_{h+1:T}$:

$$\mathcal{L}_{\text{reg}} = \frac{1}{T} \sum_{t=h+1}^{T} \sum_{c=1}^{HW} \operatorname{smooth}_{l_1}(O_{tc}, \hat{O}_{tc}) \tag{8}$$

where $O_{tc} = L_t - Q_c$ is the delta between the ground true location and the center of the c-th grid cell. The final loss is then calculated using

$$\mathcal{L}(\theta) = \mathcal{L}_{\text{cls}} + \lambda_1 \mathcal{L}_{\text{reg}} + \lambda_2 \|\theta\|_2^2 \tag{9}$$

where λ_2 controls the ℓ_2 regularization (weight decay), and $\lambda_1 = 0.5$ is used to balance the regression and classification losses.

4   Experiments

In this section, we evaluate various methods, including our *SimAug* method, on three public video benchmarks of real-world videos captured under different camera views and scenes: the VIRAT/ActEV [2,47] dataset, the Stanford Drone Dataset (SDD) [53], and the autonomous driving dataset Argoverse [8]. We demonstrate the efficacy of our method for unseen cameras in Sect. 4.2 and how our method can also improve state-of-the-art when fine-tuned on the real training data in Sect. 4.3 and Sect. 4.4.

4.1   Evaluation Metrics

Following prior works [1,37], we utilize two common metrics for trajectory prediction evaluation. Let $L^i = L_{t=(h+1)\cdots T}^i$ be the true future trajectory for the ith test sample, and $\hat{L}^{ik}$ be the corresponding k^{th} prediction sample, for $k \in [1, K]$.

i) *Minimum Average Displacement Error Given K Predictions* (minADE$_K$): for each true trajectory sample i, we select the closest K predictions, and then measure its average error:

$$\text{minADE}_K = \frac{\sum_{i=1}^{N} \min_{k=1}^{K} \sum_{t=h+1}^{T} \|L_t^i - \hat{L}_t^{ik}\|_2}{N \times (T - h)} \tag{10}$$

ii) *Minimum Final Displacement Error Given K Predictions* (minFDE$_K$): similar to minADE$_K$, but we only consider the predicted points and the ground truth point at the final prediction time instant:

$$\text{minFDE}_K = \frac{\sum_{i=1}^N \min_{k=1}^K \|L_T^i - \hat{L}_T^{ik}\|_2}{N} \tag{11}$$

iii) *Grid Prediction Accuracy* (Grid_Acc): As our base model also predicts coarse grid locations as described in Sect. 3.4, we also evaluate the accuracy between the predicted grid $\hat{y}_t$ and the ground truth grid y_t. This is an intermediate metric and hence is less indicative than the minADE$_K$ and minFDE$_K$.

4.2   Main Results

Dataset and Setups. We compare *SimAug* with classical data augmentation methods as well as adversarial learning methods to train robust representations. All methods are trained using the same backbone on the same *simulation training data* described in Sect. 3.2, and tested on the same benchmarks. Real videos are not allowed to be used during training except in our finetuning experiments. For VIRAT/ActEV and SDD, we use the standard test split as in [37,38] and [13,56], respectively. For Argoverse, we use the official validation set from the 3D tracking task, and the videos from the "ring_front_center" camera are used.

These datasets have different levels of difficulties. VIRAT/ActEV is the easiest one because its training trajectories have been projected in the simulation training data. SDD is more difficult as its camera positions and scenes are different from the training data. Argoverse is the most challenging one with distinct scenes, camera views, and ego-motions.

Following the setting in previous works [1,1,13,19,19,37,38,44,56], the models observe 3.2 s (8 frames) of every pedestrian and predict the future 4.8 s (12 frames) of the person trajectory. We use the pixel values for the trajectory coordinates as it is done in [4,7,13,21,31,33,38,44,73]. By default, we evaluate the top $K = 1$ future trajectory prediction of all models.

Baseline Methods. We compare *SimAug* with the following baseline methods for learning robust representations. All methods are built on the same backbone network and trained using the same simulation training data. *Base Model* is the trajectory prediction model proposed in [37]. *Standard Aug* is the base model trained with standard data augmentation techniques including horizontal flipping and random input jittering. *Fast Gradient Sign Method (FGSM)* is the base model trained with adversarial examples generated by the targeted-FGSM attack method [18]. Random labels are used for the targeted-FGSM attack. *Projected Gradient Descent (PGD)* is learned with an iterative adversarial learning method [43,70]. The number of iterations is set to 10 and other hyper-parameters following [70].

Implementation Details. We use $\alpha = 0.2$ for the Beta distribution in Eq. (3) and we use $\epsilon = \delta = 0.1$ in Eq. (2). As the random perturbation is small, we do not normalize the perturbed features and the normalized features yield comparable results. All models are trained using Adadelta optimizer [75] with an initial learning rate of 0.3 and a weight decay of 0.001. Other hyper-parameters for the baselines are the same as the ones in [37].

Quantitative Results. Table 1 shows the evaluation results. Our method performs favorably against other baseline methods across all evaluation metrics on all three benchmarks. In particular, "Standard Aug" seems to be not generalizing well to unseen cameras. FGSM improves significantly on the "Grid_Acc" metric but fails to translate the improvement to final location predictions. *SimAug* is able to improve the model overall stemming from the effective use of multi-view simulation data. All other methods are unable to improve trajectory prediction on Argoverse, whose data characteristics include ego-motions and distinct dashboard-view cameras. The results substantiate the efficacy of *SimAug* for future trajectory prediction in unseen cameras. Note as the baseline methods use the same features as ours, the results indicate the use of segmentation features is insufficient for learning robust representations.

Qualitative Analysis. We visualize outputs of the base model with and without *SimAug* in Fig. 4. We show visualizations on all three datasets. In each image, the yellow trajectories denote historical trajectories and the green ones are ground truth future trajectories. Outputs of the base model without SimAug are colored with blue heatmaps and the yellow-orange heatmaps are from the same model with SimAug. As we see, the base model with SimAug augmentation yields more accurate trajectories for turnings (Fig. 4 1a, 3a) while without it the model sometimes predicts the wrong turns (Fig. 4 1b, 1c, 2a, 3a, 3b). In addition, the length of SimAug predictions is more accurate (Fig. 4 1d, 2b, 2c, 2d).

Table 1. Comparison to the standard data augmentation method and recent adversarial learning methods on three datasets. We report three metrics: Grid_Acc($\uparrow$)/minADE$_1$($\downarrow$)/minFDE$_1$($\downarrow$). The units of ADE/FDE are pixels. All methods are built on the same backbone model in [37] and trained using the same multi-view simulation data described in Sect. 3.2.

Method	VIRAT/ActEV	Stanford drone	Argoverse
Base model [37]	44.2%/26.2/49.7	31.4%/21.9/42.8	26.6%/69.1/183.9
Standard Aug	45.5%/25.8/48.3	21.3%/23.7/47.6	28.9%/70.9/183.4
PGD [43,70]	47.5%/25.1/48.4	28.5%/21.0/42.2	25.9%/72.8/184.0
FGSM [18]	48.6%/25.4/49.3	42.3%/19.3/39.9	29.2%/71.1/185.4
SimAug	**51.1%/21.7/42.2**	**45.4%/15.7/30.2**	**30.9%/67.9/175.6**

4.3 State-of-the-Art Comparison on Stanford Drone Dataset

In this section, we compare our *SimAug* model with the state-of-the-art generative models, including Social-LSTM [1], Social-GAN [19], DESIRE [31], and

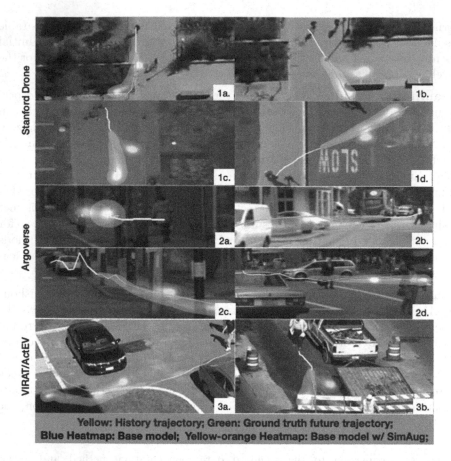

Fig. 4. Qualitative analysis. Trajectory predictions from different models are colored and overlaid in the same image. See text for details. (Color figure online)

SoPhie [56]. We also compare with the imitation learning model, IDL [33], and the inverse reinforcement learning model, P2T$_{IRL}$ [13] for trajectory prediction on the Stanford Drone Dataset. Following previous works, we evaluate the minimal errors over $K = 20$ predictions.

Results and Analysis. The results are shown in Table 2(a), where *SimAug* is built on top of the *Multiverse* model. As it shows, *SimAug* model trained only on the simulation data (second to the last row) achieves comparable or even better performance than other state-of-the-art models that are trained on in-domain real videos. By further fine-tuning on the learned representations of *SimAug*, we achieve the state-of-the-art performance on the Stanford Drone Dataset. The promising results demonstrate the efficacy of *SimAug* for future trajectory prediction in unseen cameras.

Table 2. State-of-the-art comparison on the Stanford Drone Dataset (SDD) and on the VIRAT/ActEV dataset. Numbers are minimal errors over 20 predictions for SDD and minimal errors over the top prediction for VIRAT/ActEV. Baseline models are all trained on real videos and their numbers are taken from [13,56]. "SimAug" is trained only using simulation data and "SimAug*" is further finetuned on the real training videos. "Multiverse" in the bottom rows is trained only with simulation data.

(a) Stanford Drone Dataset

Method	$minADE_{20}(\downarrow)$	$minFDE_{20}$ $(\downarrow)$
Social-LSTM [1]	31.19	56.97
Social-GAN [19]	27.25	41.44
DESIRE [31]	19.25	34.05
SoPhie [56]	16.27	29.38
Multiverse [37]	14.78	27.09
IDL [33]	13.93	24.40
P2T$_{IRL}$ [13]	12.58	22.07
SimAug	12.03	23.98
SimAug*	**10.27**	**19.71**

(b) VIRAT/ActEV

Method	$minADE_1(\downarrow)$	$minFDE_1$ $(\downarrow)$
Social-LSTM [1]	23.10	44.27
Social-GAN [19]	30.42	60.70
Next [38]	19.78	42.43
Multiverse [37]	18.51	35.84
Multiverse [37]	22.94	43.35
SimAug	21.73	42.22
SimAug*	**17.96**	**34.68**

4.4 State-of-the-Art Comparison on VIRAT/ActEV

In this section, we compare our *SimAug* model with state-of-the-art models on VIRAT/ActEV. Following the previous work [37], we compute the errors for the top $K = 1$ prediction. Experimental results are shown in Table 2(b), where all models in the top four rows are trained on the real-world training videos in VIRAT/ActEV. Our model trained on simulation data achieves competitive performance and outperforms *Multiverse* [37] model that is trained on the same data. With fine-tuning, which means using exactly the same training data without any extra annotation of real trajectories compared to [1,19,37,38], we achieve the best performance on the VIRAT/ActEV benchmark.

4.5 Ablation Experiments

We test various ablations of our approach to validate our design decisions. Results are shown in Table 3, where the top-1 prediction is used in the evaluation. We verify four key design choices by removing each, at a time, from the full model. The results show that by introducing viewpoint selection (Eq. (1)) and adversarial perturbation (Eq. (2)), our method improves model generalization.

(1) *Multi-view data:* Our method is trained on multi-view simulation data and we use 4 camera views in our experiments. We test our method without the top-down view because it is similar to the ones in the SDD dataset. As we see, the performance drops due to the fewer number of data and less diverse views, suggesting that we should use more views in augmentation (which is effortless to do in 3D simulators).

(2) *Random perturbation:* We test our model without random perturbation on the original view trajectory samples by setting $\delta = 0$ in Eq. (1). This leads to the performance drop on all three datasets and particularly on the more difficult Argoverse dataset.

(3) *Adversarial attack:* We test our model without adversarial attack by replacing Eq. (2) with $V_{1:h}^{adv} = V_{1:h}$. This is similar to applying the Mixup method [77] to two views in the feature space. The performance drops across all three benchmarks.

(4) *View selection:* We replace Eq. (1) with random search to see the effect of view selection. As we see, the significant performance drops, especially on the Stanford Drone dataset, verifying the effectiveness of this design.

Table 3. Performance on ablated versions of our method on three benchmarks. We report the $minADE_1(\downarrow)/minFDE_1(\downarrow)$ metrics.

Method	VIRAT/ActEV	Stanford Drone	Argoverse
SimAug full model	21.7/42.2	15.7/30.2	67.9/175.6
- top-down view data	22.8/43.6	18.4/35.6	68.4/178.3
- random perturbation	23.6/43.8	18.7/35.6	69.1/180.2
- adversarial attack	23.1/43.8	17.4/32.9	68.0/177.5
- view selection	23.0/42.9	19.6/38.2	68.6/177.0

5   Conclusion

In this paper, we have introduced *SimAug*, a novel simulation data augmentation method to learn robust representations for trajectory prediction. Our model is trained only on 3D simulation data and applied out-of-the-box to a wide variety of real video cameras with novel views or scenes. We have shown that our method achieves competitive performance on three public benchmarks with and without using the real-world training data. We believe our approach will facilitate future research and applications on learning robust representation for trajectory prediction with limited or zero training data. Other directions to deal with camera view dependence include using a homography matrix, which may require an additional step of manual or automatic calibration of multiple cameras. We leave them for future work.

Acknowledgements. We would like to thank the anonymous reviewers for their useful comments, and Google Cloud for providing GCP research credits. This research was supported by NSF grant IIS-1650994, the financial assistance award 60NANB17D156 from NIST, and the Baidu Scholarship. This work was also supported by IARPA via DOI/IBC contract number D17PC00340. The views and conclusions contained herein are those of the authors and should not be interpreted as necessarily representing the official policies or endorsements, either expressed or implied, of IARPA, NIST, DOI/IBC, the National Science Foundation, or the U.S. Government.

References

1. Alahi, A., Goel, K., Ramanathan, V., Robicquet, A., Fei-Fei, L., Savarese, S.: Social LSTM: human trajectory prediction in crowded spaces. In: CVPR (2016)
2. Awad, G., et al.: TRECVID 2018: benchmarking video activity detection, video captioning and matching, video storytelling linking and video search. In: TRECVID (2018)
3. Bąk, S., Carr, P., Lalonde, J.-F.: Domain adaptation through synthesis for unsupervised person re-identification. In: Ferrari, V., Hebert, M., Sminchisescu, C., Weiss, Y. (eds.) ECCV 2018. LNCS, vol. 11217, pp. 193–209. Springer, Cham (2018). https://doi.org/10.1007/978-3-030-01261-8_12
4. Bansal, M., Krizhevsky, A., Ogale, A.: ChauffeurNet: learning to drive by imitating the best and synthesizing the worst. arXiv preprint arXiv:1812.03079 (2018)
5. Bousmalis, K., Silberman, N., Dohan, D., Erhan, D., Krishnan, D.: Unsupervised pixel-level domain adaptation with generative adversarial networks. In: CVPR (2017)
6. Caesar, H., et al.: nuScenes: a multimodal dataset for autonomous driving. arXiv preprint arXiv:1903.11027 (2019)
7. Chai, Y., Sapp, B., Bansal, M., Anguelov, D.: MultiPath: multiple probabilistic anchor trajectory hypotheses for behavior prediction. arXiv preprint arXiv:1910.05449 (2019)
8. Chang, M.F., et al.: Argoverse: 3D tracking and forecasting with rich maps. In: CVPR (2019)
9. Chen, H., et al.: Data-free learning of student networks. In: ICCV (2019)
10. Chen, L.C., Papandreou, G., Kokkinos, I., Murphy, K., Yuille, A.L.: DeepLab: semantic image segmentation with deep convolutional nets, atrous convolution, and fully connected CRFs. IEEE Trans. Pattern Anal. Mach. Intell. **40**(4), 834–848 (2017)
11. Cheng, Y., Jiang, L., Macherey, W.: Robust neural machine translation with doubly adversarial inputs. In: ACL (2019)
12. Cheng, Y., Jiang, L., Macherey, W., Eisenstein, J.: AdvAug: robust data augmentation for neural machine translation. In: ACL (2020)
13. Deo, N., Trivedi, M.M.: Trajectory forecasts in unknown environments conditioned on grid-based plans. arXiv preprint arXiv:2001.00735 (2020)
14. Dosovitskiy, A., Ros, G., Codevilla, F., Lopez, A., Koltun, V.: CARLA: an open urban driving simulator. arXiv preprint arXiv:1711.03938 (2017)
15. Gaidon, A., Wang, Q., Cabon, Y., Vig, E.: Virtual worlds as proxy for multi-object tracking analysis. In: CVPR (2016)
16. Ganin, Y., et al.: Domain-adversarial training of neural networks. J. Mach. Learn. Res. **17**(1), 2096-2030 (2016)
17. Goodfellow, I., et al.: Generative adversarial nets. In: NeurIPS (2014)
18. Goodfellow, I.J., Shlens, J., Szegedy, C.: Explaining and harnessing adversarial examples. arXiv preprint arXiv:1412.6572 (2014)
19. Gupta, A., Johnson, J., Savarese, S., Fei-Fei, L., Alahi, A.: Social GAN: socially acceptable trajectories with generative adversarial networks. In: CVPR (2018)
20. Heess, N., et al.: Emergence of locomotion behaviours in rich environments. arXiv preprint arXiv:1707.02286 (2017)
21. Hong, J., Sapp, B., Philbin, J.: Rules of the road: predicting driving behavior with a convolutional model of semantic interactions. In: CVPR (2019)
22. Jiang, L., Huang, D., Liu, M., Yang, W.: Beyond synthetic noise: deep learning on controlled noisy labels. In: ICML (2020)

23. Jiang, L., Meng, D., Zhao, Q., Shan, S., Hauptmann, A.G.: Self-paced curriculum learning. In: AAAI (2015)
24. Jiang, L., Zhou, Z., Leung, T., Li, L.J., Fei-Fei, L.: MentorNet: learning data-driven curriculum for very deep neural networks on corrupted labels. In: ICML (2018)
25. Kang, G., Jiang, L., Yang, Y., Hauptmann, A.G.: Contrastive adaptation network for unsupervised domain adaptation. In: CVPR (2019)
26. Kar, A., et al.: Meta-Sim: learning to generate synthetic datasets. In: ICCV (2019)
27. Kitani, K.M., Ziebart, B.D., Bagnell, J.A., Hebert, M.: Activity forecasting. In: Fitzgibbon, A., Lazebnik, S., Perona, P., Sato, Y., Schmid, C. (eds.) ECCV 2012. LNCS, vol. 7575, pp. 201–214. Springer, Heidelberg (2012). https://doi.org/10.1007/978-3-642-33765-9_15
28. Kooij, J.F.P., Schneider, N., Flohr, F., Gavrila, D.M.: Context-based pedestrian path prediction. In: Fleet, D., Pajdla, T., Schiele, B., Tuytelaars, T. (eds.) ECCV 2014. LNCS, vol. 8694, pp. 618–633. Springer, Cham (2014). https://doi.org/10.1007/978-3-319-10599-4_40
29. Kurakin, A., Goodfellow, I., Bengio, S.: Adversarial examples in the physical world. In: ICLR (2017)
30. Lambert, J., Sener, O., Savarese, S.: Deep learning under privileged information using heteroscedastic dropout. In: CVPR (2018)
31. Lee, N., Choi, W., Vernaza, P., Choy, C.B., Torr, P.H., Chandraker, M.: DESIRE: distant future prediction in dynamic scenes with interacting agents. In: CVPR (2017)
32. Lerner, A., Chrysanthou, Y., Lischinski, D.: Crowds by example. In: Computer Graphics Forum, pp. 655–664. Wiley Online Library (2007)
33. Li, Y.: Which way are you going? Imitative decision learning for path forecasting in dynamic scenes. In: CVPR (2019)
34. Liang, J., et al.: An event reconstruction tool for conflict monitoring using social media. In: AAAI (2017)
35. Liang, J., Jiang, L., Cao, L., Kalantidis, Y., Li, L.J., Hauptmann, A.G.: Focal visual-text attention for memex question answering. IEEE Trans. Pattern Anal. Mach. Intell. 41(8), 1893–1908 (2019)
36. Liang, J., Jiang, L., Meng, D., Hauptmann, A.G.: Learning to detect concepts from webly-labeled video data. In: IJCAI (2016)
37. Liang, J., Jiang, L., Murphy, K., Yu, T., Hauptmann, A.: The garden of forking paths: towards multi-future trajectory prediction. In: CVPR (2020)
38. Liang, J., Jiang, L., Niebles, J.C., Hauptmann, A.G., Fei-Fei, L.: Peeking into the future: predicting future person activities and locations in videos. In: CVPR (2019)
39. Lopez-Paz, D., Bottou, L., Schölkopf, B., Vapnik, V.: Unifying distillation and privileged information. arXiv preprint arXiv:1511.03643 (2015)
40. Luber, M., Stork, J.A., Tipaldi, G.D., Arras, K.O.: People tracking with human motion predictions from social forces. In: ICRA (2010)
41. Luo, Z., Hsieh, J.-T., Jiang, L., Niebles, J.C., Fei-Fei, L.: Graph distillation for action detection with privileged modalities. In: Ferrari, V., Hebert, M., Sminchisescu, C., Weiss, Y. (eds.) Computer Vision – ECCV 2018. LNCS, vol. 11218, pp. 174–192. Springer, Cham (2018). https://doi.org/10.1007/978-3-030-01264-9_11
42. Ma, W.C., Huang, D.A., Lee, N., Kitani, K.M.: Forecasting interactive dynamics of pedestrians with fictitious play. In: CVPR (2017)
43. Madry, A., Makelov, A., Schmidt, L., Tsipras, D., Vladu, A.: Towards deep learning models resistant to adversarial attacks. arXiv preprint arXiv:1706.06083 (2017)

44. Makansi, O., Ilg, E., Cicek, O., Brox, T.: Overcoming limitations of mixture density networks: a sampling and fitting framework for multimodal future prediction. In: CVPR (2019)

45. Mangalam, K., Adeli, E., Lee, K.H., Gaidon, A., Niebles, J.C.: Disentangling human dynamics for pedestrian locomotion forecasting with noisy supervision. arXiv preprint arXiv:1911.01138 (2019)

46. Northcutt, C.G., Jiang, L., Chuang, I.L.: Confident learning: estimating uncertainty in dataset labels. arXiv preprint arXiv:1911.00068 (2019)

47. Oh, S., et al.: A large-scale benchmark dataset for event recognition in surveillance video. In: CVPR (2011)

48. Qiu, W., et al.: UnrealCV: virtual worlds for computer vision. In: ACM Multimedia (2017)

49. Ren, M., Zeng, W., Yang, B., Urtasun, R.: Learning to reweight examples for robust deep learning. In: ICML (2018)

50. Rhinehart, N., Kitani, K.M.: First-person activity forecasting with online inverse reinforcement learning. In: ICCV (2017)

51. Rhinehart, N., Kitani, K.M., Vernaza, P.: R2P2: a reparameterized pushforward policy for diverse, precise generative path forecasting. In: Ferrari, V., Hebert, M., Sminchisescu, C., Weiss, Y. (eds.) ECCV 2018. LNCS, vol. 11217, pp. 794–811. Springer, Cham (2018). https://doi.org/10.1007/978-3-030-01261-8_47

52. Richter, S.R., Vineet, V., Roth, S., Koltun, V.: Playing for data: ground truth from computer games. In: Leibe, B., Matas, J., Sebe, N., Welling, M. (eds.) ECCV 2016. LNCS, vol. 9906, pp. 102–118. Springer, Cham (2016). https://doi.org/10.1007/978-3-319-46475-6_7

53. Robicquet, A., Sadeghian, A., Alahi, A., Savarese, S.: Learning social etiquette: human trajectory understanding in crowded scenes. In: Leibe, B., Matas, J., Sebe, N., Welling, M. (eds.) ECCV 2016. LNCS, vol. 9912, pp. 549–565. Springer, Cham (2016). https://doi.org/10.1007/978-3-319-46484-8_33

54. Ros, G., Sellart, L., Materzynska, J., Vazquez, D., Lopez, A.M.: The synthia dataset: a large collection of synthetic images for semantic segmentation of urban scenes. In: CVPR (2016)

55. Ruiz, N., Schulter, S., Chandraker, M.: Learning to simulate. arXiv preprint arXiv:1810.02513 (2018)

56. Sadeghian, A., Kosaraju, V., Sadeghian, A., Hirose, N., Savarese, S.: SoPhie: an attentive GAN for predicting paths compliant to social and physical constraints. arXiv preprint arXiv:1806.01482 (2018)

57. Sadeghian, A., Legros, F., Voisin, M., Vesel, R., Alahi, A., Savarese, S.: CAR-Net: clairvoyant attentive recurrent network. In: Ferrari, V., Hebert, M., Sminchisescu, C., Weiss, Y. (eds.) ECCV 2018. LNCS, vol. 11215, pp. 162–180. Springer, Cham (2018). https://doi.org/10.1007/978-3-030-01252-6_10

58. Shah, S., Dey, D., Lovett, C., Kapoor, A.: AirSim: high-fidelity visual and physical simulation for autonomous vehicles. In: Hutter, M., Siegwart, R. (eds.) Field and Service Robotics. SPAR, vol. 5, pp. 621–635. Springer, Cham (2018). https://doi.org/10.1007/978-3-319-67361-5_40

59. Souza, C.R., Gaidon, A., Cabon, Y., López, A.M.: Procedural generation of videos to train deep action recognition networks. In: CVPR (2017)

60. Styles, O., Ross, A., Sanchez, V.: Forecasting pedestrian trajectory with machine-annotated training data. In: 2019 IEEE Intelligent Vehicles Symposium (IV), pp. 716–721. IEEE (2019)

61. Styles, O., Guha, T., Sanchez, V.: Multiple object forecasting: predicting future object locations in diverse environments. arXiv preprint arXiv:1909.11944 (2019)

62. Sun, C., Karlsson, P., Wu, J., Tenenbaum, J.B., Murphy, K.: Stochastic prediction of multi-agent interactions from partial observations. arXiv preprint arXiv:1902.09641 (2019)
63. Sun, S.-H., Huh, M., Liao, Y.-H., Zhang, N., Lim, J.J.: Multi-view to novel view: synthesizing novel views with self-learned confidence. In: Ferrari, V., Hebert, M., Sminchisescu, C., Weiss, Y. (eds.) ECCV 2018. LNCS, vol. 11207, pp. 162–178. Springer, Cham (2018). https://doi.org/10.1007/978-3-030-01219-9_10
64. Tramèr, F., Kurakin, A., Papernot, N., Goodfellow, I., Boneh, D., McDaniel, P.: Ensemble adversarial training: attacks and defenses. arXiv preprint arXiv:1705.07204 (2017)
65. Tzeng, E., Hoffman, J., Saenko, K., Darrell, T.: Adversarial discriminative domain adaptation. In: CVPR (2017)
66. Vapnik, V., Izmailov, R.: Learning using privileged information: similarity control and knowledge transfer. J. Mach. Learn. Res. 16(2023–2049), 2 (2015)
67. Varol, G., Laptev, I., Schmid, C., Zisserman, A.: Synthetic humans for action recognition from unseen viewpoints. arXiv preprint arXiv:1912.04070 (2019)
68. Wang, Y., Jiang, L., Yang, M.H., Li, L.J., Long, M., Fei-Fei, L.: Eidetic 3D LSTM: a model for video prediction and beyond. In: ICLR (2019)
69. Wu, Y., Jiang, L., Yang, Y.: Revisiting embodiedqa: a simple baseline and beyond. IEEE Trans. Image Process. 29, 3984–3992 (2020)
70. Xie, C., Wu, Y., van der Maaten, L., Yuille, A.L., He, K.: Feature denoising for improving adversarial robustness. In: CVPR (2019)
71. Xingjian, S., Chen, Z., Wang, H., Yeung, D.Y., Wong, W.K., Woo, W.C.: Convolutional LSTM network: a machine learning approach for precipitation nowcasting. In: NeurIPS (2015)
72. Xue, H., Huynh, D.Q., Reynolds, M.: SS-LSTM: a hierarchical LSTM model for pedestrian trajectory prediction. In: WACV (2018)
73. Yagi, T., Mangalam, K., Yonetani, R., Sato, Y.: Future person localization in first-person videos. In: CVPR (2018)
74. Yu, F., et al.: BDD100K: a diverse driving video database with scalable annotation tooling. arXiv preprint arXiv:1805.04687 (2018)
75. Zeiler, M.D.: ADADELTA: an adaptive learning rate method. arXiv preprint arXiv:1212.5701 (2012)
76. Zeng, X., et al.: Adversarial attacks beyond the image space. In: CVPR (2019)
77. Zhang, H., Cisse, M., Dauphin, Y.N., Lopez-Paz, D.: mixup: Beyond empirical risk minimization. In: ICLR (2018)
78. Zhang, P., Ouyang, W., Zhang, P., Xue, J., Zheng, N.: SR-LSTM: state refinement for LSTM towards pedestrian trajectory prediction. In: CVPR (2019)
79. Zhang, Y., Wei, X., Qiu, W., Xiao, Z., Hager, G.D., Yuille, A.: RSA: randomized simulation as augmentation for robust human action recognition. arXiv preprint arXiv:1912.01180 (2019)
80. Zhang, Y., Gibson, G.M., Hay, R., Bowman, R.W., Padgett, M.J., Edgar, M.P.: A fast 3D reconstruction system with a low-cost camera accessory. Sci. Rep. 5, 10909 (2015)
81. Zhao, T., et al.: Multi-agent tensor fusion for contextual trajectory prediction. In: CVPR (2019)
82. Zhou, B., Zhao, H., Puig, X., Fidler, S., Barriuso, A., Torralba, A.: Scene parsing through ADE20K dataset. In: CVPR (2017)
83. Zhu, Y., et al.: Target-driven visual navigation in indoor scenes using deep reinforcement learning. In: ICRA (2017)

ScribbleBox: Interactive Annotation Framework for Video Object Segmentation

Bowen Chen[1(✉)], Huan Ling[1,2,3(✉)], Xiaohui Zeng[1,2(✉)], Jun Gao[1,2,3],
Ziyue Xu[1(✉)], and Sanja Fidler[1,2,3(✉)]

[1] University of Toronto, Toronto, Canada
{chenbowen,linghuan,xiaohui,jungao,fidler}@cs.toronto.edu,
ziyue.xu@mail.utoronto.ca
[2] Vector Institute, Toronto, Canada
[3] NVIDIA, Santa Clara, USA

Abstract. Manually labeling video datasets for segmentation tasks is extremely time consuming. We introduce ScribbleBox, an interactive framework for annotating object instances with masks in videos with a significant boost in efficiency. In particular, we split annotation into two steps: annotating objects with tracked boxes, and labeling masks inside these tracks. We introduce automation and interaction in both steps. Box tracks are annotated efficiently by approximating the trajectory using a parametric curve with a small number of control points which the annotator can interactively correct. Our approach tolerates a modest amount of noise in box placements, thus typically requiring only a few clicks to annotate a track to a sufficient accuracy. Segmentation masks are corrected via scribbles which are propagated through time. We show significant performance gains in annotation efficiency over past work. We show that our ScribbleBox approach reaches 88.92% J&F on DAVIS2017 with an average of 9.14 clicks per box track, and only 4 frames requiring scribble annotation in a video of 65.3 frames on average.

1 Introduction

Video is one of the most common forms of visual media. It is used to entertain us (film, tv series), inform us (news), educate us (video lectures), connect us (video conferencing), and attract our interest via TV commercials and social media posts. Video is also a crucial modality for robotic applications such as self-driving cars, security applications, and patient monitoring in healthcare.

B. Chen and H. Ling—Authors contributed equally.

Electronic supplementary material The online version of this chapter (https://doi.org/10.1007/978-3-030-58601-0_18) contains supplementary material, which is available to authorized users.

A. Vedaldi et al. (Eds.): ECCV 2020, LNCS 12358, pp. 293–310, 2020.
https://doi.org/10.1007/978-3-030-58601-0_18

One of the fundamental tasks common to a variety of applications is the ability to segment and track individual objects across the duration of the video. However, the success of existing methods in this task is limited due to the fact that training data is hard to obtain. Labeling only a single object in a single frame can take up to a minute [7,8], thus annotating the full video is prohibitively time consuming. This fact also presents a major roadblock for video content editing where end-users may want to segment a particular object/person and replace the background with an alternative. Most film studios thus still mainly resort to the use of "green-screen" during recording. Our interest here is in interactive annotation to assist human users in segmenting objects in videos (Fig. 1).

Prior work on human assisted interactive annotation has addressed both the image [1,23,26,27,33,41] and video domains [4,6,9,18,24,30]. The prevailent image-based approaches employ grabCut-like techniques using scribbles as human feedback [33], track object boundaries via intelligent scissors [27], interactively edit predicted vertices of a polygon outlining the object [1,23], and providing human clicks on the erroneously predicted object boundary as a heatmap to a DeepLab-like architecture [26,41]. In video, methods either use online fine-tuning [22,29] of the model given a new user-annotated frame, or propose ways to propagate scribbles provided by the user in one frame to other frames. However, in current scribble propagation approaches a human-provided scribble typically only affects neighboring frames, and oftentimes the scribbles are ignored entirely by the neural network that processes them.

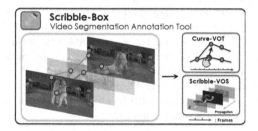

Fig. 1. ScribbleBox: interactive framework for annotating object masks in videos. Our approach splits annotation into two steps: interactive box tracking where the user corrects keyframe boxes (Curve-VOT), and interactive segmentation inside tracked boxes with human-provided scribbles (Scribble-VOS). (Color figure online)

In this paper, we introduce ScribbleBox, a novel approach to interactive annotation of object instances in videos. In particular, we propose to split the task of segmenting objects into two simpler tasks: annotating and tracking a loose box around each object across frames, and segmenting the object in each tracked box. We make both steps interactive. For tracking, we represent object's motion using a sequence of linear motions. Our key contribution is to optimize for the control points defining these motions, and allow the user to interactively correct the erroneous control points. We perform local adjustments to allow for the boxes to slightly deviate from the piece-wise linearly interpolated track. To segment an object inside each tracked box, we exploit scribbles as a form of human input. We present a new scribble propagation network and a simulation scheme that encourages the network to accurately propagate human input through the video. In a user study, we show that our approach achieves about 4% higher J&F score compared to the current state-of-the-art interactive baseline IPN [30] given the same amount of annotation time.

Online demo and tool will be released at Project Page.

2 Related Work

Literature on object tracking/segmentation is vast. Since automatic tracking and segmentation is not our contribution we limit our review to interactive methods.

Interactive Visual Object Tracking (VOT): In the traditional tracking annotation protocol, annotators are asked to determine keyframes and label the object's box in these frames. Other frames are then automatically annotated via either linear interpolation [15], or performing a shortest-path interpolation between manual annotations [37]. The annotator typically needs to go back and forth in determining the keyframes such that the final full track is accurate. To introduce intelligence in video annotation protocol and reduce cost, [38] exploits active learning to choose which frames to annotate. More recent and related to our method, PathTrack [25] presents an efficient framework to annotate tracking by tracing each object with a mouse cursor as the video plays. However, there is an ambiguity in determining the scale of the object which they try to automatically account for. In our work, the annotator does not need to watch the full video, and is only asked to inspect the automatically determined keyframes. While playing the in between segments in fast-forward mode is desired for verification, we experimentally show that no further inspection is typically needed, as our full method deals with a substantial amount of noise.

Interactive Video Object Segmentation (VOS): With the recently introduced datasets [6], there has been an increased interest in designing both automatic and interactive methods for video object segmentation. An interactive method expects user input, either clicks or scribbles, to refine the predicted output masks. For efficiency, human feedback is propagated to nearby frames.

Several earlier approaches employed graph cut techniques [3,20,32,39]. In [39], user's input spans three dimensions. Video is treated as a spatiotemporal graph and a preprocessing step is required to reduce the number of nodes for the min-cut problem. A much faster method is LIVEcut [32] where the user selects and corrects frames which are propagated forward frame by frame. In [2], an image with foreground and background scribble annotations is converted into a weighted graph, where the weights between nodes (pixels) are computed based on features like color or location. A pixel is classified based on its shortest geodesic distance to scribbles. JFS [28] propagates user annotations through the computed point trajectory and classifies the remaining pixels with a random walk algorithm. Modern methods [4,6,9,26,29,30] employ neural networks for interactive VOS. [9] formulates the segmentation task as a pixel-wise retrieval problem and supports different kinds of user input such as masks, clicks and scribbles. [6] proposes an Interactive Segmentation Track for the DAVIS2018 Challenge along with baselines. The first baseline is based on an online-learning VOS model OSVOS [5], while the second baseline trains a SVM classifier on pixels that are annotated with scribbles. Top performers in the challenge include SiamDLT [29] which performs similarity learning together with online fine-tuning on the user-provided scribbles and dense CRF as post-processing.

The winner of the DAVIS2018 Challenge, IPN [30] proposes an interactive framework by employing scribbles to correct masks and propagate corrections to the neighboring frames implicitly. Different from IPN, we incorporate tracking in the annotation process, and model scribble propagation explicitly: we directly predict scribbles for other frames based on the user's input, and employ a training strategy that encourages our network to utilize scribbles effectively. Note that our mask propagation module shares similarity with the recent mask propagation model Space-Time Memory Networks [31]. We employ Graph Convolutional Networks while they adopt a memory-network architecture.

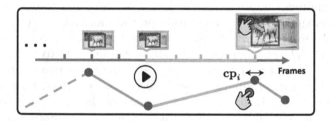

Fig. 2. Curve-VOT: annotators inspect automatically determined keyframes and adjust control points of a parametric curve. They can fast-forward the video in between keyframes to ensure the object is adequately tracked.

3   Our Approach

The goal of our work is to efficiently label object tracks in videos with accurate masks. We split annotation into two steps: 1) box tracking, and 2) mask labeling given the tracked boxes. We argue that it is easier to segment the object inside cropped regions rather than the full image both for the human labeler as well as automatic methods as they can more explicitly exploit shape priors and correlations of motion across time.

We introduce automation and human-in-the-loop interaction in both stages, aiming to achieve the highest level of labeling efficiency. We represent the box track with a parametric curve (polygon or spline [12,23]) exploiting the fact that many motions are roughly linear locally. The curve is represented with a small set of control points which are obtained automatically. The annotator is then only shown the frames closest to the control points, and in case of errors a control point can be adjusted. We exploit this information to re-estimate the control points in the subsequent parts of the video. This process can be done iteratively. Importantly, the annotated tracked boxes obtained from this step can be quite loose, and mainly serve to roughly delineate where the object is in the frames. Our second step, the mask labeling step, is able to tolerate such noise and produces tracked masks with very few interactions with the annotator.

In the second annotation step, we first automatically label the object's masks. The annotator then inspects the video of the segmented object and provides feedback for the frames where errors occur by drawing scribbles in the erroneous areas. We automatically re-predict the frame and propagate this information to the subsequent frames. We explain both steps in more detail next.

3.1 Interactive Tracking Annotation

We here introduce *Curve-VOT*, our interactive approach for tracking annotation which tries to reduce the number of clicks required to annotate boxes around an object of interest in a video. We approximate the trajectory of the box using a parametric curve which is estimated interactively. Specifically, we approximate a M-frame trajectory J as a polygonal curve P with a fixed number of control points, N. We obtain this curve automatically, and allow the annotator to edit the control points by moving them in space and time, and add or remove points.

Note that our approximation assumes that the motion of the box between two control points is linear. This assumption typically holds locally, but may be violated if the temporal gap between the two control points is large. We allow slight deviations by locally searching for a better box. We explicitly do not require this step to give us perfect boxes, but rather "good enough" region proposals. We defer the final accuracy to an automatic refinement step, and our interactive segmentation annotation module. Note that in practice $N \ll M$, resulting in a huge saving in annotation time. We illustrate our interface in Fig. 2.

We now describe how we obtain the curve for the object's trajectory. Our approach is optimization based: given the last annotated frame, we track the object using any of the existing trackers. In our work, we employ SiamMask [35] for its speed and accuracy. We then take the tracked box and fit a polygonal curve with N control points.

Let $\mathbf{cp}_i = [t_i, x_i, y_i, w_i, h_i]^T$ denote the ith control point, where t represents continuous time, and $[x_i, y_i, w_i, h_i]$ denotes the center of the box and its width and height, respectively. Let $P = \{\mathbf{cp}_1, \mathbf{cp}_1, \cdots, \mathbf{cp}_N\}$ to be the sequence of all control points. Note that our curve is continuous and parametric, i.e., $P(t)$, with $t_i \leq t \leq t_{i+1}$, we define $P(t) = [(t - t_i)\mathbf{cp}_i + (t_{i+1} - t)\mathbf{cp}_{i+1}]/(t_{i+1} - t_i)$.

Curve Fitting: To fit the curve to the observed boxes (obtained by the tracker), we initialize the control points by uniformly selecting key frames and placing points in the center of each frame, and run optimization. We uniformly sample K points along both the parametric curve P and the observed object track J, and optimize the following cost:

$$L_{\text{match}}(\{\mathbf{cp}_i\}) = \sum_{k=1}^{K} \| [t_k^P, x_k^P, y_k^P, w_k^P, h_k^P]^T - [t_k^J, x_k^J, y_k^J, w_k^J, h_k^J]^T \|_1 \qquad (1)$$

Note that each $[t_k^P, x_k^P, y_k^P, w_k^P, h_k^P]^T$ is a linear function of its neighboring control points, allowing us to compute the gradients with respect to $\{\mathbf{cp}_i\}$. We use gradient descent to optimize our objective. In our experiments, we choose $N = 10$ and we set K to be 300 to ensure number of sampled points is greater than number of frames. We run optimization for 100 steps.

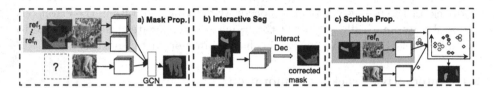

Fig. 3. Modules in our model: a) Given user annotated reference frames, our mask propagation module predicts object masks in subsequent frames. b) Interactive segmentation module takes user scribbles as input (red and green scribbles indicate false positive and false negative regions, respectively), and returns the corrected mask for the chosen frame. c) We propagate scribbles to correct masks in nearby frames. (Color figure online)

Interactive Annotation: We pop the frames closest to the estimated control points, and allow the user to make adjustments if necessary. In particular, each control point can be adjusted both in space and time to accurately place its corresponding box around the object. The user is also asked to fast-forward the video between the control points, making sure that the object is loosely tracked in each interval. In case the interpolation loses the object, the annotator is able to add an additional control point. We then take the last annotated frame and re-run the tracker in the subsequent video. In our case, the last annotated box is used to compute correlation using SiamMask in the following frames. We re-fit the remaining control points to the subsequent track. The interactive process is repeated until the annotator deems the object to be well tracked.

Box Refinement: After interactive annotation, we get a curve which models piece-wise linear motions. To refine the linearly interpolated box in the frames in between every two control points, we crop the images based on the size of the box following SiamRPN [19] and re-run the SiamMask tracker by constraining it to these crops. This in practice produces significantly more accurate boxes that we exploit further in our interactive segmentation module.

3.2   Interactive Segmentation Annotation

Given the annotated tracked box from Sect. 3.1, we now aim to interactively segment the object across the video with minimal human labour. We make use of the SiamMask's mask prediction in the first frame and predict masks for the rest of the video by our *mask propagation module*. If errors occur, the user can edit the inaccurate masks by drawing positive and negative scribbles. Here, positive scribbles indicate missing regions, while negative scribbles indicate false positive regions. To best utilize human's feedback, our method propagates both the corrected mask as well as the input scribbles to the subsequent frames. We refer to our interactive segmentation module as *Scribble-VOS*.

Network Design. Our interactive segmentation approach consists of three different modules: a *mask propagation module* to propagate segmentation masks, an *interactive segmentation module* for single image editing via scribbles, and a *scribble propagation module* that propagates user's feedback across video. Overview is in Fig. 3. We explain each module in detail next.

Image Encoder: We crop the image inside the box and encode it with ResNet50 [14] pre-trained on ImageNet. We extract image features from the Conv4 layer and denote it as $F_t \in \mathbb{R}^{W \times H \times D}$, where t is the time step in the video, and W and H are the width and height of the feature map. Note that unlike most previous works that concatenate images with additional information including masks/scribbles as input to the encoder, our encoder only takes images as input, which allows us to share the encoder among different modules and use an encoder pre-trained on any (large) image dataset.

Mask Decoder: There are two decoders in our framework. *Interactive decoder* is used to produce a refined mask of single frame based on the human interaction. We also have a *propagation decoder* which is shared by both the mask and scribble propagation modules. We describe the structure of the decoder next, and specify the input feature for the two decoders later in the section.

Our decoder consists of three refinement heads [42] that upsample image features (1/16 resolution wrt input) by 8x to produce the object mask. Sizes of the output channels of the refinement heads are 224, 224, 128. We also remove the skip connection for the last refinement head as it yields better results.

Interactive Segmentation Module: To correct errors produced by the model, our interactive module takes user's scribbles for the chosen frame and outputs a refined mask. Specifically, we first convert user's scribbles into two binary maps, one for positive and the other for negative scribbles. The input to the *interactive decoder* concatenates 2-channel scribble input, image features, and the mask of the frame that we want to correct, as shown in Fig. 3b.

To force the model to behave consistently with the user's scribbles, we utilize a *scribble consistency loss*. And, to prevent the predicted mask from being modified in regions where the initial mask was accurate, we restrict the network to only affect a local neighbourhood surrounding the scribbles. In particular, we mask out new predictions that are more than 10 pixels away from the scribble areas.

Note that in [30], both scribbles and masks are encoded along with the raw image, which requires an additional encoding for each interaction. Here, we only run the encoding once and re-use the image feature for each interaction.

Mask Propagation Module: Given the user-annotated object masks, our mask propagation module aims at re-predicting the masks for the subsequent frames. We rely on a Graph Convolutional Network (GCN) [17] to perform this propagation, and additionally employ a decoder which produces the segmentation mask based on the GCN features. Let R denotes the set of user-annotated frames, which serve as reference frames for propagation, and let c denotes the current frame that we wish to predict the mask for. We build a graph $G = (V, E)$, where V denotes nodes and E denotes edges to encode the structure between frames in R and the current frame c. In particular, we make every location in the $W \times H$ feature map of every frame a node in the graph, i.e., there are $(|R| + 1) \times W \times H$ nodes in total. Each node in frame c is connected to all the nodes in frames $\in R$ via an edge. An example of the graph is illustrated in Fig. 3a.

As input to our GCN, we concatenate the image feature with corresponding masks for each frame in R. We perform a similar concatenation operation for c but use a uniform "mask" instead. The input feature f_u for vertex u in GCN is computed as $f_u = \text{concat}\{F(x, y), M(x, y)\} \in \mathbb{R}^{(D+1)}$, where F and M are the image feature and the corresponding mask at time step t_u, respectively, and D is dimension. Here, (x, y) is the coordinate of the node u in the feature map.

We assign a weight $w_e(u, v) = \frac{\exp(f_u \cdot f_v)}{\sum_{v' \in \mathcal{N}(u)} \exp(f_u \cdot f_{v'})}$ to each edge (u, v) in the graph. The following propagation step is performed for node u:

$$f'_u = W_0 f_u + \sum_{v \in \mathcal{N}(u)} w_e(u, v) W_1 f_v, \tag{2}$$

where $\mathcal{N}(u)$ denotes neighbours of u in the graph, and W_0, W_1 are the weight matrices of the GCN layers. We take the feature $f'_u \in \mathbb{R}^K$ for all nodes u in current frame c as the input feature $F_c^g \in \mathbb{R}^{W \times H \times D'}$ to the *propagation decoder* which predicts the refined mask. We use D' to denote the output dimension of the GCN feature, and it is also the dimension of the input feature for the decoder. The superscript g stands for GCN. The feature, F_c^g, is used by the Scribble Propagation module described next.

Scribble Propagation Module: Most existing works employ user's corrections by only propagating the annotated masks to other frames. We found that propagating the scribbles explicitly produces notably better results. By feeding scribble information explicitly to the network, we are providing useful information about the regions it should pay attention to. Qualitatively, without providing this information (see Fig. 9), we notice that the propagation module typically ignores the corrections and repeats its mistakes in the subsequent frames.

As shown in Fig. 3c, inspired by [9], we formulate scribble propagation problem as a pixel-wise retrieval problem. For each pixel in current frame c, we find the pixel in the reference frame with the most similar embedding and assign the label of that pixel to the pixel in c. In the scribble propagation stage, we choose the reference frame as the annotated frame that is closest to the current time step. Formally, we first project the encoded pixel features into an embedding space and adopt the label of the nearest neighbour in this space. Pixels in the reference frame can be classified into three classes: background (regions with no scribbles), negative, and positive scribbles, respectively. We first project image features $F \in \mathbb{R}^{W \times H \times D}$ of the reference and current frames into a $d < D$ dimensional space using a shared embedding head. We use $d = 128$ and a 3×3 convolutional layer for the projection. We denote the transferred label for frame c as $S_c \in \mathbb{R}^{W \times H \times 2}$. To get the final mask, we concatenate S_c with F_c^g, i.e., the feature obtained from the GCN, reduce the dimension of the concatenation to D', and then feed it to the *propagation decoder*. Here, we employ a 3×3 convolution layer to perform the dimension reduction. Thus, the input feature to the *propagation decoder* is

$$F_c^{gs} = M(\text{concat}\{F_c^g, S_c\}) \in \mathbb{R}^{W \times H \times D'}, \qquad (3)$$

where M is the conv layer for dimensionality reduction. Superscript gs denotes merging GCN's output and the predicted scribbles. The *propagation decoder* is shared for mask and scribble propagation. The decoder takes the encoded feature (either the feature F_c^g from the mask propagation module or the feature F_c^{gs} from the scribble propagation stage), and outputs an object mask. This scribble network propagation is designed for propagating local errors within a short range and thus is different in purpose from the mask propagation module.

Network Training: All networks are trained end-to-end using binary cross entropy loss for mask prediction. To better supervise our model, we further use Scribble Consistency Loss for training the *interactive segmentation module*, and Batch Hard Triplet Loss [9] for training the *scribble propagation module*. We first describe how we synthesize scribbles and then specify the scribble consistency loss in the following paragraphs. We defer the Batch Hard Triplet Loss and implementation details to the appendix.

Scribble Correspondence: A big challenge of training the scribble propagation module is the lack of ground-truth pixel-wise correspondences between the scribbles in frame r and scribbles in frame c. To solve this problem, we create the ground-truth correspondences by synthesizing new frames: we augment the reference frame r to obtain the current frame c. The same augmentation is applied on the scribble map which gives us ground-truth correspondences between scribbles. Specifically, we use thin-plate spline transformation with 4 control points for the augmentation.

Scribble Consistency Loss: Typically, a user, who draws the scribble, would expect the network to behave consistently with the annotation, i.e., expects to see positive predictions around positive scribbles and vice versa for the negative. To encourage this behavior, we employ a scribble consistency loss:

$$L_{sc} = \sum_{i,j} -S_p(i,j) \log M_{pred}(i,j) - S_n(i,j) \log(1 - M_{pred}(i,j)), \qquad (4)$$

where S_p and S_n are the positive and negative scribble maps, (i,j) is the coordinate on the mask. Here, M_{pred} denotes the predicted object mask. Without this loss, the model in many cases ignores the user's input.

Table 1. Ablation study (DAVIS'17). Round 0 means mask prop. with predicted first frame mask.

Correction rounds	0	4	6	9
IPN-Box & Line-Scrib.	76.93	78.89	79.73	80.88
GCN Mask Prop. & Line-Scrib.	79.33	86.70	87.48	88.48
GCN Mask Prop. & Area-Scrib.	79.33	87.62	89.07	89.75
+ Scribble Prop.	–	88.92	90.90	91.16
+ GT First Frame	85.14	89.61	90.28	90.91

Table 2. Running time. Numbers are reported in ms per frame.

Model	IPN	Ours-256	Ours-512
Interaction	18	10.5	12
Curve Fitting	–	12	12
Mask Prop.	15	29	54
w/Cache	–	8	26
Scribble Prop.	–	15	28

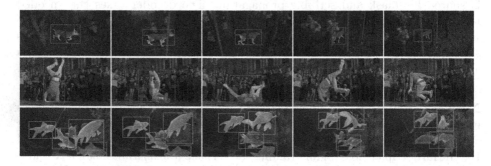

Fig. 4. Qualitative results on DAVIS2017 val set using our full annotation framework. 5 rounds of scribble correction + 8.85 box corrections were used.

4   Experimental Results

We perform extensive evaluation of ScribbleBox for video object annotation. To test generalization capabilities, we evaluate our approach both in the same domain, as well as in the out-of-domain datasets. For the In-Domain experiment, following IPN [30], we show results on DAVIS2017 [16] validation set, which has 65.3 frames per object on average. For the Out-of-Domain experiment, we show-case our results on MOTS-KITTI [36] which is a recent multi-object tracking and segmentation subset of KITTI [13]. We evaluate on a subset of 514 objects from the training and validation set where video length is between 20 and 150 frames. The average video length is 48.8 frames per object. We also perform a user study with real annotators labeling videos with our annotation tool.

Baseline: We use IPN [30] as our baseline, which ranks first in DAVIS'18 Interactive Challenge. Note that the official benchmark is not applicable in our case since our method is a two-stage method and the DAVIS-Agent does not support bounding box correction. Thus, we evaluate against the baseline by reporting box correction and scribble drawing effort v.s J&F via simulation (Table 1, Fig. 6) and annotation time v.s J&F through a user study (Fig. 7).

Scribbles: DAVIS Interactive Challenge [6] defines scribbles as thin skeletons inside erroneous areas, which we refer to as Thin-Line-Scribble. We instead propose to use more informative scribbles, where we ask the user to roughly trace the erroneous area with a cursor. We name our scribbles as Area-Scribble. While this may require slightly more effort, we show significant performance gains in our ablation study for both types of scribbles.

To simulate the Area-Scribble, given a previously predicted object mask and the ground-truth mask, we sample positive and negative scribbles from the false negative and false positive areas, respectively. To simulate realistic "trace" scribbles that a human would provide, we perform a binary erosion to the erroneous area and take the resulting regions as our simulated scribbles.

Details: We use the official SiamMask [40] tracker provided by the authors which was trained on COCO [21], ImageNetVID [34] and YouTubeVOS [43]. We perform inference for each object in the video. In Scribble-VOS, we propagate the corrected mask using mask propagation network to the end of the video. In addition, we propagate scribbles in two directions (forward and backward) for at most n frames (we use $n = 5$ in experiments).

4.1 In-Domain Annotation

Tracking Annotation: We compare Curve-VOT with a brute-force baseline which also uses SiamMask [40]. Instead of manipulating trajectories via curves, the user watches the video and corrects a box when it significantly deviates from the object. We use this correction as a new reference and run the tracker again starting from this frame. We simulate the user by correcting frames with IOU lower than a threshold, where we evaluate different thresholds from 0.4 to 0.8, representing different effort levels by the users. We treat each user's correction as two clicks, i.e., representing two corners of the box.

We first compare our approach with the baseline in terms of box IOU. As shown in the top-left of Fig. 5, our Curve-VOT requires fewer clicks to achieve the same IOU. In the bottom-left of Fig. 5, we provide a comparison in terms of segmentation J&F. We take the corrected bounding boxes and expand them to crop image. We report results with different expansion sizes. Since tracking

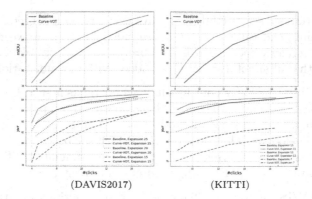

(DAVIS2017)   (KITTI)

Fig. 5. Interactive-VOT: (top) Box IoU vs number of simulated clicks (we report IoU averaged across frames), (bottom) Segmentation J&F. Note that in this experiment segmentation is automatic using annotated boxes, i.e., there are no clicks to improve masks, only to improve boxes.

the box only acts as a region proposal for VOS, we evaluate tolerance for tracking noise. As shown in the bottom-left of Fig. 5, using a 25 pixels expansion, J&F converges at around 9 clicks. This plot also emphasizes the importance of Scribble-VOS since additional box clicks only increase the accuracy marginally, which is a wasted effort. We instead turn to Scribble Annotation to further improve results.

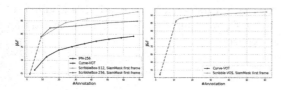

Fig. 6. Simulated full annotation workflow on (left) DAVIS2017, (right) KITTI. Dashed blue lines denote Curve-VOT, continuing lines Scribble-VOS annotation. (Color figure online)

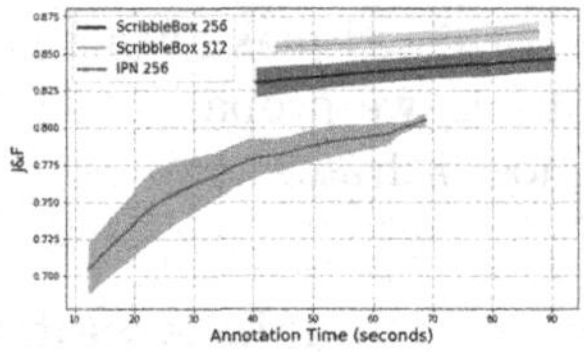

Fig. 7. Real annotator user study on DAVIS'17. Filled area denotes variance.

Mask Annotation: We first conduct an ablation study on individual components in Scribble-VOS in Table 1. Following IPN [30], we use the ground truth box in the first frame. To remove the effect of box annotation, we modify the IPN baseline to work on boxes. We name this baseline as IPN-box, where we use the officially released code from [30] and take box-cropped image as input. Same as our model, we first pre-train IPN-box on synthetic video clips, then fine-tune it on DAVIS2017. We add GCN-Mask Propagation module and multi-reference frames for interactions to the IPN-box baseline. It gives 2.4%, 7.81%, 7.75%,

7.6% improvements, respectively. To ablate our human interaction, we replace Thin-Line-Scribble with Area-Scribble. Our Area-Scribble yields 0.92%, 1.59% and 1.33% improvements, respectively. Results of ScribbleBox without scribble propagation also indicate that our *scribble propagation module* plays an important role in improving J&F (1.3%, 1.83%, and 1.41%, respectively). We further analyze impact on quality of the first frame's mask. As shown in the last line of Table 1, ground truth first frame mask gives 5.81% improvement without interactions but the improvement becomes marginal after more rounds of interaction. These demonstrate the effectiveness of our interaction model.

Full Framework Comparison: We conduct a full framework analysis in a simulated environment. We compare with previous work in terms of the number of human interactions. For a baseline, we run the officially released DAVIS Interactive agent locally and evaluate upon IPN's checkpoint which achieved the first place in DAVIS2018 Interactive Challenge. Each correction round returned by the DAVIS-Agent consists of multiple scribbles. We count each scribble as one annotation. Our results are conducted on the annotated tracked boxes after 9.14 box clicks (J&F 78.64%, i.e., second point on the dashed line in Fig. 6). Figure 6 reports a comparison of our framework with IPN [30]. Note that our model with only Curve-VOT interaction already performs better than baseline with mask annotation. We also ablate the impact of different image resolutions.

Auto   + Box   + Scribble   Auto   + Box   + Scribble

Fig. 8. Qualitative results on DAVIS2017 val. **Auto:** SiamMask, **Box:** Results after box correct. (Curve-VOT), **Scribble:** Results after Scribble-VOS.

Qualitative Results: We show qualitative results on DAVIS2017 val in Fig. 4. All results shown are annotated via Curve-VOT (9.14 clicks on average) following 5 rounds of scribble correction. Qualitative examples are in Fig. 8. Results indicate that Curve-VOT corrects large errors and Scribble-VOS further refines them. Figure 9 shows an example indicating the importance of our scribble propagation and differences between Thin-Line-Scribble and our Area-Scibble.

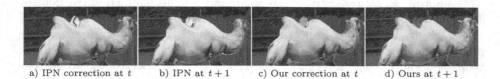

a) IPN correction at t b) IPN at $t+1$ c) Our correction at t d) Ours at $t+1$

Fig. 9. Qualitative example demonstrating **effectiveness of our scribble propagation**. a) & c): user draws a scribble in frame t. Note that IPN uses skeleton-like scribbles while we use trace scribbles. b) & d): results after scribble propagation at frame t+1.

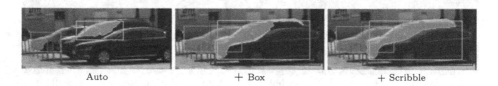

Fig. 10. Qualitative results on MOTS-KITTI [36] using our full annotation framework. 5 rounds of scribble correction + 11.2 box corrections were used.

Auto   + Box   + Scribble

Fig. 11. Qualitative results on MOTS-KITTI [36]. **Auto**: SiamMask, **Box**: Results after box correct. (Curve-VOT), **Scribble**: Results after Scribble-VOS. (Color figure online)

Fig. 12. Example annotations using our annotation tool on the EPIC-Kitchen dataset. Each object in a 100-frame video requiring on average 69.87s of annotation time (including inference time). The first column indicates target objects.

4.2   Out-of-Domain Annotation

We now run inference of our model on an unseen dataset (MOTS-KITTI). As shown in Fig. 5 (right), Curve-VOT outperforms the baseline by a large margin. Note that objects in KITTI are typically smaller than DAVIS, and so we adopt a smaller expansion size. Qualitative interactive tracking results are shown in Fig. 10 and Fig. 11. The car with blue mask in Fig. 11 also shows our intuition about why we need two-stage annotation. Curve-VOT first ensures that the intended annotated object is not lost. This usually happens when multiple small and similar objects are adjacent.

4.3   User Study

We put our framework to practice and show annotation results using human annotators with a simple tool that runs our models in the backend. All human experiments were done on the same desktop with a Nvidia-Titan Xp GPU.

In-Domain: We conduct a user study on the DAVIS2017 validation set. We randomly select one object per video which adds up to 1999 frames including blank frames. We employed four in-house annotators. Each was asked to annotate the same videos using both the baseline (IPN) and our method. For our method, we evaluate two models trained and tested at different resolutions: 256 (same as IPN) and 512, and we refer to them as ScibbleBox-256, ScibbleBox-512, respectively. For fairness, annotators first annotate with our model so that they gain familiarity with the data before using the baseline method. We ask annotators to annotate until there is no visible improvement. We show the mean curve for J&F v.s annotation time in seconds in Fig. 7. We include the data processing and model running times in the cumulative annotation time. We use filled area to denote variance between annotators. Note that the starting point of our model is to the right of our baseline because we only calculate J&F after Curve-VOT corrections and their corresponding J&F have already outperformed baseline's converging performance by a large margin. We also calculate mean J&F in the overlapping time interval, which gives IPN: 79.25%, ScribbleBox-256: 83.62% and ScribbleBox-512: 85.66%.

We further report model running times in Table 2. We report times with feature cache as "Mask Prop. w/Cache". Although our model with 512-resolution is slower, it outperforms both 256-resolution model and baseline given the same annotation time budget.

Annotating New Datasets: We annotate a subset of the EPIC-Kitchen [10,11] dataset using our tool. As shown in Fig. 12, without any finetuning on out of domain data, our method generates high-quality masks with only a few annotations. We plan to annotate and make available a large portion of the dataset.

5   Conclusion

We introduced a novel video annotation framework that splits annotation into two steps: annotating box tracks, and labeling masks inside these tracks. Box tracks are annotated efficiently by approximating the trajectory using a parametric curve with a small number of control points which the annotator can interactively correct. Segmentation masks are corrected via scribbles which are efficiently propagated through time. We showed significant performance gains in annotation efficiency over past work in two major benchmarks.

Acknowledgments. This work was supported by NSERC. SF acknowledges the Canada CIFAR AI Chair award at the Vector Institute.

References

1. Acuna, D., Ling, H., Kar, A., Fidler, S.: Efficient interactive annotation of segmentation datasets with Polygon-RNN++. In CVPR (2018)
2. Bai, X., Sapiro, G.: A geodesic framework for fast interactive image and video segmentation and matting. In: IEEE 11th International Conference on Computer Vision, ICCV 2007, Rio de Janeiro, Brazil, 14–20 October 2007, pp. 1–8. IEEE Computer Society (2007)
3. Bai, X., Wang, J., Simons, D., Sapiro, G.: Video SnapCut: robust video object cutout using localized classifiers. ACM Trans. Graph. **28**(3) (2009). Article no. 70
4. Benard, A., Gygli, M.: Interactive video object segmentation in the wild. ArXiv, abs/1801.00269 (2018)
5. Caelles, S., Maninis, K., Pont-Tuset, J., Leal-Taixé, L., Cremers, D., Gool, L.V.: One-shot video object segmentation. In 2017 IEEE Conference on Computer Vision and Pattern Recognition, CVPR 2017, Honolulu, HI, USA, 21–26 July 2017, pp. 5320–5329. IEEE Computer Society (2017)
6. Caelles, S., et al.: The 2018 DAVIS challenge on video object segmentation. arXiv:1803.00557 (2018)
7. Castrejon, L., Kundu, K., Urtasun, R., Fidler, S.: Annotating object instances with a Polygon-RNN. In: CVPR (2017)
8. Chen, L.-C., Fidler, S., Yuille, A., Urtasun, R.: Beat the MTurkers: automatic image labeling from weak 3D supervision. In: CVPR (2014)
9. Chen, Y., Pont-Tuset, J., Montes, A., Van Gool, L.: Blazingly fast video object segmentation with pixel-wise metric learning. In: Computer Vision and Pattern Recognition (CVPR) (2018)
10. Damen, D., et al.: Scaling egocentric vision: the EPIC-KITCHENS dataset. In: Ferrari, V., Hebert, M., Sminchisescu, C., Weiss, Y. (eds.) ECCV 2018. LNCS, vol. 11208, pp. 753–771. Springer, Cham (2018). https://doi.org/10.1007/978-3-030-01225-0_44
11. Damen, D., et al.: The EPIC-KITCHENS dataset: collection, challenges and baselines. IEEE Trans. Pattern Anal. Mach. Intell. (2020)
12. Gao, J., Tang, C., Ganapathi-Subramanian, V., Huang, J., Su, H., Guibas, L.J.: DeepSpline: data-driven reconstruction of parametric curves and surfaces. arXiv preprint arXiv:1901.03781 (2019)
13. Geiger, A., Lenz, P., Urtasun, R.: Are we ready for autonomous driving? The KITTI vision benchmark suite. In: 2012 IEEE Conference on Computer Vision and Pattern Recognition, pp. 3354–3361, June 2012
14. He, K., Zhang, X., Ren, S., Sun, J.: Deep residual learning for image recognition. In: Proceedings of the IEEE Conference on Computer Vision and Pattern Recognition, pp. 770–778 (2016)

15. Yuen, J., Russell, B., Liu, C., Torralba, A.: LabelMe video: building a video database with human annotations. In: 2009 IEEE 12th International Conference on Computer Vision, pp. 1451–1458, September 2009

16. Khoreva, A., Rohrbach, A., Schiele, B.: Video object segmentation with language referring expressions. In: Jawahar, C.V., Li, H., Mori, G., Schindler, K. (eds.) ACCV 2018. LNCS, vol. 11364, pp. 123–141. Springer, Cham (2019). https://doi.org/10.1007/978-3-030-20870-7_8

17. Kipf, T.N., Welling, M.: Semi-supervised classification with graph convolutional networks. In: 5th International Conference on Learning Representations, ICLR 2017, Toulon, France, 24–26 April 2017, Conference Track Proceedings (2017)

18. Levinkov, E., Tompkin, J., Bonneel, N., Kirchhoff, S., Andres, B., Pfister, H.: Interactive multicut video segmentation. In: PG 2016 (2016)

19. Li, B., Yan, J., Wu, W., Zhu, Z., Hu, X.: High performance visual tracking with siamese region proposal network. In: 2018 IEEE/CVF Conference on Computer Vision and Pattern Recognition, pp. 8971–8980, June 2018

20. Li, Y., Sun, J., Shum, H.: Video object cut and paste. ACM Trans. Graph. **24**(3), 595–600 (2005)

21. Lin, T.-Y., et al.: Microsoft COCO: common objects in context. In: Fleet, D., Pajdla, T., Schiele, B., Tuytelaars, T. (eds.) ECCV 2014. LNCS, vol. 8693, pp. 740–755. Springer, Cham (2014). https://doi.org/10.1007/978-3-319-10602-1_48

22. Lin, Z., Xie, J., Zhou, C., Hu, J., Zheng, W.: Interactive video object segmentation via spatio-temporal context aggregation and online learning. In: The 2019 DAVIS Challenge on Video Object Segmentation - CVPR Workshops (2019)

23. Ling, H., Gao, J., Kar, A., Chen, W., Fidler, S.: Fast interactive object annotation with Curve-GCN. In: CVPR, June 2019

24. Mahadevan, S., Voigtlaender, P., Leibe, B.: Iteratively trained interactive segmentation. arXiv preprint arXiv:1805.04398 (2018)

25. Manen, S., Gygli, M., Dai, D., Van Gool, L.: PathTrack: fast trajectory annotation with path supervision. arXiv:1703.02437 (2017)

26. Maninis, K.-K., Caelles, S., Pont-Tuset, J., Van Gool, L.: Deep extreme cut: from extreme points to object segmentation. In: CVPR (2018)

27. Mortensen, E.N., Barrett, W.A.: Intelligent scissors for image composition. In: SIGGRAPH, pp. 191–198 (1995)

28. Nagaraja, N.S., Schmidt, F.R., Brox, T.: Video segmentation with just a few strokes. In: 2015 IEEE International Conference on Computer Vision, ICCV 2015, Santiago, Chile, 7–13 December 2015, pp. 3235–3243. IEEE Computer Society (2015)

29. Najafi, M., Kulharia, V., Ajanthan, T., Torr, P.H.S.: Similarity learning for dense label transfer. In: The 2018 DAVIS Challenge on Video Object Segmentation - CVPR Workshops (2018)

30. Oh, S.W., Lee, J.-Y., Xu, N., Kim, S.J.: Fast user-guided video object segmentation by interaction-and-propagation networks. In: Proceedings of the IEEE Conference on Computer Vision and Pattern Recognition, pp. 5247–5256 (2019)

31. Oh, S.W., Lee, J.-Y., Xu, N., Kim, S.J.: Video object segmentation using space-time memory networks. In: Proceedings of the IEEE International Conference on Computer Vision, pp. 9226–9235 (2019)

32. Price, B.L., Morse, B.S., Cohen, S.: LIVEcut: learning-based interactive video segmentation by evaluation of multiple propagated cues. In: IEEE 12th International Conference on Computer Vision, ICCV 2009, Kyoto, Japan, 27 September–4 October 2009, pp. 779–786. IEEE Computer Society (2009)

33. Rother, C., Kolmogorov, V., Blake, A.: GrabCut: interactive foreground extraction using iterated graph cuts. In: SIGGRAPH (2004)

34. Russakovsky, O., et al.: ImageNet large scale visual recognition challenge. Int. J. Comput. Vis. **115**(3), 211–252 (2015). https://doi.org/10.1007/s11263-015-0816-y

35. Tao, R., Gavves, E., Smeulders, A.W.M.: Siamese instance search for tracking. In: 2016 IEEE Conference on Computer Vision and Pattern Recognition (CVPR), June 2016

36. Voigtlaender, P., et al.: MOTS: multi-object tracking and segmentation (2019)

37. Vondrick, C., Patterson, D., Ramanan, D.: Efficiently scaling up crowdsourced video annotation. Int. J. Comput. Vis. **101**(1), 184–204 (2013). https://doi.org/10.1007/s11263-012-0564-1

38. Vondrick, C., Ramanan, D.: Video annotation and tracking with active learning. In: Proceedings of the 24th International Conference on Neural Information Processing Systems, NIPS 2011, USA, pp. 28–36. Curran Associates Inc. (2011)

39. Wang, J., Bhat, P., Colburn, A., Agrawala, M., Cohen, M.F.: Interactive video cutout. ACM Trans. Graph. **24**(3), 585–594 (2005)

40. Wang, Q., Zhang, L., Bertinetto, L., Hu, W., Torr, P.H.: Fast online object tracking and segmentation: a unifying approach. In: CVPR (2019)

41. Wang, Z., Ling, H., Acuna, D., Kar, A., Fidler, S.: Object instance annotation with deep extreme level set evolution. In: CVPR (2019)

42. Wug Oh, S., Lee, J.-Y., Sunkavalli, K., Joo Kim, S.: Fast video object segmentation by reference-guided mask propagation. In: Proceedings of the IEEE Conference on Computer Vision and Pattern Recognition, pp. 7376–7385 (2018)

43. Xu, N., et al.: YouTube-VOS: sequence-to-sequence video object segmentation. In: Ferrari, V., Hebert, M., Sminchisescu, C., Weiss, Y. (eds.) ECCV 2018. LNCS, vol. 11209, pp. 603–619. Springer, Cham (2018). https://doi.org/10.1007/978-3-030-01228-1_36

Rethinking Pseudo-LiDAR Representation

Xinzhu Ma[1], Shinan Liu[2], Zhiyi Xia[3], Hongwen Zhang[4], Xingyu Zeng[2], and Wanli Ouyang[1(✉)]

[1] SenseTime Computer Vision Research Group, The University of Sydney, Sydney, Australia
xima0693@uni.sydney.edu.au, wanli.ouyang@sydney.edu.au
[2] SenseTime Research, Beijing, China
{liushinan,zengxingyu}@sensetime.com
[3] Dalian University of Technology, Dalian, China
xiazhiyi99@mail.dlut.edu.cn
[4] Institute of Automation, Chinese Academy of Sciences, Beijing, China
hongwen.zhang@cripac.ia.ac.cn

Abstract. The recently proposed pseudo-LiDAR based 3D detectors greatly improve the benchmark of monocular/stereo 3D detection task. However, the underlying mechanism remains obscure to the research community. In this paper, we perform an in-depth investigation and observe that the efficacy of pseudo-LiDAR representation comes from the coordinate transformation, instead of data representation itself. Based on this observation, we design an image based CNN detector named Patch-Net, which is more generalized and can be instantiated as pseudo-LiDAR based 3D detectors. Moreover, the pseudo-LiDAR data in our PatchNet is organized as the image representation, which means existing 2D CNN designs can be easily utilized for extracting deep features from input data and boosting 3D detection performance. We conduct extensive experiments on the challenging KITTI dataset, where the proposed PatchNet outperforms all existing pseudo-LiDAR based counterparts. Code has been made available at: https://github.com/xinzhuma/patchnet.

Keywords: Image-based 3D detection · Data representation · Image · pseudo-LiDAR · Coordinate transformation

1 Introduction

3D object detection has received increasing attention from both industry and academia because of its wide applications in various fields such as autonomous driving and robotics. Existing algorithms largely rely on LiDAR sensors, which

Electronic supplementary material The online version of this chapter (https://doi.org/10.1007/978-3-030-58601-0_19) contains supplementary material, which is available to authorized users.

© Springer Nature Switzerland AG 2020
A. Vedaldi et al. (Eds.): ECCV 2020, LNCS 12358, pp. 311–327, 2020.
https://doi.org/10.1007/978-3-030-58601-0_19

provide accurate 3D point clouds of the surrounding environment. Although these approaches achieve impressive performance, the excessive dependence on expensive equipment restricts their application prospects.

Compared with fast developing LiDAR-based algorithms, 3D detection [6,7,20] results produced from only RGB images lag considerably behind. This can be attributed to the ill-posed nature of the problem, where a lack of explicit knowledge about the unobserved depth dimension significantly increases the task complexity. An intuitive solution is that we can use a Convolutional Neural Network (CNN) to predict the depth map [1,10,13] and then use it to augment the input data if we do not have the available depth information. Although the estimated depth map is helpful to 3D scene understanding, the performance improvement brought by it is still limited.

Several recently proposed algorithms [24,35,36] transform the estimated depth map into pseudo-LiDAR representation, and then apply LiDAR based methods to the transformed data. Surprisingly, this simple yet effective method achieves significant improvement in detection accuracy on the challenging KITTI dataset. However, it is unclear why such a representation can bring so much performance improvement. According to the empirical explanation of proponents, the choice of representations is the critical success factor of 3D detection systems. Compared with image representation, they believe that pseudo-LiDAR is more suitable for describing the 3D structure of objects, which is the main reason for performance improvement. However, in the absence of direct evidence, the correctness of this statement is still open to doubt.

In this paper, we aim to explore the essential reasons of this phenomenon. Specifically, on the basis of prior works, we carefully construct an image representation based detector named PatchNet-vanilla, which is an equivalent implementation of pseudo-LiDAR [35] except for the representation of input data. With this detector, we can compare the influence of these two kinds of representations on 3D detection task in depth. Different from the arguments of other works [24,35,36], we observe that the performances of PatchNet-vanilla and pseudo-LiDAR [35] are completely matched, which means that data representation has no effect on 3D detection performance. Moreover, we perform ablation studies on the input data, and observe that the real thing matters is coordinate transformation from image coordinate system to the LiDAR coordinate system, which implicitly encodes the camera calibration information into input data.

PatchNet-vanilla also hints us that pseudo-LiDAR representation is not necessary to improve the accuracy of image based 3D detection. By integrating the generated 3D coordinates as additional channels of input data, our 3D detector gets promising performance. More importantly, this approach can be easily generalized to other image based detectors. Also notice that, as a kind of non-grid structured data, pseudo-LiDAR signals commonly need point-wise CNNs [29,30] to process. However, the development of these technologies still lags behind the standard CNNs. From this point of view, the image-based detectors should outperform their counterparts based on pseudo-LiDAR. To confirm this hypothesis,

PatchNet was proposed by extending our original model (e.g., using more powerful backbone network [15,16]), and outperforms other pseudo-LiDAR based detectors on KITTI dataset. In addition, there are other benefits from using images directly as the network's inputs, such as allowing us to train an end-to-end 3D detector. Based on above reasons, we argue that image representation based 3D detectors have greater development potential.

To summarize, the contributions of this paper are as follows: First, through sufficient experimental demonstration, we confirm that the reason why the pseudo-LiDAR representation is effective is not the data representation itself, but the coordinate system transformation. Second, we find that pseudo-LiDAR representation is not necessary to improve detection performance. After integrating spatial coordinates, image representation based algorithms can also achieve the competitive if not superior the same performance. Third, thanks to more powerful image-based deep learning technologies, we achieve the state-of-the-art performance and show the potential of image representation based 3D detectors.

2   Related Work

2.1   3D Detectors Based on Image Representation

Most of the early works in this scope share the same paradigm with 2D detectors [9,12,14,21,22,32,40]. However, estimating the 3D coordinates (x, y, z) of the object center is much more complicated since there is ambiguity to locate the absolute physical position from only image appearances. Mono3D [6] focus on 3D object proposals generation using prior knowledge (e.g., object size, ground plane). Deep3DBox [26] introduces geometric constraints based on the fact that the 3D bounding box should fit tightly into 2D detection bounding box. Deep-MANTA [4] encodes 3D vehicle information using key points, since vehicles are rigid objects with well known geometry. Then the vehicle recognition in Deep-MANTA can be considered as key points detection. An expansion stage of ROI-10D [25] takes the advantage of depth information provided by an additional depth estimator [5,10], which itself is learned in a self-supervised manner. In Multi-Fusion [38], a multi-level fusion approach is proposed to exploit disparity estimation results from a pre-trained module for both the 2D box proposal generation and the 3D prediction part of their network. MonoGRNet [31] consists of four subnetworks for progressive 3D localization and directly learning 3D information based on solely semantic cues. MonoDIS [34] disentangles the loss for 2D and 3D detection and jointly trains these two tasks in an end-to-end manner. M3D-RPN [2] is the current state-of-the-art with image representation as input, using multiple 2D convolutions of non-shared weights to learn location-specific features for joint prediction of 2D and 3D boxes. The above approaches utilize various prior knowledge, pre-train models or more powerful CNN designs, but they do not try to use pseudo-LiDAR data to improve their performance. Our work aims to improve the detection accuracy of image-based methods by extracting useful information from pseudo-LiDAR data, which is complementary to these approaches.

2.2   3D Detectors Based on Pseudo-LiDAR Representation

Recently, several approaches [24,35,36,39] greatly boost the performance of monocular 3D detection task. What they have in common is that they first estimate the depth map from the input RGB image and transform it into pseudo-LiDAR (point cloud) by leveraging the camera calibration information. Specifically, [35] adopt off-the-shelf LiDAR-based 3D detectors [18,28] to process the generated pseudo-LiDAR signals directly. AM3D [24] proposes a multi-modal features fusion module to embed the complementary RGB cues into the generated pseudo-LiDAR representation. Besides, [24] also proposes a depth prior based background points segmentation module to avoid the problems caused by the inaccuracy of point cloud annotation. [36] proposes a 2D-3D bounding box consistency loss which can alleviate the local misalignment issue. However, such methods rely heavily on the accuracy of depth map. Overall, pseudo-LiDAR based detectors achieve impressive accuracy in 3D detection task, however, the underlying mechanism is still obscure to the research community. In this paper, we perform an in-depth investigation on this issue. Besides, pseudo-LiDAR based detectors treat generated 3D data as point cloud and use PointNet for processing the point cloud, while our PatchNet organizes them as image and facilitates the use of 2D CNN for processing the data.

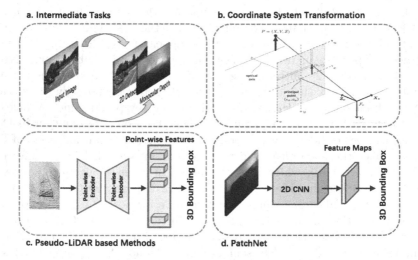

Fig. 1. Comparison of pseudo-LiDAR based methods [24,35,36] and Patch-Net. They both generate intermediate tasks using off-the-shelf models (a), and project the image coordinates to the world coordinates (b). Pseudo-LiDAR based methods treat these data as LiDAR signals, and use point-wise network to predict results from them (c). However, PatchNet organizes them as image representation for subsequent processing (d).

3 Delving into Pseudo-LiDAR Representation

In this section, we investigate the influence of pseudo-LiDAR representation on 3D detection accuracy. In particular, we first give a brief review of pseudo-LiDAR based detectors and introduce the technical details of its image based equivalent detector. Then, we analyse whether data representation is the internal reason of performance improvement by comparing the performance of these two detectors.

3.1 Review of Pseudo-LiDAR Based Detectors

Here we take pseudo-LiDAR [35] as example for analysis, and the paradigm of [35] can be summarized as follows:

Step 1: Depth estimation. Given a single monocular image (or stereo pairs) as input, [35] predict the depth d for each image pixel (u, v) using a stand alone CNN (Fig. 1(a)).

Step 2: 2D detection. Another CNN is adopted to generate 2D object region proposals (Fig. 1(a)).

Step 3: 3D data generation. First, regions of interests (RoIs) are cropped from the depth map generated from Step 1, according to the region proposals generated from Step 2. Then, the 3D coordinates of pixels of each RoI can be recovered by:

$$\begin{cases} z = d, \\ x = (u - C_x) \times z/f, \\ y = (v - C_y) \times z/f, \end{cases} \tag{1}$$

where f is the focal length of the camera, (C_x, C_y) is the principal point (Fig. 1(b)).

Step 4: 3D object detection. Pseudo-LiDAR based approaches treat the 3D data generated from Step 3 as LiDAR signals, and use point-wise CNN to predict result from them (Fig. 1(c)). In particular, they are treated as an unordered point set $\{x_1, x_2, ..., x_n\}$ with $x_i \in \mathbb{R}^d$, and processed by PointNet, which defines a set function f that maps a set of points to a output vector:

$$f(x_1, x_2, ..., x_n) = \gamma \left(\underset{i=1,...,n}{\mathbf{MAX}} \{h(x_i)\} \right) \tag{2}$$

where γ and h are implemented by multi-layer perceptron (MLP) layers.

3.2 PatchNet-Vanilla: Equivalent Implementation of Pseudo-LiDAR

Analysis. The most significant difference between the pseudo-LiDAR based approaches [24,35] and other approaches lies in the representation of depth map. The authors of [24,35] argue that pseudo-LiDAR representation is more suitable for describing the 3D structure of objects, which is the main reason behind the high accuracy of their models. To verify this, we conduct an image representation based detector, i.e., PatchNet-vanilla, which is identical to pseudo-LiDAR [35] except for the input representation.

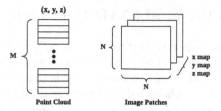

Fig. 2. Illustration of input data. Pseudo-LiDAR based approaches use point cloud (*left*) as input, while PatchNet use image patches (*right*) as input. We set $M = N \times N$ so that these two kinds of input data contain the same amount of information.

Implementation. The steps 1, 2 and 3 in PatchNet-vanilla are the same as that in the pseudo-LiDAR based detectors. Therefore, they have the same estimated depth, 2D detection results and generated 3D data. The main difference is the Step 4, which will be analyzed in details. Specifically, in PatchNet-vanilla, the generated 3D data is organized as image representation (see Fig. 2), where each pixel location with 3 channels, i.e. (x, y, z) in Eq. 1. Different from pointwise CNN used in pseudo-LiDAR counterparts, 2D CNN is used for processing the input data in PatchNet-vanilla (Fig. 1(d)). Note that we can define a same function as Eq. 2 using 2D convolution with 1×1 receptive field and global max pooling. This scheme is also adopted in the official implementation[1] of PointNet.

Table 1. Comparison of different input representation. Experiments are conducted on KITTI *validation* set. * indicates the method is reproduced by ourself. Metric is $AP|_{R_{11}}$ of the **Car** category.

Method	Modality	3D detection			BEV detection		
		Easy	Moderate	Hard	Easy	Moderate	Hard
pseudo-LiDAR [35]	pseudo-LiDAR	28.2	18.5	16.4	40.6	26.3	22.9
pseudo-LiDAR*	pseudo-LiDAR	28.9	18.4	16.2	41.0	26.2	22.8
PatchNet-vanilla	Image	28.7	18.4	16.4	40.8	26.1	22.8

3.3 Preliminary Conclusion

The performances of PatchNet-vanilla and pseudo-LiDAR are reported in Table 1, where we reproduce pseudo-LiDAR to eliminate the impact of implementation details. As can be seen, PatchNet-vanilla achieves almost the same accuracy as pseudo-LiDAR, which means the choice of data representation has no substantial impact on 3D detection tasks. Moreover, we perform ablation studies on data content, and observe that coordinate transform is the key factor

---

[1] https://github.com/charlesq34/pointnet.

for performance improvement (experimental results and analysis can be found in Sect. 5.2).

Above observations reveal that pseudo-LiDAR representation is not necessary, and after integrating the generated 3D information, image representation has the same potential. More importantly, compared with point-wise CNNs [29,30], image based representation can utilize the well-studied 2D CNNs for developing high-performance 3D detectors. Along this direction, we show how the proposed PatchNet framework is used to further improve the detection performance in Sect. 4.

4   PatchNet

In PatchNet, we first train two deep CNNs on two intermediate prediction tasks (i.e., 2D detection and depth estimation) to obtain position and depth information, which are the same as PatchNet-vanilla and pseudo-LiDAR based detectors (Fig. 1(a)). Then, as shown in Fig. 3, for each detected 2D object proposal, we crop the corresponding region from the depth map, and recover its spatial information using Eq. 1. Next, deep features of RoIs are extracted by backbone network, and filtered by the mask global pooling and foreground mask. Finally, we use a detection head with difficulty assignment mechanism to predict the 3D bounding box parameterized by $(x, y, z, h, w, l, \theta)$.

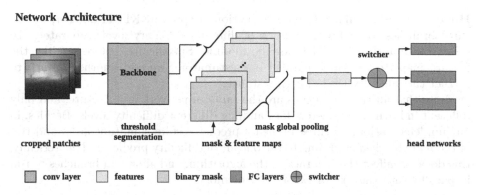

Fig. 3. Illustration of the network architecture. Given an input patch with $\{x, y, z\}$ channels, we first generate a binary mask according to mean depth, and use it to guide pooling layer to extract the features corresponding to foreground object. Then, we assign examples to different head networks according to the prediction difficulty of them.

Backbone. Most of existing backbone networks can be used in our method to extract image features. In our implementation, we use the ResNet-18 [15] with Squeeze-and-Excitation (SE) block [16] as the 3D detection backbone. Moreover, we remove all pooling layers in the original SE-ResNet-18 so that its output features have the same size as input image patches. Then we use mask global pooling operation and generated mask to extract features from foreground object.

Mask Global Pooling. The feature maps $\mathbf{X}$ output from the backbone network will be converted to a feature vector by global pooling. Conventional global pooling takes features of all positions into account and output the global feature. To obtain more robust features, we perform global pooling only on those features within foreground regions so that the final feature is corresponding to those pixels of interest. Specifically, we additionally generate a binary mask $\mathbf{M}$ which indicates the foreground region. This masks will be applied to the feature maps $\mathbf{X}$ to select foreground features before global pooling. Such a mask global pooling encourages the final feature to focus on the regions of interest.

Mask Generation. Following the prior work [24], the fore/background binary mask $\mathbf{M}$ is obtained by setting a threshold to the depth map. Specifically, we empirically add an offset on the mean depth of each patch and set it as the threshold. The regions with the depth values smaller than this threshold will be regarded as the foreground regions. The binary mask $\mathbf{M}$ has the same resolution as the input image with its values corresponding to foreground regions set as 1 and otherwise 0.

Head. Inspired by difficulty-wise evaluation adopted by KITTI dataset, we use three branches to deal with samples of different difficulty levels separately. To select the branch, we need a specific module. Specifically, before sending the feature maps to the three parallel box estimators, we add another branch to predict the difficulty level of each instance.

Note that all three branches are the same in network architecture, and only different in learned parameters for handling different difficulty levels. Besides, in our implementation, all three branches predict results simultaneously, and two of them are blocked according to the output of difficulty predictor. Theoretically, this does not affect the accuracy of the algorithm, and allows all branches to run in parallel with the cost of extra GPU memory.

Loss Function. The ground truth box is parameterized by center (x, y, z), size (w, h, l) and heading angle θ. We adopted the loss function proposed by [28] to our baseline model:

$$\mathcal{L} = \mathcal{L}_{center} + \mathcal{L}_{size} + \mathcal{L}_{heading} + \lambda \cdot \mathcal{L}_{corner} \tag{3}$$

where $\mathcal{L}_{center}, \mathcal{L}_{size}$, and $\mathcal{L}_{heading}$ respectively denote the loss function for the center, size, and heading angle. λ is an empirical weight, and $\mathcal{L}_{corner}$ is used to alleviate the potential sub-optimal problem. Please refer to [28] for details.

5 Experiments

5.1 Setup

Dataset. We evaluate our approach on the challenging KITTI dataset [11], which provides 7,481 images for training and 7,518 images for testing. Detection and localization (i.e., bird's-eye-view detection) tasks are evaluated in three different subsets: *easy*, *moderate* and *hard*, according to the occlusion and truncation levels of objects. Since the ground truth for the test set is not available and the access to the test server is limited, we follow the protocol of prior works [6–8] to divide the training data into a training set (3,712 images) and a validation set (3,769 images). We will conduct ablation studies based on this split and also report final results on the testing set provided by KITTI server. Due to space limitations, we only report the **Car** detection results of **monocular images** in the main paper. More results about **stereo pairs** and **Pedestrian/Cyclist** can be found in Appendix.

Metric. Most of previous works use 11-point interpolated average precision (IAP) metric [11] as follows:

$$AP|_{R_{11}} = \frac{1}{11} \sum_{r \in R_{11}} \max_{\tilde{r} \geq r} \rho(\tilde{r}). \tag{4}$$

Recently, to avoid ostensible boost in performance, KITTI and [34] call for a new 40-point IAP ($AP|_{R_{40}}$) with the exclusion of "0" and four-times denser interpolated prediction for better approximation of the area under the Precision/Recall curve. For fair and comprehensive comparisons with previous and future works, we show both $AP|_{R_{11}}$ and $AP|_{R_{40}}$ in the following experiments.

Table 2. 3D object detection results on KITTI *validation* set. Metrics are AP_{3D} and AP_{BEV} of the **Car** category with 11 recall positions. * indicates method is reproduced by ourselves.

Method	Modality	3D detection			BEV detection		
		Easy	Moderate	Hard	Easy	Moderate	Hard
pseudo-LiDAR [35]	pseudo-LiDAR	28.2	18.5	16.4	40.6	26.3	22.9
pseudo-LiDAR*	pseudo-LiDAR	28.9	18.4	16.2	41.0	26.2	22.8
AM3D [24]	pseudo-LiDAR	32.2	21.1	17.3	43.8	28.4	23.9
PatchNet-vanilla	Image	28.7	18.4	16.4	40.8	26.1	22.8
PatchNet-AM3D	Image	32.8	20.9	17.3	43.5	28.2	23.6
PatchNet	Image	35.1	22.0	19.6	44.4	29.1	24.1
Improvement	–	+2.9	+0.9	+2.3	+0.6	+0.7	+0.2

5.2   Investigation of Pseudo-LiDAR Representation

Analysis of Data Representation. As shown in Table 2, PatchNet-vanilla shows a comparable results with pseudo-LiDAR, which indicates that *data representation is not the key factor to improve the performance of 3D detectors.* To further validate this claim, we also adjust our image representation based detector based on AM3D, where we achieve a matched performance again.

Table 3. Comparison between different input data on KITTI *validation* set. Metrics are AP_{3D} and AP_{BEV} of the **Car** category with 11 recall positions.

Input	AP_{3D}			AP_{BEV}		
	Easy	Moderate	Hard	Easy	Moderate	Hard
$\{z\}$	4.51	3.48	3.03	6.31	4.50	3.98
$\{x, z\}$	27.1	18.3	15.8	35.9	23.4	18.3
$\{x, y, z\}$	35.1	22.0	19.6	44.4	29.1	24.1
$\{u, v, z\}$	24.6	15.7	14.6	33.2	21.3	16.7

Analysis of Data Content. We conduct an ablation study on the effect of input channels and report the results in Table 3. We can see from the results that, using only depth as an input, it is almost impossible to obtain accurate 3D bounding boxes. If other coordinates are used, the accuracy of predicted boxes improves greatly, which validates the importance of generated spatial features. It should be noted that in the absence of y-axis data, this detection accuracy is much worse than our full model. This is shows that all coordinates are useful for the 3D detection.

In pseudo-LiDAR, the coordinate (u, v) for images is projected to the world coordinate (x, y) using the camera information. Experimental results in Table 3 also compares the effectiveness of different coordinate systems. According to experimental results, world coordinate (x, y), which utilizes the camera information, performs much better than image coordinate (u, v). Through the above experiments, we can observe that *that real thing matters is coordinate system transformation, instead of data representation itself.*

5.3   Boosting the Performance of PatchNet

Backbone. Compared with point-wise backbone nets commonly used in (pseudo) LiDAR based methods, standard 2D backbones such as [15,16,37] can extract more discriminative features, which is a natural advantage of image based detectors. We investigate the impact of different backbones on proposed Patch-Net, and the experimental results are summarized in Table 4 (*left*). The original PointNet has only 8 layers. For fair comparison, we construct a PointNet with 18 layers, which is denoted by PointNet-18 in Table 4. Compared with PointNet-18, using 2D convolution backbones can improve the accuracy of 3D boxes, especially for *hard* setting. This is because these cases are usually occluded/truncated or far away from the camera, and estimating the pose of them is more dependent on context information. However, it is evident that the point-wise CNNs are hard to extract local features of data efficiently. From this perspective, image representation based detectors have greater development potentials. Besides, we can see from Table 4 (*right*) that the accuracy does not improve much when the CNN has more layers from ResNeXt-18 to ResNeXt-50. Compared with ResNeXt-50, ResNeXt-101 performs worse, which can be attributed to over-fitting. All the CNNs are trained from scratch.

Table 4. Comparisons of different backbone nets on KITTI *validation* set. Metrics are $AP_{3D}|_{R_{11}}$ for 3D detection task of the **Car** category with IoU threshold $= 0.7$. Other settings are same as PatchNet-vanilla.

Backbone	Easy	Moderate	Hard
PointNet-18	31.1	20.5	17.0
ResNet-18	33.2	21.3	19.1
ResNeXt-18	33.4	21.2	19.2
SE-ResNet-18	33.7	21.5	19.2

Backbone	Easy	Moderate	Hard
ResNeXt-18	32.7	21.2	19.2
ResNeXt-50	32.9	21.4	17.3
ResNeXt-101	31.1	20.9	17.0

Mask Global Pooling. In the PatchNet, we design the mask global pooling operation to force the feature maps must be extracted from a set of pixels of interests, which can be regarded as a hard attention mechanism. Table 5 shows the effectiveness of this operation, e.g., mask global pooling (max) can improve $AP_{3D}|_{11}$ by 1.4% for moderate setting and by 2.7% for easy setting, and max pooling is slightly better than avg pooling. Besides, the visualization result shown in Fig. 4 intuitively explains the reason for the performance improvement. Specifically, most activation units filtered by mask global pooling correspond to foreground goals, while the ones from standard global max pooling will have many activation units on the background.

It should be noted that the background points provide contextual information in our model, but they are not involved in [28,35] as input for PointNet.

Instance Assignment. We use a stand alone module to predict the 'difficulty' of each instance, and assign it to its corresponding head network. Table 6 shows the ablation study of this mechanism. First, we can find that the accuracy of outputs increases with instance assignment. Interestingly, considering that not all cases we can get the annotations of 'difficulty', we use a simple alternative: using the distance from object to camera to represent the 'difficulty' of objects

Table 5. Ablation study of mask global pooling on KITTI *validation* set. Metrics are AP_{3D} and AP_{BEV} of the **Car** category with 11 recall positions. Other settings are same as PatchNet (full model).

Pooling	Type	AP_{3D}			AP_{BEV}		
		Easy	Moderate	Hard	Easy	Moderate	Hard
Standard	Max	32.4	20.6	17.7	41.3	27.0	21.6
Mask	Avg	34.6	21.6	19.3	43.5	28.7	23.3
Mask	Max	35.1	22.0	19.6	44.4	29.1	24.1

Fig. 4. Qualitative comparison of max global pooling on KITTI *validation* set. The left/right image in each image pair marks the units activated by mask/standard global pooling.

(our default setting), and the threshold used in this experiment is $(30, 50)$. Experiment shows that this scheme get a similar performance as predicted difficulty levels.

Table 6. Ablation study of instance assignment on KITTI *validation* set. Metrics are AP_{3D} and AP_{BEV} of the **Car** category with 11 recall positions.

Assignment	Switcher	AP_{3D}			AP_{BEV}		
		Easy	Moderate	Hard	Easy	Moderate	Hard
–	–	33.7	21.5	19.2	42.5	28.2	23.5
✓	Difficulty	34.7	22.1	19.5	44.1	29.0	24.2
✓	Distance	35.1	22.0	19.6	44.4	29.1	24.1

5.4   Comparing with State-of-the-Art Methods

As shown in Table 7, we report our 3D detection results on the car category on KITTI dataset, where the proposed PatchNet ranks 1st among all published methods (ranked by *moderate* setting). Overall, our method achieves superior result over other state-of-the-art methods across all settings except for *easy* level of *testing* set. For instance, we outperform the current state-of-the-art AM3D [24] by **0.65/1.56/2.34** under *hard* setting on the listed three metrics, which is the

Table 7. 3D detection performance of the **Car** category on KITTI dataset. For *testing* set, only $AP|_{R_{40}}$ is provided by the official leaderboard. For *validation* set, we report both $AP|_{R_{40}}$ and $AP|_{R_{11}}$ for better comparisons. IoU threshold is set to 0.7. * indicates method is based on pseudo-LiDAR data. Methods are ranked by *moderate* setting (same as KITTI leaderboard). We highlight the best results in **bold**.

Method	Testing ($AP|_{40}$)			Validation ($AP|_{40}$)			Validation ($AP|_{11}$)		
	Easy	Mod	Hard	Easy	Mod	Hard	Easy	Mod	Hard
OFTNet [33]	1.61	1.32	1.00	–	–	–	4.07	3.27	3.29
FQNet [23]	2.77	1.51	1.01	–	–	–	5.98	5.50	4.75
ROI-10D [25]	4.32	2.02	1.46	–	–	–	10.25	6.39	6.18
GS3D [19]	4.47	2.90	2.47	–	–	–	13.46	10.97	10.38
Shift R-CNN [27]	6.88	3.87	2.83	–	–	–	13.84	11.29	11.08
Multi-Fusion [38]	7.08	5.18	4.68	–	–	–	22.03	13.63	11.60
MonoGRNet [31]	9.61	5.74	4.25	–	–	–	13.88	10.19	7.62
Decoupled-3D* [3]	11.08	7.02	5.63	–	–	–	26.95	18.68	15.82
MonoPSR [18]	10.76	7.25	5.85	–	–	–	12.75	11.48	8.59
MonoPL* [36]	10.76	7.50	6.10	–	–	–	31.5	21.00	17.50
SS3D [17]	10.78	7.68	6.51	–	–	–	14.52	13.15	11.85
MonoDIS [34]	10.37	7.94	6.40	11.06	7.60	6.37	18.05	14.98	13.42
M3D-RPN [2]	14.76	9.71	7.42	–	–	–	20.27	17.06	15.21
PL-AVOD* [35]	–	–	–	–	–	–	19.5	17.2	16.2
PL-FPointNet* [35]	–	–	–	–	–	–	28.2	18.5	16.4
AM3D* [24]	**16.50**	10.74	9.52	28.31	15.76	12.24	32.23	21.09	17.26
PatchNet	15.68	**11.12**	**10.17**	**31.6**	**16.8**	**13.8**	**35.1**	**22.0**	**19.6**

most challenging cases in the KITTI dataset. Besides, the proposed method outperforms existing pseudo-LiDAR based approaches. Note we use the same depth estimator (DORN) as [3,24,35,39] and the pipeline of proposed method is much simpler than pseudo-LiDAR based counterparts [3,39]. This shows the effectiveness of our design. We also observe that proposed model lags behind AM3D [24] under the *easy* setting on *testing* set. This may be attributed to the differences of the 2D detectors. We emphasize that *easy* split contains the least number of examples, so the performance of this setting is prone to fluctuations. Also note that these three splits are containment relationships (e.g., *hard* split contains all instances belong to *easy* and *moderate* setting).

5.5   Qualitative Results

We visualize some representative outputs of our PatchNet model in Fig. 5. We can observe that for simple cases in reasonable distance, our model outputs remarkably accurate 3D bounding boxes. Relatively, for distant objects, our

Fig. 5. Qualitative results on KITTI *validation* set. Red boxes represent our predictions, and green boxes come from ground truth. LiDAR signals are only used for visualization. Best viewed in color with zoom in. (Color figure online)

estimates of their size and heading angle are still accurate, although it is difficult to determine its center.

On the other hand, we do observe several failure patterns, which indicate possible directions for future efforts. First, our method often makes mistakes with truncated/occluded objects, and often manifests itself as inaccurate heading estimates. Second, sometimes our 2D detector misses object due to strong occlusion, which will cause these samples to be ignored in subsequ.

6   Conclusions

In this paper, a novel network architecture, namely PatchNet, is proposed to explore the fundamental cause why pseudo-LiDAR representation based 3D detectors achieve promising performance. Different from other works, we argue that the key factor is projecting the image coordinates to the world coordinates by the camera parameters, rather than the point cloud representation itself. More importantly, the world coordinate representation can be easily integrated into image representation, which means we can further boost the performance of 3D detector using more flexible and mature 2D CNN technologies. Experimental results on KITTI dataset demonstrate our argument and show potential of image representation based 3D detector. We hope these novel viewpoints provide insights to monocular/stereo 3D object detection community, and promote the development of new 2D CNN designs for image based 3D detection.

Acknowledgement. This work was supported by SenseTime, the Australian Research Council Grant DP200103223, and Australian Medical Research Future Fund MRFAI000085.

References

1. Alhashim, I., Wonka, P.: High quality monocular depth estimation via transfer learning. arXiv e-prints abs/1812.11941 (2018)
2. Brazil, G., Liu, X.: M3D-RPN: monocular 3D region proposal network for object detection. In: The IEEE International Conference on Computer Vision (ICCV), October 2019
3. Cai, Y., Li, B., Jiao, Z., Li, H., Zeng, X., Wang, X.: Monocular 3D object detection with decoupled structured polygon estimation and height-guided depth estimation. arXiv preprint arXiv:2002.01619 (2020)
4. Chabot, F., Chaouch, M., Rabarisoa, J., Teuliere, C., Chateau, T.: Deep MANTA: a coarse-to-fine many-task network for joint 2D and 3D vehicle analysis from monocular image. In: The IEEE Conference on Computer Vision and Pattern Recognition (CVPR), pp. 2040–2049 (2017)
5. Chang, J.R., Chen, Y.S.: Pyramid stereo matching network. In: Proceedings of the IEEE Conference on Computer Vision and Pattern Recognition, pp. 5410–5418 (2018)
6. Chen, X., Kundu, K., Zhang, Z., Ma, H., Fidler, S., Urtasun, R.: Monocular 3D object detection for autonomous driving. In: The IEEE Conference on Computer Vision and Pattern Recognition (CVPR), pp. 2147–2156 (2016)
7. Chen, X., et al.: 3D object proposals for accurate object class detection. In: Advances in Neural Information Processing Systems, pp. 424–432 (2015)
8. Chen, X., Ma, H., Wan, J., Li, B., Xia, T.: Multi-view 3D object detection network for autonomous driving. In: The IEEE Conference on Computer Vision and Pattern Recognition (CVPR), July 2017
9. Dai, J., Li, Y., He, K., Sun, J.: R-FCN: object detection via region-based fully convolutional networks. In: Advances in Neural Information Processing Systems, pp. 379–387 (2016)
10. Fu, H., Gong, M., Wang, C., Batmanghelich, K., Tao, D.: Deep ordinal regression network for monocular depth estimation. In: Proceedings of the IEEE Conference on Computer Vision and Pattern Recognition, pp. 2002–2011 (2018)
11. Geiger, A., Lenz, P., Urtasun, R.: Are we ready for autonomous driving? The KITTI vision benchmark suite. In: 2012 IEEE Conference on Computer Vision and Pattern Recognition, pp. 3354–3361. IEEE (2012)
12. Girshick, R.: Fast R-CNN. In: Proceedings of the IEEE International Conference on Computer Vision, pp. 1440–1448 (2015)
13. Godard, C., Mac Aodha, O., Brostow, G.J.: Unsupervised monocular depth estimation with left-right consistency. In: Proceedings of the IEEE Conference on Computer Vision and Pattern Recognition, pp. 270–279 (2017)
14. He, K., Gkioxari, G., Dollár, P., Girshick, R.: Mask R-CNN. In: Proceedings of the IEEE International Conference on Computer Vision, pp. 2961–2969 (2017)
15. He, K., Zhang, X., Ren, S., Sun, J.: Deep residual learning for image recognition. In: The IEEE Conference on Computer Vision and Pattern Recognition (CVPR), June 2016
16. Hu, J., Shen, L., Sun, G.: Squeeze-and-excitation networks. In: The IEEE Conference on Computer Vision and Pattern Recognition (CVPR), June 2018

17. Jörgensen, E., Zach, C., Kahl, F.: Monocular 3D object detection and box fitting trained end-to-end using intersection-over-union loss. CoRR abs/1906.08070 (2019). http://arxiv.org/abs/1906.08070
18. Ku, J., Mozifian, M., Lee, J., Harakeh, A., Waslander, S.L.: Joint 3D proposal generation and object detection from view aggregation. In: 2018 IEEE/RSJ International Conference on Intelligent Robots and Systems (IROS), pp. 1–8. IEEE (2018)
19. Li, B., Ouyang, W., Sheng, L., Zeng, X., Wang, X.: GS3D: an efficient 3D object detection framework for autonomous driving. In: Proceedings of the IEEE Conference on Computer Vision and Pattern Recognition, pp. 1019–1028 (2019)
20. Li, P., Chen, X., Shen, S.: Stereo R-CNN based 3D object detection for autonomous driving. In: Proceedings of the IEEE/CVF Conference on Computer Vision and Pattern Recognition (CVPR), June 2019
21. Lin, T.Y., Dollar, P., Girshick, R., He, K., Hariharan, B., Belongie, S.: Feature pyramid networks for object detection. In: Proceedings of the IEEE Conference on Computer Vision and Pattern Recognition (CVPR), July 2017
22. Lin, T.Y., Goyal, P., Girshick, R., He, K., Dollár, P.: Focal loss for dense object detection. In: Proceedings of the IEEE International Conference on Computer Vision, pp. 2980–2988 (2017)
23. Liu, L., Lu, J., Xu, C., Tian, Q., Zhou, J.: Deep fitting degree scoring network for monocular 3D object detection. In: Proceedings of the IEEE Conference on Computer Vision and Pattern Recognition, pp. 1057–1066 (2019)
24. Ma, X., Wang, Z., Li, H., Zhang, P., Ouyang, W., Fan, X.: Accurate monocular 3D object detection via color-embedded 3D reconstruction for autonomous driving. In: The IEEE International Conference on Computer Vision (ICCV), October 2019
25. Manhardt, F., Kehl, W., Gaidon, A.: ROI-10D: monocular lifting of 2D detection to 6D pose and metric shape. In: The IEEE Conference on Computer Vision and Pattern Recognition (CVPR), June 2019
26. Mousavian, A., Anguelov, D., Flynn, J., Kosecka, J.: 3D bounding box estimation using deep learning and geometry. In: Proceedings of the IEEE Conference on Computer Vision and Pattern Recognition, pp. 7074–7082 (2017)
27. Naiden, A., Paunescu, V., Kim, G., Jeon, B., Leordeanu, M.: Shift R-CNN: deep monocular 3D object detection with closed-form geometric constraints. In: 2019 IEEE International Conference on Image Processing (ICIP), pp. 61–65. IEEE (2019)
28. Qi, C.R., Liu, W., Wu, C., Su, H., Guibas, L.J.: Frustum PointNets for 3D object detection from RGB-D data. In: The IEEE Conference on Computer Vision and Pattern Recognition (CVPR), June 2018
29. Qi, C.R., Su, H., Mo, K., Guibas, L.J.: PointNet: deep learning on point sets for 3D classification and segmentation. In: Proceedings of the IEEE Conference on Computer Vision and Pattern Recognition, pp. 652–660 (2017)
30. Qi, C.R., Yi, L., Su, H., Guibas, L.J.: PointNet++: deep hierarchical feature learning on point sets in a metric space. In: Advances in Neural Information Processing Systems, pp. 5099–5108 (2017)
31. Qin, Z., Wang, J., Lu, Y.: MonoGRNet: a geometric reasoning network for monocular 3D object localization. In: Proceedings of the AAAI Conference on Artificial Intelligence, vol. 33, pp. 8851–8858 (2019)
32. Ren, S., He, K., Girshick, R., Sun, J.: Faster R-CNN: towards real-time object detection with region proposal networks. In: Advances in Neural Information Processing Systems, pp. 91–99 (2015)

33. Roddick, T., Kendall, A., Cipolla, R.: Orthographic feature transform for monocular 3D object detection. arXiv preprint arXiv:1811.08188 (2018)
34. Simonelli, A., Bulo, S.R., Porzi, L., Lopez-Antequera, M., Kontschieder, P.: Disentangling monocular 3D object detection. In: The IEEE International Conference on Computer Vision (ICCV), October 2019
35. Wang, Y., Chao, W.L., Garg, D., Hariharan, B., Campbell, M., Weinberger, K.Q.: Pseudo-lidar from visual depth estimation: bridging the gap in 3D object detection for autonomous driving. In: The IEEE Conference on Computer Vision and Pattern Recognition (CVPR), June 2019
36. Weng, X., Kitani, K.: Monocular 3D object detection with pseudo-lidar point cloud. In: IEEE International Conference on Computer Vision (ICCV) Workshops, October 2019
37. Xie, S., Girshick, R., Dollár, P., Tu, Z., He, K.: Aggregated residual transformations for deep neural networks. In: Proceedings of the IEEE Conference on Computer Vision and Pattern Recognition, pp. 1492–1500 (2017)
38. Xu, B., Chen, Z.: Multi-level fusion based 3D object detection from monocular images. In: The IEEE Conference on Computer Vision and Pattern Recognition (CVPR), June 2018
39. You, Y., et al.: Pseudo-LiDAR++: accurate depth for 3D object detection in autonomous driving. arXiv preprint arXiv:1906.06310 (2019)
40. Zhou, D., Zhou, X., Zhang, H., Yi, S., Ouyang, W.: Cheaper pre-training lunch: an efficient paradigm for object detection. arXiv preprint arXiv:2004.12178 (2020)

Deep Multi Depth Panoramas
for View Synthesis

Kai-En Lin[1]([✉]), Zexiang Xu[1,3], Ben Mildenhall[2], Pratul P. Srinivasan[2],
Yannick Hold-Geoffroy[3], Stephen DiVerdi[3], Qi Sun[3], Kalyan Sunkavalli[3],
and Ravi Ramamoorthi[1]

[1] UC San Diego, San Diego, USA
k2lin@ucsd.edu
[2] UC Berkeley, Berkeley, USA
[3] Adobe Research, San Jose, USA

Abstract. We propose a learning-based approach for novel view synthesis for multi-camera 360° panorama capture rigs. Previous work constructs RGBD panoramas from such data, allowing for view synthesis with small amounts of translation, but cannot handle the disocclusions and view-dependent effects that are caused by large translations. To address this issue, we present a novel scene representation—Multi Depth Panorama (MDP)—that consists of multiple RGBDα panoramas that represent both scene geometry and appearance. We demonstrate a deep neural network-based method to reconstruct MDPs from multi-camera 360° images. MDPs are more compact than previous 3D scene representations and enable high-quality, efficient new view rendering. We demonstrate this via experiments on both synthetic and real data and comparisons with previous state-of-the-art methods spanning both learning-based approaches and classical RGBD-based methods.

Keywords: 360° panoramas · View synthesis · Image-based rendering · Virtual reality

1 Introduction

Panoramic images have been widely used to create immersive experiences in virtual environments. Recently, commercial 360° cameras like the Yi Halo and GoPro Odyssey have made panoramic imaging practical. However, the classical panoramic representation only allows for a 3-DoF experience with purely rotational movements; it does not support translational motion, which is necessary for a true 6-DoF immersive experience. While recent work has leveraged panoramic depth to generate 6-DoF motion [23,27], it is highly challenging for these RGBD-based methods to handle extensive disocclusions and

Electronic supplementary material The online version of this chapter (https://doi.org/10.1007/978-3-030-58601-0_20) contains supplementary material, which is available to authorized users.

A. Vedaldi et al. (Eds.): ECCV 2020, LNCS 12358, pp. 328–344, 2020.
https://doi.org/10.1007/978-3-030-58601-0_20

view-dependent effects caused by large movements. Meanwhile, deep learning techniques for view synthesis have demonstrated photo-realistic results [20,34,37]; however, these methods are not designed for panoramic inputs and rely on per-viewpoint scene representations that are expensive to store and render.

Our goal is to enable realistic, practical and efficient novel view synthesis that supports translational motion with parallax for complex real scenes. To this end, we propose Multi Depth Panoramas (MDPs)—a novel, compact, geometry-aware panoramic representation inspired by classical layered depth images (LDIs) [28] and learning-based multiple plane images (MPIs) [37]. MDPs consist of a small set of multi-layer RGBDα (RGB pixel intensity, depth, opacity) panoramas that fully express complex scene geometry and appearance.

Fig. 1. We use 360° image data captured from a Yi-Halo camera (a), which consists of a ring of cameras as shown in (b). We present a learning based approach to reconstruct novel Multi Depth Panoramas (MDP) from these multi-view images, which can synthesize novel view images with both rotational and translational motions. We show panorama results using our MDPs from the center of the device (c) like the standard panorama synthesis, and also from a translated position (d) out of the rig. Note how the camera moves toward the counter. Our method accurately reproduces challenging disocclusion effects as shown in the cropped insets, which are significantly better than previous state-of-the-art methods that are based on RGBD representations [1,27]. For better details on all the figures, please view the electronic version of this paper.

We demonstrate the use of MDPs for novel view synthesis from images captured by commercial 360° camera rigs such as the Yi Halo that consist of a sparse array of outward-facing cameras placed in a ring. Previous work proposes limited translational motion [27] using RGBD panoramas reconstructed from this setup [1]. In contrast, we propose an efficient MDP-based rendering scheme that handles challenging occlusions and reflections that cannot be reproduced by state-of-the-art RGBD-based methods (see Fig. 1). Our flexible MDP representation can encode an arbitrary number of layers, degrading gracefully to a regular

RGBD panorama when using a single layer. MDPs are also much more compact than previous representations, providing either a similar or significantly better view synthesis quality using fewer layers, as shown in our experiments in Table 2. Finally, by encoding the entire 360° panorama in a global representation, MDPs allow for complete panoramic view synthesis, unlike previous methods that focus on synthesizing limited field-of-view images (see Fig. 2).

Our contributions can be summarized as:

- a 360° layered scene representation called Multi Depth Panorama (MDP), offering a more compact and versatile 3D representation than previous work (Sect. 3);
- a learning-based method to convert images from common 360° camera setups into our MDP representation (Sect. 4.1–4.3);
- an efficient novel view synthesis method based on MDP (Sect. 4.4);
- experiments to demonstrate the advantages of the MDP compared to existing representations (Sect. 6).

2 Related Work

View Synthesis. Novel view synthesis has been extensively studied in computer vision and graphics [7], and has been performed via approaches such as light fields [12,18] and image-based rendering [5,10,29]. Recently, deep learning has been applied in many view synthesis problems; the most successful ones leverage plane sweep volumes to infer depth and achieve realistic geometric-aware view synthesis [9,11,16,34,37]. We leverage plane sweep volumes to construct per-view MPIs, similar to [37]. By merging multiple MPIs from multiple views in a 360° camera, we construct MDPs for 6-DoF view synthesis.

Layered Representation. Layered and volumetric representations have been applied in 3D and view synthesis applications [4,8,26,28,35,37]. Unlike a single RGBD image, layered representations make the scene content occluded behind the foreground viewable from side views. In their seminal work, Shade et al. [28] introduce the Layered Depth Images (LDIs) and Sprites with Depth (SwD) representations to render scenes using multiple RGBD images. Our methods shares the RGBDα concept used in SwD, with the distinction that we reason holistically on the 360° scene while SwD decomposes it into multiple independent sprites. LDIs has been extended to a panoramic case [36], where multiple concentric RGBD panoramas are reconstructed. In addition, Zitnick et al. [38] utilizes multiple layers with alpha matting to produce interactive viewpoint videos. In concurrent work, Broxton et al. [3] propose the multi-sphere image (MSI) representation for 6-DoF light field video synthesis, yielding accurate results but involving a memory-heavy process. In contrast with previous representations, we propose a learning-based method to reconstruct multiple memory-efficient RGBDα panoramic images for 6-DoF rendering. Our method uses differentiable rendering to recover smooth object boundaries and specularities that are hard to reproduce by RGBD representations alone.

Zhou et al. [37] leverage a deep network to predict multi plane images (MPIs) [31] for realistic view extrapolation. These MPIs are a dense set of fronto parallel planes with RGBA images at an input view, which enable rendering novel view images locally for the view. Some recent works have extended this local view synthesis technique for large viewing ranges [20,30]. Mildenhall et al. [20] reconstruct MPIs at multiple views and fuse the 2D renderings from multiple MPIs to enable large viewpoint motion [20]. However, such a 2D image-level fusion technique requires expensively storing and rendering multiple view-dependent MPIs. We leverage MPIs for panorama rendering and introduce multi depth panoramas (MDPs) that are view-independent RGBDα images. We propose to fuse per-view MPIs in a canonical 3D space for MDP reconstruction, which allows for efficient view synthesis from a sparse set of RGBDα images.

6-DoF Rendering. Standard 360° panoramic rendering only allows for 2D experience with 3-DoF rotational motion. Omni-directional stereo [15,21] has been introduced to provide 3D stereo effects by leveraging panoramic depth [1]. More advanced capture hardware can support 6-DoF rendering of 360° video [23], but there is also research to enable 6-DoF for more accessible hardware. Researchers have designed systems to acquire static scenes with different camera motions over time [2,13,14,19] but they are unable to capture dynamic scenes without artifacts. Other works use ring cameras to capture dynamic scenes and store the scene model in single layer panoramas [32] or as a panorama with a static background [27], but still have significant artifacts around object boundaries, areas of poor depth reconstruction, and for large viewer head motions.

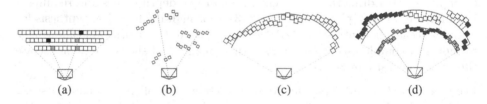

Fig. 2. 3D scene representations: the multiplane image (a) proposes a planar representation of the scene. In contrast, the layered depth image (b) encodes multiple depth pixels along a ray. RGBD panoramas (c) encode the scene distance per-pixel from a reference cylinder. Our multi depth panorama (d) takes inspiration from those previous representations, where depth is encoded on each cylindrical shell.

3   Multi Depth Panoramas

Given a 360° camera setup with k cameras, our goal is to infer a layered scene representation that allows for high-quality 6-DoF novel view rendering. To achieve this, we propose the multi depth panorama (MDP) representation.

The MDP representation is inspired by Layered Depth Images (LDI) [28] and Multiplane Images (MPI) [20,30,37] (shown in Fig. 2(a) and (b) respectively). LDIs and MPIs have been previously used as *image-based* representations and encode only a limited field-of-view; instead, we are interested in representing the entire 360° scene. Previous work has used RGBD panoramas (Fig. 2(c)) for novel view synthesis for panoramas [27] but this does not encode sufficient information to render the disocclusions that are produced at large translations.

Motivated by these limitations of previous representations, we propose the MDP. An MDP consists of a sparse set of RGBDα panoramas that divide the 3D space into annulus-like cylindrical regions, as shown in Fig. 2(d). Each layer l encodes color C_l, depth D_l and pixel transparency α_l of its corresponding region. Consequently, the MDP representation can be denoted by a set of RGBDα layers as $(C_0, D_0, \alpha_0), ..., (C_L, D_L, \alpha_L)$, where L specifies the maximum number of cylindrical shells. This representation can be thought of as a set of cylindrical shells representing the 3D scene, where in each shell, a pixel is composed of five channels—diffuse RGB color, an alpha channel for occupancy, and a depth channel for finer control over 3D geometry. These components allow for both a more accurate and a more compact representation than previous work. In order to synthesize novel views, we can forward splat each layer onto the target image plane and then perform the standard "over" alpha compositing operation [22].

While similar to an MPI in its use of RGB and α layers, our representation provides the following main benefits over the MPI:

Compactness. The main advantage of the proposed MDP is its compactness, yielding an appreciable compression ratio over existing representations. For example, an MPI discretizes the scene into multiple depth planes and requires a large number of such planes (32–128 [20,37]) for high-quality view synthesis for complex scenes. In contrast, an MDP explicitly stores the depth value allowing it to represent complex scene geometry with a small set of shells; we demonstrate this experimentally in Sect. 6.

Free of Depth Conflicts. Our MDP representation offers a canonical scene representation for merging different views and resolving depth conflicts. MPI planes are created in the viewing frustum of each input camera. In our 360° setup, where individual cameras are placed in an outward-facing ring, there are significant differences between these planes, making it difficult to blend between adjacent per-view MPIs. To address this issue, we adopt a canonical cylindrical coordinate system across all viewpoints, allowing a neural network to automatically resolve depth conflicts and blend viewpoints. This also allows us to construct a single global MDP instead of storing multiple per-view MPIs [20].

Geometry Accuracy. The depth component grants the MDP the same 3D representational accuracy as a point cloud. This increased accuracy over MPI's equidistant planes prevents depth quantization artifacts [28], which are typically more noticeable when the scene geometry is observed from grazing angles, and leads to view synthesis results with fewer visual artifacts around geometry edges.

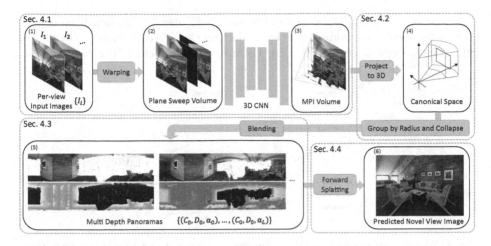

Fig. 3. Overview of our pipeline. Our network first warps multi-view images to each view to construct per-view PSVs, and leverages a 3D CNN to predict per-view MPIs. These MPIs are projected to a canonical cylindrical coordinate in the world space. We group these per-view MPIs by different radius ranges and collapse them to reconstruct per-view MDPs. The per-view MDPs are finally blended into a single global MDP, which can be used to render new novel view images using forward splatting.

4   Reconstructing and Rendering MDPs

In this section, we describe our method to a) construct MDPs from images captured with a 360° camera setup, and b) render novel viewpoints from this representation. An overview of the full pipeline is shown in Fig. 3.

Given multiple images and their corresponding camera parameters, we first construct per-view MPI volumes (Sect. 4.1). We then project these MPI volumes to a canonical space—a cylindrical coordinate system centered at the center of the 360° camera—and collapse them into a compact per-view MDP (Sect. 4.2). Finally, we blend the different per-view MDPs into a single MDP representation (Sect. 4.3). Given the reconstructed MDP representation, we can render novel views efficiently using forward splatting (Sect. 4.4).

4.1   Reconstructing Per-View MPIs from Images

In the following, we describe our pipeline for predicting per-view MPI volumes from a 360° camera setup. Our pipeline takes k input views and their corresponding camera parameters as input. For each viewpoint, we create a plane-sweep volume (PSV) by warping images from the four nearest neighboring cameras as shown in Fig. 3. Following previous work [20], we sample the depths linearly in disparity to ensure that the resulting PSV covers accurate object depths.

These PSVs are processed by a 3D CNN that predicts an MPI volume. Please see the supplementary material for a full description of our 3D CNN. Taken as is, these MPI volumes require a large amount of memory to perform novel view synthesis. For example, Mildenhall et al. [20] use 32–128 depth planes for their experiments. We address this by projecting these MPI volumes to canonical cylindrical coordinates and collapsing them into a compact MDP representation.

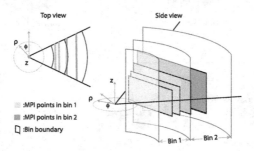

Fig. 4. We show an example of MPI collapsing at a view. In particular, we show three cylindrical shells that divide the space into two bins, and five MPIs in these bins. We mark the MPI points that belong to different bins with different colors.

4.2   Per-View MPIs to Per-View MDPs

The previous step gives us, for every input view v, an L-layer MPI volume. Our goal is to convert these multiple limited field-of-view volumes into a compact and unified representation. We do this by projecting each MPI volume to a canonical cylindrical coordinate system with its origin at the center of projection of the entire camera rig. Concretely, for a pixel (x_s, y_s) on layer l of the MPI for view v, its corresponding 3D point in the global world coordinates is given by:

$$\begin{bmatrix} x_w \\ y_w \\ z_w \\ 1 \end{bmatrix} = E_w E_v^{-1} I_v^{-1} \begin{bmatrix} x_s \\ y_s \\ 1/d_l \\ 1 \end{bmatrix}, \tag{1}$$

where d_l represents the depth of layer l, I_v and E_v are the intrinsic and extrinsic matrices of the camera view v, and E_w is the extrinsic matrix for the geometric center of our camera rig. Once projected to the world coordinates, we can calculate their cylindrical coordinates (ρ, ϕ, z) as:

$$\rho_w = \sqrt{x_w^2 + y_w^2}, \quad \phi_w = \arctan(y_w/x_w). \tag{2}$$

Applying the above operation to an MPI volume produces a point cloud of 3D points each with the color, depth, and opacity. Moreover, since each pixel coordinate in the MPI volume has multiple points at different depths, in the cylindrical coordinate system this leads to a set of multiple points along rays originating from the origin. We collapse this large set of points into a more compact set. More specifically, we divide the 3D space into a small number

$M \ll L$ of annulus-like 3D cylindrical regions with equidistant radius ranges that cover the entire scene from the nearest to the farthest radius. We bin the 3D MPI points into these M bins based on the radius ρ_w (see Fig. 4).

For each subset of points within the same bin, we use a back-to-front "over" alpha compositing operation (as is used to render novel views with MPIs [20,37]) to compute a *single* RGBDα value. Because the over operator is associative, we can process each bin individually. Thus, this operation replaces a large set of RGBα values with a single RGBDα value, thereby significantly reducing the data footprint of the representation. In practice, as demonstrated in Table 2, we find that even 2–4 layer MDPs produce results better in visual quality than MPIs with 32 layers, leading to a significant compression.

4.3 Per-View MDP Blending

The previous step produces k per-view MDPs with M layers each. Next we blend them all into a single global MDP. Since all the MDPs are in a canonical cylindrical representation, we can blend the individual corresponding layers. If layer m for the view-v MDP is represented as $(C_m^v, D_m^v, \alpha_m^v)$, the blended global MDP is given by:

$$(C_m, D_m, \alpha_m) = \frac{\sum_v w^v \alpha_m^v (C_m^v, D_m^v, \alpha_m^v)}{\sum_i w^v \alpha_m^v}. \tag{3}$$

This represents a weighted average of the color, depth, and opacity of the per-view MDPs where the weights are a product of the opacity and a per-view weight, w^v that we set to the cosine of the angular difference from the optical axis, which gets lower the further a pixel is away from the principal point.

4.4 Differentiable MDP Rendering with Forward Splatting

In this section, we describe our differentiable rendering module. It is achieved by forward splatting and utilizing soft z-buffering to resolve depth conflicts.

One distinction from previous MPI methods is that we cannot do planar homography warping for each layer to synthesize a novel view since each layer now lies on a cylindrical shell with a depth component. In order to render novel viewpoints, we treat the predicted MDP representation as a set of RGBα point clouds and forward-project each point onto the target image plane. Concretely, we can get the world coordinates (x_w, y_w, z_w) by doing the inverse of the cylindrical coordinate transformation (Eq. 2) and then splat these points onto the target image plane with a bilinear kernel.

Directly projecting the points to their corresponding target location might result in depth conflicts. Similar to rasterization, when a query ray passes through several surfaces along its direction, the resulting pixel might simultaneously have different color information. To ensure only the closest pixel is selected, we use z-buffering to resolve the conflicts. Since z-buffering is non-differentiable, we instead employ soft z-buffering [24,33] to compute the weighted average pixel value $\bar{C}(x,y)$ of all conflicting pixels. Soft z-buffering can be formulated as:

$$\bar{C}(x,y) = \frac{\sum C(x,y)e^{(d(x,y)-d_{max})\tau}}{\sum e^{(d(x,y)-d_{max})\tau}}, \tag{4}$$

where $C(x,y)$ and $d(x,y)$ denote the pixel value and inverse depth value at (x,y) of a layer, respectively. τ is a scale factor to control the discriminative power of soft z-buffering. The maximum inverse depth across the image d_{max} is subtracted to prevent overflow. As a pixel gets closer, its inverse depth d increases, thus increasing the weight for this pixel. Finally, by resolving the self-occlusion depth conflicts within each layer via soft z-buffering, we can then alpha-composite the projected maps from back to front to produce the final rendering (see Fig. 3).

5   Implementation Details

In the following, we describe the datasets used and the training procedure to learn to project images from a 360° camera setup to the MDP representation.

5.1   Dataset

Throughout our experiments, we assume the number of cameras $k = 16$, each with a 100° field of view, similar to commercial cameras such as the Yi Halo and GoPro Odyssey. Each camera viewing direction is 22.5° apart horizontally. This configuration yields a stereo overlap of over 50% between neighboring cameras.

In order to create photorealistic training data, we chose the Unreal Engine as our renderer since it offers complex effects and high quality rendering. We create two datasets of different camera configurations with UnrealCV [25]: the first with a similar sampling scheme as in [20], and the second with a ring-like camera setup similar to the Yi Halo and GoPro Odyssey. Both datasets are generated from the same 21 large-scale scenes, which consist of indoor and outdoor scenes modeled with high resolution textures and complex scene geometry. These datasets offer a large variety of albedo, depth complexity and non-Lambertian specular effects. The first dataset contains thousands of points of interest, from each of which we sample 6 images with a random baseline to ensure various levels of disparity. Image resolution ranges from 320×240 to 640×480 to allow the network to generalize on various resolutions. In the second dataset, the input images follow the predefined 16-camera configuration, while the output images have a random look-at direction and translational movement with a maximum radius of 25 cm. Image resolution for the second dataset is adjusted to range from 320×320 to 512×512 in order to better match the field-of-view of 360° cameras.

5.2   Training

To train our method, we adopt a two-step training scheme. During the first step, we train the 3D CNN on the first dataset to output a per-view MPI volume.

The first step is performed by selecting 6 neighboring views, using a random set of 5 as inputs and using the last image as a target view for supervision. During the second step, the 3D CNN is fine-tuned end-to-end with our second dataset by synthesizing a target view from its closest 5 cameras. The network is trained using the perceptual loss from [6] and a learning rate of 2×10^{-4} for roughly 600 k and 70 k iterations for each respective phase.

6   Results

We now evaluate and compare our MDP representation and panorama-based novel view synthesis method.

Evaluation of the Numbers of Layers. Our approach works for an arbitrary numbers of MDP layers. In this section, we evaluate how the number of layers impact the representation accuracy using a synthetic test set that consists of two large indoor scenes different from our training set. Several hundreds viewpoints are randomly sampled within each scene. Table 1 shows the quantitative results of our method when varying the number of layers from one to five. Our method consistently improves with an increasing number of layers. This increase typically allows a more accurate representation of scenes with more complex geometry and appearance. Note that an MDP reverts to a standard RGBD panorama when its number of layers is one (see the first row of Table 1). In fact, the depth obtained using an MDP with a single layer are significantly better than a state-of-the-art depth estimation method [17] (see Table 3). The number of layers is a user-tunable parameter that provides a trade-off between representation accuracy and memory usage. We use five layers for the remaining experiments in this paper. Note that, even with five layers, our MDPs are still compact and more memory-efficient than previous learning-based methods (see Table 2).

Table 1. Quantitative evaluation of the number of MDP layers. Please see the supplementary material for additional qualitative results.

Layers	PSNR↑	SSIM↑	L1↓
1	25.75	0.8565	0.0269
2	26.17	0.8628	0.0254
3	26.27	0.8655	0.0251
4	26.35	0.8661	0.0251
5	**26.39**	**0.8664**	**0.0251**

Comparison with MPIs. Our method effectively converts the costly per-view MPIs to the novel compact view-independent MDPs. MPIs consist of dense planes and only support local view extrapolation, which requires rendering multiple dense sets of planes from multiple views to enable arbitrary rotational motion.

In contrast, our MDPs are in a canonical world space, which only requires splatting a single sparse set of depth layers for 360° 6-DoF view synthesis. In Table 2, we show the quantitative results of our method with 2 and 5 layer MDPs. We also compare against a naive solution that directly uses the per-view MPIs to do view synthesis with 16-view MPIs and 32 planes per MPI. For this, following the method of Mildenhall et al. [20], we linearly blend the five neighboring per-view MPI renderings with the pixel-wise cosines of the angles between the per-pixel viewing directions and the central direction of each camera. The corresponding memory usage of these MPIs and MDPs are shown in the table. The naive MPI method is not able to effectively blend the multi-view renderings; training it end-to-end to learn the 2D blending process may improve the quality. In contrast, our approach can leverage its priors learned during training to merge the per-view MPIs, which leads to a method that outperforms the MPI approach. Moreover, our method is significantly more memory-efficient, taking an order of magnitude less memory than the MPI method.

Table 2. Quantitative results of our method compared to a MPI-based method on synthetic scenes, along with their memory usages. Please see the supplementary material for more qualitative results.

Methods	PSNR↑	SSIM↑	L1↓	Dimension	Storage
MPI	24.75	0.8278	0.0306	$16 \times 640 \times 640 \times 32 \times 4$	3.355 GB
Ours - 2 layers	26.17	0.8628	0.0254	$2560 \times 640 \times 2 \times 5$	**0.066 GB**
Ours - 5 layers	**26.39**	**0.8664**	**0.0251**	$2560 \times 640 \times 5 \times 5$	0.165 GB

Comparisons with Other Methods on Synthetic Scenes. We now compare our method with other 360° view synthesis techniques that allow for translational motion and demonstrate quantitative comparisons on our synthetic testing set. The most popular way to do 360° rendering is to reconstruct the depth of a panorama and render the RGBD panorama as a point cloud or mesh, as introduced in [1,23]. These techniques rely on a pre-computed depth map, and we use a state-of-the-art deep learning based depth estimation method [17] to generate depth for input panoramas. This depth map is used to generate a corresponding RGBD point cloud and mesh that are used in turn to render novel views. We also compare against a state-of-the-art method [27] that is designed to improve the 2D images rendered from the RGBD panorama mesh by resolving the disocclusions around the geometric boundaries.

Table 3 shows the quantitative results of these methods. Our MDPs generate significantly better results than the other comparison methods as reflected by the highest PSNRs and SSIMs and the lowest L1 loss. We also show our single layer MDP result in Table 3, which is essentially doing single RGBD panorama-based point cloud rendering. Interestingly, even this performs better than the point cloud rendering using the prior state-of-the-art depth estimation method.

Table 3. Comparison on synthetic scenes. We compare with other methods that use a single RGBD panorama for 6DoF rendering. We show results of SSIMs, PSNRs and L1 loss of these methods.

Methods	PSNR↑	SSIM↑	L1↓
Depth [17] as points	23.06	0.766	0.047
Depth [17] as mesh	23.75	0.780	0.040
Depth [17] + [27]	23.20	0.767	0.043
Our depth + [27]	24.98	0.827	0.031
Our single layer MDP	25.75	0.857	0.027
Our MDPs (5 layers)	**26.39**	**0.866**	**0.025**

Table 4. Quantitative comparison on maximum disparity. Our method consistently outperforms [27] on image quality over all tested disparity levels.

Disparity (PSNR/SSIM)	32	64	128
Depth [17] + [27]	22.40/0.7490	20.20/0.6911	18.17/0.6322
Our MDPs (5 layers)	26.90/0.8839	24.96/0.8436	21.94/0.7579

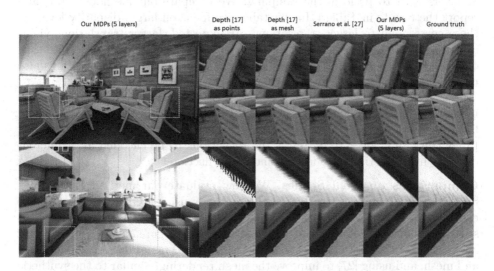

Fig. 5. Visualization of synthetic results. We show two examples of synthetic results to illustrate the visual quality corresponding to the numbers in Table 3.

This demonstrates that our method can be used as an effective panorama depth estimation technique by estimating a single MDP. We also show that, by giving the depth from our single MDP as input to Serrano et al.'s enhancing technique [27], it improves their result over using the depth from Lee et al. [17]. Note that, Serrano et al. [27] focus on improving user experience and mitigate unpleasant artifacts, which may decrease the accuracy of direct mesh rendering.

To visualize the comparisons, we show two results on synthetic data in Fig. 5. Our results offers increased visual quality than all other comparison methods, especially around object boundaries. Our results are also the most similar to the ground truth images, which is consistent with the quantitative results in Table 3. Note that, a single RGBD representation used in other methods is very limited and cannot well reproduce the challenging disocclusion effects. This leads to holes in the point cloud rendering, and noisy and stretched boundaries in the mesh rendering; Serrano et al. [27] smooth out the boundaries in the mesh rendering, which in turn introduces blurriness and distortion. Our MDPs can describe complex scenes with multiple objects on the line-of-sight and effectively handle challenging boundaries, disocclusions and other appearance effects.

We now analyze the robustness of our method on large disparities. To do so, we translate the target viewpoints in our test set and record the amount of maximum scene disparity with respect to the reference viewpoint. We use a 32-layers MPI to perform the sampling. We compare our method to [27] and report the results in Table 4. In this table, we focus on larger disparity levels as these correspond to larger translations. As expected, larger translations yields a more difficult task, which reduces the novel view visual quality. Despite this, our method outperforms [27] across all disparity levels. These observations also match the sampling guidelines in Mildenhall et al. [20].

We also show an example of specular reflection in Fig. 6. Note that the other methods use a single depth, which bakes the reflections in the object color and fails to accurately capture the motion of reflections from different viewpoints. In contrast, our novel MDP allows the reflections to be encoded at a different depth, which effectively models the moving reflection.

Comparisons on Real Scenes. We now evaluate our method on complex real scenes and compare them with the methods using RGBD panoramas. We captured these real scenes with a Yi Halo and used Google Jump Manager [1] to stitch the multi-view images and generate the depth. Figure 7 shows the results of our method with 5-layers MDPs, rendering an RGBD panorama as a point cloud and mesh, and using [27] to improve the mesh rendering. Similar to the synthetic comparisons, our method produces more realistic results than the comparison ones. Note that, the disocclusion effects introduce obvious holes and significant discontinuous noise in the baseline point cloud rendering and mesh rendering techniques. While [27] resolves the noisy boundaries in the mesh rendering for better user experience, the edges are in fact distorted in many regions and still look physically implausible. Our results are significantly more photorealistic. Please refer to supplementary material for more experiments and ablation study on end-to-end training.

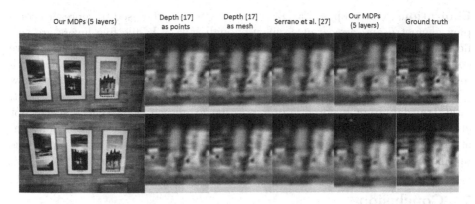

Fig. 6. Reflection effects. We show one example of specular reflection with zoomed-in insets. Note that, our method recovers the specular reflection motion that matches the ground truth very well, while the reflections in the comparison methods do not move.

Fig. 7. Qualitative results on complex real scenes. We show results on novel viewpoints comparing our 5-layers MDP (leftmost) to RGBD based methods.

Limitations. Our proposed MDP representation can be used to represent complex geometry and appearance, given enough layers. While five layers are sufficient for most cases as previously shown, it might not be adapted to more complex and challenging scenes and can exhibit blurriness or distortion. Increasing the number of layers can potentially address this. Besides, our novel view synthesis method is limited to relatively small motions for two reasons. First, large translations will potentially expose large unseen parts of the scene, not encoded in the MDP representation. We hypothesize that future work on generative models might provide a solution to this issue. Second, moving past the first concentric sphere of the MDP would break the alpha ordering.

7   Conclusion

We presented a novel 3D scene representation—Multi Depth Panoramas, or MDP—that represents complex scenes using multiple layers of concentric RGBDα panoramas. MDPs are more compact than prior scene representations such as MPIs. As such, they can be used to generate high-quality novel view synthesis results with translational motion parallax, using our proposed forward-splatting rendering method. Furthermore, we presented a learning-based method to accurately reconstruct MDPs from commercial 360° camera rigs.

Acknowledgements. We would like to thank In-Kyu Park for helpful discussion and comments. This work was supported in part by ONR grants N000141712687, N000141912293, N000142012529, NSF grant 1617234, Adobe, the Ronald L. Graham Chair and the UC San Diego Center for Visual Computing.

References

1. Anderson, R., et al.: Jump: virtual reality video. ACM Trans. Graph. (TOG) **35**(6), 1–13 (2016)
2. Bertel, T., Campbell, N.D.F., Richardt, C.: MegaParallax: casual 360° panoramas with motion parallax. IEEE Trans. Vis. Comput. Graph. **25**(5), 1828–1835 (2019). https://doi.org/10.1109/TVCG.2019.2898799
3. Broxton, M., et al.: Immersive light field video with a layered mesh representation. ACM Trans. Graph. **39**(4), 86:1–86:15 (2020)
4. Brunet, T., et al.: Soft 3D acoustic metamaterial with negative index. Nat. Mater. **14**(4), 384–388 (2015)
5. Buehler, C., Bosse, M., McMillan, L., Gortler, S., Cohen, M.: Unstructured lumigraph rendering. In: Proceedings of the 28th Annual Conference on Computer Graphics and Interactive Techniques, pp. 425–432. ACM (2001)
6. Chen, Q., Koltun, V.: Photographic image synthesis with cascaded refinement networks. In: Proceedings of the IEEE International Conference on Computer Vision, pp. 1511–1520 (2017)
7. Chen, S.E., Williams, L.: View interpolation for image synthesis. In: Proceedings of SIGGRAPH, pp. 279–288 (1993)
8. Cheng, S., et al.: Deep stereo using adaptive thin volume representation with uncertainty awareness. arXiv preprint arXiv:1911.12012 (2019)

9. Choi, I., Gallo, O., Troccoli, A., Kim, M.H., Kautz, J.: Extreme view synthesis. In: Proceedings of the IEEE International Conference on Computer Vision, pp. 7781–7790 (2019)
10. Debevec, P.E., Taylor, C.J., Malik, J.: Modeling and rendering architecture from photographs: a hybrid geometry-and image-based approach. In: Proceedings of the 23rd Annual Conference on Computer Graphics and Interactive Techniques, pp. 11–20. ACM (1996)
11. Flynn, J., Neulander, I., Philbin, J., Snavely, N.: DeepStereo: learning to predict new views from the world's imagery. In: Proceedings of the IEEE Conference on Computer Vision and Pattern Recognition, pp. 5515–5524 (2016)
12. Gortler, S.J., Grzeszczuk, R., Szeliski, R., Cohen, M.F.: The lumigraph. In: Proceedings of the 23rd Annual Conference on Computer Graphics and Interactive Techniques, pp. 43–54. ACM (1996)
13. Hedman, P., Alsisan, S., Szeliski, R., Kopf, J.: Casual 3D photography. ACM Trans. Graph. $36(6)$, 234:1–234:15 (2017)
14. Huang, J., Chen, Z., Ceylan, D., Jin, H.: 6-DOF VR videos with a single 360-camera. In: 2017 IEEE Virtual Reality (VR), pp. 37–44, March 2017. https://doi.org/10.1109/VR.2017.7892229
15. Ishiguro, H., Yamamoto, M., Tsuji, S.: Omni-directional stereo. IEEE Trans. Pattern Anal. Mach. Intell. $2(2)$, 257–262 (1992)
16. Kalantari, N.K., Wang, T.C., Ramamoorthi, R.: Learning-based view for light field cameras. ACM Trans. Graph. (TOG) $35(6)$, 193 (2016)
17. Lee, J.H., Han, M.K., Ko, D.W., Suh, I.H.: From big to small: multi-scale local planar guidance for monocular depth estimation. arXiv preprint arXiv:1907.10326 (2019)
18. Levoy, M., Hanrahan, P.: Light field rendering. In: Proceedings of the 23rd Annual Conference on Computer Graphics and Interactive Techniques, pp. 31–42. ACM (1996)
19. Luo, B., Xu, F., Richardt, C., Yong, J.H.: Parallax360: stereoscopic 360° scene representation for head-motion parallax. IEEE Trans. Vis. Comput. Graph. $24(4)$, 1545–1553 (2018). https://doi.org/10.1109/TVCG.2018.2794071
20. Mildenhall, B., et al.: Local light field fusion: practical view synthesis with prescriptive sampling guidelines. ACM Trans. Graph. (TOG) $38(4)$, 1–14 (2019)
21. Peleg, S., Ben-Ezra, M., Pritch, Y.: Omnistereo: panoramic stereo imaging. IEEE Trans. Pattern Anal. Mach. Intell. $23(3)$, 279–290 (2001)
22. Porter, T., Duff, T.: Compositing digital images. In: Proceedings of the 11th Annual Conference on Computer Graphics and Interactive Techniques, pp. 253–259 (1984)
23. Pozo, A.P., et al.: An integrated 6DoF video camera and system design. ACM Trans. Graph. (TOG) $38(6)$, 1–16 (2019)
24. Pulli, K., Hoppe, H., Cohen, M., Shapiro, L., Duchamp, T., Stuetzle, W.: View-based rendering: visualizing real objects from scanned range and color data. In: Dorsey, J., Slusallek, P. (eds.) EGSR 1997. E, pp. 23–34. Springer, Vienna (1997). https://doi.org/10.1007/978-3-7091-6858-5_3
25. Qiu, W., et al.: UnrealCV: Virtual worlds for computer vision. In: ACM Multimedia Open Source Software Competition (2017)
26. Richter, S.R., Roth, S.: Matryoshka networks: predicting 3D geometry via nested shape layers. In: Proceedings of the IEEE Conference on Computer Vision and Pattern Recognition, pp. 1936–1944 (2018)
27. Serrano, A., et al.: Motion parallax for 360 RGBD video. IEEE Trans. Vis. Comput. Graph. $25(5)$, 1817–1827 (2019)

28. Shade, J., Gortler, S., He, L.W., Szeliski, R.: Layered depth images. In: Proceedings of the 25th Annual Conference on Computer Graphics and Interactive Techniques, pp. 231–242. Association for Computing Machinery, Inc., July 1998. https://www.microsoft.com/en-us/research/publication/layered-depth-images/
29. Sinha, S., Steedly, D., Szeliski, R.: Piecewise planar stereo for image-based rendering. In: 12th International Conference on Computer Vision (ICCV), pp. 1881–1888. IEEE (2009)
30. Srinivasan, P.P., Tucker, R., Barron, J.T., Ramamoorthi, R., Ng, R., Snavely, N.: Pushing the boundaries of view extrapolation with multiplane images. In: Conference on Computer Vision and Pattern Recognition (CVPR) (2019)
31. Szeliski, R., Golland, P.: Stereo matching with transparency and matting. Int. J. Comput. Vis. **32**(1), 45–61 (1999). https://www.microsoft.com/en-us/research/publication/stereo-matching-with-transparency-and-matting/
32. Thatte, J., Boin, J.B., Lakshman, H., Girod, B.: Depth augmented stereo panorama for cinematic virtual reality with head-motion parallax. In: 2016 IEEE International Conference on Multimedia and Expo (ICME), pp. 1–6. IEEE (2016)
33. Tulsiani, S., Tucker, R., Snavely, N.: Layer-structured 3D scene inference via view synthesis. In: Ferrari, V., Hebert, M., Sminchisescu, C., Weiss, Y. (eds.) ECCV 2018. LNCS, vol. 11211, pp. 311–327. Springer, Cham (2018). https://doi.org/10.1007/978-3-030-01234-2_19
34. Xu, Z., Bi, S., Sunkavalli, K., Hadap, S., Su, H., Ramamoorthi, R.: Deep view synthesis from sparse photometric images. ACM Trans. Graph. **38**(4), 76 (2019)
35. Yao, Y., Luo, Z., Li, S., Fang, T., Quan, L.: MVSNet: depth inference for unstructured multi-view stereo. In: Proceedings of the European Conference on Computer Vision (ECCV), pp. 767–783 (2018)
36. Zheng, K.C., Kang, S.B., Cohen, M.F., Szeliski, R.: Layered depth panoramas. In: 2007 IEEE Conference on Computer Vision and Pattern Recognition, pp. 1–8. IEEE (2007)
37. Zhou, T., Tucker, R., Flynn, J., Fyffe, G., Snavely, N.: Stereo magnification: learning view synthesis using multiplane images. In: SIGGRAPH (2018)
38. Zitnick, C.L., Kang, S.B., Uyttendaele, M., Winder, S., Szeliski, R.: High-quality video view interpolation using a layered representation. ACM Trans. Graph. (TOG) **23**(3), 600–608 (2004)

MINI-Net: Multiple Instance Ranking Network for Video Highlight Detection

Fa-Ting Hong[1,4,5], Xuanteng Huang[1], Wei-Hong Li[3], and Wei-Shi Zheng[1,2,5]($\boxtimes$)

[1] School of Data and Computer Science, Sun Yat-sen University, Guangzhou, China
{hongft3,huangxt57}@mail2.sysu.edu.cn, wszheng@ieee.org
[2] Peng Cheng Laboratory, Shenzhen 518005, China
[3] VICO Group, University of Edinburgh, Edinburgh, UK
w.h.li@ed.ac.uk
[4] Pazhou Lab, Guangzhou, China
[5] Key Laboratory of Machine Intelligence and Advanced Computing,
Ministry of Education, Guangzhou, China

Abstract. We address the weakly supervised video highlight detection problem for learning to detect segments that are more attractive in training videos given their video event label but without expensive supervision of manually annotating highlight segments. While manually averting localizing highlight segments, weakly supervised modeling is challenging, as a video in our daily life could contain highlight segments with multiple event types, *e.g.*, skiing and surfing. In this work, we propose casting weakly supervised video highlight detection modeling for a given specific event as a multiple instance ranking network (MINI-Net) learning. We consider each video as a bag of segments, and therefore, the proposed MINI-Net learns to enforce a higher highlight score for a positive bag that contains highlight segments of a specific event than those for negative bags that are irrelevant. In particular, we form a max-max ranking loss to acquire a reliable relative comparison between the most likely positive segment instance and the hardest negative segment instance. With this max-max ranking loss, our MINI-Net effectively leverages all segment information to acquire a more distinct video feature representation for localizing the highlight segments of a specific event in a video. The extensive experimental results on three challenging public benchmarks clearly validate the efficacy of our multiple instance ranking approach for solving the problem.

1 Introduction

In our daily life, people like to share their shining moments by posting videos on social media platforms, such as *YouTube* and *Instagram*. These well-edited videos in the social media platforms can quickly attract audience and convey an owner's experience. However, behind a well-credited video, there is the owner's heavy workload, as producing highlight clips from a lengthy video by hand is

Electronic supplementary material The online version of this chapter (https://doi.org/10.1007/978-3-030-58601-0_21) contains supplementary material, which is available to authorized users.

a time-consuming and laborious task. Therefore, it would be highly demanded for developing an automated tool to cut out highlights from a lengthy video, automatically generating a highlight short-form video.

Recently, video highlight detection has attracted an increasing amount of attention. Existing methods are mainly divided into two strategies. The first category casts the video highlight detection into a supervised learning problem [9,12,31]. Given both unedited videos and their highlight annotations labelled manually, a ranking net is trained to score segments in videos such that the highlight segments have higher highlight scores than those non-highlight segments in the video. For example, in [9], they proposed a robust deep RankNet to generate a rank list of segments according to their suitability as graphic interchange format (GIF) and designed an adaptive Huber loss to resist the noise effect caused by the outlier data. However, these methods work in the supervised learning manner and requires massive annotation on highlights in the training videos, which is hard and costly to be collected.

The second strategy treats video highlight detection as a weakly supervised recognition task [25,27,30]. Given certain events' videos, they treat short-form videos as a collection of highlights, while long-form videos contain a high proportion of non-highlights. Specially, Xiong et al. [27] designed a model that learns to predict the relations between highlight segments and non-highlight segments of the same event such that the highlight segments would have higher scores than non-highlight segments in the same event. Additionally, the work [30] employs the auto-encoder structure to narrow the reconstruction error of segments in short-form videos, which are considered as highlights. However, video highlight detection remains as a challenging problem, as in real-world scenarios an unedited video in social media platforms may contain highlights of more than one event, and the above mentioned detectors that are trained on videos of target event cannot well filter out the highlights of the other events. Without such human annotation, it is hard and indeed challenging to locate the real highlight of a target event in a video and perform specific learning.

In this work, we provide a new and effective approach for solving the weakly supervised setting: even though the exact highlight annotations of a video are not available, the label whether a video has a type of highlight is provided. In such a weakly supervised setting, we know that there exists a segment of a video that corresponds to a target highlight, but we also understand that there exist other segments of the video that do not correspond to the target highlight. To cope with this setting, we consider each video as a bag, and each bag contains a set of segments of the video (i.e., the video segments are treated as instances in each bag). Therefore, we cast the weakly supervised highlight detection as a multiple instance learning problem and proposed a Multiple InstaNce rankIng NETwork (MINI-Net) for video highlight detection. As shown in Fig. 1, for each type of highlight event, we construct positive bags using the videos that that contain the target highlights (e.g., surfing), and the videos that contain other irrelevant highlight events but not the target event (e.g., dog show) are used to form the negative bags. For such bag-level classification, we introduce two objective functions, i.e., max-max ranking loss and binary bag event classification loss, to effectively train the MINI-Net. In particular, the max-max ranking loss is designed to acquire a reliable relative

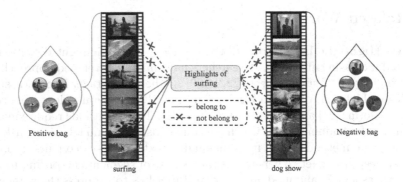

Fig. 1. To train a model to detect surfing's highlights, we can collect unannotated videos of various events from the internet using query tags. Although the highlight annotations (*i.e.*, labels telling which segments are highlights) are not available, we know that the videos with the "surfing" tag (*e.g.*, the left video) potentially contain "surfing" highlights, while the videos of other event tags would not have highlights about surfing (*e.g.*, videos of "dog show" shown on the right side would not have highlights of surfing). We cast video highlight detection as a multiple instance learning problem, where we can treat videos of "surfing" as positive bags as they contain highlights of "surfing", while videos of other events are negative bags as they do not have highlights of "surfing".

comparison between the most likely positive segment instance and the most hard negative segment instance. And meanwhile, minimizing the binary bag event classification loss enforces model to produce more informative bag representation for the specific event. To our best knowledge, this is the first to develop a multiple instance learning approach for weakly supervised video highlight detection.

In addition to the bag classification module, our MINI-Net al.so consists of two other modules: vision-audio fusion module and highlight estimation module. The vision-audio fusion module leverages both vision features and audio features, which is beneficial as, inspired by [1] learning about video segments both visually and aurally can produce more informative features. The highlight estimation module utilizes these features to estimate the highlight score for them. We aggregate all instance features weighted by their immediate highlight scores to generate the bag feature for the bag classification module.

In our experiments, we compared the proposed model with other related methods for three challenging public video highlight detection benchmarks. *i.e.*, YouTube Highlights dataset [21], TVSum dataset [19] and CoSum dataset [4]. Additionally, we have conducted an ablation study to investigate the effect of the proposed max-max ranking loss and bag classification module and validate the use of audio features and vision features. The experimental results show that our proposed model achieves a state-of-the-art performance for three public datasets and verify its efficacy for video highlight detection.

2 Related Work

- Video Highlight Detection. In recent years, video highlight detection has attracted increasing attention. Researchers have mainly developed approaches to detect highlights of sport videos [22,24,29] in the early stage. Recently, supervised video highlight detection has been proposed for general videos from social media platforms [21] and first-person videos [31]. These methods require massive annotations for training videos which is a time-consuming and laborious task. The Video2GIF [9] method, learns from manually created GIF-video pairs, proposed a robust deep RankNet to generate a ranked list of segments according to their suitability as a GIF, and used an adaptive Huber loss to suppress the noise effect caused by outlier data. Weakly supervised methods on video highlight detection can effectively reduce the pressure of manual labeling. More recently, methods that trained on a collection of videos of the same topic [27,30] gain a satisfactory performance. They leverage category-aware reconstruction loss [30] to identify the highlights or exploit the video duration as an implicit supervision [27].

Like these weakly supervised video highlight detection methods, our approach also tailors highlights to the topic event. However, existing methods cannot filter the highlights of irrelevant events as they are trained on specific event videos. Unlike existing methods, our approach formulates a multiple instance learning framework to tackle the video highlight detection problem. Treating videos of other events as negative bags in our framework and using proposed max-max ranking loss to enlarge the gap between instances of target event and those of other events in terms of highlight scores can help to filter the segments of irrelevant events and detect the highlights of the target event in a general video.

- Video Summarization. Video summarization [2,14,19,28], which is highly related to video highlight detection, outputs a video summary by the estimated importance of segments. Different from video highlight detection, video summarization focuses on the integrity of the video story. Mahasseni et al. [14] proposed an adversarial long short-term memory (LSTM) network, consisting of a summarizer and a discriminator, to regularize the consistency between the story of the summary and the original video. In addition, by using deep reinforcement learning, [33] formulated video summarization as a sequential decision-making process, rewarded by the diversity and representativeness of the generated video summaries. Recently, [2] presented a generative modeling framework, which contains two important components: a variational auto-encoder for learning the latent semantics from web videos and an encoder-attention-decoder for saliency estimation of the raw video and the summary generation, to learn the latent semantic video representations to bridge the benchmark data and web data. Different from video summarization, our approach selects the highlight segments by comparing the instances in the training pair, which consists of one most likely highlight an instance from the positive bag and one hard non-highlight instance from the negative bag. The inherent characteristics that there is at least one positive instance in the positive bag and instances are all negative in negative bag improve our MINI-Net's distinguishing power for detecting highlights.

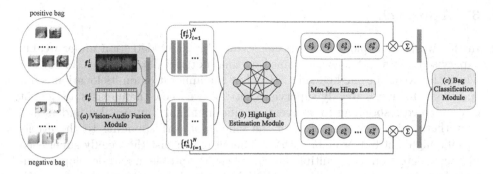

Fig. 2. Illustration of our proposed MINI-Net. We feed two bags, positive bag and negative bag, into vision-audio Fusion Module (Figure (a)) to encode the vision-audio fusion feature. The highlight estimation module (Figure (b)) takes as input these features to estimate the highlight scores. Beyond this, the immediate highlight scores and vision-audio fusion features are fed into the bag classification module (Figure (c)) for bags' event category classification. The max-max ranking loss is designed to ensure that the score of the segment in the positive bag with highest score is higher than the score of the segment in the negative bag with the highest score with a margin. Beyond this, the binary cross entropy loss is adopted for bags' event classification.

- Multiple Instance Learning. The multiple instance learning (MIL) is a form of weakly supervised learning in which the training instances are arranged in sets, called bags, and a label is provided for the entire bag. The field of MIL has generated a large amount of interest and is still growing [3,5,11,15,20,23,26]. Ilse et al. [11] proposed a neural-network-based permutation-invariant aggregation operator, a gated attention mechanism that provides insight into the contribution of each instance to the bag label, to produce bag features. Considering normal and anomalous videos as bags and video segments as instances in multiple instance learning framework, the work in [20] develops a deep multiple instance ranking framework to predict high anomaly scores for anomalous video segments.

In this work, the objective of multiple instance learning is different from the above, and ours is for solving weakly supervised video highlight detection, which has not been attempted before, and some of the above MIL methods may not be applicable or effective for our problem. In addition, unlike the above MIL methods that only explore the relations among instances of a bag to encode informative bag representation and the bag classification for learning, we introduce a max-max ranking loss to acquire a reliable relative comparison between the most likely positive segment instance and the hardest negative segment instance. This enables our method for more effectively distinguishing highlight from videos, which is verified in our experiments.

3   Approach

In this work, we explore event-specific[1] video highlight detection under weakly supervised setting; that is we trained on unannotated data samples, in each of which the event-specific highlight exists but the annotation on its location is not specified. In such a weakly supervised setting, we know there exists a segment of a video corresponding to an event-specific highlight, but we also understand that there exist other segments of the video not corresponding to the event-specific highlight but probably others. Therefore, we cast the weakly supervised highlight detection as a multiple instance learning problem, and develop a Multiple InstaNce rankIng NETwork (MINI-Net) for video highlight detection. We consider each video as a bag, and each bag contains a set of segments of the video (i.e., the video segments are treated as instances in each bag). We denote the event of interest as *interest event* and the other as *non-interest events*, and therefore a video contains the event of interest is called a *positive video* and a video that does not is called a *negative video*.

More specifically, we represent a positive video as a bag $\mathcal{B}_p = \{\mathcal{I}_p^i\}_{i=1}^N$, namely a positive bag. The positive bag contains N individual instances $\{\mathcal{I}_p^i\}_{i=1}^N$ (i.e., segments of the positive video). Similarly, the negative bag $\mathcal{B}_n$ contains N different segments $\{\mathcal{I}_n^i\}_{i=1}^N$ from a negative video. Our model learns the highlights of interest event through positive bag; and through the learning of negative bag, the segments of the videos in non-interest events are treated as non-highlights for the specific event.

Given a pair of bags (i.e., a positive bag $\mathcal{B}_p$ and a negative bag $\mathcal{B}_n$), we first pre-extract the vision features $\{\mathbf{f}_v^i\}_{i=1}^N$ and audio features $\{\mathbf{f}_a^i\}_{i=1}^N$ using pretrained models. We then feed the pre-extracted features of both the positive bag and negative bag into the proposed model to estimate the highlight scores of instances (i.e., $\{\mathcal{E}_p^i\}_{i=1}^N, \{\mathcal{E}_n^i\}_{i=1}^N$) and event prediction (i.e., interest event or non-interest event) of two bags (i.e., $y_{\mathcal{B}_p}, y_{\mathcal{B}_n}$) as follows:

$$
\begin{aligned}
\{\mathbf{f}_p^i\}_{i=1}^N, \{\mathbf{f}_n^i\}_{i=1}^N &= f^F(\{\mathcal{I}_p^i\}_{i=1}^N, \{\mathcal{I}_n^i\}_{i=1}^N | \theta^F), \\
\{\mathcal{E}_p^i\}_{i=1}^N, \{\mathcal{E}_n^i\}_{i=1}^N &= f^E(\{\mathbf{f}_p^i\}_{i=1}^N, \{\mathbf{f}_n^i\}_{i=1}^N | \theta^E), \\
y_{\mathcal{B}_p}, y_{\mathcal{B}_n} &= f^C(\{\mathbf{f}_p^i\}_{i=1}^N, \{\mathbf{f}_n^i\}_{i=1}^N, \{\mathcal{E}_p^i\}_{i=1}^N, \{\mathcal{E}_n^i\}_{i=1}^N | \theta^C),
\end{aligned}
\tag{1}
$$

where $f^F(\cdot)$ is the vision-audio fusion module parameterized by θ^F. The vision-audio fusion module takes each segment's vision feature and audio feature as input to encode the vision-audio fusion feature that contains both vision information and audio information (i.e., $\{\mathbf{f}_p^i\}_{i=1}^N, \{\mathbf{f}_n^i\}_{i=1}^N$ are vision-audio fusion features for the positive bag and negative bag). The encoded fusion features are input into the highlight estimation module $f^E(\cdot)$ parameterized by θ^E to predict their highlight scores. The bag classification module $f^C(\cdot)$ takes as input the vision-audio fusion features of all segments and their immediate highlight score to estimate the event category of both the positive bag and the negative bag.

---

[1] We use the term event-specific to mean that there is event/category of interest specified by keyword(s) like "surfing", following [27,30].

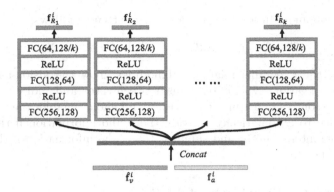

Fig. 3. Illustration of the vision-audio fusion submodule. The dimension of both vision feature $\hat{\mathbf{f}}_v^i$ and audio feature $\mathbf{f}_a^i$ are 128. k is the number of fusion submodule. The "FC" and "ReLU" represent fully connection and rectified linear unit activation, respectively.

To facilitating distinguishing positive bags from negative bags, we introduce two loss functions, *i.e.*, the max-max ranking loss and the binary bag event classification loss, to effectively train the whole multiple instance learning framework. The illustration shown in Fig. 2 provides an overview of our proposed method.

3.1   Vision-Audio Fusion Module $f^F(\cdot)$

Given a bag of segments, instead of using the visual information to estimate the highlight score individually, we consider using both visual and audio information as visual and audio events tend to occur together, and it has been shown that audio can be adopted to assist computer vision tasks[1,10,25]. For instance, a scene of people surfing is usually accompanied by the sound of waves. To this end, we design a vision-audio fusion module to encode visual-audio fusion representations for video highlight detection.

Given the pre-extracted vision feature $\mathbf{f}_v^i \in \mathbb{R}^{512}$ and audio feature $\mathbf{f}_a^i \in \mathbb{R}^{128}$ of a segment $\mathcal{I}_i$ in a bag (*i.e.*, positive bag or negative bag), as the dimensions of both features are not the same, we first employ two fully connected layers to transform $\mathbf{f}_v^i$ to a 128-dimensional vector, denoted as $\hat{\mathbf{f}}_v^i$. We then encode the vision-audio relation feature $\mathbf{f}_R^i$ and employ the residual connection to merge the vision-audio relation feature and vision feature $\hat{\mathbf{f}}_v^i$, yielding the vision-audio fusion feature $\mathbf{f}^i = \hat{\mathbf{f}}_v^i + \mathbf{f}_R^i$.

To encode $\mathbf{f}_R^i$, we concatenate the vision feature $\hat{\mathbf{f}}_v^i$ and audio feature $\mathbf{f}_a^i$ and feed the concatenated feature into k parallel fusion submodules to transform the concatenated feature to k relation features $\mathbf{f}_{R_k}^i$. We then concatenate the k relation feature to form the vision-audio relation feature $\mathbf{f}_R^i$.

We show the architecture of the submodules in Fig. 3. Each fusion submodule contains 3 fully connected layers and two activation operators to transform a 256-dimensional concatenated feature into a $\frac{128}{k}$-dimensional relation feature. In this way, the vision-audio fusion feature can be rewritten as follows:

$$\mathbf{f}^i = \hat{\mathbf{f}}^i_v + Concat[\mathbf{f}^i_{R_1}, \ldots, \mathbf{f}^i_{R_k}], (i = 1, \ldots, N). \tag{2}$$

In this way, the k parallel relation submodules allow the vision-audio fusion module to learn various types of relations between vision and audio. Additionally, encoding two sources of features (*i.e.*, vision and audio) enables the vision-audio fusion module to automatically activate the audio information if the audio is useful for the interest event and suppress the audio information if the audio is noisy or not helpful.

3.2 Highlight Estimation Module $f^E(\cdot)$

To predict the highlight score, we feed the vision-audio fused feature $\mathbf{f}^i$ into the highlight estimation module, where we transform $\mathbf{f}^i$ into a score value that will be used for bag classification and computing the proposed max-max ranking loss in later sections. More specifically, we first compute the initial highlight score by:

$$\hat{\mathcal{E}}^i = W_H(ReLU(W_S\mathbf{f}^i)), \tag{3}$$

where W_S is a matrix projecting the vision-audio fusion feature into a subspace, the ReLU activation operator activates the effective elements, and the matrix W_H is applied to measure the highlight score.

Rather than simply using $\hat{\mathcal{E}}^i$ as the highlight score, we consider estimating the final highlight score using the scores of all segments in a bag since the highlight score of one segment is related to other segments in the same video. Therefore, we formulate the final score as:

$$\mathcal{E}^i = \left(\sum_{t=1}^{N} exp(\hat{\mathcal{E}}^t)\right)^{-1} exp(\hat{\mathcal{E}}^i), \tag{4}$$

In this way, $\mathcal{E}^i$ is normalized in a bag and can be compared with the score of a segment in another bag.

3.3 Bag Classification Module $f^C(\cdot)$

Apart from estimating highlight scores of individual segments, we find that the event category can also be used as a supervision signal for training. The event category label can be more easily collected as all videos can be collected by specific query tags, and the tags can be used to generate the binary event label (*i.e.*, interest event or non-interest events). In addition, it is the fact that a video may contain highlights of various events while we are only interested in a specific event's highlights. This means that correctly classifying the event category (interest event or non-interest events) can be a useful inductive bias for event-specific highlight detection.

More specifically, we first label positive videos (videos of interest event) as 1 and negative videos (videos of non-interest events) as 0, *i.e.*, $Y_{\mathcal{B}_p} = 1$ for $\mathcal{B}_p$

and $Y_{\mathcal{B}_n} = 0$ for $\mathcal{B}_n$. To classify the event category of each bag, we aggregate the vision-audio fusion features of all instances weighted by their immediate estimated highlight scores to generate the bag representation:

$$\mathbf{f}_{\mathcal{B}} = \sum_{i=1}^{N} \mathcal{E}^i \mathbf{f}^i. \tag{5}$$

In this way, the generated bag representation could be highly informative for the event classification of each bag, as it mainly relies on the vision-audio fusion feature of the instance with high highlight scores.

We then feed the generated bag feature $\mathbf{f}_{\mathcal{B}}$ into an event classifier that consists of two fully connected layers. We apply the softmax function to estimate the event categories for both the positive bag $y_{\mathcal{B}_p}$ and the negative bag $y_{\mathcal{B}_n}$.

3.4 Objective Functions

After obtaining the predicted highlight scores of segments and the estimated event categories of the positive bag and negative bag, we introduce two objective functions (*i.e.*, max-max ranking loss and bag event classification loss) to effectively train our MINI-Net.

- **"max-max" ranking loss (MM-RL).** To learn the highlight detection model, we expect that the highlight score of a ground-truth highlight segment is higher than the score of a non-highlight segment:

$$\mathcal{E}_{gt-H} > \mathcal{E}_{gt-N}, \tag{6}$$

where $\mathcal{E}_{gt-H}$ is the highlight score of a ground-truth highlight segment and $\mathcal{E}_{gt-N}$ is the score of a non-highlight segment.

However, the highlight annotations are not available during training. Considering that the positive video contains at least one highlight segment, and the negative video does not have any highlights of the interest event, we thus believe the segment from a positive video with the highest score is the most likely to be a highlight, and the segment from the negative bag with the highest score can be assigned as a hardest non-highlight. We adapt Eq. 6 as follows for acquiring a reliable relative comparison between mostly likely positive instance and hardest negative instance:

$$\max_{\mathcal{I}_p^i \in \mathcal{B}_p} \mathcal{E}_p^i > \max_{\mathcal{I}_n^i \in \mathcal{B}_n} \mathcal{E}_n^i, \tag{7}$$

where *max* operators pick the maximum value from the highlight scores of all segments in a bag. Here, the highlights in the non-interest events' videos are viewed as non-highlights for the interest event. Using the segments of the non-interest events as a negative instance is more reliable than using the segment from the long-form interest event's video [27].

To instantiate Eq. 7, we introduce the max-max ranking loss (MM-RL) as:

$$\mathcal{L}_{MM}(\mathcal{B}_p, \mathcal{B}_n) = \max(0, \epsilon - \max_{\mathcal{I}_p^i \in \mathcal{B}_p} \mathcal{E}_p^i + \max_{\mathcal{I}_n^i \in \mathcal{B}_n} \mathcal{E}_n^i), \tag{8}$$

where $\mathcal{L}_{AH}$ is applied to ensure that $\max_{\mathcal{I}_p^i \in \mathcal{B}_p} \mathcal{E}_p^i$ is larger than $\max_{\mathcal{I}_n^i \in \mathcal{B}_n} \mathcal{E}_n^i$ with a margin of ϵ. ϵ is a hyperparameter and is equal to 1 in this work.

- **Bag Event Classification Loss.** As mentioned in Sect. 3.3, in addition to the MM-RL loss, we expect the bag event classification loss can enforce the model to produce more informative bag representation for the specific event. To this end, we apply the binary cross entropy loss function to the estimated event categories of both positive bag and negative bag for bag event classification. Finally, we add up both the MM-RL and the bag event classification loss to form the final loss:

$$\mathcal{L} = \mathcal{L}_{MM}(\mathcal{B}_p, \mathcal{B}_n) + \mathcal{L}_{CE}(y_{\mathcal{B}_p}, Y_{\mathcal{B}_p}) + \mathcal{L}_{CE}(y_{\mathcal{B}_n}, Y_{\mathcal{B}_n}), \quad (9)$$

where $\mathcal{L}_{CE}(\cdot)$ is the binary cross entropy loss function.

4   Experiments

In this section, we conduct extensive experiments on three public datasets to investigate the effectiveness of the proposed model. More experimental results and details are reported and analyzed in the Supplementary Material.

4.1   Datasets and Metrics

We evaluate our method on three public benchmarks datasets, *i.e.*, YouTube Highlights [21], TVSum [19] and CoSum [4], for video highlight detection.

- **YouTube Highlights.** contains six evnet-specific categories, *i.e.*, dogs, gymnastics, parkour, skating, skiing and surfing, and there are approximately 100 videos in each event. The given label for YouTube highlights indicates whether a segment is a ground-truth highlight segment.

- **TVSum.** is an available video summarization benchmark dataset that is collected from *YouTube* and crawled by an event-specific queried tag. The dataset consists of 50 videos grouped by 10 categories (5 videos per category). We follow [2,27] and select the top 50% shots in terms of the score provided by annotators for each video as a human-created summary.

- **CoSum.** has 51 videos covering 10 events. We follow [2,16] and compare each generated highlights with three human-created summaries.

4.2   Compared Methods

To further demonstrate the capacity of our method, we compare our method with numerous different methods on three datasets for video highlight detection.

- **Weakly Supervised Methods.** The compared methods include RRAE [30], MBF [4], SMRS [6], Quasi [13], CVS [17], SG [14], and LIM-s [27], and two weakly supervised methods, VESD [2] and DSN [16]. Although most of these methods are used for video summarization, their performance is evaluated using the same metrics as the metrics used in this study.

- **Supervised Methods** Additionally, there are several supervised methods (*i.e.*, GIFs [9],LSVM [21], KVS [18], DPP [7], sLstm [32] and SM [8]) that are applied in video highlight detection and video summarization. We compare these methods using the same matrices mentioned above.

Table 1. Experimental results (mAP) on the YouTube Highlights dataset. Our method outperforms all of the compared methods, including the state-of-the-art weakly supervised ranking-based method [27].

Topic	Supervised Methods		Weakly supervised Methods		Weakly supervised	
	GIFs	LSVM	RRAE	LIM-s	MINI-Net[w/o audio]	MINI-Net
dog	0.308	**0.60**	0.49	0.579	0.5368	0.5816
gymnastics	0.335	0.41	0.35	0.417	0.5281	**0.6165**
parkour	0.540	0.61	0.50	0.670	0.6888	**0.7020**
skating	0.554	0.62	0.25	0.578	0.7094	**0.7217**
skiing	0.328	0.36	0.22	0.486	0.5834	**0.5866**
surfing	0.541	0.61	0.49	0.651	0.6383	**0.6514**
Average	0.464	0.536	0.383	0.564	0.6138	**0.6436**

Table 2. Experimental results (top-5 mAP score) on the TVsum dataset. Our method outperforms all of the compared methods by a large margin.

Topic	Supervised Methods					Weakly supervised/Un Methods							Weakly supervised	
	KVS	DPP	sLstm	SM	SMRS	Quasi	MBF	CVS	SG	LIM-s	DSN	VESD	MINI-Net[w/o audio]	MINI-Net
VT	0.353	0.399	0.411	0.415	0.272	0.336	0.295	0.328	0.423	0.559	0.373	0.447	0.8028	**0.8062**
VU	0.441	0.453	0.462	0.467	0.324	0.369	0.357	0.413	0.472	0.429	0.441	0.493	0.6527	**0.6832**
GA	0.402	0.457	0.463	0.469	0.331	0.342	0.325	0.379	0.475	0.612	0.428	0.496	0.7535	**0.7821**
MS	0.417	0.462	0.477	0.478	0.362	0.375	0.412	0.398	0.489	0.540	0.436	0.503	0.8128	**0.8183**
PK	0.382	0.437	0.448	0.445	0.289	0.324	0.318	0.354	0.456	0.604	0.411	0.478	0.7801	**0.7807**
PR	0.403	0.446	0.461	0.458	0.276	0.301	0.334	0.381	0.473	0.475	0.417	0.485	0.5446	**0.6584**
FM	0.397	0.442	0.452	0.451	0.302	0.318	0.365	0.365	0.464	0.432	0.412	0.487	0.5586	**0.5780**
DK	0.342	0.395	0.406	0.407	0.297	0.295	0.313	0.326	0.417	0.663	0.368	0.441	0.7174	**0.7502**
BT	0.419	0.464	0.471	0.473	0.314	0.327	0.365	0.402	0.483	0.691	0.435	0.492	0.7686	**0.8019**
DS	0.394	0.449	0.455	0.453	0.295	0.309	0.357	0.378	0.466	0.626	0.416	0.488	0.5911	**0.6551**
Average	0.398	0.447	0.451	0.461	0.306	0.329	0.345	0.372	0.462	0.563	0.424	0.481	0.6979	**0.7324**

4.3   Highlight Detection Results

- Result for the YouTube Highlights Dataset: We report our results in comparison with other researches[2]. For the sake of fairness, we also reported the results of a MINI-Net's variant, *i.e.*, MINI-Net[w/o audio], which removes the audio feature from the MINI-Net and replace the vision-audio fusion feature with vision feature (more analysis about MINI-Net[w/o audio] is reported in Sect. 4.4). We find that our method achieves the best result in terms of the average mAP over all events. Compared to the ranking-based weakly supervised method LIM-s and auto-encoder-based weakly supervised method RRAE, MINI-Net's average gains in mAP are 7.96% and 26.06%, respectively. The result strongly verifies that our weakly supervised method based on multiple instance learning has better capacity than the compared methods. It is noteworthy that the our result is even better than that achieved by supervised methods, *i.e.*, GIFs and LSVM, which are trained with event-specific manually annotated data. These results indicate that our MINI-Net can leverage unlabeled videos for video highlight

---

[2] The compared results are from original papers.

Table 3. Experimental results (top-5 mAP score) on the CoSum dataset. Our method outperforms all of the compared methods by a large margin. The entries with "–" mean per-class results are not available for that method.

Topic	Supervised Methods					Weakly supervised							Weakly supervised	
	KVS	DPP	sLstm	SM	SMRS	Quasi	MBF	CVS	SG	LIM-s	VESD	DSN	MINI-Net$^{\text{w/o audio}}$	MINI-Net
BJ	0.662	0.672	0.683	0.692	0.504	0.561	0.631	0.658	0.698	–	0.685	0.715	0.7756	**0.8450**
BP	0.674	0.682	0.701	0.722	0.492	0.625	0.592	0.675	0.713	–	0.714	0.746	0.9628	**0.9887**
ET	0.731	0.744	0.749	0.789	0.556	0.575	0.618	0.722	0.759	–	0.783	0.813	0.7864	**0.9156**
ERC	0.685	0.694	0.717	0.728	0.525	0.563	0.575	0.693	0.729	–	0.721	0.756	0.9525	**1.0000**
KP	0.701	0.705	0.714	0.745	0.521	0.557	0.594	0.707	0.729	–	0.742	0.772	0.9585	**0.9611**
MLB	0.668	0.677	0.714	0.693	0.543	0.563	0.624	0.679	0.721	–	0.687	0.727	0.8686	**0.9353**
NFL	0.671	0.681	0.681	0.727	0.558	0.587	0.603	0.674	0.693	–	0.724	0.737	0.8972	**1.0000**
NDC	0.698	0.704	0.722	0.759	0.496	0.617	0.594	0.702	0.738	–	0.751	0.782	0.8901	**0.9536**
SL	0.713	0.722	0.721	0.766	0.525	0.551	0.624	0.715	0.743	–	0.763	0.794	0.7865	**0.8896**
SF	0.642	0.648	0.653	0.683	0.533	0.562	0.603	0.647	0.681	–	0.674	0.709	0.7272	**0.7897**
Average	0.684	0.692	0.705	0.735	0.525	0.576	0.602	0.687	0.720	–	0.721	0.755	0.8605	**0.9278**

Fig. 4. The example of bag in our approach, and the highlight scores of each instance estimated by our MINI-Net trained for detecting "base jump" highlight.

detection more effectively than other methods without the need to spend a lot of manual labor on data annotation. We also find that our MINI-Net$^{\text{w/o audio}}$ outperforms all compared methods without audio feature. Such results indicate that proposed objective functions can improve the ability to distinguish of our model.

- Result on TVSum Dataset and CoSum Dataset: The experimental results for our method on the TVSum dataset and the CoSum dataset are shown in Table 2 and Table 3, respectively. TVsum and CoSum are more challenging datasets as they have diverse videos. However, our method outperforms all of the baselines by a large margin on both the TVSum dataset and the CoSum dataset. Note that LIM-s [27], which is the most competitive ranking-based weakly supervised method, provides the average top-5 mAP, which is 16.94% less than the value achieved with our MINI-Net on the TVSum dataset. Our approach achieves

Table 4. Comparisions with related multiple instance learning methods.

Dataset	Gated-Attention [11]	DMIL-RM [20]	MINI-Net
YouTube	0.6289	0.6357	**0.6436**
TVSum	0.6533	0.6895	**0.7324**
Cosum	0.7516	0.7943	**0.9278**

a significant and consistent improvement over all the events in the two datasets. (*e.g.*, the top-5 mAP of our MINI-Net vs. that of VESD are 84.50% vs. 68.5% on the BJ event of CoSum dataset). These results show that the training model based on multiple instance learning using both interest events video data and non-interest events video data is more useful for video highlight detection. As these two datasets consist of long-form videos crawled from social media platforms, in addition to the highlights of the interest event, these videos inevitably contain video information of other events. Figure 4 shows segments and their highlight scores. We can determine that the segments in the non-interest event (*i.e.*, negative bag) are assigned low highlight scores (the segments (e)-(h) in Fig. 4) and the highlights of the interest event achieve the highest scores (the segment (d) in Fig. 4). The performances on the TVsum and CoSum datasets indicate that our model has the capacity to treat segments from non-interest events as non-highlights and only detect highlights from the interest event.

- Comparison with Other Multiple Instance Learning Methods. To further prove that our proposed multiple instance learning framework is suitable for video highlight detection, we compare the other two multiple instance learning frameworks, *i.e.*, Gated-Attention [11] and DMIL-AM [20], which are adapted to video highlight detection. It is clearly shown in Table 4 that our method performs the best. *e.g.*, MINI-Net outperforms Gate-Attention and DMIL-RM by 17.62% and 13.35% on CoSum dataset, respectively. The results in Table 4 demonstrate that the architecture of MINI-Net is more suitable for video highlight detection.

4.4 Ablation Studies

We present an ablation study to evaluate each component of our model.

- Effect of Bag Modeling. Firstly, we evaluate the effect of bag classification module on the proposed model by removing the module, *i.e.*, MINI-Net$^{w/o \; BCM}$. Comparing the full model and our model without bag classification module, we clearly observe that the bag classification improves the performance (*e.g.*, "MINI-Net" improves the performance of "MINI-Net$^{w/o \; BCM}$" from 65.58% to 73.24% for TVSum dataset). This implies that our bag classification module is able to help select as many ground-truth highlights from the video as possible, which benefits video highlight detection.

- Effect of max-max Ranking Loss (MM-RL). Secondly, we evaluate the impact of MM-RL on our approach. MINI-Net$^{w/o \; MM-RL}$ indicates that we have removed the MM-RL from the Eq. 9. From Table 5, we also observe that adding

Table 5. Ablation study on three datasets.

Dataset	MINI-Net$^{w/o\ vision}$	MINI-Net$^{w/o\ audio}$	MINI-Net$^{w/o\ MM\text{-}RL}$	MINI-Net$^{w/o\ BCM}$	MINI-Net
YouTube	0.5223	0.6138	0.6166	0.6113	**0.6436**
TVSum	0.5972	0.6979	0.6495	0.6558	**0.7324**
Cosum	0.6914	0.8605	0.7759	0.7823	**0.9278**

max-max ranking loss can consistently boost the performance (*e.g.*, the results of "MINI-Net" vs. those of "MINI-Net$^{w/o\ MM\text{-}RL}$" are 92.78% vs. 77.59% for the CoSum dataset). This result indicates that forcing the most likely highlight segment and the hard non-highlight segment to be far apart in terms of highlight score can help the potential ground-truth highlight segment of the interest event obtain a relatively high score .

- Effect of Audio Features. Finally, to verify that audio is beneficial in our work, we conduct an experiment that trains our model without audio features, *i.e.*, MINI-Net$^{w/o\ audio}$ in Table. 5, and MINI-Net$^{w/o\ vision}$ indicates that we have removed the vision feature. More specifically, we use the audio or vision features after several layers of fully connected layers (we make the number of parameters consistent) to replace the fused features that are input to the subsequent network. In Table 5, we can find that our full method outperforms the alternative variants. In particular, comparing MINI-Net$^{w/o\ audio}$ and MINI-Net$^{w/o\ vision}$ for the three datasets, the MINI-Net$^{w/o\ vision}$ outperforms MINI-Net$^{w/o\ audio}$ by 9.15%, 10.07% and 16.91% for YouTube Highlights dataset, TVSum dataset and CoSum dataset, respectively. These results indicate that: 1) Even using only vision features, our method outperforms the compared methods in Table 1, Table 2 and Table 3. 2) Using audio alone can degrade the performance more than using video alone, as audio is sometimes not native, and music or a voiceover is applied by the video owner. Such audio cannot be utilized to improve the performance and introduce noise; 3) It is also verified that the combination of audio and vision can improve the performance of the model.

5   Conclusion

Compared to related work, to our best knowledge, this work is the first to cast the weakly supervised video highlight detection problem as a multiple instance ranking approach. The bag modeling in our multiple instance ranking network (MINI-Net) particularly solves the difficulty of localization of highlight segments of a specific event during training, because MINI-Net works on bag level, where it is only required to ensure a positive bag having a highlight segment of that event and a negative bag having relevant ones. Based on such bag setting, with a max-max ranking loss, our MINI-Net is able to effectively leverage and quantify all segment information of a video, and therefore the proposed MINI-Net manages to acquire reliable higher highlight scores for positive bags as compared to negative bags. The experimental results have validated the effectiveness of our approach.

Acknowledgements. This work was supported partially by the National Key Research and Development Program of China (2018YFB1004903), NSFC(U19-11401,U1811461), Guangdong Province Science and Technology Innovation Leading Talents (2016TX03X157), Guangdong NSF Project (No. 2018B030312002), Guangzhou Research Project (201902010037), and Research Projects of Zhejiang Lab (No. 2019KD0AB03).

References

1. Arandjelovic, R., Zisserman, A.: Look, listen and learn. In: International Conference on Computer Vision (2017)
2. Cai, S., Zuo, W., Davis, L.S., Zhang, L.: Weakly-supervised video summarization using variational encoder-decoder and web prior. In: European Conference on Computer Vision (2018)
3. Carbonneau, M.A., Cheplygina, V., Granger, E., Gagnon, G.: Multiple instance learning: a survey of problem characteristics and applications. Pattern Recogn. **77**, 329–353 (2018)
4. Chu, W.S., Song, Y., Jaimes, A.: Video co-summarization: video summarization by visual co-occurrence. In: Computer Vision and Pattern Recognition (2015)
5. Cinbis, R.G., Verbeek, J., Schmid, C.: Weakly supervised object localization with multi-fold multiple instance learning. Trans. Pattern Anal. Mach. Intell. **39**(1), 189–203 (2016)
6. Elhamifar, E., Sapiro, G., Vidal, R.: See all by looking at a few: sparse modeling for finding representative objects. In: Computer Vision and Pattern Recognition (2012)
7. Gong, B., Chao, W.L., Grauman, K., Sha, F.: Diverse sequential subset selection for supervised video summarization. In: Advances in Neural Information Processing Systems (2014)
8. Gygli, M., Grabner, H., Van Gool, L.: Video summarization by learning submodular mixtures of objectives. In: Computer Vision and Pattern Recognition (2015)
9. Gygli, M., Song, Y., Cao, L.: Video2gif: automatic generation of animated gifs from video. In: Computer Vision and Pattern Recognition (2016)
10. Hori, C., et al.: Attention-based multimodal fusion for video description. In: International Conference on Computer Vision (2017)
11. Ilse, M., Tomczak, J.M., Welling, M.: Attention-based deep multiple instance learning. arXiv preprint arXiv:1802.04712 (2018)
12. Jiao, Y., Li, Z., Huang, S., Yang, X., Liu, B., Zhang, T.: Three-dimensional attention-based deep ranking model for video highlight detection. Trans. Multimedia **20**(10), 2693–2705 (2018)
13. Kim, G., Sigal, L., Xing, E.P.: Joint summarization of large-scale collections of web images and videos for storyline reconstruction. In: Computer Vision and Pattern Recognition (2014)
14. Mahasseni, B., Lam, M., Todorovic, S.: Unsupervised video summarization with adversarial lstm networks. In: Computer Vision and Pattern Recognition (2017)
15. Meng, J., Wu, S., Zheng, W.S.: Weakly supervised person re-identification. In: Computer Vision and Pattern Recognition (2019)
16. Panda, R., Das, A., Wu, Z., Ernst, J., Roy-Chowdhury, A.K.: Weakly supervised summarization of web videos. In: International Conference on Computer Vision (2017)

17. Panda, R., Roy-Chowdhury, A.K.: Collaborative summarization of topic-related videos. In: Computer Vision and Pattern Recognition (2017)
18. Potapov, D., Douze, M., Harchaoui, Z., Schmid, C.: Category-specific video summarization. In: Fleet, D., Pajdla, T., Schiele, B., Tuytelaars, T. (eds.) ECCV 2014. LNCS, vol. 8694, pp. 540–555. Springer, Cham (2014). https://doi.org/10.1007/978-3-319-10599-4_35
19. Song, Y., Vallmitjana, J., Stent, A., Jaimes, A.: Tvsum: summarizing web videos using titles. In: Computer Vision and Pattern Recognition (2015)
20. Sultani, W., Chen, C., Shah, M.: Real-world anomaly detection in surveillance videos. In: Computer Vision and Pattern Recognition (2018)
21. Sun, M., Farhadi, A., Seitz, S.: Ranking domain-specific highlights by analyzing edited videos. In: Fleet, D., Pajdla, T., Schiele, B., Tuytelaars, T. (eds.) ECCV 2014. LNCS, vol. 8689, pp. 787–802. Springer, Cham (2014). https://doi.org/10.1007/978-3-319-10590-1_51
22. Tang, H., Kwatra, V., Sargin, M.E., Gargi, U.: Detecting highlights in sports videos: cricket as a test case. In: International Conference on Multimedia and Expo (2011)
23. Ulges, A., Schulze, C., Breuel, T.: Multiple instance learning from weakly labeled videos. In: Workshop on Cross-media Information Analysis and Retrieval (2008)
24. Wang, J., Xu, C., Chng, E., Tian, Q.: Sports highlight detection from keyword sequences using hmm. In: International Conference on Multimedia and Expo (2004)
25. Wang, L., Sun, Z., Yao, W., Zhan, H., Zhu, C.: Unsupervised multi-stream highlight detection for the game "honor of kings". arXiv preprint arXiv:1910.06189 (2019)
26. Wu, J., Yu, Y., Huang, C., Yu, K.: Deep multiple instance learning for image classification and auto-annotation. In: Computer Vision and Pattern Recognition (2015)
27. Xiong, B., Kalantidis, Y., Ghadiyaram, D., Grauman, K.: Less is more: learning highlight detection from video duration. In: Computer Vision and Pattern Recognition (2019)
28. Xiong, B., Kim, G., Sigal, L.: Storyline representation of egocentric videos with an applications to story-based search. In: International Conference on Computer Vision (2015)
29. Xiong, Z., Radhakrishnan, R., Divakaran, A., Huang, T.S.: Highlights extraction from sports video based on an audio-visual marker detection framework. In: International Conference on Multimedia and Expo (2005)
30. Yang, H., Wang, B., Lin, S., Wipf, D., Guo, M., Guo, B.: Unsupervised extraction of video highlights via robust recurrent auto-encoders. In: International Conference on Computer Vision (2015)
31. Yao, T., Mei, T., Rui, Y.: Highlight detection with pairwise deep ranking for first-person video summarization. In: Computer Vision and Pattern Recognition (2016)
32. Zhang, K., Chao, W.-L., Sha, F., Grauman, K.: Video summarization with long short-term memory. In: Leibe, B., Matas, J., Sebe, N., Welling, M. (eds.) ECCV 2016. LNCS, vol. 9911, pp. 766–782. Springer, Cham (2016). https://doi.org/10.1007/978-3-319-46478-7_47
33. Zhou, K., Qiao, Y., Xiang, T.: Deep reinforcement learning for unsupervised video summarization with diversity-representativeness reward. In: AAAI Conference on Artificial Intelligence (2018)

ContactPose: A Dataset of Grasps with Object Contact and Hand Pose

Samarth Brahmbhatt[1]([✉])(iD), Chengcheng Tang[3], Christopher D. Twigg[3],
Charles C. Kemp[1], and James Hays[1,2]

[1] Georgia Tech, Atlanta, GA, USA
{samarth.robo,hays}@gatech.edu, charlie.kemp@bme.gatech.edu
[2] Argo AI, Pittsburgh, USA
[3] Facebook Reality Labs, Pittsburgh, USA
{chengcheng.tang,cdtwigg}@fb.com

Abstract. Grasping is natural for humans. However, it involves complex hand configurations and soft tissue deformation that can result in complicated regions of contact between the hand and the object. Understanding and modeling this contact can potentially improve hand models, AR/VR experiences, and robotic grasping. Yet, we currently lack datasets of hand-object contact paired with other data modalities, which is crucial for developing and evaluating contact modeling techniques. We introduce ContactPose, the first dataset of hand-object contact paired with hand pose, object pose, and RGB-D images. ContactPose has 2306 unique grasps of 25 household objects grasped with 2 functional intents by 50 participants, and more than 2.9 M RGB-D grasp images. Analysis of ContactPose data reveals interesting relationships between hand pose and contact. We use this data to rigorously evaluate various data representations, heuristics from the literature, and learning methods for contact modeling. Data, code, and trained models are available at https:// contactpose.cc.gatech.edu.

Keywords: Contact modeling · Hand-object contact · Functional grasping

1 Introduction

A person's daily experience includes numerous and varied hand-object interactions. Understanding and reconstructing hand-object interaction has received growing attention from the computer vision, computer graphics, and robotics communities. Most research has focused on hand pose estimation [14,46,50,52], realistic hand and body reconstruction [21,22,54,58], and robotic grasp prediction for anthropomorphic hands [4,31]. In this paper, we address the underexplored problem of *hand-object contact modeling i.e.* predicting object contact

Electronic supplementary material The online version of this chapter (https:// doi.org/10.1007/978-3-030-58601-0_22) contains supplementary material, which is available to authorized users.

© Springer Nature Switzerland AG 2020
A. Vedaldi et al. (Eds.): ECCV 2020, LNCS 12358, pp. 361–378, 2020.
https://doi.org/10.1007/978-3-030-58601-0_22

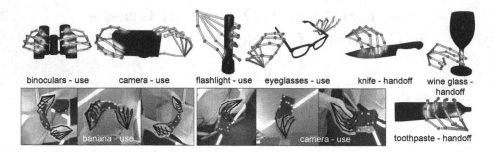

binoculars - use   camera - use   flashlight - use   eyeglasses - use   knife - handoff   wine glass - handoff

banana - use   camera - use   toothpaste - handoff

Fig. 1. Examples from ContactPose, a dataset capturing grasps of household objects. ContactPose includes high-resolution contact maps (object meshes textured with contact), 3D joints, and multi-view RGB-D videos of grasps. Left hand joints are green, right hand joints are red. (Color figure online)

with the hand, based on other information about the grasp, such as the 3D hand pose and grasp images. Accurate contact models have numerous applications in computer interfaces, understanding social interaction, object manipulation, and safety. For example, a hand contact model could interpret computer commands from physical interactions with a 3D printed replica object, or estimate if pathogens from a contaminated surface were transmitted through contact. More broadly, accurate contact modeling can improve estimation of grasp dynamics [11,32,35,41], which can lead to better VR simulations of grasping scenarios and grasping with soft robotic hands [8,25].

Lack of ground-truth data has likely played a role in the under-exploration of this problem. Typically, the contacting surfaces of a grasp are occluded from direct observation with visible light imaging. Approaches that instrument the hand with gloves [48,55] can subtly influence natural grasping behavior, and do not measure contact on the object surface. Approaches that intersect hand models with object models require careful selection of proximity thresholds or specific contact hand points [22,54]. They also cannot account for soft hand tissue deformation, since existing state-of-the-art hand models [44] are rigid.

Brahmbhatt et al. [3] recently introduced thermal cameras as sensors for capturing detailed ground-truth contact. Their method observes the heat transferred from the (warm) hand to the object through a thermal camera after the grasp. We adopt their method because it avoids the pitfalls mentioned above and allows for evaluation of contact modeling approaches with ground-truth data. However, it also imposes some constraints. 1) Objects have a plain visual texture since they are 3D printed to ensure consistent thermal properties. This does not affect 3D hand pose-based contact modeling methods and VR/robotic grasping simulators, since they rely on 3D shape and not texture. It does limit the generalization ability of RGB-based methods, which can potentially be mitigated by using depth images and synthetic textures. 2) The grasps are static, because in-hand manipulation results in multiple overlapping thermal hand-prints that depend on timing and other factors. Contact modeling for static grasps is still an unsolved problem, and forms the basis for future work on dynamic grasps. The methods we present here could be applied to dynamic scenarios frame-by-frame.

In addition, we develop a data collection protocol that captures multi-view RGB-D videos of the grasp, and an algorithm for 3D reconstruction of hand joints (Sect. 3.1). To summarize, we make the following contributions:

- **Data**: Our dataset (ContactPose) captures 50 participants grasping 25 objects with 2 functional intents. It includes high-quality contact maps for each grasp, over 2.9 M RGB-D images from 3 viewpoints, and object pose and 3D hand joints for each frame. We will make it publicly available to encourage research in hand-object interaction and pose estimation.
- **Analysis**: We dissect this data in various ways to explore the interesting relationship between contact and hand pose. This reveals some surprising patterns, and confirms some common intuitions.
- **Algorithms**: We explore various representations of object shape, hand pose, contact, and network architectures for learning-based contact modeling. Importantly, we rigorously evaluate these methods (and heuristic methods from the literature) against ground-truth unique to ContactPose.

2   Related Work

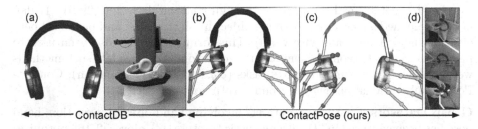

Fig. 2. Comparison to ContactDB [3]. It includes contact maps and turntable RGB-D images (a), which are often not enough to fully interpret the grasp e.g. it is not clear which fingers generated the contact. In contrast, ContactPose includes 3D joint locations (b), which allows association of contacted areas to hand parts (c), and multi-view RGB-D grasp images (d). These data enable a more comprehensive interpretation of the grasp.

Capturing and Modeling Contact: Previous works have instrumented hands and/or objects to capture contact. Bernardin *et al.* [2] and Sundaram *et al.* [48] used a tactile glove to capture hand contact during grasping. Brahmbhatt *et al.* [3] used a thermal camera after the grasp to observe the heat residue left by the warm hand on the object surface. However, these datasets lacked either hand pose or grasp images, which are necessary for developing applicable contact models (Fig. 2). Pham *et al.* [39,40] and Ehsani *et al.* [9] tracked hands and objects in videos, and trained models to predict contact forces and locations at

Table 1. Comparison with existing hand-object datasets. ContactPose stands out for its size, and paired hand-object contact, hand pose and object pose.

Feature	FPHA [14]	HO-3D [20]	FreiHand [62]	STAG [48]	ContactDB [3]	Ours
3D joints	✓	✓	✓	×	×	✓
Object pose	✓	✓	×	×	✓	✓
Grasp RGB images	✓	✓	✓	✓	×	✓
Grasp Depth images	✓	✓	×	×	×	✓
Natural hand appearance	×	✓	✓	×	×	✓
Natural object appearance	×	✓	✓	✓	×	×
Naturally situated	✓	×	×	×	×	×
Multi-view images	×	×	✓	×	×	✓
Functional intent	✓	×	×	×	✓	✓
Hand-object contact	×	×	×	✓	✓	✓
# Participants	6	8	32	1	50	50
# Objects	4	8	35	26	50	25

fingertips that explain observed object motion. In contrast, we focus on detailed contact modeling for complex objects and grasps, evaluated against contact maps over the entire object surface.

Contact Heuristics: Heuristic methods to detect hand-object contact are often aimed at improving hand pose estimation. Hamer *et al.* [18] performed joint hand tracking and object reconstruction [19], and inferred contact only at fingertips using proximity threshold. In simulation [56] and robotic grasping [33,35], contact is often determined similarly, or through collision detection [29,51]. Ballan *et al.* [1] defined a cone circumscribing object mesh triangles, and penalized penetrating hand points (and vice versa). This formulation has also been used to penalize self-penetration and environment collision [38,54]. While such methods were evaluated only through proxy tasks (*e.g.* hand pose estimation), Contact-Pose enables evaluation against ground-truth contact (Sect. 6).

Grasp Datasets: Focusing on datasets involving hand-object interaction, hand pose has been captured in 3D with magnetic trackers [14], gloves [2,16], optimization [20], multi-view boot-strapping [46], semi-automated human-in-the-loop [62], manually [47], synthetically [22], or as instances of a taxonomy [5,10,43] along with RGB-D images depicting the grasps. However, none of these have contact annotations (see Table 1), and suffer additional drawbacks like lack of object information [46,62] and simplistic objects [14,47] and interactions [22,47], which make them unsuitable for our task. In contrast, ContactPose has a large amount of ground-truth contact, and real RGB-D images of complex (including bi-manual) functional grasps for complex objects. The plain object texture is a drawback of ContactPose. Tradeoffs for this in the context of contact modeling are discussed in Sect. 1.

3   The ContactPose Dataset

In ContactPose, hand-object contact is represented as a contact map on the object mesh surface, and observed through a thermal camera. Hand pose is represented as 3D hand(s) joint locations in the object frame, and observed through multi-view RGB-D video clips. The cameras are calibrated and object pose is known, so that the 3D joints can be projected into images (examples shown in supplementary material). Importantly, we avoid instrumenting the hands with data gloves, magnetic trackers or other sensors. This has the dual advantage of not interfering with natural grasping behavior and allowing us to use the thermal camera-based contact capture method from [3]. We develop a computational approach (Sect. 3.2) that optimizes for the 3D joint locations by leveraging accurate object tracking and aggregating over multi-view and temporal information. Our data collection protocol, described below, facilitates this approach.

3.1   Data Capture Protocol and Equipment

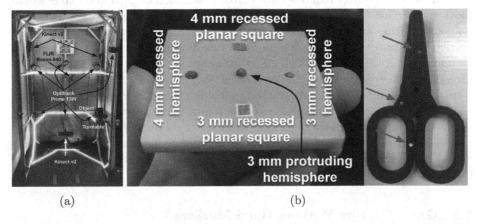

(a)   (b)

Fig. 3. (a) Our setup consists of 7 Optitrack Prime 13W tracking cameras, 3 Kinect v2 RGB-D cameras, a FLIR Boson 640 thermal camera, 3D printed objects, and a turntable. (b) **Left**: Different object tracking marker configurations we investigate. **Right**: 3D printed object with recessed 3 mm hemispherical markers (highlighted by red arrows) offer a good compromise between unobtrusiveness and tracking performance (Color figur online).

We invite able-bodied participants to our laboratory and collect data through the following IRB-approved protocol. Objects are placed at random locations on a table in orientation normally encountered in practice. Participants are instructed to grasp an object with one of two functional intents (either using the object, or handing it off). Next, they stand in the data collection area (Fig. 3a) and move the object for 10–15 s in the cubical space. They are instructed to hold their hand joints steady, but are free to arbitrarily rotate the wrist and elbow, and to grasp objects with both hands or their dominant hand. This motion is recorded by 3 Kinect v2 RGB-D cameras (used for hand pose) and an Optitrack motion capture (mocap) system (used for object pose). Next, they hand the object to a researcher, who places it on a turntable, handling it with gloved hands. The object is recorded with the mocap system, Kinect v2, and a FLIR Boson 640 thermal camera as the turntable rotates a circle.

Contact Capture: Thermal images are texture-mapped to the object mesh using Open3D [59,60]. As shown in [3] and the supp. mat., the resulting mesh textures (called contact maps) accurately capture hand-object contact.

Object Selection and Fabrication: We capture grasps on a subset of 25 objects from [3] that are applicable for both 'use' and 'hand-off' grasping (see supp. mat. for a list). The objects are 3D printed in blue for good contrast with hands and the green background of our capture area. 3D printing the objects ensures consistent thermal properties and ensures geometric consistency between real world objects in capture sessions and the 3D models in our dataset.

Mocap recovers the object pose using retro-reflective markers, whose the placement on the object requires some care. Attaching a large 'marker tree' would block interactions with a significant area of the surface. Placing hemispherical markers on the surface is more promising, but a sufficient number (8+) are needed to ensure visibility during hand occlusion and the resulting 'bumps' can be uncomfortable to touch, which might influence natural grasping behavior. We investigate a few alternative marker configurations (Fig. 3b). Flat pieces of tape were more comfortable but only tracked well when the marker was directly facing the camera. A good compromise is to use 3 mm hemispherical markers but to recess them into the surface by adding small cut-outs during 3D printing. These are visible from a wide range of angles but do not significantly affect the user's grip. Fixing the marker locations also allows for simple calibration between the Optitrack rigid body and the object's frame.

3.2   Grasp Capture Without Hand Markers

Each grasp is observed through N frames of RGB-D images from C cameras. We assume that the hand is fixed relative to the object, and the 6-DOF object pose for each frame is given. So instead of estimating 3D joints separately in each frame, we can aggregate the noisy per-frame 2D joint detections into a single set of high-quality 3D joints, which can be transformed by the frame's object pose.

For each RGB frame, we use Detectron [23] to locate the wrist, and run the OpenPose hand keypoint detector [46] on a 200×200 crop around the wrist. This produces 2D joint detections $\{\mathbf{x}^{(i)}\}_{i=1}^{N}$ and confidence values $\{\mathbf{w}^{(i)}\}_{i=1}^{N}$, following the 21-joint format from [46]. One option is to lift these 2D joint locations to 3D using the depth image [52], but that biases the location toward the camera and the hand surface (our goal is to estimate joint locations internal to the hand). Furthermore, the joint detections at any given frame are unreliable. Instead, we use our hand-object rigidity assumption to estimate the 3D joint locations $^o\mathbf{X}$ in the object frame that are consistent with all NC images. This is done by minimizing the average re-projection error:

$$\min_{^o\mathbf{X}} \sum_{i=1}^{N} \sum_{c=1}^{C} \mathcal{D}\left(\mathbf{x}_c^{(i)}, \pi\left(^o\mathbf{X}; K_c, {}^cT_w {}^wT_o^{(i)}\right); \mathbf{w}_c^{(i)}\right) \tag{1}$$

where $\mathcal{D}$ is a distance function, and $\pi(\cdot)$ is the camera projection function using camera intrinsics K_c and object pose w.r.t. camera at frame i, ${}^cT_o^{(i)} = {}^cT_w {}^wT_o^{(i)}$. Our approach requires the object pose w.r.t. world at each frame ${}^wT_o^{(i)}$ i.e. object tracking. This is done using an Optitrack motion capture system tracking markers embedded in the object surface.

In practice, the 2D joint detections are noisy and object tracking fails in some frames. We mitigate this by using the robust Huber function [26] over Mahalanobis distance ($\mathbf{w}^{(i)}$ acting as variance) as $\mathcal{D}$, and wrapping Eq. 1 in a RANSAC [13] loop. A second pass targets frames that fail the RANSAC inlier test due to inaccurate object pose. Their object pose is estimated through the correspondence between their 2D detections and the RANSAC-fit 3D joint locations, and they are included in the inlier set if they pass the inlier test (re-projection error less than a threshold). It is straightforward to extend the optimization described above to bi-manual grasps. We manually curated the dataset, including clicking 2D joint locations to aid the 3D reconstruction in some cases, and discarding some obviously noisy data.

Hand Mesh Models: In addition to capturing grasps, hand shape information is collected through palm contact maps on a flat plate, and multi-view RGB-D videos of the participant performing 7 known hand gestures (shown in the supplementary material). Along with 3D joints, this data can potentially enable fitting of the MANO hand mesh model [44] to each grasp [36]. In this paper, we use meshes fit to 3D joints (Fig. 4, see supp. mat. for details) for some of the analysis and learning experiments discussed below.

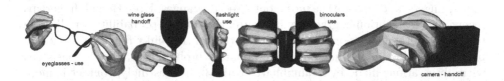

Fig. 4. MANO hand meshes [44] fit to ContactPose data. Both hand pose and shape parameters are optimized to minimize the distance of MANO joints from ContactPose 3D joint annotations.

4   Data Analysis

Contact maps are $[0, 1]$ normalized following the sigmoid fitting procedure from [3].

Association of Contact to Hand Parts: It has been observed that certain fingers and parts (e.g. fingertips) are contacted more frequently than others [5,6]. ContactPose allows us to quantify this. This can potentially inform anthropomorphic robotic hand design and tactile sensor (e.g. BioTac [49]) placement in robotic hands. For each grasp, we threshold the contact map at 0.4 and associate each contacted object point with its nearest hand point from the fitted MANO hand mesh. A hand point is considered to be contacted if one or more contacted object points are associated with it. A coarser analysis at the phalange level is possible by modeling phalanges as line segments connecting joints. In this case, the distance from an object point to a phalange is the distance to the closest point on the line segment.

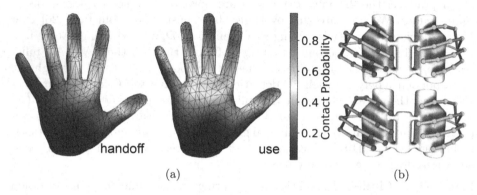

Fig. 5. (a) Hand contact probabilities estimated from the entire dataset. (b) Association of contacted binoculars points with fingers (top) and sets of phalanges at the same level of wrist proximity (bottom), **indicated** by different colors.

Figure 5a shows the contact probabilities averaged over 'use' and 'hand-off' grasps. Not surprisingly, the thumb, index, and middle finger are the most contacted fingers, and tips are the most contacted phalanges. Even though fingertips receive much attention in grasping literature, the contact probability for all three phalanges of the index finger is *higher* than that of the pinky fingertip. Proximal phalanges and palm also have significant contact probabilities. This is consistent with observations made by Brahmbhatt et al. [3]. Interestingly, contact is more concentrated at the thumb and index finger for 'hand-off' than 'use'. 'Use' grasps have an average contact area of $35.87\,\mathrm{cm}^2$ compared to $30.58\,\mathrm{cm}^2$ for 'hand-off'. This analysis is similar to that in Fig. 3 of Hasson *et al.* [22], but supported by ground-truth contact rather than synthetic grasps.

Comparison of the average fingertip vs. whole-hand contact areas (Figure 6) shows that non-fingertip areas play a significant role in grasp contact, confirming the approximate analysis in [3].

Automatic Active Area Discovery: Brahmbhatt et al. [3] define active areas as regions on the object highly likely to be contacted. While they manually

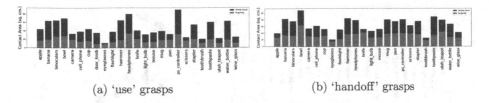

(a) 'use' grasps   (b) 'handoff' grasps

Fig. 6. Comparing average fingertip (red) vs. whole-hand (blue) contact areas. (Color figure online)

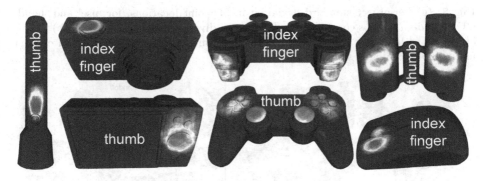

Fig. 7. Automatic 'active area' discovery: Contact probability for various hand parts on the object surface.

selected active areas and measured their probability of being contacted by *any* part of the hand, ContactPose allows us to 'discover' active areas automatically and for *specific* hand parts. We use the object point-phalange association described above (*e.g.* Fig. 5b) to estimate the probability of each object point being contacted by a given hand part (e.g. index finger tip), which can be thresholded to segment the active areas. Figure 7 shows this probability for the index fingertip and thumb, for 'use' grasps of some objects. This could potentially inform locations for placing contact sensors (real [40] or virtual for VR) on objects.

Grasp Diversity: We further quantify the effect of intent on grasping behavior by measuring the standard deviation of 3D joint locations over the dataset. The mean of all 21 joint standard deviations is shown in Fig. 8a. It shows that 'hand-off' grasps are more diverse than 'use' grasps in terms of hand pose. We accounted for symmetrical objects (e.g. wine glass) by aligning the 6 palm joints (wrist + 5 knuckles) of all hand poses for that object to a single set of palm joints, where the only degree of freedom for alignment is rotation around the symmetry axis. Hand size is normalized by scaling all joint location such that the distance from wrist to middle knuckle is constant.

Organizing the grasps by clustering these aligned 3D joints (using L2 distance and HDBSCAN [7]) reveals the diversity of grasps captured in ContactPose (Fig. 9). 'Hand-off' grasps exhibit a more continuous variation than 'use' grasps,

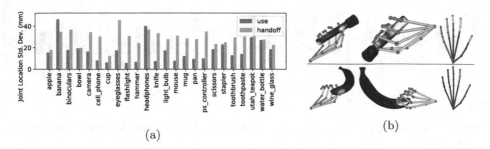

(a)   (b)

Fig. 8. (a) Per-object standard deviation in 3D joint locations, for 'use' and 'hand-off'. 'Hand-off' grasps consistently exhibit more diversity than 'use' grasps. (b) A pair of grasps with similar hand pose but different contact characteristics. Hand contact feature color-coding is similar to Fig. 5a.

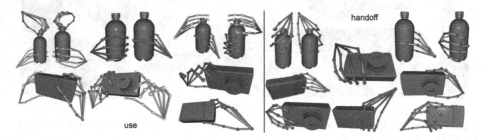

Fig. 9. Examples from hand pose clusters for 'use' and 'hand-off' grasps. Grasps from different clusters are shown with different colors (some grasps are bi-manual). Left hand joints are green, right hand joints are red (Color figure online).

which are tied more closely to the function of the object. The average intra-cluster distance for 'use' grasps is 32.5% less than that for 'handoff' grasps.

Figure 8b shows pair of grasps found by minimizing hand pose distance and maximizing hand contact distance. We use the phalange-level contact association described above. Summing the areas of all object mesh triangles incident to all vertices associated with a phalange creates a 20-dimensional vector. We use L2 distance over this vector as contact distance. It shows that grasps with similar hand pose can contact different parts of the object and/or hand, inducing different forces and manipulation possibilities [14] and emphasizing that hand pose alone provides an inadequate representation of grasping.

5   Contact Modeling Experiments

This section describes our experiments on *contact modeling* given the hand pose or RGB grasp image(s), assuming known object geometry and pose. Our experiments focus on finding good data representations and learning algorithms, and evaluating techniques against ground-truth. By providing high-quality contact output from readily available input modalities, such models can enable better hand-object dynamics simulation in AR/VR and soft robotic grasping.

Object Shape Representation: We represent the object shape through either a pointcloud densely sampled from the surface (1K-30K points based on size), or a 64^3 voxel occupancy grid. Features encoding the input hand pose are associated with individual points (voxels). The entire pointcloud (voxel grid) is then processed to predict contact values for points (surface voxels).

Hand Pose Representation: Features relating object shape to hand pose are computed for each point or voxel. These features have varying levels of richness of hand shape encoding. To simulate occlusion and noisy pose perception for the first 4 features, we sample a random camera pose and drop (set to 0) all features associated with the farthest 15% of the joints from the camera.

- `simple-joints`: We start by simply using the 21 3D joint locations w.r.t. the object coordinate system as 63-dimensional features for every point. For bi-manual grasps, points use the hand with the closest joint.
- `relative-joints`: Since contact at an object surface point depends on the *relative* position of the finger, we next calculate relative vectors from an object point to every joint of the hand closest to it. Contact also depends on the surface geometry: a finger is more likely to contact an object point if the vector to it is parallel to the surface normal at that point. Hence we use unit-norm surface normals and the relative joint vectors to form $63+3 = 66$-dimensional features for every point.
- `skeleton`: To better capture hand joint connectivity, we compute relative vectors from an object point to the nearest point on phalanges, modeled as line segments. 40-dimensional features for each object point are constructed by concatenating the lengths of 20 such vectors (one for each phalange), and their dot product with the surface normal at that object point.
- `mesh`: These features leverage the rich MANO hand model geometry. A relative vector is constructed from the object point to its closest hand mesh point. 23-dimensional features are constructed from the length of this vector, its dot product with the surface normal, and distances to 21 hand joints.
- Grasp Image(s): To investigate if CNNs can extract relevant information directly from images, we extract dense 40-dimensional features from 256 × 256 crops of RGB grasp images using a CNN encoder-decoder inspired by U-Net [45] (see supplementary material for architecture). These images come from the same time instant. We investigate both 3-view and 1-view settings, with feature extractor being shared across views for the former. Features are transferred to corresponding 3D object points using the known object pose and camera intrinsics, averaging the features if multiple images observe the same 3D point (Fig. 11a). Points not visible from any image have all features set to 0. Image backgrounds are segmented by depth thresholding at the 20th percentile, and the foreground pixels are composited onto a random COCO [30] image. This investigation is complementary to recent work on image-based estimation of object geometry [17,61], object pose [15,53], and hand pose [20,46,50,58,62].

Contact Representation: We observed in early experiments that the mean squared error loss resulted in blurred and saturated contact predictions. This might be due to contact value occurrence imbalance and discontinuous contact boundaries for smooth input features. Hence, we discretize the $[0, 1]$ normalized values into 10 equal bins and treat contact prediction as a classification problem, inspired by Zhang et al. [57]. We use the weighted cross entropy loss, where the weight for each bin is proportional to a linear combination of the inverse occurrence frequency of that bin and a uniform distribution (Eq. 4 from [57] with $\lambda = 0.4$). Following [57], we derive a point estimate for contact in $[0, 1]$ from classification outputs using the annealed mean ($T = 0.1$).

Learning Algorithms: Given the hand pose features associated with points or voxels, the entire pointcloud or voxel grid is processed by a neural network to predict the contact map. We use the PointNet++ [42] architecture implemented in pytorch-geometric [12,37] (modified to reduce the number of learnable parameters) for pointclouds, and the VoxNet [34]-inspired 3D CNN architecture from [3] for voxel grids (see the supplementary material for architectures). For voxel grids, a binary feature indicating voxel occupancy is appended to hand pose features. Following [3], hand pose features are set to 0 for voxels inside the object. Because the features are rich and provide fairly direct evidence of contact, we include a simple learner baseline of a multi-layer perceptron (MLP) with 90 hidden nodes, parametric ReLU [24] and batchnorm [27].

Contact Modeling Heuristics: We also investigate the effectiveness of heuristic techniques, given detailed hand geometry through the MANO hand mesh. Specifically, we use the conic distance field Ψ from [1,54] as a proxy for contact intensity. To account for imperfections in hand modelling (due to rigidity of the MANO mesh) and fitting, we compute Ψ not only for collisions, but also when the hand and object meshes are closer than 1 cm. Finally, we calibrate Ψ to our ground truth contact through least-squares linear regression on 4700 randomly sampled contact points. Both these steps improve the technique's performance.

6   Results

In this section, we evaluate various combinations of features and learning algorithms described in Sect. 5. The metric for quantitative evaluation is the area under the curve formed by calculating accuracy at increasing contact difference thresholds. Following [57], this value is re-balanced to account for varying occurrence frequencies of values in the 10 contact bins. We create two data splits: the *object split* holds out mug, pan and wine glass following [3], and the *participant split* holds out participants 5, 15, 25, 35, and 45. The held out data is used for evaluation, and models are trained on the rest.

Table 2 shows the re-balanced AuC values averaged over held out data for the two splits. We observe that features capturing richer hand shape information perform better (*e.g.* simple-joints vs. skeleton and mesh). Learning-based techniques with mesh features that operate on pointclouds are able to outperform

Table 2. Contact prediction re-balanced AuC (%) (higher is better) for various combinations of features and learning methods.

Learner	Features	Participant split		Object split	
		AuC (%)	Rank	AuC (%)	Rank
None	Heuristic [1, 54]	78.31	5	81.11	4
VoxNet [3, 34]	skeleton	77.94		79.99	
MLP	simple-joints	75.11		77.83	
	relative-joints	75.39		78.83	
	skeleton	80.78	3	80.07	
	mesh	79.89	4	**84.74**	1
PointNet++	simple-joints	71.61		73.67	
	relative-joints	74.51		77.10	
	skeleton	81.15	2	81.49	3
	mesh	**81.29**	1	84.18	2
Image enc-dec,	images (1-view)	72.89		77.09	
PointNet++	images (3-view)	78.06		80.80	5

heuristics, even though the latter has access to the full high-resolution object mesh, while the former makes predictions on a pointcloud. Learning also enables skeleton features, which have access to only the 3D joint locations, to perform competitively against mesh-based heuristics and features. While image-based techniques are not yet as accurate as the hand pose-based ones, a significant boost is achieved with multi-view inputs.

Figure 10 shows contact prediction results from hand pose for mug, an unseen object. Predictions are transferred from the pointcloud to high-resolution meshes for better visualization. The skeleton-PointNet++ combination is able to predict plausible contact patterns for dropped-out parts of the hand, and capture some of the nuances of palm contact. The mesh-PointNet++ combination captures more nuances, especially at the thumb and bottom of the palm. In contrast, relative-joints features-based predictions are diffused, lack finer details, and have high contact probability in the gaps between fingers, possibly due to lack of access to information about joint connectivity and hand shape.

Figure 11b shows contact prediction results from RGB images for mug, an unseen object. These predictions have less high-frequency details compared to hand pose based predictions. They also suffer from depth ambiguity – the proximal part of the index finger appears to be in contact from the mug images, but is actually not. This can potentially be mitigated by use of depth images.

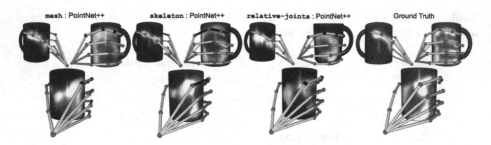

Fig. 10. Contact prediction for mug (an unseen object) from hand pose. All input features related to black line segments and joints were dropped (set to 0). Notice how the `mesh`- and `skeleton`-PointNet++ predictors is able to capture nuances of palm contact, thumb and finger shapes.

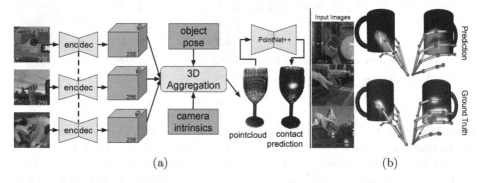

Fig. 11. (a) Image-based contact prediction architecture. (b) Contact prediction for mug (an unseen object) from RGB images, using networks trained with 3 views. Hand poses shown only for reference.

7   Conclusion and Future Work

We introduced ContactPose, the first dataset of paired hand-object contact, hand pose, object pose, and RGB-D images for functional grasping. Data analysis revealed some surprising patterns, like higher concentration of hand contact at the first three fingers for 'hand-off' vs. 'use' grasps. We also showed how learning-based techniques for geometry-based contact modeling can capture nuanced details missed by heuristic methods.

Using this contact ground-truth to develop more realistic, deformable hand mesh models could be an interesting research direction. State-of-the-art models (*e.g.* [28,44]) are rigid, while the human hand is covered with soft tissue. As the Future Work section of [44] notes, they are trained with meshes from which objects are manually removed, and do not explicitly reason about hand-object contact. ContactPose data can potentially help in the development and evaluation of hand mesh deformation algorithms.

Acknowledgements. We are thankful to the anonymous reviewers for helping improve this paper. We would also like to thank Elise Campbell, Braden Copple, David Dimond, Vivian Lo, Jeremy Schichtel, Steve Olsen, Lingling Tao, Sue Tunstall, Robert Wang, Ed Wei, and Yuting Ye for discussions and logistics help.

References

1. Ballan, L., Taneja, A., Gall, J., Van Gool, L., Pollefeys, M.: Motion capture of hands in action using discriminative salient points. In: Fitzgibbon, A., Lazebnik, S., Perona, P., Sato, Y., Schmid, C. (eds.) ECCV 2012. LNCS, vol. 7577, pp. 640–653. Springer, Heidelberg (2012). https://doi.org/10.1007/978-3-642-33783-3_46
2. Bernardin, K., Ogawara, K., Ikeuchi, K., Dillmann, R.: A sensor fusion approach for recognizing continuous human grasping sequences using hidden Markov models. IEEE Trans. Robot. **21**(1), 47–57 (2005)
3. Brahmbhatt, S., Ham, C., Kemp, C.C., Hays, J.: ContactDB: analyzing and predicting grasp contact via thermal imaging. In: The IEEE Conference on Computer Vision and Pattern Recognition (CVPR), June 2019
4. Brahmbhatt, S., Handa, A., Hays, J., Fox, D.: ContactGrasp: functional multi-finger grasp synthesis from contact. In: IEEE/RSJ International Conference on Intelligent Robots and Systems (IROS) (2019)
5. Bullock, I.M., Feix, T., Dollar, A.M.: The yale human grasping dataset: grasp, object, and task data in household and machine shop environments. Int. J. Robot. Res. **34**(3), 251–255 (2015)
6. Bullock, I.M., Zheng, J.Z., De La Rosa, S., Guertler, C., Dollar, A.M.: Grasp frequency and usage in daily household and machine shop tasks. IEEE Trans. Haptics **6**(3), 296–308 (2013)
7. Campello, R.J.G.B., Moulavi, D., Zimek, A., Sander, J.: Hierarchical density estimates for data clustering, visualization, and outlier detection. ACM Trans. Knowl. Discov. Data, **10**(1), 5:1–5:51 (2015). https://doi.org/10.1145/2733381.
8. Deimel, R., Brock, O.: A novel type of compliant and underactuated robotic hand for dexterous grasping. Int. J. Robot. Res. **35**(1–3), 161–185 (2016)
9. Ehsani, K., Tulsiani, S., Gupta, S., Farhadi, A., Gupta, A.: Use the force, luke! learning to predict physical forces by simulating effects. In: Proceedings of the IEEE/CVF Conference on Computer Vision and Pattern Recognition (CVPR), June 2020
10. Feix, T., Romero, J., Schmiedmayer, H.B., Dollar, A.M., Kragic, D.: The grasp taxonomy of human grasp types. IEEE Trans. Hum.-Mach. Syst. **46**(1), 66–77 (2015)
11. Ferrari, C., Canny, J.: Planning optimal grasps. In: Proceedings IEEE International Conference on Robotics and Automation, pp. 2290–2295. IEEE (1992)
12. Fey, M., Lenssen, J.E.: Fast graph representation learning with PyTorch geometric. In: ICLR Workshop on Representation Learning on Graphs and Manifolds (2019)
13. Fischler, M.A., Bolles, R.C.: Random sample consensus: a paradigm for model fitting with applications to image analysis and automated cartography. Commun. ACM **24**(6), 381–395 (1981)
14. Garcia-Hernando, G., Yuan, S., Baek, S., Kim, T.K.: First-person hand action benchmark with RGB-D videos and 3D hand pose annotations. In: Proceedings of Computer Vision and Pattern Recognition (CVPR) (2018)
15. Garon, M., Lalonde, J.F.: Deep 6-dof tracking. IEEE Trans. Vis. Comput. Graph. **23**(11), 2410–2418 (2017)

16. Glauser, O., Wu, S., Panozzo, D., Hilliges, O., Sorkine-Hornung, O.: Interactive hand pose estimation using a stretch-sensing soft glove. ACM Trans. Graph. (TOG) **38**(4), 1–15 (2019)
17. Groueix, T., Fisher, M., Kim, V.G., Russell, B.C., Aubry, M.: A papier-mâché approach to learning 3D surface generation. In: Proceedings of the IEEE conference on computer vision and pattern recognition, pp. 216–224 (2018)
18. Hamer, H., Gall, J., Weise, T., Van Gool, L.: An object-dependent hand pose prior from sparse training data. In: IEEE Computer Society Conference on Computer Vision and Pattern Recognition, pp. 671–678. IEEE (2010)
19. Hamer, H., Schindler, K., Koller-Meier, E., Van Gool, L.: Tracking a hand manipulating an object. In: 2009 IEEE 12th International Conference on Computer Vision, pp. 1475–1482. IEEE (2009)
20. Hampali, S., Rad, M., Oberweger, M., Lepetit, V.: Honnotate: a method for 3D annotation of hand and object poses. In: IEEE/CVF Conference on Computer Vision and Pattern Recognition (CVPR), June 2020
21. Hassan, M., Choutas, V., Tzionas, D., Black, M.J.: Resolving 3D human pose ambiguities with 3D scene constraints. In: The IEEE International Conference on Computer Vision (ICCV), October 2019
22. Hasson, Y., et al.: Learning joint reconstruction of hands and manipulated objects. In: Proceedings of the IEEE Conference on Computer Vision and Pattern Recognition, pp. 11807–11816 (2019)
23. He, K., Gkioxari, G., Dollár, P., Girshick, R.: Mask R-CNN. In: IEEE International Conference on Computer Vision (ICCV), pp. 2980–2988, October 2017
24. He, K., Zhang, X., Ren, S., Sun, J.: Delving deep into rectifiers: surpassing human-level performance on imagenet classification. In: Proceedings of the IEEE International Conference on Computer Vision, pp. 1026–1034 (2015)
25. Homberg, B.S., Katzschmann, R.K., Dogar, M.R., Rus, D.: Haptic identification of objects using a modular soft robotic gripper. In: IEEE/RSJ International Conference on Intelligent Robots and Systems (IROS), pp. 1698–1705. IEEE (2015)
26. Huber, P.J.: Robust Estimation of a location parameter. In: Kotz, S., Johnson, N.L., (eds) Breakthroughs in Statistics. Springer Series in Statistics (Perspectives in Statistics). Springer, New York, NY (1992) https://doi.org/10.1007/978-1-4612-4380-9_35
27. Ioffe, S., Szegedy, C.: Batch normalization: accelerating deep network training by reducing internal covariate shift. In: International Conference on Machine Learning, pp. 448–456 (2015)
28. Joo, H., Simon, T., Sheikh, Y.: Total capture: a 3D deformation model for tracking faces, hands, and bodies. In: Proceedings of the IEEE Conference on Computer Vision and Pattern Recognition, pp. 8320–8329 (2018)
29. Larsen, E., Gottschalk, S., Lin, M.C., Manocha, D.: Fast distance queries with rectangular swept sphere volumes. In: IEEE International Conference on Robotics and Automation. Symposia Proceedings (Cat. No. 00CH37065), vol. 4, pp. 3719–3726. IEEE (2000)
30. Lin, T.-Y., et al.: Microsoft COCO: common objects in context. In: Fleet, D., Pajdla, T., Schiele, B., Tuytelaars, T. (eds.) ECCV 2014. LNCS, vol. 8693, pp. 740–755. Springer, Cham (2014). https://doi.org/10.1007/978-3-319-10602-1_48
31. Lu, Q., Chenna, K., Sundaralingam, B., Hermans, T.: Planning multi-fingered grasps as probabilistic inference in a learned deep network. In: International Symposium on Robotics Research (2017)
32. Mahler, J., et al.: Learning ambidextrous robot grasping policies. Sci. Robot. **4**(26), eaau4984 (2019)

33. Mahler, J., et al.: Dex-net 1.0: a cloud-based network of 3D objects for robust grasp planning using a multi-armed bandit model with correlated rewards. In: IEEE International Conference on Robotics and Automation (ICRA), pp. 1957–1964. IEEE (2016)

34. Maturana, D., Scherer, S.: Voxnet: a 3D convolutional neural network for real-time object recognition. In: IEEE/RSJ International Conference on Intelligent Robots and Systems (IROS), pp. 922–928. IEEE (2015)

35. Miller, A.T., Allen, P.K.: Graspit! a versatile simulator for robotic grasping. IEEE Robot. Autom. Mag. **11**(4), 110–122 (2004)

36. Moon, G., Yong Chang, J., Mu Lee, K.: V2V-posenet: voxel-to-voxel prediction network for accurate 3D hand and human pose estimation from a single depth map. In: Proceedings of the IEEE Conference on Computer Vision and Pattern Recognition, pp. 5079–5088 (2018)

37. Paszke, A., et al.: Automatic differentiation in PyTorch. In: NIPS Autodiff Workshop (2017)

38. Pavlakos, G., et al.: Expressive body capture: 3D hands, face, and body from a single image. In: Proceedings IEEE Conference on Computer Vision and Pattern Recognition (CVPR), June 2019. http://smpl-x.is.tue.mpg.de

39. Pham, T.H., Kheddar, A., Qammaz, A., Argyros, A.A.: Towards force sensing from vision: observing hand-object interactions to infer manipulation forces. In: Proceedings of the IEEE Conference on CComputer Vision and Pattern Recognition, pp. 2810–2819 (2015)

40. Pham, T.H., Kyriazis, N., Argyros, A.A., Kheddar, A.: Hand-object contact force estimation from markerless visual tracking. IEEE Trans. Pattern Anal. Mach. Intell. **40**, 2883–2896 (2018)

41. Pollard, N.S.: Parallel methods for synthesizing whole-hand grasps from generalized prototypes. Tech. rep, MASSACHUSETTS INST OF TECH CAMBRIDGE ARTIFICIAL INTELLIGENCE LAB (1994)

42. Qi, C.R., Yi, L., Su, H., Guibas, L.J.: Pointnet++: deep hierarchical feature learning on point sets in a metric space. In: Advances in neural information processing systems, pp. 5099–5108 (2017)

43. Rogez, G., Supancic, J.S., Ramanan, D.: Understanding everyday hands in action from rgb-d images. In: Proceedings of the IEEE international conference on computer vision, pp. 3889–3897 (2015)

44. Romero, J., Tzionas, D., Black, M.J.: Embodied hands: modeling and capturing hands and bodies together. ACM Trans. Graph. (TOG) **36**(6), 245 (2017)

45. Ronneberger, O., Fischer, P., Brox, T.: U-Net: convolutional networks for biomedical image segmentation. In: Navab, N., Hornegger, J., Wells, W.M., Frangi, A.F. (eds.) MICCAI 2015. LNCS, vol. 9351, pp. 234–241. Springer, Cham (2015). https://doi.org/10.1007/978-3-319-24574-4_28

46. Simon, T., Joo, H., Matthews, I., Sheikh, Y.: Hand keypoint detection in single images using multiview bootstrapping. In: CVPR (2017)

47. Sridhar, S., Mueller, F., Zollhöfer, M., Casas, D., Oulasvirta, A., Theobalt, C.: Real-time joint tracking of a hand manipulating an object from RGB-D input. In: Leibe, B., Matas, J., Sebe, N., Welling, M. (eds.) ECCV 2016. LNCS, vol. 9906, pp. 294–310. Springer, Cham (2016). https://doi.org/10.1007/978-3-319-46475-6_19

48. Sundaram, S., Kellnhofer, P., Li, Y., Zhu, J.Y., Torralba, A., Matusik, W.: Learning the signatures of the human grasp using a scalable tactile glove. Nature **569**(7758), 698 (2019)

49. SynTouch LLC: BioTac. https://www.syntouchinc.com/robotics/. Accessed 5 March 2020

50. Tekin, B., Bogo, F., Pollefeys, M.: H+ o: unified egocentric recognition of 3D hand-object poses and interactions. In: Proceedings of the IEEE Conference on Computer Vision and Pattern Recognition, pp. 4511–4520 (2019)
51. Teschner, M., et al.: Collision detection for deformable objects. In: Computer Graphics Forum, vol. 24, pp. 61–81. Wiley Online Library (2005)
52. Tompson, J., Stein, M., Lecun, Y., Perlin, K.: Real-time continuous pose recovery of human hands using convolutional networks. ACM Trans. Graph. (ToG) $33(5)$, 169 (2014)
53. Tremblay, J., To, T., Sundaralingam, B., Xiang, Y., Fox, D., Birchfield, S.: Deep object pose estimation for semantic robotic grasping of household objects. In: Conference on Robot Learning (CoRL) (2018). https://arxiv.org/abs/1809.10790
54. Tzionas, D., Ballan, L., Srikantha, A., Aponte, P., Pollefeys, M., Gall, J.: Capturing hands in action using discriminative salient points and physics simulation. Int. J. Comput. Vis. $118(2)$, 172–193 (2016)
55. Wade, J., Bhattacharjee, T., Williams, R.D., Kemp, C.C.: A force and thermal sensing skin for robots in human environments. Robot. Auton. Syst. 96, 1–14 (2017)
56. Ye, Y., Liu, C.K.: Synthesis of detailed hand manipulations using contact sampling. ACM Trans. Graph. (TOG) $31(4)$, 41 (2012)
57. Zhang, R., Isola, P., Efros, A.A.: Colorful image colorization. In: Leibe, B., Matas, J., Sebe, N., Welling, M. (eds.) ECCV 2016. LNCS, vol. 9907, pp. 649–666. Springer, Cham (2016). https://doi.org/10.1007/978-3-319-46487-9_40
58. Zhang, X., Li, Q., Mo, H., Zhang, W., Zheng, W.: End-to-end hand mesh recovery from a monocular RGB image. In: The IEEE International Conference on Computer Vision (ICCV), October 2019
59. Zhou, Q.Y., Koltun, V.: Color map optimization for 3D reconstruction with consumer depth cameras. ACM Trans. Graph. (TOG) $33(4)$, 1–10 (2014)
60. Zhou, Q.Y., Park, J., Koltun, V.: Open3D: a modern library for 3D data processing. arXiv:1801.09847 (2018)
61. Zhou, X., Leonardos, S., Hu, X., Daniilidis, K.: 3D shape estimation from 2D landmarks: a convex relaxation approach. In: proceedings of the IEEE Conference on Computer Vision and Pattern Recognition, pp. 4447–4455 (2015)
62. Zimmermann, C., Ceylan, D., Yang, J., Russell, B., Argus, M., Brox, T.: Freihand: a dataset for markerless capture of hand pose and shape from single RGB images. In: The IEEE International Conference on Computer Vision (ICCV), October 2019

API-Net: Robust Generative Classifier via a Single Discriminator

Xinshuai Dong[1], Hong Liu[1], Rongrong Ji[1(✉)], Liujuan Cao[1], Qixiang Ye[2], Jianzhuang Liu[3], and Qi Tian[4]

[1] Media Analytics and Computing Lab, Department of Artificial Intelligence, School of Informatics, Xiamen University, Xiamen, China
rrji@xmu.edu.cn
[2] University of Chinese Academy of Sciences, Beijing, China
[3] Noah's Ark Lab, Huawei Technologies, Shenzhen, China
[4] Huawei Cloud BU, Shenzhen, China

Abstract. Robustness of deep neural network classifiers has been attracting increased attention. As for the robust classification problem, a generative classifier typically models the distribution of inputs and labels, and thus can better handle off-manifold examples at the cost of a concise structure. On the contrary, a discriminative classifier only models the conditional distribution of labels given inputs, but benefits from effective optimization owing to its succinct structure. This work aims for a solution of generative classifiers that can profit from the merits of both. To this end, we propose an *Anti-Perturbation Inference* (API) method, which searches for anti-perturbations to maximize the lower bound of the joint log-likelihood of inputs and classes. By leveraging the lower bound to approximate Bayes' rule, we construct a generative classifier *Anti-Perturbation Inference Net* (API-Net) upon a single discriminator. It takes advantage of the generative properties to tackle off-manifold examples while maintaining a succinct structure for effective optimization. Experiments show that API successfully neutralizes adversarial perturbations, and API-Net consistently outperforms state-of-the-art defenses on prevailing benchmarks, including CIFAR-10, MNIST, and SVHN.(Our code is available at github.com/dongxinshuai/API-Net.).

Keywords: Deep learning · Neural networks · Adversarial defense · Adversarial training · Generative classifier

1 Introduction

Deep neural networks (DNNs) have achieved unprecedented success in a wide range of applications [11,14,18,34,40,48]. However, they are strikingly susceptible to adversarial examples [41]. The latest attack techniques can generate adversarial perturbations that are seemingly innocuous to humans but easily

Electronic supplementary material The online version of this chapter (https://doi.org/10.1007/978-3-030-58601-0_23) contains supplementary material, which is available to authorized users.

© Springer Nature Switzerland AG 2020
A. Vedaldi et al. (Eds.): ECCV 2020, LNCS 12358, pp. 379–394, 2020.
https://doi.org/10.1007/978-3-030-58601-0_23

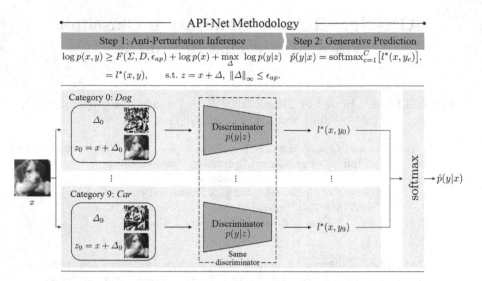

Fig. 1. Overview of our inference procedure. 1) For each sample, search for the anti-perturbation Δ to maximize the lower bound of the joint log-likelihood. 2) Leverage the lower bound $l^*(x,y)$ as an approximation of the log-likelihood for generative prediction using Bayes' rule (best view in color with zooming in)

fool DNNs [4,12,33], raising grand challenges to advanced machine learning systems where DNNs are widely deployed [1,5,19,27].

This phenomenon has attracted increased attention, with focuses on both attack methods and defenses. Attack methods intend to cause the failure of DNNs in their task, by maliciously modifying the input data. Such methods include Fast Gradient Sign Method (FGSM) [12], DeepFool [30], Projected Gradient Descent (PGD) attack [27], C&W attack [4], Universal Perturbations [24,29], and Wasserstein distance-based attack [43]. The prevailing "off-manifold" conjecture deems adversarial examples as outliers near but away from a class-related manifold [10,12,39,41], though challenged by [10].

To defend against adversarial attacks, several methods have been proposed. Some focus on the detection [21,23,25,26,28]. Another prominent category aims to enhance the accuracy of DNNs under attacks, which is the focus of this study. Among the work concerning the robust accuracy of classifiers, adversarial training is currently one of the most reliable [2]. Instead of minimizing the loss evaluated at vanilla inputs, adversarial training augments the training data with adversarially perturbed inputs, and builds defense that is shown to be the few resistant to the newest attacks [2,12,27,41].

While the robustness of discriminative classifiers is extensively investigated, few works involve the robustness of generative classifiers [32]. Generative classifiers are intuitively more robust to adversarial examples in that they learn the distribution of inputs and classes, and thus can make meaningful predictions by checking whether the class-specific features are present in the inputs. By comparing the joint log-likelihood of a given input and each class, which relates to the "distance" of the input to a class-specific data manifold, a generative classifier can estimate the prediction probabilities well even when its inputs are off-manifold examples. However, the classical generative classifiers, *e.g.*, naive Bayes, and linear discriminant analysis [8], perform poorly even on vanilla image classifications, failing to illustrate the robustness of generative classifiers.

Recent advances have been filling up this vacancy. For example, leveraging deep Latent Variable Model (LVM) to construct generative adversarial defense and detection [22]. However, the inference model of the deep LVM is itself a neural network and can be vulnerable. To tackle this problem, [37] proposed optimization-based inference, which substitutes the expectation under the inference model with a maximum likelihood sample to avoid stochastic sampling and to bypass the vulnerabilities. Though effective, current generative solutions are still perplexed by two problems: 1) To learn the joint distribution of samples and classes, a generative classifier often contains multiple components, which brings difficulties to optimization. 2) Adversarial training, which is very useful to build robustness for discriminative classifiers, is hard to apply to current generative models directly. On the contrary, a discriminative classifier only models the distribution of classes conditioned on inputs, and thus takes advantage of its succinctness for effective optimization. Hence, the main question this work aims to address is: is there a solution that can benefit from the merits of both types?

Inspired by [36], which illustrates that a single robust discriminator can be a powerful tool to perform low-level image synthesis tasks, such as inpainting and denoising, we propose to construct a structurally concise generative classifier based on such generative capabilities of a robust discriminator. Specifically, we propose an *Anti-Perturbation Inference* (API) approach and derive a tractable lower bound of the joint log-likelihood of inputs and classes. We use API to search for the anti-perturbation that neutralizes the potential perturbation to maximize the lower bound, and then leverage the lower bound to approximate Bayes' rule for generative predictions. Hence we build a generative classifier, API-Net, upon a single discriminator. API-Net benefits from the merits of both discriminative models and generative models: 1) Its generative properties facilitate modeling class-related manifolds to handle off-manifold examples. 2) Its concise structure ensures effective optimization and thus helps it make full use of adversarial training to gain robustness. We show the inference framework of API-Net in Fig. 1 and summarize the major contributions of this paper as follows:

- We propose a novel anti-perturbation inference approach and derive a lower bound of the joint log-likelihood of inputs and classes. By maximizing the lower bound, we obtain the anti-perturbation that can neutralize adversarial noise.

- Based on the proposed API method, we leverage the lower bound to approximate Bayes' rule and hence build API-Net, a novel generative classifier upon a single discriminator. API-Net takes advantage of both generative and discriminative classifiers to achieve robustness.

- Experiments on multiple prevailing benchmarks show that our approach consistently outperforms state-of-the-art methods with significant margins (*e.g.*, we achieve 63.13% accuracy under PGD-40 attacks on CIFAR-10, while the state-of-the-art is 55.40%).

2   Related Work

For a large amount of work, we focus on the most related ones, which can be classified into three categories, adversarial training, preprocessing-based defenses, and robust generative classifiers.

Adversarial Training. Adversarial training can be regarded as a special kind of data augmentation by generating and leveraging adversarial examples during training [12,19]. For each mini-batch of samples, adversarial images are generated, and further utilized to update the neural networks' parameters [12,31]. [27] suggests using Projected Gradient Descent (PGD) for adversary generation and currently it is one of the most effective ways to defend against adversarial attacks.

Preprocessing-based Defenses. This line of methods aims to destroy the structure of adversarial noise or project the adversarial examples into a learned manifold. Typical methods include image discretization [7], re-scaling [44], feature squeezing [45], thermometer encoding [3], neural-based transformations [35,38], and matrix estimation [46]. However, most of these defenses rely on obfuscated gradients which can be circumvented by applying the Backward Pass Differentiable Approximation (BPDA) based attacks [2]. Our approach can also be deemed as having non-differentiable preprocessing and should be tested under BPDA-based attacks for rigorous evaluations.

Robust Generative Classifiers. Generative classifiers are considered more robust if the "off-manifold" conjecture on adversarial examples holds. Following this line, there is a trend of study on the robustness of generative classifiers. Deep Bayes examines the robustness of different factorization structures of deep LVM [22] and builds generative adversarial defense and detection. [37] leverages Variational Auto-Encoder (VAE) [16] to approximate the joint log-likelihood and proposes an optimization-based inference method to circumvent the vulnerable inference model. Despite the effectiveness, existing generative classifiers are puzzled by their complicated structures, which impedes not only effective optimization but also obtaining further robustness through adversarial training.

3   The Proposed Method

In this section, we first introduce the basic task setting and the underlying motivation of our method. We then propose the API approach, which leads to our generative classifier, API-Net. Finally, we present the objective function and specify the optimization procedure for API-Net.

3.1   Motivation

Denote adversarial or vanilla examples as $x \in \mathbb{R}^D$ and class labels as $y \in \{y_c | c = 1, ..., C\}$, where y_c is the one-hot encoding vector for class c. The focus of this work is to build a robust classifier that can maintain high accuracy under adversarial attacks. The attacks aim at generating a perturbation δ given x such that $x + \delta$ can fool a classifier while the perturbation keeps quasi-imperceptible to humans. To guarantee the perturbation to be quasi-imperceptible, δ is usually bounded by $\|\delta\|_p \leq \epsilon$, where ϵ is a small constant and $\|\cdot\|_p$ is the l_p norm. In this paper, we mainly focus on defense against l_∞-bounded attacks, though our method can also be extended to other l_p-bounded scenario.

To solve the classification problem under attacks, recent research has explored the potential of generative classifiers [22,37]. Instead of building $p(y|x)$ directly, a generative classifier typically predicts labels using Bayes' rule:

$$p(y|x) = \frac{p(x,y)}{p(x)} = \text{softmax}_{c=1}^{C}\left[\log p(x, y_c)\right], \tag{1}$$

where $\text{softmax}_{c=1}^{C}$ denotes the softmax operation over the C axes. Generative classifiers can better estimate the prediction probabilities to handle off-manifold examples, in that they model the joint distribution and then explicitly consider the distance between the sample and each class-related manifold.

However, though considered to be robust owing to such merit, generative classifiers are often perplexed by their complicated structure. To model the joint log-likelihood for a generative classifier, it often necessitates introducing a latent variable z; the resulting probabilistic graphical model contains multiple components, which not only complicates the implementation but also hinders effective optimization [42]. On the contrary, a discriminative classifier directly models the conditional distribution $p(y|x)$, and thus takes advantage of keeping a concise structure as well as optimizing the quantity of direct interest. Hence, for a better solution of robust generative classifiers, this work makes an attempt in providing a design that can merit from both types.

Inspired by [36] which shows the capabilities of a single robust discriminator to perform image synthesis, we propose to leverage such generative capabilities to build API-Net, a structurally succint generative classifier. To be concrete, a robust conditional distribution of classes given inputs can be leveraged to generate gradients in the input space, and to direct a searching procedure to approach a class-related data manifold. Based on such properties, we derive a tractable lower bound of the joint log-likelihood, which can be further used by API-Net to approximate Bayes' rule for generative predictions. Different from [37], a generative classifier that customizes a VAE for each class, the structure of API-Net entails parameterizing only a single discriminator. The overall process, as shown in Fig. 1, is detailed in what follows.

3.2 Anti-Perturbation Inference Net

To learn the joint distribution $p(x, y)$, we leverage variational inference [16] to introduce a latent variable z and a inference model $q(z|x,y)$. Therefore, a lower bound of the joint log-likelihood can be formulated as (please see Appendix A.1

for the full derivation):

$$\log p(x, y) \geq \mathop{\mathbb{E}}_{q(z|x,y)} [\log p(x, y, z)]. \tag{2}$$

Anti-Perturbation Inference. We then introduce anti-perturbation inference, whose foundation falls in the definition of the latent variable z. We define z as the vanilla sample without any noise, which is in contrast to x that might contain adversarial perturbation (we never know in advance). We aim at an inference procedure: it generates Δ that can nullify the potential adversarial noise, and $z = x + \Delta$ can approach the unpolluted input. Therefore, we term this method *anti-perturbation inference*.

According to the meaning of each variable, we define a directed-graph model with structure:

$$p(x, y, z) = p(y|z)p(z|x)p(x), \tag{3}$$

which suggests that the unpolluted sample z depends on input x, and the class y depends on the unpolluted sample z. Similar to manifold projection defenses [35,38], we can parameterize the inference model $q(z|x, y)$ by a neural network to calculate the expectation in Eq. 2. Nonetheless, such an inference model is itself a neural network and thus vulnerable [2].

To bypass the vulnerabilities, we follow [37] to leverage optimization-based inference to substitute the expectation under the inference model $q(z|x, y)$:

$$\log p(x, y) \geq \max_{\Delta} \ \log p(y|z)p(z|x)p(x), \tag{4}$$

$$\text{s.t. } z = x + \Delta, \ \|\Delta\|_{\infty} \leq \epsilon_{ap}, \tag{5}$$

where the small constant ϵ_{ap} bounds the anti-perturbation Δ. This is because we have the prior that the anti-perturbation does not need to be very large to counter the potential adversarial perturbation which is bounded by l_{∞} with a small constant ϵ (Sect. 4.2 shows our defense does not over-fit ϵ).

Besides, owing to the restricted anti-perturbation, we can further simplify the lower bound in Eq. 4 by leveraging the following Lemma (the proof of which and the specific definition of F can be found in Appendix A.2.):

Lemma 1. *Let $p(z|x)$ be a Gaussian, $\mathcal{N}(z|x, \Sigma)$. If $\|z - x\|_{\infty} \leq \epsilon_{ap}$, then we have $\log p(z|x) \geq F(\Sigma, D, \epsilon_{ap})$, where D denotes the dimension of x and z, and F is a function irrelevant to y.*

According to Lemma 1, a new lower bound $l^*(x, y)$ of the joint log-likelihood can be obtained as follows:

$$\log p(x, y) \geq F(\Sigma, D, \epsilon_{ap}) + \log p(x) + \max_{\Delta} \ \log p(y|z) \tag{6}$$

$$= l^*(x, y), \tag{7}$$

$$\text{s.t. } z = x + \Delta, \ \|\Delta\|_{\infty} \leq \epsilon_{ap}. \tag{8}$$

Generative Prediction. To make generative predictions, we take $l^*(x, y)$ into Eq. 1 to approximate Bayes' rule. We can rule out the label-irrelevant terms and formulate the generative prediction as:

$$p(y|x) \approx \text{softmax}_{c=1}^{C} \left[l^*(x, y_c) \right] \tag{9}$$

$$= \text{softmax}_{c=1}^{C} \left[\max_{\Delta} \ \log p(y_c|z) \right], \tag{10}$$

$$\text{s.t. } z = x + \Delta, \ \|\Delta\|_{\infty} \leq \epsilon_{ap}. \tag{11}$$

Based on Eqs. 10 and 11, we here construct the generative classifier API-Net. We parameterize $p(y|z)$ with an adversarially robust neural network with parameter θ as $p_{\theta}(y|z)$, and the resulting generative classifier $\hat{p}(y|x; \theta)$ based on $p_{\theta}(y|z)$ is formulated as:

$$\hat{p}(y|x; \theta) = \text{softmax}_{c=1}^{C} \left[\max_{\Delta} \ \log p_{\theta}(y_c|z) \right], \tag{12}$$

$$\text{s.t. } z = x + \Delta, \ \|\Delta\|_{\infty} \leq \epsilon_{ap}, \tag{13}$$

where $\hat{p}(y|x; \theta)$ depends on the underlying $p_{\theta}(y|z)$ thus conditioned on θ.

Equations 12 and 13 define the proposed API-Net. As a generative classifier, API-Net makes generative predictions by comparing between log-likelihood of classes, which facilitates tackling off-manifold examples. In contrast to previous solutions of generative classifier [22,37], API-Net can be implemented with rather minimal effort and can take advantage of effective optimization, since it is built upon only a single conditional distribution $p_{\theta}(y|z)$. Besides, by maximizing the lower bound of the joint log-likelihood, Δ strives to neutralize the adversarial noise and $z = x + \Delta$ seeks to approach the vanilla sample to defend against attacks (the effectiveness of which is shown in Sect. 4.3).

3.3 Optimization

A key ingredient of API-Net is the image synthesis ability, which is achieved by making the underlying $p_{\theta}(y|z)$ robust [36]. By building API-Net upon an off-the-shelf robust discriminator, we can achieve additional robustness without training (validated in Sect. 4.3). Next, we introduce the training objective function of API-Net towards further robustness.

Objective Function. A typical objective function for generative models is to maximize the joint log-likelihood. However, the essential performance we consider in this work is the classification accuracy, which can often be enhanced by training models discriminatively to gain more powerful discrimination [15,20]. We thereby treat API-Net as a whole and minimize the expectation of cross-entropy loss under the data distribution $\mathcal{D}$ to optimize θ:

$$\min_{\theta} \left[\ \mathbb{E}_{(x,y) \sim \mathcal{D}} [- \log \hat{p}(y|x; \theta)] \right]. \tag{14}$$

Algorithm 1. API-Net Training

Input: dataset $\mathcal{D}$, number of categories C, ϵ_{ap} for anti-perturbation, ϵ_{train} for adversarial training, parameters of PGD for anti-perturbation and for adversarial training.
Output: Parameters θ.

1: **repeat**
2:   **for** random mini-batch $\{x_i, y_i\}_{i=1}^n \sim \mathcal{D}$ **do**
3:     **for** every x_i, y_i in the mini-batch (in parallel) **do**
4:       Solve δ in Eqs. 15 and 16 by PGD using gradient approximation;
5:       **for** $c = 1$ to C **do**
6:         Solve Δ_c in Eqs. 12 and 13 by PGD for anti-perturbation inference;
7:       **end for**
8:     **end for**
9:     Compute the loss defined in Eqs. 15 and 16 and then update θ;
10:   **end for**
11: **until** the training converges.

This objective function is also beneficial for API-Net to incorporate adversarial training, which is initially designed for a discriminative loss, to gain further robustness. We absorb adversarial training as a data augmentation technique to formulate the final objective function of API-Net:

$$\min_{\theta} \Big[\mathbb{E}_{(x,y)\sim\mathcal{D}} [\max_{\delta} - \log \hat{p}(y|x + \delta; \theta)] \Big], \tag{15}$$

$$\text{s.t. } \|\delta\|_{\infty} \leq \epsilon_{train}, \tag{16}$$

where ϵ_{train} sets the allowed perturbation budget for adversarial training (different from ϵ_{ap} which bounds the anti-perturbation).

Optimization Procedure. We show the overall training process of API-Net in Algorithm 1. Projected gradient descent (PGD) [6,9,27] is employed for the optimization of Δ and δ. For the adversarial training defined in Eqs. 15 and 16 and the evaluation of our method under gradient-based attacks, as $\hat{p}(y|x; \theta)$ is non-differentiable with respect to x, we leverage the following two strategies to approximate the gradients:

(1) Backward Pass Differentiable Approximation (BPDA) [2]. Since ϵ_{ap} is a small constant, we approximate the derivative of z with respect to x as the derivative of the identity function: $\nabla_x z \approx \nabla_x x = 1$ for backward passes.

(2) Forward and Backward Differentiable Approximation. As ϵ_{ap} is small, we simply set $z = x$ to calculate the gradient for both forward and backward passes.

During training, the second strategy is used considering the computational efficiency. For evaluation, we conduct attacks based on both strategies for a rigorous examination of the proposed method.

4   Experiments

In this section, we first present the experimental settings. We then evaluate the overall robustness of the proposed API-Net and compare it with state-of-the-arts in Sect. 4.2. We finally conduct ablation studies in Sect. 4.3.

Table 1. Accuracy (%) under white-box attacks on CIFAR-10 with $\epsilon = 8/255$

Method	Architecture	Clean	FGSM	PGD-40	PGD-100	C&W-40	C&W-100
Standard	ResNet18	**94.46**	24.24	0.00	0.00	0.00	0.00
Madry	ResNet18	82.15	61.83	47.52	47.29	46.78	46.66
ME-Net	ResNet18	84.00	–	55.40	53.50	–	–
Trades	ResNet18	82.83	64.14	52.08	51.97	49.05	48.94
API-Net	ResNet18	81.25	**65.71**	**63.13**	**62.87**	**55.73**	**54.57**

Table 2. Accuracy (%) under white-box attacks on SVHN with $\epsilon = 8/255$

Method	Architecture	Clean	FGSM	PGD-40	PGD-100	C&W-40	C&W-100
Standard	ResNet18	**96.62**	45.23	0.84	0.52	0.90	0.62
Madry	ResNet18	94.30	74.55	53.37	52.91	51.95	51.83
ME-Net	ResNet18	87.60	–	71.90	69.80	–	–
Trades	ResNet18	91.06	72.83	58.21	57.83	54.71	54.65
API-Net	ResNet18	87.72	**80.34**	**74.36**	**73.68**	**62.51**	**60.25**

4.1 Experimental Settings

Datasets. The experiments are performed on CIFAR-10, SVHN, and MNIST.

Compared Methods. *Standard:* standard training approach using clean images [17]. *Madry:* adversarial training based defense using PGD [27]. *ME-Net:* preprocessing-based defense with Matrix-Estimation [46]. We plot its accuracy under BPDA-based attacks. *Trades:* adversarial training based approach with KL-divergence-based adversarial examples generation and regularization [47]. We plot the performance of Trades under its best setting where $\frac{1}{\lambda} = 6$.

Implementation Details. We implement the Standard, Madry, and Trades methods, and report the robust accuracy of ME-Net according to [46]. We set the pixel values in $[0, 1]$, and use PGD [27] of 7 iterations with $\epsilon_{train} = 8/255$ and step-size 0.007 on CIFAR-10 and SVHN, and PGD of 40 iterations with $\epsilon_{train} = 76.5/255$ and step-size 0.01 on MNIST for adversarial training. We first leverage Madry's method to train the underlying $p_\theta(y|z)$ for a guarantee of generative capabilities and then train API-Net following Eqs. 15 and 16. To align with past work, we apply data augmentation on CIFAR-10 and SVHN datasets following [13] and do not apply any data augmentation on MNIST.

Parameters of API. We set $\epsilon_{ap} = 14/255$ for CIFAR-10, and $\epsilon_{ap} = 12/255$ for SVHN and MNIST. We use PGD of 8 iterations with step-size 0.007 for CIFAR-10 and SVHN, and PGD of 8 iterations with step-size 0.01 for MNIST.

Table 3. Accuracy (%) under white-box attacks on MNIST with $\epsilon = 76.5/255$

Method	Architecture	Clean	FGSM	PGD-40	PGD-100	C&W-40	C&W-100
Standard	LeNet	**99.16**	–	0.15	0.05	–	–
ME-Net	LeNet	97.40	–	94.00	91.80	–	–
API-Net	LeNet	98.30	–	**94.22**	**92.09**	–	–
Standard	SmallCNN	**99.41**	50.72	1.50	0.00	0.10	0.00
Madry	SmallCNN	99.31	97.86	96.64	95.68	96.77	95.62
Trades	SmallCNN	99.15	97.95	96.81	96.02	96.91	95.98
API-Net	SmallCNN	99.21	**98.39**	**97.10**	**96.35**	**97.17**	**96.34**

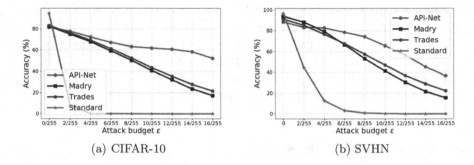

(a) CIFAR-10 (b) SVHN

Fig. 2. Accuracy under PGD-40 attacks with ϵ varying from 0/255 to 16/255

Attack Details. We mainly focus on l_∞-bounded white-box attacks. The white-box attacks are deemed as the most powerful attacks since the attacker has full information about the defense model under this setting. We leverage FGSM [12] and two currently strongest gradient-based attacks: PGD and C&W (l_∞-bounded, $k{=}50$) with T iterations (PGD-T and C&W-T) and random restart [4,27]. Aligned with past work, we mainly focus on the performance under attacks with $\epsilon = 8/255$ on CIFAR-10 and SVHN, and $\epsilon = 76.5/255$ on MNIST. As defined in Sect. 3.3, we use two strategies to approximate the gradient for the attacks and report the worst accuracy for strict evaluation.

4.2   Robustness

Accuracy Under Attacks Across Datasets. We compare the robust accuracy of API-Net with those of state-of-the-art defense methods. The results on CIFAR-10, SVHN and MNIST are respectively shown in Table 1, Table 2, and Table 3, which clearly show that API-Net surpasses the state-of-the-art methods against multiple white-box attacks of different iterations. In particular, we surpass the runner-up method by 8% under the most prevailing PGD attack on CIFAR-10 and by 4% on SVHN. These quantitative results demonstrate the outstanding robust performance of API-Net.

Table 4. Ablation study on training and initialization. The accuracy (%) is reported under the PGD-40 attack with $\epsilon = 8/255$

Initialization	Dataset	Learning rate	Trades	ME-Net
Random	CIFAR-10	0.1	**52.08**	**55.40**
From Madry	CIFAR-10	0.1	50.08	52.92
From Madry	CIFAR-10	0.01	47.24	48.55
From Madry	CIFAR-10	0.001	50.52	50.03
Method	Dataset	Initialization	w.o. train	with train
API-Net	CIFAR-10	Madry	52.08	**63.13**
API-Net	SVHN	Madry	58.58	**74.36**

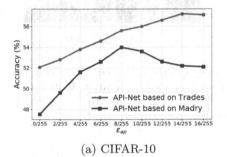

(a) CIFAR-10

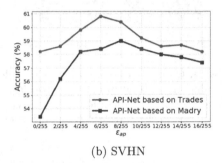

(b) SVHN

Fig. 3. Robustness of API-Net based on off-the-shelf robust discriminators without further training under the PGD-40 attack with $\epsilon = 8/255$

Accuracy under Attacks with Different ϵ. In this section, we evaluate the accuracy under the PGD-40 attack with ϵ varying from 0 to 16/255 with interval 2. As shown in Fig. 2, the proposed API-Net achieves leading robustness. It verifies that the robustness of API-Net is not based on over-fitting a specific attack ϵ. Rather, when ϵ increases, the accuracy of our method declines at a slower rate compared to the state-of-the-arts, though all the methods are trained with the same $\epsilon_{train} = 8/255$. This experiment demonstrates the potential of our method to be more applicable to real-life machine learning systems where the bound on perturbations cannot be known in advance.

4.3 Ablation Study

API-Net Based on Off-the-Shelf Robust Discriminator. In this section, we investigate the robustness gain merely owing to the design of API-Net. To this end, we initialize the underlying $p_\theta(y|z)$ of API-Net with off-the-shelf robust models, Madry, and Trades, and then test the accuracy under attacks without any training. We plot the accuracy under PGD-40 attacks with ϵ_{ap} varying from 0 to 16/255. We note that when $\epsilon_{ap} = 0$, API-Net degenerates to the original discriminative classifier and its accuracy corresponds to the off-the-shelf model.

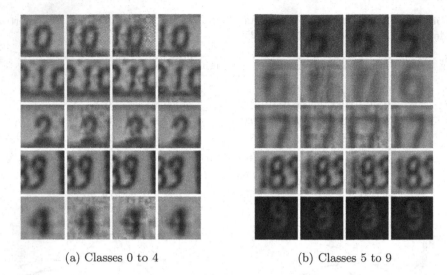

(a) Classes 0 to 4   (b) Classes 5 to 9

Fig. 4. Qualitative results to show the effectiveness of the proposed API. **Column 1:** vanilla images. **Column 2:** adversarially perturbed images as input x. **Column 3:** z generated by API conditioned on $y_{(t+1) \bmod C}$. **Column 4:** z generated conditioned on true label y_t (best view in color with zooming in)

As shown in Fig. 3, our proposed API-Net can be directly deployed to the off-the-shelf robust discriminators to obtain additional robustness. Specifically, API-Net provides additional gains of approximate 5% robust accuracy on CIFAR-10 and 4% on SVHN. It demonstrates that the proposed API-Net makes better use of the underlying discriminative distribution to build robustness.

Training and Initialization. We here investigate the effectiveness of the proposed API-Net training schedule. We compare the robust accuracy between API-Net initialized with Madry without training and API-Net initialized with Madry plus training. As shown in Table 4, the training schedule contributes to about 11% gain in robust accuracy on CIFAR-10 and 15% on SVHN. We also examine the effect of initialization. We train Trades and ME-Net on CIFAR-10 with initialization from Madry's model and try different learning rates to ensure a good convergence. As shown in Table 4, the initializations do not advance the robustness neither for Trades nor ME-Net.

Visualization of API. To emphasize the consistency, we use ten images chosen from the first one of each class in the test set of SVHN. We aim to qualitatively demonstrate how anti-perturbations work. To this end, we apply PGD attacks to generate adversarial examples as inputs and conduct API with $\epsilon_{ap} = 12/255$ to obtain z. As shown in Fig. 4, when conditioned on the true label y_t, $t \in [C]$, the anti-perturbation effectively counters the adversarial noise, leading to z (Fig. 4 column 4) that is very similar to the vanilla image (Fig. 4, column 1).

Table 5. Ablation study on the optimal ϵ_{ap}. The accuracy (%) is reported under the PGD-40 attack

ϵ_{ap}	6/255	8/255	10/255	12/255	14/255	16/255
CIFAR-10	55.09	58.68	60.90	62.32	**63.13**	62.83
SVHN	61.14	69.20	72.45	**74.40**	73.98	73.39
MNIST	96.23	96.49	96.72	**97.12**	96.32	96.69

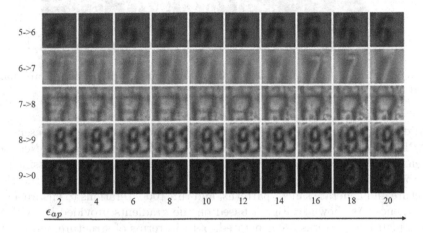

Fig. 5. Visualization of how z changes with ϵ_{ap} conditioned on $y_{(t+1) \bmod C}$. From left to right, ϵ_{ap} varies from 2 to 20 (best view in color with zooming in)

On the contrary, when conditioned on a wrong label, *e.g.*, $y_{(t+1) \bmod C}$, the resulting z would be dubious (Fig. 4 column 3). This is beneficial since it would lead to a low $p_\theta(y|z)$ and thus a low $l^*(x,y)$, which results in a low prediction probability for this wrong class. We also notice that some images in the column 3 of Fig. 4 start to generate features of the wrong class $y_{(t+1) \bmod C}$. This reveals the importance of an appropriate value of ϵ_{ap}, which should be dataset-related, to preserve the original global structure of each image.

Optimal Searching Scope of Anti-Perturbation. Intuitively, we consider two points concerning the optimal value of ϵ_{ap}: 1) it should be large enough to ensure a powerful Δ to counter potential perturbations. 2) it should be limited to prevent z from being a plausible image of a wrong class. To qualitatively analyze, we change ϵ_{ap} from 2 to 20 and visualize z conditioned on $y_{(t+1) \bmod C}$. As shown in Fig. 5, when ϵ_{ap} increases to 12/255, z begins to contain plausible features of class $y_{(t+1) \bmod C}$, which indicates ϵ_{ap} should be no more than 12/255. We then quantitatively analyze. As shown in Table 5, on SVHN, API-Net performs the best when $\epsilon_{ap} = 12/255$, which is consistent with the qualitative results.

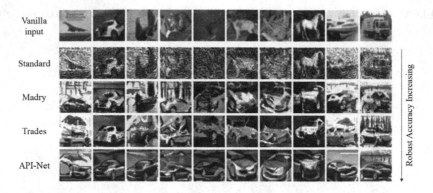

Fig. 6. Visualization of large-ε adversarial examples on CIFAR-10. Images are manipulated into being classified as a car (best view in color with zooming in)

Hidden Representation. We here explore the learned hidden representation of API-Net by leveraging the gradients and see what convinces API-Net most. We employ PGD to manipulate images from CIFAR-10 into being classified as a car from each model's perspective. We set a large $\epsilon = 80/255$ to alter the global structure and generate salient patterns, and run 1000 iterations to ensure a good convergence. As shown in Fig. 6, based on the gradients provided by API-Net, highly plausible patterns are generated, both in terms of structure and texture. These suggest that API-Net does not rely on obfuscated gradients. Rather, API-Net has learned representations consistent best with human perception.

5   Discussion and Conclusion

Despite the success in numerous applications, DNNs' performance is far from robust compared to that of a human. In this work, we made an attempt in providing a solution, API-Net, that can profit from the merits of both discriminative and generative classifiers to improve the robustness. The experiments showed that API-Net outperforms state-of-the-art defenses and generates gradients that result in perceptually meaningful representations. We hope that this work can be a stepping stone towards reliable DNNs for real-life machine learning applications.

Acknowledgements. This work is supported by the Nature Science Foundation of China (No.U1705262, No.6177244, No.61572410, No.61802324 and No.61702136), National Key R&D Program (No.2017YFC0113000, and No.2016YFB1001503), Key R&D Program of Jiangxi Province (No. 20171ACH80022) and Natural Science Foundation of Guangdong Provice in China (No.2019B1515120049).

References

1. Alzantot, M., Sharma, Y., Elgohary, A., Ho, B.J., Srivastava, M., Chang, K.W.: Generating natural language adversarial examples. In: EMNLP (2018)

2. Athalye, A., Carlini, N., Wagner, D.: Obfuscated gradients give a false sense of security: circumventing defenses to adversarial examples. In: ICML (2018)
3. Buckman, J., Roy, A., Raffel, C., Goodfellow, I.: Thermometer encoding: one hot way to resist adversarial examples. In: ICLR (2018)
4. Carlini, N., Wagner, D.: Towards evaluating the robustness of neural networks. In: SP. IEEE (2017)
5. Carlini, N., Wagner, D.: Audio adversarial examples: targeted attacks on speech-to-text. In: SPW. IEEE (2018)
6. Cauchy, A.: Méthode générale pour la résolution des systemes d'équations simultanées. Comp. Rend. Sci. Paris **25**(1847), 536–538 (1847)
7. Chen, J., Wu, X., Liang, Y., Jha, S.: Improving adversarial robustness by data-specific discretization. CoRR, abs/1805.07816 (2018)
8. Fisher, R.A.: The use of multiple measurements in taxonomic problems. Ann. Eugenics **7**(2), 179–188 (1936)
9. Frank, M., Wolfe, P.: An algorithm for quadratic programming. Naval Res. Logist. Q. **3**(1–2), 95–110 (1956)
10. Gilmer, J., et al.: Adversarial spheres. arXiv preprint arXiv:1801.02774 (2018)
11. Goodfellow, I., Bengio, Y., Courville, A.: Deep Learning. MIT press, United States (2016)
12. Goodfellow, I.J., Shlens, J., Szegedy, C.: Explaining and harnessing adversarial examples. In: ICLR (2015)
13. He, K., Zhang, X., Ren, S., Sun, J.: Deep residual learning for image recognition. In: CVPR (2016)
14. Hinton, G., et al.: Deep neural networks for acoustic modeling in speech recognition: the shared views of four research groups. IEEE Signal Process. Mag. **29**(6), 82–97 (2012)
15. Holub, A., Perona, P.: A discriminative framework for modelling object classes. In: CVPR (2005)
16. Kingma, D.P., Welling, M.: Auto-encoding variational bayes. arXiv preprint arXiv:1312.6114 (2013)
17. Krizhevsky, A., et al.: Learning multiple layers of features from tiny images. Tech. rep, Citeseer (2009)
18. Krizhevsky, A., Sutskever, I., Hinton, G.E.: Imagenet classification with deep convolutional neural networks. In: NeurIPS (2012)
19. Kurakin, A., Goodfellow, I., Bengio, S.: Adversarial examples in the physical world. arXiv preprint arXiv:1607.02533 (2016)
20. Lasserre, J.A., Bishop, C.M., Minka, T.P.: Principled hybrids of generative and discriminative models. In: CVPR (2006)
21. Li, X., Li, F.: Adversarial examples detection in deep networks with convolutional filter statistics. In: ICCV (2017)
22. Li, Y., Bradshaw, J., Sharma, Y.: Are generative classifiers more robust to adversarial attacks? In: ICML (2019)
23. Li, Y., Gal, Y.: Dropout inference in bayesian neural networks with alpha-divergences. In: ICML (2017)
24. Liu, H., et al.: Universal adversarial perturbation via prior driven uncertainty approximation. In: ICCV (2019)
25. Louizos, C., Welling, M.: Multiplicative normalizing flows for variational bayesian neural networks. In: ICML (2017)
26. Lu, J., Issaranon, T., Forsyth, D.: Safetynet: detecting and rejecting adversarial examples robustly. In: ICCV (2017)

27. Madry, A., Makelov, A., Schmidt, L., Tsipras, D., Vladu, A.: Towards deep learning models resistant to adversarial attacks. In: ICLR (2018)
28. Metzen, J.H., Genewein, T., Fischer, V., Bischoff, B.: On detecting adversarial perturbations. In: ICLR (2017)
29. Moosavi-Dezfooli, S.M., Fawzi, A., Fawzi, O., Frossard, P.: Universal adversarial perturbations. In: CVPR (2017)
30. Moosavi-Dezfooli, S.M., Fawzi, A., Frossard, P.: Deepfool: a simple and accurate method to fool deep neural networks. In: CVPR (2016)
31. Na, T., Ko, J.H., Mukhopadhyay, S.: Cascade adversarial machine learning regularized with a unified embedding. arXiv preprint arXiv:1708.02582 (2017)
32. Ng, A.Y., Jordan, M.I.: On discriminative vs. generative classifiers: a comparison of logistic regression and naive bayes. In: NeurIPS (2002)
33. Papernot, N., McDaniel, P., Jha, S., Fredrikson, M., Celik, Z.B., Swami, A.: The limitations of deep learning in adversarial settings. In: EuroS&P. IEEE (2016)
34. Ren, S., He, K., Girshick, R., Sun, J.: Faster r-cnn: towards real-time object detection with region proposal networks. In: NeurIPS (2015)
35. Samangouei, P., Kabkab, M., Chellappa, R.: Defense-gan: Protecting classifiers against adversarial attacks using generative models. arXiv preprint arXiv:1805.06605 (2018)
36. Santurkar, S., Ilyas, A., Tsipras, D., Engstrom, L., Tran, B., Madry, A.: Image synthesis with a single (robust) classifier. In: NeurIPS (2019)
37. Schott, L., Rauber, J., Bethge, M., Brendel, W.: Towards the first adversarially robust neural network model on mnist. In: ICLR (2019)
38. Song, Y., Kim, T., Nowozin, S., Ermon, S., Kushman, N.: Pixeldefend: leveraging generative models to understand and defend against adversarial examples. In: ICLR (2018)
39. Stutz, D., Hein, M., Schiele, B.: Disentangling adversarial robustness and generalization. In: CVPR (2019)
40. Sutskever, I., Vinyals, O., Le, Q.V.: Sequence to sequence learning with neural networks. In: NeurIPS (2014)
41. Szegedy, C., et al.: Intriguing properties of neural networks. In: ICLR (2013)
42. Tramer, F., Carlini, N., Brendel, W., Madry, A.: On adaptive attacks to adversarial example defenses. arXiv preprint arXiv:2002.08347 (2020)
43. Wong, E., Schmidt, F.R., Kolter, J.Z.: Wasserstein adversarial examples via projected sinkhorn iterations. In: ICML (2019)
44. Xie, C., Wang, J., Zhang, Z., Ren, Z., Yuille, A.: Mitigating adversarial effects through randomization. In: ICLR (2018)
45. Xu, W., Evans, D., Qi, Y.: Feature squeezing: Detecting adversarial examples in deep neural networks. arXiv preprint arXiv:1704.01155 (2017)
46. Yang, Y., Zhang, G., Katabi, D., Xu, Z.: Me-net: towards effective adversarial robustness with matrix estimation. In: ICML (2019)
47. Zhang, H., Yu, Y., Jiao, J., Xing, E.P., Ghaoui, L.E., Jordan, M.I.: Theoretically principled trade-off between robustness and accuracy. In: ICML (2019)
48. Zhang, X., Wan, F., Liu, C., Ji, R., Ye, Q.: Freeanchor: learning to match anchors for visual object detection. In: NeurIPS (2019)

Bias-Based Universal Adversarial Patch Attack for Automatic Check-Out

Aishan Liu[1], Jiakai Wang[1], Xianglong Liu[1,2(✉)], Bowen Cao[1],
Chongzhi Zhang[1], and Hang Yu[1]

[1] State Key Lab of Software Development Environment,
Beihang University, Beijing, China
xlliu@nlsde.buaa.edu.cn
[2] Beijing Advanced Innovation Center for Big Data-Based Precision Medicine,
Beihang University, Beijing, China

Abstract. Adversarial examples are inputs with imperceptible perturbations that easily misleading deep neural networks (DNNs). Recently, adversarial patch, with noise confined to a small and localized patch, has emerged for its easy feasibility in real-world scenarios. However, existing strategies failed to generate adversarial patches with strong generalization ability. In other words, the adversarial patches were input-specific and failed to attack images from all classes, especially unseen ones during training. To address the problem, this paper proposes a bias-based framework to generate class-agnostic universal adversarial patches with strong generalization ability, which exploits both the perceptual and semantic bias of models. Regarding the perceptual bias, since DNNs are strongly biased towards textures, we exploit the hard examples which convey strong model uncertainties and extract a textural patch prior from them by adopting the style similarities. The patch prior is more close to decision boundaries and would promote attacks. To further alleviate the heavy dependency on large amounts of data in training universal attacks, we further exploit the semantic bias. As the class-wise preference, prototypes are introduced and pursued by maximizing the multi-class margin to help universal training. Taking Automatic Check-out (ACO) as the typical scenario, extensive experiments including white-box/black-box settings in both digital-world (RPC, the largest ACO related dataset) and physical-world scenario (Taobao and JD, the worlds largest online shopping platforms) are conducted. Experimental results demonstrate that our proposed framework outperforms state-of-the-art adversarial patch attack methods.(Our code can be found at https://github.com/liuaishan/ModelBiasedAttack.)

Keywords: Universal adversarial patch · Automatic Check-Out · Bias-based attack

---

A. Liu and J. Wang—These authors contributed equally to this work.

Electronic supplementary material The online version of this chapter (https://doi.org/10.1007/978-3-030-58601-0_24) contains supplementary material, which is available to authorized users.

A. Vedaldi et al. (Eds.): ECCV 2020, LNCS 12358, pp. 395–410, 2020.
https://doi.org/10.1007/978-3-030-58601-0_24

1 Introduction

Deep learning has demonstrated remarkable performance in a wide spectrum of areas, including computer vision [14], speech recognition [21] and natural language processing [27]. Recently, deep learning strategies have been introduced into the check-out scenario in supermarkets and grocery stores to revolutionize the way people shopping (*e.g.*, Amazon Go). Automatic Check-Out (ACO) [4,16,30] is a visual item counting system that takes images of shopping items as input and generates output as a tally of different categories. Customers are not required to put items on the conveyer belt and wait for salesclerks to scan them. Instead, they can simply collect the chosen items and a deep learning based visual recognition system will classify them and automatically process the purchase.

Fig. 1. In the real-world scenario like Automatic Check-Out, items (*e.g.*, fruits and chocolates) are often tied with patch-like stickers or tags.

Though showing significant achievements in our daily lives, unfortunately, deep learning is vulnerable to adversarial examples [11,28]. These small perturbations are imperceptible to human but easily misleading DNNs, which creates potential security threats to practical deep learning applications, *e.g.*, autodriving and face recognition systems [18]. In the past years, different types of techniques have been developed to attack deep learning systems [2,7,9,11,28]. Though challenging deep learning, adversarial examples are also valuable for understanding the behaviors of DNNs, which could provide insights into the blind-spots and help to build robust models [19,31,32].

Besides the well-designed perturbations, the adversarial patch serves as an alternative way to generate adversarial examples and enjoy the advantages of being input-independent and scene-independent. [1,12,18]. In real-world scenarios, patches could be often observed which are quasi-imperceptible to humans. For example, as shown in Fig.1, the tags and brand marks on items in the supermarket. Thus, it is convenient for an adversary to attack a real-world deep learning system by simply generate and stick adversarial patches on the items. However, existing strategies [1,6] generate adversarial patches with weak generalization abilities and are not able to perform universal attacks [22]. In other words, these adversarial patches are input-specific and fail to attack images from all classes, especially unseen ones during training.

To address the problem, this paper proposes a bias-based framework to generate class-agnostic universal adversarial patches with strong generalization ability, which exploits both the perceptual and semantic bias. Regarding the **perceptual bias**, motivated by the studies [10,32] that DNNs are more perceptually biased towards texture information than shape when making predictions, we first generate textural priors by extracting textural information from multiple hard examples with style similarities. Our priors contain plenty of textural information from hard examples, thus they are more likely to reveal model uncertainties since DNNs are perceptually biased towards textures. By exploiting perceptual biases of a model, our textural prior is more close to decision boundaries which would promote the universal attack to different classes. As for the **semantic bias**, since models have semantic preference and bias for different classes, *e.g.*, model prefers wheel for car and fur for dog, we then generate prototypes to help training. A prototype is considered to contain the most representative semantics for a class. Thus, we generate a small number of prototypes by maximizing the corresponding model logits for each class to represent the original images. By exploiting the semantic bias of a model for each class, the prototypes contain more representative features. Thus, training with prototypes will alleviate the heavy dependency on large amounts of data in training universal attacks [24]. Extensive experiments including both the white-box and black-box settings in both the digital-world (RPC, the largest ACO related dataset) and physical-world scenario (Taobao and JD, the worlds largest online shopping platforms) are conducted. Experimental results demonstrate that our proposed framework outperforms state-of-the-art adversarial patch attack methods.

To the best of our knowledge, we are the first to generate class-agnostic universal adversarial patches by exploiting the perceptual and semantic biases of models. With strong generalization ability, our adversarial patches could attack images from unseen classes of the adversarial patch training process or target models. To validate the effectiveness, we choose the automatic check-out scenario and successfully attack the **Taobao** and **JD** platform, which are among the world's largest e-commerce platforms and the ACO-like scenarios.

2   Related Work

2.1   Adversarial Attacks

Adversarial examples, which are intentionally designed inputs misleading deep neural networks, have attracted research focus in many scenarios [11,15,17,28]. Szegedy *et al.* [28] first introduced adversarial examples and used the L-BFGS method to generate them. By leveraging the gradients of the target model, Goodfellow *et al.* [11] proposed the Fast Gradient Sign Method (FGSM) which could generate adversarial examples quickly. To improve the generalization ability to different classes, Moosavi *et al.* [22] first proposed an algorithm to compute universal adversarial perturbations for DNNs for object recognition tasks. Mopuri *et al.* [23] proposed a data-free objectives to generate universal adversarial perturbations by maximizing the neuron activation. Further, Reddy *et al.* [24] generated data-free universal adversarial perturbations using class impressions.

Besides, adversarial patch [1], with noise confined to a small and localized patch, emerged for its easy accessibility in real-world scenarios. Karmon *et al.* [12] created adversarial patches using an optimization-based approach with a modified loss function. In contrast to the prior research, they concentrated on investigating the blind-spots of state-of-the-art image classifiers. Eykholt *et al.* [6] adopted the traditional perturbation techniques to generate attacking noises, which can be mixed into the black and white stickers to attack the recognition of the stop sign. To improve visual fidelity, Liu *et al.* [18] proposed the PS-GAN framework to generate scrawl-like adversarial patches to fool autonomous-driving systems. Recently, adversarial patches have been used to attack person detection systems and fool automated surveillance cameras [29].

2.2 Automatic Check-Out

The bedrock of an Automatic Check-out system is visual item counting that takes images of shopping items as input and generates output as a tally of different categories [30]. However, different from other computer vision tasks such as object detection and recognition, the training of deep neural networks for visual item counting faces a special challenge of domain shift. Wei *et al.* [30] first tried to solve the problem using the data argumentation strategy. To improve the realism of the target images, through a CycleGAN framework [33], images of collections of objects are generated by overlaying images of individual objects randomly. Recently, Li *et al.* [16] developed a data priming network by collaborative learning to determine the reliability of testing data.

3 Proposed Framework

In this section, we will first give the definition of the problem and then elaborate on our proposed framework.

3.1 Problem Definition

Assuming $\mathcal{X} \subseteq \mathbb{R}^n$ is the feature space with n the number of features. Supposing (x_i, y_i) is the i-th instance in the data with feature vector $x_i \in \mathcal{X}$ and $y_i \in \mathcal{Y}$ the corresponding class label. The deep learning classifier attempts to learn a classification function $F: \mathcal{X} \to \mathcal{Y}$. Specifically, in this paper we consider the visual recognition problem.

An adversarial patch δ is a localized patch that is trained to fool the target model F to wrong predictions. Given an benign image x with its ground truth label y, we form an adversarial example x' which is composed of the original image x, an additive adversarial patch $\delta \in \mathbb{R}^z$ and a location mask $M \in \{0,1\}^n$:

$$x' = (1 - M) \odot x + M \odot \delta, \tag{1}$$

where $\odot$ is the element-wise multiplication.

The prediction result of x'_δ by model F is $y' = F(x'_\delta)$. The adversarial patch makes the model predict the incorrect label, namely $y' \neq y$.

To perform universal attacks, we generate a universal adversarial patch δ that could fool the classifier F on items sampled from distribution μ from *almost all* classes:

$$F(x) \neq F(x + \delta) \quad \text{for } almost\ all \quad x \sim \mu. \tag{2}$$

3.2 The Framework

We propose a bias-based attack framework to generate universal adversarial patches with strong generalization ability. The overall framework can be found in Fig.2.

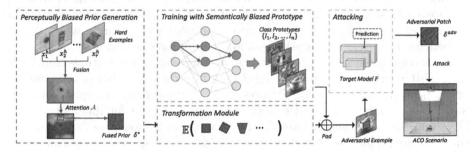

Fig. 2. Our bias-based framework to generate universal adversarial patches. We first generate a perceptually biased prior by fusing textural features from multiple hard examples. Then, we generate semantically biased prototypes to help training universal adversarial patches with a target model F

Recent studies have revealed that DNNs are strongly biased towards texture features when making predictions [10]. Deep learning models are still performing well on patch-shuffled images where local object textures are not destroyed drastically [32].

Thus, we first exploit the perceptual bias of deep models by **generating perceptually biased priors from multiple hard example set** $\mathcal{X}^h = \{x_i^h | i=1, ...r\}$. Textural features are extracted by an attention module $\mathcal{A}$ to fuse a more powerful prior δ^*. We believe the fused prior are more close to decision boundaries of different classes and would boost universal attacks.

Meanwhile, as models have preferences and impressions for different classes, we further exploit the semantic bias of models for each class. To alleviate the heavy dependency on a large amount of data suffered to train universal attacks, we **generate semantically biased prototypes to help training**. As the class-wise preference, prototypes contain the most representative semantics for a class. Semantics for each class. Thus, prototypes are generated by maximizing the multi-class margin and used to represent instances from each class. Training with prototypes would reduce the amount of training data required. Thus, we generate prototypes $\{I_1, I_2, ..., I_n\}$ and use them as training data to learn our final adversarial patch δ^{adv} from δ^*.

3.3 Perceptually Biased Prior Generation

Motivated by the fact that deep learning models are strongly biased towards textural features, we first proposed to extract textural features as priors. To fully exploit the statistic uncertainty of models, we borrow textural features from *hard examples*.

Hard examples appear as instances that are difficult for models to classify correctly. Techniques like hard example mining are used to improve training [8], in which "hard" hence informative examples are spotted and mined. Given a hard example x^h with ground truth label y, assuming that $y^h = F(x^h)$ is the prediction of the model F. The hard example suffices the constraint that $y^h \neq y$ or with relatively low classification confidence. Obviously, a hard example is an instance lying closely to model decision boundaries, and are more likely to cross the prediction surfaces. Thus, using the features from a hard example x^h to train adversarial patches is like "standing on the shoulders of a giant", which would be beneficial to overcome local-optima and gain strong attacking abilities.

To further motivate universal attacks, we extract textural features from multiple hard examples with different labels and fuse them together into a stronger prior. Intuitively, by studying features from multiple hard examples with different labels, our prior would contain more uncertainties for different classes. However, simply learning at pixel-level makes it difficult to extract and fuse textural features. Thus, we introduce the style loss which specifically measures the style differences and encourages the reproduction of texture details:

$$
\begin{aligned}
\mathcal{L}_s &= \mathbb{E}_k \left[\left\| \mathbf{G}(x^*) - \mathbf{G}(x_k^h) \right\|_F^2 \right], \\
\mathbf{G}_{ij}(x) &= \sum_k F_{ik}^l(x) \cdot F_{jk}^l(x),
\end{aligned}
\tag{3}
$$

where $\mathbf{G}$ is the Gram matrix of the features extracted from certain layers of the network. $F_{\cdot k}^l$ is the activation of a specific filter at position k in the layer l. x^* is the fused example, and x_k^h is the hard example where $k = 1, 2, ..., r$.

Besides, entropy has been widely used to depict the uncertainty of a system or distribution. To further improve universal attacks to different classes, we introduce the class-wise uncertainty loss. We increase model prediction uncertainties by minimizing the negative of entropy. Thus, the fused example would be much closer to decision boundaries and obtain low confidence for different classes. It can be written as:

$$
\mathcal{L}_u = \mathbb{E}_i \left[\log y^{h,i} \right],
\tag{4}
$$

where $y^{h,i}$ denotes the model confidence of the i-th class with the fused input x^*.

Thus, to fully exploit the perceptual bias, we optimize the fusion loss function $\mathcal{L}_f$ as follows:

$$
\mathcal{L}_f = \mathcal{L}_s + \lambda \cdot \mathcal{L}_u,
\tag{5}
$$

where λ controls the balance between the two terms.

However, the fused example x^* has a different size with our patches. Thus, an attention module has been introduced to eliminate redundant pixels and generate a textural prior δ^* from the fused example x^*.

$$\delta^* = \mathcal{A}(x^*; F), \tag{6}$$

where $\mathcal{A}(\cdot)$ is a visual attention module that selects a set of suitable visual pixels from the fused sample. These pixels contain the highest stimuli towards model predictions and would be used as textural priors.

Inspired by [25], given a hard example x^h, we compute the gradient of normalized feature maps Z of a specific hidden layer in the model w.r.t. y^h. These gradients are global-average-pooled to get the weight matrix which is a weighted combination of feature maps to the hard example x^h :

$$a_{ij} = \sum_{k=1}^{w} \frac{\partial y^h}{\partial Z_{ij}^k} Z_{ij}^k, \tag{7}$$

where a_{ij} represents the weight at position (i, j), Z_{ij}^k is the pixel value in position (i, j) of k-th feature map, and w represents the total feature map number. Note that $i \in [0, u - 1]$ and $j \in [0, v - 1]$ where u, v are the width and height of Z, respectively. Then, we can combine the pixels with the highest weight to get our textural prior δ^*.

3.4 Training with Semantically Biased Prototypes

With the textural priors generated at the previous stage, we continue to optimize and generate our adversarial patch. To generate universal adversarial perturbations, most of the strategies require a lot of training data [24]. To alleviate the heavy dependency on large amounts of training data, we further exploit the semantic bias.

A *prototype* is an instance that contains the most representative semantics for a class [13]. Prototypes have provided quantitative benefits to interpret and improve deep learning models. Thus, we further exploit the semantic bias of models (*i.e.*, prototypes)for each class. In this stage, we generate class prototypes and use them during training to effectively reduce the amount of training data required.

Thus, inspired by [26], to generate prototypes I representing the semantic preference of a model for each class, we maximize the logits of one specific class. Formally, let $S_t(I)$ denote the logits of class t, computed by the classification layer of the target model. By optimizing the *MultiMarginLoss*, the prototype I_t of class t is obtained:

$$I_t = \underset{x}{\operatorname{argmax}} \frac{1}{C} \sum_{c \neq t} \max(0, margin - S_t(x) + S_c(x))^p, \tag{8}$$

where x is the input and satisfies the constraint of an RGB image, C denotes the total number of classes and *margin* is a threshold that controls the multi-class margin. In practice, Adam optimizer is applied to find the optimal proto-type of class c with $p = 1$ and $margin = 10$.

To generate adversarial patches misleading to deep models, we introduce the adversarial attack loss. Specifically, we push the prediction label y' of the adversarial example x' (*i.e.*, a clean prototype I appended with the adversarial patch δ^{adv}) away from its original prediction label y. Therefore, adversarial attack loss can be defined as:

$$\mathcal{L}_t = \mathbb{E}_{I,\delta^{adv}}[P(c = t|I') - \max(P(c \neq t|I'))], \tag{9}$$

where δ^{adv} is the adversarial patch which is initialized as the textural prior δ^*, $P(\cdot)$ is the prediction of the target model to the input, I' is the adversarial example which is composed of the prototype I and adversarial patch δ^{adv}, c means the class, and t denotes the class label of I.

Moreover, recent studies showed that adversarial examples are ineffective to environmental conditions, *e.g.*, different views, illuminations, *etc.* In the ACO scenario, the items are often scanned from different views with different lighting conditions, which would impair the attack ability of our patches. Thus, we further introduce the idea of expectation of transformations to enhance the attack success rate of our adversarial patches in different conditions, as shown in the expectation of conditions **c** in Eqn (9).

In conclusion, we first exploit the perceptual bias of models and extract a textural prior from hard examples by adopting the style similarities. To further alleviate the heavy dependency on large amounts of data in training universal attacks, we further exploit the semantic bias to alleviate the heavy dependency on data. As the class-wise preference, prototypes are introduced and pursued by maximizing the multi-class margin. Using the textural prior as initialization, we train our adversarial patches using the prototypes as training data. The illustration of our two-staged adversarial patch attack algorithm can be found in supplementary.

4 Experiments

In this section, we will illustrate the attack effectiveness of our proposed method in different settings in the ACO scenario.

4.1 Dataset and Evaluation Metrics

As for the dataset, we use RPC [30], which is the largest grocery product dataset so far for the retail ACO task. It contains 200 product categories and 83,739 images, including 53,739 single-product exemplary images. Each image is a particular instance of a type of product, which is then divided into 17 sub-categories (*e.g.*, puffed food, instant drink, dessert, gum, milk, personal hygiene, *etc.*).

To evaluate our proposed method, we choose classification accuracy as the metric. Specifically, we further report *top*-1, *top*-3 and *top*-5 accuracy in our experiments. Note that the goal of adversarial attacks is compromising the performance of the model, *i.e.*, leading to worse values of the evaluation metrics above.

4.2 Experimental Settings

The input image is resized to 512×512 and the patch size is fixed at 32×32. The size of patches only accounts for 0.38% of the size of images. To optimize the loss, we use Adam optimizer with a learning rate of 0.01, a weight decay of 10^{-4}, and a maximum of 50 epochs. To get hard examples, we first run the target model over the training set once to get model predictions for each instance. Then, we select 200 images that are misclassified by the model with the lowest confidence as our hard examples. All of our code is implemented in Pytorch. The training and inference processes are finished on an NVIDIA Tesla k80 GPU cluster.

As for the compared methods, we choose the state-of-art adversarial patch attack methods including AdvPatch [1], RP$_2$ [5], and PSGAN [18]. We follow their implementations and parameter settings. To conduct fair comparisons, we adopt the same backbone models for our method and the compared ones in our experiments. Similar to [22], we use 50 item samples per class (10,000 in total) as the training data for the compared methods. We also extract 15 prototypes for each class (3,000 in total) as the training data for our method. With respect to the models, we follow [16] for the ACO task and use ResNet-152 as the backbone. As for the *margin*, we set the it as 10 since we found the model is insensitive to it (we tested 2, 4, 6, 8, 10, and 12 for *margin* and found similar results). To further improve the attack success rate of adversarial patches against different environments, we introduce transformations as follows:

- **Rotation**. The rotation angle is limited in $[-30°, 30°]$.
- **Distortion**. The distortion rate, *i.e.*, the control argument, moves in $[0, 0.1]$.
- **Affine Transformation**. The affine rate changes between 0 and 4.

4.3 Digital-World Attack

In this section, we evaluate the performance of our generated adversarial patches on the ACO task in the digital-world in both white-box and black-box settings. We also use a white patch to test the effectiveness of the adversarial attack (denoted as "White").

As for the **white-box** attack, we generate adversarial patches based on a ResNet-152 model and then attack it. As shown in Fig.3(a), our method outperforms other compared strategies with large margins. In other words, our adversarial patches obtain stronger attacking abilities with lower classification accuracy contrast to others, i.e., **5.42%** to 21.10%, 19.78%, and 38.89% in *top*-1 accuracy.

As for the **black-box** attack, we generate adversarial patches based on ResNet-152, then use them to attack other models with different architectures

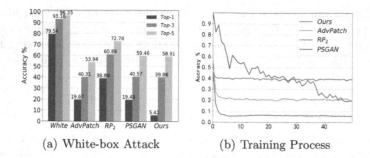

(a) White-box Attack   (b) Training Process

Fig. 3. (a) shows the White-box attack experiment in the digital-world with ResNet-152. Our method generates the strongest adversarial patches with the lowest classification accuracy. (b) denotes the training process of different methods

and unknown parameters (*i.e.*, VGG-16, AlexNet, and ResNet-101). As illustrated in Table 1, our generated adversarial patches enjoy stronger attacking abilities in the black-box setting with lower classification accuracy for different models.

Besides the classification accuracy, Fig.3(b) shows the training process of adversarial patches using different methods. After several training epochs, the attacking performance of our generated patches becomes stable and keeps the best among all. However, the performance of other methods still vibrates sharply. It is mainly due to the weak generalization ability of other methods. Thus, they achieve different accuracy when attacking different classes showing sharp vibrations.

4.4   Real-World Attack

To further validate the practical effectiveness of our generated adversarial patches, a real-world attack experiment is conducted on several online shopping platforms to simulate the ACO scenario. We use **Taobao** and **JD**, which are among the biggest e-commerce platforms in the world. We take 80 pictures of 4 different real-world products with different environmental conditions (*i.e.*, angles {-30°, -15°, 0°, 15°, 30°} and distances {0.3m, 0.5m, 0.7m, 1m}). The *top*-1 classification accuracy of these images is 100% on Taobao and 95.00% on JD, respectively. Then, we print our adversarial patches by an HP Color Laser-Jet Pro MFP M281fdw printer, stick them on the products and take photos with the combination of different distances and angles using a Canon D60 camera. A significant drop in accuracy on both platforms can be witnessed with low classification accuracy (*i.e.*, **56.25%** on Taobao, **55.00%** on JD), which is much lower than the compared methods, concretely 66.25%, 61.25%, and 66.25% on Taobao, 72.50%, 68.75%, and 63.75% on JD (the results of compared methods are in following orders: AdvPatch, RP$_2$, and PSGAN). The results demonstrate the strong attacking ability of our adversarial patches in real-world scenarios on practical applications. Visualizations can be found in Fig.4.

Table 1. Black-box attack experiment in the digital-world with VGG-16, AlexNet, and ResNet-101. Our method generates adversarial patches with strong transferability among different models

Model	Method	top-1	top-3	top-5
VGG-16	AdvPatch	73.82	**90.73**	**94.99**
	RP$_2$	81.25	94.65	97.10
	PSGAN	74.69	91.25	96.12
	Ours	**73.72**	**91.53**	**95.43**
AlexNet	AdvPatch	51.11	72.37	79.79
	RP$_2$	68.27	86.49	91.08
	PSGAN	49.39	72.85	82.94
	Ours	**31.68**	**50.92**	**60.19**
ResNet-101	AdvPatch	56.19	80.99	91.52
	RP$_2$	73.52	93.75	98.13
	PSGAN	51.26	79.22	90.47
	Ours	**22.24**	**51.32**	**60.28**

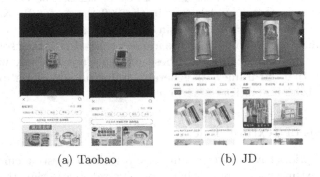

(a) Taobao   (b) JD

Fig. 4. Attack Taobao and JD platform with our adversarial patches. The `milk` in (a) and the `plastic cup` in (b) are recognised as the `decorations` and the `aluminum foil` when we stick our adversarial patches, respectively

4.5 Generalization Ability

In this section, we further evaluate the generalization ability of adversarial patches on unseen classes. We perform two experiments using the backbone model (ResNet-152), including attacking unseen item classes of adversarial patch training process and target models. For attacking unseen classes of the patch training process, we first train patches on a subset of the dataset, *i.e.*, only images from 100 classes are used *w.r.t.* 200 classes (we use prototypes for our method and item images for compared methods). According to the results in Table 2, our framework generates adversarial patches with strong generalization ability and outperforms other compared methods with huge margins (*i.e.*, **7.23%** to 40.28%, 31.62%, and 60.87%).

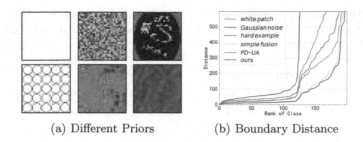

(a) Different Priors   (b) Boundary Distance

Fig. 5. (a) shows different priors used to generate adversarial patches. They are white patch, Gaussian noise, hard example, PD-UA, simple fusion, and **textural prior** respectively, from up to down, left to right. (b) is the decision boundary distance analysis, where fused prior achieves the smallest decision boundary distances for each class.

Meanwhile, we also tested the generalization ability on classes that have never been "seen" by the target model. Specifically, we train our patches on the RPC dataset and test them on the Taobao platform. We select 4 items and stick adversarial patches on them and take 64 pictures. The categories of the items are unseen to target models (not in the 200 classes for ResNet-152), but known to the Taobao platform. Interestingly, after attacks, the *top*-1 accuracy on Taobao is **65.63%**. Though our patches are not trained to attack some specified classes, they still generalize well to these unseen classes. Thus, we can draw the conclusion that our framework generates universal adversarial patches with strong generalization abilities to even unseen classes.

4.6   Analysis of Textural Priors

Since textural priors have improved universal attacks, a question emerges: "Why and how the textural priors are beneficial to universal adversarial attacks?" Thus, in this section, we further study the effectiveness of our textural priors.

Training from Different Priors. To demonstrate the effectiveness of our textural priors, we begin to study by initializing patches through different priors, *e.g.*, white patch, Gaussian noise, hard example, PD-UA [20], simple fusion, and our textural prior (denoted as "ours"). In contrast to our textual prior, we use the same amount of simple examples to generate the simple version of fused prior

Table 2. Attack on unseen classes. Our method generates adversarial patches with the strongest generalization abilities showing lowest accuracy compared with other methods

Method	AdvPatch	RP$_2$	PSGAN	**Ours**
top-1	40.28	60.87	31.62	**7.23**

(denoted as "simple fusion"). Other experimental settings are the same as the settings of the digital-world attack. The visualization of them can be found in Fig.5(a). We train 6 adversarial patches with all the same experimental settings except for the initialization. The corresponding accuracy after attacking are 17.67% (white patch), 18.96% (Gaussian noise), 16.11% (hard example), 21.10% (PD-UA), 24.09% (simple fusion), **5.42%** (ours). It shows that our fused priors offer adversarial patches the strongest attacking ability.

Decision Boundary Distance Analysis. The minimum distance to the decision boundary among the data points reflects the model robustness to small noises [3]. Similarly, the distance to decision boundaries for an instance characterizes the feasibility performing attack from it. Due to the computation difficulty of decision boundary distance for deep models, we calculate the distance of an instance x to specified classes $w.r.t.$ the model prediction to represent the decision boundary distance. Given a learnt model F and point x_i with class label y_i $(i = 1, \ldots, N)$, for each direction $(y_j, i \neq j)$ we estimate the smallest step numbers moved as the distance. We use the L_2 norm Projected Gradient Descent (PGD) until the model's prediction changes, i.e., $F(x_i) \neq y_i$.

As shown in Fig.5(b), our textural priors obtain the minimum distance in each direction compared to other initialization strategies. It explains the reason that our textural prior performs stronger adversarial attacks because it is more close to the decision boundaries.

4.7 Ablation Study

In this section, we investigate our method through ablation study. Due to the limitation of paper length, we put more ablations in the supplementary.

The Effectiveness of Class Prototypes. We first investigate the amount of data required with our framework to train adversarial patches by solely using prototypes or item images, respectively. Specifically, we first train adversarial patches with 1000 prototypes as $Ours_{P1000}$. Then, we randomly select 1000, 2000, 4000, 10000 item images from the RPC dataset to train adversarial patches, respectively (denoted by $Ours_{I1000}$, $Ours_{I2000}$, $Ours_{I4000}$, and $Ours_{I10000}$). The results in Table 3 show that to achieve the approximate attacking ability in $Ours_{P1000}$ setting, twice more items images are required. It indicates the representative ability of class prototypes for different classes. Besides, we also study

Table 3. The *top*-1 accuracy of the adversarial patches obtained using different amount of training data. Our prototypes need only half the data to achieve a similar performance compared to original method.

Settings	$Ours_{P1000}$	$Ours_{I1000}$	$Ours_{I2000}$	$Ours_{I4000}$	$Ours_{I10000}$
top-1	**6.51**	12.43	6.57	6.10	5.40

the time efficiency of generating prototypes. In our practice, it takes 1.8 h to generate 1000 prototypes, and another 3.3 h to train the model (**5.1 h in total**). To achieve similar performance, it takes 6.6 h to train a model using 2000 original images, which indeed spends more time. Also, it's time-consuming to collect original images in practice, let al.one the cost of preprocessing, etc.

The Effectiveness of Fusion Loss. We further analyze the effectiveness of fusion loss by using $\mathcal{L}_u$ only or $\mathcal{L}_s$ only respectively for the fusion loss $\mathcal{L}_f$ in 5. As shown in Table 4, the original $\mathcal{L}_f$ achieves better performance in both white-box (ResNet-152) and black-box (VGG-16, AlexNet, ResNet-101) settings. We believe that the adversarial patch benefits both attacking ability and generalization ability from the $\mathcal{L}_f$ loss. As for λ, we achieve the best performance when it is around 1. The accuracy with different λ values (0.1, 1, and 10) are 5.47%, **5.42%**, and 12.01% respectively.

Table 4. Ablation study on fusion loss. The original $\mathcal{L}_f$ achieves the best results.

Method	White-box	Black-box		
	ResNet-152	VGG-16	AlexNet	ResNet-101
$\mathcal{L}_u$only	5.47%	75.21%	49.42%	61.82%
$\mathcal{L}_s$only	15.73%	77.05%	72.65%	72.55%
$\mathcal{L}_f$	**5.42%**	**73.72%**	**31.68%**	**22.24%**

5   Conclusions

In this paper, we proposed a bias-based attack framework to generate class-agnostic universal adversarial patches, which exploits both the perceptual and semantic bias of models. Regarding the perceptual bias, since DNNs are strongly biased towards textures, we exploit the hard examples which convey strong model uncertainties and extract a textural patch prior from them by adopting the style similarities. The patch prior is more close to decision boundaries and would promote attacks. To further alleviate the heavy dependency on large amounts of data in training universal attacks, we further exploit the semantic bias. As the class-wise preference, prototypes are introduced and pursued by maximizing the multi-class margin to help universal training. Taking ACO as the typical scenario, extensive experiments are conducted which demonstrate that our proposed framework outperforms state-of-the-art adversarial patch attack methods.

Model biases, especially texture-based features, has been used to perform adversarial attacks. In contrast, can we improve model robustness by eliminating the textural features from the training data? We leave it as future work.

Acknowledgement. This work was supported by National Natural Science Foundation of China (61872021, 61690202), Beijing Nova Program of Science and Technology (Z191100001119050), and Fundamental Research Funds for Central Universities (YWF-20-BJ-J-646).

References

1. Brown, T.B., Mané, D., Roy, A., Abadi, M., Gilmer, J.: Adversarial patch. arXiv preprint arXiv:1712.09665 (2017)
2. Chen, W., Zhang, Z., Hu, X., Wu, B.: Boosting decision-based black-box adversarial attacks with random sign flip. In: Proceedings of the European Conference on Computer Vision (2020)
3. Cortes, C., Vapnik, V.: Support-vector networks. Mach. Learn. **20**, 273–297 (1995). https://doi.org/10.1007/BF00994018
4. Ekanayake, P., Deng, Z., Yang, C., Hong, X., Yang, J.: Naïve approach for bounding box annotation and object detection towards smart retail systems. In: Wang, G., Feng, J., Bhuiyan, M.Z.A., Lu, R. (eds.) SpaCCS 2019. LNCS, vol. 11637, pp. 218–227. Springer, Cham (2019). https://doi.org/10.1007/978-3-030-24900-7_18
5. Eykholt, K., et al.: Robust physical-world attacks on deep learning models. arXiv preprint arXiv:1707.08945 (2017)
6. Eykholt, K., et al.: Robust physical-world attacks on deep learning models. In: Proceedings of the IEEE Conference on Computer Vision and Pattern Recognition, pp. 1625–1634 (2018)
7. Fan, Y., et al.: Sparse adversarial attack via perturbation factorization. In: European Conference on Computer Vision (2020)
8. Felzenszwalb, P., McAllester, D., Ramanan, D.: A discriminatively trained, multiscale, deformable part model. In: 2008 IEEE conference on computer vision and pattern recognition, pp. 1–8. IEEE (2008)
9. Gao, L., Zhang, Q., Song, J., Liu, X., Shen, H.: Patch-wise attack for fooling deep neural network. In: Vedaldi, A., Bischof, H., Brox, T., Frahm, J.M.: (eds.) Computer Vision–ECCV 2020. ECCV 2020. Lecture Notes in Computer Science, vol 12373. Springer, Cham (2020). https://doi.org/10.1007/978-3-030-58604-1_19
10. Geirhos, R., Rubisch, P., Michaelis, C., Bethge, M., Wichmann, F.A., Brendel, W.: Imagenet-trained cnns are biased towards texture; increasing shape bias improves accuracy and robustness. arXiv preprint arXiv:1811.12231 (2018)
11. Goodfellow, I.J., Shlens, J., Szegedy, C.: Explaining and harnessing adversarial examples. arXiv preprint arXiv:1412.6572 (2014)
12. Karmon, D., Zoran, D., Goldberg, Y.: Lavan: localized and visible adversarial noise. arXiv preprint arXiv:1801.02608 (2018)
13. Kim, B., Rudin, C., Shah, J.A.: The bayesian case model: a generative approach for case-based reasoning and prototype classification. In: Advances in neural information processing systems (pp. 1952-1960)In Advances in neural information processing systems, pp. 1952-1960 (2014)
14. Krizhevsky, A., Sutskever, I., Hinton, G.E.: Imagenet classification with deep convolutional neural networks. Commun. ACM **60**(6), 84–90 (2012)
15. Kurakin, A., Goodfellow, I., Bengio, S.: Adversarial examples in the physical world. arXiv preprint arXiv:1607.02533 (2016)
16. Li, C., et al.: Data priming network for automatic check-out. arXiv preprint arXiv:1904.04978 (2019)

17. Liu, A., et al.: Spatiotemporal attacks for embodied agents. In: European Conference on Computer Vision (2020)
18. Liu, A., et al.: Perceptual-sensitive GAN for generating adversarial patches. In: Proceedings of the AAAI Conference on Artificial Intelligence, pp. 1028–1035 (2019)
19. Liu, A., et al.: Training robust deep neural networks via adversarial noise propagation. arXiv preprint arXiv:1909.09034 (2019)
20. Liu, H., et al.: Universal adversarial perturbation via prior driven uncertainty approximation. In: Proceedings of the IEEE International Conference on Computer Vision, pp. 2941–2949 (2019)
21. Mohamed, A.R., Dahl, G.E., Hinton, G.: Acoustic modeling using deep belief networks. IEEE Trans. Audio, Speech Lang. Process. **20**(1), 14–22 (2011)
22. Moosavi-Dezfooli, S.M., Fawzi, A., Fawzi, O., Frossard, P.: Universal adversarial perturbations. In: Proceedings of the IEEE Conference on Computer Vision and Pattern Recognition, pp. 1765–1773 (2017)
23. Mopuri, K.R., Ganeshan, A., Radhakrishnan, V.B.: Generalizable data-free objective for crafting universal adversarial perturbations. IEEE Trans. Pattern Anal. Mach. Intell. **41**(10), 2452–2465 (2018)
24. Reddy Mopuri, K., Krishna Uppala, P., Venkatesh Babu, R.: Ask, acquire, and attack: data-free uap generation using class impressions. In: Proceedings of the European Conference on Computer Vision (ECCV), pp. 19–34 (2018)
25. Selvaraju, R.R., Das, A., Vedantam, R., Cogswell, M., Parikh, D., Batra, D.: Gradcam: why did you say that? arXiv preprint arXiv:1611.07450 (2016)
26. Simonyan, K., Vedaldi, A., Zisserman, A.: Deep inside convolutional networks: visualising image classification models and saliency maps. arXiv preprint arXiv:1312.6034 (2013)
27. Sutskever, I., Vinyals, O., Le, Q.: Sequence to sequence learning with neural networks. In: Advances in Neural Information Processing Systems, pp. 3104–3112 (2014)
28. Szegedy, C., et al.: Intriguing properties of neural networks. arXiv preprint arXiv:1312.6199 (2013)
29. Thys, S., Van Ranst, W., Goedemé, T.: Fooling automated surveillance cameras: adversarial patches to attack person detection. In: Proceedings of the IEEE Conference on Computer Vision and Pattern Recognition Workshops (2019)
30. Wei, X.S., Cui, Q., Yang, L., Wang, P., Liu, L.: Rpc: a large-scale retail product checkout dataset. arXiv preprint arXiv:1901.07249 (2019)
31. Zhang, C., et al.: Interpreting and improving adversarial robustness of deep neural networks with neuron sensitivity. arXiv preprint arXiv:1909.06978 (2019)
32. Zhang, T., Zhu, Z.: Interpreting adversarially trained convolutional neural networks. arXiv preprint arXiv:1905.09797 (2019)
33. Zhu, J.Y., Park, T., Isola, P., Efros, A.A.: Unpaired image-to-image translation using cycle-consistent adversarial networks. In: Proceedings of the IEEE International Conference on Computer Vision, pp. 2223–2232 (2017)

Imbalanced Continual Learning
with Partitioning Reservoir Sampling

Chris Dongjoo Kim, Jinseo Jeong, and Gunhee Kim[✉]

Neural Processing Research Center, Seoul National University, Seoul, Korea
{cdjkim,jinseo}@vision.snu.ac.kr, gunhee@snu.ac.kr
http://vision.snu.ac.kr/projects/PRS

Abstract. Continual learning from a sequential stream of data is a crucial challenge for machine learning research. Most studies have been conducted on this topic under the single-label classification setting along with an assumption of balanced label distribution. This work expands this research horizon towards multi-label classification. In doing so, we identify unanticipated adversity innately existent in many multi-label datasets, the *long-tailed* distribution. We jointly address the two independently solved problems, Catastropic Forgetting and the long-tailed label distribution by first empirically showing a new challenge of destructive forgetting of the minority concepts on the tail. Then, we curate two benchmark datasets, *COCOseq* and *NUS-WIDEseq*, that allow the study of both *intra-* and *inter-*task imbalances. Lastly, we propose a new sampling strategy for replay-based approach named *Partitioning Reservoir Sampling* (PRS), which allows the model to maintain a balanced knowledge of both head and tail classes. We publicly release the dataset and the code in our project page.

Keywords: Imbalanced learning · Continual learning · Multi-label classification · Long-tailed distribution · Online learning

1 Introduction

Sequential data streams are among the most natural forms of input for intelligent agents abiding the law of time. Recently, there has been much effort to better learn from these types of inputs, termed *continual learning* in machine learning research. Specifically, there have been many ventures into but not limited to single-label text classification [17], question answering [17], language instruction and translation [39], object detection [41,61], captioning [51] and even video representation learning [53,54]. Surprisingly, we have yet to see continual learning for multi-label classification, a more general and practical form of classification tasks since most real-world data are typically associated with several semantic concepts.

In order to study continual learning for multi-label classification, the first job would be to construct a research benchmark for it. We select two of the most popular multi-label datasets, MSCOCO [40] and NUS-WIDE [15], and tailor them into a sequence of mutually exclusive tasks, *COCOseq* and *NUS-WIDEseq*. In the process, we recognize that large-scale multi-label datasets inevitably follow

© Springer Nature Switzerland AG 2020
A. Vedaldi et al. (Eds.): ECCV 2020, LNCS 12358, pp. 411–428, 2020.
https://doi.org/10.1007/978-3-030-58601-0_25

a *long-tailed* distribution where a small number of categories contain a large number of samples while most have only a small amount of samples. This naturally occurring phenomenon is widely observed in vision and language datasets [50,56,62], with a whole other branch of machine learning that has focused solely on this topic. Consequently, to effectively perform continual learning on multi-label data, two major obstacles should be overcome simultaneously: (i) the infamous *catastrophic forgetting* problem [23,49,55] and (ii) the long-tailed distribution problem [14,29,43,66], which we jointly address in this work.

We adopt the replay-based approach [3,28,38,44,58,60] to tackle continual learning, which explicitly stores the past experiences into a memory or a generative model, and rehearses them back with the new input samples. Although there also exists the prior-focused (*i.e.* regularization-based) [2,35,71] and expansion-based methods [59,70], the replay-based approaches have often shown superior results in terms of performance and memory efficiency. Specifically, the replay memory with *reservoir sampling* [64] has been a strong baseline, especially in the task-free continual setting [3,37] that does not require explicit task labels during the training nor test phase. It is an optimistic avenue of continual learning that we also undertake.

To conclude the introduction, we outline the contributions of this work:

I. To the best of our knowledge, this is the first work to tackle the continual learning for multi-label classification. To this end, we reveal that it is critical to correctly address the intra- and inter-task imbalances along with the prevailing catastrophic forgetting problem of continual learning.
II. For the study of this new problem, we extend the existing multi-label datasets into their continual versions called *COCOseq* and *NUS-WIDEseq*.
III. We propose a new replay method named *Partitioning Reservoir Sampling* (PRS) for continual learning in heterogeneous and long-tailed data streams. We discover that the key to success is to allocate a sufficient portion of memory to the moderate and minority classes to retain a balanced knowledge of present and past experiences.

2   Motivation: Fatal Forgetting on the Tail Classes

The long-tailed data distribution is both an enduring and pervasive problem in machine learning [29,33], as most real-world datasets are inherently imbalance [50,52,56,62,74]. Wang *et al.* [66], for example, stated that minimizing the skew in the data distribution by collecting more examples in the tail classes is an arduous task and even if one manages to balance them along one dimension, they can become imbalanced in another.

We point out that the long-tailed distribution further aggravates the problem in continual learning, as a destructive amount of forgetting occurs on the tail classes. We illustrate this with experiments on two existing continual learning approaches: a prior-focused EWC [35] and a replay-based reservoir sampling [6,44,58]. The experiments are carried out in an online setting on our *COCOseq* dataset, whose detail will be presented in Sect. 5. Figure 1 shows the results.

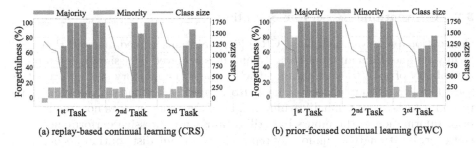

(a) replay-based continual learning (CRS)   (b) prior-focused continual learning (EWC)

Fig. 1. The forgetfulness of the majority and minority classes for two popular continual learning approaches over three sequential tasks. We test (a) replay-based reservoir sampling [6,44,58] and (b) EWC [35] with a shared output head and a memory size of 1000. We measure the forgetfulness using the metric proposed in [10] (Higher is more forgetful). The green line indicates the size of each class. More severe forgetting occurs for the minority classes in each task. (Color figur online)

We plot the forgetting metric proposed in [10], which measures the difference between the peak performance and the performance at the end of the sequence. For illustrative purposes, we sort the classes per task in decreasing order of the number of classes. In both approaches, the minority (tail) classes experience more forgetting compared to the majority (head) classes. We observe that the imbalance of sample distribution in the memory causes this phenomenon in accordance with the input distribution, as we will further discuss in Fig. 5.

3 Approach

The goal of this work is to overcome two inevitable obstacles of multi-label task-free continual learning: (i) catastrophic forgetting and (ii) long-tail input data distribution. Since we adopt the replay-based approach, we focus on a new sampling strategy to reserve past experiences into a fixed memory. We first clarify the problem (Sect. 3.1), and discuss conventional reservoir sampling (Sect. 3.2) and their fundamental limitations in this context (3.3). Finally, we propose our sampling method named *Partitioning Reservoir Sampling* (Sect. 3.4).

3.1 Problem Formulation

We formulate our multi-label task-free continual learning as follows. The input is a data stream S, which consists of an unknown set of data points (x, y), where y is a multi-hot label vector representing k arbitrary number of classes. Except for the datapoint (x, y) that enters in an online-manner, no other information (*e.g.* the task boundaries or the number of classes) is available even during training. Given an input stream, the goal of the model is to allocate the fixed memory $\mathcal{M}$ with a size of m: $\sum_{i=1}^{u} m_i \leq m$, where m_i denotes the partitioned memory size for class c_i, and u is the unique number of classes observed so far at time t.

3.2 Conventional Reservoir Sampling

Conventional reservoir sampling (CRS) [64] maintains a fixed memory that uniformly samples from an input data stream. It is achieved by assigning a sampling probability of m/n to each datapoint where m is the memory size and n is the total number of samples seen so far. CRS is used as a standard sampling approach for task-free continual learning [11,44,57,58], since it does not require any prior information of the inputs but still attains an impressive performance [12]. However, its strength to uniformly represent the input distribution becomes its Achilles-heel in a long-tailed setting as the memory distribution also becomes long-tailed, leading to the realm of problems experienced in imbalanced training.

3.3 Fundamental Problems in Imbalanced Learning

Imbalanced data induce severe issues in learning that are primarily attributed to gradient dominance and under-representation of the minority [19,36,62,74].

(1) **Gradient dominance.** The imbalance in the minibatch causes the majority classes dominating the gradient updates, which ultimately lead to the neglect of the minority classes.

(2) **Under-representation of the minority.** Mainly due to the lack of data, the minority classes are much under-represented within the learned features relative to the majority [19,69]. We empirically confirm this in Fig. 7, where the minority classes do not formulate a discernable pattern in the feature space but are sparsely distributed by conventional methods.

There have been data processing or algorithmic approaches to tackle these problems by promoting balance during training. Data processing methods such as oversampling or undersampling [5,7,52] explicitly simulate the input balance, while cost-sensitive approaches [16,31,66] adjust the update via regularizing the objective. More aggressively, there have also been directions that populate the minority samples via generation to avoid overfitting in the minority [13,20,46]. Most research in imbalanced learning shares the consensus that the *balance* during training is critical to success, which is the underlying emphasis on the design of our algorithm.

3.4 Partitioning Reservoir Sampling

Since a continual replay algorithm has no information about future input, the memory must maintain well-rounded knowledge in an online manner. To that end, we provide an online memory maintenance algorithm called *Partitioning Reservoir Sampling* (PRS) that consists of two fundamental operations: *partition* and *maintenance*. The PRS is overviewed in Fig. 2 and Algorithm 1.

The Partition. During the training phase, the model only has access to the stream of data (x, y). While it is impractical to store all examples, caching the running statistics is a more sensible alternative. Thus, the model uses the running

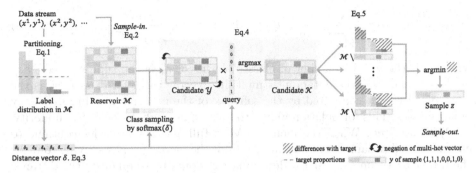

Fig. 2. Overview of Partitioning Reservoir Sampling. Based on the current data stream statistics, the target partition ratios are first obtained based on Eq. 1. We maintain the memory by iterating between the processes of *sample-in* and sample-out. The sample-in decides whether a new datapoint is stored into the memory or not, while the sample-out selects which example is removed from the memory. If the model allows to sample-in the datapoint, the algorithm traverses a process of candidate selection to sample-out an example by selecting the one that advances the memory towards the target partitions the most.

class frequency to set the target proportion of classes in the memory. This is achieved by a variant of the proportional allocation [4,8,22]:

$$p_i = \frac{n_i^\rho}{\sum_j n_j^\rho},\qquad(1)$$

where ρ is a power of allocation, and n_i is the running frequency of class i. At $\rho = 0$, all classes are equally allocated, which may be the most favorable scenario for the minority as it shares the same amount of memory with the majority. At $\rho = 1$, classes are allocated proportionally to their frequencies, which is identical to the conventional sampling in Sect. 3.2. ρ is chosen a value between 0 and 1 to compromise between the two extremes. For a given ρ, we can define the *target partition quota* for class i as $m_i = m \cdot p_i$ where p_i is defined by Eq. 1. Collectively, the target partition is represented as a vector $\mathbf{m} = [m_1, \cdots, m_u]$, whose sum is m. We will explore the effect of ρ in Fig. 6.

The Maintenance. The goal of maintenance is to allow every *class i* (not every sample as in CRS) to have a fair chance of entering the memory according to the target partition m_i. To maintain a well-rounded knowledge of the past and present experiences, we iterate between the processes of *sample-in* and *sample-out*. The sample-in decides whether a new input datapoint is reserved into the memory or not, while the sample-out selects which example is removed from the memory when it becomes full and new samples continue to enter.

1) *Sample-in.* For an incoming datapoint, we assign a sampling probability s to be reserved in the memory. We compute s with two desiderata: (i) it needs to comply with the target partition, and (ii) for better balancing, it is biased towards the minority classes with respect to the current running statistics.

$$s = \sum_{i \in \{i,...,u\}} \frac{m_i}{n_i} \cdot w_i, \quad \text{where } w_i = \frac{y_i e^{-n_i}}{\sum_{j=1} y_j e^{-n_j}} \tag{2}$$

where u is the unique number of classes observed, n_i is the running frequency of class i, and y_i is the datapoint's multi-hot vector value for class i. w_i is the normalized weight computed by the softmax of the negative running frequency of the classes. This formulation allows to bias w_i strongly towards the minority.

2) *Sample-out.* When the memory $\mathcal{M}$ is full and new samples continue to enter, we need to sample out an example from the memory while striving towards the target partition. The first order of matter would be to quantify the distance from the current memory partition to our target partition. To do so, we define a u-dimensional vector δ with each element as

$$\delta_i = l_i - p_i \cdot \sum_j l_j, \tag{3}$$

where l_i is the number of examples of class i in the memory and p_i is the partition ratio from Eq. 1. Note that we multiply p_i by $\sum_j l_j$ rather than the memory size m, due to the multiple labels on each datapoint.

In order to fulfill our objective (*i.e.* achieve the target partitions), we greedily select and remove the sample that best satisfies the following two desiderata: (i) include the classes that occupy more memory than their quota, *i.e.* $\delta_i > 0$ and (ii) exclude the classes that under-occupy or already satisfy the target, $\delta_i \leq 0$.

To this end, we devise a two-stage candidate selection process. For desideratum (i), we define a set of candidate sample $\mathcal{Y} \subset \mathcal{M}$ as follows. Among the classes with $\delta_i > 0$, we randomly sample a class with a probability of softmax(δ_i). This sampling is highly biased toward the class with the maximum δ_i value (*i.e.* the class to be reduced the most). We found this to be more robust in practice than considering multiple classes with $\delta_i > 0$. Then, $\mathcal{Y}$ contains all samples labeled with this selected class in the memory. For desideratum (ii), we define a u-dimensional indicator vector q where $q_i = 0$ if $\delta_i > 0$ and $q_i = 1$ otherwise. That is, q_i indicates the classes that do not over-occupy the memory.

Finally, the set of candidate samples $\mathcal{K}$ is obtained by

$$\mathcal{K} = \{n^* | n^* = \arg\max_{n \in \mathcal{Y}} (\neg y^n \cdot q)\}, \tag{4}$$

where $\neg y^n$ is the negation of the multi-hot label vector of sample n (*i.e.* $0 \rightarrow 1$ and $1 \rightarrow 0$). That is, $\mathcal{K}$ is a subset of $\mathcal{Y}$ that does not contain sample(s) for the under-occupied (or already-satisfied) classes as possible. $\mathcal{K}$ may include multiple samples while the samples with fewer labels are more likely to be selected.

Finally, amongst $\mathcal{K}$, we select example z to be removed as it is the one that advances the memory towards the target partition the most:

$$z = \arg\min_{k \in \mathcal{K}} \sum_{i \in \{1,..,u\}} \left| \mathcal{C}_{ki} - p_i \cdot \sum_{l \in \{1,..,u\}} \mathcal{C}_{kl} \right|, \text{where } \mathcal{C}_{ki} = \sum_{n \in \mathcal{M} \backslash k} y_i^n. \tag{5}$$

Algorithm 1. Partitioning Reservoir Sampling Pseudo-code

Require: (i) data $(x_t, y_t), ..., (x_T, y_T)$, (ii)   11:   // Partition
     power param ρ, (iii) memory size m.   12: $Partitioning(\mathcal{M}, \psi, q)$ // Eq. 1
1: $\mathcal{M} = \{\}$ // memory   13:   // Maintenance
2: $\psi = \emptyset$ // running statistics   14:   // class-indep reservoir sampling
3: $u = 0$ // number of unique classes
4: **for** $t = 1$ **to** T **do**   15: $sample\_in(\mathcal{M}_u, y_{t,u}, \psi)$ // Eq. 2
5:    $update(\psi)$ // update running stats   16:   **if** sample-in success **then**
6:    **if** $t \leq |m|$ **then**   17: $sample\_out(\mathcal{M}, \psi, q)$ // Eq. 5
7:      // fill memory   18:   **end if**
8:      $\mathcal{M}_u \leftarrow \mathcal{M}\{y_t\}$ // sub memory   19:   **end if**
9:      $\mathcal{M}_u \leftarrow \{x_t, y_t\} \cup \mathcal{M}_u$ 20: **end for**
10:   **else**

$\mathcal{C}_{ki}$ is the current number of class i in the memory after the removal of sample k from memory $\mathcal{M}$, p_i is the partition ratio of class i from Eq. 1, and y_i^n is a binary value for class i of the label vector of sample n. Equation 5 finds the sample z that minimizes the distance (defined in Eq. 3) towards the target partition before and after the removal of sample k.

4 Related Work

There have been three main branches in continual learning, which are regularization, expansion and replay methods. Here we focus on the replay-based approaches and present a more comprehensive survey in the Appendix.

Replay-based Approaches. They explicitly maintain a fixed-sized memory in the form of generative weights or explicit data to rehearse it back to the model during training. Many recent works [6,11,12,32,44,57,58] employ a memory that reserves the data samples of prior classes in an offline setting. For example, GEM [44] uses the memory to constrain the gradient direction that prevents forgetting, and this idea becomes more efficient in AGEM [11]. Chaudhry et al. [12] explore tiny episodic memory, which shows improved overall performance when training repetitively from only a few examples. Riemer et al. [57] introduce a method that combines rehearsal with meta-learning to find the right balance between transfer and interference. Since our approach uses no prior knowledge other than the given input stream, it is orthogonally integrable with many aforementioned methods.

Online Sequential Learning. Recently, there have been some approaches to *online* continual learning where each training sample is seen only once. *ExStream* [28] is an online stream clustering reservoir method, but it requires prior knowledge about the number of classes to pre-allocate the memory. As new samples enter, the sub-memory is filled based on a distance measure and merged in the feature space when the memory is full. GSS [3] may be one of the most

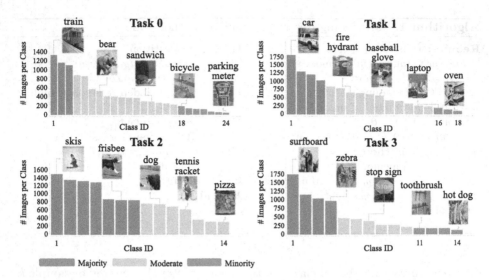

Fig. 3. Statistics of *COCOseq* dataset consisting of four tasks.

similar works to ours. It formulates the sample selection as a constraint reduction problem, intending to select a fixed subset of constraints that best approximate the feasible region. They perform miniaturized MNIST experiments with different task sizes (*e.g.* 2000 instances for one task and 200 for the others). However, this setting is difficult to represent practical long-tailed or imbalanced problems, since only a single task is much larger than the other same-sized tasks.

Multi-label Classification. There have been many works handling the vital problem of multi-label classification [25,47]. Recently, recurrent approaches [65, 67] and attention-based methods [26,73] are proposed to correlate the labels during predictions. Wei *et al.* [68] employ the prior task knowledge to perform graph-based learning that aids the correlation representation of multiple labels. While all the works in the past have focused on the offline multi-label classification, we take on its online task-free continual learning problem. Moreover, our approach is orthogonally applicable to these methods as we select some of them as the base model in our experiments.

5   The Multi-label Sequential Datasets

To study the proposed problem, we transform two multi-label classification datasets into their continual versions: *COCOseq* and *NUS-WIDEseq*. It is a non-trivial mission since the data must be split into tasks with exclusive class labels where each datapoint is associated with multiple labels.

5.1 The *COCOseq*

There have been two previous works that curate the MSCOCO dataset [40] for continual learning. Shmelkov *et al.* [61] select 20 out of 80 classes to create 2 tasks, each with 10 classes by grouping them based on alphabetical ordering. They also create an incremental version with 25 classes, where 15 classes are used for the model to obtain the base knowledge via normal batch training, and the other 10 classes are sequentially learned one at a time. These 10 classes are selected so that each image has only a *single* class label. Nguyen *et al.* [51] tailor MSCOCO for continual learning of captioning. They use 24 out of 80 classes and discarded all the images that contain multiple class labels. Similar to [61], they create 2 tasks where one task has 5 classes, and the other has 19 classes. Also, a sequential version is made using the 19 classes for base knowledge learning and the remaining 5 for incremental learning.

Different from previous works, we curate 4 tasks with multi-label images. To accurately measure the training performance on the intra-task imbalance, we make sure that the test set is *balanced*; the test set size per class is identical even though its training set size is imbalanced and long-tailed. This is a common practice in imbalanced classification benchmarks, including [66] that uses 40 test images per class in the SUN-LT dataset and the largest OLTR benchmark [43] that assigns 50 and 100 balanced test images per class for ImageNet-LT and Places-LT dataset, respectively. While referring to the Appendix for more details of dataset construction, we build a 4-way split MSCOCO dataset called *COCOscq* (Fig. 3), consisting of 70 object classes with 35072 training and 6346 test data. The test set contains one-hundred images per class. Note that $6346 \neq 70 \times 100$ due to the multi-label property.

To the best of our knowledge, there is no strict consensus to divide the majority and minority classes in long-tailed datasets. For instance, Liu *et al.* [43] define the classes with more than 100 training examples as many-shot, 20–100 as medium-shot, and less than 20 as few-shot classes. Other works such as [27] and [72] define the minority classes as less than 100 or 200 samples in the training set, respectively. Accordingly, we define classes with less than 200 training examples as the minority classes, 200–900 as moderate and >900 as the majority.

5.2 The *NUS-WIDEseq*

We further curate a sequential dataset from NUS-WIDE [15], containing 6 mutually exclusive and increasingly difficult tasks. Its novelty lies in having both inter- and intra-task imbalance; the skewness exists not only within each task but amongst the tasks as well. More details can be found in the Appendix.

NUS-WIDE [15] is a raw web-crawled multi-label image dataset. It provides a human-annotated version with 150531 images of 81 labels[1]. However, the dataset by nature exhibits a very severe long-tail property. For instance, MSCOCO's top

---

[1] The original number of images is 210832, but many URLs are no longer available.

20% classes are responsible for 50.7% of the total data, while NUS-WIDE's top 20% surmount to 76.3% of the whole data. Since the original test set is highly long-tailed, we balance it for more accurate evaluation as done for *COCOseq*. Finally, *NUS-WIDEseq* contains 49 classes with 48724 training and 2367 test data with 50 samples per class.

6   Experiments

In our evaluation, we explore how effective our PRS is for both inter- and intra-task imbalances in task-free multi-label continual learning tasks compared to the state-of-the-art models. We also analyze the importance of a balanced memory from many aspects. The task that we solve is mostly close to but more difficult than the scenario of *class-incremental learning* [63] in that the task label is not available at training as well as at test time.

6.1   Experimental Design

Previous continual learning research has shown a high amount of disparity in evaluation. As we are the first to explore multi-label continual learning, we explicitly ground our experimental setting based on [1,21,63] as follows:

- *Cross-task resemblance*: Consecutive tasks in COCOseq and NUS-WIDEseq are partly correlated to contain neighboring domain concepts.
- *Shared output heads*: Since we solve multi-label classification without task labels, the level of difficulty of our task is comparable to using a shared output head for single-label classification.
- *No test-time task labels*: Our approach does not require explicit task labels during both training and test phase, often coined as *task-free continual learning* in [3,37].
- *More than two tasks*: COCOseq and NUS-WIDEseq contain four and six tasks, respectively.
- *Online learning*: The algorithm learns from a continuous stream of data without a separate offline batch training stage such as [3,28,37].

Base Models. In recent multi-label image classification [26,42,65,67,68], it is a common practice to fine-tune a pre-trained model to a target dataset. We thus employ ResNet101 [30] pre-trained on ImageNet [18] as our base classifier. Additionally, we test two multi-label classification approaches that *do not* require any prior information about the input to train: Recurrent Attention (RNN-Attention) [67] and the more recent Attention Consistency (AC) algorithm [26]. Due to its superior performance, we choose ResNet101 as the base model for the experiments in the main draft. We report the results of RNN-Attention and AC methods in the Appendix.

Evaluation Metrics. Following the convention of multi-label classification [24, 65,73], we report the average overall F1 (O-F1), per-class F1 (C-F1) as well

Table 1. Results on *COCOseq* **and** *NUS-WIDEseq*. We report accuracy metrics for multi-label classification after the whole data stream is seen once. Similar to [43], the majority, moderate and minority are distinguished to accurately assess the long-tail performances. The memory size is fixed at 2000, with {0,3,1,2} task schedule for *COCOseq* and {3,1,0,5,4,2} for *NUS-WIDEseq*. The results are the means of five experiments except those of GSS-Greedy [3] which are the mean of three due to its computational complexity. The best and the second best methods are respectively marked in red and blue fonts, excluding the MULTITASK that is offline trained as the upper-bound. FORGET refers to the normalized forgetting measure of [10].

COCOseq	Majority			Moderate			Minority			Overall		
	C-F1	O-F1	mAP	C-F1	O-F1	mAP	C-F1	O-F1	mAP	C-F1	O-F1	mAP
Multitask [9]	72.9	70.9	77.3	53.2	51.4	55.0	12.7	13.6	24.2	51.2	52.1	53.9
Finetune	18.5	27.9	29.8	6.7	16.7	14.1	0.0	0.0	5.2	8.5	18.4	16.4
Forget	100.0	100.0	65.8	100.0	100.0	73.5	100.0	100.0	67.4	100.0	100.0	70.1
EWC [35]	60.0	53.4	64.1	37.3	38.1	47.5	7.5	8.2	21.5	38.9	40.0	46.6
Forget	24.2	24.0	0.8	35.1	33.9	3.0	56.3	56.1	9.0	32.8	32.0	3.2
CRS [64]	67.0	62.5	67.9	47.8	45.2	50.4	14.5	15.6	26.9	47.5	46.6	50.2
Forget	15.0	13.6	8.9	32.8	32.0	15.6	55.58	54.92	23.2	32.2	30.1	15.3
GSS [3]	59.3	56.7	59.6	44.9	43.0	46.0	10.5	11.0	18.6	42.8	42.7	44.0
Forget	20.2	18.8	10.3	36.4	35.3	13.6	67.4	68.4	26.1	35.1	35.3	13.6
ExStream [28]	58.8	52.0	62.5	49.2	47.3	52.7	26.4	26.6	36.6	47.8	43.9	51.1
Forget	41.8	40.2	17.7	33.9	32.9	14.7	47.0	33.4	15.5	40.5	39.6	16.2
PRS(ours)	65.4	59.3	67.5	52.5	49.7	55.2	34.5	34.6	39.7	53.2	50.3	55.3
Forget	22.0	21.7	8.5	27.2	26.8	11.5	26.2	26.3	10.5	25.6	25.2	10.2

NUS-WIDEseq	Majority			Moderate			Minority			Overall		
	C-F1	O-F1	mAP	C-F1	O-F1	mAP	C-F1	O-F1	mAP	C-F1	O-F1	mAP
Multitask [9]	33.7	30.8	32.8	29.3	28.7	28.9	9.7	11.8	25.8	24.6	24.9	28.4
Finetune	0.6	4.6	4.1	2.3	2.8	6.0	5.2	7.4	9.4	4.2	5.1	7.1
Forget	100.0	100.0	47.3	100.0	100.0	39.3	100.0	100.0	44.6	100.0	100.0	44.4
EWC [35]	15.7	9.9	15.8	16.3	12.6	19.4	12.3	13.9	24.1	17.1	11.4	20.7
Forget	18.4	15.4	7.8	64.6	63.7	7.3	63.4	63.4	4.8	36.4	31.5	7.3
CRS [64]	28.4	17.8	21.9	13.6	14.2	18.5	10.4	11.8	20.6	16.8	15.0	20.1
Forget	33.6	29.2	14.7	67.8	66.7	18.1	96.5	96.2	20.3	61.5	57.8	18.7
GSS [3]	24.6	13.5	19.0	14.8	15.5	17.9	15.9	17.6	24.5	17.9	15.3	20.9
Forget	46.8	43.9	16.6	59.6	58.3	11.7	82.8	82.0	18.6	54.8	49.8	13.0
ExStream [28]	15.6	9.2	15.3	12.4	12.8	17.6	24.6	24.1	26.7	18.7	16.0	21.0
Forget	80.7	77.6	24.0	81.0	80.6	23.3	77.2	76.7	21.8	81.0	79.3	23.4
PRS(ours)	26.7	17.9	21.2	19.2	19.3	21.5	27.5	26.8	31.0	24.8	21.7	25.5
Forget	45.8	43.0	15.7	59.0	58.4	13.4	60.6	60.3	15.5	55.3	53.5	13.9

as the mAP. Additionally, we include the forgetting metric [10] to quantify the effectiveness of continual learning techniques. However, since this is a self-relative metric on the best past and present performance of the method, comparisons between different methods could be misleading (*e.g.* if a model performs poorly throughout training, small forgetting metric values can be observed as it has

Table 2. Results according to memory sizes and schedule permutations on *COCOseq*. We fix the memory size of 2000 for schedule experiments and the schedule of {0,3,1,2} for memory experiments. Refer to Table 1 for the nomenclatures.

COCOseq	Overall C-F1	O-F1	mAP	Overall C-F1	O-F1	mAP
	Schedule: 0, 1, 3, 2			Memory: 1000		
CRS [64]	49.2	46.9	50.8	44.2	41.6	47.1
GSS [3]	42.1	41.4	44.0	40.6	39.0	42.1
ExStream [28]	47.3	42.9	50.5	41.6	37.6	47.0
PRS(ours)	52.6	50.5	55.2	47.4	43.4	51.2
	Schedule: 2, 3, 0, 1			Memory: 2000		
CRS [64]	45.4	44.3	48.2	47.5	46.6	50.2
GSS [3]	33.5	33.9	38.5	43.2	43.0	44.4
ExStream [28]	41.6	35.2	45.7	47.8	43.9	51.1
PRS(ours)	50.4	47.7	53.1	53.2	50.3	55.3
	Schedule: 3, 1, 0, 2			Memory: 3000		
CRS [64]	47.7	45.9	49.7	49.4	48.6	51.1
GSS [3]	37.8	38.8	40.2	42.2	43.0	44.3
ExStream [28]	45.4	41.8	49.2	49.7	46.8	52.2
PRS(ours)	51.4	48.9	54.1	54.9	53.4	56.7

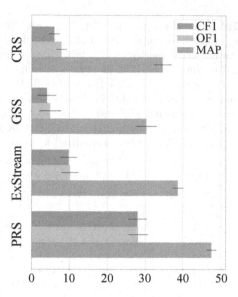

Fig. 4. Inter-task imbalance analysis on *NUS-WIDEseq*. We compare the performance for the smallest Task 3, for which our PRS robustly outperforms all the baselines.

little information to forget from the beginning). It is the reason for the absence of color for the best models with respect to this metric in the tables. In the Appendix, we also report the overall precision (O-P), recall (O-R), per-class precision (C-P) and recall (C-R) metrics.

Baselines. We compare our approach with six baselines including four state-of-the-art continual learning methods: EWC [35], CRS [64], GSS-Greedy [3] and ExStream [28]. In addition, the Multitask [9] can be regarded as an upper-bound performance as it is learned offline with minibatch training for a single epoch. The Finetune performs online training without any continual learning technique, and thus it can be regarded as a lower-bound performance. For training EWC, we fix the ResNet up to the penultimate layer in order to obtain sensible results; otherwise, it works poorly. More details for baselines are presented in the Appendix.

We use a fixed online input batch size of 10 and a replay-batch size of 10 in accordance with [3]. We use Adam [34] optimizer with $\beta_1 = 0.9$, $\beta_2 = 0.999$ and $\epsilon = 1e - 4$, and finetune all the layers unless stated otherwise. Furthermore, we set ρ between the range of $[-0.2, 0.2]$, and fix the memory size to 2000 (as done in [48]), which are 5.7% and 4.7% of the overall training data for *COCOseq* and *NUS-WIDEseq*, respectively.

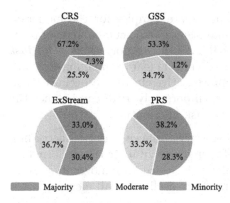

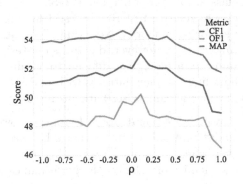

Fig. 5. The resulting memory distribution of the *COCOseq* tests in Table 1. ExStream [28] is the only *task-aware* method that knows the task distribution beforehand.

Fig. 6. Performance of PRS with different ρ in the range of $[-1, +1]$ on *COCOseq*. All results are the averages of 5 different random seeds.

6.2   Results

Table 1 compares continual learning performance between our PRS method and baselines on *COCOseq* and *NUS-WIDEseq*. In all comparable metrics of C-F1, O-F1 and mAP, PRS outperforms CRS [57], GSS [3] and even ExStream [28] that uses prior task information to pre-allocate the memory.

Schedule and Memory Permutations. Table 2 compares the robustness of PRS through random permutations of task schedule as well as different memory sizes. Interestingly, the performances of CRS, GSS and ExStream fluctuates depending on the permuted schedule, while our PRS is comparatively robust thanks to the balanced emphasis on all the learned classes. Moreover, PRS outperforms all the baselines with multiple memory sizes of $1000, 2000, 3000$.

Intra- and Inter-task Imbalance. Table 1 shows that PRS is competitive on the majority classes (*e.g.* marked in blue as the runner-up) and performs the best on both moderate and minority classes, showing its compelling robustness for the intra-task imbalances. Furthermore, Fig. 4 validates the robustness of PRS in the inter-task imbalance setting. As shown in Fig. 1 of the Appendix, tasks of NUS-WIDEseq are *imbalanced* in that the smallest Task 3 is 9.6 times smaller than that of the largest Task 1. Figure 4 compares the performances of all methods for the minority Task 3, for which PRS performs overwhelmingly better than the other baselines in all the metrics.

Memory Distribution After Training. Figure 5 compares the normalized memory distribution of the experiments in Table 1. CRS dominantly uses the memory for the majority classes while reserving only a small portion for the minority. This explains why CRS may perform better than PRS for the majority in Table 1, while sacrificing performance largely for the moderate and minority classes. On the other hand, GSS saves much more samples for the moderate classes relative to CRS, but still fails to maintain a sufficient number of samples for the minority. Note that Exstream balances the memory using *prior task information*. However, due to its clustering scheme via feature merging to maintain the memory, it is difficult to obtain representative clusters, especially when handling complex datasets with multi-labels. Importantly, PRS can balance the memory for all classes without any auxiliary task information.

Power of Allocation ρ. Figure 6 shows the performance variation according to different ρ. It confirms that a balance of memory is vital for the performance even when the input stream is highly imbalanced. Notice, as ρ moves away from the vicinity of balance, the performance gradually declines in all metrics.

Feature Analysis. Figure 7 shows the feature projections of CRS and PRS for test samples of MNIST and COCOseq using t-SNE [45]. PRS can represent the minority classes more discriminatively than CRS on both single-label MNIST and multi-label COCOseq experiments.

In the Appendix, we include more experimental results, including analysis on the memory gradients and performance on single-label classification and many more.

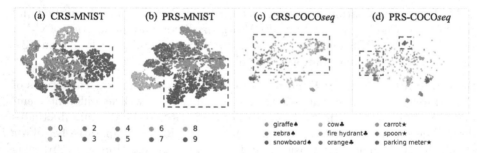

Fig. 7. t-SNE feature projection of CRS and PRS trained features for test samples of (a)–(b) MNIST and (c)–(d) COCOseq. We use the penultimate features of a 2-layer feedforward for MNIST and ResNet101 for COCOseq. As with the single-label experiments in the Appendix, we curate a sequential MNIST that follows a Pareto distribution [56] with a power value $\alpha=0.6$, which becomes increasingly long-tailed from 0 to 9. For COCOseq, we use the symbols of {Minority: ★, Moderate: ♣, Majority: ♠}. We emphasize that PRS represents the minority classes (in the blue box) much more discriminatively than the corresponding class features (in the red box) for CRS. (Color figure online)

7 Conclusion

This work explored a novel problem of multi-label continual learning, which naturally requires the model to learn from imbalanced data streams. We contributed two datasets and an effective memory maintenance algorithm, called *Partitioning Reservoir Sampling* to tackle this new challenge. Our results showed the importance of maintaining a well-rounded knowledge through balanced replay memory. As a future direction of research, the ability to learn online while automatically tuning the target partitions would be an exciting avenue to explore.

Acknowledgements. We express our gratitude for the helpful comments on the manuscript by Soochan Lee, Junsoo Ha and Hyunwoo Kim. This work was supported by Samsung Advanced Institute of Technology, Institute of Information & communications Technology Planning & Evaluation (IITP) grant (No.2019-0-01082, SW StarLab) and the international cooperation program by the NRF of Korea (NRF-2018K2A9A2A11080927).

References

1. Aljundi, R.: Continual Learning in Neural Networks. Ph.D. thesis, Department of Electrical Engineering, KU Leuven (2019)
2. Aljundi, R., Marcus, R., Tuytelaars, T.: Selfless sequential learning. arXiv preprint arXiv:1806.05421 (2019)
3. Aljundi, R., Lin, M., Goujaud, B., Bengio, Y.: Gradient based sample selection for online continual learning. In: Advances in Neural Information Processing Systems, pp. 11816–11825 (2019)
4. Bankier, M.: Power allocations: determining sample sizes for subnational areas. Am. Stat. **42**(3), 174–177 (1988)
5. Batista, G., Prati, R., Monard, M.: A study of the behavior of several methods for balancing machine learning training data. SIGKDD Explor **6**, 20–29 (2004)
6. Brahma, P.P., Othon, A.: Subset replay based continual learning for scalable improvement of autonomous systems. In: 2018 IEEE/CVF Conference on Computer Vision and Pattern Recognition Workshops (CVPRW), pp. 1179–11798. IEEE (2018)
7. Buda, M., Maki, A., Mazuorowski, M.: A systematic study of the class imbalance problem in convolutional neural networks. Neural Netw. **106**, 249–259 (2018)
8. Carroll, J.: Allocation of a sample between states. Australian Bureau of Census and Statistics (1970)
9. Caruaca, R.: Multitask learning. Mach. Learn. **28**, 41–75 (1997)
10. Chaudhry, A., Dokania, P.K., Ajanthan, T., Torr, P.H.: Riemannian walk for incremental learning: Understanding forgetting and intransigence. In: Proceedings of the European Conference on Computer Vision (ECCV), pp. 532–547 (2018)
11. Chaudhry, A., Ranzato, M., Rohrbach, M., Elhoseiny, M.: Efficient lifelong learning with a-gem. arXiv preprint arXiv:1812.00420 (2019)
12. Chaudhry, A., et al.: On tiny episodic memories in continual learning. arXiv preprint arXiv:1902.10486v4 (2019)
13. Chawla, N.V., Bowyer, K.W., Hall, L.O., Kegelmeyer, W.P.: Smote: synthetic minority over-sampling technique. J. Artif. Intell. Res. **16**, 321–357 (2002)
14. Chen, C., Liaw, A., Breiman, L., et al.: Using random forest to learn imbalanced data. Univ. Calif. Berkeley **110**(1–12), 24 (2004)
15. Chua, T.S., Tang, J., Hong, R., Li, H., luo, Z., Zheng, Y.: Nus-wide: a real-world web image database from national university of singapore. In: Proceedings of the ACM International Conference on Image and Video Retrieval, pp. 1–9 (2009)
16. Cui, Y., Jia, M., Lin, T., Song, Y., Belongie, S.: Class-balanced loss based on effective number of samples. In: Proceedings of the IEEE Conference on Computer Vision and Pattern Recognition, pp. 9268–9277 (2019)

17. d'Autume, C., Ruder, S., Kong, L., Yogatama, D.: Episodic memory in lifelong language learning. In: Advances in Neural Information Processing Systems, pp. 13143–13152 (2019)
18. Deng, J., Dong, W., Socher, R., Li, L.J., Li, K., Li, F.: Imagenet: a large-scale hierarchical image database. In: 2009 IEEE Conference on Computer Vision and Pattern Recognition, pp. 248–255. IEEE (2009)
19. Dong, Q., Gong, S., Zhu, X.: Imbalanced deep learning by minority class incremental rectification. TPAMI **41**, 1367–1381 (2019)
20. Douzas, G., Bacao, F.: Effective data generation for imbalanced learning using conditional generative adversarial networks. Expert Syst. Appl. **91**, 464–471 (2018)
21. Farquhar, S., Gal, Y.: Towards robust evaluations of continual learning. arXiv preprint arXiv:1805.09733 (2019)
22. Fellegi, I.P.: Should the Census Counts Be Adjusted for Allocation Purposes?-Equity Considerations. In: Current Topics in Survey Sampling, pp. 47–76 (1981)
23. French, R.: Catastrophic forgetting in connectionist networks. Trends Cogn. Sci. **3**(4), 128–135 (1999)
24. Ge, W., Yang, S., Yu, Y.: Multi-evidence filtering and fusion for multi-label classification, object detection and semantic segmentation based on weakly supervised learning. In: Proceedings of the IEEE Conference on Computer Vision and Pattern Recognition, pp. 1277–1286 (2018)
25. Guillaumin, M., Mensink, T., Verbeek, J., Schmid, C.: Tagprop: discriminative metric learning in nearest neighbor models for image auto-annotation. In: 2009 IEEE 12th International Conference on Computer Vision, pp. 309–316. IEEE (2009)
26. Guo, H., Zheng, K., Fan, X., Yu, H., Wang, S.: Visual attention consistency under image transforms for multi-label image classification. In: Proceedings of the IEEE Conference on Computer Vision and Pattern Recognition, pp. 729–739 (2019)
27. Han, X., Yu, P., Liu, Z., Sun, M., Li, P.: Hierarchical relation extraction with coarse-to-fine grained attention. In: Proceedings of the 2018 Conference on Empirical Methods in Natural Language Processing, pp. 2236–2245 (2018)
28. Hayes, T.L., Cahill, N.D., Kanan, C.: Memory efficient experience replay for streaming learning. In: 2019 International Conference on Robotics and Automation (ICRA), pp. 9769–9776. IEEE (2019)
29. He, H., Garcia, E.A.: Learning from imbalanced data. IEEE Trans. Knowl. Data Eng. **9**, 1263–1284 (2008)
30. He, K., Zhang, X., Ren, S., Sun, J.: Deep residual learning for image recognition. In: Proceedings of the IEEE Conference on Computer Vision and Pattern Recognition, pp. 770-778 (2016)
31. Huang, C., Li, Y., Change Loy, C., Tang, X.: Learning deep representation for imbalanced classification. In: Proceedings of the IEEE Conference on Computer Vision and Pattern Recognition, pp. 5375–5384 (2016)
32. Isele, D., Cosgun, A.: Selective experience replay for lifelong learning. arXiv preprint arXiv:1802.10269 (2018)
33. Japkowicz, N., Stephen, S.: The class imbalance problem: a systematic study. Intell. Data Anal. **6**, 429–449 (2002)
34. Kingma, D., Ba, J.: Adam: A method for stochastic optimization. arXiv preprint arXiv:1412.6980 (2015)
35. Kirkpatrick, J., et al.: Overcoming catastrophic forgetting in neural networks. In: Proceedings of the National Academy of Sciences (2017)
36. Krawczyk, B.: Learning from imbalanced data: open challenges and future directions. Progress Artif. Intell. **5**, 221–232 (2016)

37. Lee, S., Ha, J., Zhang, D., Kim, G.: A neural dirichlet process mixture model for task-free continual learning. arXiv preprint arXiv:2001.00689 (2020)
38. Lesort, T., Gepperth, A., Stoian, A., Filliat, D.: Marginal replay vs conditional replay for continual learning. In: Tetko, I.V., Kůrková, V., Karpov, P., Theis, F. (eds.) ICANN 2019. LNCS, vol. 11728, pp. 466–480. Springer, Cham (2019). https://doi.org/10.1007/978-3-030-30484-3_38
39. Li, Y., Zhao, L., Church, K., Elhoseiny, M.: Compositional continual language learning. In: International Conference on Learning Representations (2020)
40. Lin, T.Y., et al.: Microsoft COCO: common objects in context. In: Fleet, D., Pajdla, T., Schiele, B., Tuytelaars, T. (eds.) ECCV 2014. LNCS, vol. 8693, pp. 740–755. Springer, Cham (2014). https://doi.org/10.1007/978-3-319-10602-1_48
41. Liu, Y., Cong, Y., Sun, G.: L3doc: lifelong 3D object classification. arXiv preprint arXiv:1912.06135 (2019)
42. Liu, Y., Sheng, L., Shao, J., Yan, J., Xiang, S., Pan, C.: Multi-label image classification via knowledge distillation from weakly-supervised detection. In: Proceedings of the 26th ACM international conference on Multimedia, pp. 700–708 (2018)
43. Liu, Z., Miao, Z., Zhan, X., Wang, J., Gong, B., Yu, S.X.: Large-scale long-tailed recognition in an open world. In: Proceedings of the IEEE Conference on Computer Vision and Pattern Recognition, pp. 2537–2546 (2019)
44. Lopez-Paz, D., Ranzato, M.: Gradient episodic memory for continual learning. In: Advances in Neural Information Processing Systems, pp. 6467–6476 (2017)
45. van der Maaten, L., Hinton, G.: Visualizing data using t-sne. J. Mach. Learn. Res. **9**, 2579–2605 (2008)
46. Maciejewski, T., Stefanowski, J.: Local neighbourhood extension of smote for mining imbalanced data. In: 2011 IEEE Symposium on Computational Intelligence and Data Mining (CIDM), pp. 104–111. IEEE (2011)
47. Makadia, A., Pavlovic, V., Kumar, S.: A new baseline for image annotation. In: Forsyth, D., Torr, P., Zisserman, A. (eds.) ECCV 2008. LNCS, vol. 5304, pp. 316–329. Springer, Heidelberg (2008). https://doi.org/10.1007/978-3-540-88690-7_24
48. Maltoni, D., Lomonaco, V.: Continuous learning in single-incremental-task scenarios. Elsevier Neural Netw. J. **116**, 56–73 (2019)
49. McCloskey, M., Cohen, N.J.: Catastrophic interference in conncectionist networks. Psychol. Learn. Motiv. **24**, 109–265 (1989)
50. Newman, M.: Power laws, pareto distributions and zipf's law. Contemp. Phys. **46**, 323–351 (2005)
51. Nguyen, G., Jun, T.J., Tran, T., Kim, D.: Contcap: a comprehensive framework for continual image captioning. arXiv preprint arXiv:1909.08745 (2019)
52. Ouyang, W., Wang, X., Zhang, C., Yang, X.: Factors in finetuning deep model for object detection with long-tail distribution. In: Proceedings of the IEEE Conference on Computer Vision and Pattern Recognition, pp. 864–873 (2016)
53. Parisi, G.I., Tani, J., Weber, C., Wermter, S.: Lifelong learning of human actions with deep neural network self-organization. Neural Netw. **96**, 137–149 (2017)
54. Parisi, G.I., Tani, J., Weber, C., Wermter, S.: Lifelong learning of spatiotemporal representations with dual-memory recurrent self-organization. Front. Neurorobotics **12**, 78 (2018)
55. Ratcliff, R.: Conncectionist models of recognition memory: constraints imposed by learning and forgetting functions. Pscyhol. Rev. **97**(2), 285–308 (1990)
56. Reed, W.J.: The pareto, zipf and other power laws. Econ. Lett. **74**, 15–19 (2001)
57. Riemer, M., et al.: Learning to learn without forgetting by maximizing transfer and minimizing interference. arXiv preprint arXiv:1810.11910 (2019)

58. Rolnick, D., Ahuja, A., Schwarz, J., Lillicrap, T.P., Wayne, G.: Experience replay for continual learning. In: Advances in Neural Information Processing Systems, pp. 350–360 (2019)
59. Rusu, A.A., et al.: Progressive neural networks. arXiv preprint arXiv:1606.04671 (2016)
60. Shin, H., Lee, J.K., Kim, J., Kim, J.: Continual learning with deep generative replay. In: Advances in Neural Information Processing Systems, pp. 2990–2999 (2017)
61. Shmelkov, K., Schmid, C., Alahari, K.: Incremental learning of object detectors without catastrophic forgetting. In: Proceedings of the IEEE International Conference on Computer Vision, pp. 3400–3409 (2017)
62. Van Horn, G., Perona, P.: The devil is in the tails: fine-grained classification in the wild. arXiv preprint arXiv:1709.01450 (2017)
63. van de Ven, G.M., Andreas, S.T.: Three scenarios for continual learning. In: NeurIPS Continual Learning workshop (2019)
64. Vitter, J.S.: Random sampling with a reservoir. ACM Trans. Math. Softw. (TOMS) **11**(1), 37–57 (1985)
65. Wang, J., Yang, Y., Mao, J., Huang, Z., Huang, C., Xu, W.: Cnn-rnn: a unified framework for multi-label image classification. In: Proceedings of the IEEE Conference on Computer Vision and Pattern Recognition, pp. 2285–2294 (2016)
66. Wang, Y., Ramana, D., Hebert, M.: Learning to model the tail. In: Advances in Neural Information Processing Systems, pp. 7029–7039 (2017)
67. Wang, Z., Chen, T., Li, G., Xu, R., Lin, L.: Multi-label image recognition by recurrently discovering attentional regions. In: Proceedings of the IEEE International Conference on Computer Vision, pp. 464–472 (2017)
68. Wei, Z.M.C.X.S., Wang, P., Guo, Y.: Multi-label image recognition with graph convolutional networks. In: Proceedings of the IEEE Conference on Computer Vision and Pattern Recognition, pp. 5177–5186 (2019)
69. Yin, X., Yu, X., Sohn, K., Liu, X., Chandraker, M.: Feature transfer learning for deep face recognition with under-represented data. arXiv preprint arXiv:1803.09014 (2019)
70. Yoon, J., Yang, E., Lee, J., Hwang, S.J.: Lifelong learning with dynamically expandable networks. arXiv preprint arXiv:1708.01547 (2018)
71. Zenke, F., Poole, B., Ganguli, S.: Continual learning through syanptic intelligence. Proc. Mach. Learn. Res. **70**, 3987 (2017)
72. Zhang, N., et al.: Long-tail relation extraction via knowledge graph embeddings and graph convolution networks. arXiv preprint arXiv:1903.01306 (2019)
73. Zhu, F., Li, H., Ouyang, W., Yu, N., Wang, X.: Learning spatial regularization with imagelevel supervisions for multi-label image classification. In: Proceedings of the IEEE Conference on Computer Vision and Pattern Recognition, pp. 5513–5522 (2017)
74. Zhu, X., Anguelov, D., Ramanan, D.: Capturing long-tail distributions of object subcategories. In: Proceedings of the IEEE Conference on Computer Vision and Pattern Recognition, pp. 915–922 (2014)

Guided Collaborative Training
for Pixel-Wise Semi-Supervised Learning

Zhanghan Ke[1,2]($\boxtimes$), Di Qiu[2], Kaican Li[2], Qiong Yan[2], and Rynson W.H. Lau[1]

[1] Department of Computer Science, City University of Hong Kong,
Hong Kong, China
kezhanghan@outlook.com, rynson.lau@cityu.edu.hk
[2] SenseTime Research, Hong Kong, China
{kezhanghan,qiudi,likaican,yanqiong}@sensetime.com

Abstract. We investigate the generalization of semi-supervised learning (SSL) to diverse pixel-wise tasks. Although SSL methods have achieved impressive results in image classification, the performances of applying them to pixel-wise tasks are unsatisfactory due to their need for dense outputs. In addition, existing pixel-wise SSL approaches are only suitable for certain tasks as they usually require to use task-specific properties. In this paper, we present a new SSL framework, named Guided Collaborative Training (GCT), for pixel-wise tasks, with two main technical contributions. First, GCT addresses the issues caused by the dense outputs through a novel flaw detector. Second, the modules in GCT learn from unlabeled data collaboratively through two newly proposed constraints that are independent of task-specific properties. As a result, GCT can be applied to a wide range of pixel-wise tasks without structural adaptation. Our extensive experiments on four challenging vision tasks, including semantic segmentation, real image denoising, portrait image matting, and night image enhancement, show that GCT outperforms state-of-the-art SSL methods by a large margin.

Keywords: Semi-supervised learning · Pixel-wise vision tasks

1 Introduction

Deep learning has been remarkably successful in many vision tasks. Nonetheless, collecting a large amount of labeled data for training is costly, especially for pixel-wise tasks that require a precise label for each pixel, *e.g.*, the category mask in semantic segmentation and the clean picture in image denoising. Recently, semi-supervised learning (SSL) has become an important research direction to alleviate the lack of labels, by appending unlabeled data for training. Many SSL methods have been proposed for image classification with impressive results, including adversarial-based methods [11,25,39,43], consistent-based

Electronic supplementary material The online version of this chapter (https:// doi.org/10.1007/978-3-030-58601-0_26) contains supplementary material, which is available to authorized users.

© Springer Nature Switzerland AG 2020
A. Vedaldi et al. (Eds.): ECCV 2020, LNCS 12358, pp. 429–445, 2020.
https://doi.org/10.1007/978-3-030-58601-0_26

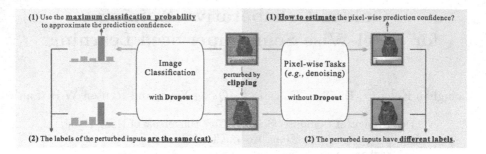

Fig. 1. Difficulties of Pixel-wise SSL. The dense outputs in pixel-wise tasks causes unsatisfactory SSL performances since (1) it is difficult to estimate the pixel-wise prediction confidence and (2) existing perturbations designed for SSL are not suitable for dense outputs.

methods [21,23,36,41], and methods that are combined with self-supervised learning [42,46]. In contrast, only a few works have applied SSL to specific pixel-wise tasks [7,19,20,30], and they mainly focus on semantic segmentation.

In this work, we investigate the generalization of SSL to diverse pixel-wise tasks. Such generalization is important in order for SSL to be used in new vision tasks with minimal efforts. However, generalizing existing pixel-wise SSL methods is not straightforward since they are designed for certain tasks by using task-specific properties (Sect. 2.2), *e.g.*., assuming similar semantic contents between the input and output. Another possible generalization approach is to apply SSL methods designed for image classification to pixel-wise tasks. But there are two critical issues caused by the dense outputs, as illustrated in Fig. 1, leading to unsatisfactory performances of these methods on pixel-wise tasks.

First, dense outputs require pixel-wise prediction confidences (Sect. 2.3), which are difficult to estimate. Pixel-wise tasks are either pixel-wise classification (*e.g.*., semantic segmentation and shadow detection) or pixel-wise regression (*e.g.*., image denoising and matting). Although we may use the maximum classification probability to represent the prediction confidence in pixel-wise classification, it is unavailable in pixel-wise regression. Second, existing perturbations designed for SSL (Sect. 2.4) are not suitable for dense outputs. In pixel-wise tasks, strong perturbations in the input, *e.g.*., clipping in Mean Teacher [41], will change the input image and its labels. As a result, the perturbed inputs from the same original image have different labels, which is undesirable in SSL. Besides, the perturbations through Dropout [40] are disabled in most pixel-wise tasks. Although Dual Student [21] proposes to create perturbations through different model initializations, its training strategy can only be used in image classification.

To address the above two issues caused by dense outputs, we propose a new SSL framework, named Guided Collaborative Training (GCT), for pixel-wise tasks. It includes three modules – two models for the specific task (the task models) and a novel flaw detector. GCT overcomes the two issues by: (1) approximating the pixel-wise prediction confidence by the output of the flaw detector, *i.e.*, a flaw probability map, and (2) extending the perturbations used in Dual Student to pixel-wise tasks. Since different model initializations lead to inconsistent predictions for the same input, we can ensemble the reliable pixels, *i.e.*, the pixels with lower flaw probabilities, in the predictions. In addition, minimizing the flaw probability map should help correct the unreliable pixels in the predictions. Motivated by these ideas, we introduce two SSL constraints, a dynamic consistency constraint between the task models and a flaw correction constraint between the flaw detector and each of the task models, to allow the modules in GCT to learn from unlabeled data collaboratively under the guidance of the flaw probability map rather than the task-specific properties. As a result, GCT can be applied to diverse pixel-wise tasks, simply by replacing the task models without structural adaptations.

We evaluate GCT on the standard benchmarks for semantic segmentation (pixel-wise classification) and real image denoising (pixel-wise regression). We also conduct experiments on our own practical datasets, *i.e.*, the datasets with a large proportion of unlabeled data, for portrait image matting and night image enhancement (both are pixel-wise regression) to demonstrate the generalization of GCT on real applications. GCT surpasses start-of-the-art SSL methods [19,41,46] that can be applied to these four challenging pixel-wise tasks. We envision that this work will contribute to future research and development of new vision tasks with scarce labels.

2   Related Work

2.1   SSL for Image Classification

Our work is related to two main branches of SSL methods designed for image classification. The adversarial-based methods [11,25,39,43] assemble the discriminator from GAN [14], and try to match the latent distributions between labeled and unlabeled data through the image-level adversarial constraint. The consistent-based methods [21,23,36,41] learn from unlabeled data by applying a consistency constraint to the predictions under different perturbations. Apart from them, some latest works combine self-supervised learning with SSL [42,46] or expand the training set by interpolating labeled and unlabeled data [5,6].

2.2   SSL for Pixel-Wise Tasks

Existing research on pixel-wise SSL mainly focuses on semantic segmentation. GANs dominate in this topic through the combination with the SSL methods derived from image classification. For example, Hung *et al.* [19] extract reliable predictions to generate pseudo labels for training. Mittal *et al.* [30] modify Mean Teacher [41] to a multi-label classifier and use it as a filter to remove uncertain categories. Besides, Lee *et al.* [18] and Huang *et al.* [24] study weak-supervised learning in the SSL context. However, these works require pre-defined categories, which is a general property of classification-based tasks. Chen *et al.* [7] apply SSL in face sketc.h synthesis, which belongs to pixel-wise regression. It regards the pre-trained VGG [38] network as a feature extractor to impose a perceptual constraint on the unlabeled data. Unfortunately, the perceptual constraint can only be used in tasks that have similar semantic contents between the inputs and outputs. For example, it does not work on segmentation since the semantic content of the category mask is different from the input image.

2.3   Prediction Confidence in SSL

Prediction confidence is necessary for computing the SSL constraints, which consider the predictions with higher confidence values as the targets, *i.e.*, pseudo labels. Earlier works show that the averaged targets are more confident. For example, Temporal Model [23] accumulates the predictions over epochs as the targets; Mean Teacher [41] defines an explicit model by exponential moving average to generate the targets; FastSWA [4] further averages the models between epochs to produce better targets. Others [25,28,39] regard the maximum classification probability as the prediction confidence.

In pixel-wise SSL, the outputs of the discriminator are used to approximate the prediction confidence [19,30]. Instead, we propose the flaw detector to estimate the prediction confidence, with two key differences. First, the flaw detector predicts a dense probability map with location information while the discriminator predicts an image-level probability. Second, we use the ground truth of the labeled data to generate the targets of the flaw detector.

2.4   Perturbations in SSL

Many SSL methods heavily rely on perturbations for training. The consistent-based methods [23,35,41] utilize data augmentations to alter the inputs. To further improve the inconsistency, VAT [31] generates virtual adversarial noises while S4L [46] adds a rotation operation to the inputs. Others such as MixMatch [6] and ReMixMatch [5] generate perturbed samples by data interpolation. Apart from the perturbations in the inputs, Dropout perturbs the predictions through a random selection of nodes [34]. The models in Dual Student [21] have inconsistent predictions for the same input due to different initializations.

Since the perturbations from both data augmentations and Dropout are not suitable for dense outputs, GCT follows Dual Student in creating perturbations. However, unlike Dual Student, GCT learns from unlabeled data through the two SSL constraints based on the flaw detector, allowing GCT to be applicable to diverse pixel-wise tasks.

3   Guided Collaborative Training

3.1   Overview of GCT

In this section, we first present an overview of GCT. We then introduce the flaw detector and the two proposed SSL constraints. Figure 2 shows the GCT framework. T^1 and T^2 are the two task models, which are referred to as T^k

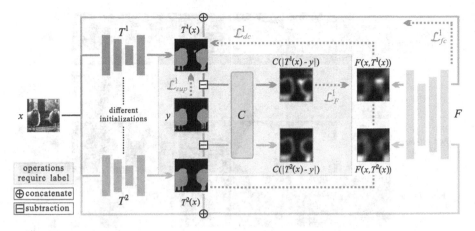

Fig. 2. The GCT Framework. It consists of two task models T^1, T^2 and a flaw detector F. Since T^1 and T^2 have different initializations, their predictions for the same x are inconsistent. These two task models learn from the unlabeled data through $\mathcal{L}_{dc}$ and $\mathcal{L}_{fc}$ under the guidance of the outputs of F. The ground truth of F is calculated on the labeled subset by an image processing pipeline C, which takes $T^1(x)$ (or $T^2(x)$) and y as the input. Here we take semantic segmentation as an example.

($k \in \{1, 2\}$) in the following context. The architecture of T^k is arbitrary, and GCT allows the task models to have different architectures. The only requirement is that T^1 and T^2 should have different initializations to form the perturbations between them (which is the same as Dual Student). F denotes the flaw detector. In SSL, we have a dataset consisting of a labeled subset $\mathcal{X}_l$ with labels $\mathcal{Y}$ and an unlabeled subset $\mathcal{X}_u$. The inputs $\mathcal{X} = \mathcal{X}_l \cup \mathcal{X}_u$ for both T^1 and T^2 are exactly the same. Given an $x \in \mathcal{X}$, the GCT framework first predicts $T^k(x)$ of size $H \times W \times O$, where the value of O is defined by the specific task. Then, the concatenation of x and $T^k(x)$ is processed by F to estimate the flaw probability map $F(x, T^k(x))$ of size $H \times W \times 1$. The prediction confidence map can be approximated by $1 - F(x, T^k(x))$. We train GCT iteratively in two steps like GAN [14].

In the first step, we train T^k with fixed F. For the labeled data, the prediction $T^k(x_l)$ is supervised by its corresponding label y as:

$$\mathcal{L}^k_{sup}(x_l, y) = \sum_{h,w,o} \mathcal{R}(T^k(x_l)^{(h,w,o)}, y^{(h,w,o)}), \tag{1}$$

where $\mathcal{R}(\cdot, \cdot)$ is a task-specific constraint, and (h, w, o) is a pixel index. To learn the unlabeled data, we propose a dynamic consistency constraint $\mathcal{L}_{dc}$ and a flaw correction constraint $\mathcal{L}_{fc}$, which are guided by the flaw probability map and will be described in Sect. 3.3 and Sect. 3.4, respectively. The final constraint for T^k is a combination of three constraints as:

$$\mathcal{L}^k_T(\mathcal{X}, \mathcal{Y}) = \sum_{\{x_l, y\}} \mathcal{L}^k_{sup}(x_l, y) + \sum_{x} \left(\lambda_{dc} \mathcal{L}^k_{dc}(x) + \lambda_{fc} \mathcal{L}^k_{fc}(x) \right), \tag{2}$$

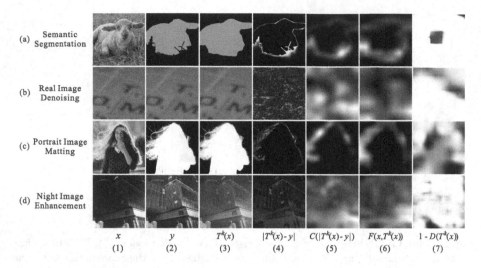

(a)	Semantic Segmentation						
(b)	Real Image Denoising						
(c)	Portrait Image Matting						
(d)	Night Image Enhancement						
	x (1)	y (2)	$T^k(x)$ (3)	$\lvert T^k(x)-y\rvert$ (4)	$C(\lvert T^k(x)-y\rvert)$ (5)	$F(x,T^k(x))$ (6)	$1-D(T^k(x))$ (7)

Fig. 3. Flaw Detector *vs.* Discriminator. The flaw detector F outputs $F(x,T^k(x))$ that highlights the flaw regions of $T^k(x)$ correctly. However, the fully convolutional discriminator D tends to activate all small errors. We show $1-D(T^k(x))$ that activates the fake probability of each pixel, which has a similar meaning to the flaw probability. Since $\lvert T^k(x)-y\rvert$ is sparse and sharp, we use $C(\lvert T^k(x)-y\rvert)$ as the ground truth of F.

where $\{x_l, y\}$ is a pair of labeled data. λ_{dc} and λ_{fc} are hyper-parameters to balance the two SSL constraints.

In the second step, F learns from the labeled subset. We calculate the ground truth of F through a classical image processing pipeline C based on $T^k(x_l)$ and y. In our framework, F is trained by using Mean Square Error (MSE) as:

$$\mathcal{L}_F^k(\mathcal{X}_l, \mathcal{Y}) = \sum_{\{x_l, y\}} \left(\frac{1}{2} \sum_{h,w} \left(F(x_l, T^k(x_l))^{(h,w)} - C(\lvert T^k(x_l) - y\rvert)^{(h,w)} \right)^2 \right), \quad (3)$$

where $C(\lvert T^k(x_l) - y\rvert)$ is the ground truth of F, which will be discussed in Sec. 3.2.

3.2   Flaw Detector

On the labeled subset, the goal of the flaw detector F is to learn the flaw probability map $F(x_l, T^k(x_l))$ that indicates the difference between $T^k(x_l)$ and y, i.e., the flaw regions in $T^k(x_l)$. One simple way to find the flaw regions is $\lvert T^k(x_l) - y\rvert$. However, it is difficult to learn many tasks since it is sparse and sharp (column (4) of Fig. 3). To address this problem, we introduce an image processing pipeline C that converts $\lvert T^k(x_l) - y\rvert$ to a dense probability map (column (5) of Fig. 3). C consists of three basic image processing operations: dilation, blurring and normalization. To estimate the flaw probability map $F(x_u, T^k(x_u))$ for the unlabeled data, we apply a common SSL assumption [48]: the distribution of unlabeled data is the same as that of the labeled data. Therefore, F trained on the labeled subset should also work well on the unlabeled subset.

The architecture of the flaw detector is similar to the fully convolutional discriminator D in [19]. However, D averages all predicted pixels to get a single confidence value during training, as its target is an image-level real or fake probability. In pixel-wise tasks, the prediction is usually accurate for some pixels but not the others, and pixels of higher accuracy should have higher confidence. Using an average confidence to represent the overall confidence is not appropriate. For example, $T^1(x)$ may be more confident (more accurate) than $T^2(x)$ in a small local region although the average prediction confidence of $T^1(x)$ is lower than $T^2(x)$. Therefore, the per-pixel prediction confidence (from the flaw detector) is more meaningful than the average prediction confidence (from the discriminator) in pixel-wise tasks. Figure 3 visualizes the results of F and D in the four validated tasks.

3.3   Dynamic Consistency Constraint

The two task models in GCT have inconsistent predictions for the same input x due to the perturbations between them. We use the dynamic consistency constraint $\mathcal{L}_{dc}$ to ensemble the reliable pixels in $T^1(x)$ and $T^2(x)$. Typically, the standard consistency constraint [23,41] is unidirectional, e.g.., from the ensemble model to the temporary model. Here, "dynamic" indicates that our $\mathcal{L}_{dc}$ is bidirectional and its direction changes with the flaw probability (Fig. 4(a)). Intuitively, if a pixel in $T^1(x)$ has a lower flaw probability, we treat it as the pseudo label to the corresponding pixel in $T^2(x)$. To assure the quality of the pseudo label, we introduce a flaw threshold $\xi \in [0,1]$ to disable $\mathcal{L}_{dc}$ for the pixels that have higher flaw probability values than ξ in both $T^1(x)$ and $T^2(x)$. Through this process, there is an effective knowledge exchange between the task models, making them collaborators.

Formally, given a sample $x \in \mathcal{X}$, GCT outputs $T^1(x)$, $T^2(x)$, and their corresponding flaw probability maps $F(x, T^1(x))$, $F(x, T^2(x))$ through forward propagation. We first normalize the values in $F(x, T^k(x))$ to $[0,1]$, and then set the pixels that are larger than ξ to 1 as:

$$F(x, T^k(x))^{(h,w)} \leftarrow \max \left(F(x, T^k(x))^{(h,w)}, \left\{ F(x, T^k(x))^{(h,w)} > \xi \right\}_1 \right). \quad (4)$$

$\{condition\}_1$ is a boolean-to-integer function, which outputs 1 when the condition is true and 0 otherwise. We define the dynamic consistency constraint for T^k as:

$$\mathcal{L}_{dc}^k(x) = \frac{1}{2} \sum_{h,w} \left(m_{dc}^k(x)^{(h,w)} \sum_o \left(T^k(x)^{(h,w,o)} - T^{\tilde{k}}(x)^{(h,w,o)} \right)^2 \right),$$

$$\text{where} \quad m_{dc}^k(x)^{(h,w)} = \left\{ F(x, T^k(x))^{(h,w)} > F(x, T^{\tilde{k}}(x))^{(h,w)} \right\}_1. \tag{5}$$

$\tilde{k}$ represents the other task model, e.g.., $\tilde{k} = 2$ when $k = 1$. If a flaw probability value in $F(x, T^{\tilde{k}}(x))$ is smaller than both ξ and the corresponding pixel in $F(x, T^k(x))$, T^k will learn this pixel from $T^{\tilde{k}}$ through $\mathcal{L}_{dc}^k$. We use MSE since it is

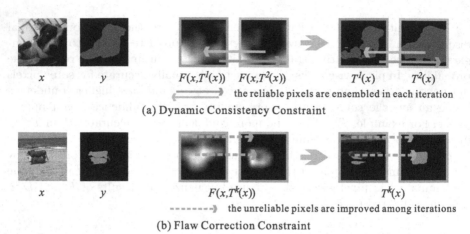

the reliable pixels are ensembled in each iteration

(a) Dynamic Consistency Constraint

the unreliable pixels are improved among iterations

(b) Flaw Correction Constraint

Fig. 4. Proposed SSL Constraints. (a) The dynamic consistency constraint exchanges the confident knowledge between the task models. (b) The flaw correction constraint minimizes the flaw probability map for each task model.

widely used in SSL and is general enough for many tasks. To prevent unreliable knowledge exchange at the beginning of training, we apply a cosine ramp-up operation with η epochs (from the standard consistency constraint) to $\mathcal{L}_{dc}$.

3.4   Flaw Correction Constraint

Apart from $\mathcal{L}_{dc}$, the flaw correction constraint $\mathcal{L}_{fc}$ attempts to correct the unreliable predictions of the task models (Fig. 4(b)). The key idea behinds $\mathcal{L}_{fc}$ is to force the values in the flaw probability map to become zero. We define $\mathcal{L}_{fc}$ for T^k (with F being fixed) as:

$$\mathcal{L}_{fc}^k(x) = \frac{1}{2} \sum_{h,w} \left(m_{fc}(x)^{(h,w)} \left(F(x, T^k(x))^{(h,w)} - 0 \right)^2 \right). \tag{6}$$

We use a binary mask $m_{fc}(x)$ to enable $\mathcal{L}_{fc}$ on the pixels without $\mathcal{L}_{dc}$, i.e., the pixels with unreliable predictions in both task models:

$$m_{fc}(x)^{(h,w)} = \left\{ F(x, T^1(x))^{(h,w)} > \xi \text{ AND } F(x, T^2(x))^{(h,w)} > \xi \right\}_1. \tag{7}$$

We consider that the flaw detector F helps improve the task models through $\mathcal{L}_{fc}$. For a system containing only one task model and the flaw detector, the objectives can be derived from Eq. (3) and (6) as:

$$\min_F V_{GCT}(F) = \frac{1}{2} \mathbb{E}_{\{x_l,y\} \sim P_{\mathcal{X}_l,\mathcal{Y}}} [(F(x_l, T^k(x_l)) - C(|T^k(x_l) - y|))^2],$$
$$\min_T V_{GCT}(T^k) = \frac{1}{2} \mathbb{E}_{x \sim P_{\mathcal{X}}} [(F(x, T^k(x)) - 0)^2], \tag{8}$$

where $\mathcal{X}_l$ and $\mathcal{X}$ have the same distribution. We simplify Eq. (8) by removing the pixel summation operation. In such situation, F learns the flaw probability map while T^k optimizes it with a zero label. If we assume that the training process converges to an optimal solution in iteration t^*, we have:

$$\lim_{t \to t^*} C(|T^k(x_l) - y|) = 0 \quad \Rightarrow \quad \lim_{t \to t^*} V_{GCT}(F) = V_{GCT}(T^k), \quad (9)$$

where t is the current iteration. Hence, the objective $V_{GCT}(F)$ changes during the training process and is equal to $V_{GCT}(T^k)$ when $t = t^*$. The alignment in the objectives indicates that F and T^k are collaborative to some degree.

To illustrate the difference between $\mathcal{L}_{fc}$ and the adversarial constraint, we compare Eq. (8) with the objectives of LSGAN [29]. If we modify LSGAN for SSL, its objectives should be:

$$\min_{D} V_{LSGAN}(D) = \frac{1}{2}\mathbb{E}_{x \sim P_\mathcal{X}}\left[(D(T^k(x)) - 1)^2\right] + \frac{1}{2}\mathbb{E}_{y \sim P_y}\left[(D(y)) - 0)^2\right],$$
$$\min_{T^k} V_{LSGAN}(T^k) = \frac{1}{2}\mathbb{E}_{x \sim P_\mathcal{X}}\left[(D(T^k(x)) - 0)^2\right], \quad (10)$$

where D is the standard discriminator that tries to differentiate $T^k(x)$ and y. In contrast, T^k tries to match the distributions between $T^k(x)$ and y. Here we reverse the labels, $i.e.$, 1 for fake and 0 for real, to be consistent with Eq. (8). Since the targets of D are constants, we have:

$$\lim_{t \to t^*} V_{LSGAN}(D) \neq V_{LSGAN}(T^k), \quad (11)$$

which means that D and T^k are adversarial during the whole training process.

4 Experiments

In order to evaluate our framework under different ratios of the labeled data, we experiment on the standard benchmarks for semantic segmentation and real image denoising. We also experiment on the practical datasets created for portrait image matting and night image enhancement to demonstrate the generalization of GCT in real applications. We further conduct ablation experiments to analyze various aspects of GCT.

Implementation Details. We compare GCT with the model trained by the labeled data only (SupOnly) and several state-of-the-art SSL methods that can be applied to various pixel-wise tasks: (1) the adversarial-based method proposed in [19] (AdvSSL); (2) the consistent-based Mean Teacher (MT) [41]; (3) the self-supervised SSL (S4L) [46]. For AdvSSL, we remove the constraint that requires classification probability to make it compatible with pixel-wise regression. For MT, we use MSE for the consistency constraint. We do not add Gaussian noise as extra perturbations since it will degrade the performance. For S4L, a four-category classifier trained by Cross Entropy is added to the end of the task model to predict the rotation angles. ($0°$, $90°$, $180°$, $270°$).

Experimental Setup. We notice that existing works of pixel-wise SSL usually report a fully supervised baseline with a lower performance than the original paper due to inconsistent hyper-parameters. In image classification, a similar situation has been discussed by [32]. To fairly evaluate the performance of SSL, we define some training rules to improve the SupOnly baselines. We denote the total number of trained samples as $N = S*T*b$, where S is the training epochs, T is the number of iterations in each epoch, and b is the batch size, which is fixed in each task. For the experiments performed on the standard benchmarks:

(1) We train the fully supervised baseline according to the hyper-parameters from the original paper to achieve a comparable result. The same hyper-parameters (except S) are used in (2) and (3).
(2) We use the same S as in (1) to train the models supervised by the labeled subset (SupOnly). Although T decreases as the labeled data reduces, to prevent overfitting, we do not increase N by training more epochs.
(3) We adjust S to ensure that N in SSL experiments is the same as (1). In SSL experiments, each batch contains both labeled and unlabeled data. We define "epoch" as going through the unlabeled subset for once. Meanwhile, the labeled subset is repeated several times inside an epoch.

By following these rules, the SupOnly baselines obtain good enough performance and do not overfit. The models trained by SSL methods have the same computational overhead, *i.e.*, the same N, as the fully supervised baseline. For experiments on the practical datasets, we first train S epochs for the SupOnly baselines. Afterwards, we train the SSL models with the same S. We use the grid search to find suitable hyper-parameters for all SSL methods.

4.1   Semantic Segmentation Experiments

Semantic segmentation [9,10,27] takes an image as input and predicts a series of category masks, which link each pixel in the input image to a class (Fig. 3(a)). We conduct experiments on the Pascal VOC 2012 dataset [12], which comprises 20 foreground classes along with 1 background class. The extra annotation set from the Segmentation Boundaries Dataset (SBD) [16] is combined to expand the dataset. Therefore, we have 10,582 training samples and 1,449 validation samples. During training, the input images are cropped to 321 × 321 after random scaling and horizontal flipping. Following previous works [19,30], we use DeepLab-v2 [9] with the ResNet-101 [17] backbone as the SupOnly baselines and as the task model in SSL methods. The same configurations as the original paper of DeepLab-v2 are applied, except the multi-scale fusion trick.

For SSL, we randomly extract 1/16, 1/8, 1/4, 1/2 samples as the labeled subset, and use the rest of the training set as the unlabeled subset. Note that the same data splits are used in all SSL methods. Table 1 shows the mean Intersection-over-Union (mIOU) on the PASCAL VOC 2012 dataset with pre-training on the Microsoft COCO dataset [26]. GCT achieves a performance increase of 1.26% (under 1/2 labels) to 3.76% (under 1/8 labels) over the

Table 1. Results of Semantic Segmentation. We report mIOU (%) on the validation set of Pascal VOC 2012 averaged over 3 runs. The task model is DeepLab-v2.

Methods	1/16 labels	1/8 labels	1/4 labels	1/2 labels	Full labels
SupOnly	64.55	68.38	70.69	73.56	75.32
MT [41]	66.08	69.81	71.28	73.23	75.28
S4L [46]	64.71	68.65	70.97	73.43	75.38
AdvSSL [19]	65.67	69.89	71.53	74.48	**75.86**
GCT (Our)	**67.19**	**72.14**	**73.62**	**74.82**	75.73

Table 2. Results of Real Image Denoising. We report PSNR (dB) on the validation set of SIDD averaged over 3 runs. The task model is DHDN.

Methods	1/16 labels	1/8 labels	1/4 labels	1/2 labels	Full labels
SupOnly	37.52	38.16	38.74	39.14	39.38
MT [41]	37.73	38.22	38.64	39.08	39.43
S4L [46]	37.81	38.32	38.88	39.21	39.16
AdvSSL [19]	37.85	38.28	38.83	39.18	39.47
GCT (Our)	**38.13**	**38.56**	**38.96**	**39.30**	**39.51**

SupOnly baselines. Moreover, our fully supervised baseline (75.32%) is comparable with the original paper of DeepLab-v2 (75.14%), which is better than the result reported in [19] (73.6%). Therefore, all SSL methods only have slight improvement under the full labels.

4.2 Real Image Denoising Experiments

Real image denoising [3,15,47] is a task that devotes to removing the real noise, rather synthetic noise, from an input natural image (Fig. 3(b)). We conduct experiments on the SIDD dataset [1], which is one of the largest benchmarks on real image denoising. It contains 160 image pairs (noisy image and clean image) for training and 40 image pairs for validation. We split each image pair into multiple patches with size 256×256 for training. The total training samples is about 30,000. We use DHDN [33], a method that won the second place in the NTRIE 2019 real image denoising challenge [2], as the task model since the code for the first place winner has not been published. The peak-signal-to-noise-ratio (PSNR) is used as the validation metric.

In image denoising, even small errors between the prediction and the ground truth can result in obvious visual artifacts. It means that the reliable pseudo labels are difficult to obtain, *i.e.*, this task is difficult for SSL. We notice that the task models with the same architecture in GCT have similar predictions. Therefore, the perturbations from different initializations are not strong enough. To alleviate this problem, we replace one of the task models with DIDN [45]

Table 3. Results of Portrait Image Matting and Night Image Enhancement. We report PSNR (dB) on the validation set of the practical datasets averaged over 3 runs. In the table, "L" means labeled data while "U" means unlabeled data.

Methods	Portrait Image Matting		Night Image Enhancement
	100L + 3,850U	100L + 7,700U	200L + 1,500U
SupOnly	25.39	25.39	18.72
MT [41]	26.60	27.63	19.93
S4L [46]	26.87	28.24	19.63
AdvSSL [19]	26.52	27.57	19.59
GCT (Our)	**27.35**	**29.38**	**20.14**

that won the third place in the NTRIE 2019 challenge. We still use DHDN for validation.

We extract 1/16, 1/8, 1/4, 1/2 labeled image pairs randomly for SSL. As shown in Table 2, our fully supervised baseline achieves 39.38dB (PSNR), which is comparable with the top-level results on the SIDD benchmark. Although SSL shows limited performance in this difficult task, GCT surpasses other SSL methods under all labeled ratios. Notably, GCT improves on PSNR by 0.61dB with 1/16 labels (only 10 labeled image pairs) while the previous SSL methods improve on PSNR by 0.33dB at most.

4.3   Portrait Image Matting Experiments

Image Matting [37, 44] predicts a foreground mask (matte) from an input image and a pre-defined trimap. Each pixel value in the matte is a probability between [0, 1]. We focus on the matting of portrait images here, which has important applications on smartphone, *e.g..*, blurring the background of an image. In Fig. 3(c), the trimap is merged into x for visualization by setting the pixels inside the unknown region of the trimap to gray. Since there are no open-source benchmarks, we first collected 8,000 portrait images from Flickr. We then generate the trimaps from the results of a pre-trained segmentation model. After that, we select 300 images with fine details and label them by Photoshop ($\sim$20min per image). Finally, we combine 100 labeled images with 7,700 unlabeled images as the training set, while the remaining 200 labeled images are used as the validation set. For each labeled image, we generate 15 samples by random cropping and 35 samples by background replacement (with the OpenImage dataset [22]). For each unlabeled image, we generate 5 samples by random cropping. The structure of our task model is derived from [44], which is a milestone in image matting.

In this task, we verify the impact of increasing the amount of unlabeled data on SSL by experimenting on two configurations. With 100 labeled images, (1) we randomly select half (3,850) of unlabeled images for training, and (2) we use all (7,700) unlabeled images for training. As shown in Table 3, GCT yields an improvement over the SupOnly baselines by 1.96dB and 3.99dB for 3,850

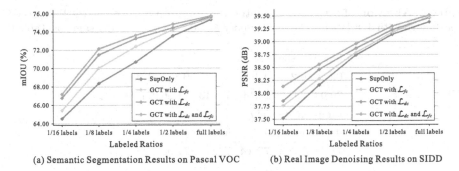

(a) Semantic Segmentation Results on Pascal VOC   (b) Real Image Denoising Results on SIDD

Fig. 5. Ablation of the Proposed SSL Constraints. We compare the performance of $\mathcal{L}_{dc}$ and $\mathcal{L}_{fc}$ on (a) the Pascal VOC benchmark and (b) the SIDD benchmark. The results of SupOnly (red) and GCT with two SSL constraints (green) are the same as (a) Table 1 and (b) Table 2.

and 7,700 unlabeled images respectively. This indicates that the SSL performance can be effectively improved by increasing the amount of unlabeled data. In addition, doubling the amount of unlabeled images achieves a more significant improvement (2.03dB) with GCT, compared with existing SSL methods.

4.4 Night Image Enhancement Experiments

Night Image Enhancement [8,13] is another common vision application. This task adjusts the coefficients of the channels in a night image to show more details (Fig. 3(d)). Our dataset contains 1,900 night images captured by smartphones, of which 400 images are labeled using Photoshop (~15min per image). We combine 200 labeled images with 1,500 unlabeled images for training and use another 200 labeled images for testing. We use horizontal flipping, slight rotation, and random cropping (to 512×512) as data augmentations during training. We regard HDRNet [13] as the task model. Since the dataset is small, we experimented with only one SSL configuration (Table 3). Similar to the experiments in the other three tasks, GCT outperforms existing SSL methods.

4.5 Ablation Experiments

We conduct ablation studies to analyze the proposed SSL constraints, the hyperparameters in GCT, and the combination of the flaw detector and Mean Teacher.

Effect of the SSL Constraints. By default, GCT learns from the unlabeled data through the two SSL constraints simultaneously. In Fig. 5, we compare the experiments of training GCT with only one SSL constraint on the benchmarks for semantic segmentation and real image denoising. The results demonstrate that both $\mathcal{L}_{dc}$ and $\mathcal{L}_{fc}$ are effective. GCT with $\mathcal{L}_{dc}$ boosts the performance impressively, proving that the knowledge exchange between the two task models is reliable and effective. Meanwhile, the curve of GCT with $\mathcal{L}_{fc}$ indicates that

Table 4. Ablation of Hyper-Parameters. We report mIOU (%) on the Pascal VOC benchmark with 1/8 labels. The result under $\xi = 0.4$ or $\eta = 3$ is the same as Table 1.

flaw threshold ξ					
0.0	0.2	0.4	0.6	0.8	1.0
70.04	70.92	72.14	**72.43**	71.96	71.49

ramp-up epochs η					
0	1	3	5	10	
71.34	72.03	**72.14**	72.06	71.95	

the flaw detector also plays a vital role in learning the unlabeled data. Moreover, combining $\mathcal{L}_{dc}$ and $\mathcal{L}_{fc}$ allows GCT to achieve the optimal performance.

Hyper-parameters in GCT. We analyze the two hyper-parameters required by GCT (mentioned in Sec. 3.3), the flaw threshold ξ and the cosine ramp-up epochs η of $\mathcal{L}_{dc}$, on the Pascal VOC benchmark for semantic segmentation with 1/8 labels. Table 4 (left) shows the results under different ξ, which controls the combination of the two SSL constraints. Specifically, only $\mathcal{L}_{fc}$ is applied when $\xi = 0.0$, and only $\mathcal{L}_{dc}$ is applied when $\xi = 1.0$. Our experiments show that ξ can be set roughly, e.g.., $\xi \in [0.4, 0.8]$ is suitable for semantic segmentation. The cosine ramp-up with η epochs prevents exchanging unreliable knowledge due to the non-convergent flaw detector in the early training stage. The results in Table 4 (right) indicate that GCT is robust to η, even though the cosine ramp-up is necessary for the best performance.

Combination of the Flaw Detector and MT. The consistency constraint in MT is applied from the teacher model to the student model. However, the teacher model may be worse than the student model on some pixels, which may cause a performance degradation. To avoid this problem, we use the flaw detector to disable the consistency constraint when the flaw probability of the teacher's prediction is larger than the student's prediction. Under 1/8 labels, this method improves the mIOU value of MT from 69.81% to 70.47% on Pascal VOC and improves the PSNR value of MT from 38.22dB to 38.42dB on SIDD.

5   Conclusions

We have studied the generalization of SSL to diverse pixel-wise tasks and indicated the drawbacks of existing SSL methods in these tasks, which to the best of our knowledge is the first. We have presented a new general framework, named GCT, for pixel-wise SSL. Our experiments have proved its effectiveness in a variety of vision tasks. Meanwhile, we also note that SSL still has limited performance for tasks that require highly precise pseudo labels, such as image denoising. A possible future work is to investigate this problem and explore ways to create more accurate pseudo labels.

References

1. Abdelhamed, A., Lin, S., Brown, M.S.: A high-quality denoising dataset for smartphone cameras. In: Proceedings of the IEEE Conference on Computer Vision and Pattern Recognition, pp. 1692–1700 (2018)
2. Abdelhamed, A., Timofte, R., Brown, M.S.: Ntire 2019 challenge on real image denoising: methods and results. In: Proceedings of the IEEE Conference on Computer Vision and Pattern Recognition Workshops (2019)
3. Anwar, S., Barnes, N.: Real image denoising with feature attention. In: Proceedings of the IEEE International Conference on Computer Vision, pp. 3155–3164 (2019)
4. Athiwaratkun, B., Finzi, M., Izmailov, P., Wilson, A.G.: There are many consistent explanations of unlabeled data: why you should average. arXiv preprint arXiv:1806.05594 (2019)
5. Berthelot, D., et al.: Remixmatch: semi-supervised learning with distribution matching and augmentation anchoring. In: International Conference on Learning Representations (2020)
6. Berthelot, D., Carlini, N., Goodfellow, I.G., Papernot, N., Oliver, A., Raffel, C.: Mixmatch: a holistic approach to semi-supervised learning. In: Advances in Neural Information Processing Systems, pp. 5049–5059 (2019)
7. Chen, C., Liu, W., Tan, X., Wong, K.-Y.K.: Semi-supervised learning for face sketch synthesis in the wild. In: Jawahar, C.V., Li, H., Mori, G., Schindler, K. (eds.) ACCV 2018. LNCS, vol. 11361, pp. 216–231. Springer, Cham (2019). https://doi.org/10.1007/978-3-030-20887-5_14
8. Chen, C., Chen, Q., Xu, J., Koltun, V.: Learning to see in the dark. In: Proceedings of the IEEE Conference on Computer Vision and Pattern Recognition, pp. 3291–3300 (2018)
9. Chen, L.C., Papandreou, G., Kokkinos, I., Murphy, K., Yuille, A.L.: Deeplab: semantic image segmentation with deep convolutional nets, atrous convolution, and fully connected crfs. IEEE Trans. Pattern Anal. Mach. Intell. **40**(4), 834–848 (2017)
10. Chen, L.C., Zhu, Y., Papandreou, G., Schroff, F., Adam, H.: Encoder-decoder with atrous separable convolution for semantic image segmentation. In: Proceedings of the European Conference on Computer Vision (ECCV), pp. 801–818 (2018)
11. Dai, Z., Yang, Z., Yang, F., Cohen, W.W., Salakhutdinov, R.R.: Good semi-supervised learning that requires a bad gan. In: Advances in Neural Information Processing Systems, pp. 6510–6520 (2017)
12. Everingham, M., Eslami, S.M.A., Van Gool, L., Williams, C.K.I., Winn, J., Zisserman, A.: The PASCAL visual object classes challenge: a retrospective. Int. J. Comput. Vis. **111**(1), 98–136 (2014). https://doi.org/10.1007/s11263-014-0733-5
13. Gharbi, M., Chen, J., Barron, J.T., Hasinoff, S.W., Durand, F.: Deep bilateral learning for real-time image enhancement. ACM Trans. Graph. (TOG) **36**(4), 1–12 (2017)
14. Goodfellow, I.J., et al.: Generative adversarial nets. In: Advances in Neural Information Processing Systems, pp. 2672–2680 (2014)
15. Guo, S., Yan, Z., Zhang, K., Zuo, W., Zhang, L.: Toward convolutional blind denoising of real photographs. In: Proceedings of the IEEE Conference on Computer Vision and Pattern Recognition, pp. 1712–1722 (2019)
16. Hariharan, B., Arbelaez, P., Bourdev, L., Maji, S., Malik, J.: Semantic contours from inverse detectors. In: 2011 International Conference on Computer Vision, pp. 991–998. IEEE (2011)

17. He, K., Zhang, X., Ren, S., Sun, J.: Deep residual learning for image recognition. In: Proceedings of the IEEE Conference on Computer Vision and Pattern Recognition, pp. 770–778 (2016)
18. Huang, Z., Wang, X., Wang, J., Liu, W., Wang, J.: Weakly-supervised semantic segmentation network with deep seeded region growing. In: Proceedings of the IEEE Conference on Computer Vision and Pattern Recognition, pp. 7014–7023 (2018)
19. Hung, W.C., Tsai, Y.H., Liou, Y.T., Lin, Y.Y., Yang, M.H.: Adversarial learning for semi-supervised semantic segmentation. arXiv preprint arXiv:1802.07934 (2018)
20. Kalluri, T., Varma, G., Chandraker, M., Jawahar, C.V.: Universal semi-supervised semantic segmentation. In: Proceedings of the IEEE International Conference on Computer Vision, pp. 5259–5270 (2019)
21. Ke, Z., Wang, D., Yan, Q., Ren, J., Lau, R.W.: Dual student: breaking the limits of the teacher in semi-supervised learning. In: Proceedings of the IEEE International Conference on Computer Vision, pp. 6728–6736 (2019)
22. Kuznetsova, A., et al.: The open images dataset v4: unified image classification, object detection, and visual relationship detection at scale. arXiv preprint arXiv:1811.00982 (2018)
23. Laine, S., Aila, T.: Temporal ensembling for semi-supervised learning. arXiv preprint arXiv:1610.02242 (2017)
24. Lee, J., Kim, E., Lee, S., Lee, J., Yoon, S.: Ficklenet: weakly and semi-supervised semantic image segmentation using stochastic inference. In: Proceedings of the IEEE Conference on Computer Vision and Pattern Recognition, pp. 5267–5276 (2019)
25. LI, C., Xu, T., Zhu, J., Zhang, B.: Triple generative adversarial nets. In: Advances in Neural Information Processing Systems, pp. 4088–4098 (2017)
26. Lin, T.-Y., et al.: Microsoft COCO: common objects in context. In: Fleet, D., Pajdla, T., Schiele, B., Tuytelaars, T. (eds.) ECCV 2014. LNCS, vol. 8693, pp. 740–755. Springer, Cham (2014). https://doi.org/10.1007/978-3-319-10602-1_48
27. Long, J., Shelhamer, E., Darrell, T.: Fully convolutional networks for semantic segmentation. In: Proceedings of the IEEE Conference on Computer Vision and Pattern Recognition, pp. 3431–3440 (2016)
28. Luo, Y., Zhu, J., Li, M., Ren, Y., Zhang, B.: Smooth neighbors on teacher graphs for semi-supervised learning. In: Proceedings of the IEEE Conference on Computer Vision and Pattern Recognition, pp. 8896–8905 (2018)
29. Mao, X., Li, Q., Xie, H., Lau, R.Y.K., Wang, Z.: Least squares generative adversarial networks. In: Proceedings of the IEEE International Conference on Computer Vision, pp. 2794–2802 (2017)
30. Mittal, S., Tatarchenko, M., Brox, T.: Semi-supervised semantic segmentation with high- and low-level consistency. IEEE Trans. Pattern Anal. Mach. Intell. (2019)
31. Miyato, T., Maeda, S.I., Ishii, S., Koyama, M.: Virtual adversarial training: a regularization method for supervised and semi-supervised learning. IEEE Trans. Pattern Anal. Mach. Intell. 41(8), 1979–1993 (2018)
32. Oliver, A., Odena, A., Raffel, C., Cubuk, E., Goodfellow, I.: Realistic evaluation of semi-supervised learning algorithms. In: NeurIPS (2018)
33. Park, B., Yu, S., Jeong, J.: Densely connected hierarchical network for image denoising. In: Proceedings of the IEEE Conference on Computer Vision and Pattern Recognition Workshops (2019)
34. Park, S., Park, J., Shin, S., Moon, I.: Adversarial dropout for supervised and semi-supervised learning. arXiv preprint arXiv:1707.03631 (2018)

35. Qiao, S., Shen, W., Zhang, Z., Wang, B., Yuille, A.L.: Deep co-training for semi-supervised image recognition. In: Proceedings of the European Conference on Computer Vision (ECCV), pp. 135–152 (2018)
36. Rasmus, A., Berglund, M., Honkala, M., Valpola, H., Raiko, T.: Semi-supervised learning with ladder networks. In: Advances in Neural Information Processing Systems, pp. 3546–3554 (2015)
37. Shen, X., Tao, X., Gao, H., Zhou, C., Jia, J.: Deep automatic portrait matting. In: Leibe, B., Matas, J., Sebe, N., Welling, M. (eds.) ECCV 2016. LNCS, vol. 9905, pp. 92–107. Springer, Cham (2016). https://doi.org/10.1007/978-3-319-46448-0_6
38. Simonyan, K., Zisserman, A.: Very deep convolutional networks for large-scale image recognition. arXiv preprint arXiv:1409.1556 (2014)
39. Springenberg, J.T.: Unsupervised and semi-supervised learning with categorical generative adversarial networks. arXiv preprint arXiv:1511.06390 (2015)
40. Srivastava, N., Hinton, G., Krizhevsky, A., Sutskever, I., Salakhutdinov, R.: Dropout: a simple way to prevent neural networks from overfitting. J. Mach. Learn. Res. **15**(1), 1929–1958 (2014)
41. Tarvainen, A., Valpola, H.: Mean teachers are better role models: weight-averaged consistency targets improve semi-supervised deep learning results. In: Advances in neural Information Processing Systems, pp. 1195–1204 (2017)
42. Tran, P.V.: Exploring self-supervised regularization for supervised and semi-supervised learning. arXiv preprint arXiv:1906.10343 (2019)
43. Wang, Q., Li, W., Van Gool, L.: Semi-supervised learning by augmented distribution alignment. In: Proceedings of the IEEE International Conference on Computer Vision, pp. 1466–1475 (2019)
44. Xu, N., Price, B.L., Cohen, S., Huang, T.S.: Deep image matting. In: Proceedings of the IEEE Conference on Computer Vision and Pattern Recognition, pp. 2970–2979 (2017)
45. Yu, S., Park, B., Jeong, J.: Deep iterative down-up cnn for image denoising. In: Proceedings of the IEEE Conference on Computer Vision and Pattern Recognition Workshops (2019)
46. Zhai, X., Oliver, A., Kolesnikov, A., Beyer, L.: S4l: self-supervised semi-supervised learning. In: Proceedings of the IEEE International Conference on Computer Vision, pp. 1476–1485 (2019)
47. Zhang, K., Zuo, W., Zhang, L.: FFDnet: toward a fast and flexible solution for cnn based image denoising. IEEE Trans. Image Process **27**(9), 4608–4622 (2018)
48. Zhu, X.: Semi-supervised learning literature survey. University of Wisconsin-Madison Department of Computer Sciences (2006)

Stacking Networks Dynamically for Image Restoration Based on the Plug-and-Play Framework

Haixin Wang[1,2], Tianhao Zhang[1], Muzhi Yu[1], Jinan Sun[1(✉)], Wei Ye[1], Chen Wang[1], and Shikun Zhang[1]

[1] Peking University, Beijing, China
{wang.hx,tianhao_z,muzhi.yu,sjn,wye,wangchen,zhangsk}@pku.edu.cn
[2] University of Science and Technology Beijing, Beijing, China

Abstract. Recently, stacked networks show powerful performance in Image Restoration, such as challenging motion deblurring problems. However, the number of stacking levels is a hyper-parameter fine-tuned manually, making the stacking levels static during training without theoretical explanations for optimal settings. To address this challenge, we leverage the iterative process of the traditional plug-and-play method to provide a dynamic stacked network for Image Restoration. Specifically, a new degradation model with a novel update scheme is designed to integrate the deep neural network as the prior within the plug-and-play model. Compared with static stacked networks, our models are stacked dynamically during training via iterations, guided by a solid mathematical explanation. Theoretical proof on the convergence of the dynamic stacking process is provided. Experiments on the noise dataset BSD68, Set12, and motion blur dataset GoPro demonstrate that our framework outperforms the state-of-the-art in terms of PSNR and SSIM score without extra training process.

Keywords: Low-level vision · Image restoration · Plug-and-play

1 Introduction

Image Restoration (IR) is a classic yet hot task in low-level vision for its high application value. It aims to recover the clean image x from its corrupted observation y. Classic degradation model is $y = Ax + n$, where A is a degradation matrix referred to as the identity matrix in image denoising or the blurring matrix in image deblurring. n is often regarded as additive white Gaussian noise.

Solutions to this ill-posed inverse model include two main categories: model-based and learning-based. Model-based methods estimate A and n in the degradation model by a series of constraints and regularizations, and then iteratively

Electronic supplementary material The online version of this chapter (https://doi.org/10.1007/978-3-030-58601-0_27) contains supplementary material, which is available to authorized users.

© Springer Nature Switzerland AG 2020
A. Vedaldi et al. (Eds.): ECCV 2020, LNCS 12358, pp. 446–462, 2020.
https://doi.org/10.1007/978-3-030-58601-0_27

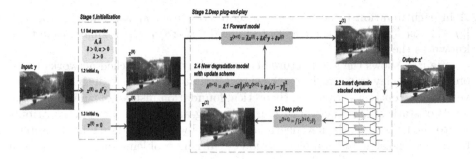

Fig. 1. The architecture of our proposed deep plug-and-play framework with dynamic stacked networks.

solve for the latent clean image supported with strong mathematical theory. But they rely heavily on fixed and handcrafted priors that certainly are insufficient in characterizing clean images. Learning-based methods gradually show superiority to learn the regression between the corrupted input image and the latent clean image directly. Meanwhile, new tricks, like the network stacking diagram, are borrowed to further improve performance. However, networks are with too many static hyper-parameters, and the learning performance depends seriously on carefully tuning of them. These facts make the training very tricky, let alone hard process and GPU limit, but also theoretical analysis difficult.

To address this challenge, we propose to stack networks dynamically for IR based on the plug-and-play framework. First, by plugging the pre-trained deep prior into our framework, we can iteratively reuse the prior knowledge like stacking deep networks without increasing parameter size. More importantly, a new degradation model $y = A^{(t)}x + n$ with update scheme is designed, and solved for the theoretical optima guided by strong explanations on the convergence. Thus, our dynamic stacking diagram not only leverages the iterations to the maximum extent, but also plays the role of shifting focus for better performance level-by-level in training stacked networks.

In this paper, we solve for the latent clean image in image denoising and extend the idea to complex motion deblurring tasks. The framework consisting a new degradation model and pre-trained deep prior is formalized as

$$x^* = x^{(t+1)} = \arg\min_{x^{(t)}} ||y - A^{(t)}x^{(t)}||^2 + \lambda f(x^{(t)}; \theta) \tag{1}$$

where y is the noisy or blurry image need to be restored, x is the latent clean solution, and θ is the parameter of plugged deep denoiser or deblurrer. Unlike the basic degradation model, A is no longer a specific degradation matrix fixed in a specific task. We note that previous works' results are superior level-by-level which means more stacked sub-models after training will focus on more blurry details spatially. But simple iterations cannot shift the focus of pre-trained networks on more blurry cues. Based on these observations, we propose to update

A in each iteration to shift focus on more corrupted areas. Thus, in Eq. (1), $||y - A^{(t)}x||^2$ represents the fidelity term, and $\lambda f(x; \theta)$ is the regularization term known as the prior.

Figure 1 shows the architecture of our novel dynamic stacked networks based on plug-and-play framework. The key point is that our dynamic diagram can converge to the optima with a firm theoretical foundation instead of tuning stacking levels of static stacked networks. Our deep plug-and-play framework, contributing to the leverage of the new degradation model with an update scheme, applies to image denoising and complex motion deblurring problems successfully first of the time to our best knowledge. We conduct extensive experiments to demonstrate the superior results of our framework, compared with the static networks who set the state-of-the-art on famous noise dataset BSD68, Set12, and motion blur dataset GoPro. Both objective evaluating metrics PSNR, SSIM and visualization in the following section help to prove that we effectively improve the performance in both image denoising and motion deblurring tasks.

Our contributions are summarized as follows:

1) We propose a dynamic stacked networks for IR based on the plug-and-play framework to solve the new degradation model. Compared with static stacking diagrams, our framework leverages the iteration process to dynamically reuse the prior knowledge.
2) Theoretical analysis is provided to show that our framework with a new degradation model inside is able to solve for the optima with fast convergence by means of iterating the output dynamically.
3) To our best knowledge, our framework exploits both the merits of model-based and learning-based methods for image denoising and non-uniform blind motion deblurring for the first time.
4) Experiments on datasets BSD68, Set12, and GoPro have proven that our framework outperforms existing methods on PSNR, SSIM, and visualization.

The remainder of the paper is organized as follows. In Sect. 2, we give an overview of the related work. In Sect. 3, we provide a detailed description of the proposed method. Finally, in Sect. 4, we perform an evaluation of our framework on image denoising and motion deblurring tasks, and compare it to the state-of-the-art. Meanwhile, mathematical explanations are provided. Section 5 concludes this paper.

2   Related Work

2.1   Plug-and-Play Methods

The plug-and-play method was first introduced to solve IR tasks in [8,27,35]. Its core idea is to decouple the fidelity term and regularization term in the energy function by splitting techniques, as well as to replace the prior associated sub-problem by any off-the-shelf Gaussian denoiser. For its flexibility and good performance, a set of work have been done mainly in three aspects:

1) various priors, including conventional priors such as the well-known BM3D [7], Gaussian mixture model [35] and the state-of-the-art CNN denoiser such as [34] as well as their combination [11]; 2) various variable splitting algorithms, such as half-quadratic splitting (HQS) algorithm [1], alternating direction method of multipliers (ADMM) algorithm [3] and primal-dual algorithm [19]; 3) theoretical analysis on the convergence from the aspect of fixed point [5,17]. In [31], priors have been proved not limited to Gaussian denoiser. In this paper, priors can transfer to be image deblurrer.

2.2   Image Denoising

Image denoising is a classic low-level vision task. DNN has been exploited since 2009, which has developed the solution in two aspects: 1) learn the clean target. MLP [4] has been adopted to learn the mapping from noise patch to clean pixel. In [6], a trainable nonlinear reaction diffusion (TNRD) model has been proposed and it can be expressed as a feed-forward deep network by unfolding a fixed number of gradient descent inference steps. Santhanam et al. [23] introduce a recursively branched deconvolutional network (RBDN), where pooling/unpooling is adopted to obtain and aggregate multi-context; 2) learn the noise. Residual learning with batch normalization (DnCNN) was first proposed by Zhang et al. [33] which outperforms other methods. A set of frameworks take advantage of DnCNN as a denoising network for various applications [28]. In [14], only noisy inputs are exploited to train in the network with L2 loss function which outputs the mean of all results. By observing the noisy inputs twice during training on a big enough dataset, the network can estimate the noise distribution in an unsupervised manner. Inspired by the success of DNN-based method, many work [16,20,34] attempted to integrate the conventional method like BM3D, wavelet transformation, including plug-and-play with DNN.

2.3   Non-uniform Blind Deblurring

The goal of non-uniform blind image deblurring is to remove the undesired blur caused by camera motion and scene dynamics [24,32]. Conventional methods used to employ a variety of constraints or regularizations to approximate the motion blur filters, involving an expensive non-convex non-linear optimization. Moreover, the commonly used assumption of spatially-uniform blur kernel is overly restrictive, resulting in a poor deblurring of complex blur patterns.

CNN-based methods have shown a powerful ability to deal with the complex motion blur in a time-efficient manner. They are developed in two main respects: 1) Learning the blur kernel. [29] proposed a deconvolutional CNN which removes blur in a non-blind setting by recovering a sharp image given the estimated blur kernel. Their network uses separable kernels which can be decomposed into a small set of filters. [25] estimated and removed a non-uniform motion blur from an image by learning the regression between image patches and their corresponding kernels. 2) Learning the sharp Image. In [32], Recurrent Neural Network (RNN) is applied as a deconvolutional decoder on feature maps extracted by the first CNN module. Another CNN module learns weights for each layer of RNN. The last CNN module reconstructs images from deblurred feature maps.

3   Proposed Methods

3.1   Overview

As shown in Fig. 1, the pre-trained stacked network is plugged into the framework dynamically in Stage 2.2–2.3. Different from existing deep plug-and-play methods [34], we solve our new degradation model by transforming the forward model into a single step of gradient descent in Stage 2.1, which not only provides fast convergence but also keeps remarkable performance with theoretical support. Ahead of the implementation, the degradation matrix $A^{(t)}$ and other parameters are initialized in Stage 1. Furthermore, an optimization target is set in Stage 2.4, which will be solved to update the variable $A^{(t)}$ in $y = A^{(t)}x + n$ in each iteration adaptively to adjust the focus of deblurring networks.

3.2   Deep Plug-and-Play

In IR, A in the basic model is reasonably equal to the blur kernel. However, the blur kernel is hard to know in complex application situations. Therefore, our new degradation model is designed, in which we no longer need to know or to estimate the blur kernel but initialize it as an identity matrix before the adaptive updating scheme. Based on the new degradation model, we can utilize the deep prior as denoiser for denoising tasks. Furthermore, we transfer the deep plug-and-play framework to complex deblurring problems by the other deep prior. Basically, to plug the deep prior into the optimization procedure of Eq. (1), the variable splitting technique is usually adopted to decouple the fidelity term and regularization term. In Half Quadratic Splitting (HQS) method, by introducing an auxiliary variable v, Eq. (1) can be reformulated as a constrained optimization problem which is given by

$$(x^*, v^*) \leftarrow \arg \min_{x,v} \frac{1}{2}||y - A^{(t)}x||^2 + \lambda f(v; \theta)$$

$$s.t. \quad x = v \qquad (2)$$

Then, standard optimization algorithms are able to be used to solve the problem. The equally constrained optimization problem can be converted into a non-constrained optimization problem,

$$\mathcal{L}(x, v) = \frac{1}{2}||y - A^{(t)}x||^2 + \lambda f(v; \theta) + \frac{\mu}{2}||v - x||^2 \qquad (3)$$

where μ is a penalty parameter which varies iteratively in a non-descending order. Eq. (3) can be solved via the following iterative scheme,

$$\begin{cases} x^{(t+1)} = \arg \min_{x} ||y - A^{(t)}x||^2 + \mu||x - v^{(t)}||^2 & (4) \\ v^{(t+1)} = \arg \min_{v} \frac{\mu}{2}||v - x^{(t+1)}||^2 + \lambda f(v; \theta) & (5) \end{cases}$$

The first step only depends on the choice of a forward model, while the second step only depends on the choice of prior and can be interpreted as a denoising operation [27]. However, it is not limited in denoiser and can be extended to be deblurrer in our paper. Typically, Eq. (4) is a quadratic optimization problem that can be solved in closed-form, as $x^{(t+1)} = W^{-1}x_t$, where W is a matrix related to the degradation matrix A. It is time-consuming to compute like this while Fast Fourier Transformation (FFT) is often applied as a feasible implementation [34]. However, FFT methods still cannot solve for answers efficiently. In our framework, we propose to take advantage of iterative classic conjugate gradient (CG) algorithm, which is a common optimization algorithm. More briefly, we only compute with a single step of gradient descent for an inexact solution,

$$x^{(t+1)} = x^{(t)} - \delta[A^{(t)^T}(A^{(t)}x^{(t)} - y) + \mu(x^{(t)} - v^{(t)})]$$
$$= [(1 - \delta\mu)I - \delta A^{(t)^T}A^{(t)}]x^{(t)} + \delta A^{(t)^T}y + \delta v^{(t)} \qquad (6)$$

where δ is the step size. It is proven that this single descent step is sufficient for convergence which follows the idea of [9] shown in Sect. 4. Equation (5) is considered to be a task-dependent denoiser or deblurrer in our framework. In this paper, inspired by the success of deep learning-based methods for IR tasks, we plug in the pre-trained deep neural network model to replace the proximity operator of conventional priors.

$$v^{(t+1)} = f(x^{(t+1)}; \theta) \qquad (7)$$

Equation (7) is just the solution of Eqn. (5). After several alternating iterations, it is expected that the final reconstructed image attains the high-quality restoration.

3.3 Deep Prior

Denoiser. In order to exploit the merits of learning-based methods, we need to specify the denoiser network according to Eqn. (7). Inspired by [10], we only need to modify most of the existing learning-based denoisers. The pretrained prior we adopt is the variational denoising network (VDN), which efficiently approximates the true posterior with the latent variables. The framework includes two subnets standing for noise estimation and noise removal separately.

The weights of VDN are initialized according to [12]. In each epoch, we randomly crop $N = 64 \times 5000$ patches with size 128×128 from the images for training. The Adam algorithm [13] is adopted to optimize the network parameters through minimizing the proposed negative lower bound objective. The initial learning rate is set as 2e–4 and linearly decayed in half every 10 epochs to 1e–6.

Deblurrer. We base our deep deblurrer on DMPHN [31] including its stacked versions which is the state-of-the-art. It processes images of different scales by dividing into different numbers of image patches from the coarsest to the finniest level. This end-to-end network can be stacked as a part with more stacks. Since the network is determined by the stacking level, this static stacking diagram is hard to find the optimal form in two-fold: 1) It has to stack many filters since their weights are fixed and spatially invariant; 2) A geometrically uniform receptive field without adaption is sub-optimal for the real-world scene. Therefore, limit to the GPU memory and long training time, there exists no performance of deeper stacked networks. After we plugging pre-trained shallow stacked models into our framework, they can explore the solution effectively dynamically.

Inside the DMPHN, there is an encoder and decoder of each layer. The encoder consists of 15 convolutional layers, 6 residual links, and 6 ReLU units. The layers of decoder and encoder are identical except that two convolutional layers are replaced by deconvolutional layers to generate images. The input of each layer is the blurry image divided into specific image patches. The output of both encoder and decoder from a lower level (corresponds to the finer grid) will be added to the upper level (one level above) so that the top level contains all information inferred in the finer levels.

3.4   Adaptive Update Scheme

Previous work has shown that the performance of stacked networks is superior level-by-level, which means more stacked sub-models will focus on more blurry details spatially. Since pre-trained networks focus on several severe blurriness are constructed from coarse-to-fine, the restoration image tends to induce undesired local blurriness after a few simple iterations especially when the motion blur is distributed all over the image. Since simple iterations cannot shift the focus of networks on more blurry cues, we design the adaptive update scheme in our degradation model to shift the focus adaptively. To be specific, A will be used as the adaptive optimized variable to complete our design. We find that networks trained under MSE loss all try to do one thing essentially: learning the mapping from corrupted images y to latent clean images x with a network $g_\theta(\cdot)$.

$$\arg\min_x ||g_\theta(y) - x||^2$$
$$= \arg\min_x ||g_\theta(Ax + n) - x||^2 \qquad (8)$$

A precondition that cannot be ignored is that deep plug-and-play framework should follow the basic degradation model $y = Ax + n$ with unknown variables in IR tasks. That means the network aims to complete the fitting task $g_\theta(y) = A^{-1}[(Ax+n)-n]$ by training on big data. However, the network cannot fit to the uncertain targets and may be trained as $g_\theta(y) = H^{-1}[(Ax+n)-\varepsilon] = H^{-1}Ax-\eta$ with deblurring ability to a certain extent. When we suppose $A = I$ in a learning-based method where H^{-1} may not be A^{-1}, the final solution must be over-blurred by an operation that is uncertain. That means that simple iterations with pre-trained deblurrers cannot improve the deblurring performance for over-blur.

Therefore, we propose a new degradation model $y = A^{(t)}x + n$ with update scheme to battle the operation H^{-1} fixed in the pre-trained deep prior which may cause undesired blurriness. Our purpose is to let $H^{-1} = A^{-1}$ and $\eta = 0$.

This idea is equal to make the basic degradation model $y = Ax + n$ reasonable in each iteration. So we set the optimization target after implementing Eq. (7).

$$\arg\min_{A^{(t)}} ||A^{(t)}x^{(t)} + n - y||^2$$

$$= \arg\min_{A^{(t)}} ||A^{(t)}x^{(t)} + g_\theta(y) - y||^2 \tag{9}$$

where noise n in the optimization target is estimated by the pre-trained deep denoiser. This optimization target will update $A^{(t)}$ in each iteration between Eq. (5) and Eq. (4) after the end of an epoch. This step of adaption can shift the focus of the deep deblurrer and pass the adjusted matrix $A^{(t)}$ to the forward model.

As for the solution, we tackle this optimization target in the similar way of the forward model. Hence, the matrix $A^{(t)}$ will be updated in a single step of gradient descent

$$A^{(t+1)} = A^{(t)} - \alpha x^{(t+1)^T} A^{(t)} x^{(t+1)} - \alpha(g_\theta(y) - y) \tag{10}$$

where α is the step size of gradient descent, and $g_\theta(\cdot)$ is the pre-trained deep prior to estimate the noise. We train a common deep denoiser DnCNN [33] as the $g_\theta(\cdot)$ due to its success. According to the deductive optimization target Eq. (10), we make $A^{(t)}$ adaptively fit to the degradation model and consequently focus on more corrupted areas.

4   Experiments

Our deep priors are based on their released version without retraining with a single NVIDIA Titan RTX GPU. In the alternating iterations between Eq. (4) and Eq. (5), we need to tune μ and set λ to make the performances satisfying. In addition, the step size of gradient descent δ in the forward model Eq. (4) and α in the update step are also needed to set previously. Actually, the step size varies with different datasets and different deep priors for different convergence speed. Although setting such parameters has been considered as a non-trivial task [21], the parameters of our framework are easy to be obtained with the following principles. Firstly, λ is fixed associated with noise level in denoising, we can instead multiply noise level by a scalar λ and therefore ignore the λ in Eq. (5). And the noise level in deblurring is 0. Secondly, the step size is tuned from 1e–3 to 1e–5 for a total of 2 to 4 iterations.

4.1   Image Denoising

Datasets. The denoising prior is trained on the famous BSD500. We test our framework on two widely used datasets BSD68 and Set12. BSD68 [22] contains of 68 nature images subtracted from Berkeley segmentation dataset. The common data augmentation operations such as flip and rotations are implemented to it. Another famous dataset we exploit contains 12 famous gray images for Image

Table 1. Average PSNR(dB)/SSIM results of the competing methods for image denoising with noise levels $\sigma = 15$, 25 and 50 on datasets Set12 and BSD68. Outperforming results are noted red bold while the second best results are blue bold.

Dataset	σ	DnCNN [33]		IRCNN [34]		MWCNN [16]		NLRN [15]		DPDD [9]		VDN [30]		Proposed	
Set12	15	32.86	0.903	32.77	0.901	33.15	0.909	33.16	0.907	32.91	0.889	33.33	0.912	33.44	0.912
	25	30.44	0.862	30.38	0.860	30.79	0.871	30.80	0.869	30.54	0.811	30.90	0.875	31.04	0.875
	50	27.18	0.783	27.14	0.780	27.74	0.806	27.64	0.798	27.50	0.739	28.00	0.816	28.27	0.816
BSD68	15	31.73	0.891	31.63	0.888	31.86	0.895	31.88	0.893	32.29	0.888	32.22	0.917	32.42	0.918
	25	29.23	0.828	29.15	0.825	29.41	0.836	29.41	0.833	29.88	0.827	30.03	0.851	30.17	0.851
	50	26.23	0.719	26.19	0.717	26.53	0.737	26.47	0.730	27.02	0.754	27.18	0.754	27.64	0.754

Processing tasks. Note that all those images are widely used for the evaluation of Gaussian denoising methods and they are not included in the training dataset. To evaluate our framework, we consider three common noise levels of additive white Gaussian noise with $\sigma = 15, 25, 50$. Noise is randomly added to the image before testing .

Baselines. We compare the proposed framework with six methods, including four learning-based methods (*i.e.*, DnCNN [33], MWCNN [16], NLRN [15], VDN [30]) as well as two methods combing conventional models and deep priors (*i.e.*, DPDD [9], IRCNN [34]). DnCNN consists of 17 layers of ResNet for learning the noise of the degraded images; NLRN integrates non-local self-similarity in natural images as an effective prior into existing deep networks for end-to-end training to capture deep feature correlation between each location and its neighborhood. A similar method is applied in MWCNN for transforming the convolutional neural networks in view of multi-level wavelet. VDN proposes a new variational inference method and integrates both noise estimation and image denoising into a unique Bayesian framework for blind denoising. IRCNN and DPDD both combine the deep neural networks and conventional models, while the former is based on a model and the latter transforms the model into several layers in a network. Our proposed framework is fairly compared to them.

Denoising Results. The PSNR and SSIM results of different methods for image denoising on the dataset BSD68 and Set12 are shown in Table 1, from which we have several observations. Firstly, VDN which set the state-of-the-art currently shows great lift with about 1.2–2.1 dB on PSNR and 0.06–0.11 on SSIM on Set12, about 0.2–1.9 dB on PSNR and 0.08–0.15 on SSIM on BSD68, which may be attributed to simultaneously implementing both noise estimation and blind image denoising tasks in a unique Bayesian framework. Secondly, IRCNN and DPDD are both superior to the methods they are based on which inspire more work to focus on deep plug-and-play methods including us. Last, our proposed framework outperforms existing best method, VDN, 0.1–0.27 dB on PSNR on Set12 and 0.18–0.5 dB on BSD68 but no obvious lift on SSIM due to no difference on variance. Our framework is based on deep priors but surpasses them for the unique combination of both the advantages of model- and learning-based method with self-adaption.

Fig. 2. Denoising results of one image from BSD68 with noise level 50. (a) Noisy, 14.76 dB. (b) BM3D, 26.21 dB. (c) WNNM, 26.51 dB. (d) DnCNN-B, 26.92 dB. (e) MLP, 26.54 dB. (f) TNRD, 26.59 dB. (g) DnCNN-S, 26.90 dB. (h) **Proposed, 28.47 dB**

Figure 2 shows the visual comparison of different methods for Gaussian denoising with $\sigma = 50$ on dataset BSD68. Conventional model methods like BM3D, WNNM cannot restore the latent image as clean as learning-based methods such as MLP, TNRD and DnCNN. DnCNN_S produces better results than similar methods. However, all these methods cause the local blurriness with error, especially the edges of the castle in Fig. 2. Our proposed method shows powerful abilities to overcome the tendency of blurriness and reduce the local error, so that the edge of the castle can be seen clearly. As we all know, PSNR evaluates the distance of all the pixels which stands for the error between two images. Our proposed framework performs the best naturally for improving the quality of reconstruction.

4.2   Image Deblurring

Datasets. GoPro dataset [18] consists of 3214 pairs of blurred and clean images extracted from 33 sequences captured at 720×1280 resolution. The blurred images are generated by averaging varying number (7–13) of successive latent frames to produce varied blur. For a fair comparison, we follow the protocol in [18], which uses 2103 image pairs for training and the remaining 1111 pairs for

Table 2. Quantitative analysis of our framework on the GoPro dataset compared with baselines. PSNR and SSIM are common evaluating metrics for image restoration tasks. Each of our proposed frameworks are based on the deep deblurreres marked in the notation. Outperforming results in the specific stacking diagram are noted red bold while the second best results are blue bold.

Models	PSNR (dB)	SSIM	Size (MB)
Sun et al. [25]	24.64	0.8429	54.1
Nah et al. [18]	29.23	0.9162	303.6
Zhang et al. [32]	29.19	0.9306	37.1
Tao et al. [26]	30.10	0.9323	33.6
DMPHN(1-2)	29.77	0.9286	14.5
DMPHN(1-2-4)	30.21	0.9345	21.7
Proposed(DMPHN(1-2-4))	**30.32**	**0.9358**	21.7
DMPHN(1-2-4-8-16)	29.87	0.9305	36.2
DMPHN(1-2-4-8)	30.25	0.9351	29.0
Proposed(DMPHN(1-2-4-8))	30.40	0.9400	29.0
Stack(2)-DMPHN	30.71	0.9403	43.4
Proposed(Stack(2)-DMPHN)	30.92	0.9478	43.4
Stack(3)-DMPHN	31.16	0.9451	65.1
Proposed(Stack(3)-DMPHN)	**31.32**	**0.9510**	65.1
Stack(4)-DMPHN	31.20	0.9453	86.8
Proposed(Stack(4)-DMPHN)	31.44	0.9530	86.8
VMPHN	30.90	0.9419	43.4
Stack(2)-VMPHN	**31.50**	**0.9483**	86.4
Proposed(Stack(2)-VMPHN)	31.72	0.9567	86.4

testing. To make the fair comparison with DMPHN itself, we follow the principle that randomly crop images to 256 × 256 pixel size. The batch size is set to 6 during training and the Adam solver is used to train the model for 3000 epochs. The initial learning rate is set to 0.0001 and the decay rate is 0.1. Then we normalize image to range the [0, 1] and subtract 0.5. Finally, we plug the deep prior into our framework.

Baselines. We compare our proposed framework with 5 competing motion deblurring methods. [25] proposed to deal with the complex motion blur using CNN in an early time by learning the regression between 30 × 30 image patches and their corresponding kernels. To exploit the deblurring cues at different processing levels, the "coarse-to-fine" scheme has been extended to deep CNN scenarios by a multi-scale network architecture and a scale-recurrent architecture. For multi-scale architecture, [18] exploited a multi-scale CNN to restore sharp images in an end-to-end fashion from images whose blur is caused by various factors. A multi-scale loss function is employed to mimic the coarse-to-fine pipeline

Fig. 3. Deblurring performance on the blurry images from the GoPro dataset. The first column contains the original blurry images, the second column is the result of [26], the third column is the result of [31]. Our results are presented in the last column which achieve the best performance across different scenes.

in conventional deblurring approaches. For RNN architecture, proposed by [32], a network consisting of three deep CNNs and one RNN, is a prominent example. The RNN is applied as a deconvolutional decoder on feature maps extracted by the first CNN module. As for [31], it successfully improves the deblurring performance by using localization deblurring cues via a fine-to-coarse hierarchical representation.

Deblurring Results. The PSNR and SSIM results of competing methods for non-uniform blind motion deblurring on the dataset GoPro are shown in Table 2, from which we have several observations. Firstly, recent studies on non-uniform blind motion deblurring focus on deep end-to-end networks all reach relatively excellent performance. Secondly, our proposed framework outperforms the based deep network [31] in all of the stacking diagrams about 0.15–0.24 dB on PSNR without extra parameters. Furthermore, we find that our framework based on shallow stacked networks tend to outperform deeper stacked networks themselves (*i.e.*, Our proposed Stack(3)-DMPHN outperforms Stack(4)-DMPHN 0.12 dB on PSNR) which shows that we successfully design the deep plug-an-play deblurring framework with dynamic stacked networks to explore more optimal clean images. Thirdly, since we can improve deblurring performance simply with whatever pre-trained deep deblurrers both on PSNR and SSIM, deep plug-and-play framework show the feasibility to combine both the advantages of model-based and learning-based IR methods.

Besides, stacked variant Stack(4)-DMPHN (including our framework based on deep deblurrers) outperformed shallower model DMPHN by 1 % PSNR, VMPHN outperformed DMPHN by 0.7% PSNR while stacked variant Stack(2)-

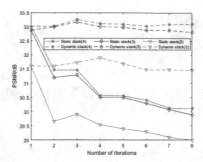

Fig. 4. Comparison between our dynamic stacking diagrams with iterating static pre-trained stacked networks simply. One can see that our framework reaches optimal solution within 4 iterations.

(a) **Input** (b) **I1(31.89)** (c) **I2(31.94)** (d) **I3(32.06)** (e) **I4(32.16)** (f) **I5(31.98)**

Fig. 5. Outputs and PSNR of different iterations of our proposed framework based on Stack(4)-DMPHN. From left to right and up to bottom are the images of different iterations denoted by I with concrete epochs.

VMPHN outperformed shallower DMPHN by 1.3% PSNR. SSIM scores also indicate the same trend. Part of the results are visualized in Fig. 3.

4.3   Analysis of Convergence

To evaluate the superiority of convergence, we compare our dynamic stacked networks with three static stacked networks with the same parameters in complex motion deblurring. In Fig. 4, we represent the deblurring performance of our dynamic diagram varying with iteration numbers in solid lines and the performance of simply iterating static stacked networks in dotted lines. From the results we have several observations: 1) Compared to static ones whose performance decrease gradually, our dynamic stacking diagram can leverage the prior to improve performance by iterations effectively; 2) Our dynamic stacking diagram is able to solve for the optimal result with fast convergence, superior to conventional models, which need large numbers of iterations and lack the reasonable stop criterion [5], as well as existing deep plug-and-play methods, which need at least 15 iterations based on Fast Fourier Transform (FFT) [34]. The visualization of the iteration process in our dynamic stacking diagram is shown in Fig. 5, which is an instance to prove that our frameworks attain the cleaner image gradually within 4 iterations indicated by PSNR. As far as we are concerned, two main reasons contribute to fast convergence: 1) We exploit the pre-trained stacked networks as the deep prior, which goes through large numbers of modulation on parameters to explore the latent clean images similar to the process of iterations in conventional models; 2) We solve the forward model with a single step of gradient descent, which improves the computation efficiency and still attains the good results. However, the drawback of the fast convergence is that our framework may cause over-fitting due to the gradient descent. That's why we can see the decrease in performance with more iterations.

4.4   Mathematical Explanations

Compared to the static stacking diagram, dynamic stacking levels are determined by the iteration number based on deep plug-and-play model. Furthermore, the iteration convergence is supported by theoretical explanations below. Since $\nabla_x \mathcal{L}(x, v)$ according to Eqn. (3) is Lipschitz continuous and our forward model is a single step of gradient descent, we have the property

$$\mathcal{L}(x^{(t)}, v^{(t)}) - \mathcal{L}(x^{(t+1)}, v^{(t)}) \geq C_1 ||x^{(t)} - x^{(t+1)}||_2^2 \tag{11}$$

where C_1 is a positive constant related to Lipschitz constant and step size. According to [2], our deep prior can be regarded as a approximately orthogonal projection of the blurry input y to the manifold of clean images. Therefore, we have

$$\mathcal{L}(x^{(t+1)}, v^{(t)}) - \mathcal{L}(x^{(t+1)}, v^{(t+1)}) \geq C_2 ||\tilde{\nabla}_v \mathcal{L}(x^{(t+1)}, v^{(t)})||_2^2 \tag{12}$$

where $C_2 > 0$ and $\tilde{\nabla}_v \mathcal{L}(x^{(t+1)}, v^{(t)})$ is a continuous limiting subgradient of $\mathcal{L}$. Therefore, by adding Eqn. (11) and Eqn. (12), the sequence $(x^{(t)}, v^{(t)})$ is proved to be bounded and has a convergent subsequence to (x^*, v^*). Then, telescopic summing over $t = 0, 1, \dots$ and by monotonicity and boundedness of $\mathcal{L}(x^{(t)}, v^{(t)})$, we have the summability property

$$\lim_{t \to \infty} ||x^{(t)} - x^{(t+1)}||_2 = 0 \tag{13}$$

$$\lim_{t \to \infty} ||\tilde{\nabla}_v \mathcal{L}(x^{(t+1)}, v^{(t)})||_2 = 0 \tag{14}$$

Thus, $\nabla_x \mathcal{L}(x^*, v^*)$ and $\nabla_v \mathcal{L}(x^*, v^*)$ all equal to 0 which makes (x^*, v^*) a stationary point standing for the optima. Above all, our framework can find for the optimal clean restoration image.

5   Conclusion

In this paper, we have stacked networks dynamically for IR based on the plug-and-play framework. Different from static stacked networks, our framework not only shows the performance improvement but also finds for the optimal solution with solid theoretic support. In addition, we have designed a new degradation model with a novel update scheme to better integrate the model-based and learning-based methods. We have also transformed the forward model into a single step of gradient descent effectively for faster convergence. Simply based on pre-trained networks, our framework can remove noise and complex motion blur beyond networks themselves. Experiments on the noise dataset BSD68, Set12, and motion blur dataset GoPro have proven the effectiveness of our framework. In the future, more research on the architecture of deep end-to-end networks will boost the use of our framework.

Acknowledgement. This work was supported in part by grants from the National Natural Science Foundation of China (NSFC, No. 61973007, 61633002).

References

1. Afonso, M.V., Bioucas-Dias, J.M., Figueiredo, M.A.: Fast image recovery using variable splitting and constrained optimization. IEEE Trans. Image Process. **19**(9), 2345–2356 (2010)
2. Alain, G., Bengio, Y.: What regularized auto-encoders learn from the data-generating distribution. J. Mach. Learn. Res. **15**(1), 3563–3593 (2014)
3. Boyd, S., et al.: Distributed optimization and statistical learning via the alternating direction method of multipliers. Found. Trends® Mach. Learn. **3**(1), 1–122 (2011)
4. Burger, H.C., Schuler, C.J., Harmeling, S.: Image denoising: can plain neural networks compete with BM3D? In: 2012 IEEE Conference on Computer Vision and Pattern Recognition, pp. 2392–2399. IEEE (2012)
5. Chan, S.H., Wang, X., Elgendy, O.A.: Plug-and-play ADMM for image restoration: fixed-point convergence and applications. IEEE Trans. Comput. Imaging **3**(1), 84–98 (2016)
6. Chen, Y., Pock, T.: Trainable nonlinear reaction diffusion: a flexible framework for fast and effective image restoration. IEEE Trans. Pattern Anal. Mach. Intell. **39**(6), 1256–1272 (2016)
7. Dabov, K., Foi, A., Katkovnik, V., Egiazarian, K.: Image denoising by sparse 3-D transform-domain collaborative filtering. IEEE Trans. Image Process. **16**(8), 2080–2095 (2007)
8. Danielyan, A., Katkovnik, V., Egiazarian, K.: Image deblurring by augmented Lagrangian with BM3D frame prior. In: Workshop on Information Theoretic Methods in Science and Engineering (WITMSE), Tampere, Finland, pp. 16–18 (2010)
9. Dong, W., Wang, P., Yin, W., Shi, G., Wu, F., Lu, X.: Denoising prior driven deep neural network for image restoration. IEEE Trans. Pattern Anal. Mach. Intell. **41**(10), 2305–2318 (2018)
10. Gharbi, M., Chaurasia, G., Paris, S., Durand, F.: Deep joint demosaicking and denoising. ACM Trans. Graph. (TOG) **35**(6), 191 (2016)
11. Gu, S., Timofte, R., Van Gool, L.: Integrating local and non-local denoiser priors for image restoration. In: 2018 24th International Conference on Pattern Recognition (ICPR), pp. 2923–2928. IEEE (2018)
12. He, K., Zhang, X., Ren, S., Sun, J.: Delving deep into rectifiers: surpassing human-level performance on imagenet classification. In: Proceedings of the IEEE International Conference on Computer Vision, pp. 1026–1034 (2015)
13. Kingma, D.P., Ba, J.: Adam: a method for stochastic optimization. arXiv preprint arXiv:1412.6980 (2014)
14. Lehtinen, J., et al.: Noise2noise: learning image restoration without clean data. arXiv preprint arXiv:1803.04189 (2018)

15. Liu, D., Wen, B., Fan, Y., Loy, C.C., Huang, T.S.: Non-local recurrent network for image restoration. In: Advances in Neural Information Processing Systems, pp. 1673–1682 (2018)
16. Liu, P., Zhang, H., Zhang, K., Lin, L., Zuo, W.: Multi-level wavelet-CNN for image restoration. In: Proceedings of the IEEE Conference on Computer Vision and Pattern Recognition Workshops, pp. 773–782 (2018)
17. Liu, R., Fan, X., Cheng, S., Wang, X., Luo, Z.: Proximal alternating direction network: a globally converged deep unrolling framework. In: Thirty-Second AAAI Conference on Artificial Intelligence (2018)
18. Nah, S., Hyun Kim, T., Mu Lee, K.: Deep multi-scale convolutional neural network for dynamic scene deblurring. In: Proceedings of the IEEE Conference on Computer Vision and Pattern Recognition, pp. 3883–3891 (2017)
19. Ono, S.: Primal-dual plug-and-play image restoration. IEEE Sig. Process. Lett. **24**(8), 1108–1112 (2017)
20. Plötz, T., Roth, S.: Neural nearest neighbors networks. In: Advances in Neural Information Processing Systems, pp. 1087–1098 (2018)
21. Reehorst, E.T., Schniter, P.: Regularization by denoising: clarifications and new interpretations. IEEE Trans. Comput. Imaging **5**(1), 52–67 (2018)
22. Roth, S., Black, M.J.: Fields of experts. Int. J. Comput. Vis. **82**(2), 205 (2009)
23. Santhanam, V., Morariu, V.I., Davis, L.S.: Generalized deep image to image regression. In: Proceedings of the IEEE Conference on Computer Vision and Pattern Recognition, pp. 5609–5619 (2017)
24. Sellent, A., Rother, C., Roth, S.: Stereo video deblurring. In: Leibe, B., Matas, J., Sebe, N., Welling, M. (eds.) ECCV 2016. LNCS, vol. 9906, pp. 558–575. Springer, Cham (2016). https://doi.org/10.1007/978-3-319-46475-6_35
25. Sun, J., Cao, W., Xu, Z., Ponce, J.: Learning a convolutional neural network for non-uniform motion blur removal. In: Proceedings of the IEEE Conference on Computer Vision and Pattern Recognition, pp. 769–777 (2015)
26. Tao, X., Gao, H., Shen, X., Wang, J., Jia, J.: Scale-recurrent network for deep image deblurring. In: Proceedings of the IEEE Conference on Computer Vision and Pattern Recognition, pp. 8174–8182 (2018)
27. Venkatakrishnan, S.V., Bouman, C.A., Wohlberg, B.: Plug-and-play priors for model based reconstruction. In: 2013 IEEE Global Conference on Signal and Information Processing, pp. 945–948. IEEE (2013)
28. Wang, S., Wen, B., Wu, J., Tao, D., Wang, Z.: Segmentation-aware image denoising without knowing true segmentation. arXiv preprint arXiv:1905.08965 (2019)
29. Xu, L., Ren, J.S., Liu, C., Jia, J.: Deep convolutional neural network for image deconvolution. In: Advances in Neural Information Processing Systems, pp. 1790–1798 (2014)
30. Yue, Z., Yong, H., Zhao, Q., Zhang, L., Meng, D.: Variational denoising network: toward blind noise modeling and removal. arXiv preprint arXiv:1908.11314 (2019)
31. Zhang, H., Dai, Y., Li, H., Koniusz, P.: Deep stacked hierarchical multi-patch network for image deblurring. In: Proceedings of the IEEE Conference on Computer Vision and Pattern Recognition, pp. 5978–5986 (2019)
32. Zhang, J., Pan, J., Ren, J., Song, Y., Bao, L., Lau, R.W., Yang, M.H.: Dynamic scene deblurring using spatially variant recurrent neural networks. In: Proceedings of the IEEE Conference on Computer Vision and Pattern Recognition, pp. 2521–2529 (2018)
33. Zhang, K., Zuo, W., Chen, Y., Meng, D., Zhang, L.: Beyond a Gaussian denoiser: residual learning of deep CNN for image denoising. IEEE Trans. Image Process. **26**(7), 3142–3155 (2017)

34. Zhang, K., Zuo, W., Gu, S., Zhang, L.: Learning deep CNN denoiser prior for image restoration. In: Proceedings of the IEEE Conference on Computer Vision and Pattern Recognition, pp. 3929–3938 (2017)
35. Zoran, D., Weiss, Y.: From learning models of natural image patches to whole image restoration. In: 2011 International Conference on Computer Vision, pp. 479–486. IEEE (2011)

Efficient Transfer Learning via Joint Adaptation of Network Architecture and Weight

Ming Sun[✉][ID], Haoxuan Dou[ID], and Junjie Yan

SenseTime Group Limited, Beijing, China
sunming1@sensetime.com

Abstract. Transfer learning can boost the performance on the target task by leveraging the knowledge of the source domain. Recent works in neural architecture search (NAS), especially one-shot NAS, can aid transfer learning by establishing sufficient network search space. However, existing NAS methods tend to approximate huge search spaces by explicitly building giant super-networks with multiple sub-paths, and discard super-network weights after a child structure is found. Both the characteristics of existing approaches causes repetitive network training on source tasks in transfer learning. To remedy the above issues, we reduce the super-network size by randomly dropping connection between network blocks while embedding a larger search space. Moreover, we reuse super-network weights to avoid redundant training by proposing a novel framework consisting of two modules, the neural architecture search module for architecture transfer and the neural weight search module for weight transfer. These two modules conduct search on the target task based on a reduced super-networks, so we only need to train once on the source task. We experiment our framework on both MS-COCO and CUB-200 for the object detection and fine-grained image classification tasks, and show promising improvements with only $O(C^N)$ super-network complexity.

Keywords: Neural architecture search · Transfer learning · Weight sharing

1 Introduction

Deep neural networks have achieved significant successes in computer vision tasks like image classification [16,18,45,55]. However, the success of deep networks tend to highly depend on a large amount of training data to ensure optimal training [32]. Therefore, insufficient training data can be an inescapable issue for tasks without a huge dataset, such as segmentation, object detection or medical image analysis. Deep transfer learning was proposed to alleviate the data insufficiency by leveraging a massive source datasets to assist training on the target

© Springer Nature Switzerland AG 2020
A. Vedaldi et al. (Eds.): ECCV 2020, LNCS 12358, pp. 463–480, 2020.
https://doi.org/10.1007/978-3-030-58601-0_28

tasks [43]. Most existing deep transfer learning methods apply transfer on networks of fixed architectures, with regularization on instance, feature or weight spaces [34,43], and the result of transfer learning is reflected only through the model weights. We argue that the architecture engineering also plays a vital role in the outcome of the knowledge transfer. We perform direct finetuning on ImageNet [7] pre-trained ResNet-50 [15] models of different architectures on a fine-grained classification dataset CUB-200-2011 [49]. We plot their performances on source and target tasks in Fig. 1. We see that far from the ideal that better source models leads to better target models, when the model architecture is taken into consideration we see certain architecture is related to higher performance on target while suffering on source compared to models of different architecture, such as the yellow triangle in Fig. 1. Therefore we argue that the potential of architecture engineering in the transfer learning process can be great, which is also recognized and explored in recent literature [24].

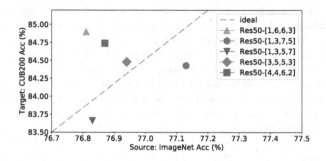

Fig. 1. The plot shows the performances on target and source tasks for models of same size but different architectures. The numbers inside the brackets behind each *ResNet-50* in the legend are the block numbers for each of the four stages of ResNet. The five ResNet-50 models have different block allocations but the same model size.

For architecture engineering, neural architecture search (NAS) methods have shown promising results. NAS methods can be roughly divided into two categories: reinforcement learning (RL) based and gradient based [1,3,27,44,53,60]. RL based NAS methods tend to be computationally expensive and not naturally fit for transfer learning, while gradient based methods, in particular single-shot NAS methods show robust and efficient search process [2,12,24]. Single-shot NAS methods often use a super-network structure, which is a giant network subsuming a great collection of child network structures. These methods provide fast architecture search and one may propose to utilize them for transfer learning. However, we argue that existing methods cause inefficient transfer due to two reasons. First,the super-networks employed in previous literature tend to be massive in size and result in slow training, which is insufficient since normally in transfer learning the size of the source task dataset is also huge. Moreover, existing approaches discard super-networks after an ideal child architecture is found and child models are used to be retrained. While in transfer learning discarding the super-network weights is not economical since the super-network weights can be inherited onto the child model for weight transfer.

To amend the aforementioned issues, we propose to first reduce the super-network size. Inspired by [24] we use the allocation of networks among stages as our search space. But unlike the multi-path super-network utilized in [24], we adopt a single-path super-network, which in-explicitly embeds a rich search space by sharing blocks among potential paths. Specifically, each potential path can be obtained by dropping blocks in different stages of the super-network. We train it by randomly dropping connection between network blocks during training iterations. In this way we create a super-network of reasonable size yet with a rich search space, and therefore limit the computational expenses for training on source. For instance, the super-network utilized in [24] is equivalent to a ResNet-923 [15], while the reduced version is only equivalent to a ResNet-182 while embedding a richer search space. Second, we aim to reuse the super-network weight by proposing a framework consisting of two modules: the neural architecture search module and the neural weight search module. In the neural architecture search module, given the trained super-network we conduct architecture transfer by greedily searching for the target structure on target. For the neural weight search module, the target structure reuse the network weights inherited from the super-network and fine-tune on target. By reusing weights from the super-network, we avoid repetitive retraining. Combining these two modules, we are able to effectively incorporate architecture engineering into the transfer learning process.

Our contributions are as following:

- We demonstrate that the network architecture is crucial in the outcome of transfer learning, and therefore propose to incorporate architecture engineering into the pipeline of transfer learning for modern computer vision tasks such as image classification, object detection and instance segmentation.
- We propose a novel transfer learning framework, which adopts a single-path super-network for fast source training and incorporates both architecture and weight transfer for effective and fast transfer learning.
- Our experiments on various tasks including object detection and fine-grained classification show that our framework's robustness to diverse tasks. Moreover, our experiments on segmentation shows the good transfer ability of target models our method generates. Our method is able to boost the model performance on these tasks while keeping almost the same FLOPs.

2   Related Work

2.1   Transfer Learning

Transfer learning addresses the problem of training with insufficient training data on a target task, by leveraging a massive dataset from a source domain [34,43]. Transfer learning focuses on what and how to transfer between the source and target domain, and different methods aim to address the two concerns in different forms such as the feature space, the instance space or the model weights. In terms of the model weights, one popular method called fine-tuning is to directly adapt the network pre-trained on a large scale source dataset to the target domain, or take the pre-trained network as backbone and add high-level layers for different target tasks such as recognition [5,22,32], object detection [20,41], and segmentation [14]. This method is shown to be more effective than a randomly initialized networks [8]. On the hand, transfer learning methods also utilize regularization on the instance space and feature space to promote efficient transfer from source to target, by either re-weighting or re-sampling data from source domain to aid target domain learning [6,28,35,50,57], or by regularizing target domain learning through minimizing distance between the feature spaces of target and source [29,48,59]. Moreover, adversarial learning is adopted to create domain-invariant models for robust transfer learning [9,10,46,47]. Recently, [21] propose to use meta-learning to do transfer learning between networks of heterogeneous structures and tasks, by learning a meta-model deciding what layer and feature should be paired for transfer.

However, the aforementioned methods mostly care about transferring knowledge between networks of fixed architectures. We instead incorporate the network architecture as a variable in the transfer process, to allow the target model to adapt its architecture to the target task.

2.2 Neural Architecture Search

Neural architecture search methods search network architecture on a fixed task, normally an image classification task [44,61]. Early NAS methods often conduct search in a nested manner, where numerous architecture is sampled from a large search space and trained from scratch, during which reinforcement learning [1,44,60] or evolution [33,38,39,54] are used. These methods usually require a giant amount of computational resources. Recent NAS methods adopt the weight-sharing protocol to reduce computational intensity by leveraging a super-network which subsume all architecture [3,27,37,53,56]. In particular one-shot NAS methods train the super-network with stochastic path [2,11,11,19], and then search for the optimal architecture from the trained super-network in a separate step [2,12,24]. They normally use super-network with multiple paths, different paths consist of different kernel sizes, dilation ratios, channel numbers and block allocations in order to achieve good adaption to fixed tasks. Even greatly reduced in recent works [24], the search spaces of recent NAS methods are still large and fine-grained. We instead use a single long path with skip connection to in-explicitly embed a large collection of possible sub-paths, which limits our complexity compared to existing methods.

3   Method

In this section, we first introduce our problem setting, and then describe the super network, which provides a strong source model for later transfer. We then

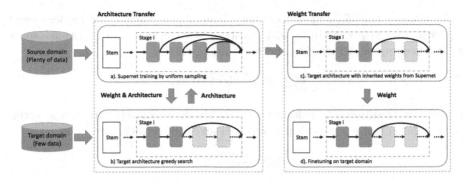

Fig. 2. Our transfer learning framework consists of the architecture transfer and the weight transfer. For the architecture transfer on the left part of the figure, the super-network is trained on source domain and passed to target domain for the greedy search, and the searched architecture is passed back to inherit weight from the super-network. For the weight transfer network on the right, the target architecture with inherited weights is fine-tuned on source and target.

introduce the neural architecture search module to optimize the structure of the target model and the neural weight search module for weight transfer. Finally we demonstrate the potential of our transferred neural network to combine with various network blocks or hand-designed modules. The overview of our method is shown in Fig. 2

3.1 Problem Setting

We consider transfer learning from the source domain and task $\{\mathcal{D}_s, \mathcal{T}_s\}$ to the target domain and task $\{\mathcal{D}_t, \mathcal{T}_t\}$, where the target can come from a diverse set of domains. We follow the definitions from [34,43] and denote domain as $\mathcal{D} = \{\mathcal{X}, P(X)\}$ with $\mathcal{X}$ as the data space and $P(X)$ as the conditional probability where $X = \{x_i, \ldots, x_n\} \in \mathcal{X}$ is the domain data. We also define task as $\mathcal{T} = \{\mathcal{Y}, f(\cdot)\}$ with $\mathcal{Y}$ as the label space and $f(\cdot)$ being an objective predictive function that maps $x \in X$ to $y \in \mathcal{Y}$ and is learnt during training. In transfer learning in general, $\mathcal{D}_s \neq \mathcal{D}_t$, $\mathcal{T}_s \neq \mathcal{T}_t$, and the size of source data is usually much larger than the size of the target data, that is $|D_s| \gg |D_t|$.

We define the backbone network by $\mathcal{N}(\phi, w_\phi)$ as a transformation from the data space to the feature space, where $\phi \in \mathcal{A}$ denotes the model architecture and $w_\phi \in \mathcal{W_A}$ denotes the model weight. $\mathcal{A}$ and $\mathcal{W_A}$ respectively define the architecture search space and corresponding weight space. We aim to find a model $\mathcal{N}(\phi_t, w_{\phi_t})$ on target to maximize performance on target domain validation set given the source $\{\mathcal{D}_s, \mathcal{T}_s\}$,

$$(\phi_t, w_{\phi_t}) = \underset{(\phi, w_\phi) \in (\mathcal{A}, \mathcal{W_A})}{\arg\min} \mathcal{L}_{val}^{target}(\mathcal{N}(\phi, w_\phi)) \tag{1}$$

where $\mathcal{L}_{val}$ represents the validation loss on the target domain.

Traditional transfer learning methods focus on optimizing the model weight w_{ϕ_t} with a fixed ϕ_t by training with constraints on feature space, instance space or by inheriting model weights and fine-tuning, that is

$$\min_{w_{\phi_t} \in \mathcal{W}_{\mathcal{A}}} \mathcal{L}_{val}^{target}(\mathcal{N}(\phi_t, w_{\phi_t})) \tag{2}$$

Here unlike traditional transfer learning methods we incorporate neural architecture search and can turn Eq. 1 into a bi-level optimization problem,

$$\min_{w_{\phi_t} \in \mathcal{W}_{\mathcal{A}}} \mathcal{L}_{val}^{target}(\mathcal{N}(\phi_t, w_{\phi_t}))$$
$$\text{s.t. } \phi_t = \arg\min_{\phi \in \mathcal{A}} \mathcal{L}_{val}^{target}(\mathcal{N}(\phi, w_{\phi}^s)) \tag{3}$$

where w_{ϕ}^s is the optimized weights on source given a super-network architecture ϕ. As we introduce NAS into the process of transfer learning, it becomes non-trivial to accommodate NAS approaches for efficient transfer. In particular we need our architecture search step to take the difference between sizes of source and target datasets into consideration during transfer learning.

3.2   Source Super-Network Training

The ideal super-network for transfer learning should contain three qualities. Firstly, the super-network should embed a rich search space for finding a powerful network structure. Secondly, the super-network size should be small for efficient training. Finally, the super-network should have the similar network hierarchy as the potential child model for weight sharing. Previous NAS approaches adopting weight sharing protocols [2,3,12,27,53] often establish giant super-networks with complex structures, which violates the second quality. In addition, the search space they embed tend to be complicated.

Inspired by recent work on single-shot NAS [24], we utilize the allocation of network blocks among different stages as the search space for its efficacy and simplicity. However, we find that the multi-branches of different numbers of blocks often utilized in these one-shot NAS methods cause the model size to significantly increase with depth. We instead just use one branch of the maximum amount of blocks, which contains all possible paths as its sub-paths. By sharing blocks among potential paths, we reduce the super-network size while maintaining a powerful search space.

To sufficiently train the super-network such that each child model represented by its sub-paths can provide robust weight for neural architecture search on target, we randomly drops networks blocks from the forward and backward pass during training. Specifically, a stage in the super-network consists of N blocks in a sequential order. During each iteration in training we uniformly sample S from $[1, N]$, and only keep the first S block for this round of training. In this way, different combination of sub-paths are trained and excessive co-adaptation between blocks are avoided. The super-network is able to still embed a powerful search space while being small in size.

3.3 Neural Architecture Search on Target

Given the super-network from the source and the required model size constraint C, we first fine-tune the super-network on the target task and then search for a robust architecture. We first define our super-network and the corresponding search space. We can represent the super-network architecture as $\phi_s = [N_1^s, \cdots, N_{ns}^s]$ where N_i refers to the number of blocks at the i_{th} stage. Normally the number of stages $ns = 4$ for most of networks. For instance, we can define ResNet50 as $\phi_{res50} = [3, 4, 6, 3]$. With the super-network and the required model size constraint C, we can define the architecture search space under model size C as,

$$\mathcal{A}_C = \{\phi_t | \phi_t \in \Gamma(\phi_s), sum(\phi_t) = C\} \tag{4}$$

where $\Gamma(\phi_s) = \{\phi_t = [N_1^t, \cdots, N_{ns}^t] | N_i^t \in [1, \cdots, N_i^s]\}$ denotes the search space of all possible child models.

Random search or evolution are often applied for specified computation limitation. However, instead of having a fixed computation limits like previous approaches often do, we aim to search for optimal allocation for all possible model sizes. Here we make the assumption that given a model size c and the corresponding optimal target architecture ϕ_c^*, the optimal architecture ϕ_{c+1}, corresponding to model size $c + 1$, contains ϕ_c as a sub-graph. Here we denote the search space of ϕ_{c+1} conditional on an optimal ϕ_c^* as $\mathcal{A}_{c+1}^*$,

$$\mathcal{A}_{c+1}^* = \{\phi_{c+1} | \phi_c^* \subset \phi_{c+1}, \phi_{c+1} \in \mathcal{A}_{c+1}\} \tag{5}$$

Based on this greedy assumption, we can inductively search for optimal target network architecture ϕ_t starting from the minimal architecture $\phi_{ns} = [1, \cdots, 1]$, where ns is the number of stages. In the inductive search step, given optimal ϕ_c, we find ϕ_{c+1} by adding one more block that maximize the resulting model's performance on the target validation set, that is

$$\phi_{c+1}^* = \underset{\phi_{c+1} \in \mathcal{A}_{c+1}^*}{\arg\max} \ \mathcal{L}_{val}(\mathcal{N}(\phi_{c+1}, w_{\phi_{c+1}}^s)) \tag{6}$$

ϕ_{c+1}^* can be found by running network evaluation for ns times, where the evaluated network is obtained by appending the next block to its path at each stage. We repeat the induction step for several times until we reach the model size constraint C, and we have the optimal architectures for models whose sizes ranges from ns to C. In detail, this algorithm is shown in Algorithm 1 and left bottom of Fig. 2.

3.4 Neural Weight Search on Target

After we have a optimized neural architecture ϕ_t, we focus on the transfer of network weights. Existing NAS methods [2,12,24] often discard the network weights after search and retrain, which is time-consuming. We reuse the weight inherited from the super-network through the neural weight search, which save time used in repetitive training. Specifically for the neural weight search we

---

Algorithm 1: Greedy Block Search

    Input   : Model size constraint $C \geq ns$, super-network $\mathcal{N}(\phi_s, w_s)$
    Output : Target architecture ϕ_t^* with $sum(\phi_t) = C$
1 initialize start network $\phi_{ns} = [1, \cdots, 1]$, $c = ns + 1$;
2 while $c \leq C$ do
3 | $\phi_c^* = \arg\max_{\phi_c \in \mathcal{A}_c^*} \mathcal{L}_{val}(\mathcal{N}(\phi_c, w_{\phi_c}))$;
4 | $c = c + 1$;
5 end
6 return $\phi_t^* = \phi_C^*$

---

apply the fine-tuning method often employed in the transfer learning. Given the searched target network $\{\phi_t, w_{\phi_t}^s\}$, where $w_{\phi_t}^s$ is directly inherited from the source super-network, we first fine-tune it on the source domain to obtain robust source network weights, and then we fine-tune the resulting network on the target domain to get $\{\phi_t, w_{\phi_t}\}$.

In this way, we ensure a sufficient transfer of network weight based on the target architecture. The process is shown in the right part of Fig. 2. Note that the weight transfer step can be extended to use other knowledge transfer methods beyond weight fine-tuning, such as knowledge distillation [17] or feature mimicking [23].

3.5 Generalization over Diverse Structures

Generalization over Diverse Blocks. Our transfer learning framework can generalize to a diverse collection of network blocks, hand-designed or generated using NAS. We first experiment on blocks of the widely used hand-designed MobileNetV2 [42] and ResNet [15]. Moreover, we apply our method using blocks of MnasNet-b0 [44], which is generated through neural architecture search using reinforcement learning on ImageNet [7]. Table 1 shows that on detection task, our framework transfers well on all three network blocks for the object detection task with a universal performance improvement.

Generalization over Hand-Designed Modules. Our framework also generalizes well over network blocks enhanced by hand-designed modules. We apply our method to two widely recognized modules. The Squeeze-Excitation module [18] improves network performances through a channel-wise attention mechanism, while ResNeXt [55] achieves improvements by multi-branching a ResNet block in order to increase the computational cardinallity. We show the robustness of our method to block enhancements by enhancing a transferred ResNet-50 model with the two modules described above on object detection task. As is shown in Table 1, the transferred ResNet-50 architecture still has 1 point improvement in mAP on the basis of SE-block and ResNeXt.

Table 1. Performance of different network configures for object detection on MS-COCO [26] dataset using Faster-RCNN with FPN [25,40].

Method	mAP	FLOPS
ResNet50 [24]	36.4	3.991G
CR-ResNet50 [24]	37.4	3.991G
Transfer-ResNet50	37.8	3.991G
ResNet101	38.5	7.62G
CR-ResNet101 [24]	39.5	7.62G
Transfer-ResNet101	39.8	7.62G
MobileNetV2	32.2	312.34M
CR-MobileNetV2 [24]	33.5	329.21M
Transfer-MobileNetV2	34.0	311.68M
MnasNet-b0	34.2	313.14M
Transfer-MnasNet-b0	34.7	318.37M
SE-ResNeXt50	38.9	4.130G
Transfer-SE-ResNeXt50	39.9	4.132G
Grid-RCNN-ResNet50	39.5	3.991G
Gird-RCNN-Transfer-ResNet50	40.3	3.991G
Cascade-MaskRCNN-ResNet101	43.3	7.62G
Cascade-MaskRCNN-Transfer-ResNet101	44.1	7.62G

4   Experiment

For all our experiments we implement our methods using the Pytorch framework [36], and in this section we describe the tasks we experimented on and the corresponding results.

4.1   Objection Detection

For the object detection task, we conduct experiments on the MS-COCO dataset [26], which 118K training images 5K validate images (*minival*) for 80 classes. The evaluation metric is the mean average precision (mAP).

We conduct experiments on three types of network blocks: the ResNet [15] bottleneck block, the MobileNetV2 [42] block and the MnasNet [44] block. For the super-network consisting of ResNet bottleneck blocks [15], we set the block allocation to be $T_s = [8, 10, 36, 14]$, whose FLOPs is roughly equal to that of ResNet-200. For the super-network consisting of MobileNetV2 block [42], we set the block allocation to be $T_s = [5, 6, 8, 7, 7]$ with 5 stages. For the super-network consisting of MnasNet blocks [44], the configuration is same to that of MobileNetV2.

We use the ImageNet dataset [7] as the source domain and train our super-networks on it for 100 epochs with label smoothing of 0.1 and 5 epochs of warmup. We use 32 GPU cards with a total batch size of 2048, and the base learning rate is 0.01. For the learning rate we conduct the step decay scheme, where we drop the learning rate by 10 at epoch of 30, 60, 80. The weight decay is set to be 0.0001.

For the object detection task on MS-COCO dataset, we adopt Faster-RCNN [41] in combination with the feature pyramid network (FPN) [25]. For finetuning, the base learning rate and weight decay are set to be 0.04 and 0.0001 respectively. We use 32 GPU cards with a total batch size of 64. Note that different to ResNet models, where the network blocks at the adjacent stages share the same FLOPs, the MobileNetV2 models' blocks need to be re-weighted during the architecture search. Specifically, the block number at each stage is re-weighted according to that stage's computation FLOPs, and then we do the greedy search until the sum of the re-weighted block numbers reaches the computational limits. We apply the same re-weighting to the architecture search with MnasNet, too.

Results on Different Network Blocks. To demonstrate the effectiveness of our proposed method, we conduct transfer learning on ResNet, MobileNetV2 and MnasNet-b0 with configurations described above. The results are shown in Table 1. For ResNet, we search the best network architecture for the popular ResNet-50, which has 16 blocks in total. The best architecture is $[1, 3, 7, 5]$, which get 37.8% mAP and 1.4% higher than default $[3, 4, 6, 3]$ configuration on MS-COCO. We also transfer the ResNet-101 model, and our transferred model reach 39.8% mAP surpassing the default configure by 1.3%, with the optimal architecture as $[2, 5, 19, 7]$. For the MobileNetV2 and the MnasNet-b0, their searched best architectures are $[2, 2, 2, 3, 5]$ and $[3, 3, 2, 3, 4]$ respectively. Also, their performances are better than baselines' on MS-COCO *minival* while keeping almost the same backbone FLOPs. Furthermore, we show better results compared to [24] on all three network blocks above. We think the reason for the better results lie in the richness of our search space, as our search space contains all sub-structures fulfilling the model size constraint. However, the search space adopted in [24] skips certain sub-structures since paths with certain number of blocks are not built in the super-network to prevent its size from being computationally unbearable.

Moreover, we show that the boosted SE-ResNeXt-50, enhancing the transferred ResNet-50 blocks with multi-branching [55] and SE-module [18], also shows solid performance improvement on MS-COCO *minival*, compared to the original SE-ResNeXt-50. Furthermore, we show that our transferred ResNet backbones also outperform their default counterparts when combined with the Grid-RCNN framework [30] and the Cascade-MaskRCNN framework [4], with both 0.8% improvements in mAP on the MS-COCO *minival*.

These results demonstrate the robustness of our methods over various types of network blocks with or without hand-designed module or strong frameworks for enhancements.

Results on Different Computation Constraints. Apart from the common network architecture configures like ResNet-50, we also explore the potential of our framework on a series of target model architectures optimized under different

Table 2. Transferred ResNet on MS-COCO. The colored numbers indicate that adding one block respectively in the third (red & blue) and fourth (green) stages seems to increase performance the most on small (red), medium (blue) and large (green) objects.

Method	mAP	Block	FLOPS(G)	Box_s	Box_m	Box_l
Transfer-ResNet37	36.4	[1, 3, 4, 4]	3.138	0.2089	0.3987	0.4747
Transfer-ResNet41	36.7	[1, 3, 5, 4]	3.352	0.2178	0.4031	0.4608
Transfer-ResNet44	37.0	[1, 3, 5, 5]	3.565	0.2128	0.4051	0.4805
Transfer-ResNet47	37.4	[1, 3, 6, 5]	3.777	0.2153	0.4117	0.4836
Transfer-ResNet50	37.8	[1, 3, 7, 5]	3.991	0.2158	0.4180	0.4925
Transfer-ResNet53	38.0	[1, 3, 7, 6]	4.205	0.2168	0.4148	0.4958

computational constraints, such as ResNet-37, ResNet-41 and so on. With the pre-trained super-network, we can search for models of different size on the target task by assigning different computation requirements. For example, you can set 15 for searching a best ResNet47 network configuration. Also, thanks to our greedy search algorithm, we can efficiently search for models of larger size on the basis of previously transferred smaller-sized model without starting from scratch. On Table 2, we show some the ResNet configurations of different computational complexity and their corresponding performances on MS-COCO *minival*. For example, $T^*_{res47} = [1, 3, 6, 5]$, $T^*_{res50} = [1, 3, 7, 5]$, $T^*_{res53} = [1, 3, 7, 6]$ are generated from the super-network.

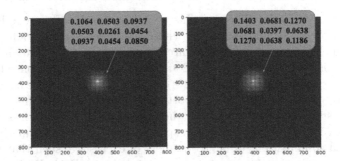

Fig. 3. The effective receptive fields of the baseline network and our transferred network from the last convolution layer. The left part is the baseline and the right part is our transferred network.

Visualization. To further understand the transferred backbone, we visualize the backbone effective receptive filed (ERF), which is the key to the objection detection task. Based on the method proposed in [31], the receptive fields of the center neuron on the last convolution layer are visualized in Fig. 3. In detail, the figure is generated by setting input values to 1 and propagating using the neuron

Table 3. CUB-200-2011 fine-grained classification with 5799 training images.

Method	mAP	Block number	ImageNet
ResNet50 [58]	84.05	[3, 4, 6, 3]	76.72
ResNet50+NL [51]	84.79	[3, 4, 6, 3]	–
ResNet50+CGNL [58]	85.14	[3, 4, 6, 3]	–
Transfer-ResNet50	**84.98**	[1, 6, 6, 3]	76.81
Transfer-ResNet50+NL [51]	**85.42**	[1, 6, 6, 3]	–
Transfer-ResNet50	84.95	[2, 4, 7, 3]	**77.06**
Transfer-ResNet50	84.76	[2, 3, 7, 4]	76.78
Transfer-ResNet50	84.74	[4, 4, 6, 2]	76.87
Transfer-ResNet50	84.64	[1, 4, 8, 3]	76.93

in the center of the last convolution layer. ReLU operations are abandoned to better visualize the intensity of connections. As shown in the Fig. 3, the ERF size of our transferred network is larger than that of the baseline network. We also calculate the outer response number, as shown in the green box on right top of the ERF figures. Except the stronger intensities of center region, the intensities of outer region from the ERF of our transferred is also stronger than that of the default baseline network. The strong intensity of ERF is important for the object detection task which contains higher scale variance compared with the classification task, and our transferred network manages to capture this characteristics through the architecture engineering on the target task.

Complexity Analysis. The one-shot NAS methods often employ super-networks made up of multi-branches while our super-network only keeps the longest path. For our super-network architecture $[8, 10, 36, 14]$ with the block sum with 68 is equal to the ResNet-206, while the equivalent one-shot super-network using multi-branches needs to contain 862 blocks to capture all the potential sub-paths. Since a ResNet bottleneck block contains three layers and the network stem contains two layers, the one-shot super-network is equivalent to a ResNet-2588. Moreover the search space of regular one-shot methods needs to contain all combinations of block numbers of each stage such that the model size requirement is met, leading to a space of order $O(C^{ns})$. While our search space, thanks to the greedy search algorithm, is only of order $O(C \times ns)$

4.2 Fine-Grained Classification

In the fine-grained image classification task, since the data collecting and labeling is time-consuming, fine-grained image classification task dataset is often small. For example, the commonly used dataset is CUB-200-2011 [49], which contains 200 classes and 5994 training images in total.

We experiment on CUB-200-2011 following [58] using the input size of 448 with ImageNet [7] dataset as the source domain. When finetuning on target,

Table 4. CUB-200-2010 fine-grained classification with total 3000 training images.

Method	mAP	Block number	ImageNet
ResNet50	68.01	[3, 4, 6, 3]	76.72
Transfer-ResNet50	**71.35**	[1, 6, 6, 3]	76.81
Transfer-ResNet50	68.02	[3, 5, 5, 3]	76.94
Transfer-ResNet50	67.72	[2, 4, 7, 3]	77.06
Transfer-ResNet50	67.66	[1, 3, 7, 5]	**77.13**
Transfer-ResNet50	67.23	[1, 4, 8, 3]	76.93

Table 5. Instance Segmentation Results on MS-COCO. Here we show comparison between our transferred network and baseline networks. We also demonstrate higher performance over more complex networks such as Cascade-MaskRCNN in the object detection task as shown in Table 1

Backbone	Seg	Seg_s	Seg_m	Seg_l	Box	Box_s	Box_m	Box_l
ResNet50	33.9	17.4	37.3	46.6	37.6	21.8	41.2	48.9
Ours	34.8(+0.9)	17.9 (+0.5)	38.3(+1.0)	48.1(+1.5)	38.6(+1.0)	22.5(+0.7)	42.2(+1.0)	50.6(+1.7)
ResNet101	35.6	18.6	39.2	49.5	39.7	23.4	43.9	51.7
Ours	36.4(+0.8)	18.7(+0.1)	40.0(+0.8)	50.6(+1.1)	40.6(+0.9)	23.5(+0.1)	44.5(+0.6)	53.4(+1.7)
MobileNetV2	30.6	15.3	33.2	44.1	33.1	18.8	35.8	43.3
Ours	31.8(+1.2)	16.0(+0.7)	34.6(+1.4)	43.8(−0.3)	34.8(+1.7)	19.7(+0.9)	37.6(+2.8)	45.6(+2.3)

all models are trained for 100 epochs with an initial learning rate of 0.01 and a step decay scheme dropping the learning rate by 10 at the epoch of 30, 60, 80. We use one GPU card with the batch size of 64 samples.

We show the performances of transferred models on both CUB-200-2011 and ImageNet datasets in Table 3, and we can see the best transferred network architecture is $[1, 6, 6, 3]$ with more than 0.9 point higher than the baseline. We also include the several other top performing transferred networks in Table 3. Note that the top performing transferred network on the CUB-200-2011 task shows worse performances on the ImageNet dataset, compared to the other transferred model with the architecture $[2, 4, 7, 3]$ that achieve 77.06 accuracy on ImageNet while performing less optimal on target. Moreover, the rest of the transferred models also demonstrate the inconsistency between source and target performances when the models are of different architectures. This fact shows that finding a suitable architecture for a target model can play a role in transfer learning as vital as the weight transfer, if not more. In addition, we conduct transfer experiments using ResNet-50 with the non-local module, showing better results than both the original and compact generalized non-local baselines [51,58].

We also conduct experiments on CUB-200-2010 [52], which is an older and smaller version of CUB-200-2011. We report the performances both on CUB-200-2010 and ImageNet in Table 4. We observe that the optimal transferred network architecture on CUB-200-2010 vary from that of CUB-200-2011, but we also observe a 60% overlap of the top 5 performing architectures on CUB-200-2011 and CUB-200-2010.

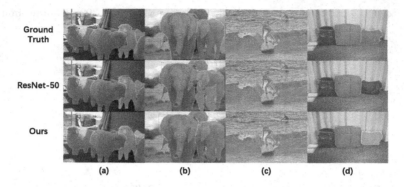

Fig. 4. Some hard segmentation cases not handled well by baseline ResNet-50 but fixed by our transferred ResNet-50. a). Our model shows tighter instance masks. b). Our model shows more consistent masks. c). Our method successfully detects the small person behind the surfer, missed by the regular ResNet-50. d). Our models captures the bag on the right while the baseline misses it.

4.3   Semantic Segmentation

We wish to explore the potential of our transferred model to transfer further to other target tasks without modification to the architecture. We conduct experiments on the MS-COCO instance segmentation task with the transferred models obtained from the object detection task. In particular, we take the Mask-RCNN [13] and replace the backbone with the transferred model, and then we directly finetune on MS-COCO instance segmentation dataset.

We report performances of our models in Table 5. Our transfer-ResNet-50 with architecture of $[1, 3, 7, 5]$ outperforms its counterparts on both segmentation and detection with various object scales. In Fig. 4 we show some of the cases from MS-COCO dataset that the traditional ResNet-50 handles badly while our transferred model handles well. For Transfer-ResNet-101, its segmentation and detection mAP are better than its default counterpart by 0.8% and 0.9%, and it also shows improvement on objects of all scales. For Transfer-MobileNetV2, the mAP of detection and segmentation are better by 1.2% and 1.7% respectively. Interestingly, the segmentation of larger object is inferior to baseline by 0.3% while detection on larger object better by 2.3%.

5   Conclusion

In this paper, we propose a novel transfer framework containing a neural architecture search module and a neural weight search module. In the architecture transfer we design a block-level search space and accordingly build an powerful super network on source, and search for the optimal architecture through a greedy algorithm on the target task. For the neural weight search module, we adopt weight fine-tuning, which can be smoothly replaced by other existing transfer learning methods to push the performance even higher. Extensive experiments of our framework on various tasks show promising results.

References

1. Baker, B., Gupta, O., Naik, N., Raskar, R.: Designing neural network architectures using reinforcement learning. CoRR abs/1611.02167 (2016). http://arxiv.org/abs/1611.02167

2. Bender, G., Kindermans, P.J., Zoph, B., Vasudevan, V., Le, Q.: Understanding and simplifying one-shot architecture search. In: Dy, J., Krause, A. (eds.) Proceedings of the 35th International Conference on Machine Learning. Proceedings of Machine Learning Research, vol. 80, pp. 550–559. PMLR, Stockholmsmüssan, Stockholm Sweden, 10–15 July 2018. http://proceedings.mlr.press/v80/bender18a.html

3. Cai, H., Zhu, L., Han, S.: ProxylessNAS: direct neural architecture search on target task and hardware. In: International Conference on Learning Representations (2019). https://openreview.net/forum?id=HylVB3AqYm

4. Cai, Z., Vasconcelos, N.: Cascade R-CNN: delving into high quality object detection. CoRR abs/1712.00726 (2017). http://arxiv.org/abs/1712.00726

5. Cui, Y., Song, Y., Sun, C., Howard, A., Belongie, S.: Large scale fine-grained categorization and domain-specific transfer learning. In: The IEEE Conference on Computer Vision and Pattern Recognition (CVPR), June 2018

6. Dai, W., Yang, Q., Xue, G.R., Yu, Y.: Boosting for transfer learning. In: Proceedings of the 24th International Conference on Machine Learning, ICML 2007, pp. 193–200. ACM, New York (2007). https://doi.org/10.1145/1273496.1273521. http://doi.acm.org/10.1145/1273496.1273521

7. Deng, J., Dong, W., Socher, R., Li, L.J., Li, K., Fei-Fei, L.: ImageNet: a large-scale hierarchical image database. In: CVPR 2009 (2009)

8. Erhan, D., Bengio, Y., Courville, A., Manzagol, P.A., Vincent, P., Bengio, S.: Why does unsupervised pre-training help deep learning? J. Mach. Learn. Res. **11**, 625–660 (2010). http://dl.acm.org/citation.cfm?id=1756006.1756025

9. Ganin, Y., Lempitsky, V.: Unsupervised domain adaptation by backpropagation. In: Proceedings of the 32nd International Conference on International Conference on Machine Learning, ICML 2015, vol. 37, pp. 1180–1189. JMLR.org (2015). http://dl.acm.org/citation.cfm?id=3045118.3045244

10. Ganin, Y., et al.: Domain-adversarial training of neural networks. J. Mach. Learn. Res. **17**(1), 2096–2030 (2016). http://dl.acm.org/citation.cfm?id=2946645.2946704

11. Ghiasi, G., Lin, T.Y., Le, Q.V.: Dropblock: a regularization method for convolutional networks. In: Proceedings of the 32nd International Conference on Neural Information Processing Systems, NIPS 2018, pp. 10750–10760. Curran Associates Inc., USA (2018). http://dl.acm.org/citation.cfm?id=3327546.3327732

12. Guo, Z., et al.: Single path one-shot neural architecture search with uniform sampling. CoRR abs/1904.00420 (2019). http://arxiv.org/abs/1904.00420

13. He, K., Gkioxari, G., Dollár, P., Girshick, R.: Mask R-CNN. In: Proceedings of the IEEE International Conference on Computer Vision, pp. 2961–2969 (2017)

14. He, K., Gkioxari, G., Dollár, P., Girshick, R.B.: Mask R-CNN. CoRR abs/1703.06870 (2017). http://arxiv.org/abs/1703.06870

15. He, K., Zhang, X., Ren, S., Sun, J.: Deep residual learning for image recognition. CoRR abs/1512.03385 (2015). http://arxiv.org/abs/1512.03385

16. He, T., Zhang, Z., Zhang, H., Zhang, Z., Xie, J., Li, M.: Bag of tricks for image classification with convolutional neural networks. In: The IEEE Conference on Computer Vision and Pattern Recognition (CVPR), June 2019

17. Hinton, G.E., Vinyals, O., Dean, J.: Distilling the knowledge in a neural network. arXiv abs/1503.02531 (2015)
18. Hu, J., Shen, L., Sun, G.: Squeeze-and-excitation networks. In: 2018 IEEE/CVF Conference on Computer Vision and Pattern Recognition, pp. 7132–7141, June 2018. https://doi.org/10.1109/CVPR.2018.00745
19. Huang, G., Sun, Y., Liu, Z., Sedra, D., Weinberger, K.Q.: Deep networks with stochastic depth. CoRR abs/1603.09382 (2016). http://arxiv.org/abs/1603.09382
20. Huang, J., et al.: Speed/accuracy trade-offs for modern convolutional object detectors. In: The IEEE Conference on Computer Vision and Pattern Recognition (CVPR), July 2017
21. Jang, Y., Lee, H., Hwang, S.J., Shin, J.: Learning what and where to transfer. In: Proceedings of the 36th International Conference on Machine Learning, ICML 2019, Long Beach, California, USA, 9–15 June 2019, pp. 3030–3039 (2019). http://proceedings.mlr.press/v97/jang19b.html
22. Kornblith, S., Shlens, J., Le, Q.V.: Do better imagenet models transfer better? In: The IEEE Conference on Computer Vision and Pattern Recognition (CVPR), June 2019
23. Li, Q., Jin, S., Yan, J.: Mimicking very efficient network for object detection. In: The IEEE Conference on Computer Vision and Pattern Recognition (CVPR), July 2017
24. Liang, F., et al.: Computation reallocation for object detection. In: International Conference on Learning Representations (2020). https://openreview.net/forum?id=SkxLFaNKwB
25. Lin, T., Dollár, P., Girshick, R., He, K., Hariharan, B., Belongie, S.: Feature pyramid networks for object detection. In: 2017 IEEE Conference on Computer Vision and Pattern Recognition (CVPR), pp. 936–944, July 2017. https://doi.org/10.1109/CVPR.2017.106
26. Lin, T.-Y., et al.: Microsoft COCO: common objects in context. In: Fleet, D., Pajdla, T., Schiele, B., Tuytelaars, T. (eds.) ECCV 2014. LNCS, vol. 8693, pp. 740–755. Springer, Cham (2014). https://doi.org/10.1007/978-3-319-10602-1_48
27. Liu, H., Simonyan, K., Yang, Y.: DARTS: differentiable architecture search. In: International Conference on Learning Representations (2019). https://openreview.net/forum?id=S1eYHoC5FX
28. Liu, X., Liu, Z., Wang, G., Cai, Z., Zhang, H.: Ensemble transfer learning algorithm. IEEE Access 6, 2389–2396 (2018). https://doi.org/10.1109/ACCESS.2017.2782884
29. Long, M., Wang, J.: Learning transferable features with deep adaptation networks. CoRR abs/1502.02791 (2015). http://arxiv.org/abs/1502.02791
30. Lu, X., Li, B., Yue, Y., Li, Q., Yan, J.: Grid R-CNN. In: The IEEE Conference on Computer Vision and Pattern Recognition (CVPR), June 2019
31. Luo, W., Li, Y., Urtasun, R., Zemel, R.: Understanding the effective receptive field in deep convolutional neural networks. In: Advances in Neural Information Processing Systems, pp. 4898–4906 (2016)
32. Mahajan, D., et al.: Exploring the limits of weakly supervised pretraining. CoRR abs/1805.00932 (2018). http://arxiv.org/abs/1805.00932
33. Miikkulainen, R., et al.: Evolving deep neural networks. CoRR abs/1703.00548 (2017). http://arxiv.org/abs/1703.00548
34. Pan, S.J., Yang, Q.: A survey on transfer learning. IEEE Trans. Knowl. Data Eng. 22(10), 1345–1359 (2010). https://doi.org/10.1109/TKDE.2009.191

35. Pardoe, D., Stone, P.: Boosting for regression transfer. In: Proceedings of the 27th International Conference on International Conference on Machine Learning, ICML 2010, Omnipress, USA, pp. 863–870 (2010). http://dl.acm.org/citation.cfm?id=3104322.3104432
36. Paszke, A., et al.: Automatic differentiation in pytorch (2017)
37. Pham, H., Guan, M.Y., Zoph, B., Le, Q.V., Dean, J.: Efficient neural architecture search via parameter sharing. CoRR abs/1802.03268 (2018). http://arxiv.org/abs/1802.03268
38. Real, E., Aggarwal, A., Huang, Y., Le, Q.V.: Regularized evolution for image classifier architecture search (2018). https://arxiv.org/pdf/1802.01548.pdf
39. Real, E., et al.: Large-scale evolution of image classifiers. In: Proceedings of the 34th International Conference on Machine Learning, ICML 2017, vol. 70, pp. 2902–2911. JMLR.org (2017). http://dl.acm.org/citation.cfm?id=3305890.3305981
40. Ren, S., He, K., Girshick, R., Sun, J.: Faster R-CNN: towards real-time object detection with region proposal networks. In: Advances in Neural Information Processing Systems, pp. 91–99 (2015)
41. Ren, S., He, K., Girshick, R.B., Sun, J.: Faster R-CNN: towards real-time object detection with region proposal networks. CoRR abs/1506.01497 (2015). http://arxiv.org/abs/1506.01497
42. Sandler, M., Howard, A.G., Zhu, M., Zhmoginov, A., Chen, L.: Inverted residuals and linear bottlenecks: Mobile networks for classification, detection and segmentation. CoRR abs/1801.04381 (2018). http://arxiv.org/abs/1801.04381
43. Tan, C., Sun, F., Kong, T., Zhang, W., Yang, C., Liu, C.: A survey on deep transfer learning. CoRR abs/1808.01974 (2018). http://arxiv.org/abs/1808.01974
44. Tan, M., et al.: Mnasnet: platform-aware neural architecture search for mobile. In: The IEEE Conference on Computer Vision and Pattern Recognition (CVPR), June 2019
45. Tan, M., Le, Q.V.: Efficientnet: rethinking model scaling for convolutional neural networks. CoRR abs/1905.11946 (2019). http://arxiv.org/abs/1905.11946
46. Tzeng, E., Hoffman, J., Darrell, T., Saenko, K.: Simultaneous deep transfer across domains and tasks. In: The IEEE International Conference on Computer Vision (ICCV), December 2015
47. Tzeng, E., Hoffman, J., Saenko, K., Darrell, T.: Adversarial discriminative domain adaptation. In: The IEEE Conference on Computer Vision and Pattern Recognition (CVPR), July 2017
48. Tzeng, E., Hoffman, J., Zhang, N., Saenko, K., Darrell, T.: Deep domain confusion: maximizing for domain invariance. CoRR abs/1412.3474 (2014). http://arxiv.org/abs/1412.3474
49. Wah, C., Branson, S., Welinder, P., Perona, P., Belongie, S.: The Caltech-UCSD Birds-200-2011 Dataset. Technical report (2011)
50. Wang, C., Wu, Y., Liu, Z.: Hierarchical boosting for transfer learning with multi-source. In: Proceedings of the International Conference on Artificial Intelligence and Robotics and the International Conference on Automation, Control and Robotics Engineering, ICAIR-CACRE 2016, pp. 15:1–15:5. ACM, New York (2016). https://doi.org/10.1145/2952744.2952756. http://doi.acm.org/10.1145/2952744.2952756
51. Wang, X., Girshick, R., Gupta, A., He, K.: Non-local neural networks. In: The IEEE Conference on Computer Vision and Pattern Recognition (CVPR), June 2018
52. Welinder, P., et al.: Caltech-UCSD Birds 200. Technical report, CNS-TR-2010-001, California Institute of Technology (2010)

53. Wu, B., et al.: FBNet: hardware-aware efficient convnet design via differentiable neural architecture search. In: The IEEE Conference on Computer Vision and Pattern Recognition (CVPR), June 2019
54. Xie, L., Yuille, A.: Genetic CNN. In: The IEEE International Conference on Computer Vision (ICCV), October 2017
55. Xie, S., Girshick, R., Dollar, P., Tu, Z., He, K.: Aggregated residual transformations for deep neural networks. In: The IEEE Conference on Computer Vision and Pattern Recognition (CVPR), July 2017
56. Xie, S., Zheng, H., Liu, C., Lin, L.: SNAS: stochastic neural architecture search. In: International Conference on Learning Representations (2019). https://openreview.net/forum?id=rylqooRqK7
57. Xu, Y., et al.: A unified framework for metric transfer learning. IEEE Trans. Knowl. Data Eng. **29**(6), 1158–1171 (2017). https://doi.org/10.1109/TKDE.2017.2669193
58. Yue, K., Sun, M., Yuan, Y., Zhou, F., Ding, E., Xu, F.: Compact generalized non-local network. In: Advances in Neural Information Processing Systems, pp. 6510–6519 (2018)
59. Zhang, J., Li, W., Ogunbona, P.: Joint geometrical and statistical alignment for visual domain adaptation. In: The IEEE Conference on Computer Vision and Pattern Recognition (CVPR), July 2017
60. Zoph, B., Le, Q.V.: Neural architecture search with reinforcement learning. CoRR abs/1611.01578 (2016). http://arxiv.org/abs/1611.01578
61. Zoph, B., Vasudevan, V., Shlens, J., Le, Q.V.: Learning transferable architectures for scalable image recognition. CoRR abs/1707.07012 (2017). http://arxiv.org/abs/1707.07012

Spatial Attention Pyramid Network
for Unsupervised Domain Adaptation

Congcong Li[1], Dawei Du[2], Libo Zhang[3(✉)], Longyin Wen[4], Tiejian Luo[1],
Yanjun Wu[3], and Pengfei Zhu[5]

[1] University of Chinese Academy of Sciences, Beijing, China
[2] University at Albany, State University of New York, Albany, NY, USA
[3] State Key Laboratory of Computer Science, Institute of Software Chinese
Academy of Sciences, Beijing, China
libo@iscas.ac.cn
[4] JD Finance America Corporation, Mountain View, CA, USA
[5] Tianjin University, Tianjin, China

Abstract. Unsupervised domain adaptation is critical in various computer vision tasks, such as object detection, instance segmentation, and semantic segmentation, which aims to alleviate performance degradation caused by domain-shift. Most of previous methods rely on a single-mode distribution of source and target domains to align them with adversarial learning, leading to inferior results in various scenarios. To that end, in this paper, we design a new spatial attention pyramid network for unsupervised domain adaptation. Specifically, we first build the spatial pyramid representation to capture context information of objects at different scales. Guided by the task-specific information, we combine the dense global structure representation and local texture patterns at each spatial location effectively using the spatial attention mechanism. In this way, the network is enforced to focus on the discriminative regions with context information for domain adaptation. We conduct extensive experiments on various challenging datasets for unsupervised domain adaptation on object detection, instance segmentation, and semantic segmentation, which demonstrates that our method performs favorably against the state-of-the-art methods by a large margin. Our source code is available at https://isrc.iscas.ac.cn/gitlab/research/domain-adaption.

Keywords: Unsupervised domain adaptation · Spatial attention pyramid · Object detection · Semantic segmentation · Instance segmentation

1 Introduction

Over the past few years, deep neural network (DNN) significantly pushed forward the state-of-the-art in several tasks in computer vision field, such as object detec-

Electronic supplementary material The online version of this chapter (https://doi.org/10.1007/978-3-030-58601-0_29) contains supplementary material, which is available to authorized users.

A. Vedaldi et al. (Eds.): ECCV 2020, LNCS 12358, pp. 481–497, 2020.
https://doi.org/10.1007/978-3-030-58601-0_29

tion [31,44], instance segmentation [10,11], and semantic segmentation [2,27]. Notably, the DNN-based methods rely on large-scale annotated training data, which is difficult to cover diverse application domains. That is, the feature distributions (e.g., local texture, object appearance and global structure) between source domain and target domain are dissimilar or even completely different. To avoid expensive and time-consuming human annotation, unsupervised domain adaptation is proposed to learn discriminative cross-domain representation in such domain shift circumstance [30].

Most of previous methods [15,16,26] attempt to globally align the entire distributions between the source and target domains. However, it is challenging to generate a unified adaptation function for various scene layouts and appearance variation of different objects. Recent methods focus on transferring texture and color statistics within object instances or local patches. To deal with domain adaptation in the object detection and instance segmentation tasks, the basic idea in [4,45] is to exploit discriminative features in bounding boxes of objects and attempt to align them across both source and target domains. However, the context information around the objects is not fully exploited, causing inferior results in some scenarios. Meanwhile, some domain adaptation methods for semantic segmentation [28,40] enforce the semantic consistency between the pixels or local patches of the two domains, leading to deficiencies of critical information from object-level patterns. To that end, recent methods [34,36] concatenate global context feature and instance-level feature for distribution alignment, and optimize the model based on several loss terms for global-level and local-level features with pre-set weights. However, this method fails to exploit the context information of objects, which is not optimal in challenging scenarios.

In this paper, we design the spatial attention pyramid network (SAPNet) to solve unsupervised domain adaptation for object detection, instance segmentation, and semantic segmentation. Inspired by spatial pyramid pooling [12], we construct the spatial pyramid representation with multi-scale feature maps, which integrates full of holistic (image-level) and local (regions of interest) semantic information. Meanwhile, we design a task-specific guided spatial attention mechanism to capture multi-scale context information. In this way, discriminative semantic regions are attended in a soft manner to extract features for adversarial learning. Extensive experiments are conducted on various challenging domain-shift datasets, such as Cityscapes [5] to FoggyCityscapes [35], PASCAL VOC [7] to Clipart [18], and GTA5 [32] to Cityscapes [5]. It is worth mentioning that the proposed method surpasses the state-of-the-art methods on various tasks, i.e., object detection, instance segmentation, and semantic segmentation. For example, our SAPNet improves from Cityscapes [5] to FoggyCityscapes [35] by 3% mAP in terms of object detection, and achieves comparable accuracy from GTA5 [32] to Cityscapes [5] in terms of semantic segmentation.

Contributions. 1) We propose a new spatial attention pyramid network to solve the unsupervised domain adaptation task for object detection, instance segmentation, and semantic segmentation. 2) We develop a task-specific guided spatial attention pyramid learning strategy to merge multi-level semantic information in feature maps of the pyramid. 3) Extensive experiments conducted on various challenging domain-shift datasets for object detection, instance segmentation, and semantic segmentation, demonstrate the effectiveness of the proposed method, surpassing the state-of-the-art methods.

2   Related Works

Unsupervised Domain Adaptation. Several methods have been proposed for unsupervised domain adaptation in terms of several tasks such as object detection [4,34,36], instance segmentation [45] and semantic segmentation [16,28,40]. For object detection domain adaptation, Chen *et al.* [4] align source and target domain both on image level and instance level using the gradient reverse layer [8]. Zhu *et al.* [45] mine the discriminative regions (pertinent to object detection) using k-means clustering and align them across both domains, which is applied in object detection and instance segmentation. Recently, the strong-weak adaptation method is proposed in [34]. It focuses the adversarial alignment loss toward images that are globally similar, and away from images that are globally dissimilar by employing focal loss [25]. Shen *et al.* [36] propose a gradient detach based stacked complementary losses method that adapt source domain and target domain on multiple layers. On the other hand, Hoffman *et al.* [16] perform global domain alignment in a novel semantic segmentation network with fully convolutional domain adversarial learning. Tsai *et al.* [40] learn discriminative feature representations of patches in the source domain by discovering multiple modes of patch-wise output distribution through the construction of a clustered space. Luo *et al.* [28] introduce a category-level adversarial network to enforce local semantic consistency on the output space using two distinct classifiers. However, the aforementioned methods only consider domain adaptation in two levels, *i.e.*, aligning the feature maps of the whole image or local regions with a fixed scale. Different from them, we design the spatial pyramid representation to capture multi-level semantic patterns within the image for better adaptation between the source domain and target domain.

Attention Mechanism. To focus on the most discriminative features, various attention mechanisms have been explored. SENet [17] develops the Squeeze-and-Excitation (SE) block that adaptively recalibrates channel-wise feature responses. Non-local networks [41] capture long-range dependencies by computing the response at a position as a weighted sum of the features at all positions in the input feature maps. SKNet [23] uses softmax attention to fuse multiple feature maps of different kernel sizes in a weighted manner to adaptively adjust the receptive field size of the input feature map. Except channel-wise attention, CBAM [43] introduce spatial attention by calculating the inter-spatial relation of features. To highlight transferable regions in domain adaptation, Wang *et al.* [42] use multiple region-level domain discriminators and single image-level domain discriminator to generate transferable local and global attention, respectively. Sun and Wu [38] integrates atrous spatial pyramid, cascade attention mechanism and residual connections for image synthesis and image-to-image translation. As previous works [24,37] have shown the importance of multi-scale information,

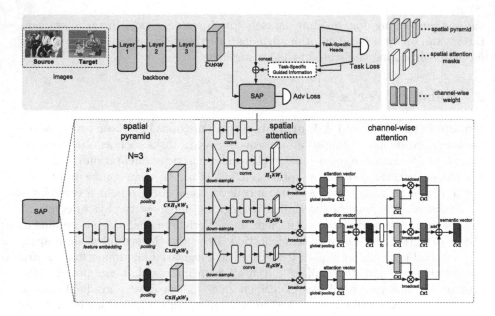

Fig. 1. The framework of spatial attention pyramid network. For clarity, we only show $N = 3$ levels in the spatial pyramid.

we propose the attention pyramid learning to better adapt the source domain and target domain. Specifically, we employ the task-specific information to guide pyramid attention to make full use of semantic information of different feature maps at different levels.

Detection and Segmentation Networks. The performance of object detection and segmentation has boosted with the development of deep convolutional neural networks. Faster R-CNN [31] is an object detection framework that predicts class-agnostic coarse object proposals using a region proposal network (RPN) and then extract fix-sized object features to classify object category and refine object location. Moreover, He *et al.* [11] extend Faster R-CNN by adding a branch for predicting instance segmentation results. For semantic segmentation, the DeepLab-v2 method [1] develops atrous spatial pyramid pooling (ASPP) modules to segment objects at multiple scales. For fair comparison, we propose the spatial attention pyramid network based on the same detection and segmentation frameworks as that in the previous domain adaptation methods.

3   Spatial Attention Pyramid Network

We design a spatial attention pyramid network (SAPNet) to solve various computer vision tasks, such as object detection, instance segmentation, and semantic segmentation. First of all, we define the labeled source domain $\mathcal{D}_s$ and the unlabeled target domain $\mathcal{D}_t$, which are subject to the complex and unknown distributions in the source and target domains. Our goal is to find discriminative representation for the distributions of both source and target domains to capture various semantic information and local patterns in different tasks. The architecture of SAPNet is presented in Fig. 1.

Spatial Pyramid Representation. According to [12,22], spatial pyramid pooling can maintain spatial information by pooling in local spatial bins. To better adapt source and target domains, we develop a spatial pyramid representation to exploit the underlying distribution within an image.

Specifically, as shown in Fig. 1, the feature map $\hat{f} \in \mathbb{R}^{\hat{C} \times H \times W}$ is extracted from the backbone G of the network, where $\hat{C}$, H and W are the channel dimension, height, width of feature maps respectively. To improve efficiency, we first reduce the number of channels in $\hat{f}$ to $\bar{f} \in \mathbb{R}^{C \times H \times W}$ gradually by using three 1×1 convolutional layers, $i.e.$, we set $C = 256$ in all our experiments. Second, we use multiple average pooling layers with different sizes to operate upon the feature map $\bar{f}$ separately. The sizes of the pooling operation are $\{k^n\}_{n=1}^N$, where N is the number of pooling layers. That is, the rectangular pooling region with the size k^n at each location of $\bar{f}$ is down-sampled to the average value of each region, resulting in the pyramid of N pooled feature maps $\{f^1, \ldots, f^N\}$. In this way, every pooled feature map $f^n \in \mathbb{R}^{C \times H_n \times W_n}$ in the pyramid can encode different semantic information of objects or layouts within the image.

It is worth mentioning that the proposed spatial pyramid representation is related with spatial pyramid pooling (SPP) for visual recognition [12]. While they share the pooling concept, we would like to highlight two important differences. First, we use average pooling instead of max pooling to construct the spatial pyramid representation. It can better capture the overall strength of local patterns such as edges and textures, which is demonstrated in the ablation study. Second, SPP pools the features with just a few window sizes and concatenates them to generate fixed-length representation; while SAP is designed to capture multi-scale context information of all levels in the pyramid. Thus, it is difficult to use a large number of windows with different sizes for SPP due to computational complexity.

Attention Mechanism. Moreover, we integrate the spatial attention pyramid strategy to enforce the network to focus on the most discriminative semantic regions and feature maps. There are mainly two advantages of introducing the attention mechanism in the spatial pyramid architecture. First, there exist different local patterns in each spatial location of feature maps. Second, different feature maps in the pyramid have different contributions to the semantic representation. The detailed learning method is described in two aspects as follows.

To facilitate highlighting the most discriminative semantic regions, the spatial attention masks for the pyramid $\{f^1, \ldots, f^N\}$ are learned based on the guided information from the task-specific heads ($i.e.$, object detection, instance segmentation and semantic segmentation). For object detection and instance segmentation, the guided information is the output map with the size of $A \times H \times W$ from the classification head of region proposal network (RPN). It can predict object's confidence in terms of the locations in feature maps for all the number

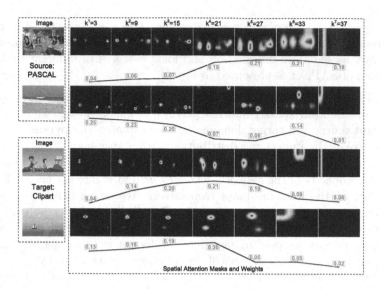

Fig. 2. Visualization of spatial attention masks and corresponding weights (blue lines) for the spatial pyramid. The attention masks of different feature maps are resized by the same scale for better visualization (Color figure online).

of anchors A. That is, it encodes the distribution of objects which is suitable for object detection and instance segmentation problem. For semantic segmentation, the guided information is the output map with the size of $C_{sem} \times H \times W$ from the segmentation head, where C_{sem} is the number of semantic categories. We denote the guided map as $\hat{\mathcal{P}}$.

Then, we concatenate the guided map $\hat{\mathcal{P}}$ and feature map $\hat{f}$ to generate guided feature map $\bar{\mathcal{P}}$ followed by 3 convolutional layers. The guided feature map $\bar{\mathcal{P}}$ is shared for all N scales. To adjust each scale of feature map f^n in the spatial pyramid, we resize $\bar{\mathcal{P}}$ to the size $C \times H_n \times W_n$ at each level. The spatial attention mask $\mathcal{P}^n \in \mathbb{R}^{H_n \times W_n}$ can be predicted by the followed 3 convolutional layers. Finally, $\mathcal{P}^n$ is normalized using the softmax function to compute the spatial attention, *i.e.*,

$$\omega^n(x,y) = \frac{e^{\mathcal{P}^n(x,y)}}{\sum_{i=1}^{H_n} \sum_{j=1}^{W_n} e^{\mathcal{P}^n(i,j)}}, \tag{1}$$

where $\omega^n(i,j)$ indicates the value of the attention mask ω^n at (i,j). Thus, we have $\sum_{i=1}^{H_n} \sum_{j=1}^{W_n} \omega^n(i,j) = 1$. As shown in Fig. 2, we provide some examples with normalized attention masks ω^n for different feature maps in the spatial pyramid when $N = 7$. We can conclude that the feature map with different scale k^n focuses on different semantic regions. For example, in the forth row, the feature map with smaller pooling size ($k = 3$) pays more attention on the seagull, while the feature map with larger pooling size ($k = 21$) focuses on the sail boat and the neighbouring context. Based on different guided information, ω^n recalibrates spatial responses in feature map f^n adaptively.

On the other hand, it can be seen that not all the attention masks correspond to meaningful regions (see the attention mask with pooling size $k = 37$ in the forth row). Inspired by [23], we develop a dynamic weight selection mechanism to adjust the channel-wise weight of feature maps in the pyramid adaptively. To consider feature maps with different size, we normalize f^n to an attention vector $V^n \in \mathbb{R}^{C \times 1}$ using the corresponding spatial attention weight ω^n as:

$$V^n = \sum_{i=1}^{H_n} \sum_{j=1}^{W_n} f^n \cdot \omega^n, \tag{2}$$

where i and j enumerate all spatial positions of weighted feature map $f^n \cdot \omega^n$. Thus the attention vectors have the same size for all the feature maps in the pyramid. Given attention vectors $\{V^1, \ldots, V^N\}$, we first fuse these vectors via an element-wise addition, $i.e.$, $v = \sum_{n=1}^{N} V^n$. Then, a compact feature $\mathbf{z} \in \mathbb{R}^{d \times 1}$ is created to enable the guidance for adaptive selections by the batch normalization layer, where d is the dimension of the compact feature $\mathbf{z}$, and we set it to $\frac{C}{2}$ in all experiments. After that, for each attention vector V^n, we compute the channel-wise attention weight $\phi^n \in \mathbb{R}^{C \times 1}$ as

$$\phi^n = \frac{e^{a_n \cdot \mathbf{z}}}{\sum_{i=1}^{N} e^{a_i \cdot \mathbf{z}}}, \tag{3}$$

where $\{a_i, \ldots, a_N\}$ are learnable parameters of fully connected layers for each scale. We have $\sum_{c=1}^{N} \phi^n(c) = 1$, where $\phi^n(c)$ is the c-th element of ϕ^n. In Fig. 2, we show the corresponding weights of each feature map in the spatial pyramid. Specifically, we compute the mean of channel-wise attention weight ϕ^n for each scale in each image. Finally, the fused semantic vector $\mathcal{V} \in \mathbb{R}^{C \times 1}$ is obtained through the channel-wise attention weight as $\mathcal{V} = \sum_{n=1}^{N} V^n \cdot \phi^n$, where $\mathcal{V}$ is a highly embedded vector in the latent space that encodes the semantic information of different spatial locations, different channels and the relations among them.

Optimization. The whole network is trained by minimizing two loss terms, $i.e.$, adversarial loss and task-specific loss. The adversarial loss is used to determine whether the sample comes from the source domain or target domain. Specifically, we calculate the probability x_i of the sample belonging to the target domain based on the fused semantic vector $\mathcal{V}$ using a simple fully-connected layer. The proposed SAPNet is denoted as D. Then, the adversarial loss is computed as

$$\mathcal{L}_{\text{adv}}(G, D) = \frac{1}{|\mathcal{D}_s \cup \mathcal{D}_t|} \sum_{x_i \in \mathcal{D}_s \cup \mathcal{D}_t} \mathcal{H}(D(G(x_i)), y_i), \tag{4}$$

where y_i is the domain label (0 for source domain and 1 for target domain) and $\mathcal{H}$ is the cross-entropy loss function. On the other hand, the task loss $\mathcal{L}_{\text{task}}$ is determined by the specific task, $i.e.$, object detection, instance segmentation, and semantic segmentation. The loss is computed as

Fig. 3. Adaptation object detection results. From left to right: Foggy Cityscapes, Watercolor and Clipart.

$$\mathcal{L}_{\text{task}}(G, R) = \frac{1}{|\mathcal{D}_s|} \sum_{x_i \in \mathcal{D}_s} \mathcal{L}_{\text{task-specific}}(R(G(x_i)), y_i^s), \tag{5}$$

where G and R are the backbone and task-specific components of the network, respectively. y_i^s is the ground-truth label of sample i in the source domain. We have $\mathcal{L}_{\text{task-specific}} = \{\mathcal{L}_{\text{det}}, \mathcal{L}_{\text{ins}}, \mathcal{L}_{\text{seg}}\}$. Taking object detection as an example, we denote the objective of Faster R-CNN as $\mathcal{L}_{\text{det}}$, which contains classification loss of object categories and regression loss of object bounding boxes. In summary, the overall objective is formulated as

$$\max_{D} \min_{G,R} \mathcal{L}_{\text{task}}(G, R) - \lambda \mathcal{L}_{\text{adv}}(G, D), \tag{6}$$

where λ controls the trade-off between task-specific loss and adversarial training loss. Following [4,34], we use gradient reverse layer (GRL) [8] to enable adversarial training where the gradient is reversed before back-propagating to G from D. We first train the networks with only source domain to avoid initially noisy predictions. Then we train the whole model with Adam optimizer and the initial learning rate is set to 10^{-5}, then divided by 10 at $70,000$, $80,000$ iterations. The total number of training iterations is $90,000$.

4   Experiment

We implement our SAPNet method with PyTorch [29], which is evaluated in three domain adaptation tasks, including object detection, instance segmentation, and semantic segmentation. For fair comparison, we set the shorter side of the image to 600 following the implementation of [34,36] with RoIAlign [11] in object detection; for instance segmentation and semantic segmentation, we

Table 1. Adaptation detection results from Cityscapes to FoggyCityscapes.

Method	Person	Rider	Car	Truck	Bus	Train	Cycle	Bicycle	mAP
Faster R-CNN (w/o)	24.1	33.1	34.3	4.1	22.3	3.0	15.3	26.5	20.3
DA-Faster [4]	25.0	31.0	40.5	22.1	35.3	20.2	20.0	27.1	27.6
SCDA [45]	33.5	38.0	48.5	26.5	39.0	23.3	28.0	33.6	33.8
Strong-Weak [34]	29.9	42.3	43.5	24.5	36.2	32.6	30.0	35.3	34.3
Diversify and match [21]	30.8	40.5	44.3	27.2	38.4	34.5	28.4	32.2	34.6
MAF [14]	28.2	39.5	43.9	23.8	39.9	33.3	29.2	33.9	34.0
SCL [36]	31.6	44.0	44.8	**30.4**	41.8	**40.7**	**33.6**	36.2	37.9
SAPNet	**40.8**	**46.7**	**59.8**	24.3	**46.8**	37.5	30.4	**40.7**	**40.9**

use the same settings as previous methods. To consider the trade-off between accuracy and complexity, the number of pyramid levels is set to $N = 13$ for object detection and instance segmentation, $i.e.$, we have the spatial pooling size set $K = \{3, 6, 9, 12, 15, 18, 21, 24, 27, 30, 33, 35, 37\}$. Note that we start from the initial pooling size 3×3 with the step of 3, and the last two pooling sizes are reduced from $\{38, 41\}$ to $\{35, 37\}$ because of the width limit of feature map. For semantic segmentation, the number of pyramid levels is set to $N = 9$ since semantic segmentation involves feature maps with higher resolution, $i.e.$, $K = \{3, 9, 15, 21, 27, 33, 39, 45, 51\}$. The hyper-parameter λ is used to control the adaptation between source and target domains. Thus, we use different λ in different tasks. Empirically, we set a larger λ for adaptation between similar domains ($e.g.$, Cityscapes→FoggyCityscapes), and set a smaller λ for adaptation between dissimilar domains ($e.g.$, PASCAL VOC→WaterColor). We choose λ based on the performance on the validation set.

4.1   Domain Adaptation for Detection

For object detection task, we conduct our experiments in 3 domain shift scenarios: (1) similar domains; (2) dissimilar domains; and (3) from synthetic to real images. We compare our model to the state-of-the-art methods on 6 domain shift datasets: Cityscapes [5] to FoggyCityscapes [35], Cityscapes [5] to KITTI [9], KITTI [9] to Cityscapes [5], PASCAL VOC [7] to Clipart [18], PASCAL VOC [7] to Watercolor [18], Sim10 K [19] to Cityscapes [5]. For fair comparison, we use ResNet101 and VGG-16 as the backbone and the last convolutional layer to enable domain adaptation as similar as that in [34,36]. Some qualitative adaptation results of object detection are shown in Fig. 3.

Cityscapes→FoggyCityscapes. Notably, we evaluate our model between Cityscapes [5] and FoggyCityscapes [35] (simulated attenuation coefficient $\beta = 0.02$) at the most difficult level. Specifically, Cityscapes is the source domain, while the target domain FoggyCityscape (Foggy for short) is rendered from the same images in Cityscape using depth information. We set $\lambda = 1.0$ in (6) empirically. As shown in Table 1, our SAPNet gains 3.0% average accuracy

Table 2. Adaptation detection results between KITTI and Cityscapes. We report AP scores in terms of the car category on both directions, including KITTI → Cityscapes and Cityscapes → KITTI.

Method	KITTI → Cityscapes	Cityscapes → KITTI
Faster RCNN	30.2	53.5
DA-Faster [4]	38.5	64.1
Strong-Weak (impl. of [36])	37.9	71.0
SCL [36]	41.9	72.7
SCDA [45]	42.5	–
SAPNet	**43.4**	**75.2**

improvement compared with the previous state-of-the-art methods. Specifically, in terms of *person* and *car* categories, our method outperforms the second performer with a huge margin (about 9% and 15% higher, respectively).

Cityscapes↔KITTI. As shown in Table 2, we present the comparison between our model and state-of-the-art on domain adaptation between Cityscapes [5] and KITTI [9]. Similar to the works in [4,36], we use KITTI training set that contains 7, 481 images. We set $\lambda = 0.01$ for Cityscapes → KITTI and $\lambda = 0.2$ for KITTI → Cityscapes in (6) empirically. The Strong-Weak and SCL [36] methods only employ multi-stage feature maps from the backbone to align holistic features, resulting in inferior performance than our method on both directions. In summary, our method achieves 1.5% and 2.5% accuracy improvement of KITTI → Cityscapes and Cityscapes → KITTI, respectively.

PASCAL VOC→Clipart/WaterColor. Moreover, we evaluate our method on dissimilar domains, *i.e.*, from real images to artistic images. According to [34], PASCAL VOC [7] is the source domain, where the PASCAL VOC 2007 and 2012 training and validation sets are used for training. For the target domain, we use Clipart [18] and Watercolor [18] as that in [34]. ResNet-101 [13] pre-trained on ImageNet [6] is used as the backbone network following [34,36]. We set $\lambda = 0.1$ and $\lambda = 0.01$ for Clipart [18] and Watercolor [18] respectively. As shown in Table 3 and Table 4, our model obtains comparable results with SCL [36].

Sim10K→Cityscapes. In addition, we evaluate our model in the synthetic to real scenario. Following [4,34], we use Sim10 K [19] as the source domain that contains 10, 000 training images collected from the computer game Grand Theft Auto 5 (GTA5). We set $\lambda = 0.1$ in (6) empirically. As shown in Table 5, our SAPNet obtains 3.3% improvement in terms of AP score compared with state-of-the-art methods.

It is worth mentioning that BDC-Faster [34] is also trained using cross-entropy loss but the performance is significantly decreased. Therefore, The Strong-Weak method [34] adapts the focal loss [25] to balance different regions. Compared with [34,36], our proposed attention mechanism is much more effective and thus the focal loss module is no longer needed.

Table 3. Adaptation detection results from PASCAL VOC to Clipart.

Method	Aero	Bicycle	Bird	Boat	Bottle	Bus	Car	Cat	Chair	Cow	
FRCNN [31]	35.6	52.5	24.3	23.0	20.0	43.9	32.8	10.7	30.6	11.7	
BDC-Faster [34]	20.2	46.4	20.4	19.3	18.7	41.3	26.5	6.4	33.2	11.7	
DA-Faster [4]	15.0	34.6	12.4	11.9	19.8	21.1	23.2	3.1	22.1	26.3	
WST-BSR [20]	28.0	64.5	23.9	19.0	21.9	**64.3**	43.5	16.4	42.2	25.9	
Strong-Weak [34]	26.2	48.5	32.6	**33.7**	38.5	54.3	37.1	18.6	34.8	58.3	
SCL [36]	**44.7**	50.0	**33.6**	27.4	42.2	55.6	38.3	**19.2**	37.9	**69.0**	
Ours	27.4	**70.8**	32.0	27.9	**42.4**	63.5	**47.5**	14.3	**48.2**	46.1	
	Table	Dog	Horse	Bike	Person	Plant	Sheep	Sofa	Train	Tv	mAP
FRCNN [31]	13.8	6.0	36.8	45.9	48.7	41.9	16.5	7.3	22.9	32.0	27.8
BDC-Faster [34]	26.0	1.7	36.6	41.5	37.7	44.5	10.6	20.4	33.3	15.5	25.6
DA-Faster [4]	10.6	10.0	19.6	39.4	34.6	29.3	1.0	17.1	19.7	24.8	19.8
WST-BSR [20]	30.5	7.9	25.5	67.6	54.5	36.4	10.3	31.2	**57.4**	43.5	35.7
Strong-Weak [34]	17.0	12.5	33.8	65.5	61.6	52.0	9.3	24.9	54.1	49.1	38.1
SCL [36]	30.1	**26.3**	34.4	67.3	61.0	47.9	**21.4**	**26.3**	50.1	47.3	41.5
Ours	**31.8**	17.9	**43.8**	**68.0**	**68.1**	**49.0**	18.7	20.4	55.8	**51.3**	**42.2**

Table 4. Adaptation detection results from PASCAL VOC to WaterColor.

Method	Bike	Bird	Car	Cat	Dog	Person	mAP
Faster RCNN	68.8	46.8	37.2	32.7	21.3	60.7	44.6
DA-Faster [4]	75.2	40.6	48.0	31.5	20.6	60.0	46.0
Strong-Weak [34]	**82.3**	**55.9**	46.5	32.7	35.5	66.7	53.3
SCL [36]	82.2	55.1	51.8	**39.6**	38.4	64.0	**55.2**
Ours	81.1	51.1	**53.6**	34.3	**39.8**	71.3	**55.2**

4.2 Domain Adaptation for Segmentation

Instance Segmentation. For instance segmentation task, we evaluate our model from Cityscapes [5] to FoggyCityscapes [35]. Similar to [45], we use the VGG16 as the backbone network and add the segmentation head similar to that in Mask R-CNN [11]. From Table 6, we can conclude that our method outperforms SCDA [45] significantly, *i.e.*, 39.4 vs. 31.4. Some visual examples of adaptation instance segmentation results are shown in Fig. 4.

Semantic Segmentation. For semantic segmentation task, we conduct experiments from GTA5 [32] to Cityscapes [5] and SYNTHIA [33] to Cityscapes. Following [28], we use the DeepLab-v2 [1] framework with ResNet-101 backbone that is pre-trained on ImageNet. Notably, the task-specific guided map for semantic segmentation naturally comes from the predicted output with the shape of $C_{sem} \times H \times W$, where C_{sem} is the number of semantic categories. As presented in Table 7 and Table 8, our method achieves comparable segmentation accuracy with state-of-the-arts on the domain adaptation from GTA5 [32] to

Table 5. Adaptation detection results from Sim10k to Cityscapes.

Method	AP on Car
Faster R-CNN	34.6
DA-Faster [4]	38.9
Strong-Weak [34]	40.1
SCL [36]	42.6
SCDA [45]	43.0
Ours	**44.9**

Table 6. Adaptation instance segmentation results from Cityscapes to FoggyCityscapes.

Method	mAP
Source only	26.6
SCDA [45]	31.4
Ours	**39.4**

Fig. 4. Instance segmentation results for Cityscapes → Foggy Cityscapes.

Cityscapes [5], and from SYNTHIA [33] to Cityscapes. Some visual examples of adaptation semantic segmentation results are shown in Fig. 5.

4.3 Ablation Study

We further perform experiments to study the effect of important aspects in SAP-Net, *i.e.*, task-specific guided map and spatial attention pyramid. Since PASCAL VOC → Clipart, Sim10 k → Cityscapes and Cityscapes → Foggy represent three different domain shift scenarios, we perform ablation study in terms of object detection datasets for comprehensive analysis.

Task-Specific Guided Information: To investigate the importance of task-specific guided information, we remove the task-specific guidance to generate the spatial attention mask, which is denoted as "w/o GM". In this way, the number of channels of the first convolutional layer after concatenation of feature maps in layer 3 and task-specific guided information is reduced (see Fig. 1). However, the impact is negligible since the channel number of guided map is small. As presented in Table 9, the task-specific guided information improves the accuracy, especially for dissimilar domains PASCAL VOC and Clipart (42.2 vs. 37.1).

Table 7. Adaptation semantic segmentation results from GTA5 to Cityscapes.

Method	Road	Side	Buil.	Wall	Fence	Pole	Light	Sign	Vege.	Terr.
Source	75.8	16.8	77.2	12.5	21.0	25.5	30.1	20.1	81.3	24.6
ROAD [3]	76.3	36.1	69.6	28.6	22.4	**28.6**	29.3	14.8	82.3	**35.3**
TAN [39]	86.5	25.9	**79.8**	22.1	20.0	23.6	33.1	21.8	81.8	25.9
CLAN [28]	87.0	27.1	79.6	27.3	23.3	28.3	**35.5**	**24.2**	**83.6**	27.4
Ours	**88.4**	**38.7**	79.5	**29.4**	**24.7**	27.3	32.6	20.4	82.2	32.9

	Sky	Pers.	Rider	Car	Truck	Bus	Train	Motor	Bike	mIoU
Source	70.3	53.8	26.4	49.9	17.2	25.9	6.5	25.3	**36.0**	36.6
ROAD [3]	72.9	54.4	17.8	78.9	27.7	30.3	4.0	24.9	12.6	39.4
TAN [39]	**75.9**	57.3	26.2	76.3	29.8	32.1	**7.2**	29.5	32.5	41.4
CLAN [28]	74.2	**58.6**	**28.0**	76.2	**33.1**	36.7	6.7	**31.9**	31.4	43.2
Ours	73.3	55.5	26.9	**82.4**	31.8	**41.8**	2.4	26.5	24.1	**43.2**

Table 8. Adaptation semantic segmentation results from SYNTHIA to Cityscapes.

Method	Road	Side	Buil.	Light	Sign	Vege.	Sky	Pers.	Rider	Car	Bus	Motor	Bike	mIoU
Source	55.6	23.8	74.6	6.1	12.1	74.8	79.0	55.3	19.1	39.6	23.3	13.7	25.0	38.6
TAN [39]	79.2	37.2	78.8	9.9	10.5	78.2	80.5	53.5	19.6	67.0	29.5	21.6	31.3	45.9
CLAN [28]	81.3	37.0	80.1	16.1	13.7	78.2	81.5	53.4	21.2	73.0	32.9	22.6	30.7	47.8
Ours	81.7	33.5	75.9	7.0	6.3	74.8	78.9	52.1	21.3	75.7	30.6	10.8	28.0	44.3

We speculate that such guidance can facilitate focusing on the most discriminative semantic regions for domain adaptation.

Spatial Attention Pyramid: To investigate the effectiveness of spatial attention pyramid, we construct the "w/o SA" variant of SAPNet, which indicates that we remove the spatial attention masks and global attention pyramid (since no multi-scale vectors are available) in Fig. 1. As shown in Table 9, the performance drops dramatically without spatial attention pyramid. On the other hand, along with the increasing number of pooled feature maps in the pyramid, the performance is gradually improved. Specifically, we use the spatial pooling size set $K = \{3, 6, 9, 12, 15, 18, 21, 24, 27, 30, 33, 35, 37\}$ when $N = 13$, $K = \{3, 9, 15, 21, 27, 33, 37\}$ when $N = 7$ and $K = \{3, 21, 37\}$ when $N = 3$. It indicates that the spatial pyramid with deep levels contains more discriminative semantic information for domain adaptation and our method can make full use of it. In addition, we compare average pooling and maximal pooling operations in spatial attention pyramid. We can conclude that average pooling achieves better performance in different datasets, which demonstrates the effectiveness of average pooling to capture discriminative local patterns for domain adaptation.

Channel-Wise Attention: To verify the effectiveness of channel-wise attention, we conduct two variants to compute the embedded vector $\mathcal{V}$, where weighted summation $\mathcal{V} = \sum_{n=1}^{N} V^n \cdot w^n$ and equal summation $\mathcal{V} = \frac{1}{N} \sum_{n=1}^{N} V^n$ are

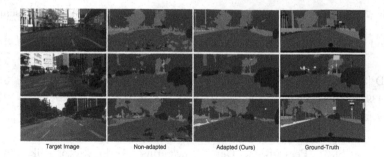

Fig. 5. Semantic segmentation results for GTA5 → Cityscapes.

Table 9. Effectiveness of important aspects in SAPNet.

Variant	PASCAL VOC→Clipart	Sim10k→Cityscapes	Cityscapes→Foggy
w/o GM	37.1	43.8	38.3
w/ GM	**42.2**	**44.9**	**40.9**
w/o CA	37.7	45.6	40.4
w/ CA	**42.2**	**44.9**	**40.9**
w/o SA	35.4	38.3	36.6
w/ SA($N = 3$)	39.6	43.9	39.0
w/ SA($N = 7$)	40.2	**45.9**	40.5
w/ SA($N = 13$)	**42.2**	44.9	**40.9**
max pooling	37.5	43.1	34.9
avg pooling	**42.2**	**44.9**	**40.9**

denoted as "w/ CA" and "w/o CA" respectively. The results are shown in Table 9. Notably, for similar domains (*e.g.*, Sim10k to Cityscapes or Cityscapes to Foggy Cityscapes), we obtain very similar result without channel-wise attention; while for dissimilar domains (*e.g.*, PASCAL to Clipart or PASCAL to Watercolor), we observe an obvious drop in performance, *i.e.*, 4.5% vs. 2.9%. This is maybe because similar/dissimilar domains share similar/different semantic information in each feature map of the spatial pyramid.

5   Conclusions

In this work, we propose a general unsupervised domain adaptation framework for various computer vision tasks including object detection, instance segmentation and semantic segmentation. Given target-specific guided information, our method can make full use of feature maps in the spatial attention pyramid, which enforces the network to focus on the most discriminative semantic regions for domain adaptation. Extensive experiments conducted on various challenging domain adaptation datasets demonstrate the effectiveness of the proposed, which performs favorably against the state-of-the-art methods.

Acknowledgement. This work was supported by the Key Research Program of Frontier Sciences, CAS, Grant No. ZDBS-LY-JSC038, the National Natural Science Foundation of China, Grant No. 61807033 and National Key Research and Development Program of China (2017YFB0801900). Libo Zhang was supported by Youth Innovation Promotion Association, CAS (2020111), and Outstanding Youth Scientist Project of ISCAS.

References

1. Chen, L., Papandreou, G., Kokkinos, I., Murphy, K., Yuille, A.L.: Deeplab: semantic image segmentation with deep convolutional nets, atrous convolution, and fully connected crfs. TPAMI **40**(4), 834–848 (2018)
2. Chen, L., Papandreou, G., Schroff, F., Adam, H.: Rethinking atrous convolution for semantic image segmentation. CoRR abs/1706.05587 (2017)
3. Chen, Y., Li, W., Gool, L.V.: ROAD: reality oriented adaptation for semantic segmentation of urban scenes. In: CVPR, pp. 7892–7901 (2018)
4. Chen, Y., Li, W., Sakaridis, C., Dai, D., Gool, L.V.: Domain adaptive faster R-CNN for object detection in the wild. In: CVPR, pp. 3339–3348 (2018)
5. Cordts, M., et al.: The cityscapes dataset for semantic urban scene understanding. In: CVPR, pp. 3213–3223 (2016)
6. Deng, J., Dong, W., Socher, R., Li, L.J., Li, K., Fei-Fei, L.: Imagenet: a large-scale hierarchical image database. In: CVPR, pp. 248–255 (2009)
7. Everingham, M., Gool, L.V., Williams, C.K.I., Winn, J.M., Zisserman, A.: The pascal visual object classes (VOC) challenge. IJCV **88**(2), 303–338 (2010)
8. Ganin, Y., Lempitsky, V.S.: Unsupervised domain adaptation by backpropagation. In: Bach, F.R., Blei, D.M. (eds.) ICML, vol. 37, pp. 1180–1189 (2015)
9. Geiger, A., Lenz, P., Urtasun, R.: Are we ready for autonomous driving? the KITTI vision benchmark suite. In: CVPR, pp. 3354–3361 (2012)
10. Hayder, Z., He, X., Salzmann, M.: Boundary-aware instance segmentation. In: CVPR, pp. 587–595 (2017)
11. He, K., Gkioxari, G., Dollár, P., Girshick, R.B.: Mask R-CNN. In: ICCV, pp. 2980–2988 (2017)
12. He, K., Zhang, X., Ren, S., Sun, J.: Spatial pyramid pooling in deep convolutional networks for visual recognition. TPAMI **37**(9), 1904–1916 (2015)
13. He, K., Zhang, X., Ren, S., Sun, J.: Deep residual learning for image recognition. In: CVPR, pp. 770–778 (2016)
14. He, Z., Zhang, L.: Multi-adversarial faster-RCNN for unrestricted object detection. CoRR abs/1907.10343 (2019)
15. Hoffman, J., et al.: CyCADA: cycle-consistent adversarial domain adaptation. In: ICML, pp. 1994–2003 (2018)
16. Hoffman, J., Wang, D., Yu, F., Darrell, T.: FCNS in the wild: Pixel-level adversarial and constraint-based adaptation. CoRR abs/1612.02649 (2016)
17. Hu, J., Shen, L., Sun, G.: Squeeze-and-excitation networks. In: CVPR, pp. 7132–7141 (2018)
18. Inoue, N., Furuta, R., Yamasaki, T., Aizawa, K.: Cross-domain weakly-supervised object detection through progressive domain adaptation. In: CVPR, pp. 5001–5009 (2018)
19. Johnson-Roberson, M., Barto, C., Mehta, R., Sridhar, S.N., Rosaen, K., Vasudevan, R.: Driving in the matrix: can virtual worlds replace human-generated annotations for real world tasks? In: ICRA, pp. 746–753 (2017)

20. Kim, S., Choi, J., Kim, T., Kim, C.: Self-training and adversarial background regularization for unsupervised domain adaptive one-stage object detection. CoRR abs/1909.00597 (2019)
21. Kim, T., Jeong, M., Kim, S., Choi, S., Kim, C.: Diversify and match: a domain adaptive representation learning paradigm for object detection. In: CVPR, pp. 12456–12465 (2019)
22. Lazebnik, S., Schmid, C., Ponce, J.: Beyond bags of features: spatial pyramid matching for recognizing natural scene categories. In: CVPR, pp. 2169–2178 (2006)
23. Li, X., Wang, W., Hu, X., Yang, J.: Selective kernel networks. In: CVPR, pp. 510–519 (2019)
24. Lin, T., Dollár, P., Girshick, R.B., He, K., Hariharan, B., Belongie, S.J.: Feature pyramid networks for object detection. In: CVPR, pp. 936–944 (2017)
25. Lin, T., Goyal, P., Girshick, R.B., He, K., Dollár, P.: Focal loss for dense object detection. In: ICCV, pp. 2999–3007. IEEE Computer Society (2017)
26. Liu, M., Breuel, T., Kautz, J.: Unsupervised image-to-image translation networks. In: NeurIPS, pp. 700–708 (2017)
27. Long, J., Shelhamer, E., Darrell, T.: Fully convolutional networks for semantic segmentation. In: CVPR, pp. 3431–3440 (2015)
28. Luo, Y., Zheng, L., Guan, T., Yu, J., Yang, Y.: Taking a closer look at domain shift: category-level adversaries for semantics consistent domain adaptation. In: CVPR, pp. 2507–2516 (2019)
29. Paszke, A., et al.: Automatic differentiation in pytorch (2017)
30. Quiñonero-Candela, J., Sugiyama, M., Schwaighofer, A., Lawrence, N.: Covariate shift and local learning by distribution matching (2008)
31. Ren, S., He, K., Girshick, R.B., Sun, J.: Faster R-CNN: towards real-time object detection with region proposal networks. TPAMI **39**(6), 1137–1149 (2017)
32. Richter, S.R., Vineet, V., Roth, S., Koltun, V.: Playing for data: ground truth from computer games. In: Leibe, B., Matas, J., Sebe, N., Welling, M. (eds.) ECCV 2016. LNCS, vol. 9906, pp. 102–118. Springer, Cham (2016). https://doi.org/10.1007/978-3-319-46475-6_7
33. Ros, G., Sellart, L., Materzynska, J., Vázquez, D., López, A.M.: The SYNTHIA dataset: a large collection of synthetic images for semantic segmentation of urban scenes. In: CVPR, pp. 3234–3243 (2016)
34. Saito, K., Ushiku, Y., Harada, T., Saenko, K.: Strong-weak distribution alignment for adaptive object detection. In: CVPR, pp. 6956–6965 (2019)
35. Sakaridis, C., Dai, D., Gool, L.V.: Semantic foggy scene understanding with synthetic data. IJCV **126**(9), 973–992 (2018)
36. Shen, Z., Maheshwari, H., Yao, W., Savvides, M.: SCL: towards accurate domain adaptive object detection via gradient detach based stacked complementary losses. CoRR abs/1911.02559 (2019)
37. Singh, B., Davis, L.S.: An analysis of scale invariance in object detection SNIP. In: CVPR, pp. 3578–3587 (2018)
38. Sun, W., Wu, T.: Learning spatial pyramid attentive pooling in image synthesis and image-to-image translation. CoRR abs/1901.06322 (2019)
39. Tsai, Y., Hung, W., Schulter, S., Sohn, K., Yang, M., Chandraker, M.: Learning to adapt structured output space for semantic segmentation. In: CVPR, pp. 7472–7481 (2018)
40. Tsai, Y., Sohn, K., Schulter, S., Chandraker, M.: Domain adaptation for structured output via discriminative patch representations. CoRR abs/1901.05427 (2019)
41. Wang, X., Girshick, R.B., Gupta, A., He, K.: Non-local neural networks. In: CVPR, pp. 7794–7803 (2018)

42. Wang, X., Li, L., Ye, W., Long, M., Wang, J.: Transferable attention for domain adaptation. In: AAAI, pp. 5345–5352 (2019)
43. Woo, S., Park, J., Lee, J.-Y., Kweon, I.S.: CBAM: convolutional block attention module. In: Ferrari, V., Hebert, M., Sminchisescu, C., Weiss, Y. (eds.) ECCV 2018. LNCS, vol. 11211, pp. 3–19. Springer, Cham (2018). https://doi.org/10.1007/978-3-030-01234-2_1
44. Zhang, S., Wen, L., Bian, X., Lei, Z., Li, S.Z.: Single-shot refinement neural network for object detection. In: CVPR, pp. 4203–4212 (2018)
45. Zhu, X., Pang, J., Yang, C., Shi, J., Lin, D.: Adapting object detectors via selective cross-domain alignment. In: CVPR, pp. 687–696 (2019)

GSIR: Generalizable 3D Shape Interpretation and Reconstruction

Jianren Wang[✉][iD] and Zhaoyuan Fang[iD]

Carnegie Mellon University, Pittsburgh, USA
{jianrenw,zhaoyuaf}@andrew.cmu.edu

Abstract. 3D shape interpretation and reconstruction are closely related to each other but have long been studied separately and often end up with priors that are highly biased towards the training classes. In this paper, we present an algorithm, *Generalizable 3D Shape Interpretation and Reconstruction (GSIR)*, designed to jointly learn these two tasks to capture generic, class-agnostic shape priors for a better understanding of 3D geometry. We propose to recover 3D shape structures as cuboids from partial reconstruction and use the predicted structures to further guide full 3D reconstruction. The unified framework is trained simultaneously offline to learn a generic notion and can be fine-tuned online for specific objects without any annotations. Extensive experiments on both synthetic and real data demonstrate that introducing 3D shape interpretation improves the performance of single image 3D reconstruction and vice versa, achieving the state-of-the-art performance on both tasks for objects in both seen and unseen categories.

Keywords: Shape interpretation · 3D reconstruction

1 Introduction

Single image 3D geometry has attracted much attention in recent years due to its numerous applications, such as robotics, medicine and film industry. To fully understand 3D geometry, it is essential to know structure properties (*e.g.*, symmetry, compactness, planarity, and part to part relations) [8,30,43] and surface properties (*e.g.*, texture and curvature). In this paper, we address these problems simultaneously, i.e., 3D shape interpretation and reconstruction, in which these two tasks have been known to be closely related to each other [28,55].

For single image 3D reconstruction, the difficulty is mainly reflected in two aspects: how to extract geometric information from high dimensional images and how to utilize prior shape knowledge to pick the most reasonable prediction from many 3D explanations. Recent research tackles these problems through deep learning [13,18,56], since it has shown great success in image information distillation tasks like classification [27], detection [24] and segmentation [22]. Many algorithms have explored ways to utilize shape prior knowledge. For example, *ShapeHD* [61] integrated deep generative models with adversarially learned shape priors and penalized the model only if its outputs were unrealistic.

© Springer Nature Switzerland AG 2020
A. Vedaldi et al. (Eds.): ECCV 2020, LNCS 12358, pp. 498–514, 2020.
https://doi.org/10.1007/978-3-030-58601-0_30

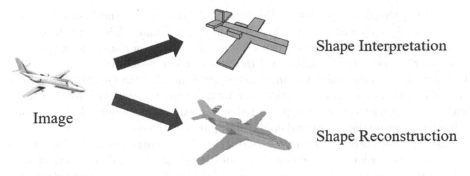

Fig. 1. We present Generalizable 3D Shape Interpretation and Reconstruction (*GSIR*) to learn 3D shape interpretation and reconstruction jointly

Many existing methods do not enforce explicit 3D representation in the model, which leads to overfitting. As a result, they suffer when reconstructing the unobservable parts of objects, especially under self-occlusions. Recently, methods that encode shapes in a function [38, 40] take a step toward better generalization. In this paper, we approach the problem by enforcing explicit 3D representation in the model. Inspired by pose-guided person generation [7, 34], we propose a structure-guided shape generation that explicitly uses the structure to guide shape completion and reconstruction. The key idea of our approach is to guide the reconstruction process explicitly by an appropriate representation of the object structure to enable direct control over the generation process. More specifically, we propose to condition the reconstruction network on both the observable parts of the object and a predicted structure. From the observable parts, the model obtains sufficient information about the visible surface of the object. The guidance given by the predicted structure is both explicit and flexible. There are many other interesting downstream applications. For example, we later show that we can design new objects by keeping the original surface details and manipulate the size and orientation of each part of the object by changing the guidance.

On the other hand, single image 3D structure interpretation itself is challenging and often inaccurate. Therefore, the derived structure information does not always help reconstruction. More specifically, when an image is captured from accidental views, the structure interpretation methods are not effective to predict landmarks positions [3] or primitive orientations [39]. To overcome this problem, we bring reconstructed 3D information to help the algorithm predict more accurate interpretations (cuboid position, orientation, and size in our case).

Based on the above observations, we propose to jointly reason about single image *generalizable 3D shape interpretation and reconstruction (GSIR)*. Building upon GenRe [64], we first project a predicted 2.5D sketch into a partial 3D model. We then generate geometrically interpretable representations of the partial 3D model through oriented cuboids, where symmetry, compactness, planarity, and part-to-part relations are taken into consideration. Instead of performing shape completion in the 3D voxel grid, our method completes the shape based on spherical maps since mapping a 2D image/2.5D sketch to a 3D shape involves complex but deterministic geometric projections. Using spherical map, our neural modules only need to model object geometry, without having to learn projections, which enhances generalizability. Unlike *GenRe*, we perform the completion in a structure-guided manner. Fusing information from both the visible object surfaces and the projected spherical maps of oriented cuboids and edges, we can further complete non-visible parts of the object.

Our model consists of four learnable modules: single-view depth estimation module, structure interpretation module, structure-guided spherical map inpainting module, and voxel refinement module. In addition, geometric projections form the links between those modules. Furthermore, we propose an interpretation consistency between the predicted structure and the partial 3D reconstruction.

Our approach offers three unique advantages. First, our estimated 3D structure encodes symmetry, compactness, planarity, and part-to-part relations of the given objects explicitly, which help us understand the reconstruction in a more transparent way. Second, we reason about 3D structure from partial observable voxel grid to alleviate the burden on domain transfer in previous single image 3D structure interpretation algorithms [39,59], which enhances generalizability. Third, our interpretation consistency can be used to fine-tune the system for specific objects without any annotations, which further enables the communication between two branches (the consistency can be jointly optimized with the model).

We evaluate our method on both synthetic images of objects from the ShapeNet dataset, and real images from the PASCAL 3D+ dataset. We show that our method performs well on 3D shape reconstruction, both qualitatively and quantitatively on novel objects from unseen categories. We also show the method's capacity to generate new objects given modified shape guidance.

To summarize, this paper makes four contributions: we propose an end-to-end trainable model *(GSIR)* to jointly reason 3D shape interpretation and reconstruction; we develop a structure-guided 3D reconstruction algorithm; we develop a novel end-to-end trainable loss that ensures consistency between estimated structure and partially reconstructed model; we demonstrate that exploiting symmetry, compactness, planarity, and part-to-part relations inside object can significantly improve both shape interpretation and reconstruction accuracy and help with generalization.

2   Related Work

Single Image 3D Reconstruction. Lots of work have been done on 3D reconstruction from single images. Early works can be traced back to Hoiem *et al.* [26] and Saxena *et al.* [49]. Theoretically, recovering 3D shapes from single-view images is an ill-posed problem. To alleviate the ill-posedness, these methods rely heavily on the knowledge of shape priors, which require large amount of data.

With the releasing of IKEA [32] and ShapeNet [9], many learning-based methods begin to dominate the trend. Choy *et al.* [13] apply a CNN to the input image, then pass the resulting features to a 3D deconvolutional network, that maps them to an occupancy grid of 32^3 voxels. Girdhar *et al.* [18] and Wu *et al.* [60] proceed similarly, but pre-train a model to encode or generate 3D shapes respectively, and regress images to the latent features of the model. Instead of directly producing voxels, Arsalan Soltani *et al.* [2], Shin *et al.* [50], Wu *et al.* [58] and Richter *et al.* [44] output multiple depth-maps and/or silhouettes, which are subsequently fused for voxel reconstruction. Although we focus on reconstructing 3D voxels, there are many other works that reconstruct 3d objects using pointcloud [16,29,35], meshes [21,25,33,55,57], octrees [45,46,54], and functions [14,38,51,63]. [25] presents a general framework to learn reconstruction and generation of 3D shapes with 2D supervision, using an assembly from cuboidal primitives as a compact representation. To encode both geometry and appearance, [51] encodes a feature and RGB representation for each point and predicts the surface location with a ray marching LSTM network. [63] combines 3D point features with image features from the projected query patch and significantly improves on 3D reconstruction. [38] represents the 3D surface as continuous decision boundaries and shows robust results.

3D Structure Interpretation. Different from 3D reconstruction, 3D structure interpretation focuses on understanding structure properties instead of dense representations, which is broadly defined based on positions and relationships among semantic (the vertical part), functional (support and stability), economic (repeatable and easy to fabricate) parts. Among all ways to abstract object structures, a 3d skeleton is most common in use because of its simplicity, especially in human pose estimation [1,6,42,65]. 3D-INN [59] estimate 3D object skeletons through 2D keypoints and achieve a promising result on chairs and cars. Another way is to represent the method using volumetric primitives, which can date to the very beginnings of the computer vision. There are many attempts to represent shapes as a collection of components or primitives, such as geons [5], block world [47] and cylinders [36]. Recently, more compact and parametric representations are introduced using LSTM [66] or set of primitives [55].

Structure-Aware Shape Processing Previous studies have recognized the value of structure-guided shape processing, editing, and synthesis, mainly in computer graphics [17] and geometric modeling [19]. For shape synthesis, many approaches have been proposed based on fixed relationships such as regular structures [41], symmetries [52], probabilistic assembly-based modeling [10]. Wu *et al.* [62] encode the structure into an embedding vector. The work that is most similar to ours is probably SASS proposed by Balashova *et al.* [3]. SASS extracts landmarks from a 3D shape and adds a shape-structure consistency loss to better align shape with predicted landmarks. Our model has two advantages over SASS. First, instead of using a fixed number of landmarks, we abstract primitives of any given object. This gives more freedom to the objects that can be constructed. Second, our proposed method deeply integrates shape interpretation and reconstruction through structure-guided inpainting and the interpretation consistency other than just force the alignment.

Depth Prediction. The ability to learn depth using a deep learning framework was introduced by [15], who uses a dataset of ground truth depth and RGB image pairs to train a network to predict depth. This has been further improved through better architecture [11,31] and larger datasets [37].

3   Approach

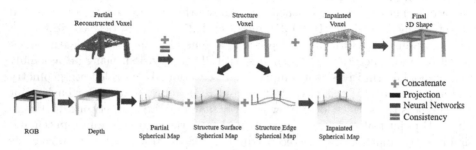

Fig. 2. Our model contains four learnable functions and five deterministic projection functions.

Our whole model (Fig. 2) consists of four learnable functions (f) connected by five deterministic projection functions (p). The model is summarized below and each module is discussed in details in the subsections:

1. The model begins with a **single-view depth estimation module**: with a color image (RGB) as input, the module estimates its depth map $D = f(RGB)$. We then convert the depth estimation D into partial reconstructed voxel grid $V_p = p(D)$, which reflects only visible surfaces.
2. Our second learnable function is the **structure interpretation module**: the partial voxel grid (V_p) is taken as input and parsed by the module into compact cuboid-based representations $S = f(V_p)$. We then project the resulting structure surfaces and edges into spherical maps: $M_{ss} = p(surface(S)), M_{se} = p(egde(S))$.
3. Along with projected spherical maps from depth estimation $M_p = p(D)$, the **structure-guided shape completion module** can predict the inpainted spherical map $M_i = f(M_p, M_{ss}, M_{se})$, which is then projected back into voxel space $V_i = p(M_i)$.
4. Since spherical maps only capture the outermost surface towards the sphere, they cannot handle self-occlusion along the sphere's radius. To mitigate this problem, we adopt the **voxel refinement module** that takes all predicted voxels as input and outputs the final reconstruction $V = f(V_p, V_i, S)$.

3.1 Single-View Depth Estimation Module

Since depth estimation is a class-agnostic task, we use depth as an intermediate representation like many other methods [44,58]. Previous research shows that depth estimation can be generalized well into different classes despite their distinct visual appearances and can even be applied in the wild [11]. Our module takes a color image (RGB) as input and estimates its depth map (D) through an encoder-decoder network. More details can be viewed in Sect. 3.6.

3.2 Structure Interpretation Module

To better represent the symmetry, compactness, planarity, and part-to-part relations, we adopt a recursive neural network as the 3D structure interpreter like in [28]. However, unlike [39], we encode the structure embedding from V_p to alleviate the domain adaptation. The encoder is achieved by a 3D convolutional network that encodes V_p into a bottleneck feature, then the decoder recursively decodes it into a hierarchy of part boxes.

Starting from the root feature code, the RNN recursively decodes it into a hierarchy of features until reaching the leaf nodes which each can be further decoded into a vector of box parameters. There are three types of nodes in our hierarchy: leaf node, adjacency node, and symmetry node. During the decoding, two types of part relations are recovered as the class of internal nodes: adjacency and symmetry. Thus, each node can be decoded by one of the three decoders below, based on its type (adjacency node, symmetry node or box node):

Adjacency Decoder. The adjacency decoder split a single part into two adjacent parts. Formally, it splits a parent n-D code p into two child n-D codes c_1 and c_2, using the mapping function with a weight matrix $W_{ad} \in \mathbb{R}^{2n \times n}$ and a bias vector $b_{ad} \in \mathbb{R}^{2n}$:

$$[c_1, c_2] = tanh(W_{ad} \cdot p + b_{ad}) \tag{1}$$

Symmetry Decoder. The symmetry decoder recovers a n-D code for a symmetry group g in the form of a n-D code for the symmetry generator s and a m-D code for the symmetry parameters z. The transformation has a weight matrix $W_{sd} \in \mathbb{R}^{n \times (n+m)}$ and a bias vector $b_{sd} \in \mathbb{R}^{n+m}$:

$$[s, z] = tanh(W_{sd} \cdot g + b_{sd}) \tag{2}$$

The symmetry parameters are represented as a 8-dim vector ($m = 8$) containing: symmetry type (1D); number of repetitions for rotation and translation symmetries (1D); and the reflection plane for reflection symmetry, rotation axis for rotation symmetry, or position and displacement for translation symmetry (6D).

Box Decoder. The box decoder converts the n-D code of a leaf node l to a 12-D box parameters defining the center, axes, and sizes of a 3D oriented box. It has a weight matrix $W_{ld} \in \mathbb{R}^{12 \times n}$ and a bias vector $b_{ld} \in \mathbb{R}^{12}$:

$$[x] = tanh(W_{ld} \cdot l + b_{ld}) \tag{3}$$

These decoders are recursively applied during decoding. We also need to distinguish p, g and l since they require different decoders. This is achieved by learning a node classifier where the ground-truth box structure is known. The node classifier is jointly trained with the three decoders. We refer the readers to [28] for a better understanding.

3.3   Structure-Guided Shape Completion Module

The problem of 3D surface completion was first cast into 2D spherical map inpainting by *GenRe* [64], showing better performance than surface completion in the voxel space. However, the original spherical inpainting network takes only the partially observable depth map M_p as input and encode the shape prior implicitly in their neural network. We use an encoder-decoder network and concatenate M_p, M_{ss}, M_{se} channel-wise as input: structure surface map M_{ss} provides the reference depth as it shows the planar tilt; structure edges M_{se} handles self-occlusion as edges do not have volume. Thus, structure information is explicitly embedded into the network. Note both structure and depth map are viewer-centered and are automatically aligned.

3.4   Voxel Refinement Module

We adopt a voxel refinement module to recover the lost information caused by spherical projection, similar to *GenRe*. This module takes all voxels (one projected from the estimated depth map V_p and the other from the inpainted spherical map V_i) as well as the voxelized structure S as input, and predict the final reconstruction.

3.5   Interpretation Consistency

There have been works attempting to enforce the consistency between estimated 3D shape and 2D representations or 2.5D sketches [58] in a neural network. Here, we propose a consistency loss between structure interpretation S and partial reconstruction V_p.

Similar to [55], our consistency loss contains both sub loss and super loss. The former evaluates if the interpretation cuboids are completely inside the target object, the latter evaluates if the target object is completely covered by the interpretation cuboids.

Formally, sub loss L_{sub} and super loss L_{sup} are defined as

$$L_{sub} = E_{p \sim V_p} \|C(p; S)\|^2 \tag{4}$$

$$L_{sup} = E_{p \sim S} \|C(p; V_p)\|^2 \tag{5}$$

$$L = L_{sub} + L_{sup} \tag{6}$$

where the points p are sampled from either the structure interpretation or the partial reconstruction, and $C(\cdot; O)$ computes the distance to the closest point on the object and equals to zero in the object interior.

$$C(p; O) = \min_{p' \in O} \|p - p'\|^2 \tag{7}$$

Note that the reconstruction V_p only contains observable parts, so it is not reasonable to force consistency in the occluded region. Therefore, we only calculate the consistency loss of structure primitive where the volume occupied by V_p is larger than a threshold α. We fix the three decoders mentioned in Sect. 3.2 during testing and only fine-tune the node codes and parameters. During inference, our method can be self-supervised.

3.6 Technical Details

Network Parameters. Following *GenRe* [64], we use a U-Net structure [48] for both single-view depth estimation module and structure-guided shape completion module. The encoder is a ResNet-18 [23], encoding a 256×256 image into 512 feature maps of size 1×1. The decoder is a mirrored version of the encoder, replacing all convolution layers with transposed convolution layers. The decoder outputs the depth map/inpainted map in the original view at the resolution of 256×256. We use a $L2$ loss between predicted and target images. Our structure interpretation module takes the $128 \times 128 \times 128$ dimensional V_p as input and output a 128D latent vector, which is then fed into the RNN decoder. The node classifier and the decoders for both adjacency and symmetry are two-layer networks, with the hidden layer and output layer having 256 and 128 units, respectively. Our voxel refinement module is also a U-Net, which takes a three-channel $128 \times 128 \times 128$ voxel grid (V_p, V_i, S) as input, encode it into a 320D latent vector and then decode the latent vector into the $128 \times 128 \times 128$ dimensional final reconstruction.

Geometric Projections. We use five deterministic projection functions: a depth to voxel projection, a depth to spherical map projection, a structure surfaces to spherical map projection, a structure edges to spherical map projection, and a spherical map to voxel projection. We use the same method as described in *GenRe*. All projections are differentiable, thus the pipeline is end-to-end trainable.

Training. We first train each module separately with fully labelled ground truth for 250 epochs, all rendered with synthetic ShapeNet objects [9]. We then jointly fine-tune our whole model together with both 3D shape and 3D structure supervision for another 250 epochs. In practice, we fine-tuned our model using consistency loss on each image for 30 iterations. We used adam optimizer with a learning rate of 1×10^{-4}.

4   Experiments

4.1   3D Shape Interpretation

Table 1. Comparison of performance on the structure recovery task.

Method	Hausdorff Error	Thresholded Acc.	
		$\delta < 0.2$	$\delta < 0.1$
im2struct (Mask + VGG-19) [39]	0.1096	91.2%	66.7%
GSIR (without consistency)	0.0798	93.3%	79.6%
GSIR (With consistency)	0.0731	97.4%	84.8%

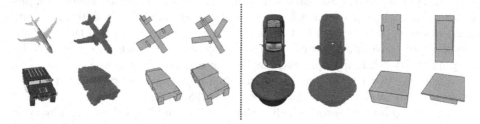

Fig. 3. Example results of 3D shape interpretation. From left to right: RGB input image, partial voxel grid, *im2struct*, Ours *(GSIR)*.

We present results on 3D shape interpretation for generalizing to novel objects unseen in training. All models are trained on cars, chairs, airplanes, tables, and motorcycles and tested on unseen objects from the same categories. Same as in *im2struct* [39], we use two measures to evaluate the performance of our 3D Shape Interpretation: *Hausdorff Error* and *Thresholded Accuracy*. The results are presented in Table 1. We compare our method with the current best method (*im2struct*). In "*GSIR* without consistency", the structure is estimated using only the structure interpretation module. In "*GSIR* with consistency", the structure is esimated using the structure interpretation module followed by a refinement using the proposed interpretation consistency. The result demonstrates that recovering structure significantly benefits from infusing information of partially reconstructed voxel grid. Figure 3 gives a visual comparison of our method and *im2struct*, which directly recover 3D shape from single-view RGB image. As can be seen, our method produces part structures that are more faithful to the input. This is because 1) we reason about 3D structure from predicted 3D voxels, which alleviates the domain adaptation, and 2) our model is end-to-end trainable, the performance of structure recovery gets better as richer information gets distilled for 3D reconstruction.

4.2   Structure-Guided Shape Completion

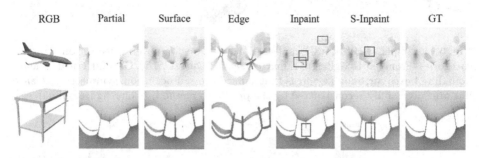

| RGB | Partial | Surface | Edge | Inpaint | S-Inpaint | GT |

Fig. 4. Visualization of example spherical maps at each stage of our method, with a comparison of structure guided inpainting and normal inpainting. From left to right: RGB (original), partial map from depth estimation, surface map from structure prediction, edge map from structure prediction, inpainted map without structure guidance, inpainted map with structure guidance, ground truth. (Color figure online)

We present qualitative results on structure-guided shape completion in Fig. 4. The contribution of each element in our method is visualized in the figure. We show that with structure guidance, the missing or unobservable parts can be well completed, hence leading a more faithful reconstruction. However, without structure information, the inpainting network can only recover incomplete unobservable parts (*e.g.*, the wing of the airplane bounded by the green boxes) or even ignore the unobservable parts directly (*e.g.*, the engine of the airplane and the leg of the table bounded by the red boxes). In contrast, structure guidance enables the model to fully reconstruct unobservable parts. More quantitative results are shown in Sect. 4.3.

4.3   3D Shape Reconstruction

In Table 2, we present results on generalizing to novel objects from both training and testing classes. All models are trained on ShapeNet cars, chairs, airplanes, tables, and motorcycles while tested on novel objects from the same categories (denoted as Seen) and unseen categories (denoted as Unseen) including benches, sofa, beds and vessels. Since our model only focuses on surface voxel reconstruction, we evaluate reconstruction quality using Chamfer distance (CD) [4]. We sweep voxel thresholds from 0.3 to 0.7 with a step size of 0.05 for isosurfaces, compute CD with 1,024 points sampled from all isosurfaces, and report the best average CD for each object class. For seen categories, our method beats all other viewer-centered methods, performing on par with most object-centered methods. For unseen objects, our model outperforms all objected-centered and viewer-centered methods by a large margin, demonstrating its capacity to generalize to objects with new shapes from completely unseen classes.

Fig. 5. Example results of 3D shape reconstruction for novel objects from training categories. From left to right: RGB image, *GenRe*, Ours*(GSIR)*, Ground Truth. The red bounding boxes surround key areas that suffer from self-occlusion/symmetry in *GenRe* but are successfully reconstructed by the proposed method. (Color figure online)

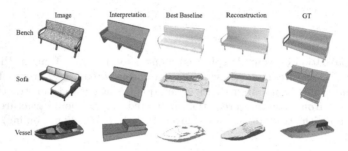

Fig. 6. Example results of 3D shape reconstruction for novel objects from testing categories. From left to right: RGB image, structural interpretation, *GenRe* (Best Baseline), Ours*(GSIR)*, Ground Truth.

We give a visual comparison of our method and the state-of-the-art method on novel objects from seen categories in Fig. 5. The red bounding boxes surround key areas that suffer from self-occlusion/symmetry in *GenRe* but are successfully reconstructed by the proposed method. These results show that our method significantly improves the reconstruction performance under self-

Table 2. Comparison of performance on the shape reconstruction task.

Method		CD	
		Seen	Unseen
Object-Centered	*IM-NET* [12]	0.055	0.119
	ONet [38]	0.060	0.128
	DeepSDF [40]	**0.053**	0.115
	AtlasNet [20]	0.063	0.126
Viewer-Centered	*DRC* [56]	0.097	0.127
	MarrNet [58]	0.081	0.116
	GenRe [64]	0.068	0.108
	Ours	0.057	**0.099**

occlusion/symmetry. We also present some visualizations on novel objects from unseen categories in Fig. 6. It can be observed that compared to the best previous method, our method better preserves the structural properties of the objects in the input images and closely reconstructs various details of the objects (*e.g.*, the middle leg of the bench, the armrest of the sofa, and the ceiling of the vessel, *etc*).

4.4   Shape Interpretation with Consistency

By reasoning the consistency between the partial voxel grid and object structure, we can obtain better structure interpretation by fine-tuning on one object while preserving good shape prior knowledge. As shown in Fig. 7, the tilt and size of each cuboid can be rectified even if the initial structure interpretation is coarse and distorted (as shown in the red boxes). Furthermore, since our structure model utilizes symmetry explicitly, the unobservable parts can also be better reconstructed through forcing consistency with observable parts.

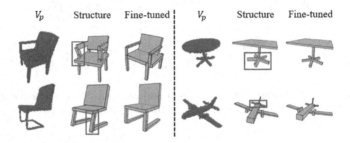

Fig. 7. Example results that demonstrates the efficacy of the proposed interpretation consistency. From left to right: partial voxel grid (V_p), coarsely reconstructed structure (Structure), fine-tuned structure with consistency (Fine-tuned).

4.5   Generalization to Real Images

In this subsection, we extend our experiments from rendered images to real images. Our experiments show that the proposed network's capability to robustly reconstruct objects of unseen classes from real images, both qualitatively and quantitatively. For example, all models are trained on rendered images of chairs, airplanes, and cars from ShapeNet, while tested on real images of beds, bookcases, desks, sofas, tables, and wardrobes from another dataset, Pix3D [53]. Quantitative results evaluated by Chamfer Distance are presented in Table 3. While *AtlasNet* achieves a smaller error on seen objects (chairs & tables), our model outperforms both other methods across all novel classes, which demonstrate its generalization abilities on cross-domain shape interpretation and reconstruction. We also present qualitative visualizations in Fig. 8. Both our interpretation network and reconstruction network produce high-fidelity results, preserving both the overall structure and fine-grained details.

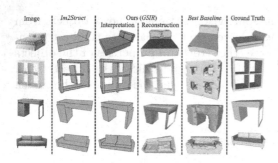

Fig. 8. Example results of 3D shape interpretation and reconstruction on real images of objects from unseen classes in Pix3D (the model is trained on ShapeNet).

Table 3. Reconstruction errors (in CD) for seen (chairs, tables) and unseen classes (beds, bookcases, sofas, wardrobes) on real images from Pix3D.

	AtlasNet	GenRe	Ours
Chair	**0.083**	0.095	0.091
Table	**0.092**	0.099	0.094
Bed	0.115	0.111	**0.107**
Bookcase	0.137	0.101	**0.095**
Desk	0.124	0.107	**0.100**
Sofa	0.096	0.085	**0.083**
Wardrobe	0.119	0.111	**0.103**

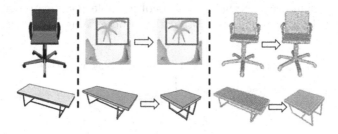

Fig. 9. Examples of structure-guided shape manipulation. We change the leg number of a swivel chair from five to six and shorten the length of a table.

4.6   Ablation Study

To investigate the effectiveness of each module in our model design, we perform an ablation study to quantify the performance of different module design configurations.

Table 4. Ablation Study. All annotations are consistent with Sect. 3.

Method	Seen	Unseen
Encoder Decoder	0.127	0.196
Depth + Decoder	0.088	0.131
Depth + Multi-view + V_i	0.075	0.123
Depth + Multi-view + Guided + V_i	0.072	0.121
Depth + Spherical Map + V_i	0.073	0.119
Depth + Spherical Map + Guided + V_i	0.069	0.113
Depth + Spherical Map + Guided + V_i + V_p	0.064	0.106
Ours (w.o. consistency loss)	0.060	0.103
Ours (w. consistency loss)	**0.057**	**0.099**

For each projection representation in our model, there could be alternative choices: instead of using spherical map, we can instead use a multi-view representation: *e.g.*, six views depth projection as proposed by MatryoshkaNet [44]. Then we can apply structure-guided depth map inpainting on all six views (denoted as Multi-view in Table 4).

In the ablation study, we gradually add more representations and more projective losses. The baseline method is a single vanilla 3D autoencoder (denoted as Encoder Decoder). Then, each module added sequentially, bearing the same name as mentioned in Sect. 3. We adopt the same experimental settings as in Sect. 4.3 and the results are shown in Table 4. Results suggest that spherical maps lead to better performance than multi-view ensemble, which justify our choice of design. This ablation study also suggests that each module in our model contributes to the improved performance. Our full model design benefits from joint learning of interpretation and reconstruction, significantly improving the baseline network performance.

4.7 Shape Manipulation

Another unique advantage of our method is that it provides explicit and flexible ways to manipulate the underlying objects while maintaining good surface details. We can modify the symmetry groups (*e.g.*, changing the number of legs of a chair from five to six) in structure-guided shape completion step (as shown in the first row of Fig. 9), and/or apply rotation, translation or scaling to the primitives (as shown in the second row of Fig. 9). As shown in Fig. 9, our model smoothly modifies the output of reconstruction according to the structure guidance.

5 Conclusion

We jointly learned single image 3D shape interpretation and reconstruction. We propose *GSIR*, an novel end-to-end trainable viewer-centered model that integrates both shape structure and surface details, for a better understanding of 3D geometry. Extensive experiments on both synthetic and real data demonstrate that with this joint structure, both interpretation and reconstruction results can be improved. We hope our work will inspire future research in this direction.

References

1. Akhter, I., Black, M.J.: Pose-conditioned joint angle limits for 3D human pose reconstruction. In: CVPR (2015)
2. Arsalan Soltani, A., Huang, H., Wu, J., Kulkarni, T.D., Tenenbaum, J.B.: Synthesizing 3D shapes via modeling multi-view depth maps and silhouettes with deep generative networks. In: CVPR (2017)
3. Balashova, E., Singh, V., Wang, J., Teixeira, B., Chen, T., Funkhouser, T.: Structure-aware shape synthesis. In: 3DV (2018)

4. Barrow, H.G., Tenenbaum, J.M., Bolles, R.C., Wolf, H.C.: Parametric correspondence and chamfer matching: two new techniques for image matching. In: IJCAI (1977)
5. Biederman, I.: Recognition-by-components: a theory of human image understanding. Psychol. Rev. **94**, 115 (1987)
6. Bogo, F., Kanazawa, A., Lassner, C., Gehler, P., Romero, J., Black, M.J.: Keep it SMPL: automatic estimation of 3D human pose and shape from a single image. In: Leibe, B., Matas, J., Sebe, N., Welling, M. (eds.) ECCV 2016. LNCS, vol. 9909, pp. 561–578. Springer, Cham (2016). https://doi.org/10.1007/978-3-319-46454-1_34
7. Chan, C., Ginosar, S., Zhou, T., Efros, A.A.: Everybody dance now. arXiv preprint arXiv:1808.07371 (2018)
8. Chan, M.W., Stevenson, A.K., Li, Y., Pizlo, Z.: Binocular shape constancy from novel views: the role of a priori constraints. Percept. Psychophysics **68**(7), 1124–1139 (2006)
9. Chang, A.X., et al.: Shapenet: an information-rich 3D model repository. arXiv preprint arXiv:1512.03012 (2015)
10. Chaudhuri, S., Kalogerakis, E., Guibas, L., Koltun, V.: Probabilistic reasoning for assembly-based 3D modeling. In: ACM TOG, vol. 30, p. 35 (2011)
11. Chen, W., Fu, Z., Yang, D., Deng, J.: Single-image depth perception in the wild. In: NeurIPS (2016)
12. Chen, Z., Zhang, H.: Learning implicit fields for generative shape modeling. In: CVPR (2019)
13. Choy, C.B., Xu, D., Gwak, J.Y., Chen, K., Savarese, S.: 3D-R2N2: a unified approach for single and multi-view 3D object reconstruction. In: Leibe, B., Matas, J., Sebe, N., Welling, M. (eds.) ECCV 2016. LNCS, vol. 9912, pp. 628–644. Springer, Cham (2016). https://doi.org/10.1007/978-3-319-46484-8_38
14. Deng, B., Genova, K., Yazdani, S., Bouaziz, S., Hinton, G.E., Tagliasacchi, A.: Cvxnets: Learnable convex decomposition (2020)
15. Eigen, D., Puhrsch, C., Fergus, R.: Depth map prediction from a single image using a multi-scale deep network. In: NeurIPS (2014)
16. Fan, H., Su, H., Guibas, L.J.: A point set generation network for 3D object reconstruction from a single image. In: CVPR (2017)
17. Ganapathi-Subramanian, V., Diamanti, O., Pirk, S., Tang, C., Niessner, M., Guibas, L.: Parsing geometry using structure-aware shape templates. In: 3DV (2018)
18. Girdhar, R., Fouhey, D.F., Rodriguez, M., Gupta, A.: Learning a predictable and generative vector representation for objects. In: Leibe, B., Matas, J., Sebe, N., Welling, M. (eds.) ECCV 2016. LNCS, vol. 9910, pp. 484–499. Springer, Cham (2016). https://doi.org/10.1007/978-3-319-46466-4_29
19. Golovinskiy, A., Funkhouser, T.: Consistent segmentation of 3D models. Comput. Graph. **33**(3), 262–269 (2009)
20. Groueix, T., Fisher, M., Kim, V.G., Russell, B., Aubry, M.: AtlasNet: a papier-mâché approach to learning 3D surface generation. In: CVPR (2018)
21. Groueix, T., Fisher, M., Kim, V.G., Russell, B.C., Aubry, M.: A papier-mâché approach to learning 3D surface generation. In: CVPR (2018)
22. He, K., Gkioxari, G., Dollar, P., Girshick, R.: Mask R-CNN. In: ICCV (2017)
23. He, K., Zhang, X., Ren, S., Sun, J.: Deep residual learning for image recognition. In: CVPR (2016)
24. He, Y., Zhu, C., Wang, J., Savvides, M., Zhang, X.: Bounding box regression with uncertainty for accurate object detection. In: CVPR (2019)

25. Henderson, P., Ferrari, V.: Learning single-image 3D reconstruction by generative modelling of shape, pose and shading. In: IJCV, October 2019

26. Hoiem, D., Efros, A.A., Hebert, M.: Recovering surface layout from an image. IJCV **75**(1), 151–172 (2007)

27. Krizhevsky, A., Sutskever, I., Hinton, G.E.: Imagenet classification with deep convolutional neural networks. In: NeurIPS (2012)

28. Li, J., Xu, K., Chaudhuri, S., Yumer, E., Zhang, H., Guibas, L.: Grass: Generative recursive autoencoders for shape structures. In: ACM TOG (Proceedings of SIGGRAPH 2017), vol. 36(4) (2017)

29. Li, K., Pham, T., Zhan, H., Reid, I.: Efficient dense point cloud object reconstruction using deformation vector fields. In: ECCV (2018)

30. Li, Y., Pizlo, Z.: Reconstruction of 3D symmetrical shapes by using planarity and compactness constraints. J. Vis. **7**(9), 834–834 (2007)

31. Li, Z., Snavely, N.: Megadepth: learning single-view depth prediction from internet photos. In: CVPR (2018)

32. Lim, J.J., Pirsiavash, H., Torralba, A.: Parsing ikea objects: fine pose estimation. In: ICCV (2013)

33. Litany, O., Bronstein, A., Bronstein, M., Makadia, A.: Deformable shape completion with graph convolutional autoencoders. In: CVPR (2018)

34. Ma, L., Jia, X., Sun, Q., Schiele, B., Tuytelaars, T., Van Gool, L.: Pose guided person image generation. In: NeurIPS (2017)

35. Mandikal, P., Navaneet, K.L., Agarwal, M., Babu, R.V.: 3D-LMNet: latent embedding matching for accurate and diverse 3D point cloud reconstruction from a single image. In: Proceedings of the British Machine Vision Conference (BMVC) (2018)

36. Marr, D.: Vision: A Computational Investigation Into the Human Representation and Processing of Visual Information. Ph.D. thesis (1982)

37. McCormac, J., Handa, A., Leutenegger, S., Davison, A.J.: Scenenet RGB-D: Can 5m synthetic images beat generic imagenet pre-training on indoor segmentation? In: ICCV (2017)

38. Mescheder, L., Oechsle, M., Niemeyer, M., Nowozin, S., Geiger, A.: Occupancy networks: learning 3D reconstruction in function space. In: CVPR (2019)

39. Niu, C., Li, J., Xu, K.: Im2struct: Recovering 3D shape structure from a single RGB image. In: CVPR (2018)

40. Park, J.J., Florence, P., Straub, J., Newcombe, R., Lovegrove, S.: Deepsdf: learning continuous signed distance functions for shape representation. In: CVPR (2019)

41. Pauly, M., Mitra, N.J., Wallner, J., Pottmann, H., Guibas, L.J.: Discovering structural regularity in 3D geometry. In: ACM TOG, vol. 27 (2008)

42. Pavlakos, G., Zhu, L., Zhou, X., Daniilidis, K.: Learning to estimate 3D human pose and shape from a single color image. In: CVPR (2018)

43. Pizlo, Z.: 3D Shape: Its Unique Place in Visual Perception. MIT Press, Cambridge (2010)

44. Richter, S.R., Roth, S.: Matryoshka networks: predicting 3D geometry via nested shape layers. In: CVPR (2018)

45. Riegler, G., Osman Ulusoy, A., Geiger, A.: Octnet: learning deep 3D representations at high resolutions. In: CVPR (2017)

46. Riegler, G., Ulusoy, A.O., Bischof, H., Geiger, A.: Octnetfusion: learning depth fusion from data. In: 3DV (2017)

47. Roberts, L.G.: Machine perception of three-dimensional solids. Ph.D. thesis, Massachusetts Institute of Technology (1963)

48. Ronneberger, O., Fischer, P., Brox, T.: U-net: convolutional networks for biomedical image segmentation. In: MICCAI (2015)

49. Saxena, A., Sun, M., Ng, A.Y.: Make3d: learning 3D scene structure from a single still image. IEEE TPAMI **31**(5), 824–840 (2009)
50. Shin, D., Fowlkes, C.C., Hoiem, D.: Pixels, voxels, and views: a study of shape representations for single view 3D object shape prediction. In: CVPR (2018)
51. Sitzmann, V., Zollhöfer, M., Wetzstein, G.: Scene representation networks: continuous 3D-structure-aware neural scene representations. In: NeurIPS (2019)
52. Št'ava, O., Beneš, B., Měch, R., Aliaga, D.G., Krištof, P.: Inverse procedural modeling by automatic generation of l-systems. Comput. Graph. Forum **29**, 665–674 (2010)
53. Sun, X., et al.: Pix3d: dataset and methods for single-image 3D shape modeling. In: CVPR (2018)
54. Tatarchenko, M., Dosovitskiy, A., Brox, T.: Octree generating networks: efficient convolutional architectures for high-resolution 3D outputs. In: ICCV (2017)
55. Tulsiani, S., Su, H., Guibas, L.J., Efros, A.A., Malik, J.: Learning shape abstractions by assembling volumetric primitives. In: CVPR (2017)
56. Tulsiani, S., Zhou, T., Efros, A.A., Malik, J.: Multi-view supervision for single-view reconstruction via differentiable ray consistency. In: CVPR (2017)
57. Wang, N., Zhang, Y., Li, Z., Fu, Y., Liu, W., Jiang, Y.G.: Pixel2mesh: generating 3D mesh models from single RGB images. In: ECCV (2018)
58. Wu, J., Wang, Y., Xue, T., Sun, X., Freeman, B., Tenenbaum, J.: Marrnet: 3D shape reconstruction via 2.5 d sketches. In: NeurIPS (2017)
59. Wu, J., et al.: 3D interpreter networks for viewer-centered wireframe modeling. In: IJCV (2018)
60. Wu, J., Zhang, C., Xue, T., Freeman, B., Tenenbaum, J.: Learning a probabilistic latent space of object shapes via 3D generative-adversarial modeling. In: NeurIPS (2016)
61. Wu, J., Zhang, C., Zhang, X., Zhang, Z., Freeman, W.T., Tenenbaum, J.B.: Learning shape priors for single-view 3D completion and reconstruction. In: ECCV (2018)
62. Wu, Z., Wang, X., Lin, D., Lischinski, D., Cohen-Or, D., Huang, H.: Structure-aware generative network for 3D-shape modeling. arXiv preprint arXiv:1808.03981 (2018)
63. Xu, Q., Wang, W., Ceylan, D., Mech, R., Neumann, U.: Disn: deep implicit surface network for high-quality single-view 3D reconstruction (2019)
64. Zhang, X., Zhang, Z., Zhang, C., Tenenbaum, J., Freeman, B., Wu, J.: Learning to reconstruct shapes from unseen classes. In: NeurIPS (2018)
65. Zhou, X., Zhu, M., Leonardos, S., Derpanis, K.G., Daniilidis, K.: Sparseness meets deepness: 3D human pose estimation from monocular video. In: CVPR (2016)
66. Zou, C., Yumer, E., Yang, J., Ceylan, D., Hoiem, D.: 3D-PRNN: generating shape primitives with recurrent neural networks. In: ICCV (2017)

Weakly Supervised 3D Object Detection from Lidar Point Cloud

Qinghao Meng[1], Wenguan Wang[2(✉)], Tianfei Zhou[3], Jianbing Shen[1,3],
Luc Van Gool[2], and Dengxin Dai[2]

[1] School of Computer Science, Beijing Institute of Technology, Beijing, China
[2] ETH Zurich, Zurich, Switzerland
wenguanwang.ai@gmail.com
[3] Inception Institute of Artificial Intelligence, Abu Dhabi, UAE
https://github.com/hlesmqh/WS3D

Abstract. It is laborious to manually label point cloud data for training high-quality 3D object detectors. This work proposes a *weakly supervised* approach for 3D object detection, only requiring a small set of
weakly annotated scenes, associated with a few precisely labeled object
instances. This is achieved by a two-stage architecture design. Stage-
1 learns to generate cylindrical object proposals under weak supervision, *i.e.*, only the horizontal centers of objects are click-annotated in
bird's view scenes. Stage-2 learns to refine the cylindrical proposals to
get cuboids and confidence scores, using a few well-labeled instances.
Using only 500 weakly annotated scenes and 534 precisely labeled vehicle instances, our method achieves $85-95\%$ the performance of current
top-leading, fully supervised detectors (requiring $3,712$ exhaustively and
precisely annotated scenes with $15,654$ instances). Moreover, with our
elaborately designed network architecture, our trained model can be
applied as a 3D object annotator, supporting both automatic and active
(human-in-the-loop) working modes. The annotations generated by our
model can be used to train 3D object detectors, achieving over 94% of
their original performance (with manually labeled training data). Our
experiments also show our model's potential in boosting performance
when given more training data. Above designs make our approach highly
practical and introduce new opportunities for learning 3D object detection at reduced annotation cost.

Keywords: 3d object detection · Weakly supervised learning

1 Introduction

Over the past several years, extensive industry and research efforts have been
dedicated to autonomous driving. Significant progress has been made in key

Electronic supplementary material The online version of this chapter (https://
doi.org/10.1007/978-3-030-58601-0_31) contains supplementary material, which is
available to authorized users.

© Springer Nature Switzerland AG 2020
A. Vedaldi et al. (Eds.): ECCV 2020, LNCS 12358, pp. 515–531, 2020.
https://doi.org/10.1007/978-3-030-58601-0_31

technologies for innovative autonomous driving functions, with 3D object detection being one representative example. Almost all recent successful 3D object detectors are built upon *fully supervised* frameworks. They provided various solutions to problems arising from monocular images [1,2], stereo images [3] or point clouds [4–7]; gave insight into point cloud representation, introducing techniques such as voxelization [8,9] and point-wise operation [10]; and greatly advanced the state-of-the-arts. However, these methods necessitate *large-scale, precisely-annotated* 3D data to reach performance saturation and avoid overfitting. Unfortunately, such data requirement involves an astonishing amount of manual work, as it takes hundreds of hours to annotate just one hour of driving data. The end result is that a corpus of 3D training data is not only costly to create, but also limited in size and variety. In short, the demand for massive, high-quality yet expensive labeled data has become one of the biggest challenges faced by 3D object detection system developers.

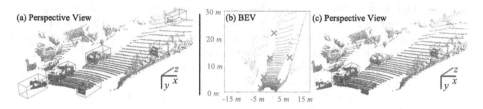

Fig. 1. Comparison between the *full* supervision used in prior arts (**a**) and our *inaccurate, inexact* (**b**) and *incomplete* (**c**) supervision. Previous fully supervised methods are trained from massive, exhaustively-labeled scenes (3, 712 precisely annotated scenes with 15, 654 vehicle instances), while our model uses only 500 weakly annotated scenes with center-annotated BEV maps as well as 534 precisely labeled vehicle instances.

In order to promote the deployment of 3D object detection systems, it is necessary to decrease the heavy annotation burden. However, this essential issue has not received due attention so far. To this end, we propose a weakly supervised method that learns 3D object detection from less training data, with more easily-acquired and cheaper annotations. Specifically, our model has two main stages. Stage-1 learns to predict the object centers on the (x, z)-plane and identity foreground points. The training in this stage only requires a small set of weakly annotated bird's eye view (BEV) maps, where the horizontal object centers are labeled (Fig. 1(b)). Such *inexact* and *inaccurate* supervision greatly saves annotation efforts. Since the height information is missing in BEV maps, we generate a set of cylindrical proposals whose extent along the y-axis is unlimited. Then, Stage-2 learns to estimate 3D parameters from these proposals and predict corresponding confidence scores. The learning paradigm in this stage is achieved by a few, precisely-annotated object instances as *incomplete* supervision (Fig. 1(c)), in contrast to prior arts [5,11], which consume massive, exhaustively-labeled scenes (*full* ground-truth labels, Fig. 1(a)).

Our weakly supervised framework provides two appealing characteristics. First, it learns 3D object detection by making use of a small amount of weakly-labeled BEV data and precisely-annotated object instances. The weak supervision from BEV maps is in the form of click annotations of the horizontal object centers. This enables much faster data labeling compared to strong supervision requiring cuboids to be elaborately annotated on point clouds (about 40~50× faster; see Sect. 3). For the small set of well-annotated object instances, we only label 25% of objects in the weakly-labeled scenes, which is about 3% of the supervision used in current leading models. Such a weakly supervised 3D object detection paradigm not only provides the opportunity to reduce the strong supervision requirement in this field, but also introduces immediate commercial benefits.

Second, once trained, our detector can be applied as an annotation tool to assist the laborious labeling process. Current popular, supervised solutions eagerly consume all the training data to improve the performance, while pay little attention to how to facilitate the training data annotation. Our model design allows both automatic and active working modes. In the automatic mode (no annotator in the loop), after directly applying our model to automatically re-annotate KITTI dataset [12], re-trained PointPillars [7] and PointRCNN [13] can maintain more than 94% of their original performance. In the active setting, human annotators first provide center-click supervision on the BEV maps, which is used as privileged information to guide our Stage-2 for final cuboid prediction. Under such a setting, re-trained PointPillars and PointRCNN reach above 96% of their original performance. More essentially, compared with current strongly supervised annotation tools [14,15], our model is able to provide more accurate annotations with much less and weaker supervision, at higher speed (Sect. 5.4).

For KITTI [12], the experiments on **Car** class show that, using only 500 weakly annotated scenes and 534 precisely labeled vehicle instances, we achieve 85−95% of the performance of fully supervised state-of-the-arts (which require 3,712 precisely annotated scenes with 15,654 vehicle instances). When using more training data, our performance is further boosted (Fig. 2). For **Pedestrian** class with fewer annotations, our method even outperforms most existing meth-

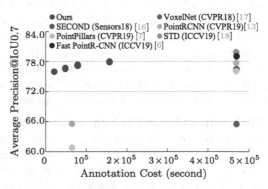

Fig. 2. Performance *vs.* annotation efforts, tested on KITTI [12] val set (**Car**), under the *moderate* regime. Our model yields promising results with far less annotation demand (Sect. 5.2).

ods, clearly demonstrating the effectiveness of our proposed weakly supervised learning paradigm.

2   Related Work

Learning Point Cloud Representations: Processing sparse, unordered point cloud data from LiDAR sensors is a fundamental problem in many 3D related areas. There are two main paradigms for this: voxelization or point based methods. The first type of methods [8,9,19,20] voxelize point clouds into volumetric grids and apply 2D/3D CNNs for prediction. Some of them [4,11,21,22] further improve volumetric features with multi-view representations of point clouds. Voxel based methods are computationally efficient but suffer from information loss (due to quantitization of point clouds with coarse voxel resolution). The second-type, point based methods [10,13,17,23–25], which directly operate on raw point clouds and preserve the original information, recently became popular.

3D Object Detection: A flurry of techniques have been explored for 3D object detection in driving scenarios, which can be broadly categorized into three classes. (1) 2D image based methods focus on camera based solutions with monocular or stereo images, by exploring geometries between 3D and 2D bounding boxes [1,3,26,27], or similarities between 3D objects and CAD models [2,28]. Though efficient, they struggle against the inherent difficulty of directly estimating depth information from images. *(2) 3D point cloud based methods* rely on depth sensors such as LiDAR. Some representative ones project point clouds to bird's view and use 2D CNNs [4,5] to learn the point cloud features. Some others [17,21] apply 3D CNNs over point cloud voxels to generate cuboids. They tend to capture local information, due to the limited receptive fields of CNN kernels. Thus sparse convolutions [16] with enlarged receptive fields are adopted later. To avoid losing information during voxelization, some efforts learn point-wise features directly from raw point clouds, using PointNet [10]-like structures [6,7]. *(3) Fusion-based methods* [10,13,24,25,29,30] attempt to fuse information from different sensors, such as cameras and LiDAR. The basic idea is to leverage the complementary information of camera images and point clouds, *i.e.*, rich visual information of images and precise depth details of point clouds, to improve the detection accuracy. However, fusion-based methods typically run slowly due to the need of processing multi-modal inputs [16].

Click Supervision: Click annotation schemes were used to reduce the burden of collecting segmentation/bounding box annotations at a large scale. Current efforts typically leverage center-click [31,32], extreme-point [33,34], or corrective-click [31] supervision for semantic segmentation [31,35] or object detection [32–34] in 2D visual scenarios. However, in this work, we explore center clicks, located on BEV maps, as weak supervision signals for 3D object detection.

3D Object Annotation: Very few attempts were made to scale up 3D object annotation pipelines [14,15]. [15] lets an annotator place 2D seeds from which to infer 3D segments and centroid parameters, using fully supervised learning. [14] suggests a differentiable template matching model with curriculum learning. In addition to different annotation paradigms, model designs and level of human interventions, our model is also unique in its weakly supervised learning strategy and dual-work mode, and achieves stronger performance.

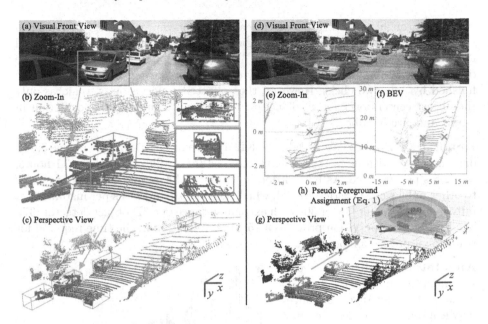

Fig. 3. (a-c): Precise annotations require extensive labeling efforts (see Sect. 3). **(d-f)**: Our weak supervision is simply obtained by clicking object centers (denoted by ✖) on BEV maps (see Sect. 3). **(g-h)**: Our pseudo groundtruths for fore-/background segmentation (yellower indicates higher foreground score; see Sect. 4.1). (Color figure online)

3   Data Annotation Strategy for Our Weak Supervision

Before detailing our model, we first discuss how to get our weakly supervised data.

Traditional Precise But Laborious Labeling Strategy: Current popular 3D object detectors are fully supervised deep learning models, requiring precisely annotated data. However, creating a high-quality 3D object detection dataset is more complex than creating, for example, a 2D object detection dataset. For precise labeling [36,37], annotators first navigate the 3D scene to find an object with the help of visual content from the camera image (Fig. 3 (a)). Later, an initial rough cuboid and orientation arrow (Fig. 3 (b)) are placed. Finally, the optimal annotation (Fig. 3 (c)) is obtained by gradually adjusting the 2D boxes projected in orthographic views. As can be seen, although this labeling procedure generates high-quality annotations, it contains several subtasks with gradual corrections and 2D-3D view switches. It is thus quite laborious and expensive.

Our Weak But Fast Annotation Scheme: Our model is learned from a small set of weakly annotated BEV maps, combined with a few precisely labeled 3D object instances. The weakly annotated data only contains object center-annotated BEV maps, which can be easily obtained. Specifically, human annotators first roughly click a target on the camera front-view map (Fig. 3 (d)). Then the BEV map is zoomed in and the region around the initial click is presented for a more accurate center-click (Fig. 3 (e)). Since our annotation procedure does not refer to any 3D view, it is very easy and fast; most annotations can be finished by only two clicks. However, the collected supervision is weak, as only the object centers over (x, z)-plane are labeled, without height information in y-axis and size of cuboids.

Annotation Speed: We re-labeled KITTI `train` set [12], which has 3,712 driving scenes with more than 15K vehicle instances. This took about 11 hours, *i.e.*, 2.5 s per instance. As KITTI does not report the annotation time, we refer to other published statistics [37,38], which suggest around 114 s per instance in a fully manual manner [38] or 30s with extra assistance of a 3D object detector [37]. Thus our click supervision provides a 15~45× reduction in the time required for traditional precise annotations.

Annotation Quality: To assess our annotation quality, Fig. 4 depicts the average distance between our annotated centers and the KITTI groundtruths on BEV maps. The average errors on x- and z-axes are about 0.25 m and 0.75 m, respectively, bringing out the limitation of LiDAR sensors in capturing the object better to its side than the back.

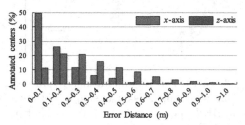

Fig. 4. Distance distributions (**Car**) on x- and z-axes of our weak BEV annotations.

4   Proposed Algorithm

Our object detector takes raw point clouds as input and outputs oriented 3D boxes. It has a cylindrical 3D proposal generation stage (Sect. 4.1, Fig. 5(a-b)), learning from click supervision, and a subsequent, proposal-based 3D object localization stage, learning from a few, well-annotated object instances (Sect. 4.2, Fig. 5(c-d)). Below we will focus on **Car** class. However, as evidenced in our experiments (Sect. 5.2), our model can also easily be applied to other classes, such as **Pedestrian**.

4.1   Learn to Generate Cylindrical Proposals from Click Annotations

There are two goals in our first stage: 1) to generate foreground point segmentation; and 2) to produce a set of cylinder-shaped 3D object proposals. The fore-/background separation is helpful for the proposal generation and provides useful information for the second stage. Because only the horizontal centers of objects are labeled on the BEV maps, our proposals are cylinder-shaped.

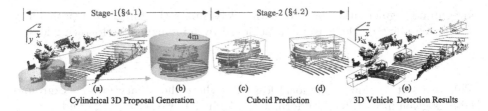

Fig. 5. Our 3D object detection pipeline (Sect. 4). (a-b) Cylindrical 3D proposal generation results from Stage-1 (Sect. 4.1). Yellower colors correspond to higher foreground probabilities. (c-d) Cuboid prediction in Stage-2 (Sect. 4.2). (e) Our final results.

Pseudo Groundtruth Generation. Since the annotations in the BEV maps are weak, proper modifications should be made to produce pseudo, yet stronger supervision signals. Specifically, for a labeled vehicle center point $o \in \mathcal{O}$, its horizontal location (x_o, z_o) in the LiDAR coordinate system can be inferred according to the projection from BEV to point cloud. We set its height y_o (over y-axis) to the LiDAR sensor's height (the height of the ego-vehicle), i.e., $y_o = 0$. The rationale behind such a setting will be detailed later. Then, for each unlabeled point p, its pseudo foreground value $f^p \in [0, 1]$ is defined as:

$$f^p = \max_{o \in \mathcal{O}}(\iota(p, o)), \quad \text{where} \quad \iota(p, o) = \begin{cases} 1 & \text{if } d(p, o) \leq 0.7, \\ \dfrac{1}{\kappa}\mathcal{N}(d(p, o)) & \text{if } d(p, o) > 0.7. \end{cases} \tag{1}$$

Here, $\mathcal{N}$ is a 1D Gaussian distribution with mean 0.7 and variance 1.5, and $\kappa = \mathcal{N}(0.7)$ is a normalization factor. And $d(p, o)$ is a distance function: $d(p, o) = [(x_p - x_o)^2 + \frac{1}{2}(y_p - y_o)^2 + (z_p - z_o)^2]^{\frac{1}{2}}$, where (x_p, y_p, z_p) is the 3D coordinate of p. The coefficient $(= \frac{1}{2})$ is used to due to the large uncertainty over y-axis. The foreground probability assignment function $\iota(p, o)$ gives high confidence $(= 1)$ for those points close to o (i.e., $d(p, o) \leq 0.7$), and attenuates the confidence for distant ones (i.e., $d(p, o) > 0.7$) by following the Gaussian distribution $\mathcal{N}$. The reason why we set the heights of the labeled center points $\mathcal{O}$ as 0 is because most object points are at lower altitudes than the LiDAR sensor (at the top of the ego-vehicle) and they will gain high foreground values in this way. For those background points even with similar altitudes to the LiDAR sensor, they are very sparse and typically far away from the vehicle centers in (x, z)-plane (see Fig. 3(h)), and can thus be ignored. Plane detection [3] can be used for more accurate height estimation, but in practice we find our strategy is good enough.

Point Cloud Representation. Several set-abstraction layers with multi-scale grouping are applied to directly learn discriminative point-wise features from raw point cloud input [24]. Then, two branches are placed over the backbone for foreground point segmentation and vehicle (x, z)-center prediction, respectively.

Foreground Point Segmentation. With the point-wise features extracted from the backbone network and pseudo groundtruth f^p generated in Eq. 1, the foreground segmentation branch learns to estimate the foreground probability $\hat{f}^p$ of each point p. The learning is achieved by minimizing the following loss:

$$\mathcal{L}_{\text{seg}} = \alpha(1 - \hat{f}^p)^\gamma \log(\hat{f}^p), \quad \text{where } \hat{f}^p = \tilde{f}^p \cdot f^p + (1 - \tilde{f}^p) \cdot (1 - f^p). \quad (2)$$

This is a soft version of the focal loss [39], where the binary fore-/background label is given in a probability formation. As in [39], we set $\alpha = 0.25$ and $\gamma = 2$.

Object (x, z)-Center Prediction. The other branch is for object (x, z)-center regression, as the weakly annotated BEV maps only contain horizontal information. As in [13], a bin-based classification strategy is adopted. For each labeled object center $o \in \mathcal{O}$, we set the points within $4\,\text{m}$ distance as *support points* (whose pseudo foreground probabilities ≥ 0.1). These support points are used to estimate the horizontal coordinates of o. For each support point p, its surrounding area $(L \times L \text{ m}^2)$ along x- and z-axes is the searching space for o, which is split into a series of discrete bins. Concretely, for x- and z-axis, the search range $L(= 8 \text{ m})$ is divided into 10 bins of uniform length $\delta(= 0.8 \text{ m})$. Therefore, for a support point p and the corresponding center o, the target bin assignments (b_x, b_z) along x- and z-axis can be formulated as:

$$b_x = \lfloor \frac{x_p - x_o + L}{\delta} \rfloor, \quad b_z = \lfloor \frac{z_p - z_o + L}{\delta} \rfloor. \quad (3)$$

Residual (r_x, r_z) is computed for further location refinement within each assigned bin:

$$r_{u \in \{x,z\}} = \frac{u}{\varepsilon}(u_p - u_o + L - (b_u \cdot \delta + \frac{\delta}{2})), \quad \text{where } \varepsilon = \frac{\delta}{2}. \quad (4)$$

For a support point p, the center localization loss $\mathcal{L}_{\text{bin}}$ is designed as:

$$\mathcal{L}_{\text{bin}} = \sum_{u \in \{x,z\}} \mathcal{L}_{\text{cls}}(\tilde{b}_u, b_u) + \mathcal{L}_{\text{reg}}(\tilde{r}_u, r_u), \quad (5)$$

where $\tilde{b}$ and $\tilde{r}$ are predicted bin assignments and residuals, and b and r are the targets. $\mathcal{L}_{\text{cls}}$ is a cross-entropy loss for bin classification along the (x, z)-plane, and $\mathcal{L}_{\text{reg}}$ refers to the $\ell 1$ loss for residual regression w.r.t the target bins.

Cylindrical 3D Proposal Generation. During inference, the segmentation branch estimates the foreground probability of each point. Then, we only preserve the points whose foreground scores are larger than 0.1. As we only have horizontal coordinates of the centers, we cannot directly generate 3D bounding box proposals. Instead, for each center, we generate a cylindrical proposal with a 4 m radius over (x, z)-plane and unlimited extent along y-axis (Fig. 5 (a, b)).

Center-Aware Non-maximum Suppression. To eliminate redundant proposals, we propose a center-aware non-maximum suppression (CA-NMS) strategy. The main idea is that, it is easier to predict centers from center-close points than far ones, and center-close points gain high foreground scores under our pseudo groundtruth generation strategy. Thus, for a predicted center, we use the foreground probability of its sourced (support) point, as its confidence score.

That means we assume that a point with a higher foreground score is more center-close and tends to make a more confident center prediction. Then we rank all the predicted centers according to their confidence, from large to small. For each center, if its distance to any other pre-selected centers is larger than 4 m on the (x, z)-plane, its proposal will be preserved; otherwise it is removed.

4.2   Learn to Refine Proposals from a Few Well-Labeled Instances

Stage-2 is to estimate cuboids from proposals and recognize false estimates. We achieve this by learning a proposal refinement model from a few well-annotated instances, motivated by two considerations. **(i)** The proposal refinement is performed instance-wise, driving us to consume instance-wise annotations. **(ii)** Our initial cylindrical proposals, though rough, contain rich useful information, which facilitates cuboid prediction especially when training data is limited.

Overall Pipeline. Our method carries out refinement of cuboid predictions over two steps. First, an initial cuboid generation network takes cylindrical proposals as inputs, and outputs initial cuboid estimations (Fig. 5 (b-c)). Then, a final cuboid refinement network takes the initial cuboid estimations as inputs, and outputs final cuboid predictions (Fig. 5 (c-d)) as well as confidence.

Initial Cuboid Generation. The initial cuboid generation network stacks several set abstraction layers, intermediated with a single-scale grouping operation, to collect contextual and pooled point features as the cylindrical proposal representations [24]. Then, a multilayer perceptron based branch is appended for initial cuboid estimation. Let us denote the groundtruth of an input cuboid as $(x, y, z, h, w, l, \theta)$, where (x, y, z) are the object-center coordinates, (h, w, l) object size, and θ orientation from BEV. A bin-based regression loss $\mathcal{L}_{bin}$ is applied for estimating θ, and a smooth $\ell 1$ loss $\mathcal{L}_{reg}$ is used for other parameters:

$$\mathcal{L}_{ref} = \mathcal{L}_{bin}(\tilde{\theta}, \theta) + \sum\nolimits_{u \in \{x,y,z,h,w,l\}} \mathcal{L}_{reg}(\tilde{u}, u), \tag{6}$$

where $(\tilde{x}, \tilde{y}, \tilde{z}, \tilde{h}, \tilde{w}, \tilde{l}, \tilde{\theta})$ are the estimated cuboid parameters.

Final Cuboid Refinement. The final cuboid refinement network has the similar network architecture of the initial cuboid generation network. It learns to refine initial cuboid estimations with the same loss design in Eq. 6. In addition, to predict cuboid's confidence, an extra confidence estimation head is added, which is supervised by an IoU-based regression loss [27,40]:

$$\mathcal{L}_{con} = \mathcal{L}_{reg}(\tilde{C}_{IoU}, C_{IoU}), \tag{7}$$

where the targeted confidence score C_{IoU} is computed as the largest IoU score between the output cuboid and groundtruths.

In the first cuboid generation step, for each groundtruth 3D bounding box, cylindrical proposals whose center-distances (on (x, z)-plane) are less than 1.4 m away are selected as the training samples. Then, the output cuboids from those cylindrical proposals are further used as the training samples for the groundtruth in the final refinement step.

4.3   Implementation Detail

Detailed Network Architecture. In Stage-1 (Sect. 4.1), to align the network input, 16K points are sampled from each point-cloud scene. Four set-abstraction layers with multi-scales are stacked to sample the points into groups with sizes (4096, 1024, 256, 64). Four feature propagation layers are then used to obtain point-wise features, as the input for the segmentation and center prediction branches. The segmentation branch contains two FC layers with 128 and 1 neuron(s), respectively. The (x, z)-center prediction branch has two FC layers with 128 and 40 neurons, respectively. In Stage-2 (Sect. 4.2), 512 points are sampled from each cylindrical proposal/cuboid, and each point is associated with a 5D feature vector, *i.e.*, a concatenation of 3D point coordinates, 1D laser reflection intensity, and foreground score. Before feeding each proposal/cuboid into the generation/refinement network, the coordinates of points are canonized to guarantee their translation and rotation invariance [6]. The corresponding groundtruth is modified accordingly. In addition, for cylindrical proposals, only a translation transformation is performed over (x, z)-plane, *i.e.*, the horizontal coordinates of the proposal center are set as $(0, 0)$. For each cuboid, the coordinates of points within a 0.3 m radius are cropped to include more context. For the cuboid generation/refinement network, four set-abstraction layers with single-scale grouping are used to sample the input points into groups with sizes (256, 128, 32, 1). Finally, a 512D feature is extracted for cuboid and confidence estimation.

Data Preparation. KITTI `train` set has 3, 712 precisely annotated training scenes with 15, 654 vehicle instances. Unless otherwise noted, we use the following training data setting. The first 500 scenes with our weakly annotated BEV maps are used for training our Stage-1 model, and 25% of the vehicle instances (=534) in the 500 scenes are associated with precise 3D annotations and used for training our Stage-2 model[1]. We make use of this weak and limited training data to better illustrate the advantage of our model. This also allows us to investigate the performance when using our model as an annotation tool (see Sect. 5.4).

Data Augmentation. During training, we adopt several data augmentation techniques to avoid overfitting and improve the generalization ability. In Stage-1, left-right flipping, scaling from [0.95, 1.05], and rotation from $[-10°, 10°]$ are randomly applied for each scene. In addition, to diversify training scenarios, we randomly sample a few annotated vehicle centers with surrounding points within a cylinder with a 4 m radius, and insert them into the current sample. Furthermore, to increase the robustness to distant vehicles, which typically contain very few points, we randomly drop the points within the cylindrical space (with a 4 m radius) of labeled centers. In Stage-2, for each proposal, we randomly conduct left-right flipping, scaling from [0.8, 1.2], and rotation from $[-90°, 90°]$. We shift each proposal by small translations, following a Gaussian distribution with mean 0 and variance 0.1, for x-, y-, and z-axis each individually. We randomly change the foreground label of the points. To address large occlusions, we randomly omit

---

[1] The instances are randomly selected and the list will be released.

part of a proposal (1/4−3/4 of the area in BEV). Finally, for each proposal, we randomly remove the inside points (at least 32 points remain).

Inference. After applying CA-NMS for the cylindrical proposals generated in Stage-1 (Sect. 4.1), we feed the remaining ones to Stage-2 (Sect. 4.2) and get final 3D predictions. We then use an oriented NMS with a BEV IoU threshold of 0.3 to reduce redundancy. Our model runs at about 0.2 s per scene, which is on par with MV3D [4] (0.36 s), VoxelNet [17] (0.23 s) and F-PointNet [25] (0.17 s).

5 Experiment

5.1 Experimental Setup

Dataset. Experiments are conducted on KITTI [12], which contains 7, 481 images for train/val and 7, 518 images for testing. The `train/val` set has 3D bounding box groundtruths and is split into two sub-sets [4,17]: `train` (3, 712 images) and `val` (3, 769 images). We train our detector only on a weakly labeled subset of `train` set, while the `val` set is used for evaluation only. Detection outcomes are evaluated in the three standard regimes: *easy, moderate, hard*.

Evaluation Metric. Following [4], average precisions for BEV and 3D boxes are reported. Unless specified, the performance is evaluated with a 0.7 IoU threshold.

Table 1. Evaluation results on KITTI `val` set (Car). See Sect. 5.2 for details.

Learning Paradigm	Detector	Modality	BEV@0.7			3D Box@0.7		
			Easy	Moderate	Hard	Easy	Moderate	Hard
Trained with the whole KITTI `train` set: 3, 712 precisely labeled scenes with 15, 654 vehicle instances								
Fully supervised	VeloFCN [11]	LiDAR	40.14	32.08	30.47	15.20	13.66	15.98
	PIXOR [5]	LiDAR	86.79	80.75	76.60	-	-	-
	VoxelNet [17]	LiDAR	89.60	84.81	78.57	81.97	65.46	62.85
	SECOND [16]	LiDAR	89.96	87.07	79.66	87.43	76.48	69.10
	PointRCNN [13]	LiDAR	-	-	-	88.45	77.67	76.30
	PointPillars [7]	LiDAR	89.64	86.46	84.22	85.31	76.07	69.76
	Fast PointR-CNN [6]	LiDAR	90.12	88.10	86.24	89.12	79.00	77.48
	STD [18]	LiDAR	90.50	88.50	88.10	89.70	79.80	79.30
Trained with a part of KITTI `train` set: 500 precisely labeled scenes with 2, 176 vehicle instances								
Fully supervised	PointRCNN [13]	LiDAR	87.21	77.10	76.63	79.88	65.50	64.93
	PointPillars [7]	LiDAR	86.27	77.13	75.91	72.36	60.75	55.88
Trained with a part of KITTI `train` set: 125 precisely labeled scenes with 550 vehicle instances								
Fully supervised	PointRCNN [13]	LiDAR	85.09	74.35	67.68	67.54	54.91	51.96
	PointPillars [7]	LiDAR	85.76	75.30	73.29	65.51	51.45	45.53
Trained with a part of KITTI `train` set: 500 weakly labeled scenes with 534 precisely annotated instances								
Weakly supervised	**Ours**	LiDAR	88.56	84.99	84.74	84.04	75.10	73.29

5.2 Quantitative and Qualitative Performance

Quantitative Results on KITTI `val` Set (Car). In Table 1, we compare our method with several leading methods, which all use fully-labeled training

Table 2. Evaluation results on KITTI test set (Car). See Sect. 5.2 for details.

Learning Paradigm	Detector	Modality	BEV@0.7			3D Box@0.7		
			Easy	Moderate	Hard	Easy	Moderate	Hard
Trained with the whole KITTI **train** set: 3, 712 precisely annotated scenes with 15, 654 vehicle instances								
	PIXOR [5]	LiDAR	87.25	81.92	76.01	-	-	-
	VoxelNet [17]	LiDAR	89.35	79.26	77.39	77.47	65.11	57.73
	SECOND [16]	LiDAR	88.07	79.37	77.95	83.13	73.66	66.20
Fully supervised	PointRCNN [13]	LiDAR	89.47	85.68	79.10	85.94	75.76	68.32
	PointPillars [7]	LiDAR	88.35	86.10	79.83	79.05	74.99	68.30
	Fast PointR-CNN [6]	LiDAR	88.03	86.10	78.17	84.28	75.73	67.39
	STD [18]	LiDAR	94.74	89.19	86.42	87.95	79.71	75.09
Trained with a part of KITTI **train** set: 500 weakly labeled scenes + 534 precisely annotated instances								
Weakly supervised	**Ours**	LiDAR	90.11	84.02	76.97	80.15	69.64	63.71

data (*i.e.*, 3, 712 precisely-labeled scenes with 15, 654 vehicle instances). However, despite using far less, weakly labeled data, our method yields comparable performance. In addition, as there is no other weakly supervised baseline, we retrain two outstanding detectors, PointRCNN [13] and PointPillars [7], under two relatively comparable settings, *i.e.*, using **(i)** 500 precisely labeled scenes (containing 2,176 well-annotated vehicle instances); and **(ii)** 125 precisely labeled scenes (containing 550 well-annotated instances). This helps further assess the efficacy of our method. Note that, for training our method, we use 500 scenes with center-click labels and 534 precisely-annotated instances. We find that our method significantly outperforms re-trained PointRCNN and PointPillars, using whether the same amount of well-annotated scenes (500; setting **(i)**) or the similar number of well-annotated instances (534; setting **(ii)**).

Fig. 6. Qualitative results of 3D object detection (Car) on KITTI val set (Sect. 5.2). Detected 3D bounding boxes are shown in yellow; images are used only for visualization.

Quantitative Results on KITTI test Set (Car). We also evaluate our algorithm on KITTI test set, by submitting our results to the official evaluation server. As shown in Table 2, though current top-performing methods use much stronger supervision, our method still gets competitive performance against some of them, such as PIXOR [5] and VoxelNet [17]. We can also observe that there is still room for improvement between weakly- and strong-supervised methods.

Qualitative Results. Figure 6 depicts visual results of a few representative scenes from KITTI val set, showing that our model is able to produce high-

Table 3. Evaluation results on KITTI val set (Pedestrian). See Sect. 5.2 for details.

Learning Paradigm	Detector	Modality	BEV@0.5			3D Box@0.5		
			Easy	Moderate	Hard	Easy	Moderate	Hard
Trained with: 951 precisely labeled scenes with 2, 257 pedestrian instances								
Fully supervised	PointPillars [7]	LiDAR	71.97	67.84	62.41	66.73	61.06	56.50
	PointRCNN [13]	LiDAR	68.89	63.54	57.63	63.70	69.43	58.13
	Part-A^2 [40]	LiDAR	-	-	-	70.73	64.13	57.45
	VoxelNet [17]	LiDAR	70.76	62.73	55.05	-	-	-
	STD [18]	LiDAR	75.90	69.90	66.00	73.90	66.60	62.90
Trained with: 951 weakly labeled scenes with 515 pedestrian instances								
Weakly supervised	**Ours**	LiDAR	74.79	70.17	66.75	74.65	69.96	66.49

quality 3D detections of vehicles that are highly occluded or far away from the ego-vehicle.

Quantitative Results on KITTI val Set (Pedestrian). We also report our performance on **Pedestrian** class (with 0.5 IoU threshold). In this case, our model is trained with 951 click-labeled scenes and 25% (515) of precisely annotated pedestrian instances. More training details can be found in the supplementary material. As shown in Fig. 3, our method shows very promising results, demonstrating its good generalizability and advantages when using less supervision.

5.3 Diagnostic Experiment

As the ground-truth for KITTI test set is not available and the access to the test server is limited, ablation studies are performed over the val set (see Table 4).

Table 4. Ablation study on KITTI val set (Car). See Sect. 5.3 for details.

Aspects		Training Setting	BEV@0.7			3D Box@0.7		
			Easy	Moderate	Hard	Easy	Moderate	Hard
Full model		500 weakly labeled scenes +25% (534) precisely annotated instances	88.56	84.99	84.74	84.04	75.10	73.29
More precisely annotated BEV maps		500 weakly labeled scenes +25% (534) more precisely annotated instances	88.52	84.57	85.02	85.67	75.13	73.92
	More training data	3,712 weakly labeled scenes +534 precisely annotated instances	88.81	86.98	85.76	86.08	76.04	74.97
		1,852 weakly labeled scenes +25% precisely annotated instances	89.11	85.95	85.52	87.14	76.78	76.56
		3,712 weakly labeled scenes +25% precisely annotated instances	89.32	86.17	86.31	87.57	77.62	76.94

Robustness to Inaccurate BEV Annotations. As discussed in Sect. 3, the annotations over the BEV maps are weak and inaccurate. To examine our robustness to inaccurate BEV annotations, we retrain our model with precise BEV annotations inferred from groundtruth 3D annotations. From Table 4, only marginal improvements are observed, verifying our robustness to noisy BEV annotations.

More Training Data. To demonstrate the potential of our weakly supervised 3D object detection scheme, we probe the upper bound by training on additional data. As evidenced by the results in the last three rows in Table 4, with the use of more training data, gradual performance boosts can indeed be achieved.

5.4   Performance as an Annotation Tool

Our model, once trained, can be used as an 3D object annotator. It only consumes part of KITTI train set, allowing us to explore its potential for assisting annotation. Due to its specific network architecture and click-annotation guided learning paradigm, it supports both automatic and active annotation modes.

Automatic Annotation Mode. For a given scene, it is straightforward to use our predictions as pseudo annotations, resulting in an automatic working mode. In such a setting, our method takes around 0.1 s for per car instance annotation. Previous 3D detection methods can also work as automatic annotators in this way. However, as they are typically trained with the whole KITTI train set, it is hard to examine their annotation quality.

Active Annotation Mode. In the active mode, human annotators first click on object centers in BEV maps, following the labeling strategy detailed in Sect. 3. Then, for each annotated center, 25 points are uniformly sampled from the surrounding 0.4 m × 0.4 m region (0.1 m interval). These points are used as the centers of cylindrical proposals and the foreground masks around them are generated according to Eq. 1. Then, we use our Stage-2 model to predict the cuboids, from which the one with largest confidence score is selected as the final annotation. About 2.6 s is needed for annotating each car instance in our active annotation mode, whereas humans take 2.5 s for center-click annotation on average.

Table 5. Comparison of annotation quality on KITTI val set (see Sect. 5.4).

Learning Paradigm	Method	Mode	Speed (sec./inst.)	BEV@0.5			3D Box@0.5		
				Easy	Moderate	Hard	Easy	Moderate	Hard
Trained with the whole KITTI train set: 3,712 well-labeled scenes with 15.654 vehicle instances									
Fully Supervised	[15]	Active	3.8	-	-	-	-	-	88.33
Trained with KITTI train+val: 7,481 scenes (implicitly using 2D instance segmentation annotations)									
Fully-Supervised	[14]	Auto	8.0	80.70	63.36	52.47	63.39	44.79	37.47
Trained with a part of KITTI train set: 500 weakly labeled scenes + 534 precisely annotated instances									
Weakly Supervised	**Ours**	Auto	0.1	96.33	89.01	88.52	95.85	89.14	88.32
		Active	2.6	99.99	99.92	99.90	99.87	90.78	90.14

Annotation Quality. Table 5 reports the evaluation results for our annotation quality on KITTI val set. Two previous annotation methods [14,15] are included. [15] is a fully supervised deep learning annotator, trained with the whole KITTI train set. It only works as an active model, where humans are required to provide object anchor clicks. [14] requires synthetic data for training and relies on MASK-RCNN [41], so it implicitly uses 2D instance segmentation annotations. It works in an automatic mode. The scores for these models are borrowed from the literature, as their implementations are not released. Following their settings [14, 15], scores with 0.5 3D IoU criterion are reported. As seen, our model produces high-quality annotations, especially in the active mode. Our annotations are

Table 6. Performance of PointRCNN [13] and PointPillars [7] when trained using different annotations sources. Results are reported on KITTI **val** set (Sect. 5.4).

Detector	Annotation Source	BEV@0.7			3D Box@0.7		
		Easy	Moderate	Hard	Easy	Moderate	Hard
PointRCNN [13]	Manual	90.21	87.89	85.51	88.45	77.67	76.30
	Automatic (ours)	88.02	85.75	84.27	83.22	74.54	73.29
	Active (ours)	88.64	85.41	84.94	84.21	76.08	74.91
PointPillars [7]	Manual	89.64	86.46	84.22	85.31	76.07	69.76
	Automatic (ours)	88.55	85.62	83.84	84.79	74.18	68.52
	Active (ours)	88.94	85.88	83.86	84.53	75.03	68.63

more accurate than [14,15], with much less and weak supervision. Considering our fast annotation speed (0.1−2.6 s per instance), the results are very significant.

Suitability for 3D Object Detection. To investigate the suitability of our labels for 3D object detection, we use our re-labeled KITTI **train** set (**Car**) to re-train PointPillars [7] and PointRCNN [13], which show leading performance with released implementations. During training, we use their original settings. From Table 6, we can observe that the two methods only suffer from small performance drops when using our labels.

6   Conclusion and Discussion

This work has made an early attempt to train a 3D object detector using limited and weak supervision. In addition, our detector can be extended as an annotation tool, whose performance was fully examined in both automatic and active modes. Extensive experiments on KITTI dataset demonstrate our impressive results, but also illustrate that there is still room for improvement. Given the massive number of algorithmic breakthroughs over the past few years, we can expect a flurry of innovation towards this promising direction.

References

1. Chen, X., Kundu, K., Zhang, Z., Ma, H., Fidler, S., Urtasun, R.: Monocular 3D object detection for autonomous driving. In: CVPR (2016)
2. Chabot, F., Chaouch, M., Rabarisoa, J., Teuliere, C., Chateau, T.: Deep MANTA: a coarse-to-fine many-task network for joint 2D and 3D vehicle analysis from monocular image. In: CVPR (2017)
3. Chen, X., et al.: 3D object proposals for accurate object class detection. In: NeurIPS (2015)
4. Chen, X., Ma, H., Wan, J., Li, B., Xia, T.: Multi-view 3D object detection network for autonomous driving. In: CVPR (2017)
5. Yang, B., Luo, W., Urtasun, R.: Pixor: real-time 3D object detection from point clouds. In: CVPR (2018)
6. Chen, Y., Liu, S., Shen, X., Jia, J.: Fast point R-CNN. In: ICCV (2019)

7. Lang, A.H., Vora, S., Caesar, H., Zhou, L., Yang, J., Beijbom, O.: Pointpillars: fast encoders for object detection from point clouds. In: CVPR (2019)
8. Maturana, D., Scherer, S.: Voxnet: a 3D convolutional neural network for real-time object recognition. In: IROS (2015)
9. Wu, Z., et al.: 3D shapenets: a deep representation for volumetric shapes. In: CVPR (2015)
10. Qi, C.R., Su, H., Mo, K., Guibas, L.J.: Pointnet: deep learning on point sets for 3D classification and segmentation. In: CVPR (2017)
11. Li, B., Zhang, T., Xia, T.: Vehicle detection from 3D Lidar using fully convolutional network. In: Robotics: Science and Systems (2016)
12. Geiger, A., Lenz, P., Urtasun, R.: Are we ready for autonomous driving? the KITTI vision benchmark suite. In: CVPR (2012)
13. Shi, S., Wang, X., Li, H.: PointRCNN: 3D object proposal generation and detection from point cloud. In: CVPR (2019)
14. Zakharov, S., Kehl, W., Bhargava, A., Gaidon, A.: Autolabeling 3D objects with differentiable rendering of SDF shape priors. arXiv preprint arXiv:1911.11288 (2019)
15. Lee, J., Walsh, S., Harakeh, A., Waslander, S.L.: Leveraging pre-trained 3D object detection models for fast ground truth generation. In: ITSC (2018)
16. Yan, Y., Mao, Y., Li, B.: Second: sparsely embedded convolutional detection. Sensors (2018)
17. Zhou, Y., Tuzel, O.: Voxelnet: end-to-end learning for point cloud based 3D object detection. In: CVPR (2018)
18. Yang, Z., Sun, Y., Liu, S., Shen, X., Jia, J.: STD: sparse-to-dense 3D object detector for point cloud. In: ICCV (2019)
19. Xiang, Y., Choi, W., Lin, Y., Savarese, S.: Data-driven 3D voxel patterns for object category recognition. In: CVPR (2015)
20. Xie, J., Zheng, Z., Gao, R., Wang, W., Zhu, S.C., Nian Wu, Y.: Learning descriptor networks for 3D shape synthesis and analysis. In: CVPR (2018)
21. Su, H., Maji, S., Kalogerakis, E., Learned-Miller, E.: Multi-view convolutional neural networks for 3D shape recognition. In: ICCV (2015)
22. Qi, C.R., Su, H., Niessner, M., Dai, A., Yan, M., Guibas, L.J.: Volumetric and multi-view CNNs for object classification on 3D data. In: CVPR (2016)
23. Rethage, D., Wald, J., Sturm, J., Navab, N., Tombari, F.: Fully-convolutional point networks for large-scale point clouds. In: ECCV (2018)
24. Qi, C.R., Yi, L., Su, H., Guibas, L.J.: Pointnet++: deep hierarchical feature learning on point sets in a metric space. In: NeurIPS (2017)
25. Qi, C.R., Liu, W., Wu, C., Su, H., Guibas, L.J.: Frustum pointnets for 3D object detection from RGB-D data. In: CVPR (2018)
26. Mousavian, A., Anguelov, D., Flynn, J., Kosecka, J.: 3D bounding box estimation using deep learning and geometry. In: CVPR (2017)
27. Li, B., Ouyang, W., Sheng, L., Zeng, X., Wang, X.: GS3D: an efficient 3D object detection framework for autonomous driving. In: CVPR (2019)
28. Mottaghi, R., Xiang, Y., Savarese, S.: A coarse-to-fine model for 3D pose estimation and sub-category recognition. In: CVPR (2015)
29. Liang, M., Yang, B., Wang, S., Urtasun, R.: Deep continuous fusion for multi-sensor 3D object detection. In: ECCV (2018)
30. Liang, M., Yang, B., Chen, Y., Hu, R., Urtasun, R.: Multi-task multi-sensor fusion for 3D object detection. In: CVPR (2019)
31. Bearman, A., Russakovsky, O., Ferrari, V., Fei-Fei, L.: What's the point: semantic segmentation with point supervision. In: ECCV (2016)

32. Papadopoulos, D.P., Uijlings, J.R., Keller, F., Ferrari, V.: Training object class detectors with click supervision. In: CVPR (2017)
33. Maninis, K.K., Caelles, S., Pont-Tuset, J., Van Gool, L.: Deep extreme cut: from extreme points to object segmentation. In: CVPR (2018)
34. Papadopoulos, D.P., Uijlings, J.R., Keller, F., Ferrari, V.: Extreme clicking for efficient object annotation. In: ICCV (2017)
35. Benenson, R., Popov, S., Ferrari, V.: Large-scale interactive object segmentation with human annotators. In: CVPR (2019)
36. Xie, J., Kiefel, M., Sun, M.T., Geiger, A.: Semantic instance annotation of street scenes by 3D to 2D label transfer. In: CVPR (2016)
37. Wang, P., Huang, X., Cheng, X., Zhou, D., Geng, Q., Yang, R.: The apolloscape open dataset for autonomous driving and its application. IEEE TPAMI (2019)
38. Song, S., Lichtenberg, S.P., Xiao, J.: SUN RGB-D: a RGB-D scene understanding benchmark suite. In: CVPR (2015)
39. Lin, T.Y., Goyal, P., Girshick, R., He, K., Dollar, P.: Focal loss for dense object detection. In: ICCV (2017)
40. Shi, S., Wang, Z., Shi, J., Wang, X., Li, H.: From points to parts: 3D object detection from point cloud with part-aware and part-aggregation network. IEEE TPAMI (2020)
41. He, K., Gkioxari, G., Dollár, P., Girshick, R.: Mask R-CNN. In: ICCV (2017)

Two-Phase Pseudo Label Densification for Self-training Based Domain Adaptation

Inkyu Shin, Sanghyun Woo, Fei Pan, and In So Kweon$^{(\boxtimes)}$

KAIST, Daejeon, South Korea
{dlsrbgg33,shwoo93,feipan,iskweon77}@kaist.ac.kr

Abstract. Recently, deep self-training approaches emerged as a powerful solution to the unsupervised domain adaptation. The self-training scheme involves iterative processing of target data; it generates target pseudo labels and retrains the network. However, since only the confident predictions are taken as pseudo labels, existing self-training approaches inevitably produce sparse pseudo labels in practice. We see this is critical because the resulting insufficient training-signals lead to a sub-optimal, error-prone model. In order to tackle this problem, we propose a novel **T**wo-phase **P**seudo **L**abel **D**ensification framework, referred to as **TPLD**. In the first phase, we use sliding window voting to propagate the confident predictions, utilizing intrinsic spatial-correlations in the images. In the second phase, we perform a confidence-based easy-hard classification. For the easy samples, we now employ their full pseudo-labels. For the hard ones, we instead adopt adversarial learning to enforce hard-to-easy feature alignment. To ease the training process and avoid noisy predictions, we introduce the bootstrapping mechanism to the original self-training loss. We show the proposed TPLD can be easily integrated into existing self-training based approaches and improves the performance significantly. Combined with the recently proposed CRST self-training framework, we achieve new state-of-the-art results on two standard UDA benchmarks.

Keywords: Unsupervised domain adaptataion · Self-training

1 Introduction

Unsupervised domain adaptation (UDA) aims to transfer knowledge learned from the label-rich source domain to an unlabeled new target domain. It is a practical and crucial problem as it could be beneficial for various label-scarce real-world scenarios, e.g., simulated learning for robots [11] or autonomous driving [31]. In this paper, we focus on the UDA for semantic segmentation, aiming to adopt a source segmentation model to a target domain without any labels.

Electronic supplementary material The online version of this chapter (https://doi.org/10.1007/978-3-030-58601-0_32) contains supplementary material, which is available to authorized users.

The dominant paradigm in UDA is based on ***adversarial learning*** [5,17, 19,25,36,37]. In particular, it minimizes both (source domain) task-specific loss and domain adversarial loss. The method thus retains good performance on the source domain task, and at the same time, can bridge the gap between source and target feature distributions. While the adversarial learning has achieved great success in UDA, recently another line of studies using ***self-training*** emerged [39,40]. Self-training generates a set of pseudo labels corresponding to high prediction scores in the target domain and then re-trains the network based on the generated pseudo labels. Recently, Zou & Yu have proposed two seminal works on CNN-based self-training methods; class balanced self-training (CBST) [39], and confidence regularized self-training (CRST) [40]. Unlike adversarial learning methods which utilize two separate losses, CBST presents a single unified self-training loss. It allows learning of domain-invariant features and classifiers in an end-to-end manner, both from labeled source data and pseudo labeled target data. CRST further generalizes the feasible space of pseudo labels and adopts regularizer. These self-training methods show state-of-the-art results in multiple UDA settings. However, we observe that its internal pseudo label selection tends to excessively cut-out the predictions, which often leads to sparse pseudo labels. We argue that sparse pseudo labels significantly miss meaningful training signals, and thus, the final model may deviate from the optimal solution eventually. A natural way to obtain dense pseudo labels is by lowering the selection threshold. However, we observe this naive approach brings noisy, unconfident predictions at an early stage, and this accumulates and propagates the errors.

To effectively address this issue, we present a two-step, gradual pseudo label densification method. The overview is shown in Fig. 1. In the first phase, we use sliding window voting to propagate the confident predictions, utilizing the intrinsic spatial correlations in the images. In the second phase, we perform an easy-hard classification using a proposed image-level confidence score. Our intuition is simple: As the model improves over time, its predictions can be trusted more. Thus, if the model in the second stage is confident with their prediction, we now do not zero out them. Indeed, we empirically observe that the confident, easy samples are near to the ground truth and vice versa. This motivates us to utilize full pseudo labels for the easy samples, while for the hard samples, we enforce adversarial loss to learn hard-to-easy adaption. Meanwhile, to tackle noisy labels effectively for both first and second phase training, we introduce the bootstrapping mechanism into the self-training loss function. By connecting all together, we build a two-phase pseudo label densification framework called TPLD. Since our method is general, we can easily apply TPLD to the existing self-training based approaches. We show consistent improvements over the strong baselines. Finally, we achieve new state-of-the-art performances on two standard UDA benchmarks.

We summarize our contributions as follows:

1. To our best knowledge, it is the first time that pseudo label densification is formally defined and explored in the self-training based domain adaptation.

2. We present a novel two-phase pseudo label densification framework, called **TPLD**. In particular, for the first phase, we introduce voting-based densification method. For the second phase, we propose an easy-hard classification-based densification method. Both phases are complementary in constructing an accurate self-training model.
3. We propose a new objective function to ease the training. Specifically, we re-formulate the original self-training loss function by incorporating the bootstrapping mechanism.
4. We conduct extensive ablation studies to thoroughly investigate the impact of our proposals. We apply TPLD to the various existing self-training approaches and achieve new state-of-the-art results on two standard UDA benchmarks.

2 Related Works

Domain Adaptation is a classic problem in computer vision and machine learning. It aims to alleviate the performance drop caused by the distribution mismatch in cross-domains. It is mostly investigated in image classification problems by both conventional methods [8,12,13,20,22] and deep CNN-based methods [9,10,21,24,27,29,33]. Besides image recognition, domain adaptation is recently being applied other vision tasks such as object detection [4], depth estimation [1], and semantic segmentation [17]. In this work, we are particularly interested in *unsupervised* domain adaptation for the task of semantic segmentation. The primary approach is to minimize the discrepancy between source and target feature distribution using adversarial learning. This type of approaches is studied on three different levels in practice: input-level alignment [5,17,28,34], intermediate feature-level alignment [18,19,23,25,37], and output-level alignment [36]. Although these methods are proven to be effective, the potentially meaningful training signals from the target domain are under-utilized. Therefore, self-training based UDA approaches [39,40], described next, emereged recently and came to dominate the performance quickly.

Self-training has been initially explored in semi-supervised method [14,38]. Recently, two seminar works [39,40] have been presented for UDA semantic segmentation. Unlike adversarial learning approaches, these methods explicitly explore the supervision signals from the target domain. The key idea is to use the prediction from the source-trained model as pseudo-labels for the unlabeled data and re-trains the current model in the target domain. CBST [39] extends this basic idea with class balancing strategy and spatial priors. CRST [40] further adds regularization term in the loss function to prevent overconfident predictions. In this paper, we also investigate the self-training framework. However, different from the previous studies, we see that the spare pseudo label problem is a fundamental limitation of self-training. We empirically found that these sparse pseudo-labels inhibit effective learning; thus, the model significantly deviates from the optimal. We, therefore, propose to densify the sparse pseudo-labels in a two-step gradually. Also, we present a new loss function to handle noisy pseudo labels and reduce optimization difficulties during training. We empirically confirm that our proposals greatly improve the strong state-of-the-art baselines with healthy margins.

3   Preliminaries

3.1   Problem Setting

Following the common UDA setting, we have full access to the data and labels, $(\mathbf{x_s}, \mathbf{y_s})$, in the labeled source domain. In contrast, in the unlabeled target domain, we can only utilize the data, $\mathbf{x_t}$. In self-training, we thus train the network to infer pseudo target label, $\hat{\mathbf{y}}_\mathbf{t} = (\hat{y}_t^{(1)}, ..., \hat{y}_t^{(K)})$, where K denotes the total number of classes.

3.2   Self-training for UDA

We first revisit the general self-training loss function [40] below:

$$\min_{\mathbf{w}, \hat{\mathbf{Y}}_\mathbf{T}} \mathcal{L}_{st}(\mathbf{w}, \hat{\mathbf{Y}}_\mathbf{T}) = -\sum_{s \in S} \sum_{k=1}^{K} y_s^{(k)} \log p(k|\mathbf{x_s}; \mathbf{w})$$

$$-\sum_{t \in T} [\sum_{k=1}^{K} \hat{y}_t^{(k)} \log \frac{p(k|\mathbf{x_t}; \mathbf{w})}{\lambda_k} - \alpha r_c(\mathbf{w}, \hat{\mathbf{Y}}_\mathbf{T})] \tag{1}$$

$$s.t. \, \hat{y}^t \in \Delta^{K-1} \cup \{\mathbf{0}\}, \forall t$$

$\mathbf{x_s}$ denotes an image in source domain indexed by $s = 1, 2, ..., S$, and $\mathbf{x_t}$ is an image in target domain indexed by $t = 1, 2, ..., T$. $y_s^{(k)}$ is ground truth source label for class k, and $\hat{y}_t^{(k)}$ is generated pseudo target label. Note that feasible set of pseudo-label is the union of $\{\mathbf{0}\}$ and a probability simplex Δ^{K-1} (i.e., continuous). $\mathbf{w}$ is the network weights, and $p(k|\mathbf{x}; \mathbf{w})$ indicates the classifier's softmax probability for class k. λ_k is a parameter, controlling pseudo-label selection [39]. $\sum_{t \in T} r_c(\mathbf{w}, \hat{\mathbf{Y}}_\mathbf{T})$ is the confidence regularizer and $\alpha \geq 0$ is the weight coefficient.

We can better understand the Eq. (1) by dividing it into three terms; The first term is model training on source domain with source labels, y_s. The second term is model re-training on target domain with generated target pseudo labels, $\hat{y}_t$. The last term is confidence regularization, $\alpha r_c(\mathbf{w}, \hat{\mathbf{Y}}_\mathbf{T})$, which prevents overconfident predictions of target pseudo-labels. The first two terms are equivalent to the CBST formula [39]. With the additional confidence regularization term, we come up with the CRST formula [40]. In general, there are two types of regularization: label-regularization (e.g., LRENT) and model regularization (e.g., MRKLD).

To minimize Eq. (1), the optimization algorithm alternatively takes block coordinate descent on both 1) pseudo-label generation and 2) network retraining.

For solving step 1), there is an optimizer formulated as:

$$some = \begin{cases} 1, & \text{if } k = \arg\max_k\{\frac{p(k|\mathbf{x_t};\mathbf{w})}{\lambda_k}\} \\ & \text{and } p(k|\mathbf{x_t};\mathbf{w}) > \lambda_k \\ 0, & \text{otherwise.} \end{cases} \tag{2}$$

If the prediction is confident, $p(k|\mathbf{x_t};\mathbf{w}) > \lambda_k$, it is selected and labeled as a class $k^* = \arg\max_k\{\frac{p(k|\mathbf{x_t};\mathbf{w})}{\lambda_k}\}$. Otherwise, the less confident predictions are set to zero vector $\mathbf{0}$. For each class k, we determine λ_k by the confidence value that is selected from the most confident p portion of class k predictions in the entire target set [39]. To avoid selecting unconfident predictions at the early stage, the hyperparameter p is usually set to a low value (i.e., 0.2), and is gradually increased for each additional round. To solve step 2), we use typical gradient-based methods (e.g., SGD). For more details, please refer to the original papers [39, 40].

We see the current self-training approach simply zeroes out the less confident predictions and in turn generates sparse pseudo labels. We argue that this limits the power of model representations and could produce sub-optimal model. Motivated by our empirical observations, we attempt to densify the sparse pseudo labels gradually, and avoid noisy predictions. In this work, we propose TPLD, which alleviates these fundamental issues successfully. We show the TPLD can be applied to any type of existing self-training based frameworks, and can consistently boost the performance significantly.

3.3   Noisy Label Handling

To handle noisy predictions, Reed et al. [30] proposed bootstrapping loss. It is a weighted sum of the standard cross-entropy loss and the (self) entropy loss. In this work, we apply it to the self-training formula as:

$$\sum_{t \in T} \sum_{k=1}^{K} [\beta \hat{y}_t^{(k)} + (1 - \beta)\frac{p(k|\mathbf{x_t};\mathbf{w})}{\lambda_k}] \log \frac{p(k|\mathbf{x_t};\mathbf{w})}{\lambda_k} \tag{3}$$

Intuitively, it simultaneously encourages the model to predict the correct (pseudo) target label and have high confidence on its prediction.

4   Method

The overview of our two-phase pseudo-label densification algorithm is shown in Fig. 1. For the first phase, we design a sliding window-based voting method to propagate the confident predictions. After enough training, we enter the second phase. Here, we present confidence based easy-hard classification and hard/easy adversarial learning. For both phases, we use the proposed bootstrapped self-training loss (Eq. (3)). We detail each phase below.

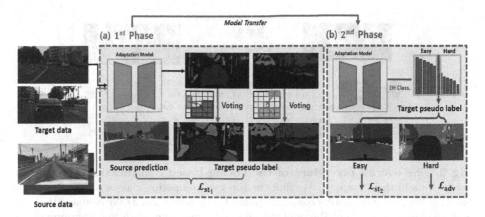

Fig. 1. The overview of the proposed two-phase pseudo-label densification framework. (a) *The first phase* utilizes the sliding window based voting in which it propagates neighbor confident predictions to fill in the unlabeled pixels. We use $\mathcal{L}_{st_1}$ to train the model in the first phase. (b) *The second phase* employs confidence-based easy-hard classification (EH class.) along with the hard-to-easy adversarial learning. This allows the model to utilize full pseudo labels for easy samples while pushing hard samples to be like easy. We use both $\mathcal{L}_{st_2}$ and $\mathcal{L}_{adv}$ to train the model in the second phase.

4.1   1st Phase: Voting Based Densification

As mentioned above, pseudo labels are generated only when the sample's prediction is confident (Eq. (2)). Specifically, the most confident p portion of predictions are selected class-wise. Because the hyperparameter p is set to a low value in practice, pseudo labels are inherently sparse during training. To overcome this issue, we present a sliding window-based voting, in which it relaxes the current hard-thresholding and propagates the confident predictions based on the intrinsic spatial correlations in the image. We attempt to utilize the fact that neighboring pixels tend to be alike. To efficiently employ this local spatial regularity in the image, we adopt the sliding-window approach. We detail the process in Fig. 2. Given the window with the unlabeled pixel at the center, we gather the neighboring confident prediction values (voting). To be more specific, for the unlabeled pixel, we first obtain the top two competing classes (i.e., classes with highest and second-highest prediction values, which would have caused ambiguity in deciding the correct label) (Fig. 2-1), and then pool the neighboring confident values for these classes (Fig. 2-2). The spatially-pooled prediction values are then weighted sum with the original prediction values (Fig. 2-3). Among the two values, we choose the bigger one. Finally, if it is above the threshold, we select the according class as a pseudo label. Note that, we use normalized prediction values (i.e., $\frac{p(k|\mathbf{x_t};\mathbf{w})}{\lambda_k}$) during the voting process, thus the thresholding criteria is $\frac{p(k|\mathbf{x_t};\mathbf{w})}{\lambda_k} > 1$. Otherwise, it continues to be a zero vector.

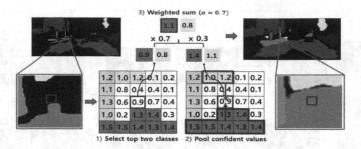

Fig. 2. The overall procedure of the voting-based densification. We describe the process in three steps. 1) We find the top two competing classes on the unlabeled pixel, 2) We pool neighboring confident values for these classes, 3) We combine the original prediction values and the pooled values (weighted-sum with hyperparameter α). We pick the bigger one and assign the corresponding class if it passes the thresholding criteria. We repeat this process by sliding the window across the images.

We call the above whole process voting-based densification. We abbreviate it as **Voting**. We iterate over total 3 times with the window size of 57×57. Those hyperparameters are set through the parameter analysis (see Table 4b). The qualitative voting results are shown in Fig. 3. We can clearly see that the initial sparse pseudo label gradually becomes dense. The pseudo label generation in the 1st phase can be summarized as:

$$
\hat{y}_t^{(k)*} = \begin{cases} 1, & \text{if } k = \arg\max_k \{ \frac{p(k|\mathbf{x_t};\mathbf{w})}{\lambda_k} \} \\ & \text{and } p(k|\mathbf{x_t};\mathbf{w}) > \lambda_k \\ \mathbf{Voting}(\frac{p(k|\mathbf{x_t};\mathbf{w})}{\lambda_k}), & \text{otherwise} \end{cases} \tag{4}
$$

Objective Function for the 1st Phase. To effectively train the model under the existence of noisy pseudo labels, we introduce bootstrapping (Eq. (3)) in our final objective function. The original self-training objective function can be re-formulated as the following:

$$
\min_{\mathbf{w}, \hat{\mathbf{Y}}_\mathbf{T}} \mathcal{L}_{st_1}(\mathbf{w}, \hat{\mathbf{Y}}_\mathbf{T}) = - \sum_{s \in S} \sum_{k=1}^{K} y_s^{(k)} \log p(k|\mathbf{x_s}; \mathbf{w})
$$

$$
- \sum_{t \in T} [\sum_{k=1}^{K} \{\beta \hat{y}_t^{(k)} \log + (1 - \beta) \frac{p(k|\mathbf{x_t}; \mathbf{w})}{\lambda_k}\} \log \frac{p(k|\mathbf{x_t}; \mathbf{w})}{\lambda_k} \tag{5}
$$

$$
- \alpha r_c(\mathbf{w}, \hat{\mathbf{Y}}_\mathbf{T})]
$$

$$
s.t. \hat{y}^t \in \Delta^{K-1} \cup \{\mathbf{0}\}, \forall t
$$

As a result, the target domain training benefits from both densified pseudo label and bootstrapped training.

Fig. 3. Voting based densification results by iteration. We can see the initial sparse pseudo label becomes dense as iteration number increases. Though it may bring noisy predictions. We set the total iteration number to 3 after conducting parameter analysis in Table 4.

4.2   2nd Phase: Easy-Hard Classification Based Densification

As the predictions of model can be trusted more over time, we now attempt to use full pseudo-labels. One may attempt to use voting multiple times for full densificaiton. However, the experimental evidence shown in Table 4b proves that it is hard for voting to generate fully densified pseudo labels. By construction, the voting is operated with a local window, which can only capture and process local predictions. Thus, iterating the voting process multiple times brings some extent of smoothing effect and noisy predictions. We, therefore, present another phase which enables full-pseudo label training. Our key idea is to consider the confidence on image-level and classify the images into two groups: easy and hard. For the easy, confident samples, we utilize their full predictions, while for the hard samples, we instead enforce hard-to-easy adaption. Indeed, we observe that the easy samples are near to the ground truth and vice versa (see Fig. 4).

To reasonably categorize target samples into easy and hard, we present effective criteria. For a particular image t, we define a confidence score as $conf_t = \frac{1}{K'}\sum_{k=1}^{K'}\frac{N_t^{k*}}{N_t^k}\cdot\frac{1}{\lambda_k}$, where N_t^k is the total number of pixels predicted as class k. Among N_t^k, we count the number of pixels that have higher prediction values than the class-wise thresholding value λ_k [39], and is set to N_t^{k*}. As a result, the ratio $\frac{N_t^{k*}}{N_t^k}$ indicates how well the model predicts confident values for each class k. We average these values with K', which is the total number of (predicted) confident classes. Thus, the higher the value, we can say that the model is more confident with that target image (i.e., easy). Note that, we multiply $\frac{1}{\lambda_k}$ to avoid sampling too easy images and instead encourage sampling of images with rare classes. We compute these confidence scores for every target image. In practice, we picked up the top q portion as easy samples and consider the rest as hard samples for the training. We initially set q to 30% and add 5% in each round.

Objective Function for the 2nd Phase. After classifying target images into easy and hard samples, we apply different objective functions to each. For the easy samples, we utilize full pseudo label predictions and employ bootstrapping loss for training (Eq. 3). For the hard samples, we instead adopt adversarial learning to push hard examples to be like easy samples (i.e., feature alignment). We describe the details below.

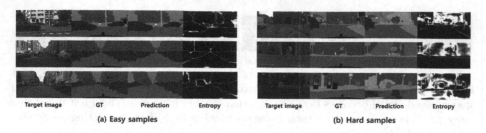

(a) Easy samples   (b) Hard samples

Fig. 4. Qualitative easy and hard samples. For the illustration, we randomly selected three samples from each. Note that easy samples are near to the ground truth with low entropy values, whereas hard samples are far from the ground truth and have high entropy values. Therefore, in the second phase, we train easy samples with their full-pseudo labels and make hard samples to be easy using adversarial loss.

Easy Sample Training. To effectively generate full pseudo labels, we calibrate the prediction values. Specifically, the full pseudo-label generation of easy samples is formulated as:

$$
\hat{y}_{t_e}^{(k)*} = \begin{cases} 1, & \text{if } k = \arg\max_{k}\{\frac{p(k|x_t;w)}{\lambda_k}\} \\ & \text{and } p(k|x_t;w) > \lambda_k \\ \left(\frac{p(k|x_t;w)}{\lambda_k}\right)^{\gamma}, & \text{otherwise.} \end{cases} \tag{6}
$$

Note that the prediction value is calibrated with the hyper parameter γ, which is set to 2 empirically (see Table 4e). We then train the model using the following bootstrapping loss:

$$
\min_{\mathbf{w},\hat{\mathbf{Y}}_\mathbf{T}} \mathcal{L}_{st_2}(\mathbf{w}, \hat{\mathbf{Y}}_\mathbf{T})
$$
$$
= -\sum_{t \in T}[\sum_{k=1}^{K}\{\beta\hat{y}_t^{(k)}\log + (1-\beta)\frac{p(k|\mathbf{x_t};\mathbf{w})}{\lambda_k}\}\log\frac{p(k|\mathbf{x_t};\mathbf{w})}{\lambda_k} \tag{7}
$$
$$
s.t.\,\hat{y}^t \in \Delta^{K-1} \cup \{\mathbf{0}\}, \forall t
$$

Hard Sample Training. To minimize the gap between easy (e) and hard (h) samples in the target domain, we propose intra-domain adversarial loss, $\mathcal{L}_{adv}$. In order to align the feature from hard to easy, the discriminator D_{intra} is trained to discriminate that the target weighted self-information map I_t [37] is whether from easy samples or hard samples. The learning objective of the discriminator is:

$$
\min_{\theta_{D_{intra}}} \frac{1}{|e|}\sum_{e} L_{D_{intra}}(I_e, 1) + \frac{1}{|h|}\sum_{h} L_{D_{intra}}(I_h, 0) \tag{8}
$$

and the adversarial objective to train the segmentation network is:

$$
\min_{\theta_{seg}} \frac{1}{|h|}\sum_{h} L_{D_{intra}}(I_h, 1) \tag{9}
$$

5   Experiments

5.1   Dataset

We evaluate our model on the most common adaptation benchmarks. 1) GTA5 [31] to Cityscapes [6] and 2) SYNTHIA [32] to Cityscapes. GTA5 and SYNTHIA contain 24966 and 9,400 synthetic images, respectively. Following the standard protocols, we adapt the model to the Cityscapes training set and evaluate the performance on the validation set.

5.2   Implementation Details

To push the state-of-the-art benchmark performances, we apply TPLD to the CRST-MRKLD framework [40]. For the backbones, we use VGG-16 [35] and ResNet-101 [15]. For the segmentation models, we adopt different versions of deeplab; deeplab-v2 [2] and deeplab-v3 [3]. We pretrain the model on ImageNet [7] and fine-tune on source domain images using SGD. We train the model total 9 rounds: 6 rounds for the first phase training and 3 rounds for the second phase training. The detailed training settings are the followings: For the source domain pre-training, we use learning rate of 2.5×10^{-4}, weight decay of 5×10^{-4}, momentum of 0.9, batch size of 2, patch size of 512×1024, multiscale training augmentation (0.5–1.5), and horizontal flipping. For the self-training, we adopt SGD with the learning rate of 5×10^{-5}.

5.3   Main Results

GTA5 $\rightarrow$ Cityscapes: Table 1 summarizes the adaptation performance of TPLD and other state-of-the-art methods [25,36,37,39,40]. We can obviously see that TPLD outperforms state-of-the-art approaches in all cases. For example, with Deeplab-v2 and ResNet-101 backbone, our TPLD significantly outperforms CRST by 4.2%. Moreover, to analyze the effect on rare classes, we also put rare-class mIoU. With the R-mIoU metric, we see the improvement is even much higher; 4.8%. We provide qualitative results in Fig. 5. Clearly, our final model generates the most visually pleasurable results.

SYNTHIA $\rightarrow$ Cityscapes: Table 2 shows the adaptation results with SYNTHIA. Our approach again achieves the best performance among all the other methods. Specifically, with Deeplab-v3 and ResNet101 backbone, we greatly improve the baseline performance of 48.1% mIoU to 55.7% mIoU.

Combining with Existing Self-training Methods. We see the proposed TPLD is general, thus can be easily applied to the existing self-training based methods. In this experiment, we combine the TPLD with three different self-training approaches: CBST [39], CRST with label regularization (LRENT) [40], and CRST with model regularization (MRKLD) [40]. The results are summarized in Table 3. We observe that TPLD consistently improves the performance of

Table 1. Experimental results on GTA5 → Cityscapes. "V" and "R" denote VGG-16 and ResNet-101 respectively. We highlight the rare classes [25] and compute Rare class mIoU (R-mIoU) as well.

Method	Seg Model	Road	SW	Build	Wall	Fence	Pole	TL	TS	Veg	Terrain	Sky	PR	Rider	Car	Truck	Bus	Train	Motor	Bike	mIoU	R-mIoU
Source		52.6	20.7	56.0	6.0	9.8	22.9	8.1	1.4	77.2	11.0	35.0	41.5	2.7	52.1	2.1	0.0	0.0	4.7	0.3	21.3	5.8
CBST [39]	Deeplabv2-V	84.2	41.4	71.9	15.5	18.1	30.8	25.4	9.2	77.6	15.2	29.6	49.3	6.0	78.0	4.0	4.5	0.3	10.4	11.6	30.7	12.6
CRST(MRKLD) [40]		81.7	46.1	70.2	10.7	11.2	30.4	26.9	15.8	75.4	18.3	24.8	48.6	10.9	77.8	2.9	13.3	1.1	10.7	31.4	32.0	15.3
CRST(MRKLD) + TPLD		83.5	49.9	72.3	17.6	10.7	29.6	28.3	9.0	78.2	20.1	25.7	47.4	13.3	79.6	3.3	19.3	1.3	14.3	33.5	34.1	16.7
Adapt-SegMap [36]		86.5	36.0	79.9	23.4	23.3	35.2	14.8	14.8	83.4	33.3	75.6	58.5	27.6	73.7	32.5	35.4	3.9	30.1	28.1	42.4	25.2
CLAN [25]	Deeplabv2-R	87.0	27.1	79.6	27.3	23.3	28.3	35.5	24.2	83.6	27.4	74.2	58.6	28.0	76.2	33.1	36.7	6.7	31.9	31.4	43.2	27.8
ADVENT [37]		89.9	36.5	81.2	29.2	25.2	28.5	32.3	22.4	83.9	34.0	77.1	57.4	27.9	83.7	29.4	39.1	1.5	28.4	23.3	43.8	25.8
Source		71.3	19.2	69.1	18.4	10.0	35.7	27.3	6.8	79.6	24.8	72.1	57.6	19.5	55.5	15.5	15.1	11.7	21.1	12.0	33.3	18.2
CBST [39]	Deeplabv2-R	91.8	53.5	80.5	32.7	21.0	34.0	28.9	20.4	83.9	34.2	80.9	53.1	24.0	82.7	30.3	35.9	16.0	25.9	42.8	45.9	28.9
CRST(MRKLD) [40]		91.3	56.1	79.8	30.6	18.9	39.0	35.1	24.0	84.2	30.0	74.0	62.1	28.2	82.6	23.6	31.8	24.2	32.2	46.3	47.0	30.3
CRST(MRKLD) + TPLD		94.2	60.5	82.8	36.6	16.6	39.3	29.0	25.5	85.6	44.9	84.4	60.6	27.4	84.1	37.0	47.0	31.2	36.1	50.3	51.2	35.1
Source		80.3	17.6	75.8	18.0	24.5	19.7	34.9	19.0	83.2	15.8	83.7	57.2	22.8	73.4	36.6	21.0	0.0	19.0	0.1	35.9	19.3
CBST [39]	Deeplabv3-R	86.9	33.9	80.0	28.8	26.2	30.2	36.0	20.4	84.6	16.3	72.1	53.3	19.8	82.8	34.1	43.8	0.0	13.0	0.0	40.2	22.5
CRST(MRKLD) [40]		85.9	40.4	76.9	27.5	21.6	35.0	39.0	25.6	84.0	20.2	71.8	55.3	23.2	83.2	38.8	43.2	0.0	10.3	0.0	41.2	23.7
CRST(MRKLD) + TPLD		83.2	46.3	74.9	29.8	21.3	33.1	36.0	24.2	86.7	43.2	87.1	58.7	24.0	84.0	36.9	49.7	0.0	29.7	0.0	44.7	27.3

Table 2. Experimental results on SYNTHIA → Cityscapes. mIoU* is computed with 13 classes out of total 16 classes except the classes with *.

Method	Seg Model	Road	SW	Build	Wall*	Fence*	Pole*	TL	TS	Veg	Sky	PR	Rider	Car	Bus	Motor	Bike	mIoU	mIoU*	R-mIoU
Source		41.5	16.6	38.3	0.2	0.0	22.6	0.1	4.9	66.5	64.7	44.9	1.7	60.7	3.3	0.0	0.6	22.9	26.4	4.3
CBST [39]	Deeplabv2-V	75.7	32.3	70.2	3.5	0.0	28.6	1.4	9.0	79.8	65.6	52.9	13.7	65.8	9.1	1.5	36.4	34.1	39.5	11.5
CRST(MRKLD) [40]		75.1	33.5	70.8	5.6	0.0	28.7	2.0	9.7	78.9	72.5	51.7	11.6	63.4	7.3	1.4	38.6	34.4	39.7	11.7
CRST(MRKLD) + TPLD		81.3	34.5	73.3	11.9	0.0	26.9	0.2	6.3	79.9	71.2	55.1	14.2	73.6	5.7	0.5	41.7	36.0	41.3	11.9
Adapt-SegMap [36]		84.3	42.7	77.5	-	-	-	4.7	7.0	77.9	82.5	54.3	21.0	72.3	32.2	18.9	32.3	-	46.7	-
ADVENT [37]	Deeplabv2-R	87.0	44.1	79.7	9.6	0.6	24.3	4.8	7.2	80.1	83.6	56.4	23.7	72.7	32.6	12.8	33.7	40.8	47.6	16.6
CLAN [25]		81.3	37.3	80.1	-	-	-	16.1	13.7	78.2	81.5	53.4	21.2	73.0	32.9	22.6	30.7	-	47.8	-
Source		45.9	21.4	63.0	7.3	0.0	33.6	4.5	14.4	81.6	79.7	55.3	16.7	67.5	21.3	7.5	19.0	33.7	38.3	13.8
CBST [39]	Deeplabv2-R	68.0	29.9	76.3	10.8	1.4	33.9	22.8	29.5	77.6	78.3	60.6	28.3	81.6	23.5	18.8	39.8	42.6	48.9	23.2
CRST(MRKLD) [40]		67.7	32.2	73.9	10.7	1.6	37.4	22.2	31.2	80.8	80.5	60.8	29.1	82.8	25.0	19.4	45.3	43.8	50.1	24.7
CRST(MRKLD) + TPLD		80.9	44.3	82.2	19.9	0.3	40.6	20.5	30.1	77.2	80.9	60.6	25.5	84.8	41.1	24.7	43.7	47.3	53.5	27.4
Source		45.5	19.0	71.3	6.2	0.0	27.4	11.3	15.3	79.4	79.4	58.3	9.2	79.7	33.0	6.0	8.8	34.4	39.7	13.0
CBST [39]	Deeplabv3-R	45.2	19.4	81.8	15.7	0.2	33.3	20.8	24.9	85.0	82.2	64.6	26.7	84.8	48.8	22.9	43.9	43.8	50.1	26.4
CRST(MRKLD) [40]		52.3	21.9	80.0	17.2	0.8	32.4	17.9	31.1	84.8	83.5	63.7	28.5	83.1	37.2	19.1	52.5	44.1	50.4	26.3
CRST(MRKLD) + TPLD		70.9	29.5	80.6	18.4	0.4	26.6	19.9	30.9	85.5	86.3	66.0	32.9	84.4	51.1	29.3	56.2	48.1	55.7	29.5

all the baselines. The positive results imply that the sparse pseudo-label is indeed a fundamental problem in self-training, and the previous works notably overlooked this problem. We show that the proposed concept of two-phase pseudo-label densificaiton effectively addresses the issue.

5.4 Ablation Study

Lowering the Selection Threshold of CRST. A straightforward way to generate dense pseudo labels is by lowering the selection threshold (i.e., increasing p) of self-training models. We summarize the results in Table 4a. Since the scheme brings unconfident predictions at an early stage, either limited improvement ($p = 0.4$, $47.0 \to 47.1$ mIoU) or worse performance is obtained ($p = 0.6$, $47.0 \to 45.7$ mIoU). Compared to these naive baselines, our TPLD shows significant improvement ($47.0 \to 51.2$ mIoU).

Table 3. Performance improvements in mIoU of integrating our TPLD with existing self-training adaptation approaches. We use the Deeplabv2-R segmentation model.

GTA5 → Cityscapes (19 categories)				SYNTHIA → Cityscapes (16 categories)			
Method	Base+	TPLD	△	Method	Base+	TPLD	△
CBST [39]	45.9	47.8	+1.9	CBST [39]	42.6	45.6	+3.0
CRST(LRENT) [40]	45.9	47.3	+1.4	CRST(LRENT) [40]	42.7	47.0	+4.3
CRST(MRKLD) [40]	47.0	51.2	+4.2	CRST(MRKLD) [40]	43.8	47.3	+3.5

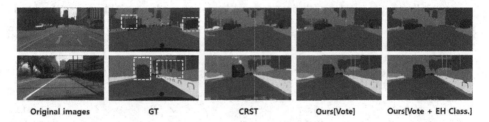

Original images   GT   CRST   Ours[Vote]   Ours[Vote + EH Class.]

Fig. 5. Qualitative results on GTA5 → Cityscapes. We can clearly see that our full model generates the most visually pleasable results.

Framework Design Choices. The main components of our framework design are the two-phase pseudo label densification. The ablation results are shown in Table 4a. If we drop the voting stage, the model is trained alone with the easy-hard classification stage. However, using full pseudo labels without any proper early-stage training introduces too noisy training signals ($51.2 \rightarrow 38.1$ mIoU). If we drop the easy-hard classification stage, the model misses a chance to receive rich training signals from the full pseudo labels ($51.2 \rightarrow 49.5$ mIoU). We also explore the effect of ordering. We observe that the voting-first method performs better than the easy-hard classification-first method (51.2 vs. 49.1 mIoU). This implies that gradual densification is indeed important for stable model training.

Effect of $\frac{1}{\lambda_k}$ in Confidence Score $conf_t$**.** We suggest to multiply $\frac{1}{\lambda_k}$ in computing the confidence score $conf_t$. The rationale behind this is to oversample the images, which include rare classes, and thus prevent the learning from being biased by images composed of obvious frequent classes. The results without and with the $\frac{1}{\lambda_k}$ are (50.5 vs 51.2 mIoU) and (33.7 vs 35.1 R-mIoU). This demonstrates the efficacy of incorporating $\frac{1}{\lambda_k}$.

5.5 Parameter Analysis

Here, we conduct experiments to decide optimal hyper-parameters in our framework. For the first phase, we have a total of three hyper-parameters; voting field size, voting iteration number, and α. In Table 4b, we conduct a grid search on the first two, and we obtain the best result with voting field 57, and voting

Table 4. Results of ablation studies.

GTA5 → Cityscapes

(a) Framework design choices

Model	p	Voting	EH	Class.	mIoU
CRST	0.2	✗			47.0
	0.4	✗			47.1
	0.6	✗			45.7
TPLD	0.2			✓	38.1
		✓			49.5
		✓₂	✓₁		49.1
		✓₁		✓₂	51.2

(b) Voting field / number

Voting Num ╲ Voting Field	37	57	77
1	48.61	48.95	48.57
3	49.49	49.52	48.37
5	48.72	48.00	48.63

(c) α

α	mIoU
0.6	48.34
0.7	49.52
0.8	49.25

(d) q

q	mIoU
1.00	48.44
0.40	50.15
0.35	50.27
0.30	51.20
0.25	49.81
0.20	50.02

(e) γ

γ	mIoU
1.5	50.0
2	51.2
2.5	48.6

Table 5. Detailed analysis on the proposed objective functions. We note the corresponding equations for each proposals. *Adv.* denotes adversarial loss term for hard sample training.

	Bootstrap Eq.(5)	Voting Eq.(4)	mIoU		EH Cls. Eq.(6) + Eq.(7)	Adv. Eq.(8)+Eq.(9)	mIoU
$\mathcal{L}_{st}$ [40]			47.00	$\mathcal{L}_{st1}$			49.51
	✓		48.47		✓		50.11
$\mathcal{L}_{st1}$	✓	✓	49.52	$\mathcal{L}_{st1} + \mathcal{L}_{st2}$	✓	✓	51.20

number 3. The hyperparameter α controls how much to maintain the initial prediction value, and we observe that 0.7 produces the best result (see Table 4c). We see that the results are in the same line with the residual learning [16]. Providing residual features (i.e., pooled neighboring confident prediction values) while securing the initial behavior (i.e., initial prediction values) is important. For the second phase, we have a total of two hyper-parameters; q and γ. The hyperparameter q controls the 'easy' portions in the target images. For example, if we increase the value, more images will be used as easy samples for the training. We observe that setting q to 0.3 provides the best result (see Table 4d). Note that if we set q to 1 (i.e., making all the target images to be trained with the full pseudo labels), we instead obtain degraded performance. This implies that a proper portion of easy and hard samples are need to be set, and both the full pseudo label training and hard-to-easy feature alignment are important. The hyperparameter γ is related to the calibration degree of the prediction values in generating full pseudo labels (see Eq. (6)). We obtain the best result when γ equals 2.

5.6   Loss Function Analysis

Finally, we explore the impact of loss functions in Table 5. We begin with the standard self-training loss, $\mathcal{L}_{st}$. Introducing the bootstrapping mechanism boosts the performance significantly, from 47.00 to 48.47 mIoU. This implies that explicitly handling noisy pseudo labels is crucial but lacking in the original formulation. Also, using *voting* to densify the sparse pseudo labels further pushes the performance from 48.47 to 49.52 mIoU. The densified pseudo labels

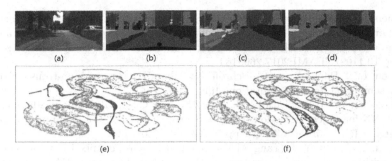

Fig. 6. A contrastive analysis of with and without hard sample training (Eq.(8)+Eq.(9)). (a): target image, (b): ground truth, (c): prediction result without hard sample training, (d): prediction result with hard sample training. We map high-dimensional features of (c) and (d) to 2-D space features of (e) and (f) respectively using t-SNE [26].

help model learning due to the increased training-signals and are complementary to the bootstrapping effect. In the second phase, we investigate the impact of both easy sample training (EH Cls.) and hard sample training (Adv.). The easy sample training pushes the performance from 49.52 to 50.11 mIoU, and the hard sample training further increases the performance from 50.11 to 51.20. The results demonstrate that the full-pseudo label training is indeed important and the hard-to-easy feature alignment further enhances the model learning. Especially for the hard sample training, we conduct a contrastive analysis in Fig. 6. We observe that hard sample training improves category-level feature alignment (Fig. 6 (e)→Fig. 6 (f)), and thus the prediction values become more accurate and clean (Fig. 6 (c) → Fig. 6 (d)).

6 Conclusions

In this paper, we point out that self-training methods for UDA suffer from the sparse pseudo label during training. Therefore, we present a novel two-phase pseudo label densification method. Combined with recently proposed CRST framework, we achieve new state-of-the-art results on UDA benchmarks.

Acknowledgement. This research is supported by the National Cancer Center(NCC).

References

1. Atapour-Abarghouei, A., Breckon, T.P.: Real-time monocular depth estimation using synthetic data with domain adaptation via image style transfer. In: Proceedings of the IEEE Conference on Computer Vision and Pattern Recognition, pp. 2800–2810 (2018)

2. Chen, L.C., Papandreou, G., Kokkinos, I., Murphy, K., Yuille, A.: Deeplab: semantic image segmentation with deep convolutional nets, atrous convolution, and fully connected CRFs. IEEE Trans. Pattern Anal. Mach. Intell., June 2016. https://doi.org/10.1109/TPAMI.2017.2699184

3. Chen, L.C., Papandreou, G., Schroff, F., Adam, H.: Rethinking atrous convolution for semantic image segmentation, June 2017

4. Chen, Y., Li, W., Sakaridis, C., Dai, D., Van Gool, L.: Domain adaptive faster R-CNN for object detection in the wild. In: Proceedings of Computer Vision and Pattern Recognition (CVPR), pp. 3339–3348 (2018)

5. Chen, Y.C., Lin, Y.Y., Yang, M.H., Huang, J.B.: Crdoco: pixel-level domain transfer with cross-domain consistency. In: Proceedings of Computer Vision and Pattern Recognition (CVPR), June 2019

6. Cordts, M., et al.: The cityscapes dataset for semantic urban scene understanding. In: Proceedings of the IEEE Conference on Computer Vision and Pattern Recognition (CVPR) (2016)

7. Deng, J., Dong, W., Socher, R., Li, L.J., Li, K., Li, F.F.: Imagenet: a large-scale hierarchical image database, pp. 248–255, June 2009. https://doi.org/10.1109/CVPR.2009.5206848

8. Fernando, B., Habrard, A., Sebban, M., Tuytelaars, T.: Unsupervised visual domain adaptation using subspace alignment. In: Proceedings of International Conference on Computer Vision (ICCV), pp. 2960–2967 (2013)

9. Ganin, Y., Lempitsky, V.: Unsupervised domain adaptation by backpropagation. arXiv preprint arXiv:1409.7495 (2014)

10. Ghifary, M., Kleijn, W.B., Zhang, M., Balduzzi, D., Li, W.: Deep reconstruction-classification networks for unsupervised domain adaptation. In: Leibe, B., Matas, J., Sebe, N., Welling, M. (eds.) ECCV 2016. LNCS, vol. 9908, pp. 597–613. Springer, Cham (2016). https://doi.org/10.1007/978-3-319-46493-0_36

11. Golemo, F., Taiga, A.A., Courville, A., Oudeyer, P.Y.: Sim-to-real transfer with neural-augmented robot simulation. In: Billard, A., Dragan, A., Peters, J., Morimoto, J. (eds.) Proceedings of the 2nd Conference on Robot Learning. Proceedings of Machine Learning Research, vol. 87, pp. 817–828. PMLR, 29–31 October 2018. http://proceedings.mlr.press/v87/golemo18a.html

12. Gong, B., Shi, Y., Sha, F., Grauman, K.: Geodesic flow kernel for unsupervised domain adaptation. In: Proceedings of Computer Vision and Pattern Recognition (CVPR), pp. 2066–2073. IEEE (2012)

13. Gopalan, R., Li, R., Chellappa, R.: Domain adaptation for object recognition: an unsupervised approach. In: Proceedings of International Conference on Computer Vision (ICCV), pp. 999–1006. IEEE (2011)

14. Grandvalet, Y., Bengio, Y.: Semi-supervised learning by entropy minimization, pp. 529–536 (2005)

15. He, K., Zhang, X., Ren, S., Sun, J.: Deep residual learning for image recognition. In: 2016 IEEE Conference on Computer Vision and Pattern Recognition (CVPR), pp. 770–778, June 2016. https://doi.org/10.1109/CVPR.2016.90

16. He, K., Zhang, X., Ren, S., Sun, J.: Deep residual learning for image recognition. In: Proceedings of the IEEE Conference on Computer Vision and Pattern Recognition, pp. 770–778 (2016)

17. Hoffman, J., et al.: CyCADA: cycle-consistent adversarial domain adaptation. In: Proceedings of International Conference on Machine Learning (ICML), pp. 1989–1998 (2018)

18. Hoffman, J., Wang, D., Yu, F., Darrell, T.: FCNS in the wild: Pixel-level adversarial and constraint-based adaptation. arXiv preprint arXiv:1612.02649 (2016)

19. Hong, W., Wang, Z., Yang, M., Yuan, J.: Conditional generative adversarial network for structured domain adaptation. In: Proceedings of Computer Vision and Pattern Recognition (CVPR), June 2018
20. Kulis, B., Saenko, K., Darrell, T.: What you saw is not what you get: domain adaptation using asymmetric kernel transforms. In: Proceedings of Computer Vision and Pattern Recognition (CVPR), pp. 1785–1792. IEEE (2011)
21. Li, D., Yang, Y., Song, Y.Z., Hospedales, T.M.: Deeper, broader and artier domain generalization. In: Proceedings of International Conference on Computer Vision (ICCV), pp. 5542–5550 (2017)
22. Li, W., Xu, Z., Xu, D., Dai, D., Van Gool, L.: Domain generalization and adaptation using low rank exemplar SVMs. In: IEEE Trans. Pattern Anal. Mach. Intell. (TPAMI), **40**, 1114–1127. IEEE (2017)
23. Long, M., Cao, Y., Cao, Z., Wang, J., Jordan, M.I.: Transferable representation learning with deep adaptation networks. IEEE Trans. Pattern Anal. Mach. Intell. (TPAMI) **41**, 3071–3085 (2019). https://doi.org/10.1109/TPAMI.2018.2868685
24. Long, M., Cao, Y., Wang, J., Jordan, M.I.: Learning transferable features with deep adaptation networks. arXiv preprint arXiv:1502.02791 (2015)
25. Luo, Y., Zheng, L., Guan, T., Yu, J., Yang, Y.: Taking a closer look at domain shift: category-level adversaries for semantics consistent domain adaptation. In: Proceedings of Computer Vision and Pattern Recognition (CVPR) (2019)
26. van der Maaten, L., Hinton, G.: Visualizing data using t-sne. J. Mach. Learn. Res. **11**, 2579–2605 (2008)
27. Motiian, S., Piccirilli, M., Adjeroh, D.A., Doretto, G.: Unified deep supervised domain adaptation and generalization. In: Proceedings of International Conference on Computer Vision (ICCV), pp. 5715–5725 (2017)
28. Murez, Z., Kolouri, S., Kriegman, D., Ramamoorthi, R., Kim, K.: Image to image translation for domain adaptation. In: Proceedings of Computer Vision and Pattern Recognition (CVPR), pp. 4500–4509, June 2018. https://doi.org/10.1109/CVPR.2018.00473
29. Panareda Busto, P., Gall, J.: Open set domain adaptation. In: Proceedings of International Conference on Computer Vision (ICCV), pp. 754–763 (2017)
30. Reed, S., Lee, H., Anguelov, D., Szegedy, C., Erhan, D., Rabinovich, A.: Training deep neural networks on noisy labels with bootstrapping, December 2014
31. Richter, S.R., Vineet, V., Roth, S., Koltun, V.: Playing for data: ground truth from computer games. In: Leibe, B., Matas, J., Sebe, N., Welling, M. (eds.) ECCV 2016. LNCS, vol. 9906, pp. 102–118. Springer, Cham (2016). https://doi.org/10.1007/978-3-319-46475-6_7
32. Ros, G., Sellart, L., Materzynska, J., Vazquez, D., Lopez, A.M.: The synthia dataset: a large collection of synthetic images for semantic segmentation of urban scenes. In: Proceedings of Computer Vision and Pattern Recognition (CVPR), pp. 3234–3243 (2016)
33. Sener, O., Song, H.O., Saxena, A., Savarese, S.: Learning transferrable representations for unsupervised domain adaptation. pp. 2110–2118 (2016)
34. Shrivastava, A., Pfister, T., Tuzel, O., Susskind, J., Wang, W., Webb, R.: Learning from simulated and unsupervised images through adversarial training. In: Proc. of Computer Vision and Pattern Recognition (CVPR), pp. 2107–2116 (2017)
35. Simonyan, K., Zisserman, A.: Very deep convolutional networks for large-scale image recognition. arXiv 1409.1556, September 2014

36. Tsai, Y.H., Hung, W.C., Schulter, S., Sohn, K., Yang, M.H., Chandraker, M.: Learning to adapt structured output space for semantic segmentation. In: Proceedings of Computer Vision and Pattern Recognition (CVPR), pp. 7472–7481 (2018)
37. Vu, T.H., Jain, H., Bucher, M., Cord, M., Pérez, P.: Advent: adversarial entropy minimization for domain adaptation in semantic segmentation. In: Proceedings of Computer Vision and Pattern Recognition (CVPR), pp. 2517–2526 (2019)
38. Zhu, X.: Semi-supervised learning tutorial. In: Proceedings of International Conference on Machine Learning (ICML) (2007)
39. Zou, Y., Yu, Z., Kumar, B.V., Wang, J.: Unsupervised domain adaptation for semantic segmentation via class-balanced self-training. In: Proceedings of European Conf. on Computer Vision (ECCV), pp. 289–305 (2018)
40. Zou, Y., Yu, Z., Liu, X., Kumar, B.V., Wang, J.: Confidence regularized self-training. In: Proceedings of International Conference on Computer Vision (ICCV), October 2019

Adaptive Offline Quintuplet Loss for Image-Text Matching

Tianlang Chen[1]([✉]) [iD], Jiajun Deng[2], and Jiebo Luo[1]

[1] University of Rochester, Rochester, USA
tchen45@cs.rochester.edu, djiajun1206@gmail.com
[2] University of Science and Technology of China, Hefei, China
jluo@cs.rochester.edu

Abstract. Existing image-text matching approaches typically leverage triplet loss with online hard negatives to train the model. For each image or text anchor in a training mini-batch, the model is trained to distinguish between a positive and the most confusing negative of the anchor mined from the mini-batch (*i.e.* online hard negative). This strategy improves the model's capacity to discover fine-grained correspondences and non-correspondences between image and text inputs. However, the above approach has the following drawbacks: (1) the negative selection strategy still provides limited chances for the model to learn from very hard-to-distinguish cases. (2) The trained model has weak generalization capability from the training set to the testing set. (3) The penalty lacks hierarchy and adaptiveness for hard negatives with different "hardness" degrees. In this paper, we propose solutions by sampling negatives offline from the whole training set. It provides "harder" offline negatives than online hard negatives for the model to distinguish. Based on the offline hard negatives, a quintuplet loss is proposed to improve the model's generalization capability to distinguish positives and negatives. In addition, a novel loss function that combines the knowledge of positives, offline hard negatives and online hard negatives is created. It leverages offline hard negatives as the intermediary to adaptively penalize them based on their distance relations to the anchor. We evaluate the proposed training approach on three state-of-the-art image-text models on the MS-COCO and Flickr30K datasets. Significant performance improvements are observed for all the models, proving the effectiveness and generality of our approach. Code is available at https://github.com/sunnychencool/AOQ.

Keywords: Image-text matching · Triplet loss · Hard negative mining

Electronic supplementary material The online version of this chapter (https://doi.org/10.1007/978-3-030-58601-0_33) contains supplementary material, which is available to authorized users.

A. Vedaldi et al. (Eds.): ECCV 2020, LNCS 12358, pp. 549–565, 2020.
https://doi.org/10.1007/978-3-030-58601-0_33

1   Introduction

Image-text matching is the core task in cross-modality retrieval to measure the similarity score between an image and a text. By image-text matching, a system can retrieve the top corresponding images of a sentence query, or retrieve the top corresponding sentences of an image query.

To train an image-text matching model to predict accurate similarity score, triplet loss is widely used [5,6,14,15,23]. Each given image or text of a training mini-batch is referred to as an *anchor*. For each image/text anchor, a text/image that corresponds to the anchor is called a *positive* while one that does not correspond to the anchor is called a *negative*. The anchor and its positives/negatives belong to two modalities. A triplet loss is applied to encourage the model to predict higher similarity scores between the anchor and its positives (*i.e.* positive pairs) than those between the anchor and its negatives (*i.e.* negative pairs).

To utilize negative pairs to train the model, early approaches [5,10,23] adopt an all-in strategy. For each anchor, all its negatives in the mini-batch participate in the loss computing process. However, in most situations, the semantic meanings of an anchor and its negatives are totally different. With this strategy, the overall training difficulty is relatively low for the model to distinguish between positive and negative pairs. The model only needs to focus on each pair's global semantic meaning difference and may ignore the local matching details. Faghri et al. [6] propose a triplet loss with online hard negatives (*i.e.* online triplet loss) as a more effective training approach. Specifically, for each anchor in a mini-batch, the model computes its similarity score to all the negatives in the same mini-batch online, and selects the negative with the highest score to the anchor as online hard negative of the anchor. The new triplet loss guides the model to only distinguish between the positives and online hard negatives of the anchor. Compared with the all-in strategy, the models trained by this approach commonly achieve better performance in distinguishing between positives and confusing negatives that have similar semantic meanings to the anchor. This training approach is employed by all the state-of-the-art models [14,15,18,27].

Even with its effectiveness, we argue that the online triplet loss still have three drawbacks in negative selection strategy, distinguishing strategy, and penalization strategy: (1) for the negative selection strategy, the "hardness" degree of online hard negatives is still not sufficient. Given the MS-COCO dataset as example, the training set contains 500K corresponding image-text pairs. When we set the mini-batch size to 128 as in [14,15,18,27], for each online hard negative of an anchor mined from the mini-batch, we prove that its similarity score rank expectation to the anchor in the whole training set is about 4000 (*i.e.* $\frac{500K}{128}$). The probability of its rank in the top-100 is only about 2.2%. In other words, a very hard negative with a top-100 similarity score rank for the anchor will rarely be sampled to train the model. This decreases the model's capacity to distinguish between the positives and those very confusing negatives. Increasing the mini-batch size could be helpful. However, the mini-batch computational complexity grows sharply. (2) For the distinguishing strategy, the triplet loss only focuses on obtaining the correct rank orders between the positives and negatives of the

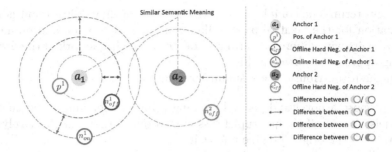

Similar Semantic Meaning

a_1	Anchor 1
p^1	Pos. of Anchor 1
n_{off}^1	Offline Hard Neg. of Anchor 1
n_{on}^1	Online Hard Neg. of Anchor 1
a_2	Anchor 2
n_{off}^2	Offline Hard Neg. of Anchor 2
⟷	Difference between ○/ ○
⟷	Difference between ○/ ○
⟷	Difference between ○/ ○
⟷	Difference between ○/ ●

Fig. 1. Overview of the proposed training approach. For each anchor, we sample its positives, offline hard negatives and online hard negatives. The training approach gives adaptive penalties to enlarge the similarity score differences among positive pairs, offline hard negative pairs and online hard negative pairs (*i.e.* the blue, green and brown arrows). On the other hand, extra penalties are added to enlarge the similarity score difference between positive pairs and offline hard negative pairs with different anchors that share similar semantic meanings (*i.e.* the cyan arrow) (Color figure online).

same anchor. However, it does not guide the model to rank among positive pairs and negative pairs that contain no common samples. Actually, this guidance is essential to improve the model's generalization capability from training to testing, especially when we apply the guidance on the very hard negative pairs. (3) For the penalization strategy, the triplet loss lacks a hierarchy. Ideally, the loss function should guide the model to maintain remarkable score gaps among the pairs of different classes. For example, the positive pairs should obtain far higher similarity scores than very hard negative pairs, and the very hard negative pairs should also obtain far higher similarity scores than ordinary hard negative pairs. When a pair's predicted score is close or beyond the boundary of its pair class, the loss function should give it a larger penalty to update the model. However, the current online triplet loss only defines positive and online hard negative pairs. More importantly, it gives an equal penalty to all the pairs when the margin conditions are not satisfied.

To overcome the above drawbacks, we propose a new training approach that can be generally applied on *all* existing models. Specifically, we utilize a two-round training to additionally sample "harder" negatives offline. In the first round, we train the model by the original online triplet loss. After that, for each image and text anchor in the training set, the model predicts its similarity score to all its negatives in the training set and ranks them. In the second round, given each anchor in a mini-batch, we sample its offline hard negatives directly from its top negative list with the highest similarity score in the whole training set. In this process, multiple kinds of offline hard negative pairs are constructed which share/do not share common elements with the positive pairs. The model is trained by a combination of online triplet loss and offline quintuplet loss to overcome the first two drawbacks successfully. Furthermore, we modify the loss function and feed information of offline hard negative pairs into the online triplet loss term. The complete training loss achieves hierarchical and adaptive penalization for the positive pairs, offline hard negative pairs, and online hard negative pairs with different "hardness" degrees. The framework of the proposed training approach is shown in Fig. 1.

Our main contributions are summarized as follows:

- We propose a novel and general training approach for image-text matching models. A new offline quintuplet loss is introduced that can effectively cooperate with the original online triplet loss.
- We skillfully feed the similarity score of offline hard negative pair into online loss term. It serves as a criterion to adaptively penalize different kinds of pairs. We analyze how it works mathematically.
- We evaluate our training approach on three state-of-the-art image-text matching models. Quantitative and qualitative experiments conducted on two publicly available datasets demonstrate its strong generality and effectiveness.

2   Related Work

Image-text matching has received much attention in recent years. Most of the previous works focus on the improvement of feature extraction and model design. Early image-text matching approaches [6,7,13,35] directly capture the visual-textual alignment at the level of image and text. Typically, they extract the global image feature by convolutional neural network (CNN), and extract the global text feature by language model such as Skip-gram model [22] or recurrent neural network (RNN). The image-text similarity score is then computed as the inner product [6,7,13] or cosine similarity [35] of the image and text features. The success of attention models for joint visual-textual learning tasks, such as visual question answering (VQA) [12,21,30,34] and image captioning [3,20,24,29,31], leads to the transition to capture image-text correspondence at the level of image regions and words [10,16,23,36]. Typically, these approaches extract the image region feature and word feature from the last pooling layer of CNN and temporal outputs of RNN. They focus on designing effective upper networks that can automatically find, align and aggregate corresponding regions and words to compute the final similarity score. Recently, Anderson et al. [1] extract the image object features by the combination of Faster R-CNN [25] and ResNet [8] for VQA. Based on [1], recent approaches [11,14,15,18,27] further construct the connection between words and image objects. They either propose new mechanisms for object feature extraction, such as feeding saliency information [11] or extracting joint features among objects by constructing object graph [15], or propose different cross-modality aggregation networks [2,9,14,18,27] to improve the aggregation process from object and word features to the final score.

Even though the network design is widely studied, relatively fewer works focus on the training approach. Early image-text matching approaches [5,7,13,32] commonly apply a standard triplet loss whose early form can be found in [28] for word-image embedding. On the other hand, Zhang et al. [35] improve the triplet

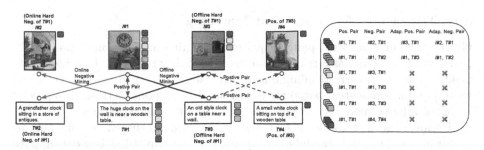

Fig. 2. Training process illustration. Given a positive image-text pair $(I\#1, T\#1)$, 6 margin-based ranking losses are applied to enlarge its similarity score differences from the online hard negative pairs $(I\#2, T\#1)$, $(I\#1, T\#2)$, the offline hard negative pairs $(I\#3, T\#1)$, $(I\#1, T\#3)$ (with the common anchor), and the derived offline hard negative pairs $(I\#3, T\#3)$, $(I\#4, T\#4)$ (without the common anchor). Adaptive penalization is imposed via the online losses to adaptively penalize positive and negative pairs with different strengths and directions. The involved samples of each loss are marked by the corresponding squares.

loss and propose a norm-softmax loss to achieve cross-modal projection. For both losses, all the negatives of an anchor in the same mini-batch are utilized for loss computing. Significant improvement is observed as Faghri et al. [6] propose the triplet loss with online hard negatives. Online triplet mining is first introduced in [26] for face recognition. For image-text matching, it mines the online hard negatives of the anchors from the mini-batch and makes the model only pay attention to these confusing negatives. Almost all the current models [14,15,18,27] apply this online triplet loss. To the best of our knowledge, our work is the first that introduces offline hard negatives for image-text matching. They are mined offline from the whole training set. Motivated by [4] for person re-identification, we propose a quintuplet loss based on offline hard negatives to effectively cooperate with an online triplet loss, leading to significant improvement. It should be noticed that Liu et al. [19] explicitly feed adaptive penalty weight into triplet loss for image-text matching. However, they use it to solve the hubness problem, while we implicitly feed hierarchical information into the model to enlarge the similarity score differences among different pair classes.

3 Methods

In this section, we formally present our training approach for image-text matching. In Sect. 3.1, we introduce the margin-based standard and online triplet losses that are used in previous works. In Sect. 3.2, we present offline quintuplet loss as an effective complement to online triplet loss to significantly improve the performance. In Sect. 3.3, we propose our final loss function with adaptive penalization and mathematically show how it works. The overall training process and the involved pairs are illustrated in Fig. 2.

3.1   Triplet Loss for Image-Text Matching

Given an input image-text pair, image-text matching models aim to predict the pair's similarity score as a criterion for cross-modality retrieval. To achieve this, positive pairs (*i.e.* corresponding image-text pairs) and negative pairs (*i.e.* non-corresponding image-text pairs) are constructed. The model is trained to predict higher similarity score for the positive pairs than the negative ones.

Because the metrics of cross-modality retrieval are based on the ranking performance of multiple candidates on a single query, triplet loss is widely applied to train the model. It holds a common sample for each positive pair and negative pair as an *anchor*. The other sample in the positive pair is called the anchor's *positive* while the other sample in the negative pair is called the anchor's *negative*. In essence, triplet loss encourages the model to predict higher similarity scores from the anchor to its positives. This is consistent with the retrieval process of finding the corresponding candidates of a query with the high similarity scores.

Early image-text matching works [5,7,13,32] typically apply a standard triplet loss without hard negative mining. Given a training mini-batch that contains a set of positive pairs, the standard triplet loss is defined as:

$$\mathcal{L}_{std} = \sum_{(i,t)\in P} (\sum_{\bar{t}\in T/t} [\gamma - S(i,t) + S(i,\bar{t})]_+ + \sum_{\bar{i}\in I/i} [\gamma - S(i,t) + S(\bar{i},t)]_+) \tag{1}$$

Here γ is the margin of the triplet loss, $[x]_+ \equiv max(x,0)$. I, T and P are the image, text and positive pair sets of the mini-batch, respectively. i and t are the anchors of the two terms, respectively. (i,t) represents the positive pair, while $(i,\bar{t})$ and $(\bar{i},t)$ represent the negative pairs available in the mini-batch.

On the other hand, to overcome the drawback of standard triplet loss mentioned in Sect. 1, Faghri et al. [6] present triplet loss with online hard negatives (*i.e.* online triplet loss). In particular, for a positive pair (i,t) in a mini-batch, the hard negatives of the anchor i and t are given by $\bar{t}_{on} = argmax_{c\in T/t}S(i,c)$ and $\bar{i}_{on} = argmax_{b\in I/i}S(b,t)$, respectively. The online triplet loss is defined as:

$$\mathcal{L}_{online} = \sum_{(i,t)\in P} ([\gamma - S(i,t) + S(i,\bar{t}_{on})]_+ + [\gamma - S(i,t) + S(\bar{i}_{on},t)]_+) \tag{2}$$

Compared with the standard triplet loss, online triplet loss forces the model to only learn to distinguish between the positive and the most confusing negative of an anchor in the mini-batch. This guides the model to not only consider the overall semantic meaning difference of a pair, but also discover correspondences and non-correspondences from the details hidden in local regions and words.

3.2   Offline Quintuplet Loss

One problem of online triplet loss in Sect. 3.1 is that the "hardness" degree of most online hard negatives is still not sufficient, especially when the training involves a large-scale training set and a relatively small batch size. As mentioned

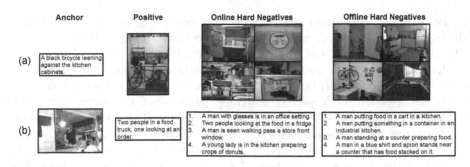

Fig. 3. Two example anchors, their corresponding positives, their sampled online hard negatives and offline hard negatives.

in Sect. 1, the rank of an anchor's online hard negative in the whole training set is commonly not very high. Qualitatively, as shown in Fig. 3, the online hard negatives of an anchor typically contain a few related words, objects or scenes to the anchor. However, there exist obvious non-correspondences between the anchor and the negatives. Indeed, the model only needs to find these non-correspondences and strengthen their influence, which is sufficient for the score difference between the positive pair and negative pair to exceed the margin γ in Eq. 2. However, during inference, when the model encounters "harder" negatives like the offline hard negative examples of Fig. 3, the model may not be able to distinguish them from the positives. The non-corresponding parts of these "harder" negatives to the anchor are subtle, and their influence on the predicted score can be offset by the perfectly corresponding parts.

To overcome the problem, we additionally mine "harder" negatives in an offline fashion. In particular, it involves a two-round training. In the first round, the model is trained by the online triplet loss. After that, it performs global similarity score prediction – for each image/text in the training set, the model predicts its similarity score to all its non-corresponding texts/images in the training set, ranks them by their scores and stores the list of the top-h. In the second round, for each anchor in a mini-batch, its offline hard negatives are uniformly sampled from the top-h negatives of the anchor in the whole training set. The model is trained from scratch again by the following loss function:

$$\mathcal{L} = \sum_{(i,t)\in P} (([\gamma_1 - S(i,t) + S(i,\bar{t}_{on})]_+ + [\gamma_2 - S(i,t) + S(i,\bar{t}_{off})]_+)$$
$$+([\gamma_1 - S(i,t) + S(\bar{i}_{on},t)]_+ + [\gamma_2 - S(i,t) + S(\bar{i}_{off},t)]_+)) \tag{3}$$

Here $\bar{t}_{off}$ and $\bar{i}_{off}$ are the offline hard negatives of i and t, γ_1 and γ_2 are the margins of the online and offline triplet losses. It should be noticed that for models with relatively low inference speed, the above mentioned global similarity score prediction step can be time-consuming. In Sect. 4, we demonstrate that a model can safely utilize the prediction of another efficient model to mine offline hard negatives, which still sharply benefits the training process.

Because the offline hard negatives are very confusing, to make them benefit the training, we should set γ_2 to a lower margin than γ_1, *e.g.* 0. However, in this situation, if the positive and offline hard negative pairs share a same anchor, the model will merely learn how to find the subtle non-corresponding parts of the offline hard negative pair, but still does not learn how to deal with the situation when the negative pair's perfect matching parts offset the score influence of non-corresponding parts. We attribute it to the fact that the positive and offline hard negative get close similarity score for their corresponding parts to the same anchor. The model only needs to find the non-corresponding parts of the negative pair to satisfy the margin condition of γ_2. Also, as claimed in [4], this setting weakens the model's generalization capability from training to testing.

Considering this, we additionally derive two offline hard negative pairs and modify Eq. 3 for the second-round training as follows:

$$
\mathcal{L} = \sum_{(i,t)\in P} (([\gamma_1 - S(i,t) + S(i,\bar{t}_{on})]_+ + [\gamma_2 - S(i,t) + S(i,\bar{t}_{off})]_+ + [\gamma_2 - S(i,t) + S(\bar{i}_{off},\bar{t}_{off})]_+)
$$

$$
+([\gamma_1 - S(i,t) + S(\bar{i}_{on},t)]_+ + [\gamma_2 - S(i,t) + S(\bar{i}_{off},t)]_+ + [\gamma_2 - S(i,t) + S(\tilde{\bar{i}}_{off},\tilde{\bar{t}}_{off})]_+))
$$

$$(4)$$

Here $\tilde{i}_{off}$ and $\tilde{t}_{off}$ are the corresponding image and text of $\bar{t}_{off}$ and $\bar{i}_{off}$, respectively. Because $\bar{t}_{off}$ and $\bar{i}_{off}$ are offline hard negatives of corresponding i and t, both $(\bar{i}_{off},\tilde{t}_{off})$ and $(\tilde{\bar{i}}_{off},\bar{t}_{off})$ can be also regarded as offline hard negative pairs (we re-sample $\tilde{i}_{off}$ and $\tilde{t}_{off}$ if they occasionally correspond to each other). The samples of each pair are non-corresponding but share very similar semantic meanings to each other, and also to i and t. This two new terms guide the model to distinguish between positive and negative pairs without common elements. In Sect. 4, we prove the effectiveness of deriving the new terms based on $\bar{i}_{off}$, $\bar{t}_{off}$ instead of $\bar{i}_{on}$, $\bar{t}_{on}$. The complete offline loss terms based on anchor i and t contain 4 and 5 elements. Following [4], we define it as an offline quintuplet loss.

3.3   Adaptive and Hierarchical Penalization

In Sect. 3.2, we introduce offline hard negatives which cooperate with online hard negatives to train the model as Eq. 4. During the training process, it is natural that we should give different penalty weights to negative pairs with different "hardness" degrees. For example, if the similarity score between a positive pair and a hard negative pair is close, both pairs should obtain higher penalty weight which guides the model to distinguish between them better. However, when we derive each loss term with respect to its contained pairs' similarity scores, the gradients are always constant. This indicates that when the margin condition is not satisfied, the penalty weight is consistent regardless of the closeness degree between the positive and negative pairs.

One simple solution is modifying each loss term to a form of square so that the penalty weight is related to the score difference between the positive and negative pairs. However, we find that the improvement is limited as there are no hierarchical knowledge provided by the loss function. Ideally, we expect that the positive pairs to obtain higher scores than offline hard negative pairs, and that the offline hard negative pairs obtain higher scores than online hard negative pairs. To this end, we feed the information of offline hard negatives into the online loss term. The final loss function for the second-round training is as follows:

$$
\begin{aligned}
\mathcal{L} = \sum_{(i,t)\in P} (((\beta - \frac{S(i,\bar{t}_{off}) - S(i,\bar{t}_{on})}{\alpha})[\gamma_1 - S(i,t) + S(i,\bar{t}_{on})]_+ \\
+ [\gamma_2 - S(i,t) + S(i,\bar{t}_{off})]_+ + [\gamma_2 - S(i,t) + S(\bar{i}_{off},\bar{t}_{off})]_+) \\
+ ((\beta - \frac{S(\bar{i}_{off},t) - S(\bar{i}_{on},t)}{\alpha})[\gamma_1 - S(i,t) + S(\bar{i}_{on},t)]_+ \\
+ [\gamma_2 - S(i,t) + S(\bar{i}_{off},t)]_+ + [\gamma_2 - S(i,t) + S(\widetilde{\bar{i}_{off}},\widetilde{\bar{t}_{off}})]_+))
\end{aligned}
\tag{5}
$$

Here α and β are hyper-parameters. In Sect. 4, we present that they can be set to consistent values for different models on different datasets.

To better understand how the proposed loss function works, we focus on the first part (line) of Eq. 5 which is symmetrical to the second part, and compute its gradient with respect to $S(i,t)$, $S(i,\bar{t}_{off})$ and $S(i,\bar{t}_{on})$ as follows:

$$
\begin{aligned}
\frac{\partial \mathcal{L}}{\partial S(i,t)} &= (\frac{S(i,\bar{t}_{off}) - S(i,\bar{t}_{on})}{\alpha} - \beta)\mathbb{I}(\gamma_1 - S(i,t) + S(i,\bar{t}_{on}) > 0) - \mathbb{I}(\gamma_2 - S(i,t) + S(i,\bar{t}_{off}) > 0) \\
&\quad - \mathbb{I}(\gamma_2 - S(i,t) + S(\bar{i}_{off},\bar{t}_{off}) > 0), \\
\frac{\partial \mathcal{L}}{\partial S(i,\bar{t}_{off})} &= (\frac{S(i,t) - S(i,\bar{t}_{on})}{\alpha} - \frac{\gamma_1}{\alpha}))\mathbb{I}(\gamma_1 - S(i,t) + S(i,\bar{t}_{on}) > 0) + \mathbb{I}(\gamma_2 - S(i,t) + S(i,\bar{t}_{off}) > 0), \\
\frac{\partial \mathcal{L}}{\partial S(i,\bar{t}_{on})} &= (\frac{2 S(i,\bar{t}_{on}) - S(i,t) - S(i,\bar{t}_{off})}{\alpha} + \beta + \frac{\gamma_1}{\alpha})\mathbb{I}(\gamma_1 - S(i,t) + S(i,\bar{t}_{on}) > 0)
\end{aligned}
\tag{6}
$$

Here $\mathbb{I}(A)$ is the indicator function: $\mathbb{I}(A) = 1$ if A is true, and 0 otherwise.

When the margin conditions are not satisfied, the gradient of $\mathcal{L}$ with respect to $S(i,\bar{t}_{on})$ becomes larger when $S(i,\bar{t}_{on})$ is close to the average of $S(i,\bar{t}_{off})$ and $S(i,t)$, which indicates a larger penalty to make $S(i,\bar{t}_{on})$ lower. For the gradient of $\mathcal{L}$ with respect to $S(i,t)$, the second and third terms indicate a negative constant which pushes $S(i,t)$ to be higher than $S(i,\bar{t}_{off})$. In addition, the first term indicates an additional adaptive penalty for $S(i,t)$ to be far away from $S(i,\bar{t}_{on})$. When $S(i,\bar{t}_{on})$ is remarkably lower than $S(i,\bar{t}_{off})$, the penalty drops since $S(i,\bar{t}_{on})$ is sufficiently lower. As for the gradient of $\mathcal{L}$ with respect to $S(i,\bar{t}_{off})$, it is subtle as the second term indicates a positive constant that penalizes $S(i,\bar{t}_{off})$ to be lower than $S(i,t)$. However, this penalty could be neutralized when $S(i,t)$ and $S(i,\bar{t}_{on})$ are close to each other. In this situation, it prevents the penalty from incorrectly making $S(i,\bar{t}_{off})$ lower than $S(i,\bar{t}_{on})$.

Overall, the proposed loss function applies adaptive and hierarchical penalties to the positive, offline hard negative and online hard negative pairs based on the differences among their predicted scores. Essentially, the pairs that are close to the boundary of its pair class obtain larger penalty weights, the inter-class score gaps can thus be enlarged among these three kinds of pairs. In Sect. 4, we demonstrate its strong effectiveness to improve the model's performance.

4 Experiments

Extensive experiments are performed to evaluate the proposed training app-roach. The performance of retrieval is evaluated by the standard recall at K (R@K). It is defined as the fraction of queries for which the correct item belongs to the top-K retrieval items. We first present the datasets, experiment settings and implementation details. We then compare and analyze the performance of the proposed approach with others quantitatively and qualitatively.

4.1 Dataset and Experiment Settings

We evaluate our model on two well-known datasets, MS-COCO and Flickr30K. The original MS-COCO dataset [17] contains 82,783 training and 40,504 valida-tion images. Each image is annotated with five descriptions. Following the splits of [14,15,18], we divide the dataset into 113,283 training images, 5,000 valida-tion images and 5,000 test images. Following [6,14,15], we report the results by averaging over 5 folds of 1K test images or testing on the full 5K test images. Flickr30k [33] consists of 31K images collected from the Flickr website. Each image also corresponds to five human-annotated sentences. Following the split of [14,15,18], we randomly select 1,000 images for validation and 1,000 images for testing and use other images to train the model.

To evaluate the effectiveness and generality of the proposed approach, we apply it to the following current state-of-the-art image-text matching models:

- **SCAN** [14]. The first model that captures image-text correspondence at the level of objects and words. The word and object features are extracted by bi-directional GRU and the combination of Faster R-CNN [25] and ResNet-101 [8], respectively. Stacked cross attention is fed into the network to discover the full latent alignments using both objects and words as context.
- **BFAN** [18]. A novel Bidirectional Focal Attention Network based on SCAN that achieves remarkable improvement. Compared with SCAN, it focuses additionally on eliminating irrelevant fragments from the shared semantics.
- **VSRN** [15]. The current state-of-the-art image-text matching models with-out leveraging extra supervision (the model in [11] is trained by extra saliency-annotated data). It generates object representation by region relationship reasoning and global semantic reasoning.

All the three models are originally trained by triplet loss with online hard negatives. We replace it with the proposed training approach for comparison.

4.2 Implementation Details

To perform a fair comparison, for SCAN, BFAN and VSRN, we completely pre-serve their network structures and model settings (*e.g.* training batch size, fea-ture dimension and other model-related hyper-parameter settings) as described in their original work. We only replace the online triplet loss by the proposed one to train them. For all the situations, the margins for online and offline ranking losses γ_1 and γ_2 are set to 0.2 and 0, the hyper-parameters β and α in Eq. 5 are set to 1.5 and 0.3. The top list size h is set to 300 and 60 to sample offline hard negative texts and images (the training texts are 5 times as many training images for both datasets). As mentioned in Sect. 3.2, for VSRN, it takes 3,400s/620s to perform global similarity score prediction on MS-COCO/Flickr30K. However, for SCAN and BFAN, they hold complex upper networks which make this step extremely time-consuming. Therefore, we skip the first-round training of SCAN and BFAN. The similarity scores predicted by VSRN are also used as a basis for the second-round training of SCAN and BFAN to sample offline hard negatives. We consider this setting valid because, after the second-round training, the final prediction is still made by SCAN or BFAN without the participating of VSRN, which can be regarded as a teacher model. For the first-round training on MS-COCO/Flickr30K, as [15], VSRN is trained by a start learning rate of 0.0002 for 15/10 epochs, and then trained by a lower learning rate of 0.00002 for another 15/10 epochs. For the second-round training on both datasets, SCAN, BFAN and VSRN are trained by a start learning rate of 0.0005, 0.0005 and 0.0002 for 10 epochs, and then trained by a lower learning rate of 0.00005, 0.00005 and 0.00002 for another 5, 5 and 10 epochs, respectively.

4.3   Results on MS-COCO and Flickr30K

Table 1. Quantitative evaluation results of image-to-text (sentence) retrieval and text-to-image (image) retrieval on MS-COCO 1K/5K test set. The baseline models (first row) are trained by the triplet loss with online hard negatives. "+ OffTri", "+ OffQuin", "+ AdapOffQuin" represent training the model by Eqs. 3, 4, 5, respectively.

Model	Sentence retrieval			Image retrieval			
	R@1	R@5	R@10	R@1	R@5	R@10	rsum
1K Test Images							
SCAN [14]	72.7	94.8	98.4	58.8	88.4	94.8	507.9
SCAN + OffTri	73.1	94.8	98.2	59.3	88.3	94.8	508.5
SCAN + OffQuin	73.6	95.0	98.4	59.6	**88.6**	**95.0**	510.2
SCAN + AdapOffQuin	**74.1**	**95.2**	**98.5**	**59.8**	88.6	95.0	**511.2**
BFAN [18]	74.9	95.2	98.3	59.4	88.4	94.5	510.7
BFAN + OffTri	75.8	95.6	98.4	60.1	88.8	94.7	513.4
BFAN + OffQuin	76.3	95.7	98.4	60.5	89.0	94.8	514.7
BFAN + AdapOffQuin	**77.3**	**96.0**	**98.5**	**61.2**	**89.2**	**95.0**	**517.2**
VSRN [15]	76.2	94.8	98.2	62.8	89.7	95.1	516.8
VSRN + OffTri	76.8	95.2	98.4	63.1	89.9	95.2	518.6
VSRN + OffQuin	76.9	95.3	98.4	63.3	90.2	95.5	519.7
VSRN + AdapOffQuin	**77.5**	**95.5**	**98.6**	**63.5**	**90.5**	**95.8**	**521.4**
5K Test Images							
SCAN [14]	50.4	82.2	90.0	38.6	69.3	**80.4**	410.9
SCAN + AdapOffQuin	**51.2**	**82.5**	**90.1**	**39.4**	**69.7**	80.4	**413.3**
BFAN [18]	52.9	82.8	90.6	38.3	67.8	79.3	411.7
BFAN + AdapOffQuin	**57.3**	**84.5**	**91.7**	**40.1**	**69.2**	**80.1**	**422.9**
VSRN [15]	53.0	81.1	89.4	40.5	70.6	81.1	415.7
VSRN + AdapOffQuin	**55.1**	**83.3**	**90.8**	**41.1**	**71.5**	**82.0**	**423.8**

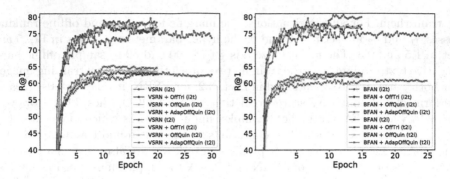

Fig. 4. Plotting training epoch against R@1 on the MS-COCO validation set for different training approaches applied on VSRN and BFAN. For the proposed approaches, the training curves correspond to the second-round training. "t2i" and "i2t" represents image retrieval and sentence retrieval, respectively.

Table 1 shows the performance comparison of models trained by different approaches on MS-COCO. We can see that all the three models are significantly improved on all the settings when trained by our proposed training approach. As mentioned in Sect. 4.2, for all the models, the offline hard negatives in their second-round training are sampled from the prediction of the first-round trained VSRN. It indicates that the proposed training approach is insensitive to the model consistency of the two-round training. When the global similarity score prediction step is intractable for the current model, we can train it by sampling offline hard negatives based on the prediction of another more efficient model. Overall, we achieve the most significant improvement on BFAN. In particular, on the more reliable 5K test set, it outperforms the baseline by 8.3% and 4.7% in top-1 sentence retrieval and top-1 image retrieval.

Table 2 shows the performance comparison on Flickr30K. It should be noted that Flickr30K is much smaller than MS-COCO as it contains fewer very confus-

Table 2. Quantitative evaluation results of sentence retrieval and image retrieval on the Flickr30K test set.

Model	Sentence retrieval			Image retrieval			
	R@1	R@5	R@10	R@1	R@5	R@10	rsum
1K Test Images							
SCAN [14]	67.4	90.3	**95.8**	48.6	77.7	85.2	465.0
SCAN + AdapOffQuin	**70.3**	**92.0**	95.5	**50.0**	**79.2**	**86.2**	**473.2**
BFAN [18]	68.1	91.4	95.9	50.8	78.4	85.8	470.4
BFAN + AdapOffQuin	**73.2**	**94.5**	**97.0**	**54.0**	**80.3**	**87.7**	**486.7**
VSRN [15]	71.3	90.6	**96.0**	54.7	81.8	88.2	482.6
VSRN + AdapOffQuin	**72.8**	**91.8**	95.8	**55.3**	**82.2**	**88.4**	**486.3**

Fig. 5. Qualitative image retrieval and sentence retrieval comparison between the baseline training approach and ours on the MS-COCO test set.

ing negative image-text pairs to be served as high-quality offline hard negative pairs. However, significant improvements are still observed for all the models. In Sect. 4.4, we show that our proposed training approach has strong robustness for the quality of offline hard negatives.

We look deeper into different training approaches by examining VSRN and BFAN's training behaviours[1] on the widely-used MS-COCO 1K validation set [6,14,15] (*i.e.* the first fold of the 5K validation set). As shown in Fig. 4, both models' performance obtains continuous improvement as we feed different proposed mechanisms into the training process. When the models are trained by Eq. 5, they converge significantly faster than the baselines as it takes less than 10 epochs for them to outperform the highest R@1 of their baselines.

4.4 Ablation Study and Visualization

First, we validate whether the offline hard negatives can completely replace online hard negatives to train the model. Specifically, we remove the online loss term in Eq. 4 to train VSRN and BFAN. As shown in Table 3, the training process fails as it is too difficult for the model to directly learn to distinguish between the positive pairs and these extremely confusing negative pairs. Also, we demonstrate the usefulness of re-training the model from scratch in the second round. As shown in Table 3, when we apply Eq. 5 to fine-tune the model that has already been trained by the online triplet loss and get trapped in a local optimum, it cannot obtain additional improvement. In Eq. 4, we create two new terms based on offline negatives. Indeed, we can instead apply them based on online negatives. However, the performance of "OnlineQuin" models are remarkably worse than the models train by Eq. 4, this supports our claim of

---

[1] The final BFAN model is an ensemble of two independently trained models BFAN-equal and BFAN-prob [18], here we show the behaviours of BFAN-prob.

Table 3. Performance of different training approach variants on MS-COCO 1K test set. "OnlyOffline" represents the model that is only trained by the offline term. "Fine-tune" represents the model that is fine-tuned in the second-round instead of re-trained from scratch. "OnlineQuin" indicates that we apply online quintuplet loss instead of offline in Eq. 4 (*i.e* replace $S(\bar{i}_{off}, \bar{t}_{off})))$, $S(\widetilde{i}_{off}, \widetilde{t}_{off}))$ with $S(\bar{i}_{on}, \bar{t}_{on})))$, $S(\widetilde{i}_{on}, \widetilde{t}_{on})))$ to train the model. "w/o OfflineAdap" represents that we replace $S(i, \bar{t}_{off})$ and $S(\bar{i}_{off}, t)$ by $S(i, t)$ for the new added terms in Eq. 5 to train the model. Performance of selecting different top list size h for offline hard negative text sampling is also studied. The values in parentheses indicate the performance difference between the models trained by the variant and by the proposed approach with the final settings.

Model	Sentence retrieval			Image retrieval		
	R@1	R@5	R@10	R@1	R@5	R@10
1K Test Images						
BFAN (OnlyOffline)	1.1 (−76.2)	2.5 (−93.5)	4.9 (−93.6)	0.5 (−60.7)	1.4 (−87.8)	2.6(−92.4)
VSRN (OnlyOffline)	0.7 (−76.8)	2.1 (−93.4)	3.8 (−94.8)	0.4 (−63.1)	1.2 (−89.3)	2.3(−93.5)
BFAN (Fine-tune)	74.3 (−3.0)	94.7 (−1.3)	98.2 (−0.3)	58.7 (−2.5)	88.1 (−1.1)	94.2 (−0.8)
VSRN (Fine-tune)	74.5 (−3.0)	94.3 (−1.2)	98.1 (−0.5)	62.0 (−1.5)	89.3 (−1.2)	94.8 (−1.0)
BFAN (OnlineQuin)	75.3 (−2.0)	95.8 (−0.2)	98.5 (+0.0)	59.8 (−1.4)	88.6 (−0.6)	94.6 (−0.4)
VSRN (OnlineQuin)	76.4 (−1.1)	94.9 (−0.6)	98.2 (−0.4)	62.8 (−0.7)	89.9 (−0.6)	95.2(−0.6)
BFAN (w/o OfflineAdap)	76.6 (−0.7)	95.8 (−0.2)	98.4 (−0.1)	60.8 (−0.4)	89.1 (−0.1)	94.8 (−0.2)
VSRN (w/o OfflineAdap)	77.1 (−0.4)	95.4(−0.1)	98.4 (−0.2)	63.4 (−0.1)	90.2 (−0.3)	95.5 (−0.3)
VSRN (h = 200)	77.1 (−0.4)	95.3 (−0.2)	98.4 (−0.2)	63.3 (−0.2)	90.4 (−0.1)	95.6 (−0.2)
VSRN (h = 500)	77.4 (−0.1)	95.6 (+0.1)	98.6 (+0.0)	63.5 (+0.0)	90.4 (−0.1)	95.7 (−0.1)
VSRN (h = 1000)	77.3 (−0.2)	95.4 (−0.1)	98.6 (+0.0)	63.3 (−0.2)	90.3 (−0.2)	95.6 (−0.2)

the second problem in Sect. 1. On the other hand, in Eq. 5, we feed the offline hard negative information into the online term for hierarchical penalization. To validate its effectiveness, we replace $S(i, \bar{t}_{off})$ and $S(\bar{i}_{off}, t)$ by $S(i, t)$ for the new added terms in Eq. 5 to break this hierarchical relation. α and β are re-adjusted to achieve the best performance on the validation set. The performance drops to the same level of using Eq. 4 to train the models, indicating the effectiveness. In the end, for VSRN, we present the model's performance when selecting different top list size h for offline hard negative text sampling (we always keep it 5 times larger than the top list size for offline hard negative image sampling). We can find that even when h is set to 1000 which indicates significant drops of "hardness" degree of offline hard negatives, the model still achieves great performance. This is consistent with the excellent performance on Flickr30K and proves the robustness of our training approach on smaller datasets when very confusing hard negative pairs are limited.

Figure 5 shows the qualitative comparison between the models trained by different approaches on MS-COCO. For sentence retrieval, given an image query, we show the top-5 retrieved sentences. For image retrieval, given a sentence query, we show the top-3 retrieved images. The correct retrieval items for each query are ticked off. Overall, our training approach guides the model to better find and attend to the detailed non-correspondences of negative image-text pairs such as "snow covered field", "rhiho", "blowing out a candle" and "poster".

5 Conclusion

We present a novel training approach for image-text matching. It starts by mining "harder" negatives offline from the whole training set. Based on the mined offline hard negatives, an effective quintuplet loss is proposed to complement the online triplet loss to better distinguish positive and negative pairs. Furthermore, we take the distance relations among positive, offline hard negative and online hard negative pairs into consideration and effectively achieve adaptive penalization for different pairs. Extensive experiments demonstrate the effectiveness and generality of the proposed approach.

Acknowledgment. This work is supported in part by NSF awards IIS-1704337, IIS-1722847, and IIS-1813709, as well as our corporate sponsors.

References

1. Anderson, P., et al.: Bottom-up and top-down attention for image captioning and visual question answering. In: Proceedings of the IEEE Conference on Computer Vision and Pattern Recognition. pp. 6077–6086 (2018)
2. Chen, T., Luo, J.: Expressing objects just like words: Recurrent visual embedding for image-text matching. arXiv preprint arXiv:2002.08510 (2020)
3. Chen, T., et al.: "factual"or"emotional": Stylized image captioning with adaptive learning and attention. In: Proceedings of the European Conference on Computer Vision (ECCV). pp. 519–535 (2018)
4. Chen, W., Chen, X., Zhang, J., Huang, K.: Beyond triplet loss: a deep quadruplet network for person re-identification. In: Proceedings of the IEEE Conference on Computer Vision and Pattern Recognition. pp. 403–412 (2017)
5. Eisenschtat, A., Wolf, L.: Linking image and text with 2-way nets. In: Proceedings of the IEEE Conference on Computer Vision and Pattern Recognition. pp. 4601–4611 (2017)
6. Faghri, F., Fleet, D.J., Kiros, J.R., Fidler, S.: Vse++: Improved visual-semantic embeddings. arXiv preprint arXiv:1707.05612 2(7), 8 (2017)
7. Frome, A., et al.: Devise: A deep visual-semantic embedding model. In: Advances in Neural Information Processing Systems. pp. 2121–2129 (2013)
8. He, K., Zhang, X., Ren, S., Sun, J.: Deep residual learning for image recognition. In: Proceedings of the IEEE Conference on Computer Vision and Pattern Recognition. pp. 770–778 (2016)
9. Huang, Y., Wang, L.: Acmm: aligned cross-modal memory for few-shot image and sentence matching. In: Proceedings of the IEEE International Conference on Computer Vision. pp. 5774–5783 (2019)
10. Huang, Y., Wang, W., Wang, L.: Instance-aware image and sentence matching with selective multimodal lstm. In: Proceedings of the IEEE Conference on Computer Vision and Pattern Recognition. pp. 2310–2318 (2017)
11. Ji, Z., Wang, H., Han, J., Pang, Y.: Saliency-guided attention network for image-sentence matching. arXiv preprint arXiv:1904.09471 (2019)

12. Kim, J.H., et al.: Multimodal residual learning for visual qa. In: Advances in Neural Information Processing Systems. pp. 361–369 (2016)
13. Kiros, R., Salakhutdinov, R., Zemel, R.S.: Unifying visual-semantic embeddings with multimodal neural language models. arXiv preprint arXiv:1411.2539 (2014)
14. Lee, K.H., Chen, X., Hua, G., Hu, H., He, X.: Stacked cross attention for image-text matching. In: Proceedings of the European Conference on Computer Vision (ECCV). pp. 201–216 (2018)
15. Li, K., Zhang, Y., Li, K., Li, Y., Fu, Y.: Visual semantic reasoning for image-text matching. In: Proceedings of the IEEE International Conference on Computer Vision. pp. 4654–4662 (2019)
16. Li, S., Xiao, T., Li, H., Yang, W., Wang, X.: Identity-aware textual-visual matching with latent co-attention. In: Proceedings of the IEEE International Conference on Computer Vision. pp. 1890–1899 (2017)
17. Lin, T.-Y., et al.: Microsoft COCO: common objects in context. In: Fleet, D., Pajdla, T., Schiele, B., Tuytelaars, T. (eds.) ECCV 2014. LNCS, vol. 8693, pp. 740–755. Springer, Cham (2014). https://doi.org/10.1007/978-3-319-10602-1_48
18. Liu, C., Mao, Z., Liu, A.A., Zhang, T., Wang, B., Zhang, Y.: Focus your attention: a bidirectional focal attention network for image-text matching. In: Proceedings of the 27th ACM International Conference on Multimedia. pp. 3–11 (2019)
19. Liu, F., Ye, R., Wang, X., Li, S.: Hal: Improved text-image matching by mitigating visual semantic hubs. arXiv preprint arXiv:1911.10097 (2019)
20. Lu, J., Xiong, C., Parikh, D., Socher, R.: Knowing when to look: Adaptive attention via a visual sentinel for image captioning. In: Proceedings of the IEEE Conference on Computer Vision and Pattern Recognition (CVPR). vol. 6 (2017)
21. Lu, J., Yang, J., Batra, D., Parikh, D.: Hierarchical question-image co-attention for visual question answering. In: Advances In Neural Information Processing Systems. pp. 289–297 (2016)
22. Mikolov, T., Chen, K., Corrado, G., Dean, J.: Efficient estimation of word representations in vector space. arXiv preprint arXiv:1301.3781 (2013)
23. Nam, H., Ha, J.W., Kim, J.: Dual attention networks for multimodal reasoning and matching. In: Proceedings of the IEEE Conference on Computer Vision and Pattern Recognition. pp. 299–307 (2017)
24. Pedersoli, M., Lucas, T., Schmid, C., Verbeek, J.: Areas of attention for image captioning. In: Proceedings of the IEEE International Conference on Computer Vision. pp. 1242–1250 (2017)
25. Ren, S., He, K., Girshick, R., Sun, J.: Faster r-cnn: Towards real-time object detection with region proposal networks. In: Advances in Neural Information Processing Systems. pp. 91–99 (2015)
26. Schroff, F., Kalenichenko, D., Philbin, J.: Facenet: a unified embedding for face recognition and clustering. In: Proceedings of the IEEE Conference on Computer Vision and Pattern Recognition. pp. 815–823 (2015)
27. Wang, Z., et al.: Camp: Cross-modal adaptive message passing for text-image retrieval. In: Proceedings of the IEEE International Conference on Computer Vision. pp. 5764–5773 (2019)
28. Weston, J., Bengio, S., Usunier, N.: Large scale image annotation: learning to rank with joint word-image embeddings. Mach. Learn. **81**(1), 21–35 (2010)
29. Xu, K., et al.: Show, attend and tell: neural image caption generation with visual attention. In: International Conference on Machine Learning. pp. 2048–2057 (2015)
30. Yang, Z., He, X., Gao, J., Deng, L., Smola, A.: Stacked attention networks for image question answering. In: Proceedings of the IEEE Conference on Computer Vision and Pattern Recognition. pp. 21–29 (2016)

31. You, Q., Jin, H., Wang, Z., Fang, C., Luo, J.: Image captioning with semantic attention. In: Proceedings of the IEEE Conference on Computer Vision and Pattern Recognition. pp. 4651–4659 (2016)
32. You, Q., Zhang, Z., Luo, J.: End-to-end convolutional semantic embeddings. In: Proceedings of the IEEE Conference on Computer Vision and Pattern Recognition. pp. 5735–5744 (2018)
33. Young, P., Lai, A., Hodosh, M., Hockenmaier, J.: From image descriptions to visual denotations: New similarity metrics for semantic inference over event descriptions. Trans. Assoc. Comput. Ling. **2**, 67–78 (2014)
34. Yu, D., Fu, J., Mei, T., Rui, Y.: Multi-level attention networks for visual question answering. In: Proceedings of the IEEE Conference on Computer Vision and Pattern Recognition. pp. 4709–4717 (2017)
35. Zhang, Y., Lu, H.: Deep cross-modal projection learning for image-text matching. In: Proceedings of the European Conference on Computer Vision (ECCV). pp. 686–701 (2018)
36. Zheng, Z., Zheng, L., Garrett, M., Yang, Y., Shen, Y.D.: Dual-path convolutional image-text embedding with instance loss. arXiv preprint arXiv:1711.05535 (2017)

Learning Object Placement by Inpainting for Compositional Data Augmentation

Lingzhi Zhang[1](✉), Tarmily Wen[1](✉), Jie Min[1](✉), Jiancong Wang[1](✉), David Han[2](✉), and Jianbo Shi[1](✉)

[1] University of Pennsylvania, Philadelphia, USA
{zlz,went,minjie,jshi}@seas.upenn.edu,
jiancong.wang@pennmedicine.upenn.edu
[2] Army Research Laboratory, Maryland, USA
ctmkhan@gmail.com

Abstract. We study the problem of common sense placement of visual objects in an image. This involves multiple aspects of visual recognition: the instance segmentation of the scene, 3D layout, and common knowledge of how objects are placed and where objects are moving in the 3D scene. This seemingly simple task is difficult for current learning-based approaches because of the lack of labeled training pair of foreground objects paired with cleaned background scenes. We propose a self-learning framework that automatically generates the necessary training data without any manual labeling by detecting, cutting, and inpainting objects from an image. We propose a PlaceNet that predicts a diverse distribution of common sense locations when given a foreground object and a background scene. We show one practical use of our object placement network for augmenting training datasets by recomposition of object-scene with a key property of contextual relationship preservation. We demonstrate improvement of object detection and instance segmentation performance on both Cityscape [4] and KITTI [9] datasets. We also show that the learned representation of our PlaceNet displays strong discriminative power in image retrieval and classification.

Keywords: Object placement · Inpainting · Data augmentation

1 Introduction

Studies in humans and animals suggest that the mental replay of past experiences is essential for enhancing visual procession as well as making action decisions [3]. We ask the question: can developing a computational mental replay model help to improve AI visual perception tasks such as recognition and segmentation? More specifically, would the mental replay of object placement and scene affordance boost visual recognition systems?

Electronic supplementary material The online version of this chapter (https://doi.org/10.1007/978-3-030-58601-0_34) contains supplementary material, which is available to authorized users.

A. Vedaldi et al. (Eds.): ECCV 2020, LNCS 12358, pp. 566–581, 2020.
https://doi.org/10.1007/978-3-030-58601-0_34

Fig. 1. Given a foreground object and a background scene, we aim to learn a set of reasonable and diverse locations and scales to insert the object into the scene.

This is not only a scientific question, but also a highly practical one for training a deep learning network. Most AI systems based on deep learning have a large appetite for a vast quantity of human-labeled training dataset, and all modern deep learning based algorithms implicitly use contextual cue for recognition tasks. Several recent works demonstrated 'copy-paste' like data augmentation by inserting objects into a background image in order to boost object recognition performance [5–7,10,30]. If the mental replay of object placement could be carried out reliably with the preservation of contextual relationship, this method leads to a new way of data augmentation by utilizing self-supervised learning of object placement.

Motivated by vast amount of driving scenes in public datasets, we create a self-supervised mental replay task of learning object placements into street scenes. Our system starts by observing many street scene images along with instance segmentation labels. It learns to mental replay: transferring objects from one scene and composite them into other plausible scenes at plausible new locations. This task has many useful side-effects: 1) it encourages the algorithm to discover functionality based object and scene features, and their contextual dependency; 2) it helps to create new object-scene compositions that could potentially balance out biases or augment hard examples in the training dataset.

The self-learning can also come for 'free' just by observing unlabeled scenes. Our insight is that we can generate 'free' labeled training data using an instance segmentation network [11] to cut out objects and fill in the holes using an image inpainting network [31]. The 'free' labeled object-background pairs tell us *what* the object looks like and *where* it is placed.

The 'free' labeled object-background pairs are then fed into our proposed PlaceNet, which predicts the location and scale to insert the object into the background. The key challenge is to learn diverse yet plausible object placements. There is a many-to-many mapping between the objects/scenes with plausible placement solutions. For example, one object-scene image pair can correspond to many different object placements (one-to-many). At the same time, similar object-scene pairs can correspond to the same object placement (many-to-one). The two key properties we want are 1) *diversity*: learns a many-to-many mapping, where images consisting of similar object-scene pairs can share the similar distributions of solutions; and 2) *modularity*: the objects and scenes are represented modularly to allow for maximal composition possibility for inserting objects into scenes.

We demonstrate that our PlaceNet can outperform strong baselines in terms of plausibility and diversity in object placement learning. In addition, we show two useful applications of our object placement learning. First, we use the learned PlaceNet to insert objects from one scene into many other scenes with natural object-context relationship in order to augment training data for boosting object detection and instance segmentation. Our hypothesis is that by compositing scenes that model the distribution of any object, we are able to improve the detection and segmentation performance by allowing the detectors [11,25] see more object-context relationships. Second, we show that our self-learning PlaceNet can learn meaningful features for object/scene retrieval as well as image classification.

2   Related Work

2.1   Learning Object Placements

There have been several attempts to solve the task of object placement with deep learning. Tan et al. [27] proposed a branching CNN to jointly predict the location and size for inserting person into a scene. Lin et al. [18] proposed Spatial Transformer Generative Adversarial Networks (ST-GAN) that iteratively warps a foreground instance into a background scene with a spatial transformer network via adversarial training against geometric and natural image manifolds. Similarly to [18], Tripathi et al. [29] proposed to composite synthetic images with STN [13] by discriminating them from the natural image datasets. Azadi et al. [1] proposed a self-consistent composition-by-decomposition network named Compositional GAN to composite a pair of objects. The insight is that the composite images should not only look realistic in appearance but also be decomposable back into individual objects, which provides the self-consistent supervisory signal for training the composition network. Li et al. [17] focused on predicting a distribution of locations and poses of humans in 3D indoor environments using Variational Auto-Encoders [14].

The work closest to ours is Lee et al. [16], where they proposed a two-step model that predicts a distribution of possible locations where a specific class of objects (person/car) could be placed and how the shape of the class of objects could look like using semantic maps. In contrast with [16], we learn object placements using images of objects and backgrounds as input without compressing them to abstract category names. Using image appearances as input is much harder due to large feature dimensionality, but it allows us to create more contextually natural scenes compared to using GAN generated objects.

2.2   Data Augmentation for Object Detection

There have been many efforts to improve performance of object detection or instance segmentation through data augmentation. The most straightforward method to accomplish this is through geometric transformations of the images [8,11,20,26] such as scale changes, horizontal flips, cropping, and rotations. By varying the levels of context around objects, the orientation, and the size of objects, their aim is to augment the data distribution that better matches the natural distribution of objects. Another method includes adjusting the signal-to-noise ratio to model the uncertainty in object boundaries and other possible sampling noises [8] by distorting the color information.

It has been demonstrated that context plays a key role in vision recognition systems [24,28]. Having contextually related objects in a scene has more of an multiplicative effect than an additive one. That is, a scene composed of contextually sound objects is more than the sum of the constituent parts. Both [24,28] validate that having contextually related objects provides more evidence for recognition than beyond just the local evidence of the object instance itself.

Instead of operating on the original data, one way to generate new images is to cut-and-paste object instances onto an image [5–7,10,30]. This has been shown to be effective for both object detection and instance segmentation.

The context-based cut-and-paste method most related to our work is [5], in that placement is learned based on context. But [5] does not condition the placement of the object on both the context and the appearance of the instance itself like ours. Instead the locations are classified on which class is most likely to be present in each location given the context. The method used is unable to distinguish if specific object instances of the same semantic class actually belong in the scene given the context.

Another closely related work is [7], which perturbs the object locations in the original image to augment object-context relationships. In contrast with this work [7], we can sample directly from the joint distribution of three disjoint variables: object appearance, scene appearance, and stochastic variations of object-scene interaction, without being forced in the original background context. This allows us to generate a far greater diversity of scene compositions.

3   Methods

Our work aims to learn the placement of foreground objects into background scenes without heavy human labeling. To do so, we first propose a novel data acquisition technique to generate training data for free. Then, we propose a generative model PlaceNet to predict a set of diverse and plausible locations and scales to insert foreground object into background scene. With the learned PlaceNet, we further propose a data augmentation pipeline to shuffle foreground objects into many different background scenes to composite new training data in order to boost object detection and instance segmentation performance.

3.1   Data Acquisition by Inpainting

What kind of data do we need in order to learn common sense object placements? Intuitively, our training set needs to contain paired examples of a foreground

Fig. 2. In our data acquisition pipeline, we first cut out the object region with the instance segmentation mask, and save the original bounding boxes as the ground truth plausible placement locations and scales. In the meantime, we crop out segmented objects corresponding to the bounding boxes. Finally, we use inpainting network to fill the holes of the occluded region and generate the clean background.

object, a cleaned background scene without objects, and labeled plausible locations to place the object. While such labeled data would be extremely difficult and expensive to obtain, we propose a novel data acquisition system. Our system leverages existing instance segmentation dataset and a self-supervised image inpainting network to generate the necessary training data for learning object placement.

Our insight is that we can generate such training data by removing objects from the background scenes. With an instance segmentation mask, we first cut out the object regions and then fill in the holes with an image inpainting network. After that, we simultaneously obtain a clean background scene without objects in it and the corresponding ground truth plausible placement locations and scales for placing these objects into the scene. The overall process is described in Fig. 2. The instance segmentation can be obtained from labeled data or a pretrained Mask R-CNN network [11]. The inpainting network [31] is trained by randomly cropping out regions in the street scene images. After the training, the inpainting network learns a prior to fill the holes with background information even if the holes were previously occupied by some objects, which has been studied in [2]. Overall, our proposed data acquisition technique provides a way to generate large-scale training data for learning object placement without any human labeling.

3.2 Learning Object Placements

Objects can have a multitude of possible placements in a given scene. For example, a person could stand on the left or right side of the street, walk across the street, or stand besides a car. To model such diverse and dense object placements is challenging, since the observation of real-world object placements could be sparse. In order to tackle this problem, we design our PlaceNet to achieve two major properties. First, our model is able to share information across sparse observations of foreground and background affordance in order to accumulate knowledge for dense placement predictions. Second, our model has the ability to actively explore diverse possible solutions for object placements.

To share information across sparse observations, our insight is that objects with similar poses and background with similar layouts could share the observed

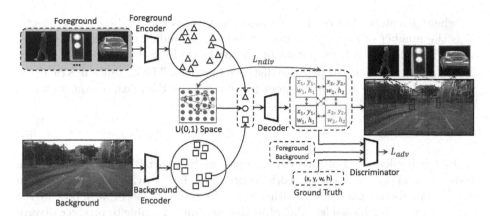

Fig. 3. This is an overview of our PlaceNet. We first encode foreground and backgroud into compact feature vectors, combine them with a random variable sampled from a $U(1,0)$ uniform space, and finally decode to the predicted object placement. The plausibility of predicted placement is checked by a discriminator conditioned on the foreground and the background. The diversity of object placement is achieved by preserving the pairwise distance between predicted placements and the corresponding random variables. The green, blue, yellow, purple circles and boxes denote the sampled random variables and the corresponding predicted placements respectively, and the red dashed double-arrow lines denote the pairwise distance. (Color figure online)

object placement with each other. Therefore, we encode foreground objects and background scenes into two compact feature vectors, where the foreground feature encodes the object semantics and pose and the background feature encodes background layout. We demonstrate that the learned features can indeed encode such information through image retrieval and feature visualization in Sect. 4.7. With the foreground and background features, we further concatenate them with a random variable sampled from $U(1,0)$ uniform distribution, and finally decode to a predicted object placement. In this work, we parameterize object placement as normalized horizontal and vertical locations and scales in the range of $0 \sim 1$.

To achieve active exploration of object placements, our insight is that we can enforce the sampled random variables to generate unique and diverse placement solutions. This is achieved by preserving the pairwise distance of the predicted placements with respect to the pairwise distance of the corresponding random variables in the sampling space [19]. To be more specific, we define the diversity loss as follows in Eq. (1).

$$\mathcal{L}_{ndiv}(y, z) = \frac{1}{N^2 - N} \sum_{i=1}^{N} \sum_{i \neq j}^{N} max(0, \alpha D_{ij}^z - D_{ij}^y) \qquad (1)$$

$$D_{ij}^z = \frac{d_z(z_i, z_j)}{\sum_j d_z(z_i, z_j)} \quad , \quad D_{ij}^y = \frac{d_y(y_i, y_j)}{\sum_j d_y(y_i, y_j)} \qquad (2)$$

where z denotes the random variable, y denotes the predicted placements, N is the number of sampled random variables, i, j indicate the sample indices, and α is a relaxation hyperparameter in the hinge loss. In Eq. (2), D_{ij}^z, $D_{ij}^y \in \mathbb{R}^{N \times N}$ are the normalized pairwise distance matrices. The distance metric $d(\cdot, \cdot)$ for random variable z and placement y is simply the Euclidean distance, which is defined as follows.

$$d_z(z_i, z_j) = ||z_i - z_j|| \quad , \quad d_y(y_i, y_j) = ||y_i - y_j|| \tag{3}$$

In our implementation, we sample four random variables ($N = 4$) at each iteration, and optimize the network to preserve the pairwise distance between the four predicted placements with respect to the four latent variables in the uniform space. With such learning objective, our model is able to produce diverse placement solutions for each pair of foreground and background inputs.

While the diversity loss L_{ndiv} encourages the network to sample diverse placements, we use a conditional GAN loss [22] to check whether the predicted placements are plausible in the meantime. We train a discriminator that takes foreground, background, and object placement as inputs and computes the probability of whether the predicted placement is realistic conditioned on the foreground and background. This conditional adversarial loss is defined as follows,

$$\mathcal{L}_{adv} = E_{x \sim p_{data}(x)} \left[log(D(y|f,b)) \right] + E_{z \sim p(z)} \left[log(1 - D(G(z|f,b)|f,b)) \right] \tag{4}$$

where D is discriminator, G is generator, f is foreground, b is background, y is ground truth placement, z is the random variable, and $G(z|f,b)$ is the predicted placement. To stabilize training, we apply the spectral normalization [23] to scale down the weight matrices in the discriminator by their largest singular values, which effectively restricts the Lipschitz constant of the network.

3.3 Data Augmentation

We randomly select a background to start placing objects, but the starting background could be completely empty and filled in with inpainting or only a few objects removed. This allows us to combine the natural distribution of the object placements with our own generated ones. This essentially can generate more contextually natural and more varied scenes around objects. The overall pipeline is shown in Fig. 4.

After selecting the background, we then choose objects that are semantically similar to the ones previously removed from the scene. This is done because there can be multiple reasons why two instances of the same class might not belong in the same scenes. The most obvious reason why an object might not belong is that some instances are occluded. For example there are many "floating heads" in Cityscapes [4] because cars are in front of the person. This is done by selecting top K nearest neighbors from the foreground database for each of the previously existing objects in the scene. We use our pretrained encoder to extract features of foregrounds and use cosine similarity as a distance metric to

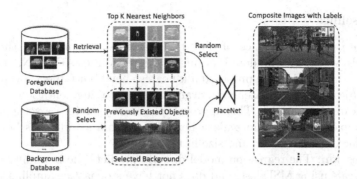

Fig. 4. In our data augmentation pipeline, the foreground database contains masked foreground objects and the background database contains "cleaned" backgrounds with no objects. To make sure the selected foregrounds semantically make sense to be placed into a background, we retrieve top K nearest neighbors of foregrounds with respect to the objects that were previously in the background scene. Then, we randomly select several foregrounds in the retrieved subset of foregrounds and copy-and-paste them into a selected background with predicted locations and scales from our PlaceNet.

find top K neighbors. Basically, the K nearest neighbors search finds a plausible subset of foregrounds to add into a specific background.

From there, we randomly select an object from a retrieved foreground subset and feed them into PlaceNet together with a background image one at a time. From the predicted locations and scales, we simply cut and paste to synthesize the new image. The method of cut-and-paste has been demonstrated by previous works [5,7,30] to not be detrimental for detection or instance segmentation despite the visual flaws at the borders.

Due to the diversity property of the PlaceNet, we are better able to model the probability distribution map of objects in a scene. The modularity of our data composition design allows us to generate any pair of object-context images. These two properties combine to generate novel scenes with contextually related objects that appear sufficiently different yet natural. Another effect of this is that we can decorrelate instances from a specific scene and location using diversity and modularity since objects can be naturally shuffled into different background scenes.

4   Experiments

We evaluate the performance of our method through comparison between strong baselines and the state-of-the-arts in three sub-tasks: object placement, data augmentation for object detection and instance segmentation, and feature learning. In the following sub-sections, we first elaborate our baseline methods and implementation details. Then, we dive into the detailed evaluation and discussion for all the experiments.

4.1   Baselines

To evaluate the performance of object placements, we proposed three baseline models, which are Random Placement, Regression, cVAE-GAN, and cVAE-GAN+Div. In addition, we proposed a k-nearest-neighbor Object Swap baseline and an Object Jitter [7] baseline to evaluate the data augmentation.

Random Placement: This approach places objects into a scene with randomly sampled location and scale, where the random sampling is bounded by the extreme object location and size in the dataset.

Regression: The regression model directly predicts the bounding box location and scale using MSE loss, and does not have stochastic sampling property.

cVAE-GAN [15]: The name of cVAE-GAN is conditional Variational Auto-Encoder with Generative Adversarial Network. This model contains a cVAE to stochastically sample outputs, which are followed by a discriminator to check the plausibility of the outputs.

cVAE-GAN+Div [15,21]: This model is simply the cVAE-GAN model with an additional diversity regularization loss [21].

Object Swap: For each segmented object in the scene, we swap the object with one randomly chosen object from the k-nearest-neighbors in the foreground object database.

Object Jitter [7]: This method proposed to inpaint the segmented object and randomly perturb its original locations with a learned probability heatmap to augment the training data variation.

For our baselines regression, cVAE-GAN and cVAE-GAN+Div, we use the same network architectures for the encoder, decoder, and discriminator modules, and different loss functions. For example, the regression baseline uses MSE loss only. The cVAE-GAN baseline uses KL-Divergence, MSE and adversarial loss with weights of 0.01, 1, 1 respectively. On top of cVAE-GAN, the cVAE-GAN+Div baseline uses an additional diversity loss [21] with weight of 1 that maximize the ratio of the distance between sampled outputs with respect to the corresponding latent codes. The implementation details in the supplementary.

4.2   Object Placements

We evaluate object placement in two criterion: plausibility and diversity. While there is generally a trade-off between plausibility and diversity in generative models [19,21,32], we emphasize that our model aims to produce diverse results without sacrificing the plausibility in the meantime.

For the placement plausibility, we conduct user study that asks user whether the sampled bounding boxes are reasonable for a pair of foreground and background. The final result is averaged across 200 testing examples from ten subjects. In addition, we quantify placement plausibility by computing the Frechet Inception Distance (FID) [12] between composite and real images. Lower FID indicates that the composite distributions are more similar to the real distribution, and that object placements are more realistic and plausible. On the other hand, we compute the diversity of placement by calculating the pairwise

Euclidean distance between pairs of sampled object bounding boxes. Overall, the results indicate that our model can generate much more diverse composite locations with even better plausibility scores, as shown in Table 1 and Fig. 5.

Table 1. Quantitative evaluation of object placements. Our method achieves the highest diversity as well as the best plausibility.

Models	Plausibility (User Study) ↑	Plausibility (FID) ↓	Diversity ↑
Random	22.4%	70.36	0
Regression	73.1%	57.86	0
cVAE-GAN [15]	75.9%	52.13	0.0219
cVAE-GAN+Div [15, 21]	74.5%	53.54	0.0335
PlaceNet (Ours)	**76.4%**	**48.15**	**0.0392**

Fig. 5. This is a qualitative comparison of object placement predictions between two baseline models and our PlaceNet. Our method can generate the most diverse object placements in the comparison.

4.3 Overfitting Inpainting Artifacts?

We study whether the our PlaceNet will overfit to the inpainting artifacts. Theoretically, since many different objects are inpainted at the same time in an image, the network can not use the artifacts as cues to find reasonable placements for a specific class of objects. For example, artifacts of inpainted cars do not provide cues for placements of traffic lights, and vice versa. Empirically, we evaluate how many generated boxes are covering the original object locations. With a Intersection-over-Union (IoU) threshold of 0.5, we observe that only 37.62% of generated boxes are covering the original locations by sampling across 1,000 examples. In Fig. 6, we show four examples that the predicted locations (purple boxes) are not covering the original inpainting object locations (white boxes).

Fig. 6. Inpainting locations (white boxes) and predicted locations (purple boxes). The predicted locations do not covering the inpainting locations most of the time, this indicates that our PlaceNet does not overfit to the inpainting artifacts. (Color figure online)

4.4 Data Augmentation for Object Detection

To evaluate the data augmentation performance for object detection, we use the same detector YOLOv3 [25] on all augmented datasets and use mean average precision (mAP) as the evaluation metric. The baseline is the model trained with the original dataset only. Compared to this baseline, our method can boost the object detection for all the classes except for car, as shown in the last row of Table 2. This comparison shows that our data augmentation can boost the rare and hard class detection by an obvious margin, such as rider and truck, by generating more rare object-and-context scenes to balance out the original data bias.

Compared to the other methods, our method can achieve the best overall mAP performance boosting on both Cityscape [4] and KITTI [9] dataset. From the random placement baseline, we can see that introducing any wrong contextual relationship could harm the data augmentation and perform even worse than the baseline. By looking at the comparison between cVAE-GAN/cVAE-GAN+Div between our method, we can see that by generating more diverse composite scenes, as shown in Table 1, our method can further boost the data augmentation performance. From the visual comparison in Fig. 7, we can see that our method is able to identify bicycle, person, and cars with better precision and recall.

4.5 Data Augmentation for Instance Segmentation

Similarly to object detection, we use the instance segmentation algorithm Mask R-CNN [11] and train it on all the augmented datasets with mAP as the evaluation metric. The quantitative evaluation is shown in Table 3. We show that our method can boost individual class mAP for rider, car, bus, train and motorcycle compared to the baseline. Our method can also achieve the best overall mAP compared to all other methods in both Cityscape [4] and KITTI [9] datasets. Overall, we can see similar performance trend as we have seen in object detection. From the quantitative results of both tasks, we can conclude that generating rare object-and-context scenes could alleviate dataset bias, which boosts the recogni-

Table 2. Object detection on Cityscape [4] and KITTI [9]. We run YOLOv3 [25] detector on all the data augmentation methods, and evaluate the results using mean average precision (mAP).

Object Detection	Cityscape [4]									K ITTI [9]
	Person	Rider	Car	Truck	Bus	Train	Motorcycle	Bicycle	Overall ↑	Overall ↑
Baseline	0.412	0.238	0.754	0.154	0.153	0.105	0.080	0.224	0.265	0.359
Random	0.454	0.278	0.738	0.104	0.135	0.099	0.058	0.218	0.260	0.203
cVAE-GAN [15]	0.441	0.323	0.745	0.154	0.203	0.105	0.104	0.223	0.287	0.274
cVAE-GAN+Div [15,21]	0.462	0.293	0.753	0.214	0.170	0.145	0.059	0.248	0.293	0.322
Object Swap	0.437	0.303	0.757	0.162	0.160	0.123	0.082	0.244	0.283	0.275
Object Jitter [7]	0.441	0.323	0.744	0.154	0.202	0.105	0.104	0.223	0.278	0.354
Object Placement (Ours)	0.448	0.381	0.749	0.200	0.179	0.140	0.088	0.227	**0.302**	**0.371**
Improvement over Baseline	0.036	0.143	-0.005	0.046	0.026	0.035	0.008	0.003	0.037	0.012

Fig. 7. A visual comparison that shows the results from the baseline (top row) and the results from our approach (bottom row) using YOLOv3 [25].

tion performance on the rare classes. In addition, the more diverse the composite scenes could boost more recognition performance.

From the visual comparison in Fig. 8, in the first image, there is a small car clearly ahead of the ego vehicle yet the baseline fails to capture it. In the second picture we detect all the bikes on the bike rack. For the third picture, the baseline has a difficult time in crowded scenes, and it misses multiple people. The motorcycle in the last image is completely missed probably due to its low class appearance. Overall, we can detect more highly occluded and small instances where context is more important for identifying them.

4.6 Feature Representation Learning

A key property of our PlaceNet is to share information across sparse observations such that we can learn a dense distribution of diverse object placements. This property is achieved in that our foreground and background encoders are able to learn feature representations that can cluster foreground and background based on their semantics and functionality. By clustering objects and scenes in the latent space, our network can then share the object-and-context relationships from the sparse observations of objects/scenes pairs.

We run the k-nearest-neighbor image retrieval on the foreground and background images using the learned encoders. As shown in Fig. 9, foreground

Table 3. Instance segmentation on Cityscape [4] and KITTI [9]. We run Mask R-CNN [11] detector on all the data augmentation methods, and evaluate the results using mean average precision (mAP).

Instance Segmentation	Cityscape [4]									KITTI [9]
	Person	Rider	Car	Truck	Bus	Train	Motorcycle	Bicycle	Overall ↑	Overall ↑
Baseline	0.202	0.069	0.620	0.495	0.493	0.156	0.133	0.118	0.286	0.235
Random	0.210	0.097	0.619	0.449	0.471	0.143	0.128	0.118	0.279	0.228
cVAE-GAN [15]	0.210	0.093	0.616	0.477	0.460	0.162	0.112	0.113	0.281	0.243
cVAE-GAN+Div [15,21]	0.213	0.090	0.620	0.496	0.478	0.187	0.133	0.104	0.291	0.247
Object Swap	0.221	0.087	0.621	0.481	0.481	0.155	0.129	0.117	0.287	0.254
Object Jitter [7]	0.202	0.164	0.627	0.465	0.479	0.196	0.143	0.121	0.300	0.281
Object Placement (Ours)	0.198	0.080	0.621	0.487	0.512	0.264	0.143	0.109	**0.302**	**0.307**
Improve over Baseline	−0.004	0.011	0.001	-0.008	0.019	0.108	0.010	−0.009	0.016	0.072

Fig. 8. A visual comparison that shows the results from the baseline (top row) and the results from our approach (bottom row) using Mask R-CNN [11].

features can cluster object pose regardless of appearance and the background features can cluster background scenes with similar scene layouts. We further visualize the feature activation of background encoders, and find that the background features implicitly segments the street and non-street regions, which encode the street scene layout, as shown in Fig. 10.

In addition to image retrieval and feature visualization, we test out how well the pretrained encoder can be used for foreground image classification. In this experiment, we collect 10K foreground images for training and 1K foreground images for testing, and we aim to classify eight classes of semantic objects in Cityscape [4]. We set up three experiment trials, where we use 1K, 5K ,and 10K training images in each of the three trials. We compare the model trained from scratch and the model that fine-tunes on the learned foreground encoder from PlaceNet. As shown in Table 4, the PlaceNet encoder can consistently outperform the model trained from scratch. This experiment, once again, shows that our PlaceNet can learn meaningful and discriminative feature representation.

Table 4. Comparison between model trained from scratch and model fine-tuned on the foreground encoder on image classification. The numbers in the 2nd and 3rd columns are the classification accuracy on 1K testing images when using different amount of training data.

Number of Training Images	Classifier Trained from Scratch	PlaceNet foreground encoder
1,000	34.3%	46.5%
5,000	52.5%	74.8%
10,000	67.7%	86.3%

Fig. 9. Foreground and background image retrieval. The foreground encoder can retrieve the objects based on the semantics and pose regardless of color. The background encoder can retrieve the scene based on the street layouts.

Fig. 10. Visualization of feature activation from the background encoder. This shows that the features fire on street segments and non-street segments, which encode the street layout.

5   Conclusion

We formulated the self-learning task of object placement. We first proposed a novel data generation technique that can generate large-scale training data for 'free'. Then, we proposed PlaceNet that can learn the distribution of diverse and plausible locations to place a given object into a background. We show that our object placement provides two useful side-effects. First, our learned PlaceNet can be used to shuffle segmented objects into different background scenes to enrich object-context variations for boosting object detection and segmentation. Second, we show that our self-learning PlaceNet can learn meaningful feature representations for object/scene retrieval and classification. Extensive experiments have been conducted to demonstrate the effectiveness of our method for data augmentation.

References

1. Azadi, S., Pathak, D., Ebrahimi, S., Darrell, T.: Compositional gan: Learning image-conditional binary composition. arXiv preprint arXiv:1807.07560 (2019)
2. Bau, D., et al.: Seeing what a gan cannot generate. In: Proceedings of the IEEE International Conference on Computer Vision. pp. 4502–4511 (2019)
3. Carr, M.F., Jadhav, S.P., Frank, L.M.: Hippocampal replay in the awake state: a potential substrate for memory consolidation and retrieval. Nat. Neurosci. **14**(2), 147 (2011)
4. Cordts, M., et al.: The cityscapes dataset for semantic urban scene understanding. In: Proceedings of the IEEE Conference on Computer Vision and Pattern Recognition. pp. 3213–3223 (2016)
5. Dvornik, N., Mairal, J., Schmid, C.: Modeling visual context is key to augmenting object detection datasets. In: Proceedings of the European Conference on Computer Vision (ECCV). pp. 364–380 (2018)
6. Dwibedi, D., Misra, I., Hebert, M.: Cut, paste and learn: Surprisingly easy synthesis for instance detection. In: Proceedings of the IEEE International Conference on Computer Vision. pp. 1301–1310 (2017)
7. Fang, H.S., Sun, J., Wang, R., Gou, M., Li, Y.L., Lu, C.: Instaboost: boosting instance segmentation via probability map guided copy-pasting. arXiv preprint arXiv:1908.07801 (2019)
8. Fu, C.Y., Liu, W., Ranga, A., Tyagi, A., Berg, A.C.: Dssd: deconvolutional single shot detector. arXiv preprint arXiv:1701.06659 (2017)
9. Geiger, A., Lenz, P., Stiller, C., Urtasun, R.: Vision meets robotics: the kitti dataset. In: International Journal of Robotics Research (IJRR) (2013)
10. Georgakis, G., Mousavian, A., Berg, A.C., Kosecka, J.: Synthesizing training data for object detection in indoor scenes. arXiv preprint arXiv:1702.07836 (2017)
11. He, K., Gkioxari, G., Dollár, P., Girshick, R.: Mask r-cnn. In: Proceedings of the IEEE International Conference on Computer Vision. pp. 2961–2969 (2017)
12. Heusel, M., Ramsauer, H., Unterthiner, T., Nessler, B., Hochreiter, S.: Gans trained by a two time-scale update rule converge to a local nash equilibrium. In: Advances in Neural Information Processing Systems. pp. 6626–6637 (2017)
13. Jaderberg, M., Simonyan, K., Zisserman, A., et al.: Spatial transformer networks. In: Advances in Neural Information Processing Systems. pp. 2017–2025 (2015)
14. Kingma, D.P., Welling, M.: Auto-encoding variational bayes. arXiv preprint arXiv:1312.6114 (2013)
15. Larsen, A.B.L., Sønderby, S.K., Larochelle, H., Winther, O.: Autoencoding beyond pixels using a learned similarity metric. arXiv preprint arXiv:1512.09300 (2015)
16. Lee, D., Liu, S., Gu, J., Liu, M.Y., Yang, M.H., Kautz, J.: Context-aware synthesis and placement of object instances. In: Advances in Neural Information Processing Systems. pp. 10393–10403 (2018)
17. Li, X., Liu, S., Kim, K., Wang, X., Yang, M.H., Kautz, J.: Putting humans in a scene: Learning affordance in 3d indoor environments. In: Proceedings of the IEEE Conference on Computer Vision and Pattern Recognition. pp. 12368–12376 (2019)
18. Lin, C.H., Yumer, E., Wang, O., Shechtman, E., Lucey, S.: St-gan: Spatial transformer generative adversarial networks for image compositing. In: Proceedings of the IEEE Conference on Computer Vision and Pattern Recognition. pp. 9455–9464 (2018)
19. Liu, S., Zhang, X., Wangni, J., Shi, J.: Normalized diversification. In: Proceedings of the IEEE Conference on Computer Vision and Pattern Recognition. pp. 10306–10315 (2019)

20. Liu, W., Anguelov, D., Erhan, D., Szegedy, C., Reed, S., Fu, C.-Y., Berg, A.C.: SSD: single shot multibox detector. In: Leibe, B., Matas, J., Sebe, N., Welling, M. (eds.) ECCV 2016. LNCS, vol. 9905, pp. 21–37. Springer, Cham (2016). https://doi.org/10.1007/978-3-319-46448-0_2

21. Mao, Q., Lee, H.Y., Tseng, H.Y., Ma, S., Yang, M.H.: Mode seeking generative adversarial networks for diverse image synthesis. In: Proceedings of the IEEE Conference on Computer Vision and Pattern Recognition. pp. 1429–1437 (2019)

22. Mirza, M., Osindero, S.: Conditional generative adversarial nets. arXiv preprint arXiv:1411.1784 (2014)

23. Miyato, T., Kataoka, T., Koyama, M., Yoshida, Y.: Spectral normalization for generative adversarial networks. arXiv preprint arXiv:1802.05957 (2018)

24. Oliva, A., Torralba, A.: The role of context in object recognition. Trends Cogn. Sci. 11(12), 520–527 (2007)

25. Redmon, J., Farhadi, A.: Yolov3: An incremental improvement. arXiv preprint arXiv:1804.02767 (2018)

26. Ren, S., He, K., Girshick, R., Sun, J.: Faster r-cnn: towards real-time object detection with region proposal networks. In: Advances in Neural Information Processing Systems. pp. 91–99 (2015)

27. Tan, F., Bernier, C., Cohen, B., Ordonez, V., Barnes, C.: Where and who? automatic semantic-aware person composition. In: 2018 IEEE Winter Conference on Applications of Computer Vision (WACV). pp. 1519–1528. IEEE (2018)

28. Torralba, A., Murphy, K.P., Freeman, W.T., Rubin, M.A.: Context-based vision system for place and object recognition (2003)

29. Tripathi, S., Chandra, S., Agrawal, A., Tyagi, A., Rehg, J.M., Chari, V.: Learning to generate synthetic data via compositing. In: Proceedings of the IEEE Conference on Computer Vision and Pattern Recognition. pp. 461–470 (2019)

30. Wang, H., Wang, Q., Yang, F., Zhang, W., Zuo, W.: Data augmentation for object detection via progressive and selective instance-switching (2019)

31. Yu, J., Lin, Z., Yang, J., Shen, X., Lu, X., Huang, T.S.: Generative image inpainting with contextual attention. In: Proceedings of the IEEE Conference on Computer Vision and Pattern Recognition. pp. 5505–5514 (2018)

32. Zhu, J.Y., et al.: Toward multimodal image-to-image translation. In: Advances in Neural Information Processing Systems. pp. 465–476 (2017)

Deep Vectorization of Technical Drawings

Vage Egiazarian[1]([✉])(iD), Oleg Voynov[1](iD), Alexey Artemov[1](iD),
Denis Volkhonskiy[1](iD), Aleksandr Safin[1](iD), Maria Taktasheva[1](iD),
Denis Zorin[1,2], and Evgeny Burnaev[1](iD)

[1] Skolkovo Institute of Science and Technology,
3 Nobel Street, Skolkovo 143026, Russian Federation
{vage.egiazarian,oleg.voinov,a.artemov,denis.volkhonskiy,
aleksandr.safin,maria.taktasheva,e.burnaev}@skoltech.ru
[2] New York University, 70 Washington Square South, New York, NY 10012, USA
dzorin@cs.nyu.edu
http://adase.group/3ddl/projects/vectorization

Abstract. We present a new method for vectorization of technical line drawings, such as floor plans, architectural drawings, and 2D CAD images. Our method includes (1) a deep learning-based cleaning stage to eliminate the background and imperfections in the image and fill in missing parts, (2) a transformer-based network to estimate vector primitives, and (3) optimization procedure to obtain the final primitive configurations. We train the networks on synthetic data, renderings of vector line drawings, and manually vectorized scans of line drawings. Our method quantitatively and qualitatively outperforms a number of existing techniques on a collection of representative technical drawings.

Keywords: Transformer network · Vectorization · Floor plans · Technical drawings

1 Introduction

Vector representations are often used for technical images, such as architectural and construction plans and engineering drawings. Compared to raster images, vector representations have a number of advantages. They are scale-independent, much more compact, and, most importantly, support easy primitive-level editing. These representations also provide a basis for higher-level semantic structure in drawings (*e.g.*, with sets of primitives hierarchically grouped into semantic objects).

However, in many cases, technical drawings are available only in raster form. Examples include older drawings done by hand, or for which only the hard copy

---

V. Egiazarian and O. Voynov—Equal contribution.
A. Artemov—Technical lead.

Electronic supplementary material The online version of this chapter (https://doi.org/10.1007/978-3-030-58601-0_35) contains supplementary material, which is available to authorized users.

A. Vedaldi et al. (Eds.): ECCV 2020, LNCS 12358, pp. 582–598, 2020.
https://doi.org/10.1007/978-3-030-58601-0_35

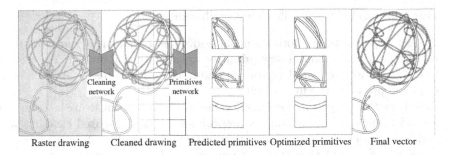

Raster drawing   Cleaned drawing   Predicted primitives Optimized primitives   Final vector

Fig. 1. An overview of our vectorization method. First, the input image is cleaned with a deep CNN. Then, the clean result is split into patches, and primitive placement in each patch is estimated with a deep neural network. After that, the primitives in each patch are refined via iterative optimization. Finally, the patches are merged together into a single vector image.

is available, and the sources were lost, or images in online collections. When the vector representation of a drawing document is unavailable, it is reconstructed, typically by hand, from scans or photos. Conversion of a raster image to a vector representation is usually referred to as *vectorization.*

While different applications have distinct requirements for vectorized drawings, common goals for vectorization are:

- approximate the semantically or perceptually important parts of the input image well;
- remove, to the extent possible, the artifacts or extraneous data in the images, such as missing parts of line segments and noise;
- minimize the number of used primitives, producing a compact and easily editable representation.

We note that the first and last requirements are often conflicting. *E.g.*, in the extreme case, for a clean line drawing, 100% fidelity can be achieved by "vectorizing" every pixel with a separate line.

In this paper, we aim for geometrically precise and compact reconstruction of vector representations of technical drawings in a fully automatic way. Distinctive features of the types of drawings we target include the prevalence of simple shapes (line segments, circular arcs, etc.) and relative lack of irregularities (such as interruptions and multiple strokes approximating a single line) other than imaging flaws. We develop a system which takes as input a technical drawing and vectorizes it into a collection of line and curve segments (Fig. 1). Its elements address vectorization goals listed above. The central element is a deep-learning accelerated optimization method that matches geometric primitives to the raster image. This component addresses the key goal of finding a compact representation of a part of the raster image (a *patch*) with few vector primitives. It is preceded by a learning-based image preprocessing stage, that removes background and noise and performs infill of missing parts of the image, and is followed by a simple heuristic postprocessing stage, that further reduces the number of primitives by merging the primitives in adjacent patches.

Our paper includes the following contributions:

1. We develop a novel vectorization method. It is based on a learnable deep vectorization model and a new primitive optimization approach. We use the model to obtain an initial vector approximation of the image, and the optimization produces the final result.
2. Based on the proposed vectorization method, we demonstrate a complete vectorization system, including a preprocessing learning-based cleaning step and a postprocessing step aiming to minimize the number of primitives.
3. We conduct an ablation study of our approach and compare it to several state-of-the-art methods.

2   Related Work

Vectorization. There is a large number of methods for image and line drawing vectorization. However, these methods solve somewhat different, often imprecisely defined versions of the problem and target different types of inputs and outputs. Some methods assume clean inputs and aim to faithfully reproduce all geometry in the input, while others aim, *e.g.*, to eliminate multiple close lines in sketches. Our method is focused on producing an accurate representation of input images with mathematical primitives.

One of the widely used methods for image vectorization is Potrace [33]. It requires a clean, black-and-white input and extracts boundary curves of dark regions, solving a problem different from ours (*e.g.*, a single line or curve segment is always represented by polygon typically with many sides). Recent works [21,27] use Potrace as a stage in their algorithms.

Another widely used approach is based on curve network extraction and topology cleanup   [3,5,6,11,17,28,29]. The method of [11] creates the curve network with a region-based skeleton initialization followed by morphological thinning. It allows to manually tune the simplicity of the result trading off its fidelity. The method of [3] uses a polyvector field (crossfield) to guide the orientation of primitives. It applies a sophisticated set of tuneable heuristics which are difficult to tune to produce clean vectorizations of technical drawings with a low number of primitives. The authors of [28] focus on speeding up sketch vectorization without loss of accuracy by applying an auxiliary grid and a summed area table. We compare to [3] and [11] which we found to be the best-performing methods in this class.

Neural Network-based Vectorization. To get the optimal result, the methods like [3,11] require manual tuning of hyper-parameters for each individual input image. In contrast, the neural network-based approach that we opt for is designed to process large datasets without tuning.

The method of [24] generates vectorized, semantically annotated floor plans from raster images using neural networks. At vectorization level, it detects a limited set of axis-aligned junctions and merges them, which is specific to a subset of floor plans (*e.g.*, does not handle diagonal or curved walls).

In [10] machine learning is used to extract a higher-level representation from a raster line drawing, specifically a program generating this drawing. This approach does not aim to capture the geometry of primitives faithfully and is restricted to a class of relatively simple diagrams.

A recent work [13] focuses on improving the accuracy of topology reconstruction. It extracts line junctions and the centerline image with a two headed convolutional neural network, and then reconstructs the topology at junctions with another neural network.

The algorithm of [12] has similarities to our method: it uses a neural network-based initialization for a more precise geometry fit for Bézier curve segments. Only simple input data (MNIST characters) are considered for line drawing reconstruction. The method was also applied to reconstructing 3D surfaces of revolution from images.

An interesting recent direction is generation of sketches using neural networks that learn a latent model representation for sketch images [14,18,39]. In principle, this approach can be used to approximate input raster images, but the geometric fidelity, in this case, is not adequate for most applications. In [38] an algorithm for generating collections of color strokes approximating an input photo is described. While this task is related to line drawing vectorization it is more forgiving in terms of geometric accuracy and representation compactness.

We note that many works on vectorization focus on sketches. Although the line between different types of line drawings is blurry, we found that methods focusing exclusively on sketches often produce less desirable results for technical line drawings (*e.g.*, [11] and [9]).

Vectorization Datasets. Building a large-scale real-world vectorization dataset is costly and time-consuming [23,35]. One may start from raster dataset and create a vector ground-truth by tracing the lines manually. In this case, both location and the style may be difficult to match to the original drawing. Another way is to start from the vector image and render the raster image from it. This approach does not necessarily produce realistic raster images, as degradation suffered by real-world documents are known to be challenging to model [20]. As a result, existing vectorization-related datasets either lack vector annotation (*e.g.*, CVC-FP [16], Rent3D [25], SydneyHouse [7], and Raster-to-Vector [24] all provide semantic segmentation masks for raster images but not the vector ground truth) or are synthetic (*e.g.*, SESYD [8], ROBIN [34], and FPLAN-POLY [31]).

Image Preprocessing. Building a complete vectorization system based on our approach requires the initial preprocessing step that removes imaging artefacts. Preprocessing tools available in commonly used graphics editors require manual parameter tuning for each individual image. For a similar task of conversion of hand-drawn sketches into clean raster line drawings the authors of [32,35] use convolutional neural networks trained on synthetic data. The authors of [23] use a neural network to extract structural lines (*e.g.*, curves separating image regions) in manga cartoon images. The general motivation behind the network-based approach is that a convolutional neural network automatically adapts to different types of images and different parts of the image, without individual parameter tuning. We build our preprocessing step based on the ideas of [23,35].

Other Related Work. Methods solving other vectorization problems include, *e.g.*, [19,37], which approximate an image with adaptively refined constant color regions with piecewise-linear boundaries; [26] which extracts a vector representation of road networks from aerial photographs; [4] which solves a similar problem and is shown to be applicable to several types of images. These methods use strong build-in priors on the topology of the curve networks.

3   Our Vectorization System

Our vectorization system, illustrated in Fig. 1, takes as the input a raster technical drawing cleared of text and produces a collection of graphical primitives defined by the control points and width, namely line segments and quadratic Bézier curves. The processing pipeline consists of the following steps:

1. We preprocess the input image, removing the noise, adjusting its contrast, and filling in missing parts;
2. We split the cleaned image into patches and for each patch estimate the initial primitive parameters;
3. We refine the estimated primitives aligning them to the cleaned raster;
4. We merge the refined predictions from all patches.

3.1   Preprocessing of the Input Raster Image

The goal of the preprocessing step is to convert the raw input data into a raster image with clear line structure by eliminating noise, infilling missing parts of lines, and setting all background/non-ink areas to white. This task can be viewed as semantic image segmentation in that the pixels are assigned the background or foreground class. Following the ideas of [23,35], we preprocess the input image with U-net [30] architecture, which is widely used in segmentation tasks. We train our preprocessing network in the image-to-image mode with binary cross-entropy loss.

3.2   Initial Estimation of Primitives

To vectorize a clean raster technical drawing, we split it into patches and for each patch independently estimate the primitives with a feed-forward neural network. The division into patches increases efficiency, as the patches are processed in parallel, and robustness of the trained model, as it learns on simple structures.

We encode each patch $I_p \in [0,1]^{64 \times 64}$ with a ResNet-based [15] feature extractor $X^{\mathrm{im}} = \mathrm{ResNet}\,(I_p)$, and then decode the feature embeddings of the primitives X_i^{pr} using a sequence of n_{dec} Transformer blocks [36]

$$X_i^{\mathrm{pr}} = \mathrm{Transformer}\left(X_{i-1}^{\mathrm{pr}}, X^{\mathrm{im}}\right) \in \mathbb{R}^{n_{\mathrm{prim}} \times d_{\mathrm{emb}}}, \qquad i = 1, \ldots, n_{\mathrm{dec}}. \qquad (1)$$

Each row of a feature embedding represents one of the n_{prim} estimated primitives with a set of d_{emb} hidden parameters. The use of Transformer architecture allows to vary the number of output primitives per patch. The maximum number of primitives is set with the size of the 0th embedding $X_0^{\mathrm{pr}} \in \mathbb{R}^{n_{\mathrm{prim}} \times d_{\mathrm{emb}}}$, initialized with positional encoding, as described in [36]. While the number of primitives in a patch is *a priori* unknown, more than 97% of patches in our data contain no more than 10 primitives. Therefore, we fix the maximum number of primitives and filter out the excess predictions with an additional stage. Specifically, we pass the last feature embedding to a fully-connected block, which extracts the coordinates of the control points, the widths of the primitives $\Theta = \{\boldsymbol{\theta}_k = (x_{k,1}, y_{k,1}, \dots, w_k)\}_{k=1}^{n_{\mathrm{prim}}}$, and the confidence values $\boldsymbol{p} \in [0,1]^{n_{\mathrm{prim}}}$. The latter indicate that the primitive should be discarded if the value is lower than 0.5. We detail more on the network in supplementary.

Loss Function. We train the primitive extraction network with the multi-task loss function composed of binary cross-entropy of the confidence and a weighted sum of L_1 and L_2 deviations of the parameters

$$L\left(\boldsymbol{p}, \hat{\boldsymbol{p}}, \Theta, \hat{\Theta}\right) = \frac{1}{n_{\mathrm{prim}}} \sum_{k=1}^{n_{\mathrm{prim}}} \left(L_{\mathrm{cls}}\left(p_k, \hat{p}_k\right) + L_{\mathrm{loc}}\left(\boldsymbol{\theta}_k, \hat{\boldsymbol{\theta}}_k\right)\right), \tag{2}$$

$$L_{\mathrm{cls}}\left(p_k, \hat{p}_k\right) = -\hat{p}_k \log p_k - (1 - \hat{p}_k) \log (1 - p_k), \tag{3}$$

$$L_{\mathrm{loc}}\left(\boldsymbol{\theta}_k, \hat{\boldsymbol{\theta}}_k\right) = (1 - \lambda) \|\boldsymbol{\theta}_k - \hat{\boldsymbol{\theta}}_k\|_1 + \lambda \|\boldsymbol{\theta}_k - \hat{\boldsymbol{\theta}}_k\|_2^2. \tag{4}$$

The target confidence vector $\hat{\boldsymbol{p}}$ is all ones, with zeros in the end indicating placeholder primitives, all target parameters $\hat{\boldsymbol{\theta}}_k$ of which are set to zero. Since this function is not invariant w.r.t. to permutations of the primitives and their control points, we sort the endpoints in each target primitive and the target primitives by their parameters lexicographically.

3.3   Refinement of the Estimated Primitives

We train our primitive extraction network to minimize the average deviation of the primitives on a large dataset. However, even with small average deviation, individual estimations may be inaccurate. The purpose of the refinement step is to correct slight inaccuracies in estimated primitives.

To refine the estimated primitives and align them to the raster image, we design a functional that depends on the primitive parameters and raster image and iteratively optimize it w.r.t. the primitive parameters

$$\Theta^{\mathrm{ref}} = \underset{\Theta}{\arg\min}\, E\left(\Theta, I_p\right). \tag{5}$$

We use physical intuition of attracting charges spread over the area of the primitives and placed in the filled pixels of the raster image. To prevent alignment of different primitives to the same region, we model repulsion of the primitives.

We define the optimized functional as the sum of three terms per primitive

$$E\left(\Theta^{\mathrm{pos}}, \Theta^{\mathrm{size}}, I_p\right) = \sum_{k=1}^{n_{\mathrm{prim}}} E_k^{\mathrm{size}} + E_k^{\mathrm{pos}} + E_k^{\mathrm{rdn}}, \tag{6}$$

where $\Theta^{\mathrm{pos}} = \{\theta_k^{\mathrm{pos}}\}_{k=1}^{n_{\mathrm{prim}}}$ are the primitive position parameters, $\Theta^{\mathrm{size}} = \{\theta_k^{\mathrm{size}}\}_{k=1}^{n_{\mathrm{prim}}}$ are the size parameters, and $\theta_k = \left(\theta_k^{\mathrm{pos}}, \theta_k^{\mathrm{size}}\right)$.

We define the position of a line segment by the coordinates of its midpoint and inclination angle, and the size by its length and width. For a curve arc, we define the midpoint at the intersection of the curve and the bisector of the angle between the segments connecting the middle control point and the endpoints. We use the lengths of these segments, and the inclination angles of the segments connecting the "midpoint" with the endpoints.

Charge Interactions. We base different parts of our functional on the energy of interaction of unit point charges r_1, r_2, defined as a sum of close- and far-range potentials

$$\varphi\left(r_1, r_2\right) = e^{-\frac{\|r_1 - r_2\|^2}{R_c^2}} + \lambda_{\mathrm{f}} e^{-\frac{\|r_1 - r_2\|^2}{R_f^2}}, \tag{7}$$

parameters R_c, R_f, λ_{f} of which we choose experimentally. The energy of interaction of the uniform positively charged area of the kth primitive Ω_k and a grid of point charges $q = \{q_i\}_{i=1}^{n_{\mathrm{pix}}}$ at the pixel centers r_i is then defined by the following equation, that we integrate analytically for lines

$$E_k\left(q\right) = \sum_{i=1}^{n_{\mathrm{pix}}} q_i \iint_{\Omega_k} \varphi\left(r, r_i\right) dr^2 \tag{8}$$

We approximate it for curves as the sum of integrals over the segments of the polyline flattening this curve.

In our functional we use three different charge grids, encoded as vectors of length n_{pix}: $\hat{q}$ represents the raster image with charge magnitudes set to intensities of the pixels, q_k represents the rendering of the kth primitive with its current values of parameters, and q represents the rendering of all the primitives in the patch. The charge grids q_k and q are updated at each iteration.

Energy Terms. Below, we denote the componentwise product of vectors with $\odot$, and the vector of ones of an appropriate size with $\mathbf{1}$.

The first term is responsible for growing the primitive to cover filled pixels and shrinking it if unfilled pixels are covered, with fixed position of the primitive:

$$E_k^{\mathrm{size}} = E_k\left([q - \hat{q}] \odot c_k + q_k \odot [1 - c_k]\right). \tag{9}$$

The weighting $c_{k,i} \in \{0, 1\}$ enforces coverage of a continuous raster region following the form and orientation of the primitive. We set $c_{k,i}$ to 1 inside the largest region aligned with the primitive with only shaded pixels of the raster, as we detail in supplementary. For example, for a line segment, this region is a rectangle centered at the midpoint of the segment and aligned with it.

The second term is responsible for alignment of fixed size primitives

$$E_k^{\text{pos}} = E_k \left([\boldsymbol{q} - \boldsymbol{q}_k - \hat{\boldsymbol{q}}] \odot [\boldsymbol{1} + 3\boldsymbol{c}_k] \right). \tag{10}$$

The weighting here adjusts this term with respect to the first one, and subtraction of the rendering of the kth primitive from the total rendering of the patch ensures that transversal overlaps are not penalized.

The last term is responsible for collapse of overlapping *collinear* primitives; for this term, we use $\lambda_{\text{f}} = 0$:

$$E_k^{\text{rdn}} = E_k \left(\boldsymbol{q}_k^{\text{rdn}} \right), \, q_{k,i}^{\text{rdn}} = \exp \left(- \left[|\boldsymbol{l}_{k,i} \cdot \boldsymbol{m}_{k,i}| - 1 \right]^2 \beta \right) \|\boldsymbol{m}_{k,i}\|, \tag{11}$$

where $\boldsymbol{l}_{k,i}$ is the direction of the primitive at its closest point to the ith pixel, $\boldsymbol{m}_{k,i} = \sum_{j \neq k} \boldsymbol{l}_{j,i} q_{j,i}$ is the sum of directions of all the other primitives weighted w.r.t. their "presence", and $\beta = (\cos 15° - 1)^{-2}$ is chosen experimentally.

As our functional is based on many-body interactions, we can use an approximation well-known in physics—mean field theory. This translates into the observation that one can obtain an approximate solution of (5) by viewing interactions of each primitive with the rest as interactions with a static set of charges, i.e., viewing each energy term E_k^{pos}, E_k^{size}, E_k^{rdn} as depending only on the parameters of the kth primitive. This enables very efficient gradient computation for our functional, as one needs to differentiate each term w.r.t. a small number of parameters only. We detail on this heuristic in supplementary.

We optimize the functional (6) by Adam. For faster convergence, every few iterations we join lined up primitives by stretching one and collapsing the rest, and move collapsed primitives into uncovered raster pixels.

3.4 Merging Estimations from All Patches

To produce the final vectorization, we merge the refined primitives from the whole image with a straightforward heuristic algorithm. For lines, we link two primitives if they are close and collinear enough but not almost parallel. After that, we replace each connected group of linked primitives with a single least-squares line fit to their endpoints. Finally, we snap the endpoints of intersecting primitives by cutting down the "dangling" ends shorter than a few percent of the total length of the primitive. For Bézier curves, for each pair of close primitives we estimate a replacement curve with least squares and replace the original pair with the fit if it is close enough. We repeat this operation for the whole image until no more pairs allow a close fit. We detail on this process in supplementary.

4 Experimental Evaluation

We evaluate two versions of our vectorization method: one operating with lines and the other operating with quadratic Bézier curves. We compare our method against FvS [11], CHD [9], and PVF [3]. We evaluate the vectorization performance with four metrics that capture artefacts illustrated in Fig. 2.

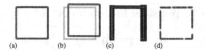

Fig. 2. (a) Ground-truth vector image, and artefacts w.r.t. which we evaluate the vectorization performance (b) skeleton structure deviation, (c) shape deviation, (d) overparameterization.

Intersection-over-Union (IoU) reflects deviations in two raster shapes or rasterized vector drawings R_1 and R_2 via $\mathrm{IoU}(R_1, R_2) = \frac{R_1 \cap R_2}{R_1 \cup R_2}$. It does not capture deviations in graphical primitives that have similar shapes but are slightly offset from each other.

Hausdorff distance

$$d_{\mathrm{H}}(X, Y) = \max \left\{ \sup_{x \in X} \inf_{y \in Y} d(x, y), \ \sup_{y \in Y} \inf_{x \in X} d(x, y) \right\}, \tag{12}$$

and **Mean Minimal Deviation**

$$d_{\mathrm{M}}(X, Y) = \frac{1}{2} \left(\widetilde{d_{\mathrm{M}}}(X \to Y) + \widetilde{d_{\mathrm{M}}}(Y \to X) \right), \tag{13a}$$

$$\widetilde{d_{\mathrm{M}}}(X \to Y) = \int_{x \in X} \inf_{y \in Y} d(x, y) dX \Big/ \int_{x \in X} dX \tag{13b}$$

measure the difference in skeleton structures of two vector images X and Y, where $d(x, y)$ is Euclidean distance between a pair of points x, y on skeletons. In practice, we densely sample the skeletons and approximate these metrics on a pair of point clouds.

Number of Primitives #P measures the complexity of the vector drawing.

4.1   Clean Line Drawings

To evaluate our vectorization system on clean raster images with precisely known vector ground-truth we collected two datasets.

To demonstrate the performance of our method with lines, we compiled **PFP vector floor plan dataset** of 1554 real-world architectural floor plans from a commercial website [2].

To demonstrate the performance of our method with curves, we compiled **ABC vector mechanical parts dataset** using 3D parametric CAD models from ABC dataset [22]. They have been designed to model mechanical parts with sharp edges and well defined surface. We prepared $\approx 10k$ vector images via projection of the boundary representation of CAD models with the open-source software Open Cascade [1].

We trained our primitive extraction network on random 64×64 crops, with random rotation and scaling. We additionally augmented PFP with synthetic data, illustrated in Fig. 3.

Fig. 3. Examples of synthetic training data for our primitive extraction network.

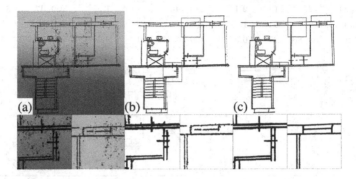

Fig. 4. Sample from DLD dataset: (a) raw input image, (b) the image cleaned from background and noise, (c) final target with infilled lines.

For evaluation, we used 40 hold-out images from PFP and 50 images from ABC with resolution $\sim 2000 \times 3000$ and different complexity per pixel. We specify image size alongside each qualitative result. We show the quantitative results of this evaluation in Table 1 and the qualitative results in Figs. 5 and 6. Since the methods we compare with produce widthless skeleton, for fair comparison w.r.t. IoU we set the width of the primitives in their outputs equal to the average on the image.

There is always a trade-off between the number of primitives in the vectorized image and its precision, so the comparison of the results with different number primitives is not to fair. On PFP, our system outperforms other methods w.r.t. all metrics, and only loses in primitive count to FvS. On ABC, PVF outperforms our full vectorization system w.r.t. IoU, but not our vectorization method without merging, as we discuss below in ablation study. It also produces much more primitives than our method.

4.2 Degraded Line Drawings

To evaluate our vectorization system on real raster technical drawings, we compiled **Degraded line drawings dataset (DLD)** out of 81 photos and scans of floor plans with resolution $\sim 1300 \times 1000$. To prepare the raster targets, we manually cleaned each image, removing text, background, and noise, and refined the line structure, inpainting gaps and sharpening edges (Fig. 4).

To train our preprocessing network, we prepared the dataset consisting of 20000 synthetic pairs of images of resolution 512×512. We rendered the ground truth in each pair from a random set of graphical primitives, such as lines,

Table 1. Quantitative results of vectorization. For our method we report two values of IoU: with the average primitive width and with the predicted.

	PFP				ABC				DLD	
	IoU,%	d_H, px	d_M, px	#P	IoU,%	d_H, px	d_M, px	#P	IoU,%	#P
FvS [11]	31	381	2.8	696	65	38	1.7	63		
CHD [9]	22	214	2.1	1214	60	9	1	109	47	329
PVF [3]	60	204	1.5	38k	89	17	0.7	7818		
Our	86/88	25	0.2	1331	77/77	19	0.6	97	79/82	452

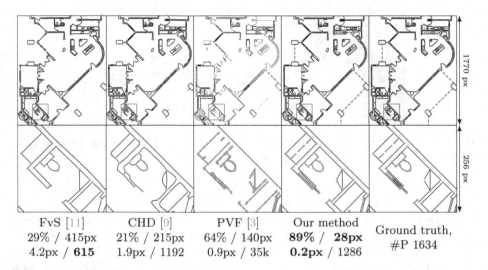

FvS [11]	CHD [9]	PVF [3]	Our method	Ground truth,
29% / 415px	21% / 215px	64% / 140px	**89%** / **28px**	#P 1634
4.2px / **615**	1.9px / 1192	0.9px / 35k	**0.2px** / 1286	

Fig. 5. Qualitative comparison on a PFP image, and values of IoU / d_H / d_M / #P with best in bold. Endpoints of the primitives are shown in orange (Color figure online).

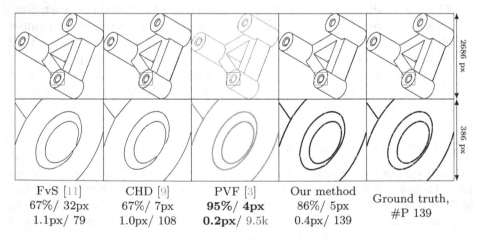

FvS [11]	CHD [9]	PVF [3]	Our method	Ground truth,
67% / 32px	67%/ 7px	**95%**/ **4px**	86%/ 5px	#P 139
1.1px/ 79	1.0px/ 108	**0.2px**/ 9.5k	0.4px/ 139	

Fig. 6. Qualitative comparison on an ABC image, and values of IoU / d_H / d_M / #P with best in bold. Endpoints of the primitives are shown in orange (Color figure online).

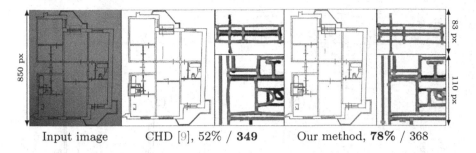

Input image   CHD [9], 52% / **349**   Our method, **78%** / 368

Fig. 7. Qualitative comparison on a real noisy image, and values of IoU / #P with best in bold. Primitives are shown in blue with endpoints in orange on top of the cleaned raster image.

Table 2. Quantitative evaluation of the preprocessing step.

	IoU,%	PSNR
MS [35]	49	15.7
Our	**92**	**25.5**

curves, circles, hollow triangles, etc. We generated the input image via rendering the ground truth on top of one of 40 realistic photographed and scanned paper backgrounds selected from images available online, and degrading the rendering with random blur, distortion, noise, etc. After that, we fine-tuned the preprocessing network on DLD.

For evaluation, we used 15 hold-out images from DLD. We show the quantitative results of this evaluation in Table 1 and the qualitative results in Fig. 7. Only CHD allows for degraded input so we compare with this method only. Since this method produces widthless skeleton, for fair comparison w.r.t. IoU we set the width of the primitives in its outputs equal to the average on the image, that we estimate as the sum of all nonzero pixels divided by the length of the predicted primitives.

Our vectorization system outperforms CHD on the real floor plans w.r.t. IoU and produces similar number of primitives.

Evaluation of Preprocessing Network. We separately evaluate our preprocessing network comparing with public pre-trained implementation of MS [35]. We show the quantitative results of this evaluation in Table 2 and qualitative results in Fig. 8. Our preprocessing network keeps straight and repeated lines commonly found in technical drawing while MS produces wavy strokes and tends to join repeated straight lines, thus harming the structure of the drawing.

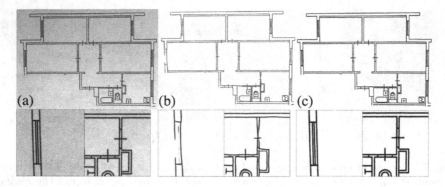

Fig. 8. Example of preprocessing results: (a) raw input image, (b) output of MS [35], (c) output of our preprocessing network. Note the tendency of MS to combine close parallel lines.

Table 3. Ablation study on ABC dataset. We compare the results of our method with and without refinement and postprocessing

	IoU,%	d_H, px	d_M, px	#P
NN	65	52	1.4	309
NN + Refinement	91	19	0.3	240
NN + Refinement + Postprocessing	77	19	0.6	97

4.3 Ablation Study

To assess the impact of individual components of our vectorization system on the results, we obtained the results on the ABC dataset with the full system, the system without the postprocessing step, and the system without the postprocessing and refinement steps. We show the quantitative results in Table 3 and the qualitative results in Fig. 9.

While the primitive extraction network produces correct estimations on average, some estimations are severely inaccurate, as captured by d_H. The refinement step improves all metrics, and the postprocessing step reduces the number of primitives but deteriorates other metrics due to the trade-off between number of primitives and accuracy.

We note that our vectorization method without the final merging step outperforms other methods on ABC dataset in terms of accuracy metrics.

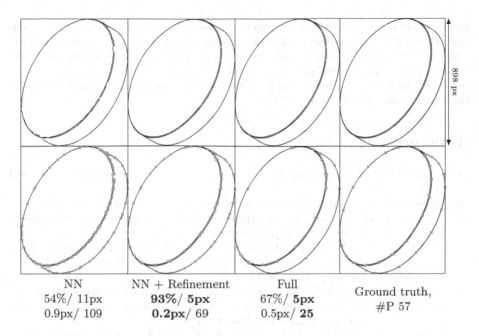

898 px

NN	NN + Refinement	Full	Ground truth,
54%/ 11px	**93%/ 5px**	67%/ **5px**	#P 57
0.9px/ 109	**0.2px/ 69**	0.5px/ **25**	

Fig. 9. Results of our method on an ABC image with and without refinement and postprocessing, and values of IoU / d_H / d_M / #P with best in bold. The endpoints of primitives are shown in orange (Color figure online).

5 Conclusion

We presented a four-part system for vectorization of technical line drawings, which produces a collection of graphical primitives defined by the control points and width. The first part is the preprocessing neural network that cleans the input image from artefacts. The second part is the primitive extraction network, trained on a combination of synthetic and real data, which operates on patches of the image. It estimates the primitives approximately in the right location most of the time, however, it is generally geometrically inaccurate. The third part is iterative optimization, which adjusts the primitive parameters to improve the fit. The final part is heuristic merging, which combines the primitives from different patches into single vectorized image. The evaluation shows that our system, in general, performs significantly better compared to a number of recent vectorization algorithms.

Modifications of individual parts of our system would allow it to be applied to different, related tasks. For example, adjustment of the preprocessing network and the respective training data would allow for application of our system to extraction of wireframe from a photo. Modification of the optimized functional and use of the proper training data for primitive extraction network would allow for sketch vectorization. Integration with an OCR system would allow for separation and enhancement of text annotations.

Acknowledgements. We thank Milena Gazdieva and Natalia Soboleva for their valuable contributions in preparing real-world raster and vector datasets, as well as Maria Kolos and Alexey Bokhovkin for contributing parts of shared codebase used throughout this project. We acknowledge the usage of Skoltech CDISE HPC cluster Zhores for obtaining the presented results. The work was partially supported by Russian Science Foundation under Grant 19–41-04109.

References

1. Open CASCADE Technology OCCT. https://www.opencascade.com/, Accessed 05 March 2005
2. PrecisionFloorplan. http://precisionfloorplan.com, Accessed 05 March 2020
3. Bessmeltsev, M., Solomon, J.: Vectorization of line drawings via polyvector fields. ACM Trans. Graph. (TOG) **38**(1), 9 (2019)
4. Chai, D., Forstner, W., Lafarge, F.: Recovering line-networks in images by junction-point processes. In: Proceedings of the IEEE Conference on Computer Vision and Pattern Recognition. pp. 1894–1901 (2013)
5. Chen, J., Du, M., Qin, X., Miao, Y.: An improved topology extraction approach for vectorization of sketchy line drawings. The Visual Comput. **34**(12), 1633–1644 (2018). https://doi.org/10.1007/s00371-018-1549-z
6. Chen, J.Z., Lei, Q., Miao, Y.W., Peng, Q.S.: Vectorization of line drawing image based on junction analysis. Sci. China Inf. Sci. **58**(7), 1–14 (2015). https://doi.org/10.1007/s11432-014-5246-x
7. Chu, H., Wang, S., Urtasun, R., Fidler, S.: HouseCraft: building houses from rental ads and street views. In: Leibe, B., Matas, J., Sebe, N., Welling, M. (eds.) ECCV 2016. LNCS, vol. 9910, pp. 500–516. Springer, Cham (2016). https://doi.org/10.1007/978-3-319-46466-4_30
8. Delalandre, M., Valveny, E., Pridmore, T., Karatzas, D.: Generation of synthetic documents for performance evaluation of symbol recognition & spotting systems. Int. J. Document Anal. Recogn. (IJDAR) **13**(3), 187–207 (2010)
9. Donati, L., Cesano, S., Prati, A.: A complete hand-drawn sketch vectorization framework. Multimed. Tools Appl. **78**(14), 19083–19113 (2019). https://doi.org/10.1007/s11042-019-7311-3
10. Ellis, K., Ritchie, D., Solar-Lezama, A., Tenenbaum, J.: Learning to infer graphics programs from hand-drawn images. In: Advances in Neural Information Processing Systems. pp. 6059–6068 (2018)
11. Favreau, J.D., Lafarge, F., Bousseau, A.: Fidelity vs. simplicity: a global approach to line drawing vectorization. ACM Trans. Graph. (TOG) **35**(4), 120 (2016)
12. Gao, J., Tang, C., Ganapathi-Subramanian, V., Huang, J., Su, H., Guibas, L.J.: Deepspline: Data-driven reconstruction of parametric curves and surfaces. arXiv preprint arXiv:1901.03781 (2019)
13. Guo, Y., Zhang, Z., Han, C., Hu, W.B., Li, C., Wong, T.T.: Deep line drawing vectorization via line subdivision and topology reconstruction. Comput. Graph. Forum **38**, 81–90 (2019)
14. Ha, D., Eck, D.: A neural representation of sketch drawings. arXiv preprint arXiv:1704.03477 (2018)
15. He, K., Zhang, X., Ren, S., Sun, J.: Deep residual learning for image recognition. In: Proceedings of the IEEE Conference on Computer Vision and Pattern Recognition. pp. 770–778 (2016)

16. de las Heras, L.-P., Terrades, O.R., Robles, S., Sánchez, G.: CVC-FP and SGT: a new database for structural floor plan analysis and its groundtruthing tool. Int. J. Document Anal. Recogn (IJDAR) **18**(1), 15–30 (2015). https://doi.org/10.1007/s10032-014-0236-5

17. Hilaire, X., Tombre, K.: Robust and accurate vectorization of line drawings. IEEE Trans. Pattern Anal. Mach. Intell. **6**, 890–904 (2006)

18. Kaiyrbekov, K., Sezgin, M.: Stroke-based sketched symbol reconstruction and segmentation. arXiv preprint arXiv:1901.03427 (2019)

19. Kansal, R., Kumar, S.: A vectorization framework for constant and linear gradient filled regions. The Visual Comput. **31**(5), 717–732 (2014). https://doi.org/10.1007/s00371-014-0997-3

20. Kanungo, T., Haralick, R.M., Baird, H.S., Stuezle, W., Madigan, D.: A statistical, nonparametric methodology for document degradation model validation. IEEE Trans. Pattern Anal. Mach. Intell. **22**(11), 1209–1223 (2000)

21. Kim, B., Wang, O., Öztireli, A.C., Gross, M.: Semantic segmentation for line drawing vectorization using neural networks. In: Computer Graphics Forum. vol. 37, pp. 329–338. Wiley Online Library (2018)

22. Koch, S., et al.: Abc: A big cad model dataset for geometric deep learning. In: Proceedings of the IEEE Conference on Computer Vision and Pattern Recognition. pp. 9601–9611 (2019)

23. Li, C., Liu, X., Wong, T.T.: Deep extraction of manga structural lines. ACM Trans. Graph. (TOG) **36**(4), 117 (2017)

24. Liu, C., Wu, J., Kohli, P., Furukawa, Y.: Raster-to-vector: revisiting floorplan transformation. In: Proceedings of the IEEE International Conference on Computer Vision. pp. 2195–2203 (2017)

25. Liu, C., Schwing, A.G., Kundu, K., Urtasun, R., Fidler, S.: Rent3d: Floor-plan priors for monocular layout estimation. In: Proceedings of the IEEE Conference on Computer Vision and Pattern Recognition. pp. 3413–3421 (2015)

26. Máttyus, G., Luo, W., Urtasun, R.: Deeproadmapper: Extracting road topology from aerial images. In: Proceedings of the IEEE International Conference on Computer Vision. pp. 3438–3446 (2017)

27. Munusamy Kabilan, V., Morris, B., Nguyen, A.: Vectordefense: Vectorization as a defense to adversarial examples. arXiv preprint arXiv:1804.08529 (2018)

28. Najgebauer, P., Scherer, R.: Inertia-based fast vectorization of line drawings. Comput. Graph. Forum **38**, 203–213 (2019)

29. Noris, G., Hornung, A., Sumner, R.W., Simmons, M., Gross, M.: Topology-driven vectorization of clean line drawings. ACM Trans. Graph. (TOG) **32**(1), 4 (2013)

30. Ronneberger, O., Fischer, P., Brox, T.: U-Net: convolutional networks for biomedical image segmentation. In: Navab, N., Hornegger, J., Wells, W.M., Frangi, A.F. (eds.) MICCAI 2015. LNCS, vol. 9351, pp. 234–241. Springer, Cham (2015). https://doi.org/10.1007/978-3-319-24574-4_28

31. Rusiñol, M., Borràs, A., Lladós, J.: Relational indexing of vectorial primitives for symbol spotting in line-drawing images. Pattern Recogn. Lett. **31**(3), 188–201 (2010)

32. Sasaki, K., Iizuka, S., SimoSerra, E., Ishikawa, H.: Learning to restore deteriorated line drawing. The Visual Comput. **34**(6–8), 1077–1085 (2018)

33. Selinger, P.: Potrace: a polygon-based tracing algorithm. Potrace. http://potrace.sourceforge.net/potrace.pdf (2003)

34. Sharma, D., Gupta, N., Chattopadhyay, C., Mehta, S.: Daniel: A deep architecture for automatic analysis and retrieval of building floor plans. In: 2017 14th IAPR International Conference on Document Analysis and Recognition (ICDAR). vol. 1, pp. 420–425. IEEE (2017)
35. Simo-Serra, E., Iizuka, S., Ishikawa, H.: Mastering sketching: adversarial augmentation for structured prediction. ACM Trans. Graph. (TOG) **37**(1), 11 (2018)
36. Vaswani, A., et al.: Attention is all you need. In: Advances in Neural Information Processing Systems. pp. 5998–6008 (2017)
37. Zhao, J., Feng, J., Zhou, B.: Image vectorization using blue-noise sampling. In: Imaging and Printing in a Web 2.0 World IV International Society for Optics and Photonics. vol. 8664, p. 86640H (2013)
38. Zheng, N., Jiang, Y., Huang, D.: Strokenet: Aneural painting environment. In: International Conference on Learning Representations (2018)
39. Zhou, T., et al.: Learning to doodle with stroke demonstrations and deep q-networks. In: BMVC. p. 13 (2018)

CAD-Deform: Deformable Fitting of CAD Models to 3D Scans

Vladislav Ishimtsev[1], Alexey Bokhovkin[1(✉)], Alexey Artemov[1],
Savva Ignatyev[1], Matthias Niessner[2], Denis Zorin[1,3], and Evgeny Burnaev[1]

[1] Skolkovo Institute of Science and Technology, Moscow, Russia
`alexey.bokhovkin@skoltech.ru`
[2] Technical University of Munich, Munich, Germany
[3] New York University, New York, USA

Abstract. Shape retrieval and alignment are a promising avenue towards turning 3D scans into lightweight CAD representations that can be used for content creation such as mobile or AR/VR gaming scenarios. Unfortunately, CAD model retrieval is limited by the availability of models in standard 3D shape collections (*e.g.*, ShapeNet). In this work, we address this shortcoming by introducing CAD-Deform (The code for the project: https://github.com/alexeybokhovkin/CAD-Deform), a method which obtains more accurate CAD-to-scan fits by non-rigidly deforming retrieved CAD models. Our key contribution is a new non-rigid deformation model incorporating smooth transformations and preservation of sharp features, that simultaneously achieves very tight fits from CAD models to the 3D scan and maintains the clean, high-quality surface properties of hand-modeled CAD objects. A series of thorough experiments demonstrate that our method achieves significantly tighter scan-to-CAD fits, allowing a more accurate digital replica of the scanned real-world environment while preserving important geometric features present in synthetic CAD environments.

Keywords: Scene reconstruction · Mesh deformation

1 Introduction

A wide range of sensors such as the Intel RealSense, Google Tango, or Microsoft Kinect can acquire point cloud data for indoor environments. These data can be subsequently used for reconstructing 3D scenes for augmented and virtual reality, indoor navigation and other applications [12,25,32,33,40,42]. However,

---

V. Ishimtsev and A. Bokhovkin—equal contribution.
A. Artemov—Technical lead.

Electronic supplementary material The online version of this chapter (https://doi.org/10.1007/978-3-030-58601-0_36) contains supplementary material, which is available to authorized users.

A. Vedaldi et al. (Eds.): ECCV 2020, LNCS 12358, pp. 599–628, 2020.
https://doi.org/10.1007/978-3-030-58601-0_36

available 3D reconstruction algorithms are not sufficient for many applied scenarios as the quality of the result may be significantly affected by noise, missing data, and other artifacts such as motion blur found in real scans, disabling reconstruction of fine-scale and sharp geometric features of objects. In most instances, reconstructions are still very distant from the clean, 3D models created manually.

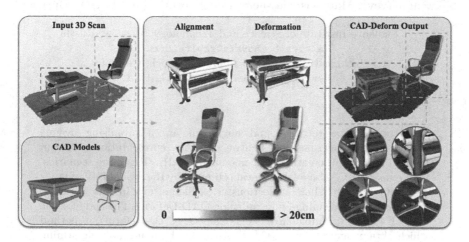

Fig. 1. CAD-Deform takes as input a set of 3D CAD models aligned on a RGB-D scan (left). In order to achieve tight fits (middle), we propose a novel part-based deformation formulation that maintains the desired CAD properties such as sharp features.

An approach to overcome these problems has been proposed in [30,36] and more recently developed using modern ML methods in [5,6]. Building on the availability of parametric (CAD) models [9,27] they perform reconstruction by finding and aligning similar CAD models from a database to each object in a noisy scan. To realize this approach, the authors of [5] introduced the Scan2CAD dataset comprising of pairwise keypoint correspondences and 9 DoF (degrees of freedom) alignments between instances of unique synthetic models from ShapeNet [9] and reconstructed scans from ScanNet [11]; in order to find and align CAD models to an input scan, they developed a deep neural model to predict correspondences, with a further optimization over potential matching correspondences for each candidate CAD model. The difference of [6] compared to the approach from [5] is an end-to-end procedure, combining initially decoupled steps to take into account additional feedback through the pipeline by learning the correspondences specifically tailored for the final alignment task.

However, geometric fidelity achieved between scans and CAD objects remains limited. CAD model geometry (clean and complete) differs significantly from scan geometry in low-level geometric features. As these methods focus on finding alignments by optimizing a small number of parameters (9 DoF), resulting alignments only roughly approximate scans, not capturing geometric details such as variation in 3D shapes of parts of individual objects.

In contrast, to improve geometric fidelity while keeping the benefit of mesh-based representations, we propose to increase the number of degrees of freedom by allowing the CAD objects to *deform* rather than stay rigid. In this work, we introduce a deformation framework CAD-Deform, which significantly increases the geometric quality of object alignment regardless of the alignment scheme. For an input scan, given object location and 9 DoF alignment of a potentially matching CAD model, we apply a specially designed mesh deformation procedure resulting in a more accurate shape representation of the underlying object. The deformation matches each semantic part of a 3D shape extracted from the PartNet [31] to the corresponding data in the scans and keeps sufficient rigidity and smoothness to produce perceptually acceptable results while minimizing the distance to scanned points. Thus, even if the initial location and alignment are not entirely accurate, the deformation can compensate to a significant extent for the discrepancy.

Our approach builds highly detailed scene descriptions with a high level of semantic accuracy for applications in 3D graphics. The approach outperforms state-of-the-art methods for CAD model alignment and mesh deformation by 2.1–6.3% for real-world 3D scans. To the best of our knowledge, the approach we propose is the first to use mesh deformation for scan-to-CAD alignment and real-world scene reconstruction. In summary, our work has several contributions:

- We developed a mesh deformation approach that 1) is computationally efficient, 2) does not require exact correspondences between each candidate CAD model and input scan, and 3) provides perceptually plausible deformation thanks to a specially introduced smoothness term and inclusion of geometric features of a CAD model in the optimization functional.
- We developed a methodology to assess the fitting accuracy and the perceptual quality of the scan-to-CAD reconstruction. The methodology includes standard data fitting criteria similar to Chamfer distance to evaluate alignment accuracy, complimentary local and global criteria for visual quality assessment of resulting deformations, and a user study.
- We performed an ablation study to assess the influence of inaccuracies in the initial object location and alignment on the final reconstruction results. For that we used both ground-truth alignments from Scan2CAD dataset [5] along with predictions of their method, and alignments trained in the end-to-end fashion [6]. We compared results with the state-of-the-art methods for mesh deformation to highlight the advantages of our approach.

2   Related Work

RGB-D Scanning and Reconstruction. RGB-D scanning and reconstruction are increasingly widely used, due to the availability of commodity range sensors and can be done both in real-time and offline modes. There are many methods for RGB-D-based real-time reconstruction such as KinectFusion [25], Voxel Hashing [33] or Bundle Fusion [12] that use the well-known volumetric fusion approach from [10]. ElasticFusion [42] is a representative offline approach to the reconstruction. These methods can produce remarkable results for large 3D environments. However, due to occlusions and imperfections of existing sensors, the reconstructed scenes contain many artifacts such as noise, missing surface parts, or over-smooth surfaces. Some methods aim to predict unobserved or corrupted parts of 3D scans from depth data. In [18], the world is modeled as a grid of voxels representing the signed distance to the nearest surface. Then structured Random Forest is used to predict the value of the signed distance function for each of the voxels computed to form a final occupancy estimate for unobserved voxels. [37] is to encode a depth map as a 3D volume and then aggregate both local geometric and contextual information via a 3D CNN to produce the probability distribution of voxel occupancy and object categories for all voxels inside the camera view frustum. Another approach is [13], where a 3D CNN architecture predicts a distance field from a partially-scanned input and finds the closest 3D CAD model from a shape database. By copying voxels from the nearest shape neighbors, they construct a high-resolution output from the low-resolution predictions, hierarchically synthesize a higher-resolution voxel output, and extracts the mesh from the implicit distance field. However, although all these methods can complete partial scans and improve 3D geometry reconstruction, the quality of the results still is far from artist-created 3D content.

CAD Model Alignment. Instead of reconstructing 3D geometry in a bottom-up manner, one can perform reconstruction by retrieving CAD models from a dataset and aligning them to the noisy scans. Matching CAD models to scans requires extracting 3D feature descriptors; thus, approaches have been proposed for 3D feature extraction. Hand-crafted features are often based on various histograms of local characteristics (*e.g.*, [16]). Such approaches do not generalize well to inherent variability and artifacts in real-world scans. Deep learning approaches lead to further improvements: *e.g.*, [43] propose a view consistency loss for a 3D keypoint prediction network based on RGB-D data; [14] develop 3D local learnable features for pairwise registration. After the descriptors are extracted, one can use a standard pipeline for CAD-to-scan alignment: first, matches between points based on 3D descriptors are identified, and then variational alignment is used to compute 6- or 9-DoF CAD model alignments. Typical examples, realizing this two-step approach, are described in [5,6,28,30,36]. The most recent ones [5,6] use learnable descriptors and differ in that the latter considers an end-to-end scan-to-CAD alignment, reconstructing a scene in a single forward pass. An obvious limitation of these two-step pipelines is that the resulting alignments approximate scans only coarsely due to a pre-defined set of available CAD models and a highly constrained range of transformations. Other approaches in this category [4,21,22], although relying on the same two-step strategy, use only a single RGB or RGB-D input.

Mesh Deformation. To improve surface reconstruction accuracy and obtain a more faithful description of geometric details (*e.g.*, preserve distinctive geometric features), it is desirable to consider a more general space of deformations than a simple non-uniform scaling. To this end, a mesh deformation approach based on Laplacian surface editing is presented in [39]. Another iterative mesh deformation scheme [38] imposes rigidity on the local transformations. Despite their conceptual simplicity, both methods require specifying correspondences between mesh vertices and scan data points. The same is true for [1,3,29] and unsuitable in our setting, due to extremely low (2–8) number of correspondences available per part, that additionally may not even be well defined for noisy and incomplete real-world scans. Many methods [1,8,15,34] focus on automatic posing of human models, dense surface tracking and similar applications. However, while producing compelling results, the methods implicitly use the assumption that a template mesh and its target shape are very similar; as a result, the semantic parts of individual 3D objects are not changed either in shape or relative scale. In our work, we are comparing to ARAP (as-rigid-as-possible) [38] and Harmonic [7,26] mesh deformation methods, however, with an added Laplacian smoothing term to leverage second-order information about the surface. This modification makes ARAP/Harmonic similar to [1,29] as far as non-data-dependent energy terms are concerned. Other methods exist that propose non-linear constraints [19,20,23]. The energy terms of our framework were designed as a natural match for our problem: we define local 3D transformations on the CAD model, mapping each subpart to the 3D scene volume, and require smooth changes of these transformations over the model. In contrast to most deformation methods, we do not aim to keep the surface close to isometric: *e.g.*, a table reference model can be stretc.hed highly anisotropically to match a different table in the data. Our energy is defined using local 3D affine transform primitives, penalizing sharp changes, without penalizing anisotropic deformations. These primitives also allow us to express 1D feature preservation simply, and the non-data terms are quadratic which is critical for our efficient preconditioned optimization. Methods in [19,20,23] propose non-linear energies, focusing on large rotations, but implicitly assuming quasi-isometry; adapting these methods is nontrivial.

3   Overview of CAD-Deform Framework

Our approach is built on top of the framework from [5,6] for CAD model retrieval and 9 DoF alignment in 3D scans. By running any of the approaches from [5,6] for an input scan, we obtain initial object locations and 9 DoF alignments of CAD models potentially matching specific parts of the scan. Next, we apply our proposed mesh deformation procedure (see Sect. 4), resulting in a more accurate shape representation of the aligned objects:

1. We segment the CAD models into semantic 3D parts following the labelling from the PartNet dataset [31].
2. For each aligned object, we select points in the scan that are the nearest (within some fixed radius) to each vertex of the CAD model. We assign a label of the nearest part of the aligned CAD model to each such point.
3. As an input to the proposed mesh deformation procedure, we use the mesh model with semantic part labels and labelled segment of the 3D scene.
4. We deform the mesh by optimizing the energy depending on the relative positions of mesh vertices and labelled points of the scene, see Sect. 4.

4 Data-Driven Shape Deformation

In this section, we describe our method for fitting a closest-match mesh from the shape dataset to the scanned data. Our algorithm assumes two inputs:

- an initial mesh M from the dataset, with part labels assigned to vertices and 9 degrees-of-freedom ($9\,\mathrm{DoF}$) transformation assigned to mesh;
- a subset of the scanned data, segmented with the same part labels as M.

Figure 2 shows an example of the input data, see also Sect. 3.

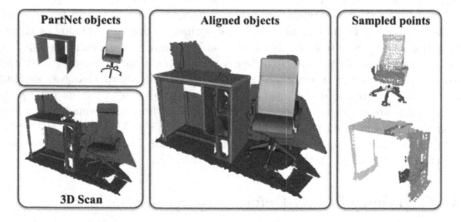

Fig. 2. Data acquisition for CAD-Deform: we project PartNet labels onto aligned ShapeNet CAD models (left), register these models to a 3D scene scan (middle), and extract points on the scene within ε-neighborhood of aligned mesh surface (we set $\varepsilon = 10\,\mathrm{cm}$), copying labels corresponding to nearest part of CAD model (right).

Notations. A mesh $\mathbf{M} = (\mathbf{V}^0, \mathbf{E}, \mathbf{F})$ consists of a set of initial 3D vertex coordinates $\mathbf{V}^0$ of size n_v, the edge set $\mathbf{E}$ of size n_e, and the triangle face set $\mathbf{F}$ of size n_f. We compute the deformed vertex positions $\mathbf{V}$ by minimizing a deformation energy. All vertices are assigned with part labels, which is a map $\mathbf{Q} : \mathbf{V}^0 \rightarrow \mathbf{C}$, where $\mathbf{C}$ is the set of labels $c_i, i = 1, \ldots, n_c$, and n_c is the number of parts in all objects in our dataset. For a mesh $\mathbf{M}_m$, $\mathbf{C}_m \subset \mathbf{C}$ is the set of labels of its parts. The set of $n_\mathbf{P}$ points $\mathbf{P}$ has the same labels as the mesh $\mathbf{M}_m$ we fit, *i.e.*, $\mathbf{C}_\mathbf{P} = \mathbf{C}_m$. In addition, we assume that for every mesh $\mathbf{M}_m$ on the scan we have a scaling transformation, represented by a 4×4 matrix T_m^0, that aligns it with voxelized points $\mathbf{P}$. In our optimization, we use *per-edge* transformations T_e, discussed below, which we use to measure the deviation from a scaled version of the original shape and deformation smoothness.

4.1   Deformation Energy

Our goal is to define a deformation energy to match the scanned data as closely as possible, while maintaining continuity and deformation smoothness, and penalizing deviation from the original shape. In addition, we include a term that preserves perceptually important linear geometric features of the mesh.

Conceptually, we follow common mesh deformation methods such as ARAP [38] which estimate a local transformation from vertex positions and penalize the deviation of this transformation from the target (*e.g.*, closest rotation). An important distinction is that the transformation we need to estimate locally is a 3D, rather than 2D transformation, and cannot be estimated from the deformed positions of vertices of a single triangle.

Edge Transformations. We associate local 3D affine transformations with mesh edges. Each transformation is defined in a standard way by a 4×4 matrix in projective coordinates, with the last row $(0, 0, 0, c)$, $c \neq 0$. The vertices of two faces (i_1, i_2, i_3) and (i_2, i_1, i_4), incident at an edge $e = (i_1, i_2)$, form a (possibly degenerate) tetrahedron. If it is not degenerate, then there is a unique linear transformation T_e mapping the undeformed positions $(v_{i_1}^0, v_{i_2}^0, v_{i_3}^0, v_{i_4}^0)$ to $(v_{i_1}, v_{i_2}, v_{i_3}, v_{i_4})$. Matrix T^0 of the affine transformation has 12 coefficients that are uniquely determined by the equations $T_e v_i^0 = v_i$, $i = 1 \ldots 4$; moreover, these are linear functions of the deformed positions v_i, as these are only present on the right-hand side of the equations. Handling of degenerate tetrahedra is discussed in Sect. 4.2.

Energy. We define the following non-linear objective for the unknown deformed vertex positions $\mathbf{V}$ and (a fixed) point set $\mathbf{P}$:

$$\mathcal{E}(\mathbf{V}, \mathbf{P}) = \underbrace{\boxed{E_{\text{shape}} + \alpha_{\text{smooth}} E_{\text{smooth}} + \alpha_{\text{sharp}} E_{\text{sharp}}}}_{\text{quadratic problem}} + \alpha_{\text{data}} E_{\text{data}} + \alpha_{\text{Lap}} E_{\text{Lap}},$$

$$E_{\text{shape}} = \underbrace{\sum_{e \in \mathbf{E}} \|T_e(\mathbf{V}) - T_e^0\|_2^2}_{\text{deviation}}; \qquad E_{\text{smooth}} = \sum_{f \in \mathbf{F}} \sum_{e_i, e_j \in f} \|T_{e_i}(\mathbf{V}) - T_{e_j}(\mathbf{V})\|_2^2;$$

$$E_{\text{sharp}} = \sum_{k=1}^{n_p} \sum_{e_s \in \mathbf{E}_{\text{sharp}}^k} \|T_{e_s}(\mathbf{V}) - T_{e_{s+1}}(\mathbf{V})\|_2^2; \qquad E_{\text{data}} = f_{\text{data}}(\mathbf{V}, \mathbf{P}). \qquad (1)$$

The first term penalizes deviations of the 3D affine transformations defined by the deformed vertex positions from the transformation (a non-uniform scale) that aligns mesh with the data. This term directly attempts to preserve the shape of the object, modulo rescaling.

As explained above, the transformations $T_e(\mathbf{V})$ are defined for non-degenerate input mesh configurations. Suppose the four initial vertex positions $(v_{i_1}^0, v_{i_2}^0, v_{i_3}^0, v_{i_4}^0)$ form a degenerate tetrahedron $\mathbf{W}$, *i.e.*, two faces incident at the edge are close to co-planar. In this case, we use an energy term consisting of two terms defined per triangle. Instead of 4×4 matrix for each non-degenerate tetrahedron, there is a 3×2 matrix for each triangular face of degenerate tetrahedron that represents a transformation restricted to the plane of this face. Note that in this case, the deformation in the direction perpendicular to the common plane of the triangles does not affect the energy, as it does not have an impact on the local shape of the deformed surface. We explain the remaining energy terms in the next sections.

To bring second-order information about mesh surface in our energy formulation, we add the Laplacian smoothness term $E_{\text{Lap}}(\mathbf{V}, \mathbf{V}') = \sum_{i=1}^{|\mathbf{V}|} \|L(v_i) - L(v_i')\|^2$, where $L(v_i) = \frac{1}{\mathcal{N}_i} \sum_{j=1}^{|\mathcal{N}(i)|} v_j$ and $\mathcal{N}(i)$ is a set of one-ring neighbors of vertex $v_i \in \mathbf{V}$ ($v_i' \in \mathbf{V}'$).

4.2   Quadratic Terms

Smoothness Term. This term can be thought of as a discrete edge-based Laplacian, applied to the transforms associated with edges: the difference of any pair of transforms for edges belonging to the same triangle is penalized.

Sharp Features Term. We have observed that a simple way to preserve some of the perceptually critical geometric aspects of the input meshes is to penalize the change of deformations T_e along sharp geometric features, effectively preserving their overall shape (although still allowing, possibly non-uniform, scaling, rotations and translations). We detect sharp edges based on a simple dihedral angle thresholding, as this is adequate for the classes of CAD models we use. Detected sharp edges are concatenated in sequences, each consisting of vertices with exactly two incident sharp edges each, except the first and the last. Those sequences are defined for each part of the mesh. Sequences of different parts has no common sharp edges or vertices belonging to them. Effectively, the sharpness term increases the weights for some edges in the smoothness term.

4.3 Data Term

We use two approaches to defining the data term, one based on screened attraction between close points in the mesh $\mathbf{M}_m$ and $\mathbf{P}$, and the other one based on attraction between *a priori* chosen corresponding points of the mesh $\mathbf{M}_m$ and data points in the set $\mathbf{P}$. We found that the former method works better globally, when the deformed mesh is still far from the target point cloud, while the latter is able to achieve a better match once a closer approximation is obtained.

Part-to-Part Mapping. We define a data-fitting term based on point proximity: we set an energy proportional to the distance between sufficiently close points. To avoid clustering of mesh points, we add a screening term that disables attraction for mesh vertices close to a given point.

We denote by $H(x)$ the Heaviside function, *i.e.*, a function with value 1 if $x \geqslant 0$ and zero otherwise. We set

$$f_{\text{data}}^{\text{p2p}}(\mathbf{V}, \mathbf{P}) = \sum_{c \in \mathbf{C}} \sum_{v \in \mathbf{V}_c} \sum_{p \in \mathbf{P}_c} \xi^\sigma(p, \mathbf{V}_c)\left(d^\varepsilon(v - p)\right)^2, \tag{2}$$

where $d^\varepsilon(v-p) = (v-p) \cdot H(\varepsilon - \|v-p\|_2^2)$, and $\xi^\sigma(p, \mathbf{V}) = H(\min_{\{v \in \mathbf{V}\}} \|v-p\| - \sigma)$ is a "screening" function. The value for σ is chosen to be the mean edge length, the value of ε is about 10 edge lengths. To make $f_{\text{data}}^{\text{p2p}}$ differentiable, instead of the Heaviside function and min, we can use their smoothed approximations.

Nearest-neighbor Mapping. Recall that the vertices $\{v_i\}$ of the mesh m and the points $\{p_i\}$ of the set $\mathbf{P}$ have the same part label sets $\mathbf{C}_m = \mathbf{C}_{\mathbf{P}}$. For each label c, we consider $\mathbf{V}_c^0$ and $\mathbf{P}_c$, the set of mesh vertices in initial positions and the set of points with the same label c in $\mathbf{P}$. Let $B_{\mathbf{V}_c}, B_{\mathbf{P}_c}$ be the bounding boxes of these sets, and consider the affine transform T_B^c that maps $B_{\mathbf{V}_c}$ to $B_{\mathbf{P}_c}$. Among all possible correspondences between corners of the boxes, we choose the one that produces the affine transform closest to identity. Then the index $i = \iota^T(p)$ of the vertex v_i, corresponding to a point $p \in \mathbf{P}_c$, is determined as $\iota^c(p) = \arg\min_{\{i, v_i \in \mathbf{V}_c\}} \|T_B^c v_i - p\|_2^2$. Then the data term is defined as

$$f_{\text{data}}^{\text{nn}}(\mathbf{V}, \mathbf{P}) = \sum_{c \in \mathbf{C}} \sum_{p \in \mathbf{P}_c} \|p - v_{\iota^c(p)}\|_2^2. \tag{3}$$

4.4 Optimization

The optimization of (1) is highly nonlinear due to the data term. However, all other terms are quadratic functions of vertex coordinates, so minimizing

$$E_{\text{quad}} = E_{\text{shape}} + \alpha_{\text{smooth}} E_{\text{smooth}} + \alpha_{\text{sharp}} E_{\text{sharp}}$$

$$= \overline{\mathbf{V}}^\top A_{\text{shape}} \overline{\mathbf{V}} + \alpha_{\text{smooth}} \overline{\mathbf{V}}^\top A_{\text{smooth}} \overline{\mathbf{V}} + \alpha_{\text{sharp}} \overline{\mathbf{V}}^\top A_{\text{sharp}} \overline{\mathbf{V}} + b^\top \overline{\mathbf{V}}$$

is equivalent to solving a system of linear equations. Denoting the sum of the matrices in the equation by A_{quad}, we obtain the optimum by solving $A_{\text{quad}} \overline{\mathbf{V}} = 0$ where the vector $\overline{\mathbf{V}}$ is a flattening of the vector $\mathbf{V}$ of 3D vertex positions to a vector of length $3n_{\mathbf{V}}$.

The data term is highly nonlinear, but solving the complete optimization problem can be done efficiently using A_{quad}^{-1} as the preconditioner. For our problem, we use the preconditioned L-BFGS optimizer summarized in Algorithm 1.

Algorithm 1: Preconditioned L-BFGS mesh optimization (PL-BFGS)

$M_{\text{precond}} = A_{\text{quad}}^{-1}$ // stored as LU decomposition

$\overline{\mathbf{V}} = T_m^0(\overline{\mathbf{V}}^0)$

for $i \leftarrow 0$ **to** N_{iter} **do**

$\quad g_{\text{tot}} = \alpha_{\text{data}} \frac{dE_{\text{data}}}{dp} + A_{\text{quad}} \overline{\mathbf{V}} + b$

$\quad \overline{\mathbf{V}} = \text{L-BFGS-step}(\overline{\mathbf{V}}, g_{\text{tot}}, M_{\text{precond}})$

end

---

5   Datasets

Our method relies on a number of publicly available datasets to compute mesh annotations for our deformations and assess fitting performance. To assess fitting performance, we use Scan2CAD dataset [5] that consists of 14225 ground-truth 9 DoF transformations between objects in 1506 reconstructions of indoor scenes from Scannet [11] and 3049 unique CAD models from ShapeNet [9].

Our deformation framework requires high-quality watertight meshes to support numerically stable optimization, which does not hold for ShapeNet CAD models. Thus, we remesh these to around 10k–15k vertices using [24], obtaining more uniform discretizations. To annotate these remeshed CAD models with semantic part labels required by our deformation procedure, we register them with the corresponding part-labeled meshes from the PartNet dataset [31] by first choosing an appropriate 90° rotation around each axis and then optimizing for a finer alignment using a point-to-point ICP algorithm [35] between vertices of the two meshes. We annotate the semantic parts for vertices in each mesh by projecting it from the respective closest vertices of the registered PartNet mesh.

The original ShapeNet meshes, however, are used to extract sharp geometric features, as these have easily detectable sharp angles between adjacent faces. We label as sharp all edges adjacent to faces with a dihedral angle smaller than the threshold $\alpha_{\text{sharp}} = 120°$. We further project vertex-wise sharpness labels from the original to the remeshed CAD models and select a sequence of edges forming the shortest paths between each pair of vertices as sharp.

6   Results

6.1   Evaluation Setup

Our performance evaluation of obtained deformations is multifaceted and addresses the following quality-related questions:

- Scan fitting performance: *How well do CAD deformations fit?*
- Perceptual performance for deformations: *How CAD-like are deformations?*
- Contributions of individual energy terms: *Which energy terms are essential?*
- Deformation flexibility: *Can better shapes be achieved by approximating clean meshes rather than noisy scans?*

Fitting and Perceptual Metrics. We quantify the deformation performance in terms of fitting quality between the scene scans and 3D CAD models using a family of related measures computed on a per-instance basis. For vertices $V = (v_i)$ of the deformed mesh M, we compute distances to their respective nearest neighbors $(\text{NN}(v_i, S))$ in the scan S. We compute per-instance Accuracy = $|V_{\text{close}}|/|V|$, reflecting the fraction of closely located vertices, and trimmed minimum matching distance tMMD = $\sum_{v_i \in V} \min(\tau, \|v_i - \text{NN}(v_i, S)\|_1)/|V|$, where $V_{\text{close}} = \{v_i \in V : \|v_i - \text{NN}(v_i, S)\|_1 < \tau\}$ is the set of vertices falling within L_1-distance τ to their nearest neighbor in the scan, and τ controls robustness w.r.t.incomplete scans. We set $\tau = 0.2$ (see supplementary) in our experiments and report Accuracy and tMMD values averaged over classes and instances.

There is no universally agreed perceptual quality measure for meshes; thus, we opted for a tripartite evaluation for our resulting deformations. First, we measure dihedral angle mesh error (DAME) [41], revealing differences in *local surface quality* between the original and the distorted meshes:

$$\text{DAME}(M, M_{\text{def}}) = \frac{1}{|E|} \sum_{\text{adjacent} f_1, f_2} |D_{f_1, f_2} - \overline{D_{f_1, f_2}}| \cdot \exp\{(Z_{\text{DAME}} D_{f_1, f_2})^2\},$$

where D_{f_1, f_2} and $\overline{D_{f_1, f_2}}$ represent oriented dihedral angles between faces f_1 and f_2 in the original and deformed meshes, respectively, and $Z_{\text{DAME}} = \frac{\sqrt{\log(100/\pi)}}{\pi}$ is a parameter scaling DAME values to $[0, 100]$.

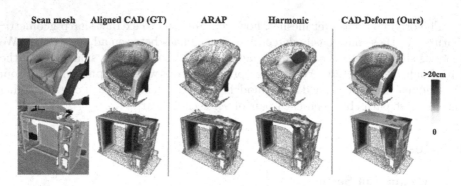

Fig. 3. Deformations obtained using our method and the baselines, with mesh colored according to the Euclidean distance to its nearest point in the scan. We note that high accuracy scores for Harmonic and ARAP deformations are achieved at the cost of destroying the initial structure of the mesh, particularly in regions where scan is missing (note that back side and armrests are gone for chairs in the first and second rows). In contrast, our method is better able to preserve smooth surfaces, sharp features, and overall mesh integrity, while keeping accurate local alignment.

Second, we assess *abnormality of deformed shapes* with respect to the distribution of the undeformed shapes, building on the idea of employing deep autoencoders for anomaly detection in structured high-dimensional data. By replicating the training instances, autoencoders learn features that minimize reconstruction error; for novel instances *similar* to those in the training set, reconstruction error is low compared to that of strong *outliers*. We train six autoencoders [2,17] for point clouds using vertices of undeformed meshes separately for the top six classes present in Scan2CAD annotation: *table, chair, display, trashbin, cabinet,* and *bookshelf.* Passing vertices $\mathbf{V}_{\text{def}}$ of a deformed shape to the respective autoencoder, one can assess how accurately deformed meshes can be approximated using features of undeformed meshes. This property can be evaluated with Earth Mover's Distance (EMD) $d_{\text{EMD}}(\mathbf{V}_{\text{def}}, \mathbf{V}'_{\text{def}}) = \min\limits_{\phi:\mathbf{V}_{\text{def}}\rightarrow\mathbf{V}'_{\text{def}}} \sum\limits_{v\in\mathbf{V}_{\text{def}}} \|v - \phi(v)\|_2$, where ϕ is a bijection, obtained as a solution to the optimal transportation problem involving $\mathbf{V}_{\text{def}}$ and $\mathbf{V}'_{\text{def}}$, that can intuitively be viewed as the least amount of work needed to transport $\mathbf{V}_{\text{def}}$ vertices to positions of $\mathbf{V}'_{\text{def}}$.

Lastly, we assess *real human perception* of deformations in a user study, detailed in Sect. 6.3.

Optimization Details. To perform quantitative comparisons, we use 299 scenes in ScanNet constituting Scan2CAD validation set [5], but with 697 shapes present in PartNet dataset, amounting to 1410 object instances. Our full experimental pipeline is a sequence of deformation stages with different optimization parameters, and Hessian being recomputed before each stage. Specifically, we perform one *part-to-part* optimization with parameters $\alpha_{\text{shape}} = 1, \alpha_{\text{smooth}} = 0, \alpha_{\text{sharp}} = 0, \alpha_{\text{data}} = 5 \times 10^4$ for 100 iterations, then we perform 5 runs of *nearest-neighbor* deformation for 50 iterations with parameters $\alpha_{\text{shape}} = 1, \alpha_{\text{smooth}} = 10, \alpha_{\text{sharp}} =$

Table 1. Comparative evaluation of our deformations to true positive (TP) alignments by non-deformable approaches in terms of Accuracy (%). Note that deformations improve performance for all considered alignment approaches.

Method	Class avg.			Instance avg.		
	GT	S2C [5]	E2E [6]	GT	S2C [5]	E2E [6]
# TPs	1410	499	882	1410	499	882
TP undeformed	89.2	83.7	88.5	90.6	79.4	93.9
Ours: NN only	89.7	84.3	89.0	91.4	84.7	94.4
Ours: p2p only	90.3	88.3	89.4	91.6	90.3	94.9
Ours: w/o smooth	90.6	**90.0**	89.6	92.3	90.3	95.0
Ours: w/o sharp	90.3	86.9	**90.6**	92.3	89.4	**95.2**
CAD-Deform	**91.7**	89.8	90.3	**93.1**	**92.8**	94.6

Table 2. Comparative evaluation of our approach to non-deformable ground-truth and baselines in terms of scan approximation Accuracy (%). We conclude that our deformations improve fitting accuracy across all object classes by 2.5 % on average.

Method	Bookshelf	Cabinet	Chair	Display	Table	Trashbin	Other	Class avg.	Avg.
# instances	142	162	322	86	332	169	197	201.4	1410
Ground-truth	88.0	75.2	94.8	98.9	89.6	96.6	81.4	89.2	90.6
Ours	**90.5**	**82.2**	**95.4**	**99.1**	**91.0**	**98.6**	**84.8**	**91.7**	**93.1**

$10, \alpha_{\text{data}} = 10^3$. More details about optimization and timings are provided in the supplementary.

6.2   Fitting Accuracy: How Well Do CAD Deformations Fit?

We first demonstrate how deformation affects scan fitting performance for meshes aligned using different methods, specifically, we use true-positive shape alignments computed using Scan2CAD (S2C) [5], End-to-End (E2E) [5], as well as ground-truth alignments. We start with an aligned mesh, copy the 9 DoF transformation to each of the mesh vertices, and optimize using our deformation method with parameters described in Sect. 6.1. We report Accuracy scores in terms of fraction of well-approximated points in the scan for aligned shapes pre- and post-optimization in Table 2, achieving improved performance across all considered alignment procedures.

Surprisingly, we improve even over ground-truth alignments by as much as 2.5 %. Thus, we compute per-class scores in Table 1 (comparison across alignments), reporting improvements of up to 7 % in average scan approximation accuracy that are consistent *across all object classes*. We visualize example deformations obtained using our approach and baselines in Fig. 3.

We have discovered our deformation framework to be robust w.r.t.level of detail in the data term in (2) and provide more detail in the supplementary.

6.3   CAD Quality: How CAD-like Are Deformed Models?

Having obtained a collection of deformed meshes, we aim to assess their visual quality in comparison to two baseline deformation methods: as-rigid-as-possible (ARAP) [38] and Harmonic deformation [7, 26], using a set of perceptual quality measures. The details of our user study design and visual assessment are provided in the supplementary.

6.4   Ablation Study

To evaluate the impact of individual energy terms in (1) on both scan fitting performance and perceptual quality, we exclude each term from the energy and compute deformations by optimizing the remaining ones. First, we exclude sharpness or smoothness terms, optimizing for deformations using the original two-stage method; second, to better understand the influence of each stage, we perform experiments with only the first or the second stage (a single run only). We aggregate results into Table 1 and display them visually in Fig. 4, concluding that our CAD-Deform maintains the right balance between fit to the scan and perceptual quality of resulting deformations.

6.5   Shape Morphing Results

To demonstrate the ability of our mesh deformation framework to perform shape interpolation, we choose two different meshes in the same ShapeNet category and optimize our energy (1) to approximate one with the other, see Fig. 5.

Table 3. Quantitative evaluation of visual quality of deformations obtained using ARAP [38], Harmonic deformation [7,26], and our CAD-Deform, using a variety of local surface-based (DAME [41]), neural (EMD [2,17]), and human measures.

Method	DAME		EMD $\times 10^{-3}$		User study	Accuracy	
	cls.	inst.	cls.	inst.		cls.	Inst
No deformation	0	0	77	77	8.6	89.2	90.6
ARAP [38]	47.1	45.7	88	87	4.0	90.8	91.8
Harmonic [7,26]	65.1	65.2	104	102	2.6	**96.2**	**96.6**
CAD-Deform	**20.5**	**17.2**	84	84	**7.7**	91.7	93.1

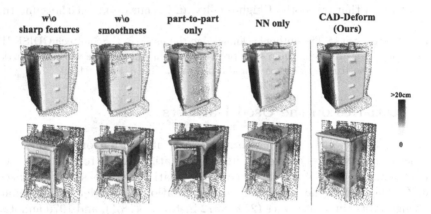

Fig. 4. Qualitative results of ablation study usind our deformation framework, with mesh coloured according to the value of the tMMD measure. Note that including smoothness term is crucial to prevent surface self-intersections, while keeping sharpness allows to ensure consistency in parallel planes and edges.

Fig. 5. Qualitative shape translation results, interpolating between the original mesh (left) and the target mesh (right).

7   Conclusion

In this work, we have presented CAD-Deform, a shape deformation-based scene reconstruction method leveraging CAD collections that is capable of improving over existing alignment methods. More specifically, we introduce a composite deformation energy formulation that achieves regularization from semantic part structures, enforces smooth transformations, and preserves sharp geometric features. As a result we obtain significantly improved perceptual quality of final 3D CAD models compared to state-of-the-art deformation formulations, such as ARAP and polyharmonic deformation frameworks. Overall, we believe that our method is an important step towards obtaining lightweight digital replica from the real world that are both of high-quality and accurate fits at the same time.

Acknowledgments. The authors acknowledge the usage of the Skoltech CDISE HPC cluster Zhores for obtaining the results presented in this paper. The work was partially supported by the Russian Science Foundation under Grant 19-41-04109.

A   Statistics on the Used Datasets

In Tables 4 and 5, we summarize statistical information on the number of instances and categories considered in our evaluation. As we require parts annotations as an important ingredient in our deformation, we only select instances in Scan2CAD [5] where the associated parts annotation in PartNet [31] is available, resulting in total in 9 categories (25%), 572 instances (18%), and 1979 annotated correspondences (14%). Note that the vast majority of cases remain within our consideration, keeping our evaluation comprehensive.

Table 4. Overall statistics on the numbers of categories, instances, and correspondences present in our datasets.

Collection	Categories	Instances	Corresp.
Scan2CAD [5]	35	3,049	14,225
w/parts annotations	24	2,477	12,246

Table 5. The top 15 most frequent ShapeNet categories in Scan2CAD dataset including a detailed information on those with the availability of the corresponding parts annotations.

Name	Scan2CAD		PartNet ∩ Scan2CAD	
	corresp.	shapes	corresp.	Shapes
Shape categories used in our evaluation:				
Chair	4677	652	4351	632
Table	2616	830	2594	822
Cabinet	1401	310	1258	294
Trash bin	1044	89	1042	88
Bookshelf	824	150	812	145
Display	770	165	762	161
Shape categories NOT used in our evaluation:				
Bed	355	50	342	47
File cabinet	294	70	290	68
Bag	165	9	165	9
Lamp	135	55	135	55
Bathtub	474	96	129	25
Microwave	99	37	98	36
Sofa	577	247	60	20
Laptop	51	24	51	24
Keyboard	62	11	48	9

We further select the most well-presented six shape categories as our core evaluation set, outlined in Table 5. Note that as our method is non-learnable, we can just as easily experiment with the remaining categories, at the cost of somewhat reduced statistical power.

B   Optimization Details

Our full experimental pipeline is a sequence of deformation stages with different optimization parameters, and Hessian being recomputed before each stage. Specifically, we perform one *part-to-part* optimization with parameters $\alpha_{\text{shape}} = 1, \alpha_{\text{smooth}} = 0, \alpha_{\text{sharp}} = 0, \alpha_{\text{data}} = 5 \times 10^4$ for 100 iterations, then we perform 5 runs of *nearest-neighbor* deformation for 50 iterations with parameters $\alpha_{\text{shape}} = 1, \alpha_{\text{smooth}} = 10, \alpha_{\text{sharp}} = 10, \alpha_{\text{data}} = 10^3$. Such number of iterations was sufficient to achieve convergence with energy changes less than 10^{-1} in our experiments. Runtime of our method breaks into cost computation (~ 0.3 s), backward (~ 0.2 s), and optimization steps containing the main bottleneck (sparse matrix-vector multiplication) (~ 1.2 s) for a typical 10^4 vertices mesh. All operations can be easily further optimized.

C   Qualitative Fitting Results

In Fig. 6, we display a series of qualitative results with a variety of shape deformations with different classes of instances. Comparing to baselines, our framework achieves accurate fit while preserving sufficient perceptual quality.

Table 6. Quantitative results of local surface quality evaluation using DAME measure [41] (the smaller, the better, normalized to a maximum score of 100), where our CAD-Deform compares favourably to the baselines across all considered categories. Note, however, how surface quality significantly decreases when smoothness and sharp feature-related terms are dropped.

Method	Bookshelf	Cabinet	Chair	Display	Table	Trash bin	Other	Class avg.	Avg.
ARAP	52.48	41.77	45.52	51.30	41.77	57.00	39.75	47.08	45.67
Harmonic	64.77	58.74	68.06	64.22	58.26	80.13	61.70	65.12	65.18
Ours: NN only	**21.54**	**23.39**	7.31	**18.37**	**18.69**	18.13	**16.07**	**17.64**	**14.14**
Ours: p2p only	22.44	24.28	9.51	21.12	18.76	**15.30**	18.34	18.54	15.57
Ours: w/o smooth	27.15	29.27	14.50	27.05	24.48	24.39	23.26	24.30	20.95
Ours: w/o sharp	26.43	25.98	13.34	24.87	22.47	21.04	21.18	22.19	19.10
CAD-Deform	24.8	24.1	11.4	24.4	21.6	19.4	17.6	20.5	17.2

Table 7. Results of LSLP-GAN reconstruction in terms of Earth-Mover's Distance between reconstructed and original point clouds of mesh vertices.

EMD $\times 10^{-3}$	Bookshelf	Cabinet	Chair	Display	Table	Trash bin	Class avg.	Avg.
Ground-truth	77.8	78.9	76.1	77.5	77.3	73.1	76.8	77.0
ARAP [38]	80.3	86.5	88.5	**85.4**	**86.8**	98.1	87.6	87.3
Harmonic [7, 26]	94.0	110.6	95.8	95.3	103.2	122.6	103.6	101.7
CAD-Deform	**79.0**	**81.1**	**80.3**	91.7	87.0	**87.4**	**84.4**	**83.8**

Table 6 reports the results of surface quality evaluation using deformations obtained with our CAD-Deform vs. the baselines, category-wise. While outperforming the baseline methods across all categories, we discover the smoothness and sharpness energy terms to be the crucial ingredients in keeping high-quality meshes.

Figure 7 displays visually the deformation results using the three distinct classes, highlighting differences in surfaces obtained using the three methods.

Table 7 reports shape abnormality evaluation results across the six considered categories. Baselines show (Fig. 8) low reconstruction quality as evidenced by a larger number of black points. In other words, comparing to CAD-Deform, the distance from these meshes to undeformed ones is mush larger.

In Fig. 9, we show a series of examples for CAD-Deform ablation study. Perceptual quality degrades when excluding every term from the energy.

D   Morphing

In this section, we present an additional series of examples of morphing properties (Fig. 10). Every iteration of optimization process gradually increases the quality of fit. With CAD-Deform we can morph each part to imitate the structure of the target shape.

E   PartNet Annotation

This set of experiments shows how quality of fitting depends on mesh vertices labelling. We can provide labels for mesh in different ways depending on the level in PartNet hierarchy [31]. We observe the increase of fitting quality with

Table 8. Comparative evaluation of our approach in terms of Accuracy on different levels of detail.

Accuracy, %	Class avg.	Avg.
Ground-truth	89.22	90.56
Level 1 (object)	89.25	90.79
Level 2	89.16	91.21
Level 3	89.40	91.05
Level 4 (parts)	**91.65**	**93.12**

Table 9. Comparative evaluation of ARAP deformations w.r.t. the change of Laplacian term weight in terms of Accuracy (%).

Lap. term weight	Class avg.			Instance avg.		
	GT	S2C [5]	E2E [6]	GT	S2C [5]	E2E [6]
$\alpha_{\mathrm{Lap}} = 10^{-2}$	90.9	81.3	90.0	92.0	80.9	90.8
$\alpha_{\mathrm{Lap}} = 10^{-1}$	91.0	81.3	90.0	92.0	80.9	90.7
$\alpha_{\mathrm{Lap}} = 1$	91.0	81.3	89.9	91.9	80.9	90.7
$\alpha_{\mathrm{Lap}} = 5$	90.9	81.2	89.9	91.9	80.9	90.7
$\alpha_{\mathrm{Lap}} = 20$	90.9	81.2	89.9	91.8	80.8	90.6

Table 10. Comparative evaluation of Harmonic deformations w.r.t. the change of Laplacian term weight in terms of Accuracy (%).

Lap. term weight	Class avg.			Instance avg.		
	GT	S2C [5]	E2E [6]	GT	S2C [5]	E2E [6]
$\alpha_{Lap} = 10^{-2}$	96.3	94.3	96.6	96.7	94.5	96.9
$\alpha_{Lap} = 10^{-1}$	96.3	94.2	96.6	96.7	94.4	96.9
$\alpha_{Lap} = 1$	96.3	94.2	96.6	96.7	94.2	96.9
$\alpha_{Lap} = 5$	96.2	94.0	96.6	96.6	94.0	96.8
$\alpha_{Lap} = 20$	96.2	93.8	96.5	96.6	93.8	96.7

greater level of detail (Table 8). Examples presented in Fig. 11 are selected as the most distinguishable deformations on different levels. There are minor visual differences in deformation performance of part labeling level.

F   Fitting Accuracy Analysis

CAD-Deform deformation framework is sensitive to Accuracy threshold τ for the distance between mesh vertices and close scan points. In Fig. 12 variation of τ threshold is presented and we selected $\tau = 0.2$ m for fitting Accuracy metric.

G   Perceptual Assessment and User Study Details

Having obtained a collection of deformed meshes, we aim to assess their visual quality in comparison to two baseline deformation methods: as-rigid-as-possible (ARAP) [38] and Harmonic deformation [7,26], using a set of perceptual quality measures. The details of our user study design and visual assessment are provided in the supplementary. To this end, we use original and deformed meshes to compute DAME and reconstruction errors, as outlined in Sect. 6.1, and complement these with visual quality scores obtained with a user study (see below). These scores, presented in Table 3, demonstrate that shapes obtained using CAD-Deform have 2× higher surface quality, only slightly deviate from undeformed shapes as viewed by neural autoencoders, and receive 2× higher ratings in human assessment, while sacrificing only 1.1–4.5 % accuracy compared to other deformation methods.

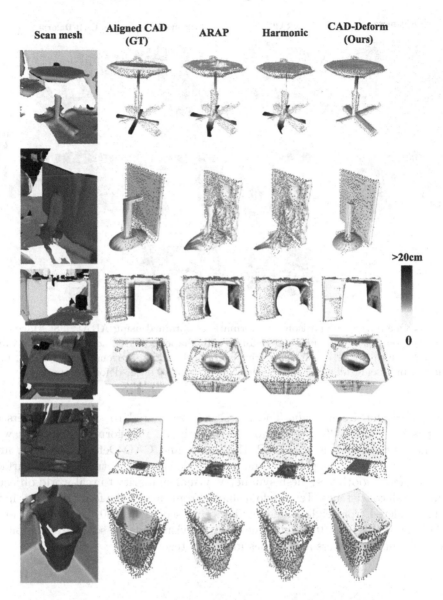

Fig. 6. Qualitative shape deformation results using obtained using ARAP [38], Harmonic deformation [7,26], and our CAD-Deform. Mesh surface is colored according to the value of tMMD measure, with darker values corresponding to the larger distance values.

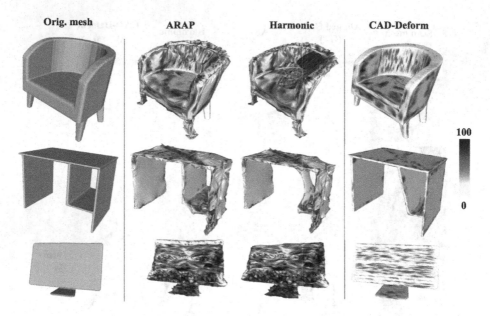

Fig. 7. Qualitative comparison of deformations obtained using ARAP [38], Harmonic deformation [7,26], and our CAD-Deform, with shapes coloured according to the value of DAME measure [41]. Our approach results in drastic improvements in local surface quality, producing higher-quality surfaces compared to other deformations.

Design of Our User Study. The users were requested to examine renders of shapes from four different categories: the original undeformed shapes as well as shapes deformed using ARAP, Harmonic, and CAD-Deform methods, and give a score to each shape according to the following perceptual aspects: surface quality and smoothness, mesh symmetry, visual similarity to real-world objects, and overall consistency. Ten random shapes from each of the four categories have been rendered from eight different views and scored by 100 unique users on a scale from 1 (bad) to 10 (good). The resulting visual quality scores are computed by averaging over users and shapes in each category.

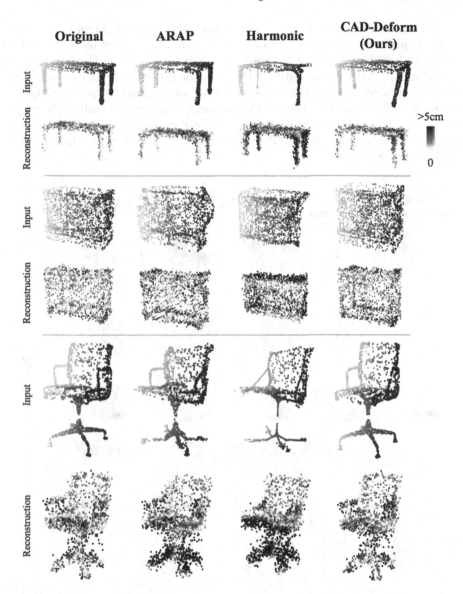

Fig. 8. Qualitative comparison of reconstruction of point clouds extracted from mesh vertices. These meshes are obtained using ARAP [38], Harmonic deformation [7,26], and our CAD-Deform, the first column corresponds to original undeformed meshes. The color of reconstructed point clouds is related to Earth-Mover's Distance between reconstructed and original point clouds of mesh vertices.

In Fig. 13, we present a distribution of user scores over different deformation methods and shapes. It can be clearly seen that users prefer our deformation results to baselines for all of the cases, which is obvious from the gap between histogram of CAD-Deform and ARAP/Harmonic histograms. At the same time, shapes deformed by CAD-Deform are close to undeformed ShapeNet shapes in terms of surface quality and smoothness, mesh symmetry, visual similarity to real-world objects, and overall consistency. Besides, in Tables 9, 10 we provide numbers for evaluation of ARAP/Harmonic deformations w.r.t. the change of Laplacian term weight.

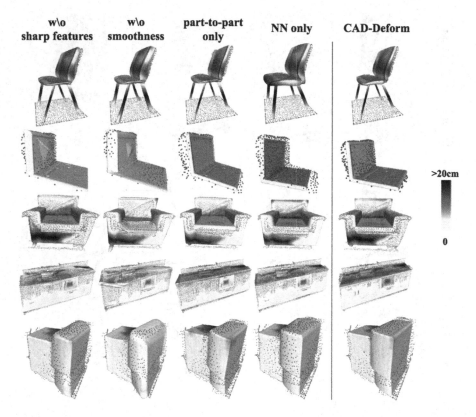

Fig. 9. Qualitative results of ablation study usind our deformation framework, with mesh coloured according to the value of the tMMD measure.

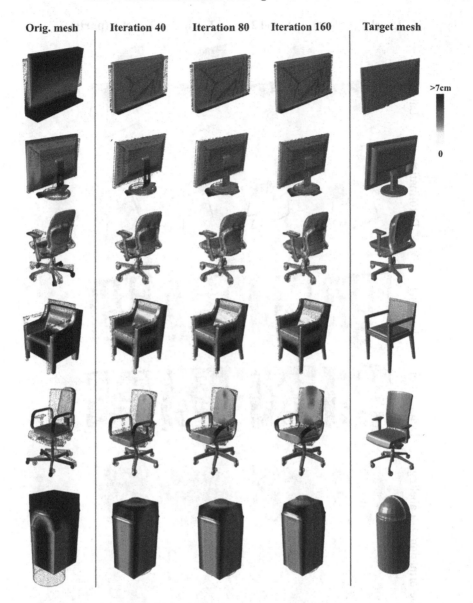

Fig. 10. Qualitative shape translation results, interpolating between the original mesh (left) and the target mesh (right).

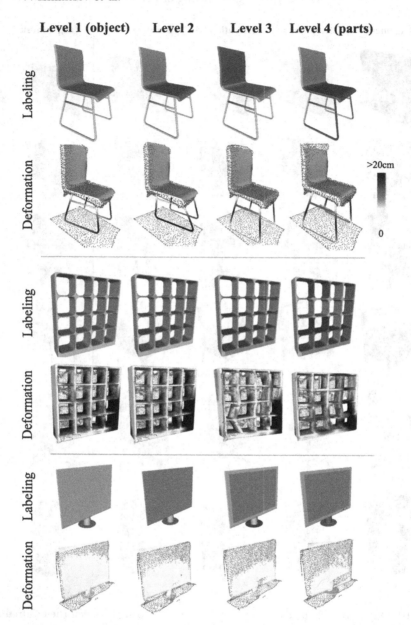

Fig. 11. Deformation performance depending on different level of labelling from the PartNet dataset [31]. Deformed mesh surfaces are colored according to the value of tMMD measure, with darker values corresponding to the larger distance values.

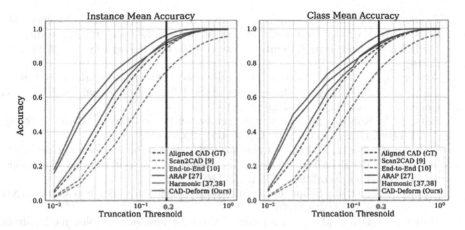

Fig. 12. Fitting Accuracy vs. varying τ threshold for the distance between mesh vertices and close scan points.

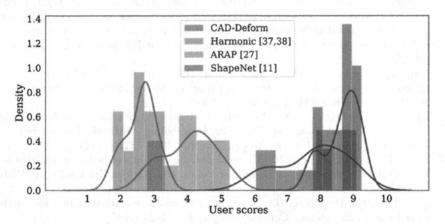

Fig. 13. Distribution of user scores averaged by ten shapes from original ShapeNet [9], meshes deformed with ARAP [38], Harmonic [7,26] and CAD-Deform.

References

1. Achenbach, J., Zell, E., Botsch, M.: Accurate face reconstruction through anisotropic fitting and eye correction. In: VMV, pp. 1–8 (2015)
2. Achlioptas, P., Diamanti, O., Mitliagkas, I., Guibas, L.: Learning representations and generative models for 3D point clouds. In: International Conference on Machine Learning, pp. 40–49 (2018)
3. Amberg, B., Romdhani, S., Vetter, T.: Optimal step nonrigid ICP algorithms for surface registration. In: 2007 IEEE Conference on Computer Vision and Pattern Recognition, pp. 1–8 (2007)
4. Aubry, M., Maturana, D., Efros, A., Russell, B., Sivic, J.: Seeing 3D chairs: exemplar part-based 2D–3D alignment using a large dataset of cad models. In: CVPR (2014)

5. Avetisyan, A., Dahnert, M., Dai, A., Savva, M., Chang, A.X., Nießner, M.: Scan2CAD: learning CAD model alignment in RGB-D scans. In: Proceedings of the IEEE Conference on Computer Vision and Pattern Recognition, pp. 2614–2623 (2019)
6. Avetisyan, A., Dai, A., Nießner, M.: End-to-end CAD model retrieval and 9DoF alignment in 3D scans. In: Proceedings of the IEEE International Conference on Computer Vision, pp. 2551–2560 (2019)
7. Botsch, M., Kobbelt, L.: An intuitive framework for real-time freeform modeling. ACM Trans. Graph. (TOG) **23**(3), 630–634 (2004)
8. Cagniart, C., Boyer, E., Ilic, S.: Iterative mesh deformation for dense surface tracking. In: 2009 IEEE 12th International Conference on Computer Vision Workshops, ICCV Workshops, pp. 1465–1472. IEEE (2009)
9. Chang, A.X., et al.: Shapenet: an information-rich 3d model repository. arXiv preprint arXiv:1512.03012 (2015)
10. Curless, B., Levoy, M.: A volumetric method for building complex models from range images. In: Proceedings of the 23rd Annual Conference on Computer Graphics and Interactive Techniques, SIGGRAPH 1996, pp. 303–312. Association for Computing Machinery, New York (1996). https://doi.org/10.1145/237170.237269
11. Dai, A., Chang, A.X., Savva, M., Halber, M., Funkhouser, T., Nießner, M.: ScanNet: richly-annotated 3D reconstructions of indoor scenes. In: Proceedings of the IEEE Conference on Computer Vision and Pattern Recognition, pp. 5828–5839 (2017)
12. Dai, A., Nießner, M., Zollöfer, M., Izadi, S., Theobalt, C.: Bundlefusion: real-time globally consistent 3D reconstruction using on-the-fly surface re-integration. In: ACM Transactions on Graphics 2017 (TOG) (2017)
13. Dai, A., Ruizhongtai Qi, C., Nießner, M.: Shape completion using 3D-encoder-predictor CNNs and shape synthesis. In: Proceedings of the IEEE Conference on Computer Vision and Pattern Recognition, pp. 5868–5877 (2017)
14. Deng, H., Birdal, T., Ilic, S.: 3D local features for direct pairwise registration. In: The IEEE Conference on Computer Vision and Pattern Recognition (CVPR), June 2019
15. Dey, T.K., Fu, B., Wang, H., Wang, L.: Automatic posing of a meshed human model using point clouds. Comput. Graph. **46**, 14–24 (2015)
16. Drost, B., Ilic, S.: 3D object detection and localization using multimodal point pair features. In: 3DIMPVT, pp. 9–16. IEEE Computer Society (2012)
17. Egiazarian, V., et al.: Latent-Space Laplacian Pyramids for Adversarial Representation Learning with 3D Point Clouds, December 2019
18. Firman, M., Mac Aodha, O., Julier, S., Brostow, G.J.: Structured prediction of unobserved voxels from a single depth image. In: Proceedings of the IEEE Conference on Computer Vision and Pattern Recognition, pp. 5431–5440 (2016)
19. Fröhlich, S., Botsch, M.: Example-driven deformations based on discrete shells. Comput. Graph. Forum **30**, 2246–2257 (2011). https://doi.org/10.1111/j.1467-8659.2011.01974.x
20. Grinspun, E., Hirani, A.N., Desbrun, M., Schröder, P.: Discrete shells. In: Proceedings of the 2003 ACM SIGGRAPH/Eurographics Symposium on Computer Animation, SCA 2003, pp. 62–67. Eurographics Association, Goslar, DEU (2003)
21. Guo, R., Zou, C., Hoiem, D.: Predicting complete 3D models of indoor scenes. arXiv preprint arXiv:1504.02437 (2015)
22. Gupta, S., Arbeláez, P., Girshick, R., Malik, J.: Aligning 3D models to RGB-D images of cluttered scenes. In: Proceedings of the IEEE Conference on Computer Vision and Pattern Recognition, pp. 4731–4740 (2015)

23. He, L., Schaefer, S.: Mesh denoising via l0 minimization. In: Proceedings of ACM SIGGRAPH, pp. 64:1–64:8, January 2013
24. Huang, J., Su, H., Guibas, L.: Robust watertight manifold surface generation method for shapenet models. arXiv preprint arXiv:1802.01698 (2018)
25. Izadi, S., et al.: Kinectfusion: real-time 3D reconstruction and interaction using a moving depth camera. In: UIST 2011 Proceedings of the 24th Annual ACM Symposium on User Interface Software and Technology, pp. 559–568. ACM (2011)
26. Jacobson, A., Tosun, E., Sorkine, O., Zorin, D.: Mixed finite elements for variational surface modeling. In: Computer Graphics Forum, vol. 29, pp. 1565–1574. Wiley Online Library (2010)
27. Koch, S., et al.: ABC: a big cad model dataset for geometric deep learning. In: The IEEE Conference on Computer Vision and Pattern Recognition (CVPR), June 2019
28. Li, Y., Dai, A., Guibas, L., Nießner, M.: Database-assisted object retrieval for real-time 3D reconstruction. Comput. Graph. Forum 34(2), 435–446 (2015)
29. Liao, M., Zhang, Q., Wang, H., Yang, R., Gong, M.: Modeling Deformable Objects from a Single Depth Camera, pp. 167–174, November 2009. https://doi.org/10.1109/ICCV.2009.5459161
30. Mattausch, O., Panozzo, D., Mura, C., Sorkine-Hornung, O., Pajarola, R.: Object detection and classification from large-scale cluttered indoor scans. In: Computer Graphics Forum, vol. 33, pp. 11–21. Wiley Online Library (2014)
31. Mo, K., et al.: PartNet: a large-scale benchmark for fine-grained and hierarchical part-level 3d object understanding. In: Proceedings of the IEEE Conference on Computer Vision and Pattern Recognition, pp. 909–918 (2019)
32. Newcombe, R.A., et al.: Kinectfusion: real-time dense surface mapping and tracking. In: IEEE ISMAR. IEEE, October 2011
33. Nießner, M., Zollhöfer, M., Izadi, S., Stamminger, M.: Real-time 3D reconstruction at scale using voxel hashing. In: ACM Transactions on Graphics (TOG) (2013)
34. Park, S.I., Lim, S.J.: Template-based reconstruction of surface mesh animation from point cloud animation. ETRI J. 36(6), 1008–1015 (2014)
35. Rusinkiewicz, S., Levoy, M.: Efficient variants of the ICP algorithm. In: Proceedings Third International Conference on 3-D Digital Imaging and Modeling, pp. 145–152. IEEE (2001)
36. Salas-Moreno, R.F., Newcombe, R.A., Strasdat, H., Kelly, P.H.J., Davison, A.J.: Slam++: simultaneous localisation and mapping at the level of objects. In: CVPR, pp. 1352–1359. IEEE Computer Society (2013)
37. Song, S., Yu, F., Zeng, A., Chang, A.X., Savva, M., Funkhouser, T.: Semantic scene completion from a single depth image. In: Proceedings of the IEEE Conference on Computer Vision and Pattern Recognition, pp. 1746–1754 (2017)
38. Sorkine, O., Alexa, M.: As-rigid-as-possible surface modeling. In: Symposium on Geometry Processing, vol. 4, pp. 109–116 (2007)
39. Stoll, C., Karni, Z., Rössl, C., Yamauchi, H., Seidel, H.P.: Template deformation for point cloud fitting. In: SPBG, pp. 27–35 (2006)
40. Sungjoon Choi, Zhou, Q., Koltun, V.: Robust reconstruction of indoor scenes. In: 2015 IEEE Conference on Computer Vision and Pattern Recognition (CVPR), pp. 5556–5565, June 2015. https://doi.org/10.1109/CVPR.2015.7299195
41. Váša, L., Rus, J.: Dihedral angle mesh error: a fast perception correlated distortion measure for fixed connectivity triangle meshes. Comput. Graph. Forum 31(5), 1715–1724 (2012). https://doi.org/10.1111/j.1467-8659.2012.03176.x, https://onlinelibrary.wiley.com/doi/abs/10.1111/j.1467-8659.2012.03176.x

42. Whelan, T., Leutenegger, S., Salas-Moreno, R.F., Glocker, B., Davison, A.J.: ElasticFusion: dense SLAM without a pose graph. In: Robotics: Science and Systems (RSS), Rome, Italy, July 2015
43. Zhou, X., Karpur, A., Gan, C., Luo, L., Huang, Q.: Unsupervised domain adaptation for 3D keypoint estimation via view consistency. In: Ferrari, V., Hebert, M., Sminchisescu, C., Weiss, Y. (eds.) ECCV 2018. LNCS, vol. 11216, pp. 141–157. Springer, Cham (2018). https://doi.org/10.1007/978-3-030-01258-8_9

An Image Enhancing Pattern-Based Sparsity for Real-Time Inference on Mobile Devices

Xiaolong Ma[1(✉)], Wei Niu[2], Tianyun Zhang[3], Sijia Liu[4], Sheng Lin[1],
Hongjia Li[1], Wujie Wen[5], Xiang Chen[6], Jian Tang[7], Kaisheng Ma[8], Bin Ren[2],
and Yanzhi Wang[1]

[1] Northeastern University, Boston, MA 02115, USA
{ma.xiaol,yanz.wang}@northeastern.edu
[2] College of William and Mary, Williamsburg, USA
[3] Syracuse University, Syracuse, USA
[4] IBM Research, Yorktown Heights, USA
[5] Lehigh University, Bethlehem, USA
[6] George Mason University, Fairfax, USA
[7] DiDi AI Labs, Mountain View, USA
[8] Tsinghua University, Beijing, China

Abstract. Weight pruning has been widely acknowledged as a straightforward and effective method to eliminate redundancy in Deep Neural Networks (DNN), thereby achieving acceleration on various platforms. However, most of the pruning techniques are essentially trade-offs between model accuracy and regularity which lead to impaired inference accuracy and limited on-device acceleration performance. To solve the problem, we introduce a new sparsity dimension, namely pattern-based sparsity that comprises pattern and connectivity sparsity, and becoming both highly accurate and hardware friendly. With carefully designed patterns, the proposed pruning unprecedentedly and consistently achieves accuracy enhancement and better feature extraction ability on different DNN structures and datasets, and our pattern-aware pruning framework also achieves pattern library extraction, pattern selection, pattern and connectivity pruning and weight training simultaneously. Our approach on the new pattern-based sparsity naturally fits into compiler optimization for highly efficient DNN execution on mobile platforms. To the best of our knowledge, it is the first time that mobile devices achieve real-time inference for the large-scale DNN models thanks to the unique spatial property of pattern-based sparsity and the help of the code generation capability of compilers.

1 Introduction

Weight pruning has been proven to be effective in eliminating redundancy in the original model [7,14,18,20,24,32], therefore accelerating DNN execution on

---

X. Ma and W. Niu—Equal Contribution.

© Springer Nature Switzerland AG 2020
A. Vedaldi et al. (Eds.): ECCV 2020, LNCS 12358, pp. 629–645, 2020.
https://doi.org/10.1007/978-3-030-58601-0_37

Fig. 1. Heat map of randomly selected convolution kernels in the third convolutional layer of a VGG-16 on ImageNet dataset. The weight values in each kernel are normalized and darker shade represents higher absolute value.

target computing platforms. Non-structured pruning [10] achieves high accuracy, but is limited by its hardware unfriendliness [14,32]. Meanwhile, structured pruning [32] is hardware friendly but suffers from accuracy loss.

It is imperative to seek an approach that can offer, or even go beyond, the best of both types of sparsity. We visualize part of the normalized heat map of a pre-trained model of VGG-16 on ImageNet in Fig. 1, we find that (i) the effective area (i.e. weights with higher absolute values) forms some specific shapes and repeatedly appears in the model, and (ii) some of the entire convolution kernels have very small weight values and make themselves void kernels. Motivated by the two observations, we introduce a new sparsity dimension – *pattern-based sparsity*, which exploits both intra-convolution and inter-convolution kernel sparsities, exhibiting both high accuracy and regularity, and revealing a previously *unknown* point in design space.

In pattern-based sparsity, we call our intra-convolution kernel sparsity *pattern sparsity* and inter-convolution kernel sparsity *connectivity sparsity*. To get pattern sparsity, we prune a fixed number of weights in each convolution kernel, and the remaining weights form specific "kernel patterns". Along this line, we find that some carefully designed kernel patterns have special vision properties that potentially enhance image quality, thereby enhancing feature extraction ability of DNNs. For connectivity sparsity, we cut the relatively unimportant connections between certain input and output channels, which is equivalent to removal of corresponding kernels. At the algorithm level, we design a novel pattern-aware network pruning framework that efficiently achieves pattern pruning and connectivity pruning without degrading accuracy. We begin by reforming the pruning problem into an ADMM optimization problem [4], and then solve the problem iteratively using a Primal-Proximal solution which decoupling the stochastic gradient descent process with regularization, enabling a progressive and gradual process of penalizing unimportant weight groups, meaning a more accurate selection of remaining weight patterns. Therefore, the framework can achieve pattern library extraction, pattern assignment, unimportant connectivity removal, as well as weight training simultaneously. Our proposed pattern-based sparsity is mobile hardware friendly with the help of *code generation* capability of compilers. More specifically, we design the *filter/kernel re-ordering* technique that enables compiler optimizations that maintain instruction-level and thread-level parallelism, and achieves the maximum possible hardware acceleration.

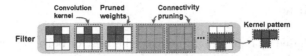

Fig. 2. Illustration of pattern-based sparsity.

Our contributions of this paper are summarized as follows:

- We design a set of patterns, namely pattern library, and prove the image enhancement property that is related to pattern pruning (Sect. 4).
- We form a novel pattern-aware network pruning framework that can extract pattern library, perform pattern and connectivity pruning and weight training at the same time (Sect. 5).
- We design the corresponding (algorithm-compiler-hardware) inference framework which fully leverages the new sparsity dimension and achieves real-time DNN execution on mobile devices (Sect. 6).

Section 7 demonstrates pattern library extraction result, pattern pruning for accuracy and image enhancement results, the overall pattern-based compression results and its acceleration results on mobile devices.

2 Background

DNN Model Pruning Techniques are studied in early work of *non-structured pruning* [10], in which an iterative, heuristic method is used with limited, non-uniform model compression rates. The irregular weight distribution causes irregular memory access and thereby execution overheads, which leads to limited acceleration performance.

Structured Pruning is pioneered by [14,32], in which regular and smaller weight matrices are generated to eliminate overhead of weight indices and achieve higher acceleration in CPU/GPU executions. However, it suffers from notable accuracy drop when the pruning rate increases.

Kernel Level Pruning is studied in [5] that the sparse complimentary kernels can save half of the weights and computations, but it is different from our approach because pattern-based sparsity is theoretically and practically improving the software and hardware performance of DNN while [5] only focuses on parameter and computation reduction without discussing on platform acceleration.

Mobile DNN Inference Frameworks are studied, including TFLite [1], TVM [6], Alibaba MNN [2], DeepCache [33] and DeepSense [34]. These works do not account for model compression techniques, and the performance is far from real-time requirement (usually 30 frames/sec). There are other researches that exploit model sparsity to accelerate DNN inference [17] [25], but they either do not target mobile platforms (require new hardware) or trade off compression rate and accuracy, thus having different challenges than our work.

3 Overview

The pattern-based sparsity should exploit the best of both non-structured and structured pruning while hiding the disadvantages. Given that, we propose two pattern-based pruning dimensions, *pattern pruning* and *connectivity pruning*.

Pattern Pruning is illustrated in Fig. 2, where the white blocks denote a fixed number of pruned weights in each kernel. The remaining (four) green blocks in each kernel have arbitrary weight values, while their locations form a specific pattern. Different kernels can have different patterns, but the total number of pattern styles (i.e., the size of the pattern library) shall be limited. We focus on 3×3 kernel pattern in this work because it is widely used in various of DNN architectures. For other kernel shape (e.g., 1×1 or 5×5), we group 1×1 kernels into 3×3 then apply patterns, or use 5×5 patterns directly (will not be discussed in this work due to space limit).

Connectivity Pruning is illustrated in Fig. 2, with gray kernels as pruned ones. Connectivity pruning is a good supplement to pattern pruning, as both can be integrated in the same algorithm-level solution and compiler-assisted mobile inference framework.

Compiler-Assisted DNN Inference Framework uniquely enables optimized code generation to guarantee end-to-end inference execution efficiency supporting pattern-based sparsity. As the computation paradigm of DNN is in a manner of layerwise execution, we convert a DNN model into computational graph, which is embodied by static C++ (for CPU execution) or OpenCL and CUDA (for GPU execution) codes. The above two pruning schemes can be naturally combined, which achieves high pruning (acceleration) rate while maintaining hardware friendliness.

4 Pattern Library – Theory and Design

4.1 A Unique Perspective on Weight Pruning

Conventionally, weight pruning is considered as a redundant information removal technique. This will inevitably omit other aspects, such as the computer vision properties of pruning. In this work, we consider weight pruning as incorporating an additional convolution mask P on an original kernel. P has the same size as original kernels and binary-valued elements (0 and 1). From our perspective, pattern pruning is an element-wise multiplication of different P's and original kernels. The set of different P's is the *pattern library*.

The multi-layer DNN are formed by cascading functional layers. Applying P on every convolution kernel across layers is intrinsically an interpolation operation of P's. Different patterns can form functional steerable filters [9] (e.g., Gaussian blur filter, sharpen filter, edge detection filter, etc.) by interpolation, and this process only needs a limited number of patterns (i.e., a small pattern library). A small pattern library has two advantages, (i) at algorithm level, an appropriate number of patterns ensures the flexible search space for achieving a solution with good performance on DNN and (ii) at compiler level, fewer patterns means fewer computation paradigms after kernel reordering and grouping, which reduces thread level divergence.

4.2 Pattern Library Design

Our designed patterns could be transformed to a series of steerable filters [9], which in our case, the Gaussian filter and Laplacian of Gaussian filter by interpolating patterns through DNN layers.

Transform Patterns to Gaussian Filter: Consider a two-dimensional Gaussian filter $\mathcal{G}$:

$$\mathcal{G}(x, y, \sigma) = \frac{1}{2\pi\sigma^2} e^{-\frac{x^2+y^2}{2\sigma^2}} \tag{1}$$

x and y are input coordinates, and σ^2 is variance.

Binomial coefficients give a compact approximation of the Gaussian coefficients using only integers. To apply the Gaussian filters with 3×3 filter size, we utilize the following approximation. According to (1) and set $\sigma^2 = \frac{1}{2}$, in the 1-D situation, the approximation of Gaussian filter $[1\ 2\ 1]$ is given by the convolution of two box filters $[1\ 1]$. Then we get the 2-D approximation of Gaussian filter by convolving $[1\ 2\ 1]$ and $[1\ 2\ 1]^T$, and the result is $\begin{bmatrix} 1 & 2 & 1 \\ 2 & 4 & 2 \\ 1 & 2 & 1 \end{bmatrix}$.

Interpolation in multi-layer DNN is proved to be convergent [30]. We can make further approximation by interpolating patterns into convolutional layers (i.e. uniformly map patterns to each kernel). In continuous probability space, interpolating patterns into convolution function is a specific Probability Density Function (PDF), so the effect of interpolating patterns is accumulating probability expectations of interpolation into n convolutional layers.

$$\underbrace{\begin{bmatrix} 1 & 1 & 0 \\ 1 & 1 & 0 \\ 0 & 0 & 0 \end{bmatrix} \cdots \begin{bmatrix} 0 & 1 & 1 \\ 0 & 1 & 1 \\ 0 & 0 & 0 \end{bmatrix} \cdots \begin{bmatrix} 0 & 0 & 0 \\ 1 & 1 & 0 \\ 1 & 1 & 0 \end{bmatrix} \cdots \begin{bmatrix} 0 & 0 & 0 \\ 0 & 1 & 1 \\ 0 & 1 & 1 \end{bmatrix}}_{n\ \text{interpolations}} = \begin{bmatrix} p & 2p & p \\ 2p & 4p & 2p \\ p & 2p & p \end{bmatrix}^n = \left[p \begin{bmatrix} 1 & 2 & 1 \\ 2 & 4 & 2 \\ 1 & 2 & 1 \end{bmatrix} \right]^n \tag{2}$$

The four pattern masks P shown in colored positions in (2) form the Gaussian filter through interpolation. The coefficient p has no effect after normalization.

Transform Patterns to Laplacian of Gaussian Filter: The Laplacian operator is a second derivative operator. According to the associative property, smoothing an image with Gaussian filter and then applying Laplacian operator is equivalent to convolve the image with the Laplacian of Gaussian (LoG) filter:

$$\nabla^2 \mathcal{G}(x, y, \sigma) = \left(\frac{x^2 + y^2}{\sigma^4} - \frac{2}{\sigma^2} \right) \mathcal{G}(x, y, \sigma) \tag{3}$$

LoG has elegant mathematical properties, and is valid for a variety of applications including image enhancement, edge detection, and stereo matching.

Taylor series expansion is utilized to determine the approximate values of the LoG filter with 3×3 filter size. First, we consider the 1-D situation. The Taylor series expansions of 1-D Gaussian filter $\mathcal{G}(x)$ are given by:

$$\mathcal{G}(x+\delta) = \mathcal{G}(x) + \delta\mathcal{G}'(x) + \frac{1}{2}\delta^2\mathcal{G}''(x) + \frac{1}{3!}\delta^3\mathcal{G}'''(x) + \mathcal{O}\left(\delta^4\right) \tag{4}$$

$$\mathcal{G}(x-\delta) = \mathcal{G}(x) - \delta\mathcal{G}'(x) + \frac{1}{2}\delta^2\mathcal{G}''(x) - \frac{1}{3!}\delta^3\mathcal{G}'''(x) + \mathcal{O}\left(\delta^4\right) \tag{5}$$

By summing (4) and (5), we have

$$[\mathcal{G}(x-\delta) - 2\mathcal{G}(x) + \mathcal{G}(x+\delta)]/\delta^2 = \nabla^2\mathcal{G}(x) + \mathcal{O}\left(\delta^2\right) \tag{6}$$

Applying central difference approximation of LoG $\nabla^2\mathcal{G}(x)$, we derive the 1-D approximation of LoG filter as $[1\ -2\ 1]$. Then we procure the 2-D approximation of LoG filter by convolving $[1\ -2\ 1]$ and $[1\ -2\ 1]^T$, and get $\begin{bmatrix} -1 & 2 & -1 \\ 2 & -4 & 2 \\ -1 & 2 & -1 \end{bmatrix}$ as the *1st approximation*. According to (6), we have

$$\nabla^2\mathcal{G}(x,y) = \left([1\ -2\ 1] + \begin{bmatrix} 1 \\ -2 \\ 1 \end{bmatrix}\right) * \mathcal{G}(x,y) \tag{7}$$

Based on (7), we derive the *2nd approximation* as $\begin{bmatrix} 0 & 1 & 0 \\ 1 & -4 & 1 \\ 0 & 1 & 0 \end{bmatrix}$.

According to the central limit theorem, the convolution of two Gaussian functions is still a Gaussian function. Hence, we convolve the above two approximations of LoG and then apply normalization, and get the *Enhanced Laplacian of Gaussian* (ELoG) filter as $\begin{bmatrix} 0 & 1 & 0 \\ 1 & 8 & 1 \\ 0 & 1 & 0 \end{bmatrix}$.

Similarly, we make the further approximation by interpolating patterns into convolutional layers.

$$\underbrace{\begin{bmatrix} 0 & 1 & 0 \\ 1 & 1 & 1 \\ 0 & 0 & 0 \end{bmatrix} \cdots \begin{bmatrix} 0 & 1 & 0 \\ 1 & 1 & 0 \\ 0 & 1 & 0 \end{bmatrix} \cdots \begin{bmatrix} 0 & 0 & 0 \\ 1 & 1 & 1 \\ 0 & 1 & 0 \end{bmatrix} \cdots \begin{bmatrix} 0 & 1 & 0 \\ 0 & 1 & 1 \\ 0 & 1 & 0 \end{bmatrix}}_{n \text{ interpolations}} = \begin{bmatrix} 0 & p & 0 \\ p & 1 & p \\ 0 & p & 0 \end{bmatrix}^n = \left[\begin{bmatrix} 0 & 1 & 0 \\ 1 & 1/p & 1 \\ 0 & 1 & 0 \end{bmatrix}\right]^n \tag{8}$$

The four pattern masks P shown in colored positions in (8) form the ELoG filter through interpolation. In order to get the best approximation to ELoG filter, we set $p = 0.75$ and $n = 8$, then the desired filter is equal to interpolating these four patterns for eight times. The coefficient p has no effect after normalization.

5   Pattern-Aware Network Pruning Framework for Pattern Library Extraction

In Sect. 4, we have determined the (eight) patterns as our pattern library through theoretical derivation. However, are these theoretically derived patterns also the most desirable at algorithm level? How to select the appropriate pattern for each kernel and train corresponding (remaining) weights? To answer these questions, we propose a novel *pattern-aware network pruning* framework, simultaneously achieving pattern library extraction (with predefined number of patterns in library), pattern assignment, and weight training.

In pattern library extraction, we start from a large library comprising all possible candidate patterns. By extending ADMM [4] and incorporating Primal-Proximal solution technique, we make convolution kernels dynamically "select" the best suited patterns within the library and train the unpruned weights. Then we delete the least selected patterns in the library, thereby updating the library. The previous step is iterated on the updated library, with a single step as shown below.

5.1   Pattern Library Extraction – A Single Step

For an N-layer DNN of interest, let $\mathbf{W}$ denote the collection of weights for all 3×3 kernels, i.e., $\mathbf{W} = \{\mathbf{W}_i\}_{i=1}^{N}$. The pattern of each kernel $\mathbf{W}_i$ is restricted to a finite pattern library $\Omega = \{\mathbf{M}_1, \ldots, \mathbf{M}_j, \ldots, \mathbf{M}_K\}$, where $\mathbf{M}_j$ denotes a binary mask, and K denotes the total number of possible patterns. We choose to reserve 4 non-zero entries in a kernel to match the SIMD (single-instruction multiple-data) architecture of embedded CPU/GPU processors, thereby maximizing throughput. As a result, the initial $K = \binom{9}{4} = 126$, and K will decrease in each step.

The purpose of each step is to select a pattern from the current library for each kernel, and train the non-zero weights. Let $f(\mathbf{W}; \mathcal{D})$ denote the training loss ($\mathcal{D}$ denotes training data), we pose the following optimization problem

$$\underset{\mathbf{W}, \mathbf{z}}{\text{minimize}} \ f(\{\mathbf{W}_i \circ (\textstyle\sum_{j=1}^{K} z_j \mathbf{M}_j)\}_{i=1}^{N}; \mathcal{D})$$
$$\text{subject to } z_j \in \{0, 1\}, \forall j, \quad \textstyle\sum_{j=1}^{K} z_j = 1, \tag{9}$$

where z_j denotes the Boolean selection variable to indicate which pattern in Ω is chosen for $\mathbf{W}_i$. The constraint $\sum_{j=1}^{K} z_j = 1$ indicates that only one pattern is selected, and thus $\mathbf{W}_i \circ (\sum_{j=1}^{K} z_j \mathbf{M}_j)$ denotes the pattern-pruned kernel using one of pruning patterns. Here $\circ$ denotes element-wise product. In (9), we have *two* types of optimization variables: (i) 3×3 kernel weights $\mathbf{W}$, (ii) pattern Boolean selection variables $\mathbf{z} \in [0, 1]^K$. The pattern selection scheme is co-optimized with non-zero weight training.

To solve the above problem analytically, we introduce auxiliary variables $\mathbf{u}$ together with constraints $\mathbf{z} = \mathbf{u}$. Based on that, we reformulate problem (9) as

$$\underset{\mathbf{W}, \mathbf{u}}{\text{minimize}} \ f(\{\mathbf{W}_i \circ (\textstyle\sum_{j=1}^{K} z_j \mathbf{M}_j)\}_{i=1}^{N}; \mathcal{D}) + \mathcal{I}(\mathbf{u})$$
$$\text{subject to } \mathbf{z} = \mathbf{u} \tag{10}$$

where $\mathcal{I}(\mathbf{u})$ is the indicator function

$$\mathcal{I}(\mathbf{u}) = \begin{cases} 0 & \text{if } u_j \in [0, 1], \forall j, \quad \textstyle\sum_{j=1}^{K} u_j = 1 \\ \infty & \text{otherwise.} \end{cases} \tag{11}$$

Here we relax the binary selection variable $z_i \in \{0, 1\}$ to the (continuous) probabilistic selection variable $u_i \in [0, 1]$.

The augmented Lagrangian function of problem (10) is given by

$$\mathcal{L}(\mathbf{W}, \mathbf{z}, \mathbf{u}, \boldsymbol{\mu}) = f\left(\{\mathbf{W}_i \circ (\sum_{j=1}^{K} z_j \mathbf{M}_j)\}_{i=1}^{N}; \mathcal{D}\right) \tag{12}$$
$$+ \mathcal{I}(\mathbf{u}) + \boldsymbol{\mu}^T(\mathbf{z} - \mathbf{u}) + \frac{\rho}{2}\|\mathbf{z} - \mathbf{u}\|_2^2$$

where $\boldsymbol{\mu}$ is Lagrangian multipliers, and $\|\cdot\|_2$ denotes the Frobenius norm. $\rho > 0$ is a given augmented penalty value, and for ease of notation we view matrices as *vectors* in optimization.

ADMM is then given by the following alternating optimization process. At iteration t, ADMM yields

$$\mathbf{W}^{(t)}, \mathbf{z}^{(t)} = \arg \min_{\mathbf{W}, \mathbf{z}} \mathcal{L}(\mathbf{W}, \mathbf{z}, \mathbf{u}^{(t-1)}, \boldsymbol{\mu}^{(t-1)}) \qquad \text{(Primal)}$$

$$\mathbf{u}^{(t)} = \arg \min_{\mathbf{u}} \mathcal{L}(\mathbf{W}^{(t)}, \mathbf{z}^{(t)}, \mathbf{u}, \boldsymbol{\mu}^{(t-1)}) \qquad \text{(Proximal)}$$

$$\boldsymbol{\mu}^{(t)} = \boldsymbol{\mu}^{(t-1)} + \rho(\mathbf{z}^{(t)} - \mathbf{u}^{(t)}), \tag{13}$$

where the initial values $\mathbf{u}^{(0)}$ and $\boldsymbol{\mu}^{(0)}$ are given.

Problem (Primal) can be simplified to

$$\text{minimize}_{\mathbf{W}, \mathbf{z}} \; f(\{\mathbf{W}_i \circ (\sum_{j=1}^{K} z_j \mathbf{M}_j)\}_{i=1}^{N}; \mathcal{D}) + \frac{\rho}{2}\|\mathbf{z} - \mathbf{a}\|_2^2 \tag{14}$$

where $\mathbf{a} := (\mathbf{u}^{(t-1)} - (1/\rho)\boldsymbol{\mu}^{(t-1)})$. In problem (14), the objective function is differentiable, and can thus be solved by standard DNN solvers in SGD.

Problem (Proximal) can be equivalently decomposed over $\mathbf{u}$. This leads to problem

$$\text{minimize}_{\mathbf{u}} \; \frac{\rho}{2}\|\mathbf{u} - \mathbf{d}\|_2^2$$
$$\text{subject to } u_j \in [0, 1], \forall j, \quad \sum_{j=1}^{K} u_j = 1, \tag{15}$$

where $\mathbf{d} := \mathbf{z}^{(t)} + (1/\rho)\boldsymbol{\mu}^{(t-1)}$.

Based on [26], the analytical solution to problem (15) is

$$\mathbf{u}^{(t)} = [\mathbf{d} - \nu \mathbf{1}]_+, \tag{16}$$

where $[x]_+ = x$ if $x \geq 0$ and 0 otherwise, ν is the root of the equation

$$\mathbf{1}^T [\mathbf{d} - \nu \mathbf{1}]_+ = 1. \tag{17}$$

Once $\mathbf{W}$ and $\mathbf{z}$ are solved, $\mathbf{z}$ is a continuous variable rather than a binary variable. We need an intermediate step to project continuous $\mathbf{z}_{\mathrm{admm}}$ to integer $\mathbf{z}_{\mathrm{binary}}$, yielding

$$\underset{\mathbf{z}_{\mathrm{binary}}}{\text{minimize}} \quad \|\mathbf{z}_{\mathrm{binary}} - \mathbf{z}_{\mathrm{admm}}\|_2^2$$
$$\text{subject to } \mathbf{1}^T \mathbf{z} = 1, z_i \in \{0, 1\}, \forall i. \tag{18}$$

The solution is given by $[\mathbf{z}_{\mathrm{binary}}]_i = 1$ if $i = \mathrm{argmax}_j [\mathbf{z}_{\mathrm{admm}}]_j$, and 0 otherwise. At this point, we have simultaneously selected pattern for each kernel and trained the non-zero weights.

5.2   Pattern Library Extraction – Overall

The overall pattern library extraction starts from $K = 126$ and decreases K in each step, with algorithm brief shown in Algorithm 1. In actual implementation we set the new K to be 12 in the first step as most of the patterns occur in very few times. We set the target K to be either 12, 8, or 4. When the type of patterns is within this range, the overhead in code generation at compiler level can be kept small and parallelism can be maximized.

Total Runtime: Despite an iterative process, the total number of epochs (and training time) can be limited. This is because except for the last step, we only need to extract a number of patterns instead of finishing the final training of non-zero weights. As a result, we can finish each step with 10% to 20% of the total epochs as training of the original DNN. In the last step, we need around 9–12 ADMM iterations, each requiring less than 20% of the total epochs of original DNN training. So the total number of training epochs using PyTorch [27] is around 300–400 for the whole process, which is even lower compared with many prior art [10,22].

Algorithm 1: Pattern library extraction process.

---

1 **Initialization:** $\Omega = \{\mathbf{M}_1, \mathbf{M}_2 \dots, \mathbf{M}_K\}$ with $K = 126$;
  Result: Subsets Ω' with $K = 12, 8$ or 4;
2 **while** *training neural network* **do**
3 | Update W by solving (Primal) ;
4 | **for** $K \leftarrow 126$ *until* $K = 12, 8$ *or* 4 **do**
5 | | Solving (Proximal) using current Ω;
6 | | Update μ in (13);
7 | | Calculate pattern distribution of current Ω ;
8 | | Removing patterns with fewest occurrences in Ω ;
9 | **end**
10 **end**

---

6   Connectivity Sparsity and the New Sparsity Induced Inference Framework

6.1   Connectivity Sparsity

Connectivity sparsity is achieved by connectivity pruning which can be integrated in the same algorithm-level solution in Sect. 5.1 and compiler-assisted mobile inference framework. Using the same notations as in Sect. 5.1, we define the collection of weights in i-th layer as $\mathbf{W}_i \in \mathbb{R}^{H_i \times W_i \times F_i \times C_i}$, where H and W denote the dimension of the convolution kernel. F and C denote the number of filters and channels, respectively. We further define critical connectivity score for each convolution kernel as

$$\gamma_{i,f,c}(\mathbf{W}_i) = ||[\mathbf{W}_i]_{:,:,f,c}||_2 \tag{19}$$

where f and c are filter and channel indices, respectively. The problem formulation and solution framework for achieving connectivity sparsity is similar with the ones in Sect. 5.1. The difference is that the constraint in the framework is related to $\gamma_{i,f,c}$. Please note that our algorithm level solution can solve the problems of pattern and connectivity pruning simultaneously or individually.

6.2   Compiler-Assisted Inference Framework for Real-Time Execution

After we obtain pattern and connectivity sparsity combined in a DNN model, we use a compiler-assisted inference framework to maximize the execution efficiency by utilizing multiple optimization techniques that are induced by pattern-based sparsity. The compiler optimizations showing in Fig. 3 target on DNN computation graph and memory access for on-device executions.

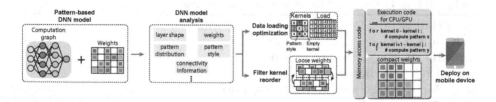

Fig. 3. Overview of the compiler level DNN inference framework.

Layerwise Optimization for DNN Computation Graph is designed to achieve the best of instruction-level and thread-level parallelism by utilizing the unique filter/kernel re-ordering technique as Fig. 3 shows. In the weight matrix illustration, the internal squares with different colors denote different pattern styles, and empty white squares denote connectivity sparsity. By filter/kernel re-ordering, we (i) organize the filters with similar kernels together to improve *inter-thread* parallelism, and (ii) group kernels with identical patterns in each filter together to improve *intra-thread* parallelism. By DNN computation graph optimization, the generated execution code eliminates all of the execution branches, implying higher instruction-level parallelism; meanwhile, similar filter groups escalate execution similarity and result in a good load balance, achieving better thread-level parallelism.

Memory Access Optimizations For Hardware Execution address the poor memory performance due to the irregular memory access. In DNN execution, the input/output data access is associated with the non-zero elements of the weights. Since in pattern-based sparse model, the non-zero pattern of each kernel is already known, we can generate data access code with this information for each kernel pattern and call them dynamically during DNN execution. With the data access code, it is possible to directly access valid input data that is associated with the non-zero elements in a pattern-based kernel. Moreover, after DNN computation graph optimization, the model weights distribution is highly compact and structured as Fig. 3 shows, which reduces the calling frequency of data access code and as a result, reduces the memory overhead.

7   Experimental Results

In our experiment, our generated pattern-based sparse models are based on four widely used network structures, VGG-16 [29], ResNet-18/50 [11] and MobileNet-V2 [15], and are trained on an eight NVIDIA RTX-2080Ti GPUs server using PyTorch [27]. We show the consistency of pattern library extraction results with the theoretically designed pattern library in Sect. 4.2, and provide the accuracy improvement and image enhancement demonstrations. We also show the overall compression results of pattern-based pruning in different DNN models. In order to show acceleration of pattern-based sparsity on mobile devices, we compare it with three state-of-the-art DNN inference acceleration frameworks, TFLite [1], TVM [6], and MNN [2]. Our experiments are conducted on a Samsung Galaxy S10 cell phone with the latest Qualcomm Snapdragon 855 mobile platform that consists of a Qualcomm Kryo 485 Octa-core CPU and a Qualcomm Adreno 640 GPU.

7.1   Pattern Library Extraction Result

We use VGG-16 on ImageNet dataset to extract pattern libraries. VGG-16 has more than 1,630,000 convolution kernels. However, patterns can be concentrated to 12 styles in only a couple of steps. Figure 4 shows the pattern styles distribution results when K decreases to 32 after two steps. We can see that most of the patterns are distributed in the top 12 styles, namely Phase 1 pattern library. If we continue to decrease K to 8, the remaining 8 patterns form Phase 2 pattern library. We can notice that Phase 2 is *exactly the same* with our derived pattern library in Sect. 4.2. Further extraction step will give us Phase 3 pattern library, which is the top-4 pattern styles. Using other DNNs and datasets gives us the

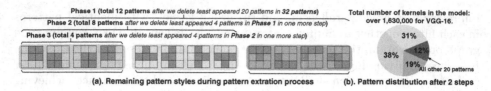

(a). Remaining pattern styles during pattern extration process   (b). Pattern distribution after 2 steps

Fig. 4. The pattern library extraction result. When $K = 32$ after two steps, the pattern distribution is shown in *(b)* with different colors representing different pattern styles in *(a)*. The 20 less significant patterns only account for 12% of the total 32 patterns, and the rest 12 patterns form the *Phase 1* pattern library. If we continue the extraction step, we can get *Phase 2* and *Phase 3* pattern libraries as *(a)* shows.

same extraction results, thereby we can conclude that the theoretically derived patterns are also the most desirable ones at algorithm level.

7.2 Visualization Demonstration and Accuracy Analysis for Pattern Pruning

After we obtain the extracted pattern libraries in three phases (i.e., containing 12, 8 or 4 patterns respectively), we need to validate the image enhancement effects and evaluate the accuracy of the pattern pruned DNN.

Visualization Comparisons of applying Phase 2 pattern library to an original DNN model (*pattern pruning*) are demonstrated in Fig. 5. To ensure the fairness in comparisons, we adopt three visualization methods to eliminate the impact of causal factors. They are (a) *Guided-backpropagation (BP)* [31], (b) *Integrated gradients* [23], and (c) *Inverted representation* [3]. Through different visualization techniques, we can see what a DNN has learned and how well it can preserve the photographically accurate information from an image.

We provide strong evidence in Fig. 5 that pattern pruned VGG-16 model can effectively capture more image details and less noise compared with the original VGG-16 model. We conclude that the accuracy improvement is attributed to the enhanced image processing ability of our designed pattern library.

Accuracy Evaluation is shown in Fig. 6 (a). Starting from the baseline accuracy results that are in many cases higher than prior works, we have the first conclusion that *the accuracy improvements are more significant when applying the designed 8 patterns (i.e., pattern library at Phase 2) on each convolution kernel*. The accuracy improvements are consistently observed on various network structures (e.g., VGG-16, ResNet-18/50, MobileNet-V2) on CIFAR-10 and ImageNet datasets.

7.3 Connectivity Pruning and Overall Model Compression Results

Combining connectivity sparsity with pattern sparsity has different DNN performances with different pattern libraries. Figure 6 (b) illustrates testing accuracies

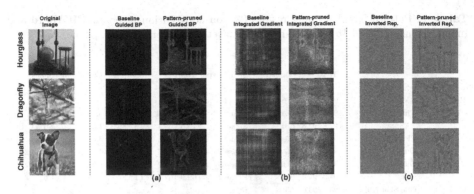

Fig. 5. Visualization comparisons of three images from ImageNet dataset on original and pattern pruned VGG-16 model using (a) guided-backpropagation (BP); (b) integrated gradients and (c) inverted representation methods.

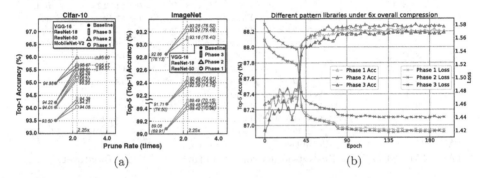

Fig. 6. (a) Accuracy improvement results from pattern pruning on different DNN models and datasets (CIFAR-10 & ImageNet). (b) Overall 6× compression for ResNet-18 on ImageNet training curves for connectivity sparsity.

of training connectivity sparsity combined with existing pattern sparsity. From diagram, we can clearly notice that by using designed pattern library (Phase 2), we can achieve better training performance, thereby higher DNN accuracy. Similar paradigm can be observed with different compression rates and on different networks/datasets. Please note that pattern sparsity already reserves 2.25× compression rate, and we add different connectivity compression rates upon it to achieve the different overall compression rates. Table 1 records the best final DNN accuracies and compression rates regarding their pattern styles, and are compared with several pruning methods with their sparsity types.

Table 1. Pattern-based pruning results (%) on convolution layer for CIFAR-10 and ImageNet using VGG-16, ResNet-18 and ResNet-50 (**O**: original, **P**: prune).

	Pruning framework	CIFAR-10				ImageNet					
		Top-1		Comp. rate	Sparse type	Top-1		Top-5		Comp. rate	Sparse type
		O	P			O	P	O	P		
ResNet-18[†]	AMC [13]	90.5	90.2	2.0×	Struct.	-	-	-	-	-	-
	Tiny [21]	94.1	93.2	15.1×	Struct.	N/A	N/A	89.1	88.4	3.3×	Struct.
	TAS [8]	92.8	92.8	1.8×	Struct.	70.6	69.1	89.8	89.2	1.5×	Struct.
	FPGM [12]	92.2	91.9	2.5×	Struct.	70.2	68.3	89.6	88.5	3.3×	Struct.
	Ours	94.0	94.7	8.0×	Phase 2	69.9	69.6	89.1	89.2	4.0×	Phase 2
	Ours	94.0	94.6	12.0×	Phase 3	69.9	68.2	89.1	88.3	6.0×	Phase 2
	Ours	94.0	94.2	16.0×	Phase 2	69.9	67.1	89.1	87.7	8.0×	Phase 2
ResNet-50*	One Shot [19]	93.8	93.6	2.5×	Irreg.	-	-	-	-	-	-
	ADMM-NN [28]	-	-	-	-	N/A	N/A	N/A	92.3	7.0×	Irreg.
	TAS [8]	94.5	93.7	2.0×	Struct.	77.5	76.2	93.5	93.1	1.7×	Struct.
	GAL [16]	93.3	90.4	2.9×	Struct.	76.4	69.3	92.8	89.1	2.5×	Struct.
	FPGM [12]	93.6	93.5	2.5×	Struct.	76.2	75.6	92.8	92.6	3.3×	Struct.
	GBN [35]	-	-	-	-	75.8	75.2	92.7	92.4	2.2×	Struct.
	Ours	94.2	95.2	8.0×	Phase 3	76.1	75.9	92.9	92.7	3.9×	Phase 2
	Ours	94.2	94.9	12.0×	Phase 3	76.1	75.8	92.9	92.8	4.9×	Phase 3
	Ours	94.2	94.5	16.0×	Phase 3	76.1	75.6	92.9	92.6	5.8×	Phase 2
VGG-16	NeST [7]	-	-	-	-	71.6	69.3	90.4	89.4	6.5×	Irreg.
	ADMM-NN [28]	-	-	-	-	69.0	68.7	89.1	88.9	10.2×	Irreg.
	DecorReg [36]	93.5	93.3	8.5×	Struct.	73.1	73.2	N/A	N/A	3.9×	Struct.
	GAL [16]	93.9	90.8	5.6×	Struct.	-	-	-	-	-	-
	Ours	93.5	93.4	8.0×	Phase 2	74.5	74.4	91.7	91.5	8.0×	Phase 2
	Ours	93.5	93.3	11.6×	Phase 2	74.5	74.1	91.7	91.3	10.0×	Phase 2
	Ours	93.5	93.2	19.7×	Phase 1	74.5	73.6	91.7	91.0	12.0×	Phase 2

† TAS, FPGM use ResNet-20 network structure on CIFAR-10 dataset.
* TAS, GAL, FPGM use ResNet-56 network structure on CIFAR-10 dataset.

7.4 Performance Evaluation on Mobile Platform

In this part, we demonstrate our evaluation results on mobile devices. To guarantee fairness, all frameworks are using the same pattern-based sparse model, and we also enable the fully optimized configurations of TFLite, TVM and MNN (e.g., Winograd optimization is turned on).

Execution Time. Figure 7 shows mobile CPU/GPU execution time of pattern-based model on different platforms. Since Phase 2 pattern library has best performance on pruning, our testing model are using Phase 2 patterns and 8× overall compression rate for ResNet-18, 5.8× for ResNet-50 and 12× for VGG-16. The inference is using images from ImageNet dataset. We can see our approach achieves significant acceleration on mobile device compared with other frameworks. Real-time execution usually requires 30 frames/sec (i.e., 33 ms/frame). From our results, all of our DNN models on ImageNet meet or far exceed this requirement, and some of them can even accomplish real-time inference on mobile CPU.

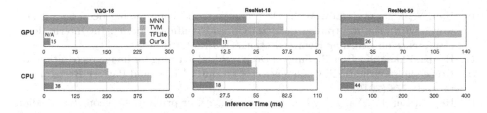

Fig. 7. Inference time (ms) comparisons for different mobile inference frameworks using image from ImageNet dataset.

8 Conclusion

This paper proposes pattern-based sparsity, along with the highly efficient algorithm level pruning framework and the novel compiler level inference framework. Pattern-based sparsity inherits the flexibility from non-structured sparsity and regularity from structured sparsity, achieving both highly accurate/compressed model and hardware friendliness. Particularly, with carefully designed pattern library, pattern pruning achieves image enhancement and accuracy improvement. The pattern-based sparsity elicits compiler optimization, achieving real-time inference on mobile devices on various representative large-scale DNNs.

Acknowledgment. This work is supported by the National Science Foundation CCF-1919117, CCF-1937500, CNS-1909172, CNS-2011260, and is sponsored by DiDi GAIA Research Collaboration Initiative. We thank all anonymous reviewers for their feedback.

References

1. https://www.tensorflow.org/mobile/tflite/
2. https://github.com/alibaba/MNN
3. Aravindh, M., Andrea, V.: Understanding deep image representations by inverting them. In: IEEE Conference on Computer Vision and Pattern Recognition, CVPR 2015 (2015)
4. Boyd, S., Parikh, N., Chu, E., Peleato, B., Eckstein, J.: Distributed optimization and statistical learning via the alternating direction method of multipliers. Found. Trends® Mach. Learn. **3**(1), 1–122 (2011)
5. Chen, C.F., Oh, J., Fan, Q., Pistoia, M.: SC-CONV: sparse-complementary convolution for efficient model utilization on CNNs. In: 2018 IEEE International Symposium on Multimedia (ISM), pp. 97–100. IEEE (2018)
6. Chen, T., et al.: TVM: an automated end-to-end optimizing compiler for deep learning. In: OSDI (2018)
7. Dai, X., Yin, H., Jha, N.K.: Nest: a neural network synthesis tool based on a grow-and-prune paradigm. IEEE Trans. Comput. **68**(10), 1487–1497 (2019)
8. Dong, X., Yang, Y.: Network pruning via transformable architecture search. In: Advances in Neural Information Processing Systems, pp. 759–770 (2019)
9. Freeman, W., Adelson, E.: The design and use of steerable filters. In: IEEE Transactions on Pattern Analysis and Machine Intelligence, vol. 13, pp. 891–906. IEEE (1991)

10. Han, S., Mao, H., Dally, W.J.: Deep compression: compressing deep neural networks with pruning, trained quantization and Huffman coding. In: International Conference on Learning Representations (ICLR) (2016)
11. He, K., Zhang, X., Ren, S., Sun, J.: Deep residual learning for image recognition. In: Proceedings of the IEEE Conference on Computer Vision and Pattern Recognition, pp. 770–778 (2016)
12. He, Y., Liu, P., Wang, Z., Hu, Z., Yang, Y.: Filter pruning via geometric median for deep convolutional neural networks acceleration. In: Proceedings of the IEEE Conference on Computer Vision and Pattern Recognition, pp. 4340–4349 (2019)
13. He, Y., Lin, J., Liu, Z., Wang, H., Li, L.-J., Han, S.: AMC: AutoML for model compression and acceleration on mobile devices. In: Ferrari, V., Hebert, M., Sminchisescu, C., Weiss, Y. (eds.) ECCV 2018. LNCS, vol. 11211, pp. 815–832. Springer, Cham (2018). https://doi.org/10.1007/978-3-030-01234-2_48
14. He, Y., Zhang, X., Sun, J.: Channel pruning for accelerating very deep neural networks. In: 2017 IEEE International Conference on Computer Vision (ICCV), pp. 1398–1406. IEEE (2017)
15. Howard, A.G., et al.: Mobilenets: efficient convolutional neural networks for mobile vision applications. arXiv preprint arXiv:1704.04861 (2017)
16. Lin, S., et al.: Towards optimal structured CNN pruning via generative adversarial learning. In: Proceedings of the IEEE Conference on Computer Vision and Pattern Recognition, pp. 2790–2799 (2019)
17. Liu, B., Wang, M., Foroosh, H., Tappen, M., Pensky, M.: Sparse convolutional neural networks. In: CVPR, pp. 806–814 (2015)
18. Liu, N., Ma, X., Xu, Z., Wang, Y., Tang, J., Ye, J.: Autocompress: an automatic DNN structured pruning framework for ultra-high compression rates. In: AAAI, pp. 4876–4883 (2020)
19. Liu, Z., Sun, M., Zhou, T., Huang, G., Darrell, T.: Rethinking the value of network pruning. In: International Conference on Learning Representations (2019)
20. Ma, X., et al.: PCONV: the missing but desirable sparsity in DNN weight pruning for real-time execution on mobile devices. In: AAAI, pp. 5117–5124 (2020)
21. Ma, X., et al.: Tiny but accurate: a pruned, quantized and optimized memristor crossbar framework for ultra efficient DNN implementation. In: ASP-DAC (2020)
22. Molchanov, P., Tyree, S., Karras, T., Aila, T., Kautz, J.: Pruning convolutional neural networks for resource efficient inference. arXiv preprint arXiv:1611.06440 (2016)
23. Mukund, S., Ankur, T., Qiqi, Y.: Axiomatic attribution for deep networks. In: 2017 International Conference on Machine Learning (ICML). ACM/IEEE (2017)
24. Niu, W., et al.: PatDNN: achieving real-time DNN execution on mobile devices with pattern-based weight pruning. In: Proceedings of the Twenty-Fifth International Conference on Architectural Support for Programming Languages and Operating Systems, pp. 907–922 (2020)
25. Parashar, A., et al.: SCNN: an accelerator for compressed-sparse convolutional neural networks. In: ISCA (2017)
26. Parikh, N., Boyd, S.: Proximal algorithms. Found. Trends® Optim. 1(3), 127–239 (2014)
27. Paszke, A., et al.: Pytorch: an imperative style, high-performance deep learning library. In: NeurIPS (2019)
28. Ren, A., et al.: ADMM-NN: an algorithm-hardware co-design framework of DNNs using alternating direction methods of multipliers. In: ASPLOS, pp. 925–938 (2019)
29. Simonyan, K., Zisserman, A.: Very deep convolutional networks for large-scale image recognition. arXiv preprint arXiv:1409.1556 (2014)

30. Siyuan, M., Raef, B., Mikhail, B.: The power of interpolation: understanding the effectiveness of SGD in modern over-parametrized learning. In: 2018 International Conference on Machine Learning (ICML). ACM/IEEE (2018)
31. Springenberg, J.T., Alexey Dosovitskiy, T.B.a.R.: Striving for simplicity: the all convolutional net. In: ICLR-2015 Workshop Track (2015)
32. Wen, W., Wu, C., Wang, Y., Chen, Y., Li, H.: Learning structured sparsity in deep neural networks. In: Advances in Neural Information Processing Systems, pp. 2074–2082 (2016)
33. Xu, M., Zhu, M., Liu, Y., Lin, F.X., Liu, X.: Deepcache: principled cache for mobile deep vision. In: Proceedings of the 24th Annual International Conference on Mobile Computing and Networking, pp. 129–144. ACM (2018)
34. Yao, S., Hu, S., Zhao, Y., Zhang, A., Abdelzaher, T.: Deepsense: a unified deep learning framework for time-series mobile sensing data processing. In: Proceedings of the 26th International Conference on World Wide Web (2017)
35. You, Z., Yan, K., Ye, J., Ma, M., Wang, P.: Gate decorator: Global filter pruning method for accelerating deep convolutional neural networks. In: Advances in Neural Information Processing Systems, pp. 2130–2141 (2019)
36. Zhu, X., Zhou, W., Li, H.: Improving deep neural network sparsity through decorrelation regularization. In: IJCAI (2018)

AutoTrajectory: Label-Free Trajectory Extraction and Prediction from Videos Using Dynamic Points

Yuexin Ma[1(✉)], Xinge Zhu[2], Xinjing Cheng[3], Ruigang Yang[3], Jiming Liu[1], and Dinesh Manocha[4]

[1] Hong Kong Baptist University, Hong Kong, China
yuexinma93@gmail.com
[2] Chinese University of Hong Kong, Hong Kong, China
[3] Inceptio, Fremont, USA
[4] University of Maryland at College Park, College Park, USA

Abstract. Current methods for trajectory prediction operate in supervised manners, and therefore require vast quantities of corresponding ground truth data for training. In this paper, we present a novel, label-free algorithm, AutoTrajectory, for trajectory extraction and prediction to use raw videos directly. To better capture the moving objects in videos, we introduce dynamic points. We use them to model dynamic motions by using a forward-backward extractor to keep temporal consistency and using image reconstruction to keep spatial consistency in an unsupervised manner. Then we aggregate dynamic points to instance points, which stand for moving objects such as pedestrians in videos. Finally, we extract trajectories by matching instance points for prediction training. To the best of our knowledge, our method is the first to achieve unsupervised learning of trajectory extraction and prediction. We evaluate the performance on well-known trajectory datasets and show that our method is effective for real-world videos and can use raw videos to further improve the performance of existing models.

1 Introduction

For intelligent agents like robots and autonomous vehicles, it is crucial to be able to forecast neighboring traffic-agents' future trajectories for navigation and planning applications. Trajectory prediction for dynamic objects has been widely studied and is an active area of research. Some traditional methods for trajectory prediction are based on motion models such as Bayesian networks [25], Kalman filters [2], Gaussian process regression models [18], etc. These methods can deal with simple scenarios with very few moving instances, but are limited in complex real-world scenarios with many instances or agents interacting with

---

Y. Ma and X. Zhu—Equal contribution.

Electronic supplementary material The online version of this chapter (https://doi.org/10.1007/978-3-030-58601-0_38) contains supplementary material, which is available to authorized users.

A. Vedaldi et al. (Eds.): ECCV 2020, LNCS 12358, pp. 646–662, 2020.
https://doi.org/10.1007/978-3-030-58601-0_38

each other. Recurrent Neural Network (RNN) and its variant long short-term Memory (LSTM) have become an effective way for trajectory prediction due to its ability to model non-linear temporal dependencies in sequence learning and generation [6,31]. Based on these networks, recent works are able to achieve good accuracy on predictig trajectories for pedestrians [1,17], vehicles [24,33], and heterogeneous traffic-agents [29]. However, all of the above methods operate in supervised manners, which rely heavily on labeled trajectory data. One general method to get a trajectory dataset [26,35] is to label consecutive positions of moving traffic-agents (pedestrians or vehicles) on fixed-view videos and then transfer the trajectory from the image coordinate system to a real-world coordinate system. Labeling consecutive objects from videos is complex and expensive [19]. There is a great demand for an unsupervised learning method to alleviate the dependence on annotations by simply taking raw videos as input and automatically extracting trajectories for training prediction network.

The most pivotal and challenging task for label-free trajectory extraction is capturing the moving objects, which we also call dynamic instances, from videos without any supervision. There are some related problems that also need to learn the motion dynamics of objects from videos, like activity prediction [27], video prediction [21,30], and object tracking [11,19]. However, we found they did not perform well for common bird's-eye view videos (sometimes, we may just see the heads and shoulders of pedestrians). For such videos, it is difficult to distinguish instances for the network just by appearance and structure features, while the above methods all rely on these features. To extract trajectories for dynamic instances in videos, we need consider not only the appearance and structure features in spatial space, but also the dynamic features (consecutive motions of objects) in temporal space. Our work is based on this consideration.

Main Results: In this paper, we propose a label-free learning-based method AutoTrajectory for trajectory extraction and prediction to overcome the above difficulties. To better capture the motion dynamics of moving objects in the video, we use the concept of *dynamic points*, which can focus on dynamic locations on images. These points are derived by keeping the spatial appearance and structure consistent via self-image reconstruction and maintaining the temporal dynamic features to be consistent in consecutive frames. Because our target is to get trajectories of instances, then we use optical flow and clustering algorithms to aggregate dynamic points to instances and extract trajectories by the matching method. Finally, we use these trajectories to train the trajectory prediction network. The whole process uses no labels. Our approach contains four main parts, including dynamic point modeling, dynamic-to-instance aggregation, trajectory extraction, and trajectory prediction. The main contributions of our work are:

- We propose a label-free trajectory extraction and prediction pipeline, which can extract trajectories of dynamic instances from raw videos directly and train a prediction network.
- We propose a novel forward-backward dynamic-point extractor, which could capture dynamic features in consecutive images.
- We propose a dynamic-to-instance mechanism, which could aggregate dynamic locations to instances.

– Our method is effective and has good scalability. With more raw videos, our method can also improve existing methods in a semi-supervised manner.

2   Related Work

2.1   Trajectory Prediction

Classical model-based approaches for trajectory prediction [2,18,25,28] focus on the inherent motion regularities of objects themselves. However, the motion of dynamic objects in the real world is diverse and can be governed by many factors, like neighboring objects' motion states and the environment. These methods are limited in modeling complex scenarios. Recently, RNN and its variant LSTM have achieved great success in modeling sequence prediction tasks [6,31]. Based on these basic networks, many prediction approaches [1,7–9,17,24,29,32,33,38,39,43,44,48] have outperformed classical methods in real-world benchmarks. However, these supervised methods require large-scale, well-annotated trajectory data. Two main ways to generate the data are labeling moving instances from fixed-view videos and LiDAR point clouds. Both ways are expensive and time-consuming. Even though there are a lot of videos captured by street or commodity cameras, they cannot be used to improve the prediction performance without annotation. We try to solve this problem by using unsupervised manners.

2.2   Supervised Multi-object Tracking

Except for manual labeling, another possible solution for getting trajectories from videos is using current SOTA trackers. However, most modern trackers [4, 5,13,40,42,46,49] follow the tracking-by-detection paradigm. The performance depends largely on the detector used to find the objects as the tracking targets and the detector requires large-scale labeled data. Besides, the tracker is always trained for fixed-categories, which is hard to adapt to other domains. Recent trend in multi-object tracking is combining both detection and tracking in one framework [3,15,37]. However, they do not overcome the above limitations. Our approach focuses on exploring the nature of video, i.e., the dynamic information, which is naturally category-free and works well on all domains.

2.3   Unsupervised Learning for Dynamic Modeling

To extract trajectories from sequential frames, a crucial step is learning the motion dynamics of the video. Many works have explored unsupervised methods for dynamic modeling for videos to solve different problems [27]. Based on keypoint-based representation [20], the video prediction approach [30] could decouple pixel generation from dynamic prediction. [21] combines keypoints and extra action classes to help generate action conditioned image sequences. Inspired by the function of keypoint on video prediction and generation, we designed dynamic point. For unsupervised tracking, unsupervised single object tracking is the mainstream [36,45,47]. However, they cannot handle the scenes with multiple objects. For unsupervised multi-object tracking, the pioneering work AIR [12] proposes a VAE-based framework to detect objects from individual images through inference, which is followed by [19,22]. [11] makes use of spatially invariant computations and representations to exploit the structure of objects in videos. In our initial attempts, we applied these unsupervised methods to locate dynamic instances on pedestrian videos directly but got poor results. The primary reason is that the above methods rely on structure and appearance features of objects, which are not applicable for trajectory extraction from bird's-eye view videos, where the these features are not very obvious.

3   Our Approach

3.1   Problem Definition

Given raw videos without any annotations, our task is to obtain a trajectory predictor in an unsupervised manner. We solve this problem by two main steps: trajectory extraction and trajectory prediction. For trajectory extraction, the input is raw videos captured by street cameras, and the output is $R = \{r_1, r_2, ..., r_n\}$, where R denotes all trajectories of moving objects in the videos. The trajectory for the ith object is defined as a set of discrete positions in the real-world coordinate system: $r_i = \{p_i^{t_{start}}, p_i^{t_{start}+1}, ..., p_i^{t_{end}}\}$, where $[t_{start}, t_{end}]$ denotes the time interval when the object occurs in the video. For the trajectory prediction, the extracted trajectories R acts as the dataset for training and validating the prediction network. The predictor observes objects' trajectories of an time interval and predicts their trajectories in the following period, like observing trajectory of 3s and predicting the trajectory for the next 5s. Without any label, we finally compute a trajectory prediction predictor.

3.2   Method Overview

We propose a label-free pipeline to generate the trajectory and then train the trajectory predictor. Specifically, our approach consists of four components: Dynamic-Point Modeling, Dynamic-to-Instance Aggregation, Instance Matching, and Trajectory Prediction. The first three parts form the unsupervised trajectory extraction. We show the pipeline in Fig. 1. In what follows, we will present these components in details.

3.3   Dynamic-Point Modeling

This part performs the unsupervised discovery of the dynamic points. Given a sequence of images, including Image$_1$ (I_1), Image$_{t-1}$ (I_{t-1}), Image$_t$ (I_t), and Image$_{t+1}$ (I_{t+1}), our objective is to capture K pixel locations, namely dynamic points $\Phi \in \mathbb{R}^{K \times 2}$, which correspond to the locations of moving regions in I_t.

The detailed networks are shown in Fig. 1(1). The first image provides the background and layout features. Two pairs of consecutive images are used to

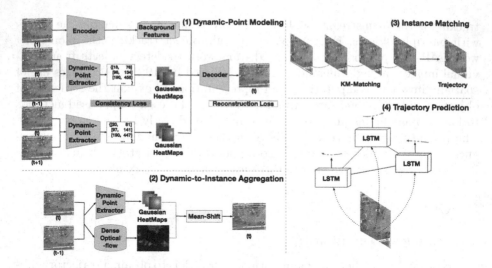

Fig. 1. Pipeline and main components of AutoTrajectory. Specifically, the first three components form the unsupervised trajectory extraction.

capture the dynamic points in I_t. Both background features and the dynamic-point gaussian heatmaps are used to reconstruct the image (I_t). The learning objective $\mathcal{L}$ then consists of two parts, consistency loss $\mathcal{L}_C$ and reconstruction loss $\mathcal{L}_R$, to regularize the dynamic points extraction and image reconstruction, respectively. The total objective is formulated as $\mathcal{L} = \mathcal{L}_R + \beta\mathcal{L}_C$.

Forward-Backward Dynamic-Point Extractors. Keypoints are known as natural representations of objects. Some methods for video prediction [21,30] encode single frames to keypoints to make the representation spatially structured and then generate videos. For the trajectory extraction from bird's eye view videos (Fig. 2(a)), the movement features in the temporal space are very important due to the limited appearance and structure features. Thus, we extend keypoints to dynamic points by utilizing more consecutive infomation in the temporal space. Dynamic-point extractors use two consecutive images to capture the dynamic points Φ. Two sets of images are applied in both forward (*i.e.* from $t-1$ to t) and backward (*i.e.* from $t+1$ to t) directions to keep the dynamic points of I_t consistent. The consistency loss is a location-wise MSE loss.

$$\mathcal{L}_C = ||(\Phi_{forward} - \Phi_{backward})||_2^2. \tag{1}$$

Gaussian Heatmaps. After obtaining dynamic points $\Phi \in \mathbb{R}^{K \times 2}$, we use gaussian heatmaps $\mathcal{H} \in \mathbb{R}^{H \times W \times K}$ to encode these points Φ into pixel representation, which is more suitable as the input for the convolutional reconstruction network. We first normalize the dynamic points via Softmax (*i.e.* Φ^* after normalization). Then each dynamic point is replaced with a gaussian function:

$$\mathcal{H} = \exp(-\frac{1}{2\sigma^2}||\Phi - \Phi^*||^2), \tag{2}$$

  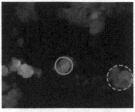

(a): Image   (b): Dynamic-Point   (c): Optical-Flow

Fig. 2. A sample of image with dynamic points and optical flow. Yellow circles denote the pedestrians. Green dashed circles denote the poor instance-level representations. Solid green circles indicate the better instance-level descriptions.

where σ is a fixed standard deviation. The result $\mathcal{H} \in \mathbb{R}^{H \times W \times K}$ is the gaussian heatmap that describes the dynamic locations; it is also used as an input to the decoder network.

Decoder. The decoder network utilizes background and layout features and dynamic-point heatmaps to reconstruct the image (*i.e.* the reconstructed image is I_t^*). The reconstruction loss is a pixel-wise L2 loss:

$$\mathcal{L}_R = \|(I_t^* - I_t)\|_2^2. \tag{3}$$

In this way, the objective could induce the representation of dynamic points for reconstructing the specific image in an unsupervised manner. Meanwhile, image reconstruction can make full use of the appearance and structure information in the spatial space, which is a complement to the focus on dynamic motions.

3.4 Dynamic-to-Instance Aggregation

Dynamic points could detect dynamic locations on images, while trajectories originate from instances. After acquiring the well-trained dynamic-point extractor in the previous step, we aim to group these dynamic points to get the instance-level location information. Intuitively, the solution is to cluster the dynamic points to instance points directly. However, the dynamic points have some characteristics: it shows better instance-level information (distinguishing different objects well) when multiple objects are close to each other while shows loose when solo object occurs.

We tackle this problem by introducing the optical flow into the instance-level information collection. An example of the dynamic points and optical flow is shown in Fig. 2. We can observe that the dynamic points correspond to a better instance-level representation, when multiple objects are in close proximity (solid green circles in (b)). The optical flow shows the compact representation for solo objects (solid green circle in (c)). It shows that dynamic points and optical flow are complementary.

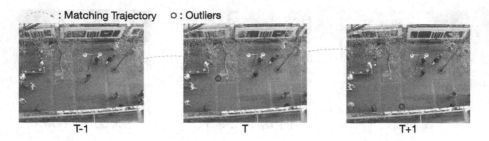

Fig. 3. An example of instance matching. Green dashed line denotes the instance points matching across timesteps. Blue circles denote the outliers of the instance points (also mean missmatching points). (Color figure online)

Specifically, we use a pair of consecutive images (I_t and I_{t-1}) to extract the dynamic point representation and optical flow, training the dynamic-point extractor in step 1 and applying unsupervised optical flow method [14]. The gaussian heatmaps are upsampled to the original image size via bilinear interpolation. Then both gaussian heatmaps and optical flow are concatenated as the input to the clustering method, *i.e.* mean-shift, to get the cluster centers, which are the coordinates of objects.

Region of Validity. Since there exist invalid regions for moving objects in images (railway in Fig. 2) and the background is static for a fixed camera, we apply the region of validity to filter these outliers located in the invalid regions. We show the details in the experiment section.

3.5 Instance Matching

The instance points obtained from the clustering method are independent across time. To obtain the trajectory, we perform cross-time instance matching. The basic idea is to establish a cost matrix between two consecutive images where each entry indicates the distance between two instance points across two images. Then we apply the Kuhn-Munkres (KM) algorithm[1] to calculate the minimum-cost matching. To better incorporate the appearance feature, we also use the RGB information as a part of distance. The final distance function is designed as $\mathcal{D}_{ij} = dist(P_i, Q_j) + \lambda rgb(P_i, Q_j)$, where P_i and Q_j are two instance points from two images. $dist(\cdot)$ is the Euclidean distance and $rgb(\cdot)$ is the L1 distance.

Specifically, the cost matrix $\mathcal{C} \in \mathbb{R}^{M \times N}$ is defined as the all-to-all distance between two images, where M and N indicate the number of instance points in two images. We use the KM algorithm with the cost matrix $\mathcal{C}$ to get the minimum-cost matching. The workflow is shown in Fig. 3. The matching pair from the KM algorithm is specified as a *true* pair if its distance is less than the pre-defined threshold $\mathbb{D}$, otherwise it is a *false* pair. Note that there exist some outliers that do not match any point. We label these outliers with blue

---

[1] http://software.clapper.org/munkres/.

circles. To handle these points, we apply some specific methods to filter them. For the points in image T, if we cannot find the former matching points in image $T - 1$ but can find the matching points in image $T + 1$, we label these points as the starting points of the sequence, otherwise we label them as outliers. This bidirectional filter benefits the precision of cross-time matching.

3.6   Trajectory Prediction

After extracting the trajectories in the pixel coordinate system, we transfer them to the real-word coordinate system and use them as the dataset to train and validate the prediction network in the last stage. At any time t, the status for the ith dynamic instance can be represented as the location $p_i = (x_i^t, y_i^t)$. The task for the prediction network is to observe the status of all the dynamic instances in the time interval $[1 : T_{obs}]$ and then predict their discrete positions at $[T_{obs} + 1 : T_{pred}]$. We have highlighted many learning-based works in Sect. 2.1 and these methods can be directly used in our approach. Because the datasets we use are human crowd videos, we utilize some classical LSTM-based approaches for pedestrian trajectory prediction in our experiments to verify the effectiveness of our unsupervised method.

3.7   Optimization

In the proposed approach, dynamic-point modeling and trajectory prediction stages have trainable parameters, and the other two stages are non-parametric. The whole workflow is stage-by-stage. We first train the dynamic-point modeling part. An ADAM optimizer with learning rate = 1e−4 is used for optimization. β is 0.5, σ is 0.1 and $\lambda = 0.2$. Then we apply the well-trained dynamic-point extractor to access the dynamic points. After dynamic-to-instance and instance matching, we get the extracted trajectories. For the trajectory prediction part, we follow the settings in the original paper to train the network optimizer, including the observation and prediction length.

3.8   Network Architecture

Dynamic-Point Modeling. For the dynamic-point extractor, we use the basic block (Conv2d + BatchNorm2d +Leaky Relu) in VGG [41] as the unit. The sizes of Conv2d are: [64, 128, 'M', 256, 256, 'M', 512, 512, 'M', 512, 512], where 'M' denotes the MaxPooling and each number indicates the size of one unit. For the encoder, we use a structure similar to the dynamic-point extractor. For the decoder part, we use the reverse setting of the encoder to keep the output and input size consistent. The detailed setting is [512, 512, 'U', 256, 256, 'U', 256, 256, 'U', 128, 64], where 'U' denotes the bilinear upsampling.

4 Experiments

4.1 Implementation Details

For trajectory prediction, we use several LSTM-based models, including Vanilla-LSTM, Occupancy-LSTM (O-LSTM), and Social LSTM (S-LSTM) [1]. They are trained by ground truth data before. In our approach, we use our extracted trajectories to train these models. Following the original setting in S-LSTM, we filter our extracted trajectories by removing the trajectories with lengths less than 20 frames (8 s). We set $K=180$ so that the dynamic points could distribute all moving objects.

Evaluation Metrics. We evaluate our performance on three aspects: detected instance points, extracted trajectories, and predicted trajectories.

We introduce recall and precision to test the quality of instance points extracted from Dynamic-to-Instance Aggregation. We give the detailed explanation as follows. (1) True-Positive instance points: instance points where the distance between detected instance points and the ground-truth points is less than the threshold $\mathcal{D}$. (2) Recall: the ratio of True-Positive points to all ground-truth points. (3) Precision: the ratio of True-Positive points to all detected instance points. We term them Ins-Recall and Ins-Precision, respectively.

We also apply recall and precision to test qualities of extracted trajectories. The True-Positive trajectories are defined as: trajectories where the average distance between extracted trajectories and ground truth trajectories across timesteps is less than the threshold $\mathcal{E}$. The definition of recall and precision is similar to the statement above. We term them Gen-Recall and Gen-Precision, respectively. Note that there exist some conditions where one detected instance point (or trajectory) corresponds to several ground truth points (or trajectories), or vice versa. We use the KM algorithm to get the minimum cost matching. Both precision and recall are calculated on average. We set $\mathcal{E} = 1.5$ and $\mathcal{D} = 1.5$.

Similar to prior work [1], we use two popular evaluation metrics for predicted trajectory evaluation: (1) Average Displacement Error (ADE): Average L2 distance between predicted trajectory and the ground truth over all timesteps. (2) Final Displacement Error (FDE): The distance between the predicted final destination and the true final destination in the ground truth. Besides the comparison between our unsupervised method and supervised methods, we also conduct semi-supervised experiments by using our extracted trajectories as extra data to train supervised models.

4.2 Datasets

For the dynamic-point modeling part, we use two publicly available datasets: ETH [34] and UCY [23] as the training data. These two datasets are captured by fixed-cameras. Although there are some other datasets containing videos of traffic scenarios such as KITTI [16] and Argoverse [10], the videos are all captured in drivers' view. The camera is moving and they do not provide the homograph matrix for each frame, which is not infeasible for our method.

We follow Social LSTM [1] to split the video to frames at every 0.4 seconds. For the trajectory prediction stage, we need to convert pixel coordinates to real-world coordinates to train these LSTM-based methods. Therefore, the extrinsic matrix is required to transfer the pixel coordinates to the real-world coordinates. From the open-source codebase[2], it can be found that only three scenes (UCY-Zara01, UCY-Zara02, and UCY-University) have complete transform matrixes. We thus use these three scenes for trajectory prediction.

Table 1. Evaluation results of detected instance points. We compare the proposed method with the unsupervised tracking [19] method and unsupervised keypoint modeling method [30]. '-' indicates the model cannot converge in the dataset

Metric	Ins-Precision					Ins-Recall				
Dataset	ETH	Hotel	Univ	Zara1	Zara2	ETH	Hotel	Univ	Zara1	Zara2
Un-Tracking [19]	8.3%	–	–	19.6%	21.4%	12.7%	–	–	10.1%	14.8%
Un-Keypoint [30]	16.8%	11.2%	–	33.1%	36.7%	14.1%	14.6%	–	39.4%	41.0%
Ours	**47.9%**	**37.1%**	**36.4%**	**58.7%**	**60.3%**	**58.3%**	**42.0%**	**31.4%**	**63.1%**	**67.9%**

4.3 Results

Experimental Results for Instance Points. We first evaluate the extracted instance points on various datasets. Since there is no annotation in any of the datasets, we use the unsupervised object tracking algorithm [19] and the keypoint-based video prediction algorithm [30] as baseline methods. From Table 1, several phenomena can be found: 1) in all datasets, the proposed dynamic-point modeling and dynamic-to-instance aggregation achieve consistently better performance than unsupervised tracking and unsupervised keypoint modeling; 2) for Hotel and Univ (where there are a large number of moving instances), unsupervised tracking method cannot converge while our method remains generalizable; 3) unsupervised keypoint modeling method without considering the sequential temporal information also performs poor (even does not converge in Univ dataset), while our method exploits the temporal consistency and achieves decent performance for all videos. Hence, for unsupervised tracking and keypoing modeling methods, it is difficult for them to extract dynamic instances from these videos, which are in bird's-eye view containing limited appearance and structure features. Instead, the proposed dynamic-point modeling and dynamic-to-instance aggregation could better handle the difficulties.

Visualization for the Decoder. To investigate the performance of the decoder part in dynamic-point modeling, we visualize the reconstructed images in Fig. 1 in the supplementary material. It can be observed that the moving pedestrians are well captured and reconstructed, even with a large number of moving objects. The reconstructed images are also real and decent. Hence, it can be

---

[2] https://github.com/trungmanhhuynh/Scene-LSTM.

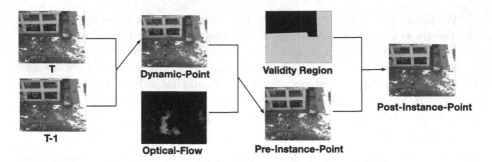

Fig. 4. Visualization for the output of each step in dynamic-to-instance aggregation. For the image of the valid region, the grey color denotes the valid part while the black color indicates the invalid region. (Color figure onine)

found that our dynamic modeling does capture the dynamic information and could reconstruct the input image.

Visualization for Each Step in Dynamic-to-Instance Aggregation. To give a more intuitive description, we visualize the output of each step during instance-point extraction in Fig. 4. Specifically, we first use Image (**T**) and Image (**T-1**) to extract the dynamic points. Then both dynamic points and optical flow are used to get the pre-instance points. Due to some invalid regions (buildings, railways) for pedestrians, we constrain these instance points with the valid region map. Because the background for a fixed-camera is static, it is easy to circle the valid region on just one frame. After that, we obtain the post-instance points.

Experimental Results for Extracted Trajectories. We use Gen-Recall and Gen-Precision to test the performance of extracted trajectories. Three datasets, including Zara1, Zara2, and Univ, are reported. The results are shown in the following; Gen-Precision of Zara1, Zara2 and Univ is 49.1%, 53.7%, and 23.7% respectively. Gen-Recall of Zara1, Zara2 and Univ is 52.9%, 54.4%, and 20.6% respectively. Our method could generate about a half number of trajectories similar to the ground truth for general videos. We visualize some extracted trajectories in Fig. 5. For very crowded scene (Univ), the performance drops due to the mismatching of instances. We show some bad cases in Fig. 2 in supplementary material. When multiple pedestrians meet, the error of instance matching occurrs and the trajectories of these pedestrians are biased in the wrong direction. It is also a fundamental obstacle for multi-object tracking methods.

Experimental Results for Trajectory Prediction. Because the datasets (Zara1, Zara2, and Univ) we use are about pedestrians, we test the extracted trajectories with three popular models for predicting trajectories of pedestrians, including LSTM, O-LSTM, and S-LSTM. We use a popular evaluation method, the leave-one-out approach, to test the trajectory prediction part, where we train on 2 scenes and test on the remaining one. We follow settings from prior works

(a)   (b)   (c)

Fig. 5. Visualization for trajectory prediction. We display three examples with the ground truth trajectory (GT in green line), the extracted trajectory by our method (ET in blue line), and the predicted trajectory by our method (PT in red dashed line). (Color figure online)

Table 2. Experimental results of trajectory prediction. We use three popular models to test the extracted trajectories, where O-LSTM and S-LSTM are both from Social-LSTM [1]. LSTM(sup), O-LSTM(sup), and S-LSTM(sup) indicate these models in a supervised manner. The unit for ADE and FDE is meters

Metric	ADE			FDE		
Dataset	Univ	Zara1	Zara2	Univ	Zara1	Zara2
LSTM	0.936	0.729	0.742	1.512	1.24	1.338
O-LSTM	0.875	0.511	0.579	1.427	0.947	1.092
S-LSTM	0.892	0.477	0.495	1.45	0.911	1.03
LSTM (sup)	0.52	0.43	0.52	1.25	0.93	1.09
O-LSTM (sup)	0.35	0.22	0.28	0.90	0.46	0.58
S-LSTM (sup)	0.27	0.22	0.25	0.77	0.48	0.50

to observe the trajectory for 8 timesteps (3.2 s) and predict the trajectory of 12 timesteps (4.8 s). We use our extracted trajectories in the training process and test with the ground truth. The results of trajectory prediction are shown in Table. 2. The performance on Univ is worse than the other two scenes because it is more complex with a crowd of moving objects. We also display the performances of LSTM, O-LSTM, and S-LSTM with supervision. We can see that the supervised method performs better than our unsupervised methods. It is mainly because our extracted trajectories are not smooth (Fig. 5) as the ground truth and sometimes we have bad cases (Fig. 2 in supplementary material). However, for our unsupervised method without any label, the ADE is about half meter and FDE is about one meter, it still has good practical significance.

Visualization for Trajectory Prediction. In Fig. 5, We show several examples to display the ground-truth trajectory, our extracted trajectory, and our predicted trajectory. From the visualization, we can find that the extracted trajectories mainly focus on the centers of moving objects, which demonstrates that our generated instance points can capture the main dynamic information of moving objects. After training on extracted trajectories, our trajectory predictor can also work on true trajectories, which also illustrates the usefulness of our extracted trajectories in an unsupervised manner.

Semi-supervised Training for Trajectory Prediction. To show the capability of our extracted trajectories in improving current supervised prediction models, we conduct semi-supervised experiments. We first use the ground truth data of Zara1 to train the model. Then we use extracted trajectories from other datasets as extra data to further train the model. Table 3 shows the results of testing on Zara2. We can see that adding more our extracted trajectories in the training process will make the prediction results more accurate. It illustrates our method is feasible in using large-scale raw videos to improve current models.

Table 3. Results of Semi-supervised training

Dataset	Zara1		+Univ(Gen)		+Univ(Gen)+Zara2(Gen)	
Method	LSTM	S-LSTM	LSTM	S-LSTM	LSTM	S-LSTM
ADE	0.598	0.347	0.578	0.341	0.521	0.320
FDE	1.25	0.69	1.157	0.687	1.094	0.659

4.4 Ablation Study

In this section, we perform several ablation studies to investigate the effectiveness of different components of the proposed approach. We train the dynamic-point modeling part with all five scenes and test the performance on Zara1 and Zara2.

Components of Clustering. For the dynamic-to-instance aggregation part, we use two types of dynamic information as the features, *i.e.* gaussian heatmaps and optical flow. From Table 4, it can be found after removing the dynamic points and optical flow, the performance of instance points is about 20% worse. Additionally, the model without dynamic points performs worse than the model without optical flow, which also demonstrates that dynamic points play a more important role in the instance-point extraction.

Forward *vs*. Backward Extractors. In the dynamic-point modeling part, we apply a forward-backward cycle extractor to keep the dynamic points consistent in cycle timesteps. We try to remove one of them to perform the ablation study. From Table 4, it can be observed that removing the forward extractor or removing the backward extractor will decrease the performance. Both forward and backward extractors are important ingredients in the instance-point extraction.

Consistency Loss. Moreover, we remove the consistency loss between the forward and backward extractors to check the effect. The results in Table 4 show that the consistency loss further boosts the forward-backward extractors (about 3%–4%) during the instance-point extraction.

Scalability. To verify the scalability of the proposed dynamic-point modeling, we compare the model trained with all five scenes to the model trained with only two scenes (Zara1 and Zara2). The results in Table 4 show that more video data improves the performance. It also demonstrates that our methods keep good scalability and take full advantage of large-scale video data.

Table 4. Ablation studies for instance-point extraction. We make several variants to investigate the effectiveness of different components

Metric	Ins-Precision		Ins-Recall	
Dataset	Zara1	Zara2	Zara1	Zara2
Ours w/o Dynamic-Point	38.3%	39.8%	44.1%	48.2%
Ours w/o Optical Flow	40.7%	43.4%	49.9%	53.1%
Ours w/o Forward Extractor	46.8%	50.1%	54.4%	59.8%
Ours w/o Backward Extractor	52.1%	56.8%	57.8%	62.2%
Ours w/o Consistency Loss	56.2%	58.0%	59.1%	60.4%
Ours w/ only-two-scenes	52.3%	53.9%	58.1%	61.6%
Ours	**58.7%**	**60.3%**	**63.1%**	**67.9%**

4.5 Limitations and Future Work

Although the proposed method works in an unsupervised manner, there also exist some limitations. 1) The whole framework is not end-to-end. We train these learnable components one by one. 2) There are some hyper-parameters, which need fine-tuning when training with different datasets. 3) Since there is no target category, our method might focus on the dynamic part of non-target category, such as a car in the pedestrian trajectory dataset. We visualize some badcases in the materials. In the future work, we aim to incorporate the category-aware memory and template into the dynamic modeling to further distinguish different categories. And we will also explore dynamic point-based approach on drivers' view videos.

5 Conclusion

In this paper, we propose a complete pipeline for label-free trajectory extraction and prediction. To our knowledge, this is the first time unsupervised trajectory extraction and prediction have been explored. We make full use of the spatial consistency by image reconstruction and the temporal dynamic consistency by sequential frames to capture moving regions in videos through dynamic points. To extract trajectories at the instance-level, we also propose a novel aggregation approach to cluster dynamic points to instance points by compensating with optical flow. Without any supervision, our method uses raw videos to extract trajectories and train trajectory prediction networks. The experiments show the effectiveness and scalability of our approach.

References

1. Alahi, A., Goel, K., Ramanathan, V., Robicquet, A., Li, F.F., Savarese, S.: Social LSTM: Human trajectory prediction in crowded spaces. 2016 IEEE Conference on Computer Vision and Pattern Recognition (CVPR), pp. 961–971 (2016)
2. Başar, T.: A new approach to linear filtering and prediction problems (2001)
3. Bergmann, P., Meinhardt, T., Leal-Taixe, L.: Tracking without bells and whistles. In: Proceedings of the IEEE International Conference on Computer Vision, pp. 941–951 (2019)
4. Bertinetto, L., Valmadre, J., Henriques, J.F., Vedaldi, A., Torr, P.H.S.: Fully-convolutional siamese networks for object tracking. In: Hua, G., Jégou, H. (eds.) ECCV 2016. LNCS, vol. 9914, pp. 850–865. Springer, Cham (2016). https://doi.org/10.1007/978-3-319-48881-3_56
5. Bewley, A., Ge, Z., Ott, L., Ramos, F., Upcroft, B.: Simple online and realtime tracking. In: 2016 IEEE International Conference on Image Processing (ICIP), pp. 3464–3468. IEEE (2016)
6. Cao, C., et al.: Look and think twice: Capturing top-down visual attention with feedback convolutional neural networks. 2015 IEEE International Conference on Computer Vision (ICCV), pp. 2956–2964 (2015)
7. Chai, Y., Sapp, B., Bansal, M., Anguelov, D.: Multipath: multiple probabilistic anchor trajectory hypotheses for behavior prediction. ArXiv abs/1910.05449 (2019)
8. Chandra, R., Bhattacharya, U., Roncal, C., Bera, A., Manocha, D.: Robusttp: End-to-end trajectory prediction for heterogeneous road-agents in dense traffic with noisy sensor inputs. In: CSCS 2019 (2019)
9. Chandra, R., et al.: Forecasting trajectory and behavior of road-agents using spectral clustering in graph-LSTMS. ArXiv abs/1912.01118 (2019)
10. Chang, M.F., et al.: Argoverse: 3D tracking and forecasting with rich maps. 2019 IEEE/CVF Conference on Computer Vision and Pattern Recognition (CVPR), pp. 8740–8749 (2019)
11. Crawford, E., Pineau, J.: Exploiting spatial invariance for scalable unsupervised object tracking. ArXiv abs/1911.09033 (2019)
12. Eslami, S.M.A., et al.: Attend, infer, repeat: Fast scene understanding with generative models. In: NIPS (2016)
13. Fang, K., Xiang, Y., Li, X., Savarese, S.: Recurrent autoregressive networks for online multi-object tracking. In: 2018 IEEE Winter Conference on Applications of Computer Vision (WACV), pp. 466–475. IEEE (2018)
14. Farnebäck, G.: Two-frame motion estimation based on polynomial expansion. In: Bigun, J., Gustavsson, T. (eds.) SCIA 2003. LNCS, vol. 2749, pp. 363–370. Springer, Heidelberg (2003). https://doi.org/10.1007/3-540-45103-X_50
15. Feichtenhofer, C., Pinz, A., Zisserman, A.: Detect to track and track to detect. In: Proceedings of the IEEE International Conference on Computer Vision, pp. 3038–3046 (2017)
16. Geiger, A., Lenz, P., Stiller, C., Urtasun, R.: Vision meets robotics: the kitti dataset. Int. J. Rob. Res. **32**, 1231–1237 (2013)
17. Gupta, A., Johnson, J.E., Fei-Fei, L., Savarese, S., Alahi, A.: Social GAN: Socially acceptable trajectories with generative adversarial networks. In: 2018 IEEE/CVF Conference on Computer Vision and Pattern Recognition, pp. 2255–2264 (2018)
18. Hall, M.A.: Correlation-based feature selection for machine learning (2003)
19. He, Z., Li, J., Liu, D., He, H., Barber, D.: Tracking by animation: unsupervised learning of multi-object attentive trackers. In: 2019 IEEE/CVF Conference on Computer Vision and Pattern Recognition (CVPR), pp. 1318–1327 (2018)

20. Jakab, T., Gupta, A., Bilen, H., Vedaldi, A.: Conditional image generation for learning the structure of visual objects. ArXiv abs/1806.07823 (2018)
21. Kim, Y., Nam, S., Cho, I.S., Kim, S.J.: Unsupervised keypoint learning for guiding class-conditional video prediction. ArXiv abs/1910.02027 (2019)
22. Kosiorek, A.R., Kim, H., Posner, I., Teh, Y.W.: Sequential attend, infer, repeat: generative modelling of moving objects. In: NeurIPS (2018)
23. Leal-Taixé, L., Fenzi, M., Kuznetsova, A., Rosenhahn, B., Savarese, S.: Learning an image-based motion context for multiple people tracking. In: 2014 IEEE Conference on Computer Vision and Pattern Recognition, pp. 3542–3549 (2014)
24. Lee, N., et al.: Desire: Distant future prediction in dynamic scenes with interacting agents. In: 2017 IEEE Conference on Computer Vision and Pattern Recognition (CVPR), pp. 2165–2174 (2017)
25. Lefevre, S., Laugier, C., Guzman, J.I.: Exploiting map information for driver intention estimation at road intersections. In: 2011 IEEE Intelligent Vehicles Symposium (IV), pp. 583–588 (2011)
26. Lerner, A., Chrysanthou, Y., Lischinski, D.: Crowds by example. Comput. Graph Forum 26, 655–664 (2007)
27. Luo, Z., Peng, B., Huang, D.A., Alahi, A., Fei-Fei, L.: Unsupervised learning of long-term motion dynamics for videos. In: 2017 IEEE Conference on Computer Vision and Pattern Recognition (CVPR), pp. 7101–7110 (2017)
28. Ma, Y., Manocha, D., Wang, W.: Autorvo: Local navigation with dynamic constraints in dense heterogeneous traffic. arXiv preprint arXiv:1804.02915 (2018)
29. Ma, Y., Zhu, X., Zhang, S., Yang, R., Wang, W., Manocha, D.: Trafficpredict: trajectory prediction for heterogeneous traffic-agents. In: Proceedings of the AAAI Conference on Artificial Intelligence, vol. 33, pp. 6120–6127 (2019)
30. Minderer, M., Sun, C., Villegas, R., Cole, F., Murphy, K., Lee, H.: Unsupervised learning of object structure and dynamics from videos. ArXiv abs/1906.07889 (2019)
31. Palaz, D.: Towards end-to-end speech recognition (2016)
32. Pan, J., Sun, H., cheng Xu, K., Jiang, Y., Xiao, X., Hu, J., Miao, J.: Lane attention: Predicting vehicles' moving trajectories by learning their attention over lanes. ArXiv abs/1909.13377 (2019)
33. Park, S., Kim, B., Kang, C.M., Chung, C.C., Choi, J.W.: Sequence-to-sequence prediction of vehicle trajectory via LSTM encoder-decoder architecture. In: 2018 IEEE Intelligent Vehicles Symposium (IV), pp. 1672–1678 (2018)
34. Pellegrini, S., Ess, A., Van Gool, L.: Improving data association by joint modeling of pedestrian trajectories and groupings. In: Daniilidis, K., Maragos, P., Paragios, N. (eds.) ECCV 2010. LNCS, vol. 6311, pp. 452–465. Springer, Heidelberg (2010). https://doi.org/10.1007/978-3-642-15549-9_33
35. Pellegrini, S., Ess, A., Schindler, K., Gool, L.V.: You'll never walk alone: modeling social behavior for multi-target tracking. In: 2009 IEEE 12th ICCV, pp. 261–268 (2009)
36. Piekniewski, F., Laurent, P.A., Petre, C., Richert, M., Fisher, D., Hylton, T.: Unsupervised learning from continuous video in a scalable predictive recurrent network. ArXiv abs/1607.06854 (2016)
37. Ren, S., He, K., Girshick, R., Sun, J.: Faster R-CNN: Towards real-time object detection with region proposal networks. In: Advances in Neural Information Processing Systems, pp. 91–99 (2015)
38. Rhinehart, N., McAllister, R., Kitani, K.M., Levine, S.: Precog: prediction conditioned on goals in visual multi-agent settings. ArXiv abs/1905.01296 (2019)

39. Sadeghian, A., Kosaraju, V., Sadeghian, A., Hirose, N., Savarese, S.: Sophie: An attentive GAN for predicting paths compliant to social and physical constraints. In: 2019 IEEE/CVF Conference on Computer Vision and Pattern Recognition (CVPR), pp. 1349–1358 (2018)

40. Sharma, S., Ansari, J.A., Murthy, J.K., Krishna, K.M.: Beyond pixels: Leveraging geometry and shape cues for online multi-object tracking. In: 2018 IEEE International Conference on Robotics and Automation (ICRA), pp. 3508–3515. IEEE (2018)

41. Simonyan, K., Zisserman, A.: Very deep convolutional networks for large-scale image recognition. CoRR abs/1409.1556 (2014)

42. Tang, S., Andriluka, M., Andres, B., Schiele, B.: Multiple people tracking by lifted multicut and person re-identification. In: Proceedings of the IEEE Conference on Computer Vision and Pattern Recognition, pp. 3539–3548 (2017)

43. Tang, Y., Salakhutdinov, R.: Multiple futures prediction. In: NeurIPS (2019)

44. Wang, M., Shi, D., Guan, N., Zhang, T., Wang, L., Li, R.: Unsupervised pedestrian trajectory prediction with graph neural networks. In: 2019 IEEE 31st International Conference on Tools with Artificial Intelligence (ICTAI), pp. 832–839 (2019)

45. Wang, N., Song, Y., Ma, C., Zhou, W., Liu, W., Li, H.: Unsupervised deep tracking. In: 2019 IEEE/CVF Conference on Computer Vision and Pattern Recognition (CVPR), pp. 1308–1317 (2019)

46. Xu, J., Cao, Y., Zhang, Z., Hu, H.: Spatial-temporal relation networks for multi-object tracking. In: Proceedings of the IEEE International Conference on Computer Vision, pp. 3988–3998 (2019)

47. Zhang, S., et al.: Tracking persons-of-interest via unsupervised representation adaptation. Int. J. Comput. Vis. **128**, 120–96 (2017)

48. Zhao, T., et al.: Multi-agent tensor fusion for contextual trajectory prediction. In: 2019 IEEE/CVF Conference on Computer Vision and Pattern Recognition (CVPR), pp. 12118–12126 (2019)

49. Zhu, J., Yang, H., Liu, N., Kim, M., Zhang, W., Yang, M.H.: Online multi-object tracking with dual matching attention networks. In: Proceedings of the European Conference on Computer Vision (ECCV), pp. 366–382 (2018)

Multi-agent Embodied Question Answering in Interactive Environments

Sinan Tan[1,2], Weilai Xiang[3], Huaping Liu[1,2(✉)], Di Guo[1,2], and Fuchun Sun[1,2]

[1] Department of Computer Science and Technology,
Tsinghua University, Beijing 100084, China
hpliu@tsinghua.edu.cn
[2] Beijing National Research Center for Information Science and Technology,
Beijing 100084, China
[3] Shenyuan Honors College, Beihang University, Beijing 100191, China

Abstract. We investigate a new AI task—Multi-Agent Interactive Question Answering—where several agents explore the scene jointly in interactive environments to answer a question. To cooperate efficiently and answer accurately, agents must be well-organized to have balanced work division and share knowledge about the objects involved. We address this new problem in two stages: Multi-Agent 3D Reconstruction in Interactive Environments and Question Answering. Our proposed framework features multi-layer structural and semantic memories shared by all agents, as well as a question answering model built upon a 3D-CNN network to encode the scene memories. During the reconstruction, agents simultaneously explore and scan the scene with a clear division of work, organized by next viewpoints planning. We evaluate our framework on the IQuADv1 dataset and outperform the IQA baseline in a single-agent scenario. In multi-agent scenarios, our framework shows favorable speedups while remaining high accuracy.

Keywords: 3D reconstruction · Embodied vision · Question answering

1 Introduction

For decades, one of our best wishes has been to develop robots that can assist humans with the ability to understand the scene, to interact with environments, and to communicate with humans. For instance, a domestic robot might be asked: *How many apples are in the house?* To answer it, the agent must explore the house, open fridges & cabinets for possibly hidden apples, check the occurrence of apples, and answer the question by natural language.

This sort of problem refers to Embodied Question Answering (EQA) [4] : Being asked *What color is the car?*, an agent navigates to the car and observes

---

S. Tan and W. Xiang—Equal contribution.

W. Xiang—This work was completed while Weilai Xiang was visiting Tsinghua University, Beijing.

© Springer Nature Switzerland AG 2020
A. Vedaldi et al. (Eds.): ECCV 2020, LNCS 12358, pp. 663–678, 2020.
https://doi.org/10.1007/978-3-030-58601-0_39

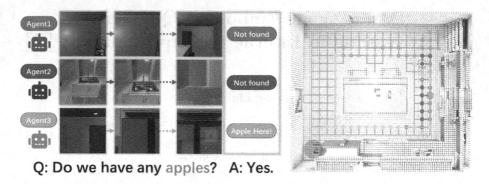

Q: **Do we have any** apples?   A: **Yes.**

Fig. 1. A demonstration of the Multi-Agent Interactive Question Answering task. Three agents search the room simultaneously with a clear division of work, enabling them to answer the question *Do we have any apples?* more efficiently.

it before it answers the question. Since the car may be out of sight initially, the agent must have common sense about possible locations of the car and a way to get there. However, point-to-point navigation is not enough—what if we want the agent to search for a missing fork which may be *anywhere* in the kitchen?

To be more practical, Interactive Question Answering (IQA) [7] takes both interactive actions (e.g., open a cabinet) and more generic questions (e.g., *existence* and *counting*) into consideration. To answer *Is there a fork in the kitchen?*, the agent must have comprehensive cognition to the kitchen, without missing any place where the target may exist, including interactive objects like containers. However, this process could be time-costing.

Parallelism has always been a fundamental but effective idea. Since several agents can search for an object simultaneously, the question will soon be answered if multiple robots can explore collaboratively. Therefore, we introduce **Multi-Agent Interactive Question Answering**, which presents additional challenges to AI systems. **First**, the multi-agent system must be well-organized to avoid duplicate work and unbalanced work. **Second**, the multi-agent QA system must integrate information from all agents and answer the question accurately without a repeat or a miss. **Third**, the multi-agent system should achieve as high speedup as possible while keeping the high accuracy.

Very few studies have looked into multi-agent embodied question answering tasks. However, active 3D reconstruction [5,24] is not a novel problem. Here we propose a two-stage framework for Multi-Agent IQA, which firstly executes a multi-agent (embodied) 3D reconstruction to construct 3D global structural and semantic memories and secondly encodes the scene via 3D memories to answer the question. To support interactive objects, we propose a multi-layer data structure as an extension to traditional voxel-based reconstructions.

We train and evaluate our proposed two-stage framework on the IQuADv1 IQA dataset [7] in both single-agent and multi-agent scenarios and observe promising results of highly effective and efficient in both cases.

Contributions. In summary, our main contributions include:

- **Problem.** We introduce the Multi-Agent IQA, the task of organizing collaborative Interactive Question Answering for several agents.
- **Method.** We propose a two-stage framework for Multi-Agent IQA, a method to efficiently construct 3D global memories via multi-agent 3D reconstruction and to answer the question by encoding the scene memories with 3D-CNN.
- **Results.** Our 3D-memory-based framework surpasses the original IQA method in both answering accuracy and episode length, with a single agent on the IQuADv1 dataset. With 2, 3, and 4 agents, we show consistent high-level parallelism and affordable speedups in average episode length.

2 Related Work

2.1 Question Answering in Embodied Environments

Visual Question Answering. VQA requires the agent to observe the given visual contents (i.e., images [1] or videos [13, 23]) and reason out the answer combining the multi-modal inputs. Common architectures for images VQA involve RNNs to encode questions, CNNs to encode images and fully connected layers to fuse language and visual features [15]. Our approach to Question Answering uses similar encoding and modality fusion strategies but uses a 3D-CNN to encode the scene with semantic memories instead of 2D-CNNs for images.

Embodied Question Answering. EQA [4] requires active perception of the environment instead of answering with images passively received. Similar to Visual Semantic Navigation [22], EQA requires the agent to navigate from the current location to the target specified by its semantic category. Some recent studies use deep Reinforcement Learning (RL) to generate navigational actions directly from visual observations [4, 25]. However, for our problems which require **holistic** scene searching, point-to-point navigation is not enough.

Interactive Question Answering. IQA is an extension of EQA with actionable environments and requires the agent to discover underlying objects. The IQuADv1 dataset [7] consists of question types including *existence, counting* and *spatial relationship*. Therefore, it requires *holistic* scene understanding to cover all occurrences of the object instead of direct navigation to a single target. The IQA baseline maintains a 2D spatial memory to encode semantic representation at each location. However, the top-down memory may fail to complex concepts like "containing". In our work, a 3D semantic memory is constructed to provide more precise records.

2.2 Multi-agent Systems

Multi-agent systems offer obvious advantages over single-agent ones including parallelism, robustness, scalability, and fitness for geographic distribution [18]. For IQA tasks, expecting a robot to visit every corner where the apple may occur is unreal, but it will be possible to have several robots to answer the question quickly with parallelism when objects are scattered throughout the house.

Multi-agent reinforcement learning is a popular topic related. Some studies involve the communication of local knowledge between agents [6,16,19]. However, designing networks and protocols for communication becomes complicated for complex tasks when the number of agents increases. Meanwhile, many traditional multi-agent systems rely on optimization-based methods such as optimal mass transport [5], which can exploit collaborations of any number of agents for the 3D reconstruction task. In this paper, we adopt the optimization-based idea and formulate the multi-agent 3D reconstruction as a Set Cover Problem.

2.3   3D Computer Vision

3D Reconstruction. With RGB-D data available, 3D reconstruction becomes fundamental to 3D machine learning tasks. KinectFusion [12] is a typical real-time 3D reconstruction framework with TSDF [3] fusion. These volumetric-based methods result in voxel-wise data representing the structure of the target, denoted as "Structural Memory" in our work.

Active 3D Reconstruction. In recent years we witnessed the development of active reconstruction by robots. Quite a few studies focus on proposing a measurement (e.g., the score of uncertainty or variance) field in the 3D space and selecting Next Best Views as targets for each time step [5,24]. Inspired by these works, we evaluate voxel coverage from each view to select the next viewpoints with a set cover algorithm and assign them to agents by clustering.

3D Semantic Segmentation. With 3D datasets, 3D deep learning has made impressive progress. 3D-SIS [10] is one of those 3D instance segmentation frameworks which proposes 3D-RPN networks. Since we use 3D-CNN in question answering stage, here we use Mask R-CNN [9] to perform 2D instance segmentation and back-project the 2D semantic map to 3D voxels as Semantic Memory.

2.4   Environments and Datasets

There are several environments for embodied agents widely used such as AI2-THOR [14], Habitat [17] (a platform supporting Matterport3D [2] and Gibson [21]) and House3D [20]. However, only AI2-THOR explicitly supports multiple agents as well as interactions with objects. Therefore, we adopt the AI2-THOR interactive environment for our embodied AIs. AI2-THOR is a photo-realistic simulation environment consists of a variety of objects. We use the IQuADv1 dataset developed on AI2-THOR to evaluate our method with questions including *counting, existence* and *spatial relationships*. In our work, the simulator settings are slightly different from IQA [7]. We perform the OpenObject/CloseObject actions by specifying the object ID and allow agents to get the IDs from the simulator in already reconstructed areas to set free from the trouble of linking each object in 3D voxels to the object ID.

3   Overview of the Proposed Framework

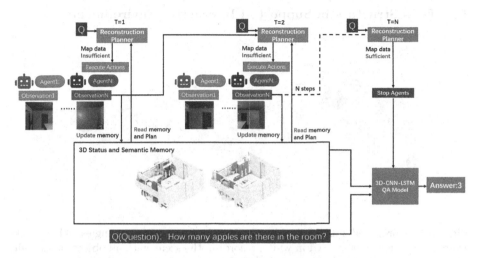

Fig. 2. Overview of the framework. The navigational actions for agents are planned step by step, according to the partially reconstructed memories. The agents execute these actions and update 3D memories along their routes. This procedure is repeated until the termination model decided there is enough data to answer the question or the whole scene is scanned. Then all agents are stopped, and the QA model encodes 3D memories and the question to predict the answer.

Our framework features enriched structural and semantic memories built along with 3D Reconstruction. Afterward, the QA model gives the answer based on memories constructed. Therefore, our framework consists of these two parts:

- **Multi-agent 3D Reconstruction in Interactive Environments:** Our agents scan and reconstruct the interactive scene via voxel-based reconstruction, resulting in a global multi-layer structural memory. To divide labor for multiple agents and avoid duplicate work, we introduce a scalable optimization-based planner to select next-step viewpoints for each agent. They are assigned to agents and agents execute actions to navigate towards these viewpoints. During this procedure, global semantic memory is being constructed as well for semantic-related questions, by back-projecting 2D instance segmentation results to the 3D volume. Meanwhile agents open every openable object they meet and a new exclusive layer in both memories is created to record the object's inside structure and contents. After the data in memories is sufficient to answer the question, the reconstruction stops.
- **Question Answering with 3D-CNN and LSTM:** A 3D-CNN network is used to encode the semantic memory and an LSTM network is used to encode questions. Then we concatenate the semantic feature and the language feature and predict the final answer by an MLP.

4   Multi-agent 3D Reconstruction in Interactive Environments

4.1   Data Structure in Support of Interactive Environments

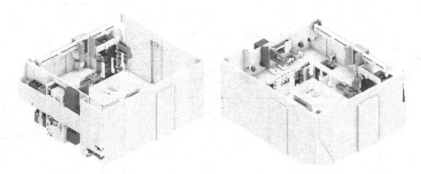

Fig. 3. The proposed multi-layer data structure from different angles. The "background" layer is demonstrated in white, recording the scene with all objects in default. The "dynamic" voxels in layers for interactive objects are shown in color. Large colored cubes represent **CONCRETE** voxels, while smaller ones are **EMPTY** voxels inside.

Traditional voxel-based reconstruction does not support interactive scenes, because voxels occupied by openable objects may be in different states when they are open and closed (denoted as "dynamic" voxels in our paper). However, we have to record both situations, otherwise, we will miss apples in cabinets/fridges. To address this issue, we develop an extended data structure for 3D reconstruction, introducing the concept of "layer".

For an interactive scene with M interactive objects, we use $M + 1$ layers to store its structure, where each layer is a $W \times L \times H$ array. Layer 0 represents the "background", i.e., the voxels when all openable objects are closed. Layer 1 to Layer M record M interactive objects to be open, in the order in which they are discovered during 3D reconstruction. In AI2Thor environments, all instances of certain categories (including "Fridge", "Cabinet" and "Microwave Oven") are guaranteed to be interactive (openable). Thus, when agents discover an object in those categories, a new layer is added.

This data structure is applied to both Structural Memory for 3D reconstruction and Semantic Memory for semantic(instance) segmentation in the scene.

4.2   Structural Memory and Semantic Memory

Each voxel in the multi-layer volume has multiple information stored, and one of the most important is its scan status. Here we call it the **Structural Memory**, which monitors and records whether a voxel is scanned. This information is crucial to plan actions for the agents. To be specific, we assign a status to each voxel in the multi-layer volume, which is one of these following statuses:

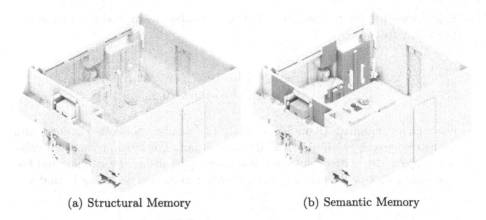

(a) Structural Memory   (b) Semantic Memory

Fig. 4. (a) Demonstration of a fully reconstructed Structural Memory in Layer 0. Large white cubes represent **CONCRETE** voxels, while small yellow cubes represent **EMPTY** voxels. The vast parts outside the volume are **UNKNOWN**. (b) Demonstration of the corresponding Semantic Memory. Each color represents one of the 20 semantic categories in the IQuADv1 dataset. White cubes represent background voxels or voxels of other unspecified semantic categories.

- **UNKNOWN**: The initial status of all voxels, representing that the voxel has not been scanned yet.
- **EMPTY**: Indicating that in all scans involving this voxel, no object is found.
- **CONCRETE**: Indicating that in at least one scan, a concrete object occupies this voxel.

Hence, the complete structure of the scene is modeled via this voxel-based memory. However, the Structural Memory itself only records the geometrical structure, which is not enough for downstream tasks (i.e. Question Answering in our case). Therefore a piece of extra information is recorded, named **Semantic Memory**.

For each scan of the 3D scene, an instance segmentation model will be applied to the observed RGB image. These semantic labels acquired is written into the Semantic Memory by back projecting labels to all "CONCRETE" voxels. The Semantic Memory provides visual information of the 3D scene, therefore it is used for question answering in our QA model.

4.3 Scanning Boundaries and Scanning Tasks

Scanning Boundaries are voxels at the border of the scanned part and the unscanned part of a layer in the 3D scene. Denoting $status(l, v)$ to be the status of a voxel with coordinate $v = (x, y, z)$ on layer l, the actions of agents are planned according to these two kinds of scanning boundaries:

– Scene Scanning Boundaries (B_S), the border between scanned and unscanned parts in Layer 0.

$$B_S = \left\{ v \;\middle|\; \begin{array}{l} v \in \mathcal{V}, \\ status(0, v) = \text{UNKNOWN}, \\ \text{CONCRETE} \in status(0, Adj(v)) \end{array} \right\} \tag{1}$$

– Interactive Scanning Boundaries (B_I), the border between scanned and unscanned voxels in an object's "dynamic" part. For example, when a cabinet is open, the border between the scanned part inside the cabinet and the unscanned part of the cabinet is considered Interactive Scanning Boundary.

$$B_I = \left\{ v \;\middle|\; \begin{array}{l} v \in \mathcal{V}, \\ status(i, v) = \text{UNKNOWN}, \\ \exists v_a \in Adj(v), \\ status(i, v_a) \neq status(0, v_a), \\ status(i, v_a) = \text{CONCRETE} \end{array} \right\} \tag{2}$$

One task for our agents is to cover voxels on scanning boundaries which represent the unfinished parts of reconstruction. Furthermore, agents must visit the unopened interactive objects (e.g. cabinets that have never been opened so far) because these unopened objects have no scanning boundaries yet. Therefore a new kind of task is created to ensure they will be opened at least once, and the **scanning tasks** are:

– Voxels on Scanning Boundaries ($B_S \cup B_I$): They need to be observed on later scans to complete the memories.
– Unopened interactive objects (T_U): These objects must be opened at least once to create new layers in memories and examine their inside.

Therefore scanning tasks can be formulated as a set of voxels to be scanned:

$$T = B_S \cup B_I \cup T_U \tag{3}$$

4.4   Viewpoint-Voxel Coverage Matrix

The target of the planning algorithm for scene reconstruction is to move the agent. Yet in our work we do not plan every single specific move, instead, we choose the target of a series of moves. To be convenient, we denote the discretized observed part of the scene as V, which contains all possible *viewpoints*. A viewpoint is the combination of position and rotation of the camera.

Then for every viewpoint, we compute the visible voxels from it according to the reconstruction of the scene. Then we construct a matrix about whether a voxel in scanning tasks T can be seen from a viewpoint in V. This is denoted as C, a $|V| \times |T|$ matrix, the **Viewpoint-Voxel Coverage Matrix**.

4.5   Termination Condition

With the definition of scanning tasks, it's obvious that, when there are no remaining tasks for interactive scene reconstruction, the reconstruction process can be terminated. Therefore, the termination condition can be formulated as:

$$T = \emptyset \tag{4}$$

Besides, for some questions, the scan can be terminated before the environment is completely scanned. We propose a special learning-based Termination Model in Sect. 5 to achieve the early stopping.

4.6   Multi-agent 3D Reconstruction

After introducing the data structures, tasks, and termination conditions, we propose the multi-agent reconstruction algorithm that repeats the routes planning procedure over and over again until either termination condition is satisfied.

In each iteration, we investigate the voxels to be scanned next and assign them to agents. They are introduced as Scanning Tasks and can be retrieved from the semi-finished Structural Memory. Afterward, we evaluate the visibility of those voxels from each possible viewpoint. To avoid duplicate work and maximize the efficiency, we expect agents to cover as more Scanning Tasks voxels as possible while having little intersection, so we convert it into a Set Cover Problem and solve it by a greedy algorithm.

To regroup the selected viewpoints into N groups (suppose that we have N agents), we use the K-means algorithm to execute a spatial clustering. Then we assign a cluster to each agent by solving a Balanced Assignment Problem to minimize the total route length from current locations to their target viewpoints. We plan the route for each agent with a TSP solver. Agents execute actions to navigate along the route and update the Structural Memory and Semantic Memory. After an agent reaches a viewpoint or when an agent gets stuck due to wrong route planning, we clear the routes and repeat the procedure to re-plan the moves.

A 2D map is maintained according to the reconstructed 3D scene, determining which location the agent can pass through. This 2D map is used for route planning. At each time step, the 2D map is updated, and all newly discovered 3D objects will be created a new layer for, and added to the multi-layer 3D data structure.

Algorithm 1: Multi-Agent 3D Reconstruction

Result: SceneMap
Initialize SceneMap;
while $T \neq \emptyset \wedge \neg\, TerminationModel(SceneMap)$ **do**
    Generate B_S, B_I, and T_U;
    Generate $T = B_S \cup B_I \cup T_U$ and Count all viewpoints V;
    Evaluate the coverage of T from each viewpoint to form matrix C;
    Choose a subset $v \subseteq V$ by running Set Cover Problem solver on C;
    Regroup v into N clusters: $v = \cup_{j=1}^{N} v_j$ by K-means Algorithm, and
    assign v_j to agent A_i by Hungarian Algorithm;
    Plan route for agent A_i to travel a series of viewpoints
    $v_j = \{v_{j,1}, v_{j,2}, ..., v_{j,n_j}\}$ with TSP solver;
    repeat
        Execute actions along the planned routes;
        Update the SceneMap for each step;
        Add new layers to for newly discovered interactive objects on
        SceneMap;
        Update the 2D Map for navigation according to SceneMap;
    until *An agent reaches a selected viewpoint $\vee$ One gets blocked*;
end

---

5   Question Answering with 3D-CNN and LSTM

5.1   3D-CNN Scene Encoder and Question Encoder

The question answering model generates the answer according to the semantic volume and the given question. Here the question, denoted as Q, is encoded with an LSTM, getting the question feature f_Q. For CNN, we first need to process all the observations we get in the process of 3D reconstruction.

Imagine a voxel $v = (x, y, z)$ in the 3D volume with shape $W \times L \times H$, where W, L, H is the size of each dimension, respectively. Then this voxel v must have been observed several times in the multi-layer Semantic Memory with shape $M \times W \times L \times H$, not only from the multi-layer scans but also within each layer. We denote the total number of observations to v in Semantic Memory layers with class label c as $N(v, c)$, and each observation has a confidence score of $s_i(v, c)$. We build a tensor $\mathcal{V}$ with shape $C \times W \times L \times H$ to integrate all information about voxel v by averaging all these observations, i.e.:

$$\mathcal{V}(c, x, y, z) = \frac{1}{N(v, c)}\left(\sum_{i=1}^{N(v,c)} s_i(v, c)\right) \tag{5}$$

We encode the semantic map with a 3D-CNN network similar to ResNet-18, yet replacing all 2D Convolution layers with 3D Convolution layers, yielding the scene feature vector f_S. Since the 3D volume can be huge, we use submanifold sparse convolutions [8] instead of traditional convolutions to process those sparse data.

5.2 Question Answering Model

Here we concatenate the scene feature vector f_S and the language feature vector f_Q and use a simple multi-layer perceptron (MLP), to get the joint representation h of the scene and the question.

$$h = \mathrm{MLP}([f_S; f_Q]) \tag{6}$$

Finally, a fully connected layer is applied to produce the probability distribution of the final answer.

$$p(ans) = \mathrm{Softmax}(W_a h + b_a) \tag{7}$$

5.3 Termination Model

Similarly, we apply another fully connect layer to predict the probability for agents to stop:

$$p(stop) = \mathrm{Softmax}(W_s h + b_s) \tag{8}$$

5.4 Training the QA Model and the Termination Model

Training the QA Model and the Termination Model is not a trivial task. Among thousands of voxels, sometimes there could be only less than ten voxels related to a given question. With such sparsity of interested voxels, end-to-end training of the QA network does not work in our experiments. Below are the steps we go through to train the QA model.

Pretraining the Instance Segmentation Model. We use Mask R-CNN for instance segmentation. The Mask R-CNN is trained on more than $10\,\mathrm{k}$ images sampled from the 3D scenes in the training set, with annotations automatically generated from the output of the simulators. The pretrained model achieves 56.7% mAP on our validation set.

Preparing Training Data. For each question in the IQuADv1 dataset, we perform scene reconstruction with the proposed interactive reconstruction algorithm to generate semantic memory for 3D scenes in the IQuADv1 dataset. Since the termination model may decide to early stop the navigation, the intermediate reconstruction results are also saved for the QA model. This provides data for pretraining the 3D-CNN. Here we use the ground truth segmentation provided by the AI2Thor simulator.

Pretraining the 3D-CNN and the LSTM. End-to-end training of the 3D-CNN & LSTM QA model from scratch is very hard to converge. Therefore, we split these two networks. For 3D-CNN network, we add three auxiliary branches, corresponding to three different kinds of questions in the IQuADv1 dataset. These branches respectively predict whether an object of a category exists, the number of objects of that category, and all containers holding that category of objects. We design loss functions for these three branches and pretrain the 3D-CNN alone. For the LSTM for language understanding, we pretrain it in the way similar to IQA, which is, using fully-connected layers on f_Q to predict the question type and all involved object categories corresponding to the type.

Training the Models. The weights of pretrained networks are transferred to the 3D-CNN-LSTM QA Network. The whole QA network is then trained with the answers as supervision. The Termination Model is trained in a similar way, with the supervision being no further exploration is needed for a given semantic memory and question (e.g. for "existence" problems, the reconstruction process can stop immediately when the object we are interested in is already found).

6   Experimental Results

6.1   Single-Agent IQA

To investigate the performance of our 3D-memory-based QA framework, we perform experiments with single-agent set-ups and compare it with the original IQA model proposed in [7]. Results are shown in Table 1. Accuracy and episode length for three question types in IQuADv1 dataset are reported separately.

Table 1. Experiment results with single-agent set-up

	Existence		Counting		Containing	
Model	Accuracy	Length	Accuracy	Length	Accuracy	Length
IQA (GT Detection) [7]	86.56%	679.70	35.31%	604.79	70.94%	311.03
IQA (Pred. Detection) [7]	68.47%	318.33	30.43%	926.11	58.67%	516.23
Human [7]	90.00%	58.40	80.00%	81.90	90.00%	43.00
Ours (GT Segmentation)	98.75%	166.31	88.28 %	237.40	91.88%	195.89
Ours (Pred. Segmentation)	79.53%	159.85	45.62%	220.95	77.50%	204.87

IQA (Pred. Detection) uses predicted depth, while others use GT depth

When ground truth (GT) semantic segmentation is available, our proposed framework not only outperforms the baseline method with GT detections, but also achieves higher accuracy than humans, showing the potential advantages of our model. Still, it takes more actions than humans to answer a question, indicating that its efficiency can be improved.

When replacing GT segmentation with results predicted by Mask R-CNN, we notice obvious performance drops. It indicates that the bottleneck of our method is the accuracy of semantic segmentation. With more advanced methods such as multi-view based image segmentation, our method may perform better.

However, even with predicted segmentation, the overall performance of our method still outperforms the IQA baseline with GT detection (better in *Counting* and *Containing*, worse in *Existence*), showing that the rest part of our model is robust enough to tolerate imperfect segmentation. Note that we use GT depth images to perform the 3D Reconstruction, but the IQA model noted as "GT Detection" uses GT depth as well. Since our method doesn't require very high reconstruction precision, noisy depth sensor is unlikely to cause severe problems. However, when it comes to predicted depth data, registration between different predicted depth frames, or MVS-based techniques like [11] would be required.

6.2   Multi-agent IQA on IQuADv1 Dataset

Table 2. Multi-agent experiments with N agents

	Existence		Counting		Containing		Overall		Overall Speedup		
N	Acc.	Length	Acc.	Length	Acc.	Length	Acc.	Length	Ideal	Actual	% of Ideal
1	79.53%	159.85	45.62%	220.95	77.50%	204.87	67.55%	195.22	1.0	1.00	100%
2	78.59%	93.99	46.56%	127.57	77.50%	116.69	67.55%	112.75	2.0	1.73	87%
3	78.28%	69.24	45.47%	90.33	77.03%	86.36	66.93%	81.98	3.0	2.38	79%
4	78.44%	60.41	43.91%	79.63	76.25%	75.46	66.20%	71.83	4.0	2.72	68%

We test the proposed framework on multi-agent set-ups. The results are shown in Table 2. There are no significant differences in *accuracy* for different numbers of agents, which indicates that our constructed semantic memory is sufficient and stable. Despite the similar accuracy, it takes much fewer steps for each agent to finish the task when more agents are available.

To examine the parallelism in our framework, we calculate the *speedup in length* with 2, 3, and 4 agents. The length is the maximum number of actions taken among all agents. When the task assignment is unbalanced, some agents may be in heavy load while other agents are idle. Therefore using the maximum number of actions as the metric can more accurately measure the speedup in terms of time consumption. As the number of agents increases, the speedup also becomes higher. However, the percentage of the actual speedup compared to the ideal speedup drops from 87% to 68%, when the number of agents increases from 2 to 4. These results show that our clustering and task assignment based multi-agent schedule algorithm is scalable, but still has room for improvement.

6.3   Qualitative Examples

To illustrate how our agents navigates in Embodied Environments, we select a question within the IQuADv1 dataset—*How many eggs are there in the room?*. The question is answered correctly with 1, 2, 3 and 4 agents set-ups. All agents are spawn at the same location as defined in the IQuADv1 dataset. We record the track of each agent and visualize it in the following figure.

As is shown in Fig. 5, the searching area of agents is relatively scattered. For example, with three agents (colored in red, yellow and blue), they act in the bottom part, the top-left part and the right part of the room respectively,

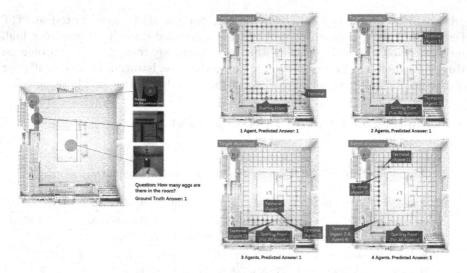

Fig. 5. A qualitative example with the question and some rendered image of the scene on the left side. The track of each agent, with single-agent set-up and multi-agent set-up with 2, 3 and 4 agents are shown on the right. (Color figure online)

indicating that the proposed task assignment algorithm is effective in allocating the scanning tasks to each agent. With more agents joining the reconstruct process, their searching area has more overlaps at the left and bottom part of the scene. That's reasonable because more interactive objects (mainly cabinets) exist in this region, and agents are required to head to this region when other parts have been fully reconstructed.

7 Conclusion

In this work, we introduce a new task of Multi-Agent Interactive Question Answering. We propose a novel two-stage framework to solve this problem, where firstly Multi-Agent 3D Reconstruction is performed to build a semantic memory, and then a 3D-CNN based QA model is used to generate the answer. Experiments show that our framework achieves high accuracy with single-agent set-up, and it is scalable to extend to multi-agent scenarios. Additionally, with GT semantic segmentation our proposed framework surpasses human performance, indicating that accurate 3D Semantic Segmentation is the bottleneck in our method.

Acknowledgements. This work was supported in part by the National Natural Science Foundation of China under Grants U1613212 and 61703284.

References

1. Antol, S., et al.: VQA: Visual question answering. In: Proceedings of the IEEE International Conference on Computer Vision, pp. 2425–2433 (2015)
2. Chang, A., et al.: Matterport3D: learning from RGB-D data in indoor environments. arXiv preprint arXiv:1709.06158 (2017)
3. Curless, B., Levoy, M.: A volumetric method for building complex models from range images. In: Proceedings of the 23rd Annual Conference on Computer Graphics and Interactive Techniques, pp. 303–312 (1996)
4. Das, A., Datta, S., Gkioxari, G., Lee, S., Parikh, D., Batra, D.: Embodied question answering. In: Proceedings of the IEEE Conference on Computer Vision and Pattern Recognition Workshops, pp. 2054–2063 (2018)
5. Dong, S., et al.: Multi-robot collaborative dense scene reconstruction. ACM Trans. Graph. (TOG) **38**(4), 1–16 (2019)
6. Foerster, J., Assael, I.A., De Freitas, N., Whiteson, S.: Learning to communicate with deep multi-agent reinforcement learning. In: Advances in Neural Information Processing Systems, pp. 2137–2145 (2016)
7. Gordon, D., Kembhavi, A., Rastegari, M., Redmon, J., Fox, D., Farhadi, A.: IQA: visual question answering in interactive environments. In: Proceedings of the IEEE Conference on Computer Vision and Pattern Recognition, pp. 4089–4098 (2018)
8. Graham, B., van der Maaten, L.: Submanifold sparse convolutional networks. arXiv preprint arXiv:1706.01307 (2017)
9. He, K., Gkioxari, G., Dollar, P., Girshick, R.: Mask R-CNN. In: The IEEE International Conference on Computer Vision (ICCV) October 2017
10. Hou, J., Dai, A., Niessner, M.: 3D-sis: 3D semantic instance segmentation of RGB-D scans. In: The IEEE Conference on Computer Vision and Pattern Recognition (CVPR) June 2019
11. Huang, P.H., Matzen, K., Kopf, J., Ahuja, N., Huang, J.B.: Deepmvs: learning multi-view stereopsis. In: Proceedings of the IEEE Conference on Computer Vision and Pattern Recognition, pp. 2821–2830 (2018)
12. Izadi, S., et al.: Kinectfusion: real-time 3D reconstruction and interaction using a moving depth camera. In: Proceedings of the 24th Annual ACM Symposium on User Interface Software and Technology, pp. 559–568 (2011)
13. Jang, Y., Song, Y., Yu, Y., Kim, Y., Kim, G.: TGIF-QA: toward spatio-temporal reasoning in visual question answering. In: The IEEE Conference on Computer Vision and Pattern Recognition (CVPR) July 2017
14. Kolve, E., et al.: Ai2-thor: an interactive 3D environment for visual AI. arXiv preprint arXiv:1712.05474 (2017)
15. Malinowski, M., Rohrbach, M., Fritz, M.: Ask your neurons: a neural-based approach to answering questions about images. In: The IEEE International Conference on Computer Vision (ICCV) December 2015
16. Mousavi, H.K., Nazari, M., Takáč, M., Motee, N.: Multi-agent image classification via reinforcement learning. arXiv preprint arXiv:1905.04835 (2019)
17. Savva, M., et al.: Habitat: a platform for embodied AI research. In: Proceedings of the IEEE International Conference on Computer Vision, pp. 9339–9347 (2019)
18. Stone, P., Veloso, M.: Multiagent systems: a survey from a machine learning perspective. Autonom. Robot. **8**(3), 345–383 (2000)
19. Sukhbaatar, S., Fergus, R., et al.: Learning multiagent communication with backpropagation. In: Advances in Neural Information Processing Systems, pp. 2244–2252 (2016)

20. Wu, Y., Wu, Y., Gkioxari, G., Tian, Y.: Building generalizable agents with a realistic and rich 3D environment. arXiv preprint arXiv:1801.02209 (2018)
21. Xia, F., et al.: Gibson Env V2: Embodied simulation environments for interactive navigation (2019)
22. Yang, W., Wang, X., Farhadi, A., Gupta, A., Mottaghi, R.: Visual semantic navigation using scene priors. arXiv preprint arXiv:1810.06543 (2018)
23. Zhao, Z., et al.: Video question answering via hierarchical spatio-temporal attention networks. In: IJCAI, pp. 3518–3524 (2017)
24. Zheng, L., et al.: Active scene understanding via online semantic reconstruction. In: Computer Graphics Forum. vol. 38, pp. 103–114. Wiley Online Library (2019)
25. Zhu, Y., et al.: Target-driven visual navigation in indoor scenes using deep reinforcement learning. In: 2017 IEEE International Conference on Robotics and Automation (ICRA), pp. 3357–3364. IEEE (2017)

Conditional Sequential Modulation for Efficient Global Image Retouching

Jingwen He[1,2], Yihao Liu[1,2,3], Yu Qiao[1,2], and Chao Dong[1,2(✉)]

[1] ShenZhen Key Lab of Computer Vision and Pattern Recognition,
SIAT - SenseTime Joint Lab, Shenzhen Institutes of Advanced Technology,
Chinese Academy of Sciences, Beijing, China
{jw.he,yh.liu4,yu.qiao,chao.dong}@siat.ac.cn
[2] SIAT Branch, Shenzhen Institute of Artificial Intelligence and Robotics
for Society, Shenzhen, China
[3] University of Chinese Academy of Sciences, Beijing, China

Abstract. Photo retouching aims at enhancing the aesthetic visual quality of images that suffer from photographic defects such as over/under exposure, poor contrast, inharmonious saturation. Practically, photo retouching can be accomplished by a series of image processing operations. In this paper, we investigate some commonly-used retouching operations and mathematically find that these pixel-independent operations can be approximated or formulated by multi-layer perceptrons (MLPs). Based on this analysis, we propose an extremely light-weight framework - Conditional Sequential Retouching Network (CSRNet) - for efficient global image retouching. CSRNet consists of a base network and a condition network. The base network acts like an MLP that processes each pixel independently and the condition network extracts the global features of the input image to generate a condition vector. To realize retouching operations, we modulate the intermediate features using Global Feature Modulation (GFM), of which the parameters are transformed by condition vector. Benefiting from the utilization of 1×1 convolution, CSRNet only contains less than 37 k trainable parameters, which is orders of magnitude smaller than existing learning-based methods. Extensive experiments show that our method achieves state-of-the-art performance on the benchmark MIT-Adobe FiveK dataset quantitively and qualitatively. Code is available at https://github.com/hejingwenhejingwen/CSRNet.

J. He and Y. Liu are co-first authors.

Electronic supplementary material The online version of this chapter (https:// doi.org/10.1007/978-3-030-58601-0_40) contains supplementary material, which is available to authorized users.

A. Vedaldi et al. (Eds.): ECCV 2020, LNCS 12358, pp. 679–695, 2020.
https://doi.org/10.1007/978-3-030-58601-0_40

1   Introduction

Photo retouching can significantly improve the visual quality of photographs through a sequence of image processing operations, such as brightness and contrast changes. Manual retouching requires specialized skills and training, thus is challenging for causal users. Even for professional retouchers, dealing with large collections requires tedious repetitive editing works. This presents the needs for automatic photo retouching. It can be equipped in smart phones to help ordinary people get visual-pleasing photos, or it can be built in photo editing softwares to provide an editing reference for experts.

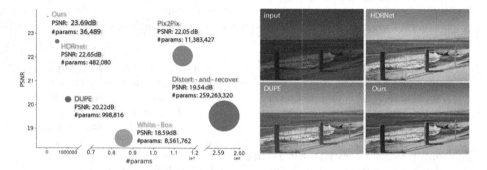

Fig. 1. Left: Compared with existing state-of-the-art methods, our method achieves superior performance with extremely few parameters (1/13 of HDRNet [10] and 1/250 of White-Box [12]). The diameter of the circle represents the amount of trainable parameters. **Right:** Image retouching examples. Please zoom in for best view. (Color figure online)

The aim of photo retouching is to generate a high quality image from a low quality input. Recent learning-based methods tend to treat photo retouching as a special case of image enhancement or image-to-image translation. They use CNNs to learn either the transformation matrix [10] or an end-to-end mapping [5,13,14] from input/output pairs. Generally, photo retouching adjusts the global color tones, without the change of high frequency components (e.g., edges), while other image enhancement/translation tasks focus more on local patterns and will even change the image textures. Moreover, photo retouching is naturally a sequential processing, which can be decomposed into several independent simple operations. This property does not always hold for image enhancement and image-to-image translation problems. As most state-of-the-art algorithms [5,10,23] are not specialized for photo retouching, they generally require extra parameters (e.g., 3×3 convolutions) to deal with local patterns, which could largely restrict their implementation efficiency. Detailed comparisons of different retouching methods are presented in the Related Work section. In real scenarios, most commonly-used operations (LUT, tone mapping, image enhancement operations in commercial software) are global adjustment. Thus in this paper, we focus on "global" photo retouching without considering local operations.

To design an efficient photo retouching algorithm, we invesigate several retouching operations adopted in [12, 19] and find that these commonly-used operations (e.g., contrast adjustment, tone mapping) are location-independent/pixel-independent. The input pixels can be mapped to the output pixels via pixel-wise mapping functions, without the need of local image features. We take a step further and show that these pixel-wise functions can be approximated by multi-layer perceptrons (MLPs). Different adjustment operations can share similar network structures but with different parameters. Then the input image can be sequentially processed by a set of neural networks to generate the final output.

Based on the above obervation, we propose an extremely light-weight network - Conditional Sequential Retouching Network (CSRNet) - for fast global photo retouching. The key idea is to mimic the sequential processing procedure and implicitly model the editing operations in an end-to-end trainable network. The framework consists of two modules - the base network and the condition network. The base network adopts a fully convolutional structure. While the unique feature is that all filters are of size 1×1, indicating that each pixel is processed independently. Therefore, the base network can be regarded as an MLP for individual pixels. To realize retouching operations, we modulate the intermediate features using Global Feature Modulation (GFM), of which the parameters are controlled by the condition network. The condition network generates a condition vector, which is then broadcasted to different layers of the base network for feature modulation. This procedure is just like a sequential editing process operated on different stages of the MLP (see Fig. 3). These two modules are jointly optimized from human-adjusted image pairs.

The proposed network enjoys a very simple architecture, which contains only six plain convolutional layers in total, without any complex building blocks. Such a compact network could achieve state-of-the-art performance on MIT-Adobe FiveK dataset [2], with less than 37 k parameters -1/13 of HDRNet [10] and 1/90 of DPE [5] (see Fig. 1 and Table 1). We have also conducted extensive ablation studies on various settings, including trying different hand-crafted global priors, network structures and feature modulation strategies.

In addition to automatic adjustment, users will desire to control the output styles according to their own preference. Even for the same style, they may also want to adjust the overall retouching strength. To meet diverse user flavors, our method enjoys the flexibility to train different condition networks for different styles, without changing the base network. For the same style, we use image interpolation between input and output images to realize the strength control.

Our contributions are three-fold. 1. We propose the Conditional Sequential Retouching Network (CSRNet) for efficient global photo retouching. The proposed method can achieve state-of-the-art performance with less than 37 k parameters. 2. We combine the idea of color decomposition and sequential processing in a unified CNN framework, which could learn implicit step-wise retouching operations without intermediate supervision. 3. We achieve continuous output effects among various retouching styles. We find that image interpolation could realize strength control between different stylized images.

2 Related Work

We briefly review the recent progress on image retouching and enhancement. Traditional algorithms have proposed various operations and filters to enhance the visual quality of images, such as histogram equalization, local Laplacian operator [1], fast bilateral filtering [7], and color correction methods based on the gray-world [8] or gray-edge [22] assumption. Since Bychkovsky et al. [2] collected a large-scale dataset MIT-Adobe FiveK, which contains input and expert-retouched image pairs, a plenty of learning-based enhancing algorithms have been developed to continuously push the performance. Generally, these learning-based methods can be divided into three groups: physical-modeling-based methods, image-to-image translation methods and reinforcement learning methods. Physical-modeling-based methods attempt to estimate the intermediate parameters of the proposed physical models or assumptions for image enhancing. Based on the Retinex theory of color vision [16], several algorithms were developed for image exposure correction by estimating the reflectance and illumination with learnable models [9,23,26,27]. By postulating that the enhanced output image can be expressed as local pointwise transformations of the input image, Gharbi et al. [10] combined bilateral grid [4] and bilateral guided upsampling models [3], then constructed a CNN model to predict the affine transformation coefficients in bilateral space for real-time image enhancement. Methods of the second group treat image enhancement as an image-to-image translation problem, which directly learn the end-to-end mapping between input and the enhanced image without modelling intermediate parameters. Ignatov et al. explored to translate ordinary photos into DSLR-quality images by residual convolutional neural networks [13] and weakly supervised generative adversarial networks [14]. Chen et al. [5] utilized an improved two-way generative adversarial network (GAN) that can be trained in an unpair-learning manner. Reinforcement learning is adopted for image retouching, which aims at explicitly simulating the step-wise retouching process. Hu et al. [12] presented a White-Box photo post-processing framework that learns to make decisions based on the current state of the image. Park et al. [19] casted the color enhancement problem into a Markov Decision Process (MDP) where each action is defined as a global color adjustment operation and selected by Deep Q-Network [18].

3 Method

Our method aims at fast automatic image retouching with low computation cost. First, we analyze several commonly-used retouching operations and gain important insights. Based on the analysis, we propose the framework – Conditional Sequential Retouching Network (CSRNet). Then we illustrate the intrinsic working mechanism of CSRNet in two perspectives. Finally, we describe how to achieve different retouching styles and control the overall enhancement strength.

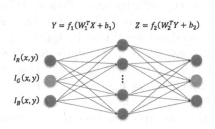

$$Y = f_1(W_1^T X + b_1) \qquad Z = f_2(W_2^T Y + b_2)$$

$I_R(x,y)$

$I_G(x,y)$

$I_B(x,y)$

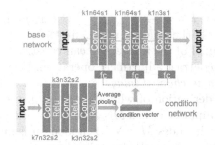

(a) An MLP on individual pixels.

(b) CSRNet. (k: kernel size; n: number of feature maps; s: stride.)

Fig. 2. (a) Illustration for MLP on a single pixel. Pixel-independent operation can be viewed as an MLP on individual pixels, such as brightness change, white-balancing, saturation controlling and tone-mapping. (b) The proposed network consists of base network, condition network and GFM.

3.1 Analysis of Retouching Operations

Image retouching is accomplished by a series of image processing operations, such as the manipulation of brightness/contrast, the adjustment in each color channel, and the controlling of saturation/hue/tones. We mathematically find that these pixel-independent operations can be approximated or formulated by multi-layer perceptrons (MLPs). Below we show two examples.

Global Brightness Change. Given an input image I, the global brightness is described as the average value of its luminance map: $I_Y = 0.299 * I_R + 0.587 * I_G + 0.114 * I_B$, where I_R, I_G, I_B represent the RGB channels, respectively. One simple way to adjust the brightness is to multiply a scalar for each pixel:

$$I_Y'(x, y) = \alpha I_Y(x, y) \tag{1}$$

where $I_Y'(x, y)$ is the adjusted pixel value, α is the scalar, and (x, y) indicates the pixel location in an $M \times N$ image. We can formulate the adjustment formula (1) into the representation of an MLP:

$$Y = f(W^T X + b) \tag{2}$$

where $X \in \mathbb{R}^{MN}$ is the vector flattened from the input image, $W \in \mathbb{R}^{MN \times MN}$ and $b \in \mathbb{R}^{MN}$ are weights and biases, and $f(.)$ is the activation function. When $W = diag\{\alpha, \alpha, \ldots, \alpha\}$, $b = \mathbf{0}$ and f is the identity mapping $f(x) = x$, the MLP (2) is equivalent to the brightness adjustment formula (1).

Contrast Adjustment. Contrast represents the difference in luminance or color maps. Among many definitions of contrast, we adopt a widely-used contrast adjustment formula:

$$I'(x, y) = \alpha I(x, y) + (1 - \alpha)\bar{I}, \tag{3}$$

where $\bar{I} = \frac{1}{M \times N} \sum_{x=0}^{M-1} \sum_{y=0}^{N-1} I(x, y)$ and α is the adjustment coefficient. When $\alpha = 1$, the image will remain the same. The above formula is applied on each channel of the image. We can construct a three-layer MLP that is equivalent to the contrast adjustment operation. For simplicity, *the following derivation is for a single-channel image,* and it can be easily generalized to RGB images (refer to the derivation of white-balancing in the supplementary material). As in Fig. 2, the input layer has $M \times N$ units covering all pixels of the input image, the middle layer includes $M \times N + 1$ hidden units and the last layer contains $M \times N$ output units. This can be formalized as:

$$Y = f_1(W_1^T X + b_1), Z = f_2(W_2^T Y + b_2) \tag{4}$$

where $X \in \mathbb{R}^{MN}$, $W_1 \in \mathbb{R}^{MN \times (MN+1)}$, $W_2 \in \mathbb{R}^{(MN+1) \times MN}$, $b_1 \in \mathbb{R}^{(MN+1)}$, $b_2 \in \mathbb{R}^{MN}$. Let $A = diag\{\alpha, \alpha, \dots, \alpha\} \in \mathbb{R}^{MN \times MN}$, $B = \frac{1}{MN}\mathbf{1} \in \mathbb{R}^{MN}$, $C = diag\{1, 1, \dots, 1\} \in \mathbb{R}^{MN \times MN}$, $D = [(1 - \alpha)\mathbf{1}]^T \in \mathbb{R}^{1 \times MN}$. When $W_1 = [A, B] \in \mathbb{R}^{MN \times (MN+1)}$, $W_2 = \begin{bmatrix} C \\ D \end{bmatrix} \in \mathbb{R}^{(MN+1) \times MN}$, $b_1 = b_2 = \mathbf{0}$ and $f_1(x) = f_2(x) = x$, the above MLP (4) is equivalent to the contrast adjustment formula (3).

Other operations, like white-balancing, saturation controlling, tone-mapping, can also be regarded as MLPs. (Please refer to the supplementary material.)

Discussions. We have shown that above the retouching operations are equivalent to classic MLPs. And the manipulation on one pixel is uncorrelated with neighboring pixels. That is why we can use a diagonal matrix as the MLP weights. Some operations, like contrast adjustment, also require global information (e.g., image mean value), which can be provided by another condition network. As shown in Fig. 2(a) the above MLPs designed for input images can be viewed as MLPs worked on *individual pixels*, which can be further formulated as 1×1 convolutions. The correlation between MLP and 1×1 convolutions has been revealed in MLPconv [17] and SRCNN [6]. According to the analysis above, we propose a comprehensible and specialized framework for efficient photo retouching.

3.2   Conditional Sequential Retouching Network

The proposed framework contains a base network and a condition network as shown in Fig. 2(b). The base network takes the low-quality image as input and generates the retouched image. The condition network estimates the global priors from the input image, and afterwards influences the base network by global feature modulation operations.

3.2.1   Network Structure

Base Network. The base network adopts a fully convolutional structure with N layers and $N - 1$ ReLU activations. One unique trait of the base network is that all the filter size is 1×1, suggesting that each pixel in the input image is manipulated independently. Hence, the base network can be regarded as an MLP, which is worked *on each pixel independently* and slides over the input image, as in [17]. Based on the analysis in Sect. 3.1, theoretically, the base network has the capability of handling all the pixel-independent retouching operations. Moreover, since all the filters are of size 1×1, the network has dramatically few parameters.

Condition Network. The global information/priors are indispensable for image retouching. For example, the contrast adjustment requires the average luminance of the image. To allow the base network to incorporate global priors, a condition network is proposed to collaborate with the base network. The condition network is like an encoder that contains three blocks, in which a series of convolutional, ReLU and downsamping layers are included. The output of the condition network is a condition vector, which will be broadcasted into the base network using the following global feature modulation. Network details are depicted in Sect. 4 and Fig. 2(b).

3.2.2   Global Feature Modulation

Our CSRNet adopts scaling and shifting operations to modulate intermediate features of the base network. First, we revisit the formulation of instance normalization [21]: $IN(x_i) = \gamma * (\frac{x_i - \mu}{\sigma}) + \beta$, where μ, β are the mean and standard deviation of the feature map x_i, γ, β are affine parameters. The proposed Global Feature Modulation (GFM) only requires γ and β to scale and shift the feature map x_i without normalizing it. Therefore, GFM can be formulated as: $GFM(x_i) = \gamma * x_i + \beta$.

GFM is also realted to Adaptive Feature Modification layer (AdaFM) [11], which can be written in the following equation: $AdaFM(x_i) = g_i * x_i + b_i$, where g_i and b_i are the filter and bias. The modulation of AdaFM is based on a local region instead of a single pixel. In another perspective, GFM is a special case of AdaFM when the filter g_i is of size 1×1.

3.2.3   Illustration

To facilitate understanding, we illustrate "how the CSRNet works" in two perspectives. We use a simple yet standard setting—$N = 3$.

Pixel-level View. We regard the base network as an MLP that works on individual pixels as shown in Fig. 3(a). From this perspective, we can explain that the base network is made up of three fully-connected layers that perform feature extraction, non-linear mapping and reconstruction, respectively. As demonstrated in Sect. 3.1, such a three-layer MLP is able to approximate most image retouching operations. Then we add the condition network, and see how these two modules work collectively. As the GFM is equivalent to a "multiply+addition" operation, it can be easily merged into filters. Then the condition network could adjust the filter weights of the base network. While for the last layer, the modulation operation can be modeled as an extra layer. This layer performs one-to-one mapping, which changes the "average intensity and dynamic

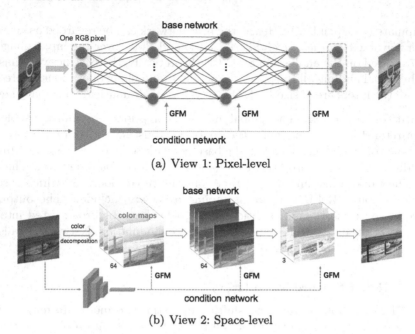

(a) View 1: Pixel-level

(b) View 2: Space-level

Fig. 3. Illustration for two perspectives of the proposed framework.

range" of the output pixel, just like "brightness/contrast adjustment". Combining the base network and the condition network, we will obtain a different MLP for a different input image, allowing image-specific photo retouching. To support this pixel-level view, we have conducted a demonstration experiment that using the proposed framework to simulate the procedures of several retouching operations. The results are shown in the supplementary material.

Space-level View. We can also regard intermediate features as color maps, while the color space transformation can be realized by linear combination of color maps (e.g., RGB to YUV). Specifically, the input image is initialized in the RGB space. As depicted in Fig. 3(b), the first and second layers of the base network project the input into high dimensional color spaces, and the last layer transforms the color maps back to the RGB space. The GFM performs linear transformation on intermediate features, thus can be regarded as a retouching operation on the mapped color space. In summary, the base network performs color decomposition, the condition network generates editing parameters, and GFM sequentially adjusts intermediate color maps.

3.2.4   Discussion

In this part, we show the merits of CSRNet by comparing with other state-of-the-art methods. First, we adopt pixel-wise operations (1×1 filters), which will preserve edges and textures. While GAN-based methods [5,15] tend to change local patterns and generate undesired artifacts (see Fig. 4, Pix2Pix). Second, we use global modulation strategy, which will maintain color consistency across the image. While HDRNet [10] predicts a transformation coefficient for each pixel, thus will lead to abrupt color changes (see Fig. 4, HDRNet). Third, we use a unified CNN framework with supervised learning, which could produce images of higher quality than RL-based methods [12,19] (see Fig. 4, White-box and Distort-and-recover). Nevertheless, as CSRNet is specially designed for global photo retouching, it cannot be generalized to other tasks (e.g., style transfer, image enhancement, unpaired learning) as the above mentioned methods.

3.2.5 Multiple Styles and Strength Control

Photo retouching is a highly ill-posed problem. Different photographers may have different preferences on retouching styles. Our method enjoys the flexibility of multiple style learning. Once the model is trained on a specific retouching style, we can easily transfer the model to another retouching style by only finetuning the condition network, which is much faster than training from scratch. While other methods all require to retrain the whole model on new datasets. Once we have obtained two stylized versions of an image, we can use "image interpolation" to produce intermediate styles between them.

$$I_{out}(x,y) = \alpha \hat{I}_1(x,y) + (1-\alpha)\hat{I}_2(x,y), \tag{5}$$

where $\hat{I}_1(x,y)$ and $\hat{I}_2(x,y)$ are two images to be interpolated, and α is the coefficient controlling the combined styles. Besides, this image interpolation strategy also allows us to control the overall retouching strength. For example, if the automatic retouched output is too bright, users may desire to decrease the overall luminance. This can be achieved by setting I_1 as the input image and I_2 as the retouched image. We can change the value of α to control the retouching strength. As shown in Fig. 6, we could achieve continuous output effects between two objectives and two input images. There are other alternatives to realize continuous output effects, such as DNI [25], AdaFM [11] and DynamicNet [20]. For pixel-wise operations, the pixels in two images on the same location are content-aligned, thus the pixel-wise blending is effective to achieve continuous imagery effects. If there are local operations, the blending should also consider neighboring pixels. As photo retouching consists of only pixel-wise operations, the simplest image interpolation is already enough to achieve satisfactory results.

4   Experiments

Dataset and Metrics. MIT-Adobe FiveK [2] is a commonly-used photo retouching dataset with 5,000 RAW images and corresponding retouched versions produced by five experts (A/B/C/D/E). We follow the previous methods [5,10,12,23] to use the retouched results of expert C as the ground truth (GT). We adopt the same pre-processing procedure as [12][1] and all the images are resized to 500px on the long edge. We randomly select 500 images for testing

---

[1] https://github.com/yuanming-hu/exposure/wiki/Preparing-data-for-the-MIT-Adobe-FiveK-Dataset-with-Lightroom.

and the remaining 4,500 images for training. We use PSNR, SSIM and the Mean L2 error in CIE L*a*b space[2] to evaluate the performance.

Implementation Details. The base network contains 3 convolutional layers with channel size 64 and kernel size 1 × 1. The condition network also contains three convolutional layers with channel size 32. The kernel size of the first convolutional layer is set to 7 × 7 to increase the receptive field, while others are 3 × 3. Each convolutional layer downsamples features to half size with a stride of 2. We use a global average pooling layer at the end of the condition network to obtain a 32-dimensional condition vector. Then the condition vector will be transformed by fully connected layers to generate the parameters of channel-wise scaling and shifting operations. In total, there are 6 fully connected layers for 3 scaling operations and 3 shifting operations. During training, the mini-batch size is set to 1. L1 loss is adopted as the loss function. The learning rate is initialized as 10^{-4} and is decayed by a factor of 2 every 10^5 iterations. All experiments run 6×10^5 iterations. We use PyTorch framework and train all models on GTX 2080Ti GPUs. It takes only 5 h for the model training.

4.1   Comparison with State-of-the-Art Methods

We compare our method with six state-of-the-art methods: DUPE [23], HDRNet [10], DPE [5], White-Box [12], Distort-and-Recover [19] and Pix2Pix [15][3].

Quantitative Comparison. We compare CSRNet with state-of-the-art methods[4] in terms of PSNR, SSIM, and the Mean L2 error in L*a*b* space. As we can see from Table 1, the proposed CSRNet outperforms all the previous state-of-the-art methods by a large margin with the fewest parameters (36,489). Specifically, White-Box and Distort-and-Recover are reinforcement-learning-based methods, which require over millions of parameters but achieve worst results. HDRNet and DUPE solve the color enhancement problem by estimating the illumination map and require relatively less parameters (less than one million).

Since the released model of DUPE is trained for under-exposed images, we can also refer to the result (23.04 dB) provided in their paper. Pix2Pix and DPE both utilize the generative adversarial networks and perform well quantitatively. Under the same experimental setting, CSRNet outperforms DPE in all three metrics with much less parameters.

---

[2] CIE L*a*b* (CIELAB) is a color space specified by the International Commission on Illumination. It describes all the colors visible to the human eye and was created to serve as a device-independent model to be used as a reference.

[3] Pix2Pix uses conditional generative adversarial networks to achieve image-to-image translation and is also applicable to image enhancement problem.

[4] For White-Box, DUPE, DPE, we directly use their released pretrained models for testing. For HDRNet, Distort-and-Recover, and Pix2Pix, we re-train their models based on their public implementations on our training dataset. The training codes of DPE is not yet accessible and their released model is trained on another input version of MIT-Adobe FiveK. For fair comparison, we additionally train our models on the same input dataset.

Table 1. Quantitative comparison with state-of-the-art methods on MIT-Adobe FiveK dataset (expert C). For L2 error in L*a*b space, lower is better.

Method	PSNR	SSIM	L2 error (Lab)	Params
White-Box [12]	18.59	0.797	13.24	8,561,762
Distort-and-Recover [19]	19.54	0.800	12.91	259,263,320
HDRNet [10]	22.65	0.880	11.64	482,080
DUPE [10]	20.22	0.829	13.38	998,816
Pix2Pix [15]	22.05	0.788	11.88	11,383,427
CSRNet (ours)	**23.69**	**0.895**	**10.86**	36,489
DPE [5]	23.76	0.881	10.50	3,335,395
CSRNet (ours)	**24.23**	**0.900**	**10.29**	36,489

Visual Comparison. The results of visual comparison[5] are shown in Fig. 4. The input images from the MIT-Adobe FiveK dataset are generally under low-light condition. Distort-and-recover tends to generate over-exposure output. It seems that White-box and DPE only increase the brightness but fail to modify the original tone, which is oversaturated. At the first glance, the outputs of the second row look more natural and vivid. However, the enhanced image obtained by Pix2Pix contains artifacts. HDRNet outputs image with unnatural color in some regions (e.g. green color on the face). In conclusion, our method is able to generate more realistic images among all methods. Please see the supplementary file for more comparisons.

User Study. We have conducted a user study with 20 participants for subjective evaluation. The participants are asked to rank four retouched image versions (HDRNet [10], DPE [5], expert-C (GT) and ours) according to the aesthetic visual quality. 50 images are randomly selected from the testing set and are shown to each participant. 4 retouched versions are displayed on the screen in random order. Users are asked to pay attention to whether the color is vivid,whether there are artifacts and whether the local color is harmonious. Since HDRNet and DPE have better quantitative and qualitative performance than other methods, we choose them to make the comparison. As suggested in Fig. 5, our results achieve better visual ranking against HDRNet and DPE with 553 images ranked first and second. 245 images of our method ranked first, second only to expert C; and 308 images are ranked second, ahead of other methods.

4.2 Multiple Styles and Strength Control

In this section, we aim to achieve different retouching styles and control retouching strength. Specifically, given an image retouching model for one style, we can

---

[5] We do not consider DUPE for visual comparison because the authors only released model trained on their collected under-exposed image pairs.

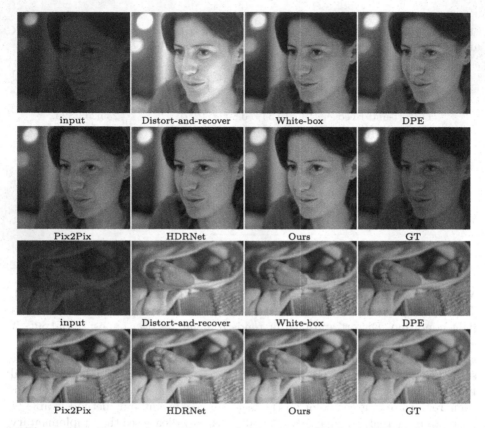

Fig. 4. Visual comparison with state-of-the-arts on MIT-Adobe FiveK data set.

easily transfer the model to other retouching styles by only finetuning the condition network. Here, we transfer the retouching model of expert C to expert A, B, D, and E. From Table 2, we can observe that finetuning the condition network can achieve comparable results with training from scratch. This indicates that the fixed base network performs like a stacked color decomposition, and have the flexibility to be modulated to different retouching styles.

Given retouched outputs of different styles, users can achieve smooth transition effects between different styles by using image interpolation. In Fig. 6, the output style changes continuously from expert A to expert B. Besides, for one certain style, users can also control the retouching strength by image interpolation between input image and the retouched one. More results can be found in the supplementary file.

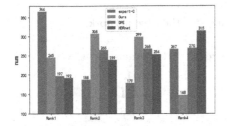

Fig. 5. Ranking results of user study. Rank 1 means the best visual quality.

Table 2. Performance for Multiple styles (A/B/D/E).

Expert	PSNR (finetune)	PSNR (scratch)
A	22.29	22.06
B	25.61	25.52
D	23.06	23.04
E	23.95	23.81

4.3 Ablation Study

In this section, we investigate our CSRNet in three aspects, base network, modulation strategy, and condition network. We present all the results in PSNR.

Base Network. The base network of our CSRNet contains 3 convolutional layers with kernel size 1×1 and channel number 64. As mentioned before, we assume that the base network with kernel size 1×1 performs like a stacked color decomposition, and each layer represents a different color space of the input image. Here, we explore the base network by changing its kernel size and increasing the number of layers. Besides, we remove the condition network to verify whether the base network could fairly deal with image retouching alone.

expert A $\alpha = 0.0$ $\alpha = 0.3$ $\alpha = 0.5$ $\alpha = 0.8$ $\alpha = 1.0$ expert B

input $\alpha = 0.0$ $\alpha = 0.3$ $\alpha = 0.5$ $\alpha = 0.8$ $\alpha = 1.0$ expert B

Fig. 6. The first row shows smooth transition effects between different styles (expert A to B) by image interpolation. In the second row, we use image interpolation to control the retouching strength from input image to the automatic retouched result. We denote the interpolation coefficient α for each image.

From Table 3, we can observe that the base network cannot solve the image retouching problem well without the condition network. Specifically, when we expand the filter size to 3×3 and increase the number of layers to 7, there is only marginal improvement (0.2 dB) in terms of PSNR.

Considering the cases with condition network, if we fix the number of layers, and expand the kernel size to 3, there is roughly no improvement. Therefore,

Table 3. Results of ablation study for the base network.

	Layers	Kernel size	PSNR	Params
w/o condition	3	1×1	20.47	4,611
	3	3×3	20.69	40,451
	7	3×3	20.67	188,163
w condition	3	1×1	23.69	36,489 (ours)
	3	3×3	23.73	72,329
	5	1×1	23.73	53,257
	5	3×3	23.70	154,633
	7	1×1	23.83	70,025
	7	3×3	23.64	236,937

the sequential processing of the base network is just pixel-independently which can be achieved by 1×1 filters. If we fix the kernel size to 1×1 and increase the number of layers, the performance improves a little bit (0.14dB). Since more layers require more parameters, we adopt a light-weight architecture with only three layers.

Modulation Strategy. Our framework adopts GFM to modulate the intermediate features under different conditions. Here, we compare different modulation strategies: concatenating, AdaFM [11], and SFTNet [24]. Specifically, we concatenate the condition vector directly with the input image. For AdaFM, we use kernel size 3×3 and 5×5. For SFTNet, we remove all the stride operations and the global average pooling in the condition network. Therefore, the modified condition network is able to generate a condition map, thus allowing spacial feature modulation on the intermediate features.

From Table 4, we observe that SFTNet obtains the worst results compared with other modulation strategies. Therefore, image retouching mainly depends on global context rather than spacial information. As for AdaFM, it is hard to achieve improvement by simply expanding its kernel size. In conclusion, conditional image retouching can be effectively achieved by GFM, which only scales and shifts the intermediate features.

Condition Network. The condition network aims to estimate a condition vector that represents global information of the input image. Alternatively, we can use other hand-crafted global priors to control the base network, such as brightness, average intensity, and histograms. Here, we investigate the effectiveness of these global priors. For brightness, we transform the RGB image to gray image, while the mean value of the gray image is regarded as the global prior. For average intensity, we compute the mean value for each channel of the RGB image. Regarding histograms, we generate the histograms for each channel of RGB image, and then concatenate them to a single vector. Besides, we combine

Table 4. Ablation study on modulation strategy.

Modulation strategies	PSNR	Params
w/o condition	20.47	4,611
concat	23.31	29,891
AdaFM 3 × 3	23.70	71,073
AdaFM 5 × 5	23.38	140,241
SFTNet	20.73	36,489
CSRNet	23.69	36,489

Table 5. Results of ablation study for the condition network

	Global prior	Dim	PSNR	Params
w/o condition	None	0	20.47	4,611
network	brightness	1	21.47	5,135
	average intensity	3	21.93	5,659
	histograms	768	22.90	206,089
w condition	None (ours)	32	23.69	36,489
network	brightness	1 + 32	23.01	36,751
	average intensity	3 + 32	23.57	37,275
	histograms	768 + 32	23.39	237,705

the global priors with our condition network to control the base network. In particular, we concatenate the global prior with the condition vector produced by the condition network. In addition, we have also explored the condition network with different hyper-parameters. The experimental results can be found in the supplementary file.

From Table 5, all three global priors can largely improve the performance compared with base network alone, which means that global priors are essential for image retouching. The ranking of their effectiveness is: histograms > average intensity > brightness. However, it seems that simply concatenating the global prior with condition vector cannot achieve improvement. In conclusion, our CSRNet can already extract effective global information.

Acknowledgement. This work is partially supported by the National Natural Science Foundation of China (61906184), Science and Technology Service Network Initiative of Chinese Academy of Sciences (KFJ-STS-QYZX-092), Shenzhen Basic Research Program (JSGG20180507182100698, CXB201104220032A), the Joint Lab of CAS-HKShenzhen Institute of Artificial Intelligence and Robotics for Society.

References

1. Aubry, M., Paris, S., Hasinoff, S.W., Kautz, J., Durand, F.: Fast local Laplacian filters: theory and applications. ACM Trans. Graph. (TOG) **33**(5), 1–14 (2014)
2. Bychkovsky, V., Paris, S., Chan, E., Durand, F.: Learning photographic global tonal adjustment with a database of input/output image pairs. In: CVPR 2011, pp. 97–104. IEEE (2011)
3. Chen, J., Adams, A., Wadhwa, N., Hasinoff, S.W.: Bilateral guided upsampling. ACM Trans. Graph. (TOG) **35**(6), 1–8 (2016)
4. Chen, J., Paris, S., Durand, F.: Real-time edge-aware image processing with the bilateral grid. ACM Trans. Graph. (TOG) **26**(3), 103-es (2007)
5. Chen, Y.S., Wang, Y.C., Kao, M.H., Chuang, Y.Y.: Deep photo enhancer: unpaired learning for image enhancement from photographs with GANS. In: Proceedings of the IEEE Conference on Computer Vision and Pattern Recognition, pp. 6306–6314 (2018)

6. Dong, C., Loy, C.C., He, K., Tang, X.: Learning a deep convolutional network for image super-resolution. In: Fleet, D., Pajdla, T., Schiele, B., Tuytelaars, T. (eds.) ECCV 2014. LNCS, vol. 8692, pp. 184–199. Springer, Cham (2014). https://doi.org/10.1007/978-3-319-10593-2_13

7. Durand, F., Dorsey, J.: Fast bilateral filtering for the display of high-dynamic-range images. In: Proceedings of the 29th Annual Conference on Computer Graphics and Interactive Techniques, pp. 257–266 (2002)

8. Finlayson, G.D., Trezzi, E.: Shades of gray and colour constancy. In: Color and Imaging Conference. vol. 2004, pp. 37–41. Society for Imaging Science and Technology (2004)

9. Fu, X., Zeng, D., Huang, Y., Zhang, X.P., Ding, X.: A weighted variational model for simultaneous reflectance and illumination estimation. In: Proceedings of the IEEE Conference on Computer Vision and Pattern Recognition, pp. 2782–2790 (2016)

10. Gharbi, M., Chen, J., Barron, J.T., Hasinoff, S.W., Durand, F.: Deep bilateral learning for real-time image enhancement. ACM Trans. Graph. (TOG) $36(4)$, 1–12 (2017)

11. He, J., Dong, C., Qiao, Y.: Modulating image restoration with continual levels via adaptive feature modification layers. In: Proceedings of the IEEE Conference on Computer Vision and Pattern Recognition, pp. 11056–11064 (2019)

12. Hu, Y., He, H., Xu, C., Wang, B., Lin, S.: Exposure: a white-box photo post-processing framework. ACM Trans. Graph. (TOG) $37(2)$, 1–17 (2018)

13. Ignatov, A., Kobyshev, N., Timofte, R., Vanhoey, K., Van Gool, L.: DSLR-quality photos on mobile devices with deep convolutional networks. In: Proceedings of the IEEE International Conference on Computer Vision, pp. 3277–3285 (2017)

14. Ignatov, A., Kobyshev, N., Timofte, R., Vanhoey, K., Van Gool, L.: Wespe: weakly supervised photo enhancer for digital cameras. In: Proceedings of the IEEE Conference on Computer Vision and Pattern Recognition Workshops, pp. 691–700 (2018)

15. Isola, P., Zhu, J.Y., Zhou, T., Efros, A.A.: Image-to-image translation with conditional adversarial networks. In: 2017 IEEE Conference on Computer Vision and Pattern Recognition (CVPR) (2017)

16. Land, E.H.: The retinex theory of color vision. Sci. Am. $237(6)$, 108–129 (1977)

17. Lin, M., Chen, Q., Yan, S.: Network in network. arXiv preprint arXiv:1312.4400 (2013)

18. Mnih, V., et al.: Human-level control through deep reinforcement learning. Nature $518(7540)$, 529–533 (2015)

19. Park, J., Lee, J.Y., Yoo, D., So Kweon, I.: Distort-and-recover: color enhancement using deep reinforcement learning. In: Proceedings of the IEEE Conference on Computer Vision and Pattern Recognition, pp. 5928–5936 (2018)

20. Shoshan, A., Mechrez, R., Zelnik-Manor, L.: Dynamic-net: tuning the objective without re-training for synthesis tasks. In: The IEEE International Conference on Computer Vision (ICCV) October 2019

21. Ulyanov, D., Vedaldi, A., Lempitsky, V.: Instance normalization: the missing ingredient for fast stylization. arXiv preprint arXiv:1607.08022 (2016)

22. Van De Weijer, J., Gevers, T., Gijsenij, A.: Edge-based color constancy. IEEE Trans. Image Process. $16(9)$, 2207–2214 (2007)

23. Wang, R., Zhang, Q., Fu, C.W., Shen, X., Zheng, W.S., Jia, J.: Underexposed photo enhancement using deep illumination estimation. In: Proceedings of the IEEE Conference on Computer Vision and Pattern Recognition, pp. 6849–6857 (2019)

24. Wang, X., Yu, K., Dong, C., Change Loy, C.: Recovering realistic texture in image super-resolution by deep spatial feature transform. In: Proceedings of the IEEE Conference on Computer Vision and Pattern Recognition, pp. 606–615 (2018)
25. Wang, X., Yu, K., Dong, C., Tang, X., Loy, C.C.: Deep network interpolation for continuous imagery effect transition. In: Proceedings of the IEEE Conference on Computer Vision and Pattern Recognition, pp. 1692–1701 (2019)
26. Ying, Z., Li, G., Ren, Y., Wang, R., Wang, W.: A new low-light image enhancement algorithm using camera response model. In: Proceedings of the IEEE International Conference on Computer Vision Workshops, pp. 3015–3022 (2017)
27. Zhang, Q., Yuan, G., Xiao, C., Zhu, L., Zheng, W.S.: High-quality exposure correction of underexposed photos. In: Proceedings of the 26th ACM International Conference on Multimedia, pp. 582–590 (2018)

Segmenting Transparent Objects in the Wild

Enze Xie[1](✉), Wenjia Wang[2], Wenhai Wang[3], Mingyu Ding[1], Chunhua Shen[4], and Ping Luo[1]

[1] The University of Hong Kong, Hong Kong, China
{xieenze,mingyuding}@hku.hk, pluo@cs.hku.hk
[2] SenseTime Research, Hong Kong, China
wangwenjia@sensetime.com
[3] Nanjing University, Nanjing, China
wangwenhai362@smail.nju.edu.cn
[4] The University of Adelaide, Adelaide, Australia
chunhua.shen@adelaide.edu.au

Abstract. Transparent objects such as windows and bottles made by glass widely exist in the real world. Segmenting transparent objects is challenging because these objects have diverse appearance inherited from the image background, making them had similar appearance with their surroundings. Besides the technical difficulty of this task, only a few previous datasets were specially designed and collected to explore this task and most of the existing datasets have major drawbacks. They either possess limited sample size such as merely a thousand of images without manual annotations, or they generate all images by using computer graphics method (*i.e.* not real image). To address this important problem, this work proposes a large-scale dataset for transparent object segmentation, named Trans10 K, consisting of 10,428 images of real scenarios with carefully manual annotations, which are 10 times larger than the existing datasets. The transparent objects in Trans10 K are extremely challenging due to high diversity in scale, viewpoint and occlusion. To evaluate the effectiveness of Trans10 K, we propose a novel boundary-aware segmentation method, termed TransLab, which exploits boundary as the clue to improve segmentation of transparent objects. Extensive experiments and ablation studies demonstrate the effectiveness of Trans10 K and validate the practicality of learning object boundary in TransLab. For example, TransLab significantly outperforms 20 recent object segmentation methods based on deep learning, showing that this task is largely unsolved. We believe that both Trans10 K and TransLab have important contributions to both the academia and industry, facilitating future researches and applications. The codes and models will be released at: https://github.com/xieenze/Segment_Transparent_Objects.

Keywords: Transparent objects · Dataset · Benchmark · Image segmentation · Object boundary

Electronic supplementary material The online version of this chapter (https://doi.org/10.1007/978-3-030-58601-0_41) contains supplementary material, which is available to authorized users.

A. Vedaldi et al. (Eds.): ECCV 2020, LNCS 12358, pp. 696–711, 2020.
https://doi.org/10.1007/978-3-030-58601-0_41

1   Introduction

Transparent objects widely exist in the real world, such as bottles, vitrines, windows, walls and many others made by glass. Transparent objects have diverse appearance inherited from their surrounding image background, making segmenting these objects challenging. The task of transparent object segmentation is important because it has many applications. For example, when a smart robot operates tasks in living rooms or offices, it needs to avoid fragile objects such as glasses, vases, bowls, bottles, and jars. In addition, when a robot navigates in factory, supermarket and hotel, its visual navigation system needs to recognize the glass walls and windows to avoid collision. Although transparent object segmentation is important in computer vision, only a few previous datasets [1,2] were specially collected to explore this task and they have major drawbacks. For example, TransCut [1] possesses limited sample size with merely 49 images. Although TOM-Net [2] has large data size of 178 K images, all the images are generated by using computer graphics method by simply overlaying a transparent object on different background images, that is, the images are not real and out of the distribution of natural images. Meanwhile, TOM-Net provides 876 real images for test, but these images do not have manual annotations and evaluation performed by user study.

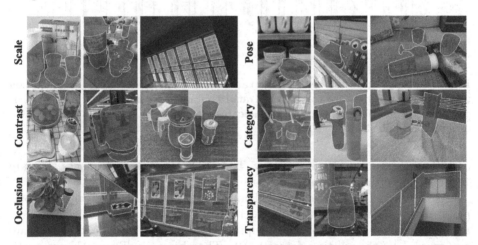

Fig. 1. This work proposes the Trans10 K dataset for transparent object segmentation, which has 10,428 manually-labeled images with high degree of variability in terms of scale, pose, contrast, category, occlusion and transparency. Objects are divided into two categories, thing and stuff, where **things** are small and movable objects (*e.g.* bottle), while **stuff** are large and fixed (*e.g.* vitrine). Example images and annotations are shown, where things and stuff are in **blue** and **brown** respectively. (Color figure online)

To address the above issues, this paper proposes a novel large-scale dataset for transparent object segmentation, named Trans10 K, containing 10,428 real-world images of transparent objects, each of which is manually labeled with segmentation mask. All images in Trans10 K are selected from complex real-world scenarios that have large variations such as scale, viewpoint, contrast,

Table 1. Comparisons between Trans10 K and previous transparent object datasets, where "Syn" represents synthetic images using computer graphics method, "Thing" represents small and movable objects, "Stuff" are large and fixed objects, and "MCC" denotes Mean Connected Components in each image. Trans10 K is much more challenging than prior arts in terms of all characteristics presented in this table.

Datasets	Image number			Objects			Height (pixels)			Properties		
	Train	Val	Test	Num	Thing	Stuff	<1 K	1 K–2 K	>2 K	MCC	Occlusion	Contrast
	Real	Syn										
TransCut [1]	0	0	0	49	7	√	×	49	0	0	1.14	×	×
TOM-Net [2]	0	178 K	900	876	18	√	×	178 K	876	0	1.33	×	×
Trans10K	5000	0	1000	4428	10 K+	√	√	1544	593	8291	3.96	√	√

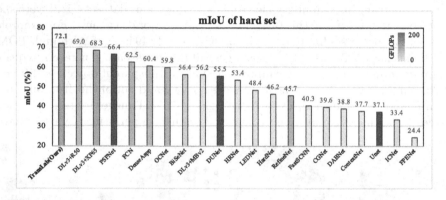

Fig. 2. Comparisons between TransLab and 20 representative semantic segmentation methods. All methods are trained on Trans10 K. mIoU on hard set of Trans10 K is chosen as the metric. Deeper color bar indicates methods with larger FLOPs. 'DLv3+' denotes DeepLabV3+.

occlusion, category and transparency. Trans10 K has rich real images that are 10 times larger than existing datasets.

As shown in Table 1 and Fig. 3, Trans10 K has three main advantages compared with existing work. **(1)** Images in Trans10 K are collected from *diverse scenes* such as living room, office, supermarket, kitchen and desks, which are not covered by the existing datasets. **(2)** The objects in Trans10 K are partitioned into two categories, **stuff** and **things**. The transparent stuff are fixed and large object such as wall and window. Segmenting stuff objects are useful for many applications, such as helping robots avoid collision during navigation. In contrast, the transparent things are small and moveable such as bottles. **(3)** As shown in Table 1, images in Trans10 K are divided into a training set of 5000 images, a validation set of 1000 images and a test set of 4428 images. Both the validation and the test sets contain two subsets, *easy and hard*. Although the overall benchmark is challenging, we carefully select a hard subset for validation and test to further evaluate different segmentation algorithms. These hard subsets may expose more flaws of semantic segmentation algorithms so as to improve the performance of transparent object segmentation.

Besides Trans10 K, we carefully design a boundary-aware object segmentation method, termed **TransLab**, which is able to "Look at boundary" to improve transparent object segmentation. As shown in Fig. 2, we train and evaluate 20 existing representative segmentation methods [3–9] on Trans10 K, and found that simply applying previous methods to this task is not sufficient. For instance, although DeepLabV3+ [10] is the state-of-the-art semantic segmentation method, it ignores the boundary information, which might be suitable for common object segmentation but not for transparent object. As a result, its mIoU is suboptimal compared to TransLab (69.0 *versus* 72.1), where the boundary prediction in TransLab is helpful due to the high contrast at the edges but diverse appearance inside a transparent object.

Specifically, TransLab has two streams including a regular stream for transparent content segmentation and a boundary stream for boundary prediction. After these two streams, a Boundary Attention Module (BAM) is devised to use the boundary map to attend both high-level and low-level features for transparent object segmentation.

To summarize, the main **contributions** of this work are three-fold. (**1**) A large-scale transparent object segmentation dataset, Trans10 K, is collected and labeled. It is 10 times larger and more challenging than previous work. (**2**) A boundary-aware approach for segmenting transparent objects, TransLab, is proposed to validate the effectiveness of Trans10 K and the boundary attention module. TransLab surpasses 20 representative segmentation approaches by training and testing them on Trans10 K for fair comparisons. For instance, TransLab outperforms DeeplabV3+, a state-of-the-art semantic segmentation method, by over 3% mIoU. (**3**) Extensive ablation studies and benchmarking results are presented by using Trans10 K and TransLab to encourage more future research efforts on this task. The data of Trans10 K and trained models are released.

2   Related Work

Semantic Segmentation. Most state-of-the-art algorithms for semantic segmentation are predominantly based on CNNs. Earlier approaches [9,11] transfer classification networks to fully convolutional networks (FCNs) for semantic segmentation, which is in an end-to-end training manner. Several works [6,12,13] propose to use structured prediction modules such as conditional random fields (CRFs) on network output for improving the segmentation performance, especially around object boundaries. To avoid costly DenseCRF, the work of [14] uses fast domain transform filtering on network output while also predicting edge maps from intermediate CNN layers. More recently, dramatic improvements in performance and inference speed have been driven by new architectural designs. For example, PSPNet [3] and DeepLab [6,10] proposed a feature pyramid pooling module that incorporates multiscale context by aggregating features at multiples scales. Some works [15–17] propose modules that use learned pixel affinities for structured information propagation across intermediate CNN representations.

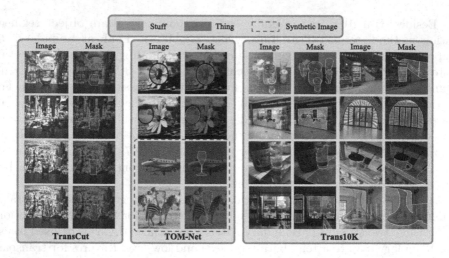

Fig. 3. Example transparent object images and masks in TransCut [1], TOM-Net [2], and our Trans10 K. We see Trans10 K has more diverse scene and challenging viewpoint, categories, occlusion than TransCut and TOM-Net.

Transparent Object Segmentation. TransCut [1] propose an energy function based on LF-linearity and occlusion detection from the 4D light-field image is optimized to generate the segmentation result. TOM-Net [2] formulate transparent object matting as a refractive ow estimation problem. This work proposed a multi-scale encoder-decoder network to generate a coarse input, and then a residual network refines it to a detailed matte. Note that TOM-Net needs a refractive flow map as label during training, which is hard to obtain from the real world, so it can **only** rely on synthetic training data.

Transparent Object Datasets. TOM-Net [2] proposed a dataset containing 876 real images and 178 K synthetic images which are generated by POV-Ray. Only 4 and 14 objects are repeatedly used in the synthetic and real data. Moreover, the test set of TOM-Net do not have mask annotation, so one cannot evaluate his algorithm quantitatively on it. TransCut [1] is proposed for the segmentation of transparent objects. It only contains 49 images. However, only 7 objects, mainly bottles and cups, are repeatedly used. The images are capture by 5 × 5 camera array in 7 different scenes. So the diversity is very limited.

Most of the background of synthetic images are chosen randomly, so the background and the objects are not semantically coordinated and reasonable. The transparent objects are usually in a unreasonable scene, *e.g.* a cup flying with a plane. Furthermore, the real data always lack in scale and complexity.

3　Trans10 K Dataset and Annotation

To tackle the transparent object segmentation problem, we build the first large-scale dataset, named Trans10 K. It contains more than 10 k pairs of images with transparent objects and their corresponding manually annotated masks, which is over 10× larger than existing real transparent object datasets.

3.1 Data Description

The Trans10 K dataset contains 10,428 images, with two categories of transparent objects: (1) Transparent things such as cups, bottles and glass, locating these things can make robots easier to grab objects. (2) Transparent stuff such as windows, glass walls and glass doors. It can make robots learn to avoid obstacles and avoid hitting these stuff. As shown in Table 2, 5000, 1000 and 4428 images are used for train, validation and test, respectively. Specifically, we keep the same ratio that these two fine-grained categories in train, validation and test set. The images are manually harvested from the internet, image library like google OpenImage [18] and our own data captured by phone cameras. As a result, the distribution of the images is various, containing different scales, born-digital, perspective distortion glass, crowded and so on. In summary, to our best knowledge, Trans10 K is the largest real dataset focus on transparent object segmentation in the wild. Moreover, due to fine-grained categories and high diversity, it is challenging enough for existing semantic segmentation methods.

3.2 Annotation

The transparent objects are manually labeled by ourselves with our labeling tool. The way of annotation is the same with semantic segmentation datasets such as ADE20 K. We set the background with 0, transparent things with 1 and transparent stuff with 2. Here are some principles: (1) Only highly transparent objects are annotated, other semi-transparent objects are ignored. Although most transparent objects are made of glass in our dataset, we also annotate those made of other materials such as plastic if they satisfy the attribute of transparent. (2) If there are things in front of the transparent objects, we will not annotate the region of the things. Otherwise, if things are behind transparent objects, we will annotate the whole region of transparent objects. (3) We further divide the validation set and test set into two parts, easy and hard according to the difficulty. The detail is shown in Sect. 3.3.

3.3 Dataset Complexity

Our dataset is diversified in scale, category, shape, color and location. We find that the segmentation difficulty varies due to these factors. So we define the easy and hard attribute of each image. The statistics are shown in Table 2. The detailed principles are shown as below:

Easy (Fig. 4 (a)): (1) Less numbered. *e.g.* most images contain a single object of the same category. (2) Regular shaped. *e.g.* there is nearly no occlusion like posters over the transparent objects and their shape is regular such as circle. (3) Salient. *e.g.* the transparent objects are salient and easy to figure out due

Table 2. Image statistics of **Trans10 K**. "MCC" denotes Mean Connected Components in each image.

Dataset		Image number				MCC
		All	Only things	Only stuff	Containing both	
Train		5000	2845	2047	108	3.87
Validation	easy	788	490	290	8	3.31
	hard	212	82	118	12	5.20
Test	easy	3491	2255	1222	14	3.15
	hard	937	337	549	51	6.29

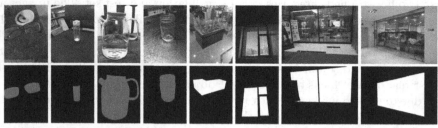

(a) Examples of easy cases. With regular shapes, less occlusion and contrast.

(b) Examples of hard cases. With irregular shapes, more occlusion and contrast.

Fig. 4. Comparisons of easy and hard samples in Trans10 K. **Red** represents things and **white** represents stuff. Best viewed in color. (Color figure online)

to the conspicuous reflection and refraction light. (4) Simply displayed. *e.g.* the transparent objects are located at a center position and spatially isolated to each other clearly.

Hard (Fig. 4 (b)): (1) More numbered. *e.g.* the images contain multiple transparent objects of different categories. (2) Irregular shaped. *e.g.* their shape is strange and without a regular pattern. (3) High Transparency. *e.g.* they are hard to figure out because they are of very high transparency and clean, even hard for people to figure. (4) Complexly displayed. *e.g.* they are located randomly and heavily occluded in a crowd scene. One transparent objects can cover, or contain part of another.

Figure 4 (a) and Fig. 4 (b) shows that our dataset contain abundant category distribution. To our knowledge, our dataset contains at least 20 different categories of objects, including but not limited to: **Stuff** such as bookshelf, showcase, freezer, window, door, glass table, vivarium, floor window, glass ceiling, glass guardrail, microwave oven and electric roaster. **Things** such as eyeglass, cup, bow, bottle, kettle, storage box, cosmetics, toys, glass chandelier. The abundant categories contain the most common transparent objects in the real world. More visualization can be found in the supplementary materials.

Figure 5 displays the statistic information of the Trans10 K dataset. (a) is the distribution of area ratio of connected components in each image, ranging from 0 to 1.0. (b) is the number of connected components of things and stuff in each image. (c) is the distribution of the image resolution of the train and validation+test set. The horizontal axis is the resolution (million pixels) of each image calculated by width × height. (d) is the distribution of the object location of the whole dataset. It shows that the stuff is more uniformly distributed while things tend to cluster near the center of the image. This is reasonable because the stuff tends to occupy the majority of the images.

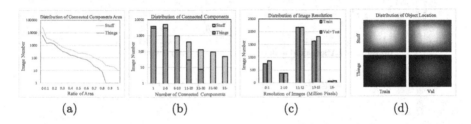

(a)   (b)   (c)   (d)

Fig. 5. Statistics of the Trans10 K dataset.

3.4 Evaluation Metrics

For a comprehensive evaluation, we apply four metrics that are widely used in semantic segmentation, salient object detection and shadow detection to benchmark the performance of transparent object segmentation. Our metrics are far more comprehensive than TransCut and TOM-Net, we hope they can expose more flaws of different methods on our dataset. Specifically, Intersection over union (**IoU**) and pixel accuracy metrics (**Acc**) are used from the semantic segmentation field as our first and second metrics. Note that we only calculate IoU of the thing and stuff, ignoring the background. Mean absolute error (**MAE**) metrics are used from the salient object detection field. Finally, Balance error rate (**BER**) is used from the shadow detection field. It considers the unbalanced areas of transparent and non-transparent regions. BER is used to evaluate binary predictions, here we change it to mean balance error rate (**mBER**) to evaluate the two fine-grained transparent categories. , it is computed as:

$$mBER = \frac{1}{C}\sum_{i=1}^{C}(1 - \frac{1}{2}(\frac{TP_i}{TP_i + FN_i} + \frac{TN_i}{TN_i + FP_i})) \times 100, \qquad (1)$$

Where C is the category of transparent objects, in this dataset C is 2.

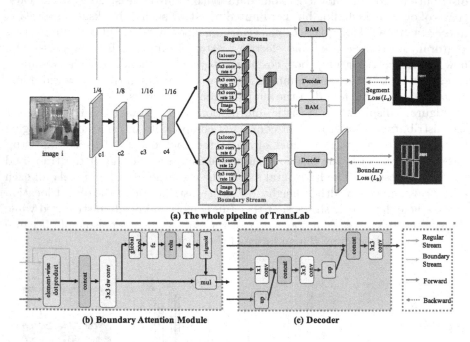

(a) The whole pipeline of TransLab

(b) Boundary Attention Module   (c) Decoder

Fig. 6. The architecture of TransLab.

4   Proposed Method

4.1   Network Architecture

Figure 6 (a) shows the overall architecture of TransLab, which is composed of two parallel stream: regular stream and boundary stream. ResNet50 [19] with dilation is used as the backbone network. The regular stream is for transparent object segmentation while the boundary stream is for boundary prediction. We argue that the boundary is easier than content to observe because it tends to have high contrast in the edge of transparent objects, which is consistent with human visual perception. So we first make the network predict the boundary, then we utilize the predicted boundary map as a clue to attend the regular stream. It is implemented by Boundary Attention Module (BAM). In each stream, we use Atrous Spatial Pyramid Pooling module (ASPP) to enlarge the receive field. Finally, we design a simple decoder to utilize both high-level feature (C4) and low-level feature (C1 and C2).

4.2   Boundary Attention Module

Figure 6 (b) illustrates the structure of the Boundary Attention Module (BAM). The boundary ground-truth is generated as a binary map with thickness 8. The channel of the predicted boundary map is 1. BAM first takes the feature map of the regular stream and the predicted boundary map as input. Then performs boundary attention with a boundary map. The two feature maps before and after boundary attention are concatenated and followed by a channel attention block. Finally, it outputs the refined feature map. BAM can be repeatedly used on the high-level and low-level features of regular stream such as C1, C2 and C4. We demonstrate that the more times of boundary attention, the better performance of segmentation results. Details are shown in Sect. 5.

4.3   Decoder

Figure 6 (c) illustrates the detailed structure of the Decoder. The input of decoder is C1, C2 and C4 (after ASPP). BAM is used to apply boundary attention to three of them. We firstly fuse the C4 and C2 by up-sampling C4 and adding 3 × 3 convolutional operation. The fused feature map is further up-sampled to fuse with C1 in the same approach. In this way, both high level and low-level feature maps are joint fused, which is beneficial for semantic segmentation.

4.4   Loss Function

We define our training loss function as follows:

$$L = L_s + \lambda L_b, \tag{2}$$

where L_s and L_b represent the losses for the segmentation text and boundary, respectively, and λ balances the importance between L_s and L_b. The trade-off parameter λ is set to 5 in our experiments. Here L_s is the standard Cross-Entropy (CE) Loss. Inspired by [20], we adopt Dice Loss in our experiment. The dice coefficient $D(S_i, G_i)$ is formulated as in Eq. (3):

$$D(S_i, G_i) = \frac{2 \sum_{x,y}(S_{i,x,y} \times G_{i,x,y})}{\sum_{x,y} S_{i,x,y}^2 + \sum_{x,y} G_{i,x,y}^2}, \tag{3}$$

where $S_{i,x,y}$ and $G_{i,x,y}$ refer to the value of pixel (x, y) in segmentation result S_i and ground truth G_i, respectively.

5   Experiments

5.1   Implementation Details

We have implemented TransLab with PyTorch [21]. We use the pre-trained ResNet50 [19] as the feature extraction network. In the final stage, we use the dilation convolution to keep the resolution as 1/16. The remaining parts of our network are randomly initialized. For loss optimization, we use the stochastic gradient descent (SGD) optimizer with momentum of 0.9 and a weight decay of 0.0005. Batch size is set to 8 per GPU. The learning rate is initialized to 0.02 and decayed by the poly strategy [22] with the power of 0.9 for 16 epochs. We use 8 V100 GPU for all experiments. During training and inference, images are resized to a resolution of 512×512.

5.2 Ablation Studies

In this part, we demonstrate the effectiveness of boundary clues for transparent object segmentation. We report the results of the ablation study on the **hard** set of Trans10 K because it is more challenging and can clearly observe the gap of different modules. We simply use the DeeplabV3+ as our baseline. We first show only using boundary loss as auxiliary loss during training can directly improve the segmentation performance. We further show how to use a boundary map as a clue to attend the feature of regular stream. Experiments demonstrate that more boundary attention leading to better results. In summary, locating boundaries is essential for transparent object segmentation.

Boundary Loss Selection. Boundary is easier to observe than the content of the transparent object. To obtain high-quality boundary map, the loss function is essential. We choose Binary Cross-Entropy Loss, Focal Loss and Dice Loss to supervise boundary stream. As shown in Table 3, Firstly, simply using boundary loss as auxiliary loss can directly improve the performance no matter which loss function is used. We argue this is due to the benefit of multi-task learning. It means the boundary loss can help the backbone focus more on the boundary of transparent objects and extract more discriminative features. Note that under this setting, the boundary stream can be removed during inference so it will not bring computation overhead. Secondly, Focal Loss works better than Binary Cross-Entropy loss because the majority of pixels of a boundary mask are background, and the Focal Loss can mitigate the sample imbalance problem by decreasing the loss of easy samples. However, the Dice Loss achieves the best results without manually adjusting the loss hyper-parameters. Dice Loss views the pixels as a whole object and can establish the right balance between foreground and background pixels automatically. As a result, Dice Loss can improve baseline with 1.25% on mIoU and 2.31% on Acc, which is the best in three loss functions. Meanwhile, the mBer and MAE are also improved (lower is better).

Boundary Attention Module. After obtaining a high-quality boundary map, boundary attention is another key step in our algorithm. We can fuse boundary information at different levels for the regular stream. In this part, we repeatedly use BAM on C1, C2, C4 feature maps to show how boundary attention module works. To evaluate the relationship between the quantity of boundary attention and the final prediction accuracy, we vary the number of fusion levels from 1 to 3 and report the mIoU, Acc, mBer and MAE in Table 4. Note that 'BL' indicates baseline with Dice Loss. It can be observed that performance is improved

Table 3. Ablation study for different loss functions of boundary stream.

L_b	mIoU ↑	Acc ↑	mBer ↓	MAE ↓
–	69.04	78.07	17.27	0.194
BCE	69.33	78.61	16.89	0.190
Focal	69.41	78.76	16.27	0.188
Dice	**70.29**	**80.38**	**15.44**	**0.183**

Table 4. Ablation study for different setting of boundary attention module.

Method	mIoU ↑	Acc ↑	mBer ↓	MAE ↓
BL	70.29	80.38	15.44	0.183
BL + C1	71.05	81.80	13.98	0.180
BL + C1&2	71.32	82.05	13.69	0.178
BL + C1&2&4	**72.10**	**83.04**	**13.30**	**0.166**

consistently by using boundary attention module at more levels. Our final model that fuses boundary information in all three levels further improves mIoU from 70.29% to 72.10% and Acc from 80.38% to 83.04%. Meanwhile, the mBer and MAE are also improved (lower is better). By using a high-quality boundary map for attention, the feature maps of regular stream can have higher weights on the boundary region.

5.3 Comparison to the State-of-the-Arts

We select several main-stream semantic segmentation methods to evaluate on our challenging Trans10 K dataset. Specifically, we choose FPENet [23], ContextNet [24], FastSCNN [25], DeeplabV3+ with MobilenetV2 [10], CGNet [26], HRNet [27], HardNet [28], DABNet [29], LEDNet [30], ICNet [4] and BiSeNet [22] as real-time methods. DenseASPP [7], DeepLabV3+ with Resnet50[10], FCN[9], OCNet [31], RefineNet [8], DeepLabV3+ with Xception65[10], DUNet [5], UNet [32] and PSPNet [3] as regular methods. We re-train each of the models on the training set of our dataset and evaluate them on our testing set. For a fair comparison, we set the size of the input image as 512 × 512 with single scale training and testing.

Table 5 reports the overall quantitative comparison results on test set, where our TransLab outperforms all other methods in our Trans10 K in terms of all four metrics in both easy/hard set and things/stuff categories. Especially, TransLab outperforms DeepLabV3+, the sota semantic segmentation method, in a large gap on all metrics as well as both things and stuff, especially in hard set. For instance, it surpasses DeepLabV3 by 3.97% on 'Acc' (hard set). Figure 7 also shows TransLab can predict sharp boundary with high-quality masks when compared with other methods. More analysis are shown in material.

Table 5. Evaluated Semantic Segmentation methods. **Sorted by FLOPs.** Note that FLOPs is computed with one 512×512 image.

(a) Comparison between things and stuff.

Method	MAE ↓	ACC ↑	IoU ↑		BER ↓		Computation	
			Things	Stuff	Things	Stuff	FLOPs	Params
FPENet [24]	0.339	24.73	33.96	34.36	39.59	39.01	0.78G	0.11M
ContextNet [25]	0.217	62.09	56.29	56.61	22.26	22.46	0.89G	0.87M
FastSCNN [26]	0.206	64.20	58.62	59.74	20.59	23.95	1.03G	1.20M
DeepLabv3+MBv2 [10]	0.130	80.92	78.55	71.97	10.38	14.58	2.70G	1.96M
CGNet [27]	0.216	59.15	58.33	56.28	21.02	24.88	3.52G	0.49M
HRNet [28]	0.134	75.82	79.34	69.78	10.39	16.64	4.20G	1.53M
HardNet [29]	0.184	69.17	64.91	63.15	17.18	20.63	4.43G	4.11M
DABNet [30]	0.230	54.87	54.48	55.32	25.77	25.64	5.25G	0.75M
LEDNet [31]	0.168	75.70	70.37	64.68	12.68	17.62	6.32G	2.31M
ICNet [4]	0.244	52.65	53.90	47.38	19.78	29.46	10.66G	8.46M
BiSeNet [23]	0.140	77.92	77.39	70.46	10.86	17.04	19.95G	13.30M
DenseASPP [7]	0.114	81.22	81.79	74.41	9.07	15.31	36.31G	29.09M
DeepLabv3+R50 [10]	0.081	89.54	87.90	81.16	5.31	10.25	37.98G	28.74M
FCN [9]	0.108	83.79	84.40	74.92	7.30	13.36	42.35G	34.99M
OCNet [32]	0.122	80.85	80.55	73.15	8.91	16.38	43.43G	35.91M
RefineNet [8]	0.180	57.97	73.65	58.40	16.44	27.98	44.34G	29.36M
DeepLabv3+XP65 [10]	0.082	89.18	87.54	80.98	5.64	10.34	51.95G	41.05M
DUNet [5]	0.140	77.84	79.10	69.00	10.53	15.84	123.35G	31.21M
UNet [33]	0.234	51.07	54.99	52.96	27.04	25.69	124.62G	13.39M
PSPNet [3]	0.093	86.25	86.13	78.42	6.68	12.75	187.27G	50.99M
TransLab	**0.063**	**92.69**	**90.87**	**84.39**	**3.63**	**7.28**	61.60G	42.19M

(b) Comparison between Easy and Hard.

Method	MAE ↓			Acc ↑			mIoU ↑			mBER ↓		
	All	Easy	Hard	All	Easy	Hard	All	Easy	Hard	All	Easy	Hard
FPENet [24]	0.339	0.297	0.492	24.73	26.50	19.19	34.17	36.82	24.41	39.31	37.88	44.03
ContextNet [25]	0.217	0.171	0.386	62.09	67.14	46.34	56.46	61.73	37.71	22.36	18.77	34.44
FastSCNN [26]	0.206	0.161	0.373	64.20	69.42	48.01	59.18	64.63	40.27	22.27	18.74	34.22
DeepLabv3+MBv2[10]	0.130	0.091	0.275	80.92	85.90	65.43	75.27	80.55	56.17	12.49	9.08	24.47
CGNet [27]	0.216	0.173	0.379	59.15	64.57	42.26	57.31	62.41	39.56	22.95	19.67	34.33
HRNet [28]	0.134	0.092	0.291	75.82	82.17	56.04	74.56	80.43	53.42	13.52	9.95	26.17
HardNet [29]	0.184	0.141	0.345	69.17	73.83	54.67	64.03	69.11	46.18	18.91	15.58	30.52
DABNet [30]	0.230	0.187	0.391	54.87	59.29	41.07	54.90	59.45	38.77	25.71	22.63	36.15
LEDNet [31]	0.168	0.124	0.331	75.70	80.62	60.37	67.54	73.04	48.38	15.15	11.83	26.58
ICNet [4]	0.244	0.200	0.408	52.65	58.31	35.01	50.65	55.48	33.44	24.63	21.71	35.24
BiSeNet [23]	0.140	0.102	0.282	77.92	82.79	62.72	73.93	78.74	56.37	13.96	10.83	24.85
DenseAspp [7]	0.114	0.078	0.247	81.22	86.25	66.55	78.11	83.11	60.38	12.19	8.85	23.71
DeepLabv3+R50[10]	0.081	0.050	0.194	89.54	93.22	78.07	84.54	89.09	69.04	7.78	4.91	17.27
FCN [9]	0.108	0.073	0.239	83.79	88.55	68.93	79.67	84.53	62.51	10.33	7.36	20.47
OCNet [32]	0.122	0.087	0.253	80.85	85.63	65.96	76.85	81.53	59.75	12.65	9.43	23.69
RefineNet [8]	0.180	0.135	0.345	57.97	64.53	37.53	66.03	71.41	45.71	22.22	19.01	34.06
DeepLabv3+XP65 [10]	0.082	0.051	0.195	89.18	92.61	78.51	84.26	88.87	68.34	8.00	5.16	17.44
DUNet [5]	0.140	0.100	0.289	77.84	83.41	60.50	74.06	79.19	55.53	13.19	9.93	25.01
UNet [33]	0.234	0.191	0.398	51.07	55.44	37.44	53.98	58.60	37.08	26.37	23.40	36.80
PSPNet [3]	0.093	0.062	0.211	86.25	90.41	73.28	82.38	86.79	66.35	9.72	6.67	20.08
TransLab	**0.063**	**0.036**	**0.166**	**92.69**	**95.77**	**83.04**	**87.63**	**92.23**	**72.10**	**5.46**	**3.12**	**13.30**

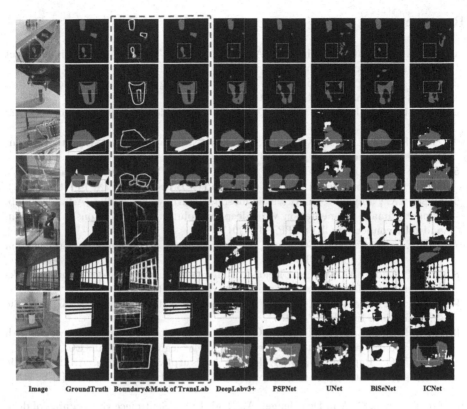

Image   GroundTruth Boundary&Mask of TransLab DeepLabv3+   PSPNet   UNet   BiSeNet   ICNet

Fig. 7. Visual comparison of TransLab to other semantic segmentation methods. Our TransLab clearly outperforms others thanks to the boundary attention, especially in yellow dash region.

6   Conclusion

In this work, we present the Trans10 K dataset, which is the largest real dataset for transparent object segmentation. We also benchmark 20 semantic segmentation algorithms on this novel dataset and shed light on what attributes are especially difficult for current methods. We suggest that transparent object segmentation in the wild is far from being solved. Finally, we propose a boundary-aware algorithm, termed TransLab, to utilize the boundary prediction to improve the segmentation performance.

Acknowledgement. This work is partially supported by the SenseTime Donation for Research, HKU Seed Fund for Basic Research, Startup Fund and General Research Fund No.27208720.

References

1. Xu, Y., Nagahara, H., Shimada, A., Taniguchi, R.: Transcut: transparent object segmentation from a light-field image. In: ICCV (2015)
2. Chen, G., Han, K., Wong, K.K.: Tom-net: learning transparent object matting from a single image. In: CVPR (2018)
3. Zhao, H., Shi, J., Qi, X., Wang, X., Jia, J.: Pyramid scene parsing network. In: CVPR (2017)
4. Zhao, H., Qi, X., Shen, X., Shi, J., Jia, J.: ICNET for real-time semantic segmentation on high-resolution images. In: ECCV (2018)
5. Jin, Q., Meng, Z., Pham, T.D., Chen, Q., Wei, L., Su, R.: Dunet: a deformable network for retinal vessel segmentation. Knowl. Based Syst. **178**, 149–162 (2019)
6. Chen, L.C., Papandreou, G., Kokkinos, I., Murphy, K., Yuille, A.L.: Deeplab: semantic image segmentation with deep convolutional nets, atrous convolution, and fully connected CRFS. TPAMI (2017)
7. Yang, M., Yu, K., Zhang, C., Li, Z., Yang, K.: Denseaspp for semantic segmentation in street scenes. In: CVPR (2018)
8. Lin, G., Milan, A., Shen, C., Reid, I.: Refinenet: multi-path refinement networks for high-resolution semantic segmentation. In: CVPR (2017)
9. Long, J., Shelhamer, E., Darrell, T.: Fully convolutional networks for semantic segmentation. In: CVPR (2015)
10. Chen, L.C., Zhu, Y., Papandreou, G., Schroff, F., Adam, H.: Encoder-decoder with atrous separable convolution for semantic image segmentation. In: ECCV (2018)
11. Chen, L.C., Papandreou, G., Kokkinos, I., Murphy, K., Yuille, A.L.: Semantic image segmentation with deep convolutional nets and fully connected CRFS. arXiv (2014)
12. Lin, G., Shen, C., Van Den Hengel, A., Reid, I.: Efficient piecewise training of deep structured models for semantic segmentation. In: CVPR (2016)
13. Zheng, S., et al.: Conditional random fields as recurrent neural networks. In: ICCV (2015)
14. Chen, L.C., Barron, J.T., Papandreou, G., Murphy, K., Yuille, A.L.: Semantic image segmentation with task-specific edge detection using CNNS and a discriminatively trained domain transform. In: CVPR (2016)
15. Gadde, R., Jampani, V., Kiefel, M., Kappler, D., Gehler, P.V.: Superpixel convolutional networks using bilateral inceptions. In: Leibe, B., Matas, J., Sebe, N., Welling, M. (eds.) ECCV 2016. LNCS, vol. 9905, pp. 597–613. Springer, Cham (2016). https://doi.org/10.1007/978-3-319-46448-0_36
16. Liu, S., De Mello, S., Gu, J., Zhong, G., Yang, M.H., Kautz, J.: Learning affinity via spatial propagation networks. In: NIPS (2017)
17. Wang, X., Girshick, R., Gupta, A., He, K.: Non-local neural networks. In: CVPR (2018)
18. Kuznetsova, A., et al.: The open images dataset v4: unified image classification, object detection, and visual relationship detection at scale. arXiv (2018)
19. He, K., Zhang, X., Ren, S., Sun, J.: Deep residual learning for image recognition. In: CVPR (2016)
20. Milletari, F., Navab, N., Ahmadi, S.A.: V-net: fully convolutional neural networks for volumetric medical image segmentation. In: IC3DV (2016)
21. Paszke, A., et al.: Automatic differentiation in pytorch (2017)
22. Yu, C., Wang, J., Peng, C., Gao, C., Yu, G., Sang, N.: Bisenet: bilateral segmentation network for real-time semantic segmentation. In: ECCV (2018)

23. Liu, M., Yin, H.: Feature pyramid encoding network for real-time semantic segmentation. arXiv (2019)
24. Poudel, R.P., Bonde, U., Liwicki, S., Zach, C.: Contextnet: exploring context and detail for semantic segmentation in real-time. arXiv (2018)
25. Poudel, R.P., Liwicki, S., Cipolla, R.: Fast-SCNN: fast semantic segmentation network. arXiv (2019)
26. Wu, T., Tang, S., Zhang, R., Zhang, Y.: CGNET: a light-weight context guided network for semantic segmentation. arXiv (2018)
27. Wang, J., et al.: Deep high-resolution representation learning for visual recognition. arXiv (2019)
28. Chao, P., Kao, C.Y., Ruan, Y.S., Huang, C.H., Lin, Y.L.: Hardnet: a low memory traffic network. In: ICCV (2019)
29. Li, G., Yun, I., Kim, J., Kim, J.: Dabnet: depth-wise asymmetric bottleneck for real-time semantic segmentation. arXiv (2019)
30. Wang, Y., et al.: Lednet: a lightweight encoder-decoder network for real-time semantic segmentation. In: ICIP (2019)
31. Yuan, Y., Wang, J.: OCNet: object context network for scene parsing. arXiv (2018)
32. Ronneberger, O., Fischer, P., Brox, T.: U-net: convolutional networks for biomedical image segmentation. In: MICCAI (2015)

Length-Controllable Image Captioning

Chaorui Deng[1], Ning Ding[1], Mingkui Tan[1(✉)], and Qi Wu[2]

[1] School of Software Engineering, South China University of Technology,
Guangzhou, China
{secrdyz,seningding}@mail.scut.edu.cn, mingkuitan@scut.edu.cn
[2] Australian Centre for Robotic Vision, University of Adelaide, Adelaide, Australia
qi.wu01@adelaide.edu.au

Abstract. The last decade has witnessed remarkable progress in the image captioning task; however, most existing methods cannot control their captions, *e.g.*, choosing to describe the image either roughly or in detail. In this paper, we propose to use a simple length level embedding to endow them with this ability. Moreover, due to their autoregressive nature, the computational complexity of existing models increases linearly as the length of the generated captions grows. Thus, we further devise a non-autoregressive image captioning approach that can generate captions in a length-irrelevant complexity. We verify the merit of the proposed length level embedding on three models: two state-of-the-art (SOTA) autoregressive models with different types of decoder, as well as our proposed non-autoregressive model, to show its generalization ability. In the experiments, our length-controllable image captioning models not only achieve SOTA performance on the challenging MS COCO dataset but also generate length-controllable and diverse image captions. Specifically, our non-autoregressive model outperforms the autoregressive baselines in terms of controllability and diversity, and also significantly improves the decoding efficiency for long captions. Our code and models are released at https://github.com/bearcatt/LaBERT.

Keywords: Controllable image captioning · Non-autoregressive model

1   Introduction

Image captioning is one of the fundamental problems of computer vision which aims to generate natural language captions for images automatically. It requires not only to recognize salient objects in an image and understand their interactions, but also to describe them using natural language, which is very challenging. Most image captioning methods adopt an Encoder-Decoder framework [39,43,47],

---

C. Deng and N. Ding—Equal contribution.

Electronic supplementary material The online version of this chapter (https://doi.org/10.1007/978-3-030-58601-0_42) contains supplementary material, which is available to authorized users.

© Springer Nature Switzerland AG 2020
A. Vedaldi et al. (Eds.): ECCV 2020, LNCS 12358, pp. 712–729, 2020.
https://doi.org/10.1007/978-3-030-58601-0_42

Reference image captions
A pizza on a pan sitting on a table.
A close up of a pizza in a pan on a table.
A pizza sits on a plate on a dark surface.
A person sitting at a table where a pizza is sitting.
A pizza topped with different toppings is brought to a table.

Predicted image captions		
Rough	VLP	A pizza sitting on top of a pan on a table.
	Ours Lv1	A pizza that is sitting on a table.
	Ours Lv2	A pizza with tomatoes and spinach on a table.
	Ours Lv3	A pizza with tomatoes cheese and toppings on it sitting on a table.
Detailed	Ours Lv4	A pizza sitting on top of a pan with a lot of cheese spinach and tomatoes on it.

Fig. 1. Illustration of image captions with different lengths. The top left image is from the MS COCO dataset. To the right of the image are five human-annotated captions. At the bottom, we show the image captions generated by an original VLP [53] model and our length-aware version of VLP. The longest caption (Ours-Lv4) involves more instances in the image and uses more adjective phrases; while in the shortest caption (Ours-Lv1), only the salient instances are mentioned in a terse style.

where the encoder, *e.g.*, a Convolutional Neural Network (CNN), first extracts features from the input image. An image caption is then decoded from the image features, one token at each time, typically using a Recurrent Neural Network (RNN). Following this, many works [20,26,53] achieve the state-of-the-art (SOTA) performance on the challenging MS COCO dataset [8], and even outperform human performance on some evaluation metrics.

Despite their remarkable performance, many advanced image captioning approaches lack the ability to control its predictions, *i.e.*, they cannot change the way they describe an image. See the example in Fig. 1, given an input image, although the caption generated by VLP [53] (a current SOTA) correctly describes the image, it also omits some informative visual concepts, such as "cheese" and "tomatoes". If we want a more detailed description, this result would be unsatisfactory. Therefore, it is desired for the image captioning task if a model can be controlled to describe the image either roughly or in detail. In this paper, we show that such an ability can be effectively acquired by directly controlling the length of the image captions.

Length is an important property of natural language since it reflects the amount of information carried by a sentence. As shown in Fig. 1, a longer image caption can describe an image more accurately, as it generally has higher fidelity for the image information. On the other hand, a shorter image caption can be generated and delivered more efficiently in practice, but with some extent of information loss. Nevertheless, the length property has not been explicitly exploited by previous image captioning approaches. Our work fills this gap by proposing a length-controllable image captioning model. Specifically, we introduce a concept of **"length level"** which refers to a specific length range of the image captions. During training, a length level embedding is learned for each level with the training data inside the length range. During inference, the image caption generation is separated into different levels, where each level is responsible for generating image captions within the corresponding length range, conditioned on the learned length level embedding.

Technically, this length control signal is able to be used in many existing image captioning approaches. However, they may encounter a problem when generating long image captions because of their *autoregressive* nature (*i.e.*, generate one token at a time conditioned on all preceding tokens): the computational complexity of autoregressive methods increase linearly as the length L of the predicted caption grows, *i.e.* a $\Theta(L)$ complexity. To tackle this, we further develop a **non-autoregressive** model for length-controllable image captions based on the idea of iterative refinement [15]. Our non-autoregressive model is inherited from BERT [12], with the input embedding layer modified to incorporate the image feature representations and the length level information. We name it as length-aware BERT (LaBERT). Moreover, we devise a non-autoregressive decoding algorithm for LaBERT to make it be able to decode image captions within a fixed number of refine steps regardless of L, *i.e.*, a *length-irrelevant* complexity.

In our experiments, we first evaluate the effectiveness of the proposed length-controllable image captioning scheme by applying it to two most recently SOTA autoregressive image captioning methods, *i.e.*, AoANet [20], which employs an LSTM [17] as the decoder, and VLP [53], which adopts a Transformer-based decoder. After incorporating the length information, these two methods successfully generate high-quality and length-controllable image captions. Specifically, on the challenging MS COCO dataset, our length-aware models not only outperform their original version in terms of CIDEr-D [42] score on a normal length level (10 to 14 tokens), but also achieve remarkable SPICE [1] scores (23.0) on longer length levels (at least 14 tokens). Afterwards, we evaluate the length level control signal on our proposed non-autoregressive image captioning model, LaBERT, which achieves competitive or even better performance compared with the two autoregressive baselines on all length levels, while also significantly improves the decoding efficiency for *long* captions. More importantly, we find that the proposed LaBERT has a better control precision than the two autoregressive models, and is also able to generate much more diverse image captions.

In summary, the main contributions of this paper are threefold:

1. We firstly introduce the design of "length level" as a control signal to learn length-aware image captioning models, which can be easily integrated into existing image captioning approaches to make them capable of generating high-quality and length-controllable image captions.
2. We devise a non-autoregressive decoder for length-controllable image captioning, which makes the decoding of long captions more efficiency. Moreover, it achieves higher control precision and produces more diverse results than the autoregressive baselines.
3. We perform extensive experiments on different kinds of image captioning models, whether they are autoregressive or non-autoregressive, and whether they use LSTM-based decoder or Transformer-based decoder, to show the effectiveness of our proposed method.

2 Background and Related Works

2.1 Autoregressive Image Captioning (AIC)

Given an image I, an image captioning model aims to describe I by a textual sentence $S = \{s_i\}_{i=1}^{L}$, where s_i is a token in S and L is the length of S. Most existing image captioning approaches operate in an autoregressive style, which factors the distribution of S into a chain of conditional probabilities with a left-to-right causal structure: $p(S|I) = \prod_{i=1}^{L} p(s_i|s_{j<i}, I)$. As a result, S must be generated sequentially, i.e., s_i cannot be generated until all preceding tokens $s_{j<i}$ are available. Assume the target image caption to be $S^* = \{s_i^*\}_{i=1}^{L^*}$. The training of AIC models typically follows the "Teacher Forcing" [5] scheme, which aims to maximize the likelihood of the ground-truth token s_i^* given all preceding *ground-truth* tokens $s_{j<i}^*$ through back-propagation:

$$\min \sum_{i=1}^{L^*} -\log p(s_i^*|s_{j<i}^*, I). \tag{1}$$

During inference, AIC models take a special [BOS] token as input to predict the first token s_1, then s_1 is fed into the model to obtain the next token s_2. Continuing like this until the special [EOS] token is predicted.

There have been many successful extensions to AIC approaches over the years. In [48], the authors proposed to integrate soft and hard attention mechanisms into the decoder, which facilitates the model to learn to focus on some specific image regions when generating the token at each decoding step. Later on, [35] developed a self-critical sequence training (SCST) strategy which directly optimizes the CIDEr [42] score of the predicted image captions through policy gradient [40] to amend the "exposure bias" problem in sequence modeling. Furthermore, instead of measuring attention over a pre-defined uniform grid of image regions as in [48], Anderson et al. [2] devised a bottom-up mechanism to enable the measurement of attention at object-level, which achieved the best results at that time and outperformed the second-best result by a large margin. Apart from this, some other works tried to improve the image caption quality by leveraging additional information, such as semantic attributes [52] and visual relations [49–51]. More recently, after witnessing the effectiveness of Deep Transformers [41] in capturing long-range dependencies in sequence modeling, many Transformer-based AIC models [20, 26, 53] have been developed to further advance the image captioning performance.

2.2 Diverse and Controllable Image Captioning

Despite the remarkable performance achieved by current SOTA AIC models, fewer efforts have been made towards improving the diversity of image captions. In [11], the authors trained a Part-of-Speech predictor and performed sampling base on its predictions to obtain diverse image captions. Chen et al. [6] proposed to control the image captions though the Abstract Scene Graph of the image.

Cornia et al. [9] used different image regions to generated region-specific image captions. However, they rely on additional tools or annotations to provide supervision. Besides, some GAN [16]-based methods have also appeared [10,36,45], most of which improve on diversity, but suffer on accuracy and do not provide controllability over the decoding process. Some other works attempted to generate image captions with controllable styles. These methods require additional training data, such as an image caption dataset with additional style annotations [7,32,37], which is scarce and expensive; or a large corpus of styled text without aligned images [13,31], which often leads to unsatisfied caption quality.

As discussed in Sect. 1, length is an important property for image captions. It is easy to acquire and is strongly associated with the structure of the image caption. Several approaches in the Natural Language Processing field have visited the length-controllable text generation setting. Kikuchi et al. [22] proposed to control the length of output in Neural Sentence Summarization task by: 1) performing beam search without [EOS] token until the desired length is reached; 2) setting a length range and manually discarding out-of-range sequences; 3) feeding an embedding into the decoder in each step to indicate the *remained length*; 4) incorporating the desired length information by multiplying the length with the initial hidden state. However, the first strategy may not produce completed sentences, and the results will have similar style since the model is not aware of the desired length during decoding. The second strategy may require a large beam size to obtain a valid result, and the diversity of the results is also limited. The last two strategies seeks to control the exact length of the output sentence, which is hard in practice and restricts the flexibility of the results. Moreover, the third strategy is only applicable in autoregressive text generation models. Similarly, Liu et al. [29] proposed to control the exact length of the output in ConvSeq2Seq models [14]. They adopted a similar way as the last strategy of [22] that incorporate the desired length information when initializing the decoder state. As a result, they face the same problems as in [22].

2.3   Non-autoregressive Text Generation

A common problem for autoregressive sequence generation models is that the decoding steps must be run sequentially, which prevents architectures like the Transformer from fully realizing their train-time performance advantage during inference. To tackle this, recent works in Neural Machine Translation have appealed to Non-Autoregressive Machine Translation (NAT), which attempts to make non-autoregressive predictions for the entire sequence with one forward pass of the decoder. However, as discussed in [18], NAT models can fail to capture the dependencies between output tokens due to the multi-modality problem, *i.e.*, multiple translations are possible for a single input sentence. To deal with this, some NAT methods relaxed the one-pass restriction and adopt multiple decoding passes to iteratively refine the generated sentences [15,19,25,38,44]. To determine the length of the output, non-autoregressive approaches either predict the length of the output sentence through a length predictor, or adopt insertion/deletion modules to automatically change the length of the output.

3   Method

In this section, we introduce our length level embedding for length-controllable image captioning. Firstly, in Sect. 3.1, we elaborate on how the length level embedding is integrated into existing autoregressive image captioning models to endow them with the ability of length controlling. Then, in Sect. 3.2, we introduce a non-autoregressive image captioning model that can decode image captions within a specific length range in a length-irrelevant complexity.

3.1   Acquisition of Length Information

Given an input image caption $S = \{s_i\}_{i=1}^{L}$, to model its length information, we assign S into a specific "length level" with the length range $[L_{low}, L_{high}]$ according to its length L. Then, we use a length level embedding matrix $W_l \in \mathbb{R}^{k \times d}$ (k is the number of levels and d is the embedding dimension) to differentiate image captions on different length levels. Let l be the length level for S, and let t_l be the one-hot representation of l. Then, the length level embedding for tokens in S is calculated by $e_l = W_l^T t_l \in \mathbb{R}^d$. The final representation of a token s_i is constructed by adding the length level embedding e_l with its word embedding $e_{w,s_i} \in \mathbb{R}^d$ and, optionally (for Transformer-based decoder), its positional embedding $e_{p,i} \in \mathbb{R}^d$:

$$x_{s_i} = e_l + e_{w,s_i} + e_{p,i}. \tag{2}$$

With the length level embedding e_l, the length information of S is explicitly incorporated into x_{s_i}. Now, given an image caption model $\mathcal{M}$, we can obtain its length-aware counterpart $\mathcal{M}'$ by simply replace their original token embeddings (*e.g.*, word embeddings) with our length-aware tokens embeddings.

When training $\mathcal{M}'$, we can directly follow the training scheme of $\mathcal{M}$, like using the Teacher Forcing scheme in Eq. (1) if $\mathcal{M}$ is autoregressive. During training, the length level embedding for level l will only be trained with captions within a particular length range, thus the "trait" of image captions with different lengths is separately captured, enabling $\mathcal{M}'$ to perform length-aware modeling. During inference, apart from the image features, the length level embedding of the desired length level is also fed into $\mathcal{M}'$ as a control signal to generate image captions within the corresponding length range.

When setting the boundary $[L_{low}, L_{high}]$ of a length level, we follow two simple principles: 1) there should be enough training data for each length level so that the length level embedding can be trained sufficiently; 2) the range of a length level should not be too narrow to ensure the flexibility of the generated captions. In our experiments, after checking the length distribution of captions in the MS COCO dataset, we explore two length level division plans which contain 4 and 5 length levels, respectively. As an example, the 4-level plan divides the image captions into 4 chunks with length inside the ranges [1,9], [10, 14], [15, 19], and [20, 25], respectively, from rough to detailed. While the 5-level plan provides more fine-grained levels.

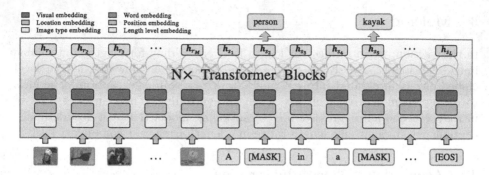

Fig. 2. The overview of LaBERT. Image regions and caption words are projected into the same dimensional space by the sum of three embeddings, respectively. All inputs are then combined together through $N\times$ Transformer blocks. The final hidden states h of [MASK] inputs are fed into a token classifier to predict their original tokens.

Length-Aware Autoregressive Caption Decoders. The decoder of most existing image captioning models can be broadly classified into two categories, *i.e.*, LSTM-based and Transformer-based. Due to its simplicity, the proposed length level embedding can be easily integrated into these models. Specifically, we implement it on AoANet [20] and VLP [53], which are the most recent SOTA image captioning models of the two decoder categories, respectively. Like many previous image captioning models, AoANet adopts an LSTM-based caption decoder. During each decoding step, the LSTM takes as input the concatenation of the word embedding of the input token and a context vector obtained from the image feature and the decoder context. On the other hand, VLP uses a BERT [12]-style decoder that consists of a stack of Transformers. Specifically, VLP follows BERT and employs three types of embeddings to embed an input token, namely the word embedding, the positional embedding, as well as the segment type embedding. To achieve length-controllable image captioning for these two methods, we directly add our length level embedding onto the word embedding of the input tokens for both AoANet and VLP, without any other modifications. Through this way, their caption decoders can explicitly model the length information of the input tokens.

3.2 Non-autoregressive Length-Controllable Decoding

To improve the decoding efficiency for long image captions, we propose a non-autoregressive length-controllable image captioning model named as LaBERT, where we modify the embedding layer of BERT [12] to incorporate the image information and the length level information, as shown in Fig. 2. Specifically, we follow [2,53] and first adopt a pre-trained object detector to detect M object proposals from I, denoted as $R = \{r_i\}_{i=1}^{M}$. The object detector is further employed to obtain the corresponding region features $F_e = \{f_{e,i}\}_{i=1}^{M}$, classification probabilities $F_c = \{f_{c,i}\}_{i=1}^{M}$, and localization features $F_l = \{f_{l,i}\}_{i=1}^{M}$ for R. Similar to [53], the input representation of r_i is constructed by:

$$\boldsymbol{x}_{r_i} = \boldsymbol{W}_e^T \boldsymbol{f}_{e,i} + \boldsymbol{W}_p^T [\text{LN}(\boldsymbol{f}_{c,i}), \text{LN}(\boldsymbol{f}_{l,i})] + \boldsymbol{e}_{img}, \tag{3}$$

where the first two term are the visual embedding and location embedding of r_i, respectively. $\boldsymbol{e}_{img} \in \mathbb{R}^d$ is a learnable embedding that differentiates the image regions from the text tokens. $[\cdot, \cdot]$ indicates the concatenate operation, and LN represents Layer Normalization [3]. $\boldsymbol{W}_e$ and $\boldsymbol{W}_p$ are two learnable projection matrices that project the corresponding features into d-D space.

Training. Given the target image caption $\boldsymbol{S}^*$, we first identify its length level l and obtain the length range $[L_{low}, L_{high}]$ of l. Then, we pad $\boldsymbol{S}^*$ with the [EOS] token to the longest length L_{high}. Following [15], we construct the input sequence $\boldsymbol{S}$ by randomly replacing m tokens in $\boldsymbol{S}^*$ with the [MASK] token, where m is also randomly selected from the range $[1, L_{high}]$. Next, LaBERT attempts to predict the original tokens at all masked positions in $\boldsymbol{S}$ conditioned only on the embeddings of input image regions (obtained by Eq. (3)) and the length-aware embeddings of the unmasked tokens in $\boldsymbol{S}$ (obtained by Eq. (2)). Hence, the predicted conditional probabilities are independent with each other, allowing them to be calculated in parallel at inference time. We train LaBERT by minimizing the cross-entropy loss over all *masked* positions:

$$\min \sum_{i=1}^{L_{high}} -\mathbb{1}(s_i) \log p(s_i = s_i^*). \tag{4}$$

$\mathbb{1}(\cdot)$ is an indicator function whose value is 1 if $s_i =$ [MASK] and 0 otherwise.

Inference. We perform parallel image caption decoding based on the idea of iterative refinement [15,25]. Specifically, at step $t = 1$, we initialize the image caption $\boldsymbol{S}$ as L_{high} consecutive [MASK] tokens. We first construct the input representations for text and image through Eq. (2) and Eq. (3), respectively. We then feed them into LaBERT to predict a probability distribution over a pre-defined vocabulary for every position in $\boldsymbol{S}$, denoted as $\boldsymbol{P} = \{p_i\}_{i=1}^{L_{high}}$. To encourage the model to predict longer captions, we propose to exponentially decay the probability of the [EOS] token by a factor γ for predictions after L_{low}:

$$p_i(s_i = \text{[EOS]}) \leftarrow \gamma^{L_{high}-i} p_i(s_i = \text{[EOS]}), \ \forall i \in [L_{low}, L_{high}]. \tag{5}$$

Then, we obtain the refined $\boldsymbol{S}$ by updating all masked position:

$$s_i \leftarrow \arg\max_s p_i(s_i = s). \tag{6}$$

Moreover, we obtain a confidence score $c_i = \max_s p_i(s_i = s)$ for each predicted token s_i, denoted as $\boldsymbol{C} = \{c_i\}_{i=1}^{L_{high}}$.

At step $t = 2$, we adopt the **mask-predict-update** procedure [15], *i.e.*, we find the lowest n confidence scores in $\boldsymbol{C}$ and **mask** the corresponding positions

Mask-predict-update process	
Step 1	[MASK] [MASK] [MASK] [MASK] [MASK] [MASK].....[MASK] [MASK] [MASK]
	A dog is on the the on a a a a a a a a a walking in the sidewalk.
	A dog laying on the side of a street with a a walking a a walking in the sidewalk.
	A dog laying on the side of a street with a woman walking on the sidewalk of the street.
Step T	A dog sitting on the side of a street with a woman walking on the sidewalk in the background.

Fig. 3. An example from our experiments that illustrates the "mask-predict-update" process of LaBERT. At each step, all red tokens are masked and re-predicted in parallel, conditioned on other tokens in the sequence and visual information from the image.

in S with [MASK]. Next, the masked S will be fed into LaBERT to **predict** all masked positions in parallel, with the probability for [EOS] decayed by Eq. (5). We **update** all masked positions in S through Eq. (6) to obtain the refined S. And we propose to update C by:

$$c_i \leftarrow \begin{cases} \max_s p_i(s_i = s), & i \text{ is a masked position,} \\ (c_i + \max_s p_i(s_i = s))/2, & \text{otherwise.} \end{cases} \tag{7}$$

The mask-predict-update procedure will be repeated until $t = T$ (T can be smaller than L_{high}). The number of masks n in each step is calculated by $n = \frac{T-t}{T}L_{high}$, which will decay linearly as the step t increases. An illustration of the mask-predict-update procedure is shown in Fig. 3.

Through iterative refinement, the computational complexity is decreased from $\Theta(L_{high})$ in autoregressive methods to $\Theta(T)$ in LaBERT. Moreover, the mistakes made at early steps in LaBERT are possible to be revised in the future steps, which is infeasible for autoregressive methods. Note that the update rule in Eq. (7) is different from the update rule in [15], which only updates the confidence scores of the masked positions. In practice, we found ours (denoted as the *global update rule*) performs much better in terms of caption quality. Besides, unlike many non-autoregressive text generation methods that rely on a length predictor to determine the length of the output at the start of decoding, our model is trained to automatically find a suitable end position within $[L_{low}, L_{high}]$ for level l, thus this length predictor is not required. Moreover, LaBERT also allows dynamic length changes during the refinement process, while not using any additional insertion/deletion modules like in [19].

4   Experiments

In this section, we first introduce the dataset and metrics we used in evaluation and the implementation details in Sect. 4.1 and Sect. 4.2, respectively. In the following sections, we verify the merit of the proposed length level embedding from two perspectives, *i.e.*, the quality of generated image captions (Sect. 4.3 and 4.4) and the controllability & diversity (Sect. 4.6). The verification is performed on two SOTA autoregressive models, and our non-autoregressive model LaBERT, to show the generalization ability of the length level embedding. Meanwhile, we analyze the performance of LaBERT and discuss how it improves the efficiency of long captions generation in Sect. 4.5.

4.1 Dataset and Metrics

We evaluate our proposed method on the popular MS COCO dataset [28] which contains 123,287 images with at least 5 ground-truth captions for each image. We adopt the Karpathy's split setting [21], which uses 113,287 images for training, 5,000 for validation and 5,000 for offline evaluation.

To evaluate the quality of the generated captions, we use standard metrics, including BLEU [33], ROUGE [27], METEOR [4], CIDEr-D [42], and SPICE [1]. All these metrics except SPICE calculate the similarity between the reference and candidate image captions by considering their n-grams similarity. On the other hand, SPICE is based on scene-graph synonym matching which considers a scene-graph representation of an image by encoding objects, attributes, and relations. According to [1,23], SPICE and METEOR correlate best with human judgments in terms of caption quality among all these metrics. Moreover, since most ground-truth image captions in the test splits are short (more than 90% contain 8–14 tokens), the performance of n-gram based metrics can be negatively affected when evaluating long candidate captions (e.g., longer than 14 tokens). Fortunately, SPICE is robust to the length of candidate captions, thus it should be the *prior metric* for the evaluation of long captions.

4.2 Implementation Details

For length-aware AoANet and VLP, we adopt their official codes as well as their experiment settings. For LaBERT, we initialize it from the official pre-trained BERT-base [12] model, which have 12 layers of Transformer, 12 attention heads, and a hidden size of 768. We represent each input image as 100 object proposals extracted by a Faster RCNN [34] pre-trained on the Visual Genome [24] dataset. We take the intermediate results at the fc6 layer (2048-D) of the Faster RCNN as the region features F_e. The classification labels F_c containing 1600 object categories are obtained from the final softmax layer. The localization feature of each proposal is a 5-tuple contains the normalized coordinates of the top-left and bottom-right corner of the proposal and its relative area to the whole image. We train LaBERT for 100,000 iterations with a batch size of 256. The AdamW [30] optimizer is used with $\beta_1 = 0.9$, $\beta_2 = 0.999$, and a weight decay of 1e-2. We linearly warm-up the learning rate from 0 to 5e-5 over the first 1,000 iterations, and cosine decay it in the rest training steps. We use a label smoothing of 0.1, and a gradient clipping threshold of 1.0. The [EOS] decay factor γ is determined by cross validation on the val splits for each level of LaBERT. Specifically, γ is set to 0.88 and 0.95 for level 2 and level 3, respectively. For other length levels, we found LaBERT performs well without [EOS] decay.

Table 1. Performance of the length-aware version of AoANet and VLP on MS COCO Karpathy's **test** split. S, C, M and B@N, are short for SPICE, CIDEr-D, METEOR, and BLEU@N scores, respectively. The original results of AoANet and VLP are obtained from models trained by ourselves with the official codes and settings provided by the authors. All values are reported as a percentage (%).

Metrics		S	C	M	B@4	S	C	M	B@4
Models			AoANet				VLP		
Original Results		21.3	118.4	28.3	**36.9**	21.2	116.9	28.5	**36.5**
4-Level	Lv 1 (1-9)	19.6	107.4	25.9	33.1	18.9	103.0	25.2	31.8
	Lv 2 (10-14)	21.7	117.6	28.6	35.8	21.4	**118.7**	28.8	36.0
	Lv 3 (15-19)	22.7	79.9	28.7	26.6	22.4	92.5	**29.3**	28.4
	Lv 4 (20-25)	22.7	29.5	27.7	20.2	22.4	40.0	28.5	21.9
5-Level	Lv 1 (1-9)	19.7	108.7	26.0	33.5	18.7	101.0	25.0	30.9
	Lv 2 (10-13)	21.6	**118.8**	28.5	36.1	21.2	117.3	28.4	35.9
	Lv 3 (14-17)	22.6	92.9	**29.0**	28.7	22.3	100.5	**29.3**	29.9
	Lv 4 (18-21)	**23.0**	48.4	28.2	22.7	22.4	60.4	28.7	24.0
	Lv 5 (22-25)	22.9	18.9	27.2	18.8	**22.5**	28.1	28.1	20.3

4.3   Performance on AoANet and VLP

We first apply our length level embedding to two current SOTA models, *i.e.*, AoANet [20] and VLP [53]. We train length-aware AoANet and VLP following their original training settings. During evaluation, we run our length-aware models on the **test** split multiple times, where each time we feed in a different length level embedding to generate the captions within different length ranges. The results are recorded in Table 1. From the table, on the normal length range (10–14 tokens), our 4-Level and 5-Level version of VLP and AoANet both achieve competitive or better performance than the original version. Our 4-level VLP even improve the CIDEr-D score by 1.8% over the original VLP. Note that, most of the image captions generated by original AoANet and VLP are inside the length range [10, 14], which indicates that our length-aware versions can maintain or even boost the performance of the original models on a normal length range.

The *n*-gram based metrics like CIDEr-D drops severely on longer length levels. However, as we discussed in Sect. 4.1, this does not mean the captions generated on these levels are bad. See Fig. 1, the 4-level VLP generates high-quality image captions on all levels. Specifically, on the shortest level, the image is concisely described, while on the longest level, 4-level VLP narrates the image in great detail, including visual concepts such as "cheese", "spinach" and "tomatoes", some are even missed in the ground-truth. Moreover, our models generally achieve remarkable SPICE scores for captions longer than 14 tokens. Our 5-level AoANet even achieves 23.0 SPICE score, which is 1.7% higher than the original result. These results indicate that the length level embedding is well-suited for existing autoregressive image captioning models and makes them capable of producing high-quality results within different length ranges.

Table 2. Performance of LaBERT on MS COCO Karpathy's `test` split. R represents ROUGE. The results of AoANet and VLP are obtained from their papers.

Metrics	S	C	M	R	B@1	B@2	B@3	B@4
State-of-the-art models								
VLP [53]	21.2	116.9	28.4	–	–	–	–	36.5
AoANet [20]	21.3	**119.8**	28.4	**57.5**	77.4	–	–	**37.2**
Single-level LaBERT								
Single Level (1–25)	21.7	116.8	27.9	57.0	77.4	61.0	46.5	35.0
4-level LaBERT								
lvl 1 (1–9)	19.5	101.6	25.4	54.7	72.5	56.3	41.8	30.0
lvl 2 (10–14)	21.8	118.2	28.4	57.4	**77.6**	**61.3**	**46.9**	35.3
lvl 3 (15–19)	**22.3**	90.5	**28.6**	53.1	66.8	50.6	37.0	26.8
lvl 4 (20–25)	22.2	39.9	27.7	46.9	56.1	40.9	28.6	19.9

4.4 Performance on LaBERT

We further apply the length level embedding to our proposed non-autoregressive image captioning model, LaBERT. To make comparisons, we implement a single-level version of LaBERT whose length range is $[1, 25]$. Moreover, the number of refine steps for 4-level LaBERT is set to 10, 15, 20 and 25, for level 1–4, respectively, so that we can compare LaBERT with the autoregressive image captioning models under roughly the same decoding complexity. Analogously, The total decoding steps of the single-level LaBERT is set to 25. The results are shown in Table 2. Compared with single-level LaBERT, 4-level LaBERT achieves clearly better performance on all metrics on the second level, which coincides with our experiments in Sect. 4.3. Moreover, 4-level LaBERT yields significantly higher SPICE scores on level 3 and level 4. These results demonstrate the advantage of the length level embedding in our non-autoregressive image caption model. Moreover, under the same computational complexity, 4-level LaBERT performs comparably with 4-level AoANet and VLP as well as the SOTA results, which verifies the effectiveness of our non-autoregressive image captioning model.

4.5 Performance Analysis of LaBERT

Here we analyze the effect of the number of refine steps T, the [EOS] decay factor γ in Eq. (5), and the global update rule in Eq. (7). To show the influence of T, we vary it from 10 to 25 for caption generation on the fourth level; to show the importance of the [EOS] decay factor γ and the global update rule, we perform ablation experiments for them on the second level. As shown in Table 3, our LaBERT can use a much smaller T to achieve comparable results with 4-Level VLP, the autoregressive baseline. We can acquire further speedup $(2.1\times)$ by setting $T = 12$, with a small sacrifice on SPICE (0.3%). Nevertheless, the performance obtain by LaBERT with 10–20 refine steps are still competitive to

Table 3. Performance analysis on 4-level LaBERT. "Speedup" indicates the relative speedup over an autoregressive baseline.

Method		S	C	M	R	B@1	B@4	Speedup
Lvl 4	10 refine steps	21.6	39.5	27.3	46.9	55.9	19.0	×2.5
	12 refine steps	21.9	39.8	27.5	46.7	56.1	19.4	×2.1
	15 refine steps	22.0	39.5	27.5	46.6	55.9	19.3	×1.67
	20 refine steps	22.4	39.9	27.8	47.0	56.1	19.8	×1.25
	25 refine steps	22.2	39.9	27.7	46.9	56.1	19.9	×1.0
	4-Level VLP	22.4	40.0	28.5	47.0	56.0	21.9	×1.0
Lvl 2	w/o global update	21.7	116.6	28.2	57.2	77.3	34.8	–
	w/o [EOS] decay	21.3	116.0	27.8	57.1	78.3	34.9	–
	Original results	21.8	118.2	28.4	57.4	77.6	35.3	–

the 25-step performance as well as the performance of the 4-level VLP, which verifies the capability of LaBERT in efficient image captioning decoding. Moreover, the global update rule and the [EOS] decay are shown to be important for LaBERT. After removing them, the CIDEr-D score of LaBERT on the second level drops by 1.6% and 2.2%, respectively.

4.6   Controllability and Diversity Analysis

In this section, we further analyze the "control precision" of the length level embedding, *i.e.*, given a length level embedding, the probability of generating image captions within the desired length range. We calculate the control precision for the 4-level version of AoANet, VLP and LaBERT, and present the results in Fig. 4(a). As shown in the figure, all methods accurately control the length of the generated image captions, and our non-autoregressive model, LaBERT, yields the best control precision (more than 95%) among all levels. This result verifies the effectiveness of the proposed length level embedding in generating length-controllable image captions. Besides, the control precision drops on longer levels, which may due to the lack of long captions in the MS COCO dataset.

We also perform diversity analysis for the image captions generated by different models, as shown in Fig. 4(b) and Table 4. From Fig. 4(b), the length of the image captions generated by our length-aware models are uniformly distributed among all length levels. On the contrary, the results of the original AoANet, VLP and the single-level LaBERT distribute mainly in the shortest two levels. We further evaluate the diversity of the image captions on n-gram diversity metrics like Div-1 and Div-2, as well as the recently proposed SelfCIDEr [46] score that focuses on semantic diversity. From Table 4, our 4-level models perform clearly better on all metrics, which means we can obtain diverse captions for an image with our length-aware image captioning models. Interestingly, our non-autoregressive model LaBERT significantly outperforms all compared autoregressive methods on all three diversity metrics.

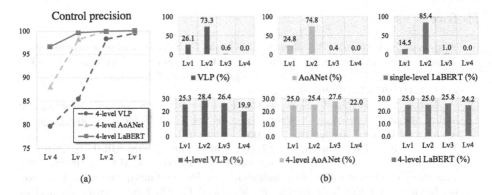

Fig. 4. Analysis of controllability and diversity on `test` split. (a) The control precision of our 4-level version of AoANet, VLP and LaBERT; (b) The length distributions of image captions generated by our 4-level length-aware models and their counterparts.

Table 4. Diversity analysis. BS denotes beam search with a beam size of 4.

Models	AoANet		VLP		LaBERT
	BS	4-Level	BS	4-Level	4-Level
SelfCIDEr [46]	0.590	0.689	0.623	0.762	**0.841**
Div-1	0.291	0.378	0.313	0.406	**0.411**
Div-2	0.462	0.523	0.470	0.559	**0.575**

5   Conclusion

In this paper, we propose to use a length level embedding for length-controllable image captioning. By simply adding our length level embedding on the word embeddings of input tokens, we endow existing image captioning methods with the ability to control the length of their predictions. To improve the decoding efficiency of long captions, we further propose a non-autoregressive image captioning model, LaBERT, that generates image captions in a length-irrelevant complexity. The experiments demonstrate the effectiveness of the proposed method.

Acknowledgments. This work was supported by the Science and Technology Program of Guangzhou, China under Grants 202007030007, Key-Area Research and Development Program of Guangdong Province (2018B010107001), National Natural Science Foundation of China 61836003 (key project), Guangdong Project 2017ZT07X183, Fundamental Research Funds for the Central Universities D2191240.

References

1. Anderson, P., Fernando, B., Johnson, M., Gould, S.: SPICE: semantic propositional image caption evaluation. In: Leibe, B., Matas, J., Sebe, N., Welling, M. (eds.) ECCV 2016. LNCS, vol. 9909, pp. 382–398. Springer, Cham (2016). https://doi.org/10.1007/978-3-319-46454-1_24
2. Anderson, P., et al.: Bottom-up and top-down attention for image captioning and visual question answering. In: Proceedings of the IEEE Conference on Computer Vision and Pattern Recognition, pp. 6077–6086 (2018)
3. Ba, J.L., Kiros, J.R., Hinton, G.E.: Layer normalization. Stat **1050**, 21 (2016)
4. Banerjee, S., Lavie, A.: Meteor: an automatic metric for MT evaluation with improved correlation with human judgments. In: Proceedings of the ACL Workshop on Intrinsic and Extrinsic Evaluation Measures for Machine Translation and/or Summarization, pp. 65–72 (2005)
5. Bengio, S., Vinyals, O., Jaitly, N., Shazeer, N.: Scheduled sampling for sequence prediction with recurrent neural networks. In: Advances in Neural Information Processing Systems, pp. 1171–1179 (2015)
6. Chen, S., Jin, Q., Wang, P., Wu, Q.: Say as you wish: fine-grained control of image caption generation with abstract scene graphs. In: Proceedings of the IEEE/CVF Conference on Computer Vision and Pattern Recognition, pp. 9962–9971 (2020)
7. Chen, T., et al.: "Factual" or "emotional": stylized image captioning with adaptive learning and attention. In: Ferrari, V., Hebert, M., Sminchisescu, C., Weiss, Y. (eds.) ECCV 2018. LNCS, vol. 11214, pp. 527–543. Springer, Cham (2018). https://doi.org/10.1007/978-3-030-01249-6_32
8. Chen, X., et al.: Microsoft coco captions: data collection and evaluation server. arXiv preprint arXiv:1504.00325 (2015)
9. Cornia, M., Baraldi, L., Cucchiara, R.: Show, control and tell: a framework for generating controllable and grounded captions. In: Proceedings of the IEEE Conference on Computer Vision and Pattern Recognition, pp. 8307–8316 (2019)
10. Dai, B., Fidler, S., Urtasun, R., Lin, D.: Towards diverse and natural image descriptions via a conditional GAN. In: Proceedings of the IEEE International Conference on Computer Vision, pp. 2970–2979 (2017)
11. Deshpande, A., Aneja, J., Wang, L., Schwing, A.G., Forsyth, D.: Fast, diverse and accurate image captioning guided by part-of-speech. In: Proceedings of the IEEE Conference on Computer Vision and Pattern Recognition, pp. 10695–10704 (2019)
12. Devlin, J., Chang, M.W., Lee, K., Toutanova, K.: Bert: pre-training of deep bidirectional transformers for language understanding. In: Proceedings of the 2019 Conference of the North American Chapter of the Association for Computational Linguistics: Human Language Technologies, Volume 1 (Long and Short Papers), pp. 4171–4186 (2019)
13. Gan, C., Gan, Z., He, X., Gao, J., Deng, L.: StyleNet: generating attractive visual captions with styles. In: Proceedings of the IEEE Conference on Computer Vision and Pattern Recognition, pp. 3137–3146 (2017)
14. Gehring, J., Auli, M., Grangier, D., Yarats, D., Dauphin, Y.N.: Convolutional sequence to sequence learning. In: International Conference on Machine Learning, pp. 1243–1252 (2017)
15. Ghazvininejad, M., Levy, O., Liu, Y., Zettlemoyer, L.: Mask-predict: parallel decoding of conditional masked language models. In: Proceedings of the 2019 Conference on Empirical Methods in Natural Language Processing and the 9th International Joint Conference on Natural Language Processing (EMNLP-IJCNLP), pp. 6114–6123 (2019)

16. Goodfellow, I., et al.: Generative adversarial nets. In: Advances in Neural Information Processing Systems, pp. 2672–2680 (2014)
17. Greff, K., Srivastava, R.K., Koutník, J., Steunebrink, B.R., Schmidhuber, J.: LSTM: a search space odyssey. IEEE Trans. Neural Netw. Learn. Syst. **28**(10), 2222–2232 (2015)
18. Gu, J., Bradbury, J., Xiong, C., Li, V.O., Socher, R.: Non-autoregressive neural machine translation. arXiv preprint arXiv:1711.02281 (2017)
19. Gu, J., Wang, C., Zhao, J.: Levenshtein transformer. In: Advances in Neural Information Processing Systems, pp. 11179–11189 (2019)
20. Huang, L., Wang, W., Chen, J., Wei, X.Y.: Attention on attention for image captioning. In: The IEEE International Conference on Computer Vision (ICCV), October 2019
21. Karpathy, A., Fei-Fei, L.: Deep visual-semantic alignments for generating image descriptions. In: Proceedings of the IEEE Conference on Computer Vision and Pattern Recognition, pp. 3128–3137 (2015)
22. Kikuchi, Y., Neubig, G., Sasano, R., Takamura, H., Okumura, M.: Controlling output length in neural encoder-decoders. In: Proceedings of the 2016 Conference on Empirical Methods in Natural Language Processing, pp. 1328–1338 (2016)
23. Kilickaya, M., Erdem, A., Ikizler-Cinbis, N., Erdem, E.: Re-evaluating automatic metrics for image captioning. In: Proceedings of the 15th Conference of the European Chapter of the Association for Computational Linguistics: Volume 1, Long Papers, pp. 199–209 (2017)
24. Krishna, R., et al.: Visual genome: connecting language and vision using crowdsourced dense image annotations. Int. J. Comput. Vis. **123**(1), 32–73 (2017)
25. Lee, J., Mansimov, E., Cho, K.: Deterministic non-autoregressive neural sequence modeling by iterative refinement. In: Proceedings of the 2018 Conference on Empirical Methods in Natural Language Processing, pp. 1173–1182 (2018)
26. Li, G., Zhu, L., Liu, P., Yang, Y.: Entangled transformer for image captioning. In: Proceedings of the IEEE International Conference on Computer Vision, pp. 8928–8937 (2019)
27. Lin, C.Y.: Rouge: a package for automatic evaluation of summaries. In: In Proceedings of the Workshop on Text Summarization Branches Out (WAS 2004) (2004)
28. Lin, T.-Y., Maire, M., Belongie, S., Hays, J., Perona, P., Ramanan, D., Dollár, P., Zitnick, C.L.: Microsoft COCO: common objects in context. In: Fleet, D., Pajdla, T., Schiele, B., Tuytelaars, T. (eds.) ECCV 2014. LNCS, vol. 8693, pp. 740–755. Springer, Cham (2014). https://doi.org/10.1007/978-3-319-10602-1_48
29. Liu, Y., Luo, Z., Zhu, K.: Controlling length in abstractive summarization using a convolutional neural network. In: Proceedings of the 2018 Conference on Empirical Methods in Natural Language Processing, pp. 4110–4119 (2018)
30. Loshchilov, I., Hutter, F.: Fixing weight decay regularization in adam (2018)
31. Mathews, A., Xie, L., He, X.: Semstyle: learning to generate stylised image captions using unaligned text. In: Proceedings of the IEEE Conference on Computer Vision and Pattern Recognition, pp. 8591–8600 (2018)
32. Mathews, A.P., Xie, L., He, X.: SentiCap: generating image descriptions with sentiments. In: Thirtieth AAAI Conference on Artificial Intelligence (2016)
33. Papineni, K., Roukos, S., Ward, T., Zhu, W.J.: Bleu: a method for automatic evaluation of machine translation. In: Proceedings of the 40th Annual Meeting on Association for Computational Linguistics, pp. 311–318. Association for Computational Linguistics (2002)

34. Ren, S., He, K., Girshick, R., Sun, J.: Faster R-CNN: towards real-time object detection with region proposal networks. In: Advances in Neural Information Processing Systems, pp. 91–99 (2015)
35. Rennie, S.J., Marcheret, E., Mroueh, Y., Ross, J., Goel, V.: Self-critical sequence training for image captioning. In: Proceedings of the IEEE Conference on Computer Vision and Pattern Recognition, pp. 7008–7024 (2017)
36. Shetty, R., Rohrbach, M., Anne Hendricks, L., Fritz, M., Schiele, B.: Speaking the same language: Matching machine to human captions by adversarial training. In: Proceedings of the IEEE International Conference on Computer Vision, pp. 4135–4144 (2017)
37. Shuster, K., Humeau, S., Hu, H., Bordes, A., Weston, J.: Engaging image captioning via personality. In: Proceedings of the IEEE Conference on Computer Vision and Pattern Recognition, pp. 12516–12526 (2019)
38. Stern, M., Chan, W., Kiros, J., Uszkoreit, J.: Insertion transformer: flexible sequence generation via insertion operations. In: International Conference on Machine Learning, pp. 5976–5985 (2019)
39. Sutskever, I., Vinyals, O., Le, Q.V.: Sequence to sequence learning with neural networks. In: Advances in Neural Information Processing Systems, pp. 3104–3112 (2014)
40. Sutton, R.S., McAllester, D.A., Singh, S.P., Mansour, Y.: Policy gradient methods for reinforcement learning with function approximation. In: Advances in Neural Information Processing Systems, pp. 1057–1063 (2000)
41. Vaswani, A., et al.: Attention is all you need. In: Advances in Neural Information Processing Systems, pp. 5998–6008 (2017)
42. Vedantam, R., Lawrence Zitnick, C., Parikh, D.: Cider: consensus-based image description evaluation. In: Proceedings of the IEEE Conference on Computer Vision and Pattern Recognition, pp. 4566–4575 (2015)
43. Vinyals, O., Toshev, A., Bengio, S., Erhan, D.: Show and tell: a neural image caption generator. In: Proceedings of the IEEE Conference on Computer Vision and Pattern Recognition, pp. 3156–3164 (2015)
44. Wang, C., Zhang, J., Chen, H.: Semi-autoregressive neural machine translation. In: Proceedings of the 2018 Conference on Empirical Methods in Natural Language Processing, pp. 479–488 (2018)
45. Wang, L., Schwing, A., Lazebnik, S.: Diverse and accurate image description using a variational auto-encoder with an additive Gaussian encoding space. In: Advances in Neural Information Processing Systems, pp. 5756–5766 (2017)
46. Wang, Q., Chan, A.B.: Describing like humans: on diversity in image captioning. In: Proceedings of the IEEE Conference on Computer Vision and Pattern Recognition, pp. 4195–4203 (2019)
47. Wu, Q., Shen, C., Wang, P., Dick, A., van den Hengel, A.: Image captioning and visual question answering based on attributes and external knowledge. IEEE Trans. Pattern Anal. Mach. Intell. **40**(6), 1367–1381 (2017)
48. Xu, K., et al.: Show, attend and tell: neural image caption generation with visual attention. In: International Conference on Machine Learning, pp. 2048–2057 (2015)
49. Yang, X., Tang, K., Zhang, H., Cai, J.: Auto-encoding scene graphs for image captioning. In: Proceedings of the IEEE Conference on Computer Vision and Pattern Recognition, pp. 10685–10694 (2019)
50. Yao, T., Pan, Y., Li, Y., Mei, T.: Exploring visual relationship for image captioning. In: Ferrari, V., Hebert, M., Sminchisescu, C., Weiss, Y. (eds.) Computer Vision – ECCV 2018. LNCS, vol. 11218, pp. 711–727. Springer, Cham (2018). https://doi.org/10.1007/978-3-030-01264-9_42

51. Yao, T., Pan, Y., Li, Y., Mei, T.: Hierarchy parsing for image captioning. In: Proceedings of the IEEE International Conference on Computer Vision, pp. 2621–2629 (2019)
52. Yao, T., Pan, Y., Li, Y., Qiu, Z., Mei, T.: Boosting image captioning with attributes. In: Proceedings of the IEEE International Conference on Computer Vision, pp. 4894–4902 (2017)
53. Zhou, L., Palangi, H., Zhang, L., Hu, H., Corso, J.J., Gao, J.: Unified vision-language pre-training for image captioning and VQA. arXiv preprint arXiv:1909.11059 (2019)

Few-Shot Semantic Segmentation with Democratic Attention Networks

Haochen Wang[1,6], Xudong Zhang[1], Yutao Hu[1], Yandan Yang[1],
Xianbin Cao[1,2,3(✉)], and Xiantong Zhen[4,5]

[1] Beihang University, Beijing, China
{haochenwang,xdzhang,huyutao,yangyandan,xbcao}@buaa.edu.cn
[2] Key Laboratory of Advanced Technology of Near Space Information System,
Ministry of Industry and Information Technology of China, Beijing, China
[3] Beijing Advanced Innovation Center for Big Data-Based Precision Medicine,
Beijing, China
[4] AIM Lab, University of Amsterdam, Amsterdam, The Netherlands
zhenxt@gmail.com
[5] Inception Institute of Artificial Intelligence, Abu Dhabi, UAE
[6] YouKu Cognitive and Intelligent Lab, Alibaba Group, Hangzhou, China

Abstract. Few-shot segmentation has recently generated great popularity, addressing the challenging yet important problem of segmenting objects from unseen categories with scarce annotated support images. The crux of few-shot segmentation is to extract object information from the support image and then propagate it to guide the segmentation of query images. In this paper, we propose the Democratic Attention Network (DAN) for few-shot semantic segmentation. We introduce the democratized graph attention mechanism, which can activate more pixels on the object to establish a robust correspondence between support and query images. Thus, the network is able to propagate more guiding information of foreground objects from support to query images, enhancing its robustness and generalizability to new objects. Furthermore, we propose multi-scale guidance by designing a refinement fusion unit to fuse features from intermediate layers for the segmentation of the query image. This offers an efficient way of leveraging multi-level semantic information to achieve more accurate segmentation. Extensive experiments on three benchmarks demonstrate that the proposed DAN achieves the new state-of-the-art performance, surpassing the previous methods by large margins. The thorough ablation studies further reveal its great effectiveness for few-shot semantic segmentation.

Keywords: Few-shot segmentation · Graph attention · Democratic attention network · Multi-scale guidance

H. Wang, X. Zhang—These authors contribute equally.

Electronic supplementary material The online version of this chapter (https://doi.org/10.1007/978-3-030-58601-0_43) contains supplementary material, which is available to authorized users.

A. Vedaldi et al. (Eds.): ECCV 2020, LNCS 12358, pp. 730–746, 2020.
https://doi.org/10.1007/978-3-030-58601-0_43

1   Introduction

Deep convolutional neural networks driven by large-scale labeled datasets [3,17] have shown great success in many visual recognition tasks, such as image classification [9,12,14,29] and semantic segmentation [8,15,18]. As for conventional semantic segmentation, training a deep neural network requires pixel-level annotation, which is costly and time consuming. In addition, once the model is learned, it is difficult to predict new classes absent in the training set. In contrast to machine learning models, humans are good at recognizing a new object even with a little guidance. Inspired by this, few-shot semantic segmentation has recently received growing interest in the computer vision community [4,27,38]. Few-shot semantic segmentation targets at learning transferable knowledge by segmenting objects of seen categories to generalize to new categories of objects, where only a few annotated support images are available.

Most of the current few-shot segmentation methods [4,24,27,39,40] are based on prototype learning, employing a two-branch encoder-decoder architecture, i.e., a support branch and a query branch. The support branch is deployed to extract a class prototype from the support images and the query branch takes the prototype as guidance for segmenting the query image. To obtain this guidance, [21,35,40] adopted global average pooling by squeezing the support feature of the support image into a vector, and based the segmentation on a specific metric, e.g., cosine similarity, between the global vector and the feature map of the query image. However, the mask average pooling operation inevitably drops the spatial information of the support images, leading to a noisy output. To solve this problem, [38] established the pixel-to-pixel connection between support and query images by leveraging the graph attention mechanism [33,36]. Nonetheless, usually only a small region of the foreground object is activated in the support image due to the biased competition among the pixels, resulting in the connection between the support and query images being dominated by a small portion of pixels, largely limiting the information to be propagated. As illustrated in Fig. 1(a), only pixels on the head region of the bird are activated. This would lead to overfitting and reduced robustness when foreground objects are partially occluded.

Furthermore, previous methods always merge the prototype and the feature map from the query branch at the highest semantic level. However, both the low-level features and the high-level features are essential for the segmentation procedure. For instance, to precisely segment a car in a query image, we require the guidance of high-level prototypes such as wheel characteristic, as well as the low-level prototypical information, such as the surface texture. A single prototypical vector would not be able to fully capture these different levels of semantic information. Therefore, it becomes essential to explicitly explore and retain different semantic levels of the prototypical information in the support image for the segmentation of query images.

In this paper, to deal with the two aforementioned problems, we propose the Democratic Attention Network (DAN) for few-shot semantic segmentation. We introduce a democratized graph attention (DGA) mechanism to estab-

(a) Graph Attention   (b) Democratized Graph Attention

Fig. 1. Graph attention (a) vs. democratized graph attention (b). The regular graph attention (GA) mechanism makes the network attentive to a dominate regains (e.g., the head of the bird in this example), which compromises the model robustness to noise, e.g., occlusion. Our DGA mechanism enables more pixels to be activated, establishing robust connections between support and query images.

lish the pixel-to-pixel correspondence between support and query images. The idea is to suppress the connections with high weights, while enhancing those with lower weights during training. This endows the network with the ability to establish robust connections by attending to larger regions of the object instead of only small specific regions. As a result, pixels on the foreground object tend to be democratized to participate in the connections. In this way, the network can propagate more guiding information from support and query images for segmentation. Once trained, the model acquires the ability to leverage more pixels from the foreground object in the support images, which enhances its robustness to occlusion and generalizability to new objects. As shown in Fig. 1(b), our proposed DGA activates the larger regions, not only the bird's head region, resulting in a more robust connection, and thus making it insensitive to the partial occlusion of foreground objects in contrast to the regular graph attention [38].

Moreover, we propose a multi-scale guidance for the segmentation of query images by constructing a hierarchical graph attention to explore multi-level semantic information. Specifically, we apply the democratized graph attention mechanism to multiple intermediate feature layers in the encoder to establish the multi-level connection between query and support images. Coupled with the hierarchical graph, we design a refinement fusion unit in the decoder to fuse the multi-level attentive information with the corresponding feature layers of the query image in the decoder for improved segmentation.

We conduct extensive experiments on three benchmarks, i.e., the PASCAL-5^i [27], COCO-20^i [11] and FSS-1000 [37] datasets, for performance evaluation. To the best of our knowledge, this is the first work that provides performance evaluation on three datasets for few-shot segmentation. The proposed DAN largely surpasses previous state-of-the-art methods. Moreover, we perform thorough ablation studies to demonstrate the benefits of the proposed democratized graph attention and the multi-scale guidance, offering more insight into its great effectiveness for few-shot semantic segmentation.

The major contributions of this work are summarized as follows:

- We propose a new, democratic attention network (DAN) for few-shot semantic segmentation. The introduced democratized graph attention mechanism can activate more pixels on the foreground object, achieving stable correspondence between a support and query image. This enables more guiding information to be propagated from support to query images, enhancing robustness and generalizability to new objects.
- We introduce multi-scale guidance by designing a refinement fusion unit to efficiently fuse multi-level semantic information of the support image to improve the segmentation of query images.
- We achieve new state-of-the-art performance on three benchmarks, largely advancing the current performance of few-shot semantic segmentation.

2 Related Work

2.1 Semantic Segmentation

Semantic segmentation is one of the most popular tasks in computer vision, which aims to classify each pixel of an image into predefined categories. Previous works [1,2,16,26] are typically based on a fully convolutional network (FCN) [18]. FCN replaces the fully connected layer with the convolution layer, which facilitates dense prediction and thus improves segmentation performance. Ronneberger et al. [26] proposed an encoder-decoder structure to produce the segmentation map with high resolution, in which the encoder network was designed to capture abstract feature representations and the decoder network is used to map the low-resolution encoder feature maps to full input resolution feature maps for pixel-wise classification. However, the traditional fully supervised segmentation methods require large amounts of pixel-level annotated images for training, which are expensive and time consuming to obtain. Additionally, once the model is trained, it cannot be generalized to unseen categories of objects.

2.2 Few-Shot Learning

Few-shot learning, which learns new concepts from a few annotated examples, has recently generated great popularity. The existing few-show learning works focus on image classification tasks, aiming to predict image class labels given only a few training examples in each category. Few-shot learning has been investigated under the meta-learning framework by exploring shared metric/similarity space [30,32,34,41], or optimization algorithms [6,22,25]. Few shot learning has also been explored in video analysis [19,20]. Recently, few-shot classification has been extended to few-shot semantic segmentation [4], a more challenging task that aims to segment objects of unseen categories with limited annotated images.

2.3 Few-Shot Semantic Segmentation

Existing deep models for few-shot semantic segmentation are mainly built upon a two-branch structure [11,24,27,39,40] which includes a support branch and a query branch. The support branch aims to extract information from the support images, which could provide guidance to the query branch for predicting segmentation maps. Most previous prototypical methods [27,35,39,40] extract a global vector from the support images to learn a class representation with limited support images. For instance, Zhang et al. [40] proposed a global average pooling operation to obtain the global vector and utilized a cosine similarity to build the relationship between support and query images. The extracted global vector can be upsampled and concatenated with the feature map of the query image to produce the segmentation map [39]. However, squeezing the support images to a global descriptor does not retain the spatial structure of the support images, which is crucial for the segmentation task. To solve this problem, Zhang et al. [38] proposed the construction of graphs to establish element-to-element connections to propagate information from the support image to query images. However, due to the limited annotation, the connections tend to be dominated by a small portion of pixels in the support images, caused by the biased competition among pixels. This compromises the robustness of the final prediction and reduces the generalization to new object classes. Moreover, they built a pyramid structure by deploying adaptive average pooling to the query feature map at the same semantic level, while the pyramid query feature maps only attend to the last single feature map of the support image, which fails to utilize multi-level semantic features.

In this work, we introduce a democratized graph attention mechanism to establish robust pixel-to-pixel connections between support and query images without falling into the centralized problem. This endows the network with the ability to extract robust categorical information from support images by constraining the connections with high weights and enhancing the remaining part. Further, we propose the multi-scale guidance by constructing hierarchical graph attentions at intermediate layers of the encoder, which offers multiple levels of semantic information to better guide the segmentation of query images.

3   Democratic Attention Network

3.1   Problem Definition

For a k-shot semantic segmentation task, the goal is to train a model to perform segmentation on new classes with scarce annotated images. Suppose we are provided with two image sets D_{train} and D_{test}, where the D_{train} is used for training the model and the D_{test} is for evaluation. Note that, in contrast to conventional semantic segmentation, there is no overlap between the categories in D_{train} and those in D_{test}. Both the training set D_{train} and testing set D_{test} are composed of several episodes. Each episode contains a support set S and a query set Q, where $S = \{\mathbf{x}_i^s, \mathbf{m}_i^s\}_{i=1}^k$ contains k images $\mathbf{x}^s$ and corresponding binary masks

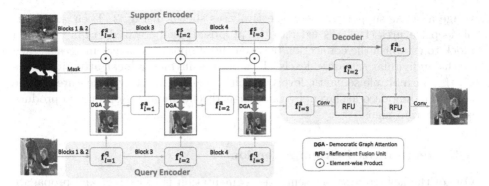

Fig. 2. Architecture of Democratic Attention Network (DAN) (illustrated in one-shot setting). Let $\{\mathbf{f}_l^s\}_{l=1}^L$ and $\{\mathbf{f}_l^q\}_{l=1}^L$ be the feature maps extracted in $L(=3)$ different layers of encoders for support and query images, respectively. The proposed democratized graph attention (DGA) mechanism is applied to those feature maps to establish the correspondence between support and query images. The obtained attentive feature maps $\{\mathbf{f}_l^a\}_{l=1}^L$ of different semantic levels are fed into the designed refinement fusion unit (RFU) to achieve multi-scale guidance for the segmentation of query images.

$\mathbf{m}^s$ for a certain category c, and $\mathcal{Q} = \{\mathbf{x}^q, \mathbf{m}^q\}$ contains query image $\mathbf{x}^q$ to be segmented and the associated ground truth mask $\mathbf{m}^q$.

The network is trained by episodically sampling support and query pairs from D_{train} to learn the mapping from $\{S, \mathbf{x}^q\}$ to the object mask $\mathbf{m}^q$. Note that once the network is learned, the mapping is fixed and requires no iterative optimization when tested on a test dataset D_{test}. The training procedure is set to be aligned with that of evaluation. Given a query image $\mathbf{x}^q$ and a support image-mask pair $(\mathbf{x}^s, \mathbf{m}^s)$ as input, our goal is to produce the segmentation map $\hat{\mathbf{m}}^q$ for query image.

3.2 Architecture Overview

As shown in Fig. 2, the proposed democratic attention network (DAN) is built upon a two-branch architecture, which is now widely used in existing few-shot segmentation networks [24,39,40]. We introduce two major innovative architectures into the two-branch network: (1) A democratized graph attention (DGA) mechanism is proposed to establish pixel-to-pixel connections between query and support images based on the graph attention. DGA constrains the connections with high weights while enhancing those with low weights during training, which endows the network with the ability to establish robust connections between support and query images. (2) We introduce a multi-scale guidance architecture by designing a refinement fusion unit, which enables multi-level semantic information into the guidance of segmenting query images.

To be more specific, we first deploy a weights-shared convolutional neural network as the feature extractor to acquire a sequence of deep features maps $(\{\mathbf{f}_l^q, \mathbf{f}_l^s\}_{l=1}^L)$ representing different semantic levels of information for the query image and the support image respectively, as shown in Fig. 2. Then, each pair of deep features $(\mathbf{f}_l^q, \mathbf{f}_l^s)$ is fed into the proposed democratized graph attention block to establish the connection between the support and query images at each of the individual semantic levels. This results in hierarchical attentive maps $\{\mathbf{f}_l^a\}_{l=1}^L$ in multiple semantic levels, which are finally fused with features in the corresponding decoder layers by the designed refinement fusion unit to produce segmentation maps.

3.3 Democratized Graph Attention

One of the keys to few-shot semantic segmentation is to extract and propagate object information from the support image to the query image. Instead of using a prototype vector that loses the essential structure information [28,39,40], we establish pixel-to-pixel dense connections between the query image and the support image based on the graph attention [33]. However, the connection provided by the regular graph attention mechanism tends to be dominated by the small most discriminative region, which is not robust and lacks generalizability to new classes of objects. We introduce the democratized graph attention (DGA) mechanism to enhance the robustness of the connection, which is easy to implement and effectively improve the performance. Moreover, in contrast to the graph attention in [38], we propose to construct a hierarchical graph based on multiple levels of semantic features, which enables more guiding information to be propagated from the support to query image for more accurate segmentation.

To be more specific, we establish the pixel-to-pixel correspondence between the query image and the support image at multiple intermediate layers of the encoder network by our democratized graph attention mechanism. In each intermediate layer, the DGA takes the feature map $\mathbf{f}^s$ from the support image and the feature map $\mathbf{f}^q$ from the query image as input. As shown in Fig. 3, two convolutional layers are applied to embed the feature maps $\mathbf{f}$ into key maps $\mathbf{k}$ and value maps $\mathbf{v}$ separately, where the $\mathbf{k}$ are used to measure the correspondence between query and support images, and the $\mathbf{v}$ restore the extracted detailed information of the feature maps. Once we obtain $\mathbf{k}^s$, $\mathbf{v}^s$ for the support image and $\mathbf{k}^q$, $\mathbf{v}^q$ for the query image, the pixel-wise connection is constructed by estimating the graph affinity between $\mathbf{k}^q$ and $\mathbf{k}^s$.

The graph affinity A is computed by measuring the similarities between all pixels of the query key map $\mathbf{k}^q$ and the support key map $\mathbf{k}^s$ with a pairwise function $g(\cdot, \cdot)$. The connection weight between the pixel i on the query image and the pixel j on the support image can be denoted as:

$$A_{i,j} = g\left(\mathbf{k}_i^q, \mathbf{k}_j^s\right) = (\mathbf{k}_i^q)^\top \times \mathbf{k}_j^s. \tag{1}$$

By applying $g(\cdot, \cdot)$ to each of the pixel pairs between the query and support image, we obtain the connection graph $A \in \mathbb{R}^{HW \times HW}$. We take the average of the graph affinity A across the first dimension to produce the attention map for the support image $A^s = \sum_{i=1}^{HW} A_i \in \mathbb{R}^{H \times W}$, in which the value measures the average connection weights between each pixel in the support image and all pixels

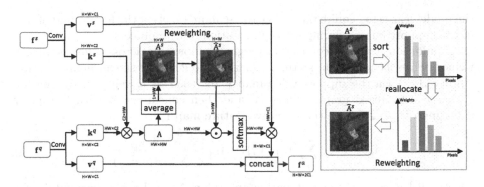

Fig. 3. Decentralized Graph Attention (DGA). The DGA weighs down the highly activated regions during training, which enables the network to leverage more informative pixels on the object for improved segmentation during testing.

in the query image. The attention map A^s generally reflects the importance of pixels in the support image in guiding the segmentation of objects on the query image. However, in the regular graph attention, activated pixels tend to fall in a small discriminative region, which dominates the connections. As shown in Fig. 3, the most of the connection weights gather on the head of the bird, caused by the biased competition among the support pixels, which limits the information to be propagated from the support to query image.

To guarantee the generalization to new objects of great variations, it is desired to leverage as many pixels as possible on the annotated object of the support image. To this end, we design a new, democratized graph attention mechanism to establish better attention maps. Specifically, we propose sorting and reallocating the affinities of each pixel in A^s during training. We sort the pixels of A^s in descending order and acquire the sorting index $\mathbf{e}_j$ for each pixel j, and then we reallocate the connection weights to pixel j according to the corresponding index by the function $\phi(A^s_j, \mathbf{e})$.

$$\hat{A}^s_j = \phi(A^s_j, \mathbf{e}) = A^s_j \times \frac{\mathbf{e}_j}{\frac{1}{HW}\sum_{j=1}^{HW} \mathbf{e}_j}, \tag{2}$$

where the H, W indicate the height and width of A^s. After this operation, the pixels with high connection weights are suppressed so that the other part of pixels are enhanced as shown in Fig. 3, where the body of the bird are activated. The reconstructed attention map $\hat{A}^s$ is used to compute the weighted graph affinity:

$$\hat{A}_{i,j} = g\left(\mathbf{k}^q_i, \mathbf{k}^s_j \cdot \hat{A}^s_j\right) = (\mathbf{k}^q_i)^{\mathrm{T}} \times (\mathbf{k}^s_j \cdot \hat{A}^s_j). \tag{3}$$

The activated pixels will expand to less discriminative regions of the foreground object and more pixels will contribute to the information propagation, which gains more robustness and generalization ability. In a similar spirit to dropout [31], the DGA is only applied to a portion of samples during training. As a result, the model learns to acquire the ability to use more pixels of the foreground object in the support images during the segmentation of new objects.

In addition, to make connection weights comparable across different pixels, we normalize them with the softmax function and generate the normalized graph affinity $\hat{A}'$. Then the support value map $\mathbf{v}^s$ is fused by a weighted summation with the normalized graph affinity $\hat{A}'$ and then concatenated with the query value map $\mathbf{v}^q$ to generate the attentive feature map $\mathbf{f}^a$:

$$\mathbf{f}_i^a = \{\mathbf{v}_i^q \| \sum_j \hat{A}'_{i,j} \cdot \mathbf{v}_j^s\}, \quad \hat{A}'_{i,j} = \frac{\exp(\hat{A}_{i,j})}{\sum_j \exp(\hat{A}_{i,j})}, \tag{4}$$

where $\{\cdot\|\cdot\}$ denotes the concatenation operation. Note that once we obtain the output attentive feature map of position i, the other positions could also be computed by applying the same operations as above.

3.4   Multi-scale Guidance

The other key step is to fully utilize the information extracted from the support image to guide the segmentation of query images. We apply the DGA blocks at the different semantic levels to generate multiple attentive feature maps $\{\mathbf{f}_l^a\}_{l=1}^L$ that contain different levels of semantic information of the foreground object. To efficiently leverage these attentive feature maps, we design a refinement fusion unit to fuse the multi-level information in $\{\mathbf{f}_l^a\}_{l=1}^L$ with the corresponding decoder layers in a sequential manner.

As shown in Fig. 2, the refinement fusion unit in the decoder network upsamples its input representation map using a bi-linear upsampling operation and the obtained representation map is concatenated with the corresponding attentive feature map processed by a residual block. The concatenated feature map is then processed by a convolutional block to produce a dense representation map. The deepest output of the final refinement fusion unit is fed into a convolutional layer and a softmax operation is applied to distinguish each pixel independently. The output of the softmax layer is a two-channel map of probabilities that indicate foreground and background, respectively. We obtain the predicted segmentation map of the query image by taking the label of the corresponding class with a maximum probability at each pixel.

4   Experiments

Implementation Details. The backbone architecture employed in our segmentation network is a resnet101 [10] that is pre-trained on ImageNet [3]. The loss function is the mean of cross-entropy loss over all pixel locations in the output segmentation map. The model is trained end-to-end by the Adam optimizer [13] using a batch size of 4 for 50000 iterations on an GeForce RTX 2080 Ti GPU. The learning rate is fixed to 1e-5 during training. We conduct multi-scale inference, where the scale rates are set to $\{0.5, 1, 1.5\}$ for both query and support images. For the k-shot setting, we concatenate the key maps and value maps produced by individual shots and acquire unified key and value maps.

Evaluation Metrics. We take the commonly-used evaluation metrics, Mean-IoU and FB-IoU, to benchmark with previous methods. Mean-IoU in [27] is defined as the average per-class foreground Intersection-over-Union (IoU) over all classes, i.e., IoU $= \frac{tp}{tp+fp+fn}$, where tp is the number of true positives, fp is the number of false positives and fn is the number of false negatives over the set of this category. In contrast, FB-IoU [24] ignores the difference among the object categories and regards all the categories as foreground class, and then averages the IoU of foreground and background over all test images.

Fig. 4. Visualization of segmentation results on Pascal-5^i. Our DAN can make accurate segmentation even when query objects exhibit great variations from support ones.

4.1 PASCAL-5^i

The PASCAL-5^i dataset combines images from the PASCAL VOC 2012 [5] and extra annotations from SDS [7]. We follow the dataset division in [27], in which the original 20 object classes in the official resealed order of PASCAL VOC are evenly divided into four folds and conduct cross-validation over all the folds.

Table 1. Performance comparison on PASCAL-5^i.

Methods	Mean-IoU(1-shot)					FB-IoU	Mean-IoU(5-shot)					FB-IoU
	s-0	s-1	s-2	s-3	Mean	(1-shot)	s-0	s-1	s-2	s-3	Mean	(5-shot)
OSLSM [27]	33.6	55.3	40.9	33.5	40.8	61.3	35.9	58.1	42.7	39.1	43.9	61.5
co-FCN [24]	36.7	50.6	44.9	32.4	41.1	60.1	37.5	50.0	44.1	33.9	41.4	60.2
AMP-2 [28]	41.9	50.2	46.7	34.7	43.4	61.9	40.3	55.3	49.9	40.1	46.4	62.1
SG-One [40]	40.2	58.4	48.4	38.4	46.3	63.1	41.9	58.6	48.6	39.4	47.1	65.9
PANet [35]	42.3	58.0	51.1	41.2	48.1	66.5	51.8	64.6	59.8	46.5	55.7	70.7
CANet [39]	52.5	65.9	51.3	51.9	55.4	66.2	55.5	67.8	51.9	53.2	57.1	69.6
PGNet [38]	**56.0**	66.9	50.6	50.4	56.0	69.9	57.7	68.7	52.9	54.6	58.5	70.5
FWB [21]	51.3	64.5	56.7	**52.2**	56.2	–	54.8	67.4	**62.2**	**55.3**	59.9	–
DAN (Ours)	54.7	**68.6**	**57.8**	51.6	**58.2**	**71.9**	**57.9**	**69.0**	60.1	54.9	**60.5**	**72.3**

Specifically, 15 object categories are used during training while the remaining 5 are used for testing for each fold. Following the settings in [27], we use 1000 support-query pairs of test support-query images for each test class.

We compare our proposed DAN with the state-of-the-art methods. As shown in Table 1, our DAN significantly outperforms all previous models under both 1-shot and 5-shot settings by large margins. Specifically, in the 1-shot setting, DAN achieves 58.2% and 71.9% in terms of Mean-IoU and FB-IoU, respectively. DAN outperforms the state-of-the-art graph-based method [38] by 2.2% in the Mean-IoU metric and 2.0% in the FB-IoU metric, which demonstrates the great benefit of our democratized graph attention mechanism. A comparison of 5-shot results is shown in Table 1, where we can see that our DAN achieves the highest performance under both evaluation metrics. Figure 4 shows some qualitative segmentation maps produced by the DAN. As can be seen, our DAN can produce accurate segmentation maps in challenging cases where the objects in the query images show great variations in both size and appearance from the annotated objects in the support images.

4.2   COCO-20^i

The COCO-20^i dataset is created for evaluation from a more challenging dataset MSCOCO [17]. The scenes in MSCOCO are more complex and the number of the categories is much higher than PASCAL-5^i. Similarly to Pascal-5^i, the 80 object categories in MSCOCO are evenly divided into four splits for cross-validation. For each split, 20 classes are sampled for testing and the remaining 60 classes are utilized for training. 1000 support-query pairs of support-query images are sampled from the 20 test classes for testing on each split.

The comparison results with previous methods are reported in Table 2. In the 1-shot setting, our DAN produces a new state-of-the-art performance, which is significantly better than the previous methods by 3.5% and 3.1% in terms of Mean-IoU and FB-IoU, respectively. The performance improvement obtained by our DAN demonstrate its great capability of handling complex scenes. In the 5-shot setting, our DAN also achieves comparable performance with the state-of-the-art method [35]. We show some qualitative visualizations in Fig. S1. Our DAN can perform very well in challenging cases. For instance, in the first and seventh cases, the objects in the query images are much smaller than those in their support images, while our DAN is still able to predict accurate segmentation maps; in the second case, the appearance of the object in query image is significantly different from that in the support image, but our DAN can still produce a segmentation result close to the ground truth.

4.3   FSS-1000

The FSS-1000 dataset contains 1000 object classes, a significant number of which have never been seen in previous datasets. Following [37], the 1000 categories are divided into three splits for training, validation and testing. The training/validation/test splits consist of 520/240/240 classes, respectively. There are only 10 support-query pairs in each category. Note that the metric on FSS-1000 is the Intersection-over-Union of positive labels (P-IoU) in binary segmentation maps as in [37]. The comparison results are shown in Table 3. As can be seen, our DAN achieves the best performance in both 1-shot and 5-shot settings, with P-IoUs of 85.2% and 88.1%, respectively, largely surpassing the previous best performance. The improvement is over 10% in the 1-shot setting, showing the great performance advantage.

Table 2. Performance comparison on COCO-20^i.

Methods	1-shot		5-shot	
	Mean	FB	Mean	FB
A-MCG [11]	–	52.0	–	54.7
FWB [21]	21.2	–	23.7	–
PANet [35]	20.9	59.2	**29.7**	63.5
DAN (Ours)	**24.4**	**62.3**	29.6	**63.9**

Table 3. Performance comparison on FSS-1000.

Methods	P-IoU	
	1-shot	5-shot
OSLSM [27]	70.3	73.0
GNet [23]	71.9	74.3
FSS [37]	73.5	80.1
DAN (Ours)	**85.2**	**88.1**

4.4 Ablation Study

We conduct extensive ablation experiments on PASCAL-5^i, results of which are reported as the average of the four folds under the Mean-IoU metric.

Backbone Network. To evaluate the influence of different backbones, we experiment with two backbone models used in previous works: ResNet-50 [38,39] and ResNet-101 [21]. The Table 4 shows the results of DAN with ResNet-50 and ResNet-101 on PASCAL-5^i.

Table 4. Results of our DAN with different backbones on PASCAL-5^i.

Backbone	Mean-IoU	
	1-shot	5-shot
ResNet-50	57.1	59.5
ResNet-101	58.2	60.5

Table 5. Influence of multi-scale evaluation on PASCAL-5^i.

Model	Mean-IoU	
	1-shot	5-shot
DAN w/o MS	57.5	60.1
DAN w/ MS	58.2	60.5

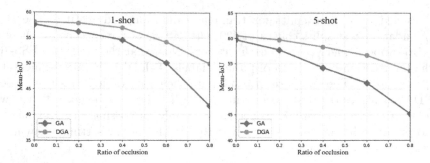

Fig. 5. Performance under different ratios of occlusion. The proposed DGA performs much better than the regular GA under occlusion.

Benefit of Democratized Graph Attention. To illustrate the improvement brought by the Democratized Graph Attention, we implement a baseline model with the regular graph attention (GA) mechanism used in PGNet [38]. We progressively mask the support images by different proportions, as shown in Fig. 6, and evaluate the Mean-IoU performance under different ratios of invisible support images. Figure 5 shows a comparison between the models with DGA and GA under different ratios of occlusion, from 0 to 0.8. Note that the result of ratio 0 is on original PASCAL-5^i. The Mean-IoU of the GA model drops rapidly from 56.6% to 41.7% in the 1-shot setting, while our proposed DGA shows relatively stable performance, dropping from just 58.1% to 49.9%. Particularly, when the occlusion rate reaches 0.8, DGA outperforms the GA with a large margin of 8.2%. This indicates the vital role of our democratized graph attention mechanism in establishing robust connections between pixels of the support and query images, resulting in more robust segmentation maps.

We show the segmentation maps with different ratios of occlusion in Fig. 6. As can be seen, the activated regions in the attention map provided by the proposed DGA are much larger than those provided by the regular GA. This makes our DGA more robust to the partial occlusion of support objects. With the increase of occlusion ratios, the performance of GA declines rapidly, while the DGA is not affected much. In particular, the regular GA misses segmenting some of the foreground objects (left) or fails to segment the whole object (right), while our DGA is still able to successfully segment all the objects (left) and most parts of the object (right).

Benefit of Multi-scale Guidance. To demonstrate the benefit of multi-scale guidance, we conduct experiments on our DAN in which we gradually remove different levels of guidance. In Table 6, we compare the performance of the variants of the models with different levels of guidance. We can see that the more levels of information used, the better the performance. The performance reaches its highest when all levels are used. It is worth mentioning that multi-scale guidance offers more benefit in the 1-shot than 5-shot setting. This is

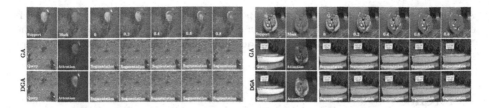

Fig. 6. One-shot segmentation maps under different ratios of occlusion. The DGA is more robust to occlusion than the regular GA.

Table 6. Benefit of multi-scale guidance. The performance is largely improved by the proposed multi-scale guidance, especially in the 1-shot setting.

Level 1	Level 2	Level 3	Mean-IoU	
			1-shot	5-shot
		✓	56.4	59.2
	✓	✓	57.8	60.2
✓		✓	56.9	59.7
✓	✓	✓	**58.2**	**60.5**

because, in the 1-shot setting, we have only one support image, from which our multi-scale guidance can extract more guiding information for segmentation.

Multi-scale Inference. We test the performance with multi-scale inference, which is adopted in [38,39]. Specifically, we rescale the query image by $\{0.5, 1, 1.5\}$ and average the predicted results. As shown in Table 5, multi-scale inference brings 0.7% and 0.4% improvements in 1-shot and 5-shot settings, respectively.

5 Conclusion

In this paper, we propose a new, democratic attention network (DAN) for few-shot semantic segmentation. We introduce a democratized graph attention mechanism to endow the network with the ability to establish robust connection between support and query images. Furthermore, we propose a multi-scale guidance structure by exploiting multiple levels of semantic information from the support images to guide the segmentation of query images. Extensive experiments on three benchmark datasets show that our DAN significantly outperforms previous works and achieves a new state-of-the-art performance. Thorough ablation studies demonstrate the benefits of the proposed democratized attention mechanism and multi-scale guidance for few-shot semantic segmentation.

Acknowledgments. This work was supported in part by the National Natural Science Foundation of China (NSFC) under grant NO. 91738301, 61871016, and the National Key Scientific Instrument and Equipment Development Project under Grant NO. 61827901.

References

1. Badrinarayanan, V., Kendall, A., Cipolla, R.: Segnet: a deep convolutional encoder-decoder architecture for image segmentation. IEEE Trans. Pattern Anal. Mach. Intell. **39**(12), 2481–2495 (2017)
2. Chen, L.C., Papandreou, G., Kokkinos, I., Murphy, K., Yuille, A.L.: Deeplab: semantic image segmentation with deep convolutional nets, atrous convolution, and fully connected CRFS. IEEE Trans. Pattern Anal. Mach. Intell. **40**(4), 834–848 (2017)
3. Deng, J., Dong, W., Socher, R., Li, L.J., Li, K., Fei-Fei, L.: Imagenet: a large-scale hierarchical image database. In: Proceedings of the IEEE Conference on Computer Vision and Pattern Recognition, pp. 248–255. IEEE (2009)
4. Dong, N., Xing, E.: Few-shot semantic segmentation with prototype learning. In: British Machine Vision Conference, vol. 1, p. 6 (2018)
5. Everingham, M., Van Gool, L., Williams, C.K., Winn, J., Zisserman, A.: The pascal visual object classes (VOC) challenge. Int. J. Comput. Vis. **88**(2), 303–338 (2010). https://doi.org/10.1007/2Fs11263-009-0275-4
6. Finn, C., Abbeel, P., Levine, S.: Model-agnostic meta-learning for fast adaptation of deep networks. In: Proceedings of the 34th International Conference on Machine Learning-Volume 70, pp. 1126–1135. JMLR. org (2017)
7. Hariharan, B., Arbeláez, P., Bourdev, L., Maji, S., Malik, J.: Semantic contours from inverse detectors. In: Proceedings of the International Conference on Computer Vision, pp. 991–998. IEEE (2011)
8. He, K., Gkioxari, G., Dollár, P., Girshick, R.: Mask R-CNN. In: Proceedings of the IEEE International Conference on Computer Vision, pp. 2961–2969 (2017)
9. He, K., Zhang, X., Ren, S., Sun, J.: Deep residual learning for image recognition. In: Proceedings of the IEEE conference on Computer Vision and Pattern Recognition, pp. 770–778 (2016)
10. He, K., Zhang, X., Ren, S., Sun, J.: Deep residual learning for image recognition. In: Proceedings of the IEEE Computer Society Conference on Computer Vision and Pattern Recognition (2016)
11. Hu, T., Yang, P., Zhang, C., Yu, G., Mu, Y., Snoek, C.G.: Attention-based multi-context guiding for few-shot semantic segmentation (2019)
12. Hu, Y., Yang, Y., Zhang, J., Cao, X., Zhen, X.: Attentional kernel encoding networks for fine-grained visual categorization. IEEE Trans. Circ. Syst. Video Technol. (2020)
13. Kingma, D., Ba, J.: Adam: a method for stochastic optimization. In: International Conference on Learning Representations (2014)
14. Krizhevsky, A., Sutskever, I., Hinton, G.E.: Imagenet classification with deep convolutional neural networks. In: Advances in Neural Information Processing Systems, pp. 1097–1105 (2012)
15. Lin, G., Milan, A., Shen, C., Reid, I.: Refinenet: multi-path refinement networks for high-resolution semantic segmentation. In: Proceedings of the IEEE conference on Computer Vision and Pattern Recognition, pp. 1925–1934 (2017)

16. Lin, G., Shen, C., Van Den Hengel, A., Reid, I.: Efficient piecewise training of deep structured models for semantic segmentation. In: Proceedings of the IEEE conference on Computer Vision and Pattern Recognition, pp. 3194–3203 (2016)

17. Lin, T.-Y., et al.: Microsoft coco: common objects in context. In: Fleet, D., Pajdla, T., Schiele, B., Tuytelaars, T. (eds.) ECCV 2014. LNCS, vol. 8693, pp. 740–755. Springer, Cham (2014). https://doi.org/10.1007/978-3-319-10602-1_48

18. Long, J., Shelhamer, E., Darrell, T.: Fully convolutional networks for semantic segmentation. In: Proceedings of the IEEE conference on Computer Vision and Pattern Recognition, pp. 3431–3440 (2015)

19. Lu, X., Wang, W., Ma, C., Shen, J., Shao, L., Porikli, F.: See more, know more: unsupervised video object segmentation with co-attention siamese networks. In: CVPR, pp. 3623–3632 (2019)

20. Lu, X., Wang, W., Shen, J., Tai, Y.W., Crandall, D.J., Hoi, S.C.: Learning video object segmentation from unlabeled videos. In: CVPR, pp. 8960–8970 (2020)

21. Nguyen, K., Todorovic, S.: Feature weighting and boosting for few-shot segmentation. In: Proceedings of the IEEE International Conference on Computer Vision, pp. 622–631 (2019)

22. Nichol, A., Schulman, J.: Reptile: a scalable metalearning algorithm. arXiv preprint arXiv:1803.02999 2, 2 (2018)

23. Rakelly, K., Shelhamer, E., Darrell, T., Efros, A.A., Levine, S.: Few-shot segmentation propagation with guided networks. arXiv preprint arXiv:1806.07373 (2018)

24. Rakelly, K., Shelhamer, E., Darrell, T., Efros, A., Levine, S.: Conditional networks for few-shot semantic segmentation (2018)

25. Ravi, S., Larochelle, H.: Optimization as a model for few-shot learning. In: International Conference on Learning Representations (2017)

26. Ronneberger, O., Fischer, P., Brox, T.: U-Net: convolutional networks for biomedical image segmentation. In: Navab, N., Hornegger, J., Wells, W.M., Frangi, A.F. (eds.) MICCAI 2015. LNCS, vol. 9351, pp. 234–241. Springer, Cham (2015). https://doi.org/10.1007/978-3-319-24574-4_28

27. Shaban, A., Bansal, S., Liu, Z., Essa, I., Boots, B.: One-shot learning for semantic segmentation. In: British Machine Vision Conference (2017)

28. Siam, M., Oreshkin, B.N., Jagersand, M.: AMP: adaptive masked proxies for few-shot segmentation. In: Proceedings of the IEEE International Conference on Computer Vision, pp. 5249–5258 (2019)

29. Simonyan, K., Zisserman, A.: Very deep convolutional networks for large-scale image recognition. arXiv preprint arXiv:1409.1556 (2014)

30. Snell, J., Swersky, K., Zemel, R.: Prototypical networks for few-shot learning. In: Advances in Neural Information Processing Systems, pp. 4077–4087 (2017)

31. Srivastava, N., Hinton, G., Krizhevsky, A., Sutskever, I., Salakhutdinov, R.: Dropout: a simple way to prevent neural networks from overfitting. J. Mach. Learn. Res. 15, 1929–1958 (2014)

32. Sung, F., Yang, Y., Zhang, L., Xiang, T., Torr, P.H., Hospedales, T.M.: Learning to compare: Relation network for few-shot learning. In: Proceedings of the IEEE conference on Computer Vision and Pattern Recognition, pp. 1199–1208 (2018)

33. Veličković, P., Cucurull, G., Casanova, A., Romero, A., Liò, P., Bengio, Y.: Graph attention networks. In: Proceedings of the International Conference on Learning Representations (2018)

34. Vinyals, O., Blundell, C., Lillicrap, T., Wierstra, D., et al.: Matching networks one shot learning. In: Advances in Neural Information Processing Systems, pp. 3630–3638 (2016)

35. Wang, K., Liew, J.H., Zou, Y., Zhou, D., Feng, J.: Panet: few-shot image semantic segmentation with prototype alignment. In: Proceedings of the IEEE International Conference on Computer Vision, pp. 9197–9206 (2019)
36. Wang, X., Girshick, R., Gupta, A., He, K.: Non-local neural networks. In: Proceedings of the IEEE conference on Computer Vision and Pattern Recognition, pp. 7794–7803 (2018)
37. Wei, T., Li, X., Chen, Y.P., Tai, Y.W., Tang, C.K.: Fss-1000: a 1000-class dataset for few-shot segmentation. arXiv preprint arXiv:1907.12347 (2019)
38. Zhang, C., Lin, G., Liu, F., Guo, J., Wu, Q., Yao, R.: Pyramid graph networks with connection attentions for region-based one-shot semantic segmentation. In: Proceedings of the IEEE International Conference on Computer Vision, pp. 9587–9595 (2019)
39. Zhang, C., Lin, G., Liu, F., Yao, R., Shen, C.: Canet: class-agnostic segmentation networks with iterative refinement and attentive few-shot learning. In: Proceedings of the IEEE conference on Computer Vision and Pattern Recognition, pp. 5217–5226 (2019)
40. Zhang, X., Wei, Y., Yang, Y., Huang, T.: Sg-one: similarity guidance network for one-shot semantic segmentation. arXiv preprint arXiv:1810.09091 (2018)
41. Zhen, X., et al.: Learning to learn kernels with variational random features. In: International Conference on Machine Learning (2020)

Defocus Blur Detection via Depth Distillation

Xiaodong Cun and Chi-Man Pun$^{(\boxtimes)}$

University of Macau, Macau, China
{yb87432,cmpun}@umac.mo

Abstract. Defocus Blur Detection (DBD) aims to separate in-focus and out-of-focus regions from a single image pixel-wisely. This task has been paid much attention since bokeh effects are widely used in digital cameras and smartphone photography. However, identifying obscure homogeneous regions and borderline transitions in partially defocus images is still challenging. To solve these problems, we introduce depth information into DBD for the first time. When the camera parameters are fixed, we argue that the accuracy of DBD is highly related to scene depth. Hence, we consider the depth information as the approximate soft label of DBD and propose a joint learning framework inspired by knowledge distillation. In detail, we learn the defocus blur from ground truth and the depth distilled from a well-trained depth estimation network at the same time. Thus, the sharp region will provide a strong prior for depth estimation while the blur detection also gains benefits from the distilled depth. Besides, we propose a novel decoder in the fully convolutional network (FCN) as our network structure. In each level of the decoder, we design the Selective Reception Field Block (SRFB) for merging multiscale features efficiently and reuse the side outputs as Supervision-guided Attention Block (SAB). Unlike previous methods, the proposed decoder builds reception field pyramids and emphasizes salient regions simply and efficiently. Experiments show that our approach outperforms 11 other state-of-the-art methods on two popular datasets. Our method also runs at over 30 fps on a single GPU, which is 2x faster than previous works. The code is available at: https://github.com/vinthony/depth-distillation.

Keywords: Defocus blur detection · Attention module · Knowledge distillation

1 Introduction

Defocus blur, which is also called the bokeh effect in photography, has been widely used in everyday photos. The focus region emphasizes the salient object

Electronic supplementary material The online version of this chapter (https://doi.org/10.1007/978-3-030-58601-0_44) contains supplementary material, which is available to authorized users.

© Springer Nature Switzerland AG 2020
A. Vedaldi et al. (Eds.): ECCV 2020, LNCS 12358, pp. 747–763, 2020.
https://doi.org/10.1007/978-3-030-58601-0_44

while the out-of-focus blur can protect the privacy of people appearing in the photo. Moreover, detecting this kind of blur is also crucial since the detected defocus region could be potentially useful in performing tasks. Such tasks include auto-refocus [1], salient object detection [14] and image retargeting [15].

Since DBD has a long history in computer vision [8,27,32,32,40], traditional methods focus on designing novel hand-crafted features such as the gradient [8, 39] or the frequency domain features [32,33,40]. However, these methods extract limited features and lack high-level semantic information. Thus, if the scene is complex, it is hard to discriminate the defocus region by particular features.

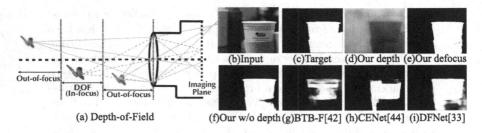

(a) Depth-of-Field   (f)Our w/o depth (g)BTB-F[42] (h)CENet[44] (i)DFNet[33]

Fig. 1. We first leverage depth into DBD since predicting defocus blur is similar to estimating the *Depth-of-Field* (DOF) from a partial defocus image as in (a). By involving depth in DBD network, our method assumes that the depths in DOF regions are similar(d) and that the region with more similar depths might be part of DOF/out-of-focus region as well(e). Thus, we obtain more accurate results than other DBD methods (f)-(i). (Color figure online)

Recently, deep learning-based methods have shown superior performance in various computer vision tasks as well as defocus blur detection. For example, Park *et al.* [27] train a CNN to classify the sharpness of each local patch in an image. Deeper fully convolutional methods [34,43–45] have been proposed by regarding the DBD as scene segmentation. Although these methods emphasize the importance of image scales in DBD, they are still considering DBD from a 2D perspective and rely solely on the power of the datasets and neural network.

In this paper, we start from the cause of defocus blur in the photography. As shown in Fig. 1(a), the sharp focus region, also called the depth-of-field (DOF [35]), is formed because the camera only images clear photo in a certain depth range[1]. When the light waves intersect behind or in front of the imaging plane (red and green lines in Fig. 1(a)), the area they originated from will be blurred in final image. Since the homogeneous region in DBD often includes multiple objects and since it is difficult to be detected by edges or semantic features, the distance between the camera and scene objects (depth) provides a strong prior for classification. However, the unconstrained depth estimation is an ill-posed problem. To evaluate on currently available DBD datasets and provide

---

[1] We simplify this model by ignoring the influence of camera parameters since we can only obtain a 2D RGB image in the dataset.

fair comparison with previous methods, we propose depth distillation by using a pre-trained network [3] as regularization and learn the defocus map simultaneously. In addition, we design a Supervision-guided Attention Block (SAB) for re-weighting the learned features based on each level of side outputs. Finally, the blur confidence is relative, which means *a sharp patch can be regarded as blurry when we enlarge it and vice versa.* Although previous methods [34,43,44] have discussed it by multi-stream or cross-layer fusion networks, we consider it in an efficient way by designing Selective Reception Field Block (SRFB) in each decoder. Our block extracts larger reception fields to build richer feature pyramids and uses a global selective attention to weight the importance of useful features. By involving depth estimation into DBD and the proposed blocks, our network outperforms other methods on the defocus detection. As shown in Fig. 1 (b)-(i), previous methods for DBD are sensitive to color, while in our network, DBD and depth estimation tasks build on each other and predict the results perfectly.

We summarize the contributions of this paper as follows:

- To the best of our knowledge, this is the first attempt to introduce depth information in DBD and distill the knowledge of pre-trained depth model as regularization of DBD network.
- In each decoder of our framework, we design the Supervision-guided Attention Block (SAB), which reuses the side depth and defocus map for spatial attention. Considering the sensitivity of scale, we also design the Selective Reception Fields Block (SRFB) to extract multiple reception field features.
- We conduct the experiments on two popular DBD benchmarks with 11 state-of-the-art methods (7 from DBD and 4 from related tasks). The results show that our proposed method can achieve much better results.

2   Related Works

Traditional Methods. Out-of-focus and DOF regions have significant visible differences in sharpness. Thus, traditional DBD methods are designed based on identifiable hand-crafted features such as gradient or edge representation [16,32]. For example, Yi *et al.* [40] use local binary patterns as focus sharpness metric. Shi *et al.* [33] use sparse representation to correlate the sparse edges and blur strength. Frequency-based methods are another noticeable trend in hand-crafted features, since the high-frequency components of the in-focus region and out-of-focus region are different. For example, Golestaneh *et al.* [8] use multi-scale high-frequency fusion and sort transform to determine the magnitudes of gradients. Although the methods based on hand-crafted features have been demonstrated to be effective in some cases, these methods are not robust enough in a broader variety of complex scenes.

Learning-Based Methods. Deep neural networks, especially CNNs, are widely used in many computer vision and image processing tasks. Park *et al.* [27] propose the first CNN based method to DBD by combining the hand-crafted features and pre-trained deep features together. In this method, the image is scanned in a patch-by-path manner to find the defocus blur. Inspired by the object detection and segmentation methods, Zhao *et al.* [43,44] firstly use the full convolutional network-based method by considering DBD to be sensitive to scale. Following this idea, Tang *et al.* [34] design a novel network structure for feature fusion and Zhao *et al.* [45] ensemble multiple networks to enhance diversity. In contrast to previous studies, Lee *et al.* [18] address the lack of datasets by learning from synthesized rendered dataset with domain adaptation. However, previous learning-based methods only focus on learning with stronger networks [43–45] or dataset [18].

Depth Estimation and Depth-Assisted Methods. Estimating the depth from a single image is ill-defined since inferring 3D information requires multi-views. However, monocular depth estimation in restricted scenes is possible, for example, with indoor scenes [5] or the road in a driving context [6,7]. In contrast, predicting the depth in the wild is still a challenge. Chen *et al.* [3] propose an end-to-end network based on point relationships. However, this network only predicts relations between the objects other than absolute depth. Li *et al.* [20] generate the multi-view disparity of humans from video of people who are frozen in place, and this task only works when the person are in the scene. Depth also plays an important role in other tasks. Most methods consider the depth to be known by the sensor. Such as RGB-D object detection [29] and RGB-D salient object detection [28]. Some methods exploit the knowledge of depth in related tasks, such as depth-assisted view synthesis [4] and depth attentional features for deraining [12].

3   Methods

We define DBD as a supervised pixel-wise binary classification problem. Rather than considering the defocus region as positive, we learn the opposite DOF (in-focus) region as previously [43–45]. Given the input image I and the corresponding ground truth DOF region M, we construct a deep convolutional network $\Phi(\cdot;\theta)$ by feeding the image I to generate the DBD maps $\Phi_{df}(I)$ and depth maps $\Phi_{dp}(I)$. Then, we optimize the parameters θ of Φ to minimize the defocus metrics L_{df} and depth metrics L_{dp}:

$$\arg\min_{\theta} L_{df}(M, \Phi_{df}(I;\theta)) + L_{dp}(\Re(I), \Phi_{dp}(I;\theta)) \tag{1}$$

where $\Re$ is a pre-trained depth estimation network [3] for depth distillation. Below, we introduce the details of depth distillation, network structure and metrics.

3.1   Depth Distillation

In general, knowledge distillation [9,24] aims to transfer the knowledge for network structure optimization. In detail, as shown in Fig. 2(a), they regularize the

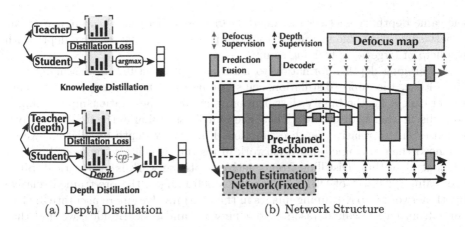

(a) Depth Distillation   (b) Network Structure

Fig. 2. (a)Comparison with knowledge distillation and the proposed depth distillation. (b)Our network structure. Under FCN framework, we distill the depth information from a pre-trained depth estimation network [3] and design novel decoders for DBD and depth estimation jointly.

compact (student) model using a larger (teacher) network in the space of **continuous** soft label(the output of Softmax), other than transferring the knowledge using predicted **discrete** hard targets.

Interestingly, we find that DBD(**discrete, classification task**) and depth estimation (**continuous, regression task**) have a similar relationship with that between hard and soft labels in knowledge distillation. In photography, the sharp focus region (DOF) is mathematically defined as [25]: $DOF \approx \frac{2NCD^2}{f^2}$, where N is the F-number of lenses, C is the circle of confusion and f is the focal length, respectively. The depth D is the only one which is not the camera parameter (cp). Thus, as shown in Fig. 2(a), we propose *depth distillation* to help defocus blur detection. In detail, we consider that the depth is the approximate soft label and distill the depth information from a pre-trained network as regularization of DBD. Instead of calculating the DOF from depth map directly and inferring the defocus map as knowledge distillation, our network can predict the defocus map and distill depth jointly because the camera parameters are unavailable. Although the structure of depth distillation and knowledge distillation are similar, the goal is totally different: We aim to involve the 3D information into DBD task other than distilling a compact model from teacher network. For implementation, we design a simple yet effective framework to achieve previous analysis. As shown in Fig. 2(b), we generate multiple outputs for depth estimation, which are supervised by a pre-trained network. Then, we fuse all the side outputs to obtain the final depth through a fusion (1×1 Conv.) block. However, single image depth estimation is ill-posed since the dense depth is hard to be collected especially in unconstrained settings. Thus, we choose the relative depth network (Chen *et al.* [3]) as teacher network. Specifically, they aim to learn the relationships between scene objects other than accurate depth values. Thus, they label the spatial relationship between 800 pairs of points (e.g., point A, B share the same depth, A is closer to camera than B and vice versa) pre-image as the supervision. Then, the neural network can predict the dense relative depth with the help of large-scale training samples.

Leveraging depth information to DBD as depth distillation has many benefits. First, the depth distillation helps our network to understand the scenes better except for the binary classification (similar to the relationships in knowledge distillation as discussed). Then, the blurriness region in the input also gives a dense hint to relative depth estimation. Finally, by depth distillation, we do not need the pre-trained depth network in testing, which also helps to build an efficient algorithm. Distilling from relative depth network is also critical. Since the training dataset of DBD only contains 600 images, the pre-trained relative depth network (421K training images in the wild) involves more accurate 3D features from larger-scale datasets to our network and task. Besides, we find that the network of Chen *et al.* automatically locates the salient object and predicts its relative depth. Luckly, DBD has a similar goal because the photographers often use the defocus blur to stress the important views.

3.2   Network Structure

Our network structure is based on *Fully Convolutional Networks* (FCN [23]). As shown in Fig. 2(b), we extract multi-scale features (5 layers in total) before each MaxPooling layer in a pre-trained ResNeXt101 [38] on ImageNet. These multi-scale features contain both high-level semantic features and low-level details for further detection. In each decoder, as shown in Fig. 3, we use the upsampling layer with convolution instead of deconvolution layer (or transpose convolution layer) to avoid checkerboard artifacts [18,26]. Then, by considering the importance of scale in DBD, we proceed using several aspects of multi-scale feature modeling and preservation. On the one hand, we design auxiliary classifiers in each level of the decoder as in [10,18,21] to prevent over-fitting and to generate multi-scale results. Differently, in each level of the decoder, we design two auxiliary classifiers for the supervision from DBD and depth distillation, respectively. Each auxiliary classifier is defined as a 1×1 convolution layer for side prediction, and we reuse these side outputs as the Supervision-guided Attention Block (SAB) for spatial attention (as shown in Fig. 3). Then, the final defocus and depth map can be generated by merging all multi-scale intermediate output maps with a 1×1 convolution layer as the PredictionFusion block in Fig. 2(b). On the other hand, we model multi-scale reception fields in each level of the decoder and propose the Selective Reception Field Block (SRFB) for efficiently selecting and merging the features in multi-contexts. Next, we provide the details of the proposed blocks.

Supervision-Guided Attention Block. Inspired by recently proposed attention mechanisms [11,36], we increase the non-linearity of network with the attention block. In detail, we generate the attention map from the side outputs since it also has a stronger prior knowledge for further feature weighting. As shown in Fig. 3, after the supervision of the auxiliary classifier, we feed the auxiliary

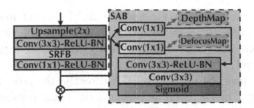

Fig. 3. The detailed structure of the proposed decoder, where the red arrows mean defocus supervision and depth distillation, respectively.

outputs of DBD and depth to the network again. Then we generate the spatial attention by two convolution blocks and a Sigmoid function. Finally, we multiply the original features by the generated attention map. These attentions rescale the features spatially before the next decoder.

Selective Reception Field Block. Since DBD needs to deal with scale carefully, previous works [34,43,44] merge multiple networks with multi-scale inputs, or recurrently and crossly fuse multi-scale features. However, these networks are still heavy and computationally inefficient. Rather than designing multi-stream networks or fusing by cross layers, we design an efficient multi-branch block for the extraction of multiple reception fields in each individual decoder.

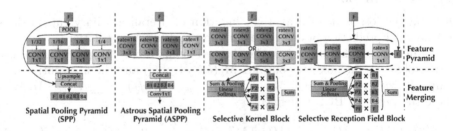

Fig. 4. Different types of multi-kernel feature pyramids. The proposed Selective Reception Field Block enlarges the reception fields of Selective Kernel Block using larger reception field pyramids. F repersents the original feature, Bx and Px are the x-th branch and the corresponding probability, respectively. rate = k means the dilation rate equals to k.

This is a natural way to extract multi-scale features using different kernel sizes. For example, the widely used (atrous) spatial pooling pyramid (SPP [42] or ASPP [2]) has been successful in semantic segmentation and other related tasks [31,41]. More recently, *Selective Kernel Networks* (SK-Block [19]) have been proposed for weighting multiple kernels in image classification. As shown in Fig. 4, we find that the SK-Block has a similar purpose to (A)SPP. Thus, we give a general formulation of these blocks by modeling them as a two stage process: *feature pyramid* and *feature merging*. The (A)SPP extracts the multi-context features by pooling or dilated convolution and then merges with convolutional block. In contrast, the SK-Block models the multi-context features using different convolution kernels (or convolution with different dilation rates). Then, it produces the probability of each branch using the global attention and uses it to weight each kernel.

However, if we insert SK-Block to FCN directly, the reception fields are still local and enlarging it needs much more memory. Thus, inspired by the (A)SPP, we design the Selective Reception Field Block with the following improvements to SK-Block: First, we add the original feature into feature pyramid and merging. By involving the original feature, other branches will try to learn the residuals of input. On the other hand, we aim to create richer and larger receptive fields in the feature pyramid. In detail, we use a sequence of convolutional layers with the growth of dilation and convolutional kernel together as feature pyramid, which is inspired by *Reception Field Block* (RFB) [22]. Note that RFB are proposed for object detection as an inception-like structure. In contrast, we build the feature pyramid, which is inspired by their intentions, and use these blocks as the decoders in the FCN framework. Thus, we have enlarged the reception field of the SK-Block substantially, which contains multi-scale features for weighting and selection. For example, when there are four branches in the block (as shown in Fig. 4), the reception field of the Sk-Block is 11 (9×9 Conv. or 3×3 Conv. dilation $= 4$) while ours is 43 (7×7 Conv. with dilation $= 7$).

3.3   Loss Function

Our training loss is defined as a combination of overall auxiliary supervisions and the final prediction of defocus estimation and depth distillation.

For defocus estimation, we use the weighed binary cross entropy (BCE) loss as in [13,46] for all the auxiliary outputs $M'_k (k \in [1,..,5])$ and the final output M_f compared with ground truth M: $\ell_{defocus} = \ell_{bce}(M, M_f) + \sum_k \alpha^k \ell_{bce}(M, M'_k)$, where the weighted BCE is defined as:

$$\ell_{bce}(M, M') = -(1 - \frac{TP}{N_p})Mlog(M') - (1 - \frac{TN}{N_n})(1 - M)log(1 - M') \quad (2)$$

TP and TN are the numbers of true positives and true negatives in the samples, N_p and N_n are the numbers of in-focus and out-of-focus pixels, respectively.

As for the depth distillation, giving the pre-trained depth estimation network as Φ_{rd}, the input image I and the predicted depth $\Phi_d(I)$ in our network, we define the depth distillation loss in level k as: $\ell^k_{depth} = ||\Phi^k_d(I) - \Phi_{rd}(I)||_2$. Similar to defocus estimation, our network predicts multi-scale depth output and fuses the side outputs to generate the final results. Thus, the full loss of depth distillation can be written as:

$$\ell_{depth} = \ell^f_{depth} + \sum_k \beta^k \ell^k_{depth} \quad (3)$$

where ℓ^f_{depth} represents the results after the final fusion layer and ℓ^k_{depth} represents the k levels of auxiliary outputs.

Overall, the total loss of our network is: $L = \ell_{defocus} + \gamma\ell_{depth}$. All the α, β are experimentally set to 1, and γ equals to 0.1.

4 Experiments

Implementation Details. We implement our method in the PyTorch framework. The parameters of the encoder backbone are initialized from the pretrained ResNeXt101 [38] on ImageNet, while the other parameters are random noise. We utilize the Stochastic Gradient Descent (SGD) algorithm to optimize the network with momentum of 0.9 and learning rate of 0.005. We resize all the images to 320 × 320 for training and evaluating the results in the same resolution as previous. Our network is trained on a computer equipped with an Intel 3.60 GHz CPU, 32G memory and a single GTX 1080 GPU. We set the batch size equals to 6, and the whole training process takes less than 2 h. Regarding interference, our network can generate a 320 × 320 image in 0.028s (**35.7 fps**), which is faster than previous DBD methods as shown in Table 1. Note that, for the training, we do not use any additional samples [44] or synthesized samples [18]. Additionally, for fair comparison, all the results are raw outputs from the network without any post-processing (such as dense conditional random fields [17]). More comparisons and experiments can be found in the supplementary materials.

Table 1. Comparisons with state-of-the-art methods on F^β and MAE score. We compare our method with 7 DBD methods [8,27,34,40,43–45] and 4 methods on the related tasks(salient object detection [30,37] and shadow detection [13,47]). Our method achieves the best performance over 11 methods on two datasets. Meanwhile, our method is 2x faster than previous DBD methods.

Datasets	Metrics	[40]	[27]	[8]	[43]	[44]	[34]	[45]	[13]	[47]	[30]	[37]	Ours
CUHK 100	F^β	.787	.477	.772	.867	.889	.818	.906	.898	.912	.922	.901	**.927**
	MAE	.136	.372	.219	.107	.082	.117	.059	.057	.046	.049	.055	**.042**
DUT 500	F^β	.719	.468	.687	.761	.827	.823	.817	.844	.877	.827	.866	**.891**
	MAE	.193	.410	.248	.194	.138	.118	.135	.109	.080	.120	.092	**.073**
–	FPS	.11	.09	.02	.04	.08	17.9	15.6	40.0	22.2	**90.9**	50.0	35.7

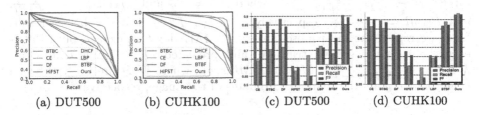

(a) DUT500   (b) CUHK100   (c) DUT500   (d) CUHK100

Fig. 5. (a) and (b) are *Precision-Recall Curves*, and (c) and (d) are the comparison of Precision, Recall and F^β on two datasets. The proposed method achieves the best performance on various metrics.

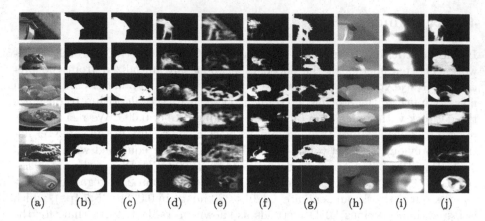

(a)   (b)   (c)   (d)   (e)   (f)   (g)   (h)   (i)   (j)

Fig. 6. Comparison with state-of-the-art DBD methods. From the left to right is: (a) Input, (b) Target, (c) Ours, (d) BTB-C [44], (e) BTB-F [43], (f) CENet [45], (g) LBP [40], (h) DHCF [27], (i) HiFST [8] and (j) DFNet [34]. Our method generates more convincing DBD maps than others.

Dataset. We evaluate our algorithm on two publicly available datasets for DBD. The first is the CUHK dataset [32], which contains 704 images with partially defocus blur. Another dataset is the DUT dataset [43], which contains 500 difficult samples with obscure homogeneous, low-contrast focal regions and background clutter. We train our network on the same split of 604 images from the CUHK dataset as previous work [43–45] and test on the remaining 100 images (CUHK100) and the whole DUT dataset (DUT500).

Metrics. We evaluate DBD on three aspects as previous works. The first metric is the *Precision-Recall (PR) Curve* for binary classification accuracy. All the results are normalized to [0, 255] and given a threshold in each integer interval. Second, we compute the mean precision, recall and F-measure scores (F^β) on the binarized results by an adaptive threshold. The threshold is determined by the 1.5 times of the mean pixel value. The F-measure is defined as: $F^\beta = \frac{(1+\beta^2) \times Precision \times Recall}{\beta^2 \times Precision + Recall}$, where $\beta^2 = 0.3$ and $Precision = \frac{TP}{TP+FP}$ and $Recall = \frac{TP}{FN+TP}$, respectively. A larger F^β indicates a better result. Last, we report the mean absolute error (MAE) for the average pixel differences between the ground truth M and predicted M'. MAE is defined as: $MAE = \frac{1}{WH} \sum_{x=0}^{W} \sum_{y=0}^{H} |M(x,y) - M'(x,y)|$, where W, H are the width and height and x, y are the spatial coordinates of the image, respectively.

4.1   Comparisons with State-of-the-Art Methods

We compare our algorithm with several state-of-the-art methods, including deep learning-based methods for DBD, such as: deep and hand-crafted features based method (DHCF [27]), multi-stream bottom-top-bottom (BTB-F [43], BTB-C [44]), network cross-ensemble (CENet [45]) and the network with recurrently feature reuse and fusion (DFNet [34]). In addition, we also conduct the experiments on state-of-the-art hand-crafted feature based methods, including local binary patterns (LBP [40]) and high-frequency multi-scale fusion and sort transform of gradient magnitudes (HiFST [8]). Note that, all the predicted maps of DBD come from the author's website or the public implementation with recommended hyper-parameters for fair comparison. For there are few learning-based DBD methods, we also compare our methods with 4 state-of-the-art learning-based methods on some relevant tasks: such as bidirectional feature pyramid network with recurrent attention (BDRAR [47]) and direction-aware attention (DSC [13]) for shadow detection, boundary-aware loss (BAS [30]) and cascaded partial decoder (CPD [37]) for salient object detection. All the networks of relevant tasks are trained on our framework with the same input resolution and batch size.

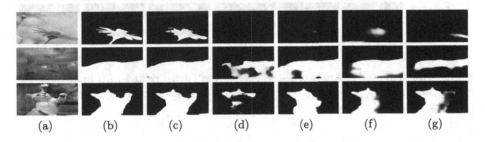

(a)   (b)   (c)   (d)   (e)   (f)   (g)

Fig. 7. The produced DBD map of our method outperforms others state-of-the-art network structures on related tasks. From the left to right is: (a)Input, (b)Target, (c)Ours, (d)BASNet [30], (e)BDRAR [47], (f)CPD [37], (g)DSC [13].

We illustrate the numerical comparison of our method and state-of-the-art methods on two public datasets in Table 1 and Fig. 5. It is clear that our method outperforms others with a larger margin on all numerical metrics. The results show that our network with depth and multi-scale features understands the complex scenes well. We also give some visual samples to compare with state-of-the-art DBD methods in Fig. 6. Our methods also show the superior visual quality. Apart from the great object awareness in examples, our network also predicts the homogeneous regions well (such as the plane in the fourth example) because of depth distillation. For comparison with related tasks, Table 1 also gives a clear result. Our network has better performance in DBD than the boundary awareness network BASNet [30] or direction awareness DSC [13] because depth is more important in our task. For example, boundary loss in BASNet [30] is benefit on CUHK100 (As Table 1) but worse in DUT500 because the homogeneous regions in DUT500 are not related to edge. As shown in Fig. 7, our method can achieve much better results than the other methods.

Table 2. Ablation study. The first two experiments use VGG19 as feature extractor while the last five experiments use ResNeXt101 as feature extractor. OursFull means the FCN+D+SRFB+SA.

Datasets	Metrics	FCN VGG	OursFull VGG	FCN ResNeXt	+D	+D +SRFB	+D +RFB+SA	OursFull ResNeXt
CUHK 100	F^β	0.911	0.919	0.917	0.922	0.926	**0.931**	0.927
	MAE	0.053	0.048	0.046	0.046	0.045	**0.040**	0.042
DUT 500	F^β	0.800	0.844	0.879	0.883	0.888	0.887	**0.891**
	MAE	0.148	0.113	0.080	0.077	0.076	0.075	**0.073**

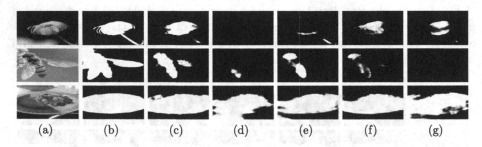

(a)   (b)   (c)   (d)   (e)   (f)   (g)

Fig. 8. Ablation study of network structure. From left to right is: (a) input, (b) Target (c) defocus+D+SRFB+SA (Our Full method) (d) defocus only, (e) defocus+D, (f) defocus+D+SRFB, (g) defocus+D+RFB+SA.

4.2   Ablation Studies of Network Structure

Backbone Choice. We choose different backbones for our network structure, especially the widely used VGG19 in previous work and ResNeXt101. For the ablation study, we use the FCN [23] with auxiliary outputs and ResNeXt101 as feature extractor and compare with our main contributions in Table 2. Since the CUHK100 dataset is small and simple, the metric differences on this dataset is not too large. While on the DUT500 dataset, ResNeXt101 can extract richer features and gain much better results. By comparing with the other state-of-the-art methods on DBD (7 DBD methods [8,27,34,40,43–45] in Table 1, and 4 related tasks in Table 1), our network can also improve the performance significantly on the similar pre-trained VGG19 backbone.

Depth Distillation (D). We test the effectiveness of depth distillation for DBD in Fig. 8(d)(e) and Table 2. It is clear that with the help of depth, our network can understand scene well and gain much better results because the depth information gives a strong prior for defocus map detection. Using Depth distillation, our network can also predict the relative depth from a single image. Although it is not our main target and our network can only predict the depth for partial defocus images, we still compare the distilled depth with our teacher network (Chen *et al.* [3]) in the supplementary materials.

Depth Distillation Hyper-Parameter γ**.** We evaluate the influence of depth distillation hyper-parameters γ on DBD. Thus, we train our full method with

Table 3. Hyper-parameters γ for depth distillation. The best and second best results are marked in bold and underline, respectively.

Datasets	Metrics	$\gamma = 0.01$	$\gamma = 0.05$	$\gamma = 0.1$	$\gamma = 1$	$\gamma = 5$
CUHK 100	F^β	<u>0.9253</u>	0.9208	**0.9267**	0.9231	0.9222
	MAE	0.0438	0.0442	**0.0424**	0.0434	<u>0.0430</u>
DUT 500	F^β	0.8844	**0.8919**	<u>0.8909</u>	0.8902	0.8818
	MAE	0.0737	0.0729	<u>0.0727</u>	**0.0696**	0.0786

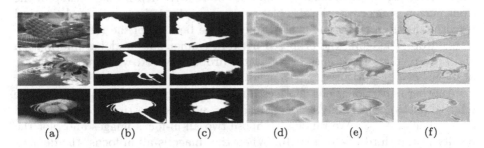

(a)   (b)   (c)   (d)   (e)   (f)

Fig. 9. Visualized attention maps in SAB. From left to right: (a) input, (b) target, (c) our final prediction, where (d)-(f) are the three attention maps in different levels of decoders. Here, we resize all the attentions to the same size for comparison. Interestingly, in high-level attention (d), our SAB generates the attention map for the whole defocus region, while in the coarser level (f), our attention map focuses on learning the edges and details.

different γ values. As shown in the Table 3, when γ is too large or too small, the performance become worse. Our network gain the best performance when γ equals to 0.1.

Selective Reception Field Block (SRFB). We evaluate the performance of the proposed SRFB by inserting the SRFB in each level of the decoder. As shown in Fig. 8 and Table 2, the SRFB models multi-scale features from the input and generate more accurate results. In addition to the necessity of our SRFB shown in Table 2 and Fig. 8, we also conduct the experiments to compare our SRFB with the model without selective attention (similar to FRB [22]). As shown in Fig. 8 and Table 2, although the FRB perform better in the CUHK100 dataset, our SRFB show a much better results in DUT500. We argue that CUHK100 is smaller and easier. Thus, the proposed SRFB is more suitable for DBD.

Supervision-guided Attention Block (SAB). In each level of auxiliary outputs, we design SAB to reuse the predicted defocus and depth map as spatial attention for further prediction. These attentions emphasize the useful features for further refinement. As shown in Fig. 8(c)(f) and Table 2, the proposed SAB also benefits blur detection. We also plot different levels of attention maps in the proposed SAB in Fig. 9. It is shown that using side outputs to generate the attention map emphasizes different features in each of their scales. Higher-level attentions stress the global features while the lower ones focus on local details.

4.3   Failure Cases

Although our network shows much better results than previous methods, there are still some failure cases. As shown in the first row of Fig. 10, when the far and near out-of-focus regions appears in a single image, the proposed network successfully predicts the defocus map but the relative depth relationship of the front person is incorrect. We also plot a more complicated example in the second row, the depth in this scene is hard to estimate because of the reflection of the water drop. Therefore, the proposed network cannot obtain global information and only predicts the scenes in the water drop. However, we argue that these problems can be mitigated by stronger networks and larger datasets.

Another limitation is our depth estimation. Our network can only predict the relative depth for partially defocused images, not depth estimation in the wild as in Chen *et al.* [3]. We randomly choose two all-in-focus images and plot the results in the third line of Fig. 10. When the image is all-in-focus, the defocus maps will not provide an effective prior for depth estimation. Thus, the apply range of our depth estimation is limited. However, our main target is DBD other than depth estimation.

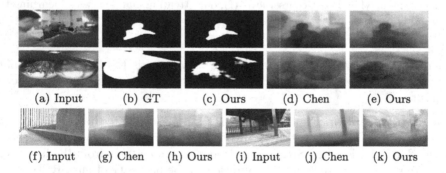

(a) Input   (b) GT   (c) Ours   (d) Chen   (e) Ours

(f) Input   (g) Chen   (h) Ours   (i) Input   (j) Chen   (k) Ours

Fig. 10. Failure cases. The top two rows show the failure examples when the scenes are complicated or when the depth is hard to predict. The thirds line shows the failed cases of predicted depth for all-in-focus image.

5   Conclusions

In this paper, we firstly discuss the role of depth in defocus blur detection and propose depth distillation for this task. In detail, we distill the relative depth as regularization for learning-based defocus blur detection in a FCN network.

Moreover, in order to build a stronger network, we design a selective reception field block because DBD is sensitive to multi-scale features, and we design a supervision-guided attention block, which serves the side outputs as spatial attention. The experimental results show the superiority of our method compared with 11 state-of-the-art methods in terms of efficiency and accuracy.

Acknowledgments. The authors would like to thanks Nan Chen for her helpful discussion. This work was partly supported by the University of Macau under Grants: MYRG2018-00035-FST and MYRG2019-00086-FST, and the Science and Technology Development Fund, Macau SAR (File no. 0034/2019/AMJ, 0019/2019/A).

References

1. Bae, S., Durand, F.: Defocus magnification. Comput. Graph. Forum **26**, 571–579 (2007). Wiley Online Library
2. Chen, L.C., Papandreou, G., Kokkinos, I., Murphy, K., Yuille, A.L.: Deeplab: semantic image segmentation with deep convolutional nets, atrous convolution, and fully connected CRFS. IEEE TPAMI **40**(4), 834–848 (2017)
3. Chen, W., Fu, Z., Yang, D., Deng, J.: Single-image depth perception in the wild. In: NeurIPS, pp. 730–738 (2016)
4. Cun, X., Xu, F., Pun, C.M., Gao, H.: Depth-assisted full resolution network for single image-based view synthesis. IEEE Comput. Graph. Appl. **39**(2), 52–64 (2018)
5. Eigen, D., Puhrsch, C., Fergus, R.: Depth map prediction from a single image using a multi-scale deep network. In: NeurIPS, pp. 2366–2374 (2014)
6. Godard, C., Mac Aodha, O., Brostow, G.J.: Unsupervised monocular depth estimation with left-right consistency. In: CVPR, pp. 270–279 (2017)
7. Godard, C., Mac Aodha, O., Firman, M., Brostow, G.J.: Digging into self-supervised monocular depth estimation. In: Proceedings of the IEEE International Conference on Computer Vision, pp. 3828–3838 (2019)
8. Golestaneh, S.A., Karam, L.J.: Spatially-varying blur detection based on multiscale fused and sorted transform coefficients of gradient magnitudes. In: CVPR, March 2017
9. Hinton, G., Vinyals, O., Dean, J.: Distilling the knowledge in a neural network. arXiv preprint arXiv:1503.02531 (2015)
10. Hou, Q., Cheng, M.M., Hu, X., Borji, A., Tu, Z., Torr, P.H.: Deeply supervised salient object detection with short connections. In: CVPR, pp. 3203–3212 (2017)
11. Hu, J., Shen, L., Sun, G.: Squeeze-and-excitation networks. In: CVPR, pp. 7132–7141 (2018)
12. Hu, X., Fu, C.W., Zhu, L., Heng, P.A.: Depth-attentional features for single-image rain removal. In: CVPR, pp. 8022–8031 (2019)
13. Hu, X., Zhu, L., Fu, C.W., Qin, J., Heng, P.A.: Direction-aware spatial context features for shadow detection. In: CVPR, pp. 7454–7462 (2018)
14. Jiang, P., Ling, H., Yu, J., Peng, J.: Salient region detection by UFO: uniqueness, focusness and objectness. In: CVPR, pp. 1976–1983 (2013)
15. Karaali, A., Jung, C.R.: Image retargeting based on spatially varying defocus blur map. In: ICIP, pp. 2693–2697. IEEE (2016)
16. Karaali, A., Jung, C.R.: Edge-based defocus blur estimation with adaptive scale selection. IEEE TIP **27**(3), 1126–1137 (2017)

17. Krähenbühl, P., Koltun, V.: Efficient inference in fully connected CRFS with gaussian edge potentials. In: NeurIPS, pp. 109–117 (2011)
18. Lee, J., Lee, S., Cho, S., Lee, S.: Deep defocus map estimation using domain adaptation. In: CVPR, pp. 12222–12230 (2019)
19. Li, X., Wang, W., Hu, X., Yang, J.: Selective kernel networks. In: CVPR, pp. 510–519 (2019)
20. Li, Z., et al.: Learning the depths of moving people by watching frozen people. In: CVPR, pp. 4521–4530 (2019)
21. Lin, T.Y., Dollár, P., Girshick, R., He, K., Hariharan, B., Belongie, S.: Feature pyramid networks for object detection. In: CVPR, pp. 2117–2125 (2017)
22. Liu, S., Huang, D., et al.: Receptive field block net for accurate and fast object detection. In: ECCV, pp. 385–400 (2018)
23. Long, J., Shelhamer, E., Darrell, T.: Fully convolutional networks for semantic segmentation. In: CVPR, June 2015
24. Lopez-Paz, D., Bottou, L., Schölkopf, B., Vapnik, V.: Unifying distillation and privileged information. arXiv preprint arXiv:1511.03643 (2015)
25. Marc, L., Andrew, A., Nora, W.: Depth of field. http://graphics.stanford.edu/courses/cs178/applets/dof.html
26. Odena, A., Dumoulin, V., Olah, C.: Distill 1(10), e3 (2016)
27. Park, J., Tai, Y.W., Cho, D., Kweon, I.S.: A unified approach of multi-scale deep and hand-crafted features for defocus estimation. In: CVPR cs.CV (2017)
28. Peng, H., Li, B., Xiong, W., Hu, W., Ji, R.: RGBD salient object detection: a benchmark and algorithms. In: Fleet, D., Pajdla, T., Schiele, B., Tuytelaars, T. (eds.) ECCV 2014. LNCS, vol. 8691, pp. 92–109. Springer, Cham (2014). https://doi.org/10.1007/978-3-319-10578-9_7
29. Qi, C.R., Liu, W., Wu, C., Su, H., Guibas, L.J.: Frustum pointnets for 3d object detection from RGB-D data. In: CVPR, pp. 918–927 (2018)
30. Qin, X., Zhang, Z., Huang, C., Gao, C., Dehghan, M., Jagersand, M.: Basnet: boundary-aware salient object detection. In: CVPR, June 2019
31. Qu, Y., Chen, Y., Huang, J., Xie, Y.: Enhanced pix2pix dehazing network. In: CVPR, pp. 8160–8168 (2019)
32. Shi, J., Li, X., Jia, J.: Discriminative blur detection features. In: CVPR (2014)
33. Shi, J., Xu, L., Jia, J.: Just noticeable defocus blur detection and estimation. In: CVPR, pp. 657–665 (2015)
34. Tang, C., Zhu, X., Liu, X., Wang, L., Zomaya, A.: Defusionnet: defocus blur detection via recurrently fusing and refining multi-scale deep features. In: CVPR, pp. 2700–2709 (2019)
35. Wikipedia contributors: Depth of field – Wikipedia, the free encyclopedia (2019). Accessed 17 Oct 2019
36. Woo, S., Park, J., Lee, J.Y., So Kweon, I.: Cbam: convolutional block attention module. In: ECCV, pp. 3–19 (2018)
37. Wu, Z., Su, L., Huang, Q.: Cascaded partial decoder for fast and accurate salient object detection. In: CVPR, pp. 3907–3916 (2019)
38. Xie, S., Girshick, R.B., Dollár, P., Tu, Z., He, K.: Aggregated residual transformations for deep neural networks. In: CVPR (2017)
39. Xu, G., Quan, Y., Ji, H.: Estimating defocus blur via rank of local patches. In: CVPR, pp. 5371–5379 (2017)
40. Yi, X., Eramian, M.: LBP-based segmentation of defocus blur. IEEE Trans. Image Process. 25(4), 1626–1638 (2016)
41. Zhang, H., Patel, V.M.: Densely connected pyramid dehazing network. In: CVPR (2018)

42. Zhao, H., Shi, J., Qi, X., Wang, X., Jia, J.: Pyramid scene parsing network. In: CVPR, pp. 2881–2890 (2017)
43. Zhao, W., Zhao, F., Wang, D., Lu, H.: Defocus blur detection via multi-stream bottom-top-bottom fully convolutional network. In: CVPR, pp. 3080–3088 (2018)
44. Zhao, W., Zhao, F., Wang, D., Lu, H.: Defocus blur detection via multi-stream bottom-top-bottom network. IEEE TPAMI **42**, 1884–1897 (2019)
45. Zhao, W., Zheng, B., Lin, Q., Lu, H.: Enhancing diversity of defocus blur detectors via cross-ensemble network. In: CVPR, June 2019
46. Zheng, Q., Qiao, X., Cao, Y., Lau, R.W.: Distraction-aware shadow detection. In: CVPR, June 2019
47. Zhu, L., et al.: Bidirectional feature pyramid network with recurrent attention residual modules for shadow detection. In: ECCV (2018)

Motion Guided 3D Pose Estimation from Videos

Jingbo Wang[1](✉)(iD), Sijie Yan[1](iD), Yuanjun Xiong[2](iD), and Dahua Lin[1](iD)

[1] The Chinese University of Hong Kong, Sha Tin, Hong Kong
{jbwang,ys016,dhlin}@ie.cuhk.edu.hk
[2] AWS/Amazon AI, Causeway Bay, Hong Kong
yuanjx@amazon.com

Abstract. We propose a new loss function, called motion loss, for supervising models for monocular 3D Human pose estimation from videos. It works by comparing the motion pattern of the prediction against ground truth key point trajectories. In computing motion loss, we introduce pairwise motion encoding, a simple yet effective representation for keypoint motion. We design a new graph convolutional network architecture, U-shaped GCN (UGCN). It captures both short-term and long-term motion information to fully leverage the supervision from the motion loss (Codes and models at http://wangjingbo.top/papers/ECCV2020-Video-Pose/MotionLossPage.html). We experiment training UGCN with the motion loss on two large scale benchmarks: Human3.6M and MPI-INF-3DHP. Our models surpass other state-of-the-art models by a large margin. It also demonstrates strong capacity in producing smooth 3D sequences and recovering keypoint motion.

Keywords: 3D pose estimation · Motion loss · Graph convolution

1 Introduction

3D human pose estimation aims at reconstructing 3D body keypoints from their 2D projections, such as images [14,24,31,34], videos [4,33], 2D pose [15,17,25], or their combination [22,32]. Unlike the 2D pose estimation, this problem is ill-posed in the sense that the lack of depth information in the 2D projections input leads to ambiguities. To obtain the perception of depth, recent works [11,26] utilized multiple synchronized cameras for observing objects from different angles and have achieved considerable progress. However, compared with monocular methods, multi-view methods are not practical in reality because of their strict prerequisites for devices and environments.

In recent years, video-based 3D human pose estimation [2,5,15,16] receives attention quickly. Taking a video as input, models are able to perceive the 3D structure of an object in motion and better infer the depth information for 3D pose estimation in each frame. Unlike image-based models, video-based models [2,15] are

Electronic supplementary material The online version of this chapter (https://doi.org/10.1007/978-3-030-58601-0_45) contains supplementary material, which is available to authorized users.

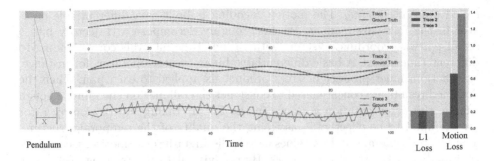

Fig. 1. A toy sample, the location estimation of pendulum motion. We show the horizontal location as time varies, a sine curve, denoted in gray, and three estimated traces, denoted in blue, orange and cyan. They have the same ℓ_1 mean distance to the groundtruth but have different temporal structure. Which estimated trace better describes the pendulum motion? The loss under different matrices is also shown in the right figure. Obviously, motion loss is good at answering the above question. (Color figure online)

supervised by a long sequence of 3D pose, which increase the dimensionality of solution space by hundreds of times. In most existing works, the common loss function for supervising 3D pose estimation models is *Minkowski Distance*, such as ℓ_1-loss and ℓ_2-loss. It independently computes the overall location error of the predicted keypoints in 3D space with respect to their ground-truth locations.

However, there is a critical limitation for the Minkowski Distance. It does not consider the similarity of temporal structure between the estimated pose sequence and the ground-truth. We illustrate this issue by a toy sample, the trace estimation of a pendulum motion. It is similar to pose estimation, but only includes one "joint". We compare three estimated trajectories of pendulum motion in Fig. 1. The first trace function has a shape similar to the ground-truth. The second one has a different tendency but still keep smoothness. And the last curve just randomly fluctuates around the ground-truth. Both of them have the same ℓ_1 mean distance to the ground-truth but have various temporal structures. Because the Minkowski Distance is calculated independently for each moment, it failed to examine the inner dependencies of a trajectory.

The keypoints in a pose sequence describe the human movement, which are strongly correlated especially in the time. Under the supervision of Minkowski Distance as the loss, same as the above toy sample, it is difficult for models to learn from the motion information in the ground-truth keypoint trajectories and thus hard to obtain natural keypoints movement in the model's prediction due to the high dimensional solution space.

We address this issue by proposing *motion loss*, a novel loss function that explicitly involves motion modeling into the learning. Motion loss works by requiring the model to reconstruct the keypoint motion trajectories in addition to the task of reconstructing 3D locations of keypoints. It evaluates the motion reconstruction quality by computing the difference between predicted keypoint locations and the ground-truth locations in the space of a specific representation called *motion encoding*. The motion encoding is built as a differentiable operator in the following manner. We first roughly decompose a trajectory into a set of pairwise coordinate vectors with various time intervals corresponding to different time scales. A basic differentiable binary vector operator, for instance, subtraction, inner product or cross product, is applied to each pair. Then the obtained results are concatenated to construct the full motion encoding. Though simple, this representation is shown in the Fig. 1 (taking subtraction operator for example) to be effective in assessing the quality of the temporal structure. The difference in motion loss values clearly distinguishes the motion reconstruction quality of the three trajectories. By applying it to the training of 3D pose estimation models, we also observe that motion loss can significantly improve the accuracy of 3D pose estimation.

To estimate the pose trajectories with reasonable human movements, the 3D pose estimation model must have the capacity to model motion in both short temporal intervals and long temporal ranges, as human actions usually have varying speeds over time. To achieve this property we propose a novel graph convolutional network based architecture for 3D pose estimation model. We start by repurposing an ST-GCN [36] model, initially proposed for skeleton-based action recognition, to take as input 2D pose sequences and output 3D pose sequences. Inspired by the success of U-shaped CNNs used in semantic segmentation and object detection, we construct a similar U-shaped structure on the temporal axis of the ST-GCN [36] model. The result is a new architecture, called *U-shaped GCN* (UGCN), with strong capacity in capturing both short-term and long-term temporal dependencies, which is essential in characterizing the keypoint motion.

We experiment the motion loss and UGCN for video-based 3D pose estimation from 2D pose on two large scale 3D human pose estimation benchmarks: Human3.6M [9] and MPI-INF-3DHP [18]. We first observe a significant boost in position accuracy when the motion loss is used in training. This corroborates the importance of motion-based supervision. When the motion loss is combined with UGCN, our model surpasses the current state of the art models in terms of location accuracy by a large margin. Besides improved location accuracy, we also observe that UGCN trained with the motion loss is able to produce smooth 3D sequences without imposing any smoothness constraint during training or inference. Our model also halves the velocity error [25] compared with other state of the art models, which again validates the importance of having motion information in the supervision. We provide detailed ablation study and visualization to further demonstrate the potential of our model.

2   Related Work

3D Pose Estimation. Before the era of deep learning, early methods for 3D human pose estimation were based on handcraft features [8,9,27]. In recent years, most works depend on powerful deep neural networks and achieve promising improvements, which can be divided into two types.

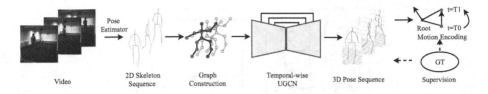

Fig. 2. Overview of our proposed pipeline for estimating 3D poses from consecutive 2D poses. We structure 2D skeletons by a spatial-temporal graph and predict 3D locations via our U-shaped Graph Convolution Networks (UGCN). The model is supervised in the space of motion encoding.

In the first type, estimators predict 3D poses from 2D image directly [24,31,33]. For example, [14] jointly regresses joint locations and detects body parts by sliding window on the image. [33] directly regresses the 3D pose from an aligned spatial-temporal feature map. [24] predicts per voxel likelihoods for each joint based on the stacked hourglass architecture. [31] utilizes an auto-encoder to learn a latent pose representation for modeling the joint dependencies.

Another typical solution builds on a two-stage pipeline [2,15,17,25]. Thereon, a 2D pose sequence is firstly predicted by a 2D pose estimator from a video frame by frame and lifted to 3D space by another estimator. For instance, [17] proposes a simple baseline composed of several fully-connected layers, which takes a single 2D pose as input. [25] generates 3D poses from 2D keypoint sequences by a temporal-convolution method. [2] introduces a local-to-global network based on graph convolution layers. [15] factorizes a 3D pose sequence into trajectory bases and train a deep network to regress the trajectory coefficient matrix.

Although the appearance information is dropped in the first stage, the data dimension is dramatically decreased as well, which makes long-term video-based 3D pose estimation possible. Our method also builds on the two-stage pipeline.

Graph Convolution. Modeling skeleton sequence via spatial-temporal graphs (st-graph) [36] and performing graph convolution thereon has significantly boosted the performance in many human understanding tasks including action recognition [36], pose tracking [21] and motion synthesis [35]. The designs for graph convolution mainly fall into two stream: spectral based [6,12] and spatial based [1,20]. They extended standard convolution to irregular graph domain by Fourier transformation and neighborhood partitioning respectively. Following [36], we perform spatial graph convolution on skeleton sequences represented by st-graphs.

3   Approach

Figure 2 illustrates our pipeline for estimating 3D pose sequences. Given the 2D projections of a pose sequence estimated from a video $P = \{\boldsymbol{p}_{t,j}|t = 1, ..., T; j = 1, ..., M\}$, we aim to reconstruct their 3D coordinates $S = \{\boldsymbol{s}_{t,j}|t = 1, ..., T; j =$

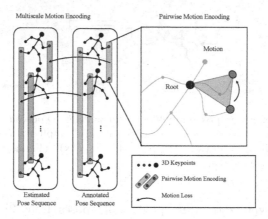

Fig. 3. Motion loss. By concatenating pairwise cross-product vectors between the coordinate vectors of the same joints across time with various intervals, we construct multi-scale motion encoding on pose sequences. The motion loss requires the model to reconstruct this encoding. It explicitly involves motion modeling into learning.

$1, ..., M\}$, where T is the number of video frames, M is the number of human joints, $p_{t,j}$ and $s_{t,j}$ are vectors respectively representing the 2D and 3D locations of joint j in the frame t. We structure these 2D keypoints by a spatial-temporal graph and predict their 3D locations via our U-shaped Graph Convolution Networks (UGCN). The model is supervised by a multiscale motion loss and trained in an end-to-end manner.

3.1   Motion Loss

In this work, motion loss is defined as the distance in the space of motion. Therefore, a motion encoder is required for projecting skeleton sequences to this space. Though there are myriad possible designs, we empirically sum up a few guiding principles: differentiability, non-independence, and multi-scale. Differentiability is the prerequisite for the end-to-end training. And the calculation should be across time for modeling the temporal dependencies, *i.e.*, non-independence. Since the speed of motion is different, multi-scale modeling is also significant. In this section, we introduce how we design a simple but effective encoding, named *pairwise motion encoding*.

Pairwise Motion Encoding. We first consider the simplest case: the length of the pose sequences is 2. The motion encoding on the joint j can be denoted as:

$$m_j = s_{0,j} \star s_{1,j}, \tag{1}$$

where $\star$ can be any differentiable binary vector operator, such as subtraction, inner-product and cross-product. In the common case, the pose sequence is longer. We can expand an extra dimension in the motion encoding:

$$m_{t,j} = s_{t,j} \star s_{t+1,j}. \tag{2}$$

Note that, this representation only models the relationship between two adjacent moments. Since the speed of human motion has a large variation range, it inspires us to encode human motion on multiple temporal scales:

$$m_{t,j,\tau} = s_{t,j} \star s_{(t+\tau),j}. \tag{3}$$

where τ is the time interval. As shown in Fig. 3, to calculate the motion loss of the full pose sequence, we compute the ℓ_1 Distance on the encoded space for all joints, moments and several time intervals. Mathematically, we have:

$$L_m = \frac{1}{\mathbb{T}} \sum_{\tau \in \mathbb{T}} \sum_{t=1}^{T-\tau} \sum_{j=1}^{M} \left\| m_{t,j,\tau} - m_{t,j,\tau}^{gt} \right\|, \tag{4}$$

where the interval set $\mathbb{T}$ includes different τ for multiple time scales. Pairwise motion encoding decomposes a trajectory into coordinate pairs and extracts features for each pair by a differentiable operation $\star$. As the first work to explore the supervision of motion for 3D pose estimation, intuitively, we choose the three most basic operations in the experiments: **subtraction, inner-product, and cross-product**. And we conducted extensive experiments to evaluate the effectiveness of these encoding methods in Sect. 4.3.

Loss Function. The motion loss only considers the second-order correlations in the formulation of pairwise motion encoding, while the absolute location information is absent. Therefore, we add a traditional reconstruction loss term to the overall training objectives:

$$L_p = \sum_{t=1}^{T} \sum_{j=1}^{M} \left\| s_{t,j} - s_{t,j}^{gt} \right\|_2^2. \tag{5}$$

The model is supervised in an end-to-end manner with the combined loss:

$$L = L_p + \lambda L_m, \tag{6}$$

where λ is a hyper parameter for balancing two objectives.

3.2   U-Shaped Graph Convolutional Networks

Intuitively, the 3D pose estimator needs stronger long-term perception for exploring the motion priors. Besides that, keeping the spatial resolution is also required by estimating 3D pose accurately. Therefore, we represent the skeleton sequence as a *spatial temporal graph* [36] to maintain their topologies, and aggregating information by an *U-shaped graph convolution network (UGCN)*.

Graph Modeling. It is an ill-posed problem to recover the 3D location of a keypoint from its 2D coordinates independently. In general, the information from other keypoints, especially the neighboring ones, play essential roles in 3D pose reconstruction. To model the relationship with these relative keypoints, it is natural to organize a skeleton sequence via a *spatial temporal graph* (st-graph) [36]. In particular, a st-graph G is determined by a node set and an edge set. The node set $V = \{v_{t,j} | t = 1, \ldots, T, j = 1, \ldots, M\}$ includes all the keypoints in a sequence of pose. And the edge set E is composed of two parts: one for connecting adjacent frames on each joint, one for the connecting endpoint of each bone in every single frame. These edges construct the temporal dependencies and spatial configuration together. Then, a series of graph convolution operations are conducted on this graph.

Graph Convolution. In this work, we adopt *spatial temporal graph convolution (st-gcn)* [36] as the basic unit to aggregate features of nodes on a st-graph. It can be regarded as a combination of two basic operations: a spatial graph convolution and a temporal convolution. The temporal convolution $Conv_t$ is a standard convolution operation applied on the temporal dimension for each joint, while the spatial graph convolution $Conv_g$ is performed on the skeleton for each time position independently. Given an input feature map f_{in}, the output of two operations can be written as:

$$f_s = Conv_g(f_{in}) \tag{7}$$

$$f_{out} = Conv_t(f_s), \tag{8}$$

where f_s is the output of the spatial graph convolution. We follow the formulation of spatial graph convolution in [36]. And more details are in our supplementary materials.

Network Structure. As shown in Fig. 4, the basic units for building networks are st-gcn blocks, which include five basic operations: a spatial graph convolution, a temporal convolution, a batch normalization, a dropout and an activation function ReLU. Our networks are composed of three stages: downsampling, upsampling, and merging.

In the downsampling stage, we utilize 9 st-gcn blocks for aggregating temporal features. In addition, we set *stride* = 2 for the second, fourth, sixth, and eighth st-gcn blocks to increase the receptive field in the time dimension. This stage embeds the global information of the full skeleton sequence.

The upsampling stage contains four st-gcn blocks. Each block is followed by an upsampling layer. Thanks to the regular temporal structure in st-graph, the upsampling in the time dimension can be simply implemented with the following formula:

$$f_{up}(v_{t,j}) = f_{in}(v_{t',i}), \tag{9}$$

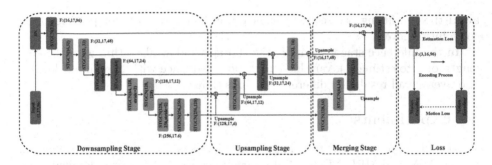

Fig. 4. Network structure. We proposed a U-shaped graph convolution network (UGCN) as the backbone of our pose estimation model to incorporate both local and global information with a high resolution. This network consists of three stages: downsampling, upsampling and merging. The network first aggregates long-range information by temporal pooling operations in the downsampling stage. And then recovers the resolution by upsampling layers. To keep the low-level information, the features in the downsampling stage are also added to the upsample branch by some shortcuts. Finally, the multi-scale feature maps are merged to predicted 3D skeletal joints. In this way, UGCN incorporates both short-term and long-term information, making it an ideal fit for the supervision of the motion loss.

where $t' = \lfloor \frac{t}{2} \rfloor$. With successive upsampling operations, the temporal resolution gradually recovers and the global information spread to the full graph. Since the 2D inputs are projections of 3D outputs, the low-level information may provide strong geometric constraints for estimating 3D pose. It motivated us to keep low-level information in the networks. Thus, we add features in the first stage to the upsampling stage with the same temporal resolution.

In the merging stage, the feature maps with various time scales in the second stage are transformed to the same shape and fused to obtain the final embedding. Obviously, this embedding contains abundant information on multiple temporal scales.

In the end, the 3D coordinate for each keypoint is estimated by a st-gcn regressor. This model is supervised by the motion loss in an end-to-end manner. Other details have been depicted in the Fig. 4.

Training and Inference. We use st-gcn blocks with the temporal kernel size of 5 and the dropout rate of 0.5 as our basic cells to construct a UGCN. The networks take as input a 2D pose sequence with 96 frames. We perform horizontal flip augmentation at the time of training and testing. Considering the various value ranges of different motion encoding in Sect. 3.1, we normalize the inner-product and cross product encoding by the temporal-wise mean value before computing motion loss. Based on this normalization, we can set $\lambda = 1$ to balance the reconstruction loss and our motion loss conveniently. We optimize the model using Adam for 110 epochs with the batch size of 256 and the initial learning rate of 10^{-2}. We decay the learning rate by 0.1 after 80, 90 and 100 epochs. To avoid the overfitting, we set the weight decay factor to 10^{-5} for parameters of convolution layers.

In the inference stage, we apply the sliding window algorithm with the step length of 5 to estimate a variable-length pose sequence with fixed input length, and average all results on different time positions.

4   Experiments

We evaluate models on two large-scale datasets for 3D pose estimation: Human3.6M and MPI-INF-3DHP. In particular, we first perform detailed ablation studies on the Human3.6M dataset to examine the effectiveness of the proposed components. To exclude the interference of 2D pose estimator, all experiments in this ablation study take 2D ground truth as input. Then, we compare the estimated results of UGCN with other state-of-the-art methods on two datasets. All experiments are conducted on PyTorch tools with one single TITANX GPU.

4.1   Dataset

Human3.6M: Human3.6M [10] is a large-scale indoor dataset for 3D human pose estimation. This widely used dataset consists of 3.6 million images which are captured from 4 different cameras. There are 11 different subjects and 15 different actions in this dataset, such as "Sitting", "Walking", and"Phoning". The 3D ground truth and all parameters of the calibrated camera systems are provided in this dataset. However, we do not exploit the camera parameters in the proposed approach. Following the recent works, we utilize (S1, S5, S6, S7, S8) for training and (S9, S11) for testing. The video from all views and all actions are trained by a single model. For this dataset, we conduct ablation studies based on the ground truth of 2D skeleton. Besides that, we also report the results of our approach taking as input predicted 2D poses. from widely used pose estimators.

Table 1. Performance of our UGCN model supervised by motion loss with different basic operators and time intervals. The empty set ∅ denotes that the motion loss is not utilized. The best MPJPE is achieved by the cross product operator with interval of 12.

Interval set $\mathbb{T}$	∅	{2}	{4}	{8}	{12}	{16}	{24}	{36}	{48}
Subtraction	32.0	31.4	30.8	29.7	**28.9**	29.3	30.6	31.8	32.8
Inner product	32.0	31.8	31.7	31.0	30.2	**29.8**	31.2	32.6	33.7
Cross product	32.0	31.2	30.4	28.2	**27.1**	28.3	30.2	31.6	32.7

MPI-INF-3DHP: MPI-INF-3DHP [18] is a recently released 3D human pose estimation dataset. And this dataset is captured in both indoor environment and in-the-wild outdoor environment. Similar to Human3.6M, this dataset al.so provides videos from different cameras, subjects, and actions.

Table 2. We select the 4 best time intervals according to the Table 1, and add them to the interval set one by one. More keypoint pairs with different intervals involve the calculation of motion encoding. The MPJPE is improved in this process.

Operator	$\tau = 8$	$\tau = 12$	$\tau = 16$	$\tau = 24$	# Time scales	MPJPE (mm)
Cross product		✓			1	27.1
Cross product	✓	✓			2	26.3
Cross product	✓	✓	✓		3	25.7
Cross product	✓	✓	✓	✓	4	**25.6**

4.2 Evaluation Metric

For both Human3.6M and MPI-INF-3DHP dataset, we report the *mean per joint position error(MPJPE)* [2,15,25] as the evaluation metric. In general, there are two protocols, *Protocol-1* and *Protocol-2*, used in the previous works to evaluate 3D pose estimation. Metric Protocol-1 first aligns the root joint(central hip) and then calculates the average Euclidean distance of the estimated joints. While in the Protocol-2, the estimated results are further aligned to the ground truth via a rigid transformation before computing distance.

In MPI-INF-3DHP, we evaluate models under two additional metrics. The first one is the area under the curve (AUC) [38] on the percentage of correct keypoints (PCK) score for different error thresholds. Besides, PCK with the threshold of 150 mm is also reported.

4.3 Ablation Study

In this section, we demonstrate the effectiveness of the proposed UGCN and our motion loss on the Human3.6M dataset. Experiments in this section directly take 2D ground-truth as input to eliminate the interference of 2D pose estimator.

Effect of Motion Loss. We start our ablation study from observing the impact of the temporal interval τ in the single scale motion loss. In other words, the interval set for motion loss has only one element. The value of this element controls the temporal scale of motion loss. We conduct experiments on three binary operators proposed in Sect. 3.1, *i.e.* subtraction, inner-product and cross-product.

As shown in Table 1, the cross-product achieves the lowest MPJPE error with almost all temporal intervals. Besides, the MPJPE error decrease first and then increase, and reduce the error by 4.9 mm (from 32.0 to 27.1) with the time interval of 12 and the cross-product encoding. There are two observations. First, compared to the result without motion term (denoted as ∅), even the temporal interval is large (24 frames), the performance gain is still positives. It implies that motion prior is not momentary. And the model might need long-term perception for better capturing the motion information. Second, motion loss boosts the performance with temporal interval τ in a large variation range (2–36 frames), which means the time scale of motion priors is also various.

Thus, it is reasonable to adopt motion loss with multiple time intervals. We select four best τ as candidates and adopt the most effective binary operator in Table 1, cross-product. The experimental results have been depicted in Table 2. Under the supervision of multiscale motion loss, our model decrease the MPJPE by $1.5\,\text{mm}$ ($27.1 \rightarrow 25.6$).

Table 3. We remove all downsampling and upsampling operations from the standard UGCN, and add them back pair by pair. The MPJPE performance of our system increases remarkably in this process. With motion loss, the achieved gain is even large.

# Downsample & Upsample	0	1	2	4	Δ
UGCN w/o Motion Loss	38.6	37.2	36.9	32.0	6.6
UGCN + Motion Loss ($\mathbb{T} = \{12\}$)	36.9	34.8	33.7	**27.1**	**9.8**
Δ	1.7	2.4	3.2	4.9	–

Table 4. We explore the importance of each individual component by removing them from standard setting. The increased MPJPE error for each module is listed below.

Backbone	MPJPE(mm)	Δ
UGCN	32.0	–
UGCN w/o Spatial graph	39.2	7.2
UGCN w/o Merging stage	32.5	0.5
UGCN + Motion loss	25.6	–
UGCN + Motion loss w/o Merging stage	28.4	2.8

Table 5. The MPJPE performance of our system with different supervision. Combining motion loss functions with different basic operators does not bring obvious improvement.

Loss function	Interval set $\mathbb{T}$	MPJPE(mm)	Δ
–	$\varnothing$	32.0	–
Derivative loss [28]	$\{1\}$	31.6	0.4
Cross product	$\{12\}$	27.1	4.9
Subtraction + Cross product	$\{12\}$	27.1	4.9
Subtraction + Inner + Cross product	$\{12\}$	27.1	4.9

Design Choices in UGCN. We first examine the impact of the U-shaped architecture. We remove all downsampling and upsampling operations from the standard UGCN, and add them back pair by pair. The experimental results have been depicted in Table 3. It can be seen that U-shaped structure brings significant improvement (6.6 mm) to UGCN. This structure even leads to a larger performance gain (9.8 mm) with the supervision of motion loss. And the gap caused by motion loss is growing with the increasing number of downsampling and upsampling. These results validate our assumption: the motion loss requires long-term perception.

We also explore other design choices in the UGCN. As shown in Table 4, the spatial configuration bring 7.2 mm improvement. Removing the merging stage only slightly enlarge the error. However, when the model is supervised by motion loss, the performance drop is more remarkable (0.5 mm vs. 2.8 mm). That is to say, multiscale temporal information is important to the learning of motion prior.

Design Choices in Motion Loss. The formula of offset encoding is similar to the Derivative Loss [28] which regularizes the joint offset between adjacent frames. This loss is under the the hypothesis that the motion is smooth between the neighborhood frames. We extend it to our motion loss formulation. Since only short-term relation is considered, the improvement achieved by Derivative Loss is minor. Then we compare the results of our method supervised by the motion loss with different combination of the proposed binary operators. The results have been shown in Table 5. The combination of these three representations is not able to bring any improvement. Therefore, we adopt cross-product as the pairwise motion encoder in the following experiments.

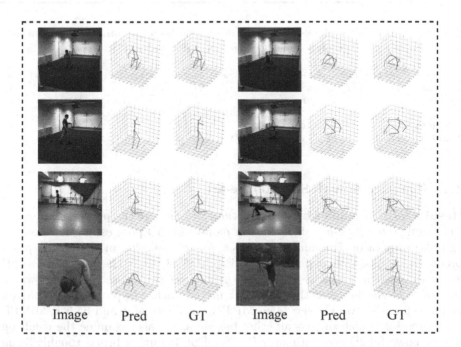

Fig. 5. Visulation results of our full system on Human3.6M and MPI-INF-3DHP.

Table 6. Results showing the errors action-wise on Human3.6M under Protocol-1 and Protocol-2. (CPN) and (HRNET) respectively indicates the model trained on 2D poses estimated by CPN [3], and HR-Net [29]. † means the methods adopt the same refine module as [2].

Protocol 1	Dir.	Disc.	Eat.	Greet	Phone	Photo	Pose	Purch.	Sit	SitD.	Somke	Wait	WalkD.	Walk	WalkT.	Ave.
Zhou [39]	54.8	60.7	58.2	71.4	62.0	65.5	53.8	55.6	75.2	111.6	64.1	66.0	51.4	63.2	55.3	64.9
Martinez [17]	51.8	56.2	58.1	59.0	69.5	78.4	55.2	58.1	74.0	94.6	62.3	59.1	65.1	49.5	52.4	62.9
Sun [32]	52.8	54.8	54.2	54.3	61.8	67.2	53.1	53.6	71.7	86.7	61.5	53.4	61.6	47.1	53.4	59.1
Fang [7]	50.1	54.3	57.0	57.1	66.6	73.3	53.4	55.7	72.8	88.6	60.3	57.7	62.7	47.5	50.6	60.4
Pavlakos [25]	48.5	54.4	54.4	52.0	59.4	65.3	49.9	52.9	65.8	71.1	56.6	52.9	60.9	44.7	47.8	56.2
Lee [13]	43.8	51.7	48.8	53.1	52.2	74.9	52.7	44.6	56.9	74.3	56.7	66.4	68.4	47.5	45.6	55.8
Hossain [30]	48.4	50.7	57.2	55.2	63.1	72.6	53.0	51.7	66.1	80.9	59.0	57.3	62.4	46.6	49.6	58.3
Lee [13](F=3)	40.2	49.2	47.8	52.6	50.1	75.0	50.2	43.0	55.8	73.9	54.1	55.6	58.2	43.3	43.3	52.8
Dabral [5]	44.8	50.4	44.7	49.0	52.9	61.4	43.5	45.5	63.1	87.3	51.7	48.5	52.2	37.6	41.9	52.1
Pavllo [27]	45.2	46.7	43.3	45.6	48.1	55.1	44.6	44.3	57.3	65.8	47.1	44.0	49.0	32.8	33.9	46.8
Cai [2]†	44.6	47.4	45.6	48.8	50.8	59.0	47.2	43.9	57.9	61.9	49.7	46.6	51.3	37.1	39.4	48.8
Lin [15]	42.5	44.8	42.6	44.2	48.5	57.1	42.6	41.4	56.5	64.5	47.4	43.0	48.1	33.0	35.1	46.6
UGCN(CPN)	41.3	43.9	44.0	42.2	48.0	57.1	42.2	43.2	57.3	61.3	47.0	43.5	47.0	32.6	31.8	45.6
UGCN(CPN)†	40.2	42.5	42.6	41.1	46.7	56.7	41.4	42.3	56.2	60.4	46.3	42.2	46.2	31.7	31.0	44.5
UGCN(HR-Net)	**38.2**	**41.0**	**45.9**	**39.7**	**41.4**	**51.4**	**41.6**	**41.4**	**52.0**	**57.4**	**41.8**	**44.4**	**41.6**	**33.1**	**30.0**	**42.6**

Protocol 2	Dir.	Disc.	Eat.	Greet	Phone	Photo	Pose	Purch.	Sit	SitD.	Somke	Wait	WalkD.	Walk	WalkT.	Ave.
Martinez [17]	39.5	43.2	46.4	47.0	51.0	56.0	41.4	40.6	56.5	69.4	49.2	45.0	49.5	38.0	43.1	47.7
Sun [32]	42.1	44.3	45.0	45.4	51.5	53.0	43.2	41.3	59.3	73.3	51.0	44.0	48.0	38.3	44.8	48.3
Fang [7]	38.2	41.7	43.7	44.9	48.5	55.3	40.2	38.2	54.5	64.4	47.2	44.3	47.3	36.7	41.7	45.7
Lee [13]	38.0	39.3	46.3	44.4	49.0	55.1	40.2	41.1	53.2	68.9	51.0	39.1	56.4	33.9	38.5	46.2
Pavlakos [25]	34.7	39.8	41.8	38.6	42.5	47.5	38.0	36.6	50.7	56.8	42.6	39.6	43.9	32.1	36.5	41.8
Hossain [30]	35.7	39.3	44.6	43.0	47.2	54.0	38.3	37.5	51.6	61.3	46.5	41.4	47.3	34.2	39.4	44.1
Pavllo [27]	34.1	36.1	34.4	37.2	36.4	42.2	34.4	33.6	45.0	52.5	37.4	33.8	37.8	25.6	27.3	36.5
Dabral [5]	**28.0**	**30.7**	39.1	34.4	37.1	44.8	**28.9**	**31.2**	**39.3**	60.6	39.3	**31.1**	37.8	25.3	28.4	36.3
Cai [2]†	35.7	37.8	36.9	40.7	39.6	45.2	37.4	34.5	46.9	50.1	40.5	36.1	41.0	29.6	33.2	39.0
Lin [15]	32.5	35.3	34.3	36.2	37.8	43.0	33.0	32.2	45.7	51.8	38.4	32.8	37.5	25.8	28.9	36.8
UGCN(CPN)	32.9	35.2	35.6	34.4	36.4	42.7	31.2	32.5	45.6	50.2	37.3	32.8	36.3	26.0	23.9	35.5
UGCN(CPN)†	31.8	34.3	35.4	33.5	35.4	41.7	31.1	31.6	44.4	49.0	36.4	32.2	35.0	**24.9**	23.0	34.5
UGCN(HR-Net)	28.4	32.5	**34.4**	**32.3**	**32.5**	40.9	30.4	29.3	42.6	**45.2**	**33.0**	32.0	**33.2**	24.2	**22.9**	**32.7**

Table 7. Results show the velocity error of our methods and other state-of-the-arts on Human3.6M. Our result without motion loss is denoted as (*).

MPJVE	Dir.	Disc.	Eat.	Greet	Phone	Photo	Pose	Purch.	Sit	SitD.	Somke	Wait	WalkD.	Walk	WalkT.	Ave.
Pavllo [25]	3.0	3.1	2.2	3.4	2.3	2.7	2.7	3.1	2.1	2.9	2.3	2.4	3.7	3.1	2.8	2.8
Lin [15]	2.7	2.8	2.1	3.1	2.0	2.5	2.5	2.9	1.8	2.6	2.1	2.3	3.7	2.7	3.1	2.7
UGCN(CPN)*	3.5	3.6	3.0	3.9	3.0	3.4	3.2	3.6	2.9	3.7	3.0	3.1	4.2	3.4	3.7	3.4
UGCN(CPN)	2.3	2.5	2.0	2.7	2.0	2.3	2.2	2.5	1.8	2.7	1.9	2.0	3.1	2.2	2.5	2.3
UGCN(GT)	1.2	1.3	1.1	1.4	1.1	1.4	1.2	1.4	1.0	1.3	1.0	1.1	1.7	1.3	1.4	1.4

4.4   Comparison with State-of-the-art

Results on Human3.6M. In this section, we compare the proposed approach to several *state-of-the-art* algorithms in monocular 3D pose estimation from an agnostic camera on Human3.6M dataset. We trained our model on 2D poses predicted by cascaded pyramid network (CPN) [3]. It is the most typical 2D estimator used in previous works. The results on two protocols are shown in the Table 6. As shown in the table, our method achieves promising results on Human3.6 under two metrics (45.6 MPJPE on *Protocol 1* and 35.5 P-MPJPE on *Protocol 2*) which surpass all other baselines. We also examine the result on a more powerful 2D pose estimator HR-Net [29]. It further brings roughly 3 mm

Table 8. Comparison with previous work on the MPI-INF-3DHP dataset. The bold-faced numbers represent the best, while underlined numbers represent the second best.

Method	PCK[↑]	AUC[↑]	MPJPE(mm)[↓]
Mehta [18]	75.7	39.3	–
Mehta (ResNet = 50) [19]	77.8	41.0	–
Mehta (ResNet = 101) [19]	79.4	41.6	–
Lin (F = 25) [15]	83.6	51.4	79.8
Lin (F = 50) [15]	82.4	49.6	81.9
UGCN w/o Motion Loss	<u>84.2</u>	<u>54.2</u>	<u>76.7</u>
UGCN	**86.9**	**62.1**	**68.1**

MPJPE improvement.Besides, we also compare our method with others based on ground-truth 2D pose. Details are illustrated in the supplementary materials.

Following [25], we evaluate the dynamic quality of predicted 3D pose sequences by Mean per Joint Velocity Error (MPJVE). This metric measures the smoothness of predicted pose sequences. As shown in Table 7, with motion loss, our method significantly reduces the MPJVE by 32% (from 3.4 mm to 2.3 mm) and outperforms other baselines.

Results on MPI-INF-3DHP. We compare the results of PCK, AUC, and MPJPE against the other state-of-the-art methods on MPI-INF-3DHP dataset with the input of ground-truth 2d skeleton sequences. As shown in Table 8, our approach achieves a significant improvement against other methods. Our method finally achieves 86.9 PCK, 62.1 AUC and 68.1 MPJPE on this dataset. The proposed motion loss significantly improves the accuracy and reduces the error.

Visualization Results. The qualitative results on Human3.6M and MPI-INF-3DHP are shown in Fig. 5. We choose samples with huge movements and hard actions to show the effectiveness of our system. More visualization results comparing with other previous works can be find in the supplementary materials.

5   Conclusion

In this work, we propose a novel objective function, motion loss. It explicitly involves motion modeling into learning. To better optimize model under the supervision of motion loss, the 3D pose estimation should have a long-term perception of pose sequences. It motivated us to design a U-shaped model to capture both short-term and long-term temporal dependencies. On two large datasets, the proposed UGCN with motion loss achieves state-of-the-art performance. The motion loss may inspire other skeleton-based tasks such as action forecasting, action generation and pose tracking.

Acknowledgment. This work is partially supported by the SenseTime Collaborative Grant on Large-scale Multi-modality Analysis (CUHK Agreement No. TS1610626 and No.TS1712093), the General Research Fund (GRF) of Hong Kong (No.14236516 and No.14203518).

References

1. Atwood, J., Towsley, D.: Diffusion-convolutional neural networks. In: Advances in Neural Information Processing Systems, pp. 1993–2001 (2016)
2. Cai, Y., et al.: Exploiting spatial-temporal relationships for 3D pose estimation via graph convolutional networks. In: Proceedings of the IEEE International Conference on Computer Vision, pp. 2272–2281 (2019)
3. Chen, Y., Wang, Z., Peng, Y., Zhang, Z., Yu, G., Sun, J.: Cascaded pyramid network for multi-person pose estimation. In: Proceedings of the IEEE Conference on Computer Vision and Pattern Recognition, pp. 7103–7112 (2018)
4. Cheng, Y., Yang, B., Wang, B., Yan, W., Tan, R.T.: Occlusion-aware networks for 3D human pose estimation in video. In: Proceedings of the IEEE International Conference on Computer Vision, pp. 723–732 (2019)
5. Dabral, R., Mundhada, A., Kusupati, U., Afaque, S., Sharma, A., Jain, A.: Learning 3D human pose from structure and motion. In: Proceedings of the European Conference on Computer Vision (ECCV), pp. 668–683 (2018)
6. Defferrard, M., Bresson, X., Vandergheynst, P.: Convolutional neural networks on graphs with fast localized spectral filtering. In: Advances in Neural Information Processing Systems, pp. 3844–3852 (2016)
7. Fang, H.S., Xu, Y., Wang, W., Liu, X., Zhu, S.C.: Learning pose grammar to encode human body configuration for 3D pose estimation. In: Thirty-Second AAAI Conference on Artificial Intelligence (2018)
8. Ionescu, C., Carreira, J., Sminchisescu, C.: Iterated second-order label sensitive pooling for 3D human pose estimation. In: Proceedings of the IEEE Conference on Computer Vision and Pattern Recognition, pp. 1661–1668 (2014)
9. Ionescu, C., Papava, D., Olaru, V., Sminchisescu, C.: Human3. 6m: large scale datasets and predictive methods for 3D human sensing in natural environments. IEEE Trans. Pattern Anal. Mach. Intell. **36**(7), 1325–1339 (2013)
10. Ionescu, C., Papava, D., Olaru, V., Sminchisescu, C.: Human3.6m: large scale datasets and predictive methods for 3D human sensing in natural environments. IEEE Trans. Pattern Anal. Mach. Intell. **36**(7), 1325–1339 (2014)
11. Iskakov, K., Burkov, E., Lempitsky, V., Malkov, Y.: Learnable triangulation of human pose. arXiv preprint arXiv:1905.05754 (2019)
12. Kipf, T.N., Welling, M.: Semi-supervised classification with graph convolutional networks. arXiv preprint arXiv:1609.02907 (2016)
13. Lee, K., Lee, I., Lee, S.: Propagating LSTM: 3D pose estimation based on joint interdependency. In: Proceedings of the European Conference on Computer Vision (ECCV), pp. 119–135 (2018)
14. Li, S., Chan, A.B.: 3D human pose estimation from monocular images with deep convolutional neural Network. In: Cremers, D., Reid, I., Saito, H., Yang, M.-H. (eds.) ACCV 2014. LNCS, vol. 9004, pp. 332–347. Springer, Cham (2015). https://doi.org/10.1007/978-3-319-16808-1_23
15. Lin, J., Lee, G.H.: Trajectory space factorization for deep video-based 3D human pose estimation. arXiv preprint arXiv:1908.08289 (2019)

16. Lin, M., Lin, L., Liang, X., Wang, K., Cheng, H.: Recurrent 3D pose sequence machines. In: Proceedings of the IEEE Conference on Computer Vision and Pattern Recognition, pp. 810–819 (2017)
17. Martinez, J., Hossain, R., Romero, J., Little, J.J.: A simple yet effective baseline for 3D human pose estimation. In: Proceedings of the IEEE International Conference on Computer Vision, pp. 2640–2649 (2017)
18. Mehta, D., et al.: Monocular 3D human pose estimation in the wild using improved CNN supervision. In: 2017 Fifth International Conference on 3D Vision (3DV). IEEE (2017). https://doi.org/10.1109/3dv.2017.00064
19. Mehta, D., et al.: Vnect: real-time 3D human pose estimation with a single RGB camera. ACM Trans. Graph. (TOG) **36**(4), 44 (2017)
20. Niepert, M., Ahmed, M., Kutzkov, K.: Learning convolutional neural networks for graphs. In: International Conference on Machine Learning, pp. 2014–2023 (2016)
21. Ning, G., Huang, H.: Lighttrack: A generic framework for online top-down human pose tracking. arXiv preprint arXiv:1905.02822 (2019)
22. Park, S., Hwang, J., Kwak, N.: 3D human pose estimation using convolutional neural networks with 2D pose information. In: Hua, G., Jégou, H. (eds.) ECCV 2016. LNCS, vol. 9915, pp. 156–169. Springer, Cham (2016). https://doi.org/10.1007/978-3-319-49409-8_15
23. Pavlakos, G., Zhou, X., Daniilidis, K.: Ordinal depth supervision for 3D human pose estimation. In: Proceedings of the IEEE Conference on Computer Vision and Pattern Recognition, pp. 7307–7316 (2018)
24. Pavlakos, G., Zhou, X., Derpanis, K.G., Daniilidis, K.: Coarse-to-fine volumetric prediction for single-image 3D human pose. In: Proceedings of the IEEE Conference on Computer Vision and Pattern Recognition, pp. 7025–7034 (2017)
25. Pavllo, D., Feichtenhofer, C., Grangier, D., Auli, M.: 3D human pose estimation in video with temporal convolutions and semi-supervised training. In: Proceedings of the IEEE Conference on Computer Vision and Pattern Recognition, pp. 7753–7762 (2019)
26. Qiu, H., Wang, C., Wang, J., Wang, N., Zeng, W.: Cross view fusion for 3D human pose estimation. In: Proceedings of the IEEE International Conference on Computer Vision, pp. 4342–4351 (2019)
27. Ramakrishna, V., Kanade, T., Sheikh, Y.: Reconstructing 3D human pose from 2D image landmarks. In: Fitzgibbon, A., Lazebnik, S., Perona, P., Sato, Y., Schmid, C. (eds.) ECCV 2012. LNCS, vol. 7575, pp. 573–586. Springer, Heidelberg (2012). https://doi.org/10.1007/978-3-642-33765-9_41
28. Rayat Imtiaz Hossain, M., Little, J.J.: Exploiting temporal information for 3D human pose estimation. In: Proceedings of the European Conference on Computer Vision (ECCV), pp. 68–84 (2018)
29. Sun, K., Xiao, B., Liu, D., Wang, J.: Deep high-resolution representation learning for human pose estimation. In: The IEEE Conference on Computer Vision and Pattern Recognition, CVPR, June 2019
30. Sun, X., Shang, J., Liang, S., Wei, Y.: Compositional human pose regression. In: Proceedings of the IEEE International Conference on Computer Vision, pp. 2602–2611 (2017)
31. Tekin, B., Katircioglu, I., Salzmann, M., Lepetit, V., Fua, P.: Structured prediction of 3D human pose with deep neural networks. arXiv preprint arXiv:1605.05180 (2016)
32. Tekin, B., Márquez-Neila, P., Salzmann, M., Fua, P.: Learning to fuse 2D and 3D image cues for monocular body pose estimation. In: Proceedings of the IEEE International Conference on Computer Vision, pp. 3941–3950 (2017)

33. Tekin, B., Rozantsev, A., Lepetit, V., Fua, P.: Direct prediction of 3D body poses from motion compensated sequences. In: Proceedings of the IEEE Conference on Computer Vision and Pattern Recognition, pp. 991–1000 (2016)
34. Tome, D., Russell, C., Agapito, L.: Lifting from the deep: convolutional 3D pose estimation from a single image. In: Proceedings of the IEEE Conference on Computer Vision and Pattern Recognition, pp. 2500–2509 (2017)
35. Yan, S., Li, Z., Xiong, Y., Yan, H., Lin, D.: Convolutional sequence generation for skeleton-based action synthesis. In: Proceedings of the IEEE International Conference on Computer Vision, pp. 4394–4402 (2019)
36. Yan, S., Xiong, Y., Lin, D.: Spatial temporal graph convolutional networks for skeleton-based action recognition. In: Thirty-Second AAAI Conference on Artificial Intelligence (2018)
37. Zhou, X., Huang, Q., Sun, X., Xue, X., Wei, Y.: Towards 3D human pose estimation in the wild: a weakly-supervised approach. In: Proceedings of the IEEE International Conference on Computer Vision, pp. 398–407 (2017)
38. Zimmermann, C., Brox, T.: Learning to estimate 3D hand pose from single RGB images. In: Proceedings of the IEEE International Conference on Computer Vision, pp. 4903–4911 (2017)

Reflection Separation via Multi-bounce Polarization State Tracing

Rui Li$^{(\boxtimes)}$, Simeng Qiu, Guangming Zang, and Wolfgang Heidrich

King Abdullah University of Science and Technology, Thuwal, Saudi Arabia
{rui.li,simeng.qiu,guangming.zang,wolfgang.heidrich}@kaust.edu.sa

Abstract. Reflection removal from photographs is an important task in computational photography, but also for computer vision tasks that involve imaging through windows and similar settings. Traditionally, the problem is approached as a single reflection removal problem under very controlled scenarios. In this paper we aim to generalize the reflection removal to real-world scenarios with more complicated light interactions. To this end, we propose a simple yet efficient learning framework for supervised image reflection separation with a polarization-guided ray-tracing model and loss function design. Instead of a conventional image sensor, we use a polarization sensor that instantaneously captures four linearly polarized photos of the scene in the same image. Through a combination of a new polarization-guided image formation model and a novel supervised learning framework for the interpretation of a ray-tracing image formation model, a general method is obtained to tackle general image reflection removal problems. We demonstrate our method with extensive experiments on both real and synthetic data and demonstrate the unprecedented quality of image reconstructions.

Keywords: Reflection removal · Polarization simulation engine · Ray-tracing · Polarization tracing

1 Introduction

There are a number of circumstances in photography as well as scientific and computer vision imaging systems in which it is unavoidable to capture images through glass windows or transparent enclosures. In these scenarios, the captured image is a mixture of transmitted and reflected light paths, which degrades both the visual quality of the scene in photography applications, as well as the performance of computer vision algorithms. Therefore, reflection removal and the separation of reflected and transmitted images are topics of considerable interest in both computational photography and computer vision.

For traditional photography, a range of different techniques have been developed to suppress reflections. These range from controlling the lighting on the

---

S. Qiu—Jointly first author.

Electronic supplementary material The online version of this chapter (https://doi.org/10.1007/978-3-030-58601-0_46) contains supplementary material, which is available to authorized users.

A. Vedaldi et al. (Eds.): ECCV 2020, LNCS 12358, pp. 781–796, 2020.
https://doi.org/10.1007/978-3-030-58601-0_46

near side of the window (the darker the better), or using a linear polarizer while shooting the image at an angle close to the Brewster angle of the reflective surface. However, even in such controlled environments, complete reflection removal is surprisingly hard in practice – for example, the angle to the glass surface varies spatially over the image plane, especially for wide-angle photography. Moreover, in many situations "in the wild" such constrained setups are simply not possible and we need to contend with bright reflections at arbitrary angles. As a result, there has been considerable interest in recovering the transmitted image by utilizing a single image as input [1–4], assuming that the reflected and transmitted scenes are independent in terms of low-level features, high-level semantics or even the motion of views. The independence assumption, however, is not always reliable or discriminating enough to solve this highly ill-posed inverse problem. Moreover, transparent windows often cause weak ghost images due to multiple reflections in the glass (Fig. 1b), which are not modeled by most prior work.

In this work, we propose a full multi-bounce reflection model for the interaction of reflected and transmitted light with the glass window. At every surface bounce, we model the full change of the polarization state due to the Fresnel equations. The spatial shift introduced by each bounce also creates weaker ghost images, especially of high-intensity light sources. The change in each bounce is influenced by unknown parameters such as the material of the transparent medium and the incident angle. The weak polarization of light from these light-surface interactions acts as an additional cue for separating the reflected and the transmitted component, and to reconstruct a clean image for both components. We design a simple yet effective deep network architecture to perform this separation and image restoration.

To separate the two independent components (i.e., reflected, transmitted) from captured polarization images efficiently, we propose a comprehensive polarization image formation model by taking into account the Stokes vector and Mueller matrices conversion, coordinate between the image sensor and transparent medium, multiple reflectances as well as transmittance, and medium thickness caused ghosts by solving an simple iterative parameter searching problem. Considering a high-quality polarization image dataset is lacking in this area, our experiment dataset includes both unpolarized and polarized cases. This carefully captured high-resolution dataset includes different polarization scenarios that are required to be solved in the real world, we will make it public for this research area. In particular, the main contributions of our works are:

- We propose a differentiable polarization simulation engine to accurately trace the polarization state of light in the transparent medium, combining it with a deep learning framework for end-to-end training.
- We design a mixed network architecture that considers a learnable forward inference model to separate reflected and transmitted scene, and a physically backward simulation loss to further verify and refine network output.
- We also release a real scene polarized image dataset with and without medium reflection, it contains a pair of clear polarized images and several reflected scenes with different scene parameters.

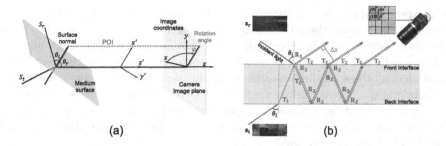

Fig. 1. Light reflection and transmission model: Incident angle θ_i, reflection angle θ_r, transmission angle θ_t, and POI. (a) Object surface and camera image plane are in different coordinate (b) Multiple light paths for reflected the (blue) and transmitted (red) scenes. The top-right is a color polarization camera with micropolarizer at four different angles and Bayer filter layout. (Color figure online)

2 Related Work

Single image reflection separation is a well-known ill-posed problem. There are two general approaches to this. One is based on handcrafted priors [5–11], while the other is based on deep learning methods [1–3]. The handcrafted priors that are based on the observations from specific natural images. Properties like gradient sparsity [5,8,11], relative smoothness [12–14], and ghosting cues [10], are leveraged in the literature. Although reasonable performance can be observed when these assumptions hold, high-level understanding for the specific input data is required for the prior based approaches. In deep learning based methods, deep convolutional neural networks (CNN) are applied to solve this inverse problem. Fan et al. [1] propose an image learning network to predict the background layer in an end-to-end approach. Yang et al. [15] estimate background and reflection in an alternating fashion, to improve the accuracy of reflection removal. Jin et al. [16] propose a neural network approach with a focus on handling color ambiguity and saturation. Wan et al. [17] applies a multi-scale strategy on the learning network to improve the target details. Wen et al. [18] synthesizes and remove reflection with a non-linear model. Perceptual loss functions have been adopted in [4]. An alignment-invariant loss is introduced in [19] to improve the performance under misaligned data.

Multiple image reflection removal is also an active research area, where some measurement diversity is introduced in the form of motion or rotating polarizers etc. By estimating the motion between the transmitted and reflected images with different strategies [20–22], researchers manage to separate them for reflection removal. Recently, there is an emerging interest in polarization guided image reflection separation [23–25]. With multiple images captured for the same scene at different polarization angles, the reflections from glasses are separated by applying independent components analysis [26]. Kong et al. [25] propose a multi-scale strategy to find the reflection separation by investigating the properties of different polarization angles. However, they failed to consider the thickness of the transparent medium, which introduced ghost images. By leveraging the properties of polarized light, the reflection and transmission images are separated with more impressive results in recent approaches [24]. Lyu et al. [23] takes unpolarized and polarized images for reflection separation. However, to the best of our knowledge, all these methods assume a simplified model with only one transmitted light path, whereas multiple reflections between the two glass surfaces are ignored. In contrast, we proposed a comprehensive polarization engine, to jointly describe polarization states for each reflection in a physical plausible way, which significantly improves our results compared to the state of the art.

3   Physically-Based Image Formation Model

When photographing in front of a double-surfaced transparent planar medium, people always capture a transmitted image with the unwanted reflected images. Therefore, we propose a comprehensive polarization-based image formation model for separating the reflection layer and transmission layer of blending scenes. Specifically, we separate the image into a reflected and a transmitted component, while taking into account multiple bounces in the glass surface and the associated ghost images (Fig. 1b).

3.1   Polarization Image Formation Model

Considering a local coordinate frame of a light ray hitting a transparent surface (Fig. 1a), a plane of incidence (POI) subsumes the transmission angle θ_t and the reflection angle θ_r, which is equal to the incident angle θ_i. The angles are related to the refractive indices via Snell's law: $n_0 \sin \theta_i = n \sin \theta_t$, where the transparent medium has refractive index n, and n_0 is the refractive index of the ambient medium (e.g. $n_0 \approx 1$ for air). An incident light passing through or reflected off a transparent media is partially polarized and consists of two orthogonal polarized components that perpendicular and parallel to the POI. This relationship is guided by the Fresnel equations, which we briefly summarize in the following. We define reflectance R and transmittance T as the intensity ratio of reflected light and transmitted light to incident light, respectively. The subscripts $\|$ and $\perp$ represent the polarized components parallel and perpendicular to the POI. R is derived from two orthogonal polarized elements of reflectance, $R = (R_\| + R_\perp)/2$. Likewise, $T = (T_\| + T_\perp)/2$.

We adopt Mueller calculus to represent the polarization state of light. The full polarization state is described by a 4D Stokes vectors $\mathbf{s} = (s_0, s_1, s_2, s_3)^T$. However, in our case we only consider linear polarization, in which case we only require a 3D vector, corresponding to the first 3 components of the full Stokes vector. In the coordinate frame of the camera sensor we perform polarization measurements with four different linear polarizer angles resulting in four images $I^{0°}$, $I^{45°}$, $I^{90°}$ and $I^{135°}$, which are acquired simultaneously with a polarization image sensor. Given the four linear polarizer images our Stokes vector in the image plane can be computed as

$$\mathbf{s} = \begin{bmatrix} s_0 \\ s_1 \\ s_2 \end{bmatrix} = \begin{bmatrix} \frac{1}{2}(I^{0°} + I^{45°} + I^{90°} + I^{135°}) \\ I^{0°} - I^{90°} \\ I^{45°} - I^{135°} \end{bmatrix}, \tag{1}$$

The change of polarization states as we propagate the light through the transparent surface can be described by Mueller matrices, which operate on the Stokes vectors. First, it is necessary to transform the vector between the local coordinate frame of the transparent surface and the coordinate frame of the camera sensor, which we also take to be the global coordinate frame for simplicity. This is achieved with a rotation Mueller matrix:

$$\mathbf{C}(\psi) = \begin{bmatrix} 1 & 0 & 0 \\ 0 & \cos 2\psi & -\sin 2\psi \\ 0 & \sin 2\psi & \cos 2\psi \end{bmatrix}, \tag{2}$$

which maps a Stokes vector $\hat{\mathbf{s}}$ in local coordinates to a Stokes vector $\mathbf{s}$ in global coordinates. $\mathbf{C}^{-1}(\psi) = \mathbf{C}(-\psi)$ is used for the reverse mapping.

Next, we need to model the Mueller matrices for the individual reflection and transmission operations along the light path (Fig. 1a,b). There are two pairs of Mueller matrices: $\mathbf{R}_1$ and $\mathbf{T}_1$ describe the reflection and transmission as the light travels from the outside (optically thinner medium) to the transparent object (optically thicker medium). When the light travels from the inside (optically thicker) to the outside (optically thinner), reflection and transmission are respectively described by $\mathbf{R}_2$ and $\mathbf{T}_2$. Please see the supplemental materials or [27,28] for the definition of these four matrices.

The contribution of the reflected scene consists of the direct reflection on the surface, as well as all possible ghost images, with the latter being characterized as all light paths transmitted into the medium, followed by an odd number of reflections, and transmission out of the medium. In the local coordinate frame of the transparent object, this can be described as

$$\hat{\mathbf{s}}_r(x) = \mathbf{R}_1 \hat{\mathbf{s}}_r^0(x) + \sum_{i=0}^{\infty} \mathbf{T}_2 \mathbf{R}_2^{2i+1} \mathbf{T}_1 \hat{\mathbf{s}}_r^0(x - i \cdot \Delta x), \tag{3}$$

where $\Delta x = 2d \tan \theta_t \sin \theta_t$ is the spatial offset between ghost images (see Fig. 1b), and $\hat{\mathbf{s}}_r^0 = \mathbf{C}(-\psi)\mathbf{s}_r^0$ describes the polarization state of the reflected scene before interacting with the transparent object.

Likewise, the total contributions of the transmitted scene are given by a transmission into the object, followed by an even number of internal reflections (possibly zero), and a transmission out of the object:

$$\hat{\mathbf{s}}_t(x) = \sum_{i=0}^{\infty} \mathbf{T}_2 \mathbf{R}_2^{2i} \mathbf{T}_1 \hat{\mathbf{s}}_t^0(x - i \cdot \Delta x), \tag{4}$$

with $\hat{\mathbf{s}}_t^0 = \mathbf{C}(-\psi)\mathbf{s}_t^0$ being the initial polarization state. The total light imaged by the camera can then be described in global/camera coordinates as

$$\mathbf{s} = \mathbf{C}(\psi)(\hat{\mathbf{s}}_r(x) + \hat{\mathbf{s}}_t(x)). \tag{5}$$

3.2   Polarization Simulation Engine

To accurately simulate the polarization state for a reflected I_r and transmitted I_t scene, our forward simulator takes RGB image pairs (I_r, I_t) that correspond to "clean" images without interaction with a transparent surface. From these inputs, the simulator generates blended images of reflected and transmitted scenes with full polarization state, i.e., simulated polarized images as described above. The initial polarization states $\mathbf{s}^0_{\{r,t\}}$ can either simply be set to unpolarized states or some other manually selected value, or it could be estimated from the reflected and transmitted scenes. Thus, our simulator can be represented as,

$$I^\phi = \mathcal{S}(I_r, I_t, \Theta), \tag{6}$$

where I^ϕ are a set of linearly polarized images corresponding to simulated sensor images. The scene parameters Θ correspond to the thickness of the transparent object d, light incident angles θ_i, and refractive index n. In our setup, the glass object has a constant thickness refractive index. The glass thickness d and incident angle θ_i, together with the corresponding transmission angle θ_t, mainly affect the spatial shift Δx in Eq. (3) of multi-bounce images (maximal bounce number is 10). Therefore, we only need to estimate the spatial shift Δx to obtain the light incident angle θ_i. The energy loss within the glass was considered, but can actually be neglected in our setting: the attenuation coefficient in glass is approximately $\alpha \approx 0.5 db/km$, corresponding to an energy loss of around 12% per km. This amounts to only a reduction by a factor of 2.4×10^{-4} per bounce for a typical glass thickness. We will show that the simulation results can verify and refine the output of recovered reflected and transmitted scenes.

4   Proposed Method

Given a set of linearly polarized images $I^\phi = \{I^{\phi_i} \mid \phi_i = 0, \cdots, N\}$, our approach first independently decomposes each polarized image into a transmitted scene $\hat{I}^\phi_t = \{I^{\phi_i}_t \mid \phi_i = 0, \cdots, N\}$ and a reflected scene $\hat{I}^\phi_r = \{I^{\phi_i}_r \mid \phi_i = 0, \cdots, N\}$ via the proposed PolarNet, then FusionNet takes all pairs of proposed separations $\hat{I}^\phi_r, \hat{I}^\phi_t$ and polarized image set I^ϕ as input to generate a refined final $\hat{I}_r$ and $\hat{I}_t$.

4.1   Network Architecture

Our pipeline mainly contains two cascade networks, PolarNet and FusionNet, for processing single polarized images and combining multiple separated results for refinement, and one polarization simulation engine (PSE) takes refined $\hat{I}_r$ and $\hat{I}_t$ as input to recover polarized image set I^ϕ by physically simulating light traveling in transparent medium. The PolarNet first decomposes each polarized image I^{ϕ_i} into two independent reflected and transmitted images $\hat{I}^{\phi_i}_r$ and $\hat{I}^{\phi_i}_t$. The encoder uses a pre-trained VGG-19 network as feature extractor with fixed parameters, and the decoder concatenates feature maps in the selected downsampling layers and upsampling layers (see Fig. 2).

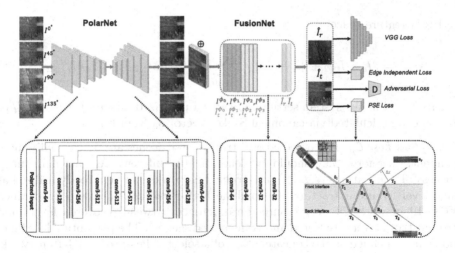

Fig. 2. Overview of system architecture.

FusionNet combines all the pairs of predicted $(\hat{I}_r^{\phi_i}, \hat{I}_t^{\phi_i})$ to have a final refined $\hat{I}_r$ and $\hat{I}_t$. Our PSE automatically estimate scene parameters and accurately simulate the polarization state of light when traveling thought transparent medium, to match the input of polarized image set I^{ϕ} by $\hat{I}_r$ and $\hat{I}_t$. For example, light travels through transparent medium will have multiple bounces between two surface of glass, for each bounce, the polarization state will change as detailed in Sect. 3. PolarNet, FusionNet, and the PSE are connected together to form a loop with an end-to-end training process.

4.2 Perceptual and Simulation-Based Loss Function

We assume that the real reflected scene I_r and transmitted scene I_t are perceptually different, and the recovered $\hat{I}_r$ and $\hat{I}_t$ can physically reconstruct the input polarized images I^{ϕ} by given the estimated scene parameter (e.g.., incident angle). Our pipeline integrates those two assumptions into the loss function and network architecture design. Our loss function contains 5 terms: a pixel-wise loss term $\mathcal{L}_d$ measures the per pixel difference between estimated $\hat{I}_r$, $\hat{I}_t$ and synthetic ground truth I_r and I_t. For real scene polarized data acquisition, I_r is hard to capture in general, so $\mathcal{L}_d$ only measures $\hat{I}_t$ and I_t for training. The perceptual loss $\mathcal{L}_p$ measures the perceptual independence of reflection and transmission, while the PSE loss $\mathcal{L}_s$ forces the output to accurately reconstruct polarized inputs. The edge independent loss $\mathcal{L}_e$ encourages the gradient of two scene to be independent, and an adversarial loss $\mathcal{L}_a$ encourages production of realistic images. Therefore, our overall loss function is,

$$\mathcal{L} = \mathcal{L}_d + \lambda_p \mathcal{L}_p + \lambda_s \mathcal{L}_s + \lambda_e \mathcal{L}_e + \lambda_a \mathcal{L}_a. \tag{7}$$

Pixelwise Loss $\mathcal{L}_d$. $\mathcal{L}_d$ compares estimated polarized images $\{\hat{I}_t^{\phi_i}\}$, $\{\hat{I}_r^{\phi_i}\}$, $\hat{I}_r$ and $\hat{I}_t$ with synthetic ground truth $\{I_r^{\phi_i}\}$, $\{I_t^{\phi_i}\}$ or camera captured scenes $\{I_t^{\phi_i}\}$, in terms of feature space,

$$\mathcal{L}_d = \|I_t - \hat{I}_t\|_2 + \|I_r - \hat{I}_r\|_2 + \sum_{i=0}^{N-1} \|I_r^{\phi_i} - \hat{I}_r^{\phi_i}\|_2 + \|I_t^{\phi_i} - \hat{I}_t^{\phi_i}\|_2, \qquad (8)$$

where $N = 4$ in our system setting indicates 4 polarized images, the target I_t or I_r could be calculated via canonical Stokes vector s_0 from Eq. (1).

Perceptual Loss $\mathcal{L}_p$. The reflected and transmitted scenes are perceptually independent, therefore, they should be semantically different. As shown in many successful applications (e.g. [4]), pre-trained networks can be directly utilized as high-level feature extractors. To combine high-level loss, we use a pre-trained VGG-19 network [29] to measure the difference between recovered layers and ground-truth layers (reflected and transmitted scenes). The perceptual loss function can be defined as the concatenation of a selected layers of VGG-19 network, and we compute the L_1 loss to measure distance in feature space as,

$$\mathcal{L}_p = \sum_l \lambda_l (\|\Phi_l(I_r) - \Phi_l(\hat{I}_r)\|_1 + \|\Phi_l(I_t) - \Phi_l(\hat{I}_t)\|_1), \qquad (9)$$

where Φ_l is the output of VGG-19, we stack 5 layers output as features: 'conv1_2', 'conv2_2', 'conv3_4', 'conv4_4', 'conv5_4', and λ_l is the weight of the layer.

PSE Loss $\mathcal{L}_s$. A good recovery of reflected or transmitted scenes could ideally recover the input polarized images using our polarization simulation engine, if scene parameters (e.g., incident angle, thickness of glass, etc.) are given or can easily be estimated. For normal reflection removal cases, the reflected and transmitted light mainly interact with double-parallel surface of transparent glass. Since the physical properties of glass are within a narrow range, the major scene parameters could be estimated by several simple line search to obtain reasonable values for the thickness and incident light angle. $\mathcal{S}(\hat{I}_r, \hat{I}_t, \Theta)$ is our polarization simulation model, it takes a predicted $\hat{I}_r$, $\hat{I}_t$ as well as scene parameters Θ as input, and traces each scene light's polarization state and spatial shift inside the two surface of transparent glass. We adopt an L_1 loss to measure the difference between ground-truth polarized images and the simulator output as,

$$\mathcal{L}_s = \sum_i \|I^{\phi_i} - \mathcal{S}(\hat{I}_r, \hat{I}_t, \Theta)\|_1. \qquad (10)$$

We implement $\mathcal{S}$ by pytorch tensor data structure, all the simulation can be computed by interior tensor operations, therefore, $\mathcal{L}_s$ can be optimized by autograd as a normal deep network training pipeline.

Edge Independent Loss $\mathcal{L}_e$. Two independent scenes are unlikely to have overlapping gradients or edges. Based on this observation, we proposed an edge independent loss to penalize those overlapping edge to recover better scenes. We formulate the $\mathcal{L}_e$ as the normalized downsampled gradient difference as,

$$\mathcal{L}_e = \sum_n \|f_n^\downarrow \nabla I_r - f_n^\downarrow \nabla \hat{I}_r\|_1 + \|f_n^\downarrow \nabla I_t - f_n^\downarrow \nabla \hat{I}_t\|_1, \qquad (11)$$

where $f_n^{\downarrow}$ is the downsampling operator with a factor of 2^{n-1}.

Adversarial Loss $\mathcal{L}_a$. To encourage realistic images, we apply normal conditional GAN's adversarial loss to avoid potential artifacts in recovered images, such as, black holes or color errors. The loss for conditional the GAN discriminator $\mathcal{D}$ is,

$$\sum_{i=0}^{N} \log D(I^{\phi_i}, I_t) - \log D(I^{\phi_i}, \hat{I}_t), \qquad (12)$$

then the adversarial loss $\mathcal{L}_a$ can be formed as,

$$\mathcal{L}_a = \sum_{i=0}^{N} - \log D(I^{\phi_i}, \hat{I}_r). \qquad (13)$$

5 Experiments

To further illustrate the superiority of this polarization-based model, we compare our proposed method with five recently published baseline reflection separation techniques. The first one is an alignment-invariant loss which is introduced in [19] (*ERRnet*) to improve the performance under misaligned data. The second one is perceptual loss functions proposed by [4] (*Zhang et al.*). Wan et al. [17] (*Wen et al.*) apply a multi-scale strategy on the learning network to improve the target details. We also compared our results with polarization guided reflection separation methods [23,24](*ReflectNet and Lyu et al.*), which are proposed most recently. They assume a simplified model with only one transmitted light path, whereas multiple reflections between the two glass surfaces are ignored.

5.1 Datasets

Synthetic Data. We generate synthetic data using our polarization simulation engine. Any pair of reflected and transmitted scene can generate a set of blended images by changing the scene parameters, e.g., incident angle, glass thickness, and refractive index. We use a widely-adopted single RGB image dataset for scene blending [4], and a proposed polarization dataset [28]. Our PSE can simulate several usual cases of reflection, e.g., strong/weak reflection, polarized incoming light, mirror reflection, etc.

Real Data. For the real data, we use a color polarization camera PHX050S-Q from Lucid Vision Labs[1]. The polarization sensor is shipped with Sony IMX250MYR CMOS with 2048×2448 pixels. Each pixel size is $3.45\,\mu\text{m} \times 3.45\,\mu\text{m}$, and every 4×4 pixels sample polarization at angles of $\{0°, 45°, 90°, 135°\}$ as well as color filter array for jointly capturing polarization and color information pixel layout shown in Fig. 1b. We use a 16mm C-mount lens for the results. To capture a clear polarized scene, we carefully select static scenes, setup camera parameters and adjust focus, and then take the clear scene

---

[1] https://thinklucid.com/phoenix-machine-vision/.

as ground truth of the current scene. To capture the blended polarized image, we set up a glass planar in the front of the lens, and adjust the angle and position of glass to capture reflected scenes with various scenarios. Our dataset contains 26 carefully captured scenes, where for each scene we captured one real ground-truth polarized transmission image and $6-12$ blended images. The resolution of the raw sensor is 2448 × 2048, while the resolution for each angle of the polarized image is 1224 × 1024. To capture high quality polarized data, we fine-tune the exposure time of polarization camera within a range of $[1 \times 10^4, 1 \times 10^5]\,\mu s$.

Training Data and Parameters. To train our proposed network, we generated 10,000 pairs of synthetic blended image from a widely-used RGB image dataset [4], with synthetic parameters $d = 10$, incident angle $\theta = [10, 40, 60, 70, 80, 85]$, refractive index $n = 1.5$, and 4 polarization angles matching the camera we use. For the training parameters, we use the Adam optimizer [30] with a learning rate of 1×10^{-4}, $\lambda_p = 0.1$, $\lambda_s = 2$, $\lambda_e = 0.1$, $\lambda_a = 0.1$. To augment the real scene dataset, we randomly sample multiple rectangle regions and resize it to 512 × 512 for each training iteration with proper flip and down-sampling operations. We use 13 real scene and synthetic data for training, and other 13 scene for testing.

5.2   Visual Comparison in Synthetic and Real Scene

We compare our method with state of the art methods [4,18,19,23,24], including single or polarization-based approaches. The implementation is based on both polarization-guided synthetic data and our delicately captured experiment data. We first show a visual comparison [4,18,19] for synthetic polarized dataset (Fig. 3). Here, our results clearly remove the reflection as well as the ghosting effect induced by the thick glass. In the second part, we compare the previous methods along with our approach on the experiment dataset (Fig. 4), which are 'pyramid', 'wood', 'DNA', and 'bird' from top to the bottom. Our proposed method yields superior results in suppressing complex reflections (row 1), or high intensity and strongly polarized reflections (row 2). It also manages to rectify color when the reflected light distorts the color of the transmitted scene (row 3), and to remove glossy reflection (row 4). In addition, we compared our results with polarization-based approaches [23,24] from real dataset (Fig. 5), which are 'violin', 'paint', 'library', and 'tea'. *ReflectNet* changes the background color of the transmitted images slightly, and *Lyu et al.* only focus on the gray scale images that captured by a monochrome polarization camera. Again, our real experiment results provide a set of distinctive transmission images.

Special Cases. Next, we test several difficult illumination scenarios, with results shown in Fig. 6. Specifically, we simulate scenes that are weakly polarized or with partially polarized illumination, which contains an LCD screen. We also simulate very bright and high contrast (HDR) scenes. The weakly polarized scene contains diffuse transmitted light with a weakly polarized reflected scene. All the competitors achieve reasonable results, and our proposed method outputs a clear transmitted scene in line with the state-of-the-art. For the fully polarized object,

Polarized   GT   ERRnet   Wen et al.   Zhang et al.   Ours

Fig. 3. Visual comparison for synthetic polarized dataset. From left to right are: polarized images (*Polarized*), transmitted scene (*GT*), ERRnet [19], *Wen et al.* [18], *Zhang et al.* [4], and our transmitted results (*Ours*), respectively.

we show a scene with an LCD screen in the transmission image. This scenario is more challenging for the competing methods, and results in incomplete removal of the reflections, whereas out approach recovers a clean transmission image. High light levels will generally lead to overexposure, and our polarized input can suppress strongly polarized reflection and recover details. Finally, the HDR scene contains non-semantic highlights, which is challenging for our competitors due to the lack of extra cues to identify the two scenes.

5.3   Quantitative Evaluation

In Table 1 we quantitatively compare our method against other state-of-the-art methods using both PSNR and SSIM. Since our approach fully utilizes polarization information, it achieves best results in most of the challenging cases. We compare *Lyu et al.* with converged gray-scale images, and our PSNR/SSIM results in Table 2 perform significantly better in each cases.

Table 1. PSNR/SSIM measurements for three approaches [4,18,19].

	Eccv	Bird	Violin	Pyramid	Wood	DNA
ERRnet	19.25/0.823	24.36/0.843	26.77/0.885	21.67/0.689	11.80/0.650	20.66 /0.314
Wen et al.	22.77/0.791	23.40/0.823	24.14/0.840	19.37/0.699	11.49/0.620	18.87/0.321
Zhang et al.	18.83/0.931	25.11/0.854	24.33/0.879	19.38/0.660	16.89/0.690	20.79/0.290
Ours	**26.14/0.83**	**26.78/0.802**	**30.34/0.877**	**27.9/0.824**	**26.79/0.79**	**28.72/0.788**

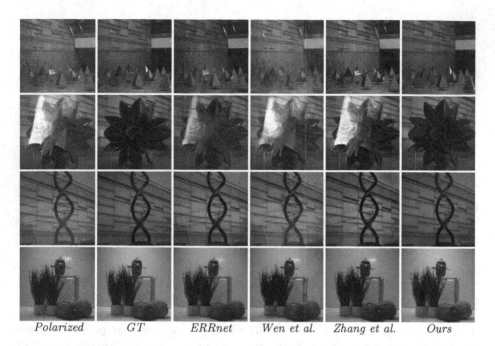

Polarized   GT   ERRnet   Wen et al.   Zhang et al.   Ours

Fig. 4. Visual comparison for our real scene dataset. From left to right are: polarized images (*Polarized*), scene without glass (*GT*), *ERRnet* [19], *Wen et al.* [18], *Zhang et al.* [4], and our transmitted results (*Ours*), respectively.

Table 2. PSNR/SSIM measurements for polarization-based approaches [23, 24].

	Violin	Paint	Library	Tea
Lyu et al.	10.56/0.519	10.31/0.267	11.10/0.425	10.33/0.450
ReflectNet	14.16/0.458	13.28/0.504	14.09/0.592	12.10/0.479
Ours	**31.08/0.911**	**25.73/0.817**	**29.16/0.907**	**22.91/0.696**

5.4 Ablation Study

In Fig. 7, we conduct a comprehensive ablation study to show the behavior of each loss term. To cancel the individual terms in the main loss function, we set the related weight parameter to 0 and re-train the model for around 100 epochs.

In Fig. 7(k), we remove our PSE loss, and observed significant artifacts in the reflection mixtures. In Fig. 7(l), the lack of $\mathcal{L}_e$ produces an overlapping gradient in the transmitted scene. In Fig. 7(m), omission of $\mathcal{L}_a$ leads to a noticeable black spot in the image. Figure 7(n) shows that replacing the VGG-19 feature map with a single L_2 loss of raw pixel values produces an over-smoothed result. We also replaced our encoder/decoder architecture with skip connections with a single multi-layer convolutional network. Figure 7(o) that these results are in poor performance and lack of local details. Our complete pipeline shows the best

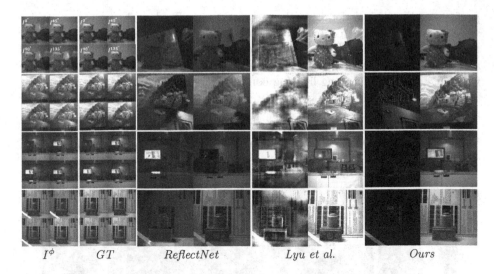

I^ϕ *GT*   *ReflectNet*   *Lyu et al.*   *Ours*

Fig. 5. Real scene comparison with polarization approaches. From left to right are: 2×2 polarized images at four angles (*Polarized I^ϕ*), 2×2 ground truth images (*GT*), *ReflectNet* [24] with reflected scene on the left and transmitted on the left, *Lyu et al.* [23], reflected and transmitted scene (*Ours*), respectively.

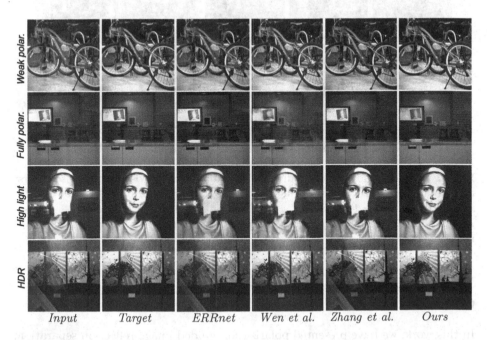

Input   *Target*   *ERRnet*   *Wen et al.*   *Zhang et al.*   *Ours*

Fig. 6. Visual comparison for special cases. From top to bottom: weak polarized diffuse scene (*Weak polar.*), fully polarized light (*Fully polar.*), high light reflection (*High light*), and dark scene with high dynamic range. From left to right: *Input*, reference image, *ERRnet* [19], *Wen et al.* [18], *Zhang et al.* [4], and *Ours*.

performance and clear details in the reconstruction. Table 3 shows a quantitative ablation study conducted by muting one of the loss terms and refining other terms weights. We compare generated polarized images with GT by using PSNR and SSIM measurements. Our GT are captured by the same polarization camera without glass while keeping lighting conditions and scenes fixed.

Table 3. PSNR/SSIM measurements for ablation study by muting loss terms.

Loss	All	$-\mathcal{L}_p$	$-\mathcal{L}_s$	$-\mathcal{L}_e$	$-\mathcal{L}_a$
PSNR/SSIM	28.3/0.889	24.1/0.797	26.4/0.842	26.6/0.809	28.1/0.878

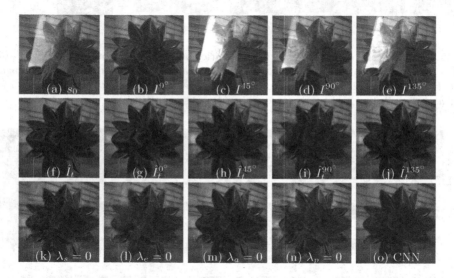

Fig. 7. Ablation study on five individual loss functions for visual comparison. First row: total intensity, 4 polarized images with polarizer angle of $\{0°, 45°, 90°, 135°\}$. Second row: recovered $\hat{I}_t$, $\hat{I}_t^{0°}$, $\hat{I}_t^{45°}$, $\hat{I}_t^{90°}$, and $\hat{I}_t^{135°}$. Third row: without $\mathcal{L}_s$, without $\mathcal{L}_e$, without $\mathcal{L}_a$, without $\mathcal{L}_p$, and replace PolarNet with a simple multi-layer CNN, respectively.

6   Conclusion

In this work, we have presented polarization guided image reflection separation. With a new image formation model where polarization information is leveraged for physically plausible measurements, we use the captured image pair as input for our designed supervised deep learning framework. Due to the natural properties of polarization for separating the reflections as well as the elegant network for training, an unprecedented quality can be achieved from our approach, which is demonstrated by the extensive experiments conducted on both synthetic data and real world captures.

References

1. Fan, Q., Yang, J., Hua, G., Chen, B., Wipf, D.: A generic deep architecture for single image reflection removal and image smoothing. In: CVPR (2017)
2. Fan, Q., Yang, J., Wipf, D., Chen, B., Tong, X.: Image smoothing via unsupervised learning. TOG **37**, 1–4 (2019)
3. Gandelsman, Y., Shocher, A., Irani, M.: Double-dip: unsupervised image decomposition via coupled deep-image-priors. In: CVPR (2019)
4. Zhang, X., Ng, R., Chen, Q.: Single image reflection separation with perceptual losses. In: CVPR (2018)
5. Levin, A., Weiss, Y.: User assisted separation of reflections from a single image using a sparsity prior. PAMI **29**, 1647–1654 (2007)
6. Li, Y., Brown, M.S.: Exploiting reflection change for automatic reflection removal. In: ICCV (2013)
7. Levin, A., Zomet, A., Weiss, Y.: Learning to perceive transparency from the statistics of natural scenes. In: NeurIPS (2003)
8. Levin, A., Zomet, A., Weiss, Y.: Separating reflections from a single image using local features. In: CVPR (2004)
9. Li, Y., Brown, M.S.: Single image layer separation using relative smoothness. In: CVPR (2014)
10. Shih, Y., Krishnan, D., Durand, F., Freeman, W.T.: Reflection removal using ghosting cues. In: CVPR (2015)
11. Arvanitopoulos, N., Achanta, R., Susstrunk, S.: Single image reflection suppression. In: CVPR (2017)
12. Long, J., Shelhamer, E., Darrell, T.: Fully convolutional networks for semantic segmentation. In: CVPR (2015)
13. Xu, L., Lu, C., Xu, Y., Jia, J.: Image smoothing via L0 gradient minimization. TOG **30**, 11 (2011)
14. Wan, R., Shi, B., Hwee, T.A., Kot, A.C.: Depth of field guided reflection removal. In: ICIP(2016)
15. Yang, J., Gong, D., Liu, L., Shi, Q.: Seeing deeply and bidirectionally: a deep learning approach for single image reflection removal. In: ECCV (2018)
16. Jin, M., Süsstrunk, S., Favaro, P.: Learning to see through reflections. In: ICCP (2018)
17. Wan, R., Shi, B., Duan, L.Y., Tan, A.H., Kot, A.C.: CRRN: multi-scale guided concurrent reflection removal network. In: CVPR (2018)
18. Wen, Q., Tan, Y., Qin, J., Liu, W., Han, G., He, S.: Single image reflection removal beyond linearity. In: CVPR (2019)
19. Wei, K., Yang, J., Fu, Y., David, W., Huang, H.: Single image reflection removal exploiting misaligned training data and network enhancements. In: CVPR (2019)
20. Xue, T., Rubinstein, M., Liu, C., Freeman, W.T.: A computational approach for obstruction-free photography. TOG **34**, 1–11 (2015)
21. Guo, X., Cao, X., Ma, Y.: Robust separation of reflection from multiple images. In: CVPR (2014)

22. Han, B.J., Sim, J.Y.: Reflection removal using low-rank matrix completion. In: CVPR (2017)
23. Lyu, Y., Cui, Z., Li, S., Pollefeys, M., Shi, B.: Reflection separation using a pair of unpolarized and polarized images. In: NeurIPS (2019)
24. Wieschollek, P., Gallo, O., Gu, J., Kautz, J.: Separating reflection and transmission images in the wild. In: ECCV (2018)
25. Kong, N., Tai, Y., Shin, J.S.: A physically-based approach to reflection separation: from physical modeling to constrained optimization. PAMI **36**, 209–221 (2014)
26. Farid, H., Adelson, E.H.: Separating reflections and lighting using independent components analysis. In: CVPR (1999)
27. Miyazaki, D., Ikeuchi, K.: Inverse polarization raytracing: estimating surface shapes of transparent objects. In: CVPR (2005)
28. Qiu, S., Fu, Q., Wang, C., Heidrich, W.: Polarization demosaicking for monochrome and color polarization focal plane arrays. In: Vision, Modeling and Visualization (2019)
29. Simonyan, K., Zisserman, A.: Very deep convolutional networks for large-scale image recognition. In: ICLR (2015)
30. Kingma, D.P., Ba, J.: Adam: a method for stochastic optimization. In: ICLR (2014)

Author Index